Merriam-Webster's
Illustrated
Spanish-English
STUDENT
Dictionary

Merriam-Webster, Incorporated

Springfield, Massachusetts

USA

Merriam-Webster Inc.

Published by Merriam-Webster Inc. 2012
Dictionary text © 2012 Merriam-Webster Inc.
Images (including associated terminology), layout, and
design copyright © 2012 QA International

ISBN: 978-0-87779-177-5

*Merriam-Webster's Illustrated Spanish-English
Student Dictionary* was created and produced by:

Merriam-Webster Inc.
P.O. Box 281; 47 Federal Street
Springfield, MA, USA 01102
Phone: 413-734-3134
Fax: 413-731-5979
Merriam-Webster.com
LearnersDictionary.com

and

QA International
7240, Saint-Hubert Street
Montreal (Quebec) H2R 2N1 Canada
Phone: +1 514.499.3000
FAX: +1 514.499.3010
ikonet.com
qa-international.com
quebec-amerique.com

Printed and bound in India. Eighth printing 2022.
13 12 11 10 09 08   24 23 22
PO 840 v.1.1

DIRECTION
Editor : Caroline Fortin
Editorial director: Martine Podesto
Artistic director: Johanne Plante

PRODUCTION
Production director: Véronique Loranger
Print production: Salvatore Parisi

EDITORIAL STAFF
Editors in chief:
Ophélie Delaunay
Hélène Mainville
Nicolas Morgantini

Editorial assistant:
Myriam Caron Belzile

Editorial consultant:
Eduardo Duque

ILLUSTRATION
Illustration Director: Anouk Noël
Jean-Yves Ahern
Pascal Bilodeau
Yan Bohler
Mélanie Boivin
François Escalmel
Alain Lemire
Rielle Lévesque
Raymond Martin
Carl Pelletier
Michel Rouleau
Claude Thivierge
Mamadou Togola

LAYOUT
Benjamin Dubé
Karine Lévesque
Fernando Salvador Marroquìn
Julie Villemaire

PROGRAMMING
Gabriel Trudeau-St-Hilaire

DATA MANAGEMENT and PREPRESS
François Hénault

MERRIAM-WEBSTER EDITORS

Susan L. Brady
Daniel B. Brandon
Rebecca R. Bryer-
    Charette
Christopher Connor

Robert Copeland
Daniel J. Hopkins
Benjamin T. Korzec
Adrienne M. Scholz

Neil S. Serven
Kory L. Stamper
Mark A. Stevens
Karen L. Wilkinson

COVER DESIGN
Lynn Stowe Tomb, Merriam-Webster Art Director

PREFACE

Merriam-Webster's Illustrated Spanish-English Student Dictionary is designed for both English-speaking students learning Spanish and Spanish-speaking students learning English. Its 45,000 entries and 50,000 translations provide up-to-date coverage of the basic vocabulary and idioms in both languages. In addition, the dictionary includes many specifically Latin American words and phrases.

This book has been created in collaboration with QA International, the creator of the family of Merriam-Webster's visual dictionaries. For this book, nearly every two-page spread includes at least one highly detailed color illustration selected to help students gain a fuller understanding of words and the concepts they represent and to add interest to the book. These illustrations are meant to encourage browsing and to help students broaden their vocabularies with interesting new words.

Users of this book are urged to explore the front and back matter of this book, especially for guidance regarding the pronunciation of English words.

PRÓLOGO

Merriam-Webster's Illustrated Spanish-English Student Dictionary está diseñado tanto para estudiantes de habla inglesa que estén aprendiendo español como para estudiantes de habla hispana que estén aprendiendo inglés. Sus 45,000 anotaciones y 50,000 traducciones proporcionan una cobertura actual del vocabulario básico y modismos en ambos idiomas. Además, el diccionario incluye muchas palabras y frases específicamente latinoamericanas.

Este libro ha sido creado en colaboración con QA International, el creador de la familia de los diccionarios visuales de Merriam-Webster. Para este libro, casi cada desplegable de dos páginas incluye, por lo menos, una ilustración en color muy detallada seleccionada para ayudar a los estudiantes a conseguir un entendimiento más completo de las palabras y los conceptos que representan y para añadir interés en el libro. Estas ilustraciones están destinadas para animar a los estudiantes a hojear el diccionario y para ayudarles a ampliar sus vocabularios con interesantes palabras nuevas.

Se ruega a los usuarios de este libro que exploren la materia en su parte inicial y final, especialmente para orientación con respecto a la pronunciación de palabras inglesas.

TABLE OF CONTENTS

ÍNDICE

HOW TO USE THIS DICTIONARY

1 **Main entries** are sorted in alphabetical order, without regard to intervening spaces or hyphens.

2 **Translations** appear in lower case, roman, light characters.

3 **Guide words** indicate the first and last main entries shown on the double page.

4 **Derivatives** are words related to the main entry. They are introduced with a dash and are in bold.

5 **Common phrases** composed of the main entry word and another word appear as run-on entries.

6 **Parts of speech indicators** provide information about the grammatical function of the word. See the list of abbreviations on page 14a.

7 **Gender** of Spanish nouns is given. See the list of abbreviations on page 14a.

8 **Inflected forms** are shown when they are irregular or when there might be a doubt about their spelling.

9 **Cross-references** lead to the appropriate main entry.

10 **Synonyms**, written in caps, may appear before the translation word(s) to clarify meaning of an entry.

11 **Title of the illustration**

12 **Terms** label specific parts of the illustration.

13 **Colored main entries** are illustrated in the double page.

14 **Homographs** are identical in spelling, but different in meaning. They can appear as run-on entries, or as separate entries if of distinctly different origin.

15 **Italic usage labels** may be added at the entry or sense as well (as **timbre** *nm* ... **4** *Lat* : postage stamp, **center** or *Brit* **centre** ...*n* ..., or **garra** *nf* ... **2** *fam* : hand, paw). These labels are also included in the translations (**bag** *n* ... **2** HANDBAG : bolso *m*, cartera *f Lat*).

---

2   9   8

1
alondra *nf* : lark
alpaca *nf* : alpaca
alpinismo *nm* : **mountain climbing**
— **alpinista** *nmf* : mountain climber
alpiste *nm* : birdseed
alquilar *vt* : rent, lease — **alquilarse** *vr* : be for rent — **alquiler** *nm* : rent, rental
alquitrán *nm, pl* **-tranes** : tar
alrededor *adv* **1** : around, about **2** alrededor de : approximately — **alrededor de** *prep phr* : around — **alrededores** *nmpl* : outskirts
alta *nf* : discharge (of a patient)
altanería *nf* : haughtiness — **altanero, -ra** *adj* : haughty
altar *nm* : altar
altavoz *nm, pl* **-voces** : loudspeaker
alterar *vt* **1** : alter, modify **2** PERTURBAR : disturb — **alterarse** *vr* : get upset
4 — **alteración** *nf, pl* **-ciones 1** : alteration **2** ALBOROTO : disturbance — **altera-do, -da** *adj* : upset
altercado *nm* : altercation, argument
alternar *vi* **1** : alternate **2** alternar con : socialize with — *vt* : alternate — **alternarse** *vr* : take turns — **alternativa** *nf* : alternative — **alternativo, -va** *adj* : alternating, alternative — **alterno, -na** *adj* : alternate
Alteza *nf* : Highness
altiplano *nm* : high plateau
altitud *nf* : altitude
altivez *nf, pl* **-veces** : haughtiness — **altivo, -va** *adj* : haughty
alto, -ta *adj* **1** : tall, high **2** RUIDOSO : loud — **alto** *adv* **1** ARRIBA : high **2** : loud, loudly — **alto, -ta** *nm* **1** ALTURA : height, elevation **2** : stop, halt — **alto** *interj* : halt!, stop! — **altoparlante** *nm Lat* : loudspeaker
altruista *adj* : altruistic — **altruismo** *nm* : altruism
altura *nf* **1** : height **2** ALTITUD : altitude **3** a la altura de : near, up by
5 **alubia** *nf* : kidney bean
alucinar *vi* : hallucinate — **alucinación** *nf, pl* **-ciones** : hallucination
alud *nm* : avalanche
aludir *vi* : allude, refer — **aludido, -da** *adj* **darse por aludido** : take it personally
alumbrar *vt* **1** : light, illuminate **2** PARIR : give birth to — **alumbrado** *nm* : (electric) lighting — **alumbramiento** *nm* : childbirth
aluminio *nm* : aluminum
alumno, -na *n* : pupil, student
alusión *nf, pl* **-siones** : allusion

aluvión *nm, pl* **-viones** : flood, barrage
alzar {21} *vt* : lift, raise — **alzarse** *vr* : rise (up) — **alza** *nf* : rise — **alzamiento** *nm* : uprising
ama → **amo**
amabilidad *nf* : kindness — **amable** *adj* : kind, nice
amaestrar *vt* : train
amagar {52} *vt* **1** : show signs of **2** AMENAZAR : threaten — *vi* : be imminent — **amago** *nm* **1** INDICIO : sign **2** AMENAZA : threat
amainar *vi* : abate
amamantar *v* : breast-feed, nurse
amanecer {53} *v impers* : dawn — *vi* : wake up — **amanecer** *nm* : dawn, daybreak
amanerado *adj* : affected, mannered
amansar *vt* **1** : tame **2** APACIGUAR : soothe — **amansarse** *vr* : calm down

faro[M] halógeno
halogen light

faro[M] estroboscópico
strobe light

equipamiento[M] de primeros auxilios[M]
first aid supplies

7   10   12

CÓMO USAR ESTE DICCIONARIO

3

amenizar **A** 11

amante *adj* **amante de** : fond
of — **amante** *nmf* : lover
amañar *vt* : rig, tamper with
amapola *nf* : poppy
amar *vt* : love
amargar {52} *vt* : make bitter —
amargado, -da *adj* : embittered
— **amargo, -ga** *adj* : bitter
— **amargo** *nm* : bitterness —
amargura *nf* : bitterness, grief
amarillo, -lla *adj* : yellow
— **amarillo** *nm* : yellow
amarrar *vt* **1** : moor **2** ATAR : tie up
amasar *vt* **1** : knead **2** :
amass (a fortune, etc.)
amateur *adj & nmf* : amateur
amatista *nf* : amethyst
ambages *nmpl* **sin ambages** : without
hesitation, straight to the point
ámbar *nm* : amber

ambición *nf, pl* **-ciones** : ambition
— **ambicionar** *vt* : aspire to —
ambicioso, -sa *adj* : ambitious
ambiente *nm* **1** AIRE : atmosphere **2**
MEDIO : environment, surroundings *pl*
— **ambiental** *adj* : environmental
ambigüedad *nf* : ambiguity —
ambiguo, -gua *adj* : ambiguous
ámbito *nm* : domain, sphere
ambos, -bas *adj & pron* : both
ambulancia *nf* : ambulance
ambulante *adj* : traveling, itinerant
ameba *nf* : amoeba
amedrentar *vt* : intimidate
amén *nm* **1** : amen **2 amén**
de : in addition to
amenazar {21} *vt* : threaten —
amenaza *nf* : threat, menace
amenizar {21} *vt* : make pleasant,
enliven — **ameno, -na** *adj* : pleasant

13

6

1 Las **anotaciones principales** son clasificadas en orden alfabético, sin considerar espacios intermedios o guiones.

2 Las **traducciones** aparecen en letra fina, minúscula y romana.

3 Las **palabras de orientación** indican la primera y la última anotación principal mostrada a doble página.

4 Las **derivadas** son palabras relacionadas con la anotación principal. Son introducidas con un guión y está en negrita.

5 **Frases comunes** que constan de la palabra de la anotación principal y otra palabra aparecen como anotaciones de texto seguido.

6 Los **indicadores de categoría gramatical** proporcionan información sobre la función gramatical de la palabra. Ver la lista de abreviaturas en página 14a.

7 Se aporta el **género** de sustantivos españoles. Ver la lista de abreviaturas en página 14a.

8 Las **conjugaciones** son mostradas cuando son irregulares o cuando puede haber una duda sobre la manera de deletrearlas.

9 Las **referencias cruzadas** dirigen a la anotación principal adecuada.

10 **Sinónimos,** escritos en mayúsculas, pueden aparecer antes de la(s) palabra(s) traducida(s) para clarificar el significado de una anotación.

11 **Título de la ilustración.**

12 **Términos** marcan partes específicas de la ilustración.

13 Las **anotaciones principales en color** son ilustradas a doble página

14 **Homógrafos** son deletreados igual, pero son distintos en significado. Pueden aparecer como anotaciones continuas, o como anotaciones separadas, si son de origen claramente diferente.

15 **Etiquetas sobre uso de cursiva** pueden ser añadidas a la anotación o en el significado también (como **timbre** *nm*...**4** *Lat* : postage stamp, **center** *or Brit* **centre**...*n*..., or **garra** *nf*... **2** *fam* : hand, paw). Estas etiquetas también se incluyen en las traducciones (**bag** *n* ... **2** HANDBAG : bolso *m*, cartera *f Lat*).

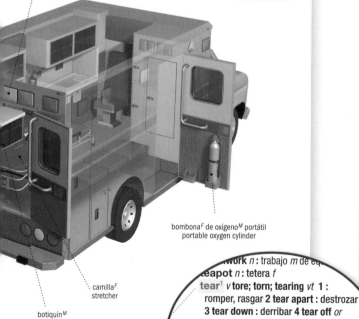

faro^M de posición^M
scene light

ambulancia^F
ambulance

11

bombona^F de oxígeno^M portátil
portable oxygen cylinder

camilla^F
stretcher

botiquín^M
drug storage

14

...**work** *n* : trabajo *m* de eq...
...**eapot** *n* : tetera *f*
tear[1] *v* tore; torn; tearing *vt* **1** :
romper, rasgar **2 tear apart** : destrozar
3 tear down : derribar **4 tear off** *or*
tear out : arrancar **5 tear up** : romper
(papel, etc.) — *vi* **1** : romperse,
rasgarse **2** RUSH : ir a toda velocidad
— **tear** *n* : desgarro *m*, rasgón *m*
tear[2] *n* : lágrima *f* — **tearful** *adj* : lloroso
tease *vt* teased; teasing **1** : tomar el
...lo a, burlarse de **2** ANNOY : fasti...
...**n 1** : cuchari...

CONJUGATION OF SPANISH VERBS

Simple Tenses

TENSE	REGULAR VERBS ENDING IN -ar hablar		REGULAR VERBS ENDING IN -er comer		REGULAR VERBS ENDING IN -ir vivir	
PRESENT INDICATIVE	hablo	hablamos	como	comemos	vivo	vivimos
	hablas	habláis	comes	coméis	vives	vivís
	habla	hablan	come	comen	vive	viven
PRESENT SUBJUNCTIVE	hable	hablemos	coma	comamos	viva	vivamos
	hables	habléis	comas	comáis	vivas	viváis
	hable	hablen	come	coman	viva	vivan
PRETERIT INDICATIVE	hablé	hablamos	comí	comimos	viví	vivimos
	hablaste	hablasteis	comiste	comisteis	viviste	vivisteis
	habló	hablaron	comió	comieron	vivió	vivieron
IMPERFECT INDICATIVE	hablaba	hablábamos	comía	comíamos	vivía	vivíamos
	hablabas	hablabais	comías	comíais	vivías	vivíais
	hablaba	hablaban	comía	comían	vivía	vivían
IMPERFECT SUBJUNCTIVE	hablara	habláramos	comiera	comiéramos	viviera	viviéramos
	hablaras	hablarais	comieras	comierais	vivieras	vivierais
	hablara	hablaran	comiera	comieran	viviera	vivieran
	or		*or*		*or*	
	hablase	hablásemos	comiese	comiésemos	viviese	viviésemos
	hablases	hablaseis	comieses	comieseis	vivieses	vivieseis
	hablase	hablasen	comiese	comiesen	viviese	viviesen
FUTURE INDICATIVE	hablaré	hablaremos	comeré	comeremos	viviré	viviremos
	hablarás	hablaréis	comerás	comeréis	vivirás	viviréis
	hablará	hablarán	comerá	comerán	vivirá	vivirán
FUTURE SUBJUNCTIVE	hablare	habláremos	comiere	comiéremos	viviere	viviéremos
	hablares	hablareis	comieres	comiereis	vivieres	viviereis
	hablare	hablaren	comiere	comieren	viviere	vivieren
CONDITIONAL	hablaría	hablaríamos	comería	comeríamos	viviría	viviríamos
	hablarías	hablaríais	comerías	comeríais	vivirías	viviríais
	hablaría	hablarían	comería	comerían	viviría	vivirían
IMPERATIVE		hablemos		comamos		vivamos
	habla	hablad	come	comed	vive	vivid
	hable	hablen	coma	coman	viva	vivan
PRESENT PARTICIPLE (GERUND)	hablando		comiendo		viviendo	
PAST PARTICIPLE	hablado		comido		vivido	

Compound Tenses

1. Perfect Tenses

The perfect tenses are formed with *haber* and the past participle:

PRESENT PERFECT
>he hablado, etc. (*indicative*);
>haya hablado, etc. (*subjunctive*)

PAST PERFECT
>había hablado, etc. (*indicative*);
>hubiera hablado, etc. (*subjunctive*)
>*or*
>hubiese hablado, etc. (*subjunctive*)

PRETERIT PERFECT
>hube hablado, etc. (*indicative*)

FUTURE PERFECT
>habré hablado, etc. (*indicative*)

CONDITIONAL PERFECT
>habría hablado, etc. (*indicative*)

2. Progressive Tenses

The progressive tenses are formed with *estar* and the present participle:

PRESENT PROGRESSIVE
>estoy llamando, etc. (*indicative*);
>esté llamando, etc. (*subjunctive*)

IMPERFECT PROGRESSIVE
>estaba llamando, etc. (*indicative*);
>estuviera llamando, etc. (*subjunctive*)
>*or*
>estuviese llamando, etc. (*subjunctive*)

PRETERIT PROGRESSIVE
>estuve llamando, etc. (*indicative*)

FUTURE PROGRESSIVE
>estaré llamando, etc. (*indicative*)

CONDITIONAL PROGRESSIVE
>estaría llamando, etc. (*indicative*)

PRESENT PERFECT PROGRESSIVE
>he estado llamando, etc. (*indicative*);
>haya estado llamando, etc. (*subjunctive*)

PAST PERFECT PROGRESSIVE
>había estado llamando, etc. (*indicative*);
>hubiera estado llamando, etc. (*subjunctive*)
>*or*
>hubiese estado llamando, etc. (*subjunctive*)

Irregular Verbs

The *imperfect subjunctive,* the *future subjunctive,* the *conditional,* and most forms of the *imperative* are not included in the model conjugations list, but can be derived as follows:

The *imperfect subjunctive* and the *future subjunctive* are formed from the third person plural form of the preterit tense by removing the last syllable (*-ron*) and adding the appropriate suffix:

PRETERIT INDICATIVE, THIRD PERSON PLURAL (querer)	quisieron
IMPERFECT SUBJUNCTIVE (querer)	quisiera, quisieras, etc. *or* quisiese, quisieses, etc.
FUTURE SUBJUNCTIVE (querer)	quisiere, quisieres, etc.

The *conditional* uses the same stem as the future indicative:

FUTURE INDICATIVE (poner)	pondré, pondrás, etc.
CONDITIONAL (poner)	pondría, pondrías, etc.

The third person singular, first person plural, and third person plural forms of the *imperative* are the same as the corresponding forms of the present subjunctive.

The second person plural (vosotros) form of the *imperative* is formed by removing the final *-r* of the infinitive form and adding a *-d* (ex.: *oír* → *oíd*).

MODEL CONJUGATIONS OF IRREGULAR VERBS

The model conjugations below include the following simple tenses: the *present indicative (IND)*, the *present subjunctive (SUBJ)*, the *preterit indicative (PRET)*, the *imperfect indicative (IMPF)*, the *future indicative (FUT)*, the second person singular form of the *imperative (IMPER)*, the *present participle* or *gerund (PRP)*, and the *past participle (PP)*. Each set of conjugations is preceded by the corresponding infinitive form of the verb, shown in bold type. Only tenses containing irregularities are listed, and the irregular verb forms within each tense are displayed in bold type. Each irregular verb entry in the Spanish-English section of this dictionary is cross-referred by number to one of the following model conjugations. These cross-reference numbers are shown in curly braces { } immediately following the entry's functional label.

1 **abolir** *(defective verb)* : *IND* abolimos, abolís *(other forms not used)*; *SUBJ (not used)*; *IMPER (only second person plural is used)*

2 **abrir** : *PP* abierto

3 **actuar** : *IND* **actúo, actúas, actúa,** actuamos, actuáis, **actúan;** *SUBJ* **actúe, actúes, actúe,** actuemos, actuéis, **actúen;** *IMPER* **actúa**

4 **adquirir** : *IND* **adquiero, adquieres, adquiere,** adquirimos, adquirís, **adquieren;** *SUBJ* **adquiera, adquieras, adquiera,** adquiramos, adquiráis, **adquieran;** *IMPER* **adquiere**

5 **airar** : *IND* **aíro, aíras, aíra,** airamos, airáis, **aíran;** *SUBJ* **aíre, aíres, aíre,** airemos, airéis, **aíren;** *IMPER* **aíra**

6 **andar** : *PRET* **anduve, anduviste, anduvo, anduvimos, anduvisteis, anduvieron**

7 **asir** : *IND* **asgo,** ases, ase, asimos, asís, asen; *SUBJ* **asga, asgas, asga, asgamos, asgáis, asgan**

8 **aunar** : IND **aúno, aúnas, aúna,** aunamos, aunáis, **aúnan;** *SUBJ* **aúne, aúnes, aúne,** aunemos, aunéis, **aúnen;** *IMPER* **aúna**

9 **avergonzar** : *IND* **avergüenzo, avergüenzas, avergüenza,** avergonzamos, avergonzáis, **avergüenzan;** *SUBJ* **avergüence, avergüences, avergüence,** avergoncemos, avergoncéis, **avergüencen;** *PRET* **avergoncé;** *IMPER* **avergüenza**

10 **averiguar** : *SUBJ* **averigüe, averigües, averigüe, averigüemos, averigüéis, averigüen;** *PRET* **averigüé,** averiguaste, averiguó, averiguamos, averiguasteis, averiguaron

11 **bendecir** : *IND* **bendigo, bendices, bendice,** bendecimos, bendecís, **bendicen;** *SUBJ* **bendiga, bendigas, bendiga, bendigamos, bendigáis, bendigan;** *PRET* **bendije, bendijiste, bendijo, bendijimos, bendijisteis, bendijeron;** *IMPER* **bendice**

12 **caber** : *IND* **quepo,** cabes, cabe, cabemos, cabéis, caben; *SUBJ* **quepa, quepas, quepa, quepamos, quepáis, quepan;** *PRET* **cupe, cupiste, cupo, cupimos, cupisteis, cupieron;** *FUT* **cabré, cabrás, cabrá, cabremos, cabréis, cabrán**

13 **caer** : *IND* **caigo,** caes, cae, caemos, caéis, caen; *SUBJ* **caiga, caigas, caiga, caigamos, caigáis, caigan;** *PRET* caí, **caíste, cayó,** caímos, **caísteis, cayeron;** *PRP* **cayendo;** *PP* **caído**

14 **cocer** : *IND* **cuezo, cueces, cuece,** cocemos, cocéis, **cuecen;** *SUBJ* **cueza, cuezas, cueza,** cozamos, cozáis, **cuezan;** *IMPER* **cuece**

15 **coger** : *IND* **cojo,** coges, coge, cogemos, cogéis, cogen; *SUBJ* **coja, cojas, coja, cojamos, cojáis, cojan**

16 **colgar** : *IND* **cuelgo, cuelgas, cuelga,** colgamos, colgáis, **cuelgan;** *SUBJ* **cuelgue, cuelgues, cuelgue, colguemos, colguéis, cuelguen;** *PRET* **colgué,** colgaste, colgó, colgamos, colgasteis, colgaron; *IMPER* **cuelga**

17 **concernir** *(defective verb; used only in the third person singular and plural of the present indicative, present subjunctive, and imperfect subjunctive)* see 25 **discernir**

18 **conocer** : *IND* **conozco,** conoces, conoce, conocemos, conocéis, conocen; *SUBJ* **conozca, conozcas, conozca, conozcamos, conozcáis, conozcan**

19 **contar** : *IND* **cuento, cuentas, cuenta,** contamos, contáis, **cuentan;** *SUBJ* **cuente, cuentes, cuente,** contemos, contéis, **cuenten;** *IMPER* **cuenta**

20 **creer** : *PRET* creí, **creíste, creyó,** creímos, **creísteis, creyeron;** *PRP* **creyendo;** *PP* **creído**

21 **cruzar** : *SUBJ* **cruce, cruces, cruce, crucemos, crucéis, crucen;** *PRET* **crucé,** cruzaste, cruzó, cruzamos, cruzasteis, cruzaron

22 **dar** : *IND* **doy,** das, da, damos, **dais,** dan; *SUBJ* **dé,** des, **dé,** demos, **deis,** den; *PRET* **di, diste, dio, dimos, disteis, dieron**

23 **decir** : *IND* **digo, dices, dice,** decimos, decís, **dicen;** *SUBJ* **diga, digas, diga, digamos, digáis, digan;** *PRET* **dije, dijiste, dijo, dijimos, dijisteis, dijeron;** *FUT* **diré, dirás, dirá, diremos, diréis, dirán;** *IMPER* **di;** *PRP* **diciendo;** *PP* **dicho**

24 **delinquir** : *IND* **delinco,** delinques, delinque, delinquimos, delinquís, delinquen; *SUBJ* **delinca, delincas, delinca, delincamos, delincáis, delincan**

25 **discernir** : *IND* **discierno, disciernes, discierne,** discernimos, discernís, **disciernen;** *SUBJ* **discierna, disciernas, discierna,** discernamos, discernáis, **disciernan;** *IMPER* **discierne**

26 **distinguir** : *IND* **distingo,** distingues, distingue, distinguimos, distinguís, distinguen; *SUBJ* **distinga, distingas, distinga, distingamos, distingáis, distingan**

27 **dormir** : *IND* **duermo, duermes, duerme,** dormimos, dormís, **duermen;** *SUBJ* **duerma, duermas, duerma, durmamos, durmáis, duerman;** *PRET* dormí, dormiste, **durmió,** dormimos, dormisteis, **durmieron;** *IMPER* **duerme;** *PRP* **durmiendo**

28 **elegir** : *IND* **elijo, eliges, elige,** elegimos, elegís, **eligen;** *SUBJ* **elija, elijas, elija, elijamos, elijáis, elijan;** *PRET* elegí, elegiste, **eligió,** elegimos, elegisteis, **eligieron;** *IMPER* **elige;** *PRP* **eligiendo**

29 **empezar** : *IND* **empiezo, empiezas, empieza,** empezamos, empezáis, **empiezan;** *SUBJ* **empiece, empieces, empiece, empecemos, empecéis, empiecen;** *PRET* **empecé,** empezaste, empezó, empezamos, empezasteis, empezaron; *IMPER* **empieza**

30 **enraizar** : *IND* **enraízo, enraízas, enraíza,** enraizamos, enraizáis, **enraízan;** *SUBJ* **enraíce, enraíces, enraíce, enraicemos, enraicéis, enraícen;** *PRET* **enraicé,** enraizaste, enraizó, enraizamos, enraizasteis, enraizaron; *IMPER* **enraíza**

31 **erguir** : *IND* **irgo** *or* **yergo, irgues** *or* **yergues, irgue** *or* **yergue,** erguimos, erguís, **irguen** *or* **yerguen;** *SUBJ* **irga** *or* **yerga, irgas** *or* **yergas, irga** *or* **yerga, irgamos, irgáis, irgan** *or* **yergan;** *PRET* erguí, erguiste, **irguió,** erguimos, erguisteis, **irguieron;** *IMPER* **irgue** *or* **yergue;** *PRP* **irguiendo**

MODEL CONJUGATIONS OF IRREGULAR VERBS

32 **errar** : *IND* **yerro, yerras, yerra,** erramos, erráis, **yerran;** *SUBJ* **yerre, yerres, yerre,** erremos, erréis, **yerren;** *IMPER* **yerra**

33 **escribir** : *PP* **escrito**

34 **estar** : *IND* **estoy, estás, está,** estamos, estáis, **están;** *SUBJ* **esté, estés, esté,** estemos, estéis, **estén;** *PRET* **estuve, estuviste, estuvo, estuvimos, estuvisteis, estuvieron;** *IMPER* **está**

35 **exigir** : *IND* **exijo,** exiges, exige, exigimos, exigís, exigen; *SUBJ* **exija, exijas, exija, exijamos, exijáis, exijan**

36 **forzar** : *IND* **fuerzo, fuerzas, fuerza,** forzamos, forzáis, **fuerzan;** *SUBJ* **fuerce, fuerces, fuerce, forcemos, forcéis, fuercen;** *PRET* **forcé,** forzaste, forzó, forzamos, forzasteis, forzaron; *IMPER* **fuerza**

37 **freír** : *IND* **frío, fríes, fríe,** freímos, freís, **fríen;** *SUBJ* **fría, frías, fría, friamos, friáis, frían;** *PRET* freí, **freíste, frió,** freímos, freísteis, frieron; *IMPER* **fríe;** *PRP* **friendo;** *PP* **frito**

38 **gruñir** : *PRET* gruñí, gruñiste, **gruñó,** gruñimos, gruñisteis, **gruñeron;** *PRP* **gruñendo**

39 **haber** : *IND* **he, has, ha, hemos,** habéis, **han;** *SUBJ* **haya, hayas, haya, hayamos, hayáis, hayan;** *PRET* **hube, hubiste, hubo, hubimos, hubisteis, hubieron;** *FUT* **habré, habrás, habrá, habremos, habréis, habrán;** *IMPER* **he**

40 **hacer** : *IND* **hago,** haces, hace, hacemos, hacéis, hacen; *SUBJ* **haga, hagas, haga, hagamos, hagáis, hagan;** *PRET* **hice, hiciste, hizo, hicimos, hicisteis, hicieron;** *FUT* **haré, harás, hará, haremos, haréis, harán;** *IMPER* **haz;** *PP* **hecho**

41 **huir** : *IND* **huyo, huyes, huye,** huimos, huís, **huyen;** *SUBJ* **huya, huyas, huya, huyamos, huyáis, huyan;** *PRET* huí, huiste, **huyó,** huimos, huisteis, **huyeron;** *IMPER* **huye;** *PRP* **huyendo**

42 **imprimir** : *PP* **impreso**

43 **ir** : *IND* **voy, vas, va, vamos, vais, van;** *SUBJ* **vaya, vayas, vaya, vayamos, vayáis, vayan;** *PRET* **fui, fuiste, fue, fuimos, fuisteis, fueron;** *IMPF* **iba, ibas, iba, íbamos, ibais, iban;** *IMPER* **ve;** *PRP* **yendo;** *PP* **ido**

44 **jugar** : *IND* **juego, juegas, juega,** jugamos, jugáis, **juegan;** *SUBJ* **juegue, juegues, juegue, juguemos, juguéis, jueguen;** *PRET* **jugué,** jugaste, jugó, jugamos, jugasteis, jugaron; *IMPER* **juega**

45 **lucir** : *IND* **luzco,** luces, luce, lucimos, lucís, lucen; *SUBJ* **luzca, luzcas, luzca, luzcamos, luzcáis, luzcan**

46 **morir** : *IND* **muero, mueres, muere,** morimos, morís, **mueren;** *SUBJ* **muera, mueras, muera, muramos, muráis, mueran;** *PRET* morí, moriste, **murió,** morimos, moristeis, **murieron;** *IMPER* **muere;** *PRP* **muriendo;** *PP* **muerto**

47 **mover** : *IND* **muevo, mueves, mueve,** movemos, movéis, **mueven;** *SUBJ* **mueva, muevas, mueva,** movamos, mováis, **muevan;** *IMPER* **mueve**

48 **nacer** : *IND* **nazco,** naces, nace, nacemos, nacéis, nacen; *SUBJ* **nazca, nazcas, nazca, nazcamos, nazcáis, nazcan**

49 **negar** : *IND* **niego, niegas, niega,** negamos, negáis, **niegan;** *SUBJ* **niegue, niegues, niegue, neguemos, neguéis, nieguen;** *PRET* **negué,** negaste, negó, negamos, negasteis, negaron; *IMPER* **niega**

50 **oír** : *IND* **oigo, oyes, oye, oímos,** oís, **oyen;** *SUBJ* **oiga, oigas, oiga, oigamos, oigáis, oigan;** *PRET* oí, oíste, oyó, oímos, oísteis, oyeron; *IMPER* **oye;** *PRP* **oyendo;** *PP* **oído**

51 **oler** : *IND* **huelo, hueles, huele,** olemos, oléis, **huelen;** *SUBJ* **huela, huelas, huela,** olamos, oláis, **huelan;** *IMPER* **huele**

52 **pagar** : *SUBJ* **pague, pagues, pague, paguemos, paguéis, paguen;** *PRET* **pagué,** pagaste, pagó, pagamos, pagasteis, pagaron

53 **parecer** : *IND* **parezco,** pareces, parece, parecemos, parecéis, parecen; *SUBJ* **parezca, parezcas, parezca, parezcamos, parezcáis, parezcan**

54 **pedir** : *IND* **pido, pides, pide,** pedimos, pedís, **piden;** *SUBJ* **pida, pidas, pida, pidamos, pidáis, pidan;** *PRET* pedí, pediste, **pidió,** pedimos, pedisteis, **pidieron;** *IMPER* **pide;** *PRP* **pidiendo**

55 **pensar** : *IND* **pienso, piensas, piensa,** pensamos, pensáis, **piensan;** *SUBJ* **piense, pienses, piense,** pensemos, penséis, **piensen;** *IMPER* **piensa**

56 **perder** : *IND* **pierdo, pierdes, pierde,** perdemos, perdéis, **pierden;** *SUBJ* **pierda, pierdas, pierda,** perdamos, perdáis, **pierdan;** *IMPER* **pierde**

57 **placer** : *IND* **plazco,** places, place, placemos, placéis, placen; *SUBJ* **plazca, plazcas, plazca, plazcamos, plazcáis, plazcan;** *PRET* plací, placiste, plació *or* **plugo,** placimos, placisteis, placieron *or* **pluguieron**

58 **poder** : *IND* **puedo, puedes, puede,** podemos, podéis, **pueden;** *SUBJ* **pueda, puedas, pueda,** podamos, podáis, **puedan;** *PRET* **pude, pudiste, pudo, pudimos, pudisteis, pudieron;** *FUT* **podré, podrás, podrá, podremos, podréis, podrán;** *IMPER* **puede;** *PRP* **pudiendo**

59 **podrir** *or* **pudrir** : *PP* **podrido** *(all other forms based on pudrir)*

60 **poner** : *IND* **pongo,** pones, pone, ponemos, ponéis, ponen; *SUBJ* **ponga, pongas, ponga, pongamos, pongáis, pongan;** *PRET* **puse, pusiste, puso, pusimos, pusisteis, pusieron;** *FUT* **pondré, pondrás, pondrá, pondremos, pondréis, pondrán;** *IMPER* **pon;** *PP* **puesto**

61 **producir** : *IND* **produzco,** produces, produce, producimos, producís, producen; *SUBJ* **produzca, produzcas, produzca, produzcamos, produzcáis, produzcan;** *PRET* **produje, produjiste, produjo, produjimos, produjisteis, produjeron**

62 **prohibir** : *IND* **prohíbo, prohíbes, prohíbe,** prohibimos, prohibís, **prohíben;** *SUBJ* **prohíba, prohíbas, prohíba,** prohibamos, prohibáis, **prohíban;** *IMPER* **prohíbe**

63 **proveer** : *PRET* proveí, **proveíste, proveyó,** proveímos, proveísteis, **proveyeron;** *PRP* **proveyendo;** *PP* **provisto**

64 **querer** : *IND* **quiero, quieres, quiere,** queremos, queréis, **quieren;** *SUBJ* **quiera, quieras, quiera,** queramos, queráis, **quieran;** *PRET* **quise, quisiste, quiso, quisimos, quisisteis, quisieron;** *FUT* **querré, querrás, querrá, querremos, querréis, querrán;** *IMPER* **quiere**

65 **raer** : *IND* **rao** *or* **raigo** *or* **rayo,** raes, rae, raemos, raéis, raen; *SUBJ* **raiga** *or* **raya, raigas** *or* **rayas, raiga** *or* **raya, raigamos** *or* **rayamos, raigáis** *or* **rayáis, raigan** *or* **rayan;** *PRET* raí, **raíste, rayó,** raímos, raísteis, **rayeron;** *PRP* **rayendo;** *PP* **raído**

MODEL CONJUGATIONS OF IRREGULAR VERBS

66 **reír** : *IND* **río, ríes, ríe, reímos,** reís, **ríen;** *SUBJ* **ría, rías, ría, riamos, riáis, rían;** *PRET* reí, **reíste, rió, reímos, reísteis, rieron;** *IMPER* **ríe;** *PRP* **riendo;** *PP* **reído**

67 **reñir** : *IND* **riño, riñes, riñe,** reñimos, reñís, **riñen;** *SUBJ* **riña, riñas, riña, riñamos, riñáis, riñan;** *PRET* reñí, reñiste, **riñó,** reñimos, reñisteis, **riñeron;** *IMPER* **riñe;** *PRP* **riñendo**

68 **reunir** : *IND* **reúno, reúnes, reúne,** reunimos, reunís, **reúnen;** *SUBJ* **reúna, reúnas, reúna,** reunamos, reunáis, **reúnan;** *IMPER* **reúne**

69 **roer** : *IND* **roo** *or* **roigo** *or* **royo,** roes, roe, roemos, roéis, roen; *SUBJ* roa *or* **roiga** *or* **roya,** roas *or* **roigas** *or* **royas,** roa *or* **roiga** *or* **roya,** roamos *or* **roigamos** *or* **royamos,** roáis *or* **roigáis** *or* **royáis,** roan *or* **roigan** *or* **royan;** *PRET* roí, **roíste, royó, roímos, roísteis, royeron;** *PRP* **royendo;** *PP* **roído**

70 **romper** : *PP* **roto**

71 **saber** : *IND* **sé,** sabes, sabe, sabemos, sabéis, saben; *SUBJ* **sepa, sepas, sepa, sepamos, sepáis, sepan;** *PRET* **supe, supiste, supo, supimos, supisteis, supieron;** *FUT* **sabré, sabrás, sabrá, sabremos, sabréis, sabrán**

72 **sacar** : *SUBJ* **saque, saques, saque, saquemos, saquéis, saquen;** *PRET* **saqué,** sacaste, sacó, sacamos, sacasteis, sacaron

73 **salir** : *IND* **salgo,** sales, sale, salimos, salís, salen; *SUBJ* **salga, salgas, salga, salgamos, salgáis, salgan;** *FUT* **saldré, saldrás, saldrá, saldremos, saldréis, saldrán;** *IMPER* **sal**

74 **satisfacer** : *IND* **satisfago,** satisfaces, satisface, satisfacemos, satisfacéis, satisfacen; *SUBJ* **satisfaga, satisfagas, satisfaga, satisfagamos, satisfagáis, satisfagan;** *PRET* **satisfice, satisficiste, satisfizo, satisficimos, satisficisteis, satisficieron;** *FUT* **satisfaré, satisfarás, satisfará, satisfaremos, satisfaréis, satisfarán;** *IMPER* **satisfaz** *or* satisface; *PP* **satisfecho**

75 **seguir** : *IND* **sigo, sigues, sigue,** seguimos, seguís, **siguen;** *SUBJ* **siga, sigas, siga, sigamos, sigáis, sigan;** *PRET* seguí, seguiste, **siguió,** seguimos, seguisteis, **siguieron;** *IMPER* **sigue;** *PRP* **siguiendo**

76 **sentir** : *IND* **siento, sientes, siente,** sentimos, sentís, **sienten;** *SUBJ* **sienta, sientas, sienta, sintamos, sintáis, sientan;** *PRET* sentí, sentiste, **sintió,** sentimos, sentisteis, **sintieron;** *IMPER* **siente;** *PRP* **sintiendo**

77 **ser** : *IND* **soy, eres, es, somos, sois, son;** *SUBJ* **sea, seas, sea, seamos, seáis, sean;** *PRET* **fui, fuiste, fue, fuimos, fuisteis, fueron;** *IMPF* **era, eras, era, éramos, erais, eran;** *IMPER* **sé;** *PRP* **siendo;** *PP* **sido**

78 **soler** *(defective verb; used only in the present, preterit, and imperfect indicative, and the present and imperfect subjunctive) see 47* **mover**

79 **tañer** : *PRET* tañí, tañiste, **tañó,** tañimos, tañisteis, **tañeron;** *PRP* **tañendo**

80 **tener** : *IND* **tengo, tienes, tiene,** tenemos, tenéis, **tienen;** *SUBJ* **tenga, tengas, tenga, tengamos, tengáis, tengan;** *PRET* **tuve, tuviste, tuvo, tuvimos, tuvisteis, tuvieron;** *FUT* **tendré, tendrás, tendrá, tendremos, tendréis, tendrán;** *IMPER* **ten**

81 **traer** : *IND* **traigo,** traes, trae, traemos, traéis, traen; *SUBJ* **traiga, traigas, traiga, traigamos, traigáis, traigan;** *PRET* **traje, trajiste, trajo, trajimos, trajisteis, trajeron;** *PRP* **trayendo;** *PP* **traído**

82 **trocar** : *IND* **trueco, truecas, trueca,** trocamos, trocáis, **truecan;** *SUBJ* **trueque, trueques, trueque, troquemos, troquéis, truequen;** *PRET* **troqué,** trocaste, trocó, trocamos, trocasteis, trocaron; *IMPER* **trueca**

83 **uncir** : *IND* **unzo,** unces, unce, uncimos, uncís, uncen; *SUBJ* **unza, unzas, unza, unzamos, unzáis, unzan**

84 **valer** : *IND* **valgo,** vales, vale, valemos, valéis, valen; *SUBJ* **valga, valgas, valga, valgamos, valgáis, valgan;** *FUT* **valdré, valdrás, valdrá, valdremos, valdréis, valdrán**

85 **variar** : *IND* **varío, varías, varía,** variamos, variáis, **varían;** *SUBJ* **varíe, varíes, varíe,** variemos, variéis, **varíen;** *IMPER* **varía**

86 **vencer** : *IND* **venzo,** vences, vence, vencemos, vencéis, vencen; *SUBJ* **venza, venzas, venza, venzamos, venzáis, venzan**

87 **venir** : *IND* **vengo, vienes, viene,** venimos, venís, **vienen;** *SUBJ* **venga, vengas, venga, vengamos, vengáis, vengan;** *PRET* **vine, viniste, vino, vinimos, vinisteis, vinieron;** *FUT* **vendré, vendrás, vendrá, vendremos, vendréis, vendrán;** *IMPER* **ven;** *PRP* **viniendo**

88 **ver** : *IND* **veo,** ves, ve, vemos, veis, ven; *PRET* **vi, viste, vio, vimos, visteis, vieron;** *IMPER* **ve;** *PRP* **viendo;** *PP* **visto**

89 **volver** : *IND* **vuelvo, vuelves, vuelve,** volvemos, volvéis, **vuelven;** *SUBJ* **vuelva, vuelvas, vuelva,** volvamos, volváis, **vuelvan;** *IMPER* **vuelve;** *PP* **vuelto**

90 **yacer** : *IND* **yazco** *or* **yazgo** *or* **yago,** yaces, yace, yacemos, yacéis, yacen; *SUBJ* **yazca** *or* **yazga** *or* **yaga, yazcas** *or* **yazgas** *or* **yagas, yazca** *or* **yazga** *or* **yaga, yazcamos** *or* **yazgamos** *or* **yagamos, yazcáis** *or* **yazgáis** *or* **yagáis, yazcan** *or* **yazgan** *or* **yagan;** *IMPER* **yace** *or* **yaz**

SOUND & SPELLING IN SPANISH

Below is a list of Spanish letters and letter combinations, with information about how those letters are pronounced. The sound for each letter or letter combination is shown using the International Phonetic Alphabet (IPA), followed by additional explanatory notes as needed. Information about the IPA symbols can be found on page 441.

VOWELS

a [a]

e [e] in open syllables (syllables ending with a vowel); [ɛ] in closed syllables (syllables ending with a consonant)

i [i]; before another vowel in the same syllable pronounced as [j] ([ʒ] or [ʃ] in Argentina and Uruguay; [dʒ] when at the beginning of a word in the Caribbean)

o [o] in open syllables (syllables ending with a vowel); [ɔ] in closed syllables (syllables ending with a consonant)

u [u]; before another vowel in the same syllable pronounced as [w]

y [i]; before another vowel in the same syllable pronounced as [j] ([ʒ] or [ʃ] in Argentina and Uruguay; [dʒ] when at the beginning of a word in the Caribbean)

CONSONANTS

b [b] at the beginning of a word or after *m* or *n*; [β] elsewhere

c [s] before *i* or *e* in Latin America and parts of southern Spain, [θ] in northern Spain; [k] elsewhere

ch [tʃ]; frequently [ʃ] in Chile and Panama; sometimes [ts] in Chile

d [d] at the beginning of a word or after *n* or *l*; [ð] elsewhere, frequently silent between vowels

f [f]; [Φ] in Honduras (no English equivalent for this sound; like [f] but made with both lips)

g [x] before *i* or *e* ([h] in the Caribbean and Central America); [g] at the beginning of a word or after *n* and not before *i* or *e*; [ɣ] elsewhere, frequently silent between vowels

gu [gw] at the beginning of a word before *a, o*; [ɣw] elsewhere before *a, o*; frequently just [w] between vowels; [g] at the beginning of a word before *i, e*; [ɣ] elsewhere before *i, e*; frequently silent between vowels

gü [gw] at the beginning of a word, [ɣw] elsewhere; frequently just [w] between vowels

h silent

j [x] ([h] in the Caribbean and Central America)

k [k]

l [l]

ll [j]; [ʒ] or [ʃ] in Argentina and Uruguay; [dʒ] when at the beginning of a word in the Caribbean; [lʲ] in Bolivia, Paraguay, Peru, and parts of northern Spain (no English equivalent; like "lli" in *million*)

m [m]

n [n]; frequently [ŋ] at the end of a word when next word begins with a vowel

ñ [ɲ]

p [p]

qu [k]

r [r] (no English equivalent; a trilled sound) at the beginning of words; [t]/[ɾ] elsewhere

rr [r] (no English equivalent; a trilled sound)

s [s]; frequently [z] before *b, d, g, m, n, l, r*; at the end of a word [h] or silent in many parts of Latin America and some parts of Spain

t [t]

v [b] at the beginning of a word or after *m* or *n*; [β] elsewhere

x [ks] or [gz] between vowels; [s] before consonants

z [s] in Latin America and parts of southern Spain, [θ] in northern Spain; at the end of a word [h] or silent in many parts of Latin America and some parts of Spain

SOUND & SPELLING IN ENGLISH

Below is a list of English letters and letter combinations, with information about how those letters are pronounced. The list shows a common English word in which the letter or letters appear and shows the pronunciation of the letters in both the traditional Merriam-Webster system and in the International Phonetic Alphabet (IPA). More information about both of these systems appears at the back of this book on page 441.

a	above	\ə\	[ə]
	cat	\a\	[æ]
	made	\ā\	[eɪ]
	father	\ä\	[ɑ]
ah	shah	\ä\	[ɑ]
	cheetah	\ə\	[ə]
ai	main	\ā\	[eɪ]
	captain	\ə\	[ə]
au	sausage	\ȯ\	[ɔ]
aw	saw	\ȯ\	[ɔ]
ay	day	\ā\	[eɪ]
b	baby	\b\	[b]
bb	rubber	\b\	[b]
c	fact	\k\	[k]
	race	\s\	[s]
	ocean	\sh\	[ʃ]
	cello	\ch\	[tʃ]
cc	soccer	\k\	[k]
ch	rich	\ch\	[tʃ]
	machine	\sh\	[ʃ]
	school	\k\	[k]
ci	special	\sh\	[ʃ]
ck	pick	\k\	[k]
cq	acquire	\k\	[k]
d	did	\d\	[d]
dd	odd	\d\	[d]
dg	budget	\j\	[dʒ]
di	soldier	\j\	[dʒ]
dj	adjective	\j\	[dʒ]
e	silent	\ə\	[ə]
	bet	\e\	[ɛ]
	me	\ē\	[i:]

ea	steak	\ā\	[eɪ]
	bread	\e\	[ɛ]
	easy	\ē\	[i:]
	ocean	\ə\	[ə]
ee	see	\ē\	[i:]
ei	vein	\ā\	[eɪ]
	receive	\ē\	[i:]
eo	luncheon	\ə\	[ə]
eu	rheumatism	\ü\	[u:]
ew	crew	\ü\	[u:]
ey	key	\ē\	[i:]
	prey	\ā\	[eɪ]
f	fan	\f\	[f]
ff	offer	\f\	[f]
g	go	\g\	[g]
	gem	\j\	[dʒ]
gg	egg	\g\	[g]
	exaggerate	\j\	[dʒ]
gh	ghost	\g\	[g]
	laugh	\f\	[f]
gi	region	\j\	[dʒ]
gn	sign	\n\	[n]
gu	guide	\g\	[g]
h	hat	\h\	[h]
i	vaccinate	\ə\	[ə]
	ski	\ē\	[i:]
	tip	\i\	[ɪ]
	fine	\ī\	[aɪ]
	opinion	\y\	[j]
ie	grief	\ē\	[i:]
	lie	\ī\	[aɪ]
ia	collegiate	\ə\	[ə]
io	cushion	\ə\	[ə]
j	joy	\j\	[dʒ]

SOUND & SPELLING IN ENGLISH

k	take	\k\	[k]			sugar	\sh\	[ʃ]
kn	knot	\n\	[n]			days	\z\	[z]
l	low	\l\	[l]		sc	science	\s\	[s]
ll	dollar	\l\	[l]			fascism	\sh\	[ʃ]
m	me	\m\	[m]		sch	schist	\sh\	[ʃ]
mb	comb	\m\	[m]		sci	conscious	\sh\	[ʃ]
mn	autumn	\m\	[m]		se	nauseous	\sh\	[ʃ]
n	no	\n\	[n]		sh	shy	\sh\	[ʃ]
	ink	\ŋ\	[ŋ]		si	vision	\zh\	[ʒ]
ng	sing	\ŋ\	[ŋ]		ss	mass	\s\	[s]
nn	banner	\n\	[n]			tissue	\sh\	[ʃ]
o	hillock	\ə\	[ə]		ssi	mission	\sh\	[ʃ]
	above	\ə\	[ʌ]		t	eat	\t\	[t]
	cot	\ä\	[ɑ]		tch	match	\ch\	[tʃ]
	bone	\ō\	[o:]		th	thin	\th\	[θ]
	do	\ü\	[u:]			this	\th\	[ð]
	woman	\u̇\	[ʊ]		ti	question	\ch\	[tʃ]
oa	boat	\ō\	[o:]			nation	\sh\	[ʃ]
oe	doe	\ō\	[o:]		tt	mattress	\t\	[t]
oh	oh	\ō\	[o:]		u	circus	\ə\	[ə]
oi	coin	\ȯi\	[ɔɪ]			hum	\ə\	[ʌ]
oo	school	\ü\	[u:]			flu	\ü\	[u:]
	wood	\u̇\	[ʊ]			pull	\u̇\	[ʊ]
ou	loud	\au̇\	[aʊ]			persuade	\w\	[w]
	boulder	\ō\	[o:]		ue	blue	\ü\	[u:]
	youth	\ü\	[u:]		v	very	\v\	[v]
	could	\u̇\	[ʊ]		vv	savvy	\v\	[v]
	famous	\ə\	[ə]		w	way	\w\	[w]
	rough	\ə\	[ʌ]		wh	whale	\w\	[w]
ow	now	\au̇\	[aʊ]		wr	write	\r\	[r]
	know	\ō\	[o:]		x	xylophone	\z\	[z]
oy	boy	\ȯi\	[ɔɪ]		y	physician	\ə\	[ə]
p	stop	\p\	[p]			pretty	\ē\	[i]
ph	telephone	\f\	[f]			myth	\i\	[ɪ]
pp	supper	\p\	[p]			sly	\ī\	[aɪ]
qu	liquor	\k\	[k]			yard	\y\	[j]
r	red	\r\	[r]		ye	dye	\ī\	[aɪ]
rh	rhyme	\r\	[r]		z	zone	\z\	[z]
rr	arrive	\r\	[r]		zi	glazier	\zh\	[ʒ]
s	say	\s\	[s]		zz	buzz	\z\	[z]

	Spanish	English		Spanish	English
adj	adjetivo	adjective	nfs & pl	sustantivo femenino invariable singular o plural	invariable singular or plural feminine noun
adv	adverbio	adverb	nm	sustantivo masculino´	masculine noun
adv phr	frase adverbial	adverbial phrase	nmf	sustantivo masculino o femenino	masculine or feminine noun
algn	alguien	someone	nmfpl	sustantivo plural invariable para género	plural noun invariable for gender
art	artículo	article	nmfs & pl	sustantivo invariable para género y número	noun invariable for both gender and number
Brit	Gran Bretaña	Great Britain	nmpl	sustantivo masculino plural	masculine plural noun
conj	conjunción	conjunction	nms & pl	sustantivo masculino invariable singular o plural	invariable singular or plural masculine noun
conj phr	frase conjuntiva	conjunctive phrase	npl	sustantivo plural	plural noun
esp	especialmente	especially	ns & pl	sustantivo invariable en plural	noun invariable for plural
etc	etcétera	et cetera	pl	plural	plural
f	femenino	feminine	pp	participio pasado	past participle
fam	familiar, informal, coloquial	familiar, informal, colloquial	prep	preposición	preposition
fpl	femenino plural	feminine plural	prep phr	frase preposicional	prepositional phrase
interj	interjección	interjection	pron	pronombre	pronoun
Lat	América Latina	Latin America	usu	normalmente	usually
m	masculino	masculine	v	verbo	verb
mf	masculino o femenino	masculine or feminine	v aux	verbo auxiliar	auxiliary verb
mpl	masculino plural	masculine plural	vi	verbo intransitivo	intransitive verb
n	sustantivo	noun	v impers	verbo impersonal	impersonal verb
nf	sustantivo femenino	feminine noun	vr	verbo reflexivo	reflexive verb
nfpl	sustantivo femenino plural	feminine plural noun	vt	verbo transitivo	transitive verb

ESPAÑOL-INGLÉS

a[1] *nf* : a, first letter of the Spanish alphabet

a[2] *prep* **1** : to **2 a las dos** : at two o'clock **3 al día siguiente** : (on) the following day **4 a pied** : on foot **5 de lunes a viernes** : from Monday until Friday **6 tres veces a la semana** : three times per week **7 a la** : in the manner of, like

abadía *nf* : abbey

abajo *adv* **1** : down, below, downstairs **2 abajo de** *Lat* : under, beneath **3 de abajo** : (at the) bottom **4 hacia abajo** : downwards

abalanzarse {21} *vr* : hurl oneself, rush

abandonar *vt* **1** : abandon, leave **2** RENUNCIAR A : give up — **abandonarse** *vr* **1** : neglect oneself **2 abandonarse a** : give oneself over to — **abandonado, -da** *adj* **1** : abandoned, deserted **2** DESCUIDADO : neglected **3** DESALIÑADO : slovenly — **abandono** *nm* **1** : abandonment, neglect **2 por abandono** : by default

abanico *nm* : fan — **abanicar** {72} *vt* : fan

abaratar *vt* : lower the price of — **abaratarse** *vr* : become cheaper

abarcar {72} *vt* **1** : cover, embrace **2** *Lat* : monopolize

abarrotar *vt* : pack, cram — **abarrotes** *nmpl Lat* **1** : groceries **2 tienda de abarrotes** : grocery store

abastecer {53} *vt* : supply, stock — **abastecimiento** *nm* : supply, provisions — **abasto** *nm* **1** : supply **2 no dar abasto a** : be unable to cope with

abatir *vt* **1** : knock down, shoot down **2** DEPRIMIR : depress — **abatirse** *vr* **1** : get depressed **2 abatirse sobre** : swoop down on — **abatido, -da** *adj* : dejected, depressed — **abatimiento** *nm* : depression, dejection

abdicar {72} *v* : abdicate — **abdicación** *nf, pl* **-ciones** : abdication

abdomen *nm, pl* **-dómenes** : abdomen — **abdominal** *adj* : abdominal

abecé *nm* : ABC — **abecedario** *nm* : alphabet

abedul *nm* : birch

abeja *nf* : bee — **abejorro** *nm* : bumblebee

aberración *nf, pl* **-ciones** : aberration

abertura *nf* : opening

abeto *nm* : fir (tree)

abierto, -ta *adj* : open

abigarrado, -da *adj* : multicolored

abismo *nm* : abyss, chasm — **abismal** *adj* : vast, enormous

abjurar *vi* **abjurar de** : abjure

ablandar *vt* : soften (up) — **ablandarse** *vr* : soften

abnegarse {49} *vr* : deny oneself — **abnegado, -da** *adj* : self-sacrificing — **abnegación** *nf, pl* **-ciones** : self-denial

abochornar *vt* : embarrass — **abochornarse** *vr* : get embarrassed

abofetear *vt* : slap

abogado, -da *n* : lawyer — **abogacía** *nf* : legal profession — **abogar** {52} *vi* **abogar por** : plead for, defend

abolengo *nm* : lineage

abolir {1} *vt* : abolish — **abolición** *nf,*

abrigos^M
coats

cazadora^F
jacket

parka^F
parka

trinchera^F
trench coat

trenca^F
duffle coat

pl **-ciones** : abolition
abollar *vt* : dent — **abolladura** *nf* : dent
abominar *vt* : abominate —
abominable *adj* : abominable —
abominación *nf, pl* **-ciones** : abomination
abonar *vt* **1** : pay (a bill, etc.) **2** :
fertilize (the soil) — **abonarse** *vr*
: subscribe — **abonado, -da** *n* :
subscriber — **abono** *nm* **1** : payment,
installment **2** FERTILIZANTE : fertilizer **3**
: season ticket (to the theater, etc.)
abordar *vt* **1** : tackle (a problem) **2**
: accost, approach (a person) **3** *Lat* :
board — **abordaje** *nm* : boarding
aborigen *nmf, pl* **-rígenes** : aborigine
— **aborigen** *adj* : aboriginal, native
aborrecer {53} *vt* : abhor, detest
— **aborrecible** *adj* : hateful —
aborrecimiento *nm* : loathing
abortar *vi* : have a miscarriage — *vt* :
abort — **aborto** *nm* : abortion, miscarriage
abotonar *vt* : button —
abotonarse *vr* : button up
abovedado, -da *adj* : vaulted
abrasar *vt* : burn, scorch — **abrasarse** *vr*
: burn up — **abrasador, -dora** *adj* : burning
abrasivo, -va *adj* : abrasive
— **abrasivo** *nm* : abrasive
abrazar {21} *vt* : hug, embrace —
abrazarse *vr* : embrace — **abrazadera** *nf*
: clamp — **abrazo** *nm* : hug, embrace
abrebotellas *nms & pl* : bottle opener
— **abrelatas** *nms & pl* : can opener
abrevadero *nm* : watering trough
abreviar *vt* **1** : shorten, abridge
2 : abbreviate (a word) —
abreviación *nf, pl* **-ciones** : shortening
— **abreviatura** *nf* : abbreviation
abridor *nm* : bottle opener, can opener
abrigar {52} *vt* **1** : wrap up (in clothing)
2 ALBERGAR : cherish, harbor —
abrigarse *vr* : dress warmly — **abrigado,
-da** *adj* **1** : sheltered **2** : warm, wrapped
up (of persons) — abrigo *nm* **1** : coat,
overcoat **2** REFUGIO : shelter, refuge
abril *nm* : April
abrillantar *vt* : polish, shine
abrir {2} *vt* **1** : open **2** : unlock, undo
— *vi* : open up — **abrirse** *vr* **1** :
open up **2** : clear up (of weather)
abrochar *vt* : button, fasten —
abrocharse *vr* : fasten, do up
abrogar {52} *vt* : annul, repeal
abrumar *vt* : overwhelm — **abrumador,
-dora** *adj* : overwhelming, oppressive

abrupto, -ta *adj* **1** ESCARPADO
: steep **2** ÁSPERO : rugged,
harsh **3** REPENTINO : abrupt
absceso *nm* : abscess
absolución *nf, pl* **-ciones 1** :
absolution **2** : acquittal (in law)
absoluto, -ta *adj* **1** : absolute,
unconditional **2 en absoluto** : not at all
— **absolutamente** *adv* : absolutely
absolver {89} *vt* **1** : absolve
2 : acquit (in law)
absorber *vt* **1** : absorb **2** : take up (time,
energy, etc.) — **absorbente** *adj* **1** :
absorbent **2** INTERESANTE : absorbing —
absorción *nf, pl* **-ciones** : absorption —
absorto, -ta *adj* : absorbed, engrossed
abstemio, -mia *adj* : abstemious
— **abstemio, -mia** *n* : teetotaler
abstenerse {80} *vr* : abstain, refrain —
abstención *nf, pl* **-ciones** : abstention
— **abstinencia** *nf* : abstinence
abstracción *nf, pl* **-ciones** : abstraction
— **abstracto, -ta** *adj* : abstract
— **abstraer** {81} *vt* : abstract —
abstraerse *vr* : lose oneself in thought
— **abstraído, -da** *adj* : preoccupied
absurdo, -da *adj* : absurd, ridiculous
— **absurdo** *nm* : absurdity
abuchear *vt* : boo, jeer —
abucheo *nm* : booing
abuelo, -la *n* **1** : grandfather,
grandmother **2** abuelos *nmpl*
: grandparents
abulia *nf* : apathy, lethargy
abultar *vi* : bulge, be bulky — *vt* : enlarge,
expand — **abultado, -da** *adj* : bulky
abundar *vi* : abound, be plentiful
— **abundancia** *nf* : abundance
— **abundante** *adj* : abundant
aburrir *vt* : bore — **aburrirse** *vr* :
get bored — **aburrido, -da** *adj* **1**
: bored **2** TEDIOSO : boring —
aburrimiento *nm* : boredom
abusar *vi* **1** : go too far **2 abusar de** :
abuse — **abusivo, -va** *adj* : outrageous,
excessive — **abuso** *nm* : abuse
abyecto, -ta *adj* : abject, wretched
acá *adv* : here, over here
acabar *vi* **1** : finish, end **2 acabar de**
: have just (done something) **3 acabar
con** : put an end to **4 acabar por** : end
up (doing something) — *vt* : finish —
acabarse *vr* : come to an end — **acabado,
-da** *adj* **1** : finished, perfect **2** AGOTADO :
old, worn-out — **acabado** *nm* : finish

academia *nf* : academy —
académico, -ca *adj* : academic
acaecer {53} *vi* : happen, occur
acallar *vt* : quiet, silence
acalorar *vt* : stir up, excite —
acalorarse *vr* : get worked up —
acalorado, -da *adj* : emotional, heated
acampar *vi* : camp — **acampada** *nf*
ir de acampar : go camping
acanalado, -da *adj* **1** : grooved
2 : corrugated (of iron, etc.)
acantilado *nm* : cliff
acaparar *vt* **1** : hoard **2**
MONOPOLIZAR : monopolize
acápite *nm Lat* : paragraph
acariciar *vt* **1** : caress **2** :
cherish (hopes, ideas, etc.)
ácaro *nm* : mite
acarrear *vt* **1** : haul, carry **2** OCASIONAR
: give rise to — **acarreo** *nm* : transport
acaso *adv* **1** : perhaps, maybe
2 por si acaso : just in case
acatar *vt* : comply with, respect —
acatamiento *nm* : compliance, respect
acatarrarse *vr* : catch a cold
acaudalado, -da *adj* : wealthy, rich
acaudillar *vt* : lead
acceder *vi* **1** : agree **2 acceder
a** : gain access to, enter
acceso *nm* **1** : access **2** ENTRADA :
entrance **3** : attack, bout (of an illness)
— **accesible** *adj* : accessible
accesorio *nm* : accessory —
accesorio, -ria *adj* : incidental
accidentado, -da *adj* **1** : eventful,
turbulent **2** : rough, uneven (of
land, etc.) **3** HERIDO : injured —
accidentado, -da *n* : accident victim
accidental *adj* : accidental —
accidentarse *vr* : have an accident
— **accidente** *nm* **1** : accident
2 : unevenness (of land)
acción *nf, pl* **-ciones 1** : action **2** ACTO :
act, deed **3** : share, stock (in finance) —
accionar *vt* : activate — *vi* : gesticulate
— **accionista** *nmf* : stockholder
acebo *nm* : holly
acechar *vt* : watch, stalk — **acecho** *nm*
estar al acecho por : be on the lookout for
aceite *nm* : oil — **aceitar** *vt* : oil
— **aceitera** *nf* **1** : oilcan **2** : cruet
(in cookery) **3** *Lat* : oil refinery
— **aceitoso, -sa** *adj* : oily
aceituna *nf* : olive
acelerar *v* : accelerate — **acelerarse** *vr*

: hurry up — **aceleración** *nf,*
pl **-ciones** : acceleration —
acelerador *nm* : accelerator
acelga *nf* : (Swiss) chard
acentuar {3} *vt* **1** : accent **2** ENFATIZAR
: emphasize, stress — **acentuarse** *vr*
: stand out — **acento** *nm* **1** : accent
2 ÉNFASIS : stress, emphasis
acepción *nf, pl* **-ciones** : sense, meaning
aceptar *vt* : accept — **aceptable** *adj* :
acceptable — **aceptación** *nf, pl* **-ciones**
1 : acceptance **2** ÉXITO : success
acequia *nf* : irrigation ditch
acera *nf* : sidewalk
acerbo, -ba *adj* : harsh, caustic
acerca *prep* **acerca de** :
about, concerning
acercar {72} *vt* : bring near or closer
— **acercarse** *vr* : approach, draw near
acero *nm* **1** : steel **2 acero**
inoxidable : stainless steel
acérrimo, -ma *adj* **1** : staunch,
steadfast **2** : bitter (of an enemy)
acertar {55} *vt* : guess correctly — *vi* **1**
ATINAR : be accurate **2 acertar a** : manage
to — **acertado, -da** *adj* : correct, accurate
acertijo *nm* : riddle
acervo *nm* : heritage
acetona *nf* : acetone, nail-polish remover
achacar {72} *vt* : attribute, impute
achacoso, -sa *adj* : sickly
achaparrado, -da *adj* : squat, stocky
achaque *nm* : aches and pains
achatar *vt* : flatten
achicar {72} *vt* **1** : make smaller **2**
ACOBARDAR : intimidate **3** : bail out (water)
— **achicarse** *vr* : become intimidated
achicharrar *vt* : scorch, burn to a crisp
achicoria *nf* : chicory
aciago, -ga *adj* : fateful, unlucky
acicalar *vt* : dress up, adorn —
acicalarse *vr* : get dressed up
acicate *nm* **1** : spur **2**
INCENTIVO : incentive
ácido, -da *adj* : acid, sour — **acidez** *nf,*
pl **-deces** : acidity — **ácido** *nm* : acid
acierto *nm* **1** : correct answer **2**
HABILIDAD : skill, sound judgment
aclamar *vt* : acclaim — **aclamación** *nf,*
pl **-ciones** : acclaim, applause
aclarar *vt* **1** CLARIFICAR : clarify,
explain **2** : rinse (clothing) **3 aclarar**
la voz : clear one's throat — *vi* : clear
up — **aclararse** *vr* : become clear —
aclaración *nf, pl* **-ciones** : explanation

— **aclaratorio, -ria** *adj* : explanatory
aclimatar *vt* : acclimatize —
aclimatarse *vr* **aclimatarse a** :
get used to — **aclimatación** *nf,*
pl **-ciones** : acclimatization
acné *nm* : acne
acobardar *vt* : intimidate —
acobardarse *vr* : become frightened
acodarse *vr* **acodarse en** :
lean (one's elbows) on
acoger {15} *vt* **1** REFUGIAR : shelter
2 RECIBIR : receive, welcome —
acogerse *vr* **1** : take refuge **2 acogerse**
a : resort to — **acogedor, -dora** *adj*
: cozy, welcoming — **acogida** *nf* **1**
: welcome **2** REFUGIO : refuge
acolchar *vt* : pad
acólito *nm* MONAGUILLO : altar boy
acometer *vt* **1** : attack **2** EMPRENDER :
undertake — *vi* **acometer contra** : rush
against — **acometida** *nf* : attack, assault
acomodar *vt* **1** ADAPTAR : adjust
2 COLOCAR : put, make a place for
— **acomodarse** *vr* **1** : settle in **2**
acomodarse a : adapt to — **acomodado,**
-da *adj* : well-to-do — **acomodaticio,**
-cia *adj* : accommodating, obliging
— **acomodo** *nm* : job, position
acompañar *vt* **1** : accompany
2 ADJUNTAR : enclose —
acompañamiento *nm* : accompaniment
— **acompañante** *nmf* **1** COMPAÑERO :
companion **2** : accompanist (in music)
acompasado, -da *adj* :
rhythmic, measured
acondicionar *vt* : fit out, equip —
acondicionado, -da *adj* : equipped
acongojar *vt* : distress, upset
— **acongojarse** *vr* : get upset
aconsejar *vt* : advise —
aconsejable *adj* : advisable
acontecer {53} *vi* : occur, happen
— **acontecimiento** *nm* : event
acopiar *vt* : gather, collect —
acopio *nm* : collection, stock
acoplar *vt* : couple, connect
— **acoplarse** *vr* : fit together —
acoplamiento *nm* : connection, coupling
acorazado, -da *adj* : armored
— **acorazado** *nm* : battleship
acordar {19} *vt* **1** : agree (on) **2** *Lat* :
award — **acordarse** *vr* : remember
acorde 1 : in agreement **2**
acorde con : in keeping with —
acorde *nm* : chord (in music)

acordeón *nm, pl* **-deones** : accordion
acordonar *vt* **1** : cordon
off **2** : lace up (shoes)
acorralar *vt* : corner, corral
acortar *vt* : shorten, cut short
— **acortarse** *vr* : get shorter
acosar *vt* : hound, harass —
acoso *nm* : harassment
acostar {19} *vt* : put to bed
— **acostarse** *vr* **1** : go to bed
2 TUMBARSE : lie down
acostumbrar *vt* : accustom — *vi*
acostumbrar a : be in the habit of —
acostumbrarse *vr* **acostumbrarse a** :
get used to — **acostumbrado, -da** *adj* **1**
HABITUADO : accustomed **2** HABITUAL : usual
acotar *vt* **1** ANOTAR : annotate
2 DELIMITAR : mark off (land) —
acotación *nf, pl* **-ciones** : marginal
note — **acotado, -da** *adj* : enclosed
acre *adj* **1** : pungent **2**
MORDAZ : harsh, biting
acrecentar {55} *vt* : increase —
acrecentamiento *nm* : growth, increase
acreditar *vt* **1** : accredit, authorize
2 PROBAR : prove — **acreditarse** *vr* :
prove oneself — **acreditado, -da** *adj* **1** :
reputable **2** : accredited (in politics, etc.)
acreedor, -dora *adj* : worthy —
acreedor, -dora *n* : creditor
acribillar *vt* **1** : riddle, pepper
2 acribillar a : harass with
acrílico *nm* : acrylic
acrimonia *nf or* acritud *nf* **1** : pungency
2 RESENTIMIENTO : bitterness, acrimony
acrobacia *nf* : acrobatics
— **acróbata** *nmf* : acrobat —
acrobático, -ca *adj* : acrobatic
acta *nf* **1** : certificate **2** :
minutes *pl* (of a meeting)
actitud *nf* **1** : attitude **2**
POSTURA : posture, position
activar *vt* **1** : activate **2** ESTIMULAR :
stimulate, speed up — **actividad** *nf*
: activity — **activo, -va** *adj* : active
— **activo** *nm* : assets *pl*
acto *nm* **1** ACCIÓN : act, deed **2** : act
(in theater) **3 en el acto** : right away
actor *nm* : actor — **actriz** *nf,*
pl **-trices** : actress
actual *adj* : present, current —
actualidad *nf* **1** : present time **2**
actuales *nfpl* : current affairs —
actualizar {21} *vt* : modernize
— **actualización** *nf, pl* **-ciones** :

guitarra^F **acústica**
acoustic guitar

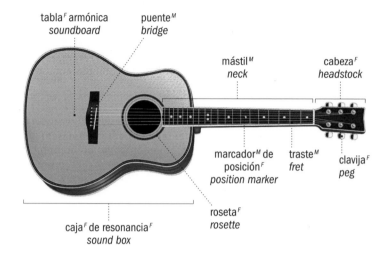

tabla^F armónica
soundboard

puente^M
bridge

mástil^M
neck

cabeza^F
headstock

marcador^M de
posición^F
position marker

traste^M
fret

clavija^F
peg

roseta^F
rosette

caja^F de resonancia^F
sound box

---

modernization — **actualmente** *adv*
: at present, nowadays
actuar {3} *vi* **1** : act, perform
2 actuar de : act as
acuarela *nf* : watercolor
acuario *nm* : aquarium
acuartelar *vt* : quarter (troops)
acuático, -ca *adj* : aquatic, water
acuchillar *vt* : knife, stab
acudir *vi* **1** : go, come **2 acudir a** : be
present at, attend **3 acudir a** : turn to
acueducto *nm* : aqueduct
acuerdo *nm* **1** : agreement **2**
de acuerdo : OK, all right **3 de**
acuerdo con : in accordance with
4 estar de acuerdo : agree
acumular *vt* : accumulate
— **acumularse** *vr* : pile up —
acumulación *nf, pl* **-ciones** : accumulation
— **acumulador** *nm* : storage battery
— **acumulativo, -va** *adj* : cumulative
acunar *vt* : rock
acuñar *vt* **1** : mint (money)
2 : coin (a word)
acuoso, -sa *adj* : watery
acupuntura *nf* : acupuncture
acurrucarse {72} *vr* : curl up, nestle
acusar *vt* **1** : accuse **2** MOSTRAR
: reveal, show — **acusación** *nf,*
pl **-ciones** : accusation, charge

— **acusado, -da** *adj* : prominent,
marked — **acusado, -da** *n* : defendant
acuse *nm* **acuse de recibo** :
acknowledgment of receipt
▸ **acústica** *nf* : acoustics —
acústico, -ca *adj* : acoustic
adagio *nm* **1** REFRÁN : adage,
proverb **2** : adagio (in music)
adaptar *vt* **1** : adapt **2** AJUSTAR : adjust,
fit — **adaptarse** *vr* **adaptarse a** : adapt
to — **adaptable** *adj* : adaptable —
adaptación *nf, pl* **-ciones** : adaptation —
adaptador *nm* : adapter (in electricity)
adecuar {8} *vt* : adapt, make suitable
— **adecuarse** *vr* **adecuarse a** :
be appropriate for — **adecuado,**
-da *adj* : suitable, appropriate
adelantar *vt* **1** : advance, move forward
2 PASAR : overtake **3** : pay in advance
— **adelantarse** *vr* **1** : move forward,
get ahead **2** : be fast (of a clock) —
adelantado, -da *adj* **1** : advanced, ahead
2 : fast (of a clock) **3 por adelantado**
: in advance — **adelante** *adv* **1** :
ahead, forward **2 ¡adelante!** : come
in! **3 más adelante** : later on, further
on — **adelanto** *nm* **1** : advance **2** *or*
adelanto de dinero : advance payment
adelgazar {21} *vt* : make
thin — *vi* : lose weight

ademán *nm, pl* **-manes 1** GESTO :
gesture **2** ademánes *nmpl* : manners
3 en ademán de : as if to
además *adv* **1** : besides, furthermore **2**
además de : in addition to, as well as
adentro *adv* : inside, within
— **adentrarse** *vr* **adentrarse**
en : go into, get inside of
adepto, -ta *n* : follower, supporter
aderezar {21} *vt* : season, dress —
aderezo *nm* : dressing, seasoning
adeudar *vt* **1** : debit **2** DEBER : owe —
adeudo *nm* **1** DÉBITO : debit **2** *Lat* : debt
adherirse {76} *vr* : adhere, stick
— **adherencia** *nf* : adherence —
adhesión *nf, pl* **-siones 1** : adhesion **2**
APOYO : support — **adhesivo, -va** *adj* :
adhesive — **adhesivo** *nm* : adhesive
adición *nf, pl* **-ciones** : addition
— **adicional** *adj* : additional
adicto, -ta *adj* : addicted —
adicto, -ta *n* : addict
adiestrar *vt* : train
adinerado, -da *adj* : wealthy
adiós *nm, pl* **adioses 1** : farewell
2 ¡adiós! : good-bye!
aditamento *nm* : attachment, accessory
aditivo *nm* : additive
adivinar *vt* **1** : guess **2** PREDECIR :
foretell — **adivinación** *nf, pl* **-ciones** :
guessing, prediction — **adivinanza** *nf* :
riddle — **adivino, -na** *n* : fortune-teller
adjetivo *nm* : adjective
adjudicar {72} *vt* : award —
adjudicarse *vr* : appropriate —
adjudicación *nf, pl* **-ciones** : awarding
adjuntar *vt* : enclose (with a letter,
etc.) — **adjunto, -ta** *adj* : enclosed,
attached — **adjunto, -ta** *n* : assistant
administración *nf, pl* **-ciones 1** :
administration **2** : administering (of a
drug, etc.) **3** DIRECCIÓN : management —
administrador, -dora *n* : administrator,
manager — **administrar** *vt* **1** : manage,
run **2** : administer (a drug, etc.) —
administrativo, -va *adj* : administrative
admirar *vt* : admire — **admirarse** *vr*
: be amazed — **admirable** *adj* :
admirable — **admiración** *nf, pl* **-ciones**
1 : admiration **2** ASOMBRO : amazement
— **admirador, -dora** *n* : admirer
admitir *vt* **1** : admit **2** ACEPTAR :
accept — **admisible** *adj* : admissible,
acceptable — **admisión** *nf, pl* **-siones 1**
: admission **2** ACEPTACIÓN : acceptance

ADN *nm* : DNA
adobe *nm* : adobe
adobo *nm* : marinade
adoctrinar *vt* : indoctrinate —
  adoctrinamiento *nm* : indoctrination
adolecer {53} *vi* **adolecer de** : suffer from
adolescente *adj & nmf* : adolescent
  — **adolescencia** *nf* : adolescence
adonde *conj* : where
adónde *adv* : where
adoptar *vt* : adopt (a child), take
  (a decision) — **adopción** *nf*,
  pl -**ciones** : adoption — **adoptivo**,
  -**va** *adj* : adopted, adoptive
adoquín *nm, pl* -**quines** : cobblestone
adorar *vt* : adore, worship —
  adorable *adj* : adorable — **adoración** *nf*,
  pl -**ciones** : adoration, worship
adormecer {53} *vt* **1** : make sleepy **2**
  ENTUMECER : numb — **adormecerse** *vr*

: doze off — **adormecimiento** *nm* :
  drowsiness — **adormilarse** *vr* : doze
adornar *vt* : decorate, adorn —
  adorno *nm* : ornament, decoration
adquirir {4} *vt* **1** : acquire **2** COMPRAR :
  purchase — **adquisición** *nf, pl* -**ciones**
  1 : acquisition **2** COMPRA : purchase
adrede *adv* : intentionally, on purpose
adscribir {33} *vt* : assign, appoint
aduana *nf* : customs (office) —
  aduanero, -ra *adj* : customs —
  aduana *n* : customs officer
aducir {61} *vt* : cite, put forward
adueñarse *vr* **adueñarse**
  de : take possession of
adular *vt* : flatter — **adulación** *nf*,
  pl -**ciones** : adulation, flattery —
  adulador, -dora *adj* : flattering —
  adulador, -dora *n* : flatterer
adulterar *vt* : adulterate

adulterio *nm* : adultery —
  adúltero, -ra *n* : adulterer
adulto, -ta *adj & n* : adult
adusto, -ta *adj* : stern, severe
advenedizo, -za *n* : upstart
advenimiento *nm* : advent, arrival
adverbio *nm* : adverb —
  adverbial *adj* : adverbial
adversario, -ria *n* : adversary,
  opponent — **adverso, -sa** *adj* :
  adverse — **adversidad** *nf* : adversity
advertir {76} *vt* **1** AVISAR : warn **2** NOTAR
  : notice — **advertencia** *nf* : warning
adviento *nm* : Advent
adyacente *adj* : adjacent
▸ **aéreo, -rea** *adj* : aerial, air
aerobic *nm* : aerobics *pl*
aerodinámico, -ca *adj* : aerodynamic
aeródromo *nm* : airfield
aerolínea *nf* : airline

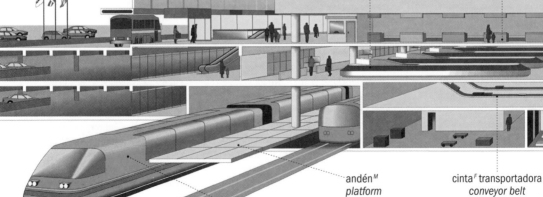
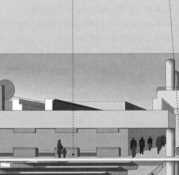

terminal^M aéreo
airport passenger terminal

control^M de seguridad^F
security check

entrega^F de equipaje^M
baggage claim area

facturación^F de equipaje^M
baggage check-in counter

andén^M
platform

cinta^F transportadora
conveyor belt

servicio^M de enlace^M ferroviario
railroad shuttle service

aeromozo, -za *n* : flight attendant, steward *m*, stewardess *f*

aeronave *nf* : aircraft

aeropuerto *nm* : airport

aerosol *nm* : aerosol, spray

afable *adj* : affable — **afabilidad** *nf* : affability

afán *nm, pl* **afanes 1** ANHELO : eagerness **2** EMPEÑO : effort, hard work — **afanarse** *vr* : toil — **afanosamente** *adv* : industriously, busily — **afanoso, -sa** *adj* **1** : eager **2** TRABAJOSO : arduous

afear *vt* : make ugly, disfigure

afección *nf, pl* -**ciones** : ailment, complaint

afectar *vt* : affect — **afectación** *nf, pl* -**ciones** : affectation — **afectado, -da** *adj* : affected

afectivo, -va *adj* : emotional

afecto *nm* : affection — **afecto, -ta** *adj* **afecto a** : fond of — **afectuoso, -sa** *adj* : affectionate, caring

afeitar *vt* : shave — **afeitarse** *vr* : shave — **afeitada** *nf* : shave

afeminado, -da *adj* : effeminate

aferrarse {55} *vr* : cling, hold on

afianzar {21} *vt* : secure, strengthen — **afianzarse** *vr* : become established

afiche *nm Lat* : poster

afición *nf, pl* -**ciones 1** : penchant, fondness **2** PASATIEMPO : hobby — **aficionado, -da** *n* **1** ENTUSIASTA : enthusiast, fan **2** AMATEUR : amateur — **aficionarse** *vr* **aficiónarse a** : become interested in

afilar *vt* : sharpen — **afilado, -da** *adj* : sharp — **afilador** *nm* : sharpener

afiliarse *vr* **afiliarse a** : join, become a member of — **afiliación** *nf, pl* -**ciones** : affiliation — **afiliado, -da** *adj* : affiliated

afín *adj, pl* **afines** : related, similar — **afinidad** *nf* : affinity, similarity

afinar *vt* **1** : tune **2** PULIR : perfect, refine

afirmar *vt* **1** : state, affirm **2** REFORZAR : strengthen — **afirmación** *nf, pl* -**ciones** : statement, affirmation — **afirmativo, -va** *adj* : affirmative

afligir {35} *vt* **1** : afflict **2** APENAR : distress — **afligirse** *vr* : grieve — **aflicción** *nf, pl* -**ciones** : grief, sorrow — **afligido -da** *adj* : sorrowful, distressed

aflojar *vt* : loosen, slacken — *vi* : ease up — **aflojarse** *vr* : become loose, slacken

aflorar *vi* : come to the surface, emerge — **afloramiento** *nm* : outcrop

afluencia *nf* : influx — **afluente** *nm* : tributary

afortunado, -da *adj* : fortunate, lucky — **afortunadamente** *adv* : fortunately

afrentar *vt* : insult — **afrenta** *nf*

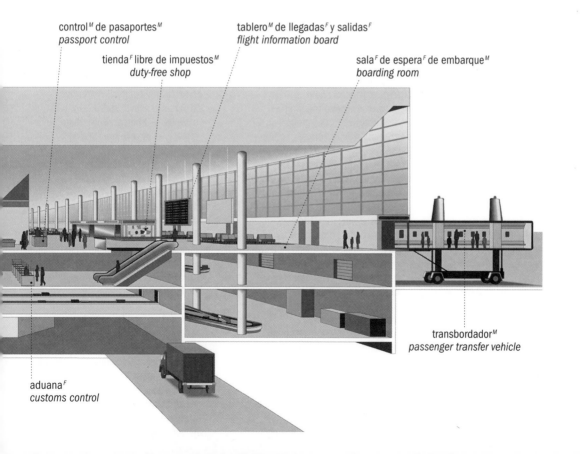

control^M de pasaportes^M
passport control

tablero^M de llegadas^F y salidas^F
flight information board

tienda^F libre de impuestos^M
duty-free shop

sala^F de espera^F de embarque^M
boarding room

transbordador^M
passenger transfer vehicle

aduana^F
customs control

: affront, insult

africano, -na *adj* : African

afrontar *vt* : confront, face

afuera *adv* **1** : out **2** : outside, outdoors — **afueras** *nfpl* : outskirts

agachar *vt* : lower — **agacharse** *vr* : crouch, stoop

agalla *nf* **1** BRANQUIA : gill **2 tener agallas** *fam* : have guts

agarrar *vt* **1** ASIR : grasp **2** *Lat* : catch — **agarrarse** *vr* : hold on, cling — **agarradera** *nf Lat* : handle — **agarrado, -da** *adj, fam* : stingy — **agarre** *nm* : grip, grasp — **agarrón** *nm, pl* **-rones** : tug, pull

agasajar *vt* : fête, wine and dine — **agasajo** *nm* : lavish attention

agave *nm* : agave

agazaparse *vr* : crouch down

agencia *nf* : agency, office — **agente** *nmf* : agent, officer

agenda *nf* **1** : agenda **2** LIBRETA : notebook

ágil *adj* : agile — **agilidad** *nf* : agility

agitar *vt* **1** : agitate, shake **2** : wave, flap (wings, etc.) **3** PERTURBAR : stir up — **agitarse** *vr* **1** : toss about **2** INQUIETARSE : get upset — **agitación** *nf, pl* **-ciones 1** : agitation, shaking **2** INTRANQUILIDAD : restlessness — **agitado, -da** *adj* **1** : agitated, excited **2** : choppy, rough (of the sea)

aglomerar *vt* : amass — **aglomerarse** *vr* : crowd together

agnóstico, -ca *adj & n* : agnostic

agobiar *vt* **1** : oppress **2** ABRUMAR : overwhelm — **agobiado, -da** *adj* : weary, weighed down — **agobiante** *adj* : oppressing, oppressive

agonizar {21} *vi* : be dying — **agonía** *nf* **1** : death throes **2** PENA : agony — **agonizante** *adj* : dying

agorero, -ra *adj* : ominous

agostar *vt* : wither

agosto *nm* : August

agotar *vt* **1** : deplete, use up **2** CANSAR : exhaust, weary — **agotarse** *vr* **1** : run out, give out **2** CANSARSE : get tired — **agotado, -da** *adj* **1** CANSADO : exhausted **2** : sold out — **agotador, -dora** *adj* : exhausting — **agotamiento** *nm* : exhaustion

agraciado, -da *adj* **1** : attractive **2** AFORTUNADO : fortunate

agradar *vi* : be pleasing — **agradable** *adj* : pleasant, agreeable — **agrado** *nm* **1** :

taste, liking **2 con agrado** : with pleasure

agradecer {53} *vt* : be grateful for, thank — **agradecido, -da** *adj* : grateful — **agradecimiento** *nm* : gratitude

agrandar *vt* : enlarge — **agrandarse** *vr* : grow larger

agrario, -ria *adj* : agrarian, agricultural

agravar *vt* **1** : make heavier **2** EMPEORAR : aggravate, worsen — **agravarse** *vr* : get worse

agraviar *vt* : insult — **agravio** *nm* : insult

agredir {1} *vt* : attack

agregar {52} *vt* : add, attach — **agregado, -da** *n* : attaché — **agregado** *nm* : aggregate

agresión *nf, pl* **-siones** : aggression, attack — **agresividad** *nf* : aggressiveness — **agresivo, -va** *adj* : aggressive — **agresor, -sora** *n* : aggressor, attacker

agreste *adj* : rugged, wild

agriar *vt* : sour — **agriarse** *vr* **1** : turn sour (of milk, etc.) **2** : become embittered

agrícola *adj* : agricultural — **agricultura** *nf* : agriculture, farming — **agricultor, -tora** *n* : farmer

agridulce *adj* **1** : bittersweet **2** : sweet-and-sour (in cooking)

agrietar *vt* : crack — **agrietarse** *vr* **1** : crack **2** : chap

agrimensor, -sora *n* : surveyor

agrio, agria *adj* : sour

agrupar *vt* : group together — **agruparse** *vr* : form a group — **agrupación** *nf, pl* **-ciones** : group, association — **agrupamiento** *nm* : grouping : group, association

agua *nf* **1** : water **2 agua oxigenada** : hydrogen peroxide **3 aguas negras** *or* **aguas residuales** : sewage

aguacate *nm* : avocado

aguacero *nm* : downpour

aguado, -da *adj* **1** : watery **2** *Lat fam* : soft, flabby — **aguar** {10} *vt* **1** : water down, dilute **2 aguar la fiesta** *fam* : spoil the party

aguafuerte *nm* : etching

aguanieve *nf* : sleet

aguantar *vt* **1** SOPORTAR : bear, withstand **2** SOSTENER : hold — *vi* : hold out, last — **aguantarse** *vr* **1** : resign oneself **2** CONTENERSE : restrain oneself — **aguante** *nm* **1** : patience **2** RESISTENCIA : endurance

aguardar *vt* : await

aguardiente *nm* : clear brandy

aguarrás *nm* : turpentine

agudo, -da *adj* **1** : acute, sharp **2** : shrill, high-pitched (in music) — **agudeza** *nf* **1** : sharpness **2** : witticism

agüero *nm* : augury, omen

aguijón *nm, pl* **-jones 1** : stinger (of an insect) **2** ESTÍMULO : goad, stimulus — **aguijonear** *vt* : goad

águila *nf* : eagle

aguja *nf* **1** : needle **2** : hand (of a clock) **3** : spire (of a church)

agujero *nm* : hole

agujeta *nf* **1** *Lat* : shoelace **2** **agujetas** *nfpl* : (muscular) stiffness

aguzar {21} *vt* **1** : sharpen **2 aguzar el oído** : prick up one's ears

ahí *adv* **1** : there **2 por ahí** : somewhere, thereabouts

ahijado, -da *n* : godchild, godson *m*, goddaughter *f*

ahínco *nm* : eagerness, zeal

ahogar {52} *vt* **1** : drown **2** ASFIXIAR : smother — **ahogarse** *vr* : drown — **ahogo** *nm* : breathlessness

ahondar *vt* : deepen — *vi* : elaborate, go into detail

ahora *adv* **1** : now **2 ahora mismo** : right now

ahorcar {72} *vt* : hang, kill by hanging — **ahorcarse** *vr* : hang oneself

ahorita *adv Lat fam* : right now

ahorrar *vt* : save, spare — *vi* : save up — **ahorrarse** *vr* : spare oneself — **ahorro** *nm* : saving

ahuecar {72} *vt* **1** : hollow out **2** : cup (one's hands)

ahumar {8} *vt* : smoke, cure — **ahumado, -da** *adj* : smoked

ahuyentar *vt* : scare away, chase away

airado, -da *adj* : irate, angry

aire *nm* **1** : air **2 aire acondicionado** : air-conditioning **3 al aire libre** : in the open air, outdoors — **airear** *vt* : air, air out

aislar {5} *vt* **1** : isolate **2** : insulate (in electricity) — **aislamiento** *nm* **1** : isolation **2** : (electrical) insulation

ajar *vt* **1** : crumple, wrinkle **2** ESTROPEAR : spoil

ajedrez *nm* : chess

ajeno, -na *adj* **1** : someone else's **2** EXTRAÑO : alien **3 ajeno, -na a** : foreign to

ajetreado, -da *adj* : hectic, busy — **ajetrearse** *vr* : bustle about — **ajetreo** *nm* : hustle and bustle

ají *nm, pl* **ajíes** *Lat* : chili pepper

ajo nm : garlic

ajustar vt **1** : adjust, adapt **2** ACORDAR : agree on **3** SALDAR : settle — **ajustarse** vr : fit, conform — **ajustable** adj : adjustable — **ajustado, -da** adj **1** : close, tight **2** CEÑIDO : tight-fitting — **ajuste** nm : adjustment

ajusticiar vt : execute, put to death

al (contraction of **a** and **el**) → **a**²

ala nf **1** : wing **2** : brim (of a hat)

alabanza nf : praise — **alabar** vt : praise

alacena nf : cupboard, larder

alacrán nm, pl **-cranes** : scorpion

alado, -da adj : winged

alambre nm : wire

alameda nf **1** : poplar grove **2** : tree-lined avenue — **álamo** nm : poplar

alarde nm : show, display — **alardear** vi : boast

alargar {52} vt **1** : extend, lengthen **2** PROLONGAR : prolong — **alargarse** vr : become longer — **alargador** nm : extension cord

alarido nm : howl, shriek

alarmar vt : alarm — **alarma** nf : alarm — **alarmante** adj : alarming

alba nf : dawn

albahaca nf : basil

albañil nm : bricklayer, mason

albaricoque nm : apricot

albedrío nm **libre albedrío** : free will

alberca nf **1** : reservoir, tank **2** Lat : swimming pool

albergar {52} vt : house, lodge — **albergue** nm **1** : lodging **2** REFUGIO : shelter **3 albergue juvenil** : youth hostel

albóndiga nf : meatball

alborear v impers : dawn — **albor** nm : dawning — **alborada** nf : dawn

alborotar vt : excite, stir up — vi : make a racket — **alborotarse** vr : get excited — **alborotado, -da** adj : excited, agitated — **alborotador, -dora** n : agitator, rioter — **alboroto** nm : ruckus

alborozar {21} vt : gladden — **alborozo** nm : joy

álbum nm : album

alcachofa nf : artichoke

alcalde, -desa n : mayor

alcance nm **1** : reach **2** ÁMBITO : range, scope

alcancía nf : money box

alcantarilla nf : sewer, drain

alcanzar {21} vt **1** : reach **2** LLEGAR A : catch up with **3** LOGRAR : achieve,

attain — vi **1** : suffice, be enough **2 alcanzar a** : manage to

alcaparra nf : caper

alcázar nm : fortress, castle

alce nm : moose, European elk

alcoba nf : bedroom

alcohol nm : alcohol — **alcohólico, -ca** adj & n : alcoholic — **alcoholismo** nm : alcoholism

aldaba nf : door knocker

aldea nf : village — **aldeano, -na** n : villager

aleación nf, pl **-ciones** : alloy

aleatorio, -ria adj : random

aleccionar vt : instruct, teach

aledaño, -ña adj : bordering — **aledaños** nmpl : outskirts

alegar {52} vt : assert, allege — vi Lat : argue — **alegato** nm **1** : allegation (in law) **2** Lat : argument

alegoría nf : allegory — **alegórico, -ca** adj : allegorical

alegrar vt : make happy, cheer up — **alegrarse** vr : be glad — **alegre** adj **1** CONTENTO : glad, happy **2** : colorful, bright — **alegremente** adv : happily — **alegría** nf : joy, cheer

alejar vt **1** : remove, move away **2** ENAJENAR : estrange — **alejarse** vr : move away, drift apart — **alejado, -da** adj : remote — **alejamiento** nm **1** : removal **2** : estrangement (of persons)

alemán, -mana adj, mpl **-manes** : German — **alemán** nm : German (language)

alentar {55} vt : encourage — **alentador, -dora** adj : encouraging

alergia nf : allergy — **alérgico, -ca** adj : allergic

alero nm : eaves pl

alertar vt : alert — **alerta** adv : on the alert — **alerta** adj & nf : alert

aleta nf **1** : fin, flipper **2** : small wing

alevosía nf : treachery — **alevoso, -sa** adj : treacherous

alfabeto nm : alphabet — **alfabético, -ca** adj : alphabetical — **alfabetismo** nm : literacy — **alfabetizar** {21} vt **1** : teach literacy **2** : alphabetize

alfalfa nf : alfalfa

alfarería nf : pottery

alféizar nm : sill, windowsill

alfil nm : bishop (in chess)

alfiler nm **1** : pin **2** BROCHE : brooch — **alfiletero** nm : pincushion

alfombra nf : carpet, rug — **alfombrilla** nf : small rug, mat

alga nf : seaweed

álgebra nf : algebra

algo pron **1** : something **2 algo de** : some, a little — **algo** adv : somewhat, rather

algodón nm, pl **-dones** : cotton

alguacil nm : constable, bailiff

alguien pron : somebody, someone

alguno, -na adj (**algún** before masculine singular nouns) **1** : some, any **2** (in negative constructions) : not any, not at all **3 algunas veces** : sometimes — **alguno, -na** pron **1** : one, someone, somebody **2 algunos, -nas** pron pl : some, a few

alhaja nf : jewel

alharaca nf : fuss

aliado, -da n : ally — **aliado, -da** adj : allied — **alianza** nf : alliance — **aliarse** {85} vr : form an alliance

alias adv & nm : alias

alicaído, -da adj : depressed

alicates nmpl : pliers

aliciente nm **1** : incentive **2** : attraction (to a place)

alienar vt : alienate — **alienación** nf, pl **-ciones** : alienation

aliento nm **1** : breath **2** ÁNIMO : encouragement, strength

aligerar vt **1** : lighten **2** APRESURAR : hasten, quicken

alimaña nf : pest, vermin

alimentar vt : feed, nourish — **alimentarse** vr **alimentar con** : live on — **alimentación** nf, pl **-ciones 1** : feeding **2** NUTRICIÓN : nourishment — **alimenticio, -cia** adj : nourishing — **alimento** nm : food, nourishment

alinear vt : align, line up — **alinearse** vr **alinear con** : align oneself with — **alineación** nf, pl **-ciones 1** : alignment **2** : lineup (in sports)

aliño nm : dressing, seasoning — **aliñar** vt : season, dress

alisar vt : smooth

alistarse vr : join up, enlist — **alistamiento** nm : enlistment

aliviar vt : relieve, soothe — **aliviarse** vr : recover, get better — **alivio** nm : relief

aljibe nm : cistern, tank

allá adv **1** : there, over there **2 más allá** : farther away **3 más allá de** : beyond

allanar vt **1** : smooth, level out **2** Spain : break into (a house) **3** Lat : raid — **allanamiento** nm **1** Spain :

alpinismo*ᴹ*: alpinista*ᶠ* y accesorios*ᴹ*
mountain climbing: mountaineer and accessories

lámpara*ᶠ* del casco*ᴹ*
headlamp

casco*ᴹ*
helmet

anorak*ᴹ*
parka

soga*ᶠ*
rope

cinturón*ᴹ* de alpinista*ᴹ*
climbing harness

mosquetón*ᴹ*
carabiner

pitón*ᴹ* de hielo*ᴹ*
ice piton

piolet*ᴹ*
ice ax

pitón*ᴹ* de hielo*ᴹ*
ice screw

polaina*ᶠ*
legging

bota*ᶠ* alpina
mountaineering boot

breaking and entering **2** *Lat*: raid
allegado, -da *n*: close friend, relation
allí *adv*: there, over there
alma *nf*: soul
almacén *nm, pl* **-cenes 1**: warehouse
2 *Lat*: shop, store **3 grandes**
almacenes: department store —
almacenamiento *or* almacenaje *nm*
: storage — **almacenar** *vt*: store
almádena *nf*: sledgehammer
almanaque *nm*: almanac
almeja *nf*: clam
almendra *nf* **1**: almond **2**:
kernel (of nuts, fruit, etc.)
almiar *nm*: haystack

almíbar *nm*: syrup
almidón *nm, pl* **-dones**: starch
— **almidonar** *vt*: starch
almirante *nm*: admiral
almohada *nf*: pillow — **almohadilla** *nf*
: small pillow, pad — **almohadón** *nm,*
pl **-dones**: bolster, large cushion
almorranas *nfpl*: hemorrhoids, piles
almorzar {36} *vi*: have lunch — *vt*:
have for lunch — **almuerzo** *nm*: lunch
alocado, -da *adj*: crazy, wild
áloe *or* aloe *nm*: aloe
alojar *vt*: house, lodge — **alojarse** *vr*
: lodge, room — **alojamiento** *nm*
: lodging, accommodations *pl*

alondra *nf*: lark
alpaca *nf*: alpaca
▸ **alpinismo** *nm*: mountain climbing
— **alpinista** *nmf*: mountain climber
alpiste *nm*: birdseed
alquilar *vt*: rent, lease — **alquilarse** *vr*
: be for rent — **alquiler** *nm*: rent, rental
alquitrán *nm, pl* **-tranes**: tar
alrededor *adv* **1**: around, about
2 alrededor de: approximately —
alrededor de *prep phr*: around —
alrededores *nmpl*: outskirts
alta *nf*: discharge (of a patient)
altanería *nf*: haughtiness —
altanero, -ra *adj*: haughty
altar *nm*: altar
altavoz *nm, pl* **-voces**: loudspeaker
alterar *vt* **1**: alter, modify **2** PERTURBAR
: disturb — **alterado** *vr*: get upset
— **alteración** *nf, pl* **-ciones 1**:
alteration **2** ALBOROTO: disturbance
— **alterado, -da** *adj*: upset
altercado *nm*: altercation, argument
alternar *vi* **1**: alternate **2 alternar**
con: socialize with — *vt*: alternate
— **alternarse** *vr*: take turns —
alternativa *nf*: alternative — **alternativo,**
-va *adj*: alternating, alternative
— **alterno, -na** *adj*: alternate
Alteza *nf*: Highness
altiplano *nm*: high plateau
altitud *nf*: altitude
altivez *nf, pl* **-veces**: haughtiness
— **altivo, -va** *adj*: haughty
alto, -ta *adj* **1**: tall, high **2** RUIDOSO:
loud — **alto** *adv* **1** ARRIBA: high **2**: loud,
loudly — **alto, -ta** *nm* **1** ALTURA: height,
elevation **2**: stop, halt — **alto** *interj*: halt!,
stop! — **altoparlante** *nm Lat*: loudspeaker
altruista *adj*: altruistic —
altruismo *nm*: altruism
altura *nf* **1**: height **2** ALTITUD: altitude
3 a la altura de: near, up by
alubia *nf*: kidney bean
alucinar *vi*: hallucinate —
alucinación *nf, pl* **-ciones**: hallucination
alud *nm*: avalanche
aludir *vi*: allude, refer — **aludido, -da** *adj*
darse por aludido: take it personally
alumbrar *vt* **1**: light, illuminate **2** PARIR:
give birth to — **alumbrado** *nm*: (electric)
lighting — **alumbramiento** *nm*: childbirth
aluminio *nm*: aluminum
alumno, -na *n*: pupil, student
alusión *nf, pl* **-siones**: allusion

aluvión *nm, pl* **-viones** : flood, barrage
alzar {21} *vt* : lift, raise — **alzarse** *vr*
: rise (up) — **alza** *nf* : rise —
alzamiento *nm* : uprising
ama → **amo**
amabilidad *nf* : kindness —
amable *adj* : kind, nice
amaestrar *vt* : train
amagar {52} *vt* **1** : show signs
of **2** AMENAZAR : threaten — *vi* :
be imminent — **amago** *nm* **1**
INDICIO : sign **2** AMENAZA : threat
amainar *vi* : abate
amamantar *v* : breast-feed, nurse
amanecer {53} *v impers* : dawn
— *vi* : wake up — **amanecer** *nm*
: dawn, daybreak
amanerado *adj* : affected, mannered
amansar *vt* **1** : tame **2** APACIGUAR :
soothe — **amansarse** *vr* : calm down

amante *adj* **amante de** : fond
of — **amante** *nmf* : lover
amañar *vt* : rig, tamper with
amapola *nf* : poppy
amar *vt* : love
amargar {52} *vt* : make bitter —
amargado, -da *adj* : embittered
— **amargo, -ga** *adj* : bitter
— **amargo** *nm* : bitterness —
amargura *nf* : bitterness, grief
amarillo, -lla *adj* : yellow
— **amarillo** *nm* : yellow
amarrar *vt* **1** : moor **2** ATAR : tie up
amasar *vt* **1** : knead **2** :
amass (a fortune, etc.)
amateur *adj & nmf* : amateur
amatista *nf* : amethyst
ambages *nmpl* **sin ambages** : without
hesitation, straight to the point
ámbar *nm* : amber

ambición *nf, pl* **-ciones** : ambition
— **ambicionar** *vt* : aspire to —
ambicioso, -sa *adj* : ambitious
ambiente *nm* **1** AIRE : atmosphere **2**
MEDIO : environment, surroundings *pl*
— **ambiental** *adj* : environmental
ambigüedad *nf* : ambiguity —
ambiguo, -gua *adj* : ambiguous
ámbito *nm* : domain, sphere
ambos, -bas *adj & pron* : both
▸ **ambulancia** *nf* : ambulance
ambulante *adj* : traveling, itinerant
ameba *nf* : amoeba
amedrentar *vt* : intimidate
amén *nm* **1** : amen **2** **amén**
de : in addition to
amenazar {21} *vt* : threaten —
amenaza *nf* : threat, menace
amenizar {21} *vt* : make pleasant,
enliven — **ameno, -na** *adj* : pleasant

ambulancia*F*
ambulance

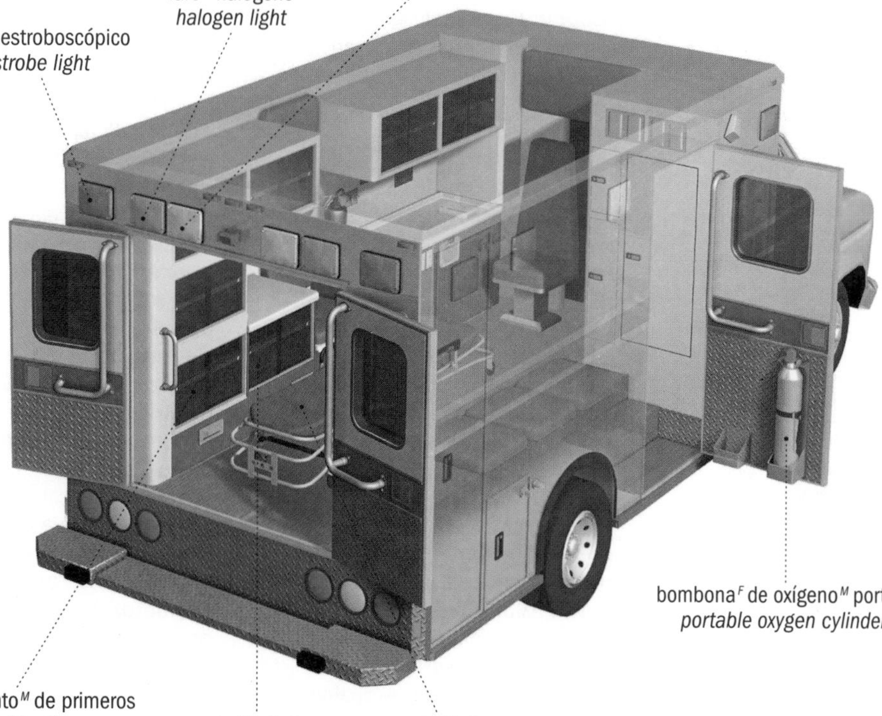

faro*M* de posición*M*
scene light

faro*M* halógeno
halogen light

faro*M* estroboscópico
strobe light

bombona*F* de oxígeno*M* portátil
portable oxygen cylinder

equipamiento*M* de primeros
auxilios*M*
first aid supplies

botiquín*M*
drug storage

camilla*F*
stretcher

ananá[M]
pineapple

americano, -na *adj* : American

ameritar *vi Lat* : deserve

ametralladora *nf* : machine gun

amianto *nm* : asbestos

amiba → **ameba**

amígdala *nf* : tonsil —
amigdalitis *nf* : tonsilitis

amigo, -ga *adj* : friendly, close — **amigo,
-ga** *n* : friend — **amigable** *adj* : friendly

amilanar *vt* : daunt —
amilanarse *vr* : lose heart

aminorar *vt* : diminish

amistad *nf* : friendship —
amistoso, -sa *adj* : friendly

amnesia *nf* : amnesia

amnistía *nf* : amnesty

amo, ama *n* **1** : master *m*, mistress *f* **2
ama de casa** : homemaker, housewife
3 ama de llaves : housekeeper

amodorrado, -da *adj* : drowsy

amolar {19} *vt* **1** : grind,
sharpen **2** MOLESTAR : annoy

amoldar *vt* : adapt, adjust —
amoldarse *vr* **amoldarse a** : adapt to

amonestar *vt* : admonish, warn
— **amonestación** *nf, pl* **-ciones**
: admonition, warning

amoníaco *or* amoniaco *nm* : ammonia

amontonar *vt* : pile up —
amontonarse *vr* : pile up (of things),
form a crowd (of persons)

amor *nm* : love

amordazar {21} *vt* : gag

amorío *nm* : love affair — **amoroso,
-sa** *adj* **1** : loving **2** *Lat* : sweet, lovable

amortado, -da *adj* : black-and-blue

amortiguar {10} *vt* : muffle, soften,
tone down — **amortiguador** *nm*
: shock absorber

amortizar {21} *vt* : pay off —
amortización *nf* : repayment

amotinar *vt* : incite (to riot) —
amotinarse *vr* : riot, rebel

amparar *vt* : shelter, protect —
ampararse *vr* **1 ampararse de** :
take shelter from **2 ampararse en**
: have recourse to — **amparo** *nm*
: refuge, protection

ampliar {85} *vt* **1** : expand **2** : enlarge
(a photograph) — **ampliación** *nf,
pl* **-ciones 1** : expansion, enlargement
2 : extension (of a building)

amplificar {72} *vt* : amplify —
amplificador *nm* : amplifier

amplio, -plia *adj* : broad, wide,
ample — **amplitud** *nf* **1** : breadth,
extent **2** ESPACIOSIDAD : spaciousness

ampolla *nf* **1** : blister **2** : vial,
ampoule — **ampollarse** *vr* : blister

ampuloso, -sa *adj* : pompous

amputar *vt* : amputate —
amputación *nf, pl* **-ciones** : amputation

amueblar *vt* : furnish (a house, etc.)

amurallar *vt* : wall in

anacardo *nm* : cashew nut

anaconda *nf* : anaconda

anacrónico, -ca *adj* : anachronistic
— **anacronismo** *nm* : anachronism

ánade *nmf* : duck

anagrama *nm* : anagram

anales *nmpl* : annals

analfabeto, -ta *adj & n* : illiterate
— **analfabetismo** *nm* : illiteracy

analgésico *nm* : painkiller, analgesic

analizar {21} *vt* : analyze —
análisis *nm* : analysis — **analítico,
-ca** *adj* : analytical, analytic

analogía *nf* : analogy —
análogo, -ga *adj* : analogous

▸ **ananá** *or* ananás *nm, pl* **-nás** : pineapple

anaquel *nm* : shelf

anaranjado, -da *adj* : orange-colored

anarquía *nf* : anarchy —
anarquista *adj & nmf* : anarchist

anatomía *nf* : anatomy — **anatómico,
-ca** *adj* : anatomic, anatomical

anca *nf* **1** : haunch **2 ancas**

de rana : frogs' legs

ancestral *adj* : ancestral

ancho, -cha *adj* : wide, broad,
ample — **ancho** *nm* : width

anchoa *nf* : anchovy

anchura *nf* : width, breadth

anciano, -na *adj* : aged, elderly —
anciano, -na *n* : elderly person

ancla *nf* : anchor — **anclar** *v* : anchor

andadas *nfpl* **1** : tracks **2 volver a las
andadas** : go back to one's old ways

andadura *nf* : walking, journey

andaluz, -luza *adj & n, mpl*
-luces : Andalusian

andamio *nm* : scaffold

andanada *nf* **1** : volley **2 soltar
una andanada** : reprimand

andanzas *nfpl* : adventures

andar {6} *vi* **1** CAMINAR : **walk 2** IR
: go, travel **3** FUNCIONAR : **run, work
4 andar en** : rummage around in **5
andar por** : be approximately — *vt* :
cover, travel — **andar** *nm* : gait, walk

andén *nm, pl* **-denes 1** : (train)
platform **2** *Lat* : sidewalk

andino, -na *adj* : Andean

andorrano, -na *adj* : Andorran

andrajos *nmpl* : tatters —
andrajoso, -sa *adj* : ragged

anécdota *nf* : anecdote

anegar {52} *vt* : flood — **anegarse** *vr* **1**
: be flooded **2** AHOGARSE : drown

anemia *nf* : anemia —
anémico, -ca *adj* : anemic

anestesia *nf* : anesthesia —
anestésico, -ca *adj* : anesthetic
— **anestésico** *nm* : anesthetic

anexar *vt* : annex, attach — **anexo,
-xa** *adj* : attached — **anexo** *nm* : annex

anfibio, -bia *adj* : amphibious
— **anfibio** *nm* : amphibian

▸ **anfiteatro** *nm* : amphitheater

anfitrión, -triona *n, mpl*
-triones : host, hostess *f*

ángel *nm* : angel — **angelical** *adj*
: angelic, angelical

angloparlante *adj* : English-speaking

anglosajón, -jona *adj, mpl*
-jones : Anglo-Saxon

angosto, -ta *adj* : narrow

anguila *nf* : eel

ángulo *nm* **1** : angle **2** ESQUINA :
corner — **angular** *adj* : angular
— **anguloso, -sa** *adj* : angular

angustiar *vt* **1** : anguish, distress **2**

INQUIETAR : **worry** — **angustiarse** *vr* :
get upset — **angustia** *nf* **1** : anguish **2**
INQUIETUD : worry — **angustioso, -sa** *adj* **1**
: anguished **2** INQUIETANTE : distressing
anhelar *vt* : yearn for, crave —
anhelante *adj* : yearning, longing
— **anhelo** *nm* : longing
anidar *vi* : nest
anillo *nm* : ring

ánima *n* : soul
animación *nf, pl* **-ciones 1** VIVEZA
: liveliness **2** BULLICIO : hustle and
bustle — **animado, -da** *adj* : cheerful,
animated — **animador, -dora** *n* **1**
: (television) host **2** : cheerleader
animadversión *nf,*
pl **-siones** : animosity
animal *nm* : animal — **animal** *nmf* :

brute, beast — **animal** *adj* : brutish
animar *vt* **1** ALENTAR : encourage **2** ALEGAR
: cheer up — **animarse** *vr* **1** : liven up
2 animarse a : get up the nerve to
ánimo *nm* **1** : spirit, soul **2** HUMOR : mood,
spirits *pl* **3** ALIENTO : encouragement
animosidad *nf* : animosity, ill will
animoso, -sa *adj* : spirited, brave
aniquilar *vt* : annihilate

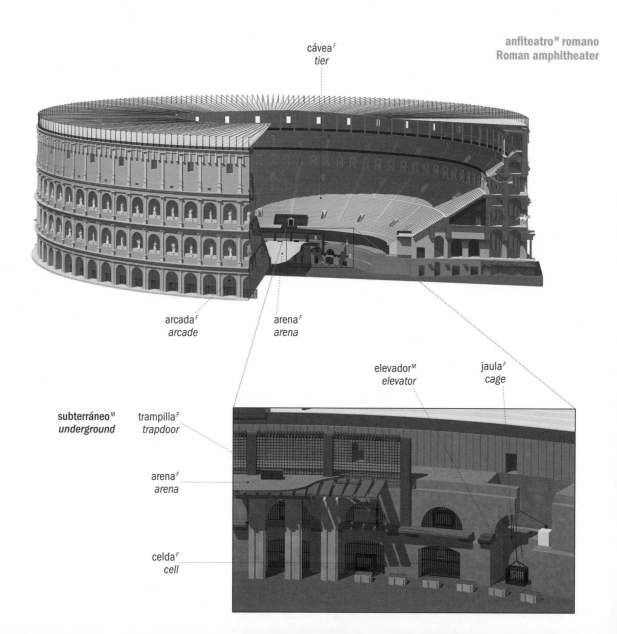

cávea*F*
tier

anfiteatro*M* romano
Roman amphitheater

arcada*F*
arcade

arena*F*
arena

elevador*M*
elevator

jaula*F*
cage

subterráneo*M*
underground

trampilla*F*
trapdoor

arena*F*
arena

celda*F*
cell

— **aniquilación** *n, pl* **-ciones** : annihilation

anís *nm* : anise

aniversario *nm* : anniversary

ano *nm* : anus

anoche *adv* : last night

anochecer {53} *vi* : get dark — **anochecer** *nm* : dusk, nightfall

anodino, -na *adj* : insipid, dull

anomalía *nf* : anomaly

anonadado, -da *adj* : dumbfounded

anónimo, -ma *adj* : anonymous — **anonimato** *nm* : anonymity

anorexia *nf* : anorexia

anormal *adj* : abnormal — **anormalidad** *nf* : abnormality

anotar *vt* **1** : annotate **2** APUNTAR : jot down — **anotación** *nf, pl* **-ciones** : annotation, note

anquilosarse *vr* **1** : become paralyzed **2** ESTANCARSE : stagnate — **anquilosamiento** *nm* **1** : paralysis **2** ESTANCAMIENTO : stagnation

ansiar {85} *vt* : long for — **ansia** *nf* **1** INQUIETUD : uneasiness **2** ANGUSTIA : anguish **3** ANHELO : longing — **ansiedad** *nf* : anxiety — **ansioso, -sa** *adj* **1** : anxious **2** DESEOSO : eager

antagónico, -ca *adj* : antagonistic — **antagonismo** *nm* : antagonism — **antagonista** *nmf* : antagonist

antaño *adv* : yesteryear, long ago

antártico, -ca *adj* : antarctic

ante¹ *nm* **1** : elk, moose **2** GAMUZA : suede

ante² *prep* **1** : before, in front of **2** : in view of **3 ante todo** : above all

anteanoche *adv* : the night before last

anteayer *adv* : the day before yesterday

antebrazo *nm* : forearm

anteceder *vt* : precede — **antecedente** *adj* : previous, prior — **anteceder** *nm* : precedent — **antecesor, -sora** *n* **1** : ancestor **2** PREDECESOR : predecessor

antedicho, -cha *adj* : aforesaid

antelación *nf, pl* **-ciones 1** : advance notice **2 con antelación** : in advance

antemano *adv* **de antemano** : beforehand

antena *nf* : antenna

antenoche → **anteanoche**

anteojos *nmpl* **1** : glasses, eyeglasses **2 anteojos bifocales** : bifocals

antepasado, -da *n* : ancestor

antepecho *nm* : ledge

antepenúltimo, -ma *adj*

: third from last

anteponer {60} *vt* **1** : place before **2** PREFERIR : prefer

anterior *adj* **1** : previous, earlier **2** DELANTERO : front — **anterioridad** *nf* **con anterioridad** : beforehand, in advance — **anteriormente** *adv* : previously

antes *adv* **1** : before, earlier **2** ANTERIORMENTE : previously **3** PRIMERO : first **4** MEJOR : rather **5 antes de** : before, previous to **6 antes que** : before

antesala *nf* : waiting room

antiaéreo, -rea *adj* : antiaircraft

antibiótico *nm* : antibiotic

anticipar *vt* **1** : move up (a date, etc.) **2** : pay in advance — **anticiparse** *vr* **1** : be early **2** ADELANTARSE : get ahead — **anticipación** *nf, pl* **-ciones 1** : anticipation **2 con anticipación** : in advance — **anticipado, -da** *adj* **1** : advance, early **2 por anticipado** : in advance — **anticipo** *nm* **1** : advance (payment) **2** : foretaste

anticoncepción *nf, pl* **-ciones** : contraception — **anticonceptivo, -va** *adj* : contraceptive — **anticonceptivo** *nm* : contraceptive

anticongelante *nm* : antifreeze

anticuado, -da *adj* : antiquated, outdated

anticuario, -ria *n* : antique dealer — **anticuario** *nm* : antique shop

anticuerpo *nm* : antibody

antídoto *nm* : antidote

antier → **anteayer**

antiestético, -ca *adj* : unsightly

antifaz *nm, pl* **-faces** : mask

antífona *nf* : anthem

antigualla *nf* : relic, old thing

antiguo, -gua *adj* **1** : ancient, old **2** ANTERIOR : former **3** ANTICUADO : old-fashioned **4 muebles antiguos** : antique furniture — **antiguamente** *adv* **1** : long ago **2** ANTES : formerly — **antigüedad** *nf* **1** : antiquity **2** : seniority (in the workplace) **3 antiguo, -guas** *nfpl* : antiques

antihigiénico, -ca *adj* : unsanitary

antihistamínico *nm* : antihistamine

antiinflamatorio, -ria *adj* : anti-inflammatory

antílope *nm* : antelope

antinatural *adj* : unnatural

antipatía *nf* : aversion, dislike — **antipático, -ca** *adj* : unpleasant

antirreglamentario, -ria *adj* : unlawful

antirrobo, -ba *adj* : antitheft

antisemita *adj* : anti-Semitic — **antisemitismo** *nm* : anti-Semitism

antiséptico, -ca *adj* : antiseptic — **antiséptico** *nm* : antiseptic

antisocial *adj* : antisocial

antítesis *nf* : antithesis

antojarse *vr* **1** APETECER : crave **2** PARECER : seem, appear — **antojadizo, -za** *adj* : capricious — **antojo** *nm* : whim, craving

antología *nf* : anthology

antorcha *nf* : torch

antro *nm* : dive, den

antropófago, -ga *nmf* : cannibal

antropología *nf* : anthropology

anual *adj* : annual, yearly — **anualidad** *nf* : annuity — **anuario** *nm* : yearbook, annual

anudar *vt* : knot — **anudarse** *vr* : tie, knot

anular *vt* : annul, cancel — **anulación** *nf, pl* **-ciones** : annulment, cancellation

anunciar *vt* **1** : announce **2** : advertise (products) — **anunciante** *nmf* : advertiser — **anuncio** *nm* **1** : announcement **2** *or* **anuncio publicitario** : advertisement

anzuelo *nm* **1** : fishhook **2 morder el anzuelo** : take the bait

añadir *vt* : add — **añadidura** *nf* **1** : additive, addition **2 por añadidura** : in addition, furthermore

añejo, -ja *adj* : aged, vintage

añicos *nmpl* **hacer(se) añicos** : smash to pieces

añil *adj & nm* : indigo (color)

año *nm* **1** : year **2 Año Nuevo** : New Year

añorar *vt* : long for, miss — **añoranza** *nf* : nostalgia

añoso, -sa *adj* : aged, old

aorta *nf* : aorta

apabullar *vt* : overwhelm

apacentar {55} *vt* : pasture, graze

apachurrar *vi Lat* : crush

apacible *adj* : gentle, mild

apaciguar {10} *vt* : appease, pacify — **apaciguarse** *vr* : calm down

apadrinar *vt* **1** : be a godparent to **2** : sponsor (an artist, etc.)

apagar {52} *vt* **1** : turn or switch off **2** EXTINGUIR : extinguish, put out — **apagarse** *vr* **1** EXTINGUIRSE : go out **2** : die down — **apagado, -da** *adj* **1** : off, out **2** : dull, subdued (of colors, sounds, etc.) — **apagador** *nm Lat* : (light) switch — **apagón** *nm, pl* **-gones** : blackout

apalancar {72} *vt* **1** LEVANTAR : jack up **2** ABRIR : pry open

— **apalancamiento** *nm* : leverage
apalear *vt* : beat up, thrash
aparador *nm* **1** : sideboard
2 *Lat* : shop window
aparato *nm* **1** : machine, appliance, apparatus **2** : system (in anatomy)
3 OSTENTACIÓN : ostentation —
aparatoso, -sa *adj* **1** : ostentatious
2 ESPECTACULAR : spectacular
aparcar {72} *v, Spain* : park
— **aparcamiento** *nm, Spain* **1**
: parking **2** : parking lot
aparcero, -ra *n* : sharecropper
aparear *vt* : mate, pair up
— **aparearse** *vr* : mate
aparecer {53} *vi* **1** : appear
2 PRESENTARSE : show up —
aparecerse *vr* : appear
aparejar *vt* **1** : rig (a ship) **2** : harness (an animal) — **aparejado, -da** *adj* **llevar aparejado** : entail — **aparejo** *nm* **1**
: equipment, gear **2** : harness (for an animal) **3** : rigging (for a ship)
aparentar *vt* **1** : seem **2** FINGIR : feign
— **aparente** *adj* : apparent, seeming
aparición *nf, pl* **-ciones 1** :
appearance **2** FANTASMA : apparition
— **apariencia** *nf* **1** : appearance, look **2 en aparición** : apparently
apartado *nm* **1** : section, paragraph
2 apartado postal : post office box
apartamento *nm* : apartment
apartar *vt* **1** ALEJAR : move away
2 SEPARAR : set aside, separate
— **apartarse** *vr* **1** : move away **2**
DESVIARSE : stray — **aparte** *adv* **1** :
apart, separately **2** ADEMÁS : besides
apasionar *vt* : excite, fascinate
— **apasionarse** *vr* : get excited —
apasionado, -da *adj* : passionate,
excited — **apasionante** *adj* : exciting
apatía *nf* : apathy — **apático,
-ca** *adj* : apathetic
apearse *vr* **1** : dismount **2** :
get out of or off (a vehicle)
apedrear *vt* : stone
apegarse {52} *vr* **apegarse a** : become
attached to, grow fond of — **apegado,
-da** *adj* : devoted — **apego** *nm* : fondness
apelar *vi* **1** : appeal **2 apelar a** : resort
to — **apelación** *nf, pl* **-ciones** : appeal
apellido *nm* : last name, surname —
apellidarse *vr* : have for a last name
apenar *vt* : sadden — **apenarse** *vr* **1**
: grieve **2** *Lat* : become embarrassed

apenas *adv* : hardly, scarcely
— **apenas** *conj* : as soon as
apéndice *nm* : appendix —
apendicitis *nf* : appendicitis
apercibir *vt* **1** : warn **2** *Lat* : notice —
apercibirse *vr* **apercibirse de** : notice
— **apercibimiento** *nm* : warning
aperitivo *nm* **1** : appetizer **2** : aperitif
apero *nm* : tool, implement
apertura *nf* : opening
apesadumbrar *vt* : sadden —
apesadumbrarse *vr* : be weighed down
apestar *vi* : stink — **apestoso,
-sa** *adj* : stinking, foul
apetecer {53} *vt* : crave, long for
— **apetecible** *adj* : appealing
apetito *nm* : appetite —
apetitoso, -sa *adj* : appetizing
ápice *nm* **1** : apex, summit
2 PIZCA : bit, smidgen
apilar *vt* : pile up — **apilarse** *vr* : pile up
apiñar *vt* : pack, cram —
apiñarse *vr* : crowd together
apio *nm* : celery
apisonadora *nf* : steamroller
aplacar {72} *vt* : appease, placate
— **aplacarse** *vr* : calm down
aplanar *vt* : flatten, level
aplastar *vt* : crush —
aplastante *adj* : overwhelming
aplaudir *v* : applaud — **aplauso** *nm* **1**
: applause **2** : acclaim
aplazar {21} *vt* : postpone, defer —
aplazamiento *nm* : postponement
aplicar {72} *vt* : apply — **aplicarse** *vr*
: apply oneself — **aplicable** *adj* :
applicable — **aplicación** *nf, pl* **-ciones** :
application — **aplicado, -da** *adj* : diligent
aplomo *nm* : aplomb
apocarse {72} *vr* : belittle oneself
— **apocado, -da** *adj* : timid —
apocamiento *nm* : timidity
apodar *vt* : nickname
apoderar *vt* : empower —
apoderarse *vr* **apoderar de** : seize
— **apoderado, -da** *n* : agent, proxy
apodo *nm* : nickname
apogeo *nm* : peak, height
apología *nf* : defense, apology
apoplegía *nf* : stroke, apoplexy
aporrear *vt* : bang on, beat
aportar *vt* : contribute — **aportación** *nf,
pl* **-ciones** : contribution
apostar[1] {19} *v* : bet, wager
apostar[2] *vt* : station, post

apostillar *vt* : annotate —
apostilla *nf* : note
apóstol *nm* : apostle
apóstrofo *nm* : apostrophe
apostura *nf* : elegance, grace
apoyar *vt* **1** : support **2** INCLINAR : lean,
rest — **apoyarse** *vr* **apoyarse en** : lean
on, rest on — **apoyo** *nm* : support
apreciar *vt* **1** ESTIMAR : appreciate **2**
EVALUAR : appraise — **apreciable** *adj* :
considerable — **apreciación** *nf, pl* **-ciones**
1 : appreciation **2** VALORACIÓN : appraisal —
aprecio *nm* **1** : appraisal **2** ESTIMA : esteem
aprehender *vt* : apprehend
— **aprehensión** *nf, pl* **-siones**
: apprehension, capture
apremiar *vt* : urge — *vi* : be urgent
— **apremiante** *adj* : pressing,
urgent — **apremio** *nm* : urgency
aprender *v* : learn —
aprenderse *vr* : memorize
aprendiz, -diza *n, mpl*
-dices : apprentice, trainee —
aprendizaje *nm* : apprenticeship
aprensión *nf, pl* **-siones** :
apprehension, dread — **aprensivo,
-va** *adj* : apprehensive
apresar *vt* : capture, seize —
apresamiento *nm* : seizure, capture
aprestar *vt* : make ready —
aprestarse *vr* : get ready
apresurar *vt* : speed up —
apresurarse *vr* : hurry —
apresuradamente *adv* : hurriedly, hastily
— **apresurado, -da** *adj* : in a rush
apretar {55} *vt* **1** : press, push (a
button) **2** : tighten (a knot, etc.) **3**
ESTRECHAR : squeeze — *vi* **1** : press
(down) **2** : fit too tightly — **apretón** *nm,
pl* **-tones 1** : squeeze **2 apretón de
manos** : handshake — **apretado,
-da** *adj* **1** : tight **2** *fam* : tightfisted
aprieto *nm* : predicament, jam
aprisa *adv* : quickly
aprisionar *vt* : imprison
aprobar {19} *vt* **1** : approve of **2** :
pass (an exam, etc.) — *vi* : pass —
aprobación *nf, pl* **-ciones** : approval
apropiarse *vr* **apropiarse de** :
take possession of, appropriate —
apropiación *nf, pl* **-ciones** : appropriation
— **apropiado, -da** *adj* : appropriate
aprovechar *vt* : take advantage of,
make good use of — *vi* : be of use —
aprovecharse *vr* **aprovecharse de** : take

araña^F
spider

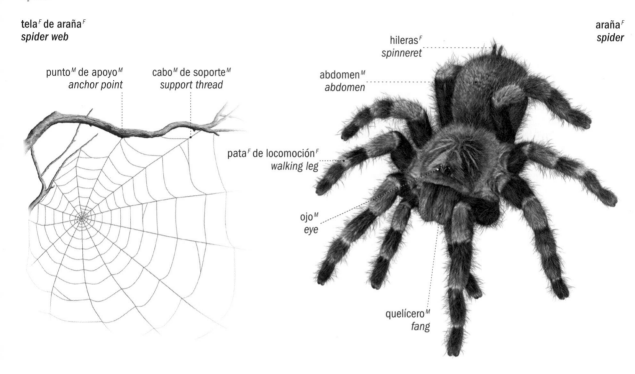

tela^F de araña^F
spider web

araña^F
spider

punto^M de apoyo^M
anchor point

cabo^M de soporte^M
support thread

hileras^F
spinneret

abdomen^M
abdomen

pata^F de locomoción^F
walking leg

ojo^M
eye

quelícero^M
fang

---

advantage of — **aprovechado, -da** *adj* **1** : diligent **2** OPORTUNISTA : opportunistic

aproximar *vt* : bring closer — **aproximarse** *vr* : approach — **aproximación** *nf, pl* **-ciones** : approximation — **aproximadamente** *adv* : approximately — **aproximado, -da** *adj* : approximate

apto, -ta *adj* **1** : suitable **2** CAPAZ : capable — **aptitud** *nf* : aptitude, capability

apuesta *nf* : bet, wager

apuesto, -ta *adj* : elegant, good-looking

apuntalar *vt* : prop up, shore up

apuntar *vt* **1** : aim, point **2** ANOTAR : jot down **3** SEÑALAR : point at **4** : prompt (in theater) — **apuntarse** *vr* **1** : sign up **2** : score, chalk up (a victory, etc.) — **apunte** *nm* : note

apuñalar *vt* : stab

apurar *vt* **1** : hurry, rush **2** AGOTAR : use up **3** PREOCUPAR : trouble — **apurarse** *vr* **1** : worry **2** *Lat* : hurry up — **apuradamente** *adv* : with difficulty

— **apurado, -da** *adj* **1** : needy **2** DIFÍCIL : difficult **3** *Lat* : rushed — **apuro** *nm* **1** : predicament, jam **2** *Lat* : hurry

aquejar *vt* : afflict

aquel, aquella *adj, mpl* aquellos : that, those

aquél, aquélla *pron, mpl* aquéllos **1** : that (one), those (ones) **2** : the former

aquello *pron* : that, that matter

aquí *adv* **1** : here **2** AHORA : now **3 por aquí** : hereabouts

aquietar *vt* : calm — **aquietarse** *vr* : calm down

ara *nf* **1** : altar **2 en aras de** : for the sake of

árabe *adj* : Arab, Arabic — **árabe** *nm* : Arabic (language)

arado *nm* : plow

arancel *nm* : tariff

arándano *nm* : blueberry

▸ **araña** *nf* **1** : spider **2** LÁMPARA : chandelier

arañar *v* : scratch, claw — **arañazo** *nm* : scratch

arar *v* : plow

arbitrar *v* **1** : arbitrate **2** : referee, umpire (in sports) — **arbitraje** *nm* : arbitration — **arbitrario, -ria** *adj* : arbitrary — **arbitrio** *nm* **1** : (free) will **2** JUICIO : judgment — **árbitro, -tra** *n* **1** : arbitrator **2** : referee, umpire (in sports)

árbol *nm* : tree — **arboleda** *nf* : grove

arbusto *nm* : shrub, bush

arca *nf* **1** : ark **2** COFRE : chest

arcada *nf* **1** : arcade **2** arcadas *nfpl* : retching

arcaico, -ca *adj* : archaic

arcano, -na *adj* : arcane, secret

arce *nm* : maple tree

archipiélago *nm* : archipelago

archivar *vt* : file — **archivador** *nm* : filing cabinet — **archivo** *nm* **1** : file **2** : archives *pl*

arcilla *nf* : clay

arco *nm* **1** : arch **2** : bow (in sports, music, etc.) **3** : arc (in geometry) **4 arco iris** : rainbow

arder *vi* : burn

ardid *nm* : scheme, ruse

ardiente *adj* **1** : burning **2** FOGOSO : ardent

ardilla *nf* **1** : squirrel **2 ardilla listada** : chipmunk

ardor *nm* **1** : burning **2** ENTUSIASMO : passion, ardor

arduo, -dua *adj* : arduous

área *nf* : area

arena *nf* **1** : sand **2** PALESTRA : arena — **arenoso, -sa** *adj* : sandy, gritty

arenque *nm* : herring

arete *nm Lat* : earring

argamasa *nf* : mortar

argentino, -na *adj* : Argentinian, Argentine

argolla *nf* : hoop, ring

argot *nm* : slang

argüir {41} *vt* **1** : argue **2** DEMOSTRAR : prove, show — *vi* : argue

argumentar *vt* : argue, contend — **argumentación** *nf, pl* **-ciones** : (line of) argument — **argumento** *nm* **1** : argument, reasoning **2** TRAMA : plot, story line

árido, -da *adj* : dry, arid — **aridez** *nf, pl* **-deces** : aridity

arisco, -ca *adj* : surly

aristocracia *nf* : aristocracy — **aristócrata** *nmf* : aristocrat — **aristocrático, -ca** *adj* : aristocratic

aritmética *nf* : arithmetic — **aritmético, -ca** *adj* : arithmetic, arithmetical

armar *vt* **1** : arm **2** MONTAR : assemble — **arma** *nf* **1** : arm, weapon **2 armar de fuego** : firearm — **armada** *nf* : navy — **armado, -da** *adj* : armed — **armadura** *nf* **1** : armor **2** ARMAZÓN : framework — **armamento** *nm* : armament, arms *pl*

armario *nm* **1** : (clothes) closet **2** : cupboard, cabinet

armazón *nmf, pl* **-zones** : frame, framework

armisticio *nm* : armistice

armonizar {21} *vt* **1** : harmonize **2** : reconcile (differences, etc.) — *vi* : harmonize, go together — **armonía** *nf* : harmony — **armónica** *nf* : harmonica — **armónico, -ca** *adj* : harmonic — **armonioso, -sa** *adj* : harmonious

arnés *nm, pl* **-neses** : harness

aro *nm* **1** : hoop, ring **2** *Lat* : earring

aroma *nm* : aroma, scent — **aromático, -ca** *adj* : aromatic

arpa *nf* : harp

arpón *nm, pl* **-pones** : harpoon

arquear *vt* : arch, bend — **arquearse** *vr* : bend, bow

arqueología *nf* : archaeology — **arqueológico, -ca** *adj* : archaeological — **arqueólogo, -ga** *n* : archaeologist

arquero, -ra *n* **1** : archer **2** PORTERO : goalkeeper, goalie

arquetipo *nm* : archetype

arquitectura *nf* : architecture — **arquitecto, -ta** *n* : architect — **arquitectónico, -ca** *adj* : architectural

arrabal *nm* **1** : slum **2** arrabales *nmpl* : outskirts

arracimarse *vr* : cluster together

arraigar {52} *vi* : take root, become established — **arraigarse** *vr* : settle down — **arraigado, -da** *adj* : deeply rooted, well established — **arraigo** *nm* : roots *pl*

arrancar {72} *vt* **1** : pull out, tear off **2** : start (an engine), boot (a computer) — *vi* **1** : start an engine **2** : get going — **arranque** *nm* **1** : starter (of a car) **2** ARREBATO : outburst **3 punto de arranque** : starting point

arrasar *vt* **1** : destroy, devastate **2** LLENAR : fill to the brim

arrastrar *vt* **1** : drag **2** ATRAER : draw, attract — *vi* : hang down, trail — **arrastrarse** *vr* **1** : crawl, creep **2** HUMILLARSE : grovel — **arrastre** *nm* **1** : dragging **2** : trawling (for fish)

arrear *vt* : urge on

arrebatar *vt* **1** : snatch, seize **2** CAUTIVAR : captivate — **arrebatarse** *vr* : get carried away — **arrebatado, -da** *adj* : hotheaded, rash — **arrebato** *nm* : outburst

arreciar *vi* : intensify, worsen

arrecife *nm* : reef

arreglar *vt* **1** COMPONER : fix **2** ORDENAR : tidy up **3** SOLUCIONAR : solve, work out — **arreglarse** *vr* **1** : get dressed (up) **2** arreglárselas *fam* : get by, manage — **arreglado, -da** *adj* **1** : fixed, repaired **2** ORDENADO : tidy **3** SOLUCIONADO : settled, sorted out **4** ATAVIADO : smart, dressed-up — **arreglo** *nm* **1** : arrangement **2** REPARACIÓN : repair **3** ACUERDO : agreement

arremangarse {52} *vr* : roll up one's sleeves

arremeter *vi* : attack, charge — **arremetida** *nf* : attack, onslaught

arremolinarse *vr* **1** : crowd around, mill about **2** : swirl (about)

arrendar {55} *vt* : rent, lease

— **arrendador, -dora** *n* : landlord, landlady *f* — **arrendamiento** *nm* : rent, rental — **arrendatario, -ria** *n* : tenant, renter

arrepentirse {76} *vr* **1** : regret, be sorry **2** : repent (for one's sins) — **arrepentido, -da** *adj* : repentant — **arrepentimiento** *nm* : regret, repentance

arrestar *vt* : arrest, detain — **arresto** *nm* : arrest

arriar *vt* : lower

arriba *adv* **1** (*indicating position*) : above, overhead **2** (*indicating direction*) : up, upwards **3** : upstairs (of a house) **4 arriba de** : more than **5 de arriba abajo** : from top to bottom

arribar *vi* **1** : arrive **2** : dock, put into port — **arribista** *nmf* : parvenu, upstart — **arribo** *nm* : arrival

arriendo → **arrendimiento**

arriesgar {52} *vt* : risk, venture — **arriesgarse** *vr* : take a chance — **arriesgado, -da** *adj* : risky

arrimar *vt* : bring closer, draw near — **arrimarse** *vr* : approach

arrinconar *vt* **1** : corner, box in **2** ABANDONAR : push aside

arrobar *vt* : entrance — **arrobarse** *vr* : be enraptured — **arrobamiento** *nm* : rapture, ecstasy

arrodillarse *vr* : kneel (down)

arrogancia *nf* : arrogance — **arrogante** *adj* : arrogant

arrojar *vt* **1** : hurl, cast **2** EMITIR : give off, spew out **3** PRODUCIR : yield — **arrojarse** *vr* : throw oneself — **arrojado, -da** *adj* : daring — **arrojo** *nm* : boldness, courage

arrollar *vt* **1** : sweep away **2** DERROTAR : crush, overwhelm **3** : run over (with a vehicle) — **arrollador, -dora** *adj* : overwhelming

arropar *vt* : clothe, cover (up) — **arroparse** *vr* : wrap oneself up

arroyo *nm* **1** RIACHUELO : stream **2** : gutter (in a street)

arroz *nm, pl* **arroces** : rice

arrugar {52} *vt* : wrinkle, crease — **arrugarse** *vr* : get wrinkled — **arruga** *nf* : wrinkle, crease

arruinar *vt* : ruin, wreck — **arruinarse** *vr* **1** : be ruined **2** EMPOBRECERSE : go bankrupt

arrullar *vt* : lull to sleep — *vi* : coo — **arrullo** *nm* **1** : lullaby **2** : cooing (of doves)

arrumbar *vt* : lay aside

arsenal *nm* : arsenal

arsénico *nm* : arsenic

arte *nmf* (*usually m in singular, f in plural*) **1** : art **2** HABILIDAD : skill **3** ASTUCIA : cunning, cleverness **4** → **bello**

artefacto *nm* : artifact, device

arteria *nf* : artery

artesanía *nm* **1** : craftsmanship **2** : handicrafts *pl* — **artesanal** *adj* : handmade — **artesano, -na** *n* : artisan, craftsman

ártico, -ca *adj* : arctic

articular *vt* : articulate — **articulación** *nf, pl* **-ciones 1** : articulation, pronunciation **2** COYUNTURA : joint

artículo *nm* **1** : article **2 artículos de primera necesidad** : essentials **3 artículos de tocador** : toiletries

artífice *nmf* : artisan, craftsman

artificial *adj* : artificial

artificio *nm* **1** HABILIDAD : skill **2** APARATO : device **3** ARDID : artifice, ruse — **artificioso, -sa** *adj* : cunning, deceptive

artillería *nf* : artillery

artilugio *nm* : gadget

artimaña *nf* : ruse, trick

artista *nmf* **1** : artist **2** ACTOR : actor, actress *f* — **artístico, -ca** *adj* : artistic

artritis *nms & pl* : arthritis — **artrítico, -ca** *adj* : arthritic

arveja *nf Lat* : pea

arzobispo *nm* : archbishop

as *nm* : ace

asa *nf* : handle

asado, -da *adj* : roasted, grilled — **asado** *nm* : roast — **asador** *nm* : spit — **asaduras** *nfpl* : offal, entrails

asalariado, -da *n* : wage earner — **asalariado, -da** *adj* : salaried

asaltar *vt* **1** : assault **2** ROBAR : mug, rob — **asaltante** *nmf* **1** : assailant **2** ATRACADOR : mugger, robber — **asalto** *nm* **1** : assault **2** ROBO : mugging, robbery

asamblea *nf* : assembly, meeting

asar *vt* : roast, grill — **asarse** *vr, fam* : roast, feel the heat

asbesto *nm* : asbestos

ascender {56} *vi* **1** : ascend, rise up **2** : be promoted (in a job) **3 ascender a** : amount to — *vt* : promote — **ascendencia** *nf* : ancestry, descent — **ascendiente** *nmf* : ancestor — **ascender** *nm* : influence — **ascensión** *nf,*

pl **-siones** : ascent — **ascenso** *nm* **1** : ascent, rise **2** : promotion (in a job) — **ascensor** *nm* : elevator

asco *nm* **1** : disgust **2 hacer ascos de** : turn up one's nose at **3 me da asco** : it makes me sick

ascua *nf* **1** : ember **2 estar en ascuas** *fam* : be on edge

asear *vt* : clean, tidy up — **asearse** *vr* : get cleaned up — **aseado, -da** *adj* : clean, tidy

asediar *vt* **1** : besiege **2** ACOSAR : harass — **asedio** *nm* **1** : siege **2** ACOSO : harassment

asegurar *vt* **1** : assure **2** FIJAR : secure **3** : insure (a car, house, etc.) — **asegurarse** *vr* : make sure

asemejarse *vr* **1** : be similar **2 asemejarse a** : look like, resemble

asentar {55} *vt* **1** : set down **2** INSTALAR : set up, establish **3** *Lat* : state — **asentarse** *vr* **1** : settle **2** ESTABLECERSE : settle down — **asentado, -da** *adj* : settled, established

asentir {76} *vi* : assent, agree — **asentimiento** *nm* : assent

aseo *nm* : cleanliness

asequible *adj* : accessible, attainable

aserrar {55} *vt* : saw — **aserradero** *nm* : sawmill — **aserrín** *nm, pl* **-rrines** : sawdust

asesinar *vt* **1** : murder **2** : assassinate — **asesinato** *nm* **1** : murder **2** : assassination — **asesino, -na** *n* **1** : murderer, killer **2** : assassin

asesorar *vt* : advise, counsel — **asesorarse** *vr* **asesorarse de** : consult — **asesor, -sora** *n* : advisor, consultant — **asesoramiento** *nm* : advice, counsel

asestar {55} *vt* **1** : aim (a weapon) **2** : deal (a blow)

aseverar *vt* : assert — **aseveración** *nf, pl* **-ciones** : assertion

asfalto *nm* : asphalt

asfixiar *vt* : asphyxiate, suffocate — **asfixiarse** *vr* : suffocate — **asfixia** *nf* : asphyxiation, suffocation

así *adv* **1** : like this, like that, thus **2 así de** : so, that (much) **3 así que** : so, therefore **4 así que** : as soon as **5 así como** : as well as — **así** *adj* : such, like that — **así** *conj* AUNQUE : even though

asiático, -ca *adj* : Asian, Asiatic

asidero *nm* : handle

asiduo, -dua *adj* : frequent, regular

asiento *nm* : seat

asignar *vt* **1** : assign, allocate **2** DESTINAR : appoint — **asignación** *nf, pl* **-ciones 1** : assignment **2** SUELDO : salary, pay — **asignatura** *nf* : subject, course

asilo *nm* **1** : asylum, home **2** REFUGIO : refuge, shelter — **asilado, -da** *n* : inmate

asimilar *vt* : assimilate — **asimilarse** *vr* **asimilar a** : resemble

asimismo *adv* **1** : similarly, likewise **2** TAMBIÉN : as well, also

asir {7} *vt* : seize, grasp — **asirse** *vr* **asirse a** : cling to

asistir *vi* **asistir a** : attend, be present at — *vt* : assist — **asistencia** *nf* **1** : attendance **2** AYUDA : assistance — **asistente** *nmf* **1** : assistant **2 los asistirs** : those present

asma *nf* : asthma — **asmático, -ca** *adj* : asthmatic

asno *nm* : ass, donkey

asociar *vt* : associate — **asociarse** *vr* **1** : form a partnership **2 asociarse a** : join, become a member of — **asociación** *nf, pl* **-ciones** : association — **asociado, -da** *adj* : associate, associated — **asociado, -da** *n* : associate, partner

asolar {19} *vt* : devastate

asomar *vt* : show, stick out — *vi* : appear, show — **asomarse** *vr* **1** : appear **2** : stick one's head out (of a window)

asombrar *vt* : amaze, astonish — **asombrarse** *vr* : be amazed — **asombro** *nm* : amazement, astonishment — **asombroso, -sa** *adj* : amazing, astonishing

asomo *nm* **1** : hint, trace **2 ni por asomo** : by no means

aspaviento *nm* : exaggerated gestures, fuss

aspecto *nm* **1** : aspect **2** APARIENCIA : appearance, look

áspero, -ra *adj* : rough, harsh — **aspereza** *nf* : roughness, harshness

aspersión *nf, pl* **-siones** : sprinkling — **aspersor** *nm* : sprinkler

aspiración *nf, pl* **-ciones 1** : breathing in **2** ANHELO : aspiration

aspiradora *nf* : vacuum cleaner

aspirar *vi* **aspirar a** : aspire to — *vt* : inhale, breathe in — **aspirante** *nmf* : applicant, candidate

aspirina *nf* : aspirin

asquear *vt* : sicken, disgust

asquerosidad *nf* : filth,

foulness — **asqueroso, -sa** *adj*
: disgusting, sickening

asta *nf* **1** : flagpole **2** CUERNO :
antler, horn **3** : shaft (of a spear)
— **astado, -da** *adj* : horned

asterisco *nm* : asterisk

asteroide *nm* : asteroid

astigmatismo *nm* : astigmatism

astillar *vt* : splinter —
astilla *nf* : splinter, chip

astillero *nm* : shipyard

astral *adj* : astral

astringente *adj & nm* : astringent

astro *nm* **1** : heavenly body
2 : star (of movies, etc.)

astrología *nf* : astrology

astronauta *nmf* : astronaut —
astronáutica *nf* : astronautics

astronave *nf* : spaceship

astronomía *nf* : astronomy —
astronómico, -ca *adj* : astronomical
— **astrónomo, -ma** *n* : astronomer

astucia *nf* **1** : astuteness **2** ARDID :
cunning, guile — **astuto, -ta** *adj* **1**
: astute **2** TAIMADO : crafty

asueto *nm* : time off, break

asumir *vt* : assume — **asunción** *nf*,
pl **-ciones** : assumption

asunto *nm* **1** : matter, affair
2 NEGOCIO : business

asustar *vt* : scare, frighten —
asustarse *vr* **asustarse de** : be frightened
of — **asustadizo, -za** *adj* : jumpy, skittish
— **asustado, -da** *adj* : frightened, afraid

atacar {72} *v* : attack —
atacante *nmf* : attacker

atado *nm* : bundle

atadura *nf* : tie, bond

atajar *vt* : block, cut off — *vi*
atajar por : take a shortcut
through — **atajo** *nm* : shortcut

atañer {79} *vi* **atañer a** :
concern, have to do with

ataque *nm* **1** : attack, assault **2**
ACCESO : fit **3** **ataque de nervios**
: nervous breakdown

atar *vt* : tie up, tie down —
atarse *vr* : tie (up)

atardecer {53} *v impers* : get dark —
atardecer *nm* : late afternoon, dusk

atareado, -da *adj* : busy

atascar {72} *vt* **1** : block, clog **2**
ESTORBAR : hinder — **atascarse** *vr* **1**
OBSTRUIRSE : become obstructed **2** :
get bogged down — **atasco** *nm* **1** :

blockage **2** EMBOTELLAMIENTO : traffic jam

ataúd *nm* : coffin

ataviar {85} *vt* : dress (up) — **ataviarse** *vr*
: dress up — **atavío** *nm* : attire

atemorizar {21} *vt* : frighten —
atemorizarse *vr* : get scared

atención *nf*, *pl* **-ciones** **1** : attention
2 **prestar atención** : pay attention **3**
llamar la atención : attract attention —
atención *interj* : attention!, watch out!

atender {56} *vt* **1** : attend to **2**
CUIDAR : look after **3** : heed (advice,
etc.) — *vi* : pay attention

atenerse {80} *vr* **atenerse a** : abide by

atentamente *adv* **1** : attentively **2 le**
saluda atentamente : sincerely yours

atentar {55} *vi* **atentar contra** : make
an attempt on — **atentado** *nm* : attack

atento, -ta *adj* **1** : attentive,
mindful **2** CORTÉS : courteous

atenuar {3} *vt* **1** : dim (lights),
tone down (colors, etc.) **2** DISMINUIR
: lessen — **atenuante** *nmf* :
extenuating circumstances

ateo, atea *adj* : atheistic
— **ateo,** *n* : atheist

aterciopelado, -da *adj* : velvety, downy

aterido, -da *adj* : frozen stiff

aterrar {55} *vt* : terrify —
aterrador, -dora *adj* : terrifying

aterrizar {21} *vi* : land —
aterrizaje *nm* : landing

aterrorizar {21} *vt* : terrify

atesorar *vt* : hoard, amass

atestar {55} *vt* **1** : crowd, pack **2**
: testify to (in law) — **atestado,**
-da *adj* : stuffed, packed

atestiguar {10} *vt* : testify to

atiborrar *vt* : stuff, cram —
atiborrarse *vr* : stuff oneself

ático *nm* **1** : penthouse **2** DESVÁN : attic

atildado, -da *adj* : smart, neat

atinar *vi* : be on target

atípico, -ca *adj* : atypical

atirantar *vt* : tighten

atisbar *vt* **1** : spy on **2** VISLUMBRAR : catch
a glimpse of — **atisbo** *nm* : sign, hint

atizar {21} *vt* **1** : poke (a fire) **2**
: rouse, stir up (passions, etc.)
— **atizador** *nm* : poker

atlántico, -ca *adj* : Atlantic

atlas *nm* : atlas

atleta *nmf* : athlete — **atlético, -ca** *adj*
: athletic — **atletismo** *nm* : athletics

atmósfera *nf* : atmosphere

— **atmosférico, -ca** *adj* : atmospheric

atolondrado, -da *adj* **1** : scatterbrained
2 ATURDIDO : bewildered, dazed

átomo *nm* : atom — **atómico, -ca** *adj*
: atomic — **atomizador** *nm* : atomizer

atónito, -ta *adj* : astonished, amazed

atontar *vt* : stun, daze

atorar *vt* : block — **atorarse** *vr* : get stuck

atormentar *vt* : torment, torture —
atormentarse *vr* : torment oneself, agonize
— **atormentador, -dora** *n* : tormenter

atornillar *vt* : screw

atorrante *nmf Lat* : bum, loafer

atosigar {52} *vt* : harass, annoy

atracar {72} *vi* : dock, land — *vt* :
hold up, mug — **atracarse** *vr, fam*
atracarse de : gorge oneself with
— **atracadero** *nm* : dock, pier —
atracador, -dora *n* : robber, mugger

atracción *nf*, *pl* **-ciones** : attraction

atraco *nm* : holdup, robbery

atractivo, -va *adj* : attractive —
atractivo *nm* : attraction, appeal

atraer {81} *vt* : attract

atragantarse *vr* : choke

atrancar {72} *vt* : block, bar —
atrancarse *vr* : get blocked, get stuck

atrapar *vt* : trap, capture

atrás *adv* **1** DETRÁS : back, behind **2**
ANTES : before, earlier **3** **para atrás**
or **hacia atrás** : backwards

atrasar *vt* **1** : put back (a clock) **2**
DEMORAR : delay — *vi* : lose time —
atrasarse *vr* : fall behind — **atrasado,**
-da *adj* **1** : late, overdue **2** : backward
(of countries, etc.) **3** : slow (of a clock)
— **atraso** *nm* **1** RETRASO : delay **2** :
backwardness **3** **atrasars** *nmpl* : arrears

atravesar {55} *vt* **1** CRUZAR : cross
2 TRASPASAR : pierce **3** : lay across (a
road, etc.) **4** : go through (a situation)
— **atravesarse** *vr* : be in the way

atrayente *adj* : attractive

atreverse *vr* : dare — **atrevido,**
-da *adj* **1** : bold **2** INSOLENTE :
insolent — **atrevimiento** *nm* **1** :
boldness **2** DESCARO : insolence

atribuir {41} *vt* **1** : attribute
2 : confer (powers, etc.) —
atribuirse *vr* : take credit for

atribular *vt* : afflict, trouble

atributo *nm* : attribute

atrincherar *vt* : entrench —
atrincherarse *vr* : dig oneself in

atrocidad *nf* : atrocity

autobús^M escolar
school bus

atronador, -dora *adj* : thunderous
atropellar *vt* 1 : run over 2 : violate,
abuse (a person) — atropellarse *vr*
: rush — atropellado, -da *adj* : hasty
— atropello *nm* : abuse, outrage
atroz *adj, pl* atroces : atrocious
atuendo *nm* : attire
atufar *vt* : vex — atufarse *vr* : get angry
atún *nm, pl* atunes : tuna
aturdir *vt* 1 : stun, shock 2
CONFUNDIR : bewilder — aturdido,
-da *adj* : dazed, bewildered
audaz *adj, pl* -daces : bold, daring
— audacia *nf* : boldness, audacity
audible *adj* : audible
audición *nf, pl* -ciones 1 : hearing
2 : audition (in theater, etc.)
audiencia *nf* : audience
audífono *nm* 1 : hearing
aid 2 audífonos *nmpl Lat* :
headphones, earphones
audiovisual *adj* : audiovisual
auditar *vt* : audit — auditor,
-tora *n* : auditor
auditorio *nm* 1 : auditorium
2 PÚBLICO : audience
auge *nm* 1 : peak 2 : (economic) boom
augurar *vt* : predict, foretell
— augurio *nm* : omen
augusto, -ta *adj* : august
aula *nf* : classroom
aullar {8} *vi* : howl — aullido *nm* : howl
aumentar *vt* : increase, raise
— *vi* : increase, grow —
aumento *nm* : increase, rise
aun *adv* 1 : even 2 aun así : even so
aún *adv* 1 : still, yet 2 más
aún : furthermore
aunar {8} *vt* : join, combine

— aunarse *vr* : unite
aunque *conj* 1 : though, although,
even if 2 aunque sea : at least
aureola *nf* 1 : halo 2 FAMA : aura
auricular *nm* 1 : telephone receiver
2 auriculares *nmpl* : headphones
aurora *nf* : dawn
ausentarse *vr* : leave, go away —
ausencia *nf* : absence — ausente *adj*
: absent — ausente *nmf* 1 : absentee
2 : missing person (in law)
auspicios *nmpl* : sponsorship, auspices
austero, -ra *adj* : austere —
austeridad *nf* : austerity
austral *adj* : southern
australiano, -na *adj* : Australian
austriaco *or* austríaco, -ca *adj* : Austrian
auténtico, -ca *adj* : authentic, genuine
— autenticidad *nf* : authenticity
auto *nm* : auto, car
autoayuda *nf* : self-help
autobiografía *nf* : autobiography —
autobiográfico, -ca *adj* : autobiographical
▶ autobús *nm, pl* -buses : bus
autocompasión *nf* : self-pity
autocontrol *nm* : self-control
autocracia *nf* : autocracy
autóctono, -na *adj* : indigenous, native
autodefensa *nf* : self-defense
autodidacta *adj* : self-taught
autodisciplina *nf* : self-discipline
autoestop → autostop
autografiar *vt* : autograph —
autógrafo *nm* : autograph
autómata *nm* : automaton
automático, -ca *adj* : automatic
— automatización *nf, pl* -ciones
: automation — automatizar
{21} *vt* : automate

automotor, -triz *adj, fpl*
-trices : self-propelled
automóvil *nm* : automobile —
automovilista *nmf* : motorist —
automovilístico, -ca *adj* : automobile, car
autonomía *nf* : autonomy —
autónomo, -ma *adj* : autonomous
autopista *nf* : expressway, highway
autopropulsado, -da *adj*
: self-propelled
autopsia *nf* : autopsy
autor, -tora *n* 1 : author 2 :
perpetrator (of a crime)
autoridad *nf* : authority —
autoritario, -ria *adj* : authoritarian
autorizar {21} *vt* : authorize, approve
— autorización *nf, pl* -ciones :
authorization — autorizado, -da *adj* 1
PERMITIDO : authorized 2 : authoritative
autorretrato *nm* : self-portrait
autoservicio *nm* 1 : self-service
restaurant 2 SUPERMERCADO : supermarket
autostop *nm* 1 : hitchhiking 2
hacer autostop : hitchhike —
autostopista *nmf* : hitchhiker
autosuficiente *adj* : self-sufficient
auxiliar *vt* : aid, assist — auxiliar *adj* :
auxiliary — auxiliar *nmf* 1 : assistant,
helper 2 auxiliar de vuelo : flight attendant
— auxilio *nm* 1 : aid, assistance
2 primeros auxiliars : first aid
avalancha *nf* : avalanche
avalar *vt* : guarantee, endorse —
aval *nm* : guarantee, endorsement
avanzar {21} *v* : advance, move
forward — avance *nm* : advance
— avanzado, -da *adj* : advanced
avaricia *nf* : greed, avarice — avaricioso,
-sa *adj* : avaricious, greedy — avaro,
-ra *adj* : miserly — avaro, -ra *n* : miser
avasallar *vt* : overpower, subjugate —
avasallador, -dora *adj* : overwhelming
ave *nf* : bird
avecinarse *vr* : approach
avecindarse *vr* : settle,
take up residence
avellana *nf* : hazelnut
avena *nf* 1 : oats *pl* 2 *or*
harina de avena : oatmeal
avenida *nf* : avenue
avenir {87} *vt* : reconcile, harmonize
— avenirse *vr* : agree, come to terms
aventajar *vt* : be ahead of, surpass
aventar {55} *vt* 1 : fan 2 : winnow
(grain) 3 *Lat* : throw, toss

aventurar *vt* : venture, risk —
aventurarse *vr* : take a risk —
aventura *nf* **1** : adventure **2** RIESGO : risk **3**
AMORÍO : love affair — **aventurado, -da** *adj*
: risky — **aventurero, -ra** *adj* : adventurous
— **aventurero, -ra** *n* : adventurer
avergonzar {9} *vt* : shame,
embarrass — **avergonzarse** *vr* :
be ashamed, be embarrassed
averiar {85} *vt* : damage — **averiarse** *vr*
: break down — **avería** *nf* **1** : damage
2 : breakdown (of an automobile) —
averiado, -da *adj* **1** : damaged, faulty
2 : broken down (of an automobile)
averiguar {10} *vt* **1** : find out **2** INVESTIGAR
: investigate — **averiguación** *nf,*
pl -**ciones** : investigation, inquiry
aversión *nf, pl* -**siones** : aversion, dislike
avestruz *nm, pl* -**truces** : ostrich
aviación *nf, pl* -**ciones** : aviation
— **aviador, -dora** *n* : aviator
aviar {85} *vt* : prepare, make ready
ávido, -da *adj* : eager, avid —
avidez *nf, pl* -**deces** : eagerness
avío *nm* **1** : preparation, provision
2 avíos *nmpl* : gear, equipment

▸ **avión** *nm, pl* **aviones** : airplane
— **avioneta** *nf* : light airplane
avisar *vt* **1** : notify **2** ADVERTIR : warn
— **aviso** *nm* **1** : notice **2** ADVERTENCIA
: warning **3** *Lat* : advertisement, ad **4**
estar sobre aviso : be on the alert
avispa *nf* : wasp — **avispón** *nm,*
pl -**pones** : hornet
avispado, -da *adj, fam* : clever, sharp
avistar *vt* : catch sight of
avivar *vt* **1** : enliven, brighten **2** : arouse
(desire, etc.) **3** : intensify (pain)
axila *nf* : underarm, armpit
axioma *nm* : axiom
ay *interj* **1** : oh! **2** : ouch!, ow!
ayer *adv* : yesterday — **ayer** *nm*
: yesteryear, days gone by
ayote *nm Lat* : pumpkin
ayudar *vt* : help, assist —
ayudarse *vr* **ayudarse de** : make use
of — **ayuda** *nf* : help, assistance —
ayudante *nmf* : helper, assistant
ayunar *vi* : fast — **ayunas** *nfpl* **en**
ayunar : fasting — **ayuno** *nm* : fast
ayuntamiento *nm* **1** : town hall, city
hall (building) **2** : town or city council

azabache *nm* : jet
azada *nf* : hoe — **azadonar** *vt* : hoe
azafata *nf* : stewardess *f*
azafrán *nm, pl* -**franes** : saffron
azalea *nf* : azalea
azar *nm* **1** : chance **2 al azar** : at
random — **azaroso, -sa** *adj* : hazardous
(of a journey, etc.), eventful (of a life)
azorar *vt* **1** : alarm **2** DESCONCERTAR
: embarrass — **azorarse** *vr*
: get embarrassed
azotar *vt* : beat, whip — **azote** *nm* **1**
LÁTIGO : whip, lash **2** CALAMIDAD : scourge
azotea *nf* : flat or terraced roof
azteca *adj* : Aztec
azúcar *nmf* : sugar — **azucarado,**
-da *adj* : sugary — **azucarera** *nf* : sugar
bowl — **azucarero, -ra** *adj* : sugar
azufre *nm* : sulphur
azul *adj & nm* : blue —
azulado, -da *adj* : bluish
azulejo *nm* **1** : ceramic
tile **2** *Lat* : bluebird
azur *n* : azure, sky blue
azuzar {21} *vt* : incite, urge on

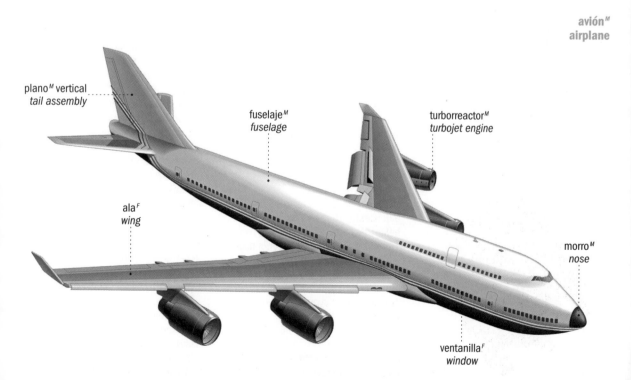

avión*M*
airplane

plano*M* vertical
tail assembly

fuselaje*M*
fuselage

turborreactor*M*
turbojet engine

ala*F*
wing

morro*M*
nose

ventanilla*F*
window

b *nf* : b, second letter of the Spanish alphabet
babear *vi* : drool, slobber — **baba** *nf* : saliva, drool
babel *nmf* : bedlam
babero *nm* : bib
babor *nm* : port (side)
babosa *nf* : slug — **baboso, -sa** *adj* **1** : slimy **2** *Lat fam* : silly
babucha *nf* : slipper
▸ **babuino** *nm* : baboon
bacalao *nm* : cod
bache *nm* **1** : pothole, rut **2** DIFICULTADES : bad time
bachiller *nmf* : high school graduate — **bachillerato** *nm* : high school diploma
bacon *nm, Spain* : bacon
bacteria *nf* : bacterium
bagaje *nm* : baggage, luggage
bagatela *nf* : trinket
bagre *nm* : catfish
bahía *nf* : bay
bailar *v* : dance — **bailarín, -rina** *n, mpl* **-rines** : dancer — **baile** *nm* **1** : dance **2** FIESTA : dance party, ball
bajar *vt* **1** : bring down, lower **2** DESCENDER : go down, come down — *vi* : descend, drop — **bajarse** *vr* **bajarse de** : get out of, get off — **baja** *nf* **1** : fall, drop **2** CESE : dismissal **3** PERMISO : sick leave **4** : (military) casualty — **bajada** *nf* **1** : descent, drop **2** PENDIENTE : slope
bajeza *nf* : lowness, meanness
bajío *nm* : sandbank, shoal
bajo, -ja *adj* **1** : low, lower **2** : short (in stature) **3** : soft, faint (of sounds)

babuino^M
baboon

4 VIL : base, vile — **bajo** *adv* **1** : low **2 habla más bajo** : speak more softly — **bajo** *nm* **1** : ground floor **2** DOBLADILLO : hem **3** : bass (in music) — **bajo** *prep* : under, below — **bajón** *nm, pl* **-jones** : sharp drop, slump
bala *nf* **1** : bullet **2** : bale (of cotton, etc.)
balada *nf* : ballad
balancear *vt* **1** : balance **2** : swing (one's arms, etc.), rock (a boat) — **balancearse** *vr* : swing, sway — **balance** *nm* **1** : balance **2** : balance sheet — **balanceo** *nm* : swaying, rocking
balancín *nm, pl* **-cines 1** : seesaw **2** MECEDORA : rocking chair
balanza *nf* : scales *pl*, balance
balar *vi* : bleat
balaustrada *nf* : balustrade, banister
balazo *nm* **1** DISPARO : shot **2** : bullet wound
balbucear *vi* **1** : stammer, stutter **2** : babble (of a baby) — **balbuceo** *nm* : stammering, muttering, babbling
balcón *nm, pl* **-cones** : balcony
balde *nm* **1** : bucket, pail **2 en balde** : in vain
baldío, -día *adj* **1** : uncultivated **2** INÚTIL : useless — **baldío** *nm* : wasteland
baldosa *nf* : floor tile
balear *vi Lat* : shoot (at) — **baleo** *nm Lat* : shot, shooting
balido *nm* : bleat
balín *nm, pl* **-lines** : pellet
balística *nf* : ballistics — **balístico, -ca** *adj* : ballistic
baliza *nf* **1** : buoy **2** : beacon (for aircraft)
ballena *nf* : whale
ballesta *nf* **1** : crossbow **2** : spring (of an automobile)
ballet *nm* : ballet
balneario *nm* : spa
balompié *nm* : soccer
balón *nm, pl* **-lones** : ball — **baloncesto** *nm* : basketball — **balonvolea** *nm* : volleyball
balsa *nf* **1** : raft **2** ESTANQUE : pond, pool
bálsamo *nm* : balsam, balm — **balsámico, -ca** *adj* : soothing
baluarte *nm* : bulwark, bastion
bambolear *vi* : sway, swing — **bambolearse** *vr* : sway, rock
bambú *nm, pl* **-búes** *or* -bús : bamboo
banal *adj* : banal
banana *nf Lat* : banana — **banano** *nm Lat* : banana

banca *nf* **1** : banking **2** BANCO : bench — **bancario, -ria** *adj* : bank, banking — **bancarrota** *nf* : bankruptcy — **banco** *nm* **1** : bank **2** BANCA : stool, bench, pew **3** : school (of fish)
banda *nf* **1** : band, strip **2** : band (in music) **3** PANDILLA : gang **4** : flock (of birds) **5 banda sonora** : sound track — **bandada** *nf* : flock (of birds), school (of fish)
bandazo *nm* : lurch
bandeja *nf* : tray, platter
bandera *nf* : flag, banner
banderilla *nf* : banderilla
banderín *nm, pl* **-rines** : pennant, small flag
bandido, -da *n* : bandit
bando *nm* **1** : proclamation, edict **2** PARTIDO : faction, side
bandolero, -ra *n* : bandit
banjo *nm* : banjo
banquero, -ra *n* : banker
banqueta *nf* **1** : stool, footstool **2** *Lat* : sidewalk
banquete *nm* : banquet
bañar *vt* **1** : bathe, wash **2** SUMERGIR : immerse **3** CUBRIR : coat, cover — **bañarse** *vr* **1** : take a bath **2** : go swimming — **bañera** *nf* : bathtub — **bañista** *nmf* : bather — **baño** *nm* **1** : bath, swim **2** BAÑERA : bathtub **3 ¿donde está el baño?** : where is the bathroom? **4 baño María** : double boiler
baqueta *nf* **1** : ramrod **2** baquetas *nfpl* : drumsticks
bar *nm* : bar, tavern
barajar *vt* **1** : shuffle (cards) **2** CONSIDERAR : consider — **baraja** *nf* : deck of cards
baranda *nf* : rail, railing — **barandal** *nm* : handrail, banister
barato, -ta *adj* : cheap — **barato** *adv* : cheap, cheaply — **barata** *nf Lat* : sale, bargain — **baratija** *nf* : trinket — **baratillo** *nm* : secondhand store, flea market
barba *nf* **1** : beard, stubble **2** BARBILLA : chin
barbacoa *nf* : barbecue
barbaridad *nf* **1** : barbarity, cruelty **2 ¡qué barbaridad!** : that's outrageous! — **barbarie** *nf* : barbarism, savagery — **bárbaro, -ra** *adj* : barbaric
barbecho *nm* : fallow land
barbero, -ra *n* : barber — **barbería** *nf* : barbershop
barbilla *nf* : chin

barbudo, -da *adj* : bearded

barca *nf* **1** : boat **2 barca de pasaje** : ferryboat — **barcaza** *nf* : barge — **barco** *nm* : boat, ship

barítono *nm* : baritone

barman *nm* : bartender

barnizar {21} *vt* **1** : varnish **2** : glaze (ceramics) — **barniz** *nm, pl* **-nices 1** : varnish **2** : glaze (on ceramics)

barómetro *nm* : barometer

barón *nm, pl* **-rones** : baron — **baronesa** *nf* : baroness

barquero *nm* : boatman

barquillo *nm* : wafer, cone

barra *nf* **1** : bar, rod, stick **2** : counter (of a bar, etc.)

barraca *nf* **1** : hut, cabin **2** CASETA : booth, stall

barranco *nm or* **barranca** *nf* : ravine, gorge, gully

barredera *nf* : street-sweeping machine

barrenar *vt* : drill — **barrena** *nf* : drill, auger

barrer *v* : sweep

barrera *nf* : barrier

barreta *nf* : crowbar

barriada *nf* : district, quarter

barrica *nf* : cask, keg

barricada *nf* : barricade

barrido *nm* : sweep, sweeping

barriga *nf* : belly

barril *nm* **1** : barrel, keg **2 de barril** : draft

barrio *nm* **1** : neighborhood **2 barrio bajo** : slums *pl*

barro *nm* **1** : mud **2** ARCILLA : clay **3** GRANO : pimple, blackhead — **barroso, -sa** *adj* : muddy

barrote *nm* : bar (on a window)

barrunto *nm* **1** : suspicion **2** INDICIO : sign, indication

bártulos *nmpl* : things, belongings

barullo *nm* : racket, ruckus

basa *nf* : base, pedestal — **basar** *vt* : base — **basarse** *vr* **basarse en** : be based on

báscula *nf* : scales *pl*

base *nf* **1** : base **2** FUNDAMENTO : basis, foundation **3 base de datos** : database — **básico, -ca** *adj* : basic

basquetbol *or* básquetbol *nm* Lat : basketball

bastar *vi* : be enough, suffice — **bastante** *adv* **1** : fairly, rather **2** SUFICIENTE : enough — **bastante** *adj* : enough, sufficient — **bastante** *pron* : enough

bastardo, -da *adj & n* : bastard

bastidor *nm* **1** : frame **2** : wing (in theater) **3 entre bastidores** : behind the scenes, backstage

bastilla *nf* : hem

bastión *nf, pl* **-tiones** : bastion, stronghold

basto, -ta *adj* : coarse, rough

bastón *nm, pl* **-tones 1** : cane, walking stick **2** : baton (in parades)

basura *nf* : garbage, rubbish — **basurero, -ra** *n* : garbage collector

bata *nf* **1** : bathrobe, housecoat **2** : smock (of a doctor, laboratory worker, etc.)

batallar *vi* : battle, fight — **batalla** *nf* **1** : battle, fight, struggle **2 de batalla** : ordinary, everyday — **batallón** *nm, pl* **-llones** : battalion

batata *nf* : yam, sweet potato

batear *v* : bat, hit — **bate** *nm* : baseball bat — **bateador, -dora** *n* : batter, hitter

batería *nf* **1** : battery **2** : drums *pl* **3 batería de cocina** : kitchen utensils *pl*

batir *vt* **1** : beat, whip **2** DERRIBAR : knock down — **batirse** *vr* : fight — **batido** *nm* : milk shake — **batidor** *nm* : eggbeater, whisk — **batidora** *nf* : electric mixer

batuta *nf* : baton

baúl *nm* : trunk, chest

bautismo *nm* : baptism — **bautismal** *adj* : baptismal — **bautizar** {21} *vt* : baptize — **bautizo** *nm* : baptism, christening

baya *nf* : berry

bayeta *nf* : cleaning cloth

bayoneta *nf* : bayonet

bazar *nm* : bazaar

bazo *nm* : spleen

bazofia *nf, fam* : rubbish, hogwash

beato, -ta *adj* : blessed

bebé *nm* : baby

beber *v* : drink — **bebedero** *nm* : watering trough — **bebedor, -dora** *n* : (heavy) drinker — **bebida** *nf* : drink, beverage — **bebido, -da** *adj* : drunk

beca *nf* : grant, scholarship

becerro, -rra *n* : calf

befa *nf* : jeer, taunt

beige *adj & nm* : beige

beisbol *or* béisbol *nm* : baseball — **beisbolista** *nmf* : baseball player

beldad *nf* : beauty

belén *nf, pl* **-lenes** : Nativity scene

belga *adj* : Belgian

beliceño, -ña *adj* : Belizean

bélico, -ca *adj* : military, war — **belicoso, -sa** *adj* : warlike

beligerancia *nf* : belligerence — **beligerante** *adj & nmf* : belligerent

belleza *nf* : beauty — **bello, -lla** *adj* **1** : beautiful **2 bellas artes** : fine arts

bellota *nf* : acorn

bemol *adj & nm* : flat (in music)

bendecir {11} *vt* **1** : bless **2 bendecir la mesa** : say grace — **bendición** *nf, pl* **-ciones** : benediction, blessing — **bendito, -ta** *adj* **1** : blessed, holy **2** DICHOSO : fortunate **3 ¡bendito sea Dios!** : thank goodness!

benefactor, -tora *n* : benefactor

beneficiar *vt* : benefit, assist — **beneficiarse** *vr* : benefit, profit — **beneficiario, -ria** *n* : beneficiary — **beneficio** *nm* **1** : gain, profit **2** BIEN : benefit — **beneficioso, -sa** *adj* : beneficial — **benéfico, -ca** *adj* : charitable

benemérito, -ta *adj* : worthy

beneplácito *nm* : approval, consent

benévolo, -la *adj* : benevolent, kind — **benevolencia** *nf* : benevolence, kindness

bengala *nf or* **luz de bengala** : flare

benigno, -na *adj* **1** : mild **2** : benign (in medicine) — **benignidad** *nf* : mildness, kindness

benjamín, -mina *n, mpl* **-mines** : youngest child

beodo, -da *adj & n* : drunk

berenjena *nf* : eggplant

berrear *vi* **1** : bellow, low **2** : bawl, howl (of a person) — **berrido** *nm* **1** : bellowing **2** : howl, scream (of a person)

berro *nm* : watercress

berza *nf* : cabbage

besar *vt* : kiss — **besarse** *vr* : kiss (each other) — **beso** *nm* : kiss

bestia *nf* : beast, animal — **bestial** *adj* : bestial, brutal — **bestialidad** *nf* : brutality

betabel *nm* Lat : beet

betún *nm, pl* **-tunes** : shoe polish

bianual *adj* : biannual

biberón *nm, pl* **-rones** : baby's bottle

Biblia *nf* : Bible — **bíblico, -ca** *adj* : biblical

bibliografía *nf* : bibliography — **bibliográfico, -ca** *adj* : bibliographic, bibliographical

biblioteca *nf* : library — **bibliotecario, -ria** *n* : librarian

bicarbonato *nm* **bicarbonato de soda** : baking soda

bicentenario *nm* : bicentennial

bíceps *nms & pl* : biceps

bicicleta^F y accesorios^M
bicycle and accessories

partes^F de una bicicleta^F
parts of a bicycle

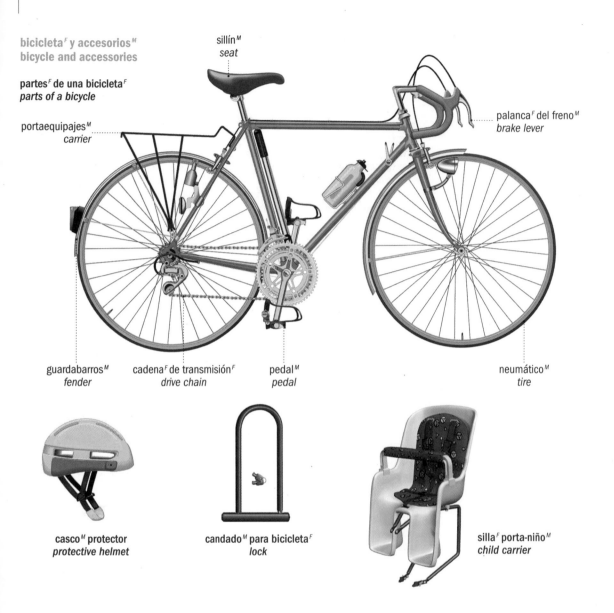

sillín^M
seat

palanca^F del freno^M
brake lever

portaequipajes^M
carrier

guardabarros^M
fender

cadena^F de transmisión^F
drive chain

pedal^M
pedal

neumático^M
tire

casco^M protector
protective helmet

candado^M para bicicleta^F
lock

silla^F porta-niño^M
child carrier

---

bicho *nm* : small animal, bug
▸ bicicleta *nf* : bicycle — **bici** *nf, fam* : bike
bicolor *adj* : two-tone
bidón *nm, pl* -dones : large can, drum
bien *adv* **1** : well, good **2** CORRECTAMENTE
: correctly, right **3** MUY : very, quite **4**
DE BUENA GANA : willingly **5 bien que**
: although **6 más bien** : rather —
bien *adj* **1** : all right, well **2** AGRADABLE :
pleasant, nice **3** SATISFACTORIO : satisfactory
4 CORRECTO : correct, right — **bien** *nm* **1**

: good **2 bienes** *nmpl* : property, goods
bienal *adj & nf* : biennial
bienaventurado, -da *adj*
: blessed, fortunate
bienestar *nm* : welfare, well-being
bienhechor, -chora *n* : benefactor
bienintencionado, -da *adj*
: well-meaning
bienvenido, -da *adj* : **welcome**
— **bienvenida** *nf* **1** : welcome **2**
dar la bienvenida a : welcome

(someone) welcome
bife *nm Lat* : steak
bifocales *nmpl* : bifocals
bifurcarse {72} *vr* : fork —
bifurcación *nf, pl* -ciones : fork, branch
bigamia *nf* : bigamy
bigote *nm* **1** : mustache **2 bigotes** *nmpl*
: whiskers (of an animal)
bikini *nm* : bikini
bilingüe *adj* : bilingual
bilis *nf* : bile

billar *nm* : pool, billiards

billete *nm* **1** : bill, banknote **2** BOLETO : ticket — **billetera** *nf* : billfold, wallet

billón *nm, pl* **-llones** : trillion

bimensual, -suale *adj* : twice a month — **bimestral** *adj* : bimonthly

binario, -ria *adj* : binary

bingo *nm* : bingo

binoculares *nmpl* : binoculars

biodegradable *adj* : biodegradable

biofísica *nf* : biophysics

biografía *nf* : biography — **biográfico, -ca** *adj* : biographical — **biógrafo, -fa** *n* : biographer

biología *nf* : biology — **biológico, -ca** *adj* : biological, biologic — **biólogo, -ga** *n* : biologist

biombo *nm* : folding screen

biomecánica *nf* : biomechanics

biopsia *nf* : biopsy

bioquímica *nf* : biochemistry — **bioquímico, -ca** *adj* : biochemical

biotecnología *nf* : biotechnology

bipartidista *adj* : bipartisan

bípedo *nm* : biped

biquini → **bikini**

birlar *vt, fam* : swipe, pinch

bis *adv* **1** : twice (in music) **2** : A (in an address) — **bis** *nm* : encore

bisabuelo, -la *n* : great-grandfather *m*, great-grandmother *f*

bisagra *nf* : hinge

bisecar {72} *vt* : bisect

biselar *vt* : bevel

bisexual *adj* : bisexual

bisiesto *adj* **año bisiesto** : leap year

bisnieto, -ta *n* : great-grandson *m*, great-granddaughter *f*

▸ **bisonte** *nm* : bison, buffalo

bisoño, -ña *n* : novice

bistec *nm* : steak

bisturí *nm* : scalpel

bisutería *nf* : costume jewelry

bit *nm* : bit (unit of information)

bizco, -ca *adj* : cross-eyed

bizcocho *nm* : sponge cake

bizquear *vi* : squint — **bizquera** *nf* : squint

blanco, -ca *adj* : white — **blanco, -ca** *n* : white person — **blanco** *nm* **1** : white **2** DIANA : target, bull's-eye **3** : blank (space) — **blancura** *nf* : whiteness

blandir {1} *vt* : wave, brandish

blando, -da *adj* **1** : soft, tender **2** DÉBIL : weak-willed **3** INDULGENTE : lenient — **blandura** *nf* **1** : softness, tenderness **2** DEBILIDAD : weakness **3** INDULGENCIA : leniency

blanquear *vt* **1** : whiten, bleach **2** : launder (money) — *vi* : turn white — **blanqueador** *nm Lat* : bleach

blasfemar *vi* : blaspheme — **blasfemia** *nf* : blasphemy — **blasfemo, -ma** *adj* : blasphemous

bledo *nm* **no me importa un bledo** *fam* : I couldn't care less

blindaje *nm* : armor, armor plating — **blindado, -da** *adj* : armored

bloc *nm, pl* **blocs** : (writing) pad

bloquear *vt* **1** OBSTRUIR : block, obstruct **2** : blockade — **bloque** *nm* **1** : block **2** : bloc (in politics) — **bloqueo** *nm* **1** OBSTRUCCIÓN : blockage **2** : blockade

blusa *nf* : blouse — **blusón** *nm, pl* **-sones** : smock

boato *nm* : showiness

bobina *nf* : bobbin, reel

bobo, -ba *adj* : silly, stupid — **bobo, -ba** *n* : fool, simpleton

boca *nf* **1** : mouth **2** ENTRADA : entrance **3 boca arriba** : faceup **4 boca abajo** : facedown, prone **5 boca de riego** : hydrant

bocacalle *nf* : entrance (to a street)

bocado *nm* **1** : bite, mouthful **2** : bit (of a bridle) — **bocadillo** *nm, Spain* : sandwich

bocajarro *nm* **a bocajarro** : point-blank

bocallave *nf* : keyhole

bocanada *nf* **1** : swallow, swig **2** : puff, gust (of smoke, wind, etc.)

boceto *nm* : sketch, outline

bochorno *nm* **1** VERGÜENZA : embarrassment **2** : muggy weather — **bochornoso, -sa** *adj* **1** VERGONZOSO : embarrassing **2** : muggy, sultry

bocina *nf* **1** : horn **2** : mouthpiece (of a telephone) — **bocinazo** *nm* : honk, toot

boda *nf* : wedding

bodega *nf* **1** : wine cellar **2** : warehouse **3** : hold (of a ship or airplane) **4** *Lat* : grocery store

bofetear *vt* : slap — **bofetada** *nf* **or bofetón** *nm* : slap (in the face)

boga *nf* : fashion, vogue

bohemio, -mia *adj & n* : bohemian

boicotear *vt* : boycott — **boicot** *nm, pl* **-cots** : boycott

boina *nf* : beret

bola *nf* **1** : ball **2** *fam* : fib

bolera *nf* : bowling alley

boleta *nf Lat* : ticket — **boletería** *nf Lat* : ticket office

boletín *nm, pl* **-tines 1** : bulletin **2 boletín de noticias** : news release

boleto *nm* : ticket

boliche *nm* **1** : bowling **2** BOLERA : bowling alley

bolígrafo *nm* : ballpoint pen

bolillo *nm* : bobbin

boliviano, -na *adj* : Bolivian

bollo *nm* : bun, sweet roll

bolo *nm* **1** : bowling pin **2 bolos** *nmpl* : bowling

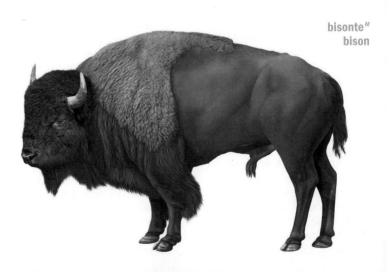

bisonte^M
bison

bolsa *nf* **1** : bag **2** *Lat* : pocketbook, purse **3 la Bolsa** : the stock market — **bolsillo** *nm* : pocket — **bolso** *nm*, *Spain* : pocketbook, handbag

bomba *nf* **1** : bomb **2 bomba de gasolina** : gas pump

bombachos *nmpl* : baggy trousers

bombardear *vt* : bomb, bombard — **bombardeo** *nm* : bombing, bombardment — **bombardero** *nm* : bomber (airplane)

bombear *vt* : pump — **bombero, -ra** *n* : firefighter

bombilla *nf* : lightbulb — **bombillo** *nm* *Lat* : lightbulb

bombo *nm* **1** : bass drum **2 a bombos y platillos** : with a great fanfare

bombón *nm*, *pl* **-bones** : candy, chocolate

bonachón, -chona *adj, mpl* **-chones** *fam* : good-natured

bonanza *nf* **1** : fair weather (at sea) **2** PROSPERIDAD : prosperity

bondad *nf* : goodness, kindness — **bondadoso, -sa** *adj* : kind, good

boniato *nm* : sweet potato

bonificación *nf, pl* **-ciones 1** : bonus, extra **2** DESCUENTO : discount

bonito, -ta *adj* : pretty, lovely

bono *nm* **1** : bond **2** VALE : voucher

boquear *vi* : gasp — **boqueada** *nf* : gasp

boquerón *nm, pl* **-rones** : anchovy

boquete *nm* : gap, opening

boquiabierto, -ta *adj* : open-mouthed, speechless

boquilla *nf* : mouthpiece (of a musical instrument)

borbollar *vi* : bubble

borbotar *or* borbotear *vi* : boil, bubble, gurgle — **borbotón** *nm, pl* **-tones 1** : spurt **2 salir a borbotones** : gush out

bordar *v* : embroider — **bordado** *nm* : embroidery, needlework

borde *nm* **1** : border, edge **2 al borde de** : on the verge of — **bordear** *vt* : border — **bordillo** *nm* : curb

bordo *nm* **a bordo** : aboard, on board

borla *nf* **1** : pom-pom, tassel **2** : powder puff

borracho, -cha *adj & n* : drunk — **borrachera** *nf* : drunkenness

borrar *vt* : erase, blot out — **borrador** *nm* **1** : rough draft **2** : eraser (for a blackboard)

borrascoso, -sa *adj* : stormy

borrego, -ga *n* : lamb, sheep — **borrego** *nm Lat* : false rumor, hoax

borrón *nm, pl* **-rrones 1** : smudge, blot **2 borrón y cuenta nueva** : let's forget about it — **borroso, -sa** *adj* **1** : blurry, smudgy **2** INDISTINTO : vague, hazy

bosque *nm* : woods, forest — **boscoso, -sa** *adj* : wooded

bosquejar *vt* : sketch (out) — **bosquejo** *nm* : outline, sketch

bostezar {21} *vi* : yawn — **bostezo** *nm* : yawn

bota *nf* : boot

botánica *nf* : botany — **botánico, -ca** *adj* : botanical

botar *vt* **1** : throw, hurl **2** *Lat* : throw away **3** : launch (a ship) — *vi* : bounce

bote *nm* **1** : small boat **2** *Spain* : can **3** TARRO : jar **4** SALTO : bounce, jump

botella *nf* : bottle

botín *nm, pl* **-tines 1** : ankle boot **2** DESPOJOS : booty, plunder

botiquín *nm, pl* **-quines 1** : medicine cabinet **2** : first-aid kit

botón *nm, pl* **-tones 1** : button **2** YEMA : bud — **botones** *nmfs & pl* : bellhop

botulismo *nm* : botulism

boutique *nf* : boutique

bóveda *nf* : vault

boxear *vi* : box — **boxeador, -dora** *n* : boxer — **boxeo** *nm* : boxing

boya *nf* : buoy — **boyante** *adj* **1** : buoyant **2** PRÓSPERO : prosperous, thriving

bozal *nm* **1** : muzzle **2** : halter (for a horse)

bracear *vi* **1** : wave one's arms **2** NADAR : swim, crawl

bracero, -ra *n* : day laborer

bragas *nf, Spain* : panties

bragueta *nf* : fly, pants zipper

braille *adj & nm* : braille

bramante *nm* : twine, string

bramar *vi* **1** : bellow, roar **2** : howl (of the wind) — **bramido** *nm* : bellow, roar

brandy *nm* : brandy

branquia *nf* : gill

brasa *nf* : ember

brasier *nm Lat* : brassiere

brasileño, -ña *adj* : Brazilian

bravata *nf* **1** : boast, bravado **2** AMENAZO : threat

bravo, -va *adj* **1** : fierce, savage **2** : rough (of the sea) **3** *Lat* : angry — **bravo, -va** *interj* : bravo!, well done! — **bravura** *nf* **1** FEROCIDAD : fierceness **2** VALENTÍA : bravery

braza *nf* **1** : breaststroke **2** : fathom

(measurement) — **brazada** *nf* : stroke (in swimming)

brazalete *nm* **1** : bracelet **2** : (cloth) armband

brazo *nm* **1** : arm **2** : branch (of a river, etc.) **3 brazo derecho** : right-hand man **4 brazos** *nmpl* : hands, laborers

brea *nf* : tar

brebaje *nm* : concoction

brecha *nf* : breach, gap

brécol *nm* : broccoli

bregar {52} *vi* **1** LUCHAR : struggle **2** TRABAJAR : work hard — **brega** *nf* **andar a la brega** : struggle

breña *nf or* breñal *nm* : scrubland, brush

breve *adj* **1** : brief, short **2 en breve** : shortly, in short — **brevedad** *nf* : brevity, shortness — **brevemente** *adv* : briefly

brezal *nm* : moor, heath — **brezo** *nm* : heather

bricolaje *or* bricolage *nm* : do-it-yourself

brida *nf* : bridle

brigada *nf* **1** : brigade **2** EQUIPO : gang, team, squad

brillar *vi* : shine, sparkle — **brilliante** *adj*

boxeador[M]
boxer

casco[M]
headgear

guante[M]
glove

pantalones[M] de boxeo[M]
boxing trunks

: brilliant, shiny — **brillante** *nm* : diamond — **brillantez** *nf* : brilliance — **brillo** *nm* **1** : luster, shine **2** ESPLENDOR : splendor — **brilloso, -sa** *adj* : shiny

brincar {72} *vi* : jump about, frolic — **brinco** *nm* : jump, skip

brindar *vi* : drink a toast — *vt* : offer, provide — **brindarse** *vr* : offer one's assistance — **brindis** *nm* : drink, toast

brío *nm* **1** : force, determination **2** ÁNIMO : spirit, verve — **brioso, -sa** *adj* : spirited, lively

brisa *nf* : breeze

británico, -ca *adj* : British

brizna *nf* **1** : strand, thread **2** : blade (of grass)

brocado *nm* : brocade

brocha *nf* : paintbrush

broche *nm* **1** : fastener, clasp **2** ALFILER : brooch

brocheta *nf* : skewer

brócoli *nm* : broccoli

bromear *vi* : joke, fool around — **broma** *nf* : joke, prank — **bromista** *adj* : fun-loving, joking

— **bromista** *nmf* : joker, prankster

bronca *nf, fam* : fight, row

bronce *nm* : bronze — **bronceado, -da** *adj* : suntanned — **bronceado** *nm* : tan — **broncearse** *vr* : get a suntan

bronco, -ca *adj* **1** : harsh, rough **2** : untamed, wild (of a horse)

bronquitis *nf* : bronchitis

broqueta *nf* : skewer

brotar *vi* **1** : bud, sprout **2** : stream, gush (of a river, tears, etc.) **3** : arise (of feelings, etc.) **4** : break out (in medicine) — **brote** *nm* **1** : outbreak **2** : sprout, bud, shoot (of plants)

brujería *nf* : witchcraft — **bruja** *nf* **1** : witch **2** *fam* : old hag — **brujo** *nm* : warlock, sorcerer — **brujo, -ja** *adj* : bewitching

brújula *nf* : compass

bruma *nf* : haze, mist — **brumoso, -sa** *adj* : hazy, misty

bruñir {38} *vt* : burnish, polish

brusco, -ca *adj* **1** SÚBITO : sudden, abrupt **2** TOSCO : brusque, rough — **brusquedad** *nf* : abruptness, brusqueness

brutal *adj* : brutal — **brutalidad** *nf* : brutality

bruto, -ta *adj* **1** : brutish, stupid **2** : crude (of petroleum, etc.), uncut (of diamonds) **3 peso bruto, -ta** : gross weight — **bruto, -ta** *n* : brute

bucal *adj* : oral

bucear *vi* **1** : dive, swim underwater **2 bucear en** : delve into — **buceo** *nm* : (underwater) diving

bucle *nm* : curl

budín *nm, pl* **-dines** : pudding

budismo *nm* : Buddhism — **budista** *adj & nmf* : Buddhist

buenamente *adv* **1** : easily **2** VOLUNTARIAMENTE : willingly

buenaventura *nf* **1** : good luck **2 decir la buenaventura a uno** : tell someone's fortune

bueno, -na *adj* (**buen** *before masculine singular nouns*) **1** : good **2** AMABLE : kind **3** APROPIADO : appropriate **4** SALUDABLE : well, healthy **5** : nice, fine (of weather) **6 buenos días** : hello, good day **7 buenas noches** : good night **8**

entrenador^M — *trainer*
boxeador^M — *boxer*
árbitro^M — *referee*
cuerda^F — *rope*
boxeo^M — *boxing*
cuadrilátero^M — *ring*
ayudante^M — *assistant*
médico^M — *physician*
lona^F — *canvas*
juez^M — *judge*

buitre^M
vulture

buenas tardes : good afternoon, good
evening — **bueno** *interj* : OK!, all right!
buey *nm* : ox, steer
búfalo *nm* : buffalo
bufanda *nf* : scarf
bufar *vi* : snort — **bufido** *nm* : snort
bufet *or* bufé *nm* : buffet-style meal
bufete *nm* **1** : law practice
  2 MESA : writing desk

bufo, -fa *adj* : comic — **bufón,**
  -fona *n, mpl* **-fones** : buffoon, jester
  — **bufonada** *nf* : wisecrack
buhardilla *nf* : attic, garret
búho *nm* : owl
▸ buitre *nm* : vulture
bujía *nf* : spark plug
bulbo *nm* : bulb (of a plant)
bulevar *nm* : boulevard
búlgaro, -ra *adj* : Bulgarian
bulla *nf* : uproar, racket
▸ bulldozer *nm* : bulldozer
bullicio *nm* **1** : uproar **2** AJETREO
  : hustle and bustle — **bullicioso,**
  -sa *adj* : noisy, boisterous
bullir {38} *vi* **1** : boil **2**
  AJETREARSE : bustle, stir
bulto *nm* **1** : package, bundle **2** VOLUMEN
  : bulk, size **3** FORMA : form, shape **4**
  PROTUBERANCIA : lump, swelling
bumerán *nm, pl* **-ranes** : boomerang
buñuelo *nm* : fried pastry
buque *nm* : ship
burbujear *vi* : bubble —
  burbuja *nf* : bubble
burdel *nm* : brothel

burdo, -da *adj* : coarse, rough
burgués, -guesa *adj & n, mpl* **-gueses**
  : bourgeois — **burguesía** *nf* : bourgeoisie
burlar *vt* : trick, deceive —
  burlarse *vr* **burlarse de** : make fun
  of — **burla** *nf* **1** MOFA : mockery,
  ridicule **2** BROMA : joke, trick
burlesco, -ca *adj* : comic, funny
burlón, -lona *adj, mpl* **-lones** : mocking
burocracia *nf* : bureaucracy —
  burócrata *nmf* : bureaucrat —
  burocrático, -ca *adj* : bureaucratic
burro, -rra *n* **1** : donkey **2** *fam* :
  dunce — **burro, -rra** *adj* : stupid —
  burro *nm* **1** : sawhorse **2** *Lat* : stepladder
bus *nm* : bus
buscar {72} *vt* **1** : look for, seek **2**
  ir a buscar a uno : fetch someone
  — *vi* : search — **busca** *nf* : search
  — **búsqueda** *nf* : search
busto *nm* : bust (in sculpture)
butaca *nf* **1** : armchair **2** : (theater) seat
butano *nm* : butane
buzo *nm* : diver
buzón *nm, pl* **-zones** : mailbox
byte *nm* : byte

bulldozer^M
bulldozer

motor^M diésel
diesel motor compartment

tubo^M de escape^M
exhaust pipe stack

cabina^F
cab

pala^F
blade

desterronadora^F
ripper

rueda^F guía^F
push frame

oruga^F
track

c *nf* : c, third letter of the Spanish alphabet

cabal *adj* **1** : exact **2** COMPLETO : complete — **cabales** *nmpl* **no estar en sus cabal** : not be in one's right mind

cabalgar {52} *vi* : ride — **cabalgata** *nf* : cavalcade

caballa *nf* : mackerel

caballería *nf* **1** : cavalry **2** CABALLO : horse, mount — **caballeriza** *nf* : stable

caballero *nm* **1** : gentleman **2** : knight (rank) — **caballerosidad** *nf* : chivalry — **caballeroso, -sa** *adj* : chivalrous

caballete *nm* **1** : ridge (of a roof) **2** : easel (for a canvas) **3** : bridge (of the nose)

caballito *nm* **1** : rocking horse **2** caballitos *nmpl* : merry-go-round

caballo *nm* **1** : horse **2** : knight (in chess) **3 caballo de fuerza** : horsepower

cabaña *nf* : cabin, hut

cabaret *nm, pl* **-rets** : nightclub, cabaret

cabecear *vi* **1** : shake one's head, nod **2** : pitch, lurch (of a boat)

cabecera *nf* **1** : head (of a bed, etc.) **2** : heading (in a text) **3 médico de cabecera** : family doctor

cabecilla *nmf* : ringleader

cabello *nm* : hair — **cabelludo, -da** *adj* : hairy

caber {12} *vi* **1** : fit, go (into) **2 no cabe duda** : there's no doubt

cabestro *nm* : halter

cabeza *nf* **1** : head **2 de cabeza** : head first — **cabezada** *nf* **1** : butt (of the head) **2 dar cabezadas** : nod off

cabezal *nm* : bolster, headrest

cabida *nf* **1** : room, capacity **2 dar cabida a** : accomodate, find room for

cabina *nf* **1** : booth **2** : cab (of a truck, etc.) **3** : cabin, cockpit (of an airplane)

cabizbajo, -ja *adj* : downcast

cable *nm* : cable

cabo *nm* **1** : end, stub **2** TROZO : bit **3** : corporal (in the military) **4** : cape (in geography) **5 al fin y al cabo** : after all **6 llevar a cabo** : carry out, do

cabra *nf* : goat

cabriola *nf* **1** : leap, skip **2 hacer cabriolas** : prance around

cabrito *nm* : kid (goat)

cacahuate *or* cacahuete *nm* : peanut

cacao *nm* **1** : cacao (tree) **2** : cocoa (drink)

cacarear *vi* : crow, cackle — *vt, fam* : boast about

cafetera*F* de filtro*M* automática
automatic drip coffeemaker

tapa*F*
lid

depósito*M* de agua*F*
reservoir

filtro*M*
basket

cafetera*F*
carafe

placa*F* térmica
warming plate

interruptor*M*
on-off switch

cacería *nf* : hunt

cacerola *nf* : pan, saucepan

cacharro *nm* **1** *fam* : thing, piece of junk **2** *fam* : jalopy **3** cacharros *nmpl* : pots and pans

cachear *vt* : search, frisk

cachemir *nm or* **cachemira** *nf* : cashmere

cachete *nm Lat* : cheek — **cachetada** *nf Lat* : slap

cacho *nm* **1** *fam* : piece, bit **2** *Lat* : horn

cachorro, -rra *n* **1** : cub **2** PERRITO : puppy

cactus *or* cacto *nm* : cactus

cada *adj* : each, every

cadalso *nm* : scaffold

cadáver *nm* : corpse

cadena *nf* **1** : chain **2** : (television) channel **3 cadena de montaje** : assembly line

cadencia *nf* : cadence

cadera *nf* : hip

cadete *nmf* : cadet

caducar {72} *vi* : expire — **caducidad** *nf* : expiration

caer {13} *vi* **1** : fall, drop **2 caer bien a uno** : be to one's liking **3 dejar caer** : drop **4 me cae bien** : I like her, I like him — **caerse** *vr* : drop, fall (down)

café *nm* **1** : coffee **2** : café — **café** *adj*

▶ *Lat* : brown — **cafetera** *nf* : coffeepot — **cafetería** *nf* : coffee shop, cafeteria — **cafeína** *nf* : caffeine

caída *nf* **1** : fall, drop **2** PENDIENTE : slope

caimán *nm, pl* **-manes** : alligator

caja *nf* **1** : box, case **2** : checkout counter, cashier's desk (in a store) **3 caja fuerte** : safe **4 caja registradora** : cash register — **cajero, -ra** *n* **1** : cashier **2** : (bank) teller — **cajetilla** *nf* : pack (of cigarettes) — **cajón** *nm, pl* **-jones 1** : drawer (in furniture) **2** : large box, crate

cajuela *nf Lat* : trunk (of a car)

cal *nf* : lime

cala *nf* : cove

calabaza *nf* **1** : pumpkin, squash, gourd **2 dar calabazas a** *fam* : give the brush-off to — **calabacín** *nm, pl* **-cines** *or* calabacita *nf Lat* : zucchini

calabozo *nm* **1** : prison **2** CELDA : cell

calamar *nm* : squid

calambre *nm* **1** ESPASMO : cramp **2** : (electric) shock

calamidad *nf* : calamity

calar *vt* **1** : soak (through) **2** PERFORAR : pierce — **calarse** *vr* : get drenched

calavera *nf* : skull

calcar {72} *vt* **1** : trace **2** IMITAR : copy, imitate

calcetín *nm, pl* **-tines** : sock

calcinar *vt* : char

calcio *nm* : calcium

calcomanía *nf* : decal

calcular *vt* : calculate, estimate — **calculador, -dora** *adj* : calculating — **calculadora** *nf* : calculator — **cálculo** *nm* **1** : calculation **2** : calculus (in mathematics and medicine) **3 cálculo biliar** : gallstone

caldera *nf* **1** : cauldron **2** : boiler (for heating, etc.) — **caldo** *nm* : broth, stock

calefacción *nf, pl* **-ciones** : heating, heat

calendario *nm* : calendar

calentar {55} *vt* : heat (up), warm (up) — **calentarse** *vr* : get warm, heat up — **calentador** *nm* : heater — **calentura** *nf* : temperature, fever

calibre *nm* **1** : caliber **2** DIÁMETRO : bore, diameter — **calibrar** *vt* : calibrate

calidad *nf* **1** : quality **2 en calidad de** : as, in the capacity of

cálido, -da *adj* : hot, warm

calidoscopio *nm* : kaleidoscope

caliente *adj* **1** : hot **2** ACALORADO : heated, fiery

calificar {72} *vt* **1** : qualify **2** EVALUAR : rate **3** : grade (an exam, etc.) — **calificación** *nf, pl* **-ciones 1** : qualification **2** EVALUACIÓN : rating **3** NOTA : grade — **calificativo, -va** *adj* : qualifying — **calificativo** *nm* : qualifier, epithet

caligrafía *nf* : penmanship

calistenia *nf* : calisthenics

cáliz *nm, pl* **-lices** : chalice

caliza *nf* : limestone

callar *vi* : keep quiet, be silent — *vt* **1** : silence, hush **2** OCULTAR : keep secret — **callarse** *vr* : remain silent — **callado, -da** *adj* : quiet, silent

calle *nf* : street, road — **callejear** *vi* : wander about the streets — **callejero, -ra** *adj* **1** : street **2 perro callejero** : stray dog — **callejón** *nm, pl* **-jones 1** : alley **2 callejón sin salida** : dead-end street

callo *nm* : callus, corn

calma *nf* : calm, quiet — **calmante** *adj* : soothing — **calma** *nm* : tranquilizer — **calmar** *vt* : calm, soothe — **calmarse** *vr* : calm down — **calmo, -ma** *adj Lat* : calm — **calmoso, -sa** *adj* **1** : calm **2** LENTO : slow

calor *nm* **1** : heat, warmth **2 tener calor** : be hot — **caloría** *nf* : calorie

calumnia *nf* : slander, libel

— calumniar *vt* : slander, libel

caluroso, -sa *adj* **1** : hot **2** : warm, enthusiastic (of applause, etc.)

calvo, -va *adj* : bald — **calvicie** *nf* : baldness

calza *nf* : wedge

calzada *nf* : roadway

calzado *nm* : footwear — **calzar** {21} *vt* **1** : wear (shoes) **2** : put shoes on (someone)

calzones *nmpl Lat* : panties — **calzoncillos** *nmpl* : underpants, briefs

cama *nf* : bed

camada *nf* : litter, brood

camafeo *nm* : cameo

cámara *nf* **1** : chamber **2** *or* **cámara fotográfica** : camera **3** : house (in government)

camarada *nmf* : comrade — **camaradería** *nf* : camaraderie

camarero, -ra *n* **1** : waiter, waitress *f* **2** : steward *m*, stewardess *f* (on a ship, etc.) — **camarera** *nf* : chambermaid *f*

camarón *nm, pl* **-rones** : shrimp

camarote *nm* : cabin, stateroom

cambiar *vt* **1** : change **2** CANJEAR : exchange — *vi* **1** : change **2** : shift gears (of an automobile) — **cambiarse** *vr* **1** : change (clothing) **2** : move (to a new address) — **cambiable** *adj* : changeable — **cambio** *nm* **1** : change **2** CANJE : exchange **3 en cambio** : on the other hand

camello *nm* : camel

camilla *nf* : stretcher — **camillero** *nm* : orderly (in a hospital)

caminar *vi* : walk — *vt* : cover (a distance) — **caminata** *nf* : hike

camino *nm* **1** : road, path **2** RUTA : way **3 a medio camino** : halfway (there) **4 ponerse en camino** : set out

camión *nm, pl* **-miones 1** : truck **2** *Lat* : bus — **camionero, -ra** *n* **1** : truck driver **2** *Lat* : bus driver — **camioneta** *nm* : light truck, van

camisa *nf* **1** : shirt **2 camisa de fuerza** : straitjacket — **camiseta** *nf* : T-shirt, undershirt — **camisón** *nm, pl* **-sones** : nightshirt, nightgown

camorra *nf, fam* : fight, trouble

camote *nm Lat* : sweet potato

campamento *nm* : camp

campana *nf* : bell — **campanada** *nf* : stroke (of a bell), peal — **campanario** *nm* : bell tower — **campanilla** *nf* : (small) bell

campaña *nf* **1** : countryside **2** : (military or political) campaign

campeón, -peona *n, mpl* **-peones** : champion — **campeonato** *nm* : championship

campesino, -na *n* : peasant, farm laborer — **campestre** *adj* : rural, rustic

camping *nm* **1** : campsite **2 hacer camping** : go camping

campiña *nf* : countryside

campo *nm* **1** : field **2** CAMPIÑA : countryside, country **3** CAMPAMENTO : camp

camuflaje *nm* : camouflage — **camuflar** *vt* : camouflage

cana *nf* : gray hair

canadiense *adj* : Canadian

canal *nm* **1** : canal **2** MEDIO : channel **3** : (radio or television) channel — **canalizar** {21} *vt* : channel

canalete *nm* : paddle (of a canoe)

canalla *nf* : rabble — **canalla** *nmf, fam* : swine, bastard

canapé *nm* **1** : canapé **2** SOFÁ : sofa, couch

canario *nm* : canary

canasta *nf* : basket — **canasto** *nm* : large basket

cancelar *vt* **1** : cancel **2** : pay off, settle (a debt) — **cancelación** *nf, pl* **-ciones 1** : cancellation **2** : payment in full (of a debt)

cáncer *nm* : cancer — **canceroso, -sa** *adj* : cancerous

cancha *nf* : court, field (for sports)

canciller *nm* : chancellor

canción *nf, pl* **-ciones 1** : song **2 canción de cuna** : lullaby — **cancionero** *nm* : songbook

candado *nm* : padlock

candela *nf* : candle — **candelabro** *nm* : candelabra — **candelero** *nm* **1** : candlestick **2 estar en el candelero** : be in the limelight

candente *adj* : red-hot

candidato, -ta *n* : candidate — **candidatura** *nf* : candidacy

cándido, -da *adj* : naïve — **candidez** *nf* **1** : simplicity **2** INGENUIDAD : naïveté

candil *nm* : oil lamp — **candilejas** *nfpl* : footlights

candor *nm* : naïveté, innocence

canela *nf* : cinnamon

▸ **cangrejo** *nm* : crab

canguro *nm* : kangaroo

caníbal *nmf* : cannibal

— **canibalismo** *nm* : cannibalism

canicas *nfpl* : (game of) marbles

canino, -na *adj* : canine —
canino *nm* : canine (tooth)

canjear *vt* : exchange —
canje *nm* : exchange, trade

cano, -na *adj* : gray, gray-haired

canoa *nf* : canoe

canon *nm, pl* **cánones** : canon

canonizar {21} *vt* : canonize

canoso, -sa *adj* : gray, gray-haired

cansar *vt* : tire (out) — *vi* : be tiring
— **cansarse** *vr* : get tired — **cansado,
-da** *adj* **1** : tired **2** PESADO : tiresome —
cansancio *nm* : fatigue, weariness

cantalupo *nm* : cantaloupe

cantar *v* : sing — **cantar** *nm* :
song — **cantante** *nmf* : singer

cántaro *nm* **1** : pitcher, jug **2 llover a
cántaros** *fam* : rain cats and dogs

cantera *nf* : quarry (excavation)

cantidad *nf* **1** : quantity, amount
2 una cantidad de : lots of

cantimplora *nf* : canteen, water bottle

cantina *nf* **1** : canteen,
cafeteria **2** *Lat* : tavern, bar

canto *nm* **1** : singing, song **2** BORDE,
LADO : edge **3 de canto** : on end,
sideways **4 canto rodado** : boulder —
cantor, -tora *adj* **1** : singing **2 pájaro
cantor** : songbird — **cantor** *n* : singer

caña *nf* **1** : cane, reed **2 caña
de pescar** : fishing pole

cáñamo *nm* : hemp

cañería *nf* : pipes, piping — **caño** *nm* **1**
: pipe **2** : spout (of a fountain) —
cañón *nm, pl* **-ñones 1** : cannon **2** : barrel
(of a gun) **3** : canyon (in geography)

caoba *nf* : mahogany

caos *nm* : chaos — **caótico,
-ca** *adj* : chaotic

capa *nf* **1** : cape, cloak **2** : coat (of paint,
etc.), coating (in cooking) **3** ESTRATO
: layer, stratum **4** : (social) class

capacidad *nf* **1** : capacity
2 APTITUD : ability

capacitar *vt* : train, qualify —
capacitación *nf, pl* **-ciones** : training

caparazón *nm, pl* **-zones** : shell

capataz *nmf, pl* **-taces** : foreman

capaz *adj, pl* **-paces 1** : capable,
able **2** ESPACIOSO : spacious

capellán *nm, pl* **-llanes** : chaplain

capilla *nf* : chapel

capital *adj* **1** : capital **2** PRINCIPAL

cangrejo^M
crab

: chief, principal — **capital** *nm*
: capital (assets) — **capital** *nf* :
capital (city) — **capitalismo** *nm*
: capitalism — **capitalista** *adj*
& nmf : capitalist, capitalistic —
capitalizar {21} *vt* : capitalize

capitán, -tana *n, mpl* **-tanes** : captain

capitolio *nm* : capitol

capitular *vi* : capitulate, surrender —
capitulación *nf, pl* **-ciones** : surrender

capítulo *nm* : chapter

capó *nm* : hood (of a car)

capote *nm* : cloak, cape

capricho *nm* : whim, caprice —
caprichoso, -sa *adj* : whimsical, capricious

cápsula *nf* : capsule

captar *vt* **1** : grasp **2** ATRAER : gain,
attract (interest, etc.) **3** : harness (waters)

capturar *vt* : capture, seize —
captura *nf* : capture, seizure

capucha *nf* : hood (of clothing)

capullo *nm* **1** : cocoon **2** : (flower) bud

caqui *adj & nm* : khaki

cara *nf* **1** : face **2** ASPECTO :
appearance **3** *fam* : nerve, gall **4
cara a** *or* **de cara a** : facing

carabina *nf* : carbine

caracol *nm* **1** : snail **2** *Lat*
: conch **3** RIZO : curl

carácter *nm, pl* **-racteres 1** :
character **2** ÍNDOLE : nature —
característica *nf* : characteristic —
característico, -ca *adj* : characteristic
— **caracterizar** {21} *vt* : characterize

caramba *interj* : oh my!, good grief!

carámbano *nm* : icicle

caramelo *nm* **1** : caramel
2 DULCE : candy

carátula *nf* **1** CARETA : mask **2** : jacket (of

a record, etc.) **3** *Lat* : face (of a watch)

caravana *nf* **1** : caravan
2 REMOLQUE : trailer

caray → **caramba**

carbohidrato *nm* : carbohydrate

carbón *nm, pl* **-bones 1** : coal **2** :
charcoal (for drawing) — **carboncillo** *nm*
: charcoal — **carbonero, -ra** *adj* :
coal — **carbonizar** {21} *vt* : char —
carbono *nm* : carbon — **carburador** *nm*
: carburetor — **carburante** *nm* : fuel

carcajada *nf* : loud laugh, guffaw

cárcel *nf* : jail, prison —
carcelero, -ra *n* : jailer

carcinógeno *nm* : carcinogen

carcomer *vt* : eat away at —
carcomido, -da *adj* : worm-eaten

cardenal *nm* **1** : cardinal
2 CONTUSIÓN : bruise

cardíaco *or* **cardiaco,
-ca** *adj* : cardiac, heart

cárdigan *nm, pl* **-gans** : cardigan

cardinal *adj* : cardinal

cardiólogo, -ga *n* : cardiologist

cardo *nm* : thistle

carear *vt* : bring face-to-face

carecer {53} *vi* **carecer de** : lack
— **carencia** *nf* : lack, want —
carente *adj* **carente de** : lacking (in)

carestía *nf* **1** : high cost **2**
ESCASEZ : dearth, scarcity

careta *nf* : mask

cargar {52} *vt* **1** : load **2** : charge (a
battery, a purchase, etc.) **3** LLEVAR :
carry **4 cargar de** : burden with — *vi* **1**
: load **2 cargar con** : pick up, carry
away — **carga** *nf* **1** : load **2** CARGAMENTO
: freight, cargo **3** RESPONSABILIDAD :
burden **4** : charge (in electricity, etc.)
— **cargado, -da** *adj* **1** : loaded,
burdened **2** PESADO : heavy, stuffy **3** :
charged (of a battery) **4** FUERTE : strong,
concentrated — **cargamento** *nm*
: cargo, load — **cargo** *nm* **1** :
charge **2** PUESTO : position, office

cariarse *vr* : decay (of teeth)

caribe *adj* : Caribbean

caricatura *nf* **1** : caricature **2** : (political)
cartoon — **caricaturizar** *vt* : caricature

caricia *nf* : caress

caridad *nf* **1** : charity **2** LIMOSNA : alms *pl*

caries *nfs & pl* : cavity (in a tooth)

cariño *nm* : affection, love — **cariñoso,
-sa** *adj* : affectionate, loving

carisma *nf* : charisma — **carismático,**

-ca adj : charismatic
caritativo, -va adj : charitable
cariz nm, pl **-rices** : appearance, aspect
carmesí adj & nm : crimson
carmín nm, pl **-mines** or
carmín de labios : lipstick
carnada nf : bait
carnal adj **1** : carnal **2 primo**

carnal : first cousin
carnaval nm : carnival
carne nf **1** : meat **2** : flesh (of persons or fruits) **3 carne de cerdo** : pork **4 carne de gallina** : goose bumps **5 carne de ternera** : veal
carné nm → **carnet**
carnero nm **1** : ram, sheep

2 : mutton (in cooking)
carnet nm **1 carnet de conducir** : driver's license **2 carnet de identidad** : identification card, ID
carnicería nf **1** : butcher shop **2** MATANZA : slaughter — **carnicero, -ra** n : butcher
carnívoro, -ra adj : carnivorous — **carnívoro** nm : carnivore

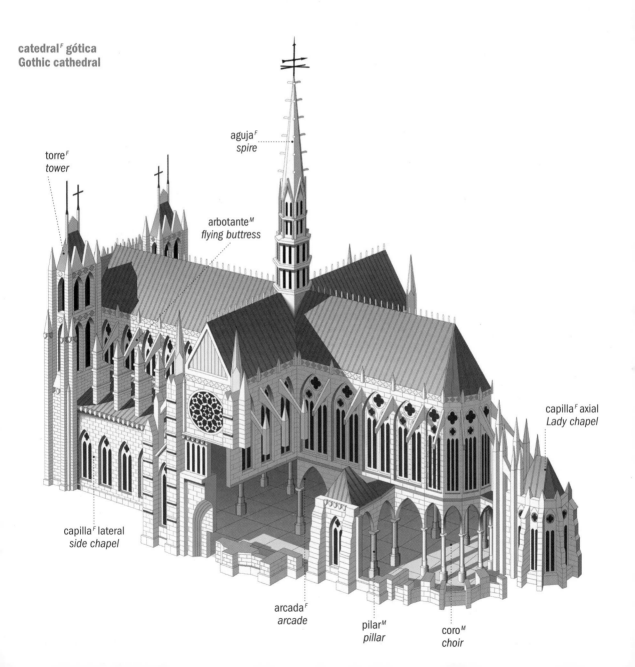

catedral^F **gótica**
Gothic cathedral

aguja^F
spire

torre^F
tower

arbotante^M
flying buttress

capilla^F axial
Lady chapel

capilla^F lateral
side chapel

arcada^F
arcade

pilar^M
pillar

coro^M
choir

carnoso, -sa *adj* : fleshy
caro, -ra *adj* **1** : expensive **2** QUERIDO
: dear — **caro** *adv* : dearly
carpa *nf* **1** : carp **2** TIENDA : tent
carpeta *nf* : folder
carpintería *nf* : carpentry —
carpintero, -ra *n* : carpenter
carraspear *vi* : clear one's throat —
carraspera *nf* **1** : hoarseness **2 tener**
carraspera : have a frog in one's throat
carrera *nf* **1** : running, run **2**
COMPETICIÓN : race **3** : course (of studies)
4 PROFESIÓN : career, profession
carreta *nf* : cart, wagon
carrete *nm* : reel, spool
carretera *nf* : highway, road
carretilla *nf* : wheelbarrow
carril *nm* **1** : lane (of a road)
2 : rail (for a railroad)
carrillo *nm* : cheek
carrito *nm* : cart, trolley
carrizo *nm* : reed
carro *nm* **1** : wagon, cart **2** *Lat* :
automobile, car — **carrocería** *nf*
: body (of an automobile)
carroña *nf* : carrion
carroza *nf* **1** : carriage **2**
: float (in a parade)
carruaje *nm* : carriage
carrusel *nm* : merry-go-round, carousel
carta *nf* **1** : letter **2** NAIPE : playing card
3 : charter (of an organization, etc.)
4 MENÚ : menu **5** MAPA : map, chart
cartel *nm* : poster, bill —
cartelera *nf* : billboard
cartera *nf* **1** : briefcase **2** BILLETERA
: wallet **3** *Lat* : pocketbook, handbag
— **carterista** *nmf* : pickpocket
cartero, -ra *nm* : mail carrier, mailman *m*
cartílago *nm* : cartilage
cartilla *nf* **1** : primer, reader **2** : booklet,
record (of a savings account, etc.)
cartón *nm, pl* **-tones 1** : cardboard
2 : carton (of cigarettes, etc.)
cartucho *nm* : cartridge
casa *nf* **1** : house **2** HOGAR : home
3 EMPRESA : company, firm **4**
casa flotante : houseboat
casar *vt* : marry — *vi* : go together,
match up — **casarse** *vr* **1** : get married
2 casarse con : marry — **casado,**
-da *adj* : married — **casamiento** *nm* **1**
: marriage **2** BODA : wedding
cascabel *nm* : small bell
cascada *nf* : waterfall

cascanueces *nms & pl* : nutcracker
cascar {72} *vt* : crack (a shell,
etc.) — **cascarse** *vr* : crack, chip
— **cáscara** *nf* : skin, peel, shell —
cascarón *nm, pl* **-rones** : eggshell
casco *nm* **1** : helmet **2** : hull (of a
boat) **3** : hoof (of a horse) **4** : fragment
(of ceramics, etc.) **5** : center (of a
town) **6** ENVASE : empty bottle
caserío *nm* **1** *Spain* : country
house **2** POBLADO : hamlet
casero, -ra *adj* **1** : homemade **2**
DOMÉSTICO : domestic, household —
casero, -ra *n* : landlord, landlady *f*
caseta *nf* : booth, stall
casete → **cassette**
casi *adv* **1** : almost, nearly **2** (*in*
negative phrases) : hardly
casilla *nf* **1** : compartment, pigeonhole
2 CASETA : booth **3** : box (on a form)
casino *nm* **1** : casino **2** : (social) club
caso *nm* **1** : case **2 en caso de** : in the
event of **3 hacer caso** : pay attention **4**
no venir al caso : be beside the point
caspa *nf* : dandruff
cassette *nmf* : cassette
casta *nf* **1** : lineage, descent **2** : breed
(of animals) **3** : caste (in India)
castaña *nf* : chestnut
castañetear *vi* : chatter (of teeth)
castaño, -ña *adj* : chestnut (color)
castañuela *nf* : castanet
castellano *nm* : Spanish,
Castilian (language)
castidad *nf* : chastity
castigar {52} *vt* **1** : punish **2** :
penalize (in sports) — **castigo** *nm* **1**
: punishment **2** : penalty (in sports)
castillo *nm* : castle
casto, -ta *adj* : chaste, pure — **castizo,**
-za *adj* : pure, traditional (in style)
castor *nm* : beaver
castrar *vt* : castrate
castrense *adj* : military
casual *adj* : chance, accidental —
casualidad *nf* **1** : coincidence **2 por**
casualidad *or* **de casualidad** : by chance
— **casualmente** *adv* : by chance
cataclismo *nm* : cataclysm
catalán, -lana *adj, mpl* **-lanes** : Catalan
— **catalán** *nm* : Catalan (language)
catalizador *nm* : catalyst
catalogar {52} *vt* : catalog, classify
— **catálogo** *nm* : catalog
catapulta *nf* : catapult

catar *vt* : taste, sample
catarata *nf* **1** : waterfall **2** :
cataract (in medicine)
catarro *nm* RESFRIADO : cold
catástrofe *nf* : catastrophe,
disaster — **catastrófico, -ca** *adj*
: catastrophic, disastrous
catecismo *nm* : catechism
cátedra *nf* : chair (at a university)
▸ **catedral** *nf* : cathedral
catedrático, -ca *n* : professor
categoría *nf* **1** : category **2** RANGO
: rank **3 de categoría** : first-rate —
categórico, -ca *adj* : categorical
católico, -ca *adj & n* : Catholic —
catolicismo *nm* : Catholicism
catorce *adj & nm* : fourteen —
catorceavo *nm* : fourteenth
catre *nm* : cot
cauce *nm* **1** : riverbed **2** VÍA
: channel, means *pl*
caucho *nm* : rubber
caución *nf, pl* **-ciones** :
security, guarantee
caudal *nm* **1** : volume of water,
flow **2** RIQUEZA : wealth
caudillo *nm* : leader, commander
causar *vt* : cause, provoke — **causa** *nf* **1**
: cause **2** RAZÓN : reason **3** : case (in
law) **4 a causar de** : because of
cáustico, -ca *adj* : caustic
cautela *nf* : caution — **cauteloso,**
-sa *adj* : cautious — **cautelosamente** *adv*
: cautiously, warily
cautivar *vt* **1** : capture **2** ENCANTAR :
captivate — **cautiverio** *nm* : captivity
— **cautivo, -va** *adj & n* : captive
cauto, -ta *adj* : cautious
cavar *v* : dig
caverna *nf* : cavern, cave
cavidad *nf* : cavity
cavilar *vi* : ponder
cayado *nm* : crook, staff
cazar {21} *vt* **1** : hunt **2** ATRAPAR
: catch, bag — *vi* : go hunting —
caza *nf* **1** : hunt, hunting **2** : game
(animals) — **cazador, -dora** *n* : hunter
cazo *nm* **1** : saucepan **2** CUCHARÓN
: ladle — **cazuela** *nf* : casserole
CD *nm* : CD, compact disc
cebada *nf* : barley
cebar *vt* **1** : bait **2** : feed, fatten (animals)
3 : prime (a firearm, etc.) — **cebo** *nm* **1**
CARNADA : bait **2** : charge (of a firearm)
cebolla *nf* : onion — **cebolleta** *nf*

: scallion, green onion —
cebollino *nm* : chive
cebra *nf* : zebra
cecear *vi* : lisp — **ceceo** *nm* : lisp
cedazo *nm* : sieve
ceder *vi* **1** : yield, give way **2** DISMINUIR :
diminish, abate — *vt* : cede, hand over
▸ **cedro** *nm* : cedar
cédula *nf* : document, certificate
cegar {49} *vt* **1** : blind **2** TAPAR :
block, stop up — *vi* : be blinded, go
blind — **ceguera** *nf* : blindness
ceja *nf* : eyebrow
cejar *vi* : give in, back down
celada *nf* : trap, ambush
celador, -dora *n* : guard, warden
celda *nf* : cell (of a jail)
celebrar *vt* **1** : celebrate **2** : hold (a
meeting), say (Mass) **3** ALEGRARSE DE :
be happy about — **celebrarse** *vr* : take
place — **celebración** *nf*, *pl* **-ciones** :
celebration — **célebre** *adj* : famous,
celebrated — **celebridad** *nf* : celebrity
celeridad *nf* : swiftness, speed
celeste *adj* **1** : celestial, heavenly
2 *or* **azul celeste** : sky blue —
celestial *adj* : celestial, heavenly
celibato *nm* : celibacy —
célibe *adj* : celibate
celo *nm* **1** : zeal **2 en celo** : in
heat **3 celos** *nmpl* : jealousy **4**
tener celos : be jealous
celofán *nm*, *pl* **-fanes** : cellophane
celoso, -sa *adj* **1** : jealous
2 DILIGENTE : zealous
célula *nf* : cell — **celular** *adj* : cellular
celulosa *nf* : cellulose
cementerio *nm* : cemetery
cemento *nm* **1** : cement **2 cemento**
armado : reinforced concrete
cena *nf* : supper, dinner
cenagal *nm* : bog, quagmire
— **cenagoso** *adj* : swampy
cenar *vi* : have dinner, have supper
— *vt* : have for dinner or supper
cenicero *nm* : ashtray
cenit *nm* : zenith
ceniza *nf* : ash
censo *nm* : census
censurar *vt* **1** : censor **2**
REPROBAR : censure, criticize
— **censura** *nf* **1** : censorship **2**
REPROBACIÓN : censure, criticism
centavo *nm* **1** : cent **2** :
centavo (unit of currency)

centellear *vi* : sparkle, twinkle —
centella *nf* **1** : flash **2** CHISPA : spark
— **centelleo** *nm* : twinkling, sparkle
centenar *nm* : hundred —
centenario *nm* : centennial
centeno *nm* : rye
centésimo, -ma *adj* : hundredth
centígrado *adj* : centigrade, Celsius
centigramo *nm* : centigram
centímetro *nm* : centimeter
centinela *nmf* : sentinel, sentry
central *adj* : central — **central** *nf*
: main office, headquarters —
centralita *nf* : switchboard —
centralizar {21} *vt* : centralize
centrar *vt* : center — **centrarse** *vr*
centrarse en : focus on — **céntrico,**
-ca *adj* : central — **centro** *nm* **1**
: center **2** : downtown (of a city) **3**
centro de mesa : centerpiece
centroamericano, -na *adj*
: Central American
ceñir {67} *vt* **1** : encircle **2** : fit (someone)
tightly — **ceñirse** *vr* **ceñirse a** : limit
oneself to — **ceñido, -da** *adj* : tight
ceño *nm* **1** : frown **2 fruncir el**
ceño : knit one's brow, frown
cepillo *nm* **1** : brush **2** : (carpenter's)
plane **3 cepillo de dientes** : toothbrush
— **cepillar** *vt* **1** : brush **2** : plane (wood)
cera *nf* **1** : wax, beeswax **2** :
floor wax, furniture wax
cerámica *nf* **1** : ceramics *pl* **2**
: (piece of) pottery
cerca[1] *nf* : fence —
cercado *nm* : enclosure
cerca[2] *adv* **1** : close, near **2 cerca**
de : near, close to **3 cerca de** :
nearly, almost — **cercano, -na** *adj*
: near, close — **cercanía** *nf* **1** :
proximity **2 cercas** *nfpl* : outskirts
cercar {72} *vt* **1** : fence in
2 RODEAR : surround
cerciorarse *vr* **cerciorarse**
de : make sure of
cerco *nm* **1** : circle, ring **2**
ASEDIO : siege **3** *Lat* : fence
cerda *nf* : bristle
cerdo *nm* **1** : pig, hog **2**
cerdo macho : boar
cereal *adj* & *nm* : cereal
cerebro *nm* : brain —
cerebral *adj* : cerebral
ceremonia *nf* : ceremony —
ceremonial *adj* : ceremonial

— **ceremonioso, -sa** *adj* : ceremonious
cereza *nf* : cherry
cerilla *nf* : match — **cerillo** *nm* *Lat* : match
cerner {56} *or* **cernir** *vt* : sift —
cernerse *vr* **1** : hover **2 cernerse sobre**
: loom over — **cernidor** *nm* : sieve
cero *nm* : zero
cerrar {55} *vt* **1** : close, shut **2** : turn
off (a faucet, etc.) **3** : bring to an end
— *vi* **1** : close up, lock up **2** : close
down (a business, etc.) — **cerrarse** *vr* **1**
: close, shut **2** TERMINAR : come to a
close, end — **cerrado, -da** *adj* **1** :
closed, shut, locked **2** : overcast (of
weather) **3** : sharp (of a curve) **4** : thick,
broad (of an accent) — **cerradura** *nf* :
lock — **cerrajero, -ra** *n* : locksmith
cerro *nm* : hill
cerrojo *nm* : bolt, latch
certamen *nm*, *pl* **-támenes**
: competition, contest
certero, -ra *adj* : accurate, precise
certeza *nf* : certainty —
certidumbre *nf* : certainty
certificar {72} *vt* **1** : certify **2** : register
(mail) — **certificado, -da** *adj* : certified,
registered — **certificado** *nm* : certificate
cervato *nm* : fawn
cerveza *nf* **1** : beer **2 cerveza de**
barril : draft beer — **cervecería** *nf* **1**
: brewery **2** BAR : beer hall, bar
cesar *vi* : cease, stop — *vt* : dismiss,
lay off — **cesación** *nf*, *pl* **-ciones** :
cessation, suspension — **cesante** *adj* **1**
: laid off **2** *Lat* : unemployed —
cesantía *nf* *Lat* : unemployment
cesárea *nf* : cesarean (section)
cese *nm* **1** : cessation, stop
2 DESTITUCIÓN : dismissal
césped *nm* : lawn, grass
cesta *nf* : basket — **cesto** *nm* **1** : (large)
basket **2 cesto de basura** : wastebasket
cetro *nm* : scepter
chabacano *nm* *Lat* : apricot
chabola *nf*, *Spain* : shack, shanty
chacal *nm* : jackal
cháchara *nf*, *fam* : gabbing, chatter
chacra *nf* *Lat* : (small) farm
chafar *vt*, *fam* : flatten, crush
chal *nm* : shawl
chaleco *nm* : vest
chalet *nm*, *Spain* : house
chalupa *nf* **1** : small boat **2**
Lat : small stuffed tortilla
chamarra *nf* : jacket

picea^F
spruce

abeto^M
fir

cedro^M del Líbano^M
cedar of Lebanon

piñón^M
pine seed

piña^F
cone

rama^F
branch

---

chamba *nf Lat fam* : job
champaña *or* champán *nm* : champagne
champiñón *nm, pl* **-ñones** : mushroom
champú *nm, pl* **-pús** *or* -púes : shampoo
chamuscar {72} *vt* : scorch
chance *nm Lat* : chance, opportunity
chancho *nm Lat* : pig
chanclos *nmpl* : galoshes
chantaje *nm* : blackmail —
　chantajear *vt* : blackmail
chanza *nf* : joke, jest
chapa *nf* **1** : sheet, plate **2** INSIGNIA :
　badge — **chapado, -da** *adj* **1** : plated **2**
　chapado a la antigua : old-fashioned
chaparrón *nm, pl* **-rrones** : downpour
chapotear *vi* : splash
chapucero, -ra *adj* : shoddy, sloppy
　— **chapuza** *nf* : botched job
chapuzón *nm, pl* **-zones**

: dip, short swim
chaqueta *nf* : jacket
charca *nf* : pond — **charco** *nm* : puddle
charlar *vi* : chat — **charla** *nf* : chat, talk
　— **charlatán, -tana** *adj* : talkative —
　charlatán, -tana *adj, mpl* **-tanes** *n* **1**
　: chatterbox **2** FARSANTE : charlatan
charol *nm* **1** : patent leather
　2 BARNIZ : varnish
chasco *nm* **1** : trick, joke **2**
　DECEPCIÓN : disappointment
chasis *nms & pl* : chassis
chasquear *vt* **1** : click (the
　tongue), snap (one's fingers) **2** :
　crack (a whip) — **chasquido** *nm* **1**
　: click, snap **2** : crack (of a whip)
chatarra *nf* : scrap (metal)
chato, -ta *adj* **1** : pug-
　nosed **2** APLANADO : flat

chauvinismo *nm* : chauvinism —
　chauvinista *adj* : chauvinist, chauvinistic
chaval, -vala *n, fam* : kid, boy *m*, girl *f*
checo, -ca *adj* : Czech —
　checo *nm* : Czech (language)
chef *nm* : chef
cheque *nm* : check —
　chequera *nf* : checkbook
chequear *vi Lat* **1** : check, inspect, verify
　2 : check in (baggage) — **chequeo** *nm* **1** :
　(medical) checkup **2** *Lat* : check, inspection
chica → **chico**
chicano, -na *adj* : Chicano,
　Mexican-American
chícharo *nm Lat* : pea
chicharrón *nm, pl* **-rrones** : pork rind
chichón *nm, pl* **-chones** : bump
chicle *nm* : chewing gum
chico, -ca *adj* : little, small — **chico,**

cine^M
movie theater

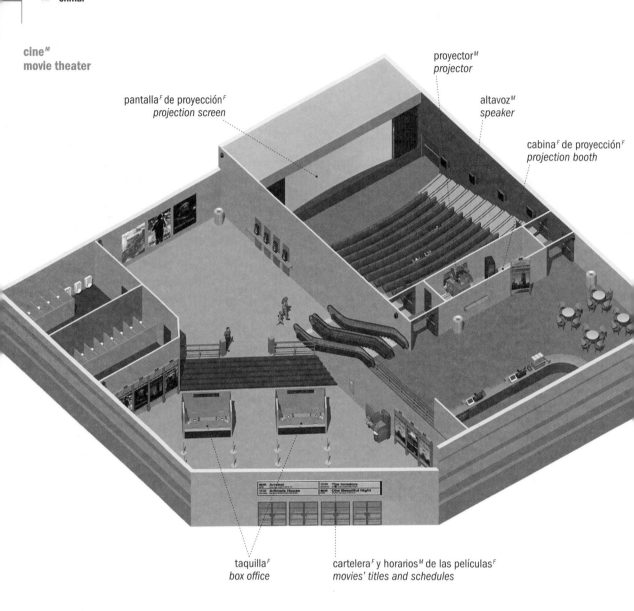

pantalla^F de proyección^F
projection screen

proyector^M
projector

altavoz^M
speaker

cabina^F de proyección^F
projection booth

taquilla^F
box office

cartelera^F y horarios^M de las películas^F
movies' titles and schedules

-ca *n* : child, boy *m*, girl *f*
chiflar *vt* : whistle at, boo — *vi Lat*
: whistle — **chiflado, -da** *adj, fam* :
crazy, nuts — **chiflido** *nm* : whistling
chile *nm* : chili pepper
chileno, -na *adj* : Chilean
chillar *vi* **1** : shriek, scream **2** CHIRRIAR
: screech, squeal — **chillido** *nm* **1** :
scream **2** CHIRRIDO : screech, squeal —
chillón, -llona *adj, mpl* **-llones** : shrill, loud
chimenea *nf* **1** : chimney

2 HOGAR : fireplace
chimpancé *nm* : chimpanzee
chinche *nf* : bedbug
chino, -na *adj* : Chinese —
chino *nm* : Chinese (language)
chiquillo, -lla *n* : kid, child
chiquito, -ta *adj* : tiny —
chiquito, -ta *n* : little child, tot
chiribita *nf* : spark
chiripa *nf* **1** : fluke **2 de**
chiripa : by sheer luck

chirivia *nf* : parsnip
chirriar {85} *vi* **1** : squeak, creak **2** :
screech (of brakes, etc.) — **chirrido** *nm* **1**
: squeak, creak **2** : screech (of brakes)
chisme *nm* : (piece of) gossip —
chismear *vi* : gossip — **chismoso,**
-sa *adj* : gossipy — **chisme** *n* : gossip
chispear *vi* : spark — **chispa** *nf* : spark
chisporrotear *vi* : crackle, sizzle
— **chisporroteo** *nm* : crackle
chiste *nm* : joke, funny story

— **chistoso, -sa** *adj* : funny, witty

chivo, -va *n* : kid, young goat

chocar {72} *vi* **1** : crash, collide **2** ENFRENTARSE : clash — **chocante** *adj* **1** : striking, shocking **2** *Lat* : unpleasant, rude

choclo *nm Lat* : ear of corn, corncob

chocolate *nm* : chocolate

chofer *or* **chófer** *nm* **1** : chauffeur **2** CONDUCTOR : driver

choque *nm* **1** : shock **2** : crash, collision (of vehicles) **3** CONFLICTO : clash

chorizo *nm* : chorizo, sausage

chorrear *vi* **1** : drip **2** BROTAR : pour out, gush — **chorro** *nm* **1** : stream, jet **2** HILO : trickle

chovinismo → **chauvinismo**

choza *nf* : hut, shack

chubasco *nm* : downpour, squall

chuchería *nf* **1** : knickknack, trinket **2** DULCE : sweet

chueco, -ca *adj Lat* : crooked

chuleta *nf* : cutlet, chop

chulo, -la *adj, fam* : cute, pretty

chupar *vt* **1** : suck **2** ABSORBER : absorb **3** *fam* : guzzle — *vi* : suckle — **chupada** *nf* : suck, sucking — **chupete** *nm* **1** : pacifier **2** *Lat* : lollipop

churro *nm* **1** : fried dough **2** *fam* : botch, mess

chusco, -ca *adj* : funny

chusma *nf* : riffraff, rabble

chutar *vi* : shoot (in soccer)

cianuro *nm* : cyanide

cicatriz *nf, pl* **-trices** : scar — **cicatrizar** {21} *vi* : form a scar, heal

cíclico, -ca *adj* : cyclical

ciclismo *nm* : cycling — **ciclista** *nmf* : cyclist

ciclo *nm* : cycle

ciclón *nm, pl* **-clones** : cyclone

ciego, -ga *adj* : blind — **ciegamente** *adv* : blindly

cielo *nm* **1** : sky **2** : heaven (in religion)

ciempiés *nms & pl* : centipede

cien *adj* : a hundred, hundred — **cien** *nm* : one hundred

ciénaga *nf* : swamp, bog

ciencia *nf* **1** : science **2 a ciencia cierta** : for a fact

cieno *nm* : mire, mud, silt

científico, -ca *adj* : scientific — **científico, -ca** *n* : scientist

ciento *adj* (used in compound numbers) : one hundred — **ciento** *nm* **1** : hundred, group of a hundred **2 por ciento** : percent

cierre *nm* **1** : closing, closure **2** BROCHE : fastener, clasp

cierto, -ta *adj* **1** : true **2** SEGURO : certain **3 por cierto** : as a matter of fact

ciervo, -va *n* : deer, stag *m*, hind *f*

cifra *nf* **1** : number, figure **2** : sum (of money, etc.) **3** CLAVE : code, cipher — **cifrar** *vt* **1** : write in code **2 cifra la esperanza en** : pin all one's hopes on

cigarrillo *nm* : cigarrette — **cigarro** *nm* **1** : cigarette **2** PURO : cigar

cigüeña *nf* : stork

cilantro *nm* : cilantro, coriander

cilindro *nm* : cylinder — **cilíndrico, -ca** *adj* : cylindrical

cima *nf* : peak, summit

címbalo *nm* : cymbal

cimbrar *or* **cimbrear** *vt* : shake, rock — **cimbrarse** *or* **cimbrearse** *vr* : sway

cimentar {55} *vt* **1** : lay the foundation of **2** : cement, strengthen (relations, etc.) — **cimientos** *nmpl* : base, foundation(s)

cinc *nm* : zinc

cincel *nm* : chisel — **cincelar** *vt* : chisel

cinco *adj & nm* : five

cincuenta *adj & nm* : fifty — **cincuentavo, -va** *adj* : fiftieth — **cincuentavo** *nm* : fiftieth

▸ **cine** *nm* : cinema, movies *pl* — **cinematográfico, -ca** *adj* : movie, film

cínico, -ca *adj* : cynical — **cínico, -ca** *n* : cynic — **cinismo** *nm* : cynicism

cinta *nf* **1** : ribbon, band **2 cinta adhesiva** : adhesive tape **3 cinta métrica** : tape measure **4 cinta magnetofónica** : magnetic tape

cinto *nm* : belt, girdle — **cintura** *nf* : waist — **cinturón** *nm, pl* **-rones 1** : belt **2 cinturón de seguridad** : seat belt

ciprés *nm, pl* **-preses** : cypress

circo *nm* : circus

circuito *nm* : circuit

circulación *nf, pl* **-ciones 1** : circulation **2** TRÁFICO : traffic — **circulaciar** *vi* **1** : circulate **2** : drive (a vehicle) — **circular** *adj* : circular

círculo *nm* : circle

circuncidar *vt* : circumcise — **circuncisión** *nf, pl* **-siones** : circumcision

circundar *vt* : surround

circunferencia *nf* : circumference

circunscribir {33} *vt* : confine, limit — **circunscribirse** *vr* **circunscribirse a** : limit oneself to — **circunscripción** *nf, pl* **-ciones** : district, constituency

circunspecto, -ta *adj* : circumspect, cautious

circunstancia *nf* : circumstance — **circunstancial** *adj* : chance — **circunstante** *nmf* **1** : bystander **2 los circunstantes** : those present

circunvalación *nf, pl* **-ciones 1** : encircling **2 carretera de circunvalación** : bypass

cirio *nm* : candle

ciruela *nf* **1** : plum **2 ciruela pasa** : prune

cirugía *nf* : surgery — **cirujano, -na** *n* : surgeon

cisma *nf* : schism

cisne *nm* : swan

cisterna *nf* : cistern

cita *nf* **1** : appointment, date **2** REFERENCIA : quote, quotation — **citación** *nf, pl* **-ciones** : summons — **citar** *vt* **1** : quote, cite **2** CONVOCAR : make an appointment with **3** : summon (in law) — **citarse** *vr* **citarse con** : arrange to meet

cítrico *nm* : citrus (fruit)

ciudad *nf* : city, town — **ciudadano, -na** *n* **1** : citizen **2** HABITANTE : resident — **ciudadanía** *nf* : citizenship

cívico, -ca *adj* : civic

civil *adj* : civil — **civil** *nmf* : civilian — **civilidad** *nf* : civility — **civilización** *nf, pl* **-ciones** : civilization — **civilizar** {21} *vt* : civilize

cizaña *nf* : discord, rift

clamar *vi* : clamor, cry out — **clamor** *nm* : clamor, outcry — **clamoroso, -sa** *adj* : clamorous, loud

clan *nm* : clan

clandestino, -na *adj* : clandestine, secret

clara *nf* : egg white

claraboya *nf* : skylight

claramente *adv* : clearly

clarear *v impers* **1** : dawn **2** ACLARAR : clear up — *vi* : be transparent

claridad *nf* **1** : clarity, clearness **2** LUZ : light

clarificar {72} *vt* : clarify — **clarificación** *nf, pl* **-ciones** : clarification

clarín *nm, pl* **-rines** : bugle

clarinete *nm* : clarinet

clarividente *adj* **1** : clairvoyant **2** PERSPICAZ : perspicacious — **clarividencia** *nf* **1** : clairvoyance **2** PERSPICACIA : farsightedness

claro *adv* **1** : clearly **2** POR SUPUESTO : of course, surely — **claro** *nm* **1** : clearing,

glade **2 claro de luna** : moonlight —
claro, -ra *adj* **1** : clear, bright **2** : light
(of colors) **3** EVIDENTE : clear, evident
clase *nf* **1** : class **2** TIPO : sort, kind
clásico, -ca *adj* : classic, classical
— **clásico** *nm* : classic
clasificar {72} *vt* **1** : classify, sort out
2 : rate, rank (a hotel, a team, etc.) —
clasificarse *vr* : qualify (in competitions)
— **clasificación** *nf, pl* **-ciones 1** :
classification **2** : league (in sports)
claudicar {72} *vi* : back down
claustro *nm* : cloister
claustrofobia *nf* : claustrophobia —
claustrofóbico, -ca *adj* : claustrophobic
cláusula *nf* : clause
clausurar *vt* : close (down) —
clausura *nf* : closure, closing
clavado *nm Lat* : dive
clavar *vt* **1** : nail, hammer **2**
HINCAR : drive in, plunge
clave *nf* **1** CIFRA : code **2** SOLUCIÓN : **key**
3 : clef (in music) — **clave** *adj* : key
clavel *nm* : carnation
clavicémbalo *nm* : harpsichord
clavícula *nf* : collarbone
clavija *nf* **1** : peg, pin **2** : (electric) plug
clavo *nm* **1** : nail **2** : clove (spice)
claxon *nm, pl* **cláxones** :
horn (of an automobile)
clemencia *nf* : clemency, mercy
— **clemente** *adj* : merciful
clerical *adj* : clerical — **clérigo, -ga** *n* :
clergyman, cleric — **clero** *nm* : clergy
cliché *nm* **1** : cliché **2** :
negative (of a photograph)
cliente, -ta *n* : customer, client —
clientela *nf* : clientele, customers *pl*
clima *nm* **1** : climate **2**
AMBIENTE : atmosphere —
climático, -ca *adj* : climatic
climatizar {21} *vt* : air-condition —
climatizado, -da *adj* : air-conditioned
clímax *nm* : climax
clínica *nf* : clinic — **clínico,
-ca** *adj* : clinical
clip *nm, pl* **clips** : (paper) clip
cloaca *nf* : sewer
cloquear *vi* : cluck —
cloqueo *nm* : cluck, clucking
cloro *nm* : chlorine
clóset *nm Lat, pl* clósets : (built-
in) closet, cupboard
club *nm* : club
coacción *nf, pl* **-ciones** : coercion

collar^M
necklaces

lazo^M
rope

collar^M de una vuelta^F, matinée^F
matinee-length necklace

collar^M de 5 vueltas^F, peto^M
bib necklace

arete^M
pendant

gargantilla^F de
terciopelo^M
velvet-band choker

— **coaccionar** *vt* : coerce
coagular *v* : clot, coagulate
— **coagularse** *vr* : coagulate
— **coágulo** *nm* : clot
coalición *nf, pl* **-ciones** : coalition
coartada *nf* : alibi
coartar *vt* : restrict, limit
cobarde *nmf* : coward — **cobarde** *adj*
: cowardly — **cobardía** *nf* : cowardice
cobaya *nf* : guinea pig
cobertizo *nm* : shelter, shed
cobertor *nm* : bedspread
cobertura *nf* **1** : cover **2** :
coverage (of news, etc.)
cobijar *vt* : shelter — **cobijarse** *vr*
: take shelter — **cobija** *nf Lat* :
blanket — **cobijo** *nm* : shelter
cobra *nf* : cobra
cobrar *vt* **1** : charge, collect **2** : earn
(a salary, etc.) **3** ADQUERIR : acquire,
gain **4** : cash (a check) — *vi* : be paid
— **cobrador, -dora** *n* **1** : collector
2 : conductor (of a bus, etc.)
cobre *nm* : copper
cobro *nm* : collection (of money),
cashing (of a check)
cocaína *nf* : cocaine
cocción *nf, pl* **-ciones** : cooking
cocear *vi* : kick
cocer {14} *vt* **1** : cook **2** HERVIR : boil
coche *nm* **1** : car, automobile **2** : coach
(of a train) **3** *or* **coche de caballos** :

carriage **4 coche fúnebre** : hearse —
cochecito *nm* : baby carriage, stroller
— **cochera** *nf* : garage, carport
cochino, -na *n* : pig, hog — **cochino,
-na** *adj, fam* : dirty, filthy — **cochinada** *nf,
fam* : dirty thing — **cochinillo** *nm* : piglet
cocido, -da *adj* **1** : boiled,
cooked **2 bien cocido, -da** : well-
done — **cocido** *nm* : stew
cociente *nm* : quotient
cocina *nf* **1** : kitchen **2** : (kitchen) stove
3 : (art of) cooking, cuisine — **cocinar** *v*
: cook — **cocinero, -ra** *n* : cook, chef
coco *nm* : coconut
cocodrilo *nm* : crocodile
coctel *or* **cóctel** *nm* **1** : cocktail
2 FIESTA : cocktail party
codazo *nm* **1** : nudge **2 dar un
codazo a** : elbow, nudge
codicia *nf* : greed — **codiciar** *vt* : covet
— **codicioso, -sa** *adj* : covetous, greedy
código *nm* **1** : code **2 código postal** :
zip code **3 código morse** : Morse code
codo *nm* : elbow
codorniz *nf, pl* **-nices** : quail
coexistir *vi* : coexist
cofre *nm* : chest, coffer
coger {15} *vt* **1** : take (hold of) **2** ATRAPAR
: catch **3** : pick up (from the ground) **4** :
pick (fruit, etc.) — **cogerse** *vr* : hold on
cohechar *vt* : bribe —
cohecho *nm* : bribe, bribery

coherencia *nf* : coherence
— **coherente** *adj* : coherent —
cohesión *nf, pl* **-siones** : cohesion
cohete *nm* : rocket
cohibir {62} *vt* 1 : restrict 2 : inhibit (a
person) — **cohibirse** *vr* : feel inhibited
— **cohibido, -da** *adj* : inhibited, shy
coincidir *vi* 1 : coincide 2
coincidir con : agree with —
coincidencia *nf* : coincidence
cojear *vi* 1 : limp 2 : wobble (of
furniture, etc.) — **cojera** *nf* : limp
cojín *nm, pl* **-jines** : cushion —
cojinete *nm* 1 : pad, cushion
2 : bearing (of a machine)
cojo, -ja *adj* 1 : lame 2 : wobbly (of
furniture) — **cojo, -ja** *n* : lame person
col *nf* 1 : cabbage 2 **col de**
Bruselas : Brussels sprout
cola *nf* 1 : tail 2 FILA : line (of people)
3 : end (of a line) 4 PEGAMENTO :
glue 5 **cola de caballo** : ponytail
colaborar *vi* : collaborate —
colaboración *nf, pl* **-ciones** : collaboration
— **colaborador, -dora** *n* 1 : collaborator
2 : contributor (to a periodical)
colada *nf, Spain* 1 : laundry 2
hacer la colada : do the washing
colador *nm* : colander, strainer
colapso *nm* : collapse
colar {19} *vt* : strain, filter —
colarse *vr* : sneak in, gate-crash
colcha *nf* : bedspread, quilt —
colchón *nm, pl* **-chones** : mattress
— **colchoneta** *nf* : mat
colear *vi* : wag its tail
colección *nf, pl* **-ciones** : collection
— **coleccionar** *vt* : collect —
coleccionista *nmf* : collector —
colecta *nf* : collection (of donations)
colectividad *nf* : community —
colectivo, -va *adj* : collective —
colectivo *nm* 1 : collective 2 *Lat* : city bus
colector *nm* : sewer
colega *nmf* : colleague
colegio *nm* 1 : school 2 :
(professional) college — **colegial,**
-giala *n* : schoolboy *m*, schoolgirl *f*
colegir {28} *vt* : gather
cólera *nm* : cholera — **cólera** *nf* :
anger, rage — **colérico, -ca** *adj* 1 :
bad-tempered 2 FURIOSO : angry
colesterol *nm* : cholesterol
coleta *nf* : pigtail
colgar {16} *vt* 1 : hang 2 : hang up

(a telephone) 3 : hang out (laundry)
— *vi* : hang up — **colgante** *adj* :
hanging — **colgante** *nm* : pendant
colibrí *nm* : hummingbird
cólico *nm* : colic
coliflor *nf* : cauliflower
colilla *nf* : (cigarette) butt
colina *nf* : hill
colindar *vi* **colindar con** : be adjacent
to — **colindante** *adj* : adjacent
coliseo *nm* : coliseum
colisión *nf, pl* **-siones** : collision —
colisionar *vi* **colisión contra** : collide with
▸ **collar** *nm* 1 : necklace 2 : collar (for pets)
colmar *vt* 1 : fill to the brim 2 : fulfill
(a wish, etc.) 3 **colmar de** : shower
with — **colmado, -da** *adj* : heaping
colmena *nf* : beehive
colmillo *nm* 1 : canine (tooth) 2 : fang
(of a dog, etc.), tusk (of an elephant)
colmo *nm* 1 : height, limit 2 ¡**eso es**
el colmo ! : that's the last straw!
colocar {72} *vt* 1 PONER : place, put
2 : find a job for — **colocarse** *vr* 1
SITUARSE : position oneself 2 : get a job —
colocación *nf, pl* **-ciones** 1 : placement,
placing 2 EMPLEO : position, job
colombiano, -na *adj* : Colombian
colon *nm* : (intestinal) colon
colonia *nf* 1 : colony 2 PERFUME : cologne
3 *Lat* : residential area — **colonial** *adj* :
colonial — **colonizar** {21} *vt* : colonize —
colonización *nf, pl* **-ciones** : colonization
— **colono, -na** *n* : settler, colonist
coloquial *adj* : colloquial —
coloquio *nm* 1 : talk, discussion
2 CONGRESO : conference
color *nm* : color — **colorado, -da** *adj* :
red — **colorear** *vt* : color — **colorete** *nm* :
rouge — **colorido** *nm* : colors *pl*, coloring
colosal *adj* : colossal
▸ **columna** *nf* 1 : column 2 **columna**
vertebral : spine, backbone —
columnista *nmf* : columnist
columpiar *vt* : push (on a swing)
— **columpiarse** *vr* : swing —
columpio *nm* : swing
coma¹ *nm* : coma
coma² *nf* : comma
comadre *nf* 1 : godmother of one's child,
mother of one's godchild 2 *fam* : (female)
friend — **comadrear** *vi, fam* : gossip
comadreja *nf* : weasel
comadrona *nf* : midwife
comandancia *nf* : command

headquarters, command —
comandante *nmf* 1 : commander 2 :
major (in the military) — **comando** *nm* 1
: commando 2 *Lat* : command
comarca *nf* : region, area
combar *vt* : bend, curve
combatir *vt* : combat, fight against
— *vi* : fight — **combate** *nm* 1
: combat 2 : fight (in boxing) —
combatiente *nmf* : combatant, fighter
combinar *vt* 1 : combine 2 : put
together, match (colors, etc.) —
combinarse *vr* : get together —
combinación *nf, pl* **-ciones** 1 :

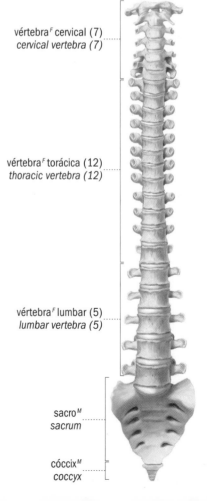

columna^F vertebral
spine

vértebra^F cervical (7)
cervical vertebra (7)

vértebra^F torácica (12)
thoracic vertebra (12)

vértebra^F lumbar (5)
lumbar vertebra (5)

sacro^M
sacrum

cóccix^M
coccyx

combination **2** : connection (in travel)
combustible *nm* : fuel —
 combustible *adj* : combustible —
 combustión *nf, pl* **-tiones** : combustion
comedia *nf* : comedy
comedido, -da *adj* : moderate
comedor *nm* : dining room
comensal *nmf* : diner, dinner guest
comentar *vt* **1** : comment on,
 discuss **2** MENCIONAR : mention
 — **comentario** *nm* **1** : comment,
 remark **2** ANÁLISIS : commentary —
 comentarista *nmf* : commentator
comenzar {29} *v* : begin, start
comer *vt* **1** : eat **2** *fam* : eat up, eat into
 — *vi* **1** : eat **2** CENAR : have a meal **3 dar**
 de comer : feed — **comerse** *vr* : eat up
comercio *nm* **1** : commerce, trade **2**
 NEGOCIO : business — **comercial** *adj* :
 commercial — **comercializar** {21} *vt* :
 market — **comerciante** *nmf* : merchant,
 dealer — **comerciar** *vi* : do business, trade
comestible *adj* : edible —
 comestibles *nmpl* : groceries, food
▸ **cometa** *nm* : comet — **cometa** *nf* : kite
cometer *vt* **1** : commit **2 cometer**
 un error : make a mistake

— **cometido** *nm* : assignment, task
comezón *nf, pl* **-zones** : itchiness, itching
comicios *nmpl* : elections
cómico, -ca *adj* : comic, comical —
 cómico, -ca *n* : comic, comedian
comida *nf* **1** ALIMENTO : food **2**
 Spain : lunch **3** *Lat* : dinner **4 tres**
 comidas al día : three meals a day
comienzo *nm* : beginning
comillas *nfpl* : quotation marks
▸ **comino** *nm* : cumin
comisario, -ria *n* : commissioner
 — **comisaría** *nf* : police station
comisión *nf, pl* **-siones 1** :
 commission **2** COMITÉ : committee
comité *nm* : committee
como *conj* **1** : as, since **2** SÍ : if —
 como *prep* **1** : like, as **2 así como**
 : as well as — **como** *adv* **1** : as **2**
 APROXIMADAMENTE : around, about
cómo *adv* **1** : how **2 cómo**
 no : by all means **3 ¿cómo te**
 llamas? : what's your name?
cómoda *nf* : chest of drawers
comodidad *nf* : comfort, convenience
comodín *nm, pl* **-dines** :
 joker (in playing cards)

cómodo, -da *adj* **1** : comfortable
 2 ÚTIL : handy, convenient
comoquiera *adv* **1** : in any way
 2 comoquiera que : however
compacto, -ta *adj* : compact
compadecer {53} *vt* : feel
 sorry for — **compadecerse** *vr*
 compadecerse de : take pity on
compadre *nm* **1** : godfather
 of one's child, father of one's
 godchild **2** *fam* : buddy
compañero, -ra *n* : companion, partner
 — **compañerismo** *nm* : companionship
compañía *nf* : company
comparar *vt* : compare —
 comparable *adj* : comparable —
 comparación *nf, pl* **-ciones** : comparison
 — **comparativo, -va** *adj* : comparative
comparecer *vt* : appear
 (before a court, etc.)
compartimiento *or*
 compartimento *nm* : compartment
compartir *vt* : share
compás *nm, pl* **-pases 1** : compass
 2 : rhythm, time (in music)
compasión *nf, pl* **-siones** :
 compassion, pity — **compasivo,**

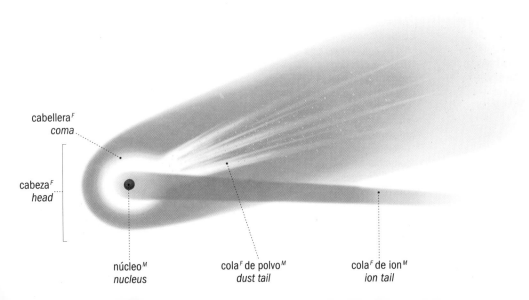

cometa^M
comet

cabellera^F
coma

cabeza^F
head

núcleo^M
nucleus

cola^F de polvo^M
dust tail

cola^F de ion^M
ion tail

-va *adj* : compassionate

compatible *adj* : compatible —
compatibilidad *nf* : compatibility

compatriota *nmf* : compatriot,
fellow countryman

compeler *vt* : compel

compendiar *vt* : summarize —
compendio *nm* : summary

compensar *vt* : compensate
for — **compensación** *nf,*
pl **-ciones** : compensation

competir {54} *vi* : compete —
competencia *nf* **1** : competition,
rivalry **2** CAPACIDAD : competence
— **competente** *adj* : competent —
competición *nf, pl* **-ciones** : competition
— **competidor, -dora** *n* : competitor

compilar *vt* : compile

compinche *nmf, fam* : friend, chum

complacer {57} *vt* : please —
complacerse *vr* **complacerse**
en : take pleasure in —
complaciente *adj* : obliging, helpful

complejidad *nf* : complexity
— **complejo, -ja** *adj* : complex
— **complejo** *nm* : complex

complementar *vt* : complement
— **complementario, -ria** *adj* :
complementary — **complemento** *nm* **1**
: complement **2** : object (in grammar)

completar *vt* : complete —
completo, -ta *adj* **1** : complete **2**
PERFECTO : perfect **3** LLENO : full —
completamente *adv* : completely

complexión *nf, pl* **-xiones**
: constitution, build

complicar {72} *vt* **1** : complicate **2**
IMPLICAR : involve — **complicación** *nf,*
pl **-ciones** : complication — **complicado,**
-da *adj* : complicated, complex

cómplice *nmf* : accomplice —
cómplice *adj* : conspiratorial, knowing

complot *nm, pl* **-plots** : conspiracy, plot

componer {60} *vt* **1** : make up, compose
2 : compose, write (a song) **3** ARREGLAR :
fix, repair — **componerse** *vr* **componerse**
de : consist of — **componente** *adj*
& nm : component, constituent

comportarse *vr* : behave —
comportamiento *nm* : behavior

composición *nf, pl* **-ciones**
: composition — **compositor,**
-tora *n* : composer, songwriter

compostura *nf* **1** : composure
2 REPARACIÓN : repair

comprar *vt* : buy, purchase
— **compra** *nf* **1** : purchase **2 ir**
de comprars : go shopping —
comprador, -dora *n* : buyer, shopper

comprender *vt* **1** : comprehend,
understand **2** ABARCAR : cover, include
— **comprensible** *adj* : understandable
— **comprensión** *nf, pl* **-siones** :
understanding — **comprensivo,**
-va *adj* : understanding

compresa *nf* **1** : compress **2** *or*
compresa higiénica : sanitary napkin

compresión *nf, pl* **-siones** :
compression — **comprimido** *nm* : pill,
tablet — **comprimir** *vt* : compress

comprobar {19} *vt* **1** VERIFICAR
: check **2** DEMOSTRAR : prove —
comprobación *nf, pl* **-ciones** : verification,
check — **comprobante** *nm* **1** :
proof **2** RECIBO : receipt, voucher

comprometer *vt* **1** : compromise
2 ARRIESGAR : jeopardize **3** OBLIGAR
: commit, put under obligation —
comprometerse *vr* **1** : commit oneself **2**
comprometerse con : get engaged to —
comprometedor, -dora *adj* : compromising
— **comprometido, -da** *adj* **1** :
compromising, awkward **2** : engaged
(to be married) — **compromiso** *nm* **1**
: obligation, commitment **2** : (marriage)
engagement **3** ACUERDO : agreement
4 APURO : awkward situation

compuesto, -ta *adj* **1** :
compound **2 compuesto, -ta de**
: made up of, consisting of —
compuesto *nm* : compound

compulsivo, -va *adj* :
compelling, urgent

computar *vt* : compute, calculate —
computadora *nf or* **computador** *nm* **1** :
computer **2 computadora portátil** : laptop
computer — **cómputo** *nm* : calculation

comulgar {52} *vi* : receive Communion

común *adj, pl* **-munes 1** : common
2 común y corriente : ordinary
3 por lo común : generally

comuna *nf* : commune —
comunal *adj* : communal

comunicar {72} *vt* : communicate
— **comunicarse** *vr* **1** : communicate
2 comunicarse con : get in touch
with — **comunicación** *nf, pl* **-ciones**
: communication — **comunicado** *nm*
: communiqué — **comunicativo,**
-va *adj* : communicative

comunidad *nf* : community

comunión *nf, pl* **-niones** :
communion, Communion

comunismo *nm* : Communism —
comunista *adj & nmf* : Communist

con *prep* **1** : with **2** A PESAR DE :
in spite of **3** (*before an infinitive*) :
by **4 con (tal) que** : so long as

cóncavo, -va *adj* : concave

concebir {54} *v* : conceive —
concebible *adj* : conceivable

conceder *vt* **1** : grant, bestow
2 ADMITIR : concede

concejal, -jala *n* : councilman, alderman

concentrar *vt* : concentrate —
concentrarse *vr* : concentrate
— **concentración** *nf,*
pl **-ciones** : concentration

concepción *nf, pl* **-ciones** :
conception — **concepto** *nm* **1**
: concept **2** OPINIÓN : opinion

concernir {17} *vi* **concernir a**
: concern — **concerniente** *adj*
concerniente a : concerning

concertar {55} *vt* **1** : arrange,
coordinate **2** (*used before an*
infinitive) : agree **3** : harmonize (in
music) — *vi* : be in harmony

concesión *nf, pl* **-siones 1** : concession
2 : awarding (of prizes, etc.)

concha *nf* : shell

conciencia *nf* **1** : conscience
2 CONOCIMIENTO : consciousness,
awareness — **concientizar** {21} *vt Lat*
: make aware — **concientizarse** *vr*
Lat **concientizarse de** : realize

concienzudo, -da *adj* : conscientious

concierto *nm* **1** : concert **2** : concerto (musical composition)

conciliar *vt* : reconcile — **conciliación** *nf, pl* **-ciones** : reconciliation

concilio *nm* : council

conciso, -sa *adj* : concise

conciudadano, -na *n* : fellow citizen

concluir {41} *vt* : conclude — *vi* : come to an end — **conclusión** *nf, pl* **-siones** : conclusion — **concluyente** *adj* : conclusive

concordar {19} *vi* : agree — *vt* : reconcile — **concordancia** *nf* : agreement — **concordia** *nf* : harmony, concord

concretar *vt* : make concrete, specify — **concretarse** *vr* : become definite, take shape — **concreto, -ta** *adj* **1** : concrete **2** DETERMINADO : specific **3 en concreto** : specifically — **concreto** *nm Lat* : concrete

concurrir *vi* **1** : come together, meet **2 concurrir a** : take part in — **concurrencia** *nf* : audience, turnout — **concurrido, -da** *adj* : busy, crowded

concursar *vi* : compete, participate — **concursante** *nmf* : competitor — **concurso** *nm* **1** : competition **2** CONCURRENCIA : gathering **3** AYUDA : help, cooperation

condado *nm* : county

conde, -desa *n* : count *m*, countess *f*

condenar *vt* **1** : condemn, damn **2** : sentence (a criminal) — **condena** *nf* **1** : condemnation **2** SENTENCIA : sentence — **condenación** *nf, pl* **-ciones** : condemnation, damnation

condensar *vt* : condense — **condensación** *nf, pl* **-ciones** : condensation

condesa *nf* → **conde**

condescender {56} *vi* **1** : acquiesce, agree **2 condescender a** : condescend to — **condescendiente** *adj* : condescending

condición *nf, pl* **-ciones** **1** : condition, state **2** CALIDAD : capacity, position — **condicional** *adj* : conditional

condimento *nm* : condiment, seasoning

condolerse {47} *vr* : sympathize — **condolencia** *nf* : condolence

condominio *nm* **1** : joint ownership **2** *Lat* : condominium

condón *nm, pl* **-dones** : condom

conducir {61} *vt* **1** DIRIGIR : direct, lead **2** MANEJAR : drive — *vi* **1** : drive **2 conducir a** : lead to — **conducirse** *vr* : behave

conducta *nf* : behavior, conduct

conducto *nm* : conduit, duct

conductor, -tora *n* : driver

conectar *vt* **1** : connect **2** ENCHUFAR : plug in — *vi* : connect

conejo, -ja *n* : rabbit — **conejera** *nf* : (rabbit) hutch

conexión *nf, pl* **-xiones** : connection — **conexo, -xa** *adj* : connected

confabularse *vr* : conspire, plot

confeccionar *vt* : make (up), prepare — **confección** *nf, pl* **-ciones** **1** : making, preparation **2** : tailoring, dressmaking

confederación *nf, pl* **-ciones** : confederation

conferencia *nf* **1** : lecture **2** REUNIÓN : conference

conferir {76} *vt* : confer, bestow

confesar {55} *v* : confess — **confesarse** *vr* : go to confession — **confesión** *nf, pl* **-siones** **1** : confession **2** CREDO : religion, creed

confeti *nm* : confetti

confiar {85} *vi* : trust — *vt* : entrust — **confiable** *adj* : trustworthy, reliable — **confiado, -da** *adj* **1** : confident **2** CRÉDULO : trusting — **confianza** *nf* **1** : trust **2** : confidence (in oneself)

confidencia *nf* : confidence, secret — **confidencial** *adj* : confidential — **confidencialidad** *nf* : confidentiality — **confidente** *nmf* **1** : confidant, confidante *f* **2** : (police) informer

configuración *nf, pl* **-ciones** : configuration, shape

confín *nm, pl* **-fines** : boundary, limit — **confinar** *vt* **1** : confine **2** DESTERRER : exile

confirmar *vt* : confirm — **confirmación** *nf, pl* **-ciones** : confirmation

confiscar {72} *vt* : confiscate

confitería *nm* : candy store

confitura *nf* : jam

conflagración *nf, pl* **-ciones** **1** : war, conflict **2** INCENDIO : fire

conflicto *nm* : conflict

confluencia *nf* : junction, confluence

conformar *vt* : shape, make up — **conformarse** *vr* **1** RESIGNARSE : resign oneself **2 conformarse con** : content oneself with — **conforme** *adj* **1** : content, satisfied **2 conforme a** : in accordance with — **conforme** *conj* : as — **conformidad** *nf* **1** : agreement **2** RESIGNACIÓN : resignation

confortar *vt* : comfort — **confortable** *adj* : comfortable

confrontar *vt* **1** : confront **2** COMPARAR : compare — *vi* : border — **confrontarse** *vr* **confrontarse con** : face up to — **confrontación** *nf, pl* **-ciones** : confrontation

confundir *vt* : confuse, mix up — **confundirse** *vr* : make a mistake, be confused — **confusión** *nf, pl* **-siones** : confusion — **confuso, -sa** *adj* **1** : confused **2** INDISTINTO : hazy, indistinct

congelar *vt* : freeze — **congelarse** *vr* : freeze — **congelación** *nf, pl* **-ciones** : freezing — **congelado, -da** *adj* : frozen — **congelador** *nm* : freezer

congeniar *vi* : get along

congestión *nf, pl* **-tiones** : congestion — **congestionado, -da** *adj* : congested

congoja *nf* : anguish, grief

congraciarse *vr* : ingratiate oneself

congratular *vt* : congratulate

congregar {52} *vt* : bring together — **congregarse** *vr* : congregate — **congregación** *nf, pl* **-ciones** : congregation, gathering

congreso *nm* : congress — **congresista** *nmf* : member of congress

conjeturar *vt* : guess, conjecture — **conjetura** *nf* : guess, conjecture

conjugar {52} *vt* : conjugate — **conjugación** *nf, pl* **-ciones** : conjugation

conjunción *nf, pl* **-ciones** : conjunction

conjunto, -ta *adj* : joint — **conjunto** *nm* **1** : collection **2** : outfit (of clothing) **3** GRUPO : band **4 en conjunto** : as a whole

conjurar *vt* : ward off — *vi* : conspire, plot

conllevar *vt* : entail

conmemorar *vt* : commemorate — **conmemoración** *nf, pl* **-ciones** : commemoration — **conmemorativo, -va** *adj* : commemorative

conmigo *pron* : with me

conminar *vt* : threaten

conmiseración *nf, pl* **-ciones** : pity, commiseration

conmocionar *vt* : shock — **conmoción** *nf, pl* **-ciones** **1** : shock, upheaval **2** *or* **conmocionar cerebral** : concussion

conmover {47} *vt* **1** : move, touch **2** SACUDIR : shake (up) — **conmoverse** *vr* : be moved — **conmovedor, -dora** *adj* : moving, touching

conmutador *nm* **1** : (electric) switch **2** *Lat* : switchboard

cono *nm* : cone
conocer {18} *vt* **1** : know **2** : meet (a person), get to know (a city, etc.) **3** RECONOCER : recognize — **conocerse** *vr* **1** : meet, get to know each other **2** : know oneself — **conocedor, -dora** *adj & n* : expert — **conocido, -da** *adj* : well-known — **conocido, -da** *n* : acquaintance — **conocimiento** *nm* **1** : knowledge **2** SENTIDO : consciousness
conque *conj* : so
conquistar *vt* : conquer — **conquista** *nf* : conquest — **conquistador, -dora** *adj* : conquering — **conquistador** *nm* : conqueror
consabido, -da *adj* **1** : well-known **2** HABITUEL : usual
consagrar *vt* **1** : consecrate **2** DEDICAR : devote — **consagración** *nf, pl* **-ciones** : consecration
consciencia *nf* → **conciencia** — **consciente** *adj* : conscious, aware
consecución *nf, pl* **-ciones** : attainment
consecuencia *nf* **1** : consequence **2 en consecuencia** : accordingly — **consecuente** *adj* : consistent
consecutivo, -va *adj* : consecutive
conseguir {75} *vt* **1** : get, obtain **2 conseguir hacer algo** : manage to do something
consejo *nm* **1** : advice, counsel **2** : council (assembly) — **consejero, -ra** *n* : adviser, counselor
consenso *nm* : consensus
consentir {76} *vt* **1** : allow, permit **2** MIMAR : pamper, spoil — *vi* : consent — **consentimiento** *nm* : consent, permission
conserje *nmf* : caretaker, janitor
conservar *vt* **1** : preserve **2** GUARDAR : keep, conserve — **conservarse** *vr* : keep — **conserva** *nf* **1** : preserve(s) **2 conservas** *nfpl* : canned goods — **conservación** *nf, pl* **-ciones** : conservation, preservation — **conservador, -dora** *adj & n* : conservative — **conservatorio** *nm* : conservatory
considerar *vt* **1** : consider **2** RESPETAR : respect — **considerable** *adj* : considerable — **consideración** *nf, pl* **-ciones** **1** : consideration **2** RESPETO : respect — **considerado, -da** *adj* **1** : considerate **2** RESPETADO : respected
consigna *nf* **1** ESLOGAN : slogan **2** ORDEN : orders **3** : checkroom (for baggage)
consigo *pron* : with her, with

him, with you, with oneself
consiguiente *adj* **1** : consequent **2 por consiguiente** : consequently
consistir *vi* **consistir en 1** : consist of **2** : lie in, consist in — **consistencia** *nf* : consistency — **consistente** *adj* **1** : firm, solid **2 consistente en** : consisting of
consolar {19} *vt* : console, comfort — **consolarse** *vr* : console oneself — **consolación** *nf, pl* **-ciones** : consolation
consolidar *vt* : consolidate — **consolidación** *nf, pl* **-ciones** : consolidation
consomé *nm* : consommé
consonante *adj* : consonant, harmonious — **consonante** *nf* : consonant
consorcio *nm* : consortium
conspirar *vi* : conspire, plot — **conspiración** *nf, pl* **-ciones** : conspiracy — **conspirador, -dora** *n* : conspirator
constancia *nf* **1** : record, evidence **2** PERSEVERANCIA : perseverance — **constante** *adj* : constant — **constantemente** *adv* : constantly, continually
constar *vi* **1** : be evident, be clear **2 constar de** : consist of
constatar *vt* **1** : verify **2** AFIRMAR : state, affirm
constelación *nf, pl* **-ciones** : constellation
consternación *nf, pl* **-ciones** : consternation
constipado, -da *adj* **estar constipado** : have a cold — **constipado** *nm* : cold — **constiparse** *vr* : catch a cold
constituir {41} *vt* **1** FORMAR : constitute, form **2** FUNDAR : establish, set up — **constituirse** *vr* **constituirse en** : set oneself up as — **constitución** *nf, pl* **-ciones** : constitution — **constitucional** *adj* : constitutional — **constitutivo, -va** *adj* : constituent — **constituyente** *adj & nm* : constituent
constreñir {67} *vt* **1** : force, compel **2** RESTRINGIR : restrict, limit
construir {41} *vt* : build, construct — **construcción** *nf, pl* **-ciones** : construction, building — **constructivo, -va** *adj* : constructive — **constructor, -tora** *n* : builder
consuelo *nm* : consolation, comfort
consuetudinario, -ria *adj* : customary
cónsul *nmf* : consul — **consulado** *nm* : consulate

consultar *vt* : consult — **consulta** *nf* : consultation — **consultor, -tora** *n* : consultant — **consultorio** *nm* : office (of a doctor or dentist)
consumar *vt* **1** : consummate, complete **2** : commit (a crime)
consumir *vt* : consume — **consumirse** *vr* : waste away — **consumición** *nf, pl* **-ciones** **1** : consumption **2** : drink (in a restaurant) — **consumido, -da** *adj* : thin, emaciated — **consumidor, -dora** *n* : consumer — **consumo** *nm* : consumption
contabilidad *nf* **1** : accounting, bookkeeping **2** : accountancy (profession) — **contable** *nmf, Spain* : accountant, bookkeeper
contactar *vi* **contactar con** : get in touch with, contact — **contacto** *nm* : contact
contado, -da *adj* : numbered, few — **contado** *nm* **al contado** : (in) cash
contador, -dora *n Lat* : accountant — **contador** *nm* : meter
contagiar *vt* **1** : infect **2** : transmit (a disease) — **contagiarse** *vr* **1** : be contagious **2** : become infected (with a disease) — **contagio** *nm* : contagion, infection — **contagioso, -sa** *adj* : contagious, infectious
contaminar *vt* : contaminate, pollute — **contaminación** *nf, pl* **-ciones** : contamination, pollution
contar {19} *vt* **1** : count **2** NARRAR : tell — *vi* **1** : count **2 contar con** : rely on, count on
contemplar *vt* **1** MIRAR : look at, behold **2** CONSIDERAR : contemplate — **contemplación** *nf, pl* **-ciones** : contemplation
contemporáneo, -nea *adj & n* : contemporary
contender {56} *vi* : contend, compete — **contendiente** *nmf* : competitor
contener {80} *vt* **1** : contain **2** RESTRINGIR : restrain, hold back — **contenerse** *vr* : restrain oneself — **contenedor** *nm* : container — **contenido, -da** *adj* : restrained — **contenido** *nm* : contents *pl*
contentar *vt* : please, make happy — **contentarse** *vr* **contentarse con** : be satisfied with — **contento, -ta** *adj* : glad, happy, contented
contestar *vt* : answer — *vi* : reply, answer back — **contestación** *nf, pl* **-ciones** : answer, reply
contexto *nm* : context

configuración^F **de los continentes**^F
configuration of the continents

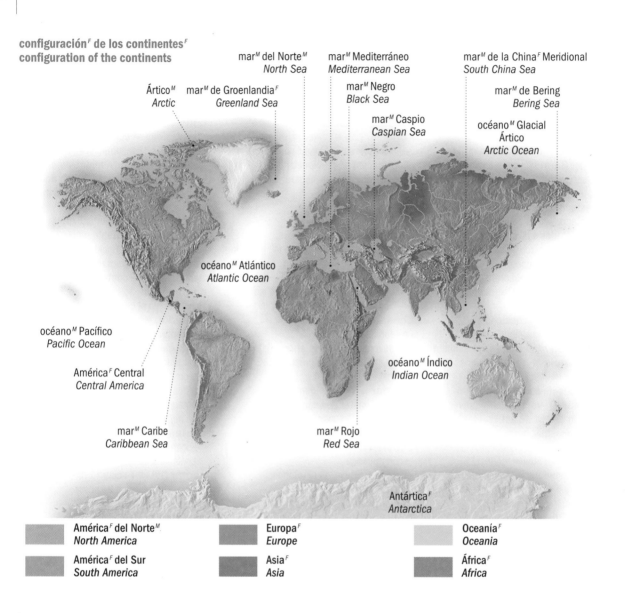

mar^M del Norte^M
North Sea

mar^M Mediterráneo
Mediterranean Sea

mar^M de la China^F Meridional
South China Sea

Ártico^M
Arctic

mar^M de Groenlandia^F
Greenland Sea

mar^M Negro
Black Sea

mar^M de Bering
Bering Sea

mar^M Caspio
Caspian Sea

océano^M Glacial
Ártico
Arctic Ocean

océano^M Atlántico
Atlantic Ocean

océano^M Pacífico
Pacific Ocean

océano^M Índico
Indian Ocean

América^F Central
Central America

mar^M Caribe
Caribbean Sea

mar^M Rojo
Red Sea

Antártica^F
Antarctica

América^F del Norte^M *North America*	Europa^F *Europe*	Oceanía^F *Oceania*
América^F del Sur *South America*	Asia^F *Asia*	África^F *Africa*

contienda *nf* **1** COMBATE : dispute, fight **2** COMPETICIÓN : contest
contigo *pron* : with you
contiguo, -gua *adj* : adjacent
▸ **continente** *nm* : continent — **continental** *adj* : continental
contingencia *nf* : contingency — **contingente** *adj & nm* : contingent
continuar {3} *v* : continue — **continuación** *nf, pl* -**ciones 1** : continuation **2 a continuación** : next, then — **continuidad** *nf* : continuity

— **continuo, -nua** *adj* **1** : continuous, steady **2** FRECUENTE : continual
contorno *nm* **1** : outline **2** contornos *nmpl* : surrounding area
contorsión *nf, pl* -**siones** : contortion
contra *prep* **1** : against **2 en contra** : against — **contra** *nm* **los pros y los contras** : the pros and cons
contraatacar {72} *v* : counterattack — **contraataque** *nm* : counterattack
contrabajo *nm* : double bass
contrabalancear *vt* : counterbalance

contrabandista *nmf* : smuggler
— **contrabando** *nm* **1** : smuggling **2** : contraband (goods)
contracción *nf, pl* -**ciones** : contraction
contrachapado *nm* : plywood
contradecir {11} *vt* : contradict
— **contradicción** *nf, pl* -**ciones** : contradiction — **contradictorio, -ria** *adj* : contradictory
contraer {81} *vt* **1** : contract **2 contraer matrimonio** : get married — **contraerse** *vr* : contract, tighten up

contrafuerte *nm* : buttress

contragolpe *nm* : backlash

contralto *nmf* : contralto

contrapartida *nf* : compensation

contrapelo: a contrapelo *adv phr* : the wrong way

contrapeso *nm* : counterbalance

contraponer {60} *vt* **1** : counter, oppose **2** COMPARAR : compare

contraproducente *adj* : counterproductive

contrariar {85} *vt* **1** : oppose **2** MOLESTAR : vex, annoy — **contrariedad** *nf* **1** : obstacle **2** DISGUSTO : annoyance — **contrario, -ria** *adj* **1** OPUESTO : opposite **2 al contrario** : on the contrary **3 ser contrario a** : be opposed to

contrarrestar *vt* : counteract

contrasentido *nm* : contradiction (in terms)

contraseña *nf* : password

contrastar *vt* **1** : check, verify **2** RESISTIR : resist — *vi* : contrast — **contraste** *nm* : contrast

contratar *vt* **1** : contract for **2** : hire, engage (workers)

contratiempo *nm* **1** : mishap **2** DIFICULTAD : setback

contrato *nm* : contract — **contratista** *nmf* : contractor

contraventana *nf* : shutter

contribuir {41} *vi* **1** : contribute **2** : pay taxes — **contribución** *nf, pl* **-ciones 1** : contribution **2** IMPUESTO : tax — **contribuyente** *nmf* **1** : contributor **2** : taxpayer

contrincante *nmf* : opponent

contrito, -ta *adj* : contrite

controlar *vt* **1** : control **2** COMPROBAR : monitor, check — **control** *nm* **1** : control **2** VERIFICACIÓN : inspection, check — **controlador, -dora** *n* : controller

controversia *nf* : controversy

contundente *adj* **1** : blunt **2** : forceful, convincing (of arguments, etc.)

contusión *nf, pl* **-siones** : bruise

convalecencia *nf* : convalescence — **convaleciente** *adj & nmf* : convalescent

convencer {86} *vt* : convince, persuade — **convencerse** *vr* : be convinced — **convencimiento** *nm* : conviction, belief

convención *nf, pl* **-ciones** : convention — **convencional** *adj* : conventional

convenir {87} *vi* **1** : be suitable, be advisable **2 convenir en** :

agree on — **conveniencia** *nf* **1** : convenience **2** : suitability (of an action, etc.) — **conveniente** *adj* **1** : convenient **2** ACONSEJABLE : suitable, advisable **3** PROVECHOSO : useful — **convenio** *nm* : agreement, pact

convento *nm* : convent, monastery

converger {15} *or* **convergir** *vi* : converge

conversar *vi* : converse, talk — **conversación** *nf, pl* **-ciones** : conversation

conversión *nf, pl* **-siones** : conversion — **converso, -sa** *n* : convert

convertir {76} *vt* : convert — **convertirse** *vr* **convertirse en** : turn into — **convertible** *adj & nm* : convertible

convexo, -xa *adj* : convex

convicción *nf, pl* **-ciones** : conviction — **convicto, -ta** *adj* : convicted

convidar *vt* : invite — **convidado, -da** *n* : guest

convincente *adj* : convincing

convite *nm* **1** : invitation **2** : banquet

convivir *vi* : live together — **convivencia** *nf* : coexistence, living together

convocar {72} *vt* : convoke, call together

convulsión *nf, pl* **-siones 1** : convulsion **2** TRASTORNO : upheaval — **convulsivo, -va** *adj* : convulsive

conyugal *adj* : conjugal — **cónyuge** *nmf* : spouse, partner

coñac *nm* : cognac, brandy

cooperar *vi* : cooperate — **cooperación** *nf, pl* **-ciones** : cooperation — **cooperativa** *nf* : cooperative, co-op — **cooperativo, -va** *adj* : cooperative

coordenada *nf* : coordinate

coordinar *vt* : coordinate — **coordinación** *nf, pl* **-ciones** : coordination — **coordinador, -dora** *n* : coordinator

copa *nf* **1** : glass, goblet **2** : cup (in sports) **3 tomar una copa** : have a drink

copia *nf* : copy — **copiar** *vt* : copy

copioso, -sa *adj* : copious, abundant

copla *nf* **1** : (popular) song **2** ESTROFA : verse, stanza

copo *nm* **1** : flake **2** *or* **copo de nieve** : snowflake

coquetear *vi* : flirt — **coqueteo** *nm* : flirting, flirtation — **coqueto, -ta** *adj* : flirtatious — **coqueto, -ta** *n* : flirt

coraje *nm* **1** : valor, courage **2** IRA : anger

coral[1] *nm* : coral

coral 2 *adj* : choral — **coral** *nf* : choir, chorale

Corán *nm* **el Corán** : the Koran

coraza *nf* **1** : armor plating **2** : shell

corazón *nm, pl* **-zones 1** : heart **2** : core (of fruit) **3 mi corazón** : my darling — **corazonada** *nf* **1** : hunch **2** IMPULSO : impulse

corbata *nf* : tie, necktie

corchete *nm* **1** : hook and eye, clasp **2** : square bracket (punctuation mark)

corcho *nm* : cork

cordel *nm* : cord, string

cordero *nm* : lamb

cordial *adj* : cordial — **cordialidad** *nf* : cordiality

cordillera *nf* : mountain range

córdoba *nf* : córdoba (Nicaraguan unit of currency)

cordón *nm, pl* **-dones 1** : cord **2 cordón policial** : (police) cordon **3 cordones** *nmpl* : shoelaces

cordura *nf* : sanity

corear *vt* : chant

coreografía *nf* : choreography

cornamenta *nf* : antlers *pl*

corneta *nf* : bugle

coro *nm* **1** : chorus **2** : (church) choir

corona *nf* **1** : crown **2** : wreath, garland (of flowers) — **coronación** *nf, pl* **-ciones** : coronation — **coronar** *vt* : crown

coronel *nm* : colonel

coronilla *nf* **1** : crown (of the head) **2 estar hasta la coronilla** : be fed up

corporación *nf, pl* **-ciones** : corporation

corporal *adj* : corporal, bodily

corporativo, -va *adj* : corporate

corpulento, -ta *adj* : stout

corral *nm* **1** : farmyard **2** : pen, corral (for animals) **3** *or* **corralito** : playpen

correa *nf* **1** : strap, belt **2** : leash (for a dog, etc.)

corrección *nf, pl* **-ciones 1** : correction **2** : correctness, propriety (of manners) — **correccional** *nm* : reformatory — **correctivo, -va** *adj* : corrective — **correcto, -ta** *adj* **1** : correct, right **2** CORTÉS : polite

corredizo, -za *adj* : sliding

corredor, -dora *n* **1** : runner, racer **2** AGENTE : agent, broker — **corredor** *nm* : corridor, hallway

corregir {28} *vt* : correct — **corregirse** *vr* : mend one's ways

correlación *nf, pl* **-ciones** : correlation

correo *nm* **1** : mail **2 correo aéreo** : airmail

correr *vi* **1** : run, race **2** : flow (of a river, etc.) **3** : pass (of time) — *vt* **1** : run **2** RECORRER : travel over, cover **3** : draw (curtains) — **correrse** *vr* **1** : move along **2** : run (of colors)

corresponder *vi* **1** : correspond **2** PERTENECER : belong **3** ENCAJAR : fit **4** **corresponder a** : reciprocate, repay — **corresponderse** *vr* : write to each other — **correspondencia** *nf* **1** : correspondence **2** : connection (of a train, etc.) — **correspondiente** *adj* : corresponding, respective — **corresponsal** *nmf* : correspondent

corretear *vi* : run about, scamper

corrida *nf* **1** : run **2** *or* **corrida de toros** : bullfight — **corrido, -da** *adj* **1** : straight, continuous **2** *fam* : worldly

corriente *adj* **1** : current **2** NORMAL : common, ordinary **3** : running (of water, etc.) — **corriente** *nf* **1** : current (of water, electricity, etc.), draft (of air) **2** TENDENCIA : tendency, trend — **corriente** *nm* **al corriente 1** : up-to-date **2** ENTERADO : aware, informed

corrillo *nm* : clique, circle — **corro** *nm* : ring, circle (of people)

corroborar *vt* : corroborate

corroer {69} *vt* **1** : corrode (of metals) **2** : erode, wear away — **corroerse** *vr* : corrode

corromper *vt* **1** : corrupt **2** PUDRIR : rot — **corrompido, -da** *adj* : corrupt

corrosión *nf, pl* **-siones** : corrosion — **corrosivo, -va** *adj* : corrosive

corrupción *nf, pl* **-ciones 1** : corruption **2** DESCOMPOSICIÓN : decay, rot — **corrupto, -ta** *adj* : corrupt

corsé *nm* : corset

cortar *vt* **1** : cut **2** RECORTAR : cut out **3** QUITAR : cut off — *vi* : cut — **cortarse** *vr* **1** : cut oneself **2** : be cut off (on the telephone) **3** : curdle (of milk) **4 cortarse el pelo** : have one's hair cut — **cortada** *nf* *Lat* : cut — **cortante** *adj* : cutting, sharp

cortauñas *nms & pl* : nail clippers

corte[1] *nm* **1** : cutting **2** ESTILO : cut, style **3 corte de pelo** : haircut

corte[2] *nf* **1** : court **2 hacer la corte a** : court, woo — **cortejar** *vt* : court, woo

cortejo *nm* **1** : entourage **2** NOVIAZGO : courtship **3 cortejo fúnebre** : funeral procession

cortés *adj* : courteous, polite — **cortesía** *nf* : courtesy

cortinas[F]
curtains

cortina[F] sujeta de doble barra[F]
attached curtain

cortina[F] abombada
balloon curtain

cortina[F] suelta corrediza
loose curtain

cortinas[F] cruzadas
crisscross curtains

corteza *nf* **1** : bark **2** : crust (of bread) **3** : rind, peel (of fruit)

▸ **cortina** *nm* : curtain

corto, -ta *adj* **1** : short **2** ESCASO : scarce **3** *fam* : timid, shy **4 corto, -ta de vista** : nearsighted — **cortocircuito** *nm* : short circuit

corvo, -va *adj* : curved, bent

cosa *nf* **1** : thing **2** ASUNTO : matter, affair **3 cosa de** : about **4 poca cosa** : nothing much

cosechar *v* : harvest, reap — **cosecha** *nf* **1** : harvest, crop **2** : vintage (of wine)

coser *v* : sew

cosmético, -ca *adj* : cosmetic

— **cosmético** *nm* : cosmetic

cósmico, -ca *adj* : cosmic

cosmopolita *adj* : cosmopolitan

cosmos *nm* : cosmos

cosquillas *nfpl* **1** : tickling **2 hacer cosquillas** : tickle — **cosquilleo** *nm* : tickling sensation, tingle

costa *nf* **1** : coast, shore **2 a toda costa** : at any cost

costado *nm* **1** : side **2 al costado** : alongside

costar {19} *v* : cost

costarricense *or* **costarriqueño, -ña** *adj* : Costa Rican

coste *nm* → **costo** — **costear** *vt* : pay for

costero, -ra *adj* : coastal

costilla *nf* **1** : rib **2** CHULETA : chop, cutlet

costo *nm* : cost, price —
costoso, -sa *adj* : costly

costra *nf* : scab

costumbre *nf* **1** : custom, habit
2 de costumbre : usual

costura *nf* **1** : sewing,
dressmaking **2** PUNTADAS : seam
— **costurera** *nf* : dressmaker

cotejar *vt* : compare

cotidiano, -na *adj* : daily

cotizar {21} *vt* : quote, set a price on
— **cotización** *nf, pl* **-ciones** : quotation,
price — **cotizado, -da** *adj* : in demand

coto *nm* : enclosure, reserve

cotorra *nf* **1** : small parrot **2**
fam : chatterbox — **cotorrear** *vi,*
fam : chatter, gab

coyote *nm* : coyote

coyuntura *nf* **1** : joint **2**
SITUACIÓN : situation, moment

coz *nm, pl* **coces** : kick (of an animal)

cráneo *nf* : cranium, skull

cráter *nm* : crater

crear *vt* : create — **creación** *nf,*
pl **-ciones** : creation — **creativo, -va** *adj*
: creative — **creador, -dora** *n* : creator

crecer {53} *vi* **1** : grow **2** AUMENTAR
: increase — **crecido, -da** *adj* **1**
: full-grown **2** : large (of numbers)
— **creciente** *adj* **1** : growing,
increasing **2** : crescent (of the
moon) — **crecimiento** *nm* **1** :

growth **2** AUMENTO : increase

credenciales *nfpl* : credentials

credibilidad *nf* : credibility

crédito *nm* : credit

credo *nm* : creed

crédulo, -la *adj* : credulous, gullible

creer {20} *v* **1** : believe **2** SUPONER :
suppose, think — **creerse** *vr* : regard
oneself as — **creencia** *nf* : belief —
creíble *adj* : believable, credible —
creído, -da *adj, fam* : conceited

crema *nf* : cream

cremación *nf, pl* **-ciones** : cremation

cremallera *nf* : zipper

cremoso, -sa *adj* : creamy

crepe *nmf* : crepe, pancake

crepitar *vi* : crackle

crepúsculo *nm* : twilight, dusk

crespo, -pa *adj* : curly, frizzy

crespón *nm, pl* **-pones** : crepe (fabric)

cresta *nf* **1** : crest **2** : comb (of a rooster)

cretino, -na *n* : cretin

creyente *nmf* : believer

criar {85} *vt* **1** : nurse (a baby) **2** EDUCAR
: bring up, rear **3** : raise, breed (animals)
— **cría** *nf* **1** : breeding, rearing **2** :
young animal — **criadero** *nm* : farm,
hatchery — **criado, -da** *n* : servant,
maid *f* — **criador, -dora** *n* : breeder
— **crianza** *nf* : upbringing, rearing

criatura *nf* **1** : creature
2 NIÑO : baby, child

crimen *nm, pl* **crímenes** : crime

— **criminal** *adj & nmf* : criminal

críquet *nm* : cricket (game)

crin *nf* : mane

criollo, -lla *adj & n* : Creole

cripta *nf* : crypt

crisantemo *nm* : chrysanthemum

crisis *nf* **1** : crisis **2 crisis**
nerviosa : nervous breakdown

crispar *vt* **1** : tense (muscles), clench
(one's fist) **2** IRRITAR : irritate, set on
edge — **crisparse** *vr* : tense up

▸ **cristal** *nm* **1** : crystal **2** VIDRIO : glass,
piece of glass — **cristalería** *nf* :
glassware — **cristalino, -na** *adj* :
crystalline — **cristalino** *nm* : lens (of the
eye) — **cristalizar** {21} *vi* : crystallize

cristiano, -na *adj & n* : Christian
— **cristianismo** *nm* : Christianity
— **Cristo** *nm* : Christ

criterio *nm* **1** : criterion **2**
JUICIO : judgment, opinion

criticar {72} *vt* : criticize — **crítica** *nf* **1**
: criticism **2** RESEÑA : review, critique
— **crítico, -ca** *adj* : critical —
crítico, -ca *n* : critic, reviewer

croar *vi* : croak

cromo *nm* : chromium, chrome

cromosoma *nm* : chromosome

crónica *nf* **1** : chronicle **2** : (news) report

crónico, -ca *adj* : chronic

cronista *nmf* : reporter, newscaster

cronología *nf* : chronology —
cronológico, -ca *adj* : chronological

cristales^M **de nieve**^F
snow crystals

columna^F
column

granizo^M
hail

cellisca^F
sleet

copo^M de nieve^F
snow pellet

aguja^F
needle

columna^F con capuchón^M
capped column

placa^F de hielo^M
plate crystal

dendrita^F espacial
spatial dendrite

cristales^M irregulares
irregular crystal

estrella^F
stellar crystal

cronometrar *vt* : time, clock —
  cronómetro *nm* : chronometer, stopwatch
croqueta *nf* : croquette
croquis *nms & pl* : (rough) sketch
cruce *nm* **1** : crossing **2** : crossroads,
  intersection **3 cruce peatonal** : crosswalk
crucero *nm* **1** : cruise **2** : cruiser (ship)
crucial *adj* : crucial
crucificar {72} *vt* : crucify —
  crucifijo *nm* : crucifix — **crucifixión** *nf,*
  pl **-fixiones** : crucifixion
crucigrama *nm* : crossword puzzle
crudo, -da *adj* **1** : harsh, crude **2** :
  raw (of food) — **crudo** *nm* : crude oil
cruel *adj* : cruel — **crueldad** *nf* : cruelty
crujir *vi* : rustle, creak, crackle, crunch
  — **crujido** *nm* : rustle, creak, crackle,
  crunch — **crujiente** *adj* : crunchy, crisp
cruzar {21} *vt* **1** : cross **2** : exchange
  (words) — **cruzarse** *vr* **1** : intersect
  2 : pass each other — **cruz** *nf,*
  pl **cruces** : cross — **cruzada** *nf*
  : crusade — **cruzado, -da** *adj* :
  crossed — **cruzado** *nm* : crusader
cuaderno *nm* : notebook
cuadra *nf* **1** : stable **2** *Lat* : (city) block

cuadrado, -da *adj* : square
  — **cuadrado** *nm* : square
cuadragésimo, -ma *adj* : fortieth,
  forty- — **cuadragésimo, -ma** *n*
  : fortieth, forty- (in a series)
cuadrar *vi* **1** : conform, agree **2** : add
  up, tally (numbers) — *vt* : square —
  cuadrarse *vr* : stand at attention
cuadrilátero *nm* **1** : quadrilateral
  2 : ring (in sports)
cuadrilla *nf* : gang, group
cuadro *nm* **1** : square **2** PINTURA
  : painting **3** DESCRIPCIÓN : picture,
  description **4** : staff, management (of
  an organization) **5** CUADRADO : check,
  square **6** : (baseball) diamond
cuadrúpedo *nm* : quadruped
cuadruple *adj* : quadruple —
  cuadruplicar {72} *vt* : quadruple
cuajar *vi* **1** : curdle **2** COAGULAR :
  clot, coagulate **3** : set (of pudding,
  etc.) **4** AFIANZARSE : catch on — *vt* **1**
  : curdle **2 cuajar de** : fill with
cual *pron* **1 el cual, la cual, los cuales,**
  las cuales : who, whom, which **2 lo**
  cual : which **3 cada cual** : everyone,

everybody — **cual** *prep* : like, as
cuál *pron* : which (one), what
  (one) — **cuál** *adj* : which, what
cualidad *nf* : quality, trait
cualquiera (cualquier *before*
  nouns) adj, pl **cualesquiera** : any,
  whatever — **cualquiera** *pron,*
  pl **cualesquiera** : anyone, whatever
cuán *adv* : how
cuando *conj* **1** : when **2** SI : since,
  if **3 cuando más** : at the most **4 de**
  vez en cuando : from time to time —
  cuando *prep* : during, at the time of
cuándo *adv* **1** : when **2 ¿desde**
  cuándo? : since when?
cuantía *nf* **1** : quantity, extent **2**
  IMPORTANCIA : importance — **cuantioso,**
  -sa *adj* : abundant, considerable
cuanto *adv* **1** : as much as **2 cuanto**
  antes : as soon as possible **3 en**
  cuanto : as soon as **4 en cuanto a** :
  as for, as regards — **cuanto, -ta** *adj* :
  as many, whatever — **cuanto** *pron* **1** :
  as much as, all that, everything **2 unos**
  cuantos, unas cuantas : a few
cuánto *adv* : how much, how many

cuarto^M **de baño**^M
bathroom

cabina^F de la ducha^F
shower stall

ducha^F de
teléfono^M portable

bañera^F
bathtub

inodoro^M
toilet

grifo^M
faucet

espejo^M
mirror

lavabo^M
sink

toallero^M
towel bar

— **cuánto, -ta** *adj* : how much, how many
— **cuánto** *pron* : how much, how many
cuarenta *adj & nm* : forty —
cuarentavo, -va *adj* : fortieth —
cuarentavo *nm* : fortieth
cuarentena *nf* : quarantine
Cuaresma *nf* : Lent
cuartear *vt* : quarter, divide up
— **cuartearse** *vr* : crack, split
cuartel *nm* **1** : barracks *pl* **2**
cuartel general : headquarters **3**
no dar cuartel : show no mercy
cuarteto *nm* : quartet
cuarto, -ta *adj* : fourth — **cuarto, -ta** *n*
: fourth (in a series) — **cuarto** *nm* **1** :
quarter, fourth **2** HABITACIÓN : room
cuarzo *nm* : quartz
cuatro *adj & nm* : four — **cuatrocientos,**
-tas *adj* : four hundred —
cuatrocientos *nms & pl* : four hundred
cuba *nf* : cask, barrel
cubano, -na *adj* : Cuban
cubeta *nf* **1** : keg, cask
2 *Lat* : pail, bucket
cúbico, -ca *adj* : cubic, cubed
— **cubículo** *nm* : cubicle
cubierta *nf* **1** : cover, covering **2** :
(automobile) tire **3** : deck (of a ship)
— **cubierto** *nm* **1** : cutlery, place
setting **2 a cubierta** : under cover
cubo *nm* **1** : cube **2** *Spain* : pail,
bucket **3** : hub (of a wheel)
cubrecama *nm* : bedspread
cubrir {2} *vt* : cover — **cubrirse** *vr* **1**
: cover oneself **2** : cloud over
cucaracha *nf* : cockroach
cuchara *nf* : spoon — **cucharada** *nf*
: spoonful — **cucharilla** *or*
cucharita *nf* : teaspoon —
cucharón *nm, pl* **-rones** : ladle
cuchichear *vi* : whisper —
cuchicheo *nm* : whisper
cuchilla *nf* **1** : (kitchen) knife **2 cuchilla**
de afeitar : razor blade — **cuchillada** *nf*
: stab, knife wound — **cuchillo** *nm* : knife
cuclillas *nfpl* **en cuclillas** :
squatting, crouching
cuco *nm* : cuckoo — **cuco,**
-ca *adj, fam* : pretty, cute
cucurucho *nm* : ice-cream cone
cuello *nm* **1** : neck **2** : collar (of clothing)
cuenca *nf* **1** : river basin **2** :
(eye) socket — **cuenco** *nm* **1** :
bowl **2** CONCAVIDAD : hollow
cuenta *nf* **1** : calculation, count **2** : (bank)

account **3** FACTURA : check, bill **4** : bead
(for a necklace, etc.) **5 darse cuenta** :
realize **6 tener en cuenta** : bear in mind
cuento *nm* **1** : story, tale **2**
cuento de hadas : fairy tale
cuerda *nf* **1** : cord, rope, string
2 cuerdas vocales : vocal cords
3 dar cuerda a : wind up
cuerdo, -da *adj* : sane, sensible
cuerno *nm* **1** : horn **2** :
antlers *pl* (of a deer)
cuero *nm* **1** : leather, hide **2** :
cuero cabelludo : scalp
cuerpo *nm* **1** : body **2** : corps
(in the military, etc.)
cuervo *nm* : crow
cuesta *nf* **1** : slope **2 a cuestas**
: on one's back **3 cuesta abajo** :
downhill **4 cuesta arriba** : uphill
cuestión *nf, pl* **-tiones** :
matter, affair — **cuestionar** *vt* :
question — **cuestionario** *nm* **1** :
questionnaire **2** : quiz (in school)
cueva *nf* : cave
cuidar *vt* **1** : take care of, look after **2**
: pay attention to (details, etc.) — *vi* **1**
cuidar de : look after **2 cuidar de que**
: make sure that — **cuidarse** *vr* : take
care of oneself — **cuidado** *nm* **1** : care
2 PREOCUPACIÓN : worry, concern **3 tener**
cuidado : be careful **4 ¡cuidado!** : watch
out!, careful! — **cuidadoso, -sa** *adj* :
careful — **cuidadosamente** *adv* : carefully
culata *nf* : butt (of a gun) —
culatazo *nm* : kick, recoil
culebra *nf* : snake
culinario, -ria *adj* : culinary
culminar *vi* : culminate —
culminación *nf, pl* **-ciones** : culmination
culo *nm, fam* : backside, bottom
culpa *nf* **1** : fault, blame **2** PECADO : sin **3**
echar la culpa a : blame **4 tener la culpa**
: be at fault — **culpabilidad** *nf* : guilt —
culpable *adj* : guilty — **culpable** *nmf* :
culprit, guilty party — **culpar** *vt* : blame
cultivar *vt* : cultivate — **cultivo** *nm* **1**
: farming, cultivation **2 cultivars** : crops
culto, -ta *adj* : cultured, educated
— **culto** *nm* **1** : worship **2** :
(religious) cult — **cultura** *nf* :
culture — **cultural** *adj* : cultural
cumbre *nf* : summit, top
cumpleaños *nms & pl* : birthday
cumplido, -da *adj* **1** : complete, full
2 CORTÉS : courteous — **cumplido** *nm*

: compliment, courtesy
cumplimentar *vt* **1** : congratulate **2**
CUMPLIR : carry out — **cumplimiento** *nm*
: carrying out, performance
cumplir *vt* **1** : accomplish, carry out
2 : keep (a promise), observe (a law,
etc.) **3** : reach (a given age) — *vi* **1** :
expire, fall due **2 cumplir con el deber**
: do one's duty — **cumplirse** *vr* **1**
: expire **2** REALIZARSE : come true
cúmulo *nm* **1** : heap, pile
2 : cumulus (cloud)
cuna *nf* **1** : cradle **2** ORIGEN : birthplace
cundir *vi* **1** PROPAGARSE : spread,
propagate **2** : go a long way
cuneta *nf* : ditch (in a road),
gutter (in a street)
cuña *nf* : wedge
cuñado, -da *n* : brother-in-
law *m*, sister-in-law *f*
cuota *nf* **1** : fee, dues **2** CUPO : quota
3 *Lat* : installment, payment
cupo *nm* **1** : quota, share
2 *Lat* : capacity, room
cupón *nm, pl* **-pones** : coupon
cúpula *nf* : dome, cupola
cura *nf* : cure, treatment — **cura** *nm* :
priest — **curación** *nf, pl* **-ciones** : healing
— **curar** *vt* **1** : cure **2** : dress (a wound) **3**
CURTIR : tan (hides) — **curarse** *vr* : get well
curiosear *vi* **1** : snoop, pry **2** : browse (in
a store) — *vt* : look over — **curiosidad** *nf*
: curiosity — **curioso, -sa** *adj* **1** : curious,
inquisitive **2** RARO : unusual, strange
currículum *nm, pl* **-lums** *or* currículo *nm*
: résumé, curriculum vitae
cursar *vt* **1** : take (a course),
study **2** ENVIAR : send, pass on
cursi *adj, fam* : affected, pretentious
cursiva *nf* : italics *pl*
curso *nm* **1** : course **2** : (school) year **3**
en curso : under way **4 en curso** : current
curtir *vt* **1** : tan **2** : harden (skin,
features, etc.) — **curtiduría** *nf* : tannery
curva *nf* **1** : curve, bend **2 curva de nivel**
: contour — **curvo, -va** *adj* : curved, bent
cúspide *nf* : apex, peak
custodia *nf* : custody —
custodiar *vt* : guard, look after —
custodio, -dia *n* : guardian
cutáneo, -nea *adj* : skin
cutícula *nf* : cuticle
cutis *nms & pl* : skin, complexion
cuyo, -ya *adj* **1** : whose, of whom, of
which **2 en cuyo caso** : in which case

damas^F
checkers

dama^F
checker

tablero^M de damas^F
checkerboard

d *nf* : d, fourth letter of the
Spanish alphabet
dádiva *nf* : gift, handout —
dadivoso, -sa *adj* : generous
dado, -da *adj* **1** : given **2 dado que** :
provided that, since — **dados** *nmpl* : dice
daga *nf* : dagger
daltónico, -ca *adj* : color-blind
▸ **dama** *nf* **1** : lady **2 damas** *nfpl* : checkers
damnificar {72} *vt* : damage, injure
danés, -nesa *adj* : Danish —
danés *nm* : Danish (language)
danzar {21} *v* : dance —
danza *nf* : dance, dancing
dañar *vt* : damage, harm — **dañarse** *vr* **1**
: be damaged **2** : hurt oneself — **dañino,
-na** *adj* : harmful — **daño** *nm* **1** : damage,
harm **2 daños y perjuicios** : damages
dar {22} *vt* **1** : give **2** PRODUCIR : yield,
produce **3** : strike (the hour) **4** MOSTRAR
: show — *vi* **1 dar como** : consider,
regard as **2 dar con** : run into, meet **3**
dar contra : knock against **4 dar para** :
be enough for — **darse** *vr* **1** : happen **2**
darse contra : bump into **3 darse por** :
consider oneself **4 dárselas de** : pose as
dardo *nm* : dart
dársena *nf* : dock
datar *vt* : date — *vi* **datar de** : date from
dátil *nm* : date (fruit)
dato *nm* **1** : fact **2 datos** *nmpl* : data
de *prep* **1** : of **2 de Managua** : from
Managua **3 de niño** : as a child **4**
de noche : at night **5 las tres de la
mañana** : three o'clock in the morning
6 más de 10 : more than 10

deambular *vi* : wander about, stroll
debajo *adv* **1** : underneath **2**
debajo de : under, underneath **3**
por debajo : below, beneath
debatir *vt* : debate — **debatirse** *vr*
: struggle — **debate** *nm* : debate
deber *vt* : owe — *v aux* **1** : have
to, should **2** (*expressing probability*)
: must — **deberse** *vr* **deberse a** :
be due to — **deber** *nm* **1** : duty **2**
deberes *nmpl* : homework — **debido,
-da** *adj* **debido a** : due to, owing to
débil *adj* : weak, feeble — **debilidad** *nf*
: weakness — **debilitar** *vt* : weaken
— **debilitarse** *vr* : get weak —
débilmente *adv* : weakly, faintly
débito *nm* **1** : debit **2** DEUDA : debt
debutar *vi* : debut — **debut** *nm, pl* **debuts**
: debut — **debutante** *nf* : debutante *f*
década *nf* : decade
decadencia *nf* : decadence —
decadente *adj* : decadent
decaer {13} *vi* : decline, weaken
decano, -na *n* : dean
decapitar *vt* : behead
decena *nf* : ten, about ten
decencia *nf* : decency
decenio *nm* : decade
decente *adj* : decent
decepcionar *vt* : disappoint —
decepción *nf, pl* **-ciones** : disappointment
decibelio *or* decibel *nm* : decibel
decidir *vt* : decide, determine — *vi*
: decide — **decidirse** *vr* : make up
one's mind — **decididamente** *adv*
: definitely, decidedly — **decidido,**

-da *adj* : determined, resolute
decimal *adj* : decimal
décimo, -ma *adj & n* : tenth
decimoctavo, -va *adj* :
eighteenth — **decimoctavo,
-va** *n* : eighteenth (in a series)
decimocuarto, -ta *adj* :
fourteenth — **decimocuarto,
-ta** *n* : fourteenth (in a series)
decimonoveno, -na *or* **decimonono,
-na** *adj* : nineteenth — **decimonoveno,
-na** *n* : nineteenth (in a series)
decimoquinto, -ta *adj* : fifteenth —
decimoquinto, -ta *n* : fifteenth (in a series)
decimoséptimo, -ma *adj* :
seventeenth — **decimoséptimo,
-ma** *n* : seventeenth (in a series)
decimosexto, -ta *adj* : sixteenth —
decimosexto, -ta *n* : sixteenth (in a series)
decimotercero, -ra *adj* :
thirteenth — **decimotercero,
-ra** *n* : thirteenth (in a series)
decir {23} *vt* **1** : say **2** CONTAR : tell **3 es
decir** : that is to say **4 querer decir** : mean
— **decirse** *vr* **1** : tell oneself **2 ¿cómo se
dice…en español?** : how do you say…in
Spanish? — **decir** *nm* : saying, expression
decisión *nf, pl* **-siones** : decision
— **decisivo, -va** *adj* : decisive
declarar *vt* : declare — *vi* : testify —
declararse *vr* **1** : declare oneself **2** :
break out (of a fire, an epidemic, etc.) —
declaración *nf, pl* **-ciones** : statement
declinar *v* : decline
declive *nm* **1** : decline **2** PENDIENTE : slope
decolorar *vt* : bleach —
decolorarse *vr* : fade
decoración *nf, pl* **-ciones** :
decoration — **decorado** *nm* : stage
set — **decorar** *vt* : decorate —
decorativo, -va *adj* : decorative
decoro *nm* : decency, decorum —
decoroso, -sa *adj* : decent, proper
decrecer {53} *vi* : decrease
decrépito, -ta *adj* : decrepit
decretar *vt* : decree —
decreto *nm* : decree
dedal *nm* : thimble
dedicar {72} *vt* : dedicate — **dedicarse** *vr*
dedicarse a : devote oneself to —
dedicación *nf, pl* **-ciones** : dedication —
dedicatoria *nf* : dedication, inscription
dedo *nm* **1** : finger **2 dedo del pie** : toe
deducir {61} *vt* **1** INFERIR : deduce **2**
DESCONTAR : deduct — **deducción** *nf,*

pl **-ciones** : deduction
defecar {72} *vi* : defecate
defecto *nm* : defect — **defectuoso,
-sa** *adj* : defective, faulty
defender {56} *vt* : defend —
defenderse *vr* : defend oneself —
defensa *nf* : defense — **defensiva** *nf* :
defensive — **defensivo, -va** *adj* : defensive
— **defensor, -sora** *n* **1** : defender **2** *or*
abogado defensor : defense counsel
deferencia *nf* : deference —
deferente *adj* : deferential
deficiencia *nf* : deficiency —
deficiente *adj* : deficient
déficit *nm, pl* **-cits** : deficit
definir *vt* : define — **definición** *nf,
pl* **-ciones** : definition —
definitivo, -va *adj* **1** : definitive
2 en definitiva : in short
deformar *vt* **1** : deform **2** : distort
(the truth, etc.) — **deformación** *nf,
pl* **-ciones** : distortion — **deforme** *adj* :
deformed — **deformidad** *nf* : deformity
defraudar *vt* **1** : defraud **2**
DECEPCIONAR : disappoint
degenerar *vi* : degenerate —
degenerado, -da *adj* : degenerate
degradar *vt* **1** : degrade **2** :
demote (in the military)
degustar *vt* : taste
dehesa *nf* : pasture
deidad *nf* : deity

dejar *vt* **1** : leave **2** ABANDONAR : abandon
3 PERMITIR : allow — *vi* **dejar de** : quit
— **dejado, -da** *adj* : slovenly, careless
dejo *nm* **1** : aftertaste **2**
: (regional) accent
delantal *nm* : apron
delante *adv* **1** : ahead **2**
delante de : in front of
delantera *nf* **1** : front **2 tomar
la delantera** : take the lead —
delantero, -ra *adj* : front, forward —
delantero, -ra *n* : forward (in sports)
delatar *vt* : denounce, inform against
delegar {52} *vt* : delegate —
delegación *nf, pl* **-ciones** : delegation —
delegado, -da *n* : delegate, representative
deleitar *vt* : delight, please
— **deleite** *nm* : delight
deletrear *vi* : spell (out)
▸ **delfín** *nm, pl* **-fines** : dolphin
delgado, -da *adj* : thin
deliberar *vi* : deliberate —
deliberación *nf, pl* **-ciones** :
deliberation — **deliberado,
-da** *adj* : deliberate, intentional
delicadeza *nf* **1** : delicacy, daintiness
2 SUAVIDAD : gentleness **3** TACTO : tact
— **delicado, -da** *adj* **1** : delicate **2**
SENSIBLE : sensible **3** DISCRETO : tactful
delicia *nf* : delight — **delicioso,
-sa** *adj* **1** : delightful **2** RICO : delicious
delictivo, -va *adj* : criminal

delimitar *vt* : define, set
the boundaries of
delincuencia *nf* : delinquency, crime
— **delincuente** *adj & nmf* : delinquent,
criminal — **delinquir** {24} *vi* : break the law
delirante *adj* : delirious — **delirar** *vi* **1**
: be delirious **2 delirante por** *fam* : rave
about — **delirio** *nm* **1** : delirium **2 delirio
de grandeza** : delusions of grandeur
delito *nm* : crime
delta *nm* : delta
demacrado, -da *adj* : emaciated
demandar *vt* **1** : sue **2** PEDIR : demand
3 *Lat* : require — **demanda** *nf* **1** :
lawsuit **2** PETICIÓN : request **3 la oferta
y la demanda** : supply and demand
— **demandante** *nmf* : plaintiff
demás *adj* : rest of the, other —
demás *pron* **1 lo (la, los, las)**
demás : the rest, others **2 por
demás** : extremely **3 por lo demás** :
otherwise **4 y demás** : and so on
demasiado *adv* **1** : too **2** : too much
— **demasiado** *adj* : too much, too many
demencia *nf* : madness —
demente *adj* : insane, mad
democracia *nf* : democracy —
demócrata *nmf* : democrat —
democrático, -ca *adj* : democratic
demoler {47} *vt* : demolish —
demolición *nf, pl* **-ciones** : demolition
demonio *nm* : devil, demon

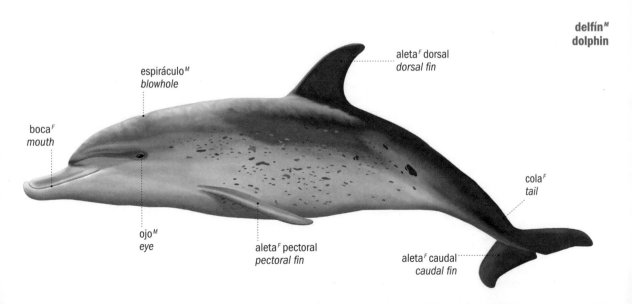

delfín^M
dolphin

aleta^F dorsal
dorsal fin

espiráculo^M
blowhole

boca^F
mouth

cola^F
tail

ojo^M
eye

aleta^F pectoral
pectoral fin

aleta^F caudal
caudal fin

demorar v : delay — **demorarse** vr :
take a long time — **demora** nf : delay
demostrar {19} vt **1** : demonstrate **2**
MOSTRAR : show — **demostración** nf,
pl -**ciones** : demonstration
demudar vt : change, alter
denegar {49} vt : deny, refuse —
denegación nf, pl -**ciones** : denial, refusal
denigrar vt **1** : denigrate
2 INJURIAR : insult
denominador nm : denominator
denotar vt : denote, show
densidad nf : density —
denso, -sa adj : dense
dental adj : dental — **dentado,
-da** adj : toothed, notched —
dentadura nf **dentadura postiza**
: dentures pl — **dentífrico** nm :
toothpaste — **dentista** nmf : dentist
dentro adv **1** : in, inside **2 dentro de
poco** : soon, shortly **3 por dentro** : inside
denuedo nm : courage
denunciar vt **1** : denounce **2** :
report (a crime) — **denuncia** nf **1**
: accusation **2** : (police) report
departamento nm **1** :
department **2** Lat : apartment
depender vi **1** : depend **2 depender
de** : depend on — **dependencia** nf **1**
: dependence, dependency **2** SUCURSAL
: branch office — **dependiente** adj
: dependent — **dependiente,
-ta** n : clerk, salesperson
deplorar vt : deplore, regret
deponer {60} vt : remove
from office, depose
deportar vt : deport — **deportación** nf,
pl -**ciones** : deportation
deporte nm : sport, sports pl —
deportista nmf : sportsman m,
sportswoman f — **deportivo,
-va** adj **1** : sporty **2 artículos
deportivos** : sporting goods
depositar vt **1** : put, place **2** : deposit
(in a bank, etc.) — **depósito** nm **1**
: deposit **2** ALMACÉN : warehouse
depravado, -da adj : depraved
depreciarse vr : depreciate —
depreciación nf : depreciation
depredador nm : predator
deprimir vt : depress — **deprimirse** vr
: get depressed — **depresión** nf,
pl -**siones** : depression
derecha nf **1** : right side **2** : right
wing (in politics) — **derechista** adj :

right-wing — **derecho** nm **1** : right **2**
LEY : law — **derecho** adv : straight —
derecho, -cha adj **1** : right, right-hand
2 VERTICAL : upright **3** RECTO : straight
deriva nf **1** : drift **2 a la deriva** :
adrift — **derivación** nf, pl -**ciones**
: derivation — **derivar** vi **1** : drift
2 derivar de : derive from
derramamiento nm **derramamiento
de sangre** : bloodshed
derramar vt **1** : spill **2** : shed
(tears, blood) — **derramarse** vr :
overflow — **derrame** nm **1** : spilling
2 : discharge, hemorrhage
derrapar vi : skid — **derrape** nm : skid
derretir {54} vt : melt, thaw —
derretirse vr **1** : melt, thaw **2**
derretirse por fam : be crazy about
derribar vt **1** : demolish **2** : bring
down (a plane, a tree, etc.) **3** :
overthrow (a government, etc.)
derrocar {72} vt : overthrow
derrochar vt : waste, squander —
derrochador, -dora n : spendthrift —
derroche nm : extravagance, waste
derrotar vt : defeat — **derrota** nf : defeat
derruir {41} vt : demolish, tear down
derrumbar vt : demolish, knock
down — **derrumbarse** vr : collapse,
break down — **derrumbamiento** nm :
collapse — **derrumbe** nm : collapse
desabotonar vt : unbutton, undo
desabrido, -da adj : bland
desabrochar vt : unbutton, undo —
desabrocharse vr : come undone
desacato nm **1** : disrespect **2** : contempt
(of court) — **desacatar** vt : defy, disobey
desacertado, -da adj : mistaken,
wrong — **desacertar** {55} vi : be mistaken
— **desacierto** nm : mistake, error
desaconsejar vt : advise against —
desaconsejable adj : inadvisable
desacreditar vt : discredit
desactivar vt : deactivate
desacuerdo nm : disagreement
desafiar {85} vt : defy, challenge
— **desafiante** adj : defiant
desafilado, -da adj : blunt
desafinado, -da adj : out-
of-tune, off-key
desafío nm : challenge, defiance
desafortunado, -da adj : unfortunate
— **desafortunadamente** adv
: unfortunately
desagradar vt : displease

— **desagradable** adj :
disagreeable, unpleasant
desagradecido, -da adj : ungrateful
desagrado nm **1** : displeasure
2 con desagrado : reluctantly
desagravio nm : amends, reparation
desagregarse {52} vr : disintegrate
desaguar {10} vi : drain, empty
— **desagüe** nm **1** : drainage
2 : drain (of a sink, etc.)
desahogar {52} vt **1** : relieve **2** : give
vent to (anger, etc.) — **desahogarse** vr
: let off steam, unburden oneself —
desahogado, -da adj **1** : roomy
2 ADINERADO : comfortable, well-
off — **desahogo** nm **1** : relief **2**
con desahogo : comfortably
desahuciar vt **1** : deprive of
hope **2** DESALOJAR : evict —
desahucio nm : eviction
desaire nm : snub, rebuff —
desairar vt : snub, slight
desalentar {55} vt : discourage —
desaliento nm : discouragement
desaliñado, -da adj : slovenly
desalmado, -da adj : heartless, cruel
desalojar vt **1** : evacuate
2 DESAHUCIAR : evict
desamparar vt : abandon —
desamparo nm : abandonment, desertion
desamueblado, -da adj : unfurnished
desangrarse vr : lose
blood, bleed to death
desanimar vt : discourage —
desanimarse vr : get discouraged
— **desanimado, -da** adj :
downhearted, despondent —
desánimo nm : discouragement
desanudar vt : untie
desaparecer {53} vi : disappear
— **desaparecido, -da** n : missing
person — **desaparición** nf,
pl -**ciones** : disappearance
desapasionado, -da adj
: dispassionate
desapego nm : indifference
desapercibido, -da adj : unnoticed
desaprobar {19} vt : disapprove of —
desaprobación nf, pl -**ciones** : disapproval
desaprovechar vt : waste
desarmar vt **1** : disarm **2**
DESMONTAR : dismantle, take apart
— **desarme** nm : disarmament
desarraigar {52} vt : uproot, root out
desarreglar vt **1** : mess up **2** : disrupt

(plans, etc.) — **desarreglado, -da** *adj*
: disorganized — **desarreglo** *nm*
: untidiness, disorder
desarrollar *vt* : develop —
desarrollarse *vr* : take place —
desarrollo *nm* : development
desarticular *vt* **1** : break up,
dismantle **2** : dislocate (a bone)
desaseado, -da *adj* **1** : dirty
2 DESORDENADO : messy
desastre *nm* : disaster —
desastroso, -sa *adj* : disastrous
desatar *vt* **1** : undo, untie
2 : unleash (passions) —
desatarse *vr* **1** : come undone **2**
DESENCADENARSE : break out, erupt
desatascar {72} *vt* : unclog
desatender {56} *vt* **1** : disregard
2 : neglect (an obligation, etc.) —
desatento, -ta *adj* : inattentive
desatinado, -da *adj* : foolish, silly
desautorizado, -da *adj* : unauthorized
desavenencia *nf* : disagreement
desayunar *vi* : have breakfast
— *vt* : have for breakfast —
desayuno *nm* : breakfast
desbancar {72} *vt* : oust
desbarajuste *nm* : disorder, confusion
desbaratar *vt* : ruin, destroy —
desbaratarse *vr* : fall apart
desbocarse {72} *vr* : run away, bolt
desbordar *vt* **1** : overflow **2** : exceed
(limits) — **desbordarse** *vr* : overflow
— **desbordamiento** *nm* : overflow
descabellado, -da *adj* : crazy
descafeinado, -da *adj* : decaffeinated
descalabrar *vt* : hit on the head —
descalabro *nm* : misfortune, setback
descalificar {72} *vt* : disqualify
— **descalificación** *nf*,
pl **-ciones** : disqualification
descalzarse {21} *vr* : take off one's
shoes — **descalzo, -za** *adj* : barefoot
descaminar *vt* : mislead, lead astray
descansar *v* : rest — **descanso** *nm* **1**
: rest **2** : landing (of a staircase) **3** :
intermission (in theater), halftime (in sports)
descapotable *adj & nm* : convertible
descarado, -da *adj* :
insolent, shameless
descargar {52} *vt* **1** : unload **2**
: discharge (a firearm, etc.) —
descarga *nf* **1** : unloading **2** : discharge
(of a firearm, of electricity, etc.) —
descargo *nm* **1** : unloading **2** : discharge

(of a duty, etc.) **3** : defense (in law)
descarnado, -da *adj* : scrawny, gaunt
descaro *nm* : insolence, nerve
descarrilar *vi* : derail —
descarrilarse *vr* : be derailed
descartar *vt* : reject —
descartarse *vr* : discard
descascarar *vt* : peel, shell, husk
descender {56} *vt* **1** : go down
2 BAJAR : lower — *vi* **1** : descend
2 descender de : be descended
from — **descendiencia** *nf* **1** :
descendants *pl* **2** LINAJE : lineage, descent
— **descendiente** *nmf* : descendant
— **descenso** *nm* **1** : descent **2** : drop,
fall (in level, in temperature, etc.)
descifrar *vt* : decipher, decode
descolgar {16} *vt* **1** : take down **2**
: pick up, answer (the telephone)
descolorarse *vr* : fade — **descolorido,
-da** *adj* : faded, discolored
descomponer {60} *vt* : break
down — **descomponerse** *vr* **1** : rot,
decompose **2** *Lat* : break down —
descompuesto, -ta *adj Lat* : out of order
descomunal *adj* : enormous
desconcertar {55} *vt* : disconcert,
confuse — **desconcertante** *adj*
: confusing — **desconcierto** *nm*
: confusion, bewilderment
desconectar *vt* : disconnect
desconfiar {85} *vi* **desconfiar de**
: distrust — **desconfiado, -da** *adj* :
distrustful — **desconfianza** *nf* : distrust
descongelar *vt* **1** : thaw,
defrost **2** : unfreeze (assets)
descongestionante *nm* : decongestant
desconocer {18} *vt* : not know, fail to
recognize — **desconocido, -da** *adj* :
unknown — **desconocer** *n* : stranger
desconsiderado, -da *adj*
: inconsiderate
desconsolar *vt* : distress —
desconsolado, -da *adj* : heartbroken
— **desconsuelo** *nm* : grief, sorrow
descontar {19} *vt* : discount
descontento, -ta *adj* : dissatisfied
— **descontento** *nm* : discontent
descontinuar *vt* : discontinue
descorazonado, -da *adj* : discouraged
descorrer *vt* : draw back
descortés *adj, pl* **-teses** : rude —
descortesía *nf* : discourtesy, rudeness
descoyuntar *vt* : dislocate
descrédito *nm* : discredit

descremado, -da *adj* : nonfat, skim
describir {33} *vt* : describe —
descripción *nf, pl* **-ciones** : description
— **descriptivo, -va** *adj* : descriptive
descubierto, -ta *adj* **1** : exposed,
uncovered **2 al descubierto** : in the open
— **descubierto** *nm* : deficit, overdraft
descubrir {2} *vt* **1** : discover **2** REVELAR :
reveal — **descubrimiento** *nm* : discovery
descuento *nm* : discount
descuidar *vt* : neglect —
descuidarse *vr* **1** : be careless **2**
ABANDONARSE : let oneself go —
descuidado, -da *adj* **1** : careless,
sloppy **2** DESATENDIDO : neglected —
descuido *nm* : neglect, carelessness
desde *prep* **1** : from (a place), since
(a time) **2 desde luego** : of course
desdén *nm* : scorn, disdain
— **desdeñar** *vt* : scorn —
desdeñoso, -sa *adj* : disdainful
desdicha *nf* **1** : misery **2** DESGRACIA
: misfortune — **desdichado,
-da** *adj* : unfortunate, unhappy
desear *vt* : wish, want —
deseable *adj* : desirable
desecar *vt* : dry up
desechar *vt* **1** : throw away **2**
RECHAZAR : reject — **desechable** *adj* :
disposable — **desechos** *nmpl* : rubbish
desembarazarse {21} *vr*
desembarazarse de : get rid of
desembarcar {72} *vi* : disembark — *vt*
: unload — **desembarcadero** *nm* : jetty,
landing pier — **desembarco** *nm* : landing
desembocar {72} *vi* **desembocar
en 1** : flow into **2** : lead to (a result)
— **desembocadura** *nf* **1** : mouth (of
a river) **2** : opening, end (of a street)
desembolsar *vt* : pay out —
desembolso *nm* : payment, outlay
desembragar *vi* : disengage the clutch
desempacar {72} *v Lat* : unpack
desempate *nm* : tiebreaker
desempeñar *vt* **1** : play (a role)
2 : redeem (from a pawnshop) —
desempeñarse *vr* : get out of debt
desempleo *nm* : unemployment —
desempleado, -da *adj* : unemployed
desempolvar *vt* : dust
desencadenar *vt* **1** : unchain **2** :
trigger, unleash (protests, crises, etc.)
— **desencadenarse** *vr* : break loose
desencajar *vt* **1** : dislocate **2**
DESCONECTAR : disconnect

desencanto *nm* : disillusionment

desenchufar *vt* : disconnect, unplug

desenfadado, -da *adj* : carefree, confident — **desenfado** *nm* : confidence, ease

desenfrenado, -da *adj* : unrestrained — **desenfreno** *nm* : abandon, lack of restraint

desenganchar *vt* : unhook

desengañar *vt* : disillusion — **desengaño** *nm* : disappointment

desenlace *nm* : ending, outcome

desenmarañar *vt* : disentangle

desenmascarar *vt* : unmask

desenredar *vt* : untangle — **desenredarse** *vr* **desenredarse de** : extricate oneself from

desenrollar *vt* : unroll, unwind

desentenderse {56} *vr* **desentenderse de** : want nothing to do with

desenterrar {55} *vt* : dig up, disinter

desentonar *vi* **1** : be out of tune **2** : clash (of colors, etc.)

desenvoltura *nf* : confidence, ease

desenvolver {89} *vt* : unfold, unwrap — **desenvolverse** *vr* : unfold, develop

desenvuelto, -ta *adj* : confident, self-assured

deseo *nm* : desire — **deseoso, -sa** *adj* : eager, anxious

desequilibrar *vt* : throw off balance — **desequilibrado, -da** *adj* : unbalanced — **desequilibrio** *nm* : imbalance

desertar *vt* : desert — **deserción** *nf, pl* **-ciones** : desertion — **desertor, -tora** *n* : deserter

desesperar *vt* : exasperate — *vi* : despair — **desesperarse** *vr* : become exasperated — **desesperación** *nf, pl* **-ciones** : desperation, despair — **desesperado, -da** *adj* : desperate, hopeless

desestimar *vt* : reject

desfalcar {72} *vt* : embezzle — **desfalco** *nm* : embezzlement

desfallecer {53} *vi* **1** : weaken **2** DESMAYARSE : faint

desfavorable *adj* : unfavorable

desfigurar *vt* **1** : disfigure, mar **2** : distort (the truth)

desfiladero *nm* : mountain pass, gorge

desfilar *vi* : march, parade — **desfile** *nm* : parade, procession

desfogar {52} *vt* : vent — **desfogarse** *vr* : let off steam

desgajar *vt* : tear off, break apart — **desgajarse** *vr* : come off

desgana *nf* **1** : lack of appetite **2** : lack of enthusiasm, reluctance

desgarbado, -da *adj* : gawky, ungainly

desgarrar *vt* : tear, rip — **desgarrador, -dora** *adj* : heartbreaking — **desgarro** *nm* : tear

desgastar *vt* : wear away, wear down — **desgaste** *nm* : deterioration, wear and tear

desgracia *nf* **1** : misfortune **2 caer en desgracia** : fall into disgrace **3 por desgracia** : unfortunately — **desgraciadamente** *adv* : unfortunately — **desgraciado, -da** *adj* : unfortunate

deshabitado, -da *adj* : uninhabited

deshacer {40} *vt* **1** : undo **2** DESTRUIR : destroy, ruin **3** DISOLVER : dissolve **4** : break (an agreement), cancel (plans, etc.) — **deshacerse** *vr* **1** : come undone **2 deshacerse de** : get rid of **3 deshacerse en** : lavish, heap (praise, etc.) — **deshecho, -cha** *adj* **1** : undone **2** DESTROZADO : destroyed, ruined

desheredar *vt* : disinherit

deshidratar *vt* : dehydrate

deshielo *nm* : thaw

deshilachar *vt* : unravel — **deshilacharse** *vr* : fray

deshonesto, -ta *adj* : dishonest

deshonrar *vt* : dishonor, disgrace — **deshonra** *nf* : dishonor — **deshonroso, -sa** *adj* : dishonorable

deshuesar *vt* **1** : pit (a fruit) **2** : bone, debone (meat)

desidia *nf* **1** : indolence **2** DESASEO : sloppiness

▸ **desierto, -ta** *adj* : deserted, uninhabited — **desierto** *nm* : desert

designar *vt* : designate — **designación** *nf, pl* **-ciones** : appointment (to an office, etc.)

designio *nm* : plan

desigual *adj* **1** : unequal **2** DISPAREJO : uneven — **desigualdad** *nf* : inequality

desilusionar *vt* : disappoint, disillusion — **desilusión** *nf, pl* **-siones** : disappointment, disillusionment

desinfectar *vt* : disinfect — **desinfectante** *adj & nm* : disinfectant

desinflar *vt* : deflate — **desinflarse** *vr* : deflate, go flat

desinhibido, -da *adj* : uninhibited

desintegrar *vt* : disintegrate — **desintegrarse** *vr* : disintegrate

— **desintegración** *nf, pl* **-ciones** : disintegration

desinteresado, -da *adj* : unselfish, generous — **desinterés** *nm* : unselfishness

desistir *vi* **desistir de** : give up

desleal *adj* : disloyal — **deslealtad** *nf* : disloyalty

desleír {66} *vt* : dilute, dissolve

desligar {52} *vt* **1** : untie **2** SEPARAR : separate — **desligarse** *vr* : extricate oneself

desliz *nm, pl* **-lices** : slip, mistake — **deslizar** {21} *vt* : slide, slip — **deslizarse** *vr* : slide, glide

deslucido, -da *adj* : dingy, tarnished

deslumbrar *vt* : dazzle — **deslumbrante** *adj* : dazzling, blinding

deslustrar *vt* : tarnish, dull

desmán *nm, pl* **-manes** : outrage, excess

desmandarse *vr* : get out of hand

desmantelar *vt* : dismantle

desmañado, -da *adj* : clumsy

desmayar *vi* : lose heart — **desmayarse** *vr* : faint — **desmayo** *nm* : faint

desmedido, -da *adj* : excessive

desmejorar *vt* : impair — *vi* : deteriorate

desmemoriado, -da *adj* : forgetful

desmentir {76} *vt* : deny — **desmentido** *nm* : denial

desmenuzar {21} *vt* **1** : crumble **2** EXAMINAR : scrutinize — **desmenuzarse** *vr* : crumble

desmerecer {53} *vt* : be unworthy of — *vi* : decline in value

desmesurado, -da *adj* : excessive

desmigajar *vt* : crumble

desmontar *vt* **1** : dismantle, take apart **2** ALLANAR : level — *vi* : dismount

desmoralizar {21} *vt* : demoralize

desmoronarse *vr* : crumble

desnivel *nm* : unevenness

desnudar *vt* : undress, strip — **desnudarse** *vr* : get undressed — **desnudez** *nf, pl* **-deces** : nudity, nakedness — **desnudo, -da** *adj* : nude, naked — **desnudo** *nm* : nude

desnutrición *nf, pl* **-ciones** : malnutrition

desobedecer {53} *v* : disobey — **desobediencia** *nf* : disobedience — **desobediente** *adj* : disobedient

desocupar *vt* : empty, vacate — **desocupado, -da** *adj* **1** : vacant **2** DESEMPLEADO : unemployed

desodorante *adj & nm* : deodorant
desolado, -da *adj* **1** : desolate **2**
DESCONSOLADO : devastated, distressed
— **desolación** *nf, pl* **-ciones** : desolation
desorden *nm, pl* **desórdenes** : disorder,
mess — **desordenado, -da** *adj* :
untidy — **desordenadamente** *adv*
: in a disorderly way
desorganizar {21} *vt* : disorganize
— **desorganización** *nf,*
pl **-ciones** : disorganization
desorientar *vt* : disorient, confuse
— **desorientarse** *vr* : lose one's way
desovar *vi* : spawn
despachar *vt* **1** : deal with (a task, etc.)
2 ENVIAR : dispatch, send **3** : wait on,
serve (customers) — **despacho** *nm* **1**
: dispatch, shipment **2** OFICINA : office
despacio *adv* : slowly
desparramar *vt* : spill, scatter, spread
despavorido, -da *adj* : terrified
despecho *nm* **1** : spite **2** a
despecho de : despite, in spite of
despectivo, -va *adj* **1** : pejorative
2 DESPRECIATIVO : contemptuous
despedazar {21} *vt* : tear apart

despedir {54} *vt* **1** : see off **2** DESTITUIR
: dismiss, fire **3** DESPRENDER : emit
— **despedirse** *vr* : say good-bye —
despedida *nf* : farewell, good-bye
despegar {52} *vt* : detach, unstick
— *vi* : take off — **despegado, -da** *adj* :
cold, distant — **despegue** *nm* : takeoff
despeinar *vt* : ruffle (hair) —
despeinado, -da *adj* : disheveled, unkempt
despejar *vt* : clear, free — *vi* :
clear up — **despejado, -da** *adj* **1** :
clear, fair **2** LÚCIDO : clear-headed
despellejar *vt* : skin (an animal)
despensa *nf* : pantry, larder
despeñadero *nm* : precipice
desperdiciar *vt* : waste —
desperdicio *nm* **1** : waste **2**
desperdicios *nmpl* : scraps
desperfecto *nm* : flaw, defect
despertar {55} *vi* : awaken,
wake up — *vt* : wake, rouse —
despertador *nm* : alarm clock
despiadado, -da *adj* :
pitiless, merciless
despido *nm* : dismissal, layoff
despierto, -ta *adj* : awake

despilfarrar *vt* : squander
— **despilfarrador, -dora** *n* :
spendthrift — **despilfarro** *nm* :
extravagance, wastefulness
despistar *vt* : throw off the track,
confuse — **despistarse** *vr* : lose
one's way — **despistado, -da** *adj* **1**
: absentminded **2** DESORIENTADO
: confused — **despiste** *nm* **1** :
absentmindedness **2** ERROR : mistake
desplazar {21} *vt* : displace
— **desplazarse** *vr* : travel
desplegar {49} *vt* : unfold, spread
out — **despliegue** *nm* : display
desplomarse *vr* : collapse
desplumar *vt* **1** : pluck **2** *fam* : fleece
despoblado, -da *adj* :
uninhabited, deserted —
despoblado *nm* : deserted area
despojar *vt* : strip, deprive —
despojos *nmpl* **1** : plunder **2**
RESTOS : remains, scraps
desportillar *vt* : chip — **desportillarse** *vr*
: chip — **desportilladura** *nf* : chip, nick
despota *nmf* : despot
despotricar *vi* : rant (and rave)

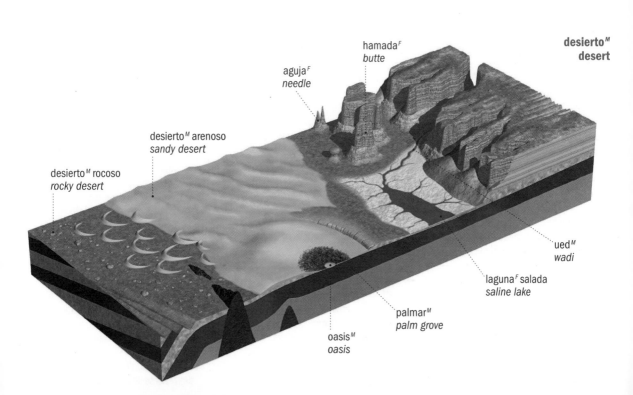

desierto^M
desert

hamada^F
butte

aguja^F
needle

desierto^M arenoso
sandy desert

desierto^M rocoso
rocky desert

ued^M
wadi

laguna^F salada
saline lake

palmar^M
palm grove

oasis^M
oasis

diamante^M
diamond

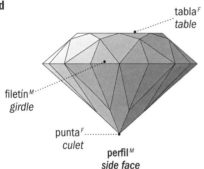

tabla^F
table

filetín^M
girdle

punta^F
culet

perfil^M
side face

cara^F superior
top face

despreciable *vt* : despise, scorn —
despreciable *adj* **1** : despicable **2 una
cantidad despreciable** : a negligible
amount — **desprecio** *nm* : disdain, scorn
desprender *vt* **1** : detach, remove **2**
EMITIR : give off — **desprenderse** *vr* **1**
: come off **2** DEDUCIRSE : be inferred,
follow — **desprendimiento** *nm*
desprendimiento de tierras : landslide
despreocupado, -da *adj* :
carefree, unconcerned
desprestigiar *vt* : discredit —
desprestigiarse *vr* : lose face
desprevenido, -da *adj* : unprepared
desproporcionado, -da
: out of proportion
despropósito *nm* : (piece
of) nonsense, absurdity
desprovisto, -ta *adj* **desprovisto,
-ta de** : lacking in
después *adv* **1** : afterward **2**
ENTONCES : then, next **3 después de**
: after **4 después (de) que** : after
5 después de todo : after all
despuntado, -da *adj* : blunt, dull
desquiciar *vt* : drive crazy
desquitarse *vr* **1** : retaliate **2
desquitarse con** : take it out on, get
back at — **desquite** *nm* : revenge
destacar {72} *vt* : emphasize — *vi* : stand
out — **destacado, -da** *adj* : outstanding
destapar *vt* : open, uncover —
destapador *nm Lat* : bottle opener
destartalado, -da *adj* : dilapidated
destellar *vi* : flash, sparkle —
destello *nm* : sparkle, twinkle, flash
destemplado, -da *adj* **1** : out

of tune **2** MAL : out of sorts **3** :
unpleasant (of weather)
desteñir {67} *vt* : fade, bleach — *vi*
: run, fade — **desteñirse** *vr* : fade
desterrar {55} *vt* : banish, exile
— **desterrado, -da** *n* : exile
destetar *vt* : wean
destiempo *adv* **a destiempo**
: at the wrong time
destierro *nm* : exile
destilar *vt* : distill —
destilería *nf* : distillery
destinar *vt* **1** : assign, allocate **2**
NOMBRAR : appoint — **destinado,
-da** *adj* : destined — **destinatario,
-ria** *n* : addressee — **destino** *nm* **1**
: destiny **2** RUMBO : destination
destituir {41} *vt* : dismiss —
destitución *nf, pl* **-ciones** : dismissal
destornillar *vt* : unscrew —
destornillador *nm* : screwdriver
destreza *nf* : skill, dexterity
destrozar {21} *vt* : destroy, wreck —
destrozos *nmpl* : damage, destruction
destrucción *nf, pl* **-ciones** : destruction
— **destructivo, -va** *adj* : destructive
— **destruir** {41} *vt* : destroy
desunir *vt* : split, divide
desusado, -da *adj* **1** : obsolete
2 INSÓLITO : unusual — **desuso** *nm*
caer en desuso : fall into disuse
desvaído, -da *adj* **1** : pale, washed-
out **2** BORROSO : vague, blurred
desvalido, -da *adj* : destitute, needy
desvalijar *vt* : rob
desván *nm, pl* **-vanes** : attic
desvanecer {53} *vt* : make

disappear — **desvanecerse** *vr* **1**
: vanish **2** DESMAYARSE : faint
desvariar {85} *vi* : be delirious
— **desvarío** *nm* : delirium
desvelar *vt* : keep awake —
desvelarse *vr* : stay awake —
desvelo *nm* **1** : sleeplessness
2 desvelars *nmpl* : efforts
desvencijado, -da *adj* :
dilapidated, rickety
desventaja *nf* : disadvantage
desventura *nf* : misfortune
desvergonzado, -da *adj* : shameless
— **desvergüenza** *nf* : shamelessness
desvestir {54} *vt* : undress —
desvestirse *vr* : get undressed
desviación *nf, pl* **-ciones 1** : deviation
2 : detour (in a road) — **desviar** {85} *vt*
: divert, deflect — **desviarse** *vr* **1**
: branch off **2** APARTARSE : stray —
desvío *nm* : diversion, detour
detallar *vt* : detail — **detallado, -da** *adj*
: detailed, thorough — **detalle** *nm* **1** :
detail **2 al detalle** : retail — **detalle** *adj*
: retail — **detalle** *nmf* : retailer
detectar *vt* : detect —
detective *nmf* : detective
detener {80} *vt* **1** : arrest, detain **2** PARAR :
stop **3** RETRASAR : delay — **detenerse** *vr* **1**
: stop **2** DEMORARSE : linger —
detención *nf, pl* **-ciones** : arrest, detention
detergente *nm* : detergent
deteriorar *vt* : damage —
deteriorarse *vr* : wear out, deteriorate —
deteriorado, -da *adj* : damaged, worn —
deterioro *nm* : deterioration, damage
determinar *vt* **1** : determine **2**
MOTIVAR : bring about **3** DECIDIR :
decide — **determinarse** *vr* : decide
— **determinación** *nf, pl* **-ciones**
1 : determination **2 tomar una
determinación** : make a decision
— **determinado, -da** *adj* **1** :
determined **2** ESPECÍFICO : specific
detestar *vt* : detest
detonar *vi* : explode, detonate —
detonación *nf, pl* **-ciones** : detonation
detrás *adv* **1** : behind **2 detrás de** : in
back of **3 por detrás** : from behind
detrimento *nm* **en detrimento
de** : to the detriment of
deuda *nf* : debt — **deudor,
-dora** *n* : debtor
devaluar {3} *vt* : devalue —
devaluarse *vr* : depreciate

devastar *vt* : devastate —
devastador, -dora *adj* : devastating
devenir {87} *vi* **1** : come about **2**
devenir en : become, turn into
devoción *nf, pl* **-ciones** : devotion
devolución *nf, pl* **-ciones** : return
devolver {89} *vt* **1** RESTITUIR : give back
2 : refund, pay back — *vi* : vomit —
devolverse *vr Lat* : return, come back
devorar *vt* : devour
devoto, -ta *adj* : devout —
devoto, -ta *n* : devotee
día *nm* **1** : day **2** : daytime **3 al día** : up-to-
date **4 en pleno día** : in broad daylight
diabetes *nf* : diabetes —
diabético, -ca *adj & n* : diabetic
diablo *nm* : devil — **diablillo** *nm* :
imp, rascal — **diablura** *nf* : prank —
diabólico, -ca *adj* : diabolic, diabolical
diafragma *nm* : diaphragm
diagnosticar {72} *vt* : diagnose
— **diagnóstico, -ca** *adj* : diagnostic
— **diagnóstico** *nm* : diagnosis
diagonal *adj & nf* : diagonal
diagrama *nm* : diagram
dial *nm* : dial (of a radio, etc.)
dialecto *nm* : dialect
dialogar {52} *vi* : have a talk
— **diálogo** *nm* : dialogue
▸ **diamante** *nm* : diamond
diámetro *nm* : diameter
diana *nf* **1** : reveille **2** BLANCO
: target, bull's-eye
diario, -ria *adj* : daily — **diario** *nm* **1**
: diary **2** PERIÓDICO : newspaper
— **diariamente** *adv* : daily
diarrea *nf* : diarrhea
dibujar *vt* **1** : draw **2** DESCRIBIR : portray
— **dibujante** *nmf* : draftsman *m*,
draftswoman *f* — **dibujo** *nm* **1** : drawing
2 dibujos animados : (animated) cartoons
diccionario *nm* : dictionary
dicha *nf* **1** ALEGRÍA : happiness **2**
SUERTE : good luck — **dicho** *nm* :
saying, proverb — **dichoso, -sa** *adj* **1**
: happy **2** AFORTUNADO : lucky
diciembre *nm* : December
dictar *vt* **1** : dictate **2** : pronounce
(a sentence), deliver (a speech)
— **dictado** *nm* : dictation —
dictador, -dora *n* : dictator —
dictadura *nf* : dictatorship
diecinueve *adj & nm* : nineteen —
diecinueveavo, -va *adj* : nineteenth
dieciocho *adj & nm* : eighteen

— **dieciochoavo, -va** *or*
dieciochavo, -va *adj* : eighteenth
dieciséis *adj & nm* : sixteen —
dieciseisavo, -va *adj* : sixteenth
diecisiete *adj & nm* : seventeen —
diecisieteavo, -va *adj* : seventeenth
▸ **diente** *nm* **1** : tooth **2** : prong, tine (of
a fork, etc.) **3 diente de ajo** : clove of
garlic **4 diente de león** : dandelion
diesel *adj & nm* : diesel
diestra *nf* : right hand — **diestro,**
-tra *adj* **1** : right **2** HÁBIL : skillful
dieta *nf* : diet — **dietético,**
-ca *adj* : dietetic, dietary
diez *adj & nm, pl* **dieces** : ten
difamar *vt* : slander, libel —
difamación *nf, pl* **-ciones** : slander, libel
diferencia *nf* : difference —
diferenciar *vt* : distinguish between
— **diferenciarse** *vr* : differ —
diferente *adj* : different
diferir {76} *vt* : postpone — *vi* : differ
difícil *adj* : difficult — **dificultad** *nf* :
difficulty — **dificultar** *vt* : hinder, obstruct
difteria *nf* : diphtheria

difundir *vt* **1** : spread (out) **2** :
broadcast (television, etc.)
difunto, -ta *adj & n* : deceased
difusión *nf, pl* **-siones** : spreading
digerir {76} *vt* : digest — **digerible** *adj*
: digestible — **digestión** *nf, pl* **-tiones** :
digestion — **digestivo, -va** *adj* : digestive
dígito *nm* : digit — **digital** *adj* : digital
dignarse *vr* **dignarse a** : deign to
dignatario, -ria *n* : dignitary
— **dignidad** *nf* : dignity —
digno, -na *adj* : worthy
digresión *nf, pl* **-ciones** : digression
dilapidar *vt* : waste, squander
dilatar *vt* **1** : expand, dilate **2** PROLONGAR
: prolong **3** POSPONER : postpone
dilema *nm* : dilemma
diligencia *nf* **1** : diligence **2** TRÁMITE :
procedure, task — **diligente** *adj* : diligent
diluir {41} *vt* : dilute
diluvio *nm* **1** : flood **2** LLUVIA : downpour
dimensión *nf, pl* **-siones** : dimension
diminuto, -ta *adj* : minute, tiny
dimitir *vi* : resign — **dimisión** *nf,*
pl **-siones** : resignation

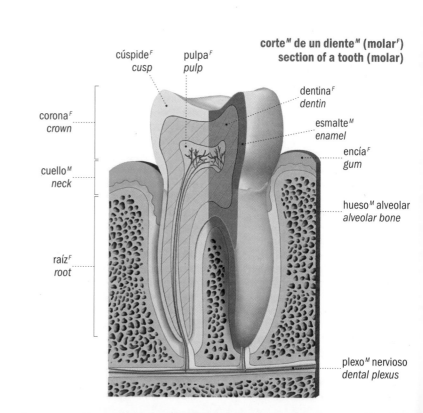

corte^M **de un diente**^M **(molar**^F**)**
section of a tooth (molar)

cúspide^F / cusp
pulpa^F / pulp
dentina^F / dentin
corona^F / crown
esmalte^M / enamel
encía^F / gum
cuello^M / neck
hueso^M alveolar / alveolar bone
raíz^F / root
plexo^M nervioso / dental plexus

disfraces^M
disguises

mago^M
magician

pirata^M
pirate

vaquero^M
cowboy

dinámico, -ca *adj* : dynamic
dinamita *nf* : dynamite
dínamo *or* dinamo *nmf* : dynamo
dinastía *nf* : dynasty
dineral *nm* : large sum, fortune
dinero *nm* : money
dinosaurio *nm* : dinosaur
diócesis *nfs & pl* : diocese
dios, diosa *n* : god, goddess *f*
— **Dios** *nm* : God
diploma *nm* : diploma — **diplomado, -da** *adj* : qualified, trained
diplomacia *nf* : diplomacy — **diplomático, -ca** *adj* : diplomatic — **diplomático, -ca** *n* : diplomat
diputación *nf, pl* **-ciones** : delegation — **diputado, -da** *n* : delegate
dique *nm* : dike
dirección *nf, pl* **-ciones 1** : address **2** SENTIDO : direction **3** GESTIÓN : management **4** : steering (of an automobile) — **direccional** *nf Lat* : turn signal, blinker — **directa** *nf* : high gear — **directiva** *nf* : board of directors — **directivo, -va** *adj* : managerial — **directivo, -va** *n* : manager, director — **directo, -ta** *adj* **1** : direct **2** DERECHO : straight — **director, -tora** *n* **1** : director, manager **2** : conductor (of an orchestra) — **directorio** *nm* : directory — **directriz** *nf, pl* **-trices** : guideline

dirigencia *nf* : leaders *pl*, leadership — **dirigente** *nmf* : director, leader
dirigible *nm* : dirigible, blimp
dirigir {35} *vt* **1** : direct, lead **2** : address (a letter, etc.) **3** ENCAMINAR : aim **4** : conduct (music) — **dirigirse** *vr* **1** **dirigirse a** : go towards **2 dirigirse a algn** : speak to someone, write to someone
discernir {25} *vt* : discern, distinguish — **discernimiento** *nm* : discernment
disciplinar *vt* : discipline — **disciplina** *nf* : discipline
discípulo, -la *n* : disciple, follower
disco *nm* **1** : disc, disk **2** : discus (in sports) **3 disco compacto** : compact disc
discordante *adj* : discordant — **discordia** *nf* : discord
discoteca *nf* : disco, discotheque
discreción *nf, pl* **-ciones** : discretion
discrepancia *nf* **1** : discrepancy **2** DESACUERDO : disagreement — **discrepar** *vi* : differ, disagree
discreto, -ta *adj* : discreet
discriminar *vt* **1** : discriminate against **2** DISTINGUIR : distinguish — **discriminación** *nf, pl* **-ciones** : discrimination
disculpar *vt* : excuse, pardon — **disculparse** *vr* : apologize — **disculpa** *nf* **1** : apology **2** EXCUSA : excuse
discurrir *vi* **1** : pass, go by **2**

REFLEXIONAR : ponder, reflect
discurso *nm* : speech, discourse
discutir *vt* **1** : discuss **2** CUESTIONAR : dispute — *vi* : argue — **discusión** *nf, pl* **-siones 1** : discussion **2** DISPUTA : argument — **discutible** *adj* : debatable
disecar {72} *vt* : dissect — **disección** *nf, pl* **-ciones** : dissection
diseminar *vt* : disseminate, spread
disentería *nf* : dysentery
disentir {76} *vi* **disentir de** : disagree with — **disentimiento** *nm* : disagreement, dissent
diseñar *vt* : design — **diseñador, -dora** *n* : designer — **diseño** *nm* : design
disertación *nf, pl* **-ciones 1** : lecture **2** : (written) dissertation
disfrazar {21} *vt* : disguise — **disfrazarse** *vr* **disfrazar de** : disguise oneself as — **disfraz** *nm, pl* **-fraces 1** : disguise **2** : costume (for a party, etc.)
disfrutar *vt* : enjoy — *vi* : enjoy oneself
disgustar *vt* : upset, annoy — **disgustarse** *vr* **1** : get annoyed **2** ENEMISTARSE : fall out (with someone) — **disgusto** *nm* **1** : annoyance, displeasure **2** RIÑA : quarrel
disidente *adj & nmf* : dissident
disimular *vt* : conceal, hide — *vi* : pretend — **disimulo** *nm* : pretense
disipar *vt* **1** : dispel **2** DERROCHAR : squander
diskette *nm* : floppy disk, diskette
dislexia *nf* : dyslexia — **disléxico, -ca** *adj* : dyslexic
dislocar {72} *vt* : dislocate — **dislocarse** *vr* : become dislocated
disminuir {41} *vt* : reduce — *vi* : decrease, drop — **disminución** *nf, pl* **-ciones** : decrease
disociar *vt* : dissociate
disolver {89} *vt* : dissolve — **disolverse** *vr* : dissolve
disparar *vi* : shoot, fire — *vt* : shoot — **dispararse** *vr* : shoot up, skyrocket
disparatado, -da *adj* : absurd — **disparate** *nm* : nonsense, silly thing
disparejo, -ja *adj* : uneven — **disparidad** *nf* : difference, disparity
disparo *nm* : shot
dispensar *vt* **1** : dispense, distribute **2** DISCULPAR : excuse
dispersar *vt* : disperse, scatter — **dispersarse** *vr* : disperse — **dispersión** *nf, pl* **-siones** : scattering

disponer {60} *vt* **1** : arrange, lay out **2** ORDENAR : decide, stipulate — *vi* **disponer de** : have at one's disposal — **disponerse** *vr* **disponerse a** : be ready to — **disponibilidad** *nf* : availability — **disponible** *adj* : available

disposición *nf, pl* **-ciones 1** : arrangement **2** APTITUD : aptitude **3** : order, provision (in law) **4 a disposición de** : at the disposal of

dispositivo *nm* : device, mechanism

dispuesto, -ta *adj* : prepared, ready

disputar *vi* **1** : argue **2** COMPETIR : compete — *vt* : dispute — **disputa** *nf* : dispute, argument

disquete → **diskette**

distanciar *vt* : space out — **distanciarse** *vr* : grow apart — **distancia** *nf* : distance — **distante** *adj* : distant

distinguir {26} *vt* : distinguish — **distinguirse** *vr* : distinguish oneself, stand out — **distinción** *nf, pl* **-ciones** : distinction — **distintivo, -va** *adj* : distinctive — **distinto, -ta** *adj* **1** : different **2** CLARO : distinct, clear

distorsión *nf, pl* **-siones** : distortion

distraer {81} *vt* **1** : distract **2** DIVERTIR : entertain — **distraerse** *vr* **1** : get distracted **2** ENTRETENERSE : amuse oneself — **distracción** *nf, pl* **-ciones 1** : amusement **2** DESPISTE : absentmindedness — **distraído, -da** *adj* : distracted, absentminded

distribuir {41} *vt* : distribute — **distribución** *nf, pl* **-ciones** : distribution — **distribuidor, -dora** *n* : distributor

distrito *nm* : district

disturbio *nm* : disturbance

disuadir *vt* : dissuade, discourage — **disuasivo, -va** *adj* : deterrent

diurno, -na *adj* : day, daytime

divagar {52} *vi* : digress

diván *nm, pl* **-vanes** : divan, couch

divergir {35} *vi* **1** : diverge **2 divergir en** : differ on

diversidad *nf* : diversity

diversificar {72} *vt* : diversify

diversión *nf, pl* **-siones** : fun, entertainment

diverso, -sa *adj* : diverse

divertir {76} *vt* : entertain — **divertirse** *vr* : enjoy oneself, have fun — **divertido, -da** *adj* : entertaining

dividendo *nm* : dividend

dividir *vt* **1** : divide **2** REPARTIR : distribute

divinidad *nf* : divinity — **divino, -na** *adj* : divine

divisa *nf* **1** : currency **2** EMBLEMA : emblem

divisar *vt* : discern, make out

división *nf, pl* **-siones** : division — **divisor** *nm* : denominator

divorciar *vt* : divorce — **divorciarse** *vr* : get a divorce — **divorciado, -da** *n* : divorcé *m*, divorcée *f* — **divorcio** *nm* : divorce

divulgar {52} *vt* **1** : divulge, reveal **2** PROPAGAR : spread, circulate

dizque *adv Lat* : supposedly, apparently

doblar *vt* **1** : double **2** PLEGAR : fold **3** : turn (a corner) **4** : dub (a film) — *vi* : turn — **doblarse** *vr* **1** : double over **2 doblarse a** : give in to — **dobladillo** *nm* : hem — **doble** *adj & nm* : double — **doble** *nmf* : stand-in, double — **doblemente** *adv* : doubly — **doblegar** {52} *vt* : force to yield — **doblegarse** *vr* : give in — **doblez** *nm, pl* **-bleces** : fold, crease

doce *adj & nm* : twelve — **doceavo, -va** *adj* : twelfth — **docena** *nf* : dozen

docente *adj* : teaching

dócil *adj* : docile

▸ **doctor, -tora** *n* : doctor — **doctorado** *nm* : doctorate

doctrina *nf* : doctrine

documentar *vt* : document — **documentación** *nf, pl* **-ciones** : documentation — **documental** *adj*

doctor^M: sala^F de examen^M
doctor: examination room

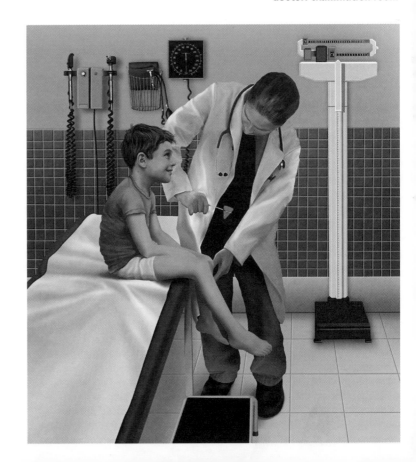

dromedario[M] **y camello**[M] **Bactriano**
dromedary camel and Bactrian camel

camello[M] Bactriano
Bactrian camel

dromedario[M]
dromedary camel

& nm : documentary —
documento *nm* : document
dogma *nm* : dogma —
dogmático, -ca *adj* : dogmatic
dólar *nm* : dollar
doler {47} *vi* **1** : hurt **2 me duelen los pies**
: my feet hurt — **dolerse** *vr* **dolerse de**
: complain about — **dolor** *nm* **1** : pain **2**
PENA : grief **3 dolor de cabeza** : headache
4 dolor de estómago : stomachache
— **dolorido, -da 1** : sore **2** AFLIGIDO :
hurt — **doloroso, -sa** *adj* : painful
domar *vt* : tame, break in
domesticar {72} *vt* : domesticate,
tame — **doméstico, -ca** *adj* : domestic
▸ **domicilio** *nm* : home, residence
dominar *vt* **1** : dominate, control **2** :
master (a subject, a language, etc.)
— **dominarse** *vr* : control oneself —
dominación *nf, pl* **-ciones** : domination
— **dominante** *adj* : dominant
domingo *nm* : Sunday — **dominical** *adj*
periódico domingo : Sunday newspaper
dominio *nm* **1** : authority **2** : mastery
(of a subject) **3** TERRITORIO : domain
dominó *nm, pl* **-nós** : dominoes *pl* (game)
don[1] *nm* : courtesy title preceding
a man's first name
don[2] *nm* **1** : gift **2** TALENTO : talent
— **donación** *nf, pl* **-ciones** : donation

— **donador, -dora** *n* : donor
donaire *nm* : grace, charm
donar *vt* : donate — **donante** *nmf* :
donor — **donativo** *nm* : donation
donde *conj* : where —
donde *prep Lat* : over by
dónde *adv* **1** : where **2 ¿de dónde**
eres? : where are you from? **3**
¿por dónde? : whereabouts?
dondequiera *adv* **1** : anywhere **2**
dondequiera que : wherever, everywhere
doña *nf* : courtesy title preceding
a woman's first name
doquier *adv* **por doquier** : everywhere
dorar *vt* **1** : gild **2** : brown (food)
— **dorado, -da** *adj* : gold, golden
dormir {27} *vt* : put to sleep — *vi* : sleep
— **dormirse** *vr* : fall asleep — **dormido,**
-da *adj* **1** : asleep **2** ENTUMECIDO : numb
— **dormilón, -lona** *n* : sleepyhead, late riser
— **dormitar** *vi* : doze — **dormitorio** *nm* **1**
: bedroom **2** : dormitory (in a college)
dorso *nm* : back
dos *adj & nm* : two — **doscientos,**
-tas *adj* : two hundred —
doscientos *nms & pl* : two hundred
dosel *nm* : canopy
dosis *nfs & pl* : dose, dosage
dotar *vt* **1** : provide, equip **2 dotar**
de : endow with — **dotación** *nf,*

pl **-ciones 1** : endowment, funding **2**
PERSONAL : personnel — **dote** *nf* **1**
: dowry **2** dotars *nfpl* : gift, talent
dragar {52} *vt* : dredge —
draga *nf* : dredge
dragón *nm, pl* **-gones** : dragon
drama *nm* : drama — **dramático,**
-ca *adj* : dramatic — **dramatizar**
{21} *vt* : dramatize — **dramaturgo,**
-ga *n* : dramatist, playwright
drástico, -ca *adj* : drastic
drenar *vt* : drain — **drenaje** *nm* : drainage
droga *nf* : drug — **drogadicto,**
-ta *n* : drug addict — **drogar** {52} *vt*
: drug — **drogarse** *vr* : take drugs
— **droguería** *nf* : drugstore
▸ **dromedario** *nm* : dromedary
dual *adj* : dual
ducha *nf* : shower —
ducharse *vr* : take a shower
ducho, -cha *adj* : experienced, skilled
duda *nf* : doubt — **dudar** *vt* :
doubt — *vi* **dudar en** : hesitate to
— **dudoso, -sa** *adj* **1** : doubtful
2 SOSPECHOSO : questionable
duelo *nm* **1** : duel **2** LUTO : mourning
duende *nm* : elf, imp
dueño, -na *n* **1** : owner **2**
: landlord, landlady *f*
dulce *adj* **1** : sweet **2** : fresh (of water)
3 SUAVE : mild, gentle — **dulce** *nm* :
candy, sweet — **dulzura** *nf* : sweetness
duna *nf* : dune
dúo *nm* : duo, duet
duodécimo, -ma *adj* : twelfth —
duodécimo, -ma *n* : twelfth (in a series)
dúplex *nms & pl* : duplex (apartment)
duplicar {72} *vt* **1** : double **2** : duplicate,
copy (a document, etc.) — **duplicado,**
-da *adj* : duplicate — **duplicado** *nm* : copy
duqe *nm* : duke — **duquesa** *nf* : duchess
durabilidad *nf* : durability
duración *nf, pl* **-ciones** : duration, length
duradero, -ra *adj* : durable, lasting
durante *prep* **1** : during **2 durante**
una hora : for an hour
durar *vi* : endure, last
durazno *nm Lat* : peach
duro *adv* : hard — **duro, -ra** *adj* **1** :
hard **2** SEVERO : harsh — **dureza** *nf* **1**
: hardness **2** SEVERIDAD : harshness

domicilios^M
residences

casa^F de dos plantas^F
two-story house

casas^F adosadas
town houses

casa^F de adobes^M
adobe house

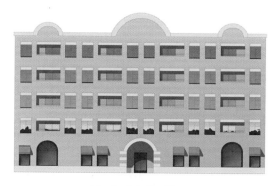

viviendas^F plurifamiliares
condominiums

casa^F de una planta^F
one-story house

bloque^M de apartamentos^M
high-rise apartment

casas^F pareadas
duplex

e[1] *nf* : e, fifth letter of the Spanish alphabet

e[2] *conj* (*used instead of* **y** *before words beginning with i or hi*) : and

ebanista *nmf* : cabinetmaker

ébano *nm* : ebony

ebrio, -bria *adj* : drunk

ebullición *nf, pl* **-ciones** : boiling

echar *vt* **1** : throw, cast **2** EXPULSAR : expel, dismiss **3** : give off, emit (smoke, sparks, etc.) **4** BROTAR : sprout **5** PONER : put (on) **6 echar a perder** : spoil, ruin **7 echar de menos** : miss — **echarse** *vr* **1** : throw oneself **2** ACOSTARSE : lie down **3 echarse a** : start (to)

eclesiástico, -ca *adj* : ecclesiastic — **eclesiástico, -ca** *nm* : clergyman

eclipse *nm* : eclipse — **eclipsar** *vi* : eclipse

eco *nm* : echo

ecología *nf* : ecology — **ecológico, -ca** *adj* : ecological — **ecologista** *nmf* : ecologist

economía *nf* **1** : economy **2** : economics (science) — **economico, -ca** *adj* **1** : economic, economical **2** BARATO : inexpensive — **economista** *nmf* : economist — **economizar** {21} *v* : save

ecosistema *nm* : ecosystem

ecuación *nf, pl* **-ciones** : equation

ecuador *nm* : equator

ecuánime *adj* **1** : even-tempered **2** : impartial (in law)

ecuatoriano, -na *adj* : Ecuadorian, Ecuadorean, Ecuadoran

ecuestre *adj* : equestrian

edad *nf* **1** : age **2 Edad Media** : Middle Ages *pl* **3 ¿qué edad tienes?** : how old are you?

edición *nf, pl* **-ciones 1** : publishing, publication **2** : edition (of a book, etc.)

edicto *nm* : edict

edificar {72} *vt* : build — **edificio** *nm* : building

editar *vt* **1** : publish **2** : edit (a film, a text, etc.) — **editor, -tora** *n* **1** : publisher **2** : editor — **editorial** *adj* : publishing — **editorial** *nm* : editorial — **editorial** *nf* : publishing house

edredón *nm, pl* **-dones** : (down) comforter, duvet

educar {72} *vt* **1** : educate **2** CRIAR : bring up, raise **3** : train (the body, the voice, etc.) — **educación** *nf, pl* **-ciones 1** : education **2** MODALES : (good) manners *pl* — **educado, -da** *adj* : polite — **educador, -dora** *n* : educator — **educativo, -va** *adj* : educational

efectivo, -va *adj* **1** : effective **2** REAL : real — **efectivo** *nm* : cash — **efectivamente** *adv* **1** : really **2** POR SUPUESTO : yes, indeed — **efecto** *nm* **1** : effect **2 en efecto** : in fact **3 efectos** *nmpl* : goods, property — **efectuar** {3} *vt* : bring about, carry out

efervescente *adj* : effervescent — **efervescencia** *nf* : effervescence

eficaz *adj, pl* **-caces 1** : effective **2** EFICIENTE : efficient — **eficacia** *nf* **1** :

effectiveness **2** EFICIENCIA : efficiency

eficiente *adj* : efficient — **eficiencia** *nf* : efficiency

efímero, -ra *adj* : ephemeral

efusivo, -va *adj* : effusive

egipcio, -cia *adj* : Egyptian

ego *nm* : ego — **egocéntrico, -ca** *adj* : egocentric — **egoísmo** *nm* : egoism — **egoísta** *adj* : egoistic — **egoísta** *nmf* : egoist

egresar *vi* : graduate — **egresado, -da** *n* : graduate — **egreso** *nm* : graduation, commencement

eje *nm* **1** : axis **2** : axle (of a wheel, etc.)

ejecutar *vt* **1** : execute, put to death **2** REALIZAR : carry out — **ejecución** *nf, pl* **-ciones** : execution

ejecutivo, -va *adj & n* : executive

ejemplar *adj* : exemplary — **ejemplar** *nm* **1** : copy, issue **2** EJEMPLO : example — **ejemplificar** {72} *vt* : exemplify — **ejemplo** *nm* **1** : example **2 por ejemplo** : for example

ejercer {86} *vt* **1** : practice (a profession) **2** : exercise (a right, etc.) — *vi* **ejercer de** : practice as, work as — **ejercicio** *nm* **1** : exercise **2** : practice (of a profession, etc.)

ejército *nm* : army

el, la *art, pl* **los, las** : the — **el** *pron* (*referring to masculine nouns*) **1** : the one **2 el, que** : he who, whoever, the one that

él *pron* : he, him

elaborar *vt* **1** : manufacture, produce **2** : draw up (a plan, etc.)

elástico, -ca *adj* : elastic — **elástico** *nm* : elastic — **elasticidad** *nf* : elasticity

elección *nf, pl* **-ciones 1** : election **2** SELECCIÓN : choice — **elector, -tora** *n* : voter — **electorado** *nm* : electorate — **electoral** *adj* : electoral

electricidad *nf* : electricity — **eléctrico, -ca** *adj* : electric, electrical — **electricista** *nmf* : electrician — **electrificar** {72} *vt* : electrify — **electrizar** {21} *vt* : electrify, thrill — **electrocutar** *vt* : electrocute

electrodo *nm* : electrode

electrodoméstico *nm* : electric appliance

electromagnético, -ca *adj* : electromagnetic

electrón *nm, pl* **-trones** : electron — **electrónico, -ca** *adj* : electronic — **electrónica** *nf* : electronics

▸ **elefante, -ta** *n* : elephant

elefante[M]
elephant

elegante adj : elegant —
  elegancia nf : elegance
elegía nf : elegy
elegir {28} vt **1** : elect **2** ESCOGER :
  choose, select — **elegible** adj : eligible
elemento nm : element —
  elemental adj **1** : elementary,
  basic **2** ESENCIAL : fundamental
elenco nm : cast (of actors)
elevar vt **1** : raise, lift **2** ASCENDER :
  elevate (in a hierarchy), promote —
  elevarse vr : rise — **elevación** nf,
  pl **-ciones** : elevation — **elevador** nm **1**
  : hoist **2** Lat : elevator
eliminar vt : eliminate — **eliminación** nf,
  pl **-ciones** : elimination
elipse nf : ellipse — **elíptico,**
  -ca adj : elliptical, elliptic
elite or **élite** nf : elite
elixir or **elíxir** nm : elixir
ella pron : she, her — **ello** pron :
  it — **ellos, ellas** pron pl **1** : they,
  them **2 de ellos, de ellas** : theirs
elocuente adj : eloquent —
  elocuencia nf : eloquence
elogiar vt : praise — **elogio** nm : praise
eludir vt : avoid, elude
emanar vi **emanar de** : emanate from
emancipar vt : emancipate
  — **emanciparse** vr : free
  oneself — **emancipación** nf,
  pl **-ciones** : emancipation
embadurnar vt : smear, daub
embajada nf : embassy —
  embajador, -dora n : ambassador
embalar vt : wrap up, pack —
  embalaje nm : packing
embaldosar vt : pave with tiles
embalsamar vt : embalm
embalse nm : dam, reservoir
embarazar {21} vt **1** : make
  pregnant **2** IMPEDIR : restrict, hamper
  — **embarazada** adj : pregnant —
  embarazo nm **1** : pregnancy **2**
  IMPEDIMENTO : hindrance, obstacle —
  embarazoso, -sa adj : embarrassing
embarcar {72} vt : load —
  embarcarse vr : embark, board —
  embarcación nf, pl **-ciones** : boat,
  craft — **embarcadero** nm : pier, jetty
  — **embarco** nm : embarkation
embargar {52} vt **1** : seize, impound
  2 : overwhelm (with emotion, etc.) —
  embargo nm **1** : embargo **2** : seizure
  (in law) **3 sin embargo** : nevertheless

embarque nm : loading (of goods),
  boarding (of passengers)
embarrancar {72} vi : run aground
embarullarse vr, fam : get mixed up
embaucar {72} vt : trick, swindle —
  embaucador, -dora n : swindler
embeber vt : absorb — vi : shrink —
  embeberse vr : become absorbed
embelesar vt : enchant, delight —
  embelesado, -da adj : spellbound
embellecer {53} vt : embellish, beautify
embestir {54} vt : attack, charge at
  — vi : charge, attack — **embestida** nf **1**
  : attack **2** : charge (of a bull)
emblema nm : emblem
embobar vt : amaze, fascinate
embocadura nf **1** : mouth (of a river,
  etc.) **2** : mouthpiece (of an instrument)
émbolo nm : piston
embolsarse vr : put in one's pocket
emborracharse vr : get drunk
emborronar vt **1** : smudge,
  blot **2** GARABATEAR : scribble
emboscar {72} vt : ambush —
  emboscada nf : ambush
embotar vt : dull, blunt
embotellar vt : bottle (up) —
  embotellamiento nm : traffic jam
embrague nm : clutch — **embragar**
  {52} vi : engage the clutch
embriagarse {52} vr : get drunk —
  embriagado, -da adj : intoxicated, drunk
  — **embriagador, -dora** adj : intoxicating
  — **embriaguez** nf : drunkenness
embrión nm, pl **-briones** : embryo
embrollo nm : tangle, confusion
embrujar vt : bewitch —
  embrujo nm : spell, curse
embrutecer vt : brutalize
embudo nm : funnel
embuste nm : lie — **embustero, -ra** adj
  : lying — **embustero, -ra** n : liar, cheat
embutir vt : stuff — **embutido** nm
  : sausage, cold meat
emergencia nf : emergency
emerger {15} vi : emerge, appear
emigrar vi **1** : emigrate **2** : migrate (of
  animals) — **emigración** nf, pl **-ciones**
  1 : emigration **2** : migration (of animals)
  — **emigrante** adj & nmf : emigrant
eminente adj : eminent —
  eminencia nf : eminence
emitir vt **1** : emit **2** EXPRESAR : express
  (an opinion, etc.) **3** : broadcast (on
  radio or television) **4** : issue (money,

stamps, etc.) — **emisión** nf, pl **-siones**
  1 : emission **2** : broadcast (on radio
  or television) **3** : issue (of money,
  etc.) — **emisora** nf : radio station
emoción nf, pl **-ciones** : emotion
  — **emocional** adj : emotional —
  emocionante adj **1** : moving, touching
  2 APASIONANTE : exciting, thrilling —
  emocionar vt **1** : move, touch **2** APASIONAR
  : excite, thrill — **emocionarse** vr **1**
  : be moved **2** APASIONARSE : get
  excited — **emotivo, -va** adj **1** :
  emotional **2** CONMOVEDOR : moving
empacar {72} vt Lat : pack
empachar vt : give indigestion to
  — **empacharse** vr : get indigestion
  — **empacho** nm : indigestion
empadronarse vr : register to vote
empalagoso, -sa adj :
  excessively sweet, cloying
empalizada nf : palisade (fence)
empalmar vt : connect, link — vi : meet,
  converge — **empalme** nm **1** : connection,
  link **2** : junction (of a railroad, etc.)
empanada nf : pie, turnover —
  empanadilla nf : meat or seafood pie
empanar vt : bread (in cooking)
empantanar vt : flood —
  empantanarse vr **1** : become
  flooded **2** : get bogged down
empañar vt **1** : steam (up) **2** :
  tarnish (one's reputation, etc.)
  — **empañarse** vr : fog up
empapar vt : soak —
  empaparse vr : get soaking wet
empapelar vt : wallpaper
empaquetar vt : pack, package
emparedado, -da adj : walled in,
  confined — **emparedado** nm : sandwich
emparejar vt : match up, pair
  — **emparejarse** vr : pair off
emparentado, -da adj : related, kindred
empastar vt : fill (a tooth)
  — **empaste** nm : filling
empatar vi : result in a draw, be
  tied — **empate** nm : draw, tie
empedernido, -da adj :
  inveterate, hardened
empedrar {55} vt : pave (with stones)
  — **empedrado** nm : paving, pavement
empeine nm : instep
empeñar vt : pawn — **empeñarse** vr **1**
  : insist, persist **2** ENDEUDARSE : go into
  debt **3 empeñarse en** : make an effort to
  — **empeñado, -da** adj **1** : determined,

committed **2** ENDEUDADO : in debt —
empeño *nm* **1** : determination, effort
2 casa de empeños : pawnshop
empeorar *vi* : get worse
— *vt* : make worse
empequeñecer {53} *vt* :
diminish, make smaller
emperador *nm* : emperor —
emperatriz *nf, pl* **-trices** : empress
empezar {29} *v* : start, begin
empinar *vt* : raise — **empinarse** *vr* : stand
on tiptoe — **empinado, -da** *adj* : steep
empírico, -ca *adj* : empirical
emplasto *nm* : poultice
emplazar {21} *vt* **1** : summon,
subpoena **2** SITUAR : place, locate —
emplazamiento *nm* **1** : location, site
2 CITACIÓN : summons, subpoena
emplear *vt* **1** : employ **2** USAR : use —
emplearse *vr* **1** : get a job **2** USARSE :
be used — **empleado, -da** *n* : employee
— **empleador, -dora** *n* : employer —
empleo *nm* **1** : occupation, job **2** USO : use
empobrecer {53} *vt* : impoverish —
empobrecerse *vr* : become poor
empollar *vi* : brood (eggs) — *vt* : incubate
empolvarse *vr* : powder one's face
empotrar *vt* : fit, build into —
empotrado, -da *adj* : built-in
emprender *vt* : undertake, begin —
emprendedor, -dora *adj* : enterprising
empresa *nf* **1** COMPAÑIA : company,
firm **2** TAREA : undertaking —
empresarial *adj* : business, managerial —
empresario, -ria *n* **1** : businessman *m*,
businesswoman *f* **2** : impresario
(in theater), promoter (in sports)
empujar *v* : push — **empuje** *nm*
: impetus, drive — **empujón** *nm,*
pl **-jones** : push, shove
empuñar *vt* : grasp, take hold of
emular *vt* : emulate
en *prep* **1** : in **2** DENTRO DE : into,
inside (of) **3** SOBRE : on **4 en avión**
: by plane **5 en casa** : at home
enajenar *vt* : alienate —
enajenación *nf, pl* **-ciones** : alienation
enagua *nf* : slip, petticoat
enaltecer {53} *vt* : praise, extol
enamorar *vt* : win the love of
— **enamorarse** *vr* : fall in love
— **enamorado, -da** *adj* : in love
— ~ *n* : lover, sweetheart
enano, -na *adj & n* : dwarf
enarbolar *vt* **1** : hoist, raise

2 : brandish (arms, etc.)
enardecer {53} *vt* : stir up, excite
encabezar {21} *vt* **1** : head, lead **2**
: put a heading on (an article, a list,
etc.) — **encabezamiento** *nm* **1** :
heading **2** : headline (in a newspaper)
encabritarse *vr* : rear up
encadenar *vt* **1** : chain, tie (up)
2 ENLAZAR : connect, link
encajar *vt* : fit (together) — *vi* **1**
: fit **2** CUADRAR : conform, tally
— **encaje** *nm* : lace
encalar *vt* : whitewash
encallar *vi* : run aground
encaminar *vt* : direct, aim —
encaminarse *vr* **encaminarse a** :
head for — **encaminado, -da** *adj*
encaminado a : aimed at, designed to
encandilar *vt* : dazzle
encanecer {53} *vi* : turn gray
encantar *vt* : enchant, bewitch — *vi*
me encanta esta canción : I love
this song — **encantado, -da** *adj* **1**
: delighted **2** HECHIZADO : bewitched
— **encantador, -dora** *adj* : charming,
delightful — **encantamiento** *nm* :
enchantment, spell — **encanto** *nm* **1**
: charm, fascination **2** HECHIZO : spell
encapotarse *vr* : cloud over —
encapotado, -da *adj* : overcast
encapricharse *vr* **encapricharse**
con : be infatuated with
encapuchado, -da *adj* : hooded
encaramar *vt* : lift up — **encaramarse** *vr*
encaramar a : climb up on
encarar *vt* : face, confront
encarcelar *vt* : imprison —
encarcelamiento *nm* : imprisonment
encarecer {53} *vt* : increase, raise
(price, value, etc.) — **encarecerse** *vr*
: become more expensive
encargar {52} *vt* **1** : put in charge
of **2** PEDIR : order — **encargarse** *vr*
encargarse de : take charge of —
encargado, -da *adj* : in charge —
encargado, -da *n* : manager, person
in charge — **encargo** *nm* **1** : errand **2**
TAREA : assignment, task **3** PEDIDO : order
encariñarse *vr* **encariñarse**
con : become fond of
encarnar *vt* : embody — **encarnación** *nf,*
pl **-ciones** : embodiment — **encarnado,**
-da *adj* **1** : incarnate **2** ROJO : red
encarnizarse {21} *vr* **encarnizarse**
con : attack viciously — **encarnizado,**

-da *adj* : bitter, bloody
encarrilar *vt* : put on the right track
encasillar *vt* : pigeonhole
encauzar {21} *vt* : channel
encender {56} *vt* **1** : light, set fire
to **2** PRENDER : switch on, start **3**
AVIVAR : arouse (passions, etc.) —
encenderse *vr* **1** : get excited **2**
RUBORIZARSE : blush — **encendedor** *nm*
: lighter — **encendido, -da** *adj* : lit, on
— **encendido** *nm* : ignition (switch)
encerar *vt* : wax, polish —
encerado, -da *adj* : waxed —
encerado *nm* : blackboard
encerrar {55} *vt* **1** : lock up, shut
away **2** CONTENER : contain
encestar *vi* : score (in basketball)
enchilada *nf* : enchilada
enchufar *vt* : plug in, connect
— **enchufe** *nm* : plug, socket
encía *nf* : gum (tissue)
encíclica *nf* : encyclical
enciclopedia *nf* : encyclopedia —
enciclopédico, -ca *adj* : encyclopedic
encierro *nm* **1** : confinement **2**
: sit-in (at a university, etc.)
encima *adv* **1** : on top **2** ADEMÁS : as
well, besides **3 encima de** : on, over, on
top of **4 por encima de** : above, beyond
encinta *adj* : pregnant
enclenque *adj* : weak, sickly
encoger {15} *v* : shrink —
encogerse *vr* **1** : shrink **2** : cower,
cringe **3 encogerse de hombros** :
shrug (one's shoulders) — **encogido,**
-da *adj* **1** : shrunken **2** TÍMIDO : shy
encolar *vt* : glue, stick
encolerizar {21} *vt* : enrage, infuriate
— **encolerizarse** *vr* : get angry
encomendar {55} *vt* : entrust
encomienda *nf* **1** : charge,
mission **2** *Lat* : parcel
encono *nm* : rancor, animosity
encontrar {19} *vt* **1** : find **2** : meet,
encounter (difficulties, etc.) —
encontrarse *vr* **1** : meet **2** HALLARSE
: find oneself, be — **encontrado,**
-da *adj* : contrary, opposing
encorvar *vt* : bend, curve —
encorvarse *vr* : bend over, stoop
encrespar *vt* **1** : curl **2** IRRITAR :
irritate — **encresparse** *vr* **1** : curl
one's hair **2** IRRITARSE : get annoyed
3 : become choppy (of the sea)
encrucijada *nf* : crossroads

encuadernar *vt* : bind (a book) — **encuadernación** *nf, pl* **-ciones** : bookbinding

encuadrar *vt* **1** : frame **2** ENCAJAR : fit **3** COMPRENDER : contain, include

encubrir {2} *vt* : conceal, cover (up) — **encubierto, -ta** *adj* : covert — **encubrimiento** *nm* : cover-up

encuentro *nm* : meeting, encounter

encuestar *vt* : poll, take a survey of — **encuesta** *nf* **1** : investigation, inquiry **2** SONDEO : survey — **encuestador, -dora** *n* : pollster

encumbrado, -da *adj* : eminent, distinguished

encurtir *vt* : pickle

endeble *adj* : weak, feeble — **endeblez** *nf* : weakness, frailty

endemoniado, -da *adj* : wicked

enderezar {21} *vt* **1** : straighten (out) **2** : put upright, stand on end

endeudarse *vr* : go into debt — **endeudado, -da** *adj* : indebted, in debt — **endeudamiento** *nm* : debt

endiablado, -da *adj* **1** : wicked, diabolical **2** : complicated, difficult

endibia *or* endivia *nf* : endive

endosar *vt* : endorse — **endoso** *nm* : endorsement

endulzar {21} *vt* **1** : sweeten **2** : soften, mellow (a tone, a response, etc.) — **endulzante** *nm* : sweetener

endurecer {53} *vt* : harden — **endurecerse** *vr* : become hardened

enema *nm* : enema

enemigo, -ga *adj* : hostile — **enemigo, -ga** *n* : enemy — **enemistad** *nf* : enmity — **enemistar** *vt* : make enemies of — **enemistarse** *vr* **enemistarse con** : fall out with

energía *nf* : energy — **enérgico, -ca** *adj* : energetic, vigorous, forceful

enero *nm* : January

enervar *vt* **1** : enervate, weaken **2** *fam* : get on one's nerves

enésimo, -ma *adj* **por enésima vez** : for the umpteenth time

enfadar *vt* : annoy, make angry — **enfadarse** *vr* : get annoyed — **enfado** *nm* : anger, annoyance — **enfadoso, -sa** *adj* : annoying

enfatizar {21} *vt* : emphasize — **énfasis** *nms & pl* : emphasis — **enfático, -ca** *adj* : emphatic

enfermar *vt* : make sick — *vi* : get sick — **enfermedad** *nf* : sickness, disease —
▶ **enfermería** *nf* : infirmary — **enfermero, -ra** *n* : nurse — **enfermizo, -za** *adj* : sickly — **enfermo, -ma** *adj* : sick — **enfermo, -ma** *n* : sick person, patient

enflaquecer {53} *vi* : lose weight

enfocar {72} *vt* **1** : focus (on) **2** : consider (a problem, etc.) — **enfoque** *nm* : focus

enfrascarse {72} *vr* **enfrascarse en** : immerse oneself in, get caught up in

enfrentar *vt* **1** : confront, face **2** : bring face to face — **enfrentarse** *vr* **enfrentar con** : confront, clash with — **enfrente** *adv* **1** : opposite

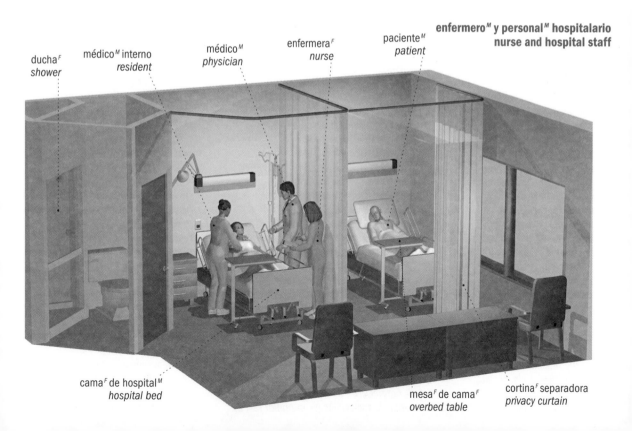

enfermero^M **y personal**^M **hospitalario**
nurse and hospital staff

ducha^F
shower

médico^M interno
resident

médico^M
physician

enfermera^F
nurse

paciente^M
patient

cama^F de hospital^M
hospital bed

mesa^F de cama^F
overbed table

cortina^F separadora
privacy curtain

2 enfrente de : in front of
enfriar {85} *vt* : chill, cool —
  enfriarse *vr* **1** : get cold **2** RESFRIARSE
  : catch a cold — **enfriamiento** *nm* **1**
  : cooling off **2** CATARRO : cold
enfurecer {53} *vt* : infuriate —
  enfurecerse *vr* : fly into a rage
enfurruñarse *vr, fam* : sulk
engalanar *vt* : decorate —
  engalanarse *vr* : dress up
enganchar *vt* : hook, snag,
  catch — **engancharse** *vr* **1** : get
  caught **2** ALISTARSE : enlist
engañar *vt* **1** EMBAUCAR : trick,
  deceive **2** : cheat on, be unfaithful
  to — **engañarse** *vr* **1** : deceive
  oneself **2** EQUIVOCARSE : be mistaken
  — **engaño** *nm* : deception, deceit —
  engañoso, -sa *adj* : deceptive, deceitful
engatusar *vt* : coax, cajole
engendrar *vt* **1** : beget **2** : engender,
  give rise to (suspicions, etc.)
englobar *vt* : include, embrace
engomar *vt* : glue
engordar *vt* : fatten — *vi* : gain weight
engorroso, -sa *adj* : bothersome
engranar *v* : mesh, engage —
  engranaje *nm* : gears *pl*
engrandecer {53} *vt* **1** :
  enlarge **2** ENALTECER : exalt
engrapar *vi Lat* : staple —
  engrapadora *nf Lat* : stapler
engrasar *vt* : lubricate, grease
  — **engrase** *nm* : lubrication
engreído, -da *adj* : conceited
engrosar {19} *vt* : swell
  — *vi* : gain weight
engrudo *nm* : paste
engullir {38} *vt* : gulp down, gobble up
enhebrar *vt* : thread
enhorabuena *nf* : congratulations *pl*
enigma *nm* : enigma —
  enigmático, -ca *adj* : enigmatic
enjabonar *vt* : soap (up), lather
enjaezar {21} *vt* : harness
enjalbegar {52} *vt* : whitewash
enjambrar *vi* : swarm —
  enjambre *nm* : swarm
enjaular *vt* **1** : cage **2** *fam* : jail
enjuagar {52} *vt* : rinse —
  enjuague *nm* **1** : rinse **2**
  enjuague bucal : mouthwash
enjugar {52} *vt* **1** : wipe away
  (tears) **2** : wipe out (debt)
enjuiciar *vt* **1** : prosecute **2** JUZGAR : try

enjuto, -ta *adj* : gaunt, lean
enlace *nm* **1** : bond, link **2** :
  junction (of a highway, etc.)
enlatar *vt* : can
enlazar {21} *vt* : join, link — *vi*
  enlazar con : link up with
enlistarse *vr Lat* : enlist
enlodar *vt* : cover with mud
enloquecer {53} *vt* : drive crazy
  — **enloquecerse** *vr* : go crazy
enlosar *vt* : pave, tile
enlutarse *vr* : go into mourning
enmarañar *vt* **1** : tangle **2** COMPLICAR
  : complicate **3** CONFUNDIR : confuse
  — **enmarañarse** *vr* **1** : get tangled up
  2 CONFUNDIRSE : become confused
enmarcar {72} *vt* : frame
enmascarar *vt* : mask
enmendar {55} *vt* **1** : amend **2** CORREGIR
  : emend, correct — **enmendarse** *vr* :
  mend one's ways — **enmienda** *nf* **1** :
  amendment **2** CORRECCIÓN : correction
enmohecerse {53} *vr* **1** : become
  moldy **2** OXIDARSE : rust
enmudecer {53} *vt* : silence
  — *vi* : fall silent
ennegrecer {53} *vt* : blacken
ennoblecer {53} *vt* : ennoble, dignify
enojar *vt* **1** : anger **2** MOLESTAR : annoy
  — **enojarse** *vr* **enojarse con** : get upset
  with — **enojo** *nm* **1** : anger **2** MOLESTIA :
  annoyance — **enojoso, -sa** *adj* : annoying
enorgullecer {53} *vt* : make
  proud — **enorgullecerse** *vr*
  enorgullecer de : pride oneself on
enorme *adj* : enormous —
  enormemente *adv* : enormously,
  extremely — **enormidad** *nf* : enormity
enraizar {30} *vi* : take root
enredadera *nf* : climbing plant, vine
enredar *vt* **1** : tangle up, entangle **2**
  CONFUNDIR : confuse **3** IMPLICAR : involve
  — **enredarse** *vr* **1** : become entangled
  2 enredarse en : get mixed up in —
  enredo *nm* **1** : tangle **2** EMBROLLO
  : confusion, mess — **enredoso,
  -sa** *adj* : tangled up, complicated
enrejado *nm* **1** : railing **2** REJILLA :
  grating, grille **3** : trellis (for plants)
enrevesado, -da *adj* : complicated
enriquecer {53} *vt* : enrich —
  enriquecerse *vr* : get rich
enrojecer {53} *vt* : redden —
  enrojecerse *vr* : blush
enrolar *vt* : enlist — **enrolarse** *vr*

enrolarse en : enlist in
enrollar *vt* : roll up, coil
enroscar {72} *vt* **1** : roll up
  2 ATORNILLAR : screw in
ensalada *nf* : salad
ensalzar {21} *vt* : praise
ensamblar *vt* : assemble, fit together
ensanchar *vt* **1** : widen **2** AMPLIAR :
  expand — **ensanche** *nm* **1** : widening
  2 : (urban) expansion, development
ensangrentado, -da *adj*
  : bloody, bloodstained
ensañarse *vr* : act cruelly
ensartar *vt* : string, thread
ensayar *vi* : rehearse — *vt* : try out,
  test — **ensayo** *nm* **1** : essay **2** PRUEBA :
  trial, test **3** : rehearsal (in theater, etc.)
enseguida *adv* : right away, immediately
ensenada *nf* : inlet, cove
enseñar *vt* **1** : teach **2** MOSTRAR :
  show — **enseñanza** *nf* **1** EDUCACIÓN
  : education **2** INSTRUCCIÓN : teaching
enseres *nmpl* **1** : equipment **2 enseres
  domésticos** : household goods
ensillar *vt* : saddle (up)
ensimismarse *vr* : lose
  oneself in thought
ensombrecer {53} *vt* : cast
  a shadow over, darken
ensoñación *nf, pl* **-ciones**
  : fantasy, daydream
ensordecer {53} *vt* : deafen
  — *vi* : go deaf — **ensordecedor,
  -dora** *adj* : deafening
ensortijar *vt* : curl
ensuciar *vt* : soil —
  ensuciarse *vr* : get dirty
ensueño *nm* : daydream, fantasy
entablar *vt* : initiate, start
entallar *vt* : tailor, fit (clothing) — *vi* : fit
entarimado *nm* : floorboards, flooring
ente *nm* **1** : being **2** ORGANISMO
  : body, organization
entender {56} *vt* **1** : understand
  2 OPINAR : think, believe — *vi* **1** :
  understand **2 entender de** : know
  about, be good at — **entenderse** *vr* **1**
  : understand each other **2** LLEVARSE BIEN
  : get along well — **entender** *nm* **a mi
  entender** : in my opinion — **entendido,
  -da** *adj* **1** : understood **2 eso se da
  por entendido** : that goes without
  saying **3 tener entendido** : be under the
  impression — **entendimiento** *nm* **1** :
  understanding **2** INTELIGENCIA : intellect

enterar *vt* : inform — **enterarse** *vr*
: find out, learn — **enterado,**
-da *adj* : well-informed

entereza *nf* **1** HONRADEZ : integrity **2**
FORTALEZA : fortitude **3** FIRMEZA : resolve

enternecer {53} *vt* : move, touch

entero, -ra *adj* **1** : whole **2** TOTAL :
absolute, total **3** INTACTO : intact —
entero *nm* : integer, whole number

enterrar {55} *vt* : bury

entibiar *vt* : cool (down) —
entibiarse *vr* : become lukewarm

entidad *nf* **1** : entity **2** ORGANIZACIÓN
: body, organization

entierro *nm* **1** : burial **2** :
funeral (ceremony)

entomología *nf* : entomology —
entomólogo, -ga *n* : entomologist

entonar *vt* : sing, intone — *vi* : be in tune

entonces *adv* **1** : then **2** **desde**
entonces : since then

entornado, -da *adj* : half-closed, ajar

entorno *nm* : surroundings *pl,*
environment

entorpecer {53} *vt* **1** : hinder, obstruct
2 : numb, dull (wits, reactions, etc.)

entrada *nf* **1** : entrance, entry **2** BILLETE
: ticket **3** COMIENZO : beginning **4** : inning
(in baseball) **5 entradas** *nfpl* : income **6**
tener entradas : have a receding hairline

entraña *nf* **1** : core, heart **2**
entrañas *nfpl* VÍSCERAS : entrails,
innards — **entrañable** *adj* : close,
intimate — **entrañar** *vt* : involve

entrar *vi* **1** : enter **2** EMPEZAR :
begin — *vt* : introduce, bring in

entre *prep* **1** : between **2** : among

entreabrir {2} *vt* : leave ajar —
entreabierto, -ta *adj* : half-open, ajar

entreacto *nm* : intermission

entrecejo *nm* **fruncir el entrecejo**
: knit one's brows, frown

entrecortado, -da *adj* : faltering (of
the voice), labored (of breathing)

entrecruzar {21} *vi* : intertwine

entredicho *nm* : doubt, question

entregar {52} *vt* : deliver, hand over —
entregarse *vr* : surrender — **entrega** *nf* **1**
: delivery **2** DEDICACIÓN : dedication,
devotion **3 entrega inicial** : down payment

entrelazar {21} *vt* : intertwine —
entrelazarse *vr* : become intertwined

entremés *nm, pl* **-meses 1** : hors
d'oeuvre **2** : short play (in theater)

entremeterse → **entrometerse**

entremezclar *vt* : mix (up)

entrenar *vt* : train, drill — **entrenarse** *vr*
: train — **entrenador, -dora** *n* : trainer,
coach — **entranamiento** *nm* : training

entrepierna *nf* : crotch

entresacar {72} *vt* : pick out, select

entresuelo *nm* : mezzanine

entretanto *adv* : meanwhile
— **entretanto** *nm* **en el**
entretanto : in the meantime

entretener {80} *vt* **1** : entertain **2**
DESPISTAR : distract **3** RETRASAR : delay,
hold up — **entretenerse** *vr* **1** : amuse
oneself **2** DEMORARSE : dawdle —
entretenido, -da *adj* : entertaining —
entretenimiento *nm* **1** : entertainment,
amusement **2** PASATIEMPO : pastime

entrever {88} *vt* : catch a
glimpse of, make out

entrevistar *vt* : interview —
entrevista *nf* : interview —
entrevistador, -dora *n* : interviewer

entristecer {53} *vt* : sadden

entrometerse *vr* : interfere —
entrometido, -da *adj* : meddling,
nosy — *n* : meddler

entroncar {72} *vi* : be
related, be connected

entumecer {53} *vt* : make numb
— **entumecerse** *vr* : go numb —
entumecido, -da *adj* **1** : numb
2 : stiff (of muscles, etc.)

enturbiar *vt* : cloud —
enturbiarse *vr* : become cloudy

entusiasmar *vt* : fill with enthusiasm
— **entusiasmarse** *vr* : get excited
— **entusiasmo** *nm* : enthusiasm
— **entusiasta** *adj* : enthusiastic
— **entusiasta** *nmf* : enthusiast

enumerar *vt* : enumerate, list
— **enumeración** *nf, pl* **-ciones**
: enumeration, count

enunciar *vt* : enunciate —
enunciación *nf, pl* **-ciones** : enunciation

envalentonar *vt* : make bold, encourage
— **envalentonarse** *vr* : be brave

envanecerse {53} *vr* : become vain

envasar *vt* **1** : package **2** : bottle,
can — **envase** *nm* **1** : packaging **2**
RECIPIENTE : container **3** : jar, bottle, can

envejecer {53} *v* : age —
envejecido, -da *adj* : aged, old —
envejecimiento *nm* : aging

envenenar *vt* : poison —
envenenamiento *nm* : poisoning

envergadura *nf* **1** ALCANCE :
scope **2** : span (of wings, etc.)

envés *nm, pl* **-veses** : reverse side

enviar {85} *vt* : send — **enviado,**
-da *n* : envoy, correspondent

envidiar *vt* : envy — **envidia** *nf*
: envy, jealousy — **envidioso,**
-sa *adj* : jealous, envious

envilecer {53} *vt* : degrade, debase
— **envilecimiento** *nm* : degradation

envío *nm* **1** : sending, shipment
2 : remittance (of funds)

enviudar *vi* : be widowed

envolver {89} *vt* **1** : wrap **2**
RODEAR : surround **3** IMPLICAR
: involve — **envoltorio** *nm* **or**
envoltura *nf* : wrapping, wrapper

enyesar *vt* **1** : plaster **2** ESCAYOLAR
: put in a plaster cast

enzima *nf* : enzyme

épico, -ca *adj* : epic — **épica** *nf* : epic

epidemia *nf* : epidemic —
epidémico, -ca *adj* : epidemic

epilepsia *nf* : epilepsy —
epiléptico, -ca *adj & n* : epileptic

epílogo *nm* : epilogue

episodio *nm* : episode

epitafio *nm* : epitaph

epíteto *nm* : epithet

época *nf* **1** : epoch, period
2 ESTACIÓN : season

epopeya *nf* : epic poem

equidad *nf* : equity, justice

equilátero, -ra *adj* : equilateral

equilibrar *vt* : balance — **equilibrado,**
-da *adj* : well-balanced — **equilibrio** *nm* **1**
: balance, equilibrium **2** JUICIO : good sense

equinoccio *nm* : equinox

equipaje *nm* : baggage, luggage

equipar *vt* : equip

equiparar *vt* **1** IGUALAR : make
equal **2** COMPARAR : compare —
equiparable *adj* : comparable

equipo *nm* **1** : equipment **2** :
team, crew (in sports, etc.)

equitación *nf, pl* **-ciones**
: horseback riding

equitativo, -va *adj* : equitable, fair, just

equivaler {84} *vi* : be equivalent
— **equivalencia** *nf* : equivalence —
equivalente *adj & nm* : equivalent

equivocar {72} *vt* : mistake, confuse
— **equivocarse** *vr* : make a mistake
— **equivocación** *nf, pl* **-ciones**
: error, mistake — **equivocado,**

escalada en roca^F
rock climbing

escalador^M
rock climber

roca^F
rock

cuerda^F de amarre^M
belay rope

pies^M de gato^M
climbing shoe

cordada^F
roped party

cabeza^F de cordada^F
leader

rocódromo^M
artificial climbing structure

viga^F de sujección^F
belay beam

juez^M de vía^F
route judge

presidente^M del
jurado^M
jury president

cronometrador^M
timekeeper

asegurador^M
belayer

-da *adj* : mistaken, wrong

equívoco, -ca *adj* : ambiguous — **equívoco** *nm* : misunderstanding

era *nf* : era

erario *nm* : public treasury, funds *pl*

erección *nf, pl* **-ciones** : erection

erguir {31} *vt* : raise, lift — **erguirse** *vr* : rise (up) — **erguido, -da** *adj* : erect, upright

erigir {35} *vt* : build, erect — **erigirse** *vr* **erigirse en** : set oneself up as

erizarse {21} *vr* : bristle, stand on end — **erizado, -da** *adj* : bristly

erizo *nm* **1** : hedgehog **2 erizo de mar** : sea urchin

ermitaño, -ña *n* : hermit

erosionar *vt* : erode — **erosión** *nf, pl* **-siones** : erosion

erótico, -ca *adj* : erotic

erradicar {72} *vt* : eradicate

errar {32} *vt* : miss — *vi* **1** : be wrong, be mistaken **2** VAGAR : wander — **errado, -da** *adj Lat* : wrong, mistaken

errata *nf* : misprint

errático, -ca *adj* : erratic

error *nm* : error — **erróneo, -nea** *adj* : erroneous, mistaken

eructar *vi* : belch, burp — **eructo** *nm* : belch, burp

erudito, -ta *adj* : erudite, learned

erupción *nf, pl* **-ciones 1** : eruption **2** SARPULLIDO : rash

esa, ésa → **ese, ése**

esbelto, -ta *adj* : slender, slim

esbozar {21} *vt* : sketch, outline — **esbozo** *nm* : sketch, outline

escabechar *vt* : pickle — **escabeche** *nm* : brine (for pickling)

escabel *nm* : footstool

escabroso, -sa *adj* **1** : rugged, rough **2** ESPINOSO : thorny, difficult **3** ATREVIDO : shocking, risqué

escabullirse {38} *vr* : slip away, escape

escalar *vt* : climb, scale — *vi* : escalate — **escala** *nf* **1** : scale **2** ESCALERA : ladder **3** : stopover (of an airplane, etc.) — **escalada** *nf* : ascent, climb — **escalador, -dora** *n* ALPINISTA : mountain climber

escaldar *vt* : scald

escalera *nf* **1** : stairs *pl*, staircase **2** ESCALA : ladder **3 escalera mecánica** : escalator

escalfar *vt* : poach

escalinata *nf* : flight of stairs

escalofrío *nm* : shiver, chill — **escalofriante** *adj* : chilling, horrifying

escalonar *vt* **1** : stagger, spread out **2** : terrace (land) — **escalón** *nm, pl* **-lones** : step, rung

escama *nf* **1** : scale (of fish or reptiles) **2** : flake (of skin) — **escamoso, -sa** *adj* : scaly

escamotear *vt* **1** : conceal **2** **escamotear algo a algn** : rob someone of something

escandalizar {21} *vt* : scandalize — **escandalizarse** *vr* : be shocked — **escándalo** *nm* **1** : scandal **2** ALBOROTO : scene, commotion — **escandaloso, -sa** *adj* **1** : shocking, scandalous **2** RUIDOSO : noisy

escandinavo, -va *adj* : Scandinavian

escáner *nm* : scanner

escaño *nm* **1** : seat (in a legislative body) **2** BANCO : bench

escapar *vi* : escape, run away — **escaparse** *vr* **1** : escape **2** : leak out (of gas, water, etc.) — **escapada** *nf* : escape

escaparate *nm* : store window

escapatoria *nf* : loophole, way out

escape *nm* **1** : leak (of gas, water, etc.) **2** : exhaust (from a vehicle)

escarabajo *nm* : beetle

escarbar *vt* **1** : dig, scratch, poke **2 escarbar en** : pry into

escarcha *nf* : frost (on a surface)

escarlata *adj & nf* : scarlet — **escarlatina** *nf* : scarlet fever

escarmentar {55} *vi* : learn one's lesson — **escarmiento** *nm* : lesson, punishment

escarnecer {53} *vt* : ridicule, mock — **escarnio** *nm* : ridicule, mockery

escarola *nf* : escarole, endive

escarpa *nf* : steep slope — **escarpado, -da** *adj* : steep

escasear *vi* : be scarce — **escasez** *nf, pl* **-seces** : shortage, scarcity — **escaso, -sa** *adj* **1** : scarce **2 escaso de** : short of

escatimar *vt* : be sparing with, skimp on

escayolar *vt* : put in a plaster cast — **escayola** *nf* **1** : plaster (for casts) **2** : plaster cast

escena *nf* **1** : scene **2** ESCENARIO : stage — **escenario** *nm* **1** : setting, scene **2** ESCENA : stage — **escénico, -ca** *adj* : scenic

escepticismo *nm* : skepticism — **escéptico, -ca** *adj* : skeptical — **escepticismo** *n* : skeptic

esclarecer {53} *vt* : shed light on, clarify

esclavo, -va *n* : slave — **esclavitud** *nf* : slavery — **esclavizar** {21} *vt* : enslave

esclerosis *nf* **esclerosis múltiple** : multiple sclerosis

esclusa *nf* : floodgate, lock (of a canal)

escoba *nf* : broom

escocer {14} *vi* : sting

escocés, -cesa *adj, mpl* **-ceses 1** : Scottish **2** : tartan, plaid — **escocés** *nm, pl* **-ceses** : Scotch (whiskey)

escoger {15} *vt* : choose — **escogido, -da** *adj* : choice, select

escolar *adj* : school — **escolar** *nmf* : student, pupil

escolta *nmf* : escort — **escoltar** *vt* : escort, accompany

escombros *nmpl* : ruins, rubble

esconder *vt* : hide, conceal — **esconderse** *vr* : hide — **escondidas** *nfpl* **1** *Lat* : hide-and-seek **2 a escondidas** : secretly, in secret — **escondite** *nm* **1** : hiding place **2** : hide-and-seek (game) — **escondrijo** *nm* : hiding place

escopeta *nf* : shotgun

escoplo *nm* : chisel

escoria *nf* **1** : slag **2** : dregs *pl* (of society, etc.)

escorpión *nm, pl* **-piones** : scorpion

escote *nm* **1** : (low) neckline **2 pagar a escote** : go Dutch

escotilla *nf* : hatchway

escribir {33} *v* : write — **escribirse** *vr* **1** : write to one another, correspond **2** : be spelled — **escribiente** *nmf* : clerk — **escrito, -ta** *adj* : written — **escritos** *nmpl* : writings — **escritor, -tora** *n* : writer — **escritorio** *nm* : desk — **escritura** *nf* **1** : handwriting **2** : deed (in law)

escroto *nm* : scrotum

escrúpulo *nm* : scruple — **escrupuloso, -sa** *adj* : scrupulous

escrutar *vt* **1** : scrutinize **2** : count (votes) — **escrutinio** *nm* **1** : scrutiny **2** : count (of votes)

escuadra *nf* **1** : square (instrument) **2** : fleet (of ships), squad (in the military) — **escuadrón** *nm, pl* **-drones** : squadron

escuálido, -da *adj* **1** : skinny **2** SUCIO : squalid

escuchar *vt* **1** : listen to **2** *Lat* : hear — *vi* : listen

escudo *nm* **1** : shield **2** *or* **escudo de armas** : coat of arms

escudriñar *vt* : scrutinize, examine

escuela *nf* : school

escueto, -ta *adj* : plain, simple

esculpir *v* : sculpt — **escultor, -tora** *n* : sculptor — **escultura** *nf* : sculpture

escupir *v* : spit

escurrir *vt* **1** : drain **2** : wring out (clothes) — *vi* **1** : drain **2** : drip-dry (of clothes) — **escurrirse** *vr* **1** : drain **2** *fam* : slip away — **escurridizo, -da** *adj* : slippery, evasive — **escurridor** *nm* **1** : dish drainer **2** COLADOR : colander

ese, esa *adj, mpl* esos : that, those

ése, ésa *pron, mpl* ésos : that one, those ones *pl*

esencia *nf* : essence — **esencial** *adj* : essential

esfera *nf* **1** : sphere **2** : dial (of a watch) — **esférico, -ca** *adj* : spherical

esfinge *nf* : sphinx

esforzar {36} *vt* : strain — **esforzarse** *vr* : make an effort — **esfuerzo** *nm* : effort

esfumarse *vr* : fade away, vanish

esgrimir *vt* **1** : brandish, wield **2** : make use of (an argument, etc.) — **esgrima** *nf* : fencing — **hacer esgrima** *vi* : fence

esguince *nm* : sprain, strain

eslabonar *vt* : link, connect — **eslabón** *nm, pl* **-bones** : link

eslavo, -va *adj* : Slavic

eslogan *nm, pl* **-lóganes** : slogan

esmaltar *vt* : enamel — **esmalte** *nm* **1** : enamel **2 esmalte de uñas** : nail polish

esmerado, -da *adj* : careful

esmeralda *nf* : emerald

esmerarse *vr* : take great care

esmeril *nm* : emery

esponja^F
sponge

esmoquin *nm, pl* **-móquines** : tuxedo

esnob *nmf, pl* **esnobs** : snob — **esnob** *adj* : snobbish

eso *pron* (*neuter*) **1** : that **2 ¡eso es!** : that's it!, that's right! **3 en eso** : at that point, then

esófago *nm* : esophagus

esos, ésos → **ese, ése**

espabilarse *vr* **1** : wake up **2** DARSE PRISA : get moving — **espabilado, -da** *adj* **1** : awake **2** LISTO : bright, clever

espaciar *vt* : space out, spread out — **espacial** *adj* : space — **espacio** *nm* **1** : space **2 espacio exterior** : outer space — **espacioso, -sa** *adj* : spacious

espada *nf* **1** : sword **2 espadas** *nfpl* : spades (in playing cards)

espagueti *nm or* **espaguetis** *nmpl* : spaghetti

espalda *nf* **1** : back **2 espaldas** *nfpl* : shoulders, back

espantar *vt* : scare, frighten — **espantarse** *vr* : become frightened — **espantajo** *nm or* **espantapájaros** *nms & pl* : scarecrow — **espanto** *nm* : fright, fear — **espantoso, -sa** *adj* **1** : frightening, horrific **2** TERRIBLE : awful, terrible

español, -ñola *adj* : Spanish — **español** *nm* : Spanish (language)

esparadrapo *nm* : adhesive bandage

esparcir {83} *vt* : scatter, spread — **esparcirse** *vr* **1** : be scattered, spread out **2** DIVERTIRSE : enjoy oneself

espárrago *nm* : asparagus

espasmo *nm* : spasm — **espasmódico, -ca** *adj* : spasmodic

espátula *nf* : spatula

especia *nf* : spice

especial *adj & nm* : special — **especialidad** *nf* : specialty — **especialista** *nmf* : specialist — **especializarse** {21} *vr* **especializarse en** : specialize in — **especialmente** *adv* : especially

▸ **especie** *nf* **1** : species **2** CLASE : type, kind

especificar {72} *vt* : specify — **especificación** *nf, pl* **-ciones** : specification — **específico, -ca** *adj* : specific

espécimen *nm, pl* **especímenes** : specimen

espectáculo *nm* **1** : show, performance **2** VISIÓN : spectacle, view — **espectacular** *adj* : spectacular

— **espectador, -dora** *n* : spectator

espectro *nm* **1** : spectrum **2** FANTASMA : ghost

especulación *nf, pl* **-ciones** : speculation

espejo *nm* : mirror — **espejismo** *nm* **1** : mirage **2** ILUSIÓN : illusion

espeluznante *adj* : terrifying, hair-raising

esperar *vt* **1** : wait for **2** CONTAR CON : expect **3 esperar que** : hope (that) — *vi* : wait — **espera** *nf* : wait — **esperanza** *nf* : hope, expectation — **esperanzado, -da** *adj* : hopeful — **esperanzar** {21} *vt* : give hope to

esperma *nmf* : sperm **2 esperma de ballena** : blubber

esperpento *nm* : (grotesque) sight, fright

espesar *vt* : thicken — **espesarse** *vr* : thicken — **espeso, -sa** *adj* : thick, heavy — **espesor** *nm* : thickness, density — **espesura** *nf* **1** ESPESOR : thickness **2** : thicket

espetar *vt* : blurt (out)

espiar {85} *vt* : spy on — *vi* : spy — **espía** *nmf* : spy

espiga *nf* : ear (of wheat, etc.)

espina *nf* **1** : thorn **2** : (fish) bone **3 espina dorsal** : spine, backbone

espinaca *nf* **1** : spinach (plant) **2** espinacas *nfpl* : spinach (food)

espinazo *nm* : spine, backbone

espinilla *nf* **1** : shin **2** GRANO : blackhead, pimple

espinoso, -sa *adj* **1** : prickly **2** : bony (of fish) **3** : difficult, thorny (of problems, etc.)

espionaje *nm* : espionage

espiral *adj & nf* : spiral

espirar *v* : breathe out, exhale

espíritu *nm* **1** : spirit **2 Espíritu Santo** : Holy Spirit — **espiritual** *adj* : spiritual — **espiritualidad** *nf* : spirituality

espita *nf* : spigot, faucet

espléndido, -da *adj* **1** : splendid **2** GENEROSO : lavish — **esplendor** *nm* : splendor

espliego *nm* : lavender

espolear *vt* : spur on

espoleta *nf* : fuse

espolvorear *vt* : sprinkle, dust

▸ **esponja** *nf* **1** : sponge **2 tirar la esponja** : throw in the towel — **esponjoso, -sa** *adj* : spongy

espontaneidad *nf* : spontaneity — **espontáneo, -nea** *adj* : spontaneous

ejemplo^M **de clasificación**^{F} **de una especie**^{F}
example of classification of a species

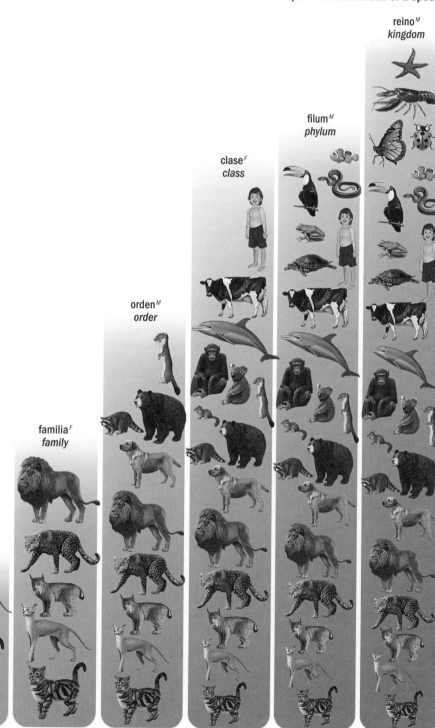

especies^F
species

género^M
genus

familia^F
family

orden^M
order

clase^F
class

filum^M
phylum

reino^M
kingdom

catus   Felis   Felidae   Carnivora   Mammalia   Chordata   Animalia

espora *nf* : spore

esporádico, -ca *adj* : sporadic

esposo, -sa *n* : spouse, wife *f*, husband *m* — **esposar** *vt* : handcuff — **esposars** *nfpl* : handcuffs

esprintar *vi* : sprint (in sports) — **esprint** *nm* : sprint

espuela *nf* : spur

espumar *vt* : skim — **espuma** *nf* **1** : foam, froth **2** : (soap) lather **3** : head (on beer) — **espumoso, -sa** *adj* **1** : foamy, frothy **2** : sparkling (of wine)

esqueleto *nm* : skeleton

esquema *nf* : outline, sketch

esquí *nm* **1** : ski **2** : skiing (sport) **3 esquí acuático** : waterskiing — **esquiador, -dora** *n* : skier — **esquiar** {85} *vi* : ski

esquilar *vt* : shear

esquimal *adj* : Eskimo

esquina *nf* : corner

esquirol *nm* : strikebreaker, scab

esquivar *vt* **1** : evade, dodge (a blow) **2** EVITAR : avoid — **esquivo, -va** *adj* : shy, elusive

esquizofrenia *nf* : schizophrenia — **esquizofrénico, -ca** *adj & n* : schizophrenic

esta, ésta → **este**[1], **éste**

estable *adj* : stable — **estabilidad** *nf* : stability — **estabilizar** {21} *vt* : stabilize

establecer {53} *vt* : establish — **establecerse** *vr* : establish oneself, settle — **establecimiento** *nm* : establishment

establo *nm* : stable

estaca *nf* : stake — **estacada** *nf* **1** : (picket) fence **2 dejar en la estacada** : leave in a lurch

estación *nf, pl* **-ciones 1** : season **2 estación de servicio** : gas station — **estacionar** *v* : park — **estacionamiento** *nm* : parking — **estacionario, -ria** *adj* : stationary

estadía *nf Lat* : stay

estadio *nm* **1** : stadium **2** FASE : phase, stage

estadista *nmf* : statesman

estadística *nf* : statistics — **estadístico, -ca** *adj* : statistical

estado *nm* **1** : state **2 estado civil** : marital status

estadounidense *adj & nmf* : American (from the United States)

estafar *vt* : swindle, defraud — **estafa** *nf* : swindle, fraud — **estafador, -dora** *n* : cheat, swindler

estallar *vi* **1** : explode **2** : break out

(of war, an epidemic, etc.) **3 estallar en llamas** : burst into flames — **estallido** *nm* **1** : explosion **2** : report (of a gun) **3** : outbreak (of war, etc.)

estampar *vt* : stamp, print — **estampa** *nf* **1** : print, illustration **2** ASPECTO : appearance — **estampado, -da** *adj* : printed

estampida *nf* : stampede

estampilla *nf* : stamp

estancarse {72} *vr* **1** : stagnate **2** : come to a halt — **estancado, -da** *adj* : stagnant

estancia *nf* **1** : stay **2** HABITACIÓN : (large) room **3** *Lat* : (cattle) ranch

estanco, -ca *adj* : watertight

estándar *adj & nm* : standard — **estandarizar** {21} *vt* : standardize

estandarte *nm* : standard, banner

estanque *nm* **1** : pool, pond **2** : reservoir (for irrigation)

estante *nm* : shelf — **estantería** *nf* : shelves *pl*, bookcase

estaño *nm* : tin

estar {34} *v aux* : be — *vi* **1** : be **2** : be at home **3** QUEDARSE : stay, remain **4 ¿cómo estás?** : how are you? **5 estar a** : cost **6 estar bien (mal)** : be well (sick) **7 estar para** : be in the mood for **8 estar por** : be in favor of **9 estar por** : be about to — **estarse** *vr* : stay, remain

estarcir {83} *vt* : stencil

estárter *nm* : choke (of an automobile)

estatal *adj* : state, national

estático, -ca *adj* **1** : static **2** INMÓVIL : unmoving, still — **estática** *nf* : static

estatua *nf* : statue

estatura *nf* : height

estatus *nm* : status, prestige

estatuto *nm* : statute — **estatutario, -ria** *adj* : statutory

este[1], **esta** *adj, mpl* **estos** : this, these

este[2] *adj* : eastern, east — **este** *nm* **1** : east **2** : east wind **3 el Este** : the Orient

éste, ésta *pron, mpl* **éstos 1** : this one, these ones *pl* **2** : the latter

estela *nf* **1** : wake (of a ship) **2** : trail (of smoke, etc.)

estera *nf* : mat

estéreo *adj & nm* : stereo — **estereofónico, -ca** *adj* : stereophonic

estereotipo *nm* : stereotype

estéril *adj* **1** : sterile **2** : infertile — **esterilidad** *nf* **1** : sterility **2** : infertility — **esterilizar** {21} *vt* : sterilize

estética *nf* : aesthetics

— **estético, -ca** *adj* : aesthetic

estiércol *nm* : dung, manure

estigma *nm* : stigma — **estigmatizar** {21} *vt* : stigmatize

estilarse {21} *vr* : be in fashion

estilo *nm* **1** : style **2** MANERA : fashion, manner — **estilista** *nmf* : stylist

estima *nf* : esteem, regard — **estimación** *nf, pl* **-ciones 1** : esteem **2** VALORACIÓN : estimate — **estimado, -da** *adj* **Estimado señor** : Dear Sir — **estimar** *vt* **1** : esteem, respect **2** VALORAR : value, estimate **3** CONSIDERAR : consider

estimular *vt* **1** : stimulate **2** ALENTAR : encourage — **estimulante** *adj* : stimulating — **estimular** *nm* : stimulant — **estímulo** *nm* : stimulus

estío *nm* : summertime

estipular *vt* : stipulate

estirar *vt* : stretch (out), extend — **estirado, -da** *adj* **1** : stretched, extended **2** ALTANERO : stuck-up, haughty — **estiramiento** *nm* **estiramiento facial** : face-lift — **estirón** *nm, pl* **-rones** : pull, tug

estirpe *nf* : lineage, stock

estival *adj* : summer

esto *pron* (*neuter*) **1** : this **2 en esto** : at this point **3 por esto** : for this reason

estofa *nf* **1** : class, quality **2 de baja estofa** : low-class

estofar *vt* : stew — **estofado** *nm* : stew

estoicismo *nm* : stoicism — **estoico, -ca** *adj* : stoic, stoical — **estoico, -ca** *n* : stoic

estómago *nm* : stomach — **estomacal** *adj* : stomach

estorbar *vt* : obstruct — *vi* : get in the way — **estorbo** *nm* **1** : obstacle **2** MOLESTIA : nuisance

estornino *nm* : starling

estornudar *vi* : sneeze — **estornudo** *nm* : sneeze

estos, éstos → **este, éste**

estrabismo *nm* : squint

estrado *nm* : platform, stage

estrafalario, -ria *adj* : eccentric, bizarre

estragar {52} *vt* : devastate — **estragos** *nmpl* **1** : ravages **2 hacer estragos en** *or* **causar estragos entre** : wreak havoc with

estragón *nm* : tarragon

estrangular *vt* : strangle — **estrangulación** *nf* : strangulation

estratagema *nf* : stratagem

estrategia *nf* : strategy

— **estratégico, -ca** *adj* : strategic

estrato *nm* : stratum

estratosfera *nf* : stratosphere

estrechar *vt* **1** : narrow **2** : strengthen (a bond) **3** ABRAZAR : embrace **4 estrechar la mano a uno** : shake someone's hand — **estrecharse** *vr* : narrow — **estrechez** *nf, pl* **-checes 1** : narrowness **2** estrecheces *nfpl* : financial problems — **estrecho, -cha** *adj* **1** : tight, narrow **2** ÍNTIMO : close — **estrecho** *nm* : strait

estrella *nf* **1** : star **2** DESTINO : destiny **3 estrella de mar** : starfish — **estrellado, -da** *adj* **1** : starry **2** : star-shaped

estrellar *v* : crash — **estrellarse** *vr* **estrellarse contra** : smash into

estremecer {53} *vt* : cause to shudder — *vi* : tremble, shake — **estremecerse** *vr* : shudder, shiver (with emotion) — **estremecimiento** *nm* : shaking, shivering

estrenar *vt* **1** : use for the first time **2** : premiere, open (a film, etc.) — **estrenarse** *vr* : make one's debut — **estreno** *nm* : debut, premiere

estreñirse {67} *vr* : be constipated — **estreñimiento** *nm* : constipation

estrépito *nm* : clamor, din — **estrepitoso, -sa** *adj* : noisy, clamorous

estrés *nm, pl* **estreses** : stress — **estresante** *adj* : stressful — **estresar** *vt* : stress (out)

estría *nf* : groove

estribaciones *nfpl* : foothills

estribar *vi* **estribar en** : stem from, lie in

estribillo *nm* : refrain, chorus

estribo *nm* **1** : stirrup **2** : running board (of a vehicle) **3** CONTRAFUERTE : buttress **4 perder los estribos** : lose one's temper

estribor *nm* : starboard

estricto, -ta *adj* : strict

estridente *adj* : strident, shrill

estrofa *nf* : stanza, verse

estropajo *nm* : scouring pad

estropear *vt* **1** : ruin, spoil **2** DAÑAR : damage — **estropearse** *vr* **1** : go bad **2** AVERIARSE : break down — **estropicio** *nm* : damage, havoc

estructura *nf* : structure — **estructural** *adj* : structural

estruendo *nm* : din, roar — **estruendoso, -sa** *adj* : thunderous

estrujar *vt* : squeeze

estuario *nm* : estuary

estuche *nm* : kit, case

estuco *nm* : stucco

estudiar *v* : study — **estudiante** *nmf* : student — **estudiantil** *adj* : student — **estudio** *nm* **1** : study **2** OFICINA : studio, office **3 estudios** *nmpl* : studies, education — **estudioso, -sa** *adj* : studious

estufa *nf* : stove, heater

estupefaciente *adj & nm* : narcotic — **estupefacto, -ta** *adj* : astonished

estupendo, -da *adj* : stupendous, marvelous

estúpido, -da *adj* : stupid — **estupidez** *nf, pl* **-deces** : stupidity

estupor *nm* **1** : stupor **2** ASOMBRO : amazement

etapa *nf* : stage, phase

etcétera : et cetera, and so on

éter *nm* : ether

etéreo, -rea *adj* : ethereal

eterno, -na *adj* : eternal — **eternidad** *nf* : eternity — **eternizarse** {21} *vr* : take forever

ética *nf* : ethics — **ético, -ca** *adj* : ethical

etimología *nf* : etymology

etíope *adj* : Ethiopian

etiqueta *nf* **1** : tag, label **2** PROTOCOLO : etiquette **3 de etiqueta** : formal, dressy — **etiquetar** *vt* : label

étnico, -ca *adj* : ethnic

eucalipto *nm* : eucalyptus

Eucaristía *nf* : Eucharist, communion

eufemismo *nm* : euphemism — **eufemístico, -ca** *adj* : euphemistic

euforia *nf* : euphoria — **eufórico, -ca** *adj* : euphoric

europeo, -pea *adj* : European

eutanasia *nf* : euthanasia

evacuar *vt* : evacuate, vacate — *vi* : have a bowel movement — **evacuación** *nf, pl* **-ciones** : evacuation

evadir *vt* : evade, avoid — **evadirse** *vr* : escape

evaluar {3} *vt* : evaluate — **evaluación** *nf, pl* **-ciones** : evaluation

evangelio *nm* : gospel — **evangélico, -ca** *adj* : evangelical — **evangelismo** *nm* : evangelism

evaporar *vt* : evaporate — **evaporarse** *vr* : evaporate, disappear — **evaporación** *nf, pl* **-ciones** : evaporation

evasión *nf, pl* **-siones 1** : evasion **2** FUGA : escape — **evasiva** *nf* : excuse, pretext — **evasivo, -va** *adj* : evasive

evento *nm* : event

eventual *adj* **1** : temporary **2** POSIBLE : possible — **eventualidad** *nf* : possibility, eventuality

evidencia *nf* **1** : evidence, proof **2 poner en evidencia** : demonstrate — **evidenciar** *vt* : demonstrate, show — **evidente** *adj* : evident — **evidentemente** *adj* : evidently, apparently

evitar *vt* **1** : avoid **2** IMPEDIR : prevent — **evitable** *adj* : avoidable

evocar {72} *vt* : evoke

evolución *nf, pl* **-ciones** : evolution — **evolucionar** *vi* : evolve

exacerbar *vt* **1** : exacerbate **2** IRRITAR : irritate

exacto, -ta *adj* : precise, exact — **exactamente** *adv* : exactly — **exactitud** *nf* : precision, accuracy

exagerar *v* : exaggerate — **exageración** *nf, pl* **-ciones** : exaggeration — **exagerado, -da** *adj* : exaggerated

exaltar *vt* **1** : exalt, extol **2** EXCITAR : excite, arouse — **exaltarse** *vr* : get worked-up — **exaltado, -da** *adj* : worked up, hotheaded

examen *nm, pl* **exámenes 1** : examination, test **2** ANÁLISIS : investigation — **examinar** *vt* **1** : examine **2** ESTUDIAR : study, inspect — **examinarse** *vr* : take an exam

exánime *adj* : lifeless

exasperar *vt* : exasperate, irritate — **exasperación** *nf, pl* **-ciones** : exasperation

excavar *v* : excavate — **excavación** *nf, pl* **-ciones** : excavation

exceder *vt* : exceed, surpass — **excederse** *vr* : go too far — **excedente** *adj & nm* : surplus, excess

excelente *adj* : excellent — **excelencia** *nf* **1** : excellence **2 Su Excelencia** : His/Her Excellency

excéntrico, -ca *adj & n* : eccentric — **excentricidad** *nf* : eccentricity

excepción *nf, pl* **-ciones** : exception — **excepcional** *adj* : exceptional

excepto *prep* : except (for) — **exceptuar** {3} *vt* : exclude, except

exceso *nm* **1** : excess **2 exceso de velocidad** : speeding — **excesivo, -va** *adj* : excessive

excitar *vt* : excite, arouse — **excitarse** *vr* : get excited — **excitable** *adj* : excitable — **excitación** *nf, pl* **-ciones** : excitement, agitation, arousal — **excitante** *adj* : exciting

exclamar *v* : exclaim — **exclamación** *nf, pl* **-ciones** : exclamation

excluir {41} *vt* : exclude —
exclusión *nf, pl* **-siones** : exclusion
— **exclusivo, -va** *adj* : exclusive
excomulgar {52} *vt* : excommunicate
— **excomunión** *nf, pl* **-niones**
: excommunication
excremento *nm* : excrement
exculpar *vt* : exonerate
excursión *nf, pl* **-siones** :
excursion — **excursionista** *nmf* **1**
: tourist, sightseer **2** : hiker
excusar *vt* **1** : excuse **2** EXIMIR :
exempt — **excusarse** *vr* : apologize —
excusa *nf* **1** : excuse **2** DISCULPA : apology
exento, -ta *adj* : exempt
exequias *nfpl* : funeral rites
exhalar *vt* **1** : exhale **2** :
give off (an odor, etc.)
exhaustivo, -va *adj* : exhaustive —
exhausto, -ta *adj* : exhausted, worn-out
exhibir *vt* : exhibit, show —
exhibición *nf, pl* **-ciones** : exhibition
exhortar *vt* : exhort, admonish
exigir {35} *vt* : demand, require —
exigencia *nf* : demand, requirement
— **exigente** *adj* : demanding
exiguo, -gua *adj* : meager
exiliar *vt* : exile — **exiliarse** *vr* :
go into exile — **exiliado, -da** *adj* :
exiled, in exile — **exiliado, -da** *n*
: exile — **exilio** *nm* : exile
eximir *vt* : exempt
existir *vi* : exist — **existencia** *nf* **1** :
existence **2** existirs *nfpl* MERCANCÍA :
goods, stock — **existente** *adj* : existing
éxito *nm* **1** : success, hit **2 tener**
éxito : be successful — **exitoso,**
-sa *adj Lat* : successful
éxodo *nm* : exodus
exorbitante *adj* : exorbitant
exorcizar {21} *vt* : exorcize —
exorcismo *nm* : exorcism
exótico, -ca *adj* : exotic
expandir *vt* : expand —
expandirse *vr* : spread —
expansión *nf, pl* **-siones** : expansion
— **expansivo, -va** *adj* : expansive
expatriarse {85} *vr* **1** : emigrate
2 EXILIARSE : go into exile —
expatriado, -da *adj & n* : expatriate
expectativa *nf* **1** : expectation, hope
2 expectativas *nfpl* : prospects
expedición *nf, pl* **-ciones** : expedition
expediente *nm* **1** : expedient
2 DOCUMENTOS : file, record **3**

INVESTIGACIÓN : inquiry, proceedings
expedir {54} *vt* **1** : issue **2** ENVIAR :
dispatch — **expedito, -ta** *adj* : free, clear
expeler *vt* : expel, eject
expendedor, -dora *n* : dealer, seller
expensas *nfpl* **1** : expenses **2 a**
expensas de : at the expense of
experiencia *nf* : experience
experimentar *vi* : experiment
— *vt* **1** : experiment with, test
out **2** SENTIR : experience, feel —
experimentado, -da *adj* : experienced
— **experimental** *adj* : experimental
— **experimento** *nm* : experiment
experto, -ta *adj & n* : expert
expiar {85} *vt* : atone for
expirar *vi* **1** : expire **2** MORIR : die
explayar *vt* : extend — **explayarse** *vr* **1**
: spread out **2** HABLAR : speak at length
explicar {72} *vt* : explain —
explicarse *vr* : understand —
explicación *nf, pl* **-ciones** : explanation
— **explicativo, -va** *adj* : explanatory
explícito, -ta *adj* : explicit
explorar *vt* : explore — **exploración** *nf,*
pl **-ciones** : exploration — **explorador,**
-dora *n* : explorer, scout —
exploratorio, -ria *adj* : exploratory
explosión *nf, pl* **-siones** **1** : explosion
2 : outburst (of anger, laughter, etc.)
— **explosivo, -va** *adj* : explosive
— **explosivo** *nm* : explosive
explotar *vt* **1** : exploit **2** : operate,
run (a factory, etc.), work (a mine)
— *vi* : explode — **explotación** *nf,*
pl **-ciones** **1** : exploitation **2** : running
(of a business), working (of a mine)
exponer {60} *vt* **1** : expose **2** :
explain, set out (ideas, theories,
etc.) **3** EXHIBIR : exhibit, display
— *vi* : exhibit — **exponerse** *vr*
exponerse a : expose oneself to
exportar *vt* : export —
exportaciones *nfpl* : exports —
exportador, -dora *n* : exporter
exposición *nf, pl* **-ciones** **1** : exposure
2 : exhibition (of objects, art, etc.) **3** :
exposition, setting out (of ideas, etc.)
— **expositor, -tora** *n* **1** : exhibitor
2 : exponent (of a theory, etc.)
exprés *nms & pl* **1** : express (train)
2 *or* **café exprés** : espresso
expresamente *adv* :
expressly, on purpose
expresar *vt* : express — **expresarse** *vr*

: express oneself — **expresión** *nf,*
pl **-siones** : expression —
expresivo, -va *adj* **1** : expressive
2 CARIÑOSO : affectionate
expreso, -sa *adj* : express —
expreso *nm* : express train, express
exprimir *vt* **1** : squeeze **2** EXPLOTAR :
exploit — **exprimidor** *nm* : squeezer, juicer
expuesto, -ta *adj* **1** : exposed **2**
PELIGROSO : risky, dangerous
expulsar *vt* : expel, eject —
expulsión *nf, pl* **-siones** : expulsion
exquisito, -ta *adj* **1** : exquisite **2**
RICO : delicious — **exquisitez** *nf* **1** :
exquisiteness **2** : delicacy, special dish
éxtasis *nms & pl* : ecstasy —
extático, -ta *adj* : ecstatic
extender {56} *vt* **1** : spread out **2** : draw
up (a document), write out (a check) —
extenderse *vr* **1** : extend, spread **2** DURAR :
last — **extendido, -da** *adj* **1** : widespread
2 : outstretched (of arms, wings, etc.)
extensamente *adv* : extensively
extensión *nf, pl* **-siones** **1** : extension
2 AMPLITUD : expanse **3** ALCANCE : range,
extent — **extenso, -sa** *adj* : extensive
extenuar {3} *vt* : exhaust, tire out
exterior *adj* **1** : exterior, external **2**
EXTRANJERO : foreign — **exterior** *nm* **1**
: outside **2 en el exterior** : abroad —
exteriorizar {21} *vt* : show, reveal —
exteriormente *adv* : outwardly, externally
exterminar *vt* : exterminate —
exterminación *nf, pl* **-ciones** :
extermination — **exterminio** *nm*
: extermination
externo, -na *adj* : external
extinguir {26} *vt* **1** : extinguish (a
fire) **2** : put an end to, wipe out —
extinguirse *vr* **1** : go out (of fire, light,
etc.) **2** : become extinct — **extinción** *nf,*
pl **-ciones** : extinction — **extinguidor** *nm*
Lat : fire extinguisher — **extinto, -ta** *adj* :
extinct — **extintor** *nm* : fire extinguisher
extirpar *vt* : remove, eradicate
extorsión *nf, pl* **-siones** **1** :
extortion **2** MOLESTIA : trouble
extra *adv* : extra — **extra** *adj* **1**
ADICIONAL : additional **2** : top-quality
— **extra** *nmf* : extra (in movies)
— **extra** *nm* : extra (expense)
extraditar *vt* : extradite
extraer {81} *vt* : extract — **extracción** *nf,*
pl **-ciones** : extraction — **extracto** *nm* **1**
: extract **2** RESUMEN : abstract, summary

explotación^F **agricola**
farm

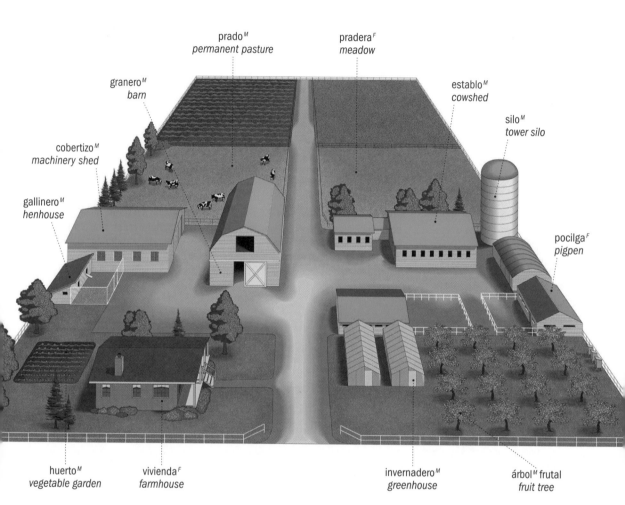

prado^M
permanent pasture

pradera^F
meadow

granero^M
barn

establo^M
cowshed

silo^M
tower silo

cobertizo^M
machinery shed

gallinero^M
henhouse

pocilga^F
pigpen

huerto^M
vegetable garden

vivienda^F
farmhouse

invernadero^M
greenhouse

árbol^M frutal
fruit tree

---

extranjero, -ra *adj* : foreign —
extranjero, -ra *n* : foreigner —
extranjero *nm* : foreign countries *pl*
extrañar *vt* : miss (someone) —
extrañarse *vr* : be surprised —
extrañeza *nf* : surprise — **extraño,
-ña** *adj* **1** : foreign **2** RARO : strange,
odd — **extraño, -ña** *n* : stranger
extraoficial *adj* : unofficial
extraordinario, -ria *adj* : extraordinary
extrasensorial *adj* : extrasensory
extraterrestre *adj & nmf*
: extraterrestrial

extravagante *adj* : extravagant,
outrageous — **extravagancia** *nf*
: extravagance, outlandishness
extraviar {85} *vt* : lose, misplace
— **extraviarse** *vr* : get lost
— **extravío** *nm* : loss
extremar *vt* : carry to extremes —
extremarse *vr* : do one's utmost —
extremadamente *adv* : extremely
— **extremado, -da** *adj* : extreme
— **extremidad** *nf* **1** : tip, end **2**
extremidades *nfpl* : extremities —
extremista *adj & nmf* : extremist

— **extremo, -ma** *adj* **1** : extreme **2**
en caso extremo : as a last resort —
extremo *nm* **1** : end **2 en extremo**
: in the extreme, extremely **3 en
ultimo extremo** : as a last resort
extrovertido -da *adj* : extroverted
— **extrovertido -da** *n* : extrovert
exuberante *adj* : exuberant —
exuberancia *nf* : exuberance
exudar *vt* : exude
eyacular *vi* : ejaculate —
eyaculación *nf, pl* **-ciones** : ejaculation

f *nf* : f, sixth letter of the Spanish alphabet
fabricar {72} *vt* **1** : manufacture **2** CONSTRUIR : build, construct **3** INVENTAR : fabricate — **fábrica** *nf* : factory — **fabricación** *nf, pl* **-ciones** : manufacture — **fabricante** *nmf* : manufacturer
fábula *nf* **1** : fable **2** MENTIRA : story, lie
fabuloso, -sa *adj* : fabulous
facción *nf, pl* **-ciones 1** : faction **2** facciónes *nfpl* RASGOS : features
faceta *nf* : facet
facha *nf* : appearance, look
fachada *nf* : façade
facial *adj* : facial
fácil *adj* **1** : easy **2** PROBABLE : likely — **facilemente** *adv* : easily, readily — **facilidad** *nf* **1** : facility, ease **2** fáciles *nfpl* : facilities, services — **facilitar** *vt* **1** : facilitate **2** PROPORCIONAR : provide, supply
facsímil *or* facsímile *nm* **1** COPIA : facsimile, copy **2** : fax
factible *adj* : feasible
factor *nm* : factor

factoría *nf* : factory
factura *nf* **1** : bill, invoice **2** HECHURA : making, manufacture — **facturar** *vt* **1** : bill for **2** : check in (baggage, etc.)
facultad *nf* **1** : faculty, ability **2** AUTORIDAD : authority **3** : school (of a university) — **facultativo, -va** *adj* : optional
faena *nf* **1** : task, job **2** faenas domésticas : housework
fagot *nm* : bassoon
faisán *nm, pl* **-sanes** : pheasant
faja *nf* **1** : sash **2** : girdle, corset **3** : strip (of land)
fajo *nm* : bundle, sheaf
falda *nf* **1** : skirt **2** : side, slope (of a mountain)
falible *adj* : fallible
fálico, -ca *adj* : phallic
fallar *vi* : fail, go wrong — *vt* **1** : pronounce judgment on **2** ERRAR : miss — **falla** *nf* **1** : flaw, defect **2** : (geological) fault
fallecer {53} *vi* : pass away, die — **fallecimiento** *nm* : demise, death

fallido, -da *adj* : failed, unsuccessful
fallo *nm* **1** : error **2** SENTENCIA : sentence, verdict
falo *nm* : phallus, penis
falsear *vt* : falsify, distort — **falsedad** *nf* **1** : falseness **2** MENTIRA : falsehood, lie — **falsificación** *nf, pl* **-ciones** : forgery, fake — **falsificador, -dora** *n* : forger — **falsificar** {72} *vt* **1** : counterfeit, forge **2** ALTERAR : falsify — **falso, -sa** *adj* **1** : false, untrue **2** FALSIFICADO : counterfeit, forged
falta *nf* **1** CARENCIA : lack **2** DEFECTO : defect, fault, error **3** AUSENCIA : absence **4** : offense, misdemeanor (in law) **5** : foul (in sports) **6** hacer falta : be lacking, be needed **7** sin falta : without fail — **faltar** *vi* **1** : be lacking, be needed **2** : be missing **3** QUEDAR : remain, be left **4** ¡no faltaba más! : don't mention it! — **falto, -ta** *adj* falto de : lacking (in)
fama *nf* **1** : fame **2** REPUTACIÓN : reputation
famélico, -ca *adj* : starving

estación^F de ferrocarril^M
passenger station

tren^M de pasajeros^M
passenger train

andén^M de pasajeros^M
passenger platform

indicador^M de hora^F de salida^F
departure time indicator

borde^M del andén^M
platform edge

sala^F de equipajes^M
baggage room

vestíbulo^M
concourse

destinos^M
destination

horarios^M
schedules

vía^F
track

revisor^M
ticket collector

familia *nf* : family — **familiar** *adj* **1**
: familial, family **2** CONOCIDO : familiar
3 : informal (of language, etc.) —
familiar *nmf* : relation, relative
— **familiaridad** *nf* : familiarity —
familiarizarse {21} *vr* **familiarizarse**
con : familiarize oneself with
famoso, -sa *adj* : famous
fanático, -ca *adj* : fanatic, fanatical
— **fanático, -ca** *n* : fanatic —
fanatismo *nm* : fanaticism
fanfarria *nf* : fanfare
fanfarrón, -rrona *adj, mpl* **-rrones** *fam*
: boastful — **fanfarrón, -rrona** *n, fam* :
braggart — **fanfarronear** *vi* : boast, brag
fango *nm* : mud, mire —
fangoso, -sa *adj* : muddy
fantasear *vi* : fantasize, daydream
— **fantasía** *nf* **1** : fantasy **2**
IMAGINACIÓN : imagination
fantasma *nm* : ghost, phantom
— **fantasmal** *adj* : ghostly
fantástico, -ca *adj* : fantastic
fardo *nm* : bundle
farfullar *v* : jabber, gabble
farmacéutico, -ca *adj* : pharmaceutical
— **farmacéutico, -ca** *n* : pharmacist
— **farmacia** *nf* : drugstore, pharmacy
faro *nm* **1** : lighthouse **2** : headlight
(of an automobile) — **farol** *nm* **1**
LINTERNA : lantern **2** FAROLA : streetlight —
farola *nf* **1** : lamppost **2** FAROL : streetlight
farsa *nf* : farce — **farsante** *nmf*
: charlatan, fraud
fascículo *nm* : installment,
part (of a publication)
fascinar *vt* : fascinate —
fascinación *nf, pl* **-ciones** : fascination
— **fascinante** *adj* : fascinating
fascismo *nm* : fascism —
fascista *adj & nmf* : fascist
fase *nf* : phase
fastidiar *vt* : annoy, bother — *vi*
: be annoying or bothersome —
fastidio *nm* : annoyance — **fastidioso,**
-sa *adj* : annoying, bothersome
fatal *adj* **1** : fateful **2** MORTAL : fatal **3**
fam : awful, terrible — **fatalidad** *nf* **1**
: fate, destiny **2** DESGRACIA : misfortune
fatídico, -ca *adj* : fateful, momentous
fatiga *nf* : fatigue — **fatigado, -da** *adj*
: weary, tired — **fatigar** {52} *vt* :
tire — **fatigarse** *vr* : get tired —
fatigoso, -sa *adj* : fatiguing, tiring
fatuo, -tua *adj* **1** : fatuous **2**

PRESUMIDO : conceited
fauna *nf* : fauna
favor *nm* **1** : favor **2 a favor de** : in favor
of **3 por favor** : please — **favorable** *adj* **1**
: favorable **2 ser favorable a** : be in favor
of — **favorecedor, -dora** *adj* : flattering
— **favorecer** {53} *vt* **1** AYUDAR : favor **2**
: look well on, suit — **favoritismo** *nm* :
favoritism — **favorito, -ta** *adj & n* : favorite
fax *nm* : fax — **faxear** *vt* : fax
faz *nf, pl* **faces** : face, countenance
fe *nf* **1** : faith **2 dar fe de** : bear witness
to **3 de buena fe** : in good faith
fealdad *nf* : ugliness
febrero *nm* : February
febril *adj* : feverish
fecha *nf* **1** : date **2 fecha de caducidad**
or **fecha de vencimiento** : expiration
date **3 fecha límite** : deadline —
fechar *vt* : date, put a date on
fechoría *nf* : misdeed
fécula *nf* : starch (in food)
fecundar *vt* **1** : fertilize (an egg) **2** :
make fertile — **fecundo, -da** *adj* : fertile
federación *nf, pl* **-ciones** :
federation — **federal** *adj* : federal
felicidad *nf* **1** : happiness **2 ¡felicidades!**
: best wishes!, congratulations!,
happy birthday! — **felicitación** *nf,*
pl **-ciones** : congratulation — **felicitar** *vt*
: congratulate — **felicitarse** *vr*
felicitarse de : be glad about
feligrés -gresa *n, mpl*
-greses : parishioner
▸ **felino, -na** *adj & n* : feline
feliz *adj, pl* **-lices 1** : happy **2**
AFORTUNADO : fortunate **3 Feliz**
Navidad : Merry Christmas
felpa *nf* **1** : plush **2** : terry
cloth (for towels, etc.)
felpudo *nm* : doormat
femenino, -na *adj* **1** : feminine **2** :
female (in biology) — **femenino** *nm* :
feminine (in grammar) — **femineidad** *nf*
: femininity — **feminismo** *nm* : feminism
— **feminista** *adj & nmf* : feminist
fenómeno *nm* : phenomenon —
fenomenal *adj* **1** : phenomenal
2 *fam* : fantastic, terrific
feo, fea *adj* **1** : ugly **2** DESAGRADABLE
: unpleasant, nasty
féretro *nm* : coffin
feria *nf* **1** : fair, market **2** FIESTA : festival,
holiday **3** *Lat fam* : small change —
feriado, -da *adj* **día feriado** : public holiday

felinos^M
felines

gato^M doméstico
cat

jaguar^M
jaguar

león^M
lion

leopardo^M
leopard

fermentar *v* : ferment —
fermentación *nf, pl* **-ciones** :
fermentation — **fermento** *nm* : ferment
feroz *adj, pl* **-roces** : ferocious, fierce
— **ferocidad** *nf* : ferocity, fierceness
férreo, -rrea *adj* **1** : iron **2**
vía férrea : railroad track
ferretería *nf* : hardware store
▸ **ferrocarril** *nm* : railroad, railway —
ferroviario, -ria *adj* : rail, railroad

follaje^M: tipos^M de hojas^F
foliage: types of leaves

estructura^F de una hoja^F
structure of a leaf

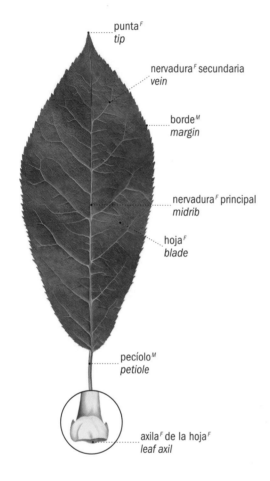

punta^F
tip

nervadura^F secundaria
vein

borde^M
margin

nervadura^F principal
midrib

hoja^F
blade

pecíolo^M
petiole

axila^F de la hoja^F
leaf axil

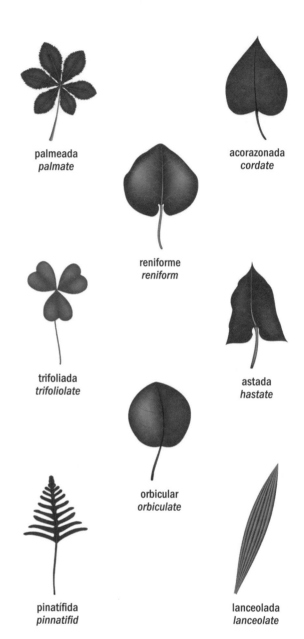

palmeada
palmate

acorazonada
cordate

reniforme
reniform

trifoliada
trifoliolate

astada
hastate

pinatífida
pinnatifid

orbicular
orbiculate

lanceolada
lanceolate

---

ferry *nm, pl* **ferrys** : ferry
fértil *adj* : fertile, fruitful — **fertilidad** *nf*
: fertility — **fertilizante** *nm* :
fertilizer — **fertilizar** *vt* : fertilize
fervor *nm* : fervor, zeal —
ferviente *adj* : fervent
festejar *vt* **1** : celebrate **2** AGASAJAR
: entertain, wine and dine —
festejo *nm* : celebration, festivity

festín *nm, pl* **-tines** : banquet, feast
festival *nm* : festival — **festividad** *nf*
: festivity — **festivo, -va** *adj* **1** :
festive **2 día festivo** : holiday
fetiche *nm* : fetish
fétido, -da *adj* : foul-smelling, fetid
feto *nm* : fetus — **fetal** *adj* : fetal
feudal *adj* : feudal
fiable *adj* : reliable

— **fiabilidad** *nf* : reliability
fiado, -da *adj* : on credit — **fiador,**
-dora *n* : bondsman, guarantor
fiambres *nfpl* : cold cuts
fianza *nf* **1** : bail, bond **2 dar**
fianza : pay a deposit
fiar {85} *vt* **1** : guarantee **2** : sell on
credit — *vi* **ser de fiar** : be trustworthy
— **fiarse** *vr* **fiarse de** : place trust in

fiasco *nm* : fiasco

fibra *nf* **1** : fiber **2 fibra de vidrio** : fiberglass

ficción *nf, pl* **-ciones** : fiction

ficha *nf* **1** : token **2** TARJETA : index card **3** : counter, chip (in games) — **fichar** *vt* : file, index — **fichero** *nm* **1** : card file **2** : filing cabinet

ficticio, -cia *adj* : fictitious

fidedigno, -na *adj* : reliable, trustworthy

fidelidad *nf* : fidelity, faithfulness

fideo *nm* : noodle

fiebre *nf* **1** : fever **2 fiebre del heno** : hay fever **3 fiebre palúdica** : malaria

fiel *adj* **1** : faithful, loyal **2** PRECISO : accurate, reliable — **fiel** *nm* **1** : pointer (of a scale) **2 los fieles** : the faithful — **fielmente** *adv* : faithfully

fieltro *nm* : felt

fiero, -ra *adj* : fierce, ferocious — **fiera** *nf* : wild animal, beast

fierro *nm Lat* : iron (bar)

fiesta *nf* **1** : party **2** DIA FESTIVO : holiday, feast day

figura *nf* **1** : figure **2** FORMA : shape, form — **figurar** *vi* **1** : figure (in), be included (among) **2** DESTACAR : stand out — *vt* : represent — **figurarse** *vr* : imagine

fijar *vt* **1** : fasten, affix **2** CONCRETAR : set, fix — **fijarse** *vr* **1** : settle **2 fijarse en** : notice, pay attention to — **fijo, -ja** *adj* **1** : fixed, firm **2** PERMANENTE : permanent

fila *nf* **1** : line, file, row **2 ponerse en fila** : line up

filantropía *nf* : philanthropy — **filantrópico, -ca** *adj* : philanthropic — **filántropo, -pa** *n* : philanthropist

filatelia *nf* : philately, stamp collecting

filete *nm* : fillet

filial *adj* : filial — **filial** *nf* : affiliate, subsidiary

filigrana *nf* **1** : filigree **2** : watermark (on paper)

filipino, -na *adj* : Filipino

filmar *vt* : film, shoot — **filme** *or* **film** *nm* : film, movie

filo *nm* **1** : edge **2 dar filo a** : sharpen

filón *nm, pl* **-lones 1** : vein (of minerals) **2** *fam* : gold mine

filoso, -sa *adj Lat* : sharp

filosofía *nf* : philosophy — **filosófico, -ca** *adj* : philosophical — **filósofo, -fa** *n* : philosopher

filtrar *v* : filter — **filtrarse** *vr* : leak out, seep through — **filtro** *nm* : filter

fin *nm* **1** : end **2** OBJETIVO : purpose, aim **3 en fin** : well, in short **4 fin de semana** : weekend **5 por fin** : finally, at last

final *adj* : final — **final** *nm* : end, conclusion — **final** *nf* : final (in sports) — **finalidad** *nf* : purpose, aim — **finalista** *nmf* : finalist — **finalizar** {21} *v* : finish, end — **finalmente** *adv* : finally

financiar *vt* : finance, fund — **financiero, -ra** *adj* : financial — **financiero, -ra** *n* : financier — **finanzas** *nfpl* : finance

finca *nf* **1** : farm, ranch **2** *Lat* : country house

fingir {35} *v* : feign, pretend — **fingido, -da** *adj* : false, feigned

finito, -ta *adj* : finite

finlandés, -desa *adj* : Finnish

fino, -na *adj* **1** : fine **2** DELGADO : slender **3** REFINADO : refined **4** AGUDO : sharp, keen — **finura** *nf* **1** : fineness **2** REFINAMIENTO : refinement

firma *nf* **1** : signature **2** : (act of) signing **3** EMPRESA : firm, company

firmamento *nm* : firmament, sky

firmar *v* : sign

firme *adj* **1** : firm, resolute **2** ESTABLE : steady, stable — **firmeza** *nf* **1** : strength, resolve **2** ESTABILIDAD : firmness, stability

fiscal *adj* : fiscal — **fiscal** *nmf* : district attorney — **fisco** *nm* : (national) treasury

fisgar {52} *vt* : pry into — *vi* : pry — **fisgón, -gona** *n, mpl* **-gones** : snoop, busybody

física *nf* : physics — **físico, -ca** *adj* : physical — **física** *n* : physicist — **físico** *nm* : physique

fisiología *nf* : physiology — **fisiológico, -ca** *adj* : physiological — **fisiólogo, -ga** *n* : physiologist

fisioterapia *nf* : physical therapy — **fisioterapeuta** *nmf* : physical therapist

fisonomía *nf* : features *pl*, appearance

fisura *nf* : fissure

fláccido, -da *or* **flácido, -da** *adj* : flaccid, flabby

flaco, -ca *adj* **1** : thin, skinny **2** DÉBIL : weak

flagrante *adj* : flagrant

flamante *adj* **1** : bright, brilliant **2** NUEVO : brand-new

flamenco, -ca *adj* **1** : flamenco (of music or dance) **2** : Flemish — **flamenco** *nm* **1** : flamingo **2** : flamenco (music or dance)

flaquear *vi* : weaken, flag

— **flaqueza** *nf* **1** : thinness **2** DEBILIDAD : weakness

flash *nm* : flash

flatulencia *nf* : flatulence

flauta *nf* **1** : flute **2 flauta dulce** : recorder — **flautín** *nm, pl* **-tines** : piccolo — **flautista** *nmf* : flutist

flecha *nf* : arrow

fleco *nm* **1** : fringe **2** *Lat* : bangs *pl*

flema *nf* : phlegm — **flemático, -ca** *adj* : phlegmatic

flequillo *nm* : bangs *pl*

fletar *vt* **1** : charter, rent **2** *Lat* : transport — **flete** *nm* **1** : charter **2** : shipping (charges) **3** *Lat* : transport, freight

flexible *adj* : flexible — **flexibilidad** *nf* : flexibility

flirtear *vi* : flirt

flojo, -ja *adj* **1** SUELTO : loose, slack **2** DÉBIL : weak **3** PEREZOSO : lazy — **flojera** *nf, fam* : lethargy

flor *nf* : flower — **flora** *nf* : flora — **floral** *adj* : floral — **floreado, -da** *adj* : flowered — **florear** *vi Lat* : flower, bloom — **florecer** {53} *vi* **1** : bloom, blossom **2** PROSPERAR : flourish — **floreciente** *adj* : flourishing — **florero** *nm* : vase — **florido, -da** *adj* : flowery — **florista** *nmf* : florist — **floritura** *nf* : frill, flourish

flota *nf* : fleet

flotar *vi* : float — **flotador** *nm* **1** : float **2** : life preserver (for a swimmer) — **flotante** *adj* : floating, buoyant — **flote** : **a flotante** *adv phr* : afloat

flotilla *nf* : flotilla, fleet

fluctuar {3} *vi* : fluctuate — **fluctuación** *nf, pl* **-ciones** : fluctuation

fluir {41} *vi* : flow — **fluidez** *nf* **1** : fluidity **2** : fluency (of language, etc.) — **fluido, -da** *adj* **1** : fluid **2** : fluent (of language) — **fluido** *nm* : fluid — **flujo** *nm* : flow

fluorescente *adj* : fluorescent

fluoruro *nm* : fluoride

fluvial *adj* : river

fobia *nf* : phobia

foca *nf* : seal (animal)

foco *nm* **1** : focus **2** : spotlight, floodlight (in theater, etc.) **3** *Lat* : lightbulb

fofo, -fa *adj* : flabby

fogata *nf* : bonfire

fogón *nm, pl* **-gones** : burner

fogoso, -sa *adj* : ardent

folklore *nm* : folklore — **folklórico, -ca** *adj* : folk, traditional

▸ **follaje** *nm* : foliage

folleto *nm* : pamphlet, leaflet
fomentar *vt* : promote, encourage —
  fomento *nm* : promotion, encouragement
fonda *nf* : boarding house
fondear *vt* : sound out,
  examine — *vi* : anchor
fondillos *nmpl* : seat (of pants, etc.)
fondo *nm* 1 : bottom 2 : rear,
  back, end 3 PROFUNDIDAD : depth 4 :
  background (of a painting, etc.) 5 *Lat*
  : slip, petticoat 6 **fondos** *nmpl* : funds,
  resources 7 **a fondo** : thoroughly, in
  depth 8 **en el fondo** : deep down
fonético, -ca *adj* : phonetic

— **fonética** *nf* : phonetics
fontanería *nf, Spain* : plumbing —
  fontanero, -ra *n, Spain* : plumber
footing *nm* 1 : jogging 2
  hacer footing : jog
forajido, -da *n* : bandit, outlaw
foráneo, -nea *adj* : foreign, strange
forastero, -ra *n* : stranger, outsider
forcejear *vi* : struggle —
  forcejeo *nm* : struggle
forense *adj* : forensic
forja *nf* : forge — **forjar** *vt* 1 : forge
  2 CREAR, FORMAR : build up, create
forma *nf* 1 : form, shape 2 MANERA

: manner, way 3 **en forma** : fit,
  healthy 4 **formas** *nfpl* : appearances,
  conventions — **formación** *nf, pl* **-ciones**
  1 : formation 2 EDUCACIÓN : training
formal *adj* 1 : formal 2 SERIO : serious
  3 FIABLE : dependable, reliable —
  formalidad *nf* 1 : formality 2 SERIEDAD
  : seriousness 3 FIABILIDAD : reliability
formar *vt* 1 : form, shape 2 CONSTITUIR
  : constitute 3 EDUCAR : train, educate —
  formarse *vr* 1 DESARROLLARSE : develop,
  take shape 2 EDUCARSE : be educated
formato *nm* : format
formidable *adj* 1 : tremendous
  2 *fam* : fantastic, terrific
fórmula *nf* : formula
formular *vt* 1 : formulate, draw up
  2 : make, lodge (a complaint, etc.)
formulario *nm* : form
fornido, -da *adj* : well-built, burly
foro *nm* : forum
forraje *nm* : forage, fodder
  — **forrajear** *vi* : forage
forrar *vt* 1 : line (a garment) 2 :
  cover (a book) — **forro** *nm* 1 :
  lining 2 CUBIERTA : book cover
fortalecer {53} *vt* : strengthen —
  fortaleza *nf* 1 : fortress 2 FUERZA
  : strength 3 : (moral) fortitude
fortificar {72} *vt* : fortify —
  fortificación *nf, pl* **-ciones** : fortification
fortuito, -ta *adj* : fortuitous, chance
fortuna *nf* 1 SUERTE : fortune,
  luck 2 RIQUEZA : wealth, fortune
  3 **por fortuna** : fortunately
forzar {36} *vt* 1 : force 2 : strain (one's
  eyes) — **forzosamente** *adv* : necessarily
  — **forzoso, -sa** *adj* : necessary, inevitable
fosa *nf* 1 : pit, ditch 2 TUMBA :
  grave 3 **fosas nasales** : nostrils
fósforo *nm* 1 : phosphorus 2
  CERILLA : match — **fosforescente** *adj*
  : phosphorescent
fósil *nm* : fossil
foso *nm* 1 : ditch 2 : pit (of a
  theater) 3 : moat (of a castle)
foto *nf* : photo
fotocopia *nf* : photocopy —
  fotocopiadora *nf* : photocopier
  — **fotocopiar** *vt* : photocopy
fotogénico, -ca *adj* : photogenic
fotografía *nf* 1 : photography
  2 : photograph, picture —
  fotografiar {85} *vt* : photograph —
  fotográfico, -ca *adj* : photographic

fregadero^M con triturador^M de basura^F
sink with garbage disposal

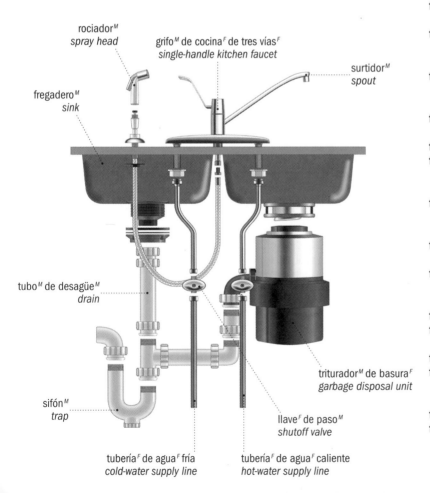

rociador^M
spray head

grifo^M de cocina^F de tres vías^F
single-handle kitchen faucet

surtidor^M
spout

fregadero^M
sink

tubo^M de desagüe^M
drain

triturador^M de basura^F
garbage disposal unit

sifón^M
trap

llave^F de paso^M
shutoff valve

tubería^F de agua^F fría
cold-water supply line

tubería^F de agua^F caliente
hot-water supply line

— **fotógrafo, -fa** *n* : photographer
fotosíntesis *nf* : photosynthesis
fracasar *vi* : fail — **fracaso** *nm* : failure
fracción *nf, pl* -**ciones 1** :
fraction **2** : faction (in politics)
— **fraccionamiento** *nm Lat*
: housing development
fractura *nf* : fracture — **fracturarse** *vr*
: fracture, break (a bone)
fragancia *nf* : fragrance, scent
— **fragante** *adj* : fragrant
fragata *nf* : frigate
frágil *adj* **1** : fragile **2** DÉBIL :
frail, delicate — **fragilidad** *nf* **1**
: fragility **2** DEBILIDAD : frailty
fragmento *nm* : fragment
fragor *nm* : clamor, din
fragoso, -sa *adj* : rough, rugged
fragua *nf* : forge — **fraguar**
{10} *vt* **1** : forge **2** IDEAR : concoct
— *vi* : harden, solidify
fraile *nm* : friar, monk
frambuesa *nf* : raspberry
francés, -cesa *adj, mpl* -**ceses** : French
— **francés** *nm* : French (language)
franco, -ca *adj* **1** : frank, candid **2** : free
(in commerce) — **franco** *nm* : franc
francotirador, -dora *n* : sniper
franela *nf* : flannel
franja *nf* **1** : stripe, band **2** FLECO : fringe
franquear *vt* **1** : clear (a path,
etc.) **2** : cross over (a doorstep,
etc.) **3** : pay postage on (mail)
— **franqueo** *nm* : postage
franqueza *nf* : frankness
frasco *nm* : small bottle, vial, flask
frase *nf* **1** : phrase **2** ORACIÓN : sentence
fraternal *adj* : brotherly, fraternal —
fraternidad *nf* : brotherhood, fraternity
— **fraternizar** {21} *vi* : fraternize —
fraterno, -na *adj* : brotherly, fraternal
fraude *nm* : fraud — **fraudulento,
-ta** *adj* : fraudulent
fray *nm* (*used in titles*) : brother, friar
frazada *nf Lat* : blanket
frecuencia *nf* **1** : frequency **2**
con frecuencia : often, frequently
— **frecuentar** *vt* : frequent, haunt
— **frecuente** *adj* : frequent
fregadero *nm* : kitchen sink
fregar {49} *vt* **1** : scrub, wash **2** *Lat
fam* : annoy — *vi Lat fam* : be a pest
freír {37} *vt* : fry
fregona *nf, Spain* : mop
frenar *vt* **1** : brake **2**

corte *M* de una fresa *F*
section of a strawberry

pedúnculo *M*
peduncle

cáliz *M*
calyx

aquenio *M*
achene

pulpa *F*
flesh

receptáculo *M*
receptacle

RESTRINGIR : curb, check
frenesí *nm* : frenzy — **frenético,
-ca** *adj* : frantic, frenzied
freno *nm* **1** : brake **2** : bit (of a bridle)
3 CONTROL : check, restraint
frente *nm* **1** : front **2** : facade (of a
building) **3** al frente de : at the head
of **4** frente a : opposite **5** de frente :
(facing) forward **6** hacer frente a : face
up to, brave — **frente** *nf* : forehead
▸ **fresa** *nf* : strawberry
fresco, -ca *adj* **1** : fresh **2** FRÍO : cool **3**
fam : insolent, nervy — **fresco** *nm* **1** :
fresh air **2** FRESCOR : coolness **3** : fresco
(art or painting) — **frescor** *nm* : coolness,
cool air — **frescura** *nf* **1** : freshness **2**
FRÍO : coolness **3** *fam* : nerve, insolence
fresno *nm* : ash (tree)
frialdad *nf* **1** : coldness **2**
INDIFERENCIA : indifference
fricción *nf, pl* -**ciones 1** : friction **2** MASAJE
: rubbing, massage — **friccionar** *vt* : rub
frigidez *nf* : frigidity
frigorífico *nm, Spain* : refrigerator
frijol *nm Lat* : bean

frío, fría *adj* **1** : cold **2** INDIFERENTE :
cool, indifferent — **frío** *nm* **1** : cold **2**
INDNDERENCIA : coldness, indifference
3 hacer frío, : be cold (outside) **4**
tener frío, : be cold, feel cold
frito, -ta *adj* **1** : fried **2** *fam* : fed up
frívolo, -la *adj* : frivolous —
frivolidad *nf* : frivolity
fronda *nf* **1** : frond **2** *or* **frondas** *nfpl* :
foliage — **frondoso, -sa** *adj* : leafy
frontera *nf* : border, frontier —
fronterizo, -za *adj* : border, on the border
— **frontero, -ra** *adj* : facing, opposite
frotar *vt* : rub — **frotarse** *vr* **frotarse
las manos** : rub one's hands
fructífero, -ra *adj* : fruitful
frugal *adj* : frugal, thrifty —
frugalidad *adj* : frugality
fruncir {83} *vt* **1** : gather (in pleats)
2 fruncir el ceño : frown **3** fruncir
la boca : purse one's lips
frustrar *vt* : frustrate — **frustrarse** *vr* : fail
— **frustración** *nf, pl* -**ciones** : frustration
— **frustrado, -da** *adj* **1** : frustrated
2 FRACASADO : failed, unsuccessful

— **frustrante** *adj* : frustrating

▸ **fruta** *nf* : fruit — **frutilla** *nf Lat* : strawberry — **fruto** *nm* **1** : fruit **2** RESULTADO : result, consequence

fucsia *adj & nm* : fuchsia

fuego *nm* **1** : fire **2** : flame, burner (on a stove) **3 fuegos artificiales** *nmpl* : fireworks **4 ¿tienes fuego?** : have you got a light?

fuelle *nm* : bellows

fuente *nf* **1** : fountain **2** MANANTIAL : spring **3** ORIGEN : source **4** PLATO : platter, serving dish

fuera *adv* **1** : outside, out **2** : abroad, away **3 fuera de** : outside of, beyond **4 fuera de** : aside from, in addition to

fuerte[1] : strong **2** : bright (of colors), loud (of sounds) **3** EXTREMO : intense **4** DURO : hard — **fuerte** *adv* **1** : strongly, hard **2** : loudly **3** MUCHO : abundantly, a lot — **fuerte** *nm* **1** : fort **2** ESPECIALIDAD : strong point

fuerza *nf* **1** : strength **2** VIOLENCIA : force **3** PODER : power, might **4 fuerzas armadas** *nfpl* : armed forces **5 a fuerza de** : by dint of **6 a la fuerza** : necessarily

fuga *nf* **1** : flight, escape **2** : fugue (in music) **3** ESCAPE : leak — **fugarse** {52} *vr* : flee, run away — **fugaz** *adj, pl* **-gaces** : fleeting — **fugitivo, -va** *adj & n* : fugitive

fulano, -na *n* : so-and-so, what's-his-name, what's-her-name

fulgor *nm* : brilliance, splendor

fulminar *vt* **1** : strike with lightning **2** : strike down (with an illness, etc.) — **fulminante** *adj* : devastating

fumar *v* : smoke — **fumarse** *vr* **1** : smoke **2** *fam* : squander — **fumador, -dora** *n* : smoker

funámbulo, -la *n* : tightrope walker

función *nf, pl* **-ciones 1** : function **2** TRABAJOS : duties *pl* **3** : performance, show (in theater) — **funcional** *adj* : functional — **funcionamiento** *nm* **1** : functioning **2 en funcionamiento** : in operation — **funcionar** *vi* **1** : function, run, work **2 no funciona** : out of order — **funcionario, -ria** *n* : civil servant, official

funda *nf* **1** : cover, sheath **2** *or* **funda de almohada** : pillowcase

fundar *vt* **1** ESTABLECER : found, establish **2** BASAR : base — **fundarse** *vr* **fundarse en** : be based on — **fundación** *nf, pl* **-ciones** : foundation — **fundador, -dora** *n* : founder

— **fundamental** *adj* : fundamental, basic — **fundamentalmente** *adv* : basically — **fundamentar** *vt* **1** : lay the foundations for **2** BASAR : base — **fundamento** *nm* **1** : foundation **2 fundamentos** *nmpl* : fundamentals

fundir *vt* **1** : melt down, smelt **2** FUSIONAR : fuse, merge — **fundirse** *vr* **1** : blend, merge **2** DERRETIRSE : melt **3** : burn out (of a lightbulb) — **fundición** *nf, pl* **-ciones 1** : smelting **2** : foundry

fúnebre *adj* **1** : funeral **2** LÚGUBRE : gloomy

funeral *adj* : funeral, funerary — **funeral** *nm* **1** : funeral **2 funerales** *nmpl* EXEQUIAS : funeral (rites) — **funeraria** *nf* : funeral home

funesto, ta *adj* : terrible, disastrous

fungir {35} *vi Lat* : act, function

furgón *nm, pl* **-gones 1** : van, truck **2** : freight car (of a train) **3 furgón de cola** : caboose — **furgoneta** *nf* : van

furia *nf* **1** CÓLERA : fury, rage **2** VIOLENCIA : violence — **furibundo, -da** *adj* : furious — **furioso, -sa** *adj* **1** : furious, irate **2** INTENSO : intense, violent — **furor** *nm* : fury

furtivo, -va *adj* : furtive

furúnculo *nm* : boil

fuselaje *nm* : fuselage

fusible *nm* : fuse

fusil *nm* : rifle — **fusilar** *vt* : shoot (by firing squad)

fusión *nf, pl* **-siones 1** : fusion **2** UNIÓN : union, merger — **fusionar** *vt* **1** : fuse **2** UNIR : merge — **fusionarse** *vr* : merge

futbol *or* **fútbol** *nm* **1** : soccer **2 futbol americano** : football — **futbolista** *nmf* : soccer player, football player

fútil *adj* : trifling, trivial

futuro, -ra *adj* : future — **futuro** *nm* : future

frutas^F: drupas^F
fruits: stone fruits

nectarina^F
nectarine

durazno^M
peach

dátil^M
date

albaricoque^M
apricot

ciruela^F
plum

cereza^F
cherry

g *nf* : g, seventh letter of the Spanish alphabet

gabán *nm, pl* **-banes** : topcoat, overcoat

gabardina *nf* **1** : trench coat, raincoat **2** : gabardine (fabric)

gabinete *nm* **1** : cabinet (in government) **2** : (professional) office

gacela *nf* : gazelle

gaceta *nf* : gazette

gachas *nfpl* : porridge

gacho, -cha *adj* : drooping

gaélico, -ca *adj* : Gaelic

gafas *nfpl* **1** : eyeglasses **2 gafas de sol** : sunglasses

gaita *nf* : bagpipes *pl*

gajo *nm* : segment (of fruit)

gala *nf* **1** : gala **2 de gala** : formal **3 hacer gala de** : display, show off **4** galas *nfpl* : finery

galáctico, -ca *adj* : galactic

galán *nm, pl* **-lanes 1** : leading man (in theater) **2** *fam* : boyfriend

galante *adj* : gallant — **galantear** *vt* : court, woo — **galantería** *nf* **1** : gallantry **2** CUMPLIDO : compliment

galápago *nm* : (aquatic) turtle

galardón *nm, pl* **-dones** : reward

▶ **galaxia** *nf* : galaxy

galera *nf* : galley

galería *nf* **1** : corridor **2** : gallery, balcony (in a theater)

galés, -lesa *adj, mpl* **-leses** : Welsh

galgo *nm* : greyhound

galimatías *nms & pl* : gibberish

gallardía *nf* **1** : bravery **2** ELEGAN-CIA : elegance — **gallardo, -da** *adj* **1** : brave **2** APUESTO : elegant, good-looking

gallego, -ga *adj* : Galician

galleta *nf* **1** : (sweet) cookie **2** : (salted) cracker

gallina *nf* **1** : hen **2 gallina de Guinea** : guinea fowl — **gallinero** *nm* : henhouse, (chicken) coop — **gallo** *nm* : rooster, cock

galón *nm, pl* **-lones 1** : gallon **2** : stripe (military insignia)

galopar *vi* : gallop — **galope** *nm* : gallop

galvanizar {21} *vt* : galvanize

gama *nf* **1** : range, spectrum **2** : scale (in music)

gamba *nf* : large shrimp, prawn

gamuza *nf* **1** : chamois (animal) **2** : chamois (leather), suede

gana *nf* **1** : desire, wish **2** APETITO : appetite **3 de buena gana** : willingly, heartily **4 de mala gana** : unwillingly **5 no**

me da la gana : I don't feel like it **6 tener ganas de** : feel like, be in the mood for

ganado *nm* **1** : cattle *pl*, livestock **2 ganado ovino** : sheep *pl* **3 ganado porcino** : swine *pl* — **ganadería** *nf* **1** : cattle raising **2** GANADO : livestock

ganador, -dora *adj* : winning — **ganador, -dora** *n* : winner

ganancia *nf* : profit

ganar *vt* **1** : earn **2** : win (in games, etc.) **3** CONSEGUIR : gain **4** ADQUERIR : get, obtain **5 ganar a algn** : win over someone, beat someone — *vi* : win — **ganarse** *vr* **1** : win, gain **2 ganarse la vida** : make a living

gancho *nm* **1** : hook **2** HORQUILLA : hairpin **3** *Lat* : (clothes) hanger

gandul, -dula *adj & n fam* : good-for-nothing — **gandul** *nm Lat* : pigeon pea

ganga *nf* : bargain

gangrena *nf* : gangrene

gángster *nmf* : gangster

ganso, -sa *n* : goose, gander *m* — **gansada** *nf* : silly thing, nonsense

gañir {38} *vi* : yelp — **gañido** *nm* : yelp

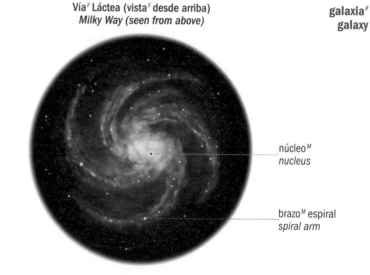

Vía*^F* Láctea (vista*^F* desde arriba)
Milky Way (seen from above)

galaxia*^F*
galaxy

núcleo*^M*
nucleus

brazo*^M* espiral
spiral arm

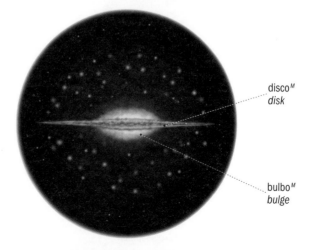

Vía*^F* Láctea (vista*^F* lateral)
Milky Way (side view)

disco*^M*
disk

bulbo*^M*
bulge

garabatear *v* : scribble —
 garabato *nm* : scribble
garaje *nm* : garage
garantizar {21} *vt* : guarantee —
 garante *nmf* : guarantor — garantía *nf* 1
 : guarantee, warranty 2 FIANZA : surety
garapiñar *vt* : candy (fruits, etc.)
garbanzo *nm* : chickpea, garbanzo
garbo *nm* : grace, elegance —
 garboso, -sa *adj* : graceful, elegant
gardenia *nf* : gardenia
garfio *nm* : hook, gaff
garganta *nf* 1 : throat 2 CUELLO :
 neck 3 DESFILADERO : ravine, gorge
 — gargantilla *nf* : necklace
gárgara *nf* 1 : gargling, gargle
 2 hacer gárgaras : gargle
gárgola *nf* : gargoyle
garita *nf* 1 : sentry box 2
 CABAÑA : cabin, hut
garito *nm* : gambling den
garra *nf* 1 : claw, talon 2 *fam* : hand, paw
garrafa *nf* : decanter, carafe
 — garrafón *nm, pl* -fones :
 large decanter or bottle
garrapata *nf* : tick
garrocha *nf* 1 : lance, pike
 2 *Lat* : pole (in sports)
garrote *nm* : club, cudgel
garúa *nf Lat* : drizzle

garza *nf* : heron
gas *nm* 1 : gas 2 gas
 lacrimógeno : tear gas
gasa *nf* : gauze
gaseosa *nf* : soda, soft drink
gasolina *nf* : gasoline, gas — gasoil *or*
 gasóleo *nm* : diesel fuel — gasolinera *nf*
 : gas station, service station
gastar *vt* 1 : spend 2 CONSUMIR :
 consume, use up 3 DESPERDICIAR :
 squander, waste — gastarse *vr* 1 : spend
 2 DETERIORARSE : wear out — gastado,
 -da *adj* 1 : spent 2 : worn-out (of clothing,
 etc.) — gastador, -dora *n* : spendthrift
 — gastos *nm* 1 : expense, expenditure
 2 gastos generales : overhead
gástrico, -ca *adj* : gastric
gastronomía *nf* : gastronomy —
 gastrónomo, -ma *n* : gourmet
gatas: a gatas *adv phr* : on all fours
gatear *vi* : crawl, creep
gatillo *nm* : trigger —
 gatillero *nm, Mex* : gunman
gato, -ta *n* : cat — gatito, -ta *n* : kitten
 — gato *nm* : jack (for an automobile)
gaucho *nm* : gaucho
gaveta *nf* : drawer
gavilla *nf* 1 : sheaf 2 PANDILLA : gang
gaviota *nf* : gull, seagull
gay *adj* : gay (homosexual)

gaza *nf* : loop
gazpacho *nm* : gazpacho
géiser *nm* : geyser
gelatina *nf* : gelatin
gema *nf* : gem
gemelo, -la *adj & n* : twin —
 gemelo *nm* 1 : cuff link 2 gemelo,
 -las *nmpl* : binoculars
gemir {54} *vi* : moan, groan, whine —
 gemido *nm* : moan, groan, whine
gen *or* gene *nm* : gene
genealogía *nf* : genealogy —
 genealógico, -ca *adj* : genealogical
generación *nf, pl* -ciones : generation
generador *nm* : generator
general *adj* 1 : general 2 en general
 or por lo general : in general,
 generally — general *nmf* : general
 — generalidad *nf* 1 : generalization
 2 MAYORÍA : majority — generalizar
 {21} *vi* : generalize — *vt* : spread (out) —
 generalizarse *vr* : become widespread
 — generalmente *adv* : usually, generally
generar *vt* : generate
género *nm* 1 : kind, sort 2 : gender (in
 grammar) 3 género humano : human
 race — genérico, -ca *adj* : generic
generoso, -sa *adj* 1 : generous,
 unselfish 2 : ample (in quantity)
 — generosidad *nf* : generosity

formas*F* geométricas: volúmenes*M*
geometrical shapes: volumes

toro*M*
torus

hemisferio*M*
hemisphere

esfera*F*
sphere

cubo*M*
cube

hélice*F*
helix

paralelepípedo*M*
parallelepiped

cilindro*M*
cylinder

pirámide*F*
pyramid

génesis *nfs & pl* : genesis
genética *nf* : genetics —
  genético, -ca *adj* : genetic
genial *adj* **1** : brilliant **2**
  ESTUPENDO : great, terrific
genio *nm* **1** : genius **2** CARÁCTER : temper,
  disposition **3** : genie (in mythology)
genital *adj* : genital —
  genitales *nmpl* : genitals
genocidio *nm* : genocide
gente *nf* **1** : people **2** *fam* :
  relatives *pl*, folks *pl* **3 ser buena**
  gente : be nice, be kind
gentil *adj* **1** AMABLE : kind **2** :
  gentile (in religion) — **gentileza** *nf*
  : kindness, courtesy
gentío *nm* : crowd, mob
gentuza *nf* : riffraff, rabble
genuflexión *nf, pl* **-xiones** : genuflection
genuino, -na *adj* : genuine
geografía *nf* : geography — **geográfico,**
  -ca *adj* : geographic, geographical
geología *nf* : geology — **geológico,**
  -ca *adj* : geologic, geological
▸ **geometría** *nf* : geometry — **geométrico,**
  -ca *adj* : geometric, geometrical
geranio *nm* : geranium
gerencia *nf* : management —
  gerente *nmf* : manager
geriatría *nf* : geriatrics —
  geriátrico, -ca *adj* : geriatric
germen *nm, pl* **gérmenes** : germ
germinar *vi* : germinate, sprout
gestación *nf, pl* **-ciones** : gestation
gesticular *vi* : gesticulate, gesture —
  gesticulación *nf, pl* **-ciones** : gesticulation
gestión *nf, pl* **-tiones** **1** : procedure,
  step **2** ADMINISTRACIÓN : management
  — **gestionar** *vt* **1** : negotiate, work
  towards **2** ADMINISTRAR : manage, handle
gesto *nm* **1** : gesture **2** : (facial)
  expression **3** MUECA : grimace
gigante *adj & nm* : giant —
  gigantesco, -ca *adj* : gigantic
gimnasia *nf* : gymnastics —
  gimnasio *nm* : gymnasium, gym
  — **gimnasta** *nmf* : gymnast
gimotear *vi* : whine, whimper
ginebra *nf* : gin
ginecología *nf* : gynecology —
  ginecólogo, -ga *n* : gynecologist
gira *nf* : tour
girar *vi* : turn (around), revolve
  — *vt* **1** : turn, twist, rotate **2** : draft
  (checks) **3** : transfer (funds)

girasol^M
sunflower

▸ **girasol** *nm* : sunflower
giratorio, -ria *adj* : revolving
giro *nm* **1** : turn, rotation **2** LOCUCIÓN
  : expression **3 giro bancario** : bank
  draft **4 giro postal** : money order
giroscopio *nm* : gyroscope
gis *nm Lat* : chalk
gitano, -na *adj & n* : Gypsy
glaciar *nm* : glacier —
  glacial *adj* : glacial, icy
gladiador *nm* : gladiator
glándula *nf* : gland
glasear *vt* : glaze, ice (cake,
  etc.) — **glaseado** *nm* : icing
glicerina *nf* : glycerin
globo *nm* **1** : globe **2** : balloon **3**
  globo ocular : eyeball — **global** *adj* **1**
  : global **2** TOTAL : total, overall
glóbulo *nm* : blood cell, corpuscle
gloria *nf* : glory
glorieta *nf* **1** : bower, arbor **2**
  Spain : rotary, traffic circle
glorificar {72} *vt* : glorify
glorioso, -sa *adj* : glorious
glosario *nm* : glossary
glotón, -tona *adj, mpl* **-tones** :
  gluttonous — **glotón, -tona** *n* :
  glutton — **glotonería** *nf* : gluttony
glucosa *nf* : glucose
gnomo *nm* : gnome
gobernar {55} *v* **1** : govern, rule **2**
  DIRIGIR : direct, manage **3** : steer (a boat,
  etc.) — **gobernación** *nf, pl* **-ciones** :
  governing, government — **gobernador,**
  -dora *n* : governor — **gobernante** *adj* :

ruling, governing — **gobernante** *n* : ruler,
  leader — **gobierno** *nm* : government
goce *nm* : enjoyment
gol *nm* : goal (in sports)
golf *nm* : golf — **golfista** *nmf* : golfer
golfo *nm* : gulf
golondrina *nf* **1** : swallow **2**
  golondrina de mar : tern
golosina *nf* : sweet, candy —
  goloso, -sa *adj* : fond of sweets
golpe *nm* **1** : blow **2** PUÑETAZO : punch
  3 : knock (on a door, etc.) **4 de golpe**
  : suddenly **5 de un golpe** : all at once
  6 golpe de estado : coup d'etat —
  golpear *vt* **1** : hit, punch **2** : slam, bang
  (a door, etc.) — *vi* : knock (at a door)
goma *nf* **1** CAUCHO : rubber **2** PEGAMENTO
  : glue **3** *or* **goma elástica** : rubber
  band **4 goma de mascar** : chewing
  gum **5 goma de borrar** : eraser
gong *nm* : gong
gordo, -da *adj* **1** : fat, plump **2** GRUESO
  : thick **3** : fatty (of meat) **4** *fam* : big,
  serious — **gordo, -da** *n* : fat person
  — **gorda** *nf Lat* : thick corn tortilla —
  gordo *nm* **1** GRASA : fat **2** : jackpot (in a
  lottery) — **gordura** *nf* : fatness, flab
gorgotear *vi* : gurgle, bubble
gorila *nm* : gorilla
gorjear *vi* **1** : chirp, tweet **2** : gurgle
  (of a baby) — **gorjeo** *nm* : chirping
gorra *nf* **1** : cap, bonnet **2**
  de gorra *fam* : for free
gorrear *vt, fam* : bum, scrounge
▸ **gorrión** *nm, pl* **-rriones** : sparrow
gorro *nm* **1** : cap, bonnet **2**
  de gorro *fam* : for free

gorrión^M
sparrow

gota *nf* 1 : drop 2 : gout (in medicine)
— **gotear** *vi* : drip, leak — **goteo** *nm*
: drip, dripping — **gotera** *nf* : leak
gótico, -ca *adj* : Gothic
gozar {21} *vi* 1 : enjoy oneself 2
gozar de algo : enjoy something
gozne *nm* : hinge
gozo *nm* 1 : joy 2 PLACER : enjoyment,
pleasure — **gozoso, -sa** *adj* : joyful, glad
grabar *vt* 1 : engrave 2 : record,
tape — **grabación** *nf, pl* -**ciones** :
recording — **grabado** *nm* : engraving
— **grabadora** *nf* : tape recorder
gracia *nf* 1 : grace 2 FAVOR : favor,
kindness 3 HUMOR : humor, wit 4
gracias *nfpl* : thanks 5 **¡(muchas)**
gracias! : thank you (very much)! —
gracioso, -sa *adj* : funny, amusing
grada *nf* 1 : step, stair 2 : row
(in a theater, etc.) 3 **gradas** *nfpl* :
bleachers, grandstand — **gradación** *nf,*
pl -**ciones** : gradation, scale —
gradería *nf* : rows *pl*, stands *pl* —
grado *nm* 1 : degree 2 : grade (in
school) 3 **de buen grado** : willingly
graduar {3} *vt* 1 : regulate, adjust 2
MARCAR : calibrate 3 : confer a degree
on (in education) — **graduarse** *vr* :
graduate (from a school) — **graduación** *nf,*
pl -**ciones** 1 : graduation 2 : alcohol
content, proof — **graduado, -da** *n* :
graduate — **gradual** *adj* : gradual —
gradualmente *adv* : little by little, gradually
gráfico, -ca *adj* : graphic —
gráfica *nf* : graph — **gráfico** *nm* 1
: graph 2 : graphic (in computers)
gragea *nf* : pill, tablet
grajo *nm* : rook (bird)
gramática *nf* : grammar —
gramatical *adj* : grammatical
gramo *nm* : gram
gran → **grande**
grana *nf* : scarlet
granada *nf* 1 : pomegranate 2
: grenade (in the military)
granate *nm* : garnet
grande *adj* (**gran** *before singular nouns*)
1 : large, big 2 ALTO : tall 3 : great (in
quality, intensity, etc.) 4 *Lat* : grown-up
— **grandeza** *nf* 1 : greatness 2 NOBLEZA :
nobility — **grandiosidad** *nf* : grandeur —
grandioso, -sa *adj* : grand, magnificent
granel: a granel *adv phr* 1 :
in bulk 2 : in abundance
granero *nm* : barn, granary

granito *nm* : granite
granizar {21} *v impers* : hail —
granizada *nf* : hailstorm — **granizado** *nm*
: iced drink — **granizo** *nm* : hail
granja *nf* : farm — **granjero, -ra** *n* : farmer
grano *nm* 1 : grain 2 SEMILLA : seed
3 : (coffee) bean 4 BARRO : pimple
granuja *nmf* : rascal
grapa *nf* : staple — **grapadora** *nf*
: stapler — **grapar** *vt* : staple
grasa *nf* 1 : grease 2 : fat (in cooking,
etc.) — **grasiento, -ta** *adj* : greasy, oily
— **graso, -sa** *adj* : fatty, greasy, oily
— **grasoso, -sa** *adj Lat* : greasy, oily
gratificar {72} *vt* 1 : give a tip or bonus
to 2 SATISFACER : gratify, satisfy —
gratificación *nf, pl* -**ciones** 1 : bonus,
tip, reward 2 SATISFACCIÓN : gratification
gratis *adv & adj* : free
gratitud *nf* : gratitude
grato, -ta *adj* : pleasant, agreeable
gratuito, -ta *adj* 1 : gratuitous,
unwarranted 2 GRATIS : free
grava *nf* : gravel
gravar *vt* 1 : tax 2 CARGAR : burden
— **gravamen** *nm, pl* -**vámenes** 1 :
burden, obligation 2 IMPUESTO : tax
grave *adj* 1 : grave, serious 2 : deep, low
(of a voice, etc.) — **gravedad** *nf* : gravity
gravilla *nf* : gravel
gravitar *vi* 1 : gravitate 2 **gravitar**
sobre : weigh on — **gravitación** *nf,*
pl -**ciones** : gravitation
gravoso, -sa *adj* : costly, burdensome
graznar *vi* : caw, quack, honk —
graznido *nm* : caw, quack, honk
gregario, -ria *adj* : gregarious
gremio *nm* : guild, (trade) union
greñas *nfpl* : shaggy hair, mop
griego, -ga *adj* : Greek —
griego *nm* : Greek (language)
grieta *nf* : crack, crevice
grifo *nm, Spain* : faucet, tap
grillete *nm* : shackle
grillo *nm* 1 : cricket 2 **grillos** *nmpl*
: fetters, shackles
grima *nf* **dar grima** : annoy, irritate
gringo, -ga *adj & n Lat*
fam : Yankee, gringo
gripe *nf or* **gripa** *nf Lat* : flu, influenza
gris *adj & nm* : gray
gritar *v* : shout, scream, cry
— **grito** *nm* 1 : shout, scream,
cry 2 **dar gritos** : shout
grosella *nf* : currant

grosería *nf* 1 : vulgar remark
2 DESCORTESÍA : rudeness —
grosero, -ra *adj* 1 : coarse,
vulgar 2 DESCORTÉS : rude
grosor *nm* : thickness
grotesco, -ca *adj* : grotesque, hideous
grúa *nf* : crane, derrick
grueso, -sa *adj* 1 : thick 2 CORPULENTO
: stout, heavy — **gruesa** *nf* : gross —
grueso *nm* 1 GROSOR : thickness 2 : main
body, mass 3 **en grueso, -sa** : wholesale
grulla *nf* : crane (bird)
grumo *nm* : lump, clot —
grumoso, -sa *adj* : lumpy
gruñir {38} *vi* 1 : growl, grunt 2 *fam* :
grumble — **gruñido** *nm* 1 : growl, grunt
2 *fam* : grumble — **gruñón, -ñona** *adj*
fam : grumpy, grouchy — **gruñón,**
-ñona *n, mpl* -**ñones** *fam* : grouch
grupa *nf* : rump, hindquarters *pl*
▸ **grupo** *nm* : group
gruta *nf* : grotto
guacamayo *nm or*
guacamaya *nf Lat* : macaw
guacamole *nm* : guacamole
guadaña *nf* : scythe
guagua *nf Lat* 1 : baby 2 AUTOBÚS : bus
guajalote, -ta *or* **guajolote,**
-ta *n Lat* : turkey
guante *nm* : glove
guapo, -pa *adj* : handsome,
good-looking
guaraní *nm* : Guarani
(language of Paraguay)
guarda *nmf* 1 : keeper, custodian
2 GUARDIÁN : security guard —
guardabarros *nms & pl* : fender —
guardabosque *nmf* : forest ranger —
guardacostas *nmfs & pl* : coast guard
vessel — **guardaespaldas** *nmfs &*
pl : bodyguard — **guardameta** *nmf*
: goalkeeper — **guardapolvo** *nm* :
overalls *pl* — **guardar** *vt* 1 : keep 2
PROTEGER : guard, protect 3 RESERVAR
: save — **guardarse** *vr* **guardase**
de 1 : refrain from 2 : guard against
— **guardarropa** *nm* 1 : cloakroom,
checkroom 2 ARMARIO : wardrobe
guardería *nf* : nursery, day-care center
guardia *nf* 1 : guard, vigilence 2 TURNO
: duty, watch — **guardia** *nmf* 1 : guard
2 *or* **guardia municipal** : police officer
— **guardián, -diana** *n, mpl* -**dianes** 1 :
guardian, keeper 2 GUARDA : security guard
guarecer {53} *vt* : shelter, protect

— **guarecerse** *vr* : take shelter

guarida *nf* **1** : den, lair (of animals) **2** : hideout (of persons)

guarnecer {53} *vt* **1** : adorn, garnish **2** : garrison (an area) — **guarnición** *nf, pl* -**ciones 1** : garnish, trimming **2** : (military) garrison

guasa *nf, fam* **1** : joke **2 de guasa** : in jest — **guasón -sona** *adj, fam* : joking, witty — **guasón, -sona** *n, mpl*-**sona** *fam* : joker

guatemalteco, -ca *adj* : Guatemalan

guayaba *nf* : guava

gubernamental *or* **gubernativo, -va** *adj* : governmental

guepardo *nm* : cheetah

güero, -ra *adj Lat* : blond, fair

guerra *nf* **1** : war, warfare **2** LUCHA : conflict, struggle — **guerrear** *vi* : wage war — **guerrero, -ra** *adj* **1** : war, fighting

2 BELICOSO : warlike — **guerrero, -ra** *n* : warrior — **guerrilla** *nf* : guerrilla warfare — **guerrillero, -ra** *adj & n* : guerrilla

gueto *nm* : ghetto

guiar {85} *vt* **1** : guide, lead **2** ACONSEJAR : advise — **guiarse** *vr* : be guided by, go by — **guía** *nf* **1** : guidebook **2** ORIENTACIÓN : guidance — **guía** *nmf* : guide, leader

guijarro *nm* : pebble

guillotina *nf* : guillotine

guinda *nf* : morello (cherry)

guiñar *vi* : wink — **guiño** *nm* : wink

guión *nm, pl* **guiones 1** : script, screenplay **2** : hyphen, dash (in punctuation) — **guionista** *nmf* : scriptwriter, screenwriter

guirnalda *nf* : garland

guisa *nf* **1** : manner, fashion **2 a guisa de** : by way of **3 de tal guisa** : in such a way

guisado *nm* : stew

guisante *nm* : pea

guisar *vt* : cook — **guiso** *nm* : stew, casserole

guitarra *nf* : guitar — **guitarrista** *nmf* : guitarist

gula *nf* : gluttony

gusano *nm* **1** : worm **2** : maggot (larva)

gustar *vt* **1** : taste **2** *Lat* : like — *vi* **1** : be pleasing **2 como guste** : as you like **3 me gustan los dulces** : I like sweets — **gusto** *nm* **1** : taste **2** PLACER : pleasure, liking **3 a gusto** : comfortable, at ease **4 al gusto** : to taste **5 mucho gusto** : pleased to meet you — **gustoso, -sa** *adj* **1** : tasty **2** AGRADABLE : pleasant **3 hacer algo gustoso** : do something willingly

gutural *adj* : guttural

grupos^{*M*} **musicales**
instrumental groups

sexteto^{*M*}
sextet

cuarteto^{*M*}
quartet

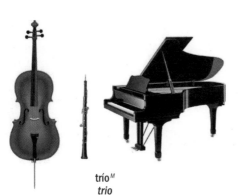

trío^{*M*}
trio

dúo^{*M*}
duo

h *nf* : h, eighth letter of the Spanish alphabet

haba *nf* : broad bean

habanero, -ra *adj* : Havanan — **habano** *nm* : Havana cigar

haber {39} *v aux* **1** : have, has **2 haber de** : must — *v impers* **1** hay : there is, there are **2 hay que** : it is necessary (to) **3 ¿qué hay?** *or* **¿qué hubo?** : how's it going? — **haber** *nm* **1** : assets *pl* **2** : credit side (in accounting) **3 haberes** *nmpl* : income, earnings

habichuela *nf* **1** : bean **2 habichuela verde** : string bean

hábil *adj* **1** : able, skillful **2** LISTO : clever **3 horas hábiles** : business hours — **habilidad** *nf* : ability, skill

habilitar *vt* **1** : equip, furnish

2 AUTORIZAR : authorize

habitar *vt* : inhabit — *vi* : reside, dwell — **habitable** *adj* : habitable, inhabitable — **habitación** *nf, pl* **-ciones 1** : room, bedroom **2** MORADA : dwelling, abode **3** : habitat (in biology) — **habitante** *nmf* : inhabitant, resident — **hábitat** *nm* : habitat

hábito *nm* : habit — **habitual** *adj* : habitual, usual — **habituar** {3} *vt* : accustom, habituate — **habituarse** *vr* **habituarse a** : get used to

hablar *vi* **1** : speak, talk **2 hablar de** : mention, talk about **3 hablar con** : talk to, speak with — *vt* **1** : speak (a language) **2** DISCUTIR : discuss — **hablarse** *vr* **1** : speak to each other **2 se habla inglés** : English spoken — **habla** *nf* **1** : speech **2** IDIOMA : language, dialect **3 de habla**

inglesa : English-speaking — **hablador, -dora** *adj* : talkative — **hablador, -dora** *n* : chatterbox — **habladuría** *nf* **1** : rumor **2 habladurías** *nfpl* : gossip — **hablante** *nmf* : speaker

hacedor, -dora *n* : creator, maker

hacendado, -da *n* : landowner, rancher

hacer {40} *vt* **1** : do, perform **2** CONSTRUIR, CREAR : make **3** OBLIGAR : force, oblige — *vi* : act — *v impers* **1 hacer calor/ viento** : be hot/be windy **2 hacer falta** : be necessary **3 hace mucho tiempo** : a long time ago **4 no lo hace** : it doesn't matter — **hacerse** *vr* **1** VOLVERSE : become **2** : pretend (to be) **3 hacerse a** : get used to **4 se hace tarde** : it's getting late

hacha *nf* **1** : hatchet, ax **2** ANTORCHA : torch

complejo^M hidroeléctrico
hydroelectric complex

aliviadero^M
spillway

tubería^F de carga^F
penstock

embalse^M
reservoir

presa^F
dam

central^F eléctrica
power plant

sala^F de máquinas^F
machine hall

boquilla^F
bushing

sala^F de control^M
control room

hachís *nm* : hashish
hacia *prep* **1** : toward, towards **2** CERCA DE : near, around, about **3 hacia abajo** : downward **4 hacia adelante** : forward
hacienda *nf* **1** : estate, ranch **2** BIENES : property **3** *Lat* : livestock **4 Hacienda** : department of revenue
hacinar *vt* : stack
hada *nf* : fairy
hado *nm* : fate
halagar {52} *vt* : flatter — **halagador, -dora** *adj* : flattering — **halago** *nm* : flattery — **halagüeño, -ña** *adj* **1** : flattering **2** PROMETEDOR : promising
halcón *nm, pl* **-cones** : hawk, falcon
halibut *nm, pl* **-buts** : halibut
hálito *nm* : breath
hallar *vt* **1** : find **2** DESCUBRIR : discover, find out — **hallarse** *vr* : be, find oneself — **hallazgo** *nm* : discovery, find
halo *nm* : halo
hamaca *nf* : hammock
hambre *nf* **1** : hunger **2** INANICIÓN : starvation, famine **3 tener hambre** : be hungry — **hambriento, -ta** *adj* : hungry, starving — **hambruna** *nf* : famine
hamburguesa *nf* : hamburger
hampa *nf* : underworld — **hampón, -pona** *n, mpl* **-pones** : criminal, thug
hámster *nm* : hamster
hándicap *nm* : handicap (in sports)
hangar *nm* : hangar
haragán, -gana *adj, mpl* **-ganes** : lazy, idle — **haragán, -gana** *n* : slacker, idler — **haraganear** : be lazy, loaf
harapiento, -ta *adj* : ragged, in rags — **harapos** *nmpl* : rags, tatters
harina *nf* : flour
hartar *vt* **1** : glut, satiate **2** FASTIDIAR : annoy — **hartarse** *vr* **1** : gorge oneself **2** CANSARSE : get fed up — **harto, -ta** *adj* **1** : full, satiated **2** CANSADO : tired, fed up — **harto** *adv* : extremely, very — **hartura** *nf* **1** : surfeit **2** ABUNDANCIA : abundance, plenty
hasta *prep* **1** : until, up until (in time) **2** : as far as, up to (in space) **3 ¡hasta luego!** : see you later! **4 hasta que** : until — **hasta** *adv* : even
hastiar {85} *vt* **1** : make weary, bore **2** ASQUEAR : sicken — **hastiarse** *vr* **hastiarse de** : get tired of — **hastío** *nm* **1** : weariness, tedium **2** REPUGNANCIA : disgust
hato *nm* **1** : flock, herd **2** : bundle (of possessions)

haya *nf* : beech
haz *nm, pl* **haces** **1** : bundle, sheaf **2** : beam (of light)
hazaña *nf* : feat, exploit
hazmerreír *nm, fam* : laughingstock
he {39} *v impers* **he aquí** : here is, here are, behold
hebilla *nf* : buckle
hebra *nf* : strand, thread
hebreo, -brea *adj* : Hebrew — **hebreo** *nm* : Hebrew (language)
hecatombe *nm* : disaster
hechizo *nm* **1** : spell **2** ENCANTO : charm, fascination — **hechicería** *nf* : sorcery, witchcraft — **hechicero, -ra** *n* : sorcerer, sorceress *f* — **hechizar** {21} *vt* **1** : bewitch **2** CAUTIVAR : charm
hecho, -cha *adj* **1** : made, done **2** : ready-to-wear (of clothing) **3 hecho, -cha y derecho** : full-fledged, mature — **hecho** *nm* **1** : fact **2** SUCESO : event **3** ACTO : act, deed **4 de hecho** : in fact — **hechura** *nf* **1** : making, creation **2** FORMA : shape, form **3** : build (of the body) **4** ARTESANÍA : workmanship
heder {56} *vi* : stink, reek — **hediondez** *nf, pl* **-deces** : stench — **hediondo, -da** *adj* : stinking — **hedor** *nm* : stench
helar {55} *v* : freeze — **helarse** *vr* : freeze up, freeze over — **helado, -da** *adj* **1** : freezing cold **2** CONGELADO : frozen — **helada** *nf* : frost — **heladería** *nf* : ice-cream parlor — **helado** *nm* : ice cream — **heladora** *nf* : freezer
helecho *nm* : fern
hélice *nf* **1** : propeller **2** ESPIRAL : spiral, helix
helicóptero *nm* : helicopter
helio *nm* : helium
hembra *nf* **1** : female **2** MUJER : woman
hemisferio *nm* : hemisphere
hemorragia *nf* **1** : hemorrhage **2 hemorragia nasal** : nosebleed
hemorroides *nfpl* : hemorrhoids, piles
henchir {54} *vt* : stuff, fill
hender {56} *vt* : cleave, split — **hendidura** *nf* : crevice, fissure
henequén *nm, pl* **-quenes** : sisal
heno *nm* : hay
hepatitis *nf* : hepatitis
heraldo *nm* : herald
herbolario, -ria *n* : herbalist
heredar *vt* : inherit — **heredad** *nm* : rural property, estate — **heredero,**

-ra *n* : heir, heiress *f* — **hereditario, -ria** *adj* : hereditary
hereje *nmf* : heretic — **herejía** *nf* : heresy
herencia *nf* **1** : inheritance **2** : heredity (in biology)
herir {76} *vt* **1** : injure, wound **2** : hurt (feelings, pride, etc.) — **herida** *nf* : injury, wound — **herido, -da** *adj* **1** : injured, wounded **2** : hurt (of feelings, pride, etc.) — **herido, -da** *n* : injured person, casualty
hermano, -na *n* : brother *m*, sister *f* — **hermanastro, -tra** *n* : half brother *m*, half sister *f* — **hermandad** *nf* : brotherhood
hermético, -ca *adj* : hermetic, watertight
hermoso, -sa *adj* : beautiful, lovely — **hermosura** *nf* : beauty
hernia *nf* : hernia
héroe *nm* : hero — **heroico, -ca** *adj* : heroic — **heroína** *nf* **1** : heroine **2** : heroin (narcotic) — **heroísmo** *nm* : heroism
herradura *nf* : horseshoe
herramienta *nf* : tool
herrero, -ra *n* : blacksmith
herrumbre *nf* : rust
hervir {76} *v* : boil — **hervidero** *nm* **1** : mass, swarm **2** : hotbed (of intrigue, etc.) — **hervidor** *nm* : kettle — **hervor** *nm* **1** : boiling **2** ENTUSIASMO : fervor, ardor
heterogéneo, -nea *adj* : heterogeneous
heterosexual *adj & nmf* : heterosexual
hexágono *nm* : hexagon — **hexagonal** *adj* : hexagonal
hez *nf, pl* **heces** : dregs *pl*, scum
hiato *nm* : hiatus
hibernar *vi* : hibernate — **hibernación** *nf, pl* **-ciones** : hibernation
híbrido, -da *adj* : hybrid — **híbrido** *nm* : hybrid
hidalgo, -ga *n* : nobleman *m*, noblewoman *f*
hidratante *adj* : moisturizing
hidrato *nm* **hidrato de carbono** : carbohydrate
hidráulico, -ca *adj* : hydraulic
hidroavión *nm, pl* **-aviones** : seaplane
▸ **hidroeléctrico, -ca** *adj* : hydroelectric
hidrofobia *nf* : rabies
hidrógeno *nm* : hydrogen
hidroplano *nm* : hydroplane
hiedra *nf* **1** : ivy **2 hiedra venenosa** : poison ivy
hiel *nm* **1** : bile **2** AMARGURA : bitterness
hielo *nm* **1** : ice **2** FRIALDAD : coldness **3 romper el hielo** : break the ice

hiena *nf* : hyena

hierba *nf* **1** : herb **2** CÉSPED : grass **3 mala hierba** : weed — **hierbabuena** *nf* : mint

hierro *nm* **1** : iron **2 hierro fundido** : cast iron

hígado *nm* : liver

higiene *nf* : hygiene — **higiénico, -ca** *adj* : hygienic

higo *nm* : fig

hijo, -ja *n* **1** : son *m*, daughter *f* **2** hijos *nmpl* : children, offspring — **hijastro, -tra** *n* : stepson *m*, stepdaughter *f*

hilar *v* **1** : spin **2 hilar delgado** : split hairs — **hilado** *nm* : yarn, thread

hilaridad *nf* : hilarity

hilera *nf* : file, row

hilo *nm* **1** : thread **2** LINO : linen **3** ALAMBRE : wire **4** : trickle (of water, etc.) **5 hilo dental** : dental floss

hilvanar *vt* **1** : baste, tack **2** : put together (ideas, etc.)

himno *nm* **1** : hymn **2 himno nacional** : national anthem

hincapié *nm* **hacer hincapié en** : emphasize, stress

hincar {72} *vt* : drive in, plunge — **hincarse** *vr* **hincarse de rodillas** : kneel (down)

hinchar *vt, Spain* : inflate, blow up — **hincharse** *vr* **1** : swell (up) **2** *Spain fam* : stuff oneself — **hinchado, -da** *adj* **1** : swollen **2** POMPOSO : pompous — **hinchazón** *nf, pl* **-zones** : swelling

hindú *adj & nmf* : Hindu — **hinduismo** *nm* : Hinduism

hinojo *nm* : fennel

hiperactivo, -va *adj* : hyperactive

hipersensible *adj* : oversensitive

hipertensión *nf, pl* **-siones** : hypertension, high blood pressure

hípico, -ca *adj* : equestrian, horse

hipil → **huipil**

hipnosis *nfs & pl* : hypnosis — **hipnótico, -ca** *adj* : hypnotic — **hipnotismo** *nm* : hypnotism — **hipnotizador, -dora** *n* : hypnotist — **hipnotizar** {21} *vt* : hypnotize

hipo *nm* **1** : hiccup, hiccups *pl* **2 tener hipo** : have hiccups

hipocondríaco, -ca *adj* : hypochondriacal — **hipocondríaco, -ca** *n* : hypochondriac

hipocresía *nf* : hypocrisy — **hipócrita** *adj* : hypocritical — **hipocresía** *nmf* : hypocrite

hipodérmico, -ca *adj* : hypodermic

hipódromo *nm* : racetrack

hipopótamo *nm* : hippopotamus

hipoteca *nf* : mortgage — **hipotecar** {72} *vt* : mortgage

hipótesis *nfs & pl* : hypothesis — **hipotético, -ca** *adj* : hypothetical

hiriente *adj* : hurtful, offensive

hirsuto, -ta *adj* **1** : hairy **2** : bristly, wiry (of hair)

hirviente *adj* : boiling

hispano, -na *or* **hispánico, -ca** *adj & n* : Hispanic — **hispanoamericano, -na** *adj* : Latin-American — **hispanoamericano, -na** *n* : Latin American — **hispanohablante** *or* hispanoparlante *adj* : Spanish-speaking

histeria *nf* : hysteria — **histérico, -ca** *adj* : hysterical — **histerismo** *nm* : hysteria

historia *nf* **1** : history **2** CUENTO : story — **historiador, -dora** *n* : historian — **historial** *nm* : record, background — **histórico, -ca** *adj* **1** : historical **2** IMPORTANTE : historic, important — **historieta** *nf* : comic strip

hito *nm* : milestone, landmark

hocico *nm* : snout, muzzle

hockey *nm* : hockey

hogar *nm* **1** : home **2** CHIMENEA : hearth, fireplace — **hogareño, -ña** *adj* **1** : home-loving **2** DOMÉSTICO : home, domestic

hoguera *nf* : bonfire

hoja *nf* **1** : leaf **2** : sheet (of paper) **3 hoja de afeitar** : razor blade — **hojalata** *nf* : tinplate — **hojaldre** *nm* : puff pastry — **hojear** *vt* : leaf through — **hojuela** *nf Lat* : flake

hola *interj* : hello!, hi!

holandés, -desa *adj, mpl* **-deses** : Dutch

holgado, -da *adj* **1** : loose, baggy **2** : comfortable (of an economic situation, a victory, etc.) — **holgazán, -zana** *adj* : lazy — **holgazán, -zana** *n, nmpl* **-zanes** : slacker, idler — **holgazanear** *vi* : laze about, loaf — **holgura** *nf* **1** : looseness **2** BIENESTAR : comfort, ease

hollín *nm, pl* **-llines** : soot

holocausto *nm* : holocaust

hombre *nm* **1** : man **2 el hombre** : mankind **3 hombre de estado** : statesman **4 hombre de negocios** : businessman

hombrera *nf* **1** : shoulder pad **2** : epaulet (of a uniform)

hombría *nf* : manliness

hombro *nm* : shoulder

hombruno, -na *adj* : mannish

homenaje *nm* **1** : homage **2 rendir**

homenaje a : pay tribute to

homeopatía *nf* : homeopathy

homicidio *nm* : homicide, murder — **homicida** *adj* : homicidal, murderous — **homicidio** *nmf* : murderer

homogéneo, -nea *adj* : homogeneous

homólogo, -ga *adj* : equivalent — **homólogo, -ga** *n* : counterpart

homosexual *adj & nmf* : homosexual — **homosexualidad** *nf* : homosexuality

hondo, -da *adj* : deep — **hondo** *adv* : deeply — **hondonada** *nf* : hollow — **hondura** *nf* : depth

hondureño, -ña *adj* : Honduran

honesto, -ta *adj* : decent, honorable — **honestidad** *nf* : honesty, integrity

hongo *nm* **1** : mushroom **2** : fungus (in botany and medicine)

honor *nm* : honor — **honorable** *adj* : honorable — **honorario, -ria** *adj* : honorary — **honorarios** *nmpl* : payment, fee — **honra** *nf* : honor — **honradez** *nf, pl* **-deces** : honesty, integrity — **honrado, -da** *adj* : honest, upright — **honrar** *vt* : honor — **honrarse** *vr* : be honored — **honroso, -sa** *adj* : honorable

hora *nf* **1** : hour **2** : (specific) time **3** CITA : appointment **4 a la última hora** : at the last minute **5 hora punta** : rush hour **6 media hora** : half an hour **7 ¿qué hora es?** : what time is it? **8 horas de oficina** : office hours **9 horas extraordinarias** : overtime

horario *nm* : schedule, timetable

horca *nf* **1** : gallows *pl* **2** : pitchfork (in agriculture)

horcajadas: a horcajadas *adv phr* : astride

horda *nf* : horde

horizonte *nm* : horizon — **horizontal** *adj* : horizontal

horma *nf* **1** : form, mold, last **2** : shoe tree

hormiga *nf* : ant

hormigón *nm, pl* **-gones** : concrete

hormigueo *nm* : tingling, pins and needles

hormiguero *nm* **1** : anthill **2** : swarm (of people)

hormona *nf* : hormone

horno *nm* **1** : oven (for cooking) **2** : small furnace, kiln — **hornada** *nf* : batch — **hornear** *vt* : bake — **hornillo** *nf* : portable stove

horóscopo *nm* : horoscope

horquilla *nf* **1** : hairpin, bobby

pin **2** HORCA : pitchfork
horrendo, -da *adj* : horrendous, awful — **horrible** *adj* : horrible — **horripilante** *adj* : horrifying — **horror** *nm* **1** : horror, dread **2** ATROCIDAD : atrocity — **horrorizar** {21} *vt* : horrify, terrify — **horrorizarse** *vr* : be horrified — **horroroso, -sa** *adj* : horrifying, dreadful
hortaliza *nf* : (garden) vegetable — **hortelano, -na** *n* : truck farmer — **horticultura** *nf* : horticulture
hosco, -ca *adj* : sullen, gloomy
hospedar *vt* : put up, lodge — **hospedarse** *vr* : stay, lodge — **hospedaje** *nm* : lodging
hospital *nm* : hospital — **hospitalario, -ria** *adj* : hospitable — **hospitalidad** *nf* : hospitality — **hospitalizar** {21} *vt* : hospitalize
hostería *nf* : small hotel, inn
hostia *nf* : host (in religion)
hostigar {52} *vt* **1** : whip **2** ACOSAR : harass, pester
hostil *adj* : hostile — **hostilidad** *nf* : hostility
hotel *nm* : hotel — **hotelero, -ra** *adj* : hotel — **hotelero, -ra** *n* : hotel manager, hotelier
hoy *adv* **1** : today **2 de hoy en adelante** : from now on **3 hoy (en) día** : nowadays **4 hoy mismo** : this very day
hoyo *nm* : hole — **hoyuelo** *nm* : dimple
hoz *nf, pl* **hoces** : sickle
huarache *nm* : huarache (sandal)
hueco, -ca *adj* **1** : hollow, empty **2** ESPONJOSO : soft, spongy **3** RESONANTE : resonant — **hueco** *nm* **1** : hollow, cavity **2** : recess (in a wall, etc.) **3 hueco de escalera** : stairwell
huelga *nf* **1** : strike **2 declararse en huelga** : go on strike — **huelguista** *nmf* : striker
huella *nf* **1** : footprint **2** VESTIGIO : track, mark **3 huella digital** *or* **huella dactilar** : fingerprint
huérfano, -na *n* : orphan — **huérfano, -na** *adj* : orphaned
huerta *nf* : truck farm — **huerto** *nm* **1** : vegetable garden **2** : (fruit) orchard
hueso *nm* **1** : bone **2** : pit, stone (of a fruit)
huésped, -peda *n* : guest — **huésped** *nm* : host (organism)
huesudo, -da *adj* : bony
▸ **huevo** *nm* **1** : egg **2 huevos estrellados** : fried eggs **3 huevos revueltos** :

scrambled eggs — **hueva** *nf* : roe
huida *nf* : flight, escape — **huidizo, -za** *adj* **1** : shy **2** FUGAZ : fleeting
huipil *nm Lat* : traditional embroidered blouse or dress
huir {41} *vi* **1** : escape, flee **2 huir de** : shun, avoid
hule *nm* **1** : oilcloth **2** *Lat* : rubber
humano, -na *adj* **1** : human **2** COMPASIVO : humane — **humano** *nm* : human (being) — **humanidad** *nf* **1** : humanity, mankind **2** BENEVOLENCIA : humaneness **3 humanidads** *nfpl* : humanities — **humanismo** *nm* : humanism — **humanista** *nmf* : humanist — **humanitario, -ria** *adj & n* : humanitarian
humear *vi* : smoke, steam — **humareda** *nf* : cloud of smoke
humedad *nf* **1** : dampness **2** : humidity (in meteorology) — **humedecer** {53} *vt* : moisten, dampen — **humedecerse** *vr* : become moist — **húmedo, -da** *adj* **1** : moist, damp **2** : humid (in meteorology)
humildad *nf* : humility — **humilde** *adj* : humble — **humillación** *nf, pl* **-ciones** : humiliation — **humillante** *adj* : humiliating — **humillar** *vt* : humiliate

— **humillarse** *vr* : humble oneself
humo *nm* **1** : smoke, steam, fumes **2 humos** *nmpl* : airs, conceit
humor *nm* **1** : mood, temper **2** GRACIA : humor **3 de buen humor** : in a good mood — **humorismo** *nm* : humor, wit — **humorista** *nmf* : humorist, comedian — **humorístico, -ca** *adj* : humorous
hundir *vt* **1** : sink **2** : destroy, ruin (a building, plans, etc.) — **hundirse** *vr* **1** : sink **2** DERRUMBARSE : collapse — **hundido, -da** *adj* : sunken — **hundimiento** *nm* **1** : sinking **2** DERRUMBE : collapse
húngaro, -ra *adj* : Hungarian
huracán *nm, pl* **-canes** : hurricane
huraño, -ña *adj* : unsociable
hurgar {52} *vi* **hurgar en** : rummage around in
hurón *nm, pl* **-rones** : ferret
hurra *interj* : hurrah!, hooray!
hurtadillas: a hurtadillas *adv phr* : stealthily, on the sly
hurtar *vt* : steal — **hurto** *nm* **1** ROBO : theft **2** : stolen property
husmear *vt* : sniff out, pry into — *vi* : nose around
huy *interj* : ow!, ouch!

huevos ᴹ
eggs

huevo ᴹ de codorniz ᶠ
quail egg

huevo ᴹ de faisán ᴹ
pheasant egg

huevo ᴹ de oca ᶠ
goose egg

huevo ᴹ de gallina ᶠ
hen egg

huevo ᴹ de avestruz ᴹ
ostrich egg

i *nf* : i, ninth letter of the Spanish alphabet
ibérico, -ca *adj* : Iberian — **ibero, -ra** *or* **íbero, -ra** *adj* : Iberian
iceberg *nm, pl* **-bergs** : iceberg
icono *nm* : icon
ictericia *nf* : jaundice
ida *nf* **1** : outward journey **2 ida y vuelta** : round-trip **3 idas y venidas** : comings and goings
idea *nf* **1** : idea **2** OPINIÓN : opinion
ideal *adj & nm* : ideal — **idealismo** *nm* : idealism — **idealista** *adj* : idealistic — **idealista** *nmf* : idealist

— **idealizar** {21} *vt* : idealize
idear *vt* : devise, think up
ídem *nm* : the same, ditto
identidad *nf* : identity — **idéntico, -ca** *adj* : identical — **identificar** {72} *vt* : identify — **identificarse** *vr* **1** : identify oneself **2 identificarse con** : identify with — **identificación** *nf, pl* **-ciones** : identification
ideología *nf* : ideology — **ideológico, -ca** *adj* : ideological
idílico, -ca *adj* : idyllic
idioma *nm* : language — **idiomático,**

-ca *adj* : idiomatic
idiosincrasia *nf* : idiosyncrasy — **idiosincrásico, -ca** *adj* : idiosyncratic
idiota *adj* : idiotic — **idiota** *nmf* : idiot — **idiotez** *nf* : idiocy
ídolo *nm* : idol — **idolatrar** *vt* : idolize — **idolatría** *nf* : idolatry
idóneo, -nea *adj* : suitable, fitting — **idoneidad** *nf* : fitness, suitability
▸ **iglesia** *nf* : church
iglú *nm* : igloo
ignición *nf, pl* **-ciones** : ignition
ignífugo, -ga *adj* :

iglesia^F
church

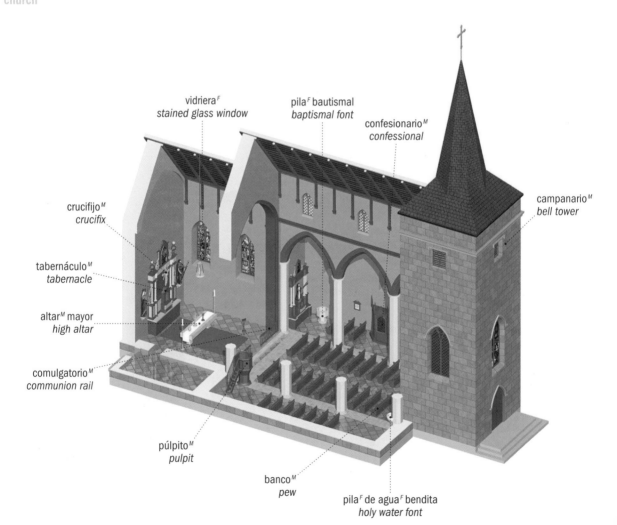

vidriera^F
stained glass window

pila^F bautismal
baptismal font

confesionario^M
confessional

crucifijo^M
crucifix

campanario^M
bell tower

tabernáculo^M
tabernacle

altar^M mayor
high altar

comulgatorio^M
communion rail

púlpito^M
pulpit

banco^M
pew

pila^F de agua^F bendita
holy water font

fire-resistant, fireproof
ignorar *vt* **1** : ignore **2** DESCONOCER
: be unaware of — **ignorancia** *nf* :
ignorance — **ignorante** *adj* : ignorant
— **ignorante** *nmf* : ignorant person
igual *adv* **1** : in the same way **2 por
igual** : equally — **igual** *adj* **1** : equal
2 IDÉNTICO : the same **3** LISO : smooth,
even **4** SEMEJANTE : similar — **igual** *nmf* :
equal, peer — **igualar** *vt* **1** : make equal
2 : be equal to **3** NIVELAR : level (off) —
igualdad *nf* **1** : equality **2** UNIFORMIDAD :
uniformity — **igualmente** *adv* : likewise
iguana *nf* : iguana
ijada *nf* : flank
ilegal *adj* : illegal
ilegible *adj* : illegible
ilegítimo, -ma *adj* : illegitimate
— **ilegitimidad** *nf* : illegitimacy
ileso, -sa *adj* : unharmed
ilícito, -ta *adj* : illicit
ilimitado, -da *adj* : unlimited
ilógico, -ca *adj* : illogical
iluminar *vt* : illuminate — **iluminarse** *vr*
: light up — **iluminación** *nf, pl* **-ciones**
1 : illumination **2** ALUMBRADO : lighting
ilusionar *vt* : excite — **ilusionarse** *vr*
: get one's hopes up — **ilusión** *nf,
pl* **-siones 1** : illusion **2** ESPERANZA :
hope — **ilusionado, -da** *adj* : excited
iluso -sa *adj* : naïve, gullible —
iluso -sa *n* : dreamer, visionary
— **ilusorio, -ria** *adj* : illusory
ilustrar *vt* **1** : illustrate **2** ACLARAR :
explain — **ilustración** *nf, pl* **-ciones**
1 : illustration **2** SABER : learning **3 la
Ilustración** : the Enlightenment —
ilustrado, -da *adj* **1** : illustrated **2** ERUDITO
: learned — **ilustrador, -dora** *n* : illustrator
ilustre *adj* : illustrious
imagen *nf, pl* **imágenes** : image, picture
imaginar *vt* : imagine — **imaginarse** *vr*
: imagine — **imaginación** *nf,
pl* **-ciones** : imagination —
imaginario, -ria *adj* : imaginary —
imaginativo, -va *adj* : imaginative
imán *nm, pl* **imanes** : magnet
— **imantar** *vt* : magnetize
imbécil *adj* : stupid, idiotic
— **imbécil** *nmf* : idiot
imborrable *adj* : indelible
imbuir {41} *vt* **imbuir de** : imbue with
imitar *vt* **1** COPIAR : imitate, copy **2** :
impersonate — **imitación** *nf, pl* **-ciones**
1 COPIA : imitation, copy **2** : impersonation

— **imitador, -dora** *n* : impersonator
impaciencia *nf* : impatience —
impacientar *vt* : make impatient,
exasperate — **impacientarse** *vr* : grow
impatient — **impaciente** *adj* : impatient
impacto *nm* : impact
impar *adj* : odd — **impar** *nm* : odd number
imparcial *adj* : impartial —
imparcialidad *nf* : impartiality
impartir *vt* : impart, give
impasible *adj* : impassive
impasse *nm* : impasse
impávido, -da *adj* : fearless
impecable *adj* : impeccable, spotless
impedir {54} *vt* **1** : prevent **2**
DIFICULTAR : impede, hinder —
impedido, -da *adj* : disabled —
impedimento *nm* : obstacle, impediment
impeler *vt* : drive, propel
impenetrable *adj* : impenetrable
impenitente *adj* : unrepentant
impensable *adj* : unthinkable —
impensado, -da *adj* : unexpected
imperar *vi* **1** : reign, rule **2** PREDOMINAR
: prevail — **imperante** *adj* : prevailing
imperativo, -va *adj* : imperative
— **imperativo** *nm* : imperative
imperceptible *adj* : imperceptible
imperdible *nm* : safety pin
imperdonable *adj* : unforgivable
imperfección *nf, pl* **-ciones** :
imperfection — **imperfecto, -ta** *adj*
: imperfect — **imperfecto** *nm*
: imperfect (tense)
imperial *adj* : imperial —
imperialismo *nm* : imperialism —
imperialista *adj & nmf* : imperialist
impericia *nf* : lack of skill
imperio *nm* **1** : empire **2** DOMINIO : rule
— **imperioso, -sa** *adj* **1** : imperious
2 URGENTE : pressing, urgent
impermeable *adj* **1** : waterproof
2 impermeable a : impervious to
— **impermeable** *nm* : raincoat
impersonal *adj* : impersonal
impertinente *adj* : impertinent —
impertinencia *nf* : impertinence
ímpetu *nm* **1** : impetus **2** ENERGÍA :
energy, vigor **3** VIOLENCIA : force —
impetuoso, -sa *adj* : impetuous —
impetuosidad *nf* : impetuosity
impío, -pía *adj* : impious, ungodly
implacable *adj* : implacable
implantar *vt* **1** : implant **2**
ESTABLECER : establish, introduce

implemento *nm Lat* : implement, tool
implicar {72} *vt* **1** : involve, implicate
2 SIGNIFICAR : imply — **implicación** *nf,
pl* **-ciones** : implication
implícito, -ta *adj* : implicit
implorar *vt* : implore
imponer {60} *vt* **1** : impose **2** :
command (respect, etc.) — *vi* : be
imposing — **imponerse** *vr* **1** : assert
oneself, command respect **2** PREVALECER
: prevail — **imponente** *adj* : imposing,
impressive — **imponible** *adj* : taxable
impopular *adj* : unpopular —
impopularidad *nf* : unpopularity
importación *nf, pl* **-ciones 1** :
importation **2** importaciones *nfpl* :
imports — **importado, -da** *adj* : imported
— **importador, -dora** *adj* : importing
— **importador, -dora** *n* : importer
importancia *nf* : importance
— **importante** *adj* : important —
importar *vi* **1** : matter, be important **2
no me importa** : I don't care — *vt* **1** :
import **2** ASCENDER A : amount to, cost
importe *nm* **1** : price **2**
CANTIDAD : sum, amount
importunar *vt* : bother —
importuno, -na *adj* **1** : inopportune
2 MOLESTO : bothersome
imposible *adj* : impossible —
imposibilidad *nf* : impossibility
imposición *nf, pl* **-ciones 1** :
imposition **2** IMPUESTO : tax
impostor, -tora *n* : impostor
impotente *adj* : powerless, impotent
— **impotencia** *nf* : impotence
impracticable *adj* **1** : impracticable
2 INTRANSITABLE : impassable
impreciso, -sa *adj* : vague, imprecise
— **imprecisión** *nf, pl* **-siones 1** :
vagueness **2** ERROR : inaccuracy
impredecible *adj* : unpredictable
impregnar *vt* : impregnate
imprenta *nf* **1** : printing **2**
: printing shop, press
imprescindible *adj* :
essential, indispensable
impresión *nf, pl* **-siones 1** : impression **2**
IMPRENTA : printing — **impresionable** *adj*
: impressionable — **impresionante** *adj* :
impressive — **impresionar** *vt* **1** : impress
2 CONMOVER : affect, move — *vi* : make an
impression — **impresionarse** *vr* **1** : be
impressed **2** CONMOVERSE : be affected
impreso, -sa *adj* : printed

impresoras^F
printers

impresora^F de líneas^F
combination printer and scanner

indicador^M de alimentación^F
power light

botón^M de avance/parada
on-off button

bandeja^F de alimentación^F
input tray

impresora^F láser
laser printer

bandeja^F de alimentación^F
output tray

guía^F papel^M
paper guide

bandeja^F de alimentación^F
input tray

— **impreso** *nm* **1** FORMULARIO : form
2 impreso, -sas *nmpl* : printed matter
— **impresor, -sora** *n* : printer —
▸ **impresora** *nf* : (computer) printer
imprevisible *adj* : unforeseeable
— **imprevisto, -ta** *adj* :
unexpected, unforeseen
imprimir {42} *vt* **1** : print
2 DAR : impart, give
improbable *adj* : improbable —
improbabilidad *nf* : improbability
improcedente *adj* : inappropriate
improductivo, -va *adj* : unproductive
improperio *nm* : insult

impropio, -pia *adj* **1** : inappropriate
2 INCORRECTO : incorrect
improvisar *v* : improvise —
improvisado, -da *adj* : improvised,
impromptu — **improvisación** *nf,*
pl **-ciones** : improvisation — **improviso**:
de improvisar *adv phr* : suddenly
imprudente *adj* : imprudent,
rash — **imprudencia** *nf* :
imprudence, carelessness
impúdico, -ca *adj* : shameless, indecent
impuesto *nm* **1** : tax **2 impuesto**
sobre la renta : income tax
impugnar *vt* : challenge, contest

impulsar *vt* : propel, drive —
impulsividad *nf* : impulsiveness
— **impulsivo, -va** *adj* : impulsive
— **impulso** *nm* **1** : drive, thrust
2 MOTIVACIÓN : impulse
impune *adj* : unpunished —
impunidad *nf* : impunity
impuro, -ra *adj* : impure —
impureza *nf* : impurity
imputar *vt* : impute, attribute
inacabable *adj* : interminable, endless
inaccesible *adj* : inaccessible
inaceptable *adj* : unacceptable
inactivo, -va *adj* : inactive —
inactividad *nf* : inactivity
inadaptado, -da *adj* : maladjusted
— **inadaptado, -da** *n* : misfit
inadecuado, -da *adj* **1** : inadequate
2 INAPROPIADO : inappropriate
inadmisible *adj* : inadmissible
inadvertido, -da *adj* **1** :
unnoticed **2** DISTRAÍDO : distracted
— **inadvertencia** *nf* : oversight
inagotable *adj* : inexhaustible
inaguantable *adj* : unbearable
inalámbrico, -ca *adj* : wireless, cordless
inalcanzable *adj* :
unreachable, unattainable
inalterable *adj* **1** : unchangeable **2** :
impassive (of character) **3** : fast (of colors)
inanición *nf, pl* **-ciones** :
starvation, famine
inanimado, -da *adj* : inanimate
inaplicable *adj* : inapplicable
inapreciable *adj* : imperceptible
inapropiado, -da *adj* : inappropriate
inarticulado, -da *adj* : inarticulate
inasequible *adj* : unattainable
inaudito, -ta *adj* : unheard-
of, unprecedented
inaugurar *vt* : inaugurate —
inauguración *nf, pl* **-ciones** : inauguration
— **inaugural** *adj* : inaugural
inca *adj* : Inca, Incan
incalculable *adj* : incalculable
incandescencia *nf* : incandescence
— **incandescente** *adj* : incandescent
incansable *adj* : tireless
incapacitar *vt* : incapacitate, disable
— **incapacidad** *nf* : incapacity, inability
— **incapaz** *adj, pl* **-paces** : incapable
incautar *vt* : confiscate, seize
incendiar *vt* : set fire to, burn (down) —
incendiarse *vr* : catch fire — **incendiario,**
-ria *adj* : incendiary — **incendiar** *n*

: arsonist — incendio *nm* **1** : fire **2**
incendiar premeditado : arson
incentivo *nm* : incentive
incertidumbre *nf* : uncertainty
incesante *adj* : incessant
incesto *nm* : incest — **incestuoso, -sa** *adj* : incestuous
incidencia *nf* **1** : impact **2** SUCESO : incident — **incidental** *adj* : incidental — **incidente** *nm* : incident
incidir *vi* **incidir en 1** : fall into (a habit, mistake, etc.) **2** INFLUIR EN : affect, influence
incienso *nm* : incense
incierto, -ta *adj* : uncertain
incinerar *vt* **1** : incinerate **2** : cremate (a corpse) — **incineración** *nf, pl* **-ciones 1** : incineration **2** : cremation (of a corpse) — **incinerador** *nm* : incinerator
incipiente *adj* : incipient
incisión *nf, pl* **-siones** : incision
incisivo, -va *adj* : incisive — **incisivo** *nm* : incisor

incitar *vt* : incite, rouse
incivilizado, -da *adj* : uncivilized
inclinar *vt* : tilt, lean — **inclinarse** *vr* **1** : lean (over) **2 inclinarse a** : be inclined to — **inclinación** *nf, pl* **-ciones 1** : inclination **2** LADEAR : incline, tilt
incluir {41} *vt* **1** : include **2** ADJUNTAR : enclose — **inclusión** *nf, pl* **-siones** : inclusion — **inclusive** *adv* : up to and including — **inclusivo, -va** *adj* : inclusive — **incluso** *adv* : even, in fact — **incluso, -sa** *adj* : enclosed
incógnito, -ta *adj* **1** : unknown **2 de incógnito, -ta** : incognito
incoherente *adj* : incoherent — **incoherencia** *nf* : incoherence
incoloro, -ra *adj* : colorless
incombustible *adj* : fireproof
incomible *adj* : inedible
incomodar *vt* **1** : inconvenience **2** ENFADAR : bother, annoy — **incomodarse** *vr* **1** : take the trouble **2** ENFADARSE : get annoyed

— **incomodidad** *nf* : discomfort — **incómodo, -da** *adj* **1** : uncomfortable **2** INCONVENIENTE : inconvenient, awkward
incomparable *adj* : incomparable
incompatible *adj* : incompatible — **incompatibilidad** *nf* : incompatibility
incompetente *adj* : incompetent — **incompetencia** *nf* : incompetence
incompleto, -ta *adj* : incomplete
incomprendido, -da *adj* : misunderstood — **incomprensible** *adj* : incomprehensible — **incomprensión** *nf, pl* **-siones** : lack of understanding
incomunicado, -da *adj* **1** : isolated **2** : in solitary confinement
inconcebible *adj* : inconceivable
inconcluso, -sa *adj* : unfinished
incondicional *adj* : unconditional
inconformista *adj & nmf* : nonconformist
inconfundible *adj* : unmistakable
incongruente *adj* : incongruous
inconmensurable *adj* : vast, immeasurable

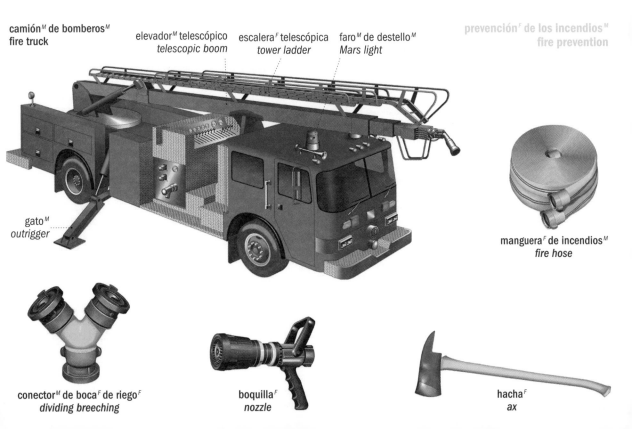

camión^M de bomberos^M
fire truck

elevador^M telescópico
telescopic boom

escalera^F telescópica
tower ladder

faro^M de destello^M
Mars light

prevención^F de los incendios^M
fire prevention

gato^M
outrigger

manguera^F de incendios^M
fire hose

conector^M de boca^F de riego^F
dividing breeching

boquilla^F
nozzle

hacha^F
ax

inconsciente *adj* **1** : unconscious, unaware **2** IRREFLEXIVO : reckless — **inconsciente** *nm* **el inconsciente** : the unconscious — **inconsciencia** *nf* **1** : unconsciousness **2** INSENSATEZ : thoughtlessness

inconsecuente *adj* : inconsistent — **inconsecuencia** *nf* : inconsistency

inconsiderado, -da *adj* : inconsiderate

inconsistente *adj* **1** : flimsy **2** : watery (of a sauce, etc.) **3** : inconsistent (of an argument) — **inconsistencia** *nf* : inconsistency

inconsolable *adj* : inconsolable

inconstante *adj* : changeable, unreliable — **inconstancia** *nf* : inconstancy

inconstitucional *adj* : unconstitutional

incontable *adj* : countless

incontenible *adj* : irrepressible

incontestable *adj* : indisputable

incontinente *adj* : incontinent — **incontinencia** *nf* : incontinence

inconveniente *adj* **1** : inconvenient **2** INAPROPIADO : inappropriate — **inconveniente** *nm* : obstacle, problem — **inconveniencia** *nf* **1** : inconvenience **2** : tactless remark

incorporar *vt* **1** AGREGAR : incorporate, add **2** : mix (in cooking) — **incorporarse** *vr* **1** : sit up **2** **incorporarse a** : join — **incorporación** *nf, pl* **-ciones** : incorporation

incorrecto, -ta *adj* **1** : incorrect **2** DESCORTÉS : impolite

incorregible *adj* : incorrigible

incrédulo, -la *adj* : incredulous — **incredulidad** *nf* : incredulity, disbelief

increíble *adj* : incredible, unbelievable

incrementar *vt* : increase — **incremento** *nm* : increase

incriminar *vt* **1** : incriminate **2** ACUSAR : accuse

incrustar *vt* : set, inlay — **incrustarse** *vr* : become embedded

incubar *vt* : incubate — **incubadora** *nf* : incubator

incuestionable *adj* : unquestionable

inculcar {72} *vt* : instill

inculpar *vt* : accuse, charge

inculto, -ta *adj* **1** : uneducated **2** : uncultivated (of land)

incumplimiento *nm* **1** : noncompliance **2** **incumplimiento de contrato** : breach of contract

incurable *adj* : incurable

incurrir *vi* **incurrir en 1** : incur (expenses, etc.) **2** : fall into, commit (crimes)

incursión *nf, pl* **-siones** : raid

indagar {52} *vt* : investigate — **indagación** *nf, pl* **-ciones** : investigation

indebido, -da *adj* : undue

indecente *adj* : indecent, obscene — **indecencia** *nf* : indecency, obscenity

indecible *adj* : inexpressible

indecisión *nf, pl* **-siones** : indecision — **indeciso, -sa** *adj* **1** : undecided **2** IRRESOLUTO : indecisive

indefenso, -sa *adj* : defenseless, helpless

indefinido, -da *adj* : indefinite — **indefinidamente** *adv* : indefinitely

indeleble *adj* : indelible

indemnizar {21} *vt* : indemnify, compensate — **indemnización** *nf, pl* **-ciones** : compensation

independiente *adj* : independent — **independencia** *nf* : independence — **independizarse** {21} *vr* : become independent

indescifrable *adj* : indecipherable

indescriptible *adj* : indescribable

indeseable *adj* : undesirable

indestructible *adj* : indestructible

indeterminado, -da *adj* : indeterminate

indicar {72} *vt* **1** : indicate **2** MOSTRAR : show — **indicación** *nf, pl* **-ciones** **1** : sign, indication **2** indicaciones *nfpl* : directions — **indicador** *nm* **1** : sign, signal **2** : gauge, dial, meter — **indicativo, -va** *adj* : indicative — **indicativo** *nm* : indicative (mood)

índice *nm* **1** : indication **2** : index (of a book, etc.) **3** : index finger **4** **índice de natalidad** : birth rate

indicio *nm* : indication, sign

indiferente *adj* **1** : indifferent **2** **me es indiferente** : it doesn't matter to me — **indiferencia** *nf* : indifference

indígena *adj* : indigenous, native — **indígena** *nmf* : native

indigente *adj & nmf* : indigent — **indigencia** *nf* : poverty

indigestión *nf, pl* **-tiones** : indigestion — **indigesto, -ta** *adj* : indigestible

indignar *vt* : outrage, infuriate — **indignarse** *vr* : become indignant — **indignación** *nf, pl* **-ciones** : indignation — **indignado, -da** *adj* : indignant — **indignidad** *nf* : indignity — **indigno, -na** *adj* : unworthy

indio, -dia *adj* **1** : American Indian **2** : Indian (from India)

indirecta *nf* **1** : hint **2** **lanzar una indirecta** : drop a hint — **indirecto, -ta** *adj* : indirect

indisciplina *nf* : lack of discipline — **indisciplinado, -da** *adj* : undisciplined

indiscreto, -ta *adj* : indiscreet — **indiscreción** *nf, pl* **-ciones 1** : indiscretion **2** : tactless remark

indiscriminado, -da *adj* : indiscriminate

indiscutible *adj* : indisputable

indispensable *adj* : indispensable

indisponer {60} *vt* **1** : upset, make ill **2** ENEMISTAR : set against, set at odds — **indisponerse** *vr* **1** : become ill **2** **indisponerse con** : fall out with — **indisposición** *nf, pl* **-ciones** : indisposition, illness — **indispuesto, -ta** *adj* : unwell, indisposed

indistinto, -ta *adj* : indistinct

individual *adj* : individual — **individualidad** *nf* : individuality — **individualizar** {21} *vt* : individualize — **individuo** *nm* : individual

indivisible *adj* : indivisible

índole *nf* **1** : nature, character **2** TIPO : type, kind

indolente *adj* : indolent, lazy — **indolencia** *nf* : indolence, laziness

indoloro, -ra *adj* : painless

indómito, -ta *adj* : indomitable

indonesio, -sia *adj* : Indonesian

inducir {61} *vt* **1** : induce **2** DEDUCIR : infer

indudable *adj* : beyond doubt — **indudablemente** *adv* : undoubtedly

indulgente *adj* : indulgent — **indulgencia** *nf* : indulgence

indultar *vt* : pardon, reprieve — **indulto** *nm* : pardon, reprieve

industria *nf* : industry — **industrial** *adj* : industrial — **industrial** *nmf* : industrialist, manufacturer — **industrialización** *nf, pl* **-ciones** : industrialization — **industrializar** {21} *vt* : industrialize — **industrioso, -sa** *adj* : industrious

inédito, -ta *adj* : unpublished

inefable *adj* : inexpressible

ineficaz *adj, pl* **-caces 1** : ineffective **2** INEFICIENTE : inefficient

ineficiente *adj* : inefficient — **ineficiencia** *nf* : inefficiency

inelegible *adj* : ineligible

ineludible *adj* : unavoidable, inescapable

inepto, -ta *adj* : inept — **ineptitud** *nf* : ineptitude

inequívoco, -ca *adj* : unequivocal

inercia *nf* : inertia

inerme *adj* : unarmed, defenseless

inerte *adj* : inert

inesperado, -da *adj* : unexpected

inestable *adj* : unstable — **inestabilidad** *nf* : instability

inevitable *adj* : inevitable

inexacto, -ta *adj* **1** : inexact **2** INCORRECTO : incorrect, wrong

inexistente *adj* : nonexistent

inexorable *adj* : inexorable

inexperiencia *nf* : inexperience — **inexperto, -ta** *adj* : inexperienced, unskilled

inexplicable *adj* : inexplicable

infalible *adj* : infallible

infame *adj* **1** : infamous, vile **2** *fam* : horrible — **infamia** *nf* : infamy, disgrace

infancia *nf* : infancy — **infanta** *nf* : infanta, princess — **infante** *nm* **1** : infante, prince **2** : infantryman (in the military) — **infantería** *nf* : infantry — **infantil** *adj* **1** : child's, children's **2** INMADURO : childish

infarto *nm* : heart attack

infatigable *adj* : tireless

infectar *vt* : infect — **infectarse** *vr* : become infected — **infección** *nf, pl* **-ciones** : infection — **infeccioso, -sa** *adj* : infectious — **infecto, -ta** *adj* **1** : infected **2** : foul, sickening

infecundo, -da *adj* : infertile

infeliz *adj, pl* **-lices** : unhappy — **infelicidad** *nf* : unhappiness

inferior *adj & nmf* : inferior — **inferioridad** *nf* : inferiority

inferir {76} *vt* **1** DEDUCIR : infer **2** : cause (harm or injury)

infernal *adj* : infernal, hellish

infestar *vt* : infest

infiel *adj* : unfaithful — **infidelidad** *nf* : infidelity

infierno *nm* **1** : hell **2 el quinto infierno** *fam* : the middle of nowhere

infiltrar *vt* : infiltrate — **infiltrarse** *vr* : infiltrate

infinidad *nf* **1** : infinity **2 una infinidad de** : countless — **infinitivo** *nm* : infinitive — **infinito, -ta** *adj* : infinite — **infinito** *nm* : infinity

inflación *nf, pl* **-ciones** : inflation — **inflacionario, -ria** *or* inflacionista *adj* : inflationary

inflamar *vt* : inflame — **inflamable** *adj* : flammable, inflammable — **inflamación** *nf, pl* **-ciones** : inflammation — **inflamatorio, -ria** *adj* : inflammatory

inflar *vt* **1** : inflate **2** EXAGERAR : exaggerate — **inflarse** *vr* **inflarse de** : swell (up) with

inflexible *adj* : inflexible — **inflexión** *nf, pl* **-xiones** : inflection

infligir {35} *vt* : inflict

influencia *nf* : influence — **influenciar** → **influir**

influenza *nf* : influenza

influir {41} *vt* : influence — *vi* **influir en** *or* **influir sobre** : have an influence on — **influjo** *nm* : influence — **influyente** *adj* : influential

información *nf, pl* **-ciones 1** : information **2** NOTICIAS : news **3** : directory assistance (on the telephone)

informal *adj* **1** : informal **2** IRRESPONSABLE : unreliable

informar *v* : inform — **informarse** *vr* : get information, find out — **informante** *nmf* : informant — **informática** *nf* : information technology — **informativo, -va** *adj* : informative — **informatizar** {21} *vt* : computerize

informe *adj* : shapeless — **informe** *nm* **1** : report **2 informes** *nmpl* : information, data **3 informes** *nmpl* : references (for employment)

infortunado, -da *adj* : unfortunate — **infortunio** *nm* : misfortune

infracción *nf, pl* **-ciones** : violation, infraction

infraestructura *nf* : infrastructure

infrahumano, -na *adj* : subhuman

infranqueable *adj* **1** : impassable **2** INSUPERABLE : insurmountable

infrarrojo, -ja *adj* : infrared

infrecuente *adj* : infrequent

infringir {35} *vt* : infringe

infructuoso, -sa *adj* : fruitless

infundado, -da *adj* : unfounded, baseless

infundir *vt* : instill, infuse — **infusión** *nf, pl* **-siones** : infusion

ingeniar *vt* : invent, think up

ingeniería *nf* : engineering — **ingeniero, -ra** *n* : engineer

ingenio *nm* **1** : ingenuity **2** AGUDEZA : wit **3** MÁQUINA : device, apparatus **4 ingenio azucarero** *Lat* : sugar refinery — **ingenioso, -sa** *adj* **1** :

ingenious **2** AGUDO : clever, witty — **ingeniosamente** *adv* : cleverly

ingenuidad *nf* : naïveté, ingenuousness — **ingenuo, -nua** *adj* : naive

ingerir {76} *vt* : ingest, consume

ingle *nf* : groin

inglés, -glesa *adj, mpl* **-gleses** : English — **inglés** *nm* : English (language)

ingrato, -ta *adj* **1** : ungrateful **2 un trabajo ingrato** : a thankless task — **ingratitud** *nf* : ingratitude

ingrediente *nm* : ingredient

ingresar *vt* : deposit — *vi* **ingresar en** : enter, be admitted into, join — **ingreso** *nm* **1** : entrance, entry **2** : admission (into a hospital, etc.) **3 ingresos** *nmpl* : income, earnings

inhábil *adj* **1** : unskillful, clumsy **2 inhábil para** : unsuited for — **inhabilidad** *nf* : unskillfulness

inhabitable *adj* : uninhabitable — **inhabitado, -da** *adj* : uninhabited

inhalar *vt* : inhale — **inhalación** *nf* : inhalation

inherente *adj* : inherent

inhibir *vt* : inhibit — **inhibición** *nf, pl* **-ciones** : inhibition

inhóspito, -ta *adj* : inhospitable

inhumano, -na *adj* : inhuman, inhumane — **inhumanidad** *nf* : inhumanity

iniciar *vt* : initiate, begin — **iniciación** *nf, pl* **-ciones 1** : initiation **2** COMIENZO : beginning — **inicial** *adj & nf* : initial — **iniciativa** *nf* : initiative — **inicio** *nm* : start, beginning

inigualado, -da *adj* : unequaled

ininterrumpido, -da *adj* : uninterrupted

injerirse {76} *vr* : interfere — **injerencia** *nf* : interference

injertar *vt* : graft — **injerto** *nm* : graft

injuriar *vt* : insult — **injuria** *nf* : insult — **injurioso, -sa** *adj* : insulting, abusive

injusticia *nf* : injustice, unfairness — **injusto, -ta** *adj* : unfair, unjust

inmaculado, -da *adj* : immaculate

inmaduro, -ra *adj* **1** : immature **2** : unripe (of fruit) — **inmadurez** *nf* : immaturity

inmediaciones *nfpl* : surrounding area

inmediato, -ta *adj* **1** : immediate **2** CONTIGUO : adjoining **3 de inmediato** : immediately, right away **4 inmediato a** : next to, close to — **inmediatamente** *adv* : immediately

inmejorable *adj* : excellent

insectos^M
insects

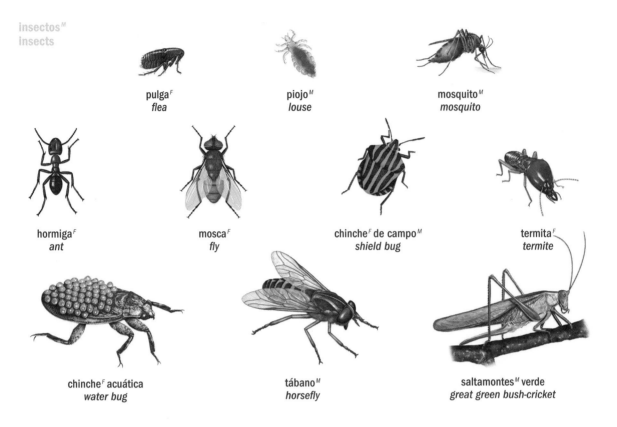

pulga^F
flea

piojo^M
louse

mosquito^M
mosquito

hormiga^F
ant

mosca^F
fly

chinche^F de campo^M
shield bug

termita^F
termite

chinche^F acuática
water bug

tábano^M
horsefly

saltamontes^M verde
great green bush-cricket

inmenso, -sa *adj* : immense, vast
— **inmensidad** *nf* : immensity
inmerecido, -da *adj* : undeserved
inmersión *nf, pl* **-siones** : immersion
inmigrar *vi* : immigrate —
inmigración *nf, pl* **-ciones** : immigration
— **inmigrante** *adj & nmf* : immigrant
inminente *adj* : imminent, impending
— **inminencia** *nf* : imminence
inmiscuirse {41} *vr* : interfere
inmobiliario, -ria *adj* :
real estate, property
inmodesto, -ta *adj* : immodest
inmoral *adj* : immoral —
inmoralidad *nf* : immorality
inmortal *adj & nmf* : immortal —
inmortalidad *nf* : immortality
inmóvil *adj* : motionless, still —
inmovilizar {21} *vt* : immobilize
inmueble *nm* : building, property
inmundicia *nf* : filth, trash —
inmundo, -da *adj* : dirty, filthy
inmunizar {21} *vt* : immunize —
inmune *adj* : immune — **inmunidad** *nf*

: immunity — **inmunización** *nf,*
pl **-ciones** : immunization
inmutable *adj* : unchangeable
innato, -ta *adj* : innate
innecesario, -ria *adj* :
unnecessary, needless
innegable *adj* : undeniable
innoble *adj* : ignoble
innovar *vt* : introduce — *vi* : innovate
— **innovación** *nf, pl* **-ciones** : innovation
— **innovador, -dora** *adj* : innovative
— **innovador, -dora** *n* : innovator
innumerable *adj* : innumerable
inocencia *nf* : innocence — **inocente** *adj*
& nmf : innocent — **inocentón,**
-tona *adj* : naive — **inocentón, -tona** *n,*
mpl **-tones** : simpleton, dupe
inocular *vt* : inoculate — **inoculación** *nf,*
pl **-ciones** : inoculation
inocuo, -cua *adj* : innocuous
inodoro, -ra *adj* : odorless
— **inodoro** *nm* : toilet
inofensivo, -va *adj* :
inoffensive, harmless

inolvidable *adj* : unforgettable
inoperable *adj* : inoperable
inoperante *adj* : ineffective
inopinado, -da *adj* : unexpected
inoportuno, -na *adj* :
untimely, inopportune
inorgánico, -ca *adj* : inorganic
inoxidable *adj* **1** : rustproof **2**
acero inoxidable : stainless steel
inquebrantable *adj* : unwavering
inquietar *vt* : disturb, worry
— **inquietarse** *vr* : worry —
inquietante *adj* : disturbing, worrisome
— **inquieto, -ta** *adj* : anxious, worried
— **inquietud** *nf* : anxiety, worry
inquilino, -na *n* : tenant
inquirir {4} *vi* : make inquiries
— *vt* : investigate
insaciable *adj* : insatiable
insalubre *adj* : unhealthy
insatisfecho, -cha *adj* **1** : unsatisfied
2 DESCONTENTO : dissatisfied
inscribir {33} *vt* **1** : enroll, register
2 GRABAR : inscribe, engrave

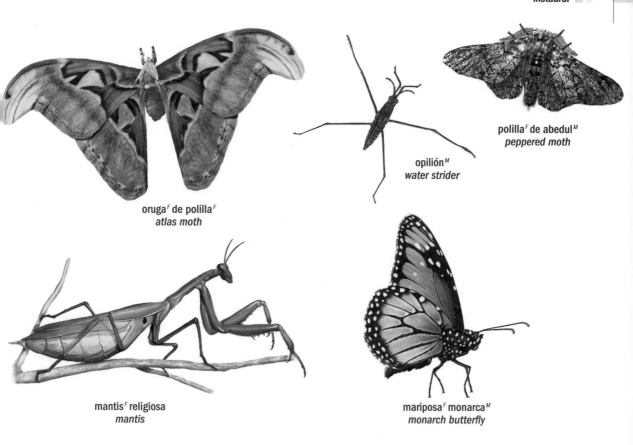

polilla^F de abedul^M
peppered moth

opilión^M
water strider

oruga^F de polilla^F
atlas moth

mantis^F religiosa
mantis

mariposa^F monarca^M
monarch butterfly

— **inscribirse** *vr* : register —
inscripción *nf, pl* **-ciones 1** :
inscription **2** REGISTRO : registration
insecto *nm* : insect —
insecticida *nm* : insecticide
inseguro, -ra *adj* **1** : insecure **2**
PELIGROSO : **unsafe 3** DUDOSO : uncertain
— **inseguridad** *nf* **1** : insecurity **2** PELIGRO
: lack of safety **3** DUDA : uncertainty
inseminar *vt* : inseminate —
inseminación *nf, pl* **-ciones** : insemination
insensato, -ta *adj* : senseless,
foolish — **insensatez** *nf* :
foolishness, thoughtlessness
insensible *adj* **1** : insensitive,
unfeeling **2** : numb (in medicine)
3 IMPERCEPTIBLE : imperceptible —
insensibilidad *nf* : insensitivity
inseparable *adj* : inseparable
insertar *vt* : insert
insidia *nf* : snare, trap —
insidioso, -sa *adj* : insidious
insigne *adj* : noted, famous
insignia *nf* **1** : insignia,

badge **2** BANDERA : flag
insignificante *adj* :
insignificant, negligible
insincero, -ra *adj* : insincere
insinuar {3} *vt* : insinuate —
insinuarse *vr* **insinuarse en** : worm
one's way into — **insinuación** *nf,
pl* **-ciones** : insinuation — **insinuante** *adj*
: insinuating, suggestive
insípido, -da *adj* : insipid
insistir *v* : insist — **insistencia** *nf* :
insistence — **insistente** *adj* : insistent
insociable *adj* : unsociable
insolación *nf, pl* **-ciones** : sunstroke
insolencia *nf* : insolence —
insolente *adj* : insolent
insólito, -ta *adj* : rare, unusual
insoluble *adj* : insoluble
insolvencia *nf* : insolvency, bankruptcy
— **insolvente** *adj* : insolvent, bankrupt
insomnio *nm* : insomnia —
insomne *nmf* : insomniac
insondable *adj* : unfathomable

insonorizado, -da *adj* : soundproof
insoportable *adj* : unbearable
insospechado, -da *adj* : unexpected
insostenible *adj* : untenable
inspeccionar *vt* : inspect —
inspección *nf, pl* **-ciones** : inspection
— **inspector, -tora** *n* : inspector
inspirar *vt* : inspire — *vi* : inhale
— **inspirarse** *vr* : be inspired
— **inspiración** *nf, pl* **-ciones 1** :
inspiration **2** RESPIRACIÓN : inhalation —
inspirador, -dora *adj* : inspirational
instalar *vt* : install — **instalarse** *vr* : settle
— **instalación** *nf, pl* **-ciones** : installation
instancia *nf* **1** : request **2 en última**
instancia : ultimately, as a last resort
instantáneo, -nea *adj* : instantaneous,
instant — **instantánea** *nf* : snapshot
— **instante** *nm* **1** : instant **2 a**
cada instante : frequently, all the
time **3 al instante** : immediately
instar *vt* : urge, press
instaurar *vt* : establish —
instauración *nf, pl* **-ciones** : establishment

instigar {52} *vt* : incite, instigate —
instigador, -dora *n* : instigator
instinto *nm* : instinct —
instintivo, -va *adj* : instinctive
institución *nf, pl* **-ciones** : institution
— **institucional** *adj* : institutional —
institucionalizar {21} *vt* : institutionalize
— **instituir** {41} *vt* : institute, establish
— **instituto** *nm* : institute —
institutriz *nf, pl* **-trices** : governess
instruir {41} *vt* : instruct —
instrucción *nf, pl* **-ciones 1** : instruction **2**
instrucciones *nfpl* : instructions, directions
— **instructivo, -va** *adj* : instructive
— **instructor, -tora** *n* : instructor
instrumento *nm* : instrument —
instrumental *adj* : instrumental
insubordinarse *vr* : rebel
— **insubordinado, -da** *adj* :
insubordinate — **insubordinación** *nf,
pl* **-ciones** : insubordination
insuficiente *adj* : insufficient,
inadequate — **insuficiencia** *nf* **1**
: insufficiency, inadequacy **2**
insuficiencia cardíaca : heart failure
insufrible *adj* : insufferable
insular *adj* : insular, island
insulina *nf* : insulin
insulso, -sa *adj* **1** : insipid,
bland **2** SOSO : dull
insultar *vt* : insult — **insultante** *adj*
: insulting — **insulto** *nm* : insult
insuperable *adj* : insurmountable
insurgente *adj & nmf* : insurgent
insurrección *nf, pl* **-ciones**
: insurrection, uprising
intachable *adj* : irreproachable
intacto, -ta *adj* : intact
intangible *adj* : intangible
integrar *vt* : integrate — **integrarse** *vr*
: become integrated — **integración** *nf,
pl* **-ciones** : integration — **integral** *adj* **1**
: integral **2 pan integral** : whole
grain bread — **íntegro, -gra** *adj* **1**
: honest, upright **2** ENTERO : whole,
complete — **integridad** *nf* **1** RECTITUD
: integrity **2** TOTALIDAD : wholeness
intelecto *nm* : intellect —
intelectual *adj & nmf* : intellectual
inteligencia *nf* : intelligence
— **inteligente** *adj* : intelligent —
inteligible *adj* : intelligible
intemperie *nf* **a la intemperie**
: in the open air, outside
intempestivo, -va *adj* :

untimely, inopportune
intención *nf, pl* **-ciones** : intention,
intent — **intencionado, -da** *adj* **1** :
intended **2 bien intencionado** : well-
meaning **3 mal intencionado** : malicious
— **intencional** *adj* : intentional
intensidad *nf* : intensity — **intensificar**
{72} *vt* : intensify — **intensificarse** *vr*
: intensify — **intensivo, -va** *adj* :
intensive — **intenso, -sa** *adj* : intense
intentar *vt* : attempt, try — **intento** *nm* **1**
: intention **2** TENTATIVA : attempt
interactuar {3} *vi* : interact —
interacción *nf, pl* **-ciones** : interaction
— **interactivo, -va** *adj* : interactive
intercalar *vt* : insert, intersperse
intercambio *nm* : exchange —
intercambiable *adj* : interchangeable
— **intercambiar** *vt* : exchange, trade
interceder *vi* : intercede
interceptar *vt* : intercept —
intercepción *nf, pl* **-ciones** : interception
intercesión *nf, pl* **-siones** : intercession
interés *nm, pl* **-reses** : interest —
interesado, -da *adj* **1** : interested **2**
EGOISTA : selfish — **interesante** *adj*
: interesting — **interesar** *vt* :
interest — *vi* : be of interest —
interesarse *vr* : take an interest
interfaz *nf, pl* **-faces** : interface
interferir {76} *vi* : interfere
— *vt* : interfere with —
interferencia *nf* : interference
interino, -na *adj* : temporary, interim
— **interiormente** *adv* : inwardly
interior *adj* : interior, inner —
interior *nm* : interior, inside —
interiormente *adv* : inwardly
interjección *nf, pl* **-ciones** : interjection
interlocutor, -tora *n* : speaker
intermediario, -ria *adj*
& *n* : intermediary
intermedio, -dia *adj* : intermediate
— **intermedio** *nm* : intermission
interminable *adj* : interminable, endless
intermisión *nf, pl* **-siones**
: intermission, pause
intermitente *adj* : intermittent —
intermitente *nm* : blinker, turn signal
internacional *adj* : international
internar *vt* : commit, confine
— **internarse** *vr* : penetrate —
internado *nm* : boarding school —
interno, -na *adj* : internal — **interno** *n* **1**
: boarder **2** : inmate (in a jail, etc.)

interponer {60} *vt* : interpose —
interponerse *vr* : intervene
interpretar *vt* **1** : interpret **2** :
play, perform (in theater, etc.)
— **interpretación** *nf, pl* **-ciones** :
interpretation — **intérprete** *nmf* **1**
TRADUCTOR : interpreter **2** :
performer (of music)
interrogar {52} *vt* : interrogate, question
— **interrogación** *nf, pl* **-ciones 1** :
interrogation **2 signo de interrogar** :
question mark — **interrogativo, -va** *adj*
: interrogative — **interrogatorio** *nm*
: interrogation, questioning
interrumpir *v* : interrupt —
interrupción *nf, pl* **-ciones** : interruption
— **interruptor** *nm* : (electrical) switch
intersección *nf, pl* **-ciones** : intersection
intervalo *nm* : interval
intervenir {87} *vi* **1** : take part **2** MEDIAR
: intervene — *vt* **1** : tap (a telephone) **2**
INSPECCIONAR : audit **3** OPERAR : operate
on — **intervención** *nf, pl* **-ciones 1** :
intervention **2** : audit (in business) **3** *or*
intervenir quirúrgica : operation —
interventor, -tora *n* : inspector, auditor
intestino *nm* : intestine —
intestinal *adj* : intestinal
intimar *vi* **intimar con** : become
friendly with — **intimidad** *nf* **1** :
private life **2** AMISTAD : intimacy
intimidar *vt* : intimidate
íntimo, -ma *adj* **1** : intimate,
close **2** PRIVADO : private
intolerable *adj* : intolerable —
intolerancia *nf* : intolerance —
intolerante *adj* : intolerant
intoxicar {72} *vt* : poison —
intoxicación *nf, pl* **-ciones** : poisoning
intranquilizar {21} *vt* : make uneasy
— **intranquilizarse** *vr* : be anxious —
intranquilidad *nf* : uneasiness, anxiety
— **intranquilo, -la** *adj* : uneasy, worried
intransigente *adj* :
unyielding, intransigent
intransitable *adj* : impassable
intransitivo, -va *adj* : intransitive
intrascendente *adj* :
unimportant, insignificant
intravenoso, -sa *adj* : intravenous
intrépido, -da *adj* : intrepid, fearless
intrigar {52} *v* : intrigue — **intriga** *nf* :
intrigue — **intrigante** *adj* : intriguing
intrincado, -da *adj* : intricate, involved
intrínseco, -ca *adj* : intrinsic

— **intrínsecament** *adv* :
intrinsically, inherently
introducción *nf, pl* **-ciones** : introduction
— **introducir** {61} *vt* **1** : introduce
2 METER : insert — **introducirse** *vr*
introducirse en : penetrate, get into —
introductorio, -ria *adj* : introductory
intromisión *nf, pl* **-siones** : interference
introvertido, -da *adj* : introverted
— **introvertido, -da** *n* : introvert
intrusión *nf, pl* **-siones** : intrusion
— **intruso, -sa** *adj* : intrusive
— **intruso, -sa** *n* : intruder
intuir {41} *vt* : sense —
intuición *nf, pl* **-ciones** : intuition
— **intuitivo, -va** *adj* : intuitive
inundar *vt* : flood — **inundarse** *vr*
inundarse de : be inundated with —
inundación *nf, pl* **-ciones** : flood
inusitado, -da *adj* : unusual, uncommon
inútil *adj* **1** : useless **2** INVÁLIDO :
disabled — **inutilidad** *nf* : uselessness
— **inutilizar** {21} *vt* **1** : make
useless **2** INCAPACITAR : disable
invadir *vt* : invade
invalidez *nf, pl* **-deces 1** : invalidity
2 : disability (in medicine) —
inválido, -da *adj & n* : invalid
invalorable *adj Lat* : invaluable
invariable *adj* : invariable
invasión *nf, pl* **-siones** : invasion
— **invasor, -sora** *adj* : invading
— **invasor, -sora** *n* : invader
invencible *adj* : invincible
inventar *vt* **1** : invent **2** : fabricate,
make up (a word, an excuse, etc.)
— **invención** *nf, pl* **-ciones 1** :
invention **2** MENTIRA : lie, fabrication
inventario *nm* : inventory
inventiva *nf* : inventiveness —
inventivo, -va *adj* : inventive —
inventor, -tora *n* : inventor
invernadero *nm* : greenhouse
invernal *adj* : winter
inverosímil *adj* : unlikely
inversión *nf, pl* **-siones 1** :
inversion, reversal **2** : investment
(of money, time, etc.)
inverso, -sa *adj* **1** : inverse **2**
CONTRARIO : opposite **3 a la inversa**
: the other way around, inversely
inversor, -sora *n* : investor
invertebrado, -da *adj* : invertebrate
— **invertebrado** *nm* : invertebrate
invertir {76} *vt* **1** : invert, reverse

2 : invest (money, time, etc.)
— *vi* : make an investment
investidura *nf* : investiture
investigar {52} *vt* **1** : investigate **2**
ESTUDIAR : research — *vi* **investigar sobre**
: do research into — **investigación** *nf,*
pl **-ciones 1** : investigation **2** ESTUDIO
: research — **investigador, -dora** *n*
: investigator, researcher
investir {54} *vt* : invest
inveterado, -da *adj* : deep-
seated, inveterate
invicto, -ta *adj* : undefeated
invierno *nm* : winter
invisible *adj* : invisible —
invisibilidad *nf* : invisibility
invitar *vt* : invite — **invitación** *nf,*
pl **-ciones** : invitation —
invitado, -da *n* : guest
invocar {72} *vt* : invoke —
invocación *nf, pl* **-ciones** : invocation
involuntario, -ria *adj* : involuntary
invulnerable *adj* : invulnerable
inyectar *vt* : inject — **inyección** *nf,*
pl **-ciones** : injection, shot — **inyectado,**
-da *adj* **ojos inyectados** : bloodshot eyes
ion *nm* : ion — **ionizar** {21} *vt* : ionize
ir {43} *vi* **1** : go **2** FUNCIONAR : work,
function **3** CONVENIR : suit **4 ¿cómo te**
va? : how are you? **5 ir con prisa** : be
in a hurry **6 ir por** : follow, go along
7 vamos : let's go — *v aux* **1 ir a** : be
going to, be about to **2 ir caminando**
: take a walk **3 vamos a ver** : we shall
see — **irse** *vr* : go away, be gone
ira *nf* : rage, anger — **iracundo,**
-da *adj* : irate, angry
iraní *adj* : Iranian
iraquí *adj* : Iraqi
iris *nms & pl* **1** : iris (of the
eye) **2 arco iris** : rainbow
irlandés, -desa *adj, mpl* **-deses** : Irish
ironía *nf* : irony — **irónico,**
-ca *adj* : ironic, ironical
irracional *adj* : irrational
irradiar *vt* : radiate, irradiate
irrazonable *adj* : unreasonable
irreal *adj* : unreal
irreconciliable *adj* : irreconcilable
irreconocible *adj* : unrecognizable
irrecuperable *adj* : irretrievable
irreductible *adj* : unyielding
irreemplazable *adj* : irreplaceable
irreflexivo, -va *adj* : rash, unthinking
irrefutable *adj* : irrefutable

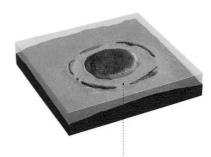

isla*ᶠ* coralina (atolón*ᴹ*)
coral island (atoll)

laguna*ᶠ*
lagoon

irregular *adj* : irregular —
irregularidad *nf* : irregularity
irrelevante *adj* : irrelevant
irreparable *adj* : irreparable
irreprimible *adj* : irrepressible
irreprochable *adj* : irreproachable
irresistible *adj* : irresistible
irresoluto, -ta *adj* : indecisive, irresolute
irrespetuoso, -sa *adj* : disrespectful
irresponsable *adj* : irresponsible —
irresponsabilidad *nf* : irresponsibility
irreverente *adj* : irreverent
irreversible *adj* : irreversible
irrevocable *adj* : irrevocable
irrigar {52} *vt* : irrigate —
irrigación *nf, pl* **-ciones** : irrigation
irrisorio, -ria *adj* : laughable, ridiculous
irritar *vt* : irritate — **irritarse** *vr* : get
annoyed — **irritable** *adj* : irritable —
irritación *nf, pl* **-ciones** : irritation
— **irritante** *adj* : irritating
irrompible *adj* : unbreakable
irrumpir *vi* **irrumpir en** : burst into
▸ **isla** *nf* : island
islámico, -ca *adj* : Islamic, Muslim
islandés, -desa *adj, mpl*
-deses : Icelandic
isleño, -ña *n* : islander
israelí *adj* : Israeli
istmo *nm* : isthmus
italiano, -na *adj* : Italian —
italiano *nm* : Italian (language)
itinerario *nm* : itinerary
izar {21} *vt* : hoist, raise
izquierda *nf* : left — **izquierdista** *adj &*
nmf : leftist — **izquierdo, -da** *adj* : left

J

j *nf* : j, tenth letter of the Spanish alphabet

jabalí *nm, pl* **-líes** : wild boar

jabalina *nf* : javelin

jabón *nm, pl* **-bones** : soap — **jabonar** *vt* : soap (up) — **jabonera** *nf* : soap dish — **jabonoso, -sa** *adj* : soapy

jaca *nf* : pony

jacinto *nm* : hyacinth

jactarse *vr* : boast, brag — **jactancia** *nf* : boastfulness, bragging — **jactancioso, -sa** *adj* : boastful

jadear *vi* : pant, gasp — **jadeante** *adj* : panting, breathless — **jadeo** *nm* : gasp, panting

jaez *nm, pl* **jaeces 1** : harness **2** jaeces *nmpl* : trappings

jaguar *nm* : jaguar

jaiba *nf Lat* : crab

jalapeño *nm Lat* : jalapeño pepper

jalar *v Lat* : pull, tug

jalea *nf* : jelly

jaleo *nm, fam* **1** : uproar, racket **2 armar un jaleo** : raise a ruckus

jalón *nm, pl* **-lones** *Lat* : pull, tug

jamaicano, -na *or* **jamaiquino, -na** *adj* : Jamaican

jamás *adv* **1** : never **2 para siempre jamás** : for ever and ever

jamelgo *nm* : nag (horse)

jamón *nm, pl* **-mones 1** : ham **2 jamón serrano** : cured ham

Januká *nmf* : Hanukkah

japonés, -nesa *adj, mpl* **-neses** : Japanese — **japonés** *nm* : Japanese (language)

jaque *nm* **1** : check (in chess) **2 jaque mate** : checkmate

jaqueca *nf* : headache, migraine

jarabe *nm* : syrup

jardín *nm, pl* **-dines 1** : garden **2 jardín infantil** *or* **jardín de niños** *Lat* : kindergarten — **jardinería** *nf* : gardening — **jardinero, -ra** *n* : gardener

jarra *nf* : pitcher, jug — **jarro** *nm* : pitcher — **jarrón** *nm, pl* **-rrones** : vase

jaula *nf* : cage

jauría *nf* : pack of hounds

jazmín *nm, pl* **-mines** : jasmine

jazz *nm* : jazz

jeans *nmpl* : jeans

jefe, -fa *n* **1** : chief, leader **2 PATRÓN** : boss **3 jefe, -fa de cocina** : chef — **jefatura** *nf* **1** : leadership **2 SEDE** : headquarters

jengibre *nm* : ginger

jeque *nm* : sheikh, sheik

jerarquía *nf* **1** : hierarchy **2 RANGO** : rank — **jerárquico, -ca** *adj* : hierarchical

jerez *nm, pl* **-reces** : sherry

jerga *nf* **1** : coarse cloth **2 ARGOT** : jargon, slang

jerigonza *nf* **1** : jargon **2 GALIMATÍAS** : gibberish

jeringa *or* jeringuilla *nf* : syringe — **jeringar** {52} *vt, fam* : annoy, pester

jeroglífico *nm* : hieroglyphic

jersey *nm, pl* **-seys** : jersey

jesuita *adj & nm* : Jesuit

Jesús *nm* : Jesus

jilguero *nm* : goldfinch

jinete *nmf* : horseman, horsewoman *f*, rider

jirafa *nf* : giraffe

jirón *nm, pl* **-rones** : shred, tatter

jitomate *nm Lat* : tomato

jockey *nmf, pl* **-keys** : jockey

jocoso, -sa *adj* : humorous, jocular

jofaina *nf* : washbowl

jolgorio *nm* : merrymaking

jornada *nf* **1** : day's journey **2** : working day — **jornal** *nm* : day's pay — **jornalero, -ra** *n* : day laborer

joroba *nf* : hump — **jorobado, -da** *adj* : hunchbacked, humpbacked — **jorobado, -da** *n* : hunchback — **jorobar** *vt, fam* : annoy

jota *nf* **1** : iota, jot **2 no veo ni jota** : I can't see a thing

joven *adj, pl* **jóvenes** : young — **joven** *nmf* : young man *m*, young woman *f*, youth

jovial *adj* : jovial, cheerful

joya *nf* : jewel — **joyería** *nf* : jewelry store — **joyero, -ra** *n* : jeweler

jabalí[M]
wild boar

— joyero *nm* : jewelry box

juanete *nm* : bunion

jubilación *nf, pl* **-ciones** : retirement — **jubilado, -da** *adj* : retired — **jubilado, -da** *nmf* : retiree — **jubilar** *vt* : retire, pension off — **jubilarse** *vr* : retire — **jubileo** *nm* : jubilee

júbilo *nm* : joy, jubilation — **jubiloso, -sa** *adj* : joyous, jubilant

judaísmo *nm* : Judaism

judía *nf* **1** : bean **2** *or* **judía verde** : green bean, string bean

judicial *adj* : judicial

judío, -día *adj* : Jewish — **judío, -día** *n* : Jew

judo *nm* : judo

juego *nm* **1** : game **2** : playing (of children, etc.) **3** *or* **juegos de azar** : gambling **4 CONJUNTO** : set **5 estar en juego** : be at stake **6 fuera de juego** : offside (in sports) **7 hacer juego** : go together, match **8 juego de manos** : conjuring trick **9 poner en juego** : bring into play

juerga *nf, fam* : spree, binge

jueves *nms & pl* : Thursday

juez *nmf, pl* **jueces 1** : judge **2 ÁRBITRO** : umpire, referee

jugar {44} *vi* **1** : play **2** : gamble (in a casino, etc.) **3 APOSTAR** : bet **4 jugar (al) tenis** : play tennis — *vt* : play — **jugarse** *vr* : risk, gamble (away) — **jugada** *nf* **1** : play, move **2 TRETA** : (dirty) trick — **jugador, -dora** *n* **1** : player **2** : gambler

juglar *nm* : minstrel

jugo *nm* **1** : juice **2 SUSTANCIA** : substance, essence — **jugoso, -sa** *adj* **1** : juicy **2 SUSTANCIAL** : substantial, important

juguete *nm* : toy — **juguetear** *vi* : play — **juguetería** *nf* : toy store — **juguetón, -tona** *adj, mpl* **-tones** : playful

juicio *nm* **1** : judgment **2 RAZÓN** : reason, sense **3 a mi juicio** : in my opinion — **juicioso, -sa** *adj* : wise, sensible

julio *nm* : July

junco *nm* : reed, rush

jungla *nf* : jungle

junio *nm* : June

juntar *vt* **1 UNIR** : join, unite **2 REUNIR** : collect — **juntarse** *vr* **1** : join (together) **2 REUNIRSE** : meet, get together — **junta** *nf* **1** : board, committee **2 REUNIÓN** : meeting **3** : (political) junta **4** : joint, gasket — **junto, -ta** *adj* **1** : joined **2 PRÓXIMO**

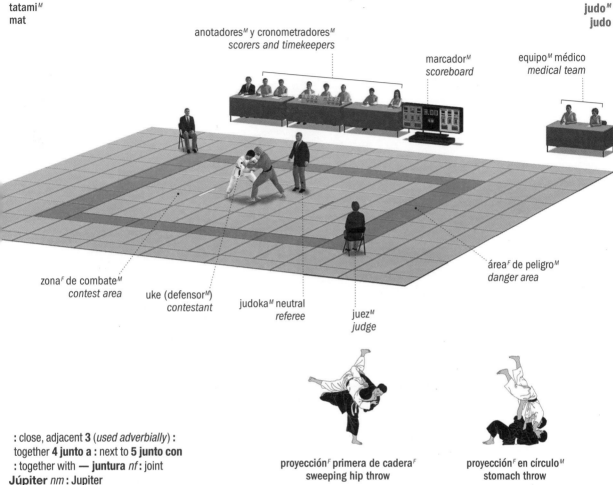

tatami^M
mat

judo^M
judo

anotadores^M y cronometradores^M
scorers and timekeepers

marcador^M
scoreboard

equipo^M médico
medical team

zona^F de combate^M
contest area

uke (defensor^M)
contestant

judoka^M neutral
referee

juez^M
judge

área^F de peligro^M
danger area

: close, adjacent **3** (*used adverbially*) :
together **4 junto a** : next to **5 junto con**
: together with — **juntura** *nf* : joint
Júpiter *nm* : Jupiter
jurar *v* **1** : swear **2 jurar en falso** : commit
perjury — **jurado** *nm* **1** : jury **2** : juror,
member of a jury — **juramento** *nm* : oath
jurídico, -ca *adj* : legal
jurisdicción *nf, pl* **-ciones** : jurisdiction
jurisprudencia *nf* : jurisprudence
justamente *adv* **1** : fairly, justly **2**
PRECISAMENTE : precisely, exactly
justicia *nf* : justice, fairness
justificar {72} *vt* **1** : justify **2**
DISCULPAR : excuse, vindicate —
justificación *nf, pl* **-ciones** : justification
justo, -ta *adj* **1** : just, fair **2** EXACTO :
exact **3** APRETADO : tight — **justo** *adv* **1** :
just, exactly **2 justo a tiempo** : just in time
juvenil *adj* : youthful — **juventud** *nf* **1**
: youth **2** JÓVENES : young people
juzgar {52} *vt* **1** : try (a case in court) **2**
ESTIMAR : judge, consider **3 a juzgar por** :
judging by — **juzgado** *nm* : court, tribunal

proyección^F primera de cadera^F
sweeping hip throw

proyección^F en círculo^M
stomach throw

inmovilización^F de brazo
arm lock

estrangulación^F
naked strangle

inmovilización^F
holding

proyección^F por encima del hombro^M con
una mano^F
one-arm shoulder throw

gran siega^F interior
major inner reaping throw

K

k *nf* : k, eleventh letter of
the Spanish alphabet
kaki → **caqui**
▸ **karate** *or* kárate *nm* : karate
kilo *nm* : kilo — **kilogramo** *nm* : kilogram
kilómetro *nm* : kilometer —
kilometraje *nm* : distance in
kilometers, mileage — **kilométrico,
-ca** *adj, fam* : end-less
kilovatio *nm* : kilowatt
kiosco *nm* → **quiosco**

karate^M
karate

karateka^M
karateka

karategi^M
karate-gi

obi^M
obi

zona^F de combate^M
contest area

línea^F de árbitro^M
referee's line

línea^F de los competidores^M
competitors' line

zona^F de competición^F
competition area

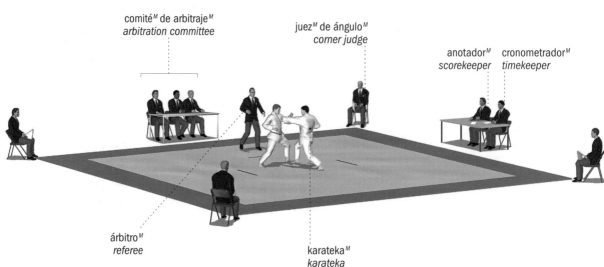

comité^M de arbitraje^M
arbitration committee

juez^M de ángulo^M
corner judge

anotador^M
scorekeeper

cronometrador^M
timekeeper

árbitro^M
referee

karateka^M
karateka

l *nf*: l, twelfth letter of the
Spanish alphabet
la *pron* **1**: her, it **2** (*formal*): you **3 la
que**: the one who — **la** *art* → **el**
laberinto *nm*: labyrinth, maze
labia *nf, fam*: gift of gab
labio *nm*: lip
labor *nf* **1**: work, labor **2** TAREA: task
3 labores domésticas: housework
— **laborable** *adj* **día laborable**:
business day — **laborar** *vi*: work
— **laboratorio** *nm*: laboratory, lab
— **laborioso, -sa** *adj*: laborious
labrar *vt* **1**: cultivate, till **2**: work
(metals), carve (stone, wood) **3** CAUSAR
: cause, bring about — **labrado,
-da** *adj* **1**: cultivated, tilled **2**: carved,
wrought — **labrador, -dora** *n*:
farmer — **labranza** *nf*: farming
laca *nf* **1**: lacquer **2**: hair spray
lacayo *nm*: lackey
lacerar *vt*: lacerate
lacio, -cia *adj* **1**: limp **2**
: straight (of hair)
lacónico, -ca *adj*: laconic
lacra *nf*: scar
lacrar *vt*: seal — **lacre** *nm*: sealing wax
lacrimógeno, -na *adj* **gas lacrimógeno**
: tear gas — **lacrimoso, -sa** *adj*: tearful
lácteo, -tea *adj* **1**: dairy **2**
Vía Láctea: Milky Way
ladear *vt*: tilt — **ladearse** *vr*: lean
ladera *nf*: slope, hillside
ladino, -na *adj*: crafty
lado *nm* **1**: side **2 al lado**: next door,
nearby **3 al lado de**: beside, next
to **4 de lado**: sideways **5 por otro
lado**: on the other hand **6 por todos
lados**: everywhere, all around
ladrar *vi*: bark — **ladrido** *nm*: bark
ladrillo *nm*: brick
ladrón, -drona *n, mpl* **-drones**: thief
lagarto *nm*: lizard —
lagartija *nf*: (small) lizard
▸ **lago** *nm*: lake
lágrima *nf*: tear
laguna *nf* **1**: lagoon **2** VACÍO: gap
laico, -ca *adj*: lay, secular — **laico,
-ca** *n*: layman *m*, layperson
lamentar *vt* **1**: regret, be sorry about **2
lo lamento**: I'm sorry — **lamentarse** *vr*
: lament — **lamentable** *adj* **1**:
deplorable **2** TRISTE: sad, pitiful —
lamento *nm*: lament, moan
lamer *vt* **1**: lick **2**: lap (against)

— **lamida** *nf*: lick
lámina *nf* **1** PLANCHA: sheet **2** DIBUJO:
plate, illustration — **laminar** *vt*: laminate
lámpara *nf*: lamp
lampiño, -ña *adj*: beardless, hairless
lana *nf* **1**: wool **2 de lana**: woolen
lance *nm* **1**: event, incident **2**:
throw (of dice, etc.) **3** RIÑA: quarrel
lanceta *nf*: lancet
lancha *nf* **1**: boat, launch **2**
lancha motora: motorboat
langosta *nf* **1**: lobster **2**: locust (insect)
— **langostino** *nm*: prawn, crayfish
languidecer {53} *vi*: languish —
languidez *nf, pl* **-deces**: languor —
lánguido, -da *adj*: languid, listless
lanilla *nf*: nap (of fabric)
lanudo, -da *adj*: woolly
lanza *nf*: spear, lance
lanzar {21} *vt* **1**: throw **2**: shoot
(a glance), give (a sigh, etc.) **3**:
launch (a missile, a project) —
lanzarse *vr*: throw oneself —
lanzamiento *nm*: throwing, launching
lapicero *nm*: (mechanical) pencil
lápida *nf*: tombstone
lapidar *vt*: stone
lápiz *nm, pl* **-pices** **1**: pencil **2**

lápiz de labios: lipstick
lapso *nm*: lapse (of time) — **lapsus** *nms
& pl*: lapse, slip (of the tongue)
largar {52} *vt* **1** AFLOJAR: loosen, slacken
2 *fam*: give — **largarse** *vr, fam*: go
away, beat it — **largo, -ga** *adj* **1**: long
2 a la larga: in the long run **3 a lo largo**
: lengthwise **4 a lo largo de**: along —
largo *nm*: length — **largometraje** *nm*:
feature film — **largueza** *nf*: generosity
laringe *nf*: larynx —
laringitis *nfs & pl*: laryngitis
larva *nf*: larva
las → **el**
lascivo, -va *adj*: lascivious, lewd
láser *nm*: laser
lastimar *vt*: hurt — **lastimarse** *vr*
: hurt oneself — **lástima** *nf* **1**:
pity **2 dar lástima**: be pitiful **3 me
dan lástima**: I feel sorry for them **4**
¡qué lástima!: what a shame! —
lastimero, -ra *adj*: pitiful, wretched —
lastimoso, -sa *adj*: pitiful, terrible
lastre *nm*: ballast
lata *nf* **1**: tinplate **2**: (tin) can **3**
fam: nuisance, bore **4 dar (la)**
lata a *fam*: bother, annoy
latente *adj*: latent

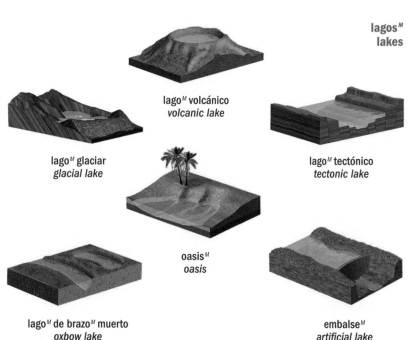

lagos^M
lakes

lago^M volcánico
volcanic lake

lago^M glaciar
glacial lake

lago^M tectónico
tectonic lake

oasis^M
oasis

lago^M de brazo^M muerto
oxbow lake

embalse^M
artificial lake

lector^M **de CD**^{M}
CD player

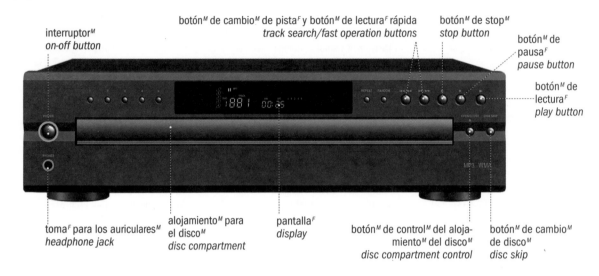

interruptor^M
on-off button

botón^M de cambio^M de pista^F y botón^M de lectura^F rápida
track search/fast operation buttons

botón^M de stop^M
stop button

botón^M de
pausa^F
pause button

botón^M de
lectura^F
play button

toma^F para los auriculares^M
headphone jack

alojamiento^M para
el disco^M
disc compartment

pantalla^F
display

botón^M de control^M del aloja-
miento^M del disco^M
disc compartment control

botón^M de cambio^M
de disco^M
disc skip

---

lateral *adj* : side, lateral

latido *nm* **1** : beat, throb **2 latido del corazón** : heartbeat

latifundio *nm* : large estate

látigo *nm* : whip — **latigazo** *nm* : lash

latín *nm* : Latin (language)

latino, -na *adj* **1** : Latin **2** : Latin-American — **latino, -na** *n* : Latin American — **latinoamericano, -na** *adj* : Latin-American — **latinoamericano, -na** *n* : Latin American

latir *vi* : beat, throb

latitud *nf* : latitude

latón *nm, pl* **-tones** : brass

latoso, -sa *adj, fam* : annoying

laúd *nm* : lute

laudable *adj* : laudable

laureado, -da *adj* : prize-winning

laurel *nm* **1** : laurel **2** : bay leaf (in cooking)

lava *nf* : lava

lavar *vt* : wash — **lavarse** *vr* **1** : wash oneself **2 lavarse las manos** : wash one's hands — **lavable** *adj* : washable — **lavabo** *nm* **1** : sink **2** RETRETE : lavatory, toilet — **lavadero** *nm* : laundry room — **lavado** *nm* : wash, washing — **lavadora** *nf* : washing machine — **lavamanos** *nms & pl* : washbowl — **lavandería** *nf* : laundry (service) —

lavaplatos *nms & pl* **1** : dishwasher **2** *Lat* : kitchen sink — **lavativa** *nf* : enema — **lavatorio** *nm* : lavatory, washroom — **lavavajillas** *nms & pl* : dishwasher

laxante *adj & nm* : laxative — **laxo, -xa** *adj* : loose

lazo *nm* **1** VÍNCULO : link, bond **2** LAZADA : bow **3** : lasso, lariat — **lazada** *nf* : bow, loop

le *pron* **1** : (to) her, (to) him, (to) it **2** *(formal)* : (to) you **3** *(as direct object)* : him, you

leal *adj* : loyal, faithful — **lealtad** *nf* : loyalty, allegiance

lebrel *nm* : hound

lección *nf, pl* **-ciones 1** : lesson **2** : lecture (in a classroom)

leche *nf* **1** : milk **2 leche descremada** *or* **leche desnatada** : skim milk **3 leche en polvo** : powdered milk — **lechera** *nf* : milk jug — **lechería** *nf* : dairy store — **lechero, -ra** *adj* : dairy — **lechero, -ra** *n* : milkman *m*, milk dealer

lecho *nm* : bed

lechón, -chona *n, mpl* **-chones** : suckling pig

lechoso, -sa *adj* : milky

lechuga *nf* : lettuce

lechuza *nf* : owl

▶ **lector, -tora** *n* : reader — **lectura** *nf* **1**

: reading **2** ESCRITOS : reading matter

leer {20} *v* : read

legación *nf, pl* **-ciones** : legation

legado *nm* **1** : legacy **2** ENVIADO : legate, emissary

legajo *nm* : dossier, file

legal *adj* : legal — **legalidad** *nf* : legality — **legalizar** {21} *vt* : legalize — **legalización** *nf, pl* **-ciones** : legalization

legar {52} *vt* : bequeath

legendario, -ria *adj* : legendary

legible *adj* : legible

legión *nf, pl* **-giones** : legion — **legionario, -ria** *n* : legionnaire

legislar *vi* : legislate — **legislación** *nf, pl* **-ciones** : legislation — **legislador, -dora** *n* : legislator — **legislatura** *nf* : legislature

legítimo, -ma *adj* **1** : legitimate **2** GENUINO : authentic — **legitimidad** *nf* : legitimacy

lego, -ga *adj* **1** : secular, lay **2** IGNORANTE : ignorant — **lego, -ga** *n* : layman *m*, layperson

legua *nf* : league

legumbre *nf* : vegetable

leído, -da *adj* : well-read

lejano, -na *adj* : distant, far away — **lejanía** *nf* : distance

lejía *nf* : bleach

lejos *adv* **1** : far (away) **2 a lo lejos**
: in the distance **3 de lejos** *or* **desde**
lejos : from afar **4 lejos de** : far from
lelo, -la *adj* : silly, stupid
lema *nm* : motto
lencería *nf* **1** : linen **2** :
(women's) lingerie
▶ **lengua** *nf* **1** : tongue **2** IDIOMA : language
3 morderse la lengua : hold one's tongue
lenguado *nm* : sole, flounder
lenguaje *nm* : language
lengüeta *nf* **1** : tongue (of a shoe)
2 : reed (of a musical instrument)
lengüetada *nf* **beber a**
lengüetadas : lap (up)
lente *nmf* **1** : lens **2 lentes** *nmpl*
: eyeglasses **3 lentes de**
contacto : contact lenses
lenteja *nf* : lentil — **lentejuela** *nf* : sequin
lento, -ta *adj* : slow — **lento** *adv* :
slowly — **lentitud** *nf* : slowness
leña *nf* : firewood — **leñador, -dora** *n* :
lumberjack, woodcutter — **leño** *nm* : log
león, -ona *n, mpl* **leones** : lion, lioness *f*
leopardo *nm* : leopard
leotardo *nm* : leotard, tights *pl*
lepra *nf* : leprosy — **leproso, -sa** *n* : leper
lerdo, -da *adj* **1** TORPE : clumsy
2 TONTO : slow-witted
les *pron* **1** : (to) them, (to) you **2**
(*as direct object*) : them, you
lesbiano, -na *adj* : lesbian
— **lesbiana** *nf* : lesbian —
lesbianismo *nm* : lesbianism
lesión *nf, pl* **-siones** : lesion, wound
— **lesionado, -da** *adj* : injured,
wounded — **lesionar** *vt* **1** : injure,
wound **2** DAÑAR : damage
letal *adj* : lethal
letanía *nf* : litany
letárgico, -ca *adj* : lethargic
— **letargo** *nm* : lethargy
letra *nf* **1** : letter **2** ESCRITURA :
handwriting **3** : lyrics *pl* (of a song) **4**
letra de cambio : bill of exchange **5**
letras *nfpl* : arts — **letrado, -da** *adj* :
learned — **letrero** *nm* : sign, notice
letrina *nf* : latrine
leucemia *nf* : leukemia
levadizo, -za *adj* **puente**
levadizo : drawbridge
levadura *nf* **1** : yeast **2 levadura**
en polvo : baking powder
levantar *vt* **1** : lift, raise **2** RECOGER : pick
up **3** CONSTRUIR : erect, put up **4** ENCENDER

: rouse, stir up **5 levantar la mesa** *Lat* :
clear the table — **levantarse** *vr* **1** : rise,
stand up **2** : get out of bed **3** SUBLEVARSE
: rise up — **levantamiento** *nm* **1** :
raising, lifting **2** SUBLEVACIÓN : uprising
levante *nm* **1** : east **2** : east wind
levar *vt* **levar anclas** : weigh anchor
leve *adj* **1** : light, slight **2** : minor,
trivial (of wounds, sins, etc.)
— **levedad** *nf* : lightness —
levemente *adv* : lightly, slightly
léxico *nm* : vocabulary, lexicon
ley *nf* **1** : law **2 de (buena) ley**
: genuine, pure (of metals)
leyenda *nf* **1** : legend **2** : caption
(of an illustration, etc.)
liar {85} *vt* **1** : bind, tie (up) **2** : roll
(a cigarette) **3** CONFUNDIR : confuse,

muddle — **liarse** *vr* : get mixed up
libanés, -nesa *adj, mpl*
-neses : Lebanese
libelo *nm* **1** : libel **2** : petition (in court)
libélula *nf* : dragonfly
liberación *nf, pl* **-ciones** :
liberation, deliverance
liberal *adj & nmf* : liberal —
liberalidad *nf* : generosity, liberality
liberar *vt* : liberate, free — **libertad** *nf* **1**
: freedom, liberty **2 libertad bajo fianza** :
bail **3 libertad condicional** : parole **4 en**
libertad : free — **libertar** *vt* : set free
libertinaje *nm* : licentiousness
— **libertino, -na** *n* : libertine
libido *nf* : libido
libio, -bia *adj* : Libyan
libra *nf* **1** : pound **2 libra**

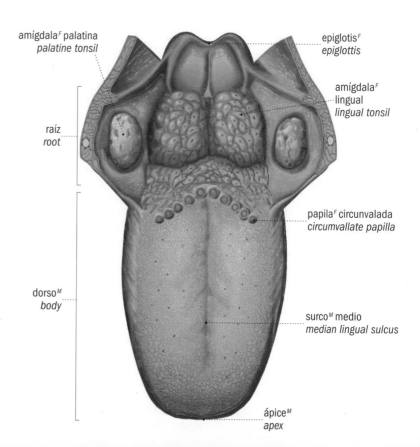

lengua^M
tongue

amígdala^F palatina
palatine tonsil

epiglotis^F
epiglottis

amígdala^F
lingual
lingual tonsil

raíz
root

papila^F circunvalada
circumvallate papilla

dorso^M
body

surco^M medio
median lingual sulcus

ápice^M
apex

libro[M] **encuadernado
bound book**

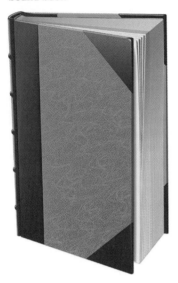

esterlina : pound sterling
librar vt **1** : free, save **2** : wage,
fight (a battle) **3** : draw, issue (a
check, etc.) — **librarse** vr **librarse
de** : free oneself from, get rid of
libre adj **1** : free **2** : unoccupied
(of space), spare (of time) **3 al
aire libre** : in the open air **4 libre
de impuestos** : tax-free
librea nf : livery
▸ **libro** nm **1** : book **2 libro de bolsillo** :
paperback — **librería** nf : bookstore —
librero, -ra n : bookseller — **librero** nm
Lat : bookcase — **libreta** nf : notebook
licencia nf **1** : license, permit **2**
PERMISO : permission **3** : (military) leave
— **licenciado, -da** n **1** : graduate **2**
Lat : lawyer — **licenciar** vt : dismiss,
discharge — **licenciarse** vr : graduate
— **licenciatura** nf : degree
licencioso, -sa adj : licentious
liceo nm : high school
licitar vt : bid for
lícito, -ta adj **1** : lawful,
legal **2** JUSTO : just, fair
licor nm **1** : liquor **2** : liqueur
— **licorera** nf : decanter
licuadora nf : blender — **licuado** nm
: milk shake — **licuar** {3} vt : liquefy

lid nf **1** : fight **2 en buena
lid** : fair and square
líder adj : leading — **líder** nmf : leader
— **liderato** or **liderazgo** nm : leadership
lidia nf : bullfight — **lidiar** v : fight
liebre nf : hare
lienzo nm **1** : cotton or linen cloth **2** :
canvas (for a painting) **3** PARED : wall
liga nf **1** : league **2** Lat : rubber band **3** :
garter (for stockings) — **ligadura** nf **1**
ATADURA : tie, bond **2** : ligature (in
medicine or music) — **ligamento** nm :
ligament — **ligar** {52} vt : bind, tie (up)
ligero, -ra adj **1** : light, lightweight
2 LEVE : slight **3** ÁGIL : agile **4** FRÍVOLO
: lighthearted, superficial —
ligeramente adv : lightly, slightly —
ligereza nf **1** : lightness **2** : flippancy
(of character), thoughtlessness
(of actions) **3** AGILIDAD : agility
lija nf : sandpaper — **lijar** vt : sand
lila nf : lilac
lima nf **1** : file **2** : lime (fruit) **3 lima
para uñas** : nail file — **limar** vt : file
limbo nm : limbo
limitar vt : limit — vi **limitar con** :
border on — **limitación** nf, pl **-ciones**
: limitation, limit — **límite** nm **1** : limit
2 CONFÍN : boundary, border **3 límite de
velocidad** : speed limit **4 fecha límite** :
deadline — **limítrofe** adj : bordering
limo nm : slime, mud
limón nm, pl **-mones 1** : lemon
2 limón verde Lat : lime —
limonada nf : lemonade
limosna nf **1** : alms **2 pedir limosna**
: beg — **limosnero, -ra** n : beggar
limpiabotas nmfs & pl : bootblack
limpiaparabrisas nms &
pl : windshield wiper
limpiar vt **1** : clean, wipe (away)
2 limpiar en seco : dry-clean —
limpieza nf **1** : cleanliness **2** : (act of)
cleaning — **limpio** adv : cleanly, fairly
— **limpio, -pia** adj **1** : clean, neat **2**
HONRADO : honest **3** NETO : net, clear
limusina nf : limousine
linaje nm : lineage, ancestry
linaza nf : linseed
lince nm : lynx
linchar vt : lynch
lindar vi **lindar con** : border on
— **lindante** adj : bordering —
linde nmf or **lindero** nm : boundary
lindo, -da adj **1** : pretty, lovely

2 de lo lindo fam : a lot
línea nf **1** : line **2 línea de conducta**
: course of action **3 en línea** :
on-line **4 guardar la línea** : watch
one's figure — **lineal** adj : linear
lingote nm : ingot
lingüista nmf : linguist —
lingüística nf : linguistics —
lingüístico, -ca adj : linguistic
linimento nm : liniment
lino nm **1** : flax (plant) **2** : linen (fabric)
linóleo nm : linoleum
linterna nf **1** FAROL : lantern **2** : flashlight
lío nm **1** : bundle **2** fam : mess,
trouble **3** fam : (love) affair
liofilizar {21} vt : freeze-dry
liquen nm : lichen
liquidar vt **1** : liquefy **2** : liquidate
(merchandise, etc.) **3** : settle, pay
off (a debt, etc.) — **liquidación** nf,
pl **-ciones 1** : liquidation **2** REBAJA :
clearance sale — **líquido, -da** adj **1** :
liquid **2** NETO : net — **líquido** nm : liquid
lira nf : lyre
lírico, -ca adj : lyric, lyrical
— **lírica** nf : lyric poetry
lirio nm : iris
lisiado, -da adj : disabled —
lisiado, -da n : disabled person
— **lisiar** vt : disable, cripple
liso, -sa adj **1** : smooth **2** PLANO
: flat **3** SENCILLO : plain **4 pelo
liso, -sa** : straight hair
lisonjear vt : flatter — **lisonja** nf : flattery
lista nf **1** : stripe **2** ENUMERACIÓN
: list **3** : menu (in a restaurant)
— **listado, -da** adj : striped
listo, -ta adj **1** : clever, smart
2 PREPARADO : ready
listón nm, pl **-tones 1** : ribbon
2 : strip (of wood)
lisura nf : smoothness
litera nf : bunk bed, berth
literal adj : literal
literatura nf : literature —
literario, -ria adj : literary
litigar {52} vi : litigate — **litigio** nm **1**
: litigation **2 en litigio** : in dispute
litografía nf **1** : lithography
2 : lithograph (picture)
▸ **litoral** adj : coastal — **litoral** nm
: shore, seaboard
litro nm : liter
liturgia nf : liturgy — **litúrgico,
-ca** adj : liturgical

liviano, -na *adj* **1** LIGERO : light **2** INCONSTANTE : fickle

lívido, -da *adj* : livid

llaga *nf* : sore, wound

llama *nf* **1** : flame **2** : llama (animal)

llamar *vt* **1** : call **2** : call up (on the telephone) — *vi* **1** : phone, call **2** : knock, ring (at the door) — **llamarse** *vr* **1** : be called **2 ¿cómo te llamas?** : what's your name? — **llamada** *nf* : call — **llamado, -da** *adj* : named, called — **llamamiento** *nm* : call, appeal

llamarada *nf* **1** : blaze **2** : flushing (of the face)

llamativo, -va *adj* : flashy, showy

llamear *vi* : flame, blaze

llano, -na *adj* **1** : flat **2** : straightforward (of a person, a message, etc.) **3** SENCILLO : plain, simple — **llano** *nm* : plain — **llaneza** *nf* : simplicity

llanta *nf* **1** : rim (of a wheel) **2** *Lat* : tire

llanto *nm* : crying, weeping

llanura *nf* : plain

llave *nf* **1** : key **2** *Lat* : faucet **3** INTERRUPTOR : switch **4 cerrar con llave** : lock **5 llave inglesa** : monkey wrench — **llavero** *nm* : key chain

llegar {52} *vi* **1** : arrive, come **2** ALCANZAR : reach **3** BASTAR : be enough **4 llegar a** : manage to **5 llegar a ser** : become — **llegada** *nf* : arrival

llenar *vt* : fill (up), fill in — **lleno, -na** *adj* **1** : full **2 de lleno** : completely — **lleno** *nm* : full house

llevar *vt* **1** : take, carry **2** CONDUCIR : lead **3** : wear (clothing, etc.) **4** TENER : have **5 llevo una hora aquí** : I've been here for an hour — **llevarse** *vr* **1** : take (away) **2 llevarse bien** : get along well — **llevadero, -ra** *adj* : bearable

llorar *vi* : cry, weep — **lloriquear** *vi* : whimper, whine — **lloro** *nm* : crying — **llorón, -rona** *n, mpl* **-rones** : crybaby, whiner — **lloroso, -sa** *adj* : tearful

llover {47} *v impers* : rain — **llovizna** *nf* : drizzle — **lloviznar** *v impers* : drizzle

lluvia *nf* : rain — **lluvioso, -sa** *adj* : rainy

lo *pron* **1** : him, it **2** (*formal, masculine*) : you **3 lo que** : what, that which — **lo** *art* **1** : the **2 lo mejor** : the best (part) **3 sé lo bueno que eres** : I know how good you are

loa *nf* : praise — **loable** *adj* : praiseworthy — **loar** *vt* : praise

lobo, -ba *n* : wolf

lóbrego, -ga *adj* : gloomy

lóbulo *nm* : lobe

local *adj* : local — **local** *nm* : premises *pl* — **localidad** *nf* : town, locality — **localizar** {21} *vt* **1** : localize **2** ENCONTRAR : locate — **localizarse** *vr* : be located

loción *nf, pl* **-ciones** : lotion

loco, -ca *adj* **1** : crazy, insane **2 a lo loco** : wildly, recklessly **3 volverse loco, -ca** : go mad — **loco, -ca** *n* **1** : crazy person, lunatic **2 hacerse el loco** : act the fool

locomoción *nf, pl* **-ciones** : locomotion — **locomotora** *nf* : engine, locomotive

locuaz *adj, pl* **-cuaces** : talkative, loquacious

locución *nf, pl* **-ciones** : expression, phrase

locura *nf* **1** : insanity, madness **2** INSENSATEZ : crazy act, folly

locutor, -tora *n* : announcer

locutorio *nm* : phone booth

lodo *nm* : mud — **lodazal** *nm* : quagmire

logaritmo *nm* : logarithm

lógica *nf* : logic — **lógico, -ca** *adj* :

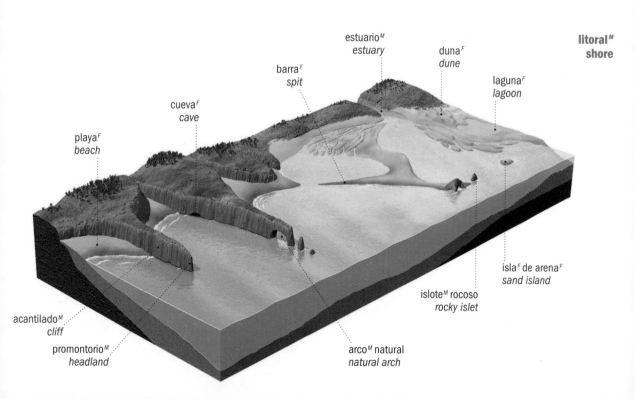

litoral^M
shore

estuario^M
estuary

duna^F
dune

laguna^F
lagoon

barra^F
spit

cueva^F
cave

playa^F
beach

isla^F de arena^F
sand island

islote^M rocoso
rocky islet

acantilado^M
cliff

promontorio^M
headland

arco^M natural
natural arch

logical — **logística** *nf* : logistics *pl*
logotipo *nm* : logo
lograr *vt* **1** : achieve, attain **2** CONSEGUIR : get, obtain **3 lograr hacer** : manage to do — **logro** *nm* : achievement, success
loma *nf* : hill, hillock
lombriz *nf, pl* **-brices** : worm
lomo *nm* **1** : back (of an animal) **2** : spine (of a book) **3 lomo de cerdo** : pork loin
lona *nf* : canvas
loncha *nf* : slice (of bacon, etc.)
lonche *nm Lat* : lunch — **lonchería** *nf*

lucha^F
wrestling

luchador^M
wrestler

Lat : luncheonette
longaniza *nf* : sausage
longevidad *nf* : longevity — **longevo, -va** *adj* : long-lived
longitud *nf* **1** : longitude **2** LARGO : length
lonja → **loncha**
loro *nm* : parrot
los, las *pron* **1** : them **2** : you **3 los que, las que** : those who, the ones who — **los** *art* → **el**
losa *nf* **1** : flagstone **2** *or* **losa sepulcral** : tombstone
lote *nm* **1** : batch, lot **2** *Lat* : plot of land
lotería *nf* : lottery
loto *nm* : lotus
loza *nf* : crockery, earthenware
lozano, -na *adj* **1** : healthy-looking, vigorous **2** : luxuriant (of plants) — **lozanía** *nf* **1** : (youthful) vigor **2** : luxuriance (of plants)
lubricar {72} *vt* : lubricate — **lubricante** *adj* : lubricating — **lubricante** *nm* : lubricant
lucero *nm* : bright star
luchar *vi* **1** : fight, struggle **2** : ▶ wrestle (in sports) — **lucha** *nf* **1** : struggle, fight **2** : wrestling (sport) — **luchador, -dora** *n* : fighter, wrestler
lucidez *nf, pl* **-deces** : lucidity — **lúcido, -da** *adj* : lucid
lucido, -da *adj* : magnificent, splendid
luciérnaga *nf* : firefly, glowworm
lucir {45} *vi* **1** : shine **2** *Lat* : appear, seem — *vt* **1** : wear, sport **2** OSTENTAR : show off — **lucirse** *vr* **1** : shine, excel **2** PRESUMIR : show off — **lucimiento** *nm* **1** : brilliance

2 ÉXITO : brilliant performance, success
lucrativo, -va *adj* : lucrative — **lucro** *nm* : profit
luego *adv* **1** : then **2** : later (on) **3 desde luego** : of course **4 ¡hasta luego!** : see you later! **5 luego que** : as soon as — **luego** *conj* : therefore
lugar *nm* **1** : place **2** ESPACIO : space, room **3 dar lugar a** : give rise to **4 en lugar de** : instead of **5 tener lugar** : take place
lugarteniente *nmf* : deputy
lúgubre *adj* : gloomy
lujo *nm* **1** : luxury **2 de lujo** : deluxe — **lujoso, -sa** *adj* : luxurious
lujuria *nf* : lust
lumbre *nf* **1** : fire **2 poner en la lumbre** : put on the stove
luminoso, -sa *adj* : shining, luminous
luna *nf* **1** : moon **2** : (window) glass **3** ESPEJO : mirror **4 luna de miel** : honeymoon — **lunar** *adj* : lunar — **lunar** *nm* : mole, beauty spot
lunes *nms & pl* : Monday
lupa *nf* : magnifying glass
lúpulo *nm* : hops
lustrar *vt* : shine, polish — **lustre** *nm* **1** BRILLO : luster, shine **2** ESPLENDOR : glory — **lustroso, -sa** *adj* : lustrous, shiny
luto *nm* **1** : mourning **2 estar de luto** : be in mourning
luxación *nf, pl* **-ciones** : dislocation
luz *nf, pl* **luces 1** : light **2** : lighting (in a room, etc.) **3** *fam* : electricity **4 a la luz de** : in light of **5 dar a luz** : give birth **6 sacar a la luz** : bring to light

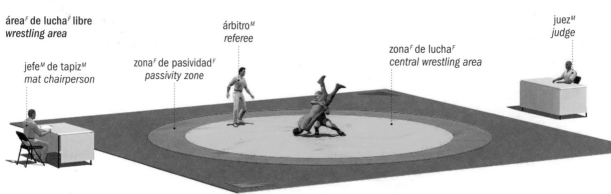

área^F **de lucha**^F **libre**
wrestling area

jefe^M **de tapiz**^M
mat chairperson

zona^F **de pasividad**^F
passivity zone

árbitro^M
referee

zona^F **de lucha**^F
central wrestling area

juez^M
judge

m *nf* : m, 13th letter of the Spanish alphabet

macabro, -bra *adj* : macabre

macarrón *nm, pl* **-rrones 1** : macaroon **2 macarrones** *nmpl* : macaroni

maceta *nf* : flowerpot

machacar {72} *vt* : crush, grind — *vi* **machacar sobre** : go on about — **machacón, -cona** *adj, mpl* **-cones** : tiresome, boring

machete *nm* : machete — **machetear** *vt* : hack with a machete

macho *adj* **1** : male **2** *fam* : macho — **macho** *nm* **1** : male **2** *fam* : he-man — **machista** *nm* : male chauvinist

machucar {72} *vt* **1** : beat, crush **2** : bruise (fruit)

macizo, -za *adj* : solid — **macizo** *nm* **macizo de flores** : flower bed

mácula *nf* : stain

madeja *nf* : skein, hank

madera *nf* **1** : wood **2** : lumber (for construction) **3 madera dura** : hardwood — **madero** *nm* : piece of lumber, plank

madre *nf* **1** : mother **2 madre política** : mother-in-law — **madrastra** *nf* : stepmother

madreselva *nf* : honeysuckle

madriguera *nf* : burrow, den

madrileño, -ña *adj* : of or from Madrid

madrina *nf* **1** : godmother **2** : bridesmaid (at a wedding)

madrugada *nf* : dawn, daybreak — **madrugador, -dora** *n* : early riser

madurar *v* **1** : mature **2** : ripen (of fruit) — **madurez** *nf, pl* **-reces 1** : maturity **2** : ripeness (of fruit) — **maduro, -ra** *adj* **1** : mature **2** : ripe (of fruit)

maestría *nf* : mastery, skill — **maestro, -tra** *adj* : masterly, skilled — **maestro, -tra** *n* **1** : teacher (in grammar school) **2** EXPERTO : expert, master

Mafia *nf* : Mafia

magia *nf* : magic — **mágico, -ca** *adj* : magic, magical

magisterio *nm* : teachers *pl*, teaching profession

magistrado, -da *n* : magistrate, judge

magistral *adj* **1** : masterful **2** : magisterial (of an attitude, etc.)

magnánimo, -ma *adj* : magnanimous — **magnanimidad** *nf* : magnanimity

magnate *nmf* : magnate, tycoon

magnesia *nf* : magnesia — **magnesio** *nm* : magnesium

magnético, -ca *adj* : magnetic —
▸ **magnetismo** *nm* : magnetism — **magnetizar** {21} *vt* : magnetize

magnetófono *nm* : tape recorder

magnificencia *nf* : magnificence — **magnífico, -ca** *adj* : magnificent

magnitud *nf* : magnitude

magnolia *nf* : magnolia

mago, -ga *n* **1** : magician **2 los Reyes Magos** : the Magi

magro, -gra *adj* **1** : lean **2** MEZQUINO : poor, meager

magullar *vt* : bruise — **magulladura** *nf* : bruise

mahometano, -na *adj* : Islamic, Muslim — **mahometano, -na** *n* : Muslim

maicena *nf* : cornstarch

maíz *nm* : corn

maja *nf* : pestle

majadero, -ra *adj* : foolish, silly — **majadero, -ra** *n* : fool

majar *vt* : crush

majestad *nf* **1** : majesty **2 Su Majestad** : His/Her Majesty

— **majestuoso, -sa** *adj* : majestic

majo, -ja *adj* **1** : nice **2** GUAPO : good-looking

mal *adv* **1** : badly, poorly **2** INCORRECTAMENTE : incorrectly **3** DIFÍCILMENTE : with difficulty, hardly **4 de mal en peor** : from bad to worse **5 menos mal** : it's just as well — **mal** *nm* **1** : evil **2** DAÑO : harm, damage **3** ENFERMEDAD : illness — **mal** *adj* → **malo**

malabarismo *nm* : juggling — **malabarista** *nmf* : juggler

malacostumbrar *vt* : spoil, pamper — **malacostumbrado, -da** *adj* : spoiled

malaria *nf* : malaria

malasio, -sia *adj* : Malaysian

malaventura *nf* : misfortune — **malaventurado, -da** *adj* : unfortunate

malayo, -ya *adj* : Malay, Malayan

malcriado, -da *adj* : bad-mannered, spoiled

maldad *nf* **1** : evil **2** : evil deed

maldecir {11} *vt* : curse, damn — *vi* **1** : curse, swear **2 maldecir de** : speak ill

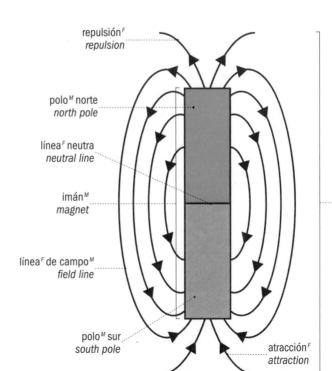

magnetismo[M]
magnetism

repulsión[F]
repulsion

polo[M] norte
north pole

línea[F] neutra
neutral line

imán[M]
magnet

línea[F] de campo[M]
field line

polo[M] sur
south pole

campo[M] magnético
magnetic field

atracción[F]
attraction

of — **maldición** *nf, pl* **-ciones** : curse
— **maldito, -ta** *adj, fam* : damned
maleable *adj* : malleable
maleante *nmf* : crook
malecón *nm, pl* **-cones** : jetty
maleducado, -da *adj* : rude
maleficio *nm* : curse — **maléfico,
-ca** *adj* : evil, harmful
malentendido *nm* : misunderstanding
malestar *nm* **1** : discomfort
2 INQUIETUD : uneasiness
maleta *nf* **1** : suitcase **2 hacer la maleta**
: pack one's bags — **maletero, -ra** *n*
: porter — **maletero** *nm* : trunk (of an
automobile) — **maletín** *nm, pl* **-tines 1**
PORTAFOLIO : briefcase **2** : overnight bag
malévolo, -la *adj* : malevolent —
malevolencia *nf* : malevolence
maleza *nf* **1** : underbrush **2**
MALAS HIERBAS : weeds *pl*
malgastar *vt* : waste, squander
malhablado, -da *adj* : foul-mouthed
malhechor, -chora *n* :
criminal, delinquent
malhumorado, -da *adj* :
bad-tempered, cross
malicia *nf* : malice — **malicioso,
-sa** *adj* : malicious
maligno, -na *adj* **1** : malignant
2 PERNICIOSO : harmful, evil
malla *nf* **1** : mesh **2 mallas** *nfpl* : tights
malo, -la *adj* **(mal** *before masculine
singular nouns*) **1** : bad **2** : poor (in
quality) **3** ENFERMO : unwell **4 estar de
malas** : be in a bad mood — **malo,
-la** *n* : villain, bad guy (in movies, etc.)
malograr *vt* : waste —
malograrse *vr* **1** FRACASAR : fail **2** :
die young — **malogro** *nm* : failure
maloliente *adj* : smelly
malpensado, -da *adj* : malicious, nasty
malsano, -na *adj* : unhealthy
malsonante *adj* : rude
malta *nf* : malt
maltratar *vt* : mistreat
maltrecho, -cha *adj* : battered
malvado, -da *adj* : evil, wicked
malvavisco *nm* : marshmallow
malversar *vt* : embezzle —
malversación *nf, pl* **-ciones**
: embezzlement
mama *nf* : teat (of an animal),
breast (of a woman)
mamá *nf, fam* : mom, mama
mamar *vi* **1** : suckle **2 dar de mamar**

a : breast-feed — *vt* **1** : suckle, nurse
2 : learn from childhood, grow up with
— **mamario, -ria** *adj* : mammary
mamarracho *nm, fam* : mess, sight
mambo *nm* : mambo
mamífero, -ra *adj* : mammalian
— **mamífero** *nm* : mammal
mamografía *nf* : mammogram
mampara *nf* : screen, room divider
mampostería *nf* : masonry
manada *nf* **1** : flock, herd, pack
2 en manada : in droves
manar *vi* **1** : flow **2 manar en**
: be rich in — **manantial** *nm* **1**
: spring **2** ORIGEN : source
manchar *vt* **1** : stain, spot,
mark **2** : tarnish (a reputation,
etc.) — **mancharse** *vr* : get
dirty — **mancha** *nf* : stain
mancillar *vt* : sully, stain
manco, -ca *adj* : one-
armed, one-handed
mancomunar *vt* : combine, join
— **mancomunarse** *vr* : unite —
mancomunidad *nf* : union
mandar *vt* **1** : command, order **2**
ENVIAR : send **3** *Lat* : hurl, throw — *vi* **1**
: be in charge **2 ¿mande?** *Lat* : yes?,
pardon? — **mandadero, -ra** *nm* :
messenger — **mandado** *nm* : errand
— **mandamiento** *nm* **1** : order, warrant
2 : commandment (in religion)
mandarina *nf* : mandarin
orange, tangerine
mandato *nm* **1** : term of office **2** ORDEN
: mandate — **mandatario, -ria** *n* **1** :
leader (in politics) **2** : agent (in law)
mandíbula *nf* : jaw, jawbone
mandil *nm* : apron
mando *nm* **1** : command, leadership
2 al mando de : in charge of **3 mando
a distancia** : remote control
mandolina *nf* : mandolin
mandón, -dona *adj, mpl* **-dones** : bossy
manecilla *nf* : hand (of a clock), pointer
manejar *vt* **1** : handle, operate **2** :
manage (a business, etc.) **3** : manipulate
(a person) **4** *Lat* : drive (a car) —
manejarse *vr* **1** : manage, get by **2** *Lat* :
behave — **manejo** *nm* **1** : handling, use
2 : management (of a business, etc.)
manera *nf* **1** : way, manner **2 de manera
que** : so that **3 de ninguna manera** : by
no means **4 de todas maneras** : anyway
manga *nf* **1** : sleeve **2** MANGUERA : hose

mango *nm* **1** : hilt, handle
2 : mango (fruit)
mangonear *vt, fam* : boss
around — *vi* **1** : be bossy **2**
HOLGAZANEAR : loaf, fool around
manguera *nf* : hose
maní *nm, pl* **-níes** *Lat* : peanut
manía *nf* **1** : mania, obsession **2**
MODA PASAJERA : craze, fad **3** ANTIPATÍA
: dislike — **maníaco, -ca** *adj* :
maniacal — **manía** *n* : maniac
maniatar *vt* : tie the hands of
maniático, -ca *adj* : obsessive, fussy —
maniático, -ca *n* : fussy person, fanatic
manicomio *nm* : insane asylum
manicura *nf* : manicure —
manicuro, -ra *n* : manicurist
manido, -da *adj* : stale, hackneyed
manifestar {55} *vt* **1** : demonstrate,
show **2** DECLARAR : express, declare
— **manifestarse** *vr* **1** : become
evident **2** : demonstrate (in politics)
— **manifestación** *nf, pl* **-ciones 1** :
manifestation, sign **2** : demonstration
(in politics) — **manifestante** *nmf*
: protester, demonstrator —
manifiesto, -ta *adj* : manifest, evident
— **manifiesto** *nm* : manifesto
manija *nf* : handle
manillar *nm* : handlebars *pl*
maniobra *nf* : maneuver —
maniobrar *v* : maneuver
manipular *vt* **1** : manipulate **2**
MANEJAR : handle — **manipulación** *nf,
pl* **-ciones** : manipulation
maniquí *nmf, pl* **-quíes** :
mannequin, model — **maniquí** *nm*
: mannequin, dummy
manirroto, -ta *adj* : extravagant
— **manirroto, -ta** *n* : spendthrift
manivela *nf* : crank
manjar *nm* : delicacy, special dish
mano *nf* **1** : hand **2** : coat (of paint,
etc.) **3 a mano** *or* **a la mano** : at hand,
nearby **4 dar la mano** : shake hands
5 de segunda mano : secondhand **6
mano de obra** : labor, manpower
manojo *nm* : bunch
manopla *nf* : mitten
manosear *vt* **1** : handle
excessively **2** : fondle (a person)
manotazo *nm* : slap
mansalva: a mansalva *adv phr*
: at close range, without risk
mansarda *nf* : attic

mansedumbre *nf* **1** : gentleness
2 : tameness (of an animal)
mansión *nf, pl* **-siones** : mansion
manso, -sa *adj* **1** : gentle
2 : tame (of an animal)
manta *nf* **1** : blanket **2** *Lat* : poncho
manteca *nf* : lard, fat —
mantecoso, -sa *adj* : greasy
mantel *nm* : tablecloth —
mantelería *nf* : table linen
mantener {80} *vt* **1** : support **2**
CONSERVAR : preserve **3** : keep up,
maintain (relations, correspondence, etc.)
4 AFIRMAR : affirm — **mantenerse** *vr* **1** :
support oneself **2 mantenerse firme** : hold
one's ground — **mantenimiento** *nm* **1**
: maintenance **2** SUSTENTO : sustenance
mantequilla *nf* : butter —
mantequera *nf* : churn —
mantequería *nf* : dairy
mantilla *nf* : mantilla
manto *nm* : cloak
mantón *nm, pl* **-tones** : shawl
manual *adj* : manual —
manual *nm* : manual, handbook
manubrio *nm* **1** : handle,
crank **2** *Lat* : handlebars *pl*
manufactura *nf* **1** : manufacture
2 FÁBRICA : factory
manuscrito *nm* : manuscript —
manuscrito, -ta *adj* : handwritten
manutención *nf, pl* **-ciones**
: maintenance
manzana *nf* **1** : apple **2** : (city) block
— **manzanar** *nm* : apple orchard
— **manzano** *nm* : apple tree
maña *nf* **1** : skill **2** ASTUCIA : cunning, guile
mañana *adv* : tomorrow —
mañana *nm* **el mañana** : the
future — **mañana** *nf* : morning
mañoso, -sa *adj* **1** :
skillful **2** *Lat* : finicky
mapa *nm* : map — **mapamundi** *nm*
: map of the world
mapache *nm* : raccoon
maqueta *nf* : model, mock-up
maquillaje *nm* : makeup —
maquillarse *vr* : put on makeup
máquina *nf* **1** : machine **2** LOCOMOTORA
: locomotive **3 a toda máquina** : at
full speed **4 máquina de escribir**
: typewriter — **maquinación** *nf,*
pl **-ciones** : machination — **maquinal** *adj*
: mechanical — **maquinaria** *nf* **1** :
machinery **2** : mechanism, works *pl*

(of a watch, etc.) — **maquinilla** *nf* :
small machine — **maquinista** *nmf* **1**
: machinist **2** : (railroad) engineer
mar *nmf* **1** : sea **2 alta mar** : high seas *pl*
maraca *nf* : maraca
maraña *nf* **1** : thicket **2**
ENREDO : tangle, mess
maratón *nm, pl* **-tones** : marathon
maravilla *nf* **1** : wonder, marvel **2** :
marigold (flower) — **maravillar** *vt* :
astonish — **maravillarse** *vr* : be amazed
— **maravilloso, -sa** *adj* : marvelous
marca *nf* **1** : mark **2** : brand (on livestock)
3 *or* **marca de fábrica** : trademark
4 : record (in sports) — **marcado,**
-da *adj* : marked — **marcador** *nm* **1** :
scoreboard **2** *Lat* : marker, felt-tipped pen
marcapasos *nms & pl* : pacemaker
marcar {72} *vt* **1** : mark **2** : brand
(livestock) **3** INDICAR : indicate,
show **4** : dial (a telephone, etc.) **5**
: score (in sports) — *vi* **1** : score
2 : dial (on the telephone, etc.)
marchar *vi* **1** : go **2** CAMINAR : walk **3**
FUNCIONAR : work, run — **marcharse** *vr* :
leave, go — **marcha** *nf* **1** : march **2** PASO
: pace, speed **3** : gear (of an automobile)
4 poner en marcha : put in motion
marchitarse *vr* : wither, wilt —
marchito, -ta *adj* : withered
marcial *adj* : martial, military
marco *nm* **1** : frame **2** : goalposts *pl* (in
sports) **3** ENTORNO : setting, framework
marea *nf* : tide — **marear** *vt* **1** :
make nauseous or dizzy **2** CONFUNDIR :
confuse — **marearse** *vr* **1** : become
nauseated or dizzy **2** CONFUNDIRSE : get

confused — **mareado, -da** *adj* **1** : sick,
nauseous **2** ATURDIDO : dazed, dizzy
maremoto *nm* : tidal wave
mareo *nm* **1** : nausea, seasickness
2 VÉRTIGO : dizziness
marfil *nm* : ivory
margarina *nf* : margarine
margarita *nf* : daisy
margen *nm, pl* **márgenes 1** : edge,
border **2** : margin (of a page, etc.) —
marginado, -da *adj* **1** : alienated **2 clases**
marginadas : underclass — **margen** *n*
: outcast — **marginal** *adj* : marginal
— **marginar** *vt* : ostracize, exclude
mariachi *nm* : mariachi musician or band
maridaje *nm* : marriage, union
— **marido** *nm* : husband
marihuana *or* mariguana *or*
marijuana *nf* : marijuana
marimba *nf* : marimba
marina *nf* **1** : coast **2** *or* **marina**
de guerra : navy, fleet
marinada *nf* : marinade —
marinar *vt* : marinate
marinero, -ra *adj* **1** : sea, marine **2** :
seaworthy (of a ship) — **marinero** *nm*
: sailor — **marino, -na** *adj* : marine
— **marino** *nm* : seaman, sailor
marioneta *nf* : puppet, marionette
mariposa *nf* **1** : butterfly **2**
mariposa nocturna : moth
mariquita *nf* : ladybug
marisco *nm* **1** : shellfish **2**
mariscos *nmpl* : seafood
marisma *nf* : salt marsh
marítimo, -ma *adj* : maritime, shipping
mármol *nm* : marble

mapache^M
raccoon

formas^F farmacéuticas de medicamentos^M
forms of medicines

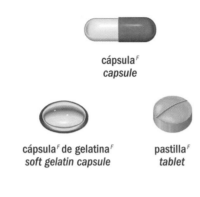

cápsula^F
capsule

cápsula^F de gelatina^F
soft gelatin capsule

pastilla^F
tablet

jarabe^M
syrup

ampolla^F
vial

inhalador^M-dosificador^M
metered dose inhaler

---

marmota *nf* **marmota de**
  América : groundhog
marquesina *nf* : marquee, (glass) canopy
marrano, -na *n* **1** : pig, hog **2** *fam* : slob
marrar *vt* : miss (a target) — *vi* : fail
marrón *adj & nm, pl* **-rrones** : brown
marroquí *adj* : Moroccan
marsopa *nf* : porpoise
marsupial *nm* : marsupial
Marte *nm* : Mars
martes *nms & pl* : Tuesday
martillo *nm* **1** : hammer **2 martillo**
  neumático : jackhammer —
  martillar *or* **martillear** *v* : hammer
mártir *nmf* : martyr — **martirio** *nm*
  : martyrdom — **martirizar** {21} *vt* **1**
  : martyr **2** ATORMENTAR : torment
marxismo *nm* : Marxism —
  marxista *adj & nmf* : Marxist
marzo *nm* : March
mas *conj* : but
más *adv* **1** : more **2 el/la/lo más** : (the)
  most **3** (*in negative constructions*) :
  (any) longer **4 ¡qué día más bonito!**
  : what a beautiful day! — **más** *adj* **1**
  : more **2** : most **3 ¿quién más?** : who
  else? — **más** *prep* : plus — **más** *pron* **1**
  a lo más : at most **2 de más** : extra,
  spare **3 más o menos** : more or less **4**

¿tienes más? : do you have more?
masa *nf* **1** : mass, volume **2** : dough (in
  cooking) **3 masas** *nfpl* : people, masses
masacre *nf* : massacre
masaje *nm* : massage —
  masajear *vt* : massage
mascar {72} *v* : chew
máscara *nf* : mask — **mascarada** *nf*
  : masquerade — **mascarilla** *nf*
  : mask (in medecine, etc.)
mascota *nf* : mascot
masculino, -na *adj* **1** :
  masculine, male **2** VARONIL : manly
  3 : masculine (in grammar) —
  masculinidad *nf* : masculinity
mascullar *v* : mumble
masilla *nf* : putty
masivo, -va *adj* : mass, large-scale
masón *nm, pl* **-sones** : Mason, Freemason
  — **masónico, -ca** *adj* : Masonic
masoquismo *nm* : masochism —
  masoquista *adj* : masochistic —
  masoquismo *nmf* : masochist
masticar {72} *v* : chew
mástil *nm* **1** : mast **2** ASTA : flagpole
  3 : neck (of a stringed instrument)
mastín *nm, pl* **-tines** : mastiff
masturbarse *vr* : masturbate
  — **masturbación** *nf,*

pl **-ciones** : masturbation
mata *nf* : bush, shrub
matadero *nm* : slaughterhouse
matador *nm* : matador, bullfighter
matamoscas *nms & pl* : flyswatter
matar *vt* **1** : kill **2** : slaughter
  (animals) — **matarse** *vr* **1** : be
  killed **2** SUICIDARSE : commit suicide
  — **matanza** *nf* : slaughter, killing
matasanos *nms & pl fam* : quack
matasellos *nms & pl* : postmark
mate *adj* : matte, dull — **mate** *nm* **1**
  : maté **2 jaque mate** : checkmate
matemáticas *nfpl* : mathematics —
  matemático, -ca *adj* : mathematical —
  matemático, -ca *n* : mathematician
materia *nf* **1** ASUNTO : matter **2**
  MATERIAL : material — **material** *adj* **1**
  : material **2 daños materials** :
  property damage — **material** *nm* **1**
  : material **2** EQUIPO : equipment, gear
  — **materialismo** *nm* : materialism
  — **materialista** *adj* : materialistic —
  materializar {21} *vt* : bring to fruition
  — **materializarse** *vr* : materialize —
  materialmente *adv* : absolutely
maternal *adj* : maternal —
  maternidad *nf* **1** : motherhood **2**
  : maternity hospital — **materno,**

-na *adj* **1** : maternal **2 lengua materna** : mother tongue

matinal *adj* : morning

matinée *or* **matiné** *nf* : matinee

matiz *nm, pl* **-tices 1** : nuance **2** : hue, shade (of colors) — **matizar** {21} *vt* **1** : blend (colors) **2** : qualify (a statement, etc.) **3 matiz de** : tinge with

matón *nm, pl* **-tones 1** : bully **2** CRIMINAL : gangster, hoodlum

matorral *nm* : thicket

matraca *nf* **1** : rattle, noisemaker **2 dar la matraca a** : pester

matriarcado *nm* : matriarchy

matrícula *nf* **1** : list, roll, register **2** INSCRIPCIÓN : registration **3** : license plate (of an automobile) — **matricular** *vt* : register — **matricularse** *vr* : register, matriculate

matrimonio *nm* **1** : marriage **2** PAREJA : (married) couple — **matrimonial** *adj* : marital

matriz *nf, pl* **-trices 1** : matrix **2** : uterus, womb (in anatomy)

matrona *nf* : matron

matutino, -na *adj* : morning

maullar {8} *vi* : meow — **maullido** *nm* : meow

maxilar *nm* : jaw, jawbone

máxima *nf* : maxim

máxime *adv* : especially

máximo, -ma *adj* : maximum, highest — **máximo** *nm* **1** : maximum **2 al máximo** : to the full

maya *adj* : Mayan

mayo *nm* : May

mayonesa *nf* : mayonnaise

mayor *adj* **1** (*comparative of* **grande**) : bigger, larger, greater, older **2** (*superlative of* **grande**) : biggest, largest, greatest, oldest **3 al por mayor** : wholesale **4 mayor de edad** : of (legal) age — **mayor** *nmf* **1** : major (in the military) **2** ADULTO : adult **3 mayores** *nmfpl* : grown-ups — **mayoral** *nm* : foreman

mayordomo *nm* : butler

mayoreo *nm Lat* : wholesale

mayoría *nf* : majority

mayorista *adj* : wholesale — **mayorista** *nmf* : wholesaler

mayormente *adv* : primarily

mayúscula *nf* : capital letter — **mayúsculo, -la** *adj* **1** : capital, uppercase **2 un fallo mayúsculo** : a terrible mistake

maza *nf* : mace (weapon)

mazapán *nm, pl* **-panes** : marzipan

mazmorra *nf* : dungeon

mazo *nm* **1** : mallet **2** MAJA : pestle

mazorca *nf* **mazorca de maíz** : corncob

me *pron* **1** (*direct object*) : me **2** (*indirect object*) : to me, for me, from me **3** (*reflexive*) : myself, to myself, for myself, from myself

mecánica *nf* : mechanics — **mecánico, -ca** *adj* : mechanical — **mecánico, -ca** *n* : mechanic

mecanismo *nm* : mechanism — **mecanización** *nf, pl* **-ciones** : mechanization — **mecanizar** {21} *vt* : mechanize

mecanografiar {85} *vt* : type — **mecanografía** *nf* : typing — **mecanógrafo, -fa** *n* : typist

mecate *nm Lat* : rope

mecedora *nf* : rocking chair

mecenas *nmfs & pl* : patron, sponsor — **mecenazgo** *nm* : patronage, sponsorship

mecer {86} *vt* **1** : rock **2** : push (on a swing) — **mecerse** *vr* : rock, swing

mecha *nf* **1** : fuse (of a bomb, etc.) **2** : wick (of a candle)

mechero *nm* **1** : burner **2** *Spain* : cigarette lighter

mechón *nm, pl* **-chones** : lock (of hair)

medalla *nf* : medal — **medallón** *nm, pl* **-llones 1** : medallion **2** : locket (jewelry)

media *nf* **1** : average **2 medias** *nfpl* : stockings **3 a medias** : by halves, halfway

mediación *nf, pl* **-ciones** : mediation

mediado, -da *adj* **1** : half full, half empty, half over **2** : halfway through — **mediados** *nmpl* **a mediados de** : halfway through, in the middle of

mediador, -dora *n* : mediator

medialuna *nf* **1** : crescent **2** : croissant (pastry)

medianamente *adv* : fairly

medianero, -ra *adj* **pared medianera** : dividing wall

mediano, -na *adj* **1** : medium, average **2** MEDIOCRE : mediocre

medianoche *nf* : midnight

mediante *prep* : through, by means of

mediar *vi* **1** : be in the middle **2** INTERVENIR : mediate **3 mediar entre** : be between

medicación *nf, pl* **-ciones** : ▸ medication — **medicamento** *nm* : medicine — **medicar** {72} *vt* : medicate — **medicarse** *vr* : take

medicine — **medicina** *nf* : medicine — **medicinal** *adj* : medicinal

medición *nf, pl* **-ciones** : measurement

médico, -ca *adj* : medical — **médico, -ca** *n* : doctor, physician

medida *nf* **1** : measurement, measure **2** MODERACIÓN : moderation **3** GRADO : extent, degree **4 tomar medidas** : take steps — **medidor** *nm Lat* : meter, gauge

medieval *adj* : medieval

medio, -dia *adj* **1** : half **2** MEDIANO : average **3 una media hora** : half an hour **4 la clase media** : the middle class — **medio** *adv* : half — **medio** *nm* **1** : half **2** MANERA : means *pl*, way **3 en medio de** : in the middle of **4 medio ambiente** : environment **5 medios** *nmpl* : means, resources

mediocre *adj* : mediocre, average — **mediocridad** *nf* : mediocrity

mediodía *nm* : noon, midday

medioevo *nm* : Middle Ages

medir {54} *vt* **1** : measure **2** CONSIDERAR : weigh, consider — **medirse** *vr* : be moderate

meditar *vi* : meditate, contemplate — *vt* **1** : think over, consider **2** PLANEAR : plan, work out — **meditación** *nf, pl* **-ciones** : meditation

mediterráneo, -nea *adj* : Mediterranean

medrar *vt* : flourish, thrive

medroso, -sa *adj* : fearful

médula *nf* **1** : marrow **2 médula espinal** : spinal cord

medusa *nf* : jellyfish

megabyte *nm* : megabyte

megáfono *nm* : megaphone

mejicano → **mexicano**

mejilla *nf* : cheek

mejillón *nm, pl* **-llones** : mussel

mejor *adv* **1** (*comparative*) : better **2** (*superlative*) : best **3 a lo mejor** : maybe, perhaps — **mejor** *adj* **1** (*comparative of* **bueno** *or* **bien**) : better **2** (*superlative of* **bueno** *or* **bien**) : best **3 lo mejor** : the best thing **4 tanto mejor** : so much the better — **mejora** *nf* : improvement

mejorana *nf* : marjoram

mejorar *vt* : improve — *vi* : improve, get better

mejunje *nm* : concoction, brew

melancolía *nf* : melancholy — **melancólico, -ca** *adj* : melancholic, melancholy

melón^M
melons

melón^M escrito
cantaloupe

sandía^F
watermelon

melón^M invernal
casaba melon

melón^M cantalupo
charentais

melón^M de miel^F
honeydew melon

melaza *nf* : molasses
melena *nf* **1** : long hair
 2 : mane (of a lion)
melindroso, -sa *adj* **1** :
 affected **2** *Lat* : finicky
mella *nf* : chip, nick — **mellado,
 -da** *adj* : chipped, jagged
mellizo, -za *adj & n* : twin
melocotón *nm, pl* **-tones** : peach
melodía *nf* : melody —
 melódico, -ca *adj* : melodic
melodrama *nm* : melodrama —
 melodramático, -ca *adj* : melodramatic
▶ **melón** *nm, pl* **-lones** : melon
meloso, -sa *adj* **1** : sweet,
 honeyed **2** EMPALAGOSO : cloying
membrana *nf* : membrane
membrete *nm* : letterhead, heading
membrillo *nm* : quince
membrudo, -da *adj* : muscular, burly
memorable *adj* : memorable
memorándum *or* memorando *nm,
 pl* **-dums** *or* **-dos** **1** : memorandum
 2 AGENDA : notebook

memoria *nf* **1** : memory **2** RECUERDO :
 remembrance **3** INFORME : report **4 de
 memoria** : by heart **5** memorias *nfpl* :
 memoirs — **memorizar** {21} *vt* : memorize
mena *nf* : ore
menaje *nm* : household
 goods *pl*, furnishings *pl*
mencionar *vt* : mention, refer to —
 mención *nf, pl* **-ciones** : mention
mendaz *adj, pl* **-daces** : lying
mendigar {52} *vi* : beg — *vt* : beg
 for — **mendicidad** *nf* : begging
 — **mendigo, -ga** *n* : beggar
mendrugo *nm* : crust (of bread)
menear *vt* **1** : move, shake **2**
 : sway (one's hips) **3** : wag (a
 tail) — **menearse** *vr* **1** : sway,
 shake, move **2** *fam* : hurry up
menester *nm* **ser menester** : be
 necessary — **menestroso, -sa** *adj* : needy
menguar *vt* : diminish, lessen — *vi* **1**
 : decline, decrease **2** : wane (of the
 moon) — **mengua** *nf* : decrease, decline
menopausia *nf* : menopause

menor *adj* **1** (*comparative of* **pequeño**)
 : smaller, lesser, younger **2** (*superlative
 of* **pequeño**) : smallest, least, youngest
 3 : minor (in music) **4 al por menor** :
 retail — **menor** *nmf* : minor, juvenile
menos *adv* **1** (*comparative*) : less **2**
 (*superlative*) : least **3 menos de** : fewer
 than — **menos** *adj* **1** (*comparative*) :
 less, fewer **2** (*superlative*) : least, fewest
 — **menos** *prep* **1** : minus **2** EXCEPTO :
 except — **menos** *pron* **1** : less, fewer **2**
 al menos *or* **por lo menos** : at least **3 a
 menos que** : unless — **menoscabar** *vt* **1**
 : lessen **2** ESTROPEAR : harm, damage
 — **menospreciar** *vt* **1** DESPRECIAR
 : scorn **2** SUBESTIMAR : undervalue
 — **menosprecio** *nm* : contempt
mensaje *nm* : message —
 mensajero, -ra *n* : messenger
menso, -sa *adj Lat fam* : foolish, stupid
menstruar {3} *vi* : menstruate —
 menstruación *nf* : menstruation
mensual *adj* : monthly —
 mensualidad *nf* **1** : monthly
 payment **2** : monthly salary
mensurable *adj* : measurable
menta *nf* **1** : mint, peppermint
 2 menta verde : spearmint
mental *adj* : mental —
 mentalidad *nf* : mentality
mentar {55} *vt* : mention, name
mente *nf* : mind
mentir {76} *vi* : lie — **mentira** *nf* : lie
 — **mentirilla** *nf* : fib — **mentiroso,
 -sa** *adj* : lying — **mentiroso, -sa** *n* : liar
mentís *nms & pl* : denial
mentol *nm* : menthol
mentón *nm, pl* **-tones** : chin
menú *nm, pl* **-nús** : menu
menudear *vi* : occur frequently —
 menudeo *nm Lat* : retail, retailing
menudillos *nmpl* : giblets
menudo, -da *adj* **1** : small,
 insignificant **2 a menudo, -da** : often
meñique *nm or* **dedo meñique**
 : little finger, pinkie
meollo *nm* **1** : marrow **2**
 ESENCIA : essence, core
mercado *nm* **1** : market **2 mercado
 de valores** : stock market —
 mercadería *nf* : merchandise, goods *pl*
mercancía *nf* : merchandise, goods *pl*
 — **mercante** *nmf* : merchant, dealer
 — **mercantil** *adj* : commercial
mercenario, -ria *adj & n* : mercenary

mercería *nf* : notions store

mercurio *nm* : mercury

Mercurio *nm* : Mercury (planet)

merecer {53} *vt* : deserve — *vi* : be worthy — **merecedor, -dora** *adj* : deserving, worthy — **merecido** *nm* **recibir su merecido** : get one's just deserts

merendar {55} *vi* : have an afternoon snack — *vt* : have as an afternoon snack — **merendero** *nm* **1** : snack bar **2** : picnic area

merengue *nm* **1** : meringue **2** : merengue (dance)

meridiano, -na *adj* **1** : midday **2** CLARO : crystal-clear — **meridiano** *nm* : meridian — **meridional** *adj* : southern

merienda *nf* : afternoon snack, tea

mérito *nm* : merit, worth — **meritorio, -ria** *adj* : deserving — **meritorio, -ria** *n* : intern, trainee

mermar *vi* : decrease — *vt* : reduce, cut down — **merma** *nf* : decrease

mermelada *nf* : marmalade, jam

mero, -ra *adj* **1** : mere, simple **2** *Lat fam* (*used as an intensifier*) : very, real — **mero** *adv Lat fam* **1** : nearly,
almost **2 aquí mero, -ra** : right here

merodear *vi* **1** : maraud **2 merodear por** : prowl about (a place)

mes *nm* : month

mesa *nf* **1** : table **2** COMITÉ : committee, board

mesarse *vr* **mesarse los cabellos** : tear one's hair

meseta *nf* : plateau

Mesías *nm* : Messiah

mesilla *nf* : small table

mesón *nm, pl* **-sones** : inn — **mesonero, -ra** *nm* : innkeeper

mestizo, -za *adj* **1** : of mixed ancestry **2** HÍBRIDO : hybrid — **mestizo, -za** *n* : person of mixed ancestry

mesura *nf* : moderation — **mesurado, -da** *adj* : moderate, restrained

meta *nf* : goal, objective

metabolismo *nm* : metabolism

metafísica *nf* : metaphysics — **metafísico, -ca** *adj* : metaphysical

metáfora *nf* : metaphor — **metafórico, -ca** *adj* : metaphoric, metaphorical

metal *nm* **1** : metal **2** : brass section (in an orchestra)

— **metálico, -ca** *adj* : metallic, metal

— **metalurgia** *nf* : metallurgy

metamorfosis *nfs & pl* : metamorphosis

metano *nm* : methane

metedura *nf* **metedura de pata** *fam* : blunder

meteoro *nm* : meteor — **meteórico, -ca** *adj* : meteoric — **meteorito** *nm* : meteorite — **meteorología** *nf* : ▸ meteorology — **meteorológico, -ca** *adj* : meteorological, meteorologic — **meteorólogo** *n* : meteorologist

meter *vt* **1** : put (in) **2** : place (in a job, etc.) **3** ENREDAR : involve **4** CAUSAR : make, cause **5** : spread (a rumor) **6** *Lat* : strike (a blow) — **meterse** *vr* **1** : get in, enter **2 meterse en** : get involved in, meddle in **3 meterse con** *fam* : pick a fight with

meticuloso, -sa *adj* : meticulous

método *nm* : method — **metódico, -ca** *adj* : methodical — **metodología** *nf* : methodology

metomentodo *nmf, fam* : busybody

metralla *nf* : shrapnel — **metralleta** *nf* : submachine gun

métrico, -ca *adj* : metric, metrical

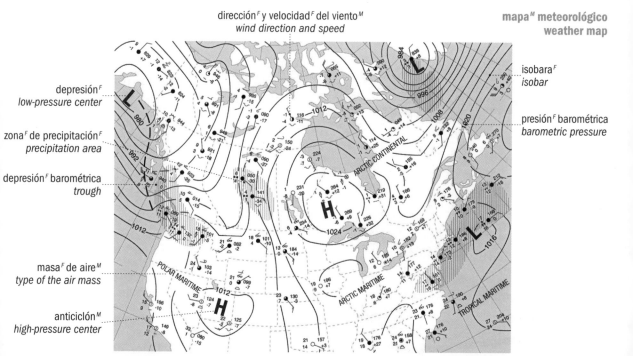

dirección^F y velocidad^F del viento^M
wind direction and speed

mapa^M meteorológico
weather map

isobara^F
isobar

depresión^F
low-pressure center

presión^F barométrica
barometric pressure

zona^F de precipitación^F
precipitation area

depresión^F barométrica
trough

masa^F de aire^M
type of the air mass

anticiclón^M
high-pressure center

metro *nm* **1** : meter **2** : subway (train)
metrópoli *nf or* **metrópolis** *nfs &*
pl : metropolis — **metropolitano,**
-na *adj* : metropolitan
mexicano, -na *adj* : Mexican
— **mexicoamericano, -na** *adj*
: Mexican-American
mezcla *nf* **1** : mixture **2** ARGAMASA
: mortar — **mezclar** *vt* **1** : mix,
blend **2** CONFUNDIR : mix up, muddle **3**
INVOLUCRAR : involve — **mezclarse** *vr* **1**
: get mixed up **2** : mingle (socially)
— **mezcolanza** *nf* : mixture
mezclilla *nf Lat* : denim
mezquino, -na *adj* **1** : mean, petty
2 ESCASO : meager — **mezquindad** *nf*
: meanness, stinginess
mezquita *nf* : mosque
mezquite *nm* : mesquite
mi *adj* : my
mí *pron* **1** : me **2** *or* **mí mismo,**
mí misma : myself **3 a mí no me**
importa : it doesn't matter to me

miajas → **migajas**
miau *nm* : meow
mica *nf* : mica
mico *nm* : (long-tailed) monkey
microbio *nm* : microbe, germ —
microbiología *nf* : microbiology
microbús *nm, pl* **-buses** : minibus
microcosmos *nms & pl* : microcosm
microfilm *nm, pl* **-films** : microfilm
micrófono *nm* : microphone
microondas *nms & pl* : microwave (oven)
microorganismo *nm* : microorganism
microscopio *nm* : microscope —
microscópico, -ca *adj* : microscopic
miedo *nm* **1** : fear **2 dar miedo** : be
frightening — **miedoso, -sa** *adj* : fearful
miel *nf* : honey
miembro *nm* **1** : member **2**
EXTREMIDAD : limb, extremity
mientras *adv or* **mientras tanto**
: meanwhile, in the meantime
— **mientras** *conj* **1** : while, as **2**
mientras que : while, whereas **3**

mientras viva : as long as I live
miércoles *nms & pl* : Wednesday
mies *nf* : (ripe) corn, grain
miga *nf* : crumb — **migajas** *nfpl* **1** :
breadcrumbs **2** SOBRAS : leftovers
migración *nf, pl* **-ciones** : migration
migraña *nf* : migraine
migrar *vi* : migrate
mijo *nm* : millet
mil *adj & nm* : thousand
milagro *nm* : miracle —
milagroso, -sa *adj* : miraculous
milenio *nm* : millennium
milésimo, -ma *adj* : thousandth
milicia *nf* **1** : militia **2** : military (service)
miligramo *nm* : milligram
mililitro *nm* : milliliter
milímetro *nm* : millimeter
militante *adj & nmf* : militant
militar *adj* : military — **militar** *nmf* :
soldier — **militarizar** {21} *vt* : militarize
milla *nf* : mile
millar *nm* : thousand
millón *nm, pl* **-llones 1** : million
2 mil millones : billion —
millonario, -ria *n* : millionaire —
millonésimo, -ma *adj* : millionth
mimar *vt* : pamper, spoil
mimbre *nm* : wicker
mímica *nf* **1** : mime, sign
language **2** IMITACIÓN : mimicry
mimo *nm* : pampering —
mimo *nmf* : mime
mina *nf* **1** : mine **2** : lead (for pencils) —
minar *vt* **1** : mine **2** DEBILITAR : undermine
mineral *adj* : mineral — **mineral** *nm* **1**
: mineral **2** : ore (of a metal)
minería *nf* : mining — **minero, -ra** *adj*
: mining — **minería** *n* : miner
miniatura *nf* : miniature
minifalda *nf* : miniskirt
minifundio *nm* : small farm
minimizar {21} *vt* : minimize
mínimo, -ma *adj* **1** : minimum
2 MINÚSCULO : minute **3 en lo más**
mínimo, -ma : in the slightest
— **mínimo** *nm* : minimum
minino, -na *n, fam* : pussycat
ministerio *nm* : ministry — **ministro,**
-tra *n* **1** : minister, secretary **2**
primer ministro : prime minister
minoría *nf* : minority
minorista *adj* : retail —
minorista *nmf* : retailer
minoritario, -ria *adj* : minority

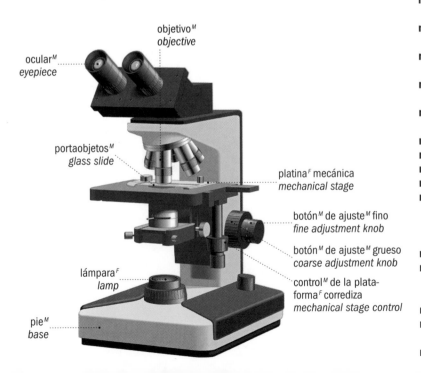

microscopio*M* binocular
binocular microscope

objetivo*M*
objective

ocular*M*
eyepiece

portaobjetos*M*
glass slide

platina*F* mecánica
mechanical stage

botón*M* de ajuste*M* fino
fine adjustment knob

botón*M* de ajuste*M* grueso
coarse adjustment knob

lámpara*F*
lamp

control*M* de la plata-
forma*F* corrediza
mechanical stage control

pie*M*
base

vagón^M de metro^M
subway passenger car

puerta^F lateral
side door

ventanilla^F
window

mapa^M de rutas^F
subway map

llanta^F neumática guía^F
inflated guiding tire

llanta^F neumática de tracción^F
inflated carrying tire

suspensión^F
suspension

---

minucia *nf* : trifle, small detail —
minucioso, -sa *adj* **1** : detailed
2 METICULOSO : thorough
minué *nm* : minuet
minúsculo, -la *adj* : minuscule, tiny
minusvalía *nf* : handicap, disability
— **minusválido, -da** *adj* : disabled
minuta *nf* **1** : bill, fee **2**
BORRADOR : rough draft
minuto *nm* : minute —
minutero *nm* : minute hand
mío, mía *adj* **1** : mine **2 una amiga
mía** : a friend of mine — **mío,** *pron*
el mío, la mía : mine, my own
miope *adj* : nearsighted
mirar *vt* **1** : look at **2** OBSERVAR : watch
3 CONSIDERAR : consider — *vi* **1** : look
2 mirar a : face, overlook **3 mirar por**
: look after — **mirarse** *vr* **1** : look at
oneself **2** : look at each other — **mira** *nf* **1**
: sight (of a firearm or instrument) **2**
INTENCIÓN : aim, objective — **mirada** *nf*

: look — **mirado, -da** *adj* **1** : careful **2**
CONSIDERADO : considerate **3 bien mirado**
: well thought of — **mirador** *nm* **1**
BALCÓN : balcony **2** : lookout, vantage
point — **miramiento** *nm* : consideration
mirlo *nm* : blackbird
misa *nf* : Mass
miscelánea *nf* : miscellany
miserable *adj* **1** : poor **2** LASTIMOSO :
miserable, wretched — **miseria** *nf* **1** :
poverty **2** DESGRACIA : misfortune, misery
misericordia *nf* : mercy —
misericordioso, -sa *adj* : merciful
mísero, -ra *adj* : wretched, miserable
misil *nm* : missile
misión *nf, pl* **-siones** : mission —
misionero, -ra *adj & n* : missionary
mismo *adv* (*used for emphasis*) : right,
exactly — **mismo, -ma** *adj* **1** : same
2 (*used for emphasis*) : very **3** : -self
4 por lo mismo : for that reason
misoginia *nf* : misogyny

— **misógino** *nm* : misogynist
misterio *nm* : mystery —
misterioso, -sa *adj* : mysterious
mística *nf* : mysticism —
místico, -ca *adj* : mystic, mystical
— **místico, -ca** *n* : mystic
mitad *nf* **1** : half **2** MEDIO : middle
mítico, -ca *adj* : mythical, mythic
mitigar {52} *vt* : mitigate
mitin *nm, pl* **mítines** : (political) meeting
mito *nm* : myth — **mitología** *nm*
: mythology — **mitológico,
-ca** *adj* : mythological
mixto, -ta *adj* **1** : mixed, joint **2**
: coeducational (of a school)
mnemónico, -ca *adj* : mnemonic
mobiliario *nm* : furniture
mocasín *nm, pl* **-sines** : moccasin
mochila *nf* : backpack, knapsack
moción *nf, pl* **-ciones** : motion
moco *nm* **1** : mucus **2 limpiarse
los mocos** : wipe one's nose

— **mocoso, -sa** *n, fam* : kid, brat
moda *nf* **1** : fashion, style **2 a la moda** *or* **de moda** : in style, fashionable **3**
moda pasajera : fad — **modal** *adj* : modal — **modales** *nmpl* : manners
— **modalidad** *nf* : type, kind
modelar *vt* : model, mold — **modelo** *adj* : model — **modelo** *nm* : model, pattern
— **modelo** *nmf* : model, mannequin
módem *or* modem *nm* : modem
moderar *vt* **1** : moderate **2** : reduce (speed, etc.) **3** PRESIDIR : chair (a meeting) — **moderarse** *vr* : restrain oneself — **moderación** *nf, pl* **-ciones** : moderation — **moderado, -da** *adj & n* : moderate — **moderador, -dora** *n* : moderator, chairperson
moderno, -na *adj* : modern — **modernismo** *nm* : modernism — **modernizar** {21} *vt* : modernize
modesto, -ta *adj* : modest — **modestia** *nf* : modesty
modificar {72} *vt* : modify, alter — **modificación** *nf, pl* **-ciones** : alteration
modismo *nm* : idiom
modista *nmf* **1** : dressmaker

2 : (fashion) designer
modo *nm* **1** : way, manner **2** : mood (in grammar) **3** : mode (in music) **4 a modo de** : by way of **5 de modo que** : so (that) **6 de todos modos** : in any case, anyway
modorra *nf* : drowsiness
modular *vt* : modulate — **modulación** *nf, pl* **-ciones** : modulation
módulo *nm* : module, unit
mofa *nf* : ridicule, mockery — **mofarse** *vr* **mofarse de** : make fun of
mofeta *nf* : skunk
moflete *nm, fam* : fat cheek — **mofletudo, -da** *adj, fam* : fat-cheeked, chubby
mohín *nm, pl* **-hines** : grimace — **mohino, -na** *adj* : sulky
moho *nm* **1** : mold, mildew **2** ÓXIDO : rust — **mohoso, -sa** *adj* **1** : moldy **2** OXIDADO : rusty
moisés *nm, pl* **-seses** : bassinet, cradle
mojar *vt* **1** : wet, moisten **2** : dunk (food) — **mojarse** *vr* : get wet — **mojado, -da** *adj* : wet, damp
mojigato, -ta *adj* : prudish — **mojigato, -ta** *n* : prude

mojón *nm, pl* **-jones** : boundary stone, marker
molar *nm* : molar
moldear *vt* : mold, shape — **molde** *nm* : mold, form — **moldura** *nf* : molding
mole[1] *nf* : mass, bulk
mole[2] *nm* **1** : Mexican chili sauce **2** : meat served with mole
molécula *nf* : molecule — **molecular** *adj* : molecular
moler {47} *vt* : grind, crush
molestar *vt* **1** : annoy, bother **2 no molestar** : do not disturb — *vi* : be a nuisance — **molestarse** *vr* **1** : bother **2** OFENDERSE : take offense — **molestia** *nf* **1** : annoyance, nuisance **2** MALESTAR : discomfort — **molesto, -ta** *adj* **1** : annoyed **2** FASTIDIOSO : annoying **3** INCÓMODO : in discomfort — **molestoso, -sa** *adj* : bothersome, annoying
molido, -da *adj* **1** : ground (of meat, etc.) **2** *fam* : worn out, exhausted
molino *nm* **1** : mill **2 molino de viento** : windmill — **molinero, -ra** *n* : miller — **molinillo** *nm* : grinder, mill
mollera *nf* **1** : crown (of the

---

moneda[F] **y formas**[F] **de pago**[M]
money and modes of payment

tarjeta[F] de débito[M]
debit card

tarjeta[F] de crédito[M]
credit card

moneda[F]
coin

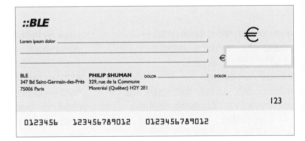

cheques[M]
checks

billete[M]
banknote

head) **2** *fam* : brains *pl*
molusco *nm* : mollusk
momento *nm* **1** : moment, instant
2 : (period of) time **3** : momentum
(in physics) **4 de momento** : for the
moment **5 de un momento a otro** : any
time now — **momentáneamente** *adv* :
momentarily — **momentáneo, -nea** *adj* **1**
: momentary **2** PASAJERO : temporary
momia *nf* : mummy
monaguillo *nm* : altar boy
monarca *nmf* : monarch —
monarquía *nf* : monarchy
monasterio *nm* : monastery —
monástico, -ca *adj* : monastic
mondadientes *nms & pl* : toothpick
mondar *vt* : peel
mondongo *nm* : innards *pl*, guts *pl*
moneda *nf* **1** : coin **2** : currency (of a
country) — **monedero** *nm* : change purse
monetario, -ria *adj* : monetary
monitor *nm* : monitor
monja *nf* : nun — **monje** *nm* : monk
mono, -na *n* : monkey — **mono,
-na** *adj, fam* : lovely, cute
monogamia *nf* : monogamy —
monógamo -ma *adj* : monogamous
monografía *nf* : monograph
monograma *nm* : monogram
monolingüe *adj* : monolingual
monólogo *nm* : monologue
monopatín *nm, pl* **-tines** :
scooter, skateboard
monopolio *nm* : monopoly —
monopolizar {21} *vt* : monopolize
monosílabo *nm* : monosyllable —
monosilábico, -ca *adj* : monosyllabic
monoteísmo *nm* : monotheism —
monoteísta *adj* : monotheistic
monotonía *nf* : monotony —
monótono, -na *adj* : monotonous
monóxido *nm* **monóxido de
carbono** : carbon monoxide
monstruo *nm* : monster —
monstruosidad *nf* : monstrosity —
monstruoso, -sa *adj* : monstrous
monta *nf* : importance, value
montaje *nm* **1** : assembly **2** : staging
(in theater), editing (of films)
montaña *nf* **1** : mountain **2**
montaña rusa : roller coaster —
montañero, -ra *n* : mountain climber
— **montañoso, -sa** *adj* : mountainous
montar *vt* **1** : mount **2** ESTABLECER :
establish **3** ENSAMBLAR : assemble, put

together **4** : stage (a performance)
5 : cock (a gun) — *vi* **1 montar a
caballo** : ride horseback **2 montar
en bicicleta** : get on a bicycle
monte *nm* **1** : mountain **2** BOSQUE :
woodland **3** *or* **monte bajo** : scrubland
4 monte de piedad : pawnshop
montés *adj, pl* **-teses** : wild
(of animals or plants)
montículo *nm* : mound, hillock
montón *nm, pl* **-tones 1** : heap, pile
2 un montón de *fam* : lots of
montura *nf* **1** : mount (horse) **2** SILLA
: saddle **3** : frame (of glasses)
monumento *nm* : monument —
monumental *adj, fam* : monumental, huge
monzón *nm, pl* **-zones** : monsoon
moño *nm* **1** : bun (of hair)
2 *Lat* : bow (knot)
mora *nf* **1** : mulberry **2**
ZARZAMORA : blackberry
morada *nf* : residence, dwelling
morado, -da *adj* : purple
— **morado** *nm* : purple
moral *adj* : moral — **moral** *nf* **1** :
ethics, morals *pl* **2** ÁNIMO : morale
— **moraleja** *nf* : moral (of a story) —
moralidad *nf* : morality — **moralista** *adj*

: moralistic — **moral** *nmf* : moralist
morar *vi* : live, reside
morboso, -sa *adj* : morbid
mordaz *adj* : caustic, scathing —
mordacidad *nf* : bite, sharpness
mordaza *nf* : gag
morder {47} *v* : bite — **mordedura** *nf*
: bite (of an animal)
mordisquear *vt* : nibble (on) —
mordisco *nm* : nibble, bite
moreno, -na *adj* **1** : dark-haired,
brunette **2** : dark-skinned — **moreno,
-na** *n* **1** : brunette **2** : dark-skinned person
moretón *nm, pl* **-tones** : bruise
morfina *nf* : morphine
morir {46} *vi* **1** : die **2** APAGARSE : die
out, go out — **morirse** *vr* **1 morirse
de** : die of **2 morirse por** : be dying
for — **moribundo, -da** *adj* : dying
moro, -ra *adj* : Moorish —
moro, -ra *n* : Moor
moroso, -sa *adj* : delinquent,
in arrears — **morosidad** *nf* :
delinquency (in payment)
morral *nm* : backpack
morriña *nf* : homesickness
morro *nm* : snout
morsa *nf* : walrus

circo^M glaciar
glacial cirque

morrena^F central
medial moraine

glaciar^M de montaña^F
mountain glacier

glaciar^M suspendido
hanging glacier

agua^F de deshielo^M
meltwater

lengua^F glaciar
glacier tongue

grieta^F
crevasse

morrena^F frontal
end moraine

moto[F]
motorcycle

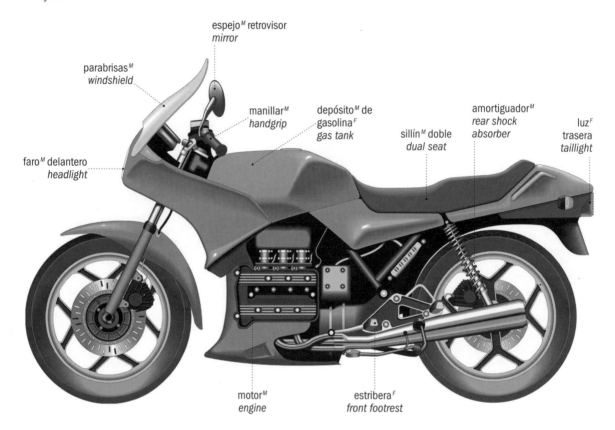

espejo[M] retrovisor
mirror

parabrisas[M]
windshield

manillar[M]
handgrip

depósito[M] de
gasolina[F]
gas tank

amortiguador[M]
*rear shock
absorber*

luz[F]
trasera
taillight

sillín[M] doble
dual seat

faro[M] delantero
headlight

motor[M]
engine

estribera[F]
front footrest

---

morse *nm* : Morse code
mortaja *nf* : shroud
mortal *adj* **1** : mortal **2** : deadly (of a
wound, an enemy, etc.) — **mortal** *nmf*
: mortal — **mortalidad** *nf* : mortality
— **mortandad** *nf* : death toll
mortero *nm* : mortar
mortífero, -ra *adj* : deadly, lethal
mortificar {72} *vt* **1** : mortify
2 ATORMENTAR : torment —
mortificarse *vr* : be distressed
mosaico *nm* : mosaic
mosca *nf* : fly
moscada *adj* → **nuez**
mosquearse *vr, fam* **1** : become
suspicious **2** ENFADARSE : get annoyed
mosquito *nm* : mosquito —
mosquitero *nm* **1** : (window)
screen **2** : mosquito net
mostachón *nm, pl* **-chones** : macaroon

mostaza *nf* : mustard
mostrador *nm* : counter (in a store)
mostrar {19} *vt* : show —
mostrarse *vr* : show oneself, appear
mota *nf* : spot, speck — **moteado,
-da** *adj* : speckled, spotted
mote *nm* : nickname
motel *nm* : motel
motín *nm, pl* **-tines 1** : riot,
uprising **2** : mutiny (of troops)
motivo *nm* **1** : motive, cause **2** : motif
(in art, music, etc.) — **motivación** *nf,
pl* **-ciones** : motivation — **motivar** *vt* **1**
: cause **2** IMPULSAR : motivate
▸ **moto** *nf* : motorcycle, motorbike
— **motocicleta** *nf* : motorcycle —
motociclista *nmf* : motorcyclist
motor, -triz *or* **-tora** *adj* :
motor — **motor** *nm* : motor,
engine — **motorista** *nmf* **1** :

motorcyclist **2** *Lat* : motorist
mover {47} *vt* **1** : move, shift **2** : shake
(the head) **3** PROVOCAR : provoke —
moverse *vr* **1** : move (over) **2** APRESURARSE
: get a move on — **movedizo, -za** *adj* :
movable, shifting — **movible** *adj* : movable
móvil *adj* : mobile — **móvil** *nm* **1** MOTIVO
: motive **2** : mobile — **movilidad** *nf* :
mobility — **movilizar** {21} *vt* : mobilize
movimiento *nm* **1** : movement,
motion **2 movimiento sindicalista**
: labor movement
mozo, -za *adj* : young — **mozo,
-za** *n* **1** : young man *m,* young
woman *f* **2** *Lat* : waiter *m,* waitress *f*
muchacho, -cha *n* : kid, boy *m,* girl *f*
muchedumbre *nf* : crowd
mucho *adv* **1** : very much, a lot **2** : long,
a long time — **mucho, -cha** *adj* **1** : a lot
of, many, much **2 muchas veces** : often

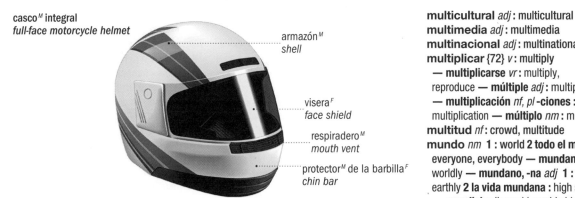

casco^M integral
full-face motorcycle helmet

armazón^M
shell

visera^F
face shield

respiradero^M
mouth vent

protector^M de la barbilla^F
chin bar

tablero^M de instrumentos^M
motorcycle dashboard

tacómetro^M
tachometer

velocímetro^M
speedometer

indicador^M del intermitente^M
turn signal indicator

indicador^M de luz^F larga
high beam warning indicator

interruptor^M de encendido^M
ignition switch

— **mucho** *pron* : a lot, many, much
mucosidad *nf* : mucus
muda *nf* **1** : molting (of animals) **2** : change (of clothing) — **mudanza** *nf* **1** : change **2** TRASLADO : move, change of residence — **mudar** *v* **1** : molt, shed **2** CAMBIAR : change — **mudarse** *vr* **1** : change (one's clothes) **2** TRASLADARSE : move (one's residence)
mudo, -da *adj* **1** : mute **2** SILENCIOSO : silent
mueble *nm* **1** : piece of furniture **2** muebles *nmpl* : furniture, furnishings
mueca *nf* **1** : grimace, face **2** **hacer muecas** : makes faces
muela *nf* **1** : tooth, molar **2** **muela de juicio** : wisdom tooth
muelle *adj* : soft — **muelle** *nm* **1** : wharf, jetty **2** RESORTE : spring
muérdago *nm* : mistletoe

muerte *nf* : death — **muerto, -ta** *adj* **1** : dead **2** : dull (of colors, etc.) — **muerte** *nm* : dead person, deceased
muesca *nf* : nick, notch
muestra *nf* **1** : sample **2** SEÑAL : sign, show
mugir {35} *vi* : moo, bellow — **mugido** *nm* : mooing, bellowing
mugre *nf* : grime, filth — **mugriento, -ta** *adj* : filthy, grimy
muguete *nm* : lily of the valley
mujer *nf* **1** : woman **2** ESPOSA : wife **3** **mujer de negocios** : businesswoman
mulato, -ta *adj & n* : mulatto
muleta *nf* **1** : crutch **2** APOYO : prop, support
mullido, -da *adj* : soft, spongy
mulo, -la *n* : mule
multa *nf* : fine — **multar** *vt* : fine
multicolor *adj* : multicolored

multicultural *adj* : multicultural
multimedia *adj* : multimedia
multinacional *adj* : multinational
multiplicar {72} *v* : multiply — **multiplicarse** *vr* : multiply, reproduce — **múltiple** *adj* : multiple — **multiplicación** *nf, pl* **-ciones** : multiplication — **múltiplo** *nm* : multiple
multitud *nf* : crowd, multitude
mundo *nm* **1** : world **2** **todo el mundo** : everyone, everybody — **mundanal** *adj* : worldly — **mundano, -na** *adj* **1** : worldly, earthly **2** **la vida mundana** : high society — **mundial** *adj* : world, worldwide
municiones *nfpl* : ammunition
municipal *adj* : municipal — **municipio** *nm* **1** : municipality **2** AYUNTAMIENTO : town council
muñeca *nf* **1** : doll **2** : wrist (in anatomy) — **muñeco** *nm* **1** : boy doll **2** MANIQUÍ : dummy, puppet
muñon *nm, pl* **-ñones** : stump (of an arm or leg)
mural *adj & nm* : mural — **muralla** *nf* : wall, rampart
murciélago *nm* : bat (animal)
murmullo *nm* **1** : murmur, murmuring **2** : rustling (of leaves, etc.)
murmurar *vi* **1** : murmur, whisper **2** CRITICAR : gossip
muro *nm* : wall
musa *nf* : muse
musaraña *nf* : shrew
músculo *nm* : muscle — **muscular** *adj* : muscular — **musculatura** *nf* : muscles *pl* — **musculoso, -sa** *adj* : muscular
muselina *nf* : muslin
museo *nm* : museum
musgo *nm* : moss — **musgoso, -sa** *adj* : mossy
música *nf* : music — **musical** *adj* : musical — **músico, -ca** *adj* : musical — **música** *n* : musician
musitar *vt* : mumble
muslo *nm* : thigh
musulmán, -mana *adj & n, mpl* **-manes** : Muslim
mutar *v* : mutate — **mutación** *nf, pl* **-ciones** : mutation — **mutante** *adj & nmf* : mutant
mutilar *vt* : mutilate — **mutilación** *nf, pl* **-ciones** : mutilation
mutuo, -tua *adj* : mutual
muy *adv* **1** : very, quite **2** DEMASIADO : too

n *nf* : n, 14th letter of the Spanish alphabet

nabo *nm* : turnip

nácar *nm* : mother-of-pearl

nacer {48} *vi* **1** : be born **2** : hatch (of an egg), sprout (of a plant) **3** SURGIR : arise, spring up — **nacido, -da** *adj & n* **recién nacer** : newborn — **naciente** *adj* **1** : new, growing **2** : rising (of the sun) — **nacimiento** *nm* **1** : birth **2** : source (of a river) **3** ORIGEN : beginning **4** BELÉN : Nativity scene

nación *nf, pl* **-ciones** : nation, country — **nacional** *adj* : national — **nacional** *nmf* : national, citizen — **nacionalidad** *nf* : nationality — **nacionalismo** *nm* : nationalism — **nacionalista** *adj & nmf* : nationalist — **nacionalizar** {21} *vt* **1** : nationalize **2** : naturalize (as a citizen) — **nacionalizarse** *vr* : become naturalized

nada *pron* **1** : nothing **2 de nada** : you're welcome **3 nada más** : nothing else, nothing more — **nada** *adv* : not at all — **nada** *nf* **la nada** : nothingness

nadar *v* : swim — **nadador, -dora** *n* : swimmer

nadería *nf* : small thing, trifle

nadie *pron* : nobody, no one

nado: a nado *adv phr* : swimming

nafta *nf Lat* : gasoline

naipe *nm* : playing card

nalgas *nfpl* : buttocks, bottom

nana *nf* : lullaby

naranja *adj & nm* : orange (color) — **naranja** *nf* : orange (fruit) — **naranjal** *nm* : orange grove — **naranjo** *nm* : orange tree

narciso *nm* : narcissus, daffodil

narcótico, -ca *adj* : narcotic — **narcótico** *nm* : narcotic — **narcotizar** {21} *vt* : drug — **narcotraficante** *nmf* : drug trafficker — **narcotráfico** *nm* : drug trafficking

nariz *nf, pl* **-rices 1** : nose **2** OLFATO : sense of smell **3 narices** *nfpl* : nostrils

narrar *vt* : narrate, tell — **narración** *nf, pl* **-ciones** : narration — **narrador, -dora** *n* : narrator — **narrativa** *nf* : narrative, storytelling

nasal *adj* : nasal

nata *nf, Spain* : cream

▸ **natación** *nf, pl* **-ciones** : swimming

natal *adj* : native, birth — **natalicio** *nm* : birthday — **natalidad** *nf* : birthrate

natillas *nfpl* : custard

natividad *nf* : birth, nativity

nativo, -va *adj & n* : native

natural *adj* **1** : natural **2** NORMAL : normal **3 natural de** : native of, from — **natural** *nm* **1** : temperament **2** NATIVO : native — **naturaleza** *nf* : nature — **naturalidad** *nf* : naturalness — **naturalista** *adj* : naturalistic — **naturalización** *nf, pl* **-ciones** : naturalization — **naturalizar** {21} *vt* : naturalize — **naturalizarse** *vr* : become naturalized — **naturalmente** *adv* **1** : naturally **2** POR SUPUESTO : of course

naufragar {52} *vi* **1** : be shipwrecked **2** FRACASAR : fail — **naufragio** *nm* : shipwreck — **náufrago, -ga** *adj* : shipwrecked — **náufrago, -ga** *n* : castaway

náusea *nf* **1** : nausea **2 dar náuseas** : nauseate **3 náuseas matutinas** : morning sickness — **nauseabundo, -da** *adj* : nauseating

náutico, -ca *adj* : nautical

navaja *nf* : pocketknife, penknife

naval *adj* : naval

nave *nf* **1** : ship **2** : nave (of a church) **3 nave espacial** : spaceship

navegar {52} *v* : navigate, sail — **navegable** *adj* : navigable — **navegación** *nf, pl* **-ciones** : navigation — **navegante** *adj* : sailing, seafaring — **navegante** *nmf* : navigator

Navidad *nf* **1** : Christmas **2 feliz Navidad** : Merry Christmas — **navideño, -ña** *adj* : Christmas

naviero, -ra *adj* : shipping

nazi *adj & nmf* : Nazi — **nazismo** *nm* : Nazism

neblina *nf* : mist

nebuloso, -sa *adj* **1** : hazy, misty, foggy **2** VAGO : vague, nebulous

necedad *nf* **1** : stupidity **2 decir necedades** : talk nonsense

necesario, -ria *adj* : necessary — **necesariamente** *adv* : necessarily — **necesidad** *nf* **1** : need, necessity **2** POBREZA : poverty **3 necesidades** *nfpl* : hardships — **necesitado, -da** *adj* : needy — **necesitar** *vt* : need — *vi* **necesitar de** : have need of

necio, -cia *adj* : silly, dumb

necrología *nf* : obituary

néctar *nm* : nectar

nectarina *nf* : nectarine

neerlandés, -desa *adj, mpl* **-deses** : Dutch — **neerlandés** *nm* : Dutch (language)

nefasto, -ta *adj* **1** : ill-fated **2** *fam* : terrible, awful

negar {49} *vt* **1** : deny **2** REHUSAR : refuse **3** : disown (a person) — **negarse** *vr* : refuse — **negación** *nf, pl* **-ciones 1** : denial **2** : negative (in grammar) — **negativa** *nf* **1** : denial **2** RECHAZO : refusal — **negativo, -va** *adj* : negative — **negativo** *nm* : negative (of a photograph)

negligente *adj* : negligent — **negligencia** *nf* : negligence

negociar *vt* : negotiate — *vi* : deal, do business — **negociable** *adj* : negotiable — **negociación** *nf, pl* **-ciones** : negotiation — **negociante** *nmf* : businessman *m*, businesswoman *f* — **negocio** *nm* **1** : business **2** TRANSACCIÓN : deal **3 negocios** : business, commerce

negro, -gra *adj* : black, dark — **negro, -gra** *n* : dark-skinned person — **negro** *nm* : black (color) — **negrura** *nf* : blackness — **negruzco, -ca** *adj* : blackish

nene, -na *n, fam* : baby, small child

nenúfar *nm* : water lily

neón *nm* : neon

neoyorquino, -na *adj* : of or from New York

nepotismo *nm* : nepotism

Neptuno *nm* : Neptune

nervio *nm* **1** : nerve **2** : sinew (in meat) **3** VIGOR : vigor, energy **4 tener nervios** : be nervous — **nerviosismo** *nf* : nervousness — **nervioso, -sa** *adj* **1** : nervous, anxious **2 sistema nervioso** : nervous system

nervudo, -da *adj* : sinewy

neto, -ta *adj* **1** : clear, distinct **2** : net (of weight, salaries, etc.)

neumático *nm* : tire

neumonía *nf* : pneumonia

neurología *nf* : neurology — **neurológico, -ca** *adj* : neurological, neurologic — **neurólogo, -ga** *n* : neurologist

neurosis *nfs & pl* : neurosis — **neurótico, -ca** *adj & n* : neurotic

neutral *adj* : neutral — **neutralidad** *nf* : neutrality — **neutralizar** {21} *vt* : neutralize — **neutro, -tra** *adj* **1** : neutral **2** : neuter (in biology and grammar)

neutrón *nm, pl* **-trones** : neutron

nevar {55} *v impers* : snow — **nevada** *nf* : snowfall — **nevado, -da** *adj* **1** : snow-covered, snowy **2** : snow-white — **nevasca** *nf* : snowstorm

nevera *nf* : refrigerator

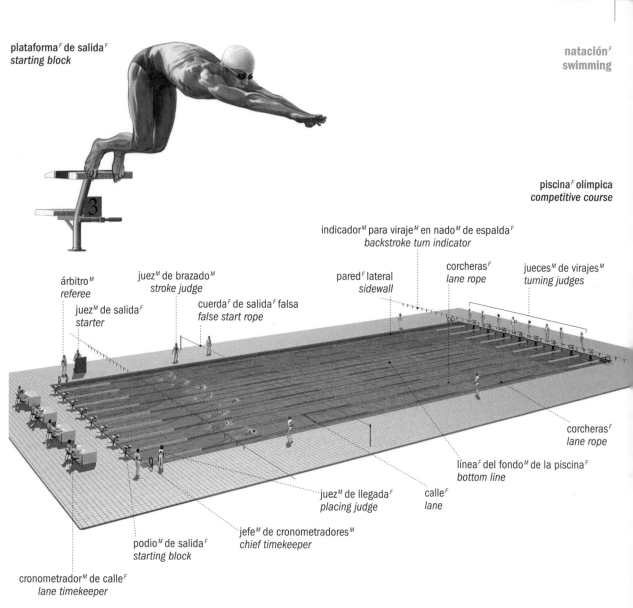

plataforma^F de salida^F
starting block

natación^F
swimming

piscina^F olímpica
competitive course

indicador^M para viraje^M en nado^M de espalda^F
backstroke turn indicator

corcheras^F
lane rope

jueces^M de virajes^M
turning judges

pared^F lateral
sidewall

árbitro^M
referee

juez^M de brazado^M
stroke judge

juez^M de salida^F
starter

cuerda^F de salida^F falsa
false start rope

corcheras^F
lane rope

línea^F del fondo^M de la piscina^F
bottom line

juez^M de llegada^F
placing judge

calle^F
lane

jefe^M de cronometradores^M
chief timekeeper

podio^M de salida^F
starting block

cronometrador^M de calle^F
lane timekeeper

---

nevisca *nf* : light snowfall, flurry
nexo *nm* : link, connection
ni *conj* **1** : neither, nor **2 ni que** : as if **3 ni siquiera** : not even
nicaragüense *adj* : Nicaraguan
nicho *nm* : niche
nicotina *nf* : nicotine
nidada *nf* : brood (of chicks, etc.)
nido *nm* **1** : nest **2** GUARIDA : hiding place, den
niebla *nf* : fog, mist
nieto, -ta *n* **1** : grandson *m*,

granddaughter *f* **2 nietos** *nmpl* : grandchildren
nieve *nf* : snow
nigeriano, -na *adj* : Nigerian
nilón *or* **nilon** *nm, pl* **-lones** : nylon
nimio, -mia *adj* : insignificant, trivial — **nimiedad** *nf* **1** : trifle **2** INSIGNIFICANCIA : triviality
ninfa *nf* : nymph
ninguno, -na (ningún *before masculine singular nouns) adj* : no, not any — **ninguno, -na** *pron* **1** :

neither, none **2** : no one, nobody
niña *nf* **1** : pupil (of the eye) **2 la niña de los ojos** : the apple of one's eye
niño, -ña *n* : child, boy *m*, girl *f* — **niño, -ña** *adj* **1** : young **2** INFANTIL : immature, childish — **niñero, -ra** *n* : baby-sitter, nanny — **niñez** *nf, pl* **-ñeces** : childhood
nipón, -pona *adj* : Japanese
níquel *nm* : nickel
nítido, -da *adj* : clear, sharp — **nitidez** *nf, pl* **-deces** : clarity, sharpness
nitrato *nm* : nitrate

nitrógeno *nm* : nitrogen
nivel *nm* **1** : level, height **2 nivel de vida** : standard of living — **nivelar** *vt* : level (out)
no *adv* **1** : not **2** (*in answer to a question*) : no **3 ¡como no!** : of course! **4 no bien** : as soon as **5 no fumador** : non-smoker — **no** *nm* : no
noble *adj & nmf* : noble — **nobleza** *nf* : nobility
noche *nf* **1** : night, evening **2 buenas noches** : good evening, good night **3 de noche** *or* **por la noche** : at night **4 hacerse de noche** : get dark — **Nochebuena** *nf* : Christmas Eve — **nochecita** *nf* : dusk — **Nochevieja** *nf* : New Year's Eve
noción *nf, pl* **-ciones 1** : notion, concept **2 nociones** *nfpl* : rudiments
nocivo, -va *adj* : harmful, noxious
nocturno, -na *adj* **1** : night **2** : nocturnal (of animals, etc.) — **nocturno** *nm* : nocturne
nogal *nm* **1** : walnut tree **2 nogal americano** : hickory
nómada *nmf* : nomad — **nómada** *adj* : nomadic
nomás *adv Lat* : only, just
nombrar *vt* **1** : appoint **2** CITAR : mention — **nombrado, -da** *adj* : famous, well-known — **nombramiento** *nm* : appointment, nomination — **nombre** *nm* **1** : name **2** SUSTANTIVO : noun **3** FAMA : fame, renown **4 nombre de pila** : first name
nómina *nf* : payroll
nominal *adj* : nominal
nominar *vt* : nominate — **nominación** *nf, pl* **-ciones** : nomination
nomo *nm* : gnome
non *adj* : odd, not even — **non** *nm* : odd number
nonagésimo, -ma *adj & n* : ninetieth
nopal *nm* : nopal, prickly pear
nordeste *or* noreste *adj* **1** : northeastern **2** : northeasterly (of wind, etc.) — **nordeste** *nm* : northeast
nórdico, -ca *adj* : Scandinavian
noreste → **nordeste**
noria *nf* **1** : waterwheel **2** : Ferris wheel (at a fair, etc.)
norma *nf* : rule, norm, standard — **normal** *adj* **1** : normal **2 escuela norma** : teacher-training college — **normalidad** *nf* : normality — **normalizar** {21} *vt* **1** : normalize **2** ESTANDARIZAR : standardize — **normalizarse** *vr* : return to normal — **normalmente** *adv* : ordinarily, generally

noroeste *adj* **1** : northwestern **2** : northwesterly (of wind, etc.) — **noroeste** *nm* : northwest
norte *adj* : north, northern — **norte** *nm* **1** : north **2** : north wind
norteamericano, -na *adj* : North American
norteño, -ña *adj* : northern
noruego, -ga *adj* : Norwegian — **noruego** *nm* : Norwegian (language)
nos *pron* **1** (*direct object*) : us **2** (*indirect object*) : to us, for us, from us **3** (*reflexive*) : ourselves **4** : each other, one another
nosotros, -tras *pron* **1** (*subject*) : we **2** (*object*) : us **3** *or* **nosotros, -tras mismos** : ourselves
nostalgia *nf* **1** : nostalgia **2 sentir nostalgia por** : be homesick for — **nostálgico, -ca** *adj* : nostalgic
nota *nf* **1** : note **2** : grade, mark (in school) **3** CUENTA : bill, check — **notable** *adj* : noteworthy, notable — **notar** *vt* : notice — **notarse** *vr* : be evident, seem
notario, -ria *n* : notary (public)
noticia *nf* **1** : news item, piece of news **2 noticias** *nfpl* : news — **noticiario** *nm* : newscast — **noticiero** *nm Lat* : newscast
notificar {72} *vt* : notify — **notificación** *nf, pl* **-ciones** : notification
notorio, -ria *adj* **1** : obvious **2** CONOCIDO : well-known — **notoriedad** *nf* : fame, notoriety
novato, -ta *adj* : inexperienced — **novato, -ta** *n* : beginner, novice
novecientos, -tas *adj* : nine hundred — **novecientos** *nms & pl* : nine hundred
novedad *nf* **1** : newness, innovation **2** NOTICIAS : news **3 novedades** : novelties, latest news — **novedoso, -sa** *adj* : original, novel
novela *nf* **1** : novel **2** : soap opera (on television) — **novelesco, -ca** *adj* **1** : fictional **2** FANTÁSTICO : fabulous — **novelista** *nmf* : novelist
noveno, -na *adj* : ninth — **noveno** *nm* : ninth
noventa *adj & nm* : ninety — **noventavo, -va** *adj* : ninetieth — **noventavo** *nm* : ninetieth
novia → **novio**
noviazgo *nm* : engagement
novicio, -cia *n* : novice
noviembre *nm* : November
novillo, -lla *n* : young bull *m*, heifer *f*
novio, -via *n* **1** : boyfriend *m*,

girlfriend *f* **2** PROMETIDO : fiancé *m*, fiancée *f* **3** : bridegroom *m*, bride *f* (at a wedding)
novocaína *nf* : novocaine
▸ **nube** *nf* : cloud — **nubarrón** *nm, pl* **-rrones** : storm cloud — **nublado, -da** *adj* **1** : cloudy **2** ENTURBIADO : clouded, dim — **nublado** *nm* : storm cloud — **nublar** *vt* **1** : cloud **2** OSCURECER : obscure — **nublarse** *vr* : get cloudy — **nuboso, -sa** *adj* : cloudy
nuca *nf* : nape, back of the neck
núcleo *nm* **1** : nucleus **2** CENTRO : center, core — **nuclear** *adj* : nuclear
nudillo *nm* : knuckle
nudismo *nm* : nudism — **nudista** *adj & nmf* : nudist
nudo *nm* **1** : knot **2** : crux, heart (of a problem, etc.) — **nudoso, -sa** *adj* : knotty, gnarled
nuera *nf* : daughter-in-law
nuestro, -tra *adj* : our — **nuestro, -tra** *pron* (*with definite article*) : ours, our own
nuevamente *adv* : again, anew
nueve *adj & nm* : nine
nuevo, -va *adj* **1** : new **2 de nuevo** : again, once more
nuez *nf, pl* **nueces 1** : nut **2** *or* **nuez de nogal** : walnut **3 nuez de Adán** : Adam's apple **4 nuez moscada** : nutmeg
nulo, -la *adj* **1** *or* **nulo, -la y sin efecto** : null and void **2** INCAPAZ : useless, inept — **nulidad** *nf* **1** : nullity **2 es una nulidad** *fam* : he's a total loss
numerar *vt* : number — **numeración** *nf, pl* **-ciones 1** : numbering **2** NÚMEROS : numbers *pl*, numerals *pl* — **numeral** *adj* : numeral — **número** *nm* **1** : number, numeral **2** : issue (of a publication) **3 sin número** : countless — **numérico, -ca** *adj* : numerical — **numeroso, -sa** *adj* : numerous
nunca *adv* **1** : never, ever **2 nunca más** : never again **3 nunca jamás** : never ever
nupcial *adj* : nuptial, wedding — **nupcias** *nfpl* : nuptials, wedding
nutria *nf* : otter
nutrir *vt* **1** ALIMENTAR : feed, nourish **2** FOMENTAR : fuel, foster — **nutrición** *nf, pl* **-ciones** : nutrition — **nutrido, -da** *adj* **1** : nourished **2** ABUNDANTE : considerable, abundant — **nutriente** *nm* : nutrient — **nutritivo, -va** *adj* : nourishing, nutritious

nubes^F
clouds

nubes^F **altas**
high clouds

cirrostratos^M
cirrostratus

cirrocúmulos^M
cirrocumulus

cirros^M
cirrus

nubes^F **medias**
middle clouds

altostratos^M
altostratus

altocúmulos^M
altocumulus

nubes^F **bajas**
low clouds

estratocúmulos^M
stratocumulus

nimbostratos^M
nimbostratus

estratos^M
stratus

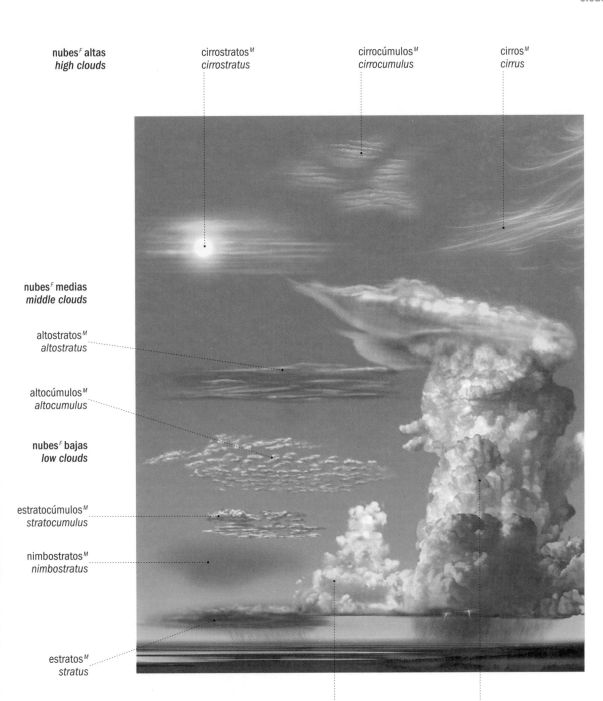

nubes^F **de desarrollo**^M **vertical**
clouds of vertical development

cúmulos^M
cumulus

cumulonimbus^M
cumulonimbus

o[1] *nf*: o, 16th letter of the Spanish alphabet

o[2] *conj* (**u** *before words beginning with o- or ho-*) **1** : or, either **2 o sea** : in other words

oasis *nms & pl* : oasis

obcecar {72} *vt* : blind (by emotions) — **obcecarse** *vr* : become stubborn

obedecer {53} *vt* : obey — *vi* **1** : obey **2 obedecer a** : respond to **3 obedecer a** : be due to — **obediencia** *nf* : obedience — **obediente** *adj* : obedient

obertura *nf* : overture

obeso, -sa *adj* : obese — **obesidad** *nf* : obesity

obispo *nm* : bishop

objetar *v* : object — **objeción** *nf, pl* **-ciones** : objection

objeto *nm* : object — **objetivo, -va** *adj* : objective — **objetivo** *nm* **1** : objective, goal **2** : lens (in photography, etc.)

objetor, -tora *n* **objetor, -tora de conciencia** : conscientious objector

oblicuo, -cua *adj* : oblique

obligar {52} *vt* : require, oblige

— **obligarse** *vr* : commit oneself (to do something) — **obligación** *nf, pl* **-ciones** : obligation — **obligado, -da** *adj* **1** : obliged **2** FORZOSO : obligatory — **obligatorio, -ria** *adj* : mandatory

oblongo, -ga *adj* : oblong

oboe *nm* : oboe — **oboe** *nmf* : oboist

obra *nf* **1** : work, deed **2** : work (of art, literature, etc.) **3** CONSTRUCCIÓN : construction work **4 obra maestra** : masterpiece **5 obras públicas** : public works — **obrar** *vt* : work, produce — *vi* : act, behave — **obrero, -ra** *adj* **la clase obrera** : the working class — **obrero, -ra** *n* : worker, laborer

obsceno, -na *adj* : obscene — **obscenidad** *nf* : obscenity

obsequiar *vt* : give, present — **obsequio** *nm* : gift, present

observar *vt* **1** : observe, watch **2** ADVERTIR : notice **3** ACATAR : observe, obey **4** COMENTAR : remark — **observación** *nf, pl* **-ciones** : observation — **observador, -dora** *adj* : observant

— **observador, -dora** *n* : observer — **observancia** *nf* : observance — **observatorio** *nm* : observatory

obsesionar *vt* : obsess — **obsesionarse** *vr* : be obsessed — **obsesión** *nf, pl* **-siones** : obsession — **obsesivo, -va** *adj* : obsessive — **obseso, -sa** *adj* : obsessed

obsoleto, -ta *adj* : obsolete

obstaculizar {21} *vt* : hinder — **obstáculo** *nm* : obstacle

obstante: no obstante *conj phr* : nevertheless, however — **obstante** *prep phr* : in spite of, despite

obstar {21} *vi* **obstar a** *or* **obstar para** : stop, prevent

obstetricia *nf* : obstetrics — **obstetra** *nmf* : obstetrician

obstinarse *vr* : be stubborn — **obstinado, -da** *adj* **1** : obstinate, stubborn **2** TENAZ : persistent

obstruir {41} *vt* : obstruct — **obstrucción** *nf, pl* **-ciones** : obstruction

obtener {80} *vt* : obtain, get

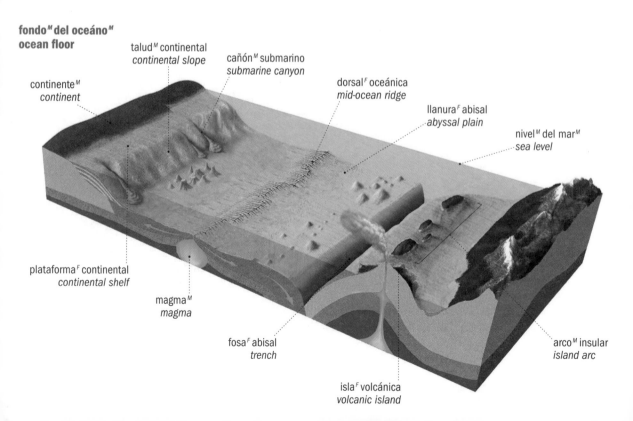

fondo*M* **del oceáno***M*
ocean floor

talud*M* continental
continental slope

cañón*M* submarino
submarine canyon

continente*M*
continent

dorsal*F* oceánica
mid-ocean ridge

llanura*F* abisal
abyssal plain

nivel*M* del mar*M*
sea level

plataforma*F* continental
continental shelf

magma*M*
magma

fosa*F* abisal
trench

isla*F* volcánica
volcanic island

arco*M* insular
island arc

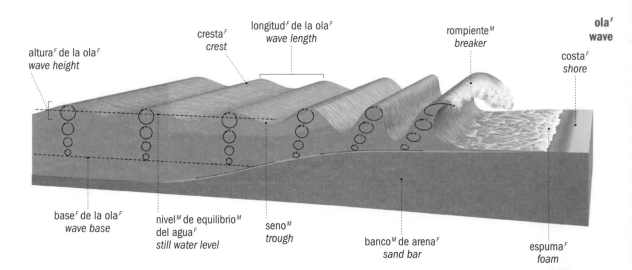

altura*F* de la ola*F*
wave height

cresta*F*
crest

longitud*F* de la ola*F*
wave length

rompiente*M*
breaker

ola*F*
wave

costa*F*
shore

base*F* de la ola*F*
wave base

nivel*M* de equilibrio*M* del agua*F*
still water level

seno*M*
trough

banco*M* de arena*F*
sand bar

espuma*F*
foam

---

obtuso, -sa *adj* : obtuse
obviar *vt* : get around, avoid
obvio, -via *adj* : obvious —
  obviamente *adv* : obviously, clearly
oca *nf* : goose
ocasión *nf, pl* -**siones 1** : occasion
  2 OPORTUNIDAD : opportunity **3** GANGA
  : bargain — **ocasional** *adj* **1** :
  occasional **2** ACCIDENTAL : accidental,
  chance — **ocasionar** *vt* : cause
ocaso *nm* **1** : sunset **2**
  DECADENCIA : decline
occidente *nm* **1** : west **2**
  el Occidente : the West —
  occidental *adj* : western, Western
▶ **océano** *nm* : ocean —
  oceanografía *nf* : oceanography
ochenta *adj & nm* : eighty
ocho *adj & nm* : eight — **ochocientos,**
  -tas *adj* : eight hundred —
  ochocientos *nms & pl* : eight hundred
ocio *nm* **1** : free time, leisure **2**
  INACTIVIDAD : idleness — **ociosidad** *nf* :
  idleness, inactivity — **ocioso, -sa** *adj* **1**
  : idle, inactive **2** INÚTIL : useless
ocre *adj & nm* : ocher
octágono *nm* : octagon —
  octagonal *adj* : octagonal
octava *nf* : octave
octavo, -va *adj & n* : eighth
octeto *nm* : byte
octogésimo, -ma *adj & n* : eightieth
octubre *nm* : October

ocular *adj* : ocular, eye —
  oculista *nmf* : ophthalmologist
ocultar *vt* : conceal, hide — **ocultarse** *vr*
  : hide — **oculto, -ta** *adj* : hidden, occult
ocupar *vt* **1** : occupy **2** : hold (a
  position, etc.) **3** : provide work for —
  ocuparse *vr* **1 ocuparse de** : concern
  oneself with **2 ocuparse de** : take care
  of (children, etc.) — **ocupación** *nf,*
  pl -**ciones 1** : occupation **2** EMPLEO : job
  — **ocupado, -da** *adj* **1** : busy **2** : occupied
  (of a place) **3 señal de occupado** : busy
  signal — **ocupante** *nmf* : occupant
ocurrir *vi* : occur, happen —
  ocurrirse *vr* **ocurrirse a** : occur to
  — **occurrencia** *nf* **1** : occurrence,
  event **2** SALIDA : witty remark, quip
oda *nf* : ode
odiar *vt* : hate — **odio** *nm* : hatred
  — **odioso, -sa** *adj* : hateful
odisea *nf* : odyssey
odontología *nf* : dentistry,
  dental surgery — **odontólogo,**
  -ga *n* : dentist, dental surgeon
oeste *adj* : west, western — **oeste** *nm* **1**
  : west **2 el Oeste** : the West
ofender *v* : offend — **ofenderse** *vr*
  : take offense — **ofensa** *nf* : offense,
  insult — **ofensiva** *nf* : offensive —
  ofensivo, -va *adj* : offensive
oferta *nf* **1** : offer **2 de oferta** : on sale **3**
  oferta y demanda : supply and demand
oficial *adj* : official — **oficial** *nmf* **1** :

skilled worker **2** : officer (in the military)
oficina *nf* : office —
  oficinista *nmf* : office worker
oficio *nm* : trade, profession —
  oficioso, -sa *adj* : unofficial
ofrecer {53} *vt* **1** : offer **2** :
  provide, present (an opportunity,
  etc.) — **ofrecerse** *vr* : volunteer
  — **ofrecimiento** *nm* : offer
ofrenda *nf* : offering
oftalmología *nf* : ophthalmology —
  oftalmólogo, -ga *n* : ophthalmologist
ofuscar {72} *vt* **1** : blind, dazzle **2**
  CONFUNDIR : confuse — **ofuscarse** *vr*
  ofuscarse con : be blinded by
  — **ofuscación** *nf, pl* -**ciones 1** :
  blindness **2** CONFUSIÓN : confusion
ogro *nm* : ogre
oír {50} *vi* : hear — *vt* **1** : hear **2** ESCUCHAR
  : listen to **3 ¡oiga!** *or* **¡oye!** : excuse
  me!, listen! — **oidas: de oír** *adv phr* : by
  hearsay — **oído** *nm* **1** : ear **2** : (sense of)
  hearing **3 duro de oír** : hard of hearing
ojal *nm* : buttonhole
ojalá *interj* : I hope so!, if only!
ojear *vt* : eye, look at —
  ojeada *nf* : glimpse, glance
ojeriza *nf* **1** : ill will **2 tener ojeriza**
  a : have a grudge against
ojo *nm* **1** : eye **2** PERSPICACIA :
  shrewdness **3** : span (of a bridge) **4**
  ¡ojo! : look out!, pay attention!
▶ **ola** *nf* : wave — **oleada** *nf* : wave, surge

estructura^F **de la oreja**^F
structure of the ear

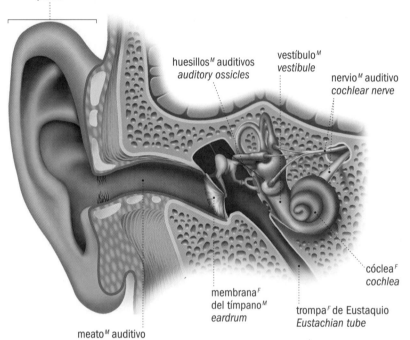

pabellón^M auricular
pinna

huesillos^M auditivos
auditory ossicles

vestíbulo^M
vestibule

nervio^M auditivo
cochlear nerve

cóclea^F
cochlea

membrana^F
del tímpano^M
eardrum

trompa^F de Eustaquio
Eustachian tube

meato^M auditivo
acoustic meatus

huesillos^M **auditivos**
auditory ossicles

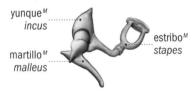

yunque^M
incus

estribo^M
stapes

martillo^M
malleus

— **oleaje** *nm* : swell (of the sea)
olé *interj* : bravo!
oleada *nf* : wave, swell —
  oleaje *nm* : waves *pl*, surf
óleo *nm* **1** : oil **2** CUADRO : oil painting
  — **oleoducto** *nm* : oil pipeline
oler {51} *vt* : smell — *vi* **1** : smell
  2 oler a : smell of — **olerse** *vr*,
  fam : have a hunch about
olfatear *vt* **1** : sniff **2** OLER : sense,
  sniff out — **olfato** *nm* **1** : sense of

smell **2** PERSPICACIA : nose, instinct
Olimpiada *or* Olimpíada *nf* :
  Olympics *pl*, Olympic Games *pl*
  — **olímpico, -ca** *adj* : Olympic
oliva *nf* : olive — **olivo** *nm* : olive tree
olla *nf* **1** : pot **2 olla podrida**
  : (Spanish) stew
olmo *nm* : elm
olor *nm* : smell — **oloroso,**
  -sa *adj* : fragrant
olvidar *vt* **1** : forget **2** DEJAR : leave
  (behind) — **olvidarse** *vr* : forget
  — **olvidadizo, -za** *adj* : forgetful
  — **olvido** *nm* **1** : forgetfulness
  2 DESCUIDO : oversight
ombligo *nm* : navel
omelette *nmf Lat* : omelet
ominoso, -sa *adj* : ominous
omitir *vt* : omit — **omisión** *nf,*
  pl **-siones** : omission
ómnibus *nm, pl* **-bus** *or* **-buses** : bus
omnipotente *adj* : omnipotent
omóplato *or* **omoplato** *nm*

: shoulder blade
once *adj & nm* : eleven —
  onceavo, -va *adj & n* : eleventh
onda *nf* : wave — **ondear** *vi* : ripple —
  ondulación *nf, pl* **-ciones** : undulation —
  ondulado, -da *adj* : wavy — **ondular** *vt*
  : wave (hair) — *vi* : undulate, ripple
ónice *nmf or* **ónix** *nm* : onyx
onza *nf* : ounce
opaco, -ca *adj* **1** : opaque
  2 DESLUSTRADO : dull
ópalo *nm* : opal
opción *nf, pl* **-ciones** : option
  — **opcional** *adj* : optional
ópera *nf* : opera
operar *vt* **1** : operate on **2** *Lat* : operate,
  run (a machine) — *vi* **1** : operate
  2 NEGOCIAR : deal, do business —
  operarse *vr* **1** : have an operation **2**
  OCURRIR : take place — **operación** *nf,*
  pl **-ciones 1** : operation **2** TRANSACCIÓN
  : transaction, deal — **operacional** *adj*
  : operational — **operador, -dora** *n* **1** :
  operator **2** : cameraman (for television, etc.)
opereta *nf* : operetta
opinar *vt* : think — *vi* : express an opinion
  — **opinión** *nf, pl* **-niones** : opinion
opio *nm* : opium
oponer {60} *vt* **1** : raise, put forward
  (arguments, etc.) **2 oponer resistencia**
  : put up a fight — **oponerse** *vr*
  oponerse a : oppose, be against
  — **oponente** *nmf* : opponent
oporto *nm* : port (wine)
oportunidad *nf* : opportunity —
  oportunista *nmf* : opportunist —
  oportuno, -na *adj* **1** : opportune,
  timely **2** APROPIADO : suitable
opositor, -tora *n* **1** : opponent
  2 : candidate (for a position) —
  oposición *nf, pl* **-ciones** : opposition
oprimir *vt* **1** : press, squeeze **2**
  TIRANIZAR : oppress — **opresión** *nf,*
  pl **-siones 1** : oppression **2 opresión**
  de pecho : tightness in the chest
  — **opresivo, -va** *adj* : oppressive
  — **opresor, -sora** *n* : oppressor
optar *vi* **1 optar a** : apply for **2**
  optar por : choose, opt for
óptica *nf* **1** : optics **2** : optician's
  (shop) — **óptico, -ca** *adj* : optical
  — **óptico, -ca** *n* : optician
optimismo *nm* : optimism —
  optimista *adj* : optimistic —
  optimismo *nmf* : optimist

optometría *nf* : optometry —
optometrista *nmf* : optometrist
opuesto *adj* **1** : opposite **2**
CONTRADICTORIO : opposed, conflicting
opulencia *nf* : opulence —
opulento, -ta *adj* : opulent
oración *nf, pl* **-ciones 1** : prayer
2 FRASE : sentence, clause
oráculo *nm* : oracle
orador, -dora *n* : speaker
oral *adj* : oral
orar *vi* : pray
órbita *nf* **1** : orbit (in astronomy) **2**
: eye socket — **orbitar** *vi* : orbit
orden *nm, pl* **órdenes 1** : order **2**
orden del día : agenda (at a meeting)
3 orden público : law and order —
orden *nf, pl* **órdenes 1** : order (of food)
2 orden religiosa : religious order **3**
orden de compra : purchase order
ordenador *nm, Spain* : computer
ordenar *vt* **1** : order, command **2**
ARREGLAR : put in order **3** : ordain
(a priest) — **ordenanza** *nm* :
orderly (in the armed forces) —
ordenanza *nf* : ordinance, regulation
ordeñar *vt* : milk
ordinal *adj & nm* : ordinal
ordinario, -ria *adj* **1** : ordinary
2 GROSERO : common, vulgar
orear *vt* : air
orégano *nm* : oregano
oreja *nf* : ear
orfanato *or* **orfelinato** *nm* : orphanage
orfebre *nmf* : goldsmith, silversmith
orgánico, -ca *adj* : organic
organigrama *nm* : flowchart
organismo *nm* **1** : organism **2**
ORGANIZACIÓN : agency, organization
organista *nmf* : organist
organizar {21} *vt* : organize —
organizarse *vr* : get organized —
organización *nf, pl* **-ciones** : organization
— **organizador, -dora** *n* : organizer
órgano *nm* : organ
orgasmo *nm* : orgasm
orgía *nf* : orgy
orgullo *nm* : pride —
orgulloso, -sa *adj* : proud
orientación *nf, pl* **-ciones 1** :
orientation **2** DIRECCIÓN : direction
3 CONSEJO : guidance
oriental *adj* **1** : eastern **2** : oriental
— **oriental** *nmf* : Oriental
orientar *vt* **1** : orient, position **2** GUIAR :

guide, direct — **orientarse** *vr* **1** : orient
oneself **2 orientarse hacia** : turn towards
oriente *nm* **1** : east, East **2**
el Oriente : the Orient
orificio *nm* : orifice, opening
origen *nm, pl* **orígenes** : origin
— **original** *adj & nm* : original —
originalidad *nf* : originality — **originar** *vt*
: give rise to — **originarse** *vr* :
originate, arise — **originario, -ria** *adj*
originario, -ria de : native of
orilla *nf* **1** : border, edge **2** : bank
(of a river), shore (of the sea)
orinar *vi* : urinate — **orina** *nf* : urine
oriol *nm* : oriole
oriundo, -da *adj* **oriundo,**
-da de : native of
orla *nf* : border
ornamental *adj* : ornamental —
ornamento *nm* : ornament
ornar *vt* : adorn
ornitología *nf* : ornithology
oro *nm* : gold
orquesta *nf* : orchestra —
orquestar *vt* : orchestrate
▸ **orquídea** *nf* : orchid
ortiga *nf* : nettle
ortodoxia *nf* : orthodoxy —
ortodoxo, -xa *adj* : orthodox
ortografía *nf* : spelling
ortopedia *nf* : orthopedics —
ortopédico, -ca *adj* : orthopedic
oruga *nf* : caterpillar
orzuelo *nm* : sty (in the eye)
os *pron pl Spain* **1** (*direct or indirect object*)
: you, to you **2** (*reflexive*) : yourselves, to
yourselves **3** : each other, to each other
osado, -da *adj* : bold, daring —
osadía *nf* **1** : boldness, daring
2 DESCARO : audacity, nerve
osamenta *nf* : skeleton
osar *vi* : dare
oscilar *vi* **1** : swing, sway **2** FLUCTUAR :
fluctuate — **oscilación** *nf, pl* **-ciones 1**
: swinging **2** FLUCTUACIÓN : fluctuation
oscuro, -ra *adj* **1** : dark **2** : obscure
(of ideas, persons, etc.) **3 a oscuras**
: in the dark — **oscurecer** {53} *vt* **1** :
darken **2** : confuse, cloud (the mind) **3**
al oscurecer : at nightfall — *v impers*
: get dark — **oscurecerse** *vr* : grow
dark — **oscuridad** *nf* **1** : darkness **2**
: obscurity (of ideas, persons, etc.)
óseo, ósea *adj* : skeletal, bony
oso, osa *n* **1** : bear **2 oso, de peluche**

or **oso, de felpa** : teddy bear
ostensible *adj* : evident, obvious
ostentar *vt* **1** : flaunt, display **2**
POSEER : have, hold — **ostentación** *nf,*
pl **-ciones** : ostentation — **ostentoso,**
-sa *adj* : ostentatious, showy
osteopatía *n* : osteopathy —
osteópata *nmf* : osteopath
osteoporosis *nf* : osteoporosis
ostra *nf* : oyster
ostracismo *nm* : ostracism
otear *vt* : scan, survey
otoño *nm* : autumn, fall —
otoñal *adj* : autumn, fall
otorgar {52} *vt* **1** : grant, award **2**
: draw up (a legal document)
otro, otra *adj* **1** : another, other **2**
otra vez : again — **otro,** *pron* **1** :
another (one), other (one) **2 los otros,**
las otras : the others, the rest
ovación *nf, pl* **-ciones** : ovation
óvalo *nm* : oval — **oval** *or*
ovalado, -da *adj* : oval
ovario *nm* : ovary
oveja *nf* **1** : sheep, ewe **2**
oveja negra : black sheep
overol *nm Lat* : overalls *pl*
ovillo *nm* **1** : ball (of yarn) **2 hacerse**
un ovillo : curl up (into a ball)
ovni *or* **OVNI** *nm* (*objeto volador*
no identificado) : UFO
ovular *vi* : ovulate — **ovulación** *nf,*
pl **-ciones** : ovulation
oxidar *vi* : rust — **oxidarse** *vr* : get rusty
— **oxidación** *nf, pl* **-ciones** : rusting —
oxidado, -da *adj* : rusty — **óxido** *nm* : rust
oxígeno *nm* : oxygen
oye → **oír**
oyente *nmf* **1** : listener **2**
: auditor (student)
ozono *nm* : ozone

orquídea^F
orchid

p *nf* : p, 17th letter of the Spanish alphabet

pabellón *nm, pl* **-llones 1** : pavilion **2** : block, building (in a hospital complex, etc.) **3** : summerhouse (in a garden, etc.) **4** BANDERA : flag

pabilo *nm* : wick

pacer {48} *v* : graze

paces → **paz**

paciencia *nf* : patience — **paciente** *adj & nmf* : patient

pacificar {72} *vt* : pacify, calm — **pacificarse** *vr* : calm down — **pacífico, -ca** *adj* : peaceful, pacific — **pacifismo** *nm* : pacifism — **pacifista** *adj & nmf* : pacifist

pacotilla *nf* **de pacotilla** : second-rate, trashy

pacto *nm* : pact, agreement — **pactar** *vt* : agree on — *vi* : come to an agreement

padecer {53} *vt* : suffer, endure — *vi* **padecer de** : suffer from — **padecimiento** *nm* : suffering

padre *nm* **1** : father **2** padres *nmpl* : parents — **padre** *adj Lat fam* : great, fantastic — **padrastro** *nm* : stepfather — **padrino** *nm* **1** : godfather **2** : best man (at a wedding)

padrón *nm, pl* **-drones** : register, roll

paella *nf* : paella

paga *nf* : pay, wages *pl* — **pagadero, -ra** *adj* : payable

pagano, -na *adj & n* : pagan, heathen

pagar {52} *vt* : pay, pay for — *vi* : pay — **pagaré** *nm* : IOU

página *nf* : page

pago *nm* : payment

país *nm* **1** : country, nation **2** REGIÓN : region, land — **paisaje** *nm* : scenery, landscape — **paisano, -na** *n* : compatriot

paja *nf* **1** : straw **2** *fam* : nonsense

pájaro *nm* **1** : bird **2 pájaro carpintero** : woodpecker — **pajarera** *nf* : aviary

pajita *nf* : (drinking) straw

pala *nf* **1** : shovel, spade **2** : blade (of an oar or a rotor) **3** : paddle, racket (in sports)

palabra *nf* **1** : word **2** HABLA : speech **3 tener la palabra** : have the floor — **palabrota** *nf* : swearword

palacio *nm* **1** : palace, mansion **2 palacio de justicia** : courthouse

paladar *nm* : palate — **paladear** *vt* : savor

palanca *nf* **1** : lever, crowbar **2** *fam* : leverage, influence **3 palanca de cambio** *or* **palanca de velocidades** : gearshift

palangana *nf* : washbowl

palco *nm* : box (in a theater)

---

palestino, -na *adj* : Palestinian

paleta *nf* **1** : small shovel, trowel **2** : palette (in art) **3** : paddle (in sports, etc.)

paletilla *nf* : shoulder blade

paliar *vt* : alleviate, ease — **paliativo, -va** *adj* : palliative

pálido, -da *adj* : pale — **palidecer** {53} *vi* : turn pale — **palidez** *nf, pl* **-deces** : paleness, pallor

palillo *nm* **1** : small stick **2** *or* **palillo de dientes** : toothpick

paliza *nf* : beating

palma *nf* **1** : palm (of the hand) **2** : palm (tree or leaf) **3 batir palmas** : clap, applaud — **palmada** *nf* **1** : pat, slap **2** palmas *nfpl* : clapping

palmera *nf* : palm tree

palmo *nm* **1** : span, small amount **2 palmo a palmo** : bit by bit

palmotear *vi* : applaud — **palmoteo** *nm* : clapping, applause

palo *nm* **1** : stick **2** MANGO : shaft, handle **3** MÁSTIL : mast **4** POSTE : pole **5** GOLPE : blow **6** : suit (of cards)

paloma *nf* : pigeon, dove — **palomilla** *nf* : moth — **palomitas** *nfpl* : popcorn

palpar *vt* : feel, touch — **palpable** *adj* : palpable

palpitar *vi* : palpitate, throb — **palpitación** *nf, pl* **-ciones** : palpitation

palta *nf Lat* : avocado

paludismo *nm* : malaria

pampa *nf* : pampa

pantalla *f* **plana**
flat screen monitor

---

pan *nm* **1** : bread **2** : loaf (of bread, etc.) **3 pan tostado** : toast

pana *nf* : corduroy

panacea *nf* : panacea

panadería *nf* : bakery, bread shop — **panadero, -ra** *n* : baker

panal *nm* : honeycomb

panameño, -ña *adj* : Panamanian

pancarta *nf* : placard, banner

pancito *nm Lat* : (bread) roll

páncreas *nms & pl* : pancreas

panda *nmf* : panda

pandemonio *nm* : pandemonium

pandero *nm* : tambourine — **pandereta** *nf* : (small) tambourine

pandilla *nf* : gang

panecillo *nm, Spain* : (bread) roll

panel *nm* : panel

panfleto *nm* : pamphlet

pánico *nm* : panic

panorama *nm* : panorama — **panorámico, -ca** *adj* : panoramic

panqueque *nm Lat* : pancake

pantaletas *nfpl Lat* : panties

▸ **pantalla** *nf* **1** : screen **2** : lampshade

pantalón *nm, pl* **-lones 1** *or* **pantalones** *nmpl* : pants *pl*, trousers *pl* **2 pantalones vaqueros** : jeans

pantano *nm* **1** : swamp, marsh **2** EMBALSE : reservoir — **pantanoso, -sa** *adj* : marshy, swampy

pantera *nf* : panther

pantimedias *nfpl Lat* : panty hose

pantomima *nf* : pantomime
pantorrilla *nf* : calf (of the leg)
pantufla *nf* : slipper
panza *nf* : belly, paunch — **panzón,**
-zona *adj, mpl* **-zones** : potbellied
pañal *nm* : diaper
paño *nm* **1** : cloth **2** TRAPO : rag, dust
cloth **3 paño de cocina** : dishcloth
4 paño higiénico : sanitary napkin
5 paños menores : underwear
pañuelo *nm* **1** : handkerchief
2 : scarf, kerchief
papa [1] *nm* : pope
papa [2] *nf Lat* **1** : potato **2 papas**
fritas : potato chips, french fries
papá *nm, fam* **1** : dad, pop **2**
papás *nmpl* : parents, folks
papada *nf* : double chin
papagayo *nm* : parrot
papal *adj* : papal
papalote *nm Lat* : kite
papanatas *nmfs & pl fam* : simpleton
papaya *nf* : papaya
papel *nm* **1** : paper, sheet of paper
2 : role, part (in theater, etc.) **3 papel**
de aluminio : aluminum foil **4 papel**
higiénico *or* **papel de baño** : toilet paper **5**
papel de lija : sandpaper **6 papel pintado**
: wallpaper — **papeleo** *nm* : paperwork,
red tape — **papelera** *nf* : wastebasket
— **papelería** *nf* : stationery store —
papeleta *nf* **1** : ticket, slip **2** : ballot (paper)
paperas *nfpl* : mumps
papilla *nf* **1** : baby food, pap **2**
hacer papilla : smash to bits
paquete *nm* **1** : package, parcel
2 : pack (of cigarettes, etc.)
paquistaní *adj* : Pakistani
par *nm* **1** : pair, couple **2** : par (in golf)
3 NOBLE : peer **4 abierto de par en par** :
wide open **5 sin par** : without equal —
par *adj* : even (in number) — **par** *nf* **1** :
par **2 a la par que** : at the same time as
para *prep* **1** : for **2** HACIA : towards
3 : (in order) to **4** : around, by (a
time) **5 para adelante** : forwards
6 para atrás : backwards **7 para**
que : so (that), in order that
parabienes *nmpl* : congratulations
parábola *nf* : parable
parabrisas *nms & pl* : windshield
paracaídas *nms & pl* : parachute
— **paracaidista** *nmf* **1** : parachutist
2 : paratrooper (in the military)
parachoques *nms & pl* : bumper

parada *nf* **1** : stop **2** : (act of) stopping
3 DESFILE : parade — **paradero** *nm* **1**
: whereabouts **2** *Lat* : bus stop —
parado, -da *adj* **1** : idle, stopped
2 *Lat* : standing (up) **3 bien (mal)**
parado : in good (bad) shape
paradoja *nf* : paradox
parafernalia *nf* : paraphernalia
parafina *nf* : paraffin
parafrasear *vt* : paraphrase —
paráfrasis *nfs & pl* : paraphrase
paraguas *nms & pl* : umbrella
paraguayo, -ya *adj* : Paraguayan
paraíso *nm* : paradise
paralelo, -la *adj* : parallel — **paralelo** *nm*
: parallel — **paralelismo** *nm* : similarity
parálisis *nfs & pl* : paralysis —
paralítico, -ca *adj* : paralytic —
paralizar {21} *vt* : paralyze
parámetro *nm* : parameter
páramo *nm* : barren plateau
parangón *nm, pl* **-gones 1** : comparison
2 sin parangón : matchless
paraninfo *nm* : auditorium, hall
paranoia *nf* : paranoia —
paranoico, -ca *adj & n* : paranoid
parapeto *nm* : parapet, rampart
parapléjico, -ca *adj & n* : paraplegic
parar *vt* **1** : stop **2** *Lat* : stand, prop
— *vi* **1** : stop **2 ir a parar** : end up, wind
up — **pararse** *vr* **1** : stop **2** *Lat* : stand up
pararrayos *nms & pl* : lightning rod
parásito, -ta *adj* : parasitic
— **parásito** *nm* : parasite
parasol *nm* : parasol
parcela *nf* : parcel, tract (of land)
— **parcelar** *vt* : parcel (up)
parche *nm* : patch
parcial *adj* **1** : partial **2 a**
tiempo parcial : part-time —
parcialidad *nf* : partiality, bias
parco, -ca *adj* : sparing, frugal
pardo, -da *adj* : brownish grey
parear *vt* : pair (up)
parecer {53} *vi* **1** : seem, look **2**
ASEMEJARSE A : look like, seem like **3**
me parece que : I think that, in my
opinion **4 ¿qué te parece?** : what do
you think? **5 según parece** : apparently
— **parecerse** *vr* **parecerse a** : resemble
— **parecer** *nm* **1** : opinion **2** ASPECTO
: appearance **3 al parecer** : apparently
— **parecido, -da** *adj* **1** : similar **2**
bien parecido : good-looking —
parecido *nm* : resemblance, similarity

pared *nf* : wall
parejo, -ja *adj* **1** : even, smooth **2**
SEMEJANTE : similar — **pareja** *nf* **1**
: couple, pair **2** : partner (person)
parentela *nf* : relatives *pl*, kin —
parentesco *nm* : relationship, kinship
paréntesis *nms & pl* **1** : parenthesis
2 DIGRESIÓN : digression **3 entre**
paréntesis : by the way
paria *nmf* : outcast
paridad *nf* : equality
pariente *nmf* : relative, relation
parir *vi* : give birth, have a
baby — *vt* : give birth to
parking *nm* : parking lot
parlamentar *vi* : discuss —
parlamentario, -ria *adj* : parliamentary
— **parlamentario, -ria** *n* : member of
parliament — **parlamento** *nm* : parliament
parlanchín, -china *adj, mpl*
-chines : talkative, chatty —
parlanchín, -china *n* : chatterbox
parlotear *vi, fam* : chatter —
parloteo *nm, fam* : chatter
paro *nm* **1** : stoppage, shutdown **2**
DESEMPLEO : unemployment **3** *Lat* : strike
4 paro cardíaco : cardiac arrest
parodia *nf* : parody —
parodiar *vt* : parody
párpado *nm* : eyelid — **parpadear** *vi* **1**
: blink **2** : flicker (of light), twinkle (of
stars) — **parpadeo** *nm* **1** : blink **2** :
flicker (of light), twinkling (of stars)
parque *nm* **1** : park **2 parque de**
atracciones : amusement park
parqué *nm* : parquet
parquear *vi Lat* : park
parquedad *nf* : frugality, moderation
parquímetro *nm* : parking meter
parra *nf* : grapevine
párrafo *nm* : paragraph
parranda *nf, fam* : party, spree
parrilla *nf* **1** : broiler, grill **2** : grate (of a
chimney, etc.) — **parrillada** *nf* : barbecue
párroco *nm* : parish priest —
parroquia *nf* **1** : parish **2** : parish
church — **parroquial** *adj* : parochial
— **parroquiano, -na** *nm* **1** :
parishioner **2** CLIENTE : customer
parsimonia *nf* **1** : calm **2** FRUGALIDAD
: thrift — **parsimonioso, -sa** *adj* **1**
: calm, unhurried **2** FRUGAL : thrifty
parte *nf* **1** : part **2** PORCIÓN : share **3**
LADO : side **4** : party (in negotiations,
etc.) **5 de parte de** : on behalf of **6 ¿de**

parte de quién? : who is speaking? **7 en
alguna parte** : somewhere **8 en todas
partes** : everywhere **9 tomar parte** :
take part — **parte** *nm* **1** : report **2 parte
meteorológico** : weather forecast
partero, -ra *n* : midwife
partición *nf, pl* **-ciones** : division, sharing
participar *vi* **1** : participate, take part
2 participar en : have a share in — *vt* :
notify — **participación** *nf, pl* **-ciones 1** :
participation **2** : share, interest (in a fund,
etc.) **3** NOTICIA : notice — **participante** *adj*
: participating — **participante** *nmf* :
participant — **partícipe** *nmf* : participant
participio *nm* : participle
partícula *nf* : particle
particular *adj* **1** : particular **2**
PRIVADO : private — **particular** *nm* **1**
: matter **2** PERSONA : individual —
particularidad *nf* : peculiarity —
particularizar {21} *vt* : distinguish,
characterize — *vi* : go into details
partir *vt* **1** : split, divide **2** ROMPER : break,
crack **3** REPARTIR : share (out) — *vi* **1** :
depart **2 partir de** : start from **3 a partir
de** : as of, from — **partirse** *vr* **1** : split
(open) **2** RAJARSE : crack — **partida** *nf* **1**
: departure **2** : entry, item (in a register,
etc.) **3** JUEGO : game **4** : group (of persons)
5 mala partida : dirty trick **6 partida
de nacimiento** : birth certificate —
partidario, -ria *n* : follower, supporter —
partido *nm* **1** : (political) party **2** : game,
match (in sports) **3** PARTIDARIOS : following
4 sacar partido de : make the most of
partitura *nf* : (musical) score
parto *nm* **1** : childbirth **2 estar
de parto** : be in labor
parvulario *nm* : nursery school
pasa *nf* **1** : raisin **2 pasa
de Corinto** : currant
pasable *adj* : passable
pasada *nf* **1** : pass, wipe, coat (of paint,
etc.) **2 de pasada** : in passing **3 mala
pasada** : dirty trick — **pasadizo** *nm*
: corridor — **pasado, -da** *adj* **1** : past
2 PODRIDO : bad, spoiled **3** ANTICUADO
: out-of-date **4 el año pasado** :
last year — **pasado** *nm* : past
pasador *nm* **1** CERROJO : bolt
2 : barrette (for the hair)
pasaje *nm* **1** : passage **2** BILLETE : ticket,
fare **3** PASILLO : passageway **4** PASAJEROS
: passengers *pl* — **pasajero, -ra** *adj* :
passing — **pasajero, -ra** *n* : passenger

pasamanos *nms & pl* : handrail, banister
pasaporte *nm* : passport
pasar *vi* **1** : pass, go (by) **2** ENTRAR : come
in **3** SUCEDER : happen **4** TERMINARSE : be
over, end **5 pasar de** : exceed **6 ¿qué
pasa?** : what's the matter? — *vt* **1** : pass
2 : spend (time) **3** CRUZAR : cross **4** TOLERAR
: tolerate **5** SUFRIR : go through, suffer **6** :
show (a movie, etc.) **7 pasarlo bien** : have
a good time **8 pasar por alto** : overlook,
omit — **pasarse** *vr* **1** : pass, go away **2**
ESTROPEARSE : spoil, go bad **3** OLVIDARSE :
slip one's mind **4** EXCEDERSE : go too far
pasarela *nf* **1** : footbridge **2**
: gangway (on a ship)
pasatiempo *nm* : pastime, hobby
Pascua *nf* **1** : Easter (Christian
feast) **2** : Passover (Jewish
feast) **3** NAVIDAD : Christmas
pase *nm* : pass
pasear *vi* : take a walk, go for a ride
— *vt* **1** : take for a walk **2** EXHIBIR
: parade, show off — **pasearse** *vr*
: go for a walk, go for a ride —
paseo *nm* **1** : walk, ride **2** *Lat* : outing
pasillo *nm* : passage, corridor
pasión *nf, pl* **-siones** : passion
pasivo, -va *adj* : passive —
pasivo *nm* : liabilities *pl*
pasmar *vt* : astonish, amaze —
pasmarse *vr* : be astonished —
pasmado, -da *adj* : stunned, flabbergasted
— **pasmo** *nm* : astonishment —
pasmoso, -sa *adj* : astonishing
paso[1] **, -sa** *adj* : dried (of fruit)
paso[2] *nm* **1** : step **2** HUELLA : footprint
3 RITMO : pace **4** CRUCE : crossing **5**
PASAJE : passage, way through **6** :
(mountain) pass **7 de paso** : in passing
▸ **pasta** *nf* **1** : paste **2** MASA : dough **3**
or **pastas** : pasta **4 pasta de dientes**
or **pasta dentífrica** : toothpaste
pastar *v* : graze
pastel *nm* **1** : cake **2** EMPANADA
: pie **3** : pastel (crayon) —
pastelería *nf* : pastry shop
pasteurizar {21} *vt* : pasteurize
pastilla *nf* **1** : pill, tablet **2** : bar (of
chocolate, soap, etc.) **3 pastilla
para la tos** : lozenge, cough drop
pasto *nm* **1** : pasture **2** *Lat* : grass, lawn
— **pastor, -tora** *n* **1** : shepherd **2** : pastor
(in religion) — **pastoral** *adj* : pastoral
pata *nf* **1** : paw, leg (of an animal) **2** :
foot, leg (of furniture) **3 meter la pata**

fam : put one's foot in it — **patada** *nf* **1**
: kick **2** : stamp (of the foot) —
patalear *vi* **1** : kick **2** : stamp (one's feet)
patata *nf, Spain* : potato
patear *vt* : kick — *vi* **1** : kick
2 : stamp (one's feet)
patentar *vt* : patent — **patente** *adj* :
obvious, patent — **patente** *nf* : patent
paternal *adj* : fatherly, paternal —
paternidad *nf* **1** : fatherhood **2** : paternity
(in law) — **paterno, -na** *adj* : paternal
patético, -ca *adj* : pathetic, moving
patillas *nfpl* : sideburns
patinar *vi* **1** : skate **2** RESBALAR : slip,
slide — **patín** *nm, pl* **-tines** : skate —
patinador, -dora *n* : skater — **patinaje** *nm*
: skating — **patinazo** *nm* **1** : skid **2** *fam*
: blunder — **patinete** *nm* : scooter
patio *nm* **1** : courtyard, patio **2** *or*
patio de recreo : playground
pato, -ta *n* **1** : duck **2 pagar el pato** *fam* :
take the blame — **patito, -ta** *n* : duckling
patología *nf* : pathology —
patológico, -ca *adj* : pathological
patraña *nf* : hoax
patria *nf* : native land
patriarca *nm* : patriarch
patrimonio *nm* **1** : inheritance **2**
: (historical or cultural) heritage
patriota *adj* : patriotic — **patriota** *nmf*
: patriot — **patriótico, -ca** *adj* : patriotic
— **patriotismo** *nm* : patriotism
patrocinador, -dora *n* : sponsor
— **patrocinar** *vt* : sponsor —
patrocinio *nm* : sponsorship
patrón, -trona *n, mpl* **-trones 1**
: patron **2** JEFE : boss **3** : landlord,
landlady *f* (of a boarding house, etc.)
— **patrón** *nm, pl* **-trones** : pattern (in
sewing) — **patronato** *nm* **1** : patronage
2 FUNDACIÓN : foundation, trust
patrulla *nf* **1** : patrol **2** : (police)
cruiser — **patrullar** *v* : patrol
paulatino, -na *adj* : gradual
pausa *nf* : pause, break — **pausado,
-da** *adj* : slow, deliberate
pauta *nf* : guideline
pavimento *nm* : pavement
— **pavimentar** *vt* : pave
pavo, -va *n* **1** : turkey **2**
pavo real : peacock
pavonearse *vr* : strut, swagger
pavor *nm* : dread, terror —
pavoroso, -sa *adj* : terrifying
payaso, -sa *n* : clown — **payasada** *nf*

pastas^F
pasta

tiburones^M
elbow macaroni

ñoquis^M
gnocchi

tortellini^M
tortellini

conchitas^F
conchiglie

penne^M
penne

canelones^M
cannelloni

lasañas^F
lasagna

raviolis^M
ravioli

espagueti^M
spaghetti

máquina^F para hacer pasta^F italiana
pasta maker

: antic, buffoonery — **payasear** *vi*
Lat fam : clown (around)

paz *nf, pl* **paces 1** : peace **2 dejar
en paz** : leave alone **3 hacer las
paces** : make up, reconcile

peaje *nm* : toll

peatón *nm, pl* **-tones** : pedestrian

peca *nf* : freckle

pecado *nm* : sin — **pecador,
-dora** *adj* : sinful — **pecado** *n* :
sinner — **pecaminoso, -sa** *adj* :
sinful — **pecar** {72} *vi* : sin

pecera *nf* : fishbowl, fish tank

pecho *nm* **1** : chest **2** MAMA : breast **3**
CORAZÓN : heart, courage **4 dar el pecho**
: breast-feed **5 tomar a pecho** : take to
heart — **pechuga** *nf* : breast (of fowl)

pecoso, -sa *adj* : freckled

pectoral *adj* : pectoral

peculiar *adj* **1** : particular
2 RARO : peculiar, odd —
peculiaridad *nf* : peculiarity

pedagogía *nf* : education, pedagogy
— **pedagogo, -ga** *n* : educator, teacher

pedal *nm* : pedal — **pedalear** *vi* : pedal

pedante *adj* : pedantic, pompous

pedazo *nm* **1** : piece, bit **2 hacerse
pedazos** : fall to pieces

pedernal *nm* : flint

pedestal *nm* : pedestal

pediatra *nmf* : pediatrician

pedigrí *nm* : pedigree

pedir {54} *vt* **1** : ask for, request **2** : order
(food, merchandise, etc.) — *vi* **1** : ask **2**
pedir prestado : borrow — **pedido** *nm* **1**
: order **2 hacer un pedido** : place an order

pedregoso, -sa *adj* : rocky, stony

pedrería *nf* : precious stones *pl*

pegar {52} *vt* **1** : stick, glue, paste **2** :
sew on (a button, etc.) **3** JUNTAR : bring
together **4** GOLPEAR : hit, strike **5** PROPINAR
: deal (a blow, etc.) **6** : transmit (an
illness) **7 pegar un grito** : let out a scream
— *vi* **1** : adhere, stick **2** GOLPEAR : hit —
pegarse *vr* **1** : hit oneself, hit each other
2 ADHERIRSE : stick, adhere **3** CONTAGIARSE
: be transmitted — **pegadizo, -za** *adj* **1**
: catchy **2** CONTAGIOSO : contagious
— **pegajoso, -sa** *adj* **1** : sticky **2** *Lat*
: catchy — **pegamento** *nm* : glue

peinar *vt* : comb — **peinarse** *vr* :
comb one's hair — **peinado** *nm* :
hairstyle, hairdo — **peine** *nm* : comb
— **peineta** *nf* : ornamental comb

pelado, -da *adj* **1** : shorn, hairless
2 : peeled (of fruit, etc.) **3** *fam* :
bare **4** *fam* : broke, penniless

pelaje *nm* : coat (of an animal), fur
pelar *vt* **1** : cut the hair of (a person)
  2 MONDAR : peel (fruit) **3** : pluck (a
  chicken, etc.), skin (an animal) —
  pelarse *vr* **1** : peel **2** *fam* : get a haircut
peldaño *nm* **1** : step (of stairs)
  2 : rung (of a ladder)
pelear *vi* **1** : fight **2** DISCUTIR : quarrel
  — **pelearse** *vr* : have a fight —
  pelea *nf* **1** : fight **2** DISCUSIÓN : quarrel
peletería *nf* : fur shop
peliagudo, -da *adj* : tricky, difficult
pelícano *nm* : pelican
película *nf* : movie, film
peligro *nm* **1** : danger **2** RIESGO : risk
  — **peligroso, -sa** *adj* : dangerous
pelirrojo, -ja *adj* : red-haired
  — **pelirrojo, -ja** *n* : redhead
pellejo *nm* : skin, hide
pellizcar {72} *vt* : pinch —
  pellizco *nm* : pinch

pelo *nm* **1** : hair **2** : coat, fur (of an
  animal) **3** : pile, nap (of fabric) **4 con
pelos y señales** : in great detail **5 no
tener pelo en la lengua** *fam* : not to
mince words **6 tomar el pelo a algn**
fam : pull someone's leg — **pelón,
-lona** *adj, fam, mpl* **-lones** : bald
pelota *nf* : ball
pelotón *nm, pl* **-tones** :
  squad, detachment
peltre *nm* : pewter
peluca *nf* : wig
peluche *nm* **1** : plush **2 oso
de peluche** : teddy bear
peludo, -da *adj* : hairy, furry
peluquería *nf* : hairdresser's,
  barber shop — **peluquero,
-ra** *n* : barber, hairdresser
pelusa *nf* : fuzz, lint
pelvis *nfs & pl* : pelvis
pena *nf* **1** : penalty **2** TRISTEZA :

sorrow **3** DOLOR : suffering, pain **4** *Lat* :
embarrassment **5 a duras penas** : with
great difficulty **6 ¡qué pena!** : what a
shame! **7 valer la pena** : be worthwhile
penacho *nm* **1** : crest, tuft
  2 : plume (ornament)
penal *adj* : penal — **penal** *nm* :
  prison, penitentiary — **penalidad** *nf* **1**
  : hardship **2** : penalty (in law) —
  penalizar {21} *vt* : penalize
penalty *nm* : penalty (in sports)
penar *vt* : punish — *vi* : suffer
pendenciero, -ra *adj* : quarrelsome
pender *vi* : hang — **pendiente** *adj* **1**
  : pending **2 estar pender de** : be
  watching out for — **pender** *nf* : slope
  — **pender** *nm, Spain* : earring
pendón *nm, pl* **-dones** : banner
péndulo *nm* : pendulum
pene *nm* : penis
penetrar *vi* **1** : penetrate **2 penetrar en**

instrumentos^M **de percusión**^F
percussion instruments

pandereta^F
tambourine

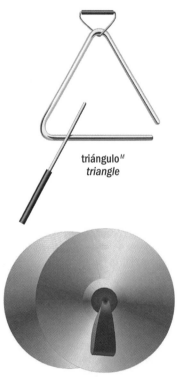

triángulo^M
triangle

castañuelas^F
castanets

bongos^M
bongos

platillos^M
cymbals

timbal^M
kettledrum

: go into — *vt* **1** : penetrate **2** : pierce
(one's heart, etc.) **3** ENTENDER : fathom,
grasp — **penetración** *nf, pl* **-ciones**
1 : penetration **2** PERSPICACIA : insight
— **penetrante** *adj* **1** : penetrating
2 : sharp (of odors, etc.), piercing (of
sounds) **3** : deep (of a wound, etc.)
penicilina *nf* : penicillin
península *nf* : peninsula —
peninsular *adj* : peninsular
penitencia *nf* **1** : penitence **2** CASTIGO :
penance — **penitenciaría** *nf* : penitentiary
— **penitente** *adj & nmf* : penitent
penoso, -sa *adj* **1** : painful, distressing
2 TRABAJOSO : difficult **3** *Lat* : shy
pensar {55} *vi* **1** : think **2** pensar en :
think about — *vt* **1** : think **2** CONSIDERAR
: think about **3** pensar hacer algo :
intend to do something — **pensador,**
-dora *n* : thinker — **pensamiento** *nm* **1**
: thought **2** : pansy (flower) — **pensativo,**

-**va** *adj* : pensive, thoughtful
pensión *nf, pl* **-siones** **1** :
boarding house **2** : (retirement)
pension **3** pensión alimenticia :
alimony — **pensionista** *nmf* **1**
: lodger **2** JUBILADO : retiree
pentágono *nm* : pentagon
pentagrama *nm* : staff (in music)
penúltimo, -ma *adj* : next
to last, penultimate
penumbra *nf* : half-light
penuria *nf* : dearth, shortage
peña *nf* : rock, crag — **peñasco** *nm*
: crag, large rock — **peñón** *nm,*
pl **-ñones** : craggy rock
peón *nm, pl* **peones** **1** : laborer,
peon **2** : pawn (in chess)
peonía *nf* : peony
peor *adv* **1** (*comparative of* **mal**) :
worse **2** (*superlative of* **mal**) : worst
— **peor** *adj* **1** (*comparative of* **malo**) :

perdiz[F]
partridge

worse **2** (*superlative of* **malo**) : worst
pepino *nm* : cucumber —
pepinillo *nm* : pickle, gherkin
pepita *nf* **1** : seed, pip **2** :
nugget (of gold, etc.)
pequeño, -ña *adj* : small, little
— **pequeñez** *nf, pl* **-ñeces** **1** :
smallness **2** NIMIEDAD : trifle
pera *nf* : pear — **peral** *nm* : pear tree
percance *nm* : mishap, setback
percatarse *vr* percatarse de : notice
percepción *nf, pl* **-ciones** : perception
— **perceptible** *adj* : perceptible
percha *nf* **1** : perch (for birds) **2** :
(coat) hanger **3** : coatrack (on a wall)
percibir *vt* **1** : perceive **2** :
receive (a salary, etc.)
▸ **percusión** *nf, pl* **-siones** : percussion
perder {56} *vt* **1** : lose **2** : miss (an
opportunity, etc.) **3** DESPERDICIAR : **waste**
(time) — *vi* : lose — **perderse** *vr* **1**
: get lost **2** DESAPARECER : disappear **3**
DESPERDICIARSE : be wasted — **perdedor,**
-dora *n* : loser — **pérdida** *nf* **1** : loss **2**
ESCAPE : leak **3** pérdida de tiempo : waste
of time — **perdido, -da** *adj* **1** : lost **2** un
caso perdido *fam* : a hopeless case
perdigón *nm, pl* **-gones** : shot, pellet
▸ **perdiz** *nf, pl* **-dices** : partridge
perdón *nm, pl* **-dones** : forgiveness,
pardon — **perdón** *interj* : sorry!
— **perdonar** *vt* **1** DISCULPAR :
forgive **2** : pardon (in law)
perdurar *vi* : last, endure —
perdurable *adj* : lasting
perecer {53} *vi* : perish, die

yembé[M]
djembe

batería[F]
drum kit

perros^M
dogs

Gran Danés^M
Great Dane

hocico^M
muzzle

belfos^M
flews

muslo^M
thigh

lomo^M
back

cola^F
tail

codo^M
elbow

rodilla^F
knee

buldog^M
bulldog

San Bernardo^M
Saint Bernard

dálmata^M
dalmatian

chow chow^M
chowchow

lebrero^M
greyhound

collie^M
collie

pastor^M **alemán**
German shepherd

— **perecedero, -ra** *adj* : perishable
peregrinación *nf, pl* **-ciones** *or*
  peregrinaje *nm* : pilgrimage —
  peregrino, -na *adj* **1** : migratory **2** RARO :
  unusual, odd — **peregrino, -na** *n* : pilgrim
perejil *nm* : parsley
perenne *adj & nm* : perennial
pereza *nf* : laziness —
  perezoso, -sa *adj* : lazy
perfección *nf, pl* **-ciones** : perfection
  — **perfeccionar** *vt* **1** : perfect **2** MEJORAR
  : improve — **perfeccionista** *nmf* :
  perfectionist — **perfecto, -ta** *adj* : perfect
perfidia *nf* : treachery —
  pérfido, -da *adj* : treacherous
perfil *nm* **1** : profile **2** CONTORNO : outline
  3 perfiles *nmpl* RASGOS : features —
  perfilar *vt* : outline — **perfilarse** *vr* **1** :
  be outlined **2** CONCRETARSE : take shape
perforar *vt* **1** : perforate **2** : drill,
  bore (a hole) — **perforación** *nf,*
  pl **-ciones** : perforation —
  perforadora *nf* : (paper) punch
perfume *nm* : perfume, scent
  — **perfumar** *vt* : perfume —
  perfumarse *vr* : put perfume on
pergamino *nm* : parchment
pericia *nf* : skill
periferia *nf* : periphery, outskirts
  (of a city, etc.) — **periférico,**
  -ca *adj* : peripheral
perilla *nf* **1** : goatee **2** *Lat* : knob **3**
  venir de perillas *fam* : come in handy
perímetro *nm* : perimeter
periódico, -ca *adj* : periodic
  — **periódico** *nm* : newspaper —
  periodismo *nm* : journalism —
  periodista *nmf* : journalist
período *or* periodo *nm* : period
periquito *nm* : parakeet
periscopio *nm* : periscope
perito, -ta *adj & n* : expert
perjudicar {72} *vt* : harm, damage
  — **perjudicial** *adj* : harmful —
  perjuicio *nm* **1** : harm, damage **2 en**
  perjudicar de : to the detriment of
perjurar *vi* : perjure oneself
  — **perjurio** *nm* : perjury
perla *nf* **1** : pearl **2 de perlas**
  fam : great, just fine
permanecer {53} *vi* : remain —
  permanencia *nf* **1** : permanence
  2 : stay, staying (in a place) —
  permanente *adj* : permanent —
  permanecer *nf* : permanent (wave)

permeable *adj* : permeable
permitir *vt* **1** : permit, allow **2 ¿me**
  permite? : may I? — **permitirse** *vr* : allow
  oneself — **permisible** *adj* : permissible,
  allowable — **permisivo, -va** *adj* :
  permissive — **permiso** *nm* **1** : permission
  2 : permit, license (document) **3** : leave (in
  the military) **4 con permiso** : excuse me
permuta *nf* : exchange
pernicioso, -sa *adj* :
  pernicious, destructive
pero *conj* : but — **pero** *nm* **1** :
  fault **2** REPARO : objection
perorar *vi* : make a speech —
  perorata *nf* : (long-winded) speech
perpendicular *adj & nf* : perpendicular
perpetrar *vt* : perpetrate
perpetuar {3} *vt* : perpetuate —
  perpetuo, -tua *adj* : perpetual
perplejo, -ja *adj* : perplexed —
  perplejidad *nf* : perplexity
▸ **perro, -rra** *n* **1** : dog, bitch *f* **2 perro**
  caliente : hot dog — **perrera** *nf* : kennel
perseguir {75} *vt* **1** : pursue,
  chase **2** ACOSAR : persecute —
  persecución *nf, pl* **-ciones 1** : pursuit,
  chase **2** ACOSO : persecution
perseverar *vi* : persevere —
  perseverancia *nf* : perseverance
persiana *nf* : (venetian) blind
persistir *vi* : persist — **persistencia** *nf* :
  persistence — **persistente** *adj* : persistent
persona *nf* : person — **personaje** *nm* **1**
  : character (in literature, etc.) **2** : important
  person, celebrity — **personal** *adj* :
  personal — **personal** *nm* : personnel,
  staff — **personalidad** *nf* : personality
  — **personificar** {72} *vi* : personify
perspectiva *nf* **1** : perspective **2** VISTA
  : view **3** POSIBILIDAD : prospect, outlook
perspicacia *nf* : shrewdness,
  insight — **perspicaz** *adj,*
  pl **-caces** : shrewd, discerning
persuadir *vt* : persuade —
  persuadirse *vr* : become convinced —
  persuasión *nf, pl* **-siones** : persuasion
  — **persuasivo, -va** *adj* : persuasive
pertenecer {53} *vi* **pertenecer a** : belong
  to — **perteneciente** *adj* **perteneciente**
  a : belonging to — **pertenencia** *nf* **1** :
  ownership **2** pertenecers *nfpl* : belongings
pertinaz *adj, pl* **-naces 1** OBSTINADO :
  obstinate **2** PERSISTENTE : persistent
pertinente *adj* : pertinent, relevant
  — **pertinencia** *nf* : relevance

pesa*F* : halterofilia*F*
barbell : weightlifting

perturbar *vt* : disturb — **perturbación** *nf,*
  pl **-ciones** : disturbance
peruano, -na *adj* : Peruvian
pervertir {76} *vt* : pervert —
  perversión *nf, pl* **-siones** : perversion
  — **perverso, -sa** *adj* : perverse
  — **pervertido, -da** *adj* : perverted,
  depraved — **pervertir** *n* : pervert
▸ **pesa** *nf* **1** : weight **2** pesas : weights
  (in sports) — **pesadez** *nf, pl* **-deces 1**
  : heaviness **2** *fam* : tediousness, drag
pesadilla *nf* : nightmare
pesado, -da *adj* **1** : heavy **2** LENTO
  : sluggish **3** MOLESTO : annoying **4**
  ABURRIDO : tedious **5** DURO : tough,
  difficult — **pesado, -da** *n, fam* : bore,
  pest — **pesadumbre** *nf* : grief, sorrow
pésame *nm* : condolences *pl*
pesar *vt* : weigh — *vi* **1** : weigh,
  be heavy **2** INFLUIR : carry weight
  3 pese a : despite — **pesar** *nm* **1**
  : sorrow, grief **2** REMORDIMIENTO :
  remorse **3 a pesar de** : in spite of
pescado *nm* : fish — **pesca** *nf* **1** :
  fishing **2** PECES : fish *pl*, catch **3 ir de**
  pesca : go fishing — **pescadería** *nf* :
  fish market — **pescador, -dora** *n, mpl*
  -dores : fisherman — **pescar** {72} *vt* **1**
  : fish for **2** *fam* : catch (a cold, etc.) **3**
  fam : catch hold of, nab — *vi* : fish
pescuezo *nm* : neck (of an animal)
pese a → **pesar**
pesebre *nm* : manger

peces^M óseos
bony fishes

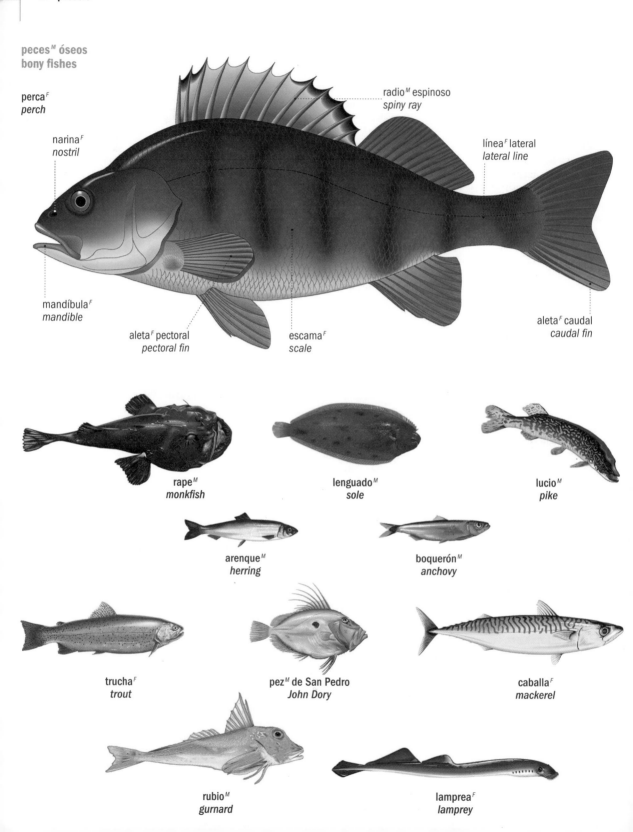

perca^F
perch

radio^M espinoso
spiny ray

narina^F
nostril

línea^F lateral
lateral line

mandíbula^F
mandible

aleta^F pectoral
pectoral fin

escama^F
scale

aleta^F caudal
caudal fin

rape^M
monkfish

lenguado^M
sole

lucio^M
pike

arenque^M
herring

boquerón^M
anchovy

trucha^F
trout

pez^M de San Pedro
John Dory

caballa^F
mackerel

rubio^M
gurnard

lamprea^F
lamprey

pesero *nm Lat* : minibus
peseta *nf* : peseta
pesimismo *nm* : pessimism —
  pesimista *adj* : pessimistic —
  pesimismo *nmf* : pessimist
pésimo, -ma *adj* : awful
peso *nm* **1** : weight **2** CARGA :
  burden **3** : peso (currency) **4**
  peso pesado : heavyweight
pesquero, -ra *adj* : fishing
pesquisa *nf* : inquiry
pestaña *nf* : eyelash — **pestañear** *vi*
  : blink — **pestañeo** *nm* : blink
peste *nm* **1** : plague **2** *fam* : stench, stink
  3 *Lat fam* : cold, bug — **pesticida** *nm*
  : pesticide — **pestilencia** *nf* **1** :

stench **2** PLAGA : pestilence
pestillo *nm* : bolt, latch
petaca *nf Lat* : suitcase
pétalo *nm* : petal
petardo *nm* : firecracker
petición *nf, pl* **-ciones** : petition, request
petirrojo *nm* : robin
petrificar {72} *vt* : petrify
petróleo *nm* : oil, petroleum — **petrolero,**
  -ra *adj* : oil — **petrolero** *nm* : oil tanker
petulante *adj* : insolent, arrogant
peyorativo, -va *adj* : pejorative
▸ **pez** *nm, pl* **peces 1** : fish **2 pez de**
  colores : goldfish **3 pez espada** :
  swordfish **4 pez gordo** *fam* : big shot
pezón *nm, pl* **-zones** : nipple

pezuña *nf* : hoof
piadoso, -sa *adj* **1** : compassionate
  2 DEVOTO : pious, devout
▸ **piano** *nm* : piano — **pianista** *nmf*
  : pianist, piano player
piar {85} *vi* : chirp, tweet
pibe, -ba *n Lat fam* : kid, child
pica *nf* **1** : pike, lance **2** :
  spade (in playing cards)
picado, -da *adj* **1** : perforated **2** :
  minced, chopped (of meat, etc.) **3** :
  decayed (of teeth) **4** : choppy (of the
  sea) **5** *fam* : annoyed — **picada** *nf* **1**
  : bite, sting **2** *Lat* : sharp descent
  — **picadillo** *nm* : minced meat —
  picadura *nf* **1** : sting, bite **2** : (moth) hole

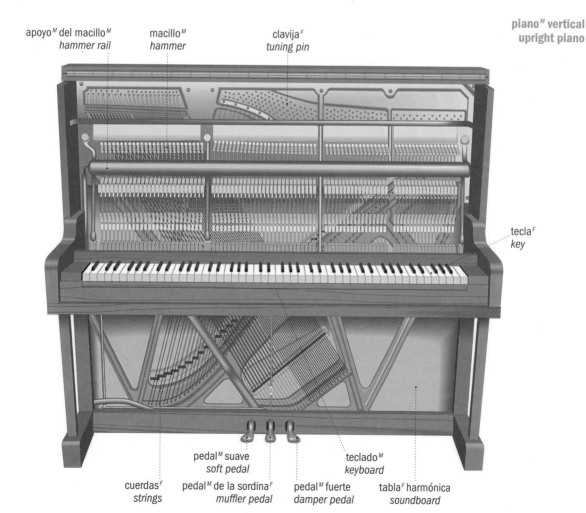

piano^M **vertical**
upright piano

apoyo^M del macillo^M
hammer rail

macillo^M
hammer

clavija^F
tuning pin

tecla^F
key

pedal^M suave
soft pedal

teclado^M
keyboard

cuerdas^F
strings

pedal^M de la sordina^F
muffler pedal

pedal^M fuerte
damper pedal

tabla^F harmónica
soundboard

huesos^M del pie^M
foot bones

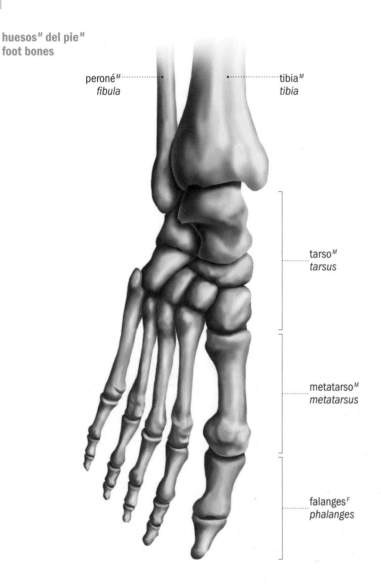

peroné^M ······· *fibula*

tibia^M ······· *tibia*

tarso^M ······· *tarsus*

metatarso^M ······· *metatarsus*

falanges^F ······· *phalanges*

---

picante *adj* : hot, spicy
picaporte *nm* **1** : door handle **2** ALDABA
: door knocker **3** PESTILLO : latch
picar {72} *vt* **1** : sting, bite **2** : peck
at, nibble on (food) **3** PERFORAR : prick,
puncture **4** TRITURAR : chop, mince
— *vi* **1** : bite, take the bait **2** ESCOCER
: sting, itch **3** COMER : nibble **4** : be
spicy (of food) — **picarse** *vr* **1** : get
a cavity **2** ENFADARSE : take offense
picardía *nf* **1** : craftiness **2**
TRAVESURA : prank — **picaresco,**
-ca *adj* **1** : picaresque **2** TRAVIESO

: roguish — **pícaro, -ra** *adj* **1** :
mischievous **2** MALICIOSO : villainous
— **pícaro, -ra** *n* : rascal, scoundrel
picazón *nf, pl* **-zones** : itch
pichón, -chona *n, mpl*
-chones : (young) pigeon
picnic *nm, pl* **-nics** : picnic
pico *nm* **1** : beak **2** CIMA : peak **3**
PUNTA : (sharp) point **4** : pick, pickax
(tool) **5 las siete y pico** : a little after
seven — **picotazo** *nm* : peck —
picotear *vt* : peck — *vi, fam* : nibble,
pick — **picudo, -da** *adj* : pointy

▶ **pie** *nm* **1** : foot (in anatomy) **2** : base,
bottom, stem **3 al pie de la letra** :
word for word **4 dar pie a** : give rise
to **5 de pie** : standing (up) **6 de pies**
a cabeza : from top to bottom
piedad *nf* **1** : pity, mercy
2 DEVOCIÓN : piety
piedra *nf* **1** : stone **2** : flint (of a
lighter) **3** GRANIZO : hailstone **4 piedra**
angular : cornerstone **5** → **pómez**
piel *nf* **1** : skin **2** CUERO :
leather **3** PELO : fur, pelt
pienso *nm* : feed, fodder
pierna *nf* : leg
pieza *nf* **1** : piece, part **2** *or* **pieza de**
teatro : play **3** HABITACIÓN : room
pigmento *nm* : pigment —
pigmentación *nf, pl* **-ciones**
: pigmentation
pigmeo, -mea *adj* : pygmy
pijama *nm* : pajamas *pl*
pila *nf* **1** : battery **2** MONTÓN
: pile **3** FREGADERO : sink **4** :
basin (of a fountain, etc.)
pilar *nm* : pillar
píldora *nf* : pill
pillar *vt* **1** : catch **2** : get (a joke, etc.)
— **pillaje** *nm* : pillage — **pillo, -lla** *adj* :
crafty — **pillo, -lla** *n* : rascal, scoundrel
piloto *nmf* : pilot — **pilotar** *vt* : pilot
pimienta *nf* : pepper (condiment)
— **pimiento** *nm* : pepper (fruit)
— **pimentero** *nm* : pepper shaker
— **pimentón** *nm, pl* **-tones 1** :
paprika **2** : cayenne pepper
pináculo *nm* : pinnacle
pincel *nm* : paintbrush
pinchar *vt* **1** : pierce, prick **2** :
puncture (a tire, etc.) **3** INCITAR :
goad — **pinchazo** *nm* **1** : prick
2 : puncture (of a tire, etc.)
pingüino *nm* : penguin
pino *nm* : pine (tree)
pintar *v* : paint — **pintarse** *vr* : put
on makeup — **pinta** *nf* **1** : spot **2** :
pint (measure) **3** *fam* : appearance —
pintada *nf* : graffiti — **pinto, -ta** *adj* :
speckled, spotted — **pintor, -tora** *n,*
mpl **-tores** : painter — **pintoresco,**
-ca *adj* : picturesque, quaint —
pintura *nf* **1** : paint **2** CUADRO : painting
pinza *nf* **1** : clothespin **2** : claw, pincer
(of a crab, etc.) **3 pinzas** *nfpl* : tweezers
pinzón *nm, pl* **-zones** : finch
piña *nf* **1** : pine cone **2** ANANÁS : pineapple

piñata *nf* : piñata

piñón *nm, pl* **-ñones** : pine nut

pío[1] , **pía** *adj* **1** : pious **2** : piebald (of a horse)

pío[2] *nm* : peep, chirp

piojo *nm* : louse

pionero, -ra *n* : pioneer

pipa *nf* **1** : pipe (for smoking) **2** *Spain* : seed, pip

pique *nm* **1** : grudge **2** RIVALIDAD : rivalry **3 irse a pique** : sink, founder

piqueta *nf* : pickax

piquete *nm* : picket (line) — **piquetear** *v* : picket

piragua *nf* : canoe

pirámide *nf* : pyramid

piraña *nf* : piranha

pirata *adj* : bootleg, pirated — **pirata** *nmf* : pirate — **piratear** *vt* **1** : bootleg, pirate **2** : hack into (a computer)

piropo *nm* : (flirtatious) compliment

pirueta *nf* : pirouette

pirulí *nm* : (cone-shaped) lollipop

pisada *nf* **1** : footstep **2** HUELLA : footprint

pisapapeles *nms & pl* : paperweight

pisar *vt* **1** : step on **2** HUMILLAR : walk all over, abuse — *vi* : step, tread

piscina *nf* **1** : swimming pool **2** : (fish) pond

piso *nm* **1** : floor, story **2** *Lat* : floor (of a room) **3** *Spain* : apartment

pisotear *vt* : trample (on)

pista *nf* **1** : trail, track **2** INDICIO : clue **3 pista de aterrizaje** : runway, airstrip **4 pista de baile** : dance floor **5 pista de hielo** : ice-skating rink

pistacho *nm* : pistachio

pistola *nf* **1** : pistol, gun **2** PULVERIZADOR : spray gun — **pistolera** *nf* : holster — **pistolero** *nm* : gunman

pistón *nm, pl* **-tones** : piston

pito *nm* **1** SILBATO : whistle **2** CLAXON : horn — **pitar** *vi* **1** : blow a whistle **2** : beep, honk (of a horn) — *vt* : whistle at — **pitido** *nm* **1** : whistle, whistling **2** : beep (of a horn) — **pitillo** *nm, fam* : cigarette

▸ **pitón** *nm, pl* **-tones** *nm* : python

pitorro *nm* : spout

pivote *nm* : pivot

piyama *nmf Lat* : pajamas *pl*

pizarra *nf* **1** : slate **2** ENCERADO : blackboard — **pizarrón** *nm, pl* **-rrones** *Lat* : blackboard

pizca *nf* **1** : pinch (of salt) **2** ÁPICE : speck, tiny bit **3** *Lat* : harvest

pizza *nf* : pizza — **pizzería** *nf* : pizzeria

placa *nf* **1** : sheet, plate **2** INSCRIPCIÓN : plaque **3** : (police) badge

placenta *nf* : placenta

placer {57} *vt* : please — **placer** *nm* : pleasure — **placentero, -ra** *adj* : pleasant, agreeable

plácido, -da *adj* : placid, calm

plaga *nf* **1** : plague **2** CALAMIDAD : disaster — **plagar** {52} *vt* : plague, infest

plagiar *vt* : plagiarize — **plagio** *nm* : plagiarism

plan *nm* **1** : plan **2 en plan de** : as **3 no te pongas en ese plan** *fam* : don't be that way

plana *nf* **1** : page **2 en primera plana** : on the front page

plancha *nf* **1** : iron (for ironing) **2** : grill (for cooking) **3** LÁMINA : sheet, plate — **planchar** *v* : iron — **planchado** *nm* : ironing

planear *vt* : plan — *vi* : glide — **planeador** *nm* : glider

planeta *nm* : planet

planicie *nf* : plain

planificar {72} *vt* : plan — **planificación** *nf, pl* **-ciones** : planning

planilla *nf Lat* : list, roster

plano, -na *adj* : flat — **plano** *nm* **1** : map, plan **2** : plane (surface) **3** NIVEL : level **4 de plano, -na** : flatly, outright **5 primer plano, -na** : foreground, close-up (in photography)

planta *nf* **1** : plant **2** PISO : floor, story **3** : sole (of the foot) — **plantación** *nf, pl* **-ciones** **1** : plantation **2** : (action of) planting — **plantar** *vt* **1** : plant **2** *fam* : deal, land — **plantarse** *vr* : stand firm

plantear *vt* **1** : expound, set forth **2** : raise (a question) **3** CAUSAR : create, pose (a problem) — **plantearse** *vr* : think about, consider

plantel *nm* **1** : staff, team **2** *Lat* : educational institution

plantilla *nf* **1** : insole **2** PATRÓN : pattern, template **3** : staff (of a business, etc.)

plasma *nm* : plasma

plástico, -ca *adj* : plastic — **plástico** *nm* : plastic

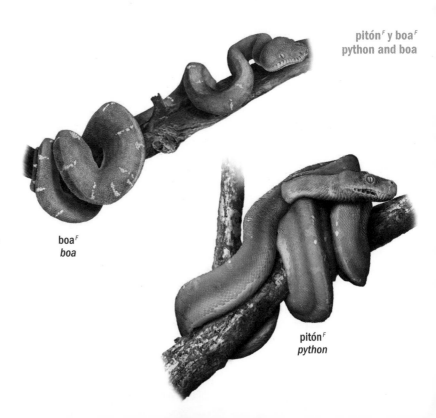

pitón[F] **y boa**[F]
python and boa

boa[F]
boa

pitón[F]
python

plata *nf* **1** : silver **2** *Lat fam* : money
3 plata de ley : sterling silver
plataforma *nf* **1** : platform **2 plataforma**
petrolífera : oil rig **3 plataforma**
de lanzamiento : launching pad
plátano *nm* **1** : banana **2** : plantain
platea *nf* : orchestra, pit (in a theater)
plateado, -da *adj* **1** : silver,
silvery (color) **2** : silver-plated
platicar {72} *vi* : talk, chat —
plática *nf* : chat, conversation
platija *nf* : flatfish, flounder
platillo *nm* **1** : saucer **2** CÍMBALO
: cymbal **3** *Lat* : dish, course
platino *nm* : platinum
plato *nm* **1** : plate, dish **2** : course (of
a meal) **3 plato principal** : entrée
platónico, -ca *adj* : platonic
playa *nf* **1** : beach, seashore **2 playa**
de estacionamiento *Lat* : parking lot
plaza *nf* **1** : square, plaza **2** : seat (in
transportation) **3** PUESTO : post, position
4 MERCADO : market, marketplace
5 plaza de toros : bullring
plazo *nm* **1** : period, term **2** PAGO :
installment **3 a largo plazo** : long-term
plazoleta *or* plazuela *nf* : small square
pleamar *nf* : high tide
plebe *nf* : common people —
plebeyo, -ya *adj & nm* : plebeian
plegar {49} *vt* : fold, bend —
plegarse *vr* **1** : give in, yield **2** :
jackknife (of a truck) — **plegable** *or*
plegadizo, -za *adj* : folding, collapsible
plegaria *nf* : prayer
pleito *nm* **1** : lawsuit **2** *Lat* : dispute, fight
plenilunio *nm* : full moon
pleno, -na *adj* **1** : full, complete
2 en plena forma : in top form **3**
en pleno día : in broad daylight —
plenitud *nf* : fullness, abundance
pleuresía *nf* : pleurisy
pliego *nm* : sheet (of paper)
— **pliegue** *nm* **1** : crease,
fold **2** : pleat (in fabric)
plisar *vt* : pleat
plomería *nf Lat* : plumbing —
plomero, -ra *n Lat* : plumber
plomo *nm* **1** : lead **2** FUSIBLE : fuse
pluma *nf* **1** : feather **2** : (fountain) pen —
plumaje *nm* : plumage — **plumero** *nm*
: feather duster — **plumilla** *nf* : nib
— **plumón** *nm, pl* **-mones** : down
plural *adj & nm* : plural —
pluralidad *nf* : plurality

pluriempleo *nm* **hacer pluriempleo**
: have more than one job
plus *nm* : bonus
plusvalía *nf* : appreciation, capital gain
plutocracia *nf* : plutocracy
Plutón *nm* : Pluto
plutonio *nm* : plutonium
pluvial *adj* : rain
poblar {19} *vt* **1** : settle, colonize **2**
HABITAR : inhabit — **poblarse** *vr* : become
crowded — **población** *nf, pl* **-ciones**
1 : city, town, village **2** HABITANTES :
population — **poblado, -da** *adj* **1** :
populated **2** : thick, bushy (of a beard,
eyebrows, etc.) — **poblado** *nm* : village
pobre *adj* **1** : poor **2 ¡pobre de mí!** :
poor me! — **pobre** *nmf* **1** : poor person
2 los pobres : the poor **3 ¡pobre!** :
poor thing! — **pobreza** *nf* : poverty
pocilga *nf* : pigsty
poción *nf, pl* **-ciones** *or* **pócima** *nf* : potion
poco, -ca *adj* **1** : little, not much,
(a) few **2 pocas veces** : rarely —
poco, -ca *pron* **1** : little, few **2 hace**
poco : not long ago **3 poco a poco**
: bit by bit, gradually **4 por poco** :
nearly, just about **5 un poco** : a little,
a bit — **poco** *adv* : little, not much
podar *vt* : prune
poder {58} *v aux* **1** : be able to, can **2**
(*expressing possibility*) : might, may **3**
(*expressing permission*) : can, may **4**
¿cómo puede ser? : how can it be?
5 ¿puedo pasar? : may I come in?
— *vi* **1** : be possible **2 poder con** : cope
with, manage **3 no poder más** : I've
had enough — **poder** *nm* **1** : power **2**
POSESIÓN : possession — **poderío** *nm* :
power — **poderoso, -sa** *adj* : powerful
podólogo, -ga *n* : chiropodist
podrido, -da *adj* : rotten
poema *nm* : poem — **poesía** *nf* **1** :
poetry **2** POEMA : poem — **poeta** *nmf*
: poet — **poético, -ca** *adj* : poetic
póker *nm* → **póquer**
polaco, -ca *adj* : Polish
polar *adj* : polar — **polarizar**
{21} *vt* : polarize
polea *nf* : pulley
polémica *nf* : controversy —
polémico, -ca *adj* : controversial
— **polemizar** *vt* : argue
polen *nm, pl* **pólenes** : pollen
▸ **policía** *nf* : police — **policía** *nmf* : police
officer, policeman *m*, policewoman *f*

— **policíaco, -ca** *adj* **1** : police **2**
novela policíaca : detective story
poliéster *nm* : polyester
poligamia *nf* : polygamy —
polígamo, -ma *n* : polygamist
polígono *nm* : polygon
polilla *nf* : moth
polio *or* **poliomielitis** *nf* :
polio, poliomyelitis
politécnico, -ca *adj* : polytechnic
política *nf* **1** : politics **2** POSTURA
: policy — **político, -ca** *adj* **1** :
political **2 hermano político** : brother-
in-law — **política** *n* : politician
póliza *nf or* **póliza de seguros**
: insurance policy
polizón *nm, pl* **-zones** : stowaway
pollo, -lla *n* **1** : chicken, chick **2** :
chicken (for cooking) — **pollera** *nf*
Lat : skirt — **pollería** *nf* : poultry
shop — **pollito, -ta** *n* : chick
polo *nm* **1** : pole **2** : polo (sport)
3 polo norte : North Pole
poltrona *nf* : easy chair
polución *nf, pl* **-ciones** : pollution
polvo *nm* **1** : powder **2** SUCIEDAD : dust **3**
polvos *nmpl* : face powder **4 hacer polvo**
fam : crush, shatter — **polvareda** *nf* :
cloud of dust — **polvera** *nf* : compact
(for powder) — **pólvora** *nf* : gunpowder
— **polvoriento, -ta** *adj* : dusty
pomada *nf* : ointment
pomelo *nm* : grapefruit
pómez *nm or* **piedra pómez** *nf* : pumice
pomo *nm* : knob, doorknob
pompa *nf* **1** : (soap) bubble **2**
ESPLENDOR : pomp **3 pompas fúnebres**
: funeral — **pomposo, -sa** *adj* **1** :
pompous **2** ESPLÉNDIDO : splendid
pómulo *nm* : cheekbone
ponchar *vi Lat* : puncture —
ponchadura *nf Lat* : puncture
ponche *nm* : punch (drink)
poncho *nm* : poncho
ponderar *vt* **1** : consider **2**
ALABAR : speak highly of
poner {60} *vt* **1** : put **2** AGREGAR : add
3 CONTRIBUIR : contribute **4** SUPONER :
suppose **5** DISPONER : arrange, set out
6 : give (a name), call **7** ENCENDER :
turn on **8** ESTABLECER : set up, establish
9 : lay (eggs) — *vi* : lay eggs —
ponerse *vr* **1** : move (into a position) **2** :
put on (clothing, etc.) **3** : set (of the sun)
4 ponerse furioso : become angry

poniente *nm* **1** OCCIDENTE
: west **2** : west wind
pontífice *nm* : pontiff
pontón *nm, pl* **-tones** : pontoon
ponzoña *nf* : poison, venom
popa *nf* **1** : stern **2 a popa** : astern
popelín *nm, pl* **-lines** : poplin
popote *nm Lat* : (drinking) straw
populacho *nm* : rabble, masses *pl*
popular *adj* **1** : popular **2** : colloquial (of
language) — **popularidad** *nf* : popularity
— **popularizar** {21} *vt* : popularize
— **populoso, -sa** *adj* : populous

póquer *nm* : poker (card game)
por *prep* **1** : for **2** (*indicating an
approximate time*) : around, during **3**
(*indicating an approximate place*) : around,
about **4** A TRAVÉS DE : through, along **5**
A CAUSA DE : because of **6** (*indicating
rate or ratio*) : per **7** *or* **por medio de** :
by means of **8** : times (in mathematics)
9 SEGÚN : as for, according to **10 estar
por** : be about to **11 por ciento** : percent
12 por favor : please **13 por lo tanto**
: therefore **14 ¿por qué?** : why?
porcelana *nf* : porcelain, china

porcentaje *nm* : percentage
porción *nf, pl* **-ciones** : portion, piece
pordiosero, -ra *n* : beggar
porfiar {85} *vi* : insist — **porfiado,
-da** *adj* : obstinate, persistent
pormenor *nm* : detail
pornografía *nf* : pornography —
pornográfico, -ca *adj* : pornographic
poro *nm* : pore — **poroso, -sa** *adj* : porous
poroto *nm Lat* : bean
porque *conj* **1** : because **2** *or* **por que**
: in order that — **porqué** *nm* : reason
porquería *nf* **1** SUCIEDAD : filth
2 : shoddy thing, junk
porra *nf* : nightstick, club —
porrazo *nm* : blow, whack
portaaviones *nms & pl* : aircraft carrier
portada *nf* **1** : facade **2** : title page
(of a book), cover (of a magazine)
portador, -dora *n* : bearer
portaequipajes *nms & pl* : luggage rack
portafolio *or* portafolios *nm, pl* **-lios**
1 : portfolio **2** MALETÍN : briefcase
portal *nm* **1** : doorway **2**
VESTÍBULO : hall, vestibule
portamonedas *nms & pl* : purse
portar *vt* : carry, bear —
portarse *vr* : behave
portátil *adj* : portable
portaviones *nm* → **portaaviones**
portavoz *nmf, pl* **-voces** : spokesperson,
spokesman *m*, spokeswoman *f*
portazo *nm* **dar un portazo**
: slam the door
porte *nm* **1** : transport, freight **2**
ASPECTO : bearing, appearance **3**
porte pagado : postage paid
portento *nm* : marvel, wonder —
portentoso, -sa *adj* : marvelous
porteño, -ña *adj* : of or
from Buenos Aires
portería *nf* **1** : superintendent's office
2 : goal, goalposts *pl* (in sports) —
portero, -ra *n* **1** : goalkeeper, goalie
2 CONSERJE : janitor, superintendent
portezuela *nf* : door (of an automobile)
pórtico *nm* : portico
portilla *nf* : porthole
portugués, -guesa *adj, mpl* **-gueses**
: Portuguese — **portugués** *nm*
: Portuguese (language)
porvenir *nm* : future
pos: en pos de *adv phr* : in pursuit of
posada *nf* : inn
posaderas *nfpl, fam* : backside, bottom

oficial*M* de policía*F*
police officer

gorra*F*
cap

insignia*F*
badge

placa*F* de identificación*F*
name tag

insignia*F* de grado*M*
rank insignia

uniforme*M*
uniform

presas^F
dams

presa^F de contrafuertes^M
buttress dam

presa^F
gravity dam

presa^F de bóveda^F
arch dam

presa^F de tierra^F
embankment dam

posar *vi* : pose — *vt* : place, lay
— **posarse** *vr* : settle, rest
posavasos *nms & pl* : coaster
posdata *nf* : postscript
pose *nf* : pose
poseer {20} *vt* : possess, own —
poseedor, -dora *n* : possessor, owner
— **poseído, -da** *adj* : possessed —
posesión *nf, pl* **-siones** : possession
— **posesionarse** *vr* **posesionarse
de** : take possession of, take over —
posesivo, -va *adj* : possessive
posguerra *nf* : postwar period
posibilidad *nf* : possibility —
posibilitar *vt* : make possible
— **posible** *adj* **1** : possible **2**
de ser posible : if possible
posición *nf, pl* **-ciones** : position
— **posicionar** *vt* : position —
posicionarse *vr* : take a stand
positivo, -va *adj* : positive

poso *nm* : sediment, (coffee) grounds
posponer {60} *vt* **1** : postpone **2**
RELEGAR : put behind, subordinate
postal *adj* : postal — **postal** *nf* : postcard
postdata → **posdata**
poste *nm* : post, pole
póster *nm, pl* **-ters** : poster
postergar {52} *vt* **1** : pass
over **2** APLAZAR : postpone
posteridad *nf* : posterity —
posterior *adj* **1** : later, subsequent
2 TRASERO : back, rear —
posteriormente *adv* : subsequently, later
postigo *nm* **1** : small door **2**
CONTRAVENTANA : shutter
postizo, -za *adj* : artificial, false
postrarse *vr* : prostrate oneself
— **postrado, -da** *adj* : prostrate
postre *nm* : dessert
postular *vt* **1** : advance, propose **2** *Lat*
: nominate — **postulado** *nm* : postulate

póstumo, -ma *adj* : posthumous
postura *nf* : position, stance
potable *adj* : drinkable, potable
potaje *nm* : thick vegetable soup
potasio *nm* : potassium
pote *nm* : jar
potencia *nf* : power — **potencial** *adj &
nm* : potential — **potente** *adj* : powerful
potro, -tra *n* : colt *m*, filly *f* —
potro *nm* : horse (in gymnastics)
pozo *nm* **1** : well **2** : shaft (in a mine)
práctica *nf* **1** : practice **2 en la práctica**
: in practice — **practicable** *adj* :
practicable, feasible — **practicante** *adj* :
practicing — **práctica** *nmf* : practitioner
— **practicar** {72} *vt* **1** : practice **2**
REALIZAR : perform, carry out — *vi* :
practice — **práctico, -ca** *adj* : practical
pradera *nf* : grassland, prairie
— **prado** *nm* : meadow
pragmático, -ca *adj* : pragmatic
preámbulo *nm* : preamble
precario, -ria *adj* : precarious
precaución *nf, pl* **-ciones 1** :
precaution **2** PRUDENCIA : caution,
care **3 con precaución** : cautiously
precaver *vt* : guard against —
precavido, -da *adj* : prudent, cautious
preceder *v* : precede —
precedencia *nf* : precedence, priority
— **precedente** *adj* : preceding, previous
— **precedente** *nm* : precedent
precepto *nm* : precept
preciado, -da *adj* : prized, valuable
— **preciarse** *vr* **preciarse de** :
pride oneself on, boast about
precinto *nm* : seal
precio *nm* : price, cost —
preciosidad *nf* **1** VALOR : value **2** :
beautiful thing — **precioso, -sa** *adj* **1**
HERMOSO : beautiful **2** VALIOSO : precious
precipicio *nm* : precipice
precipitar *vt* **1** : hasten, speed up **2**
ARROJAR : hurl — **precipitarse** *vr* **1**
APRESURARSE : rush **2** : act rashly
3 ARROJARSE : throw oneself —
precipitación *nf, pl* **-ciones 1** :
precipitation **2** PRISA : haste —
precipitadamente *adv* : in a rush,
hastily — **precipitado, -da** *adj* : hasty
preciso, -sa *adj* **1** : precise **2** NECESARIO
: necessary — **precisamente** *adv* :
precisely, exactly — **precisar** *vt* **1**
: specify, determine **2** NECESITAR :
require — **precisión** *nf, pl* **-siones 1**

: precision **2** NECESIDAD : necessity
preconcebido *adj* : preconceived
precoz *adj, pl* **-coces 1** : early
2 : precocious (of children)
precursor, -sora *n* : forerunner
predecesor, -sora *n* : predecessor
predecir {11} *vt* : foretell, predict
predestinado, -da *adj* : predestined
predeterminar *vt* : predetermine
prédica *nf* : sermon
predicado *nm* : predicate
predicar {72} *v* : preach —
predicador, -dora *n* : preacher
predicción *nf, pl* **-ciones 1** :
prediction **2** PRONÓSTICO : forecast
predilección *nf, pl* **-ciones** : preference
— **predilecto, -ta** *adj* : favorite
predisponer {60} *vt* :
predispose — **predisposición** *nf,*
pl **-ciones** : predisposition
predominar *vi* : predominate —
predominante *adj* : predominant,
prevailing — **predominio** *nm*
: predominance
preeminente *adj* : preeminent
prefabricado, -da *adj* : prefabricated
prefacio *nm* : preface
preferir {76} *vt* : prefer —
preferencia *nf* **1** : preference **2 de**
preferencia : preferably — **preferente** *adj*
: preferential — **preferible** *adj* : preferable
— **preferido, -da** *adj* : favorite
prefijo *nm* **1** : prefix **2** *Spain* : area code
pregonar *vt* : proclaim, announce
pregunta *nf* **1** : question **2 hacer**
preguntas : ask questions — **preguntar** *v*
: ask — **preguntarse** *vr* : wonder
prehistórico, -ca *adj* : prehistoric
prejuicio *nm* : prejudice
preliminar *adj & nm* : preliminary
preludio *nm* : prelude
prematrimonial *adj* : premarital
prematuro, -ra *adj* : premature
premeditar *vt* : premeditate
— **premeditación** *nf,*
pl **-ciones** : premeditation
premenstrual *adj* : premenstrual
premio *nm* **1** : prize **2** RECOMPENSA
: reward **3 premio gordo** : jackpot
— **premiado, -da** *adj* : prizewinning
— **premiar** *vt* **1** : award a prize
to **2** RECOMPENSAR : reward
premisa *nf* : premise
premonición *nf, pl* **-ciones** : premonition
premura *nf* : haste, urgency

prenatal *adj* : prenatal
prenda *nf* **1** : piece of clothing **2**
GARANTÍA : pledge **3** : forfeit (in a game)
— **prendar** *vt* : captivate — **prendarse** *vr*
prendarse de : fall in love with
prender *vt* **1** SUJETAR : pin, fasten **2**
APRESAR : capture **3** : light (a match,
etc.) **4** *Lat* : turn on (a light, etc.) — *vi* **1**
: take root **2** ARDER : catch, burn (of
fire) — **prenderse** *vr* : catch fire —
prendedor *nm* *Lat* : brooch, pin
prensa *nf* : press — **prensar** *vt* : press
preñado, -da *adj* **1** : pregnant **2**
preñado, -da de : filled with
preocupar *vt* : worry —
preocuparse *vr* **1** : worry **2**
preocuparse de : take care of —
preocupación *nf, pl* **-ciones** : worry
preparar *vt* : prepare — **prepararse** *vr* :
get ready — **preparación** *nf, pl* **-ciones**
: preparation — **preparado, -da** *adj*
: prepared, ready — **preparado** *nm*
: preparation — **preparativo,**
-va *adj* : preparatory, preliminary —
preparativos *nmpl* : preparations —
preparatorio, -ria *adj* : preparatory
preposición *nf, pl* **-ciones** : preposition
prepotente *adj* : arrogant, domineering
prerrogativa *nf* : prerogative
▸ **presa** *nf* **1** : catch, prey **2** DIQUE :
dam **3 hacer presa en** : seize
presagiar *vt* : presage, forebode
— **presagio** *nm* **1** : omen **2**
PREMONICIÓN : premonition
presbítero *nm* : presbyter, priest
prescindir *vi* **prescindir de 1** : do
without **2** OMITIR : dispense with
prescribir {33} *vt* : prescribe —
prescripción *nf, pl* **-ciones** : prescription
presencia *nf* **1** : presence **2** ASPECTO
: appearance — **presenciar** *vt*
: be present at, witness
presentar *vt* **1** : present **2** OFRECER :
offer, give **3** MOSTRAR : show **4** : introduce
(persons) — **presentarse** *vr* **1** : show
up **2** : arise, come up (of a problem, etc.)
3 : introduce oneself — **presentación** *nf,*
pl **-ciones 1** : presentation **2** : introduction
(of persons) **3** ASPECTO : appearance
— **presentador, -dora** *n* : presenter,
host (of a television program, etc.)
presente *adj* **1** : present **2**
tener presente : keep in mind —
presente *nm* **1** : present **2 entre los**
presentes : among those present

presentir {76} *vt* : have a presentiment
of — **presentimiento** *nm* : premonition
preservar *vt* : preserve, protect —
preservación *nf, pl* **-ciones** : preservation
— **preservativo** *nm* : condom
presidente, -ta *n* **1** : president **2**
: chair, chairperson (of a meeting)
— **presidencia** *nf* **1** : presidency
2 : chairmanship (of a meeting) —
presidencial *adj* : presidential
presidio *nm* : prison —
presidiario, -ria *n* : convict
presidir *vt* **1** : preside over, chair
2 PREDOMINAR : dominate
presión *nf, pl* **-siones 1** : pressure **2**
presión arterial : blood pressure **3**
hacer presión : press — **presionar** *vt* **1**
: press **2** COACCIONAR : put pressure on
preso, -sa *adj* : imprisoned
— **preso, -sa** *n* : prisoner
prestar *vt* **1** : lend, loan **2** : give (aid)
3 prestar atención : pay attention
— **prestado, -da** *adj* **1** : borrowed,
on loan **2 pedir prestado** : borrow
— **prestamista** *nmf* : moneylender
— **préstamo** *nm* : loan
prestidigitación *nf, pl* **-ciones** :
sleight of hand — **prestidigitador,**
-dora *n* : magician
prestigio *nm* : prestige —
prestigioso, -sa *adj* : prestigious
presto, -ta *adj* : prompt, ready —
presto *adv* : promptly, right away
presumir *vt* : presume — *vi* : boast, show
off — **presumido, -da** *adj* : conceited,
vain — **presunción** *nf, pl* **-ciones 1**
: presumption **2** VANIDAD : vanity —
presunto, -ta *adj* : presumed, alleged
— **presuntuoso, -sa** *adj* : conceited
presuponer {60} *vt* : presuppose
— **presupuesto** *nm* **1** : budget,
estimate **2** SUPUESTO : assumption
presuroso, -sa *adj* : hasty, quick
pretender *vt* **1** : try to **2** AFIRMAR : claim
3 CORTEJAR : court, woo **4 pretender**
que : expect — **pretencioso, -sa** *adj*
: pretentious — **pretendido** *adj* :
supposed — **pretendiente** *nmf* **1** :
candidate **2** : pretender (to a throne) —
pretendiente *nm* : suitor — **pretensión** *nf,*
pl **-siones 1** INTENCIÓN : intention,
aspiration **2** : claim (to a throne, etc.)
3 pretensiones *nfpl* : pretensions
pretérito *nm* : past (in grammar)
pretexto *nm* : pretext, excuse

prevalecer {53} *vi* : prevail —
prevaleciente *adj* : prevailing, prevalent
prevenir {87} *vt* **1** : prevent **2**
AVISAR : warn — **prevenirse** {87} *vr*
prevenirse contra *or* **prevenirse**
de : take precautions against —
prevención *nf, pl* **-ciones 1** : prevention
2 PRECAUCIÓN : precaution **3** PREJUICIO
: prejudice — **prevenido, -da** *adj* **1** :
prepared, ready **2** PRECAVIDO : cautious
— **preventivo, -va** *adj* : preventive
prever {88} *vt* **1** : foresee **2** PLANEAR : plan
previo, -via *adj* : previous, prior
previsible *adj* : foreseeable —
previsión *nf, pl* **-siones 1** : foresight
2 PREDICCIÓN : prediction, forecast —
previsor, -sora *adj* : farsighted, prudent
prieto, -ta *adj* **1** CEÑIDO : tight
2 *Lat fam* : dark-skinned
prima *nf* **1** : bonus **2** : (insurance)
premium **3** → **primo**
primario, -ria *adj* **1** : primary **2**
escuela primaria : elementary school
primate *nm* : primate
primavera *nf* **1** : spring
(season) **2** : primrose (flower)
— **primaveral** *adj* : spring
primero, -ra *adj* (**primer** *before*
masculine singular nouns) **1** : first **2** MEJOR
: top, leading **3** PRINCIPAL : main, basic **4**
de primera : first-rate — **primero, -ra** *n*
: first (person or thing) — **primero** *adv* **1**
: first **2** MÁS BIEN : rather, sooner
primitivo, -va *adj* : primitive
primo, -ma *n* : cousin
primogénito, -ta *adj & n* : firstborn
primor *nm* : beautiful thing
primordial *adj* : basic, fundamental
primoroso, -sa *adj* **1** : exquisite,
fine **2** HÁBIL : skillful
princesa *nf* : princess
principado *nm* : principality
principal *adj* : main, principal
príncipe *nm* : prince
principio *nm* **1** : principle **2**
COMIENZO : beginning, start **3** ORIGEN
: origin **4 al principio** : at first **5 a**
principios de : at the beginning of
— **principiante** *nmf* : beginner
pringar {52} *vt* : spatter (with grease)
— **pringoso, -sa** *adj* : greasy
prioridad *nf* : priority
prisa *nf* **1** : hurry, rush **2 a prisa** *or*
de prisa : quickly **3 a toda prisa** :
as fast as possible **4 darse prisa** :

hurry **5 tener prisa** : be in a hurry
prisión *nf, pl* **-siones 1** : prison **2**
ENCARCELAMIENTO : imprisonment
— **prisionero, -ra** *n* : prisoner
prisma *nm* : prism —
prismáticos *nmpl* : binoculars
privar *vt* **1** : deprive **2** PROHIBIR : forbid **3**
Lat : knock out — **privarse** *vr* : deprive
oneself — **privación** *nf, pl* **-ciones** :
deprivation — **privado, -da** *adj* : private
— **privativo, -va** *adj* : exclusive
privilegio *nm* : privilege —
privilegiado, -da *adj* : privileged
pro *prep* : for, in favor of — **pro** *nm* **1**
: pro, advantage **2 en pro de** :
for, in support of **3 los pros y los**
contras : the pros and cons
proa *nf* : bow, prow
probabilidad *nf* : probability —
probable *adj* : probable, likely —
probablemente *adv* : probably
probar {19} *vt* **1** : try, test **2** : try on
(clothing) **3** DEMOSTRAR : prove **4** DEGUSTAR
: taste — *vi* : try — **probarse** *vr* : try
on (clothing) — **probeta** *nf* : test tube
problema *nm* : problem —
problemático, -ca *adj* : problematic
proceder *vi* **1** : proceed, act **2** : be
appropriate **3 proceder de** : come from —
procedencia *nf* : origin — **procedente** *adj*
procedente de : coming from, originating
in — **procedimiento** *nm* **1** : procedure,
method **2** : proceedings *pl* (in law)
procesar *vt* **1** : prosecute **2** : process
(data) — **procesador** *nm* **procesador**
de textos : word processor —
procesamiento *nm* : processing —
procesión *nf, pl* **-siones** : procession
— **proceso** *nm* **1** : process **2** :
trial, proceedings *pl* (in law)
proclamar *vt* : proclaim — **proclama** *nf*
: proclamation — **proclamación** *nf,*
pl **-ciones** : proclamation
procrear *vi* : procreate —
procreación *nf, pl* **-ciones** : procreation
procurar *vt* **1** : try, endeavor **2**
CONSEGUIR : obtain, procure —
procurador, -dora *n* : attorney
prodigar {52} *vt* : lavish —
prodigio *nm* : wonder, prodigy —
prodigioso, -sa *adj* : prodigious
pródigo, -ga *adj* : extravagant, prodigal
producir {61} *vt* **1** : produce **2** CAUSAR
: cause **3** : yield, bear (interest,
fruit, etc.) — **producirse** *vr* : take

place — **producción** *nf, pl* **-ciones**
: production — **productividad** *nf* :
productivity — **productivo, -va** *adj* :
productive — **producto** *nm* : product
— **productor, -tora** *n* : producer
proeza *nf* : exploit
profanar *vt* : profane, desecrate —
profanación *nf, pl* **-ciones** : desecration
— **profano, -na** *adj* : profane
profecía *nf* : prophecy
proferir {76} *vt* **1** : utter **2** : hurl (insults)
profesar *vt* **1** : profess **2** : practice
(a profession, etc.) — **profesión** *nf,*
pl **-siones** : profession — **profesional** *adj*
& nmf : professional — **profesor,**
-sora *n* **1** : teacher **2** : professor (at a
university, etc.) — **profesorado** *nm* **1** :
teaching profession **2** PROFESORES : faculty
profeta *nm* : prophet — **profético, -ca** *adj*
: prophetic — **profetista** *nf* : (female)
prophet — **profetizar** {21} *vt* : prophesy
prófugo, -ga *adj & n* : fugitive
profundo, -da *adj* **1** HONDO : deep
2 : profound (of thoughts, etc.)
— **profundamente** *adv* : deeply,
profoundly — **profundidad** *nf* : depth
— **profundizar** {21} *vt* : study in depth
profuso, -sa *adj* : profuse —
profusión *nf, pl* **-siones** : profusion
progenie *nf* : progeny, offspring
programa *nm* **1** : program **2**
: curriculum (in education) —
programación *nf, pl* **-ciones** :
programming — **programador, -dora** *n*
: programmer — **programar** *vt* **1** :
schedule **2** : program (a computer, etc.)
progreso *nm* : progress —
progresar *vi* : (make) progress —
progresión *nf, pl* **-ciones** : progression
— **progresista** *adj & nmf* : progressive —
progresivo, -va *adj* : progressive, gradual
prohibir {62} *vt* : prohibit, forbid —
prohibición *nf, pl* **-ciones** : ban, prohibition
— **prohibido, -da** *adj* : forbidden —
prohibitivo, -va *adj* : prohibitive
prójimo *nm* : neighbor, fellow man
prole *nf* : offspring
proletariado *nm* : proletariat —
proletario, -ria *adj & n* : proletarian
proliferar *vi* : proliferate —
proliferación *nf, pl* **-ciones** : proliferation
— **prolífico, -ca** *adj* : prolific
prolijo, -ja *adj* : wordy, long-winded
prólogo *nm* : prologue, foreword
prolongar {52} *vt* **1** : prolong **2** ALARGAR :

lengthen — **prolongarse** *vr* : last, continue — **prolongación** *nf, pl* **-ciones** : extension
promedio *nm* : average
promesa *nf* : promise — **prometedor, -dora** *adj* : promising, hopeful — **prometer** *vt* : promise — *vi* : show promise — **prometerse** *vr* : get engaged — **prometido, -da** *adj* : engaged — **prometido, -da** *n* : fiancé *m*, fiancée *f*
prominente *adj* : prominent — **prominencia** *nf* : prominence
promiscuo, -cua *adj* : promiscuous — **promiscuidad** *nf* : promiscuity
promocionar *vt* : promote — **promoción** *nf, pl* **-ciones** : promotion
promontorio *nm* : promontory
promover {47} *vt* **1** : promote **2** CAUSAR : cause — **promotor, -tora** *n* : promoter
promulgar {52} *vt* **1** : proclaim **2** : enact (a law)
pronombre *nm* : pronoun
pronosticar {72} *vt* : predict, forecast — **pronóstico** *nm* **1** : prediction, forecast **2** : (medical) prognosis
pronto, -ta *adj* **1** : quick, prompt **2** PREPARADO : ready — **pronto** *adv* **1** : soon **2** RAPIDAMENTE : quickly, promptly **3 de pronto, -ta** : suddenly **4 por lo pronto, -ta** : for the time being **5 tan pronto, -ta como** : as soon as
pronunciar *vt* **1** : pronounce **2** : give, deliver (a speech) — **pronunciarse** *vr* **1** : declare oneself **2** SUBLEVARSE : revolt — **pronunciación** *nf, pl* **-ciones** : pronunciation
propagación *nf, pl* **-ciones** : propagation
propaganda *nf* **1** : propaganda **2** PUBLICIDAD : advertising
propagar {52} *vt* : propagate, spread — **propagarse** *vr* : propagate
propano *nm* : propane
propasarse *vr* : go too far
propensión *nf, pl* **-siones** : inclination, propensity — **propenso, -sa** *adj* : prone, inclined
propiamente *adv* : exactly
propicio, -cia *adj* : favorable, propitious
propiedad *nf* **1** : property **2** PERTINENCIA : ownership, possession — **propietario, -ria** *n* : owner, proprietor
propina *nf* : tip
propinar *vt* : give, deal (a blow, etc.)
propio, -pia *adj* **1** : own **2** APROPIADO : proper, appropriate **3** CARACTERÍSTICO : characteristic, typical **4** MISMO

: himself, herself, oneself
proponer {60} *vt* **1** : propose **2** : nominate (a person) — **proponerse** *vr* : propose, intend
proporción *nf, pl* **-ciones** : proportion — **proporcionado, -da** *adj* : proportionate — **proporcional** *adj* : proportional — **proporcionar** *vt* **1** : provide **2** AJUSTAR : adapt, proportion
proposición *nf, pl* **-ciones** : proposal, proposition
propósito *nm* **1** : purpose, intention **2 a propósito** : incidentally, by the way **3 a propósito** : on purpose, intentionally
propuesta *nf* **1** : proposal **2** : offer (of employment, etc.)
propulsar *vt* **1** : propel, drive **2** PROMOVER : promote — **propulsión** *nf, pl* **-siones** : propulsion
prorrogar {52} *vt* **1** : extend **2** APLAZAR : postpone — **prórroga** *nf* **1** : extension, deferment **2** : overtime (in sports)
prorrumpir *vi* : burst forth, break out

prosa *nf* : prose
proscribir {33} *vt* **1** : prohibit, ban **2** DESTERRAR : exile — **proscripción** *nf, pl* **-ciones 1** : ban **2** DESTIERRO : banishment — **proscrito, -ta** *adj* : banned — **proscrito** *n* : exile, outlaw
proseguir {75} *v* : continue — **prosecución** *nf, pl* **-ciones** : continuation
prospección *nf, pl* **-ciones** : prospecting, exploration
prospecto *nm* : prospectus
prosperar *vi* : prosper, thrive — **prosperidad** *nf* : prosperity — **próspero, -ra** *adj* : prosperous, flourishing
prostituir {41} *vt* : prostitute — **prostitución** *nf, pl* **-ciones** : prostitution — **prostituta** *nf* : prostitute
protagonista *nmf* : protagonist — **protagonizar** *vt* : star in
proteger {15} *vt* : protect — **protegerse** *vr* : protect oneself —
▸ **protección** *nf, pl* **-ciones** : protection — **protector, -tora** *adj* : protective

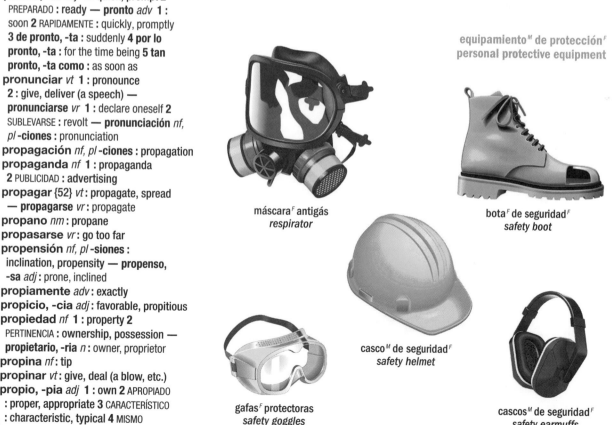

equipamiento^M **de protección**^F
personal protective equipment

máscara^F antigás
respirator

bota^F de seguridad^F
safety boot

casco^M de seguridad^F
safety helmet

gafas^F protectoras
safety goggles

cascos^M de seguridad^F
safety earmuffs

puentes*ᴹ*
bridges

puentes*ᴹ* de tirantes*ᴹ*
cable-stayed bridge

puente*ᴹ* colgante
suspension bridge

puente*ᴹ* cantilever
cantilever bridge

puente*ᴹ* de arco*ᴹ*
arch bridge

puente*ᴹ* giratorio
swing bridge

— **protector, -tora** *n* : protector
— **protegido, -da** *n* : protégé
proteína *nf* : protein
protestar *v* : protest — **protesta** *nf*
: protest — **protestante** *adj*
& *nmf* : Protestant
protocolo *nm* : protocol
prototipo *nm* : prototype
protuberancia *nf* : protuberance
— **protuberante** *adj* : protuberant
provecho *nm* **1** : benefit, advantage **2**
¡buen provecho! : enjoy your meal! —
provechoso, -sa *adj* : profitable, beneficial
proveer {63} *vt* : provide, supply
— **proveedor, -dora** *n* : supplier
provenir {87} *vi* **provenir de** : come from
proverbio *nm* : proverb —
proverbial *adj* : proverbial
providencia *nf* **1** : providence
2 PRECAUCIÓN : precaution —
providencial *adj* : providential
provincia *nf* : province — **provincial** *adj*
: provincial — **provinciano,
-na** *adj* : provincial, parochial
provisión *nf, pl* **-siones** : provision
— **provisional** *adj* : provisional
provocar {72} *vt* **1** : provoke, cause
2 IRRITAR : irritate — **provocación** *nf,
pl* **-ciones** : provocation —
provocativo, -va *adj* : provocative
próximo, -ma *adj* **1** CERCANO : near **2**
SIGUIENTE : next — **próximamente** *adv*
: shortly, soon — **proximidad** *nf* **1** :
proximity **2 proximidades** *nfpl* : vicinity
proyectar *vt* **1** : plan **2** LANZAR : throw,
hurl **3** : cast (light) **4** : show (a film) —
proyección *nf, pl* **-ciones** : projection —
proyectil *nm* : missile — **proyecto** *nm* :
plan, project — **proyector** *nm* : projector
prudencia *nf* : prudence, care —
prudente *adj* : prudent, sensible
prueba *nf* **1** : proof, evidence **2** : test (in
education, medicine, etc.) **3** : event (in
sports) **4 a prueba de agua** : waterproof
psicoanálisis *nm* : psychoanalysis —
psicoanalista *nmf* : psychoanalyst —
psicoanalizar {21} *vt* : psychoanalyze
psicología *nf* : psychology —
psicológico, -ca *adj* : psychological
— **psicólogo, -ga** *n* : psychologist
psicópata *nmf* : psychopath
psicosis *nfs & pl* : psychosis
psicoterapia *nf* : psychotherapy —
psicoterapeuta *nmf* : psychotherapist
psicótico, -ca *adj & n* : psychotic

psiquiatría *nf* : psychiatry —
psiquiatra *nmf* : psychiatrist —
psiquiátrico, -ca *adj* : psychiatric
psíquico, -ca *adj* : psychic
púa *nf* **1** : sharp point **2** : tooth (of a
comb) **3** : thorn (of a plant), quill (of
a porcupine, etc.) **4** : (guitar) pick
pubertad *nf* : puberty
publicar {72} *vt* **1** : publish **2**
DIVULGAR : divulge, disclose —
publicación *nf, pl* **-ciones** : publication
publicidad *nf* **1** : publicity **2** : advertising
(in marketing) — **publicista** *nmf* :
publicist — **publicitar** *vt* **1** : publicize
2 : advertise (a product, etc.) —
publicitario, -ria *adj* : advertising
público, -ca *adj* : public —
público *nm* **1** : public **2** : audience (of
theater, etc.), spectators *pl* (of sports)
puchero *nm* **1** : (cooking) pot **2** GUISADO
: stew **3 hacer pucheros** : pout
púdico, -ca *adj* : modest
pudiente *adj* : wealthy
pudín *nm, pl* **-dines** : pudding
pudor *nm* : modesty —
pudoroso, -sa *adj* : modest
pudrir {59} *vt* **1** : rot **2** *fam* :
annoy — **pudrirse** *vr* : rot
pueblo *nm* **1** : town, village
2 NACIÓN : people, nation
puente *nm* **1** : bridge **2 hacer**
puente : have a long weekend **3**
puente levadizo : drawbridge
puerco, -ca *n* **1** : pig **2 puerco espín** :
porcupine — **puerco, -ca** *adj* : dirty, filthy
pueril *adj* : childish
puerro *nm* : leek
puerta *nf* **1** : door, gate **2 a puerta**
cerrada : behind closed doors
puerto *nm* **1** : port **2** : (mountain)
pass **3** REFUGIO : haven
puertorriqueño, -ña *adj* : Puerto Rican
pues *conj* **1** : since, because **2**
POR LO TANTO : so, therefore **3** (*used
interjectionally*) : well, then
puesta *nf* **1 puesta a punto** : tune-
up **2 puesta de sol** : sunset **3 puesta**
en marcha : starting up — **puesto,**
-ta *adj* **1** : put, set **2** VESTIDO : dressed
— **puesto** *nm* **1** : place **2** EMPLEO :
position, job **3** : stand, stall (in a market)
4 puesto avanzado : outpost —
puesto que *conj* : since, given that
púgil *nm* : boxer
pugnar *vi* : fight — **pugna** *nf* : fight, battle

pulcro, -cra *adj* : tidy, neat
pulga *nf* **1** : flea **2 tener malas**
pulgas : have a bad temper
pulgada *nf* : inch — **pulgar** *nm* **1**
: thumb **2** : big toe
pulir *vt* **1** : polish **2** REFINAR
: touch up, perfect
pulla *nf* : cutting remark, gibe
pulmón *nm, pl* **-mones** : lung
— **pulmonar** *adj* : pulmonary —
pulmonía *nf* : pneumonia
pulpa *nf* : pulp
pulpería *nf Lat* : grocery store
púlpito *nm* : pulpit
pulpo *nm* : octopus
pulsar *vt* **1** : press (a button),
strike (a key) **2** : play (music) —
pulsación *nf, pl* **-ciones 1** : beat, throb
2 : keystroke (on a typewriter, etc.)
pulsera *nf* : bracelet
pulso *nm* **1** : pulse **2** :
steadiness (of hand)
pulular *vi* : swarm
pulverizar {21} *vt* **1** : pulverize,
crush **2** : spray (a liquid) —
pulverizador *nm* : atomizer, spray
puma *nf* : puma
punitivo, -va *adj* : punitive
punta *nf* **1** : tip, end **2** : point (of
a needle, etc.) **3 punta del dedo** :
fingertip **4 sacar punta a** : sharpen
puntada *nf* **1** : stitch **2**
puntadas *nfpl* : seam
puntal *nm* : prop, support
puntapié *nm* : kick
puntear *vt* : pluck (a guitar)
puntería *nf* : aim, marksmanship
puntiagudo, -da *adj* : sharp, pointed
puntilla *nf* **1** : lace edging **2**
de puntillas : on tiptoe
punto *nm* **1** : dot, point **2** : period (in
punctuation) **3** ASUNTO : item, question **4**
LUGAR : spot, place **5** MOMENTO : moment
6 : point (in a score) **7** PUNTADA : stitch
8 a las dos en punto : at two o'clock
sharp **9 dos puntos** : colon **10 hasta**
cierto punto : up to a point **11 punto de**
partida : starting point **12 punto muerto**
: deadlock **13 punto y coma** : semicolon
puntuación *nf, pl* **-ciones 1** :
punctuation **2** : scoring, score (in sports)
puntual *adj* **1** : prompt, punctual **2** EXACTO
: accurate, detailed — **puntualidad** *nf* **1**
: punctuality **2** EXACTITUD : accuracy
puntuar {3} *vt* : punctuate

puerro*M*
leek

— *vi* : score (in sports)
punzar {21} *vt* : prick, puncture
— **punzada** *nf* **1** PINCHAZO : prick
2 : sharp pain — **punzante** *adj* **1** :
sharp **2** MORDAZ : biting, caustic
puñado *nm* **1** : handful **2 a**
puñados : by the handful
puñal *nm* : dagger — **puñalada** *nf* : stab
puño *nm* **1** : fist **2** : cuff (of a shirt)
3 : handle, hilt (of a sword, etc.) —
puñetazo *nm* : punch (with the fist)
pupila *nf* : pupil (of the eye)
pupitre *nm* : desk
puré *nm* **1** : purée **2 puré de papas** *or*
puré de patatas *Spain* : mashed potatoes
pureza *nf* : purity
purga *nf* : purge — **purgar** {52} *vt* :
purge — **purgatorio** *nm* : purgatory
purificar {72} *vt* : purify —
purificación *nf, pl* **-ciones** : purification
puritano, -na *adj* : puritanical
— **puritano, -na** *n* : puritan
puro, -ra *adj* **1** : pure **2** SIMPLE
: plain, simple **3** *Lat fam* : only,
just — **puro** *nm* : cigar
púrpura *nf* : purple —
purpúreo, -rea *adj* : purple
pus *nm* : pus
pusilánime *adj* : cowardly
puta *nf* : whore
putrefacción *nf, pl* **-ciones**
: putrefaction, rot — **pútrido,**
-da *adj* : putrid, rotten

puerto^M
port

esclusa^F de canal^M
canal lock

puente^M de carga^F para contenedores^M
container-loading bridge

terminal^F de petróleo^M
oil terminal

dique^M seco
dry dock

depósito^M de mercancía^F en tránsito^M
transit shed

petrolero^M
tanker

grúa^F de muelle^M
dock crane

terminal^F de carga^F
bulk terminal

cámara^F frigorífica
cold shed

transbordador^M
ferryboat

compuerta^F
gate

muelle^M
wharf

faro^M
lighthouse

terminal^F de pasajeros^M
passenger terminal

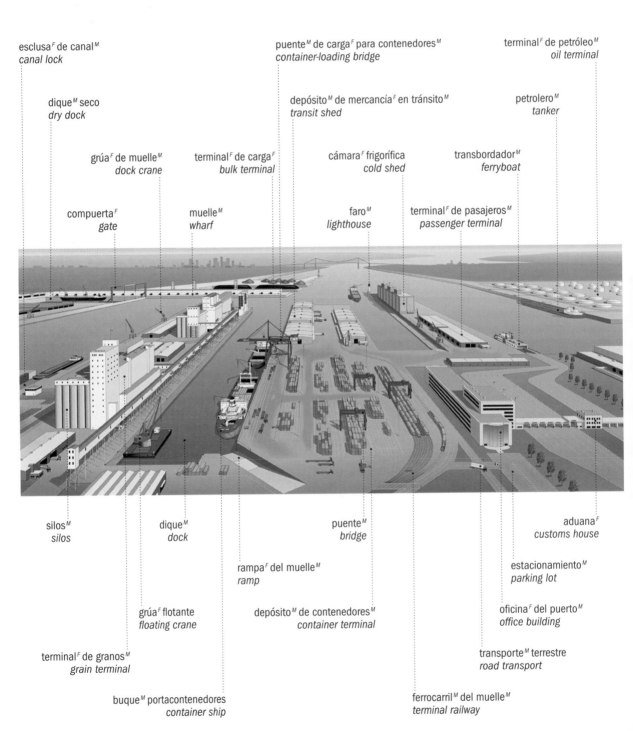

silos^M
silos

dique^M
dock

puente^M
bridge

aduana^F
customs house

rampa^F del muelle^M
ramp

estacionamiento^M
parking lot

grúa^F flotante
floating crane

depósito^M de contenedores^M
container terminal

oficina^F del puerto^M
office building

terminal^F de granos^M
grain terminal

transporte^M terrestre
road transport

buque^M portacontenedores
container ship

ferrocarril^M del muelle^M
terminal railway

q *nf* : q, 18th letter of the Spanish alphabet

que *conj* **1** : that **2** (*in comparisons*) : than **3** (*introducing a reason or cause*) : so that, or else **4 es que** : the thing is that **5 yo que tú** : if I were you —

que *pron* **1** (*referring to persons*) : who, whom **2** (*referring to things*) : that, which **3 el** (**la, lo, las, los**) **que** : he (she, it, they) who, whoever, the one(s) that

qué *adv* **1** : how, what **2 ¡qué lindo!** : how lovely! — **qué** *adj* : what, which — **qué** *pron* **1** : what **2 ¿qué crees?** : what do you think?

quebrar {55} *vt* : break — *vi* : go bankrupt — **quebrarse** *vr* : break — **quebrada** *nf* : ravine, gorge — **quebradizo, -za** *adj* : breakable, fragile — **quebrado, -da** *adj* **1** : bankrupt **2** : rough, uneven (of land, etc.) **3** ROTO : broken — **quebrado** *nm* : fraction — **quebradura** *nf* : crack, fissure — **quebrantar** *vt* **1** : break **2** DEBILITAR : weaken — **quebranto** *nm* **1** : harm, damage **2** AFLICCIÓN : grief, pain

queda *nf* → **toque**

quedar *vi* **1** PERMANECER : remain, stay **2** ESTAR : be **3** FALTAR : be left **4** : fit, look (of clothing, etc.) **5 no queda lejos** : it's not far **6 quedar en** : agree to, agree on — **quedarse** *vr* **1** : stay **2 quedarse con** : keep

quedo, -da *adj* : quiet, still — **quedo** *adv* : softly, quietly

quehacer *nm* **1** : task **2** quehaceres *nmpl* : chores

queja *nf* : complaint — **quejarse** *vr* **1** : complain **2** GEMIR : moan, groan — **quejido** *nm* : moan, whimper — **quejoso, -sa** *adj* : complaining, whining

quitanieves *M*
snowblower

quemar *vt* **1** : burn **2** MALGASTAR : squander — *vi* : burn — **quemarse** *vr* **1** : burn oneself **2** : burn (up) **3** : get sunburned — **quemado, -da** *adj* **1** : burned **2** AGOTADO : burned-out **3 estar quemado, -da** : be fed up — **quemador** *nm* : burner — **quemadura** *nf* : burn — **quemarropa** : **a quemar** *adj & adv phr* : point-blank

querella *nf* **1** : dispute, quarrel **2** : charge (in law)

querer {64} *vt* **1** : want **2** AMAR : love **3 querer decir** : mean **4 ¿quieres pasarme la leche?** : please pass the milk **5 sin querer** : unintentionally — **querer** *nm* : love — **querido, -da** *adj* : dear, beloved — **querer** *n* **1** : darling **2** AMANTE : lover

queroseno *nm* : kerosene

querubín *nm, pl* **-bines** : cherub

▸ **queso** *nm* : cheese — **quesadilla** *nf Lat* : quesadilla

quicio *nm* **1 estar fuera de quicio** : be beside oneself **2 sacar de quicio** : drive crazy

quiebra *nf* **1** : break **2** BANCARROTA : bankruptcy

quien *pron, pl* **quienes 1** (*subject*) : who **2** (*object*) : whom **3** (*indefinite*) : whoever, anyone, some people

quién *pron, pl* **quiénes 1** (*subject*) : who **2** (*object*) : whom **3 ¿de quién es este lápiz?** : whose pencil is this?

quienquiera *pron, pl* **quienesquiera** : whoever, whomever

quieto, -ta *adj* **1** : calm, quiet **2** INMÓVIL : still — **quietud** *nf* : stillness

quijada *nf* : jaw, jawbone (of an animal)

quilate *nm* : carat, karat

quilla *nf* : keel

quimera *nf* : illusion — **quimérico, -ca** *adj* : fanciful

▸ **química** *nf* : chemistry — **químico, -ca** *adj* : chemical — **química** *n* : chemist

quince *adj & nm* : fifteen — **quinceañero, -ra** *n* : fifteen-year-old, teenager — **quincena** *nf* : two-week period, fortnight — **quincenal** *adj* : semimonthly, twice a month

quincuagésimo, -ma *adj & n* : fiftieth

quinientos, -tas *adj* : five hundred — **quinientos** *nms & pl* : five hundred

quinina *nf* : quinine

quinqué *nm* : oil lamp

quinta *nf* : country house, villa

quintaesencia *nf* : quintessence

quinteto *nm* : quintet

símbolos *M* **químicos**
chemistry symbols

—

elemento *M* negativo
negative charge

+

elemento *M* positivo
positive charge

⇄

reacción *F*
reversible reaction

→

dirección *F*
reaction direction

quinto, -ta *adj & n* : fifth — **quinto** *nm* : fifth

quiosco *nm* : kiosk, newsstand

quiropráctico, -ca *n* : chiropractor

quirúrgico, -ca *adj* : surgical

quisquilloso, -sa *adj* : fastidious, fussy

quiste *nm* : cyst

quitar *vt* **1** : remove, take away **2** : take off (clothes) **3** : get rid of, relieve (pain, etc.) — **quitarse** *vr* **1** : withdraw, leave **2** : take off (one's clothes) **3 quitarse de** : give up (a habit) **4 quitarse de encima** : get rid of — **quitaesmalte** *nm* : nail-polish remover — **quitamanchas** *nms*
▸ **& pl** : stain remover — **quitanieves** *nm* : snowplow — **quitasol** *nm* : parasol

quizá *or* quizás *adv* : maybe, perhaps

quesos^M
cheeses

quesos^M frescos
fresh cheeses

queso^M cottage
cottage cheese

queso^M cremoso
cream cheese

mozzarella^F
mozzarella

quesos^M de cabra^F
goat's-milk cheeses

queso^M chèvre
Chèvre cheese

ricotta^F
ricotta

Crottin^M de Chavignol
Crottin de Chavignol

quesos^M blandos
soft cheeses

Pont-l'Évêque^M
Pont-l'Évêque

camembert^M
Camembert

brie^M
Brie

coulommiers^M
Coulommiers

munster^M
Muenster

quesos^M azules
blue cheeses

roquefort^M
Roquefort

stilton^M
Stilton

gorgonzola^M
Gorgonzola

azul danés^M
Danish blue

quesos^M prensados
pressed cheeses

raclette^F
raclette

parmesano^M
Parmesan

pecorino romano^M
Romano

gruyère^M
Gruyère

jarlsberg^M
Jarlsberg

emmenthal^M
Swiss cheese

r *nf* : r, 19th letter of the Spanish alphabet

rábano *nm* **1** : radish **2 rábano picante** : horseradish

rabí *nmf, pl* **-bíes** : rabbi

rabia *nf* **1** : rage, anger **2** : rabies (disease) — **rabiar** *vi* **1** : be furious **2** : be in great pain **3 rabiar por** : be dying for — **rabioso, -sa** *adj* **1** : enraged, furious **2** : rabid, having rabies

rabino, -na *n* : rabbi

rabo *nm* **1** : tail **2 el rabo del ojo** : the corner of one's eye

racha *nf* **1** : gust of wind **2** SERIE : series, string — **racheado, -da** *adj* : gusty

racial *adj* : racial

racimo *nm* : bunch, cluster

raciocinio *nm* : reason, reasoning

ración *nf, pl* **-ciones 1** : share, ration **2** : helping (of food)

racional *adj* : rational — **racionalizar** {21} *vt* : rationalize

racionar *vt* : ration — **racionamiento** *nm* : rationing

racismo *nm* : racism — **racista** *adj & nmf* : racist

radar *nm* : radar

radiación *nf, pl* **-ciones** : radiation

radiactivo, -va *adj* : radioactive — **radiactividad** *nf* : radioactivity

radiador *nm* : radiator

radiante *adj* : radiant

radical *adj & nmf* : radical

radicar {72} *vi* **radicar en** : lie in, be rooted in

radio *nm* **1** : radius **2** : spoke (of a wheel) **3** : radium (element) — **radio** *nmf* : radio

radioactivo, -va *adj* : radioactive — **radioactividad** *nf* : radioactivity

radiodifusión *nf, pl* **-siones** : broadcasting — **radioemisora** *nf* : radio station — **radioescucha** *nmf* : listener — **radiofónico, -ca** *adj* : radio

radiografía *nf* : X ray — **radiografiar** {85} *vt* : x-ray

radiología *nf* : radiology — **radiólogo, -ga** *n* : radiologist

raer {65} *vt* : scrape off

ráfaga *nf* **1** : gust (of wind) **2** : flash (of light)

raído, -da *adj* : worn, shabby

raíz *nf, pl* **raíces 1** : root **2** ORIGEN : origin, source **3 echar raíces** : take root

raja *nf* **1** : crack, slit **2** RODAJA : slice — **rajar** *vt* : crack, split — **rajarse** *vr* **1** : crack, split open **2** *fam* : back out

rajatabla : a rajatabla *adv phr* : strictly, to the letter

ralea *nf* : sort, kind

ralentí *nm* : neutral (gear)

rallar *vt* : grate — **rallador** *nm* : grater

rama *nf* : branch — **ramaje** *nm* : branches *pl* — **ramal** *nm* : branch (of a railroad, etc.) — **ramificarse** {72} *vr* : branch (off) — **ramillete** *nm* **1** : bouquet **2** GRUPO : cluster, bunch — **ramo** *nm* **1** : branch **2** RAMILLETE : bouquet

rampa *nf* : ramp, incline

rana *nf* **1** : frog **2 rana toro** : bullfrog

rancho *nm* : ranch, farm — **ranchero, -ra** *n* : rancher, farmer

rancio, -cia *adj* **1** : rancid **2** : aged (of wine)

rango *nm* **1** : rank **2** : (social) standing

ranúnculo *nm* : buttercup

ranura *nf* : groove, slot

rapar *vt* **1** : shave **2** : crop (hair)

rapaz *adj, pl* **-paces** : rapacious, predatory

rápido, -da *adj* : rapid, quick — **rápidamente** *adv* : rapidly, fast — **rapidez** *nf* : speed — **rápido** *adv* : quickly, fast — **rápido** *nm* **1** : express train **2 rápidos** *nmpl* : rapids

rapiña *nf* **1** : plunder **2 ave de rapiña** : bird of prey

rapsodia *nf* : rhapsody

raptar *vt* : kidnap — **rapto** *nm* : kidnapping — **raptor, -tora** *n* : kidnapper

▸ **raqueta** *nf* : racket (in sports)

raro, -ra *adj* **1** : rare **2** EXTRAÑO : odd,

raqueta^F
rackets

raqueta^F **de tenis**^M
tennis racket

raqueta^F **de bádminton**^M
badminton racket

raqueta^F **de squash**^M
squash racket

raqueta^F **de raquetball**^M
racquetball racket

strange — **raramente** adv : rarely, infrequently — **rareza** nf : rarity

ras nm **a ras de** : level with

▸ **rascacielos** nms & pl : skyscraper

rascar {72} vt **1** : scratch **2** RASPAR : scrape — **rascarse** vr : scratch oneself

rasgar {52} vt : rip, tear — **rasgarse** vr : rip

rasgo nm **1** : stroke (of a pen) **2** CARACTERÍSTICA : trait, characteristic **3** rasgos nmpl FACCIONES : features

rasguear vt : strum

rasguñar vt : scratch — **rasguño** nm : scratch

raso, -sa adj **1** : level, flat **2** : low (of a flight) **3 soldado raso** : private (in the army) — **raso** nm : satin

raspar vt **1** : scrape **2** LIMAR : file down, smooth — vi : be rough — **raspadura** nf **1** : scratch **2** **raspars** nfpl : scrapings

rastra nf **1** : rake **2 a rastras** : unwillingly — **rastrear** vt : track, trace

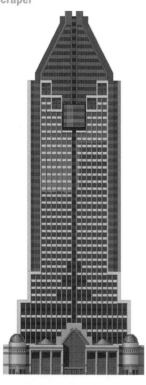
rascacielosM
skyscraper

— **rastrero, -ra** adj **1** : creeping **2** DESPRECIABLE : despicable — **rastrillar** vt : rake — **rastrillo** nm : rake — **rastro** nm **1** : trail, track **2** SEÑAL : sign

rasurar vi Lat : shave — **rasurarse** vr Lat : shave

rata nf : rat

ratear vt : steal — **ratero, -ra** n : thief

ratificar {72} vt : ratify — **ratificación** nf, pl **-ciones** : ratification

rato nm **1** : while **2 al poco rato** : shortly after **3 pasar el rato** : pass the time

ratón nm, pl **-tones** : mouse — **ratonera** nf : mousetrap

raudal nm **1** : torrent **2 a raudales** : in abundance — **raudo, -da** adj : swift

raya nf **1** : line **2** LISTA : stripe **3** : part (in the hair) — **rayar** vt : scratch — vi **1 al rayar el día** : at daybreak **2 rayar en** : border on — **rayarse** vr : get scratched

rayo nm **1** : ray, beam **2** : bolt of lightning **3 rayos X** : X rays

rayón nm : rayon

raza nf **1** : (human) race **2** : breed (of animals) **3 de raza** : thoroughbred, pedigreed

razón nf, pl **-zones 1** : reason **2 dar razón** : inform **3 en razón de** : because of **4 tener razón** : be right — **razonable** adj : reasonable — **razonamiento** nm : reasoning — **razonar** v : reason, think

reacción nf, pl **-ciones** : reaction — **reaccionar** vi : react — **reaccionario, -ria** adj & n : reactionary

reacio, -cia adj : resistant, stubborn

reactivar vt : reactivate, revive

reactor nm **1** : jet (airplane) **2 reactor nuclear** : nuclear reactor

reajustar vt : readjust — **reajuste** nm : readjustment

real adj **1** : royal **2** VERDADERO : real, true

realce nm **1** : relief **2 dar realce** : highlight

realeza nf : royalty

realidad nf **1** : reality **2 en realidad** : actually, in fact

realismo nm : realism — **realista** adj : realistic — **realismo** nmf : realist

realizar {21} vt **1** : carry out **2** : achieve (a goal) **3** : produce (a film or play) **4** : realize (a profit) — **realizarse** vr **1** : fulfill oneself **2** : come true (of a dream, etc.) — **realización** nf, pl **-ciones** : execution, realization

realmente adv : really, actually

realzar {21} vt : highlight, enhance

reanimar vt : revive

reanudar vt : resume, renew — **reanudarse** vr : resume

reaparecer {53} vi : reappear — **reaparición** nf, pl **-ciones** : reappearance

reavivar vt : revive

rebajar vt **1** : lower, reduce **2** HUMILLAR : humiliate — **rebajarse** vr **1** : humble oneself **2 rebajarse a** : stoop to — **rebaja** nf **1** : reduction **2** DESCUENTO : discount **3 rebajars** nfpl : sales

rebanada nf : slice

rebaño nm **1** : herd **2** : flock (of sheep)

rebasar vt : surpass, exceed

rebatir vt : refute

rebelarse vr : rebel — **rebelde** adj : rebellious — **rebelde** nmf : rebel — **rebeldía** nf : rebelliousness — **rebelión** nf, pl **-liones** : rebellion

reblandecer vt : soften

rebobinar vt : rewind

rebosar vi **1** : overflow **2 rebosar de** : be bursting with — vt : overflow with

rebotar vi : bounce, rebound — **rebote** nm **1** : bounce **2 de rebotar** : on the rebound

rebozar {21} vt : coat in batter

rebuscado, -da adj : pretentious

rebuznar vi : bray

recabar vt **1** : obtain, collect **2 recabar fondos** : raise money

recado nm **1** MENSAJE : message **2** Spain : errand

recaer {13} vi **1** : relapse **2 recaer sobre** : fall on — **recaída** nf : relapse

recalcar {72} vt : emphasize, stress

recalcitrante adj : recalcitrant

recalentar {55} vt **1** : overheat **2** : reheat, warm up (food) — **recalentarse** vr : overheat

recámara nf **1** : chamber (of a firearm) **2** Lat : bedroom

recambio nm **1** : spare part **2** : refill (for a pen, etc.)

recapitular vt : recapitulate, sum up — **recapitulación** nf, pl **-ciones** : recapitulation

recargar {52} vt **1** : overload **2** : recharge (a battery), reload (a firearm, etc.) — **recargado, -da** adj : overly elaborate — **recargo** nm : surcharge

recato nm : modesty — **recatado, -da** adj : modest, demure

recaudar vt : collect — **recaudación** nf,

reciclar: contenedores*M* de reciclaje*M*
recycle: recycling containers

cubo*M* de basura*F* reciclable
recycling bin

contenedor*M* de recogida*F* de papel*M*
paper collection unit

contenedor*M* de reciclado*M* de vidrio*M*
glass collection unit

contenedor*M* de recogida*F* de vidrio*M*
glass recycling container

contenedor*M* de reciclado*M* de aluminio*M*
aluminum recycling container

contenedor*M* de reciclado*M* de papel*M*
paper recycling container

---

pl **-ciones** : collection —
recaudador, -dora *n* **recaudar
de impuestos** : tax collector
recelar *vt* : distrust, fear — **recelo** *nm*
: distrust, suspicion — **receloso,
-sa** *adj* : distrustful, suspicious
recepción *nf, pl* **-ciones** : reception
— **recepcionista** *nmf* : receptionist
receptáculo *nm* : receptacle
receptivo, -va *adj* : receptive
— **receptor, -tora** *n* : recipient —
receptor *nm* : receiver (of a radio, etc.)
recesión *nf, pl* **-siones** : recession
receso *nm Lat* : recess, adjournment
receta *nf* **1** : recipe **2** :
prescription (in medicine)
rechazar {21} *vt* **1** : reject, refuse
2 REPELER : repel **3** : reflect (light)
— **rechazo** *nm* : rejection
rechinar *vi* **1** : squeak, creak **2**
: grind, gnash (one's teeth)
rechoncho, -cha *adj, fam* : chubby
recibir *vt* **1** : receive **2** ACOGER :
welcome — *vi* : receive visitors —
recibidor *nm* : vestibule, entrance
hall — **recibimiento** *nm* : reception,
welcome — **recibo** *nm* : receipt

▸ **reciclar** *vt* **1** : recycle **2** : retrain
(workers) — **reciclaje** *nm* : recycling
recién *adv* **1** : newly, recently **2 recién
casados** : newlyweds — **reciente** *adj* :
recent — **recientemente** *adv* : recently
recinto *nm* **1** : enclosure
2 ÁREA : area, site
recio, -cia *adj* : tough, strong
recipiente *nm* : container, receptacle
— **recipiente** *nmf* : recipient
recíproco, -ca *adj* : reciprocal, mutual
recitar *vt* : recite — **recital** *nm* : recital
reclamar *vt* : demand, ask for — *vi* :
complain — **reclamación** *nf, pl* **-ciones**
1 : claim, demand **2** QUEJA : complaint
— **reclamo** *nm* **1** : lure (in hunting)
2 *Lat* : inducement, attraction
reclinar *vt* : rest, lean —
reclinarse *vr* : recline, lean back
recluir {41} *vt* : confine, lock up —
recluirse *vr* : shut oneself away —
reclusión *nf, pl* **-siones** : imprisonment
— **recluso, -sa** *n* : prisoner
recluta *nmf* : recruit — **reclutamiento** *nm*
: recruitment — **reclutar** *vt* : recruit, enlist
recobrar *vt* : recover, regain
— **recobrarse** *vr* **recobrarse**

de : recover from
recodo *nm* : bend
recoger {15} *vt* **1** : collect, gather **2**
COGER : pick up **3** LIMPIAR, ORDENAR : clean
up, tidy (up) — **recogerse** *vr* : retire,
withdraw — **recogedor** *nm* : dustpan
— **recogido, -da** *adj* : quiet, secluded
recolección *nf, pl* **-ciones 1** :
collection **2** COSECHA : harvest
recomendar {55} *vt* : recommend
— **recomendación** *nf, pl* **-ciones**
: recommendation
recompensar *vt* : reward —
recompensa *nf* : reward
reconciliar *vt* : reconcile
— **reconciliarse** *vr* : be
reconciled — **reconciliación** *nf,
pl* **-ciones** : reconciliation
recóndito, -ta *adj* : hidden
reconfortar *vt* : comfort
reconocer {18} *vt* **1** : recognize **2**
ADMITIR : admit **3** EXAMINAR : examine
— **reconocible** *adj* : recognizable
— **reconocido, -da** *adj* **1** :
recognized, accepted **2** AGRADECIDO
: grateful — **reconocimiento** *nm* **1**
: recognition **2** AGRADECIMIENTO :

gratitude **3 :** (medical) examination
reconsiderar *vt* **:** reconsider
reconstruir {41} *vt* **:** reconstruct
— **reconstrucción** *nf,*
pl **-ciones :** reconstruction
recopilar *vt* **1** RECOGER **:** collect,
gather **2 :** compile — **recopilación** *nf,*
pl **-ciones :** collection, compilation
récord *nm, pl* **-cords :** record
recordar {19} *vt* **1** ACORDARSE DE **:**

remember **2 :** remind — *vi* **:** remember
— **recordatorio** *nm* **:** reminder
recorrer *vt* **1 :** travel through **2 :**
cover (a distance) — **recorrido** *nm* **1 :**
journey, trip **2** TRAYECTO **:** route, course
recortar *vt* **1 :** reduce **2** CORTAR **:** cut (out)
3 : trim (hair) — **recortarse** *vr* **:** stand out
— **recorte** *nm* **1 :** cut, cutting **2 recortes**
de periódicos : newspaper clippings
recostar {19} *vt* **:** lean, rest

— **recostarse** *vr* **:** lie down
recoveco *nm* **1 :** bend **2**
RINCÓN **:** nook, corner
recrear *vt* **1 :** recreate **2** ENTRETENER
: entertain — **recrearse** *vr* **:** to enjoy
oneself — **recreativo, -va** *adj* **:**
recreational — **recreo** *nm* **1 :** recreation,
amusement **2 :** recess, break (at school)
recriminar *vt* **:** reproach
recrudecer {53} *vi* **:** worsen

la Red
Internet

URL localizador*M* universal de recursos*M*
uniform resource locator (URL)

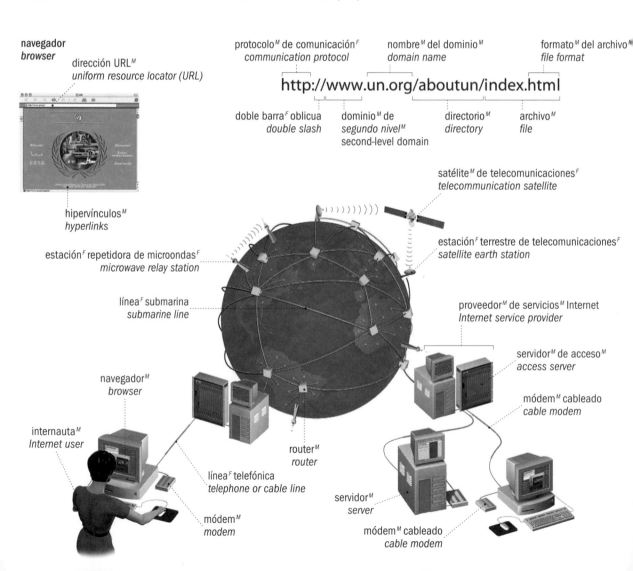

navegador
browser
dirección URL*M*
uniform resource locator (URL)

hipervínculos*M*
hyperlinks

protocolo*M* de comunicación*F*
communication protocol

nombre*M* del dominio*M*
domain name

formato*M* del archivo*M*
file format

http://www.un.org/aboutun/index.html

doble barra*F* oblicua
double slash

dominio*M* de
segundo nivel*M*
second-level domain

directorio*M*
directory

archivo*M*
file

satélite*M* de telecomunicaciones*F*
telecommunication satellite

estación*F* repetidora de microondas*F*
microwave relay station

estación*F* terrestre de telecomunicaciones*F*
satellite earth station

línea*F* submarina
submarine line

proveedor*M* de servicios*M* Internet
Internet service provider

servidor*M* de acceso*M*
access server

navegador*M*
browser

módem*M* cableado
cable modem

internauta*M*
Internet user

router*M*
router

línea*F* telefónica
telephone or cable line

servidor*M*
server

módem*M* cableado
cable modem

módem*M*
modem

— **recrudecerse** *vr* : intensify, get worse
rectángulo *nm* : rectangle —
rectangular *adj* : rectangular
rectificar {72} *vt* **1** : rectify, correct **2**
AJUSTAR : straighten (out) — **rectitud** *nf* **1**
: straightness **2** : (moral) rectitude —
recto, -ta *adj* **1** : straight **2** INTEGRO :
upright, honorable — **recto** *nm* : rectum
rector, -tora *adj* : governing,
managing — **rector, -tora** *n* :

rector — **rectoría** *nf* : rectory
recubrir {2} *vt* : cover, coat
recuento *nm* : count, recount
recuerdo *nm* **1** : memory **2** : souvenir,
remembrance (of a journey, etc.) **3**
recuerdos *nmpl* SALUDOS : **regards**
recuperar *vt* **1** : recover, retrieve **2**
recuperar el tiempo perdido : make
up for lost time — **recuperarse** *vr*
recuperarse de : recover from

— **recuperación** *nf, pl* -**ciones**
1 : recovery **2 recuperación**
de datos : data retrieval
recurrir *vi* **recurrir a** : turn to (a person),
resort to (force, etc.) — **recurso** *nm* **1**
: recourse, resort **2** : appeal (in law)
3 recursos *nmpl* : resources
red *nf* **1** : net **2** SISTEMA : network,
▸ system **3** la Red : the Internet
redactar *vt* : write (up), draft

Internet uses
usos*M* de Internet*M*

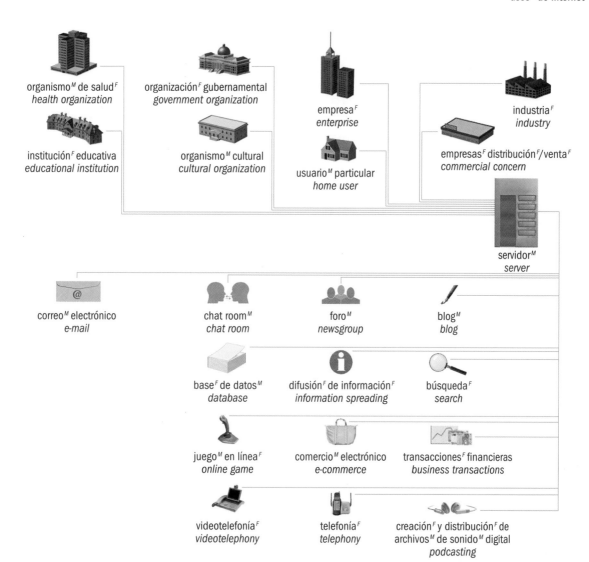

organismo*M* de salud*F*
health organization

organización*F* gubernamental
government organization

empresa*F*
enterprise

industria*F*
industry

institución*F* educativa
educational institution

organismo*M* cultural
cultural organization

usuario*M* particular
home user

empresas*F* distribución*F*/venta*F*
commercial concern

servidor*M*
server

correo*M* electrónico
e-mail

chat room*M*
chat room

foro*M*
newsgroup

blog*M*
blog

base*F* de datos*M*
database

difusión*F* de información*F*
information spreading

búsqueda*F*
search

juego*M* en línea*F*
online game

comercio*M* electrónico
e-commerce

transacciones*F* financieras
business transactions

videotelefonía*F*
videotelephony

telefonía*F*
telephony

creación*F* y distribución*F* de
archivos*M* de sonido*M* digital
podcasting

— **redacción** *nf, pl* **-ciones 1** : writing, drafting **2** : editing (of a newspaper, etc.) — **redactor, -tora** *n* : editor

redada *nf* **1** : (police) raid **2** : catch (in fishing)

redescubrir {2} *vt* : rediscover

redención *nf, pl* **-ciones** : redemption — **redentor, -tora** *adj* : redeeming

redil *nm* : fold, pen

rédito *nm* : interest, yield

redoblar *vt* : redouble

redomado, -da *adj* : out-and-out

redondear *vt* **1** : make round **2** : round off (a number, etc.) — **redonda** *nf* **1** : whole note (in music) **2 a la redonda** : in the surrounding area — **redondel** *nm* **1** : ring, circle **2** : bullring — **redondo, -da** *adj* **1** : round **2** PERFECTO : excellent

reducir {61} *vt* : reduce — **reducirse** *vr* **reducirse a** : come down to, amount to — **reducción** *nf, pl* **-ciones** : reduction — **reducido, -da** *adj* **1** : reduced, limited **2** PEQUEÑO : small

redundante *adj* : redundant — **redundancia** *nf* : redundancy

reedición *nf, pl* **-ciones** : reprint

reembolsar *vt* : refund, reimburse, repay — **reembolso** *nm* : refund, reimbursement

reemplazar {21} *vt* : replace — **reemplazo** *nm* : replacement

reencarnación *nf, pl* **-ciones** : reincarnation

reencuentro *nm* : reunion

reestructurar *vt* : restructure

refaccionar *vi Lat* : repair,

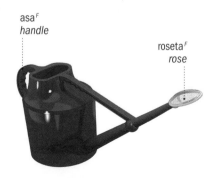

asa*F*
handle

roseta*F*
rose

renovate — **refacciones** *nfpl Lat* : repairs, renovations

referir {76} *vt* **1** : tell **2** REMITIR : refer — **referirse** *vr* **referirse a** : refer to — **referencia** *nf* **1** : reference **2 hacer referencia a** : refer to —

referéndum *nm, pl* **-dums** : referendum — **referente** *adj* **referente a** : concerning

refinar *vt* : refine — **refinado, -da** *adj* : refined — **refinamiento** *nm* : refinement — **refinería** *nf* : refinery

reflector *nm* **1** : reflector **2** : spotlight, searchlight, floodlight

reflejar *vt* : reflect — **reflejarse** *vr* : be reflected — **reflejo** *nm* **1** : reflection **2** : (physical) reflex **3 reflejos** *nmpl* : highlights (in hair)

reflexionar *vi* : reflect, think — **reflexión** *nf, pl* **-xiones** : reflection, thought — **reflexivo, -va** *adj* **1** : reflective, thoughtful **2** : reflexive (in grammar)

reflujo *nm* : ebb (tide)

reforma *nf* **1** : reform **2 reformas** *nfpl* : renovations — **reformador, -dora** *n* : reformer — **reformar** *vt* **1** : reform **2** : renovate, repair (a house, etc.) — **reformarse** *vr* : mend one's ways — **reformatorio** *nm* : reformatory

reforzar {36} *vt* : reinforce

refrán *nm, pl* **-franes** : proverb, saying

refregar {49} *vt* : scrub

refrenar *vt* **1** : rein in (a horse) **2** CONTENER : restrain — **refrenarse** *vr* : restrain oneself

refrendar *vt* : approve, endorse

refrescar {72} *vt* **1** : refresh, cool **2** : brush up on (knowledge) — *vi* : turn cooler — **refrescante** *adj* : refreshing — **refresco** *nm* : soft drink

refriega *nf* : scuffle, skirmish

refrigerar *vt* **1** : refrigerate **2** CLIMATIZAR : air-condition — **refrigeración** *nf, pl* **-ciones 1** : refrigeration **2** AIRE ACONDICIONADO : air-conditioning — **refrigerador** *nmf Lat* : refrigerator — **refrigerio** *nm* : refreshments *pl*

refrito, -ta *adj* : refried — **refrito** *nm* : rehash

refuerzo *nm* : reinforcement

refugiar *vt* : shelter — **refugiarse** *vr* : take refuge — **refugiado, -da** *n* : refugee — **refugio** *nm* : refuge, shelter

refulgir {35} *vi* : shine brightly

refunfuñar *vi* : grumble, groan

refutar *vt* : refute

▸ **regadera** *nf* **1** : watering can **2** *Lat* : shower head, shower

regalar *vt* : give (as a gift) — **regalarse** *vr* **regalarse con** : treat oneself to

regaliz *nm, pl* **-lices** : licorice

regalo *nm* **1** : gift, present **2** PLACER : pleasure, delight

regañadientes: a regañadientes *adv* *phr* : reluctantly, unwillingly

regañar *vt* : scold — *vi* **1** QUEJARSE : grumble **2** *Spain* : quarrel — **regañón, -ñona** *adj, mpl* **-ñones** *fam* : grumpy, irritable

regar {49} *vt* **1** : irrigate, water **2** ESPARCIR : scatter

regatear *vt* **1** : haggle over **2** ESCATIMAR : skimp on — *vi* : bargain, haggle

regazo *nm* : lap (of a person)

regenerar *vt* : regenerate

regentar *vt* : run, manage

régimen *nm, pl* **regímenes 1** : regime **2** DIETA : diet **3 régimen de vida** : lifestyle

regimiento *nm* : regiment

regio, -gia *adj* : royal, regal

región *nf, pl* **-giones** : region, area — **regional** *adj* : regional

regir {28} *vt* **1** : rule **2** ADMINISTRAR : manage, run **3** DETERMINAR : govern, determine — *vi* : apply, be in force — **regirse** *vr* **regirse por** : be guided by

registrar *vt* **1** : register **2** GRABAR : record, tape **3** : search (a house, etc.), frisk (a person) — **registrarse** *vr* **1** : register **2** : be recorded (of temperatures, etc.) — **registrador, -dora** *adj* **caja registradora** : cash register — **registrador, -dora** *n* : registrar — **registro** *nm* **1** : registration **2** : register (book) **3** : registry (office) **4** : range (of a voice, etc.) **5** INSPECCIÓN : search

regla *nf* **1** : rule, regulation **2** : ruler (for measuring) **3** MENSTRUACIÓN : period — **reglamentación** *nf, pl* **-ciones 1** : regulation **2** REGLAS : rules *pl* — **reglamentar** *vt* : regulate — **reglamentario, -ria** *adj* : regulation, official — **reglamento** *nm* : regulations *pl*, rules *pl*

regocijar *vt* : gladden, delight — **regocijarse** *vr* : rejoice — **regocijo** *nm* : delight, rejoicing

regodearse *vr* : be delighted — **regodeo** *nm* : delight

regordete *adj, fam* : chubby

regresar *vi* : return, come back, go back — *vt Lat* : give back — **regresión** *nf, pl* **-siones** : regression

— **regresivo, -va** *adj* : regressive
— **regreso** *nm* **1** : return **2 estar de regreso** : be back, be home again
reguero *nm* **1** : irrigation ditch **2** SEÑAL : trail, trace **3 correr como un reguero de pólvora** : spread like wildfire
regular *adj* **1** : regular **2** MEDIANO : medium, average **3 por lo regular** : in general — **regular** *vt* : regulate, control — **regulación** *nf, pl* **-ciones** : regulation, control — **regularidad** *nf* : regularity — **regularizar** {21} *vt* : normalize, make regular
rehabilitar *vt* **1** : rehabilitate **2** : reinstate (someone in a position) **3** : renovate (a building, etc.) — **rehabilitación** *nf* **1** : rehabilitation **2** : reinstatement (in a position) **3** : renovation (of a building, etc.)
rehacer {40} *vt* **1** : redo **2** REPARAR : repair — **rehacerse** *vr* **1** : recover **2 rehacerse de** : get over
rehén *nm, pl* **-henes** : hostage
rehuir {41} *vt* : avoid, shun
rehusar {8} *v* : refuse
reimprimir *vt* : reprint — **reimpresión** *nf, pl* **-siones** : reprinting, reprint
reina *nf* : queen — **reinado** *nm* : reign — **reinante** *adj* : reigning — **reinar** *vi* **1** : reign **2** PREVALECER : prevail
reincidir *vi* : backslide, relapse
reino *nm* : kingdom, realm
reintegrar *vt* **1** : reinstate **2** : refund (money), reimburse (expenses, etc.) — **reintegrarse** *vr* **reintegrarse a** : return to — **reintegro** *nm* : reimbursement
reír {66} *vi* : laugh — *vt* : laugh at — **reírse** *vr* : laugh
reiterar *vt* : repeat, reiterate
reivindicar {72} *vt* **1** : claim **2** RESTAURAR : restore
reja *nf* : grille, grating — **rejilla** *nf* : grille, grate, screen
rejuvenecer {53} *vt* : rejuvenate — **rejuvenecerse** *vr* : be rejuvenated
relación *nf, pl* **-ciones 1** : relation, connection **2** COMUNICACIÓN : relationship, relations *pl* **3** RELATO : account **4** LISTA : list **5 con relación a** *or* **en relación a** : in relation to — **relacionar** *vt* : relate, connect — **relacionarse** *vr* **relacionarse con** : be connected to, interact with
relajar *vt* : relax — **relajarse** *vr* : relax — **relajación** *nf, pl* **-ciones** : relaxation — **relajado, -da** *adj* **1** : relaxed **2** : dissolute, lax (in behavior)

relamerse *vr* : smack one's lips, lick its chops
relámpago *nm* : flash of lightning — **relampaguear** *vi* : flash
relatar *vt* : relate, tell
relativo, -va *adj* **1** : relative **2 en lo relativo a** : with regard to — **relatividad** *nf* : relativity
relato *nm* **1** : account, report **2** CUENTO : story, tale
releer {20} *vt* : reread
relegar {52} *vt* : relegate
relevante *adj* : outstanding, important
relevar *vt* **1** : relieve, take over from **2 relevar de** : exempt from — **relevo** *nm* **1** : relief, replacement **2 carrera de relevos** : relay race
relieve *nm* **1** : relief (in art, etc.) **2** IMPORTANCIA : prominence, importance **3 poner en relieve** : emphasize
religión *nf, pl* **-giones** : religion — **religioso, -sa** *adj* : religious — **religión** *n* : monk *m*, nun *f*
relinchar *vi* : neigh, whinny — **relincho** *nm* : neigh, whinny
reliquia *nf* **1** : relic **2 reliquia de familia** : family heirloom
rellenar *vt* **1** : refill **2** : stuff, fill (in cooking) — **relleno, -na** *adj* : stuffed, filled — **relleno** *nm* : stuffing, filling
reloj *nm* **1** : clock **2** *or* **reloj de pulsera** : wristwatch **3 reloj de arena** : hourglass **4 como un reloj** : like clockwork
relucir {45} *vi* **1** : glitter, shine **2 sacar a relucir** : bring up, mention — **reluciente** *adj* : brilliant, shining
relumbrar *vi* : shine brightly
remachar *vt* **1** : rivet **2** RECALAR : stress, drive home — **remache** *nm* : rivet
remanente *nm* : remainder, surplus
remanso *nm* : pool
remar *vi* : row
rematar *vt* **1** : conclude, finish up **2** MATAR : finish off **3** LIQUIDAR : sell off cheaply **4** *Lat* : auction — *vi* **1** : shoot (in sports) **2** TERMINAR : end — **rematado, -da** *adj* : utter, complete — **remate** *nm* **1** : shot (in sports) **2** FIN : end
remedar *vt* : imitate, mimic
remediar *vt* **1** : remedy, repair **2** : solve (a problem) **3** EVITAR : avoid — **remedio** *nm* **1** : remedy, cure **2** SOLUCIÓN : solution **3 sin remedio** : hopeless
rememorar *vi* : recall
remendar {55} *vt* : mend

remesa *nf* **1** : remittance **2** : shipment (of merchandise)
remezón *nm, pl* **-zones** *Lat* : mild earthquake, tremor
remiendo *nm* : mend, patch
remilgado, -da *adj* **1** : prudish **2** AFECTADO : affected — **remilgo** *nm* : primness, affectation
reminiscencia *nf* : reminiscence
remisión *nf, pl* **-siones** : remission
remiso, -sa *adj* **1** : reluctant **2** NEGLIGENTE : remiss
remitir *vt* **1** : send, remit **2 remitir a** : refer to, direct to — *vi* : subside, let up — **remite** *nm* : return address — **remitente** *nmf* : sender (of a letter, etc.)
remo *nm* : paddle, oar
remodelar *vt* **1** : remodel **2** : restructure (an organization)
remojar *vt* : soak, steep — **remojo** *nm* **poner en remojo** : soak
remolacha *nf* : beet
remolcar {72} *vt* : tow, tug — **remolcador** *nm* : tugboat
remolino *nm* **1** : whirlwind, whirlpool **2** : crowd (of people) **3** : cowlick (of hair)
remolque *nm* **1** : towing, tow **2** : trailer (vehicle)
remontar *vt* **1** : overcome **2** SUBIR : go up — **remontarse** *vr* **1** : soar **2 remontarse a** : date from, go back to
rémora *nf* : hindrance
remorder {47} *vt* : trouble, worry — **remordimiento** *nm* : remorse
remoto, -ta *adj* : remote — **remotamente** *adv* : remotely, slightly
remover {47} *vt* **1** : stir **2** : move around, turn over (earth, embers, etc.) **3** REAVIVIR : bring up again **4** DESPEDIR : fire, dismiss
remunerar *vt* : remunerate
renacer {48} *vi* : be reborn, revive — **renacimiento** *nm* **1** : rebirth, revival **2 el Renacimiento** : the Renaissance
renacuajo *nm* : tadpole, pollywog
rencilla *nf* : quarrel
renco, -ca *adj Lat* : lame
rencor *nm* **1** : rancor, hostility **2 guardar rencor** : hold a grudge — **rencoroso, -sa** *adj* : resentful
rendición *nf, pl* **-ciones** : surrender — **rendido, -da** *adj* **1** : submissive **2** AGOTADO : exhausted
rendija *nf* : crack, split
rendir {54} *vt* **1** : render, give **2** PRODUCIR : yield, produce **3** CANSAR : exhaust

reptiles^M
reptiles

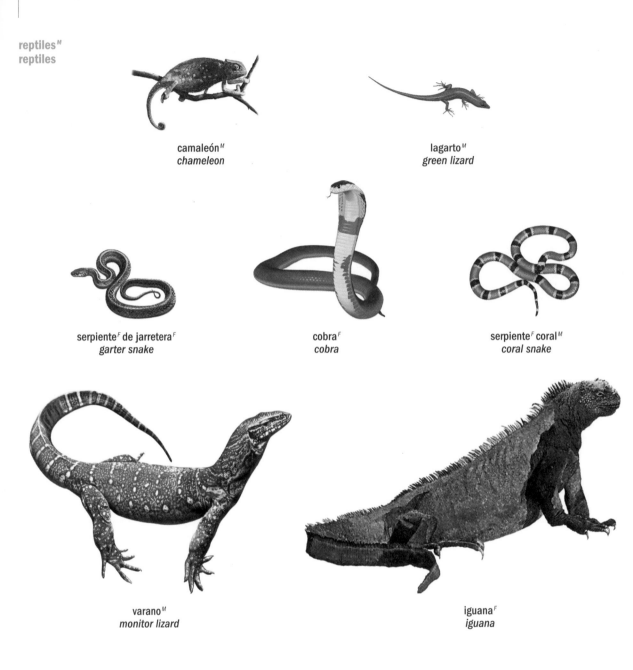

camaleón^M
chameleon

lagarto^M
green lizard

serpiente^F de jarretera^F
garter snake

cobra^F
cobra

serpiente^F coral^M
coral snake

varano^M
monitor lizard

iguana^F
iguana

— *vi* : make progress, go a long way
— **rendirse** *vr* : surrender, give up
— **rendimiento** *nm* **1** : performance
2 : yield, return (in finance, etc.)
renegar {49} *vt* : deny — *vi* **1** QUEJARSE :
grumble **2 renegar de** ABJURAR : renounce,
disown — **renegado, -da** *n* : renegade
renglón *nm, pl* **-glones 1** : line (of
writing) **2** *Lat* : line (of products)

reno *nm* : reindeer
renombre *nm* : renown — **renombrado,
-da** *adj* : famous, renowned
renovar {19} *vt* **1** : renew, restore
2 : renovate (a building, etc.) —
renovación *nf, pl* **-ciones 1** : renewal
2 : renovation (of a building, etc.)
renquear *vi* : limp, hobble
rentar *vt* **1** : produce, yield **2** *Lat* : rent

— **renta** *nf* **1** : income **2** ALQUILER : rent
3 impuesto sobre la renta : income
tax — **rentable** *adj* : profitable
renunciar *vi* **1** : resign **2 renunciar a** :
renounce, relinquish — **renuncia** *nf* **1**
: renunciation **2** DIMISIÓN : resignation
reñir {67} *vi* **reñir con** : argue with, fall
out with — *vt* **1** : scold **2** DISPUTAR :
fight — **reñido, -da** *adj* **1** : hard-fought

2 reñido con : on bad terms with
reo, rea *n* **1** : accused, defendant
2 CULPABLE : culprit
reojo *nm* **de reojo** : out of
the corner of one's eye
reorganizar {21} *vt* : reorganize
repantigarse {52} *vr* : sprawl out
reparar *vt* **1** : repair, fix **2** : make
amends for (an offense, etc.) — *vi* **1**
reparar en ADVERTIR : take notice of
2 reparar en CONSIDERAR : consider
— **reparación** *nf, pl* **-ciones 1** :
reparation, amends **2** ARREGLO : repair
— **reparo** *nm* **1** : reservation, objection
2 poner reparos a : object to
repartir *vt* **1** : allocate **2** DISTRIBUIR
: distribute **3** ESPARCIR : spread
— **repartición** *nf, pl* **-ciones** :
distribution — **repartidor, -dora** *n*
: delivery person, distributor —
reparto *nm* **1** : allocation **2** DISTRIBUCIÓN
: delivery **3** : cast (of characters)
repasar *vt* **1** : review, go over **2**
ZURCIR : mend — **repaso** *nm* **1** :
review **2** : mending (of clothes)
repeler *vt* **1** : repel **2** REPUGNAR : disgust
— **repelente** *adj* : repellent, repulsive
repente *nm* **1** : fit, outburst **2 de repente**
: suddenly — **repentino, -na** *adj* : sudden
repercutir *vi* **1** : reverberate **2**
repercutir en : have repercussions on —
repercusión *nf, pl* **-siones** : repercussion
repertorio *nm* : repertoire
repetir {54} *vt* **1** : repeat **2** : have a
second helping of (food) — **repetirse** *vr* **1**
: repeat oneself **2** : recur (of an event, etc.)
— **repetición** *nf, pl* **-ciones 1** : repetition
2 : rerun, repeat (of a program, etc.) —
repetido, -da *adj* **1** : repeated **2 repetidas
veces** : repeatedly, time and again —
repetitivo, -va *adj* : repetitive, repetitious
repicar {72} *vt* : ring — *vi* : ring out,
peal — **repique** *nm* : ringing, pealing
repisa *nf* **1** : shelf, ledge **2 repisa
de ventana** : windowsill
replegar {49} *vt* : fold —
replegarse *vr* : retreat, withdraw
repleto, -ta *adj* **1** : replete, full **2**
repleto, -ta de : packed with
replicar {72} *vt* : reply, retort — *vi* :
answer back — **réplica** *nf* **1** RESPUESTA
: reply **2** COPIA : replica, reproduction
repliegue *nm* **1** : fold **2** :
(military) withdrawal
repollo *nm* : cabbage

reponer {60} *vt* **1** : replace **2** REPLICAR
: reply — **reponerse** *vr* : recover
reportar *vt* **1** : yield, bring **2** *Lat*
: report — **reportaje** *nm* : article,
(news) report — **reporte** *nm* *Lat* :
report — **reportero, -ra** *n* : reporter
reposar *vi* **1** DESCANSAR : rest **2**
: stand, settle (of liquids, dough,
etc.) — **reposado, -da** *adj* : calm,
relaxed — **reposición** *nf, pl* **-ciones**
1 : replacement **2** : rerun, repeat (of a
program, etc.) — **reposo** *nm* : rest
repostar *vi* **1** : stock up on **2** : refuel
(an airplane, etc.) — *vi* : fill up, refuel
reprender *vt* : reprimand, scold —
reprensible *adj* : reprehensible
represalia *nf* **1** : reprisal **2**
tomar represalias : retaliate
represar *vt* : dam
representar *vt* **1** : represent **2** : perform
(a play, etc.) **3** APARENTAR : look, appear
as — **representación** *nf, pl* **-ciones**
1 : representation **2** : performance (of
a play, etc.) **3 en representar de** : on
behalf of — **representante** *nmf* **1** :
representative **2** ACTOR : performer —
representativo, -va *adj* : representative
represión *nf, pl* **-siones** : repression
reprimenda *nf* : reprimand
reprimir *vt* **1** : repress **2** :
suppress (a rebellion, etc.)
reprobar {19} *vt* **1** : reprove,
condemn **2** *Lat* : fail (an exam, etc.)
reprochar *vt* : reproach —
reprocharse *vr* : reproach oneself
— **reproche** *nm* : reproach
reproducir {61} *vt* : reproduce —
reproducirse *vr* **1** : breed, reproduce
2 : recur (of an event, etc.) —
reproducción *nf, pl* **-ciones** : reproduction
— **reproductor, -tora** *adj* : reproductive
▸ **reptil** *nm* : reptile
república *nf* : republic — **republicano,
-na** *adj & n* : republican
repudiar *vt* : repudiate
repuesto *nm* : spare (auto) part
repugnar *vt* : disgust — **repugnancia** *nf*
: disgust — **repugnante** *adj* : disgusting
repujar *vt* : emboss
repulsivo, -va *adj* : repulsive
reputar *vt* : consider, deem —
reputación *nf, pl* **-ciones** : reputation
requerir {76} *vt* **1** : require **2** :
summon, send for (a person)
requesón *nm, pl* **-sones** : cottage cheese

réquiem *nm* : requiem
requisito *nm* **1** : requirement **2**
requisito previo : prerequisite
res *nf* **1** : beast, animal **2** *Lat*
or **carne de res** : beef
resabio *nm* **1** VICIO : bad habit,
vice **2** DEJO : aftertaste
resaca *nf* **1** : undertow **2 tener
resaca** : have a hangover
resaltar *vi* **1** : stand out **2 hacer resaltar**
: bring out, highlight — *vt* : emphasize
resarcir {83} *vt* : compensate, repay —
resarcirse *vr* **resarcirse de** : make up for
resbalar *vi* **1** : slip, slide **2** : skid (of
an automobile) — **resbalarse** *vr* : slip,
skid — **resbaladizo, -za** *adj* : slippery
— **resbalón** *nm, pl* **-lones** : slip —
resbaloso, -sa *adj Lat* : slippery
rescatar *vt* **1** : rescue, ransom **2**
RECUPERAR : recover, get back —
rescate *nm* **1** : rescue **2** : ransom
(money) **3** RECUPERACIÓN : recovery
rescindir *vt* : cancel — **rescisión** *nf,
pl* **-siones** : cancellation
rescoldo *nm* : embers *pl*
resecar {72} *vt* : dry (out) — **resecarse** *vr*
: dry up — **reseco, -ca** *adj* : dry, dried-up
resentirse {76} *vr* **1** : suffer, be
weakened **2** OFENDERSE : be offended
3 resentirse de : feel the effects of
— **resentido, -da** *adj* : resentful —
resentimiento *nm* : resentment
reseñar *vt* **1** : review **2** DESCRIBIR
: describe — **reseña** *nf* **1** : review,
report **2** DESCRIPCIÓN : description
reservar *vt* **1** : reserve **2** GUARDAR : keep,
save — **reservarse** *vr* **1** : save oneself
2 : keep for oneself — **reserva** *nf* **1**
: reservation **2** PROVISIÓN : reserve
3 de reserva : spare, in reserve —
reservación *nf, pl* **-ciones** : reservation
— **reservado, -da** *adj* **1** : reserved **2**
: confidential (of a document, etc.)
resfriar {85} *vt* : cool — **resfriarse** *vr* **1**
: cool off **2** CONSTIPARSE : catch a
cold — **resfriado** *nm* CATARRO :
cold — **resfrío** *nm Lat* : cold
resguardar *vt* : protect —
resguardarse *vr* : protect
oneself — **resguardo** *nm* **1** :
protection **2** RECIBO : receipt
residir *vi* **1** : reside, live **2 residir en** :
lie in — **residencia** *nf* **1** : residence **2**
or **residencia universitaria** : dormitory
— **residencial** *adj* : residential

respirar: aparato^M respiratorio
breathe: respiratory system

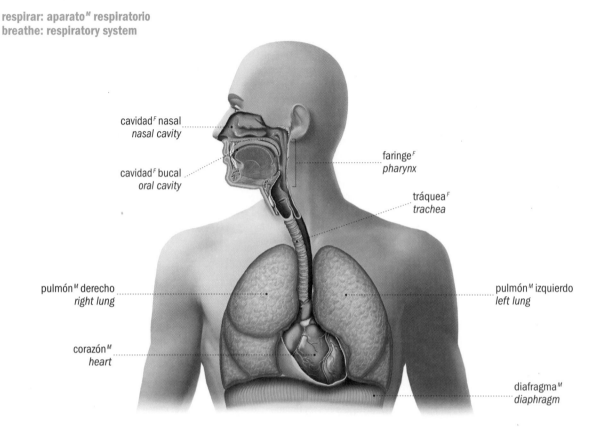

cavidad^F nasal
nasal cavity

faringe^F
pharynx

cavidad^F bucal
oral cavity

tráquea^F
trachea

pulmón^M derecho
right lung

pulmón^M izquierdo
left lung

corazón^M
heart

diafragma^M
diaphragm

— **residente** *adj & nmf* : resident
residuo *nm* **1** : residue **2** residuos *nmpl*
: waste — **residual** *adj* : residual
resignar *vt* : resign — **resignarse** *vr*
resignarse a : resign oneself to —
resignación *nf, pl* **-ciones** : resignation
resina *nf* **1** : resin **2 resina**
epoxídica : epoxy
resistir *vt* **1** AGUANTAR : stand, bear **2** :
withstand (temptation, etc.) — *vi* : resist
— **resistirse** *vr* **resistirse a** : be resistant
to — **resistencia** *nf* **1** : resistance
2 AGUANTE : endurance, stamina —
resistente *adj* : resistant, strong, tough
resma *nf* : ream
resollar {19} *vi* : breathe heavily, pant
resolver {89} *vt* **1** : resolve **2** DECIDIR
: decide — **resolverse** *vr* : make up
one's mind — **resolución** *nf, pl* **-ciones**
1 : resolution **2** DECISIÓN : decision **3**
FIRMEZA : determination, resolve
resonar {19} *vi* : resound

— **resonancia** *nf* **1** : resonance **2**
CONSECUENCIAS : impact, repercussions *pl*
— **resonante** *adj* : resonant, resounding
resoplar *vi* **1** : puff, pant **2** :
snort (with annoyance)
resorte *nm* **1** MUELLE : spring **2**
tocar resortes : pull strings
respaldar *vt* : back, endorse
— **respaldarse** *vr* : lean back —
respaldo *nm* **1** : back (of a chair,
etc.) **2** APOYO : support, backing
respectar *vt* : concern, relate to
— **respectivo, -va** *adj* : respective
— **respecto** *nm* **1 al respecto**
: in this respect **2 respecto a** :
in regard to, concerning
respetar *vt* : respect —
respetable *adj* : respectable —
respeto *nm* **1** : respect **2 presentar**
sus respetos : pay one's respects —
respetuoso, -sa *adj* : respectful
respingo *nm* : start, jump

▸ **respirar** *v* : breathe — **respiración** *nf,*
pl **-ciones** : respiration, breathing —
respiratorio, -ria *adj* : respiratory
— **respiro** *nm* **1** : breath **2**
DESCANSO : respite, break
resplandecer {53} *vi* : shine —
resplandeciente *adj* : shining, gleaming
— **resplandor** *nm* **1** : brilliance,
gleam **2** : flash (of lightning, etc.)
responder *vt* : answer, reply — *vi* **1**
: answer **2** REPLICAR : answer back **3**
responder a : respond to **4 responder**
de : answer for (something)
responsable *adj* : responsible —
responsabilidad *nf* : responsibility
respuesta *nf* **1** : answer, reply
2 REACCIÓN : response
resquebrajar *vt* : split, crack
— **resquebrajarse** *vr* : crack
resquicio *nm* **1** : crack, crevice
2 VESTIGIO : trace, glimmer
resta *nf* : subtraction

restablecer {53} *vt* : reestablish, restore — **restablecerse** *vr* : recover — **restablecimiento** *nm* : restoration, recovery

restallar *vi* : crack, crackle

restar *vt* **1** : deduct, subtract **2** DISMINUIR : minimize — *vi* : be left — **restante** *adj* **1** : remaining **2 lo restar** : the rest

restauración *nf, pl* **-ciones** : restoration

restaurante *nm* : restaurant

restaurar *vt* : restore

restituir {41} *vt* : return, restore — **restitución** *nf, pl* **-ciones** : restitution

resto *nm* **1** : rest, remainder **2 restos** *nmpl* : leftovers **3** *or* **restos mortales** : mortal remains

restregar {49} *vt* : rub, scrub — **restregarse** *vr* : rub

restringir {35} *vt* : restrict, limit — **restricción** *nf, pl* **-ciones** : restriction, limitation — **restrictivo, -va** *adj* : restrictive

resucitar *vt* : resuscitate, revive — *vi* : come back to life

resuelto, -ta *adj* : determined, resolved

resuello *nm* : heavy breathing, panting

resultar *vi* **1** : succeed, work out **2** SALIR : turn out (to be) **3 resultar de** : be the result of **4 resultar en** : result in — **resultado** *nm* : result, outcome

resumir *v* : summarize, sum up — **resumen** *nm, pl* **-súmenes 1** : summary **2 en resumir** : in short

resurgir {35} *vi* : reappear, revive — **resurgimiento** *nm* : resurgence — **resurrección** *nf, pl* **-ciones** : resurrection

retahíla *nf* : string, series

retal *nm* : remnant

retardar *vt* **1** RETRASAR : delay

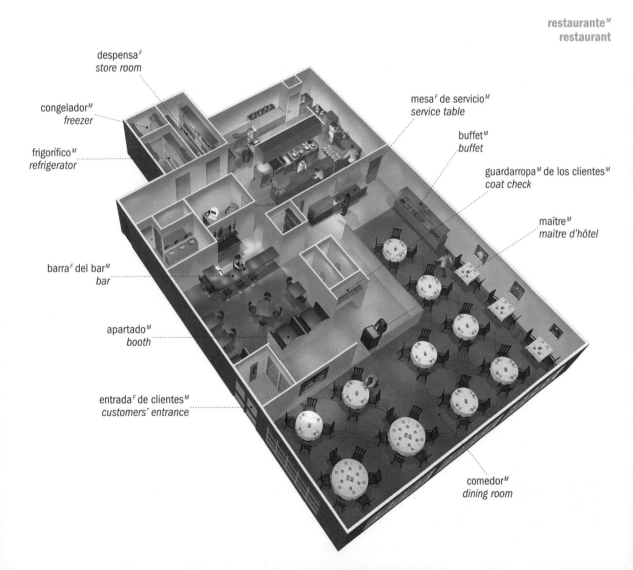

restaurante^M
restaurant

despensa^F
store room

congelador^M
freezer

frigorífico^M
refrigerator

barra^F del bar^M
bar

apartado^M
booth

entrada^F de clientes^M
customers' entrance

mesa^F de servicio^M
service table

buffet^M
buffet

guardarropa^M de los clientes^M
coat check

maître^M
maître d'hôtel

comedor^M
dining room

2 POSPONER : postpone

retazo *nm* **1** : remnant, scrap **2** : fragment (of a text, etc.)

retener {80} *vt* **1** : retain, keep **2** : withhold (funds, etc.) **3** DETENER : detain — **retención** *nf, pl* **-ciones 1** : retention **2** : deduction, withholding (of funds)

reticente *adj* : reluctant — **reticencia** *nf* : reluctance

retina *nf* : retina

retintín *nm, pl* **-tines 1** : tinkling, jingle **2 con retintín** : sarcastically

retirar *vt* **1** : remove, take away **2** : withdraw (funds, statements, etc.) — **retirarse** *vr* **1** : retreat, withdraw **2** JUBILARSE : retire — **retirada** *nf* **1** : withdrawal **2 batirse en retirada** : beat a retreat — **retirado, -da** *adj* **1** : remote, secluded **2** JUBILADO : retired — **retiro** *nm* **1** : retreat **2** JUBILACIÓN : retirement **3** *Lat* : withdrawal

reto *nm* : challenge, dare

retocar {72} *vt* : touch up

retoño *nm* : sprout, shoot

retoque *nm* **1** : retouching **2 el último retoque** : the finishing touch

retorcer {14} *vt* **1** : twist, contort **2** : wring out (clothes, etc.) — **retorcerse** *vr* **1** : get twisted up **2** : squirm, writhe (in pain) — **retorcijón** *nm, pl* **-jones** : cramp, spasm — **retorcimiento** *nm* : twisting, wringing out

retórica *nf* : rhetoric — **retórico, -ca** *adj* : rhetorical

retornar *v* : return — **retorno** *nm* : return

retozar {21} *vi* : frolic, romp — **retozón, -zona** *adj* : playful, frisky

retractarse *vr* **1** : withdraw, back down

2 retractarse de : take back, retract

retraer {81} *vt* : retract — **retraerse** *vr* : withdraw — **retraído, -da** *adj* : withdrawn, shy

retrasar *vt* **1** : delay, hold up **2** APLAZAR : postpone **3** : set back (a clock) — **retrasarse** *vr* **1** : be late **2** : fall behind (in work, etc.) — **retrasado, -da** *adj* **1** : retarded **2** : in arrears (of payments) **3** : backward (of a country) **4** : slow (of a clock) — **retraso** *nm* **1** : delay **2** SUBDESARROLLO : backwardness **3 retraso mental** : mental retardation

retratar *vt* **1** : portray **2** FOTOGRAFIAR : photograph **3** DIBUJAR : paint a portrait of — **retrato** *nm* **1** : portrayal **2** DIBUJO : portrait **3** FOTOGRAFÍA : photograph

retrete *nm* : restroom, toilet

retribuir {41} *vt* **1** : pay **2** RECOMPENSAR : reward — **retribución** *nf, pl* **-ciones 1** : payment **2** RECOMPENSA : reward

retroactivo, -va *adj* : retroactive

retroceder *vi* **1** : go back, turn back **2** CEDER : back down — **retroceso** *nm* **1** : backward movement **2** : backing down

retrógrado, -da *adj & nmf* : reactionary

retrospectiva *nf* : hindsight — **retrospectivo, -va** *adj* : retrospective

retrovisor *nm* : rearview mirror

retumbar *vi* : resound, reverberate, rumble

reumatismo *nm* : rheumatism

reunir {68} *vt* **1** : unite, join **2** TENER : have, possess **3** RECOGER : gather, collect — **reunirse** *vr* : meet, gather — **reunión** *nf, pl* **-niones 1** : meeting **2** : (social) gathering, reunion

revalidar *vt* : confirm, ratify

revancha *nf* **1** : revenge **2** : rematch (in sports)

revelar *vt* **1** : reveal, disclose **2** : develop (film) — **revelación** *nf, pl* **-ciones** : revelation — **revelado** *nm* : developing (of film) — **revelador, -dora** *adj* : revealing

reventar {55} *v* : burst, blow up — **reventarse** *vr* : burst — **reventón** *nm, pl* **-tones** : blowout, flat tire

reverberar *vi* : reverberate — **reverberación** *nf, pl* **-ciones** : reverberation

reverenciar *vt* : revere — **reverencia** *nf* **1** : bow, curtsy **2** VENERACIÓN : reverence — **reverendo, -da** *adj & nmf* : reverend — **reverente** *adj* : reverent

reversa *nf Lat* : reverse (gear)

reverso *nm* **1** : back, reverse **2 el reverso de la medalla** : the complete opposite — **reversible** *adj* : reversible

revertir {76} *vi* **1** : revert **2 revertir en** : result in

revés *nm, pl* **-veses 1** : back, wrong side **2** CONTRATIEMPO : setback **3** BOFETADA : slap **4** : backhand (in sports) **5 al revés** : the other way around, upside down, inside out

revestir {54} *vt* **1** : coat, cover **2** ASUMIR : take on, assume — **revestimiento** *nm* : covering, coating

revisar *vt* **1** : examine, inspect **2** : check over, overhaul (machinery, etc.) **3** MODIFICAR : revise — **revisión** *nf, pl* **-siones 1** : revision **2** INSPECCIÓN : inspection, check — **revisor, -sora** *n* : inspector

revistar *vt* : review, inspect (troops, etc.) — **revista** *nf* **1** : magazine, journal **2** : revue (in theater) **3 pasar revista** : review, inspect

revivir *vi* : revive, come alive again — *vt* : relive

revocar {72} *vt* : revoke

revolcar {82} *vt* : knock over, knock down — **revolcarse** *vr* : roll around

revolotear *vi* : flutter, flit — **revoloteo** *nm* : fluttering, flitting

revoltijo *nm* : mess, jumble

revoltoso, -sa *adj* : rebellious

revolución *nf, pl* **-ciones** : revolution — **revolucionar** *vt* : revolutionize — **revolucionario, -ria** *adj & n* : revolutionary

revolver {89} *vt* **1** : mix, stir **2** : upset (one's stomach) **3** DESORGANIZAR : mess up — **revolverse** *vr* **1** : toss and turn **2** VOLVERSE : turn around

revólver *nm* : revolver

revuelo *nm* : commotion

revuelta *nf* : uprising, revolt — **revuelto, -ta** *adj* **1** : choppy, rough **2** DESORDENADO : messed up **3 huevos revueltos** : scrambled eggs

rey *nm* : king

reyerta *nf* : brawl, fight

rezagarse {52} *vr* : fall behind, lag

rezar {21} *vi* **1** : pray **2** DECIR : say — *vt* : say, recite — **rezo** *nm* : prayer

rezongar {52} *vi* : gripe, grumble

rezumar *v* : ooze

ría *nf* : estuary

riachuelo *nm* : brook, stream

riada *nf* : flood

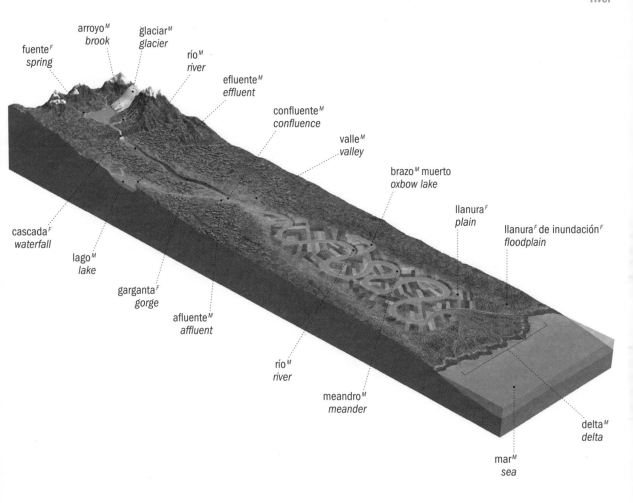

río^M
river

fuente^F
spring

arroyo^M
brook

glaciar^M
glacier

río^M
river

efluente^M
effluent

confluente^M
confluence

valle^M
valley

brazo^M muerto
oxbow lake

llanura^F
plain

llanura^F de inundación^F
floodplain

cascada^F
waterfall

lago^M
lake

garganta^F
gorge

afluente^M
affluent

río^M
river

meandro^M
meander

delta^M
delta

mar^M
sea

ribera *nf* : bank, shore
ribetear *vt* : border, trim — **ribete** *nm* **1**
: border, trim **2** : embellishment
rico, -ca *adj* **1** : rich, wealthy **2**
ABUNDANTE : **abundant 3** SABROSO : rich,
tasty — **rico, -ca** *n* : rich person
ridiculizar {21} *vt* : ridicule — **ridículo,
-la** *adj* : ridiculous — **ridículo** *nm* **1**
hacer el ridículo : make a fool of
oneself **2 poner en ridículo** : ridicule
riego *nm* : irrigation
riel *nm* : rail
rienda *nf* **1** : rein **2 dar rienda
suelta a** : give free rein to
riesgo *nm* : risk

rifa *nf* : raffle — **rifar** *vt* : raffle (off)
— **rifarse** *vr, fam* : fight over
rifle *nm* : rifle
rígido, -da *adj* **1** : rigid, stiff **2**
SEVERO : harsh, strict — **rigidez** *nf,
pl* **-deces 1** : rigidity, stiffness **2**
SEVERIDAD : harshness, strictness
rigor *nm* **1** : rigor, harshness **2** EXACTITUD
: precision **3 de rigor** : essential,
obligatory — **riguroso, -sa** *adj* : rigorous
rima *nf* **1** : rhyme **2 rimas** *nfpl* :
verse, poetry — **rimar** *vi* : rhyme
rimbombante *adj* : showy, pompous
rímel *nm* : mascara
rincón *nm, pl* **-cones** : corner, nook

▸ **rinoceronte** *nm* : rhinoceros
riña *nf* **1** : fight, brawl **2**
DISPUTA : **dispute, quarrel**
riñón *nm, pl* **-ñones** : kidney
▸ **río** *nm* **1** : river **2** TORRENTE
: torrent, stream
riqueza *nf* **1** : wealth **2** ABUNDANCIA
: richness **3 riquezas naturales**
: natural resources
risa *nf* **1** : laughter, laugh **2 dar risa
a algn** : make someone laugh **3
morirse de la risa** *fam* : die laughing
risco *nm* : crag, cliff
risible *adj* : laughable
ristra *nf* : string, series

risueño, -ña *adj* : cheerful, smiling

ritmo *nm* **1** : rhythm **2** VELOCIDAD : pace, speed — **rítmico, -ca** *adj* : rhythmical

rito *nm* : rite, ritual — **ritual** *adj & nm* : ritual

rival *adj & nmf* : rival — **rivalidad** *nf* : rivalry, competition — **rivalizar** {21} *vi* **rivalizar con** : rival, compete with

rizar {21} *vt* **1** : curl **2** : ripple (a surface) — **rizarse** *vr* : curl — **rizado, -da** *adj* **1** : curly **2** : choppy (of water) — **rizo** *nm* **1** : curl **2** : ripple (in water) **3** : loop (in aviation)

róbalo *nm* : bass (fish)

robar *vt* **1** : steal **2** : burglarize (a house, etc.) **3** SECUESTRAR : kidnap — **robo** *nm* : robbery, theft

roble *nm* : oak

robot *nm, pl* **-bots** : robot — **robótica** *nf* : robotics

robustecer {53} *vt* : make stronger, strengthen — **robusto, -ta** *adj* : robust, sturdy

roca *nf* : rock, boulder

roce *nm* **1** : rubbing, chafing **2** RASGUÑO : graze, scratch **3 tener un roce con** : have a brush with

rociar {85} *vt* : spray, sprinkle — **rocío** *nm* : dew

rocoso, -sa *adj* : rocky

rodaja *nf* : slice

rodar {19} *vi* **1** : roll, roll down, roll along **2** GIRAR : turn, go around **3** : travel (of a vehicle) **4** : film (of movies, etc.) — *vt* **1** : film, shoot **2** : break in (a vehicle) — **rodaje** *nm* **1** : filming, shooting **2** : breaking in (of a vehicle)

rodear *vt* **1** : surround, encircle **2** *Lat* : round up (cattle) — **rodearse** *vr* **rodearse de** : surround oneself with — **rodeo** *nm* **1** : rodeo, roundup **2** DESVÍO : detour **3 andar con rodeos** : beat around the bush

rodilla *nf* : knee

rodillo *nm* **1** : roller **2** : rolling pin (for pastry)

roer {69} *vt* **1** : gnaw **2** ATORMENTAR : eat away at, torment — **roedor** *nm* : rodent

rogar {16} *vt* : beg, request — *vi* : pray

rojo, -ja *adj* **1** : red **2 ponerse rojo, -ja** : blush — **rojo** *nm* : red — **rojez** *nf* : redness — **rojizo, -za** *adj* : reddish

rollizo, -za *adj* : plump, chubby

rollo *nm* **1** : roll, coil **2** *fam* : boring speech, lecture

romance *nm* **1** : romance **2** : Romance (language)

romano, -na *adj & n* : Roman

romántico, -ca *adj* : romantic — **romanticismo** *nm* : romanticism

romería *nf* : pilgrimage, procession

romero *nm* : rosemary

romo, -ma *adj* : blunt, dull

rompecabezas *nms & pl* : puzzle

romper {70} *vt* **1** : break **2** RASGAR : rip, tear **3** : break off (relations), break (a contract) — *vi* **1** : break (of the day, waves, etc.) **2 romper a** : begin to, burst out with **3 romper con** : break off with — **romperse** *vr* : break

ron *nm* : rum

roncar {72} *vi* : snore — **ronco, -ca** *adj* : hoarse

ronda *nf* **1** : rounds *pl*, patrol **2** : round (of drinks, etc.) — **rondar** *vt* **1** : patrol **2** : hang around (a place) **3** : be approximately (an age, a number, etc.) — *vi* **1** : be on patrol **2** MERODEAR : prowl about

ronquera *nf* : hoarseness

ronquido *nm* : snore

ronronear *vi* : purr — **ronroneo** *nm* : purr, purring

ronzar {21} *vt* : munch, crunch

roña *nf* **1** : mange **2** SUCIEDAD : dirt, filth — **roñoso, -sa** *adj* **1** : mangy **2** SUCIO : dirty **3** *fam* : stingy

ropa *nf* **1** : clothes *pl*, clothing **2 ropa interior** : underwear — **ropaje** *nm* : robes *pl*, regalia — **ropero** *nm* : wardrobe, closet

rosa *nf* : rose (flower) — **rosa** *adj* : rose-colored — **rosa** *nm* : rose (color) — **rosado, -da** *adj* **1** : pink **2 vino rosado** : rosé — **rosado** *nm* : pink (color) — **rosal** *nm* : rosebush

rosario *nm* : rosary

rosbif *nm* : roast beef

rosca *nf* **1** : thread (of a screw) **2** ESPIRAL : ring, coil

roseta *nf* : rosette

rosquilla *nf* : doughnut

rostro *nm* : face

rotación *nf, pl* **-ciones** : rotation — **rotativo, -va** *adj* : rotary, revolving

roto, -ta *adj* : broken, torn

rotonda *nf* : traffic circle, rotary

rótula *nf* : kneecap

rótulo *nm* **1** : heading, title **2** ETIQUETA : label, sign

rotundo, -da *adj* : categorical, absolute

rotura *nf* : break, tear, fracture

rozar {21} *vt* **1** : graze, touch lightly

2 APROXIMARSE DE : touch on, border on — *vi* : scrape, rub — **rozarse** *vr* **1** : rub, chafe **2 rozarse con** *fam* : rub elbows with — **rozadura** *nf* : scratch

rubí *nm, pl* **rubíes** : ruby

rubicundo, -da *adj* : ruddy

rubio, -bia *adj & n* : blond

rubor *nm* : flush, blush — **ruborizarse** {21} *vr* : blush

rubrica *nf* **1** : flourish (in writing) **2** TÍTULO : title, heading

rudeza *nf* : roughness, coarseness

rudimentos *nmpl* : rudiments, basics — **rudimentario, -ria** *adj* : rudimentary

rudo, -da *adj* **1** : rough, harsh **2** GROSERO : coarse, unpolished

rueda *nf* **1** : wheel **2** CORRO : circle, ring **3** RODAJA : (round) slice **4 ir sobre ruedas** : go smoothly — **ruedo** *nm* : bullring

ruego *nm* : request

rugir {35} *vi* : roar — **rugido** *nm* : roar

rugoso, -sa *adj* **1** : rough **2** ARRUGADO : wrinkled

ruibarbo *nm* : rhubarb

ruido *nm* : noise — **ruidoso, -sa** *adj* : loud, noisy

ruina *nf* **1** : ruin, destruction **2** COLAPSO : collapse **3 ruinas** *nfpl* : ruins, remains — **ruinoso, -sa** *adj* : run-down, dilapidated

ruiseñor *nm* : nightingale

ruleta *nf* : roulette

rulo *nm* : curler, roller

rumano, -na *adj* : Romanian, Rumanian

rumba *nf* : rumba

rumbo *nm* **1** : direction, course **2** ESPLENDIDEZ : lavishness **3 con rumbo a** : bound for, heading for **4 perder el rumbo** : go off course

rumiar *vt* : mull over — *vi* : chew the cud — **rumiante** *adj & nm* : ruminant

rumor *nm* **1** : rumor **2** MURMULLO : murmur — **rumorearse** *or* **rumorarse** *vr* : be rumored — **rumoroso, -sa** *adj* : murmuring, babbling

ruptura *nf* **1** : break, rupture **2** : breach (of a contract) **3** : breaking off (of relations)

rural *adj* : rural

ruso, -sa *adj* : Russian — **ruso** *nm* : Russian (language)

rústico, -ca *adj* **1** : rural, rustic **2 en rústica** : in paperback

ruta *nf* : route

rutina *nf* : routine — **rutinario, -ria** *adj* : routine

s *nf* : s, 20th letter of the Spanish alphabet
sábado *nm* : Saturday
sábana *nf* : sheet
sabandija *nf* : bug
saber {71} *vt* **1** : know **2** SER CAPAZ DE : know how to, be able to **3** ENTERARSE : learn, find out **4 a saber** : namely — *vi* **1** : taste **2 saber de** : know about — **saber** *nm* : knowledge — **sabelotodo** *nmf, fam* : know-it-all — **sabido, -da** *adj* : well-known — **sabiduría** *nf* **1** : wisdom **2** CONOCIMIENTO : learning, knowledge — **sabiendas**: **a sabiendas** *adv phr* : knowingly — **sabio, -bia** *adj* **1** :

learned **2** PRUDENTE : wise, sensible
sabor *nm* : flavor, taste — **saborear** *vt* : savor
sabotaje *nm* : sabotage — **saboteador, -dora** *n* : saboteur — **sabotear** *vt* : sabotage
sabroso, -sa *adj* : delicious, tasty
sabueso *nm* **1** : bloodhound **2** *fam* : sleuth
sacacorchos *nms & pl* : corkscrew
sacapuntas *nms & pl* : pencil sharpener
sacar {72} *vt* **1** : take out **2** OBTENER : get, obtain **3** EXTRAER : extract, withdraw

4 : bring out (a book, a product, etc.) **5** : take (photos), make (copies) **6** QUITAR : remove **7 sacar adelante** : bring up (children), carry out (a project, etc.) **8 sacar la lengua** : stick out one's tongue — *vi* : serve (in sports)
sacarina *nf* : saccharin
sacerdote, -tisa *n* : priest *m*, priestess *f* — **sacerdocio** *nm* : priesthood — **sacerdotal** *adj* : priestly
saciar *vt* : satisfy
▶ **saco** *nm* **1** : bag, sack **2** : sac (in anatomy) **3** *Lat* : jacket
sacramento *nm* : sacrament

saco*M* de dormir y equipamiento*M* para acampar
sleeping bag and camping equipment

tienda*F* de campaña*F* clásica
pup tent

saco*M* de dormir de tipo*M* momia*F*
mummy bag

sartén*F*
frying pan

cubertería*F*
cutlery set

colchoneta*F* de aire*M*
air mattress

plato*M*
plate

cantimplora*F*
canteen

hornillo*M*
single-burner camp stove

linterna*F*
lantern

muelle*M* para inflar y desinflar
inflator-deflator

salmones^M
salmon

salmón^M del Pacífico^M
Pacific salmon

salmón^M del Atlántico^M
Atlantic salmon

— **sacramental** *adj* : sacramental
sacrificar {72} *vt* : sacrifice —
sacrificarse *vr* : sacrifice oneself
— **sacrificio** *nm* : sacrifice
sacrilegio *nm* : sacrilege —
sacrílego, -ga *adj* : sacrilegious
sacro, -cra *adj* : sacred —
sacrosanto, -ta *adj* : sacrosanct
sacudir *vt* **1** : shake **2** GOLPEAR : beat
3 CONMOVER : shake up, shock —
sacudirse *vr* : shake off — **sacudida** *nf* **1**
: shaking **2** : jolt (of a train, etc.), tremor
(of an earthquake) **3** : (emotional) shock
sádico, -ca *adj* : sadistic — **sádico,
-ca** *n* : sadist — **sadismo** *nm* : sadism
saeta *nf* : arrow
safari *nm* : safari
sagaz *adj*, *pl* **-gaces** : shrewd, sagacious
— **sagacidad** *nf* : shrewdness
sagrado, -da *adj* : sacred, holy
sal *nf* : salt
sala *nf* **1** : room, hall **2** : living room (of a
house) **3 sala de espera** : waiting room
salar *vt* : salt — **salado, -da** *adj* **1** : salty **2**
GRACIOSO : witty **3 agua salada** : salt water
salario *nm* : salary, wage

salchicha *nf* : sausage — **salchichón** *nf*,
pl **-chones** : salami-like cold cut
saldar *vt* **1** : settle, pay off **2** VENDER
: sell off — **saldo** *nm* **1** : balance
(of an account) **2 saldars** *nmpl*
: remainders, sale items
salero *nm* : saltshaker
salir {73} *vi* **1** : go out, come out **2**
PARTIR : leave **3** APARECER : appear **4**
RESULTAR : turn out **5** : rise (of the sun)
6 salir adelante : get by **7 salir con** : go
out with, date **8 salir de** : come from
— **salirse** *vr* **1** : leave **2** ESCAPARSE :
leak out, escape **3** SOLTARSE : come off
4 salirse con la suya : get one's own
way — **salida** *nf* **1** : exit **2** : (action of)
leaving, departure **3** SOLUCIÓN : way out
4 : leak (of gas, liquid, etc.) **5** OCURRENCIA
: witty remark **6 salida de emergencia**
: emergency exit **7 salida del sol** :
sunrise — **saliente** *adj* **1** : departing,
outgoing **2** DESTACADO : outstanding
saliva *nf* : saliva
salmo *nm* : psalm
▸ **salmón** *nm*, *pl* **-mones** : salmon
salmuera *nf* : brine

salón *nm*, *pl* **-lones 1** : lounge, sitting
room **2 salón de belleza** : beauty
salon **3 salón de clase** : classroom
salpicar {72} *vt* **1** : splash,
spatter **2 salpicar de** : pepper
with — **salpicadera** *nf Lat* : fender
— **salpicadura** *nf* : splash
salsa *nf* **1** : sauce **2** : (meat)
gravy **3** : salsa (music)
saltamontes *nms & pl* : grasshopper
saltar *vi* **1** : jump, leap **2** REBOTAR
: bounce **3** : come off (of a button,
etc.) **4** ROMPERSE : shatter **5** ESTALLAR :
explode, blow up — *vt* **1** : jump (over)
2 OMITIR : skip, miss — **saltarse** *vr* **1**
: come off **2** OMITIR : skip, miss
saltear *vt* : sauté
saltimbanqui *nmf* : acrobat
salto *nm* **1** : jump, leap **2** : dive
(into water) **3 salto de agua** :
waterfall — **saltón, -tona** *adj*, *mpl*
-tones : bulging, protruding
salud *nf* **1** : health **2 ¡salud!** : here's
to your health! **3 ¡salud!** *Lat* : bless
you! (when someone sneezes)
— **saludable** *adj* : healthy
saludar *vt* **1** : greet, say hello to **2** :
salute (in the military) — **saludo** *nm* **1**
: greeting **2** : (military) salute **3**
saludars : best wishes, regards
salva *nf* **salva de aplausos**
: round of applause
salvación *nf*, *pl* **-ciones** : salvation
salvado *nm* : bran
salvador, -dora *n* : savior, rescuer
salvadoreño, -ña *adj* : (El) Salvadoran
salvaguardar *vt* : safeguard
salvaje *adj* **1** : wild **2** PRIMITIVO : savage,
primitive — **salvaje** *nmf* : savage
salvar *vt* **1** : save, rescue **2** RECORRER
: cover, travel **3** SUPERAR : overcome
— **salvarse** *vr* : save oneself —
salvavidas *nms & pl* **1** : life preserver
2 bote salvavidas : lifeboat
salvia *nf* : sage (plant)
salvo, -va *adj* : safe — **salvo** *prep* **1** :
except (for), save **2 salvo que** : unless
samba *nf* : samba
San → **santo**
sanar *vt* : heal, cure — *vi* : recover
— **sanatorio** *nm* **1** : sanatorium
2 HOSPITAL : clinic, hospital
sanción *nf*, *pl* **-ciones** : sanction
— **sancionar** *vt* : sanction
sandalia *nf* : sandal

sándalo *nm* : sandalwood
sandía *nf* : watermelon
sandwich *nm, pl* **-wiches** : sandwich
saneamiento *nm* : sanitation
sangrar *vt* **1** : bleed **2** : indent (a paragraph) — *vi* : bleed — **sangrante** *adj* : bleeding — **sangre** *nf* **1** : blood **2 a sangre fría** : in cold blood — **sangriento, -ta** *adj* : bloody
sanguijuela *nf* : leech
sanguinario, -ria *adj* : bloodthirsty — **sanguíneo, -nea** *adj* : blood
sano, -na *adj* **1** : healthy **2** : (morally) wholesome **3** ENTERO : intact **4 sano y salvo** : safe and sound — **sanidad** *nf* **1** : health **2** : public health, sanitation — **sanitario, -ria** *adj* : sanitary, health — **sanitario** *nm Lat* : toilet
santiamén *nm* **en un santiamén** : in no time at all
santo, -ta *adj* **1** : holy **2 Santo, Santa** (**San** *before masculine names except those beginning with D or T*) : Saint — **santo, -ta** *n* : saint — **santo** *nm* **1** : saint's day **2** *Lat* : birthday — **santidad** *nf* : holiness, sanctity — **santiguarse** {10} *vr* : cross oneself — **santuario** *nm* : sanctuary
saña *nf* **1** : fury **2** BRUTALIDAD : viciousness
sapo *nm* : toad
saque *nm* : serve (in tennis, etc.), throw-in (in soccer)
saquear *vt* : sack, loot — **saqueador, -dora** *n* : looter — **saqueo** *nm* : sacking, looting
sarampión *nm* : measles *pl*
sarape *nm Lat* : serape
sarcasmo *nm* : sarcasm — **sarcástico, -ca** *adj* : sarcastic
sardina *nf* : sardine
sardónico, -ca *adj* : sardonic
sargento *nmf* : sergeant
sarpullido *nm* : rash
sartén *nmf, pl* **-tenes** : frying pan
sastre, -tra *n* : tailor — **sastrería** *nf* **1** : tailoring **2** : tailor's shop
Satanás *nm* : Satan — **satánico, -ca** *adj* : satanic
satélite *nm* : satellite
sátira *nf* : satire — **satírico, -ca** *adj* : satirical
satisfacer {74} *vt* **1** : satisfy **2** CUMPLIR : fulfill, meet **3** PAGAR : pay — **satisfacerse** *vr* **1** : be satisfied **2** VENGARSE : take revenge — **satisfacción** *nf, pl* **-ciones** : satisfaction

— **satisfactorio, -ria** *adj* : satisfactory
— **satisfecho, -cha** *adj* : satisfied
saturar *vt* : saturate — **saturación** *nf, pl* **-ciones** : saturation
Saturno *nm* : Saturn
sauce *nm* : willow
sauna *nmf* : sauna
savia *nf* : sap
saxofón *nm, pl* **-fones** : saxophone
sazón *nf, pl* **-zones** **1** : seasoning **2** MADUREZ : ripeness **3 a la sazón** : at that time, then **4 en sazón** : ripe, in season — **sazonar** *vt* : season
se *pron* **1** (*reflexive*) : himself, herself, itself, oneself, yourself, yourselves, themselves **2** (*indirect object*) : (to) him, (to) her, (to) you, (to) them **3** : each other, one another **4 se dice que** : it is said that **5 se habla inglés** : English spoken
sebo *nm* **1** : fat **2** : tallow (for candles, etc.) **3** : suet (for cooking)
secar {72} *v* : dry — **secarse** *vr* : dry (up) — **secador** *nm* : hair dryer

— **secadora** *nf* : (clothes) dryer
sección *nf, pl* **-ciones** : section
seco, -ca *adj* **1** : dry **2** : dried (of fruits, etc.) **3** TAJANTE : sharp, brusque **4** *fam* : thin, skinny **5 a secas** : simply, just **6 en seco** : suddenly
secretar *vt* : secrete — **secreción** *nf, pl* **-ciones** : secretion
secretario, -ria *n* : secretary — **secretaría** *nf* : secretariat
secreto, -ta *adj* : secret — **secreto** *nm* **1** : secret **2 en secreto, -ta** : in confidence
secta *nf* : sect
sector *nm* : sector
secuaz *nmf, pl* **-cuaces** : follower, henchman
secuela *nf* : consequence
secuencia *nf* : sequence
secuestrar *vt* **1** : kidnap **2** : hijack (an airplane, etc.) **3** EMBARGAR : confiscate, seize — **secuestrador, -dora** *n* **1** : kidnapper **2** : hijacker (of

secador^M
hair dryer

rejilla^F de salida^F de aire^M
air-outlet grill

botón^M selector de velocidad^F
speed selector switch

interruptor^M
on-off switch

botón^M selector de temperatura^F
heat selector switch

mango^M
handle

difusor^M
diffuser

cable^M de alimentación^F
power supply cord

sedes *F*
seats

puf *M*
ottoman

escabel *M*
stool

banco *M*
bench

silla *F* **cojín** *M*
bean bag chair

an airplane, etc.) — **secuestro** *nm* **1**
: kidnapping **2** : hijacking (of an
airplane, etc.) **3** : seizure (of goods)
secular *adj* : secular
secundar *vt* : support, second —
secundario, -ria *adj* : secondary
sed *nf* **1** : thirst **2 tener sed** : be thirsty
seda *nf* : silk

sedal *nm* : fishing line
sedar *vt* : sedate — **sedante** *adj*
& *nm* : sedative
▸ **sede** *nf* **1** : seat, headquarters
2 Santa Sede : Holy See
sedentario, -ria *adj* : sedentary
sedición *nf, pl* **-ciones** : sedition
— **sedicioso, -sa** *adj* : seditious
sediento, -ta *adj* : thirsty
sedimento *nm* : sediment
sedoso, -sa *adj* : silky, silken
seducir {61} *vt* **1** : seduce **2** ATRAER
: captivate, charm — **seducción** *nf,*
pl **-ciones** : seduction — **seductor,**
-tora *adj* **1** : seductive **2** ENCANTADOR :
charming — **seductor, -tora** *n* : seducer
segar {49} *vt* : reap — **segador,**
-dora *n* : reaper, harvester
seglar *adj* : lay, secular — **seglar** *nm*
: layperson, layman *m,* laywoman *f*
segmento *nm* : segment
segregar {52} *vt* : segregate —
segregación *nf, pl* **-ciones** : segregation
seguir {75} *vt* : follow — *vi* : go on,
continue — **seguida**: **en seguida** *adv phr*
: right away — **seguido** *adv* **1** : straight
(ahead) **2** *Lat* : often — **seguido, -da** *adj* **1**
: continuous **2** CONSECUTIVO : consecutive
— **seguidor, -dora** *n* : follower
según *prep* : according to — **según** *adv*
: it depends — **según** *conj* : as, just as
segundo, -da *adj* : second —
segundo, -da *n* : second (one) —
segundo *nm* : second (unit of time)
seguro, -ra *adj* **1** : safe **2** FIRME : secure
3 CIERTO : sure, certain **4** FIABLE : reliable
— **seguramente** *adv* : for sure, surely
— **seguridad** *nf* **1** : safety **2** GARANTÍA :
security **3** CERTEZA : certainty **4** CONFIANZA
: confidence — **seguro** *adv* : certainly —
seguro *nm* **1** : insurance **2** : safety (device)
seis *adj & nm* : six — **seiscientos,**
-tas *adj* : six hundred —
seiscientos *nms & pl* : six hundred
▸ **seísmo** *nm* : earthquake
selección *nf, pl* **-ciones** : selection
— **seleccionar** *vt* : select, choose
— **selectivo, -va** *adj* : selective —
selecto, -ta *adj* : choice, select
sellar *vt* **1** : seal **2** TIMBRAR : stamp
— **sello** *nm* **1** : seal **2** TIMBRE : stamp
3 *or* **sello distintivo** : hallmark
selva *nf* **1** : jungle **2** BOSQUE : forest
semáforo *nm* : traffic light
semana *nf* : week — **semanal** *adj* :

weekly — **semanario** *nm* : weekly
semántica *nf* : semantics —
semántico, -ca *adj* : semantic
semblante *nm* **1** : countenance,
face **2** APARIENCIA : look
sembrar {55} *vt* **1** : sow **2**
sembrar de : strew with
semejar *vi* : resemble — **semejarse** *vr*
: look alike — **semejante** *adj* **1** :
similar **2** TAL : such — **semejante** *nm* :
fellowman — **semejanza** *nf* : similarity
semen *nm* : semen — **semental** *nm* **1**
: stud **2 caballo semental** : stallion
semestre *nm* : semester
semiconductor *nm* : semiconductor
semifinal *nf* : semifinal
semilla *nf* : seed — **semillero** *nm* **1**
: nursery (for plants) **2** HERVIDERO
: hotbed, breeding ground
seminario *nm* **1** : seminary
2 CURSO : seminar, course
sémola *nf* : semolina
senado *nm* : senate —
senador, -dora *n* : senator
sencillo, -lla *adj* **1** : simple **2** ÚNICO
: single — **sencillez** *nf* : simplicity
senda *nf or* **sendero** *nm* : path, way
sendos, -das *adj pl* : each, both
senil *adj* : senile
seno *nm* **1** : breast, bosom **2** : sinus
(in anatomy) **3 seno materno** : womb
sensación *nf, pl* **-ciones** : feeling,
sensation — **sensacional** *adj* :
sensational — **sensacionalista** *adj*
: sensationalistic, lurid
sensato, -ta *adj* : sensible —
sensatez *nf* : good sense
sensible *adj* **1** : sensitive **2** APRECIABLE
: considerable, significant —
sensibilidad *nf* : sensitivity — **sensitivo,**
-va *or* **sensorial** *adj* : sense, sensory
sensual *adj* : sensual, sensuous
— **sensualidad** *nf* : sensuality
sentar {55} *vt* **1** : seat, sit **2** ESTABLECER
: establish, set — *vi* **1** : suit **2**
sentar bien a : agree with (of food or
drink) — **sentarse** *vr* : sit (down) —
sentado, -da *adj* **1** : sitting, seated **2**
dar por sentado : take for granted
sentencia *nf* **1** FALLO : sentence,
judgment **2** MÁXIMA : saying —
sentenciar *vt* : sentence
sentido, -da *adj* **1** : heartfelt, sincere
2 SENSIBLE : touchy, sensitive —
sentido *nm* **1** : sense **2** CONOCIMIENTO

seísmo^M
earthquake

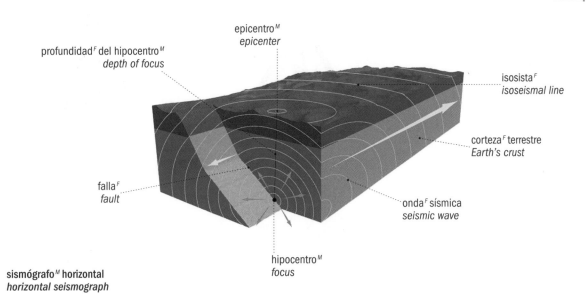

epicentro^M
epicenter

profundidad^F del hipocentro^M
depth of focus

isosista^F
isoseismal line

corteza^F terrestre
Earth's crust

falla^F
fault

onda^F sísmica
seismic wave

hipocentro^M
focus

sismógrafo^M horizontal
horizontal seismograph

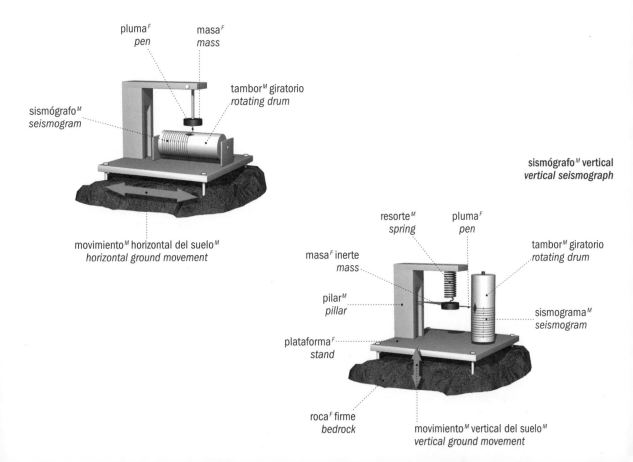

pluma^F
pen

masa^F
mass

tambor^M giratorio
rotating drum

sismógrafo^M
seismogram

movimiento^M horizontal del suelo^M
horizontal ground movement

sismógrafo^M vertical
vertical seismograph

resorte^M
spring

pluma^F
pen

tambor^M giratorio
rotating drum

masa^F inerte
mass

pilar^M
pillar

sismograma^M
seismogram

plataforma^F
stand

roca^F firme
bedrock

movimiento^M vertical del suelo^M
vertical ground movement

símbolos^M de seguridad^F
safety symbols

inflamable
flammable

alta tensión^F
high voltage

veneno^M
poison

protección^F de la cabeza^F
head protection

protección del sistema^M respiratorio
respiratory system protection

protección^F de los oídos^M
ear protection

: consciousness **3** DIRECCIÓN : direction **4 doble sentido** : double entendre **5 sentido común** : common sense **6 sentido del humor** : sense of humor **7 sentido único** : one-way
sentimiento *nm* **1** : feeling, emotion **2** PESAR : regret — **sentimental** *adj* : sentimental — **sentimentalismo** *nm* : sentimentality
sentir {76} *vt* **1** : feel **2** OÍR : hear **3** LAMENTAR : be sorry for **4 lo siento** : I'm sorry — *vi* : feel — **sentirse** *vr* : feel
seña *nf* **1** : sign **2 señas** *nfpl* DIRECCIÓN : address **3 señas particulares** : distinguishing marks
señal *nf* **1** : signal **2** AVISO, INDICIO : sign **3** DEPÓSITO : deposit **4 dar señales de** : show signs of **5 en señal de** : as a token of — **señalado, -da** *adj* : notable — **señalar** *vt* **1** INDICAR : indicate, point out **2** MARCAR : mark **3** FIJAR : fix, set — **señalarse** *vr* : distinguish oneself
señor, -ñora *n* **1** : gentleman *m*, man *m*, lady *f*, woman *f* **2** : Sir *m*, Madam *f* **3** : Mr. *m*, Mrs. *f* **4 señora** : wife *f* **5 el Señor** : the Lord — **señorial** *adj*

: stately — **señorita** *nf* **1** : young lady, young woman **2** : Miss
señuelo *nm* **1** : decoy **2** TRAMPA : **bait, lure**
separar *vt* **1** : separate **2** QUITAR : detach, remove **3** APARTAR : move away **4** DESTITUIR : dismiss — **separarse** *vr* **1** APARTARSE : separate **2** : part company — **separación** *nf, pl* **-ciones** : separation — **separado, -da** *adj* **1** : separate **2** : separated (of persons) **3 por separado** : separately
septentrional *adj* : northern
séptico, -ca *adj* : septic
septiembre *nm* : September
séptimo, -ma *adj* : seventh — **séptimo, -ma** *n* : seventh
sepulcro *nm* : tomb, sepulchre — **sepultar** *vt* : bury — **sepultura** *nf* **1** : burial **2** TUMBA : grave
sequedad *nf* : dryness — **sequía** *nf* : drought
séquito *nm* : retinue, entourage
ser {77} *vi* **1** : be **2 a no ser que** : unless **3 ¿cuánto es?** : how much is it? **4 es más** : what's more **5 ser de** : belong

to **6 ser de** : come from **7 son las diez** : it's ten o'clock — **ser** *nm* **1** ENTE : being **2 ser humano** : human being
serbio, -bia *adj* : Serb, Serbian
serenar *vt* : calm — **serenarse** *vr* : calm down — **serenata** *nf* : serenade — **serenidad** *nf* : serenity — **sereno, -na** *adj* **1** : serene, calm **2** : fair, clear (of weather) — **sereno** *nm* : night watchman
serie *nf* **1** : series **2 fabricación en serie** : mass production **3 fuera de serie** : extraordinary — **serial** *nm* : serial
serio, -ria *adj* **1** : serious **2** RESPONSABLE : reliable **3 en serio** : seriously — **seriedad** *nf* : seriousness
sermón *nm, pl* **-mones** : sermon — **sermonear** *vt* : lecture, reprimand
serpentear *vi* : twist, wind — **serpiente** *nf* **1** : serpent, snake **2 serpiente de cascabel** : rattlesnake
serrado, -da *adj* : serrated
serrano, -na *adj* **1** : mountain **2 jamón serrano** : cured ham
serrar {55} *vt* : saw — **serrín** *nm, pl* **-rrines** : sawdust — **serrucho** *nm* : saw, handsaw

servicio *nm* **1** : service **2** servicios *nmpl* : restroom — **servicial** *adj* : obliging, helpful — **servidor, -dora** *n* **1** : servant **2 su seguro servidor** : yours truly — **servidumbre** *nf* **1** : servitude **2** CRIADOS : help, servants *pl* — **servil** *adj* : servile

servilleta *nf* : napkin

servir {54} *vt* : serve — *vi* **1** : work, function **2** VALER : be of use — **servirse** *vr* **1** : help oneself **2 sírvase sentarse** : please have a seat

sesenta *adj & nm* : sixty

sesgo *nm* : bias, slant

sesión *nf, pl* **-siones 1** : session **2** : showing (of a film), performance (of a play)

seso *nm* : brain — **sesudo, -da** *adj* **1** : sensible **2** *fam* : brainy

seta *nf* : mushroom

setecientos, -tas *adj* : seven hundred — **setecientos** *nms & pl* : seven hundred

setenta *adj & nm* : seventy

setiembre *nm* → **septiembre**

seto *nm* **1** : fence **2 seto vivo** : hedge

seudónimo *nm* : pseudonym

severo, -ra *adj* **1** : harsh, severe **2** : strict (of a teacher, etc.) — **severidad** *nf* : severity

sexagésimo, -ma *adj & n* : sixtieth

sexo *nm* : sex — **sexismo** *nm* : sexism — **sexista** *adj & nmf* : sexist

sexteto *nm* : sextet

sexto, -ta *adj & n* : sixth

sexual *adj* : sexual — **sexualidad** *nf* : sexuality

sexy *adj, pl* sexy *or* sexys : sexy

si *conj* **1** : if **2** (*in indirect questions*) : whether **3 si bien** : although **4 si no** : otherwise, or else

sí[1] *adv* **1** : yes **2 creo que sí** : I think so **3 porque sí** *fam* : (just) because — **sí** *nm* : consent

sí[2] *pron* **1 de por sí** *or* **en sí** : by itself, in itself, per se **2 fuera de sí** : beside oneself **3 para sí (mismo)** : to himself, to herself, for himself, for herself **4 entre sí** : among themselves

sico- → **psico-**

SIDA *or* sida *nm* : AIDS

siderurgia *nf* : iron and steel industry

sidra *nf* : (hard) cider

siega *nf* **1** : harvesting **2** : harvest (time)

siembra *nf* **1** : sowing **2** : sowing season

siempre *adv* **1** : always **2** *Lat* : still **3 para siempre** : forever, for good **4 siempre que** : whenever, every time **5 siempre que** *or* **siempre y cuando** : provided that

sien *nf* : temple

sierra *nf* **1** : saw **2** CORDILLERA : mountain range **3 la sierra** : the mountains *pl*

siervo, -va *n* : slave

siesta *nf* : nap, siesta

siete *adj & nm* : seven

sífilis *nf* : syphilis

sifón *nm, pl* **-fones** : siphon

sigilo *nm* : secrecy

sigla *nf* : acronym, abbreviation

siglo *nm* **1** : century **2 hace siglos** : for ages

significar {72} *vt* **1** : mean, signify **2** EXPRESAR : express — **significación** *nf, pl* **-ciones 1** : significance, importance **2** : meaning (of a word, etc.) — **significado, -da** *adj* : well-known — **significado** *nm* : meaning — **significativo, -va** *adj* : significant

signo *nm* **1** : sign **2 signo de admiración** : exclamation point **3 signo de interrogación** : question mark

siguiente *adj* : next, following

sílaba *nf* : syllable

silbar *v* **1** : whistle **2** ABUCHEAR : hiss, boo — **silbato** *nm* : whistle — **silbido** *nm* **1** : whistle, whistling **2** ABUCHEO : hiss, booing

silenciar *vt* : silence — **silenciador** *nm* : muffler — **silencio** *nm* : silence — **silencioso, -sa** *adj* : silent, quiet

silicio *nm* : silicon

silla *nf* **1** : chair **2** *or* **silla de montar** : saddle **3 silla de ruedas** : wheelchair — **sillón** *nm, pl* **-llones** : armchair, easy chair

silo *nm* : silo

silueta *nf* **1** : silhouette **2** CONTORNO : outline, shape

silvestre *adj* : wild

silvicultura *nf* : forestry

▸ **símbolo** *nm* : symbol — **simbólico, -ca** *adj* : symbolic — **simbolismo** *nm* : symbolism — **simbolizar** {21} *vt* : symbolize

simetría *nf* : symmetry — **simétrico, -ca** *adj* : symmetrical, symmetric

simiente *nf* : seed

símil *nm* **1** : simile **2** COMPARACIÓN : comparison — **similar** *adj* : similar, alike

simio *nm* : ape

simpatía *nf* **1** : liking, affection **2** AMABILIDAD : friendliness — **simpático, -ca** *adj* **1** : nice, likeable **2** AMABLE : pleasant, kind — **simpatizante** *nmf* : sympathizer — **simpatizar** {21} *vi* **1** : get along, hit it off **2 simpatizar con** : sympathize with

simple *adj* **1** SENCILLO : simple **2** MERO : pure, sheer **3** TONTO : simpleminded — **simple** *n* : fool, simpleton — **simpleza** *nf* **1** : simpleness **2** TONTERÍA : silly thing — **simplicidad** *nf* : simplicity — **simplificar** {72} *vt* : simplify

simposio *or* simposium *nm* : symposium

simular *vt* **1** : simulate **2** FINGIR : feign — **simulacro** *nm* : simulation, drill

simultáneo, -nea *adj* : simultaneous

sin *prep* **1** : without **2 sin que** : without

sinagoga *nf* : synagogue

sincero, -ra *adj* : sincere — **sinceramente** *adv* : sincerely — **sinceridad** *nf* : sincerity

síncopa *nf* : syncopation

sincronizar {21} *vt* : synchronize

sindicato *nm* : (labor) union — **sindical** *adj* : union, labor

síndrome *nm* : syndrome

sinfín *nm* **1** : endless number **2 un sinfín de** : no end of

sinfonía *nf* : symphony — **sinfónico, -ca** *adj* : symphonic

singular *adj* **1** : exceptional, outstanding **2** PECULIAR : peculiar **3** : singular (in grammar) — **singular** *nm* : singular — **singularizar** {21} *vt* : single out — **singularizarse** *vr* : stand out

siniestro, -tra *adj* **1** : sinister **2** IZQUIERDO : left — **siniestro** *nm* : disaster

sinnúmero *nm* → **sinfín**

sino *conj* **1** : but, rather **2** EXCEPTO : except, save

sinónimo, -ma *adj* : synonymous — **sinónimo** *nm* : synonym

sinopsis *nfs & pl* : synopsis

sinrazón *nf, pl* **-zones** : wrong

síntaxis *nfs & pl* : syntax

síntesis *nfs & pl* : synthesis — **sintético, -ca** *adj* : synthetic — **sintetizar** {21} *vt* **1** : synthesize **2** RESUMIR : summarize

síntoma *nm* : symptom — **sintomático, -ca** *adj* : symptomatic

sintonía *nf* **1** : tuning in (of a radio) **2 en sintonía con** : in tune with — **sintonizar** {21} *vt* : tune (in) to

sinuoso, -sa *adj* : winding

sinvergüenza *nmf* : scoundrel

sionismo *nm* : Zionism

siquiera *adv* **1** : at least **2 ni siquiera** : not even — **siquiera** *conj* : even if

sirena *nf* **1** : mermaid **2** : siren
(of an ambulance, etc.)
sirio, -ria *adj* : Syrian
sirviente, -ta *n* : servant, maid *f*
sisear *vi* : hiss — **siseo** *nm* : hiss
sismo *nm* : earthquake —
sísmico, -ca *adj* : seismic
sistema *nm* **1** : system **2 por**
sistema : systematically —
sistemático, -ca *adj* : systematic
sitiar *vt* : besiege
sitio *nm* **1** : place, site **2** ESPACIO
: room, space **3** CERCO : siege **4**
en cualquier sitio : anywhere
situar {3} *vt* : situate, place —
situarse *vr* **1** : be located **2** ESTABLECERSE
: get oneself established — **situación** *nf,*
pl -**ciones** : situation, position —
situado, -da *adj* : situated, placed
slip *nm* : briefs *pl*, underpants *pl*
smoking *nm* : tuxedo
so *prep* : under
sobaco *nm* : armpit
sobar *vt* **1** : finger, handle **2** : knead
(dough) — **sobado, -da** *adj* : worn, shabby
soberanía *nf* : sovereignty —
soberano, -na *adj & n* : sovereign
soberbia *nf* : pride, arrogance —
soberbio, -bia *adj* : proud, arrogant
sobornar *vt* : bribe — **soborno** *nm* **1**
: bribe **2** : (action of) bribery
sobrar *vi* **1** : be more than enough
2 RESTAR : be left over — **sobra** *nf* **1**
: surplus **2 de sobra** : to spare **3**
sobrars *nfpl* : leftovers — **sobrado,**
-da *adj* : more than enough —
sobrante *adj* : remaining
sobre[1] *nm* : envelope
sobre[2] *prep* **1** : on, on top of **2** POR ENCIMA
DE : over, above **3** ACERCA DE : about **4**
sobre todo : especially, above all
sobrecama *nmf Lat* : bedspread
sobrecargar {52} *vt* :
overload, overburden
sobrecoger {15} *vt* : startle —
sobrecogerse *vr* : be startled
sobrecubierta *nf* : dust jacket
sobredosis *nfs & pl* : overdose
sobreentender {56} *vt* : infer,
understand — **sobreentenderse** *vr*
: be understood
sobreestimar *vt* : overestimate
sobregiro *nm* : overdraft
sobrellevar *vt* : endure, bear
sobremesa *nf* **de sobremesa**

: after-dinner
sobrenatural *adj* : supernatural
sobrenombre *nm* : nickname
sobrentender → **sobreentender**
sobrepasar *vt* : exceed
sobreponer {60} *vt* **1** :
superimpose **2** ANTEPONER :
put before — **sobreponerse** *vr*
sobreponerse a : overcome
sobresalir {73} *vi* **1** : protrude
2 DESTACARSE : stand out —
sobresaliente *adj* : outstanding
sobresaltar *vt* : startle —
sobresaltarse *vr* : start, jump up
— **sobresalto** *nm* : fright
sobrestimar → **sobreestimar**
sobretodo *nm* : overcoat
sobrevenir {87} *vi* : happen, ensue
sobrevivencia *nf* → **supervivencia**
sobreviviente *adj & nmf*
→ **superviviente**
sobrevivir *vi* : survive — *vt* : outlive
sobrevolar {19} *vt* : fly over
sobriedad *nf* **1** : sobriety **2**
MODERACIÓN : restraint
sobrino, -na *n* : nephew *m*, niece *f*
sobrio , -bria *adj* : sober
socarrón, -rrona *adj, mpl*
-**rrones** : sarcastic
socavar *vt* : undermine
sociable *adj* : sociable — **social** *adj*
: social — **socialismo** *nm* : socialism
— **socialista** *adj & nmf* : socialist —
sociedad *nf* **1** : society **2** EMPRESA
: company **3 sociedad anónima** :
incorporated company — **socio,**
-**cia** *n* **1** : partner **2** MIEMBRO :
member — **sociología** *nf* : sociology
— **sociólogo, -ga** *n* : sociologist
socorrer *vt* : help — **socorrista** *nmf*
: lifeguard — **socorro** *nm* : help
soda *nf* : soda (water)
sodio *nf* : sodium
sofá *nm* : couch, sofa
sofisticación *nf, pl* -**ciones** :
sophistication — **sofisticado,**
-**da** *adj* : sophisticated
sofocar {72} *vt* **1** : suffocate,
smother **2** : put out (a fire), stifle (a
rebellion, etc.) — **sofocarse** *vr* **1**
: suffocate **2** *fam* : get upset —
sofocante *adj* : suffocating, stifling
sofreír {66} *vt* : sauté
soga *nf* : rope
soja *nf* → **soya**

sojuzgar *vt* : subdue, subjugate
sol *nm* **1** : sun **2 hacer sol** : be sunny
solamente *adv* : only, just
solapa *nf* **1** : lapel (of a jacket) **2** :
flap (of an envelope) — **solapado,**
-**da** *adj* : secret, underhanded
solar[1] *adj* : solar, sun
solar[2] *nm* : lot, site
solariego, -ga *adj* : ancestral
solaz *nm, pl* -**laces 1** : solace **2** DESCANSO
: relaxation — **solazarse** {21} *vr* : relax
soldado *nm* **1** : soldier **2**
soldado raso : private
soldar {19} *vt* : weld, solder —
soldador *nm* : soldering iron —
soldador, -dora *n* : welder
soleado, -da *adj* : sunny
soledad *nf* : loneliness, solitude
solemne *adj* : solemn —
solemnidad *nf* : solemnity
soler {78} *vi* **1** : be in the habit of **2 suele**
llegar tarde : he usually arrives late
solicitar *vt* **1** : request, solicit **2** : apply
for (a job, etc.) — **solicitante** *nmf*
: applicant — **solícito, -ta** *adj* :
solicitous, obliging — **solicitud** *nf* **1**
: concern **2** PETICIÓN : request **3**
: application (for a job, etc.)
solidaridad *nf* : solidarity
sólido, -da *adj* **1** : solid **2** : sound (of an
argument, etc.) — **sólido** *nm* : solid —
solidez *nf* : solidity — **solidificar** {72} *vt* :
solidify — **solidificarse** *vr* : solidify, harden
soliloquio *nm* : soliloquy
solista *nmf* : soloist
solitario, -ria *adj* **1** : solitary **2**
AISLADO : lonely, deserted — **solitario,**
-**ria** *n* : recluse — **solitaria** *nf* :
tapeworm — **solitario** *nm* : solitaire
sollozar {21} *vi* : sob — **sollozo** *nm* : sob
solo, -la *adj* **1** : alone **2** AISLADO
: lonely **3 a solas** : alone, by
oneself — **solo** *nm* : solo
sólo *adv* : just, only
solomillo *nm* : sirloin
solsticio *nm* : solstice
soltar {19} *vt* **1** : release **2** DEJAR CAER
: let go of, drop **3** DESATAR : unfasten,
undo — **soltarse** *vr* **1** : break free
2 DESATARSE : come undone
soltero, -ra *adj* : single, unmarried
— **soltero, -ra** *n* **1** : bachelor *m*,
single woman *f* **2 apellido de**
soltera : maiden name
soltura *nf* **1** : looseness **2** : fluency (in

language) **3** AGILIDAD : agility, ease
soluble *adj* : soluble
solución *nf, pl* **-ciones** : solution
— **solucionar** *vt* : solve, resolve
solventar *vt* **1** : settle, pay **2** RESOLVER :
resolve — **solvente** *adj & nm* : solvent
sombra *nf* **1** : shadow **2** : shade (of a
tree, etc.) **3 sombras** *nfpl* : darkness,
shadows — **sombreado, -da** *adj* : shady
sombrero *nm* : hat
sombrilla *nf* : parasol, umbrella
sombrío, -bría *adj* : dark,
somber, gloomy
somero, -ra *adj* : superficial
someter *vt* **1** : subjugate **2** SUBORDINAR
: subordinate **3** : subject (to treatment,
etc.) **4** PRESENTAR : submit, present
— **someterse** *vr* **1** : submit, yield
2 someterse a : undergo
somnífero, -ra *adj* : soporific —
somnífero *nm* : sleeping pill —
somnoliento, -ta *adj* : drowsy, sleepy
somos → ser
son[1] → ser
son[2] *nm* **1** : sound **2 en son
de** : as, in the manner of
sonajero *nm* : (baby's) rattle
sonámbulo, -la *n* : sleepwalker
sonar {19} *vi* **1** : sound **2** : ring (as
a bell) **3** : look or sound familiar **4
sonar a** : sound like — **sonarse** *vr or*
sonarse las narices : blow one's nose
sonata *nf* : sonata
sondear *vt* **1** : sound, probe **2**
: survey, sound out (opinions,
etc.) — **sondeo** *nm* **1** : sounding,
probing **2** ENCUESTA : survey, poll
soneto *nm* : sonnet
sónico, -ca *adj* : sonic
sonido *nm* : sound
sonoro, -ra *adj* **1** : resonant,
sonorous **2** RUIDOSO : loud
sonreír {66} *vi* : smile —
sonreírse *vr* : smile — **sonriente** *adj*
: smiling — **sonrisa** *nf* : smile
sonrojar *vt* : cause to blush
— **sonrojarse** *vr* : blush —
sonrojo *nm* : blush
sonrosado, -da *adj* : rosy, pink
sonsacar {72} *vt* : wheedle (out)
soñar {19} *v* **1** : dream **2 soñar con**
: dream about **3 soñar despierto** :
daydream — **soñador, -dora** *adj* :
dreamy — **soñador, -dora** *n* : dreamer
— **soñoliento, -ta** *adj* : sleepy, drowsy

sopa *nf* : soup
sopesar *vt* : weigh, consider
soplar *vi* : blow — *vt* : blow out,
blow off, blow up — **soplete** *nm* :
blowtorch — **soplo** *nm* : puff, gust
soplón, -plona *n, pl* **-plones** *fam* : sneak
sopor *nm* : drowsiness —
soporífero, -ra *adj* : soporific
soportar *vt* **1** SOSTENER : support **2**
AGUANTAR : bear — **soporte** *nm* : support
soprano *nmf* : soprano
sor *nf* : Sister (in religion)
sorber *vt* **1** : sip **2** ABSORBER : absorb
3 CHUPAR : suck up — **sorbete** *nm*
: sherbet — **sorbo** *nm* **1** : sip,
swallow **2 beber a sorbos** : sip
sordera *nf* : deafness

sórdido, -da *adj* : sordid, squalid
sordo, -da *adj* **1** : deaf **2** : muted (of a
sound) — **sordomudo, -da** *n* : deaf-mute
sorna *nf* : sarcasm
sorprender *vt* : surprise —
sorprenderse *vr* : be surprised
— **sorprendente** *adj* : surprising
— **sorpresa** *nf* : surprise
sortear *vt* **1** : raffle off, draw
lots for **2** ESQUIVAR : dodge —
sorteo *nm* : drawing, raffle
sortija *nf* **1** : ring **2** : ringlet (of hair)
sortilegio *nm* **1** HECHIZO : spell
2 HECHICERÍA : sorcery
sosegar {49} *vt* : calm, pacify
— **sosegarse** *vr* : calm down
— **sosegado, -da** *adj* : calm,

sombreros[M]
hats

sombrero[M] de campana[F]
cloche

sombrero[M] de hongo[M]
derby

sombrero[M] de fieltro[M]
fedora

panamá[M]
panama

chistera[F]
top hat

pamela[F]
cartwheel hat

contaminación^F **del suelo**^M
soil pollution

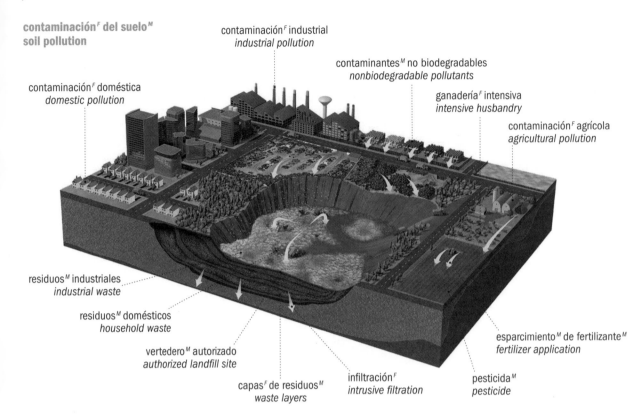

contaminación^F industrial
industrial pollution

contaminantes^M no biodegradables
nonbiodegradable pollutants

contaminación^F doméstica
domestic pollution

ganadería^F intensiva
intensive husbandry

contaminación^F agrícola
agricultural pollution

residuos^M industriales
industrial waste

residuos^M domésticos
household waste

esparcimiento^M de fertilizante^M
fertilizer application

vertedero^M autorizado
authorized landfill site

capas^F de residuos^M
waste layers

infiltración^F
intrusive filtration

pesticida^M
pesticide

---

tranquil — **sosiego** *nm* : calm
soslayo: de soslayo *adv phr*
: obliquely, sideways
soso, -sa *adj* **1** : insipid,
tasteless **2** ABURRIDO : **dull**
sospechar *vt* : suspect — **sospecha** *nf*
: suspicion — **sospechoso, -sa** *adj* :
suspicious — **sospechoso, -sa** *n* : suspect
sostener {80} *vt* **1** : support **2** SUJETAR
: hold **3** MANTENER : **sustain, maintain** —
sostenerse *vr* **1** : stand (up) **2** CONTINUAR
: remain **3** SUSTENTARSE : support oneself
— **sostén** *nm, pl* **-tenes 1** APOYO : support
2 SUSTENTO : sustenance **3** : brassiere, bra
— **sostenido, -da** *adj* **1** : sustained **2** :
sharp (in music) — **sostenido** *nm* : sharp
sótano *nm* : basement
soterrar {55} *vt* **1** : bury **2** ESCONDER : hide
soto *nm* : grove
soviético, -ca *adj* : Soviet
soy → **ser**
soya *nf* : soy
Sr. *nm* : Mr. — **Sra.** *nf* : Mrs., Ms.

— **Srta.** *or* **Srita.** *nf* : Miss, Ms.
su *adj* **1** : his, her, its, their,
one's **2** (*formal*) : your
suave *adj* **1** : soft **2** LISO : smooth
3 APACIBLE : gentle, mild —
suavidad *nf* **1** : softness, smoothness
2 APACIBILIDAD : mildness, gentleness
— **suavizar** {21} *vt* : soften, smooth
subalimentado, -da *adj* :
undernourished, underfed
subalterno, -na *adj* **1** SUBORDINADO :
subordinate **2** SECUNDARIO : secondary
— **subalterno, -na** *n* : subordinate
subarrendar {55} *vt* : sublet
subasta *nf* : auction —
subastar *vt* : auction (off)
subcampeón, -peona *n,*
mpl **-peones** : runner-up
subcomité *nm* : subcommittee
subconsciente *adj & nm* : subconscious
subdesarrollado, -da *adj*
: underdeveloped
subdirector, -tora *n* :

assistant manager
súbdito, -ta *n* : subject
subdividir *vt* : subdivide —
subdivisión *nf, pl* **-siones** : subdivision
subestimar *vt* : underestimate
subir *vt* **1** : climb, go up **2** LLEVAR : bring
up, take up **3** AUMENTAR : raise — *vi* **1** :
go up, come up **2** subir a : get in (a car),
get on (a bus, etc.) — **subirse** *vr* **1** :
climb (up) **2** subirse a : get in (a car), get
on (a bus, etc.) **3** subirse a la cabeza :
go to one's head — **subida** *nf* **1** : ascent,
climb **2** AUMENTO : rise **3** PENDIENTE :
slope — **subido, -da** *adj* **1** : bright,
strong **2** subido de tono : risqué
súbito, -ta *adj* **1** : sudden **2** de
súbito : all of a sudden, suddenly
subjetivo, -va *adj* : subjective
subjuntivo, -va *adj* : subjunctive —
subjuntivo *nm* : subjunctive (case)
sublevar *vt* : stir up, incite to rebellion —
sublevarse *vr* : rebel — **sublevación** *nf,*
pl **-ciones** : uprising, rebellion

sublime *adj* : sublime
submarino, -na *adj* : underwater
— **submarino** *nm* : submarine —
submarinismo *nm* : scuba diving
subordinar *vt* : subordinate —
subordinado, -da *adj & n* : subordinate
subproducto *nm* : by-product
subrayar *vt* **1** : underline **2**
ENFATIZAR : emphasize, stress
subrepticio, -cia *adj* : surreptitious
subsanar *vt* **1** : rectify, correct
2 : make up for (a deficiency),
overcome (an obstacle)
subscribir → **suscribir**
subsidio *nm* : subsidy, benefit
subsiguiente *adj* : subsequent
subsistir *vi* **1** : live, subsist **2** SOBREVIVIR :
survive — **subsistencia** *nf* : subsistence
substancia *nf* → **sustancia**
subterfugio *nm* : subterfuge
subterráneo, -nea *adj* : underground,
subterranean — **subterráneo** *nm*
: underground passage
subtítulo *nm* : subtitle
suburbio *nm* **1** : suburb **2** : slum (outside
a city) — **suburbano, -na** *adj* : suburban
subvencionar *vt* : subsidize —
subvención *nf, pl* **-ciones** : subsidy, grant
subvertir {76} *vt* : subvert —
subversión *nf, pl* **-siones** : subversion
— **subversivo, -va** *adj & n* : subversive
subyacente *adj* : underlying
subyugar {52} *vt* : subjugate, subdue
succión *nf, pl* **-ciones** : suction —
succionar *vt* : suck up, draw in
sucedáneo *nm* : substitute
suceder *vi* **1** : happen, occur **2 suceder
a** : follow **3 suceda lo que suceda**
: come what may — **sucesión** *nf,
pl* **-siones** : succession — **sucesivo,
-va** *adj* : successive — **suceso** *nm* **1**
: event **2** INCIDENTE : incident —
sucesor, -sora *n* : successor
suciedad *nf* **1** : dirtiness
2 MUGRE : dirt, filth
sucinto, -ta *adj* : succinct, concise
sucio, -cia *adj* : dirty, filthy
suculento, -ta *adj* : succulent
sucumbir *vi* : succumb
sucursal *nf* : branch (of a business)
sudadera *nf* : sweatshirt —
sudado, -da *adj* : sweaty
sudafricano, -na *adj* : South African
sudamericano, -na *adj*
: South American

sudar *vi* : sweat
sudeste → **sureste**
sudoeste → **suroeste**
sudor *nm* : sweat — **sudoroso,
-sa** *adj* : sweaty
sueco, -ca *adj* : Swedish —
sueco *nm* : Swedish (language)
suegro, -gra *n* **1** : father-in-law *m*,
mother-in-law *f* **2 suegros** *nmpl* : in-laws
suela *nf* : sole (of a shoe)
sueldo *nm* : salary, wage
▸ **suelo** *nm* **1** : ground **2** : floor (in
a house) **3** TIERRA : soil, land
suelto, -ta *adj* : loose, free —
suelto *nm* : loose change
sueño *nm* **1** : dream **2 coger el sueño** :
get to sleep **3 tener sueño** : be sleepy
suero *nm* **1** : whey **2** :
serum (in medicine)
suerte *nf* **1** : luck, fortune **2** AZAR : chance
3 DESTINO : fate **4** CLASE : sort, kind **5 por
suerte** : luckily **6 tener suerte** : be lucky
suéter *nm* : sweater
suficiencia *nf* **1** CAPACIDAD :
competence, proficiency **2** PRESUNCIÓN
: smugness — **suficiente** *adj* **1** :
enough, sufficient **2** PRESUNTUOSO : smug
— **suficientemente** *adv* : enough
sufijo *nm* : suffix
sufragio *nm* : suffrage, vote
sufrir *vt* **1** : suffer **2** SOPORTAR : bear,
stand — *vi* : suffer — **sufrido, -da** *adj* **1**
: long-suffering **2** : sturdy, serviceable (of
clothing) — **sufrimiento** *nm* : suffering
sugerir {76} *vt* : suggest —
sugerencia *nf* : suggestion —
sugestión *nf, pl* **-tiones** : suggestion
— **sugestionable** *adj* : impressionable
— **sugestionar** *vt* : influence —
sugestivo, -va *adj* **1** : suggestive **2**
ESTIMULANTE : interesting, stimulating
suicidio *nm* : suicide — **suicida** *adj* :
suicidal — **suicida** *nmf* : suicide (victim)
— **suicidarse** *vr* : commit suicide
suite *nf* : suite
suizo, -za *adj* : Swiss
sujetar *vt* **1** : hold (on to) **2** FIJAR : fasten
3 DOMINAR : subdue — **sujetarse** *vr* **1**
sujetarse a : hold on to, cling to **2**
sujetarse a : abide by — **sujeción** *nf,
pl* **-ciones 1** : fastening **2** DOMINACIÓN
: subjection — **sujetador** *nm, Spain* :
brassiere, bra — **sujetapapeles** *nms & pl*
: paper clip — **sujeto, -ta** *adj* **1** : fastened
2 sujeto a : subject to — **sujeto** *nm* **1**

: individual **2** : subject (in grammar)
sulfuro *nm* : sulfur —
sulfúrico, -ca *adj* : sulfuric
sultán *nm, pl* **-tanes** : sultan
suma *nf* **1** : sum, total **2** : addition (in
mathematics) **3 en suma** : in short
— **sumamente** *adv* : extremely —
sumar *vt* **1** : add (up) **2** TOTALIZAR
: add up to, total — *vi* : add up —
sumarse *vr* **sumarse a** : join
sumario, -ria *adj* : concise
— **sumario** *nm* **1** : summary
2 : indictment (in law)
sumergir {35} *vt* : submerge,
plunge — **sumergirse** *vr* : be
submerged — **sumergible** *adj* :
waterproof (of a watch, etc.)
sumidero *nm* : drain
suministrar *vt* : supply, provide —
suministro *nm* : supply, provision
sumir *vt* : plunge, immerse —
sumirse *vr* **sumirse en** : sink into
sumisión *nf, pl* **-siones** : submission
— **sumiso, -sa** *adj* : submissive
sumo, -ma *adj* **1** : highest, supreme **2 de
suma importancia** : of great importance
suntuoso, -sa *adj* : sumptuous, lavish
super *or* **súper** *nm, fam* : supermarket
superabundancia *nf* : overabundance
superar *vt* **1** : surpass,
outdo **2** VENCER : overcome —
superarse *vr* : improve oneself
superávit *nm* : surplus
superestructura *nf* : superstructure
superficie *nf* **1** : surface **2** ÁREA :
area — **superficial** *adj* : superficial
superfluo, -flua *adj* : superfluous
superintendente *nmf* :
supervisor, superintendent
superior *adj* **1** : superior **2** : upper
(of a floor, etc.) **3 superior a** : above,
higher than — **superior** *nm* : superior
— **superioridad** *nf* : superiority
superlativo, -va *adj* : superlative
— **superlativo** *nm* : superlative
supermercado *nm* : supermarket
superpoblado, -da *adj* : overpopulated
supersónico, -ca *adj* : supersonic
superstición *nf, pl* **-ciones** : superstition
— **supersticioso, -sa** *adj* : superstitious
supervisar *vt* : supervise, oversee —
supervisión *nf, pl* **-siones** : supervision
— **supervisor, -sora** *n* : supervisor
supervivencia *nf* : survival
— **superviviente** *adj* : surviving

— **supervivencia** *nmf* : survivor
suplantar *vt* : supplant, replace
suplemento *nm* : supplement —
suplementario, -ria *adj* : supplementary
suplente *adj & nmf* : substitute
suplicar {72} *vt* : beg, entreat
— **súplica** *nf* : plea, entreaty
suplicio *nm* : ordeal, torture
suplir *vt* **1** : make up for **2**
REEMPLAZAR : replace
supo, etc. → **saber**
suponer {60} *vt* **1** : suppose, assume
2 SIGNIFICAR : mean **3** IMPLICAR :
involve, entail — **suposición** *nf,*
pl **-ciones** : supposition
supositorio *nm* : suppository
supremo, -ma *adj* : supreme —
supremacía *nf* : supremacy
suprimir *vt* **1** : suppress, eliminate
2 : delete (text) — **supresión** *nf,*
pl **-siones 1** : suppression,
elimination **2** : deletion (of text)
supuesto, -ta *adj* **1** : supposed,
alleged **2 por supuesto** : of course
— **supuesto** *nm* : assumption —
supuestamente *adv* : allegedly
sur *nm* **1** : south, South **2** : south
wind **3 del sur** : south, southerly
surafricano, -na → **sudafricano**
suramericano, -na → **sudamericano**
surcar {72} *vt* **1** : plow (earth) **2**
: cut through (air, water, etc.) —
surco *nm* : groove, furrow, rut
sureño, -ña *adj* : southern, Southern
— **sureño, -ña** *n* : Southerner
sureste *adj* **1** : southeast, southeastern
2 : southeasterly (of wind, etc.) —
sureste *nm* : southeast, Southeast
▸ **surf** *or* **surfing** *nm* : surfing
surgir {35} *vi* **1** : arise **2** APARECER : appear
— **surgimiento** *nm* : rise, emergence
suroeste *adj* **1** : southwest,
southwestern **2** : southwesterly
(of wind, etc.) — **suroeste** *nm*
: southwest, Southwest
surtir *vt* **1** : supply, provide **2**
surtir efecto : have an effect —
surtirse *vr* **surtirse de** : stock up
on — **surtido, -da** *adj* **1** : assorted,
varied **2** : stocked (with merchandise)
— **surtido** *nm* : assortment, selection
— **surtidor** *nm* : gas pump
susceptible *adj* **1** : susceptible,
sensitive **2 susceptible de** : capable
of — **susceptibilidad** *nf* : sensitivity

surf^M
surfing

escarpín^M
boot

alerón^F
skeg

tabla^F de surf^M
surfboard

surfista^M
surfer

suscitar *vt* : provoke, arouse
suscribir {33} *vt* **1** : sign (a formal
document) **2** RATIFICAR : endorse
— **suscribirse** *vr* **suscribirse a**
: subscribe to — **suscripción** *nf,*
pl **-ciones** : subscription —
suscriptor, -tora *n* : subscriber
susodicho, -cha *adj* : aforementioned
suspender *vt* **1** : suspend **2** COLGAR
: hang **3** *Spain* : fail (an exam, etc.) —
suspensión *nf, pl* **-siones** : suspension
— **suspenso** *nm* **1** *Spain* : failure
(in an exam, etc.) **2** *Lat* : suspense
suspicaz *adj, pl* **-caces** : suspicious
suspirar *vi* : sigh — **suspiro** *nm* : sigh
sustancia *nf* **1** : substance **2 sin**
sustancia : shallow, lacking substance
— **sustancial** *adj* : substantial, significant
— **sustancioso, -sa** *adj* : substantial, solid
sustantivo *nm* : noun
sustentar *vt* **1** : support **2** ALIMENTAR :
sustain, nourish **3** MANTENER : maintain
— **sustentarse** *vr* : support oneself —
sustentación *nf, pl* **-ciones** : support
— **sustento** *nm* **1** : means of support,

livelihood **2** ALIMENTO : sustenance
sustituir {41} *vt* : replace, substitute —
sustitución *nf, pl* **-ciones** : replacement,
substitution — **sustituto, -ta** *n* : substitute
susto *nm* : fright, scare
sustraer {81} *vt* **1** : remove, take
away **2** : subtract (in mathematics) —
sustraerse *vr* **sustraerse a** : avoid, evade
— **sustracción** *nf, pl* **-ciones** : subtraction
susurrar *vi* **1** : whisper **2** : murmur
(of water) **3** : rustle (of leaves, etc.)
— *vt* : whisper — **susurro** *nm* **1**
: whisper **2** : murmur (of water) **3** :
rustle, rustling (of leaves, etc.)
sutil *adj* **1** : delicate, fine **2** :
subtle (of fragrances, differences,
etc.) — **sutileza** *nf* : subtlety
sutura *nf* : suture
suyo, -ya *adj* **1** : his, her, its, one's,
theirs **2** (*formal*) : yours **3 un primo**
suyo : a cousin of his/hers — **suyo,**
-ya *pron* **1** : his, hers, its (own), one's
own, theirs **2** (*formal*) : yours
switch *nm* *Lat* : switch

t *nf* : t, 21st letter of the Spanish alphabet

taba *nf* : anklebone

tabaco *nm* : tobacco — **tabacalero, -ra** *adj* : tobacco

tábano *nm* : horsefly

taberna *nf* : tavern

tabicar {72} *vt* : wall up — **tabique** *nm* : thin wall, partition

tabla *nf* **1** : board, plank **2** LISTA : table, list **3 tabla de planchar** : ironing board **4 tablas** *nfpl* : stage, boards *pl* — **tablado** *nm* **1** : flooring **2** PLATAFORMA : platform **3** : (theater) stage — **tablero** *nm* **1** : bulletin board **2** : board (in games) **3** PIZARRA : blackboard **4 tablero de instrumentos** : dashboard, instrument panel

tableta *nf* **1** : tablet, pill **2** : bar (of chocolate)

tablilla *nf* : slat — **tablón** *nm, pl* **-lones 1** : plank, beam **2 tablilla de anuncios** : bulletin board

tabú *adj* : taboo — **tabú** *nm, pl* **-búes** *or* **-bús** : taboo

tabular *vt* : tabulate

taburete *nm* : stool

tacaño, -na *adj* : stingy, miserly

tacha *nf* **1** : flaw, defect **2 sin tacha** : flawless

tachar *vt* **1** : cross out, delete **2 tachar de** : accuse of, label as

tachón *nm, pl* **-chones** : stud, hobnail — **tachuela** *nf* : tack, hobnail

tácito, -ta *adj* : tacit

taciturno, -na *adj* : taciturn

taco *nm* **1** : stopper, plug **2** *Lat* : heel (of a shoe) **3** : cue (in billiards) **4** : taco (in cooking)

tacón *nm, pl* **-cones 1** : heel (of a shoe) **2 de tacón alto** : high-heeled

táctica *nf* : tactic, tactics *pl* — **táctico, -ca** *adj* : tactical

tacto *nm* **1** : (sense of) touch, feel **2** DELICADEZA : tact

tafetán *nm, pl* **-tanes** : taffeta

tailandés, -desa *adj* : Thai

taimado, -da *adj* : crafty, sly

tajar *vt* : cut, slice — **tajada** *nf* **1** : slice **2 sacar tajada** *fam* : get one's share — **tajante** *adj* : categorical — **tajo** *nm* **1** : cut, gash **2** ESCARPA : steep cliff

tal *adv* **1** : so, in such a way **2 con tal que** : provided that, as long as **3 ¿qué tal?** : how are you?, how's it going? — **tal** *adj* **1** : such, such a **2 tal vez** : maybe,

perhaps — **tal** *pron* **1** : such a one, such a thing **2 tal para cual** : two of a kind

taladrar *vt* : drill — **taladro** *nm* : drill

talante *nm* **1** HUMOR : mood **2** VOLUNTAD : willingness

talar *vt* : cut down, fell

talco *nm* : talcum powder

talego *nm* : sack

talento *nm* : talent — **talentoso, -sa** *adj* : talented

talismán *nm, pl* **-manes** : talisman, charm

talla *nf* **1** : sculpture, carving **2** ESTATURA : height **3** : size (in clothing) — **tallar** *vt* **1** : sculpt, carve **2** : measure (someone's height)

tallarín *nf, pl* **-rines** : noodle

talle *nm* **1** : waist, waistline **2** FIGURA : figure **3** : measurements *pl* (of clothing)

taller *nm* **1** : workshop **2** : studio (of an artist)

tallo *nm* : stalk, stem

talón *nm, pl* **-lones 1** : heel (of the foot) **2** : stub (of a check) — **talonario** *nm* : checkbook

taltuza *nf* : gopher

tamal *nm* : tamale

tamaño, -ña *adj* : such a, such a big — **tamaño** *nm* **1** : size **2 de tamaño natural** : life-size

tambalearse *vr* **1** : teeter, wobble **2** : stagger, totter (of persons)

también *adv* : too, as well, also

tambor *nm* : drum — **tamborilear** *vi* : drum

tamiz *nm* : sieve — **tamizar** {21} *vt* : sift

tampoco *adv* : neither, not either

tampón *nm, pl* **-pones 1** : tampon **2** : ink pad (for stamping)

tan *adv* **1** : so, so very **2 tan pronto como** : as soon as **3 tan sólo** : only, merely

tanda *nf* **1** TURNO : turn, shift **2** GRUPO : batch, lot, series

tangente *nf* : tangent

tangible *adj* : tangible

tango *nm* : tango

tanque *nm* : tank

tantear *vt* **1** : feel, grope **2** SOPESAR : size up, weigh — *vi* : feel one's way — **tanteador** *nm* : scoreboard — **tanteo** *nm* **1** : weighing, sizing up **2** PUNTUACIÓN : scoring (in sports)

tanto *adv* **1** : so much **2** (*in expressions of time*) : so long — **tanto** *nm* **1** : certain amount **2** : goal, point (in sports)

3 un tanto : somewhat, rather — **tanto, -ta** *adj* **1** : so much, so many **2** (*in comparisons*) : as much, as many **3** *fam* : however many — **tanto, -ta** *pron* **1** : so much, so many **2 entre tanto** : meanwhile **3 por lo tanto** : therefore

tañer {79} *vt* **1** : ring (a bell) **2** : play (a musical instrument)

tapa *nf* **1** : cover, top, lid **2** *Spain* : snack

tapacubos *nms & pl* : hubcap

tapar *vt* **1** : cover, put a lid on **2** OCULTAR : block out **3** ENCUBRIR : cover up — **tapadera** *nf* **1** : cover, lid **2** : front (to hide a deception)

tapete *nm* **1** : small rug, mat **2** : cover (for a table)

tapia *nf* : (adobe) wall, garden wall — **tapiar** *vt* **1** : wall in **2** : block off (a door, etc.)

tapicería *nf* **1** : upholstery **2** TAPIZ : tapestry — **tapicero, -ra** *n* : upholsterer

tapioca *nf* : tapioca

tapiz *nm, pl* **-pices** : tapestry — **tapizar** {21} *vt* : upholster

tapón *nm, pl* **-pones 1** : cork **2** : cap (for a bottle, etc.) **3** : plug, stopper (for a sink)

tapujo *nm* **sin tapujos** : openly, outright

taquigrafía *nf* : stenography, shorthand — **taquígrafo, -fa** *n* : stenographer

taquilla *nf* **1** : box office **2** RECAUDACIÓN : earnings *pl*, take — **taquillero, -ra** *adj* **un éxito taquillero** : a box-office hit

tarántula *nf* : tarantula

tararear *vt* : hum

tardar *vi* **1** : take a long time, be late **2 a más tardar** : at the latest — *vt* : take (time) — **tardanza** *nf* : lateness, delay — **tarde** *adv* **1** : late **2 tarde o temprano** : sooner or later — **tarde** *nf* **1** : afternoon, evening **2 ¡buenas tardes!** : good afternoon!, good evening! **3 en la tarde** *or* **por la tarde** : in the afternoon, in the evening — **tardío, -día** *adj* : late, tardy — **tardo, -da** *adj* : slow

tarea *nf* **1** : task, job **2** : homework (in education)

tarifa *nf* **1** : fare, rate **2** LISTA : price list **3** ARANCEL : duty, tariff

tarima *nf* : platform, stage

tarjeta *nf* **1** : card **2 tarjeta de crédito** : credit card **3 tarjeta postal** : postcard

tarro *nm* : jar, pot

tarta *nf* **1** : cake **2** TORTA : tart

tartamudear *vi* : stammer, stutter — **tartamudeo** *nm* : stutter, stammer

teléfonos^M
telephones

teléfono^M **inalámbrico**
cordless telephone

teléfono^M **celular**
cellular telephone

teléfono^M **de teclado**^M
push-button telephone

teléfono^M **con memoria**^F
memory telephone set

teléfono^M **intelligente**
smartphone

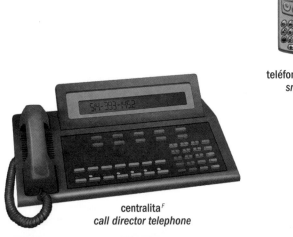

centralita^F
call director telephone

teléfono^M **público**
pay phone

tartán *nm, pl* **-tanes** : tartan, plaid
tártaro *nm* : tartar
tarugo *nm* **1** : block (of wood)
2 *fam* : blockhead, dunce
tasa *nf* **1** : rate **2** IMPUESTO : tax **3**
VALORACIÓN : appraisal — **tasación** *nf,*
pl **-ciones** : appraisal — **tasar** *vt* **1** : set
the price of **2** VALORAR : appraise, value
tasca *nf* : cheap bar, dive
tatuar {3} *vt* : tattoo —
tatuaje *nm* : tattoo, tattooing
taurino, -na *adj* : bull, bullfighting —
tauromaquia *nf* : (art of) bullfighting
taxi *nm, pl* **taxis** : taxi, taxicab
— **taxista** *nmf* : taxi driver
taza *nf* **1** : cup **2** : (toilet) bowl —
tazón *nm, pl* **-zones** : bowl
te *pron* **1** (*direct object*) : you **2**
(*indirect object*) : for you, to you,
from you **3** (*reflexive*) : yourself, for
yourself, to yourself, from yourself
té *nm* : tea
teatro *nm* : theater —
teatral *adj* : theatrical
techo *nm* **1** : roof **2** : ceiling (of a
room) **3** LÍMITE : upper limit, ceiling
— **techumbre** *nf* : roofing
tecla *nf* : key (of a musical instrument
or a machine) — **teclado** *nm* :
keyboard — **teclear** *vt* : type in, enter
técnica *nf* **1** : technique, skill
2 TECNOLOGÍA : technology —
técnico, -ca *adj* : technical —
técnico, -ca *n* : technician
tecnología *nf* : technology —
tecnológico, -ca *adj* : technological
tecolote *nm Lat* : owl
tedio *nm* : boredom — **tedioso,**
-sa *adj* : tedious, boring
teja *nf* : tile — **tejado** *nm* : roof
tejer *v* **1** : knit, crochet **2**
: weave (on a loom)
tejido *nm* **1** : fabric, cloth **2**
: tissue (of the body)
tejón *nm, pl* **-jones** : badger
tela *nf* **1** : fabric, material **2** **tela de**
araña : spiderweb — **telar** *nm* : loom
— **telaraña** *nf* : spiderweb, cobweb
tele *nf, fam* : TV, television
telecomunicación *nf, pl* **-ciones**
: telecommunication
teledifusión *nf, pl* **-siones** :
television broadcasting
teledirigido, -da *adj* : remote-controlled
telefonear *v* : telephone, call

— **telefónico, -ca** *adj* : telephone —
telefonista *nmf* : telephone operator
▸ — **teléfono** *nm* **1** : telephone **2** **llamar**
por telefonear : make a phone call
telegrafiar {85} *v* : telegraph —
telegráfico, -ca *adj* : telegraphic
— **telégrafo** *nm* : telegaph
telegrama *nm* : telegram
telenovela *nf* : soap opera
telepatía *nf* : telepathy —
telepático, -ca *adj* : telepathic
▸ **telescopio** *nm* : telescope —
telescópico, -ca *adj* : telescopic
telespectador, -dora *n*
: (television) viewer
telesquí *nm, pl* **-squís** : ski lift
televidente *nmf* : (television) viewer
televisión *nf, pl* **-siones** : television,

TV — **televisar** *vt* : televise —
televisor *nm* : television set
telón *nm, pl* **-lones** **1** : curtain (in theater)
2 **telón de fondo** : backdrop, background
tema *nm* : theme
temblar {55} *vi* **1** : tremble, shiver **2** :
shake (of a building, the ground, etc.) —
temblor *nm* **1** : shaking, trembling **2** *or*
temblor de tierra : tremor, earthquake —
tembloroso, -sa *adj* : trembling, shaky
temer *vt* : fear, dread — *vi* : be afraid
— **temerario, -ria** *adj* : reckless
— **temeridad** *nf* **1** : recklessness
2 : rash act — **temeroso, -sa** *adj* :
fearful — **temor** *nm* : fear, dread
temperamento *nm* : temperament —
temperamental *adj* : temperamental
temperatura *nf* : temperature

telescopio^M **reflector**
reflecting telescope

anteojo^M buscador
finderscope

ocular^M
eyepiece

tubo^M principal
main tube

botón^M de enfoque^M
focusing knob

cancha^F **de tenis**^M
tennis court

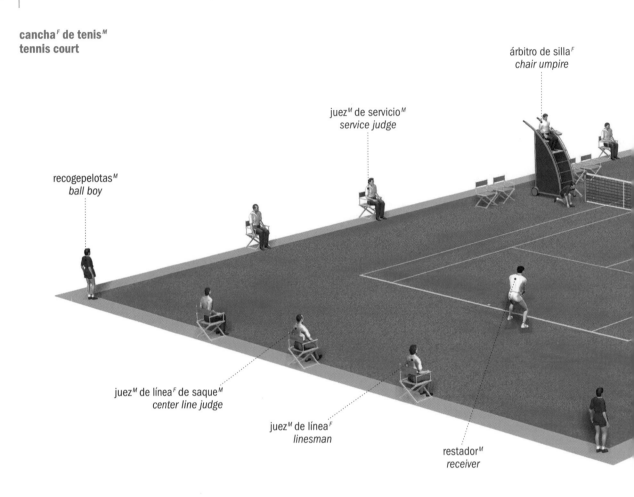

árbitro de silla^F
chair umpire

juez^M de servicio^M
service judge

recogepelotas^M
ball boy

juez^M de línea^F de saque^M
center line judge

juez^M de línea^F
linesman

restador^M
receiver

---

tempestad *nf* : storm —
  tempestuoso, -sa *adj* : stormy
templar *vt* **1** : temper (steel) **2** : moderate
  (temperature) **3** : tune (a musical
  instrument) — **templarse** *vr* : warm
  up, cool down — **templado, -da** *adj* **1**
  : temperate, mild **2** TIBIO : lukewarm **3**
  VALIENTE : courageous — **templanza** *nf* **1**
  : moderation **2** : mildness (of weather)
templo *nm* : temple, synagogue
tempo *nm* : tempo
temporada *nf* **1** : season, time **2**
  PERÍODO : period, spell — **temporal** *adj* **1**
  : temporal **2** PROVISIONAL : temporary —
  temporal *nm* : storm — **temporero,
  -ra** *n* : temporary or seasonal worker
temporizador *nm* : timer
temprano, -na *adj* : early
  — **temprano** *adv* : early

tenaz *adj, pl* **-naces** : tenacious
  — **tenaza** *nf or* **tenazas** *nfpl* **1** :
  pliers **2** : tongs (for the fireplace,
  etc.) **3** : claw (of a crustacean)
tendedero *nm* : clothesline
tendencia *nf* : tendency, trend
tender {56} *vt* **1** : spread out, stretch
  out **2** : hang out (clothes) **3** : lay
  (cables, etc.) **4** : set (a trap) — *vi*
  tender a : have a tendency towards
  — **tenderse** *vr* : stretch out, lie down
tendero, -ra *n* : shopkeeper
tendido *nm* **1** : laying (of cables, etc.)
  2 : seats *pl*, stand (at a bullfight)
tendón *nm, pl* **-dones** : tendon
tenebroso, -sa *adj* **1** : gloomy,
  dark **2** SINIESTRO : sinister
tenedor, -dora *n* **1** : holder **2**
  tenedor, -dora de libros : bookkeeper

— **tenedor** *nm* : table fork — **teneduría** *nf*
  teneduría de libros : bookkeeping
tener {80} *vt* **1** : have, possess **2**
  SUJETAR : hold **3** TOMAR : take **4 tener
  frío (hambre,** *etc.***)** : be cold (hungry,
  etc.) **5 tener ... años** : be ... years old
  6 tener por : think, consider — *v aux* **1**
  tener que : have to, ought to **2 tenía
  pensado escribirte** : I've been thinking
  of writing to you — **tenerse** *vr* **1** : stand
  up **2 tenerse por** : consider oneself
tenería *nf* : tannery
tengo → **tener**
tenia *nf* : tapeworm
teniente *nmf* : lieutenant
▸ **tenis** *nms & pl* **1** : tennis **2 tenis** *nmpl* :
  sneakers — **tenista** *nmf* : tennis player
tenor *nm* **1** : tenor **2** : tone,
  sense (in style)

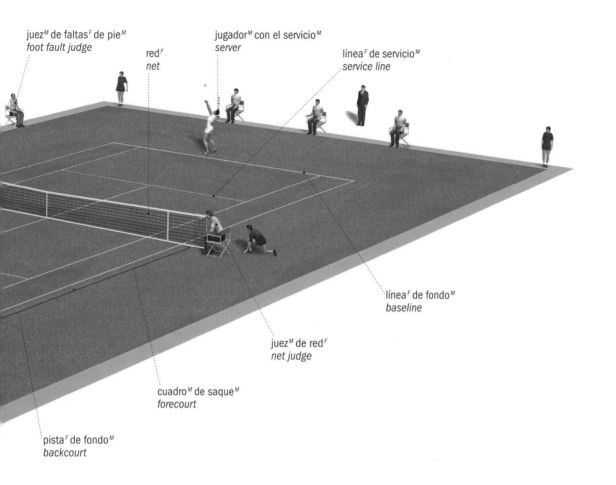

juez^M de faltas^F de pie^M
foot fault judge

jugador^M con el servicio^M
server

red^F
net

línea^F de servicio^M
service line

línea^F de fondo^M
baseline

juez^M de red^F
net judge

cuadro^M de saque^M
forecourt

pista^F de fondo^M
backcourt

tensar *vt* **1** : tense, make taut **2** : draw (a bow) — **tensarse** *vr* : become tense — **tensión** *nf, pl* **-siones 1** : tension **2 tensión arterial** : blood pressure — **tenso, -sa** *adj* : tense

tentación *nf, pl* **-ciones** : temptation

tentáculo *nm* : tentacle

tentar {55} *vt* **1** : feel, touch **2** ATRAER : tempt — **tentador, -dora** *adj* : tempting

tentativa *nf* : attempt

tentempié *nm, fam* : snack

tenue *adj* **1** : tenuous **2** : faint, weak (of sounds) **3** : light, fine (of thread, rain, etc.)

teñir {67} *vt* **1** : dye **2 teñir de** : tinge with

teología *nf* : theology — **teólogo, -ga** *n* : theologian

teorema *nm* : theorem

teoría *nf* : theory — **teórico, -ca** *adj* : theoretical

tequila *nm* : tequila

terapia *nf* **1** : therapy **2 terapia ocupacional** : occupational therapy — **terapeuta** *nmf* : therapist — **terapéutico, -ca** *adj* : therapeutic

tercermundista *adj* : third-world

tercero, -ra *adj* (**tercer** *before masculine singular nouns*) **1** : third **2 el Tercer Mundo** : the Third World — **tercero, -ra** *n* : third (in a series)

terciar *vt* : sling (something over one's shoulders), tilt (a hat) — *vi* **1** : intervene **2 terciar en** : take part in

tercio *nm* : third

terciopelo *nm* : velvet

terco, -ca *adj* : obstinate, stubborn

tergiversar *vt* : distort, twist

termal *adj* : thermal, hot — **termas** *nfpl* : hot springs

terminar *vt* : conclude, finish — *vi* **1** : finish **2** ACABARSE : come to an end — **terminarse** *vr* **1** : run out **2** ACABARSE : come to an end — **terminación** *nf, pl* **-ciones** : termination, conclusion — **terminal** *adj* : terminal, final — **terminal** *nm* (*in some regions f*) : (electric or electronic) terminal — **terminal** *nf* (*in some regions m*) : terminal, station — **término** *nm* **1** : end **2** PLAZO : period, term **3 término medio** : happy medium **4 términos** *nmpl* : terms — **terminología** *nf* : terminology

termita *nf* : termite

termo *nm* : thermos

termómetro *nm* : thermometer

termóstato *nm* : thermostat

ternero, -ra *n* : calf — **ternera** *nf* : veal

ternura *nf* : tenderness

terquedad *nf* : obstinacy, stubbornness

terracota *nf* : terra-cotta

terraplén *nm, pl* **-plenes** : embankment

terráqueo, -quea *adj* : earth, terrestrial

terrateniente *nmf* : landowner

terraza *nf* **1** : terrace **2** BALCÓN : balcony

terremoto *nm* : earthquake

terreno *nm* **1** : terrain **2** SUELO : earth, ground **3** SOLAR : plot, tract of land — **terreno, -na** *adj* : earthly — **terrestre** *adj* : terrestrial

terrible *adj* : terrible

terrier *nmf* : terrier

territorio *nm* : territory — **territorial** *adj* : territorial

terrón *nm, pl* **-rones 1** : clod (of earth) **2 terrón de azúcar** : lump of sugar

terror *nm* : terror — **terrorífico, -ca** *adj* : terrifying — **terrorismo** *nm* : terrorism — **terrorista** *adj & nmf* : terrorist

terroso, -sa *adj* : earthy

terso, -sa *adj* **1** : smooth **2** : polished, flowing (of a style) — **tersura** *nf* : smoothness

tertulia *nf* : gathering, group

tesis *nfs & pl* : thesis

tesón *nm* : persistence, tenacity

tesoro *nm* **1** : treasure **2** : thesaurus (book) **3 el Tesoro** : the Treasury — **tesorero, -ra** *n* : treasurer

testaferro *nm* : figurehead

testamento *nm* : testament, will — **testamentario, -ria** *n* : executor, executrix *f* — **testar** *vi* : draw up a will

testarudo, -da *adj* : stubborn

testículo *nm* : testicle

testificar {72} *v* : testify — **testigo** *nmf* **1** : witness **2 testigo ocular** : eyewitness — **testimoniar** *vi* : testify — **testimonio** *nm* : testimony

tétano *or* **tétanos** *nm* : tetanus

tetera *nf* : teapot

tetilla *nf* **1** : teat, nipple (of a man) **2** : nipple (of a baby bottle) — **tetina** *nf* : nipple (of a baby bottle)

tétrico, -ca *adj* : somber, gloomy

textil *adj & nm* : textile

texto *nm* : text — **textual** *adj* **1** : textual **2** EXACTO : literal, exact

textura *nf* : texture

tez *nf, pl* **teces** : complexion

ti *pron* **1** : you **2 ti mismo, ti misma** : yourself

tía → **tío**

tianguis *nms & pl Lat* : open-air market

tibio, -bia *adj* : lukewarm

tiburón *nm, pl* **-rones** : shark

tic *nm* : tic

tiempo *nm* **1** : time **2** ÉPOCA : age, period **3** : weather (in meteorology) **4** : halftime (in sports) **5** : tempo (in music) **6** : tense (in grammar)

tienda *nf* **1** : store, shop **2** *or* **tienda de campaña** : tent

tiene → **tener**

tienta *nf* **andar a tientas** : feel one's way, grope around

tierno, -na *adj* **1** : tender, fresh, young **2** CARIÑOSO : affectionate

tierra *nf* **1** : land **2** SUELO : ground, earth **3** *or* **tierra natal** : native land **4 la Tierra** : the Earth **5 por tierra** : overland **6 tierra adentro** : inland

tieso, -sa *adj* **1** : stiff, rigid **2** ERGUIDO : erect **3** ENGREÍDO : haughty

tiesto *nm* : flowerpot

tifoideo, -dea *adj* **fiebre tifoidea** : typhoid fever

tifón *nm, pl* **-fones** : typhoon

tifus *nm* : typhus

tigre, -gresa *n* **1** : tiger, tigress *f* **2** *Lat* : jaguar

tijera *nf or* **tijeras** *nfpl* : scissors — **tijeretada** *nf* : cut, snip

tildar *vt* **tildar de** : brand as, call

tilde *nf* **1** : tilde **2** ACENTO : accent mark

tilo *nm* : linden (tree)

timar *vt* : swindle, cheat

timbre *nm* **1** : bell **2** : tone, timbre (of a voice, etc.) **3** SELLO : seal, stamp **4** *Lat* : postage stamp — **timbrar** *vt* : stamp

tímido, -da *adj* : timid, shy — **timidez** *nf* : timidity, shyness

timo *nm, fam* : swindle, hoax

timón *nm, pl* **-mones 1** : rudder **2 coger el timón** : take the helm, take charge

tímpano *nm* **1** : eardrum **2 tímpanos** *nmpl* : timpani, kettledrums

tina *nf* **1** : vat **2** BAÑERA : bathtub

tinieblas *nfpl* **1** : darkness **2 estar en tinieblas sobre** : be in the dark about

tino *nm* **1** : good judgment, sense **2** TACTO : tact

tinta *nf* **1** : ink **2 saberlo de buena tinta** : have it on good authority — **tinte** *nm* **1** : dye, coloring **2** MATIZ : overtone — **tintero** *nm* : inkwell

tintinear *vi* : jingle, tinkle, clink — **tintineo** *nm* : jingle, tinkle, clink

tinto, -ta *adj* **1** : dyed, stained **2** : red (of wine)

tintorería *nf* : dry cleaner (service)

tintura *nf* **1** : dye, tint **2 tintura de yodo** : tincture of iodine

tiña *nf* : ringworm

tío, tía *n* : uncle *m*, aunt *f*

tiovivo *nm* : merry-go-round

típico, -ca *adj* : typical

tiple *nm* : soprano

tipo *nm* **1** : type, kind **2** FIGURA : figure (of a woman), build (of a man) **3** : rate (of interest, etc.) **4** : (printing) type, typeface — **tipo, -pa** *n, fam* : guy *m*, gal *f*

tipografía *nf* : typography, printing — **tipográfico, -ca** *adj* : typographical — **tipógrafo, -fa** *n* : printer

tique *or* **tíquet** *nm* : ticket — **tiquete** *nm Lat* : ticket

tira *nf* **1** : strip, strap **2 tira cómica** : comic strip

tirabuzón *nf, pl* **-zones 1** : corkscrew **2** RIZO : curl, coil

tirada *nf* **1** : throw **2** DISTANCIA : distance **3** IMPRESIÓN : printing, issue — **tirador** *nm* : handle, knob — **tirador, -dora** *n* : marksman *m*, markswoman *f*

tiranía *nf* : tyranny — **tiránico, -ca** *adj* : tyrannical — **tiranizar** {21} *vt* : tyrannize — **tirano, -na** *adj* : tyrannical — **tirano, -na** *n* : tyrant

tirante *adj* **1** : taut, tight **2** : tense (of a situation, etc.) — **tirante** *nm* **1** : (shoulder) strap **2 tirantes** *nmpl* : suspenders

tirar *vt* **1** : throw **2** DESECHAR : throw away **3** DERRIBAR : knock down **4** DISPARAR : shoot, fire **5** IMPRIMIR : print — *vi* **1** : pull **2** DISPARAR : shoot **3** ATRAER : attract **4** *fam* : get by, manage **5 tirar a** : tend towards — **tirarse** *vr* **1** : throw oneself **2** *fam* : spend (time)

tiritar *vi* : shiver

tiro *nm* **1** : shot, gunshot **2** : shot, kick (in sports) **3** : team (of horses, etc.) **4 a tiro** : within range

tiroides *nmf* : thyroid (gland)

tirón *nm, pl* **-rones 1** : pull, yank **2 de un tirón** : in one go

tirotear *vt* : shoot at — **tiroteo** *nm* : shooting

tisis *nfs & pl* : tuberculosis

títere *nm* : puppet

titilar *vi* : flicker

titiritero, -ra *n* **1** : puppeteer **2** ACRÓBATA : acrobat

titubear *vi* **1** : hesitate **2** BALBUCEAR : stutter, stammer — **titubeante** *adj* : hesitant, faltering — **titubeo** *nm* : hesitation

titular *vt* : title, call — **titularse** *vr* **1** : be called, be titled **2** LICENCIARSE : receive a degree — **titular** *adj* : titular, official — **titular** *nm* : headline — **titular** *nmf* : holder, incumbent — **título** *nm* **1** : title **2** : degree, qualification (in education)

tiza *nf* : chalk

tiznar *vt* : blacken (with soot, etc.) — **tizne** *nm* : soot

toalla *nf* : towel — **toallero** *nm* : towel rack

tobillo *nm* : ankle

tobogán *nm, pl* **-ganes 1** : toboggan, sled **2** : slide (in a playground, etc.)

tocadiscos *nms & pl* : record player

tocado, -da *adj, fam* : touched, not all there — **tocado** *nm* : headgear, headdress

tocador *nm* : dressing table

tocar {72} *vt* **1** : touch, feel **2** MENCIONAR : touch on, refer to **3** : play (a musical instrument) — *vi* **1** : knock, ring **2 tocar en** : touch on, border on

tocayo, -ya *n* : namesake

tocino *nm* **1** : bacon **2** : salt pork (for cooking) — **tocineta** *nf Lat* : bacon

tocólogo, -ga *n* : obstetrician

tocón *nm, pl* **-cones** : stump (of a tree)

todavía *adv* **1** AÚN : still **2** (*in comparisons*) : even **3 todavía no** : not yet

todo, -da *adj* **1** : all **2** CADA, CUALQUIER : every, each **3 a toda velocidad** : at top speed **4 todo el mundo** : everyone, everybody — **todo, -da** *pron* **1** : everything, all **2 todos, -das** *pl* : everybody, everyone, all — **todo** *nm* : whole — **todopoderoso, -sa** *adj* : almighty, all-powerful

toga *nf* **1** : toga **2** : gown, robe (of a judge, etc.)

toldo *nm* : awning, canopy

tolerar *vt* : tolerate — **tolerancia** *nf* : tolerance — **tolerante** *adj* : tolerant

toma *nf* **1** : capture **2** DOSIS : dose **3** : take (in film) **4 toma de corriente** : wall socket, outlet **5 toma y daca** : give-and-take — **tomar** *vt* **1** : take **2** : have (food or drink) **3** CAPTURAR : capture, seize **4 toma el sol** : sunbathe **5 toma tierra** : land — *vi* : drink (alcohol) — **tomarse** *vr* **1** : take (time, etc.) **2** : drink, eat, have (food, drink)

tomate *nm* : tomato

tomillo *nm* : thyme

tomo *nm* : volume

ton *nm* **sin ton ni son** : without rhyme or reason

tonada *nf* : tune

tonel *nm* : barrel, cask

tonelada *nf* : ton — **tonelaje** *nm* : tonnage

tónica *nf* **1** : tonic (water) **2** TENDENCIA : trend, tone — **tónico, -ca** *adj* : tonic — **tónico** *nm* : tonic (in medicine)

tono *nm* **1** : tone **2** : shade (of colors) **3** : key (in music)

tontería *nf* **1** : silly thing or remark **2** ESTUPIDEZ : foolishness **3 decir tonterías** : talk nonsense — **tonto, -ta** *adj* **1** : stupid, silly **2 a tontas y a locas** : haphazardly — **tonto, -ta** *n* : fool, idiot

topacio *nm* : topaz

toparse *vr* **toparse con** : run into, come across

tope *nm* **1** : limit, end **2** *or* **tope de puerta** : doorstop **3** *Lat* : bump — **tope** *adj* : maximum

tópico, -ca *adj* **1** : topical, external **2** MANIDO : trite — **tópico** *nm* : cliché

topo *nm* : mole (animal)

toque *nm* **1** : (light) touch **2** : ringing, peal (of a bell) **3 toque de queda** : curfew **4 toque de diana** : reveille — **toquetear** *vt* : finger, handle

tórax *nms & pl* : thorax

torbellino *nm* : whirlwind

torcer {14} *vt* **1** : twist, bend **2** : turn (a corner) **3** : wring (out) — *vi* : turn — **torcerse** *vr* **1** : twist, sprain **2** FRUSTRARSE : go wrong **3** DESVIARSE : go astray — **torcedura** *nf* **1** : twisting **2** ESGUINCE : sprain — **torcido, -da** *adj* : twisted, crooked

tordo, -da *adj* : dappled — **tordo** *nm* : thrush (bird)

torear *vt* **1** : fight (bulls) **2** ELUDIR : dodge, sidestep — *vi* : fight bulls — **toreo** *nm* : bullfighting — **torero, -ra** *n* : bullfighter

tormenta *nf* : storm — **tormento** *nm* **1** : torture **2** ANGUSTIA : torment, anguish — **tormentoso, -sa** *adj* : stormy

▸ **tornado** *nm* : tornado

tornar *vt* CONVERTIR : render, turn — *vi* : go back, return — **tornarse** *vr* : become, turn into

torneo *nm* : tournament

tornillo *nm* : screw

torniquete *nm* **1** : turnstile **2** : tourniquet (in medicine)

tornado^M
tornado

muro^M de nubes^F
wall cloud

nube^F en forma^F de embudo^M
funnel cloud

detritos^M
debris

tortuga^F
turtle

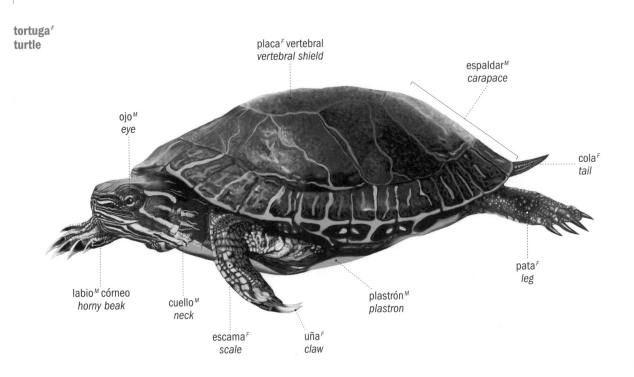

placa^F vertebral
vertebral shield

espaldar^M
carapace

ojo^M
eye

cola^F
tail

labio^M córneo
horny beak

cuello^M
neck

plastrón^M
plastron

pata^F
leg

escama^F
scale

uña^F
claw

---

torno *nm* **1** : winch **2** : (carpenter's) lathe **3 torno de alfarero** : (potter's) wheel **4 torno de banco** : vise **5 en torno a** : around, about

toro *nm* **1** : bull **2 toros** *nmpl* : bullfight

toronja *nf* : grapefruit

torpe *adj* **1** : clumsy, awkward **2** ESTÚPIDO : stupid, dull

torpedear *vt* : torpedo — **torpedo** *nm* : torpedo

torpeza *nf* **1** : clumsiness, awkwardness **2** ESTUPIDEZ : slowness, stupidity

torre *nf* **1** : tower **2** : turret (on a ship, etc.) **3** : rook, castle (in chess)

torrente *nm* **1** : torrent **2 torrente sanguíneo** : bloodstream — **torrencial** *adj* : torrential

tórrido, -da *adj* : torrid

torsión *nf*, *pl* **-siones** : twisting

torta *nf* **1** : torte, cake **2** *Lat* : sandwich

tortazo *nm*, *fam* : blow, wallop

tortícolis *nfs & pl* : stiff neck

tortilla *nf* **1** : tortilla **2** *or* **tortilla de huevo** : omelet

tórtola *nf* : turtledove

▸ **tortuga** *nf* **1** : turtle, tortoise **2 tortuga de agua dulce** : terrapin

tortuoso, -sa *adj* : tortuous, winding

tortura *nf* : torture — **torturar** *vt* : torture

tos *nf* **1** : cough **2 tos ferina** : whooping cough

tosco, -ca *adj* : rough, coarse

toser *vi* : cough

tosquedad *nf* : coarseness

tostar {19} *vt* **1** : toast **2** BRONCEAR : tan — **tostarse** *vr* : get a tan — **tostada** *nf* **1** : piece of toast **2** *Lat* : tostada — **tostador** *nm* : toaster

tostón *nm*, *pl* **-tones** *Lat* : fried plantain chip

total *adj & nm* : total — **total** *adv* : so, after all — **totalidad** *nf* : whole — **totalitario, -ria** *adj & n* : totalitarian — **totalitarismo** *nm* : totalitarianism — **totalizar** {21} *vt* : total, add up to

tóxico, -ca *adj* : toxic, poisonous — **tóxico** *nm* : poison — **toxicomanía** *nf* : drug addiction — **toxicómano, -na** *n* : drug addict — **toxina** *nf* : toxin

tozudo, -da *adj* : stubborn

traba *nf* : obstacle, hindrance

trabajar *vi* **1** : work **2** : act, perform (in theater, etc.) — *vt* **1** : work (metal) **2** : knead (dough) **3** MEJORAR : work on, work

at — **trabajador, -dora** *adj* : hard-working — **trabajador, -dora** *n* : worker — **trabajo** *nm* **1** : work **2** EMPLEO : job **3** TAREA : task **4** ESFUERZO : effort **5 costar trabajo** : be difficult **6 trabajo en equipo** : teamwork **7 trabajos** *nmpl* : hardships, difficulties — **trabajoso, -sa** *adj* : hard, laborious

trabalenguas *nms & pl* : tongue twister

trabar *vt* **1** : join, connect **2** OBSTACULIZAR : impede **3** : strike up (a conversation, etc.) **4** : thicken (sauces) — **trabarse** *vr* **1** : jam **2** ENREDARSE : become entangled **3 se le traba la lengua** : he gets tongue-tied

trabucar {72} *vt* : mix up

tracción *nf* : traction

▸ **tractor** *nm* : tractor

tradición *nf*, *pl* **-ciones** : tradition — **tradicional** *adj* : traditional

traducir {61} *vt* : translate — **traducción** *nf*, *pl* **-ciones** : translation — **traductor, -tora** *n* : translator

traer {81} *vt* **1** : bring **2** CAUSAR : cause, bring about **3** CONTENER : carry, have **4** LLEVAR : wear — **traerse** *vr* **1** : bring along **2 traérselas** : be difficult

traficar {72} *vi* **traficar en** : traffic in — **traficante** *nmf* : dealer, trafficker — **tráfico** *nm* **1** : trade (of merchandise) **2** : traffic (of vehicles)

tragaluz *nf, pl* **-luces** : skylight

tragar {52} *vt* **1** : swallow **2** *fam* : put up with — *vi* : swallow — **tragarse** *vr* **1** : swallow **2** ABSORBER : absorb, swallow up

tragedia *nf* : tragedy — **trágico, -ca** *adj* : tragic

trago *nm* **1** : swallow, swig **2** *fam* : drink, liquor — **tragón, -gona** *adj, fam* : greedy — **tragón, -gona** *nmf, fam* : glutton

traicionar *vt* : betray — **traición** *nf, pl* **-ciones 1** : betrayal **2** : treason (in law) — **traidor, -dora** *adj* : traitorous, treacherous — **traidor, -dora** *n* : traitor

trailer *nm* : trailer

traje *nm* **1** : dress, costume **2** : (man's) suit **3 traje de baño** : bathing suit

trajinar *vi, fam* : rush around — **trajín** *nm, pl* **-jines** *fam* : hustle and bustle

trama *nf* **1** : plot **2** : weave, weft (of fabric) — **tramar** *vt* **1** : plot, plan **2** : weave (fabric)

tramitar *vt* : negotiate

— **trámite** *nm* : procedure, step

tramo *nm* **1** : stretch, section **2** : flight (of stairs)

trampa *nf* **1** : trap **2 hacer trampas** : cheat — **trampear** *vt* : cheat

trampilla *nf* : trapdoor

trampolín *nm, pl* **-lines 1** : diving board **2** : trampoline (in a gymnasium, etc.)

tramposo, -sa *adj* : crooked, cheating — **tramposo, -sa** *n* : cheat, swindler

tranca *nf* **1** : cudgel, club **2** : bar (for a door or window)

trance *nm* **1** : critical juncture **2** : (hypnotic) trance **3 en trance de** : in the process of

tranquilo, -la *adj* : calm, tranquil — **tranquilidad** *nf* : tranquility, peace — **tranquilizante** *nm* : tranquilizer — **tranquilizar** {21} *vt* : calm, soothe — **tranquilizarse** *vr* : calm down

trans- *see also* **tras-**

transacción *nf, pl* **-ciones** : transaction

▸ **transatlántico, -ca** *adj* : transatlantic — **transatlántico** *nm* : ocean liner

transbordador *nm* **1** : ferry **2 transbordador espacial** : space shuttle — **transbordar** *vt* : transfer — *vi* : change (of trains, etc.) — **transbordo** *nm* **hacer transbordador** : change (trains, etc.)

transcribir {33} *vt* : transcribe — **transcripción** *nf, pl* **-ciones** : transcription

transcurrir *vi* : elapse, pass — **transcurso** *nm* : course, progression

transeúnte *nmf* : passerby

transferir {76} *vt* : transfer — **transferencia** *nf* : transfer, transference

transformar *vt* **1** : transform, change **2** CONVERTIR : convert — **transformarse** *vr* : be transformed — **transformación** *nf, pl* **-ciones** : transformation — **transformador** *nm* : transformer

transfusión *nf, pl* **-siones** : transfusion

transgredir {1} *vt* : transgress — **transgresión** *nf* : transgression

transición *nf, pl* **-ciones** : transition

transido, -da *adj* : overcome, stricken

transigir {35} *vi* : give in, compromise

transistor *nm* : transistor

tractor^M
tractor

tubo^M de escape^M / exhaust stack

cabina^F / cab

motor^M / engine compartment

faro^F delantero / headlight

guardabarros^M / fender

rueda^F delantera / front wheel

rueda^F motriz / driving wheel

buque^M trasatlántico
cruise ship

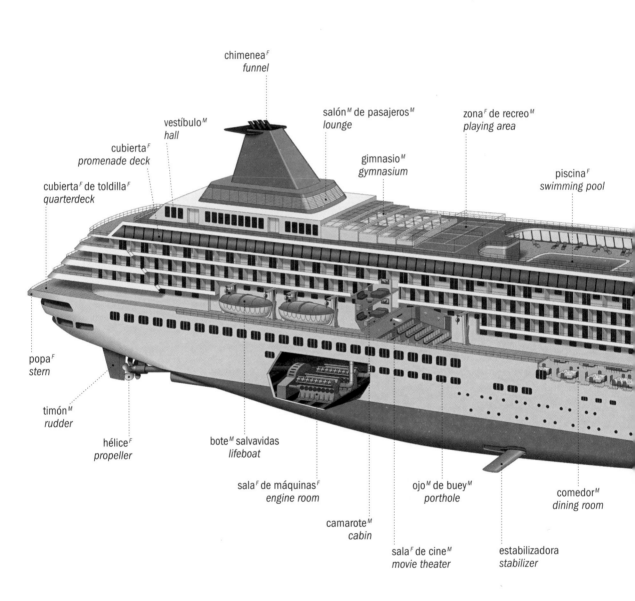

chimenea^F
funnel

salón^M de pasajeros^M
lounge

zona^F de recreo^M
playing area

vestíbulo^M
hall

gimnasio^M
gymnasium

cubierta^F
promenade deck

piscina^F
swimming pool

cubierta^F de toldilla^F
quarterdeck

popa^F
stern

timón^M
rudder

hélice^F
propeller

bote^M salvavidas
lifeboat

sala^F de máquinas^F
engine room

ojo^M de buey^M
porthole

comedor^M
dining room

camarote^M
cabin

sala^F de cine^M
movie theater

estabilizadora
stabilizer

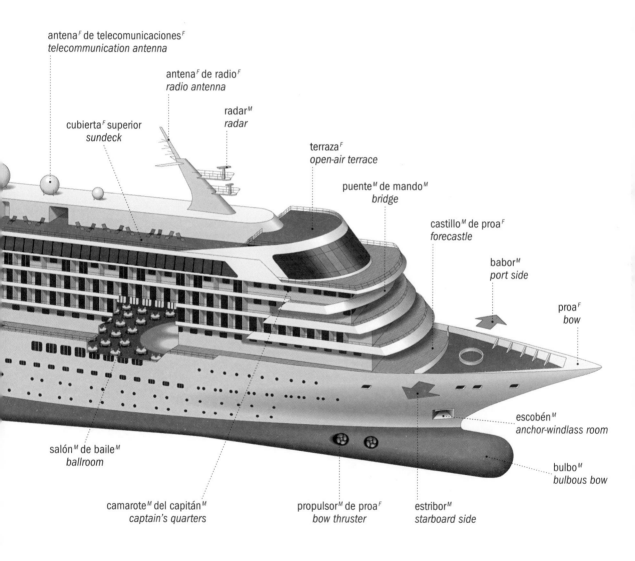

antena^F de telecomunicaciones^F
telecommunication antenna

antena^F de radio^F
radio antenna

radar^M
radar

cubierta^F superior
sundeck

terraza^F
open-air terrace

puente^M de mando^M
bridge

castillo^M de proa^F
forecastle

babor^M
port side

proa^F
bow

escobén^M
anchor-windlass room

bulbo^M
bulbous bow

salón^M de baile^M
ballroom

camarote^M del capitán^M
captain's quarters

propulsor^M de proa^F
bow thruster

estribor^M
starboard side

transitar *vi* : go, travel —
  transitable *adj* : passable
transitivo, -va *adj* : transitive
tránsito *nm* **1** : transit **2** TRÁFICO : traffic
  3 hora de máximo tránsito : rush hour
  — **transitorio, -ria** *adj* : transitory
transmitir *vt* **1** : transmit **2** : broadcast
  (radio, TV, etc.) **3** CEDER : pass on

— **transmisión** *nf, pl* **-siones 1** :
broadcast **2** TRANSFERENCIA : transfer
3 : transmission (of an automobile)
  — **transmisor** *nm* : transmitter
transparentarse *vr* : be transparent
  — **transparente** *adj* : transparent
transpirar *vi* : perspire, sweat

— **transpiración** *nf, pl* **-ciones**
  : perspiration, sweat
transponer {60} *vt* : transpose,
move — **transponerse** *vr* **1** : set (of
the sun, etc.) **2** DORMITAR : doze off
transportar *vt* : transport, carry —
  transportarse *vr* : get carried away —
  transporte *nm* : transport, transportation

tribunal^M
court

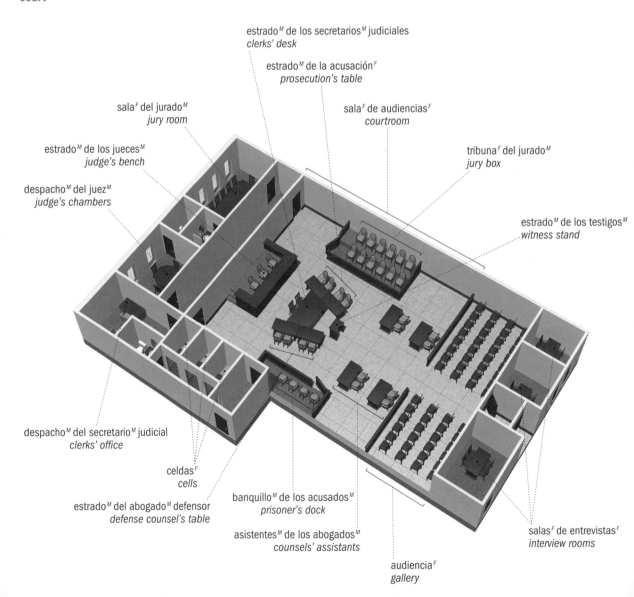

estrado^M de los secretarios^M judiciales
clerks' desk

estrado^M de la acusación^F
prosecution's table

sala^F del jurado^M
jury room

sala^F de audiencias^F
courtroom

estrado^M de los jueces^M
judge's bench

tribuna^F del jurado^M
jury box

despacho^M del juez^M
judge's chambers

estrado^M de los testigos^M
witness stand

despacho^M del secretario^M judicial
clerks' office

celdas^F
cells

estrado^M del abogado^M defensor
defense counsel's table

banquillo^M de los acusados^M
prisoner's dock

asistentes^M de los abogados^M
counsels' assistants

salas^F de entrevistas^F
interview rooms

audiencia^F
gallery

transversal *adj* **corte**
  transversal : cross section
tranvía *nm* : streetcar, trolley
trapear *vi Lat* : mop
trapecio *nm* : trapeze
trapisonda *nf* : scheme, plot
trapo *nm* **1** : cloth, rag **2**
  trapos *nmpl, fam* : clothes
tráquea *nf* : trachea, windpipe
traquetear *vi* : rattle around,
  shake — **traqueteo** *nm* : rattling
tras *prep* **1** DESPUÉS DE : after
  2 DÉTRAS DE : behind
tras- *see also* **trans-**
trascender {56} *vi* **1** : leak out,
  become known **2** EXTENDERSE : spread
  3 trascender de : transcend —
  trascendencia *nf* : importance —
  trascendental *adj* **1** : transcendental
  2 IMPORTANTE : important
trasegar *vt* : move around
trasero, -ra *adj* : rear, back —
  trasero *nm* : buttocks *pl*
trasfondo *nm* **1** : background **2** :
  undercurrent (of suspicion, etc.)
trasladar *vt* **1** : transfer, move **2**
  POSPONER : postpone — **trasladarse** *vr*
  : move, relocate — **traslado** *nm* **1**
  : transfer, move **2** COPIA : copy
traslapar *vt* : overlap —
  traslaparse *vr* : overlap
traslucirse {45} *vr* **1** : be translucent
  2 REVELARSE : be revealed —
  traslúcido, -da : translucent
trasnochar *vi* : stay up all night
traspasar *vt* **1** : pierce, go through
  2 EXCEDER : go beyond **3** ATRAVESAR :
  cross, go across **4** : transfer (a business,
  etc.) — **traspaso** *nm* : transfer, sale
traspié *nm* **1** : stumble,
  trip **2** ERROR : blunder
trasplantar *vt* : transplant —
  trasplante *nm* : transplant
trasquilar *vt* : shear
traste *nm* **1** : fret (on a guitar, etc.) **2**
  Lat : (kitchen) utensil **3 dar al traste**
  con : ruin **4 irse al traste** : fall through
trastos *nmpl, fam* : pieces of junk, stuff
trastornar *vt* **1** : disturb, disrupt **2** VOLVER
  LOCO : drive crazy — **trastornarse** *vr*
  : go crazy — **trastornado, -da** *adj* :
  disturbed, deranged — **trastorno** *nm* **1**
  : disturbance, disruption **2** : (medical
  or psychological) disorder
trastrocar *vt* : change, switch around

tratable *adj* : friendly, sociable
tratar *vi* **1 tratar con** : deal with **2**
  tratar de : try to **3 tratar de** *or* **tratar**
  sobre : be about, concern **4 tratar**
  en : deal in — *vt* **1** : treat **2** MANEJAR
  : deal with, handle — **tratarse** *vr*
  tratarse de : be about, concern —
  tratado *nm* **1** : treatise **2** CONVENIO :
  treaty — **tratamiento** *nm* : treatment —
  trato *nm* **1** : treatment **2** ACUERDO : deal,
  agreement **3 tratos** *nmpl* : dealings
trauma *nm* : trauma —
  traumático, -ca *adj* : traumatic
través *nm* **1 a través de** : across,
  through **2 de través** : sideways
travesaño *nm* : crosspiece
travesía *nf* : voyage, crossing (of the sea)
travesura *nf* **1** : prank **2**
  travesuras *nfpl* : mischief — **travieso,**
  -sa *adj* : mischievous, naughty
trayecto *nm* **1** : trajectory, path
  2 VIAJE : journey **3** RUTA : route —
  trayectoria *nf* : path, trajectory
traza *nf* **1** : design, plan **2** ASPECTO :
  appearance — **trazado** *nm* **1** : outline,
  sketch **2** DISEÑO : plan, layout — **trazar**
  {21} *vt* **1** : trace, outline **2** : draw up (a
  plan, etc.) — **trazo** *nm* : stroke, line
trébol *nm* **1** : clover, shamrock **2**
  tréboles *nmpl* : clubs (in playing cards)
trece *adj & nm* : thirteen —
  treceavo, -va *adj* : thirteenth —
  treceavo *nm* : thirteenth (fraction)
trecho *nm* **1** : stretch, period **2**
  DISTANCIA : distance **3 de trecho**
  a trecho : at intervals
tregua *nf* **1** : truce **2 sin**
  tregua : without respite
treinta *adj & nm* : thirty —
  treintavo, -va *adj* : thirtieth —
  treintavo *nm* : thirtieth (fraction)
tremendo, -da *adj* :
  tremendous, enormous
trementina *nf* : turpentine
trémulo, -la *adj* : trembling, flickering
tren *nm* **1** : train **2 tren de**
  aterrizaje : landing gear
trenza *nf* : braid, pigtail — **trenzar** {21} *vt*
  : braid — **trenzarse** *vr Lat* : get involved
trepar *vi* **1** : climb **2** : creep,
  spread (of a plant) — **treparse** *vr* :
  climb (up) — **trepador, -dora** *adj* :
  climbing — **trepadora** *nf* **1** : climbing
  plant **2** *fam* : social climber
trepidar *vi* : shake, vibrate

tres *adj & nm* : three — **trescientos,**
  -tas *adj* : three hundred —
  trescientos *nms & pl* : three hundred
treta *nf* : trick
triángulo *nm* : triangle —
  triangular *adj* : triangular
tribu *nf* : tribe — **tribal** *adj* : tribal
tribulación *nf, pl* **-ciones** : tribulation
tribuna *nf* **1** : dais, platform **2** :
  grandstand, bleachers *pl* (in a stadium)
▸ **tribunal** *nm* : court, tribunal
tributar *vt* : pay, render — *vi* : pay taxes
  — **tributo** *nm* **1** : tribute **2** IMPUESTO : tax
triciclo *nm* : tricycle
tricolor *adj* : tricolored
tridimensional *adj* : three-dimensional
trigésimo, -ma *adj & n* : thirtieth
trigo *nm* : wheat
trigonometría *nf* : trigonometry
trillado, -da *adj* : trite
trillar *vt* : thresh — **trilladora** *nf*
  : threshing machine
trillizo, -za *n* : triplet
trilogía *nf* : trilogy
trimestral *adj* : quarterly
trinar *vi* : warble
trinchar *vt* : carve
trinchera *nf* **1** : trench, ditch **2**
  IMPERMEABLE : trench coat
trineo *nm* : sled, sleigh
trinidad *nf* : trinity
trino *nm* : trill, warble
trío *nm* : trio
tripa *nf* **1** : gut, intestine **2**
  tripas *nfpl, fam* : belly, tummy
triple *adj & nm* : triple —
  triplicar {72} *vt* : triple
trípode *nm* : tripod
tripular *vt* : man — **tripulación** *nf,*
  pl **-ciones** : crew — **tripulante** *nmf*
  : crew member
tris *nm* **estar en un tris de**
  : be within an inch of
triste *adj* **1** : sad **2** SOMBRÍO : dismal,
  gloomy **3** MISERABLE : sorry, miserable
  — **tristeza** *nf* : sadness, grief
tritón *nm, pl* **-tones** : newt
triturar *vt* : crush, grind
triunfar *vi* : triumph, win — **triunfal** *adj*
  : triumphal — **triunfante** *adj* : triumphant
  — **triunfo** *nm* : triumph, victory
trivial *adj* : trivial
triza *nf* **1** : shred, bit **2 hacer**
  trizas : smash to pieces
trocar {82} *vt* **1** CONVERTIR : change

2 INTERCAMBIAR : exchange
trocha *nf* : path, trail
trofeo *nm* : trophy
trombón *nm, pl* **-bones 1** : trombone
　2 : trombonist (musician)
trombosis *nf* : thrombosis
trompa *nf* **1** : trunk (of an
　elephant), snout **2** : horn (musical
　instrument) **3** : tube (in anatomy)
trompeta *nf* : trumpet —
　trompetista *nmf* : trumpet player
trompo *nm* : top (toy)
tronada *nf* : thunderstorm — **tronar**
　{19} *vi* : thunder, rage — *vt Lat fam*
　: shoot — *v impers* : thunder
tronchar *vt* **1** : snap **2** TRUNCAR : cut short
tronco *nm* **1** : trunk (of a tree) **2** :
　torso (of a person) **3 dormir como**
　un tronco : sleep like a log
trono *nm* : throne
tropa *nf* : troops *pl*, soldiers *pl*
tropel *nm* : mob
tropezar {29} *vi* **1** : trip, stumble **2**
　tropezar con : come up against, run
　into — **tropezón** *nm, pl* **-zones 1** :
　stumble **2** EQUIVOCACIÓN : mistake, slip
trópico *nm* : tropic —
▸ **tropical** *adj* : tropical
tropiezo *nm* **1** CONTRATIEMPO : snag,
　setback **2** EQUIVOCACIÓN : mistake, slip
trotar *vi* **1** : trot **2** *fam* : rush about
　— **trote** *nm* **1** : trot **2** *fam* : rush,
　bustle **3 al trote** : at a trot, quickly
trozo *nm* : piece, bit, chunk
trucha *nf* : trout
truco *nm* **1** : knack **2** ARDID : trick
trueno *nm* : thunder
trueque *nm* : barter, exchange
trufa *nf* : truffle
truncar {72} *vt* **1** : cut short **2**
　: thwart, spoil (plans, etc.)
tu *adj* : your
tú *pron* : you
tuba *nf* : tuba
tuberculosis *nf* : tuberculosis
tubo *nm* **1** : tube, pipe **2 tubo de**
　escape : exhaust pipe (of a vehicle)
　3 tubo de desagüe : drainpipe —
　tubería *nf* : pipes *pl*, tubing
tuerca *nf* : nut (for a screw)
tuerto, -ta *adj* : one-
　eyed, blind in one eye
tuétano *nm* : marrow
tufo *nm* **1** : vapor **2** *fam* : stench, stink
tugurio *nm* : hovel

tulipán *nm, pl* **-panes** : tulip
tullido, -da *adj* : crippled, paralyzed
tumba *nf* : tomb, grave
tumbar *vt* : knock down, knock over
　— **tumbarse** *vr* : lie down — **tumbo** *nm*
　dar tumbos : jolt, bump around
tumor *nm* : tumor
tumulto *nm* **1** : commotion, tumult
　2 MOTÍN : riot — **tumultuoso,**
　-sa *adj* : tumultuous
tuna *nf* : prickly pear
túnel *nm* : tunnel
túnica *nf* : tunic
tupé *nm* : toupee
tupido, -da *adj* : dense, thick
turba *nf* **1** : peat **2** MUCHEDUMBRE
　: mob, throng
turbación *nf, pl* **-ciones 1** :
　disturbance **2** CONFUSION : confusion
turbante *nm* : turban
turbar *vt* **1** : disturb, upset **2**
　CONFUNDIR : confuse, bewilder
tubina *nf* : turbine
turbio, -bia *adj* **1** : cloudy, murky

2 : blurred (of vision, etc.) —
turbión *nm, pl* **-biones** : squall
turbulencia *nf* : turbulence —
　turbulento, -ta *adj* : turbulent
turco, -ca *adj* : Turkish —
　turco *nm* : Turkish (language)
turista *nmf* : tourist — **turismo** *nm*
　: tourism, tourist industry —
　turístico, -ca *adj* : tourist, travel
turnarse *vr* : take turns, alternate
　— **turno** *nm* **1** : turn **2 turnarse**
　de noche : night shift
turquesa *nf* : turquoise
turrón *nm, pl* **-rrones** : nougat
tutear *vt* : address as *tú*
tutela *nf* **1** : guardianship (in law) **2 bajo**
　la tutela de : under the protection of
tuteo *nm* : addressing as *tú*
tutor, -tora *n* **1** : guardian
　2 : tutor (in education)
tuyo, -ya *adj* : yours, of yours —
　tuyo, *pron* **1 el tuyo, la tuya, lo tuyo,**
　los tuyos, las tuyas : yours **2 los**
　tuyos : your family, your friends

frutas[F] **tropicales**
tropical fruits

granada[F]
pomegranate

papaya[F]
papaya

piña[F]
pineapple

mango[M]
mango

kiwi[M]
kiwi

lichi[M]
litchi

carambola[F]
carambola

banana[F]
banana

fruta[F] de la pasión[F]
passion fruit

higo[M]
fig

U

u¹ *nf* : u, 22d letter of the Spanish alphabet

u² *conj* (*used before words beginning with o- or ho-*) : **or**

uapití *nm* : American elk, wapiti

ubicar {72} *vt Lat* **1** COLOCAR : place, position **2** LOCALIZAR : find — **ubicarse** *vr* : be located

ubre *nf* : udder

Ud., Uds. → usted

ufanarse *vr* **ufanarse de** : boast about — **ufano, -na** *adj* **1** : proud **2** ENGREÍDO : self-satisfied

ujier *nm* : usher

úlcera *nf* : ulcer

ulterior *adj* : later, subsequent — **ulteriormente** *adv* : subsequently

últimamente *adv* : lately, recently

ultimar *vt* **1** : complete, finish **2** *Lat* : kill — **ultimátum** *nm, pl* -**tums** : ultimatum

último, -ma *adj* **1** : last **2** : latest, most recent (in time) **3** : farthest (in space) **4 por último** : finally

ultrajar *vt* : outrage, insult — **ultraje** *nm* : outrage, insult

ultramar *nm* **de ultramar** *or* **en ultramar** : overseas — **ultramarino, -na** *adj* : overseas — **ultramarinos** *nmpl* **tienda de ultramar** : grocery store

ultranza: a ultranza *adv phr* : to the extreme — **a ultranza** *adj phr* : out-and-out, complete

ultrasonido *nm* : ultrasound

ultravioleta *adj* : ultraviolet

ulular *vi* **1** : hoot (of an owl) **2** : howl (of a wolf, the wind, etc.) — **ululato** *nm* : hoot (of an owl)

umbilical *adj* : umbilical

umbral *nm* : threshold

un, una *art, mpl* **unos** **1** : a, an **2 unos** *or* **unas** *pl* : some, a few **3 unos** *or* **unas** *pl* : about, approximately — **un** *adj* → **uno**

unánime *adj* : unanimous — **unanimidad** *nf* : unanimity

uncir {83} *vt* : yoke

undécimo, -ma *adj & n* : eleventh

ungir {35} *vt* : anoint — **ungüento** *nm* : ointment

único, -ca *adj* **1** : only, sole **2** EXCEPCIONAL : unique — **único, -ca** *n* : only one — **únicamente** *adv* : only

unicornio *nm* : unicorn

unidad *nf* **1** : unit **2** ARMONÍA :

unity — **unido, -da** *adj* **1** : united **2** : close (of friends, etc.)

unificar {72} *vt* : unify — **unificación** *nf, pl* -**ciones** : unification

uniformar *vt* **1** : standardize **2** : put into uniform — **uniformado, -da** *adj* : uniformed — **uniforme** *adj & nm* : uniform — **uniformidad** *nf* : uniformity

unilateral *adj* : unilateral

unir *vt* **1** : unite, join **2** COMBINAR : combine, mix together — **unirse** *vr* **1** : join together **2 unirse a** : join — **unión** *nf, pl* **uniones** **1** : union **2** JUNTURA : joint, coupling

unísono *nm* **al unísono** : in unison

unitario, -ria *adj* : unitary

universal *adj* : universal

universidad *nf* : university, college — **universitario, -ria** *adj* : university, college

universo *nm* : universe

uno, una (**un** *before masculine singular nouns*) *adj* : one — **uno,** *pron* **1** : one **2 unos, unas** *pl* : some **3 uno(s) a otro(s)** : one another, each other **4 uno y otro** : both — **uno** *nm* : one (number)

untar *vt* **1** : smear, grease **2** *fam* : bribe — **untuoso, -sa** *adj* : greasy, sticky

uña *nf* **1** : nail, fingernail **2** : claw (of a cat, etc.), hoof (of a horse, etc.)

uranio *nm* : uranium

Urano *nm* : Uranus

urbano, -na *adj* : urban, city — **urbanidad** *nf* : politeness, courtesy — **urbanización** *nf, pl* -**ciones** : housing development — **urbanizar** *vt* : develop, urbanize — **urbe** *nf* : large city

urdir *vt* **1** : warp **2** PLANEAR : plot — **urdimbre** *nf* : warp (of a fabric)

urgir {35} *v impers* : be urgent, be pressing — **urgencia** *nf* **1** : urgency **2** EMERGENCIA : emergency — **urgente** *adj* : urgent

urinario, -ria *adj* : urinary — **urinario** *nm* : urinal (place)

urna *nf* **1** : urn **2** : ballot box (for voting)

urraca *nf* : magpie

uruguayo, -ya *adj* : Uruguayan

usar *vt* **1** : use **2** LLEVAR : wear — **usarse** **1** EMPLEARSE : be used **2** : be worn, be in fashion — **usado, -da** *adj* **1** : used **2** GASTADO : worn, worn-out — **usanza** *nf* : custom, usage — **uso** *nm* **1** : use **2** DESGASTE : wear and tear **3** USANZA : custom, usage

usted *pron* **1** (*used in formal address; often written as* **Ud.** *or* Vd.)

uvas*F*
grapes

: you **2 ustedes** *pl* (*often written as* **Uds.** *or* Vds.) : you (all)

usual *adj* : usual

usuario, -ria *n* : user

usura *nf* : usury — **usurero, -ra** *n* : usurer

usurpar *vt* : usurp

utensilio *nm* : utensil, tool

útero *nm* : uterus, womb

utilizar {21} *vt* : use, utilize — **útil** *adj* : useful — **útiles** *nmpl* : implements, tools — **utilidad** *nf* : utility, usefulness — **utilitario, -ria** *adj* : utilitarian — **utilización** *nf, pl* -**ciones** : utilization, use

▸ **uva** *nf* : grape

V

v *nf* : v, 23d letter of the Spanish alphabet

va → **ir**

vaca *nf* : cow

vacaciones *nfpl* **1** : vacation **2 estar de vacaciones** : be on vacation **3 irse de vacaciones** : go on vacation

vacante *adj* : vacant — **vacante** *nf* : vacancy

vaciar {85} *vt* **1** : empty (out) **2** AHUECAR : hollow out **3** : cast, mold (a statue, etc.)

vacilar *vi* **1** : hesitate, waver **2** : flicker (of light) **3** TAMBALEARSE : be

unsteady, wobble **4** *fam* : joke, fool
around — **vacilación** *nf, pl* **-ciones**
: hesitation — **vacilante** *adj* **1** :
hesitant **2** OSCILANTE : unsteady
vacío, -cía *adj* : empty —
  vacío *nm* **1** : void **2** : vacuum (in
physics) **3** HUECO : space, gap
vacuna *nf* : vaccine — **vacunación** *nf,*
pl **-ciones** : vaccination —
  vacunar *vt* : vaccinate
vacuno, -na *adj* : bovine
vadear *vt* : ford — **vado** *nm* : ford
vagabundear *vi* : wander —
  vagabundo, -da *adj* **1** : vagrant **2** :
stray (of a dog, etc.) — **vagabundear** *n*
: hobo, bum — **vagancia** *nf* **1** :
vagrancy **2** PEREZA : laziness, idleness
  — **vagar** {52} *vi* : roam, wander
vagina *nf* : vagina
vago, -ga *adj* **1** : vague **2** PEREZOSO :
lazy, idle — **vago, -ga** *n* : idler, loafer
vagón *nm, pl* **-gones** : car (of a train)
vahído *nm* : dizzy spell
vaho *nm* **1** : breath **2** VAPOR : vapor, steam
vaina *nf* **1** : sheath, scabbard **2** : pod
(in botany) **3** *Lat fam* : bother, pain
vainilla *nf* : vanilla
vaivén *nm, pl* **-venes 1** : swinging,
swaying **2** : coming and going (of people,
etc.) **3 vaivenes** *nmpl* : ups and downs
vajilla *nf* : dishes *pl*
vale *nm* **1** : voucher **2** PAGARÉ :
IOU — **valedero, -ra** *adj* : valid
valentía *nf* : courage, bravery
valer {84} *vt* **1** : be worth **2** COSTAR : cost
3 GANAR : gain, earn **4** EQUIVALER A : be
equal to — *vi* **1** : have value, cost **2** SER
VÁLIDO : be valid, count **3** SERVIR : be of use
4 hacerse valer : assert oneself **5 más**
vale : it's better — **valerse** *vr* **1 valerse**
de : take advantage of **2 valerse solo** *or*
valerse por sí mismo : look after oneself
valeroso, -sa *adj* : courageous
valga, etc. → **valer**
valía *nf* : worth
validar *vt* : validate — **validez** *nf* :
validity — **válido, -da** *adj* : valid
valiente *adj* **1** : brave **2** (*used*
ironically) : fine, great
valija *nf* : case, valise
valioso, -sa *adj* : valuable
valla *nf* **1** : fence **2** : hurdle (in sports)
  — **vallar** *vt* : put a fence around
valle *nm* : valley
valor *nm* **1** : value, worth **2** VALENTÍA

: courage, valor **3 objetos de valor**
: valuables **4 sin valor** : worthless **5**
valores *nmpl* : values, principles **6**
valores *nmpl* : securities, bonds —
valoración *nf, pl* **-ciones** : valuation
  — **valorar** *vt* : evaluate, assess
vals *nm* : waltz
válvula *nf* : valve
vamos → **ir**
vampiro *nm* : vampire
van → **ir**
vanagloriarse *vr* : boast, brag
vándalo *nm* : vandal —
  vandalismo : vandalism
vanguardia *nf* **1** : vanguard **2** :
avant-garde (in art, music, etc.) **3 a**
la vanguardia : at/in the forefront
vanidad *nf* : vanity — **vanidoso,**
-sa *adj* : vain, conceited
vano, -na *adj* **1** INÚTIL : vain,
useless **2** SUPERFICIAL : empty,
hollow **3 en vano** : in vain
vapor *nm* **1** : steam, vapor **2 al vapor** :
steamed — **vaporizador** *nm* : vaporizer
  — **vaporizar** {21} *vt* : vaporize
vaquero, -ra *n* : cowboy *m*, cowgirl *f*
  — **vaqueros** *nmpl* : jeans
vara *nf* **1** : stick, rod **2** : staff (of office)
varado, -da *adj* : stranded
variar {85} *vt* **1** : vary **2** CAMBIAR :
change, alter — *vi* : vary, change —
variable *adj & nf* : variable — **variación** *nf,*
pl **-ciones** : variation — **variado, -da** *adj*
: varied — **variante** *nf* : variant
varicela *nf* : chicken pox
varicoso, -sa *adj* : varicose
variedad *nf* : variety
varilla *nf* : rod, stick
vario, -ria *adj* **1** : varied **2**
  vario, -rias *pl* : several
varita *nf* : wand
variz *nf, pl* **-rices** *or* **várices** : varicose vein
varón *nm, pl* **-rones 1** : man, male **2**
  NIÑO : boy — **varonil** *adj* : manly
vas → **ir**
vasco, -ca *adj* : Basque —
  vasco *nm* : Basque (language)
vasija *nf* : container, vessel
vaso *nm* **1** : glass **2** : vessel (in anatomy)
vástago *nm* **1** : offspring, descendent
  2 BROTE : shoot **3** VARILLA : rod
vasto, -ta *adj* : vast
vaticinar *vt* : prophesy, predict
  — **vaticinio** *nm* : prophecy
vatio *nm* : watt

vaya, etc. → **ir**
Vd., Vds. → **usted**
ve, etc. → **ir, ver**
vecinal *adj* : local
vecino, -na *n* **1** : neighbor **2**
  HABITANTE : resident, inhabitant —
  vecino, -na *adj* : neighboring —
vecindad *nf* : neighborhood, vicinity
  — **vecindario** *nm* **1** : neighborhood
2 VECINOS : community, residents *pl*
vedar *vt* : prohibit — **veda** *nf* **1** :
prohibition, ban **2** : closed season (for
hunting and fishing) — **vedado** *nm*
: preserve (for game, etc.)
vega *nf* : fertile lowland
vegetal *nm* : vegetable, plant
  — **vegetal** *adj* : vegetable —
vegetación *nf, pl* **-ciones** : vegetation
  — **vegetar** *vi* : vegetate —
vegetariano, -na *adj & n* : vegetarian
vehemente *adj* : vehement
vehículo *nm* : vehicle
veinte *adj & nm* : twenty —
  veinteavo, -va *adj* : twentieth
  — **veinteavo** *nm* : twentieth —
veintena *nf* : group of twenty, score
vejar *vt* : mistreat, humiliate —
  vejación *nf, pl* **-ciones** : humiliation
vejez *nf* : old age
vejiga *nf* **1** : bladder **2** AMPOLLA : blister
vela *nf* **1** : candle **2** : sail (of a ship)
3 VIGILIA : vigil **4 pasar la noche en**
vela : have a sleepless night
velada *nf* : evening (party)
velar *vt* **1** : hold a wake over **2** CUIDAR
: watch over **3** : blur (a photograph)
4 OCULTAR : veil, mask — *vi* **1** : stay
awake **2 velar por** : watch over —
velado, -da *adj* **1** : veiled, hidden
2 : blurred (of a photograph)
velero *nm* : sailing ship
veleta *nf* : weather vane
vello *nm* **1** : body hair **2** PELUSA :
down, fuzz — **vellón** *nm, pl* **-llones**
: fleece — **velloso, -sa** *adj* : downy,
fluffy — **velludo, -da** *adj* : hairy
velo *nm* : veil
veloz *adj, pl* **-loces** : fast, quick —
velocidad *nf* **1** : speed, velocity **2**
  MARCHA : gear (of an automobile) —
velocímetro *nm* : speedometer
vena *nf* **1** : vein **2** : grain (of wood)
3 DISPOSICIÓN : mood **4 tener**
vena de : have a talent for
venado *nm* **1** : deer **2** :

venison (in cooking)

vencer {86} *vt* **1** : beat, defeat **2** SUPERAR : overcome — *vi* **1** : win **2** CADUCAR : expire — **vencerse** *vr* : collapse, give way — **vencedor, -dora** *adj* : winning — **vencedor, -dora** *n* : winner — **vencido, -da** *adj* **1** : beaten, defeated **2** CADUCADO : expired **3** : due, payable (in finance) **4 darse por vencido** : give up — **vencimiento** *nm* **1** : expiration **2** : maturity (of a loan)

venda *nf* : bandage — **vendaje** *nm* : bandage, dressing — **vendar** *vt* **1** : bandage **2 vendar los ojos** : blindfold

vendaval *nm* : gale

vender *vt* : sell — **venderse** *vr* **1** : be sold **2 se vende** : for sale — **vendedor, -dora** *n* **1** : seller **2** : salesman *m*, saleswoman *f* (in a store)

vendimia *nf* : grape harvest

vendrá, etc. → venir

veneno *nm* **1** : poison **2** : venom (of a snake, etc.) — **venenoso, -sa** *adj* : poisonous

venerar *vt* : venerate, revere — **venerable** *adj* : venerable — **veneración** *nf, pl* **-ciones**

: veneration, reverence

venéreo, -rea *adj* : venereal

venezolano, -na *adj* : Venezuelan

venga → venir

vengar {52} *vt* : avenge — **vengarse** *vr* : get even, take revenge — **venganza** *nf* : vengeance, revenge — **vengativo, -va** *adj* : vindictive, vengeful

venia *nf* **1** : permission **2** : pardon (in law)

venial *adj* : venial, petty

venir {87} *vi* **1** : come **2** LLEGAR : arrive **3** HALLARSE : be, appear **4** QUEDAR : fit **5 que viene** : coming, next **6 venir a ser** : turn out to be **7 venir bien** : be suitable — **venirse** *vr* **1** : come **2 venirse abajo** : fall apart, collapse — **venida** *nf* **1** : arrival, coming **2** REGRESO : return — **venidero, -ra** *adj* : coming

venta *nf* **1** : sale, selling **2 en venta** : for sale

ventaja *nf* : advantage — **ventajoso, -sa** *adj* : advantageous

▸ **ventana** *nf* **1** : window **2 ventana de la nariz** : nostril — **ventanilla** *nf* **1** : window (of a vehicle or airplane) **2** : ticket window, box office (of a theater, etc.)

ventilar *vt* : ventilate, air (out)

— **ventilación** *nf, pl* **-ciones** : ventilation — **ventilador** *nm* : fan, ventilator

ventisca *nf* : blizzard — **ventisquero** *nm* : snowdrift

ventoso, -sa *adj* : windy — **ventosidad** *nf* : wind, flatulence

ventrílocuo, -cua *n* : ventriloquist

ventura *nf* **1** : fortune, luck **2** SATISFACCIÓN : happiness **3 a la ventura** : at random — **venturoso, -sa** *adj* : fortunate, happy

ver {88} *vt* **1** : see **2** : watch (television, etc.) — *vi* **1** : see **2 a ver** *or* **vamos a ver** : let's see **3 no tener nada que ver con** : have nothing to do with **4 ya veremos** : we'll see — **verse** *vr* **1** : see oneself **2** HALLARSE : find oneself **3** ENCONTRARSE : see each other, meet

vera *nf* **1** : side, edge **2** : bank (of a river)

veracidad *nf* : truthfulness

verano *nm* : summer — **veraneante** *nmf* : summer vacationer — **veranear** *vi* : spend the summer — **veraniego, -ga** *adj* : summer

veras *nfpl* **de veras** : really

veraz *adj, pl* **-races** : truthful

verbal *adj* : verbal

ventanas^F
windows

ventana^F de librillo^M
sliding folding window

ventana^F de guillotina^F
double-hung window

ventana^F a la inglesa^F
casement window

ventana^F corredera
sliding window

ventana^F de celosía^F
louvered window

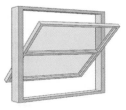

ventana^F basculante
horizontal pivoting window

ventana^F a la francesa^F
French casement window

ventana^F pivotante
vertical pivoting window

verbena *nf* : festival, fair
verbo *nm* : verb — **verboso,**
  -sa *adj* : verbose
verdad *nf* **1** : truth **2 de verdad** : really,
  truly **3 ¿verdad?** : right?, isn't that so?
  — **verdaderamente** *adv* : really, truly
  — **verdadero, -dera** *adj* : true, real
verde *adj* **1** : green **2** : dirty, risqué
  (of a joke, etc.) — **verde** *nm* :
  green — **verdor** *nm* : greenness
verdugo *nm* **1** : executioner,
  hangman **2** : cruel person, tyrant
verdura *nf* : vegetable(s), green(s)
vereda *nf* **1** : path, trail **2** *Lat* : sidewalk
veredicto *nm* : verdict
vergüenza *nf* **1** : shame **2** TIMIDEZ :
  bashfulness, shyness — **vergonzoso,**
  -sa *adj* **1** : shameful **2** TÍMIDO : bashful, shy
verídico, -ca *adj* : true, truthful
verificar {72} *vt* **1** : verify, confirm
  2 EXAMINAR : test, check out —
  verificarse *vr* **1** : take place **2** :
  come true (of a prophecy, etc.) —
  verificación *nf, pl* **-ciones** : verification
verja *nf* **1** : (iron) gate **2** : rails *pl* (of
  a fence) **3** ENREJADO : grating, grille
vermut *nm, pl* **-muts** : vermouth
vernáculo, -la *adj* : vernacular
verosímil *adj* **1** : probable,
  likely **2** CREÍBLE : credible
verraco *nm* : boar
verruga *nf* : wart
versar *vi* **versar sobre** : deal
  with, be about — **versado,**
  -da *adj* **versar en** : versed in
versátil *adj* **1** : versatile **2** VOLUBLE : fickle
versión *nf, pl* **-siones 1** : version
  2 TRADUCCIÓN : translation
verso *nm* **1** : poem, verse
  2 : line (of poetry)
vértebra *nf* : vertebra
verter {56} *vt* **1** : pour (out) **2**
  DERRAMAR : spill **3** TIRAR : dump — *vi*
  : flow — **vertedero** *nm* **1** : dump,
  landfill **2** DESAGÜE : drain, outlet
vertical *adj & nf* : vertical
vértice *nm* : vertex, apex
vertiente *nf* : slope
vértigo *nm* : vertigo, dizziness
  — **vertiginoso, -sa** *adj* : dizzy
vesícula *nf* **1** : blister **2**
  vesícula biliar : gallbladder
vestíbulo *nm* : vestibule, hall, foyer
vestido *nm* **1** : dress **2** ROPA
  : clothing, clothes *pl*

víbora[F]
viper

vestigio *nm* : vestige, trace
vestir {54} *vt* **1** : dress, clothe **2** LLEVAR
  : wear — *vi* : dress — **vestirse** *vr* : get
  dressed — **vestimenta** *nf* : clothing
  — **vestuario** *nm* **1** : wardrobe,
  clothes *pl* **2** : dressing room (in a
  theater), locker room (in sports)
veta *nf* **1** : vein, seam **2** : grain (of wood)
vetar *vt* : veto
veteado, -da *adj* : streaked, veined
veterano, -na *adj & n* : veteran
veterinaria *nf* : veterinary medicine
  — **veterinario, -ria** *adj* : veterinary
  — **veterinaria** *n* : veterinarian
veto *nm* : veto
vetusto, -ta *adj* : ancient
vez *nf, pl* **veces 1** : time **2** TURNO : turn
  3 a la vez : at the same time **4 a veces**
  : sometimes **5 de una vez** : all at once
  6 de una vez para siempre : once and
  for all **7 de vez en cuando** : from time
  to time **8 dos veces** : twice **9 en vez
  de** : instead of **1 0 una vez** : once
vía *nf* **1** : way, road, route **2** MEDIO :
  means **3** : track, line (of a railroad)
  4 : (anatomical) tract **5 en vía de** :
  in the process of — **vía** *prep* : via
viable *adj* : viable, feasible —
  viabilidad *nf* : viability
viaducto *nm* : viaduct
viajar *vi* : travel — **viajante** *nmf* : traveling
  salesperson — **viaje** *nm* : trip, journey —
  viajero, -ra *adj* : traveling — **viajar** *n* **1**
  : traveler **2** PASAJERO : passenger
vial *adj* : road, traffic

▸ **víbora** *nf* : viper
vibrar *vi* : vibrate — **vibración** *nf,
  pl* **-ciones** : vibration —
  vibrante *adj* : vibrant
vicario, -ria *n* : vicar
vicepresidente, -ta *n* : vice president
viceversa *adv* : vice versa
vicio *nm* **1** : vice **2** MALA COSTUMBRE
  : bad habit **3** DEFECTO : defect —
  viciado, -da *adj* **1** : corrupt **2** : stuffy,
  stale (of air, etc.) — **viciar** *vt* **1** :
  corrupt **2** ESTROPEAR : spoil, pollute —
  vicioso, -sa *adj* : depraved, corrupt
vicisitud *nf* : vicissitude
víctima *nf* : victim
victoria *nf* : victory — **victorioso,**
  -sa *adj* : victorious
vid *nf* : vine, grapevine
vida *nf* **1** : life **2** DURACIÓN :
  lifetime **3 de por vida** : for life
  4 estar con vida : be alive
video *or* vídeo *nm* **1** : video **2** :
  VCR, videocassette recorder
vidrio *nm* : glass — **vidriado** *nm* : glaze
  — **vidriar** *vt* : glaze — **vidriera** *nf* **1**
  : stained-glass window **2** : glass door
  3 *Lat* : shopwindow — **vidrioso,**
  -sa *adj* **1** : delicate (of a subject, etc.)
  2 ojos vidriosos : glassy eyes
vieira *nf* : scallop
viejo, -ja *adj* : old — **viejo, -ja** *n* **1**
  : old man *m,* old woman *f* **2**
  hacerse viejo, -ja : get old
viene, etc. → **venir**
viento *nm* : wind

vientre *nm* **1** : abdomen, belly **2** MATRIZ : **womb 3** INTESTINO : bowels *pl*
viernes *nms & pl* **1** : Friday **2** **Viernes Santo** : Good Friday
vietnamita *adj & nm* : Vietnamese
viga *nf* : beam, girder
vigencia *nf* **1** : validity **2 entrar en vigencia** : go into effect — **vigente** *adj* : valid, in force
vigésimo, -ma *adj & n* : twentieth
vigía *nmf* : lookout
vigilar *vt* : look after, watch over — *vi* : keep watch — **vigilancia** *nf* **1** : vigilance **2 bajo vigilancia** : under surveillance — **vigilante** *adj* : vigilant — **vigilante** *nmf* : watchman, guard — **vigilia** *nf* **1** : wakefulness **2** : vigil (in religion)
vigor *nm* **1** : vigor **2 entrar en vigor** : go into effect — **vigorizante** *adj* : invigorating — **vigoroso, -sa** *adj* : vigorous
VIH *nm* : HIV
vil *adj* : vile, despicable — **vileza** *nf* **1** : vileness **2** : despicable act — **vilipendiar** *vt* : revile
villa *nf* **1** : town, village **2** : villa (house)
villancico *nm* : (Christmas) carol
villano, -na *n* : villain
vilo *nm* **en vilo** : suspended, in the air
vinagre *nm* : vinegar — **vinagrera** *nf* : cruet — **vinagreta** *nf* : vinaigrette
vincular *vt* : tie, link — **vínculo** *nm* : link, tie, bond
vindicar *vt* **1** : vindicate **2** VENGAR : avenge
vino[1], etc. → **venir**
vino[2] *nm* : wine
viña *nf* or **viñedo** *nm* : vineyard
vio, etc. → **ver**
viola *nf* : viola
violar *vt* **1** : violate (a law, etc.) **2** : rape (a person) — **violación** *nf, pl* **-ciones 1** : violation, offense **2** : rape (of a person)
violencia *nf* : violence, force — **violentar** *vt* **1** : force **2** : break into (a house, etc.) — **violentarse** *vr* **1** : force oneself **2** AVERGONZARSE : be embarrassed — **violento, -ta** *adj* **1** : violent **2** INCÓMODO : awkward, embarrassing
violeta *adj & nm* : violet (color) — **violeta** *nf* : violet (flower)
violín *nm, pl* **-lines** : violin — **violinista** *nmf* : violinist — **violoncelista** or **violonchelista** *nmf* : cellist — **violoncelo** or **violonchelo** *nm* : cello, violoncello

virar *vi* : turn, change direction — **viraje** *nm* **1** : turn, swerve **2** CAMBIO : change
virgen *adj & nmf, pl* **vírgenes** : virgin — **virginal** *adj* : virginal — **virginidad** *nf* : virginity
viril *adj* : virile — **virilidad** *nf* : virility
virtual *adj* : virtual
virtud *nf* **1** : virtue **2 en virtud de** : by virtue of — **virtuoso, -sa** *adj* : virtuous — **virtud** *n* : virtuoso
viruela *nf* **1** : smallpox **2 picado de viruelas** : pockmarked
virulento, -ta *adj* : virulent
virus *nms & pl* : virus
visa *nf Lat* : visa — **visado** *nm, Spain* : visa
vísceras *nfpl* : entrails — **visceral** *adj* : visceral
viscoso, -sa *adj* : viscous — **viscosidad** *nf* : viscosity
visera *nf* : visor
visible *adj* : visible — **visibilidad** *nf* : visibility
visión *nf, pl* **-siones 1** : eyesight **2** APARICIÓN : vision, illusion **3** PUNTO DE VISTA : view, perspective — **visionario, -ria** *adj & n* : visionary
visitar *vt* : visit — **visita** *nf* **1** : visit **2 tener visita** : have company — **visitante** *adj* : visiting — **visitante** *nmf* : visitor
vislumbrar *vt* : make out, discern — **vislumbre** *nf* **1** : glimpse, sign **2** RESPLANDOR : glimmer, gleam
viso *nm* **1** : sheen **2 tener visos de** : seem, show signs of
visón *nm, pl* **-sones** : mink
víspera *nf* : eve, day before
vista *nf* **1** : vision, eyesight **2** MIRADA : look, gaze **3** PANORAMA : view, vista **4** : hearing (in court) **5 a primera vista** or **a simple vista** : at first sight **6 hacer la vista gorda** : turn a blind eye **7 perder de vista** : lose sight of — **vistazo** *nm* **1** : glance **2 echar un vista** : have a look
visto, -ta *adj* **1** : clear, obvious **2** COMÚN : commonly seen **3 estar bien visto** : be approved of **4 estar mal visto** : be frowned upon **5 nunca visto** : unheard-of **6 por lo visto** : apparently **7 visto que** : since, given that — **visto** *nm* **visto bueno** : approval — **visto** *pp* → **ver**
vistoso, -sa *adj* : colorful, bright
visual *adj* : visual — **visualizar** {21} *vt* : visualize

vital *adj* : vital — **vitalicio, -cia** *adj* : life, for life — **vitalidad** *nf* : vitality
vitamina *nf* : vitamin
viticultor, -tora *n* : winegrower — **viticultura** *nf* : wine growing
vitorear *vt* : cheer, acclaim
vítreo, -trea *adj* : glassy
vitrina *nf* **1** : showcase, display case **2** *Lat* : shopwindow
vituperar *vt* : censure — **vituperio** *nm* : censure
viudo, -da *n* : widower *m*, widow *f* — **viudo, -da** *adj* : widowed — **viudez** *nf* : widowerhood, widowhood
viva *nm* **dar vivas** : cheer
vivacidad *nf* : vivacity, liveliness
vivamente *adv* **1** : vividly **2** PROFUNDAMENTE : deeply, acutely
vivaz *adj, pl* **-vaces 1** : lively, vivacious **2** AGUDO : vivid, sharp
víveres *nmpl* : provisions, supplies
vivero *nm* **1** : nursery (for plants) **2** : (fish) hatchery, (oyster) bed
viveza *nf* **1** : liveliness **2** : vividness (of colors, descriptions, etc.) **3**

violín [M]
violin

ASTUCIA : sharpness (of mind)
— **vívido, -da** *adj* : vivid
vividor, -dora *n* : freeloader
vivienda *nf* **1** : housing **2**
MORADA : dwelling
viviente *adj* : living
vivificar {72} *vt* : enliven
vivir *vi* **1** : live, be alive **2 vivir de** : live
on — *vt* : experience, live (through) —
vivir *nm* **1** : life, lifestyle **2 de mal vivir** :
disreputable — **vivo, -va** *adj* **1** : alive **2**
INTENSO : intense, bright **3** ANIMADO : lively
4 ASTUTO : sharp, quick **5 en vivo** : live
vocablo *nm* : word —
vocabulario *nm* : vocabulary
vocación *nf, pl* **-ciones** : vocation
— **vocacional** *adj* : vocational
vocal *adj* : vocal — **vocal** *nmf* : member
(of a committee, etc.) — **vocal** *nf* : vowel
— **vocalista** *nmf* : singer, vocalist
vocear *v* : shout — **vocerío** *nm* : shouting
vociferar *vi* : shout

vodka *nmf* : vodka
volar {19} *vi* **1** : fly **2** : blow away (of
papers, etc.) **3** *fam* : disappear **4 irse**
volando : rush off — *vt* : blow up —
volador, -dora *adj* : flying — **volandas** :
en volar *adv phr* : in the air — **volante** *adj*
: flying — **volante** *nm* **1** : steering
wheel **2** : shuttlecock (in badminton) **3** :
flounce (of fabric) **4** *Lat* : flier, circular
volátil *adj* : volatile
▸ **volcán** *nm, pl* **-canes** : volcano —
volcánico, -ca *adj* : volcanic
volcar {82} *vt* **1** : upset, knock over
2 VACIAR : empty out — *vi* : overturn
— **volcarse** *vr* **1** : overturn, tip over
2 volcar en : throw oneself into
voleibol *nm* : volleyball
voltaje *nm* : voltage
voltear *vt* : turn over, turn upside
down — **voltearse** *vr Lat* : turn
(around) — **voltereta** *nf* : somersault
voltio *nm* : volt

voluble *adj* : fickle
volumen *nm, pl* **-lúmenes** : volume
— **voluminoso, -sa** *adj* : voluminous
voluntad *nf* **1** : will **2** DESEO : wish
3 INTENCIÓN : intention **4 a voluntad**
: at will **5 buena voluntad** : goodwill
6 mala voluntad : ill will **7 fuerza de**
voluntad : willpower — **voluntario,**
-ria *adj* : voluntary — **voluntad** *n* :
volunteer — **voluntarioso, -sa** *adj* **1**
: willing **2** TERCO : stubborn, willful
voluptuoso, -sa *adj* : voluptuous
volver {89} *vi* **1** : return, come or go back
2 volver a : return to, do again **3 volver en**
sí : come to — *vt* **1** : turn, turn over, turn
inside out **2** CONVERTIR EN : turn (into) **3**
volver loco : drive crazy — **volverse** *vr* **1**
: turn (around) **2** HACERSE : become
vomitar *vi* : vomit — *vt* **1** : vomit
2 : spew (out) — **vómito** *nm* **1** :
(action of) vomiting **2** : vomit
voraz *adj, pl* **-races** : voracious
vos *pron Lat* : you
vosotros, -tras *pron, Spain*
: you, yourselves
votar *vi* : vote — *vt* : vote for —
votación *nf, pl* **-ciones** : vote, voting
— **votante** *nmf* : voter — **voto** *nm* **1**
: vote **2** : vow (in religion)
voy → **ir**
voz *nf, pl* **voces 1** : voice **2** GRITO : shout,
yell **3** VOCABLO : word, term **4** RUMOR
: rumor **5 dar voces** : shout **6 en voz**
alta : loudly **7 en voz baja** : softly
vuelco *nm* : upset, overturning
vuelo *nm* **1** : flight **2** : (action of) flying **3** :
flare (of clothing) **4 al vuelo** : on the wing
vuelta *nf* **1** : turn **2** REVOLUCIÓN : circle,
revolution **3** CURVA : bend, curve **4**
REGRESO : return **5** : round, lap (in sports)
6 PASEO : walk, drive, ride **7** REVÉS :
back, other side **8** *Spain* : change **9**
dar vueltas : spin **10 estar de vuelta**
: be back — **vuelto** *nm Lat* : change
vuestro, -tra *adj, Spain* : your, of
yours — **vuestro, -tra** *pron, Spain*
(*with definite article*) : yours
vulgar *adj* **1** : vulgar **2** CORRIENTE :
common — **vulgaridad** *nf* **1** : vulgarity
2 BANALIDAD : banality — **vulgo** *nm* **el**
vulgar : the masses, common people
vulnerable *adj* : vulnerable —
vulnerabilidad *nf* : vulnerability

volcán^M
volcano (erupting volcano)

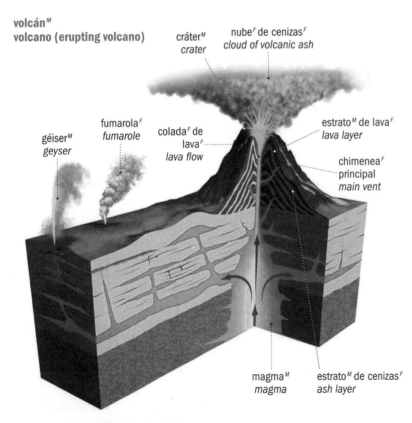

géiser^M
geyser

fumarola^F
fumarole

colada^F de
lava^F
lava flow

cráter^M
crater

nube^F de cenizas^F
cloud of volcanic ash

estrato^M de lava^F
lava layer

chimenea^F
principal
main vent

magma^M
magma

estrato^M de cenizas^F
ash layer

W

w *nf* : w, 24th letter of the Spanish alphabet
wáter *nm, Spain* : toilet
whisky *nm, pl* **-skys** *or* -skies : whiskey

X

x *nf* : x, 25th letter of the Spanish alphabet
xenofobia *nf* : xenophobia
▸ **xilófono** *nm* : xylophone

Y

y¹ *nf* : y, 26th letter of the Spanish alphabet
y² *conj* : and
ya *adv* **1** : already **2** AHORA : (right) now **3** MÁS TARDE : later, soon **4 ya no** : no longer **5 ya que** : now that, since, inasmuch as
yacer {90} *vi* : lie (on or in the ground) — **yacimiento** *nm* : bed, deposit
yanqui *adj & nmf* : Yankee
yate *nm* : yacht
yegua *nf* : mare
yelmo *nm* : helmet
yema *nf* **1** : bud, shoot **2** : yolk (of an egg) **3** *or* **yema del dedo** : fingertip
yerba *nf* **1** *or* **yerba mate** : maté **2** → **hierba**
yermo, -ma *adj* : barren, deserted — **yermo** *nm* : wasteland
yerno *nm* : son-in-law
yerro *nm* : blunder, mistake
yerto, -ta *adj* : stiff

xilófono^M
xylophone

yesca *nf* : tinder
yeso *nm* **1** : gypsum **2** : plaster (for art, construction)
yo *pron* **1** (*subject*) : I **2** (*object*) : me **3 soy yo** : it is I, it's me — **yo** *nm* : ego, self
yodo *nm* : iodine
yoga *nm* : yoga
yogurt *or* yogur *nm* : yogurt
yuca *nf* : yucca
yugo *nm* : yoke (of oxen)
yugoslavo, -va *adj* : Yugoslavian
yugular *adj* : jugular
yunque *nm* : anvil
yunta *nf* : yoke
yuxtaponer {60} *vt* : juxtapose — **yuxtaposición** *nf, pl* **-ciones** : juxtaposition

Z

z *nf* : z, 27th letter of the Spanish alphabet
zacate *nm Lat* : grass
zafar *vi Lat* : loosen, untie — **zafarse** *vr* **1** : come undone **2** : get free of (an obligation, etc.)
zafio, -fia *adj* : coarse
▸ **zafiro** *nm* : sapphire
zaga *nf* **a la zaga** *or* **en zaga** : behind, in the rear
zaguán *nm, pl* **-guanes** : (entrance) hall
zaherir {76} *vt* : hurt (someone's feelings)
zaino, -na *adj* : chestnut (color)
zalamería *nf* : flattery — **zalamero, -ra** *adj* : flattering — **zalamero, -ra** *n* : flatterer
zambullirse {38} *vr* : dive, plunge — **zambullida** *nf* : dive, plunge
zanahoria *nf* : carrot
zancada *nf* : stride, step — **zancadilla** *nf* **1** : trip, stumble **2 hacer una zancadilla a algn** : trip someone up
zancos *nmpl* : stilts
zancudo *nm Lat* : mosquito
zángano, -na *n, fam* : lazy person, slacker — **zángano** *nm* : drone (bee)
zanja *nf* : ditch, trench — **zanjar** *vt* : settle, resolve
zapallo *nm Lat* : pumpkin — **zapallito** *nm Lat* : zucchini
zapapico *nm* : pickax
zapato *nm* : shoe — **zapatería** *nf* : shoe store — **zapatero, -ra** *n* : shoemaker, cobbler — **zapatilla** *nf* **1** : slipper **2** : sneaker (for sports, etc.)
zar *nm* : czar
zarandear *vt* **1** : sift **2** SACUDIR : shake

zorro^M
fox

zarcillo *nm* : earring
zarpa *nf* : paw
zarpar *vi* : set sail, raise anchor
zarza *nf* : bramble — **zarzamora** *nf* : blackberry
zigzag *nm, pl* **-zags** *or* **-zagues** : zigzag — **zigzaguear** *vi* : zigzag
zinc *nm* : zinc
zíper *nm Lat* : zipper
zircón *nm, pl* **-cones** : zircon
zócalo *nm* **1** : base (of a column, etc.) **2** : baseboard (of a wall) **3** *Lat* : main square, plaza
zodíaco *nm* : zodiac
zona *nf* : zone, area
zoo *nm* : zoo — **zoología** *nf* : zoology — **zoológico, -ca** *adj* : zoological — **zoológico** *nm* : zoo — **zoólogo, -ga** *n* : zoologist
zopilote *nm Lat* : buzzard
zoquete *nmf, fam* : oaf, blockhead
zorrillo *nm Lat* : skunk
▸ **zorro, -rra** *n* : fox, vixen *f* — **zorro, -rra** *adj* : foxy, sly
zozobra *nf* : anxiety, worry — **zozobrar** *vi* : capsize
zueco *nm* : clog (shoe)
zumbar *vi* : buzz — *vt, fam* : hit, beat — **zumbido** *nm* : buzzing
zumo *nf* : juice
zurcir {83} *vt* : darn, mend
zurdo, -da *adj* : left-handed — **zurdo, -da** *n* : left-handed person — **zurda** *nf* : left hand
zutano, -na → **fulano**

zafiro^M **y otras piedras**^F
sapphire and other stones

piedras^F **preciosas**
precious stones

zafiro^M
sapphire

diamante^M
diamond

rubí^M
ruby

esmeralda^F
emerald

piedras^F **semipreciosas**
semiprecious stones

amatista^F
amethyst

lapislázuli^M
lapis lazuli

aguamarina^F
aquamarine

turquesa^F
turquoise

granate^M
garnet

topacio^M
topaz

turmalina^F
tourmaline

ópalo^M
opal

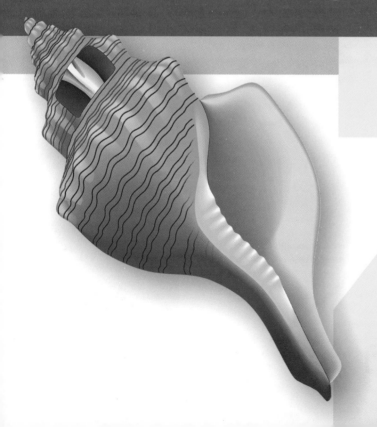

ENGLISH-SPANISH

a[1] *n, pl* **a's** *or* **as** : a *f*, primera letra del alfabeto inglés

a[2] *art* (an *before vowel or silent h*) **1** : un *m*, una *f* **2** PER : por, a la, al

aback *adv* **be taken aback** : quedarse desconcertado

abacus *n, pl* **abaci** *or* **abacuses** : ábaco *m*

abandon *vt* **1** DESERT : abandonar **2** GIVE UP : renunciar a — **abandon** *n* : desenfreno *m* — **abandonment** *n* : abandono *m*

abashed *adj* : avergonzado

abate *vi* **abated; abating** : amainar, disminuir

abattoir *n* : matadero *m*

abbey *n, pl* **-beys** : abadía *f* — **abbot** *n* : abad *m*

abbreviate *vt* **-ated; -ating** :

abreviar — **abbreviation** *n* : abreviatura *f*, abreviación *f*

abdicate *v* **-cated; -cating** : abdicar — **abdication** *n* : abdicación *f*

abdomen *n* : abdomen *m*, vientre *m* — **abdominal** *adj* : abdominal

abduct *vt* : secuestrar — **abduction** *n* : secuestro *m*

aberration *n* : aberración *f*

abet *vt* **abetted; abetting** *or* **aid and abet** : ser cómplice de

abeyance *n* : desuso *m*

abhor *vt* **-horred; -horring** : aborrecer

abide *v* **abode** *or* **abided; abiding** *vt* : soportar, tolerar — *vi* **1** DWELL : morar **2 abide by** : atenerse a

ability *n, pl* **-ties 1** CAPABILITY : aptitud *f*, capacidad *f* **2** SKILL : habilidad *f*

abject *adj* : miserable, desdichado

ablaze *adj* : en llamas

able *adj* **abler; ablest 1** CAPABLE : capaz, hábil **2** COMPETENT : competente

abnormal *adj* : anormal — **abnormality** *n, pl* **-ties** : anormalidad *f*

aboard *adv* : a bordo — **aboard** *prep* : a bordo de

abode *n* : morada *f*, domicilio *m*

abolish *vt* : abolir, suprimir — **abolition** *n* : abolición *f*

abominable *adj* : abominable, aborrecible — **abomination** *n* : abominación *f*

aborigine *n* : aborigen *mf*

abort *vt* : abortar — **abortion** *n* : aborto *m* — **abortive** *adj* UNSUCCESSFUL : malogrado

abound *vi* **abound in** : abundar en

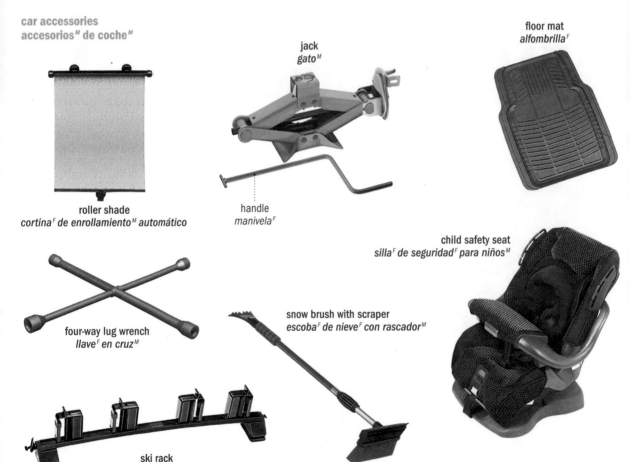

car accessories
accesorios*M* de coche*M*

jack
gato*M*

floor mat
alfombrilla*F*

roller shade
cortina*F* de enrollamiento*M* automático

handle
manivela*F*

child safety seat
silla*F* de seguridad*F* para niños*M*

four-way lug wrench
llave*F* en cruz*M*

snow brush with scraper
escoba*F* de nieve*F* con rascador*M*

ski rack
porta-esquí*M*

about *adv* **1** APPROXIMATELY :
aproximadamente, más o menos **2** AROUND
: alrededor **3 be about to** : estar a punto
de **4 be up and about** : estar levantado
— **about** *prep* **1** AROUND : alrededor
de **2** CONCERNING : acerca de, sobre
above *adv* : arriba — **above** *prep* **1**
: encima de **2 above all** : sobre todo
— **aboveboard** *adj* : honrado
abrasive *adj* **1** : abrasivo **2**
BRUSQUE : brusco, mordaz
abreast *adv* **1** : al lado **2 keep abreast
of** : mantenerse al corriente de
abridge *vt* **abridged; abridging** : abreviar
abroad *adv* **1** : en el extranjero
2 WIDELY : por todas partes **3 go
abroad** : ir al extranjero
abrupt *adj* **1** SUDDEN : repentino
2 BRUSQUE : brusco
abscess *n* : absceso *m*
absence *n* **1** : ausencia *f* **2** LACK
: falta *f*, carencia *f* — **absent** *adj* :
ausente — **absentee** *n* : ausente *mf* —
absentminded *adj* : distraído, despistado
absolute *adj* : absoluto —
absolutely *adv* : absolutamente
absolve *vt* **-solved; -solving** : absolver
absorb *vt* : absorber — **absorbent** *adj* :
absorbente — **absorption** *n* : absorción *f*
abstain *vi* **abstain from** : abstenerse
de — **abstinence** *n* : abstinencia *f*
abstract *adj* : abstracto — **abstract** *vt*
: extraer — **abstract** *n* : resumen *m*
— **abstraction** *n* : abstracción *f*
absurd *adj* : absurdo —
absurdity *n, pl* **-ties** : absurdo *m*
abundant *adj* : abundante —
abundance *n* : abundancia *f*
abuse *vt* **abused; abusing 1** MISUSE :
abusar de **2** MISTREAT : maltratar **3** REVILE :
insultar — **abuse** *n* **1** : abuso *m* **2** INSULTS
: insultos *mpl* — **abusive** *adj* : injurioso
abut *vi* **abutted; abutting
abut on** : colindar con
abyss *n* : abismo *m* —
abysmal *adj* : atroz, pésimo
academy *n, pl* **-mies** : academia *f*
— **academic** *adj* **1** : académico
2 THEORETICAL : teórico
accelerate *v* **-ated; -ating** : acelerar
— **acceleration** *n* : aceleración *f*
accent *vt* : acentuar — **accent** *n* :
acento *m* — **accentuate** *vt* **-ated;
-ating** : acentuar, subrayar
accept *vt* : aceptar — **acceptable** *adj*

: aceptable — **acceptance** *n* **1** :
aceptación *f* **2** APPROVAL : aprobación *f*
access *n* : acceso *m* — **accessible** *adj*
: accesible, asequible
▸ **accessory** *n, pl* **-ries 1** : accesorio *m* **2**
ACCOMPLICE : cómplice *mf*
accident *n* **1** MISHAP : accidente *m* **2**
CHANCE : casualidad *f* — **accidental** *adj*
: accidental — **accidentally** *adv* **1**
BY CHANCE : por casualidad **2**
UNINTENTIONALLY : sin querer
acclaim *vt* : aclamar —
acclaim *n* : aclamación *f*
acclimatize *vt* **-tized; -tizing** : aclimatar
accommodate *vt* **-dated; -dating 1**
ADAPT : acomodar, adaptar **2** SATISFY :
complacer, satisfacer **3** HOLD : tener
cabida para — **accommodation** *n* **1**
: adaptación *f* **2 accommodations** *npl*
LODGING : alojamiento *m*
accompany *vt* **-nied;
-nying** : acompañar
accomplice *n* : cómplice *mf*
accomplish *vt* : realizar, llevar
a cabo — **accomplishment** *n* **1**
COMPLETION : realización *f* **2**
ACHIEVEMENT : logro *m*, éxito *m*
accord *n* **1** AGREEMENT : acuerdo *m* **2**
of one's own accord : voluntariamente
— **accordance** *n* **in accordance
with** : conforme a, de acuerdo con

— **accordingly** *adv* : en consecuencia
— **according to** *prep* : según
▸ **accordion** *n* : acordeón *m*
accost *vt* : abordar
account *n* **1** : cuenta *f* **2** REPORT
: relato *m*, informe *m* **3** WORTH :
importancia *f* **4 on account of** : a causa
de, debido a **5 on no account** : de ninguna
manera — **account** *vi* **account for** : dar
cuenta de, explicar — **accountable** *adj*
: responsable — **accountant** *n* :
contador *m*, -dora *f Lat;* contable *mf*
Spain — **accounting** *n* : contabilidad *f*
accrue *vi* **-crued; -cruing** : acumularse
accumulate *v* **-lated; -lating** *vt*
: acumular — *vi* : acumularse —
accumulation *n* : acumulación *f*
accurate *adj* : exacto, preciso —
accuracy *n* : exactitud *f*, precisión *f*
accuse *vt* **-cused; -cusing** : acusar
— **accusation** *n* : acusación *f*
accustomed *adj* **1** : acostumbrado
2 become accustomed to
: acostumbrarse a
ace *n* : as *m*
ache *vi* **ached; aching** : doler
— **ache** *n* : dolor *m*
achieve *vt* **achieved; achieving** :
lograr, realizar — **achievement** *n*
: logro *m*, éxito *m*
acid *adj* : ácido — **acid** *n* : ácido *m*

accordion
acordeón *M*

treble register
registro M de altos M

treble keyboard
teclado M triple

bass keyboard
teclado M de bajos M

bass register
registros M de bajos M

bellows
doble fuelle M

acknowledge *vt* **-edged; -edging 1**
ADMIT : admitir **2** RECOGNIZE : reconocer
3 acknowledge receipt of : acusar
recibo de — **acknowledgment** *n* **1**
: reconocimiento *m* **2** THANKS :
agradecimiento *m* **3 acknowledgement
of receipt** : acuse *m* de recibo
acne *n* : acné *m*
acorn *n* : bellota *f*
acoustic *or* **acoustical** *adj* : acústico
— **acoustics** *ns & pl* : acústica *f*
acquaint *vt* **1 acquaint someone
with** : poner a algn al corriente de
2 be acquainted with : conocer a
(una persona), saber (un hecho) —
acquaintance *n* **1** : conocimiento *m* **2**
: conocido *m*, -da *f* (persona)
acquire *vt* **-quired; -quiring** : adquirir
— **acquisition** *n* : adquisición *f*
acquit *vt* **-quitted; -quitting** : absolver
acre *n* : acre *m* — **acreage** *n*
: superficie *f* en acres
acrid *adj* : acre
acrobat *n* : acróbata *mf* —
acrobatic *adj* : acrobático
acronym *n* : siglas *fpl*
across *adv* **1** : de un lado a otro **2**
CROSSWISE : a través **3 go across** :
atravesar — **across** *prep* **1** : a través de **2**
across the street : al otro lado de la calle
acrylic *n* : acrílico *m*
act *vi* **1** : actuar **2** PRETEND : fingir **3**
FUNCTION : funcionar **4 act as** : servir de
— *vt* : interpretar (un papel) — **act** *n* **1**
ACTION : acto *m*, acción *f* **2** DECREE : ley *f* **3**
: acto *m* (en una obra de teatro), número *m*
(en un espectáculo) — **acting** *adj* : interino
action *n* **1** : acción *f* **2** LAWSUIT :
demanda *f* **3 take action** : tomar medidas
activate *vt* **-vated; -vating** : activar
active *adj* **1** : activo **2** LIVELY : enérgico
3 active volcano : volcán *m* en actividad
— **activity** *n*, *pl* **-ties** : actividad *f*
actor *n* : actor *m* — **actress** *n* : actriz *f*
actual *adj* : real, verdadero —
actually *adv* : realmente, en realidad
acupuncture *n* : acupuntura *f*
acute *adj* **acuter; acutest 1** :
agudo **2** PERCEPTIVE : perspicaz
ad → **advertisement**
adamant *adj* : inflexible
adapt *vt* : adaptar — *vi* : adaptarse —
adaptable *adj* : adaptable — **adaptation** *n*
: adaptación *f* — **adapter** *n* : adaptador *m*
add *vt* **1** : añadir **2** *or* **add up**

: sumar — *vi* : sumar
addict *n* **1** : adicto *m*, -ta *f* **2**
or **drug addict** : drogadicto *m*,
-ta *f;* toxicómano *m*, -na *f* —
addiction *n* : dependencia *f*
addition *n* **1** : suma *f* (en matemáticas)
2 ADDING : adición *f* **3 in addition** :
además — **additional** *adj* : adicional
— **additive** *n* : aditivo *m*
address *vt* **1** : dirigirse a (una
persona) **2** : ponerle la dirección
a (una carta) **3** : tratar (un asunto)
— **address** *n* **1** : dirección *f*,
domicilio *m* **2** SPEECH : discurso *m*
adept *adj* : experto, hábil
adequate *adj* : adecuado, suficiente
adhere *vi* **-hered; -hering 1** STICK
: adherirse **2 adhere to** : observar
— **adherence** *n* **1** : adhesión *f* **2**
: observancia *f* (de una ley, etc.)
— **adhesive** *adj* : adhesivo —
adhesive *n* : adhesivo *m*
adjacent *adj* : adyacente, contiguo
adjective *n* : adjetivo *m*
adjoining *adj* : contiguo, vecino
adjourn *vt* : aplazar, suspender
— *vi* : suspenderse
adjust *vt* : ajustar, arreglar — *vi* :
adaptarse — **adjustable** *adj* : ajustable —
adjustment *n* : ajuste *m* (a una máquina,
etc.), adaptación *f* (de una persona)
ad–lib *v* **-libbed; -libbing** : improvisar
administer *vt* : administrar —
administration *n* : administración *f* —
administrative *adj* : administrativo —
administrator *n* : administrador *m*, -dora *f*
admirable *adj* : admirable
admiral *n* : almirante *m*
admire *vt* **-mired; -miring** : admirar
— **admiration** *n* : admiración *f* —
admirer *n* : admirador *m*, -dora *f*
admit *vt* **-mitted; -mitting 1** :
admitir, dejar entrar **2** ACKNOWLEDGE
: reconocer — **admission** *n* **1**
ADMITTANCE : entrada *f*, admisión *f* **2**
ACKNOWLEDGMENT : reconocimiento *m* —
admittance *n* : admisión *f*, entrada *f*
admonish *vt* : amonestar, reprender
ado *n* **1** : alboroto *m*, bulla *f* **2 without
further ado** : sin más (preámbulos)
adolescent *n* : adolescente *mf* —
adolescence *n* : adolescencia *f*
adopt *vt* : adoptar —
adoption *n* : adopción *f*
adore *vt* **adored; adoring 1** : adorar

2 LIKE, LOVE : encantarle (algo a
uno) — **adorable** *adj* : adorable
— **adoration** *n* : adoración *f*
adorn *vt* : adornar —
adornment *n* : adorno *m*
adrift *adj & adv* : a la deriva
adroit *adj* : diestro, hábil
adult *adj* : adulto — **adult** *n*
: adulto *m*, -ta *f*
adultery *n*, *pl* **-teries** : adulterio *m*
advance *v* **-vanced; -vancing** *vt* :
adelantar — *vi* : avanzar, adelantarse
— **advance** *n* **1** : avance *m* **2**
PROGRESS : adelanto *m* **3 in advance**
: por adelantado — **advancement** *n*
: adelanto *m*, progreso *m*
advantage *n* **1** : ventaja *f* **2 take
advantage of** : aprovecharse de —
advantageous *adj* : ventajoso
advent *n* **1** ARRIVAL : llegada *f*
2 Advent : Adviento *m*
adventure *n* : aventura *f* —
adventurous *adj* **1** : intrépido
2 RISKY : arriesgado
adverb *n* : adverbio *m*
adversary *n*, *pl* **-saries** :
adversario *m*, -ria *f*
adverse *adj* : adverso, desfavorable
— **adversity** *n*, *pl* **-ties** : adversidad *f*
advertise *v* **-tised; -tising** *vt* :
anunciar — *vi* : hacer publicidad
— **advertisement** *n* : anuncio *m*
— **advertiser** *n* : anunciante *mf*
— **advertising** *n* : publicidad *f*
advice *n* : consejo *m*
advise *vt* **-vised; -vising 1** COUNSEL
: aconsejar, asesorar **2** RECOMMEND
: recomendar **3** INFORM : informar
— **advisable** *adj* : aconsejable —
adviser *n* : consejero *m*, -ra *f;* asesor *m*,
-sora *f* — **advisory** *adj* : consultivo
advocate *vt* **-cated; -cating**
: recomendar — **advocate** *n*
: defensor *m*, -sora *f*
aerial *adj* : aéreo — **aerial** *n* : antena *f*
aerobics *ns & pl* : aeróbic *m*
aerodynamic *adj* : aerodinámico
aerosol *n* : aerosol *m*
aesthetic *adj* : estético
afar *adv* : lejos
affable *adj* : afable
affair *n* **1** : asunto *m*, cuestión *f* **2** *or*
love affair : amorío *m*, aventura *f*
affect *vt* **1** : afectar **2** FEIGN : fingir
— **affection** *n* : afecto *m*, cariño *m*

— **affectionate** *adj* : afectuoso, cariñoso
affinity *n, pl* **-ties** : afinidad *f*
affirm *vt* : afirmar —
  affirmative *adj* : afirmativo
affix *vt* : fijar, pegar
afflict *vt* : afligir — **affliction** *n* : aflicción *f*
affluent *adj* : próspero, adinerado
afford *vt* **1** : tener los recursos para,
  permitirse (el lujo de) **2** PROVIDE : brindar
affront *n* : afrenta *f*
afloat *adv & adj* : a flote
afoot *adj* : en marcha
afraid *adj* **1 be afraid** : tener miedo
  2 I'm afraid not : me temo que no
African *adj* : africano
after *adv* **1** AFTERWARD : después **2** BEHIND
  : detrás, atrás — **after** *conj* : después
  de (que) — **after** *prep* **1** : después
  de **2 after all** : después de todo **3 it's
  ten after five** : son las cinco y diez
aftereffect *n* : efecto *m* secundario
aftermath *n* : consecuencias *fpl*
afternoon *n* : tarde *f*
afterward *or* afterwards *adv*
  : después, más tarde
again *adv* **1** : otra vez, de nuevo **2
  again and again** : una y otra vez

3 then again : por otra parte
against *prep* : contra, en contra de
age *n* **1** : edad *f* **2** ERA : era *f*, época *f* **3
  be of age** : ser mayor de edad **4 for
  ages** : hace siglos **5 old age** : vejez *f*
  — **age** *vi* **aged; aging** : envejecer —
  aged *adj* **1** OLD : anciano, viejo **2 children
  aged 10 to 17** : niños de 10 a 17 años
agency *n, pl* **-cies** : agencia *f*
agenda *n* : orden *m* del día
agent *n* : agente *mf*, representante *mf*
aggravate *vt* **-vated; -vating 1** WORSEN
  : agravar, empeorar **2** ANNOY : irritar
aggregate *adj* : total, global
  — **aggregate** *n* : total *m*
aggression *n* : agresión *f* —
  aggressive *adj* : agresivo —
  aggressor *n* : agresor *m*, -sora *f*
aghast *adj* : horrorizado
agile *adj* : ágil — **agility** *n*,
  pl **-ties** : agilidad *f*
agitate *v* **-tated; -tating** *vt* **1** SHAKE
  : agitar **2** TROUBLE : inquietar —
  agitation *n* : agitación *f*, inquietud *f*
agnostic *n* : agnóstico *m*, -ca *f*
ago *adv* **1** : hace **2 long ago**
  : hace mucho tiempo

agony *n, pl* **-nies 1** PAIN : dolor *m* **2**
  ANGUISH : angustia *f* — **agonize** *vi*
  -nized; -nizing : atormentarse —
  agonizing *adj* : angustioso
agree *v* **agreed; agreeing** *vt* **1** : acordar
  2 agree that : estar de acuerdo de que
  — *vi* **1** : estar de acuerdo **2** CORRESPOND
  : concordar **3 agree to** : acceder a **4 this
  climate agrees with me** : este clima
  me sienta bien — **agreeable** *adj* **1**
  PLEASING : agradable **2** WILLING : dispuesto
  — **agreement** *n* : acuerdo *m*
agriculture *n* : agricultura *f* —
▸ **agricultural** *adj* : agrícola
aground *adv* **run aground** : encallar
ahead *adv* **1** IN FRONT : delante, adelante
  2 BEFOREHAND : por adelantado **3** LEADING
  : a la delantera **4 get ahead** : adelantar
  — **ahead of** *prep* **1** : delante de, antes
  de **2 get ahead of** : adelantarse a
aid *vt* : ayudar — **aid** *n* :
  ayuda *f*, asistencia *f*
AIDS *n* : SIDA *m*, sida *m*
ail *vi* : estar enfermo —
  ailment *n* : enfermedad *f*
aim *vt* : apuntar (un arma), dirigir
  (una observación) — *vi* **1** : apuntar

**agricultural machinery
maquinaria*F* agrícola*F***

**cultivator
cultivador*M***

**combine harvester
cosechadora*F* trilladora*F***

**rake
rastrillo*M***

airport
aeropuerto^M

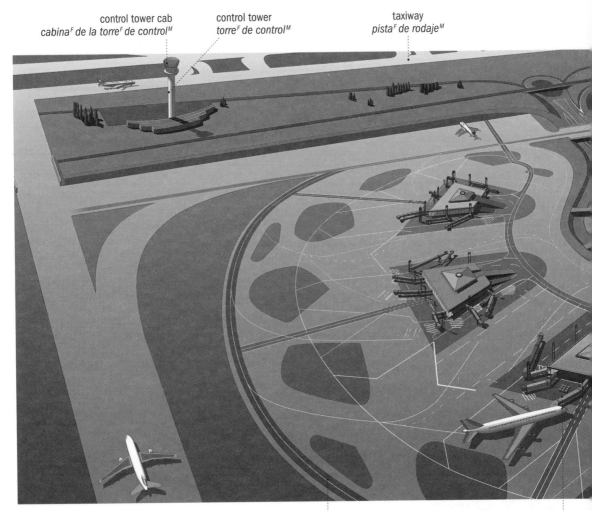

control tower cab
cabina^F de la torre^F de control^M

control tower
torre^F de control^M

taxiway
pista^F de rodaje^M

service road
ruta^F de servicio^M

jet bridge
pasarela^F telescópica

---

2 ASPIRE : aspirar — **aim** n **1** : puntería f **2** GOAL : propósito m, objetivo m — **aimless** adj : sin objetivo
air vt or **air out** : airear **2** EXPRESS : expresar **3** BROADCAST : emitir — **air** n **1** : aire m **2 be on the air** : estar en el aire — **air–conditioning** n : aire m acondicionado — **air conditioned** n : climatizado — **aircraft** ns & pl **1** : avión m, aeronave f **2 air carrier** : portaaviones m — **air**

force n : fuerza f aérea — **airline** n : aerolínea f, línea f aérea — **airliner** n : avión m de pasajeros — **airmail** n : correo m aéreo — **airplane** n : avión m — **airport** n : aeropuerto m — **airstrip** n : pista f de aterrizaje — **airtight** adj : hermético — **airy** adj **airier; -est** : aireado, bien ventilado
aisle n **1** : pasillo m **2** : nave f lateral (de una iglesia)

ajar adj : entreabierto
akin adj **akin to** : semejante a
alarm n **1** : alarma f **2** ANXIETY : inquietud f — vt : alarmar, asustar — **alarm clock** n : despertador m
alas interj : ¡ay!
album n : álbum m
alcohol n : alcohol m — **alcoholic** adj : alcohólico — **alcohol** n : alcohólico m, -ca f — **alcoholism** n : alcoholismo m

passenger terminal
terminal^F de pasajeros^M

service area
zona^F de servicio^M

boarding walkway
túnel^M de embarque^M

satellite terminal
terminal^F satélite de pasajeros^M

alcove *n* : nicho *m*, hueco *m*
ale *n* : cerveza *f*
alert *adj* **1** WATCHFUL : alerta, atento
2 LIVELY : vivo — **alert** *n* : alerta *f* —
alert *vt* : alertar, poner sobre aviso
alfalfa *n* : alfalfa *f*
alga *n, pl* **-gae** : alga *f*
algebra *n* : álgebra *f*
alias *adv* : alias — **alias** *n* : alias *m*
alibi *n* : coartada *f*

alien *adj* : extranjero — **alien** *n* **1**
FOREIGNER : extranjero *m*, -ra *f* **2**
EXTRATERRESTRIAL : extraterrestre *mf*
alienate *vt* **-ated; -ating** : enajenar
— **alienation** *n* : enajenación *f*
alight *vi* **1** LAND : posarse **2**
alight from : apearse de
align *vt* : alinear —
alignment *n* : alineación *f*
alike *adv* : igual, del mismo

modo — **alike** *adj* : parecido
alimony *n, pl* **-nies** : pensión *f* alimenticia
alive *adj* **1** LIVING : vivo, viviente
2 LIVELY : animado, activo
all *adv* **1** COMPLETELY : todo,
completamente **2 all the better** : tanto
mejor **3 all the more** : aún más, todavía
más — **all** *adj* : todo — **all** *pron* **1**
: todo, -da **2 all in all** : en general **3**
not at all : de ninguna manera — **all–**
around *adj* VERSATILE : completo
allay *vt* **1** ALLEVIATE : aliviar
2 CALM : aquietar
allege *vt* **-leged; -leging** : alegar —
allegation *n* : alegato *m*, acusación *f*
— **alleged** *adj* : presunto —
allegedly *adv* : supuestamente
allegiance *n* : lealtad *f*
allegory *n, pl* **-ries** : alegoría *f*
— **allegorical** *adj* : alegórico
allergy *n, pl* **-gies** : alergia *f*
— **allergic** *adj* : alérgico
alleviate *vt* **-ated; -ating** : aliviar
alley *n, pl* **-leys** : callejón *m*
alliance *n* : alianza *f*
alligator *n* : caimán *m*
allocate *vt* **-cated; -cating** : asignar —
allocation *n* : asignación *f*, reparto *m*
allot *vt* **-lotted; -lotting** : asignar —
allotment *n* : reparto *m*, asignación *f*
allow *vt* **1** PERMIT : permitir **2** GRANT
: dar, conceder **3** ADMIT : admitir **4**
CONCEDE : reconocer — *vi* **allow for** :
tener en cuenta — **allowance** *n* **1** :
pensión *f*, subsidio *m* **2 make allowance**
for : tener en cuenta, disculpar
alloy *n* : aleación *f*
all right *adv* **1** YES : sí, de acuerdo
2 WELL : bien **3** DEFINITELY : bien,
sin duda — **all** *adj* : bien, bueno
allude *vi* **-luded; -luding** : aludir
allure *vt* **-lured; -luring** : atraer —
alluring *adj* : atrayente, seductor
allusion *n* : alusión *f*
ally *vi* **-lied; -lying ally oneself with** :
aliarse con — **ally** *n* : aliado *m*, -da *f*
almanac *n* : almanaque *m*
almighty *adj* : omnipotente, todopoderoso
almond *n* : almendra *f*
almost *adv* : casi
alms *ns & pl* : limosna *f*
alone *adv* : sólo, solamente,
únicamente — **alone** *adj* : solo
along *adv* **1** FORWARD : adelante **2 along**
with : con, junto con **3 all along** : desde

amphibians
anfibios^M

common frog
rana^F bermeja

common toad
sapo^M común

salamander
salamandra^F

tree frog
rana^F arborícola

wood frog
rana^F de bosque^M

Northern leopard frog
rana^F leopardo^M

newt
tritón^M

---

el principio — **along** *prep* : por, a lo largo de — **alongside** *adv* : al costado — **along** *or* **along of** *prep* : al lado de

aloof *adj* : distante, reservado

aloud *adv* : en voz alta

alphabet *n* : alfabeto *m* — **alphabetical** *or* alphabetic *adj* : alfabético

already *adv* : ya

also *adv* : también, además

altar *n* : altar *m*

alter *vt* : alterar, modificar — **alteration** *n* : alteración *f*, modificación *f*

alternate *adj* : alterno — **alternate** *v* -nated; -nating : alternar — **alternating current** *n* : corriente *f* alterna — **alternative** *adj* : alternativo — **alternative** *n* : alternativa *f*

although *conj* : aunque

altitude *n* : altitud *f*

altogether *adv* **1** COMPLETELY : completamente, del todo **2** ON THE WHOLE : en suma, en general

aluminum *n* : aluminio *m*

always *adv* **1** : siempre **2** FOREVER : para siempre

am → **be**

amass *vt* : amasar, acumular

amateur *adj* : amateur — **amateur** *n* : amateur *mf*; aficionado *m*, -da *f*

amaze *vt* **amazed; amazing** : asombrar

— **amazement** *n* : asombro *m*

— **amazing** *adj* : asombroso

ambassador *n* : embajador *m*, -dora *f*

amber *n* : ámbar *m*

ambiguous *adj* : ambiguo — **ambiguity** *n*, *pl* -ties : ambigüedad *f*

ambition *n* : ambición *f* — **ambitious** *adj* : ambicioso

ambivalence *n* : ambivalencia *f* — **ambivalent** *adj* : ambivalente

amble *vi* *or* **amble along** : andar sin prisa

ambulance *n* : ambulancia *f*

ambush *vt* : emboscar — **ambush** *n* : emboscada *f*

amen *interj* : amén

amenable *adj* **amenable to** : receptivo a

amend *vt* : enmendar — **amendment** *n* : enmienda *f* — **amends** *ns & pl* **make amends for** : reparar

amenities *npl* : servicios *mpl*, comodidades *fpl*

American *adj* : americano

amethyst *n* : amatista *f*

amiable *adj* : amable, agradable

amicable *adj* : amigable, amistoso

amid *or* amidst *prep* : en medio de, entre

amiss *adv* **1** : mal **2** take **something amiss** : tomar algo a mal — **amiss** *adj* **1** WRONG : malo **2** **something is amiss** : algo anda mal

ammonia *n* : amoníaco *m*

ammunition *n* : municiones *fpl*

amnesia *n* : amnesia *f*

amnesty *n*, *pl* -ties : amnistía *f*

among *prep* : entre

amorous *adj* : amoroso

amount *vi* **1** amount to : equivaler a **2** amount to TOTAL : sumar, ascender a — **amount** *n* : cantidad *f*

▸ **amphibian** *n* : anfibio *m* — **amphibious** *adj* : anfibio

amphitheater *n* : anfiteatro *m*

ample *adj* -pler; -plest **1** SPACIOUS : amplio, extenso **2** ABUNDANT : abundante

amplify *vt* -fied; -fying : amplificar — **amplifier** *n* : amplificador *m*

amputate *vt* -tated; -tating : amputar — **amputation** *n* : amputación *f*

amuse *vt* **amused; amusing 1** : hacer reír, divertir **2** ENTERTAIN : entretener — **amusement** *n* : diversión *f* — **amusing** *adj* : divertido

an → **a**²

analogy *n*, *pl* -gies : analogía *f* — **analogous** *adj* : análogo

analysis *n*, *pl* -yses : análisis *m* — **analytic** *or* **analytical** *adj* : analítico — **analyze** *vt* -lyzed; -lyzing : analizar

anarchy *n* : anarquía *f*

anatomy *n*, *pl* -mies : anatomía *f*

— **anatomic** *or* anatomical *adj* : anatómico
ancestor *n* : antepasado *m*, -da *f* —
  ancestral *adj* : ancestral — **ancestry** *n* **1**
  DESCENT : linaje *m*, abolengo *m* **2**
  ANCESTORS : antepasados *mpl*, -das *fpl*
anchor *n* **1** : ancla *f* **2** : presentador *m*,
  -dora *f* (en televisión) — **anchor** *vt* **1** :
  anclar **2** FASTEN : sujetar — *vi* : anclar
anchovy *n, pl* **-vies** *or* **-vy** : anchoa *f*
ancient *adj* : antiguo, viejo
and *conj* **1** : y (e *before words beginning*
  with i- *or* hi-) **2 come and see** : ven a ver **3**
  more and more : cada vez más **4 try and**
  finish it soon : trata de terminarlo pronto
anecdote *n* : anécdota *f*
anemia *n* : anemia *f* —
  anemic *adj* : anémico
anesthesia *n* : anestesia *f* —
  anesthetic *adj* : anestésico —
  anesthetic *n* : anestésico *m*
anew *adv* : de nuevo, nuevamente
angel *n* : ángel *m* — **angelic**
  or angelical *adj* : angélico
anger *vt* : enojar, enfadar —
  anger *n* : ira *f*, enojo *m*, enfado *m*
angle *n* **1** : ángulo *m* **2** POINT OF VIEW
  : perspectiva *f*, punto *m* de vista —
  angler *n* : pescador *m*, -dora *f*
Anglo–Saxon *adj* : anglosajón
angry *adj* **-grier; -est** : enojado, enfadado
anguish *n* : angustia *f*
angular *adj* **1** : angular **2 angular**
  features : rasgos *mpl* angulosos
animal *n* : animal *m*
animate *adj* : animado — **animate** *vt*
  -mated; -mating : animar —
  animated *adj* **1** : animado **2 animate**
  cartoon : dibujos *mpl* animados
  — **animation** *n* : animación *f*
animosity *n, pl* **-ties** : animosidad *f*
anise *n* : anís *m*
ankle *n* : tobillo *m*
annals *npl* : anales *mpl*
annex *vt* : anexar — **annex** *n* : anexo *m*
annihilate *vt* **-lated; -lating** : aniquilar
  — **annihilation** *n* : aniquilación *f*
anniversary *n, pl* **-ries** : aniversario *m*
annotate *vt* **-tated; -tating** : anotar
  — **annotation** *n* : anotación *f*
announce *vt* **-nounced; -nouncing** :
  anunciar — **announcement** *n* : anuncio *m*
  — **announcer** *n* : locutor *m*, -tora *f*
annoy *vt* : fastidiar, molestar —
  annoyance *n* : fastidio *m*, molestia *f*
  — **annoying** *adj* : molesto, fastidioso

annual *adj* : anual — **annual** *n* : anuario *m*
annuity *n, pl* **-ties** : anualidad *f*
annul *vt* **annulled; annulling** : anular
  — **annulment** *n* : anulación *f*
anoint *vt* : ungir
anomaly *n, pl* **-lies** : anomalía *f*
anonymous *adj* : anónimo —
  anonymity *n* : anonimato *m*
another *adj* **1** : otro **2 in another**
  minute : en un minuto más —
  another *pron* : otro, otra
answer *n* **1** REPLY : respuesta *f*,
  contestación *f* **2** SOLUTION : solución *f*
  — **answer** *vt* **1** : contestar a, responder
  a **2 answer the door** : abrir la puerta
  — *vi* : contestar, responder
ant *n* : hormiga *f*
antagonize *vt* **-nized; -nizing**
  : provocar la enemistad de —
  antagonism *n* : antagonismo *m*
antarctic *adj* : antártico
▸ **antelope** *n, pl* **-lope** *or* **-lopes** : antílope *m*
antenna *n, pl* **-nae** *or* **-nas** : antena *f*
anthem *n* : himno *m*

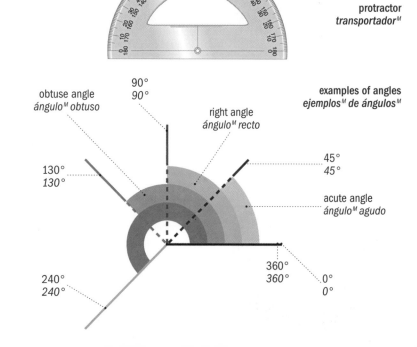

antelope
antílope*M*

anthology *n, pl* **-gies** : antología *f*
anthropology *n* : antropología *f*
antibiotic *adj* : antibiótico —
  antibiotic *n* : antibiótico *m*
antibody *n, pl* **-bodies** : anticuerpo *m*
anticipate *vt* **-pated; -pating**
  1 FORESEE : anticipar, prever **2**

angles
ángulos*M*

protractor
transportador*M*

examples of angles
ejemplos*M* de ángulos*M*

obtuse angle
ángulo*M* obtuso

90°
90°

right angle
ángulo*M* recto

130°
130°

45°
45°

acute angle
ángulo*M* agudo

360°
360°

0°
0°

240°
240°

EXPECT : esperar — **anticipation** n
: anticipación f, expectación f

antics npl : payasadas fpl

antidote n : antídoto m

antifreeze n : anticongelante m

antipathy n, pl **-thies** : antipatía f

antiquated adj : anticuado

antique adj : antiguo — **antique** n
: antigüedad f — **antiquity** n,
pl **-ties** : antigüedad f

anti–Semitic adj : antisemita

antiseptic adj : antiséptico —
antiseptic n : antiséptico m

antisocial adj 1 : antisocial 2
UNSOCIABLE : poco sociable

antithesis n, pl **-eses** : antítesis f

antlers npl : cornamenta f

antonym n : antónimo m

anus n : ano m

anvil n : yunque m

anxiety n, pl **-eties** 1 APPREHENSION :
inquietud f, ansiedad f 2 EAGERNESS :
anhelo m — **anxious** adj 1 WORRIED :
inquieto, preocupado 2 EAGER : ansioso
— **anxiously** adv : con ansiedad

any adv 1 SOMEWHAT : algo, un poco 2
it's not any good : no sirve para nada 3
we can't wait any longer : no podemos
esperar más — **any** adj 1 : alguno 2
(in negative constructions) : ningún 3
WHATEVER : cualquier 4 **in any case** :
en todo caso — **any** pron 1 : alguno,
-na 2 : ninguno, -na 3 **do you want any
more rice?** : ¿quieres más arroz?

anybody → **anyone**

anyhow adv 1 : de todas formas 2
HAPHAZARDLY : de cualquier modo

anymore adv **not anymore** : ya no

anyone pron 1 SOMEONE : alguien
2 WHOEVER : quienquiera 3 **I don't
see anyone** : no veo a nadie

anyplace → **anywhere**

anything pron 1 SOMETHING : algo, alguna
cosa 2 (in negative constructions) : nada
3 WHATEVER : cualquier cosa, lo que sea

anytime adv : en cualquier momento

anyway → **anyhow**

anywhere adv 1 : en cualquier parte,
dondequiera 2 (used in questions) : en
algún sitio 3 **I can't find it anywhere**
: no lo encuentro por ninguna parte

apart adv 1 : aparte 2 **apart from**
: excepto, aparte de 3 **fall apart** :
deshacerse, hacerse pedazos 4
live apart : vivir separados 5 **take
apart** : desmontar, desmantelar

apartment n : apartamento m

apathy n : apatía f — **apathetic** adj
: apático, indiferente

ape n : simio m

aperture n : abertura f

apex n, pl **apexes** or **apices**
: ápice m, cumbre f

apiece adv : cada uno

aplomb n : aplomo m

apology n, pl **-gies** : disculpa f —
apologetic adj : lleno de disculpas
— **apologize** vi **-gized; -gizing**
: disculparse, pedir perdón

apostle n : apóstol m

apostrophe n : apóstrofo m

appall vt : horrorizar —
appalling adj : horroroso

apparatus n, pl **-tuses**
or **-tus** : aparato m

apparel n : ropa f

apparent adj 1 OBVIOUS : claro,
evidente 2 SEEMING : aparente —
apparently adv : al parecer, por lo visto

apparition n : aparición f

appeal vi 1 **appeal for** : solicitar 2
appeal to : apelar a (la bondad de algn,
etc.) 3 **appeal to** ATTRACT : atraer a —
appeal n 1 : apelación f (en derecho) 2
REQUEST : llamamiento m 3 ATTRACTION :
atractivo m — **appealing** adj : atractivo

appear vi 1 : aparecer 2 : comparecer
(ante un tribunal), actuar (en el teatro)
3 SEEM : parecer — **appearance** n 1 :
aparición f 2 LOOK : apariencia f, aspecto m

appease vt **-peased; -peasing**
: apaciguar, aplacar

appendix n, pl **-dixes** or

-**dices** : apéndice m —
appendicitis n : apendicitis f

appetite n : apetito m — **appetizer** n :
aperitivo m — **appetizing** adj : apetitoso

applaud v : aplaudir —
applause n : aplauso m

▸ **apple** n : manzana f

appliance n : aparato m

apply v **-plied; -plying** vt 1 : aplicar
2 **apply oneself** : aplicarse — vi 1
: aplicarse 2 **apply for** : solicitar,
pedir — **applicable** adj : aplicable —
applicant n : solicitante mf; candidato m,
-ta f — **application** n 1 : aplicación f 2
: solicitud f (para un empleo, etc.)

appoint vt 1 NAME : nombrar 2 FIX SET
: fijar, señalar — **appointment** n 1
APPOINTING : nombramiento m 2
ENGAGEMENT : cita f

apportion vt : distribuir, repartir

appraise vt **-praised; -praising** : evaluar,
valorar — **appraisal** n : evaluación f

appreciate v **-ated; -ating** vt 1
VALUE : apreciar 2 UNDERSTAND :
darse cuenta de 3 **I appreciate your
help** : te agradezco tu ayuda — vi :
aumentar en valor — **appreciation** n 1
GRATITUDE : agradecimiento m 2
VALUING : apreciación f, valoración f
— **appreciative** adj 1 : apreciativo
2 GRATEFUL : agradecido

apprehend vt 1 ARREST : aprehender,
detener 2 DREAD : temer 3 COMPREHEND
: comprender — **apprehension** n 1
ARREST : detención f, aprehensión f 2
ANXIETY : aprensión f, temor m —
apprehensive adj : aprensivo, inquieto

apprentice n : aprendiz m, -diza f

approach vt 1 NEAR : acercarse a 2 :
dirigirse a (algn), abordar (un problema,
etc.) — vi : acercarse — **approach** n 1
NEARING : acercamiento m 2 POSITION
: enfoque m 3 ACCESS : acceso m —
approachable adj : accesible, asequible

appropriate vt **-ated; -ating** : apropiarse
de — **appropriate** adj : apropiado

approve vt **-proved; -proving** :
aprobar — **approval** n : aprobación f

approximate adj : aproximado —
approximate vt **-mated; -mating** :
aproximarse a — **approximately** adv
: aproximadamente

apricot n : albaricoque m,
chabacano m Lat

April n : abril m

apple
manzana^F

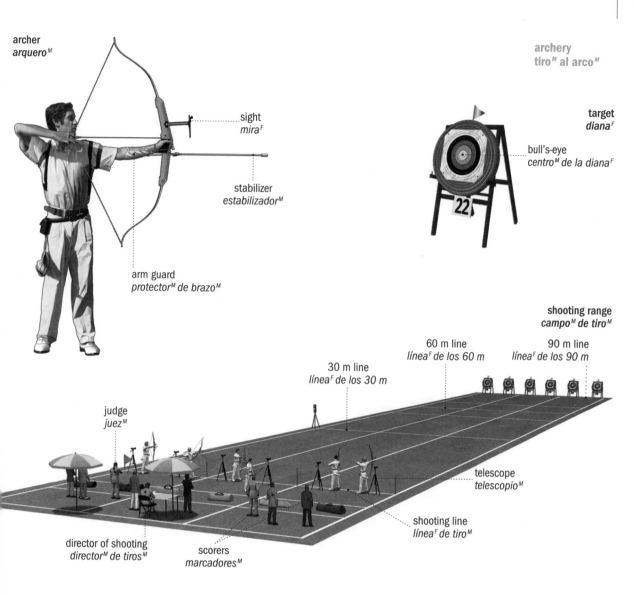

archer
arquero^M

sight
mira^F

stabilizer
estabilizador^M

arm guard
protector^M *de brazo*^M

archery
tiro^M *al arco*^M

target
diana^F

bull's-eye
centro^M *de la diana*^F

22

shooting range
campo^M *de tiro*^M

60 m line
línea^F *de los 60 m*

90 m line
línea^F *de los 90 m*

30 m line
línea^F *de los 30 m*

judge
juez^M

telescope
telescopio^M

shooting line
línea^F *de tiro*^M

director of shooting
director^M *de tiros*^M

scorers
marcadores^M

---

apron *n* : delantal *m*
apropos *adv* : a propósito
apt *adj* **1** FITTING : apto, apropiado **2** LIABLE
 : propenso — **aptitude** *n* : aptitud *f*
aquarium *n, pl* **-iums** *or* **-ia** : acuario *m*
aquatic *adj* : acuático
aqueduct *n* : acueducto *m*
Arab *adj* : árabe — **Arabic** *adj* : árabe
 — **Arab** *n* : árabe *m* (idioma)
arbitrary *adj* : arbitrario
arbitrate *v* **-trated; -trating** : arbitrar
 — **arbitration** *n* : arbitraje *m*
arc *n* : arco *m*

arcade *n* **1** : arcada *f* **2 shopping**
 arcade : galería *f* comercial
arch *n* : arco *m* — **arch** *vt* :
 arquear — *vi* : arquearse
archaeology *or* archeology *n* :
 arqueología *f* — **archaeological** *adj*
 : arque-ológico — **archaeologist** *n*
 : arqueólogo *m*, -ga *f*
archaic *adj* : arcaico
archbishop *n* : arzobispo *m*
▶ **archery** *n* : tiro *m* al arco
archipelago *n, pl* **-goes** *or*
 -gos : archipiélago *m*

architecture *n* : arquitectura *f* —
 architect *n* : arquitecto *m*, -ta *f* —
 architectural *adj* : arquitectónico
archives *npl* : archivo *m*
archway *n* : arco *m* (de entrada)
arctic *adj* : ártico
ardent *adj* : ardiente, fervoroso
 — **ardor** *n* : ardor *m*, fervor *m*
arduous *adj* : arduo
are → **be**
area *n* **1** REGION : área *f*, zona *f* **2** FIELD
 : campo *m* **3 area code** : código *m*
 de la zona *Lat*, prefijo *m Spain*

arena *n* : arena *f*, ruedo *m*
aren't (*contraction of* **are not**) → **be**
Argentine *or* Argentinean *or*
Argentinian *adj* : argentino
argue *v* **-gued; -guing** *vi* **1** QUARREL :
discutir **2 argue against** : argumentar
contra — *vt* : argumentar, sostener
— **argument** *n* **1** QUARREL : disputa *f*,
discusión *f* **2** REASONING : argumentos *mpl*
arid *adj* : árido — **aridity** *n* : aridez *f*
arise *vi* **arose; arisen; arising 1** :
levantarse **2 arise from** : surgir de
aristocracy *n*, *pl* **-cies** : aristocracia *f*
— **aristocrat** *n* : aristócrata *mf* —
aristocratic *adj* : aristocrático
arithmetic *n* : aritmética *f*
ark *n* : arca *f*

arm *n* **1** : brazo *m* **2** WEAPON : arma *f*
— **arm** *vt* : armar — **armament** *n*
: armamento *m* — **armchair** *n* :
sillón *m* — **armed** *adj* **1 armed
forces** : fuerzas *fpl* armadas **2 armed
robbery** : robo *m* a mano armada
armistice *n* : armisticio *m*
▸ **armor** *or Brit* **armour** *n* : armadura *f*
— **armored** *or Brit* **armoured** *adj*
: blindado, acorazado — **armory**
or Brit **armoury** : arsenal *m*
armpit *n* : axila *f*, sobaco *m*
army *n*, *pl* **-mies** : ejército *m*
aroma *n* : aroma *m* —
aromatic *adj* : aromático
around *adv* **1** : de circunferencia **2**

NEARBY : por ahí **3** APPROXIMATELY : más o
menos, aproximadamente **4 all around**
: por todos lados, todo alrededor **5 turn
around** : voltearse — **around** *prep* **1**
SURROUNDING : alrededor de **2** THROUGHOUT
: por **3** NEAR : cerca de **4 around the
corner** : a la vuelta de la esquina
arouse *vt* **aroused; arousing 1**
AWAKE : despertar **2** EXCITE : excitar
arrange *vt* **-ranged; -ranging**
: arreglar, poner en orden —
arrangement *n* **1** ORDER : arreglo *m* **2**
arranges *npl* : preparativos *mpl*
array *n* : selección *f*, surtido *m*
arrears *npl* **1** : atrasos *mpl* **2 be in
arrears** : estar atrasado en pagos
arrest *vt* : detener — **arrest** *n* **1**
: arresto *m*, detención *f* **2**
under arrest : detenido
arrive *vi* **-rived; -riving** : llegar
— **arrival** *n* : llegada *f*
arrogance *n* : arrogancia *f* —
arrogant *adj* : arrogante
arrow *n* : flecha *f*
arsenal *n* : arsenal *m*
arsenic *n* : arsénico *m*
arson *n* : incendio *m* premeditado
art *n* **1** : arte *m* **2 arts** *npl* : letras *fpl* (en
educación) **3 fine arts** : bellas artes *fpl*
artefact *Brit* → **artifact**
artery *n*, *pl* **-teries** : arteria *f*
artful *adj* : astuto, taimado
arthritis *n*, *pl* **-tides** : artritis *f*
— **arthritic** *adj* : artrítico
artichoke *n* : alcachofa *f*
article *n* : artículo *m*
articulate *vt* **-lated; -lating** :
articular — **articulate** *adj* **be
articulate** : expresarse bien
artifact *or Brit* **artefact** *n* : artefacto *m*
artificial *adj* : artificial
▸ **artillery** *n*, *pl* **-leries** : artillería *f*
artisan *n* : artesano *m*, **-na** *f*
artist *n* : artista *mf* —
artistic *adj* : artístico
as *adv* **1** : tan, tanto **2 as much** : tanto
como **3 as tall as** : tan alto como **4
as well** : también — **as** *conj* **1** WHILE
: mientras **2** (*referring to manner*)
: como **3** SINCE : ya que **4** THOUGH :
por más que — **as** *prep* **1** : de **2**
LIKE : como — **as** *pron* : que
asbestos *n* : asbesto *m*, amianto *m*
ascend *vi* : ascender, subir — *vt* : subir
(a) — **ascent** *n* : ascensión *f*, subida *f*

armor
armadura^F

vision slit
ranura^F de visión^F

pauldron
espaldarón^M

breastplate
peto^M

rerebrace
brafonera^F

chain mail
cota^F de malla^F

cuisse
quijote^M

poleyn
rodillera^F

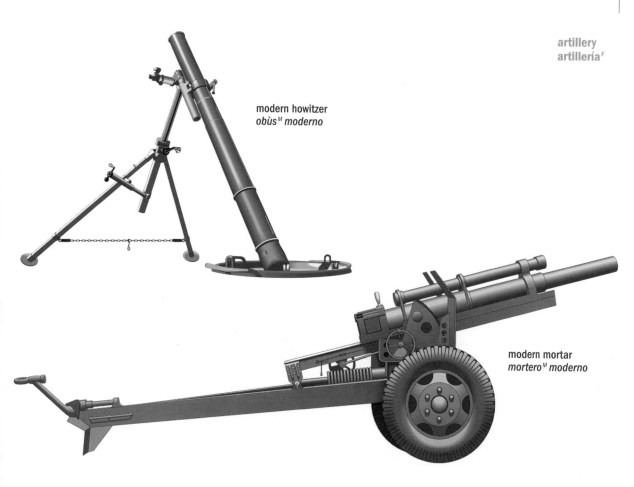

modern howitzer
obùs^M moderno

modern mortar
mortero^M moderno

ascertain *vt* : averiguar, determinar
ascribe *vt* **-cribed; -cribing** : atribuir
as for *prep* : en cuanto a
ash[1] *n* : ceniza *f*
ash[2] *n* : fresno *m* (árbol)
ashamed *adj* : avergonzado, apenado *Lat*
ashore *adv* **1** : en tierra **2 go
ashore** : desembarcar
ashtray *n* : cenicero *m*
Asian *adj* : asiático
aside *adv* **1** : a un lado **2** APART :
aparte **3 set aside** : guardar —
aside from *prep* **1** BESIDES : además
de **2** EXCEPT : aparte de, menos
as if *conj* : como si
ask *vt* **1** : preguntar **2** REQUEST : pedir
3 INVITE : invitar — *vi* : preguntar
askance *adv* **look askance**
: mirar de soslayo
askew *adj* : torcido, ladeado
asleep *adj* **1** : dormido **2 fall asleep**

: dormirse, quedarse dormido
as of *prep* : desde, a partir de
asparagus *n* : espárrago *m*
aspect *n* : aspecto *m*
asphalt *n* : asfalto *m*
asphyxiate *v* **-ated; -ating** *vt* :
asfixiar — **asphyxiation** *n* : asfixia *f*
aspire *vi* **-pired; -piring** : aspirar
— **aspiration** *n* : aspiración *f*
aspirin *n, pl* **aspirin** *or* **aspirins** : aspirina *f*
ass *n* **1** : asno *m* **2** IDIOT :
imbécil *mf*, idiota *mf*
assail *vt* : atacar, asaltar — **assailant** *n*
: asaltante *mf*, atacante *mf*
assassin *n* : asesino *m*, -na *f* —
assassinate *vt* **-nated; -nating** : asesinar
— **assassination** *n* : asesinato *m*
assault *n* **1** : ataque *m*, asalto *m* **2**
: agresión *f* (contra algn) —
assault *vt* : atacar, asaltar
assemble *v* **-bled; -bling** *vt* **1** GATHER

: reunir, juntar **2** CONSTRUCT : montar
— *vi* : reunirse — **assembly** *n, pl* **-blies**
1 MEETING : reunión *f*, asamblea *f* **2**
CONSTRUCTING : montaje *m*
assent *vi* : asentir, consentir —
assent *n* : asentimiento *m*
assert *vt* **1** : afirmar **2 assert oneself** :
hacerse valer — **assertion** *n* : afirmación *f*
— **assertive** *adj* : firme, enérgico
assess *vt* : evaluar, valorar —
assessment *n* : evaluación *f*, valoración *f*
asset *n* **1** : ventaja *f*, recurso *m* **2**
assets *npl* : bienes *mpl*, activo *m*
assiduous *adj* : asiduo
assign *vt* **1** APPOINT : designar, nombrar
2 ALLOT : asignar — **assignment** *n* **1**
TASK : misión *f* **2** HOMEWORK :
tarea *f* **3** ASSIGNING : asignación *f*
assimilate *vt* **-lated; -lating** : asimilar
assist *vt* : ayudar — **assistance** *n* :
ayuda *f* — **assistant** *n* : ayudante *mf*

associate *v* -ated; -ating *vt* : asociar
— *vi* : asociarse — **associate** *n*
: asociado *m*, -da *f*; socio *m*, -cia *f*
— **association** *n* : asociación *f*
as soon as *conj* : tan pronto como
assorted *adj* : surtido —
assortment *n* : surtido *m*, variedad *f*
assume *vt* -sumed; -suming 1
SUPPOSE : **suponer 2** UNDERTAKE :

asumir 3 TAKE ON : adquirir, tomar
— **assumption** *n* : suposición *f*
assure *vt* -sured; -suring : asegurar
— **assurance** *n* 1 CERTAINTY :
certeza *f*, garantía *f* 2 CONFIDENCE :
confianza *f*, seguridad *f* (de sí mismo)
asterisk *n* : asterisco *m*
asthma *n* : asma *m*
as though → **as if**

as to *prep* : sobre, acerca de
astonish *vt* : asombrar —
astonishing *adj* : asombroso —
astonishment *n* : asombro *m*
astound *vt* : asombrar, pasmar —
astounding *adj* : asombroso, pasmoso
astray *adv* **1 go astray** : extraviarse **2**
lead astray : llevar por mal camino
astrology *n* : astrología *f*

astronaut
astronauta^F

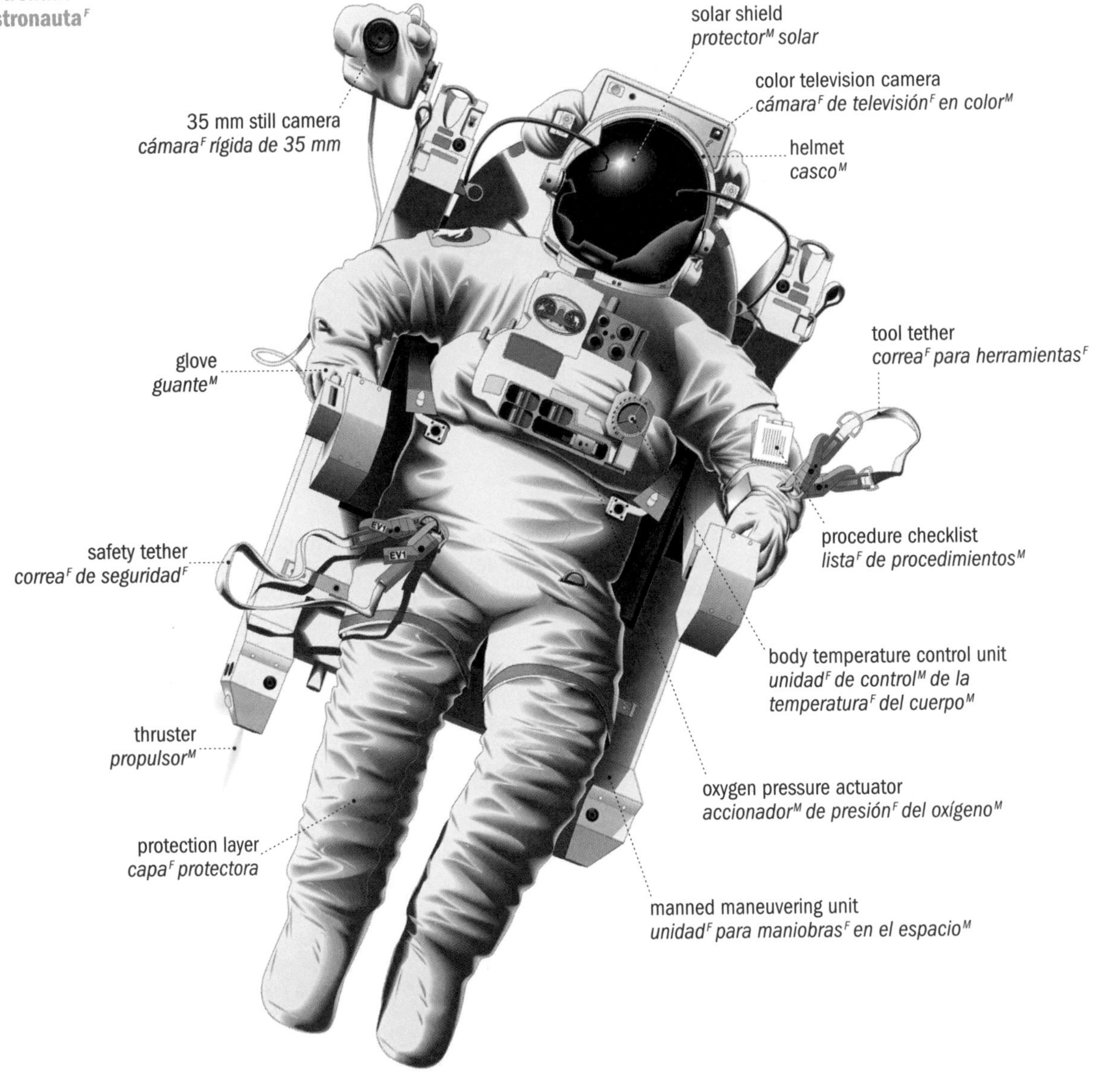

solar shield
protector^M solar

color television camera
cámara^F de televisión^F en color^M

35 mm still camera
cámara^F rígida de 35 mm

helmet
casco^M

glove
guante^M

tool tether
correa^F para herramientas^F

safety tether
correa^F de seguridad^F

procedure checklist
lista^F de procedimientos^M

body temperature control unit
unidad^F de control^M de la temperatura^F del cuerpo^M

thruster
propulsor^M

oxygen pressure actuator
accionador^M de presión^F del oxígeno^M

protection layer
capa^F protectora

manned maneuvering unit
unidad^F para maniobras^F en el espacio^M

▸ **astronaut** n : astronauta mf
astronomy n, pl **-mies** : astronomía f
— **astronomer** n : astrónomo m, -ma f
— **astronomical** adj : astronómico
astute adj : astuto, sagaz —
astuteness n : astucia f
as well as conj : tanto como —
as prep : además de, aparte de
asylum n 1 : asilo m 2 **insane**
asylum : manicomio m
at prep 1 : a 2 **at home** : en casa 3 **at**
night : en la noche, por la noche 4 **at**
two o'clock : a las dos 5 **be angry at** :
estar enojado con 6 **laugh at** : reírse de
— **at all** adv **not at** : en absoluto, nada
ate → **eat**
atheist n : ateo m, atea f —
atheism n : ateísmo m
athlete n : atleta mf — **athletic** adj :
atlético — **athletics** ns & pl : atletismo m
atlas n : atlas m
atmosphere n 1 : atmósfera f 2
AMBIENCE : ambiente m —
atmospheric adj : atmosférico
atom n : átomo m — **atomic** adj : atómico
atomizer n : atomizador m
atone vt **atoned; atoning**
atone for : expiar
atrocity n, pl **-ties** : atrocidad f
— **atrocious** adj : atroz
atrophy vi **-phied; -phying** : atrofiarse
attach vt 1 : sujetar, atar 2 : adjuntar (un
documento, etc.) 3 **attach importance**
to : atribuir importancia a 4 **become**
attached to someone : encariñarse con
algn — **attachment** n 1 ACCESSORY :
accesorio m 2 FONDNESS : cariño m
attack v : atacar — **attack** n : ataque m
— **attacker** n : agresor m, -sora f
attain vt : lograr, alcanzar —
attainment n : logro m
attempt vt : intentar —
attempt n : intento m
attend vt : asistir a — vi 1 : asistir
2 **attend to** : ocuparse de —
attendance n 1 : asistencia f 2
TURNOUT : concurrencia f — **attendant** n
: encargado m, -da f; asistente mf
attention n 1 : atención f 2 **pay**
attention : prestar atención, hacer
caso — **attentive** adj : atento
attest vt : atestiguar
attic n : desván m
attire n : atavío m
attitude n 1 : actitud f 2

POSTURE : postura f
attorney n, pl **-neys** : abogado m, -da f
attract vt : atraer — **attraction** n 1 :
atracción f 2 APPEAL : atractivo m —
attractive adj : atractivo, atrayente
attribute n : atributo m — **attribute** vt
-tributed; -tributing : atribuir, imputar
auburn adj : castaño rojizo
auction n : subasta f — **auction** vt
or **auction off** : subastar
audacious adj : audaz — **audacity** n,
pl **-ties** : audacia f, atrevimiento m
audible adj : audible
audience n 1 INTERVIEW :
audiencia f 2 PUBLIC : público m
audiovisual adj : audiovisual
audition n : audición f
auditor n 1 : auditor m, -tora f (de
finanzas) 2 STUDENT : oyente mf
auditorium n, pl **-riums**
or **-ria** : auditorio m
augment vt : aumentar
augur vi **augur well** : ser de buen agüero
August n : agosto m
aunt n : tía f
aura n : aura f
auspices npl : auspicios mpl
auspicious adj : propicio, prometedor
austere adj : austero — **austerity** n,
pl **-ties** : austeridad f
Australian adj : australiano
authentic adj : auténtico
author n : autor m, -tora f
authority n, pl **-ties** : autoridad f
— **authoritarian** adj : autoritario
— **authoritative** adj 1 RELIABLE :
autorizado 2 DICTATORIAL : autoritario
— **authorization** n : autorización f —
authorize vt **-rized; -rizing** : autorizar
autobiography n, pl **-phies** :
autobiografía f — **autobiographical** adj
: autobiográfico
autograph n : autógrafo m —
autograph vt : autografiar
automatic adj : automático —
automate vt **-mated; -mating**
: automatizar — **automation** n
: automatización f
▸ **automobile** n : automóvil m
autonomy n, pl **-mies** : autonomía f
— **autonomous** adj : autónomo
autopsy n, pl **-sies** : autopsia f
autumn n : otoño m
auxiliary adj : auxiliar —
auxiliary n, pl **-ries** : auxiliar mf

avail vt **avail oneself of** : aprovecharse
de — **avail** n **to no avail** : en vano
— **available** adj : disponible —
availability n, pl **-ties** : disponibilidad f
avalanche n : avalancha f
avarice n : avaricia f
avenge vt **avenged; avenging** : vengar
avenue n 1 : avenida f 2 MEANS : vía f
average n : promedio m —
average adj 1 MEAN : medio 2 ORDINARY
: regular, ordinario — **average** vt **-aged;**
-aging 1 : hacer un promedio de 2 or
average out : calcular el promedio de
averse adj **be averse to** : sentir aversión
por — **aversion** n : aversión f
avert vt 1 AVOID : evitar, prevenir 2
avert one's eyes : apartar los ojos
aviation n : aviación f —
aviator n : aviador m, -dora f
avid adj : ávido — **avidly** adv : con avidez
avocado n, pl **-dos** : aguacate m
avoid vt : evitar — **avoidable** adj : evitable
await vt : esperar
awake v **awoke; awoken** or **awaked;**
awaking : despertar — **awake** adj :
despierto — **awaken** v → **awake**
award vt 1 : otorgar, conceder (un
premio, etc.) 2 : adjudicar (daños
y perjuicios) — **award** n 1 PRIZE
: premio m 2 : adjudicación f
aware adj **be aware of** : estar consciente
de — **awareness** n : conciencia f
away adv 1 (referring to distance) : de
aquí, de distancia 2 **far away** : lejos 3
give away : regalar 4 **go away** : irse 5
right away : en seguida 6 **take away** :
quitar — **away** adj 1 ABSENT : ausente
2 **away game** : partido m fuera de casa
awe n : temor m reverencial —
awesome adj : imponente, formidable
awful adj 1 : terrible, espantoso
2 **an awful lot** : muchísimo —
awfully adv : terriblemente
awhile adv : un rato
awkward adj 1 CLUMSY : torpe 2
EMBARRASSING : embarazoso, delicado 3
DIFFICULT : difícil — **awkwardly** adv 1 :
con dificultad 2 CLUMSILY : de manera torpe
awning n : toldo m
awry adj 1 ASKEW : torcido
2 **go awry** : salir mal
ax or **axe** n : hacha f
axiom n : axioma m
axis n, pl **axes** : eje m
axle n : eje m

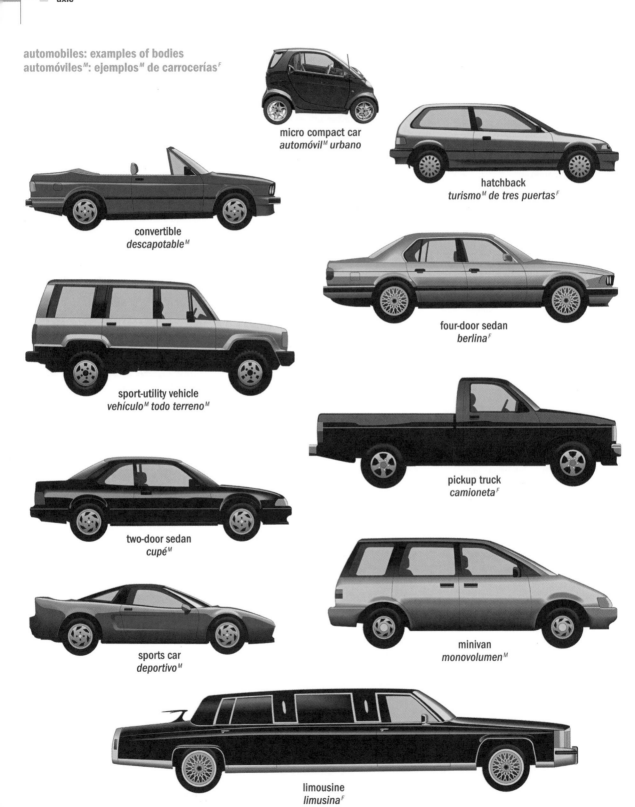

automobiles: examples of bodies
automóviles^M: ejemplos^M de carrocerías^F

micro compact car
automóvil^M *urbano*

hatchback
turismo^M *de tres puertas*^F

convertible
descapotable^M

four-door sedan
berlina^F

sport-utility vehicle
vehículo^M *todo terreno*^M

pickup truck
camioneta^F

two-door sedan
cupé^M

minivan
monovolumen^M

sports car
deportivo^M

limousine
limusina^F

b *n, pl* **b's** *or* **bs** : b, segunda
letra del alfabeto inglés

babble *vi* **-bled; -bling 1** : balbucear
2 MURMUR : murmurar — **babble** *n*
: balbuceo *m* (de bebé), murmullo *m*
(de voces, de un arroyo)

baboon *n* : babuino *m*

baby *n, pl* **-bies** : bebé *m;* niño *m*, -ña *f* —
baby *vt* **-bied; -bying** : mimar, consentir
— **babyish** *adj* : infantil — **baby–sit** *vi*
-sat; -sitting : cuidar a los niños

bachelor *n* **1** : soltero *m* **2**
GRADUATE : licenciado *m*, -da *f*

back *n* **1** : espalda *f* **2** REVERSE :
reverso *m*, dorso *m*, revés *m* **3** REAR :
fondo *m*, parte *f* trasera **4** : defensa *mf*
(en deportes) — **back** *adv* **1** : atrás **2**
be back : estar de vuelta **3 go back** :
volver **4 two years back** : hace dos años
— **back** *adj* **1** REAR : de atrás, trasero **2**
OVERDUE : atrasado — **back** *vt* **1** SUPPORT
: apoyar **2** *or* **back up** : darle marcha
atrás a (un vehículo) — *vi* **1 back down**
: volverse atrás **2 back up** : retroceder
— **backache** *n* : dolor *m* de espalda —
backbone *n* : columna *f* vertebral —
backfire *vi* **-fired; -firing** : petardear —
background *n* **1** : fondo *m* (de un cuadro,
etc.), antecedentes *mpl* (de una situación) **2**
EXPERIENCE : formación *f* — **backhand** *adv*
: de revés, con el revés — **backhanded** *adj*
: indirecto — **backing** *n* : apoyo *m*,
respaldo *m* — **backlash** *n* : reacción *f*
violenta — **backlog** *n* : atrasos *mpl* —
backpack *n* : mochila *f* — **backstage** *adv*
& adj : entre bastidores — **backtrack** *vi*
: dar marcha atrás — **backup** *n* **1**
SUPPORT : respaldo *m*, apoyo *m* **2** : copia *f*
de seguridad (para computadoras) —
backward *or* **backwards** *adv* **1** : hacia
atrás **2 do it backward** : hacerlo al revés

badger
tejón^M

---

racquetball
pelota^F de raquetball^M

baseball
pelota^F de béisbol^M

tennis ball
pelota^F de tenis^M

softball
pelota^F de softball^M

soccer ball
balón^M de fútbol^M

rugby ball
balón^M de rugby^M

football
balón^M de fútbol^M americano

volleyball
pelota^F de voleibol^M

---

3 fall backward : caer de espaldas **4**
bend over backwards : hacer todo
lo posible — **backward** *adj* **1** : hacia
atrás **2** RETARDED : retrasado **3** SHY :
tímido **4** UNDERDEVELOPED : atrasado

bacon *n* : tocino *m*, tocineta *f*
Lat, bacon *m Spain*

bacteria : bacterias *fpl*

bad *adj* **worse; worst 1** : malo **2** ROTTEN
: podrido **3** SEVERE : grave **4 from bad
to worse** : de mal en peor **5 too bad!**
: ¡qué lástima! — **bad** *adv* → **badly**

badge *n* : insignia *f*, chapa *f*

▸ **badger** *n* : tejón *m* — **badger** *vt* : acosar

badly *adv* **1** : mal **2** SEVERELY :
gravemente **3 want badly** : desear mucho

baffle *vi* **-fled; -fling** : desconcertar

bag *n* **1** : bolsa *f*, saco *m* **2** HANDBAG
: bolso *m*, cartera *f Lat* **3** SUITCASE :
maleta *f* — **bag** *vt* **bagged; bagging**
: ensacar, poner en una bolsa

baggage *n* : equipaje *m*

baggy *adj* **-gier; -est** : holgado

bail *n* : fianza *f* — **bail** *vt* **1** : achicar
(agua de un bote) **2 bail out** RELEASE
: poner en libertad bajo fianza **3 bail
out** EXTRICATE : sacar de apuros

bailiff *n* : alguacil *mf*

bait *vt* **1** : cebar **2** HARASS : acosar
— **bait** *n* : cebo *m*, carnada *f*

bake *v* **baked; baking** *vt* : cocer
al horno — *vi* : cocerse (al horno)
— **baker** *n* : panadero *m*, -ra *f* —
bakery *n, pl* **-ries** : panadería *f*

balance *n* **1** SCALES : balanza *f* **2**
COUNTERBALANCE : contrapeso *m* **3**
EQUILIBRIUM : equilibrio *m* **4** REMAINDER
: resto *m* **5** *or* **bank balance** : saldo *m*
— **balance** *v* **-anced; -ancing** *vt* **1**
: hacer el balance de (una cuenta) **2**
EQUALIZE : equilibrar **3** WEIGH : sopesar
— *vi* **1** : sostenerse en equilibrio **2**
: cuadrar (dícese de una cuenta)

balcony *n, pl* **-nies 1** : balcón *m* **2**
: galería *f* (de un teatro)

bald *adj* **1** : calvo **2** WORN : pelado
3 the bald truth : la pura verdad

bale *n* : bala *f*, fardo *m*

baleful *adj* : siniestro

balk *vi* **balk at** : resistirse a

▸ **ball** *n* **1** : pelota *f*, bola *f*,
balón *m* **2** DANCE : baile *m* **3 ball
of string** : ovillo *m* de cuerda

ballad *n* : balada *f*

ballast *n* : lastre *m*

ball bearing *n* : cojinete *m* de bola

ballerina *n* : bailarina *f*
ballet *n* : ballet *m*
ballistic *adj* : balístico
balloon *n* : globo *m*
ballot *n* **1** : papeleta *f* (de voto) **2** VOTING : votación *f*
ballpoint pen *n* : bolígrafo *m*
ballroom *n* : sala *f* de baile
balm *n* : bálsamo *m* — **balmy** *adj* **balmier; -est** : templado, agradable
baloney *n* NONSENSE : tonterías *fpl*
bamboo *n* : bambú *m*
bamboozle *vt* **-zled; -zling** : engañar, embaucar
ban *vt* **banned; banning** : prohibir — **ban** *n* : prohibición *f*
banal *adj* : banal
banana *n* : plátano *m*, banana *f* *Lat*, banano *m*, *Lat*
band *n* **1** STRIP : banda *f* **2** GROUP : banda *f*, grupo *m*, conjunto *m* — **band** *vi*

band together : unirse, juntarse
bandage *n* : vendaje *m*, venda *f* — **bandage** *vt* **-daged; -daging** : vendar
bandit *n* : bandido *m*, -da *f*
bandy *vt* **-died; -dying bandy about** : circular, repetir
bang *vt* **1** STRIKE : golpear **2** SLAM : cerrar de un golpe — *vi* **1** SLAM : cerrarse de un golpe **2 bang on** : golpear — **bang** *n* **1** BLOW : golpe *m* **2** NOISE : estrépito *m* **3** SLAM : portazo *m*
bangle *n* : brazalete *m*, pulsera *f*
bangs *npl* : flequillo *m*
banish *vt* : desterrar
banister *n* : pasamanos *m*, barandal *m*
bank *n* **1** : banco *m* **2** : orilla *f*, ribera *f* (de un río) **3** EMBANKMENT : terraplén *m* — **bank** *vt* : depositar — *vi* **1** : ladearse (dícese de un avión) **2** : tener una cuenta (en un banco) **3 bank on** : contar con — **banker** *n* :

banquero *m*, -ra *f* — **banking** *n* : banca *f*
bankrupt *adj* : en bancarrota, en quiebra — **bankruptcy** *n*, *pl* **-cies** : quiebra *f*, bancarrota *f*
banner *n* : bandera *f*, pancarta *f*
banquet *n* : banquete *m*
banter *n* : bromas *fpl* — **banter** *vi* : hacer bromas
baptize *vt* **-tized; -tizing** : bautizar — **baptism** *n* : bautismo *m*
bar *n* **1** : barra *f* **2** BARRIER : barrera *f*, obstáculo *m* **3** COUNTER : mostrador *m*, barra *f* **4** TAVERN : bar *m* **5 behind bars** : entre rejas **6 bar of soap** : pastilla *f* de jabón — **bar** *vt* **barred; barring 1** OBSTRUCT : obstruir, bloquear **2** EXCLUDE : excluir **3** PROHIBIT : prohibir — **bar** *prep* **1** : excepto **2 bar none** : sin excepción
barbarian *n* : bárbaro *m*, -ra *f*
barbecue *vt* **-cued; -cuing** : asar a la parrilla — **barbecue** *n* : barbacoa *f*

baseball field
campo^M **de béisbol**^M

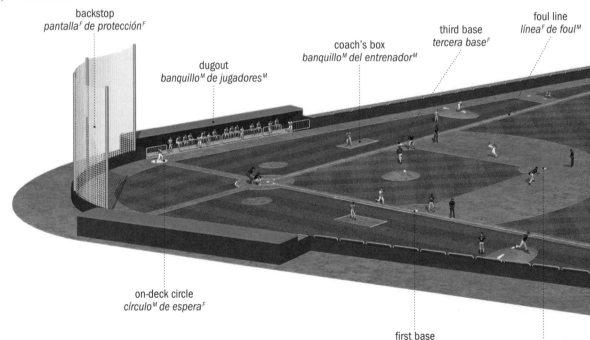

backstop
pantalla^F *de protección*^F

dugout
banquillo^M *de jugadores*^M

coach's box
banquillo^M *del entrenador*^M

third base
tercera base^F

foul line
línea^F *de foul*^M

on-deck circle
círculo^M *de espera*^F

first base
primera base^F

second base
segunda base^F

barbed wire *n* : alambre *m* de púas
barber *n* : barbero *m*, -ra *f*
bare *adj* **1** : desnudo **2** EMPTY :
vacío **3** MINIMUM : mero, esencial —
barefaced *adj* : descarado — **barefoot**
or **barefooted** *adv & adj* : descalzo
— **barely** *adv* : apenas, por poco
bargain *n* **1** AGREEMENT : acuerdo *m* **2**
BUY : ganga *f* — **bargain** *vi* **1** : regatear,
negociar **2 bargain for** : contar con
barge *n* : barcaza *f* — **barge** *vi*
barged; barging barge in :
entrometerse, interrumpir
baritone *n* : barítono *m*
bark[1] *vi* : ladrar — **bark** *n* :
ladrido *m* (de un perro)
bark[2] *n* : corteza *f* (de un árbol)
barley *n* : cebada *f*
barn *n* : granero *m* —
barnyard *n* : corral *m*
barometer *n* : barómetro *m*

baron *n* : barón *m* —
baroness *n* : baronesa *f*
barracks *ns & pl* : cuartel *m*
barrage *n* **1** : descarga *f* (de artillería)
2 : aluvión *m* (de preguntas, etc.)
barrel *n* **1** : barril *m*, tonel *m* **2** :
cañón *m* (de un arma de fuego)
barren *adj* : estéril
barricade *vt* **-caded; -cading** : cerrar con
barricadas — **barricade** *n* : barricada *f*
barrier *n* : barrera *f*
barring *prep* : salvo
barrio *n* : barrio *m*
bartender *n* : camarero *m*, -ra *f*
barter *vt* : cambiar, trocar
— **barter** *n* : trueque *m*
base *n*, *pl* **bases** : base *f* — **base** *vt*
based; basing : basar, fundamentar
— **base** *adj* **baser; basest** : vil
▸ **baseball** *n* : beisbol *m*, béisbol *m*
basement *n* : sótano *m*

bash *vt* : golpear violentamente —
bash *n* **1** BLOW : golpe *m* **2** PARTY: fiesta *f*
bashful *adj* : tímido, vergonzoso
basic *adj* : básico, fundamental —
basically *adv* : fundamentalmente
basil *n* : albahaca *f*
basin *n* **1** WASHBOWL : palangana *f*,
lavabo *m* **2** : cuenca *f* (de un río)
basis *n*, *pl* **bases** : base *f*
bask *vi* **bask in the sun** : tostarse al sol
basket *n* : cesta *f*, cesto *m* —
basketball *n* : baloncesto *m*,
basquetbol *m*, *Lat*
bass[1] *n*, *pl* **bass** *or* **basses**
: róbalo *m* (pesca)
bass[2] *n* : bajo *m* (tono, voz, instrumento)
bassoon *n* : fagot *m*
bastard *n* : bastardo *m*, -da *f*
baste *vt* **basted; basting 1** STITCH
: hilvanar **2** : bañar (carne)
bat[1] *n* : murciélago *m* (animal)

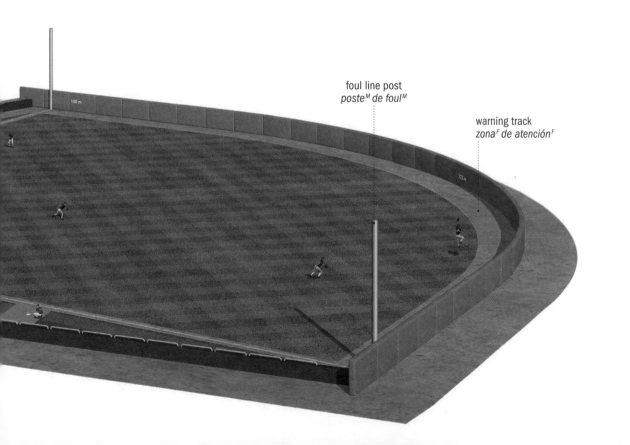

foul line post
poste[M] *de foul*[M]

warning track
zona[F] *de atención*[F]

100 m

122 m

bee
abeja^F

honeybee: worker
abeja^F: *obrera*^F

wing
ala^F

thorax
tórax^M

abdomen
abdomen^M

compound eye
ojo^M *compuesto*

mouthparts
apéndices^M *bucales*

antenna
antena^F

stinger
aguijón^M

pollen basket
cestillo^M

hind leg
pata^F *trasera*

middle leg
pata^F *media*

foreleg
pata^F *delantera*

queen
reina^F

worker
obrera^F

drone
zángano^M

---

bat^2 *n* : bate *m* — **bat** *vt*
  batted; batting : batear
batch *n* : hornada *f* (de pasteles, etc.),
  lote *m* (de mercancías), montón *m*
  (de trabajo), grupo *m* (de personas)
bath *n, pl* **baths 1** : baño *m* **2** BATHROOM
  : baño *m*, cuarto *m* de baño **3 take a
  bath** : bañarse — **bathe** *v* **bathed;
  bathing** *vt* : bañar, lavar — *vi* : bañarse
  — **bathrobe** *n* : bata *f* (de baño) —
  bathroom *n* : baño *m*, cuarto *m* de baño
  — **bathtub** *n* : bañera *f*, tina *f* (de baño)
baton *n* : batuta *f*
battalion *n* : batallón *m*
batter *vt* **1** BEAT : golpear **2** MISTREAT :
  maltratar — **batter** *n* **1** : masa *f* para
  rebozar **2** HITTER : bateador *m*, -dora *f*
battery *n, pl* **-teries** : batería *f*,
  pila *f* (de electricidad)
battle *n* **1** : batalla *f* **2** STRUGGLE :
  lucha *f* — **battle** *vi* **-tled; -tling** : luchar
  — **battlefield** *n* : campo *m* de batalla
  — **battleship** *n* : acorazado *m*
bawl *vi* : llorar a gritos

bay^1 *n* INLET : bahía *f*
bay^2 *n or* **bay leaf** : laurel *m*
bay^3 *vi* : aullar — **bay** *n* : aullido *m*
bayonet *n* : bayoneta *f*
bay window *n* : ventana *f* en saliente
bazaar *n* **1** : bazar *m* **2**
  SALE : venta *f* benéfica
be *v* **was, were; been; being; am, is,
  are** *vi* **1** : ser **2** (*expressing location*)
  : estar **3** (*expressing existence*) : ser,
  existir **4** (*expressing a state of being*) :
  estar, tener — *v impers* **1** (*indicating
  time*) : ser **2** (*indicating a condition*) :
  hacer, estar — *v aux* **1** (*expressing
  occurrence*) : ser **2** (*expressing possibility*)
  : poderse **3** (*expressing obligation*) :
  deber **4** (*expressing progression*) : estar
beach *n* : playa *f*
beacon *n* : faro *m*
bead *n* **1** : cuenta *f* **2** DROP : gota *f* **3**
  beads *npl* NECKLACE : collar *m*
beak *n* : pico *m*
beam *n* **1** : viga *f* (de madera, etc.) **2**
  RAY : rayo *m* — **beam** *vi* SHINE : brillar

— *vt* BROADCAST : transmitir, emitir
bean *n* **1** : habichuela *f*, frijol *m* **2 coffee
  bean** : grano *m* **3 string bean** : judía *f*
▸ **bear**^{1} *n, pl* **bears** *or* **bear** : oso *m*, osa *f*
bear^2 *v* **bore; borne; bearing** *vt* **1** CARRY
  : portar **2** ENDURE : soportar — *vi* **bear
  right/left** : doble a la derecha/a la
  izquierda — **bearable** *adj* : soportable
beard *n* : barba *f*
bearer *n* : portador *m*, -dora *f*
bearing *n* **1** MANNER :
  comportamiento *m* **2** SIGNIFICANCE
  : relacíon *f*, importancia *f* **3 get
  one's bearings** : orientarse
beast *n* : bestia *f*
beat *v* **beat; beaten** *or* **beat; beating** *vt* **1**
  HIT : golpear **2** : batir (huevos, etc.) **3**
  DEFEAT : derrotar — *vi* : latir (dícese
  del corazón) — **beat** *n* **1** : golpe *m* **2**
  : latido *m* (del corazón) **3** RHYTHM :
  ritmo *m*, tiempo *m* — **beating** *n* **1**
  : paliza *f* **2** DEFEAT : derrota *f*
beauty *n, pl* **-ties** : belleza *f* —
  beautiful *adj* : hermoso, lindo

— **beautifully** *adv* WONDERFULLY : maravillosamente — **beautify** *vt* -**fied**; -**fying** : embellecer

beaver *n* : castor *m*

because *conj* : porque — **because of** *prep* : por, a causa de, debido a

beckon *vt* : llamar, hacer señas a — *vi* : hacer una seña

become *v* -**came**; -**come**; -**coming** *vi* : hacerse, ponerse — *vt* SUIT : favorecer — **becoming** *adj* **1** SUITABLE : apropiado **2** FLATTERING : favorecedor

bed *n* **1** : cama *f* **2** : cauce *m* (de un río), fondo *m* (del mar) **3** : macizo *m* (de flores) **4 go to bed** : irse a la cama — **bedclothes** *npl* : ropa *f* de cama

bedlam *n* : confusión *f*, caos *m*

bedraggled *adj* : desaliñado, sucio

bedridden *adj* : postrado en cama

bedroom *n* : dormitorio *m*, recámara *f Lat*

bedspread *n* : colcha *f*

bedtime *n* : hora *f* de acostarse

▸ **bee** *n* : abeja *f*

beech *n*, *pl* **beeches** *or* **beech** : haya *f*

beef *n* : carne *f* de vaca, carne *f* de res *Lat* — **beefsteak** *n* : bistec *m*

beehive *n* : colmena *f*

beeline *n* **make a beeline for** : irse derecho a

beep *n* : pitido *m* — **beep** *v* : pitar

beer *n* : cerveza *f*

beet *n* : remolacha *f*

beetle *n* : escarabajo *m*

before *adv* **1** : antes **2 the month before** : el mes anterior — **before** *prep* **1** (*in space*) : delante de, ante **2** (*in time*) : antes de — **before** *conj* : antes de que — **beforehand** *adv* : antes

befriend *vt* : hacerse amigo de

beg *v* **begged**; **begging** *vt* **1** : pedir, mendigar **2** ENTREAT : suplicar — *vi* : mendigar, pedir limosna — **beggar** *n* : mendigo *m*, -ga *f*

begin *v* -**gan**; -**gun**; -**ginning** : empezar, comenzar — **beginner** *n* : principiante *mf* — **beginning** *n* : principio *m*, comienzo *m*

begrudge *vt* -**grudged**; -**grudging 1** : dar de mala gana **2** ENVY : envidiar

behalf *n* **on behalf of** : de parte de, en nombre de

behave *vi* -**haved**; -**having** : comportarse, portarse — **behavior** *n* : comportamiento *m*, conducta *f*

behind *adv* **1** : detrás **2 fall behind** : atrasarse — **behind** *prep* **1** : atrás de, detrás de **2 be behind schedule** : ir retrasado **3 her friends are behind her** : tiene el apoyo de sus amigos

behold *vt* -**held**; -**holding** : contemplar

beige *adj* & *nm* : beige

being *n* **1** : ser *m* **2 come into being** : nacer

belated *adj* : tardío

belch *vi* : eructar — **belch** *n* : eructo *m*

Belgian *adj* : belga

belie *vt* -**lied**; -**lying** : contradecir, desmentir

belief *n* **1** TRUST : confianza *f* **2** CONVICTION : creencia *f*, convicción *f* **3** FAITH : fe *f* — **believable** *adj* : creíble — **believe** *v* -**lieved**; -**lieving** : creer — **believer** *n* : creyente *mf*

belittle *vt* -**littled**; -**littling** : menospreciar

Belizean *adj* : beliceño *m*, -ña *f*

bell *n* **1** : campana *f* **2** : timbre *m* (de teléfono, de la puerta, etc.)

belligerent *adj* : beligerante

bellow *vi* : bramar, mugir — *vt or* **bellow out** : gritar

bellows *ns & pl* : fuelle *m*

belly *n*, *pl* -**lies** : vientre *m*

belong *vi* **1 belong to** : pertenecer a, ser propiedad de **2 belong to** : ser miembro de (un club, etc.) **3 where does it belong** : ¿dónde va? — **belongings** *npl* : pertenencias *fpl*, efectos *mpl* personales

beloved *adj* : querido, amado — **beloved** *n* : querido *m*, -da *f*

below *adv* : abajo — **below** *prep* **1** : abajo de, debajo de **2 below average** : por debajo

bears
osos^M

black bear
oso^M negro

polar bear
oso^M polar

del promedio **3 below zero :** bajo cero
belt *n* **1 :** cinturón *m* **2** BAND STRAP
: cinta *f,* correa *f* **3** AREA **:** frente *m,*
zona *f* — **belt** *vt* **1 :** ceñir con un
cinturón **2** THRASH **:** darle una paliza a
bench *n* **1 :** banco *m* **2** WORKBENCH **:**
mesa *f* de trabajo **3** COURT **:** tribunal *m*
bend *v* **bent; bending** *vt* **:** doblar,
torcer — *vi* **1 :** torcerse **2 bend over :**
inclinarse — **bend** *n* **:** curva *f,* ángulo *m*
beneath *adv* **:** abajo, debajo —
beneath *prep* **:** bajo, debajo de
benediction *n* **:** bendición *f*

benefactor *n* **:** benefactor *m,* -tora *f*
benefit *n* **1** ADVANTAGE **:** ventaja *f,*
provecho *m* **2** AID **:** asistencia *f,*
beneficio *m* — **benefit** *vt* **:** beneficiar
— *vi* **:** beneficiarse — **beneficial** *adj*
: beneficioso — **beneficiary** *n,*
pl **-ries :** beneficiario *m,* -ria *f*
benevolent *adj* **:** benévolo
benign *adj* **1** KIND **:** benévolo,
amable **2 :** benigno (en medicina)
bent *adj* **1 :** encorvado **2 be**
bent on : estar empeñado en —
bent *n* **:** aptitud *f,* inclinación *f*

bequeath *vt* **:** legar —
bequest *n* **:** legado *m*
berate *vt* **-rated; -rating :**
reprender, regañar
bereaved *adj* **:** desconsolado, a luto
beret *n* **:** boina *f*
▸ berry *n, pl* -ries **:** baya *f*
berserk *adj* **1 :** enloquecido **2**
go berserk : volverse loco
berth *n* **1** MOORING **:**
atracadero *m* **2** BUNK **:** litera *f*
beseech *vt* **-sought** *or* **-seeched;**
-seeching : suplicar, implorar

billiards
billarᴹ

chalk
tiza ᶠ

rack
triángulo ᴹ

billiard cue
taco ᴹ *de billar* ᴹ

table
mesa ᶠ

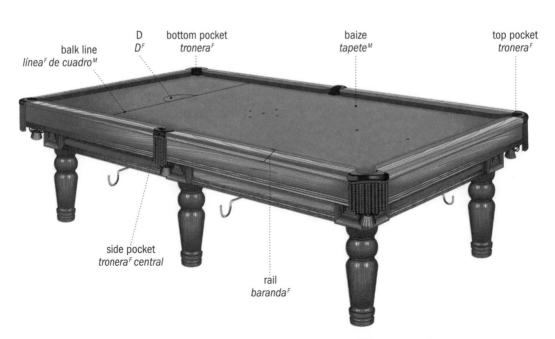

balk line
línea ᶠ *de cuadro* ᴹ

D
D ᶠ

bottom pocket
tronera ᶠ

baize
tapete ᴹ

top pocket
tronera ᶠ

side pocket
tronera ᶠ *central*

rail
baranda ᶠ

berries
bayas[F]

blueberry
arándano[M]

strawberry
fresa[M]

black currant
grosella[F] *negra*

currant
grosella[F]

raspberry
frambuesa[F]

cranberry
arándano[M] *agrio*

gooseberry
grosella[F] *espinosa*

blackberry
moras[F]

---

beset *vt* **-set; -setting 1** HARASS
: acosar **2** SURROUND : rodear
beside *prep* **1** : al lado de, junto a **2 be**
beside oneself : estar fuera de sí —
besides *adv* : además — **beside** *prep* **1**
: además de **2** EXCEPT : excepto
besiege *vt* **-sieged; -sieging** : asediar
best *adj* (*superlative of* **good**) : mejor —
best *adv* (*superlative of* **well**) : mejor —
best *n* **1 at best** : a lo más **2 do one's**
best : hacer todo lo posible **3 the best** : lo
mejor — **best man** *n* : padrino *m* (de boda)
bestow *vt* : otorgar, conceder
bet *n* : apuesta *f* — **bet** *v* **bet;**
betting *vt* : apostar — *vi* **bet on**
something : apostarle a algo
betray *vt* : traicionar —
betrayal *n* : traición *f*
better *adj* (*comparative of* **good**[1]) : mejor
2 get better : mejorar — **better** *adv*
(*comparative of* **well**) **1** : mejor **2 all**
the better : tanto mejor — **better** *n* **1**
the better : el mejor, la mejor **2 get**
the better of : vencer a — **better** *vt* **1**
IMPROVE : mejorar **2** SURPASS : superar
between *prep* : entre — **between** *adv*
or **in between** : en medio
beverage *n* : bebida *f*
beware *vi* **beware of** : tener cuidado con
bewilder *vt* : desconcertar —
bewilderment *n* : desconcierto *m*
bewitch *vt* : hechizar, encantar
beyond *adv* : más allá, más lejos

(en el espacio), más adelante (en el
tiempo) — **beyond** *prep* : más allá de
bias *n* **1** PREJUDICE : prejuicio *m* **2**
TENDENCY : inclinación *f*, tendencia *f*
— **biased** *adj* : parcial
bib *n* : babero *m* (para niños)
Bible *n* : Biblia *f* — **biblical** *adj* : bíblico
bibliography *n*, *pl* **-phies** : bibliografía *f*
bicarbonate of soda *n* :
bicarbonato *m* de soda
biceps *ns & pl* : bíceps *m*
bicker *vi* : reñir
bicycle *n* : bicicleta *f* — **bicycle** *vi*
-cled; -cling : ir en bicicleta
bid *vt* **bade** *or* **bid; bidden** *or* **bid; bidding**
1 OFFER : ofrecer **2 bid farewell** : decir
adiós — **bid** *n* **1** OFFER : oferta *f* **2**
ATTEMPT : intento *m*, tentativa *f*
bide *vt* **bode** *or* **bided; bided; biding bide**
one's time : esperar el momento oportuno
bifocals *npl* : anteojos *mpl* bifocales
big *adj* **bigger; biggest** : grande
bigamy *n* : bigamía *f*
bigot *n* : intolerante *mf* — **bigotry** *n*,
pl **-tries** : intolerancia *f*, fanatismo *m*
bike *n* **1** BICYCLE : bici *f fam* **2**
MOTORCYCLE : moto *f*
bikini *n* : bikini *m*
bile *n* : bilis *f*
bilingual *adj* : bilingüe
bill *n* **1** BEAK : pico *m* **2** INVOICE : cuenta *f*,
factura *f* **3** BANKNOTE : billete *m* **4** LAW :
proyecto *m* de ley, ley *f* — **bill** *vt* : pasarle
la cuenta a — **billboard** *n* : cartelera *f*

— **billfold** *n* : billetera *f*, cartera *f*
▸ **billiards** *n* : billar *m*
billion *n*, *pl* **billions** *or* **billion**
: mil millones *mpl*
billow *vi* : ondular, hincharse
billy goat *n* : macho *m* cabrío
bin *n* : cubo *m*, cajón *m*
binary *adj* : binario *m*
bind *vt* **bound; binding 1** TIE : atar
2 OBLIGATE : obligar **3** UNITE : unir **4**
BANDAGE : vendar **5** : encuadernar (un
libro) — **binder** *n* FOLDER : carpeta *f* —
binding *n* : encuadernación *f* (de libros)
binge *n* : juerga *f fam*
bingo *n*, *pl* **-gos** : bingo *m*
binoculars *npl* : binoculares *mpl*,
gemelos *mpl*
biochemistry *n* : bioquímica *f*
biography *n*, *pl* **-phies** : biografía *f*
— **biographer** *n* : biógrafo *m*, -fa *f*
— **biographical** *adj* : biográfico
biology *n* : biología *f* — **biological** *adj* :
biológico — **biologist** *n* : biólogo *m*, -ga *f*
birch *n* : abedul *m*
bird *n* : pájaro *m* (pequeño), ave *f* (grande)
birth *n* **1** : nacimiento *m*, parto *m* **2**
give birth to : dar a luz a — **birthday** *n*
: cumpleaños *m* — **birthmark** *n*
: mancha *f* de nacimiento —
birthplace *n* : lugar *m* de nacimiento
— **birthrate** *n* : índice *m* de natalidad
biscuit *n* : bizcocho *m*
bisect *vt* : bisecar
bisexual *adj* : bisexual

bloodstream
circulación^F **sanguínea**

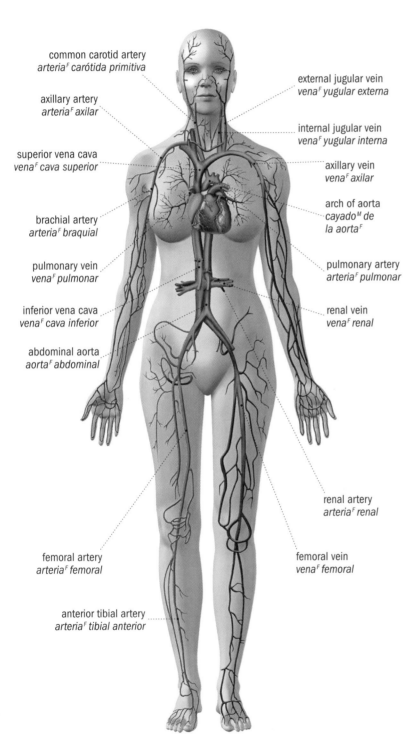

common carotid artery
arteria^F *carótida primitiva*

axillary artery
arteria^F *axilar*

superior vena cava
vena^F *cava superior*

brachial artery
arteria^F *braquial*

pulmonary vein
vena^F *pulmonar*

inferior vena cava
vena^F *cava inferior*

abdominal aorta
aorta^F *abdominal*

femoral artery
arteria^F *femoral*

anterior tibial artery
arteria^F *tibial anterior*

external jugular vein
vena^F *yugular externa*

internal jugular vein
vena^F *yugular interna*

axillary vein
vena^F *axilar*

arch of aorta
cayado^M *de
la aorta*^F

pulmonary artery
arteria^F *pulmonar*

renal vein
vena^F *renal*

renal artery
arteria^F *renal*

femoral vein
vena^F *femoral*

bishop *n* : obispo *m*
bison *ns & pl* : bisonte *m*
bit¹ *n* : bocado *m* (de una brida)
bit² **1** : trozo *m*, pedazo *m* **2** : bit *m*
  (de información) **3 a bit** : un poco
bitch *n* : perra *f* — **bitch** *vi*
  COMPLAIN : quejarse, reclamar
bite *v* **bit; bitten; biting** *vt* **1** : morder
  2 STING : picar — *vi* : morder — *n* **1** :
  picadura *f* (de un insecto), mordedura *f*
  (de un animal) **2** SNACK : bocado *m* —
  biting *adj* **1** PENETRATING : cortante,
  penetrante **2** CAUSTIC : mordaz
bitter *adj* **1** : amargo **2 it's bitter cold** :
  hace un frío glacial **3 to the bitter end** :
  hasta el final — **bitterness** *n* : amargura *f*
bizarre *adj* : extraño
black *adj* : negro — **black** *n* **1** :
  negro *m* (color) **2** : negro *m*, -gra *f*
  (persona) — **black–and–blue** *adj* :
  amoratado — **blackberry** *n*, *pl* **-ries**
  : mora *f* — **blackbird** *n* : mirlo *m* —
  blackboard *n* : pizarra *f*, pizarrón *m*,
  Lat — **blacken** *vt* : ennegrecer —
  blackmail *n* : chantaje *m* — **blackmail** *vt*
  : chantajear — **black market** *n* :
  mercado *m* negro — **blackout** *n* **1**
  : apagón *m* (de poder eléctrico) **2**
  FAINT : desmayo *m* — **blacksmith** *n* :
  herrero *m* — **blacktop** *n* : asfalto *m*
bladder *n* : vejiga *f*
blade *n* **1** : hoja *f* (de un cuchillo),
  cuchilla *f* (de un patín) **2** : pala *f* (de
  un remo, una hélice, etc.) **3 blade**
  of grass : brizna *f* (de hierba)
blame *vt* **blamed; blaming** : culpar,
  echar la culpa a — **blame** *n* : culpa *f*
  — **blameless** *adj* : inocente
bland *adj* : soso, insulso
blank *adj* **1** : en blanco (dícese de un
  papel), liso (dícese de una pared) **2** EMPTY
  : vacío — **blank** *n* : espacio *m* en blanco
blanket *n* **1** : manta *f*, cobija *f*
  Lat **2 blanket of snow** : manto *m*
  de nieve — **blanket** *vt* : cubrir
blare *vi* **blared; blaring** : resonar
blasphemy *n*, *pl* **-mies** : blasfemia *f*
blast *n* **1** GUST : ráfaga *f* **2** EXPLOSION :
  explosión *f* **3** : toque *m* (de trompeta,
  etc.) — **blast** *vt* BLOW UP : volar
  — **blast-off** *n* : despegue *m*
blatant *adj* : descarado
blaze *n* **1** FIRE : fuego *m* **2** BRIGHTNESS
  : resplandor *m*, brillantez *f* **3 blaze of**
  anger : arranque *m* de cólera — **blaze** *v*

blazed; blazing *vi* : arder, brillar — *vt*
blaze a trail : abrir un camino
blazer *n* : chaqueta *f* deportiva
bleach *vt* : blanquear, decolorar —
bleach *n* : lejía *f*, blanqueador *m*, *Lat*
bleachers *ns & pl* : gradas *fpl*
bleak *adj* **1** DESOLATE : desolado
2 GLOOMY : triste, sombrío
bleary–eyed *adj* : con los ojos nublados
bleat *vi* : balar — **bleat** *n* : balido *m*
bleed *v* **bled; bleeding** : sangrar
blemish *vt* : manchar, marcar —
blemish *n* : mancha *f*, marca *f*
blend *vt* : mezclar, combinar —
blend *n* : mezcla *f*, combinación *f*
— **blender** *n* : licuadora *f*
bless *vt* **blessed; blessing** : bendecir
— **blessed** *or* blest *adj* : bendito
— **blessing** *n* : bendición *f*
blew → **blow**
blind *adj* : ciego — **blind** *vt* **1** : cegar,
dejar ciego **2** DAZZLE : deslumbrar —
blind *n* **1** : persiana *f* (para una ventana)
2 the blind : los ciegos — **blindfold** *vt*
: vendar los ojos — **blindfold** *n* :
venda *f* (para los ojos) — **blindly** *adv* :
ciegamente — **blindness** *n* : ceguera *f*
blink *vi* **1** : parpadear **2** FLICKER
: brillar intermitentemente —
blink *n* : parpadeo *m* — **blinker** *n* :
intermitente *m*, direccional *f Lat*
bliss *n* : dicha *f*, felicidad *f*
(absoluta) — **blissful** *adj* : feliz
blister *n* : ampolla *f* —
blister *vi* : ampollarse
blitz *n* : bombardeo *m* aéreo
blizzard *n* : ventisca *f* (de nieve)
bloated *adj* : hinchado
blob *n* **1** DROP : gota *f* **2** SPOT : mancha *f*
block *n* **1** : bloque *m* **2** OBSTRUCTION :
obstrucción *f* **3** : manzana *f*, cuadra *f*
Lat (de edificios) **4** *or* **building block**
: cubo *m* de construcción — **block** *vt*
: obstruir, bloquear — **blockade** *n* :
bloqueo *m* — **blockage** *n* : obstrucción *f*
blond *or* blonde *adj* : rubio —
blond *n* : rubio *m*, -bia *f*
blood *n* : sangre *f* — **bloodhound** *n*
: sabueso *m* — **blood pressure** *n* :
tensión *f* (arterial) — **bloodshed** *n*
: derramamiento *m* de sangre —
bloodshot *adj* : inyectado de sangre —
bloodstained *adj* : manchado de sangre —
bloodstream *n* : sangre *f*, torrente *m*
sanguíneo — **bloody** *adj* **bloodier;**

-est : ensangrentado, sangriento
▸ **bloom** *n* **1** : flor *f* **2 in full bloom** : en
plena floración — **bloom** *vi* : florecer
blossom *n* : flor *f* — **blossom** *vi* : florecer
blot *n* **1** : borrón *m* (de tinta, etc.) **2**
BLEMISH : mancha *f* — **blot** *vt* **blotted;**
blotting 1 : emborronar **2** DRY : secar
blotch *n* : mancha *f*, borrón *m*
— **blotchy** *adj* **blotchier;**
-est : lleno de manchas
blouse *n* : blusa *f*
blow *v* **blew; blown; blowing** *vi* **1** :
soplar **2** SOUND : sonar **3** *or* **blow out** :
fundirse (dícese de un fusible eléctrico),
reventarse (dícese de una llanta)
— *vt* **1** : soplar **2** SOUND : tocar, sonar
3 BUNGLE : echar a perder — **blow** *n* :
golpe *m* — **blowout** *n* : reventón *m* —
blow up *vi* : estallar, hacer explosión
— *vt* **1** EXPLODE : volar **2** INFLATE : inflar
blubber *n* : esperma *f* de ballena
bludgeon *vt* : aporrear
blue *adj* **bluer; bluest 1** : azul **2**
MELANCHOLY : triste — **blue** *n* : azul *m*
— **blueberry** *n*, *pl* **-ries** : arándano *m* —
bluebird *n* : azulejo *m* — **blue cheese** *n*

: queso *m* azul — **blueprint** *n* PLAN :
proyecto *m* — **blues** *npl* **1** SADNESS
: tristeza *f* **2** : blues *m* (en música)
bluff *vi* : hacer un farol — **bluff** *n* : farol *m*
blunder *vi* : meter la pata *fam* —
blunder *n* : metedura *f* de pata *fam*
blunt *adj* **1** DULL : desafilado
2 DIRECT : directo, franco
blur *n* : imágen *f* borrosa — **blur** *vt*
blurred; blurring : hacer borroso
blurb *n* : nota *f* publicitaria
blurt *vt or* **blurt out** : espetar
blush *n* : rubor *m* — **blush** *vi* : ruborizarse
blustery *adj* : borrascoso, tempestuoso
boar *n* : cerdo *m* macho
board *n* **1** PLANK : tabla *f*, tablón *m* **2**
COMMITTEE : junta *f*, consejo *m* **3** :
tablero *m* (de juegos) **4 room and**
board : comida y alojamiento —
board *vt* **1** : subir a bordo de (una
nave, un avión, etc.), subir a (un tren) **2**
LODGE : hospedar **3 board up** : cerrar
con tablas — **boarder** *n* : huésped *mf*
boast *n* : jactancia *f* — **boast** *vi* : alardear,
jactarse — **boastful** *adj* : jactancioso

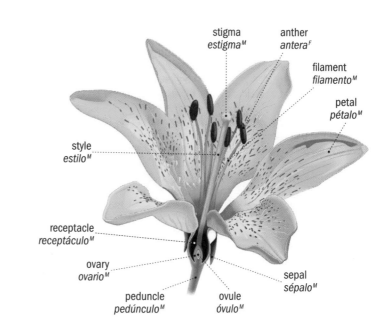

stigma
estigma^M

anther
antera^F

filament
filamento^M

petal
pétalo^M

style
estilo^M

receptacle
receptáculo^M

ovary
ovario^M

peduncle
pedúnculo^M

ovule
óvulo^M

sepal
sépalo^M

▸ boat *n* : barco *m* (grande), barca *f* (pequeña)

bob *vi* **bobbed; bobbing** *or* **bob up and down** : subir y bajar

bobbin *n* : bobina *f*, carrete *m*

bobby pin *n* : horquilla *f*

body *n, pl* **bodies 1** : cuerpo *m* **2** CORPSE : cadáver *m* **3** : carrocería (de un automóvil, etc.) **4** COLLECTION : conjunto *m* **5 body of water** : masa *f* de agua — **bodily** *adj* : corporal — **bodyguard** *n* : guardaespaldas *mf*

bog *n* : ciénaga *f* — **bog** *vt* **bogged; bogging** *or* **bog down** : empantanarse

bogus *adj* : falso

boil *v* : hervir — **boiler** *n* : caldera *f*

bold *adj* **1** DARING : audaz **2** IMPUDENT : descarado — **boldness** *n* : audacia *f*

Bolivian *adj* : boliviano *m*, -na *f*

bologna *n* : salchicha *f* ahumada

bolster *vt* **-stered; -stering** *or* **bolster up** : reforzar

bolt *n* **1** LOCK : cerrojo *m* **2** SCREW : tornillo *m* **3 bolt of lightning** : relámpago *m*, rayo *m* — **bolt** *vt* **1** FASTEN : atornillar **2** LOCK : echar el cerrojo a — *vi* FLEE : salir corriendo

bomb *n* : bomba *f* — **bomb** *vt* : bombardear — **bombard** *vt* : bombardear — **bombardment** *n* : bombardeo *m* — **bomber** *n* : bombardero *m*

bond *n* **1** TIE : vínculo *m*, lazo *m* **2** SURETY : fianza *f* **3** : bono *m* (en finanzas) — **bond** *vi* STICK : adherirse

bondage *n* : esclavitud *f*

bone *n* : hueso *m* — **bone** *vt* **boned; boning** : deshuesar

bonfire *n* : hoguera *f*

bonus *n* **1** PAY : prima *f* **2** BENEFIT : beneficio *m* adicional

bony *adj* **bonier; -est 1** : huesudo **2** : lleno de espinas (dícese de pescados)

boo *n, pl* **boos** : abucheo *m* — **boo** *vt* : abuchear

book *n* **1** : libro *m* **2** NOTEBOOK : libreta *f*, cuaderno *m* — **book** *vt* : reservar — **bookcase** *n* : estantería *f* — **bookkeeping** *n* : teneduría *f* de libros, contabilidad *f* — **booklet** *n* : folleto *m* — **bookmark** *n* : marcador *m* de libros — **bookseller** *n* : librero *m*, -ra *f* — **bookshelf** *n, pl* **-shelves** : estante *m* — **bookstore** *n* : librería *f*

boom *vi* **1** : tronar, resonar **2** PROSPER : estar en auge, prosperar — **boom** *n* **1** : bramido *m*, estruendo *m* **2** : auge *m* (económico)

boon *n* : ayuda *f*, beneficio *m*

boost *vt* **1** LIFT : levantar **2** INCREASE : aumentar — **boost** *n* **1** INCREASE : aumento *m* **2** ENCOURAGEMENT : estímulo *m*

boot *n* : bota *f*, botín *m* — **boot** *vt* **1** : dar una patada a **2** *or* **boot up** : cargar (un ordenador)

booth *n, pl* **booths** : cabina *f* (de teléfono, de votar), caseta *f* (de información)

booty *n, pl* **-ties** : botín *m*

booze *n* : trago *m*, bebida *f* (alcohólica)

border *n* **1** EDGE : borde *m*, orilla *f* **2** TRIM : ribete *m* **3** FRONTIER : frontera *f*

bore[1] *vt* **bored; boring** DRILL : taladrar

bore[2] *vt* TIRE : aburrir — **bore** *n* : pesado *m*, -da *f fam* (persona), lata *f fam* (cosa, situación) — **boredom** *n* : aburrimiento *m* — **boring** *adj* : aburrido, pesado

born *adj* **1** : nacido **2 be born** : nacer

borough *n* : distrito *m* municipal

borrow *vt* : pedir prestado, tomar prestado

Bosnian *adj* : bosnio *m*, -nia *f*

bosom *n* BREAST : pecho *m*, seno *m* — **bosom** *adj* **bosom friend** : amigo *m* íntimo

boss *n* : jefe *m*, -fa *f*; patrón *m*, -trona *f*

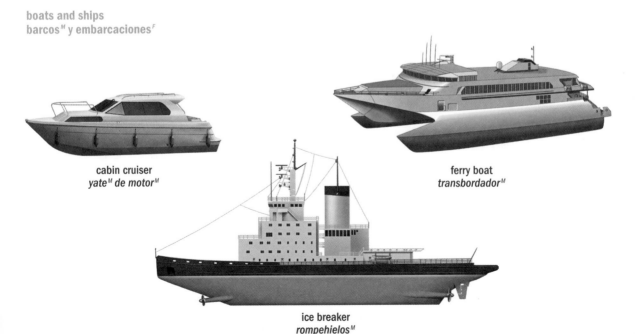

boats and ships
barcos[M] **y embarcaciones**[F]

cabin cruiser
yate[M] *de motor*[M]

ferry boat
transbordador[M]

ice breaker
rompehielos[M]

— **boss** *vt* SUPERVISE : dirigir —
bossy *adj* **bossier; -est** : autoritario
botany *n* : botánica *f* —
  botanical *adj* : botánico
botch *vt* : hacer una
  chapuza de, estropear
both *adj* : ambos, los dos, las
  dos — **both** *pron* : ambos *m*,
  -bas *f*; los dos, las dos
bother *vt* **1** TROUBLE : preocupar **2** PESTER
  : molestar, fastidiar — *vi* **bother to** :
  molestarse en — **bother** *n* : molestia *f*
bottle *n* **1** : botella *f*, frasco *m* **2** *or*
  baby bottle : biberón *m* — **bottle** *vt*
  bottled; bottling : embotellar —
  bottleneck *n* : embotellamiento *m*
bottom *n* **1** : fondo *m* (de una caja,
  del mar, etc.), pie *m* (de una escalera,
  una montaña, etc.), final *m* (de una
  lista) **2** BUTTOCKS : nalgas *fpl*, trasero *m*
  — **bottom** *adj* : más bajo, inferior, de
  abajo — **bottomless** *adj* : sin fondo
bough *n* : rama *f*
bought → **buy**
bouillon *n* : caldo *m*
boulder *n* : canto *m* rodado
boulevard *n* : bulevar *m*

bounce *v* **bounced; bouncing** *vt*
  : hacer rebotar — *vi* : rebotar
  — **bounce** *n* : rebote *m*
bound[1] *adj* **be bound for** : ir rumbo a
bound[2] *adj* **1** OBLIGED : obligado
  2 DETERMINED : decidido **3 be
  bound to** : tener que
bound[3] *n* **out of bounds** : (en) zona
  prohibida — **boundary** *n, pl* **-aries** :
  límite *m* — **boundless** *adj* : sin límites
bouquet *n* : ramo *m*
bourgeois *adj* : burgués
bout *n* **1** : combate *m* (en deportes)
  2 : ataque *m* (de una enfermedad)
  3 : período *m* (de actividad)
bow[1] *vi* : inclinarse — *vt* **bow
  one's head** : inclinar la cabeza —
  bow *n* : reverencia *f*, inclinación *f*
bow[2] *n* **1** : arco *m* **2 tie a
  bow** : hacer un lazo
bow[3] *n* : proa *f* (de un barco)
bowels *npl* **1** : intestinos *mpl* **2**
  DEPTHS : entrañas *fpl*
bowl[1] *n* : tazón *m*, cuenco *m*
bowl[2] *vi* : jugar a los bolos —
  bowling *n* : bolos *mpl*
box[1] *vi* FIGHT : boxear — **boxer** *n* :
  boxeador *m*, -dora *f* — **boxing** *n* : boxeo *m*

box[2] *n* **1** : caja *f*, cajón *m* **2** : palco *m*
  (en el teatro) — **box** *vt* : empaquetar —
  box office *n* : taquilla *f*, boletería *f Lat*
boy *n* : niño *m*, chico *m*
boycott *vt* : boicotear —
  boycott *n* : boicot *m*
boyfriend *n* : novio *m*
bra → **brassiere**
brace *n* **1** SUPPORT : abrazadera *f* **2**
  braces *npl* : aparatos *mpl* (para
  dientes) — **brace** *vi* **brace
  oneself for** : prepararse para
bracelet *n* : brazalete *m*
bracket *n* **1** SUPPORT : soporte *m* **2**
  : corchete *m* (marca de puntuación)
  3 CATEGORY : categoría *f* —
  bracket *vt* **1** : poner entre corchetes
  2 CATEGORIZE : catalogar
brag *vi* **bragged; bragging** : jactarse
braid *vt* : trenzar — **braid** *n* : trenza *f*
braille *n* : braille *m*
brain *n* **1** : cerebro *m* **2** brains *npl*
  : inteligencia *f* — **brainstorm** *n*
  : idea *f* genial — **brainwash** *vt*
  : lavar el cerebro — **brainy** *adj*
  brainier; -est : inteligente, listo
brake *n* : freno *m* — **brake** *v*
  braked; braking : frenar

trawler
trainera[F]

tugboat
remolcador[M]

houseboat
casa[F] *flotante*

breads
panes^M

bagel
rosquilla^F

tortilla
tortilla^F

croissant
cruasán^M

challah
pan^M *jalá*

brioche
pan^M *de huevo*^M

multigrain bread
pan^M *multicereales*

Greek bread
pan^M *griego*

epi bread
pan^M *espiga*^F

baguette
baguette^F

---

bramble *n* : zarza *f*

bran *n* : salvado *m*

branch *n* **1** : rama *f* (de una planta) **2** DIVISION : ramal *m* (de un camino, etc.), sucursal *f* (de una empresa), agencia *f* (del gobierno) — **branch** *vi* *or* **branch off** : ramificarse, bifurcarse

brand *n* **1** : marca *f* (de ganado) **2** *or* **brand name** : marca *f* de fábrica — **brand** *vt* **1** : marcar (ganado) **2** LABEL : tachar, tildar

brandish *vt* : blandir

brand–new *adj* : flamante

brandy *n, pl* **-dies** : brandy *m*, coñac *m*

brass *n* **1** : latón *m* **2** : metales *mpl* (de una orquesta)

brassiere *n* : sostén *m*, brasier *m*, *Lat*

brat *n* : mocoso *m*, -sa *f fam*

bravado *n, pl* **-does** *or* **-dos** : bravuconadas *fpl*

brave *adj* **braver; bravest** : valiente, valeroso — **brave** *vt* **braved; braving** : afrontar, hacer frente a — **brave** *n* : guerrero *m* indio —

bravery *n* : valor *m*, valentía *f*

brawl *n* : pelea *f*, reyerta *f*

brawn *n* : músculos *mpl* — **brawny** *adj* **brawnier; -est** : musculoso

bray *vi* : rebuznar

brazen *adj* : descarado

Brazilian *adj* : brasileño *m*, -ña *f*

breach *n* **1** VIOLATION : infracción *f*, violación *f* **2** GAP : brecha *f*

▸ **bread** *n* **1** : pan *m* **2 bread**

crumbs : migajas *fpl*

breadth *n* : anchura *f*

break *v* **broke; broken; breaking** *vt* **1** : romper, quebrar **2** VIOLATE : infringir, violar **3** INTERRUPT : interrumpir **4** SURPASS : batir (un récord, etc.) **5 break a habit** : quitarse una costumbre **6 break the news** : dar la noticia — *vi* **1** : romperse, quebrarse **2 break away** : escapar **3 break down** : estropearse (dícese de una máquina), fallar (dícese de un sistema, etc.) **4 break into** : entrar en **5 break off** : interrumpirse **6 break out of** : escaparse de **7 break up** SEPARATE : separarse — **break** *n* **1** : ruptura *f*, fractura *f* **2** GAP : interrupción *f*, claro *m* (entre las nubes) **3 lucky break** : golpe *m* de suerte **4**

take a break : tomar(se) un descanso
— **breakable** adj : quebradizo, frágil —
breakdown n **1** : avería f (de máquinas),
interrupción f (de comunicaciones),
fracaso m (de negociaciones) **2** or
nervous breakdown : crisis f nerviosa
breakfast n : desayuno m
breast n **1** : seno m (de una mujer)
2 CHEST : pecho m — **breast–feed** vt
-fed; -feeding : amamantar
breath n : aliento m, respiración f —
breathe v breathed; breathing : respirar
— **breathless** adj : sin aliento, jadeante
— **breathtaking** adj : impresionante
breed v bred; breeding vt **1** : criar
(animales) **2** ENGENDER : engendrar,
producir — vi : reproducirse —
breed n **1** : raza f **2** CLASS : clase f, tipo m
breeze n : brisa f — **breezy** adj
breezier; -est **1** WINDY : ventoso **2**
NONCHALANT : despreocupado
brevity n, pl -ties : brevedad f
brew vt : hacer (cerveza, etc.), preparar
(té) — vi **1** : fabricar cerveza **2** :
amenazar (dícese de una tormenta)
— **brewery** n, pl -eries : cervecería f
bribe n : soborno m — **bribe** vt
bribed; bribing : sobornar —
bribery n, pl -eries : soborno m
brick n : ladrillo m —
bricklayer n : albañil mf
bride n : novia f — **bridal** adj : nupcial,
de novia — **bridegroom** n : novio m
— **bridesmaid** n : dama f de honor
bridge n **1** : puente m **2** : caballete m
(de la nariz) **3** : bridge m (juego de
naipes) — **bridge** vt bridged; bridging
1 : tender un puente sobre **2 bridge
the gap** : salvar las diferencias
bridle n : brida f — **bridle** vt
-dled; -dling : embridar
brief adj : breve — **brief** n **1** : resumen m,
sumario m **2 briefs** npl UNDERPANTS :
calzoncillos mpl — **brief** vt : dar órdenes
a, instruir — **briefcase** n : portafolio m,
maletín m — **briefly** adv : brevemente
bright adj **1** : brillante, claro **2** CHEERFUL
: alegre, animado **3** INTELLIGENT :
listo, inteligente — **brighten** vi **1** :
hacerse más brillante **2** or **brighten up** :
animarse, alegrarse — vt **1** ILLUMINATE
: iluminar **2** ENLIVEN : alegrar, animar
brilliant adj : brillante — **brilliance** n **1**
BRIGHTNESS : resplandor m, brillantez f **2**
INTELLIGENCE : inteligencia f

brim n **1** : borde m (de una taza,
etc.) **2** : ala f (de un sombrero) —
brim vi brimmed; brimming or
brim over : desbordarse, rebosar
brine n : salmuera f
bring vt brought; bringing **1** : traer
2 bring about : ocasionar **3 bring
around** PERSUADE : convencer **4
bring back** : devolver **5 bring down** :
derribar **6 bring on** CAUSE : provocar
7 bring out : sacar **8 bring to an end**
: terminar (con) **9 bring up** REAR :
criar **10 bring up** MENTION : sacar
brink n : borde m
brisk adj **1** FAST : rápido
2 LIVELY : enérgico
bristle n : cerda f (de un animal),
pelo m (de una planta) — **bristle** vi
-tled; -tling : erizarse
British adj : británico
brittle adj -tler; -tlest : frágil, quebradizo
broach vt : abordar
broad adj **1** WIDE : ancho **2** GENERAL :
general **3 in broad daylight** : en pleno día
broadcast vt -cast; -casting :
emitir — **broadcast** n : emisión f
broaden vt : ampliar, ensanchar
— vi : ensancharse — **broadly** adv
: en general — **broad–minded** adj
: de miras amplias, tolerante
broccoli n : brócoli m, brécol m
brochure n : folleto m
broil vt : asar a la parrilla
broke → **break** — **broke** adj : pelado
fam — **broken** adj : roto, quebrado —
brokenhearted adj : desconsolado,
con el corazón destrozado
broker n : corredor m, -dora f
bronchitis n : bronquitis f
bronze n : bronce m
brooch n : broche m
brood n : nidada f (de pájaros),
camada f (de mamíferos) — **brood** vi **1**
INCUBATE : empollar **2 brood about** :
dar vueltas a, pensar demasiado en
brook n : arroyo m
▸ **broom** n : escoba f — **broomstick** n
: palo m de escoba
broth n, pl **broths** : caldo m
brothel n : burdel m
brother n : hermano m — **brotherhood** n
: fraternidad f — **brother–in–law** n,
pl **brothers–in–law** : cuñado m
— **brotherly** adj : fraternal
brought → **bring**

brow n **1** EYEBROW : ceja f **2** FOREHEAD
: frente f **3** : cima f (de una colina)
brown adj : marrón, castaño
(dícese del pelo), moreno (dícese
de la piel) — **brown** n : marrón m
— **brown** vt : dorar (en cocinar)
browse vi browsed; browsing
: mirar, echar un vistazo
bruise vt bruised; bruising **1** :
contusionar, magullar (a una persona)
2 : machucar (frutas) — **bruise** n
: cardenal m, magulladura f
brunch n : brunch m
brunet or **brunette** adj : moreno
— **brunet** n : moreno m, -na f
brunt n **bear the brunt of** :
aguantar el mayor impacto de

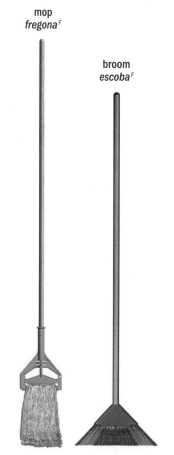

broom and mop
ecoba^F y fregona^F

mop
fregona^F

broom
escoba^F

▸ brush *n* **1** : cepillo *m*, pincel *m* (de artista), brocha *f* (de pintor) **2** UNDERBRUSH : maleza *f* — **brush** *vt* **1** : cepillar **2** GRAZE : rozar **3 brush aside** : rechazar **4 brush off** DISREGARD : hacer caso omiso de — *vi* **brush up on** : repasar — **brush–off** *n* **give the brush to** : dar calabazas a

brusque *adj* : brusco

brutal *adj* : brutal — **brutality** *n, pl* **-ties** : brutalidad *f*

brute *adj* : bruto — **brute** *n* : bestia *f*; bruto *m*, -ta *f*

bubble *n* : burbuja *f* — **bubble** *vi* **-bled; -bling** : burbujear

buck *n, pl* **buck** *or* **bucks 1** : animal *m* macho, ciervo *m* (macho) **2** DOLLAR : dólar *m* — **buck** *vi* **1** : corcovear (dícese de un caballo) **2 buck up** : animarse, levantar el ánimo — *vt* OPPOSE : oponerse a, ir en contra de

bucket *n* : cubo *m*

buckle *n* : hebilla *f* — **buckle** *v* **-led; -ling** *vt* **1** FASTEN : abrochar **2** BEND : combar, torcer — *vi* **1** : combarse, torcerse **2** : doblarse (dícese de las rodillas)

bud *n* **1** : brote *m* **2** *or* **flower bud** : capullo *m* — **bud** *vi* **budded;**

budding : brotar, hacer brotes

Buddhism *n* : budismo *m* — **Buddhist** *adj* : budista — **Buddhism** *n* : budista *mf*

buddy *n, pl* **-dies** : compañero *m*, -ra *f*

budge *vi* **budged; budging 1** MOVE : moverse **2** YIELD : ceder

budget *n* : presupuesto *m* — **budget** *vi* : presupuestar — **budgetary** *adj* : presupuestario

buff *n* **1** : beige *m*, color *m* de ante **2** ENTHUSIAST : aficionado *m*, -da *f* — **buff** *adj* : beige — **buff** *vt* POLISH : pulir

buffalo *n, pl* **-lo** *or* **-loes** : búfalo *m*

buffet *n* **1** : bufé *m* (comida) **2** SIDEBOARD : aparador *m*

bug *n* **1** INSECT : bicho *m*, insecto *m* **2** FLAW : defecto *m* **3** GERM : microbio *m* **4** MICROPHONE : micrófono *m* (oculto) — **bug** *vt* **bugged; bugging 1** PESTER : fastidiar, molestar **2** : ocultar micrófonos en (una habitación, etc.)

buggy *n, pl* **-gies 1** CARRIAGE : calesa *f* **2** *or* **baby buggy** : cochecito *m* (para niños)

bugle *n* : clarín *m*, corneta *f*

build *v* **built; building** *vt* **1** : construir **2** DEVELOP : desarrollar — *vi* **1**

or **build up** INTENSIFY : aumentar, intensificar **2** *or* **build up** ACCUMULATE : acumularse — **build** *n* PHYSIQUE : físico *m*, complexión *f* — **builder** *n* : constructor *m*, -tora *f* — **building** *n* **1** STRUCTURE : edificio *m* **2** CONSTRUCTION : construcción *f* — **built–in** *adj* : empotrado

bulb *n* **1** : bulbo *m* (de una planta) **2** LIGHTBULB : bombilla *f*

bulge *vi* **bulged; bulging** : sobresalir — **bulge** *n* : bulto *m*, protuberancia *f*

bulk *n* **1** VOLUME : volumen *m*, bulto *m* **2 in bulk** : en grandes cantidades — **bulky** *adj* **bulkier; -est** : voluminoso

bull *n* **1** : toro *m* **2** MALE : macho *m*

bulldog *n* : buldog *m*

bulldozer *n* : bulldozer *m*

bullet *n* : bala *f*

bulletin *n* : boletín *m* — **bulletin board** *n* : tablón *m* de anuncios

bulletproof *adj* : a prueba de balas

bullfight *n* : corrida *f* (de toros) — **bullfighter** *n* : torero *m*, -ra *f*; matador *m*

bullion *n* : oro *m* en lingotes, plata *f* en lingotes

bull's–eye *n, pl* **bull's–eyes** : diana *f*

bully *n, pl* **-lies** : matón *m* — **bully** *vt* **-lied; -lying** : intimidar

bum *n* : vagabundo *m*, -da *f*

bumblebee *n* : abejorro *m*

bump *n* **1** BULGE : bulto *m*, protuberancia *f* **2** IMPACT : golpe *m* **3** JOLT : sacudida *f* — **bump** *vt* : chocar contra — *vi* **bump into** MEET : encontrarse con — **bumper** *n* : parachoques *mpl* — **bumper** *adj* : extraordinario, récord — **bumpy** *adj* **bumpier; -est 1** : desigual, lleno de baches (dícese de un camino) **2 a bumpy flight** : un vuelo agitado

bun *n* : bollo *m*

bunch *n* : grupo *m* (de personas), racimo *m* (de frutas, etc.), ramo *m* (de flores), manojo *m* (de llaves) — **bunch** *vi* *or* **bunch up** : amontrase, agruparse

bundle *n* **1** : lío *m*, bulto *m*, atado *m*, haz *m* (de palos) **2** PARCEL : paquete *m* **3 bundle of nerves** : manojo *m* de nervios — **bundle** *vt* **-dled; -dling** *or* **bundle up** : liar, atar

bungalow *n* : casa *f* de un solo piso

bungle *vt* **-gled; -gling** : echar a perder

bunion *n* : juanete *m*

bunk *n* *or* **bunk bed** : litera *f*

bunny *n, pl* **-nies** : conejo *m*, -ja *f*

buoy *n* : boya *f* — **buoy** *vt* *or* **buoy up**

brushes
pinceles^M

sumi-e brush
sumie^M

fan brush
brocha^F

brush
pincel^M

flat brush
pincel^M *plano*

HEARTEN : animar, levantar el ánimo a
— **buoyant** *adj* **1** : boyante, flotante
2 LIGHTHEARTED : alegre, optimista
burden *n* : carga *f* — **burden** *vt*
burden someone with : cargar a algn
con — **burdensome** *adj* : oneroso
bureau *n* **1** : cómoda *f* (mueble)
2 : departamento *m* (del
gobierno) **3** AGENCY : agencia *f* —
bureaucracy *n, pl* -**cies** : burocracia *f*
— **bureaucrat** *n* : burócrata *mf* —
bureaucratic *adj* : burocrático
burglar *n* : ladrón *m*, -drona *f* —
burglarize *vt* -**ized; -izing** : robar —
burglary *n, pl* -**glaries** : robo *m*
burgundy *n, pl* -**dies** : borgoña *m*,
vino *m* de Borgoña
burial *n* : entierro *m*
burly *adj* -**lier; -liest** : fornido
burn *v* **burned** *or* burnt; **burning** *vt* **1**
: quemar **2** *or* **burn down** : incendiar
3 burn up : consumir — *vi* **1** : arder
(dícese de un fuego), quemarse
(dícese de la comida, etc.) **2** : estar
encendido (dícese de una luz) **3 burn
out** : apagarse — **burn** *n* : quemadura *f*
— **burner** *n* : quemador *m*
burnish *vt* : pulir
burp *vi* : eructar — **burp** *n* : eructo *m*
burro *n, pl* -**os** : burro *m*
burrow *n* : madriguera *f* — **burrow** *vi* **1**
: cavar **2 burrow into** : hurgar en
bursar *n* : tesorero *m*, -ra *f*
burst *v* **burst** *or* **bursted; bursting** *vi* :
reventarse — *vt* : reventar — **burst** *n* **1**
EXPLOSION : estallido *m*, explosión *f* **2**
OUTBURST : arranque *m*, arrebato *m* **3**
burst of laughter : carcajada *f*
bury *vt* **buried; burying 1** INTER
: enterrar **2** HIDE : esconder
bus *n, pl* **buses** *or* **busses** : autobús *m*,
bus *m* — **bus** *v* **bused** *or* **bussed;
busing** *or* **bussing** *vt* : transportar en
autobús — *vi* : viajar en autobús
bush *n* SHRUB : arbusto *m*, mata *f*
bushel *n* : medida *f* de áridos
igual a 35.24 litros
bushy *adj* **bushier; -est** : poblado, espeso
busily *adv* : afanosamente
business *n* **1** COMMERCE :
negocios *mpl*, comercio *m* **2** COMPANY
: empresa *f*, negocio *m* **3 it's none
of your business** : no es asunto
tuyo — **businessman** *n, pl* -**men** :
empresario *m*, hombre *m* de negocios

— **businesswoman** *n, pl* -**women** :
empresaria *f*, mujer *f* de negocios
bust[1] *vt* BREAK : romper
bust[2] *n* **1** : busto *m* (en la escultura)
2 BREASTS : pecho *m*, senos *mpl*
bustle *vi* -**tled; -tling** *or* **bustle about**
: ir y venir, ajetrearse — **bustle** *n or*
hustle and bustle : bullicio *m*, ajetreo *m*
busy *adj* **busier; -est 1** : ocupado
2 BUSTLING : concurrido
but *conj* **1** : pero **2 not one but two** : no
uno sino dos — **but** *prep* : excepto, menos
butcher *n* : carnicero *m*, -ra *f*
— **butcher** *vt* **1** : matar **2** BOTCH
: hacer una carnicería de
butler *n* : mayordomo *m*
butt *vt* : embestir (con los cuernos),
darle un cabezazo a — *vi* **butt in** :
interrumpir — **butt** *n* **1** BUTTING :
embestida *f* (de cuernos) **2** TARGET :
blanco *m* **3** : extremo *m*, culata *f* (de
un rifle), colilla *f* (de un cigarrillo)
butter *n* : mantequilla *f* — **butter** *vt*
: untar con mantequilla
buttercup *n* : ranúnculo *m*
▸ **butterfly** *n, pl* -**flies** : mariposa *f*
buttocks *npl* : nalgas *fpl*

button *n* : botón *m* — **button** *vt* :
abotonar — *vi or* **button up** : abotonarse
— **buttonhole** *n* : ojal *m* — **button** *vt*
-**holed; -holing** : acorralar
buy *vt* **bought; buying** : comprar
— **buy** *n* : compra *f* — **buyer** *n*
: comprador *m*, -dora *f*
buzz *vi* : zumbar — **buzz** *n* : zumbido *m*
buzzard *n* : buitre *m*
buzzer *n* : timbre *m*
by *prep* **1** NEAR : cerca de **2** VIA : por **3**
PAST : por, por delante de **4** DURING : de,
durante **5** (*in expressions of time*) : para
6 (*indicating cause or agent*) : por, de, a
— **by** *adv* **1 by and by** : poco después
2 by and large : en general **3 go by**
: pasar **4 stop by** : pasar por casa
bygone *adj* : pasado — **bygone** *n*
let bygones be bygones : lo
pasado, pasado está
bypass *n* : carretera *f* de
circunvalación — **bypass** *vt* : evitar
by–product *n* : subproducto *m*
bystander *n* : espectador *m*, -dora *f*
byte *n* : byte *m*, octeto *m*
byword *n* **be a byword for**
: estar sinónimo de

butterfly
mariposa[F]

head
cabeza[F]

compound eye
ojo[M] *compuesto*

antenna
antena[F]

proboscis
probóscide[M]

thorax
tórax[M]

foreleg
pata[F] *delantera*

middle leg
pata[F] *media*

hind leg
pata[F] *trasera*

abdomen
abdomen[M]

forewing
ala[F] *delantera*

hind wing
ala[F] *trasera*

c *n, pl* **c's** *or* **cs** : c, tercera
letra del alfabeto inglés
cab *n* **1** : taxi *m* **2** : cabina *f*
(de un camión, etc.)
cabbage *n* : col *f*, repollo *m*
cabin *n* **1** : cabaña *f* **2** : cabina *f* (de un
avión, etc.), camarote *m* (de un barco)
cabinet *n* **1** CUPBOARD : armario *m* **2**
: gabinete *m* (del gobierno) **3** *or*
medicine cabinet : botiquín *m*
cable *n* : cable *m* — **cable**
television *n* : televisión *f* por cable
cackle *vi* **-led; -ling 1** CLUCK : cacarear
2 LAUGH : reírse a carcajadas
cactus *n, pl* **cacti** *or* **-tuses** : cactus *m*
cadence *n* : cadencia *f*, ritmo *m*
cadet *n* : cadete *mf*
café *n* : café *m*, cafetería *f* — **cafeteria** *n*
: restaurante *m* autoservicio, cantina *f*

caffeine *n* : cafeína *f*
cage *n* : jaula *f* — **cage** *vt*
caged; caging : enjaular
cajole *vt* **-joled; -joling** : engatusar
▸ **cake** *n* **1** : pastel *m*, torta *f* **2** : pastilla *f*
(de jabón) **3 take the cake** : ser el colmo
— **caked** *adj* **caked with** : cubierto de
calamity *n, pl* **-ties** : calamidad *f*
calcium *n* : calcio *m*
calculate *v* **-lated; -lating** : calcular
— **calculating** *adj* : calculador
— **calculation** *n* : cálculo *m* —
calculator *n* : calculadora *f*
calendar *n* : calendario *m*
calf[1] *n, pl* **calves 1** : becerro *m*,
-rra *f*; ternero *m*, -ra *f* (de vacunos)
2 : cría *f* (de otros mamíferos)
calf[2] *n, pl* **calves** : pantorrilla *f*
(de la pierna)

caliber *or* **calibre** *n* : calibre *m*
call *vi* **1** : llamar **2** VISIT : pasar,
hacer (una) visita **3 call for** : requerir
— *vt* **1** : llamar **2 call off** : cancelar
— **call** *n* **1** : llamada *f* **2** SHOUT :
grito *m* **3** VISIT : visita *f* **4** DEMAND :
petición *f* — **calling** *n* : vocación *f*
callous *adj* : insensible, cruel
calm *n* : calma *f*, tranquilidad *f* —
calm *vt* : calmar — *vi or* **calm down**
: calmarse — **calm** *adj* : tranquilo, en
calma — **calmly** *adv* : con calma
calorie *n* : caloría *f*
came → **come**
camel *n* : camello *m*
▸ **camera** *n* : cámara *f*
camouflage *n* : camuflaje *m*
— **camouflage** *vt* **-flaged;**
-flaging : camuflar

cameras
cámara*F* fotográfica

ultracompact camera
cámara*F* ultracompacta

single-lens reflex (SLR) camera
cámara*F* reflex de un solo objetivo*M*

view camera
cámara*F* de fuelle*M*

canoe
canoa*F*

camp *n* **1** : campamento *m* **2**
FACTION : bando *m* — **camp** *vi*
: acampar, ir de camping
campaign *n* : campaña *f* —
campaign *vi* : hacer (una) campaña
camping *n* : camping *m*
campus *n* : ciudad *f* universitaria
can[1] *v aux past* **could** *present s & pl* **can**
1 (*expressing possibility or permission*) :
poder **2** (*expressing knowledge or ability*) :
saber **3 that cannot be!** : ¡no puede ser!
can[2] *n* : lata *f* — **can** *vt*
canned; canning : enlatar
Canadian *adj* : canadiense
canal *n* : canal *m*
canary *n*, *pl* **-naries** : canario *m*
cancel *vt* **-celed** *or* **-celled;**
-celing *or* **-celling** : cancelar —
cancellation *n* : cancelación *f*
cancer *n* : cáncer *m* —
cancerous *adj* : canceroso
candelabra *n*, *pl* **-bra** *or*
-bras : candelabro *m*
candid *adj* : franco
candidate *n* : candidato *m*, -ta *f* —
candidacy *n*, *pl* **-cies** : candidatura *f*
candle *n* : vela *f* —
candlestick *n* : candelero *m*
candor *or Brit* **candour** *n* : franqueza *f*
candy *n*, *pl* **-dies** : dulce *m*, caramelo *m*
cane *n* **1** : bastón *m* (para andar),
vara *f* (para castigar) **2** REED : caña *f*,
mimbre *m* — **cane** *vt* **caned; caning**
1 : tapizar con mimbre **2** FLOG : azotar
canine *n or* **canine tooth** : colmillo *m*,
diente *m* canino — **canine** *adj* : canino

canister *n* : lata *f*, bote *m Spain*
cannibal *n* : caníbal *mf*
cannon *n*, *pl* **-nons** *or* **-non** : cañón *m*
cannot (can not) → can 1
canny *adj* **cannier; -est** : astuto
▸ canoe *n* : canoa *f*, piragua *f* —
canoe *vt* **-noed; -noeing** : ir en canoa
canon *n* : canon *m* — **canonize** *vt*
-ized; -izing : canonizar
can opener *n* : abrelatas *m*
canopy *n*, *pl* **-pies** : dosel *m*
can't (*contraction of* **can not**) → can 1
cantaloupe *n* : melón *m*, cantalupo *m*
cantankerous *adj* : irritable, irascible
canteen *n* **1** FLASK : cantimplora *f* **2**
CAFETERIA : cantina *f*
canter *vi* : ir a medio galope —
canter *n* : medio galope *m*
canvas *n* **1** : lona *f* (tela) **2**
: lienzo *m* (de pintar)
canvass *vt* **1** : solicitar votos de,
hacer campaña entre **2** POLL : sondear
— **canvass** *n* **1** : solicitación *f*
(de votos) **2** POLL : sondeo *m*
canyon *n* : cañón *m*
cap *n* **1** : gorra *f*, gorro *m* **2** TOP :
tapa *f*, tapón *m* (de botellas) **3** LIMIT :
tope *m* — **cap** *vt* **capped; capping 1**
COVER : tapar, cubrir **2** OUTDO : superar
capable *adj* : capaz, competente —
capability *n*, *pl* **-ties** : capacidad *f*
capacity *n*, *pl* **-ties 1** :
capacidad *f* **2** ROLE : calidad *f*
cape[1] *n* : cabo *m* (en geografía)
cape[2] *n* CLOAK : capa *f*
caper[1] *n* : alcaparra *f*

caper[2] *n* PRANK : broma *f*, travesura *f*
capital *adj* **1** : capital **2** : mayúsculo
(dícese de las letras) — **capital** *n* **1**
or **capital city** : capital *f* **2** WEALTH :
capital *m* **3** *or* **capital letter** : mayúscula *f*
— **capitalism** *n* : capitalismo *m* —
capitalist *or* capitalistic *adj* : capitalista
— **capitalize** *vt* **-ized; -izing 1** FINANCE
: capitalizar **2** : escribir con mayúscula
— *vi* **capitalize on** : sacar partido de
capitol *n* : capitolio *m*
capitulate *vi* **-lated; -lating** : capitular
capsize *v* **-sized; -sizing** *vt* : hacer
volcar — *vi* : zozobrar, volcar(se)
capsule *n* : cápsula *f*
captain *n* : capitán *m*, -tana *f*
caption *n* **1** : leyenda *f* (al pie de una
ilustración) **2** SUBTITLE : subtítulo *m*
captivate *vt* **-vated; -vating**
: cautivar, encantar
captive *adj* : cautivo —
captive *n* : cautivo *m*, -va *f* —
captivity *n* : cautiverio *m*
capture *n* : captura *f*, apresamiento *m*
— **capture** *vt* **-tured; -turing 1** SEIZE
: capturar, apresar **2 capture one's**
interest : captar el interés de uno
car *n* **1** : automóvil *m*, coche *m*, carro *m*,
Lat **2** *or* **railroad car** : vagón *m*
carafe *n* : garrafa *f*
caramel *n* : caramelo *m*,
azúcar *f* quemada
carat *n* : quilate *m*
caravan *n* : caravana *f*
carbohydrate *n* : carbohidrato *m*,
hidrato *m* de carbono

birthday cake
torta*F* de cumpleaños*M*

carbon *n* : carbono *m* — **carbon copy** *n* : copia *f*, duplicado *m*

carburetor *n* : carburador *m*

carcass *n* : cuerpo *m* (de un animal muerto)

card *n* **1** : tarjeta *f* **2** *or* **playing card** : carta *f*, naipe *m* — **cardboard** *n* : cartón *m*

cardiac *adj* : cardíaco

cardigan *n* : cárdigan *m*

cardinal *n* : cardenal *m* — **cardinal** *adj* : cardinal, fundamental

care *n* **1** : cuidado *m* **2** WORRY : preocupación **3 take care of** : cuidar (de) — **care** *vi* **cared; caring 1** : preocuparse, inquietarse **2 care for** TEND : cuidar (de), atender **3 care for** LIKE : querer **4 I don't care** : no me importa

career *n* : carrera *f* — **career** *vi* : ir a toda velocidad

carefree *adj* : despreocupado

careful *adj* : cuidadoso — **carefully** *adv* : con cuidado, cuidadosamente — **careless** *adj* : descuidado — **carelessness** *n* : descuido *m*

caress *n* : caricia *f* — **caress** *vt* : acariciar

cargo *n*, *pl* **-goes** *or* **-gos** : cargamento *m*, carga *f*

caricature *n* : caricatura *f* — **caricature** *vt* **-tured; -turing** : caricaturizar

caring *adj* : solícito, afectuoso

carnage *n* : matanza *f*, carnicería *f*

carnal *adj* : carnal

carnation *n* : clavel *m*

carnival *n* : carnaval *m*

carol *n* : villancico *m*

carp *vi* **carp at** : quejarse de

carpenter *n* : carpintero *m*, -ra *f* — **carpentry** *n* : carpintería *f*

carpet *n* : alfombra *f*

carriage *n* **1** : transporte *m* (de mercancías) **2** BEARING : porte *m* **3** *or* **baby carriage** : cochecito *m* **4** *or* **horse-drawn carriage** : carruaje *m*, coche *m*

carrier *n* **1** : transportista *mf*, empresa *f* de transportes **2** : portador *m*, -dora *f* (de una enfermedad)

carrot *n* : zanahoria *f*

carry *v* **-ried; -rying** *vt* **1** : llevar **2** TRANSPORT : transportar **3** STOCK : vender **4** ENTAIL : acarrear, implicar **5 carry oneself** : portarse — *vi* : oírse (dícese de sonidos) — **carry away** *vt* **get carried away** : exaltarse, entusiasmarse — **carry on** *vt* CONDUCT : realizar — *vi* **1** : portarse inapropiadamente **2** CONTINUE : seguir,

cats
gatos *M*

ear *oreja* *F*

eye *ojo* *M*

whiskers *bigotes* *M*

fur *pelaje* *M*

tail *cola* *F*

continuar — **carry out** *vt* **1** PERFORM : llevar a cabo, realizar **2** FULFILL : cumplir

cart *n* : carreta *f*, carro *m* — **cart** *vt* *or* **cart around** : acarrear

cartilage *n* : cartílago *m*

carton *n* : caja *f* (de cartón)

cartoon *n* **1** : caricatura *f* **2** COMIC STRIP : historieta *f* **3** *or* **animated cartoon** : dibujos *mpl* animados

cartridge *n* : cartucho *m*

carve *vt* **carved; carving 1** : tallar, esculpir **2** : trinchar (carne)

case *n* **1** : caso *m* **2** BOX : caja *f* **3 in any case** : en todo caso **4 in case of** : en caso de **5 just in case** : por si acaso

cash *n* : efectivo *m*, dinero *m* en efectivo — **cash** *vt* : convertir en efectivo, cobrar

cashew *n* : anacardo *m*

cashier *n* : cajero *m*, -ra *f*

cashmere *n* : cachemira *f*

cash register *n* : caja *f* registradora

casino *n*, *pl* **-nos** : casino *m*

cask *n* : barril *m*

casket *n* : ataúd *m*

casserole *n* **1** *or* **casserole dish** : cazuela *f* **2** : guiso *m* (comida)

cassette *n* : cassette *mf*

cast *vt* **cast; casting 1** THROW : arrojar, lanzar **2** : depositar (un voto) **3** : repartir (papeles dramáticos) **4** MOLD : fundir — **cast** *n* **1** : elenco *m*, reparto *m* (de actores) **2** *or* **plaster cast** : molde *m* de yeso, escayola *f*

castanets *npl* : castañuelas *fpl*

castaway *n* : náufrago *m*, -ga *f*

cast iron *n* : hierro *m* fundido

castle *n* **1** : castillo *m* **2** : torre *f* (en ajedrez)

castrate *vt* **-trated; -trating** : castrar

casual *adj* **1** CHANCE : casual, fortuito **2** INDIFFERENT : despreocupado **3** INFORMAL : informal — **casually** *adv* **1** : de manera despreocupada **2** INFORMALLY : informalmente

casualty *n*, *pl* **-ties 1** : accidente *m* **2** VICTIM : víctima *f*; herido *m*, -da *f* **3**

American shorthair
*American*ᴹ *shorthair*

Persian
*persa*ᴹ

Maine coon
*Maine Coon*ᴹ

Siamese
*siamés*ᴹ

Abyssinian
*abisinio*ᴹ

casualties *npl* : bajas *fpl* (militares)

▶ **cat** *n* : gato *m*, -ta *f*

catalog *or* **catalogue** *n* : catálogo *m*
— **catalog** *vt* -**loged** *or* -**logued**;
-**loging** *or* -**loguing** : catalogar

catapult *n* : catapulta *f*

cataract *n* : catarata *f*

catastrophe *n* : catástrofe *f* —
catastrophic *adj* : catastrófico

catch *v* **caught**; **catching** *vt* **1** CAPTURE,
TRAP : capturar, atrapar **2** SURPRISE :
sorprender **3** GRASP : agarrar, captar **4**
SNAG : enganchar **5** : tomar (un tren, etc.)
6 catch a cold : resfriarse — *vi* **1** SNAG :
engancharse **2 catch fire** : prender fuego
— **catching** *adj* : contagioso — **catchy** *adj*
catchier; -**est** : pegadizo, pegajoso *Lat*

category *n*, *pl* -**ries** : categoría *f*
— **categorical** *adj* : categórico

cater *vi* **1** : proveer comida **2**
cater to : atender a — **caterer** *n* :
proveedor *m*, -dora *f* de comida

caterpillar *n* : oruga *f*

catfish *n* : bagre *m*

cathedral *n* : catedral *f*

catholic *adj* **1** : universal **2** Catholic :
católico — **catholicism** *n* : catolicismo *m*

cattle *npl* : ganado *m* (vacuno)

caught → **catch**

cauldron *n* : caldera *f*

cauliflower *n* : coliflor *f*

cause *n* **1** : causa *f* **2** REASON : motivo *m*
— **cause** *vt* **caused**; **causing** : causar

caustic *adj* : cáustico

caution *n* **1** WARNING : advertencia *f* **2**
CARE : precaución *f*, cautela *f* —
caution *vt* : advertir — **cautious** *adj*
: cauteloso, precavido —
cautiously *adv* : con precaución

cavalier *adj* : arrogante, desdeñoso

cavalry *n*, *pl* -**ries** : caballería *f*

cave *n* : cueva *f* — **cave** *vi* **caved**;
caving *or* **cave in** : hundirse

cavern *n* : caverna *f*

cavity *n*, *pl* -**ties 1** : cavidad *f* **2**
: caries *f* (dental)

cavort *vi* : brincar

CD *n* : CD *m*, disco *m* compacto

cease *v* **ceased**; **ceasing** *vt* : dejar de
— *vi* : cesar — **cease–fire** *n* : alto *m*
el fuego — **ceaseless** *adj* : incesante

cedar *n* : cedro *m*

ceiling *n* : techo *m*

celebrate *v* -**brated**; -**brating** *vt*
: celebrar — *vi* : divertirse —
celebrated *adj* : célebre —
celebration *n* **1** : celebración *f* **2**
FESTIVITY : fiesta *f* — **celebrity** *n*,
pl -**ties** : celebridad *f*

celery *n*, *pl* -**eries** : apio *m*

cell *n* **1** : célula *f* **2** : celda *f*
(en una cárcel, etc.)

cellar *n* **1** BASEMENT : sótano *m* **2**
: bodega *f* (de vinos)

cello *n*, *pl* -**los** : violoncelo *m*

cellular *adj* : celular

cement *n* : cemento *m* —
cement *vt* : cementar

cemetery *n*, *pl* -**teries** : cementerio *m*

censor *vt* : censurar — **censorship** *n* : censura *f* — **censure** *n* : censura *f* — **censor** *vt* **-sured; -suring** : censurar, criticar

census *n* : censo *m*

cent *n* : centavo *m*

centennial *n* : centenario *m*

center *or Brit* **centre** *n* : centro *m* — **center** *v* **centered** *or Brit* **centred; centering** *or Brit* **centring** *vt* : centrar — *vi* **center on** : centrarse en

centigrade *adj* : centígrado

centimeter *n* : centímetro *m*

centipede *n* : ciempiés *m*

central *adj* **1** : central **2 a central location** : un lugar céntrico — **centralize** *vt* **-ized; -izing** : centralizar

centre → **center**

century *n, pl* **-ries** : siglo *m*

ceramics *npl* : cerámica *f*

cereal *n* : cereal *m*

ceremony *n, pl* **-nies** : ceremonia *f*

— **ceremonial** *adj* : ceremonial

certain *adj* **1** : cierto **2 be certain of** : estar seguro de **3 for certain** : seguro, con toda seguridad **4 make certain of** : asegurarse de — **certainly** *adv* : desde luego, por supuesto — **certainty** *n, pl* **-ties** : certeza *f*, seguridad *f*

certify *vt* **-fied; -fying** : certificar — **certificate** *n* : certificado *m*, partida *f*, acta *f*

chafe *v* **chafed; chafing** *vi* : rozarse — *vt* : rozar

chain *n* **1** : cadena *f* **2 chain of events** : serie *f* de acontecimientos — **chain** *vt* : encadenar

chair *n* **1** : silla *f* **2** : cátedra *f* (en una universidad) — **chair** *vt* : presidir — **chairman** *n, pl* **-men** : presidente *m* — **chairperson** *n* : presidente *m*, -ta *f*

chalk *n* : tiza *f*, gis *m, Lat*

challenge *vt* **-lenged; -lenging 1** DISPUTE : disputar, poner en duda **2**

DARE : desafiar — **challenge** *n* : reto *m*, desafío *m* — **challenging** *adj* : estimulante

chamber *n* : cámara *f* — **chambermaid** *n* : camarera *f*

champagne *n* : champaña *m*, champán *m*

champion *n* : campeón *m*, -peona *f* — **champion** *vt* : defender — **championship** *n* : campeonato *m*

chance *n* **1** LUCK : azar *m*, suerte *f* **2** OPPORTUNITY : oportunidad *f* **3** LIKELIHOOD : probabilidad *f* **4 by chance** : por casualidad **5 take a chance** : arriesgarse — **chance** *vt* **chanced; chancing** RISK : arriesgar — **chance** *adj* : fortuito

chandelier *n* : araña *f* (de luces)

change *v* **changed; changing** *vt* **1** : cambiar **2** SWITCH : cambiar de — *vi* **1** : cambiar **2** *or* **change clothes** : cambiarse (de ropa) — **change** *n* : cambio *m* — **changeable** *adj* : cambiable

channel *n* **1** : canal *m* **2** : cauce *m* (de un río) **3** MEANS : vía *f*, medio *m*

chant *v* : cantar — **chant** *n* : canto *m*

chaos *n* : caos *m* — **chaotic** *adj* : caótico

chap[1] *vi* **chapped; chapping** : agrietarse

chap[2] *n* : tipo *m fam*

chapel *n* : capilla *f*

chaperon *or* chaperone *n* : acompañante *mf*

chaplain *n* : capellán *m*

chapter *n* : capítulo *m*

char *vt* **charred; charring** : carbonizar

character *n* **1** : carácter *m* **2** : personaje *m* (en una novela, etc.) — **characteristic** *adj* : característico — **character** *n* : característica *f* — **characterize** *vt* **-ized; -izing** : caracterizar

charcoal *n* : carbón *m*

charge *n* **1** : carga *f* (eléctrica) **2** COST : precio *m* **3** BURDEN : carga *f*, peso *m* **4** ACCUSATION : cargo *m*, acusación *f* **5 in charge of** : encargado de **6 take charge of** : hacerse cargo de — **charge** *v* **charged; charging** *vt* **1** : cargar **2** ENTRUST : encargar **3** COMMAND : ordenar, mandar **4** ACCUSE : acusar — *vi* **1** : cargar **2 charge too much** : cobrar demasiado

charisma *n* : carisma *m* — **charismatic** *adj* : carismático

charity *n, pl* **-ties 1** : organización *f* benéfica **2** GOODWILL : caridad *f*

charlatan *n* : charlatán *m*, -tana *f*

charm *n* **1** : encanto *m* **2** SPELL : hechizo *m* — **charm** *vt* : encantar,

chess
ajedrez[M]

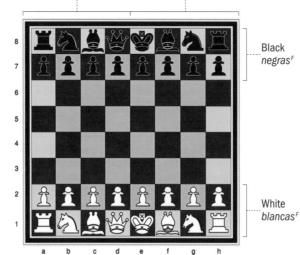

chessboard
tablero[M] *de ajedrez*[M]

queen's side
lado[M] *de la reina*[F]

king's side
lado[M] *del rey*[M]

Black
negras[F]

White
blancas[F]

pawn
peón[M]

rook
torre[F]

knight
caballo[M]

bishop
alfil[M]

king
rey[M]

queen
reina[F]

chocolate
chocolate^M

dark chocolate
chocolate^M *amargo*

cocoa
cacao^M

milk chocolate
chocolate^M *con leche*^F

white chocolate
chocolate^M *blanco*

cautivar — **charming** *adj* : encantador
chart *n* **1** MAP : carta *f* **2**
DIAGRAM : **gráfico** *m*, tabla *f* —
chart *vt* : trazar un mapa de
charter *n* : carta *f* —
charter *vt* : alquilar, fletar
chase *n* : persecución *f* — **chase** *vt*
chased; chasing 1 PURSUE : perseguir
2 or **chase away** : ahuyentar
chasm *n* : abismo *m*
chaste *adj* **chaster; -est** : casto
— **chastity** *n* : castidad *f*
chat *vi* **chatted; chatting** : charlar
— **chat** *n* : charla *f* — **chatter** *vi* **1** :
parlotear *fam* **2** : castañetear (dícese de
los dientes) — **chatter** *n* : parloteo *m*,
cháchara *f* — **chatterbox** *n* : parlanchín *m*,
-china *f* — **chatty** *adj* **chattier; chattiest**
1 : parlanchín **2** INFORMAL : familiar
chauffeur *n* : chofer *mf*
chauvinist *or* chauvinistic *adj*
: chauvinista, patriotero
cheap *adj* **1** INEXPENSIVE : barato **2**
SHODDY : de baja calidad — **cheap** *adv*
: barato — **cheapen** *vt* : rebajar —
cheaply *adv* : barato, a precio bajo
cheat *vt* : defraudar, estafar — *vi* **1**
: hacer trampa(s) **2 cheat on**
someone : engañar a algn — **cheat**
or **cheater** *n* : tramposo *m*, -sa *f*
check *n* **1** RESTRAINT : freno *m* **2**
INSPECTION : inspección *f*,
comprobación *f* **3** DRAFT : cheque *m* **4**
BILL : **cuenta** *f* **5** : jaque *m* (en ajedrez) **6**
: tela *f* a cuadros — **check** *vt* **1** RESTRAIN
: frenar, contener **2** INSPECT : revisar
3 VERIFY : comprobar **4** : dar jaque (en
ajedrez) **5 check in** : enregistrarse (en un
hotel) **6 check out** : irse (de un hotel) **7**
check out VERIFY : verificar, comprobar
checkers *n* : damas *fpl*

checkmate *n* : jaque *m* mate
checkpoint *n* : puesto *m* de control
checkup *n* : chequeo *m*,
examen *m* médico
cheek *n* : mejilla *f*
cheer *n* **1** CHEERFULNESS : alegría *f* **2**
APPLAUSE : aclamación *f* **3 cheers!**
: ¡salud! — **cheer** *vt* **1** GLADDEN :
alegrar **2** APPLAUD, SHOUT : aclamar,
aplaudir — **cheerful** *adj* : alegre
cheese *n* : queso *m*
cheetah *n* : guepardo *m*
chef *n* : chef *m*
chemical *adj* : químico —
chemical *n* : sustancia *f* química
— **chemist** *n* : químico *m*, -ca *f* —
chemistry *n*, *pl* **-tries** : química *f*
cheque *Brit* → **check**
cherish *vt* **1** : querer, apreciar **2** HARBOR :
abrigar (un recuerdo, una esperanza, etc.)
cherry *n*, *pl* **-ries** : cereza *f*
▸ **chess** *n* : ajedrez *m*
chest *n* **1** BOX : cofre *m* **2** : pecho *m* (del
cuerpo) **3** or **chest of drawers** : cómoda *f*
chestnut *n* : castaña *f*
chew *vt* : masticar, mascar —
chewing gum *n* : chicle *m*
chic *adj* : elegante
chick *n* : polluelo *m*, -la *f* — **chicken** *n*
: pollo *m* — **chicken pox** *n* : varicela *f*
chicory *n*, *pl* **-ries 1** : endivia *f* (para
ensaladas) **2** : achicoria *f* (aditivo de café)
chief *adj* : principal — **chief** *n* : jefe *m*,
-fa *f* — **chiefly** *adv* : principalmente
child *n*, *pl* **children 1** : niño *m*, -ña *f* **2**
OFFSPRING : hijo *m*, -ja *f* — **childbirth** *n*
: parto *m* — **childhood** *n* : infancia *f*,
niñez *f* — **childish** *adj* : infantil —
childlike *adj* : infantil, inocente —
childproof *adj* : a prueba de niños
Chilean *adj* : chileno

chili *or* **chile** *or* **chilli** *n*, *pl* **chilies** *or*
chiles *or* **chillies 1** *or* **chili pepper**
: chile *m* **2** : chile *m* con carne
chill *n* **1** CHILLINESS : frío *m* **2 catch**
a chill : resfriarse **3 there's a chill**
in the air : hace fresco — **chill** *adj*
: frío — **chill** *v* : enfriar — **chilly** *adj*
chillier; -est : fresco, frío
chime *vi* **chimed; chiming** : repicar,
sonar — **chime** *n* : carillón *m*
chimney *n*, *pl* **-neys** : chimenea *f*
chimpanzee *n* : chimpancé *m*
chin *n* : barbilla *f*
china *n* : porcelana *f*, loza *f*
Chinese *adj* : chino —
Chinese *n* : chino *m* (idioma)
chink *n* : grieta *f*
chip *n* **1** : astilla *f* (de madera o vidrio),
lasca *f* (de piedra) **2** : ficha *f* (de póker,
etc.) **3** NICK : desportilladura *f* **4**
or **computer chip** : chip *m* **5** →
potato chips — **chip** *v* **chipped;**
chipping *vt* : desportillar — *vi* **1** :
desportillarse **2 chip in** : contribuir
chipmunk *n* : ardilla *f* listada
chiropodist *n* : podólogo *m*, -ga *f*
chiropractor *n* : quiropráctico *m*, -ca *f*
chirp *vi* : piar, gorjear
chisel *n* : cincel *m* (para piedras,
etc.), formón *m*, escoplo *m* (para
madera) — **chisel** *vt* **-eled** *or* **-elled;**
-eling *or* **-elling** : cincelar, tallar
chit *n* : nota *f*
chitchat *n* : cháchara *f* *fam*
chivalrous *adj* : caballeroso —
chivalry *n*, *pl* **-ries** : caballerosidad *f*
chive *n* : cebollino *m*
chlorine *n* : cloro *m*
chock–full *adj* : repleto, atestado
▸ **chocolate** *n* : chocolate *m*
choice *n* **1** : elección *f*, selección *f* **2**

PREFERENCE : preferencia *f* —
choice *adj* **choicer; -est** : selecto
choir *n* : coro *m*
choke *v* **choked; choking** *vt* **1** : asfixiar,
estrangular **2** BLOCK : atascar — *vi* :
asfixiarse, atragantarse (con comida)
— **choke** *n* : estárter *m* (de un motor)
choose *v* **chose; chosen; choosing** *vt* **1**
SELECT : escoger, elegir **2** DECIDE :
decidir — *vi* : escoger — **choosy** *or*
choosey *adj* **choosier; -est** : exigente
chop *vt* **chopped; chopping 1** : cortar,
picar (carne, etc.) **2 chop down** : talar
— **chop** *n* : chuleta *f* (de cerdo, etc.) —
choppy *adj* **-pier; -est** : picado, agitado

chopsticks *npl* : palillos *mpl*
chord *n* : acorde *m* (en música)
chore *n* **1** : tarea *f* **2 household**
chores : faenas *fpl* domésticas
choreography *n, pl* **-phies**
: coreografía *f*
chortle *vi* **-tled; -tling** : reírse
(con satisfacción o júbilo)
chorus 1 : coro *m* (grupo de
personas) **2** REFRAIN : estribillo *m*
chose, chosen → **choose**
christen *vt* : bautizar —
christening *n* : bautizo *m*
Christian *n* : cristiano *m*, -na *f*
— **Christian** *adj* : cristiano

— **Christianity** *n* : cristianismo *m*
Christmas *n* : Navidad *f*
chrome *n* : cromo *m*
chronic *adj* : crónico
chronicle *n* : crónica *f*
chronology *n, pl* **-gies** : cronología *f*
— **chronological** *adj* : cronológico
chrysanthemum *n* : crisantemo *m*
chubby *adj* **-bier; -est** : regordete
fam, rechoncho *fam*
chuck *vt* : tirar, arrojar
chuckle *vi* **-led; -ling** : reírse (entre
dientes) — **chuckle** *n* : risa *f* ahogada
chum *n* : amigo *m*, -ga *f*;
compinche *mf fam* — **chummy** *adj*

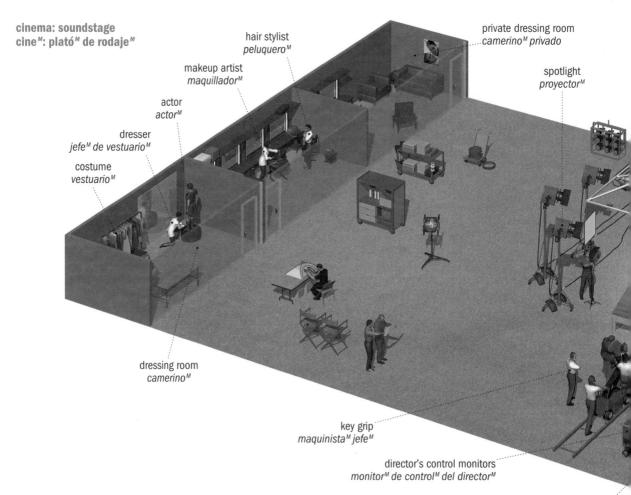

cinema: soundstage
cineᴹ**: plató**ᴹ **de rodaje**ᴹ

hair stylist
*peluquero*ᴹ

makeup artist
*maquillador*ᴹ

actor
*actor*ᴹ

dresser
*jefe*ᴹ *de vestuario*ᴹ

costume
*vestuario*ᴹ

private dressing room
*camerino*ᴹ *privado*

spotlight
*proyector*ᴹ

dressing room
*camerino*ᴹ

key grip
*maquinista*ᴹ *jefe*ᴹ

director's control monitors
*monitor*ᴹ *de control*ᴹ *del director*ᴹ

director
*director*ᴹ

-mier; -est : muy amigable
chunk *n* **:** trozo *m,* pedazo *m*
church *n* **:** iglesia *f*
churn *n* **:** mantequera *f* —
  churn *vt* **1 :** agitar **2 churn out :**
  producir en grandes cantidades
chute *n* **1 :** vertedor *m* **2**
  SLIDE **:** tobogán *m*
cider *n* **:** sidra *f*
cigar *n* **:** puro *m* — **cigarette** *n*
  : cigarrillo *m,* cigarro *m*
cinch *n* **it's a cinch :** es pan comido
▸ **cinema** *n* **:** cine *m*
cinnamon *n* **:** canela *f*
cipher *n* **1** ZERO **:** cero *m* **2** CODE **:** cifra *f*

circa *prep* **:** hacia
circle *n* **:** círculo *m* — **circle** *v* **-cled;**
  -cling *vt* **1 :** dar vueltas alrededor de
  2 : trazar un círculo alrededor de (un
  número, etc.) — *vi* **:** dar vueltas
circuit *n* **:** circuito *m* —
  circuitous *adj* **:** tortuoso
circular *adj* **:** circular —
  circular *n* LEAFLET **:** circular *f*
circulate *v* **-lated; -lating** *vt* **:**
  hacer circular — *vi* **:** circular —
  circulation *n* **1 :** circulación *f* **2**
  : tirada *f* (de una publicación)
circumcise *vt* **-cised; -cising**
  : circuncidar — **circumcision** *n*

  : circuncisión *f*
circumference *n* **:** circunferencia *f*
circumspect *adj* **:**
  circunspecto, prudente
circumstance *n* **1 :** circunstancia *f* **2**
  under no circumstances :
  bajo ningún concepto
circus *n* **:** circo *m*
cistern *n* **:** cisterna *f*
cite *vt* **cited; citing :** citar —
  citation *n* **:** citación *f*
citizen *n* **:** ciudadano *m,* -na *f* —
  citizenship *n* **:** ciudadanía *f*
citrus *n, pl* **-rus** *or* **-ruses** *or*
  citrus fruit : cítrico *m*

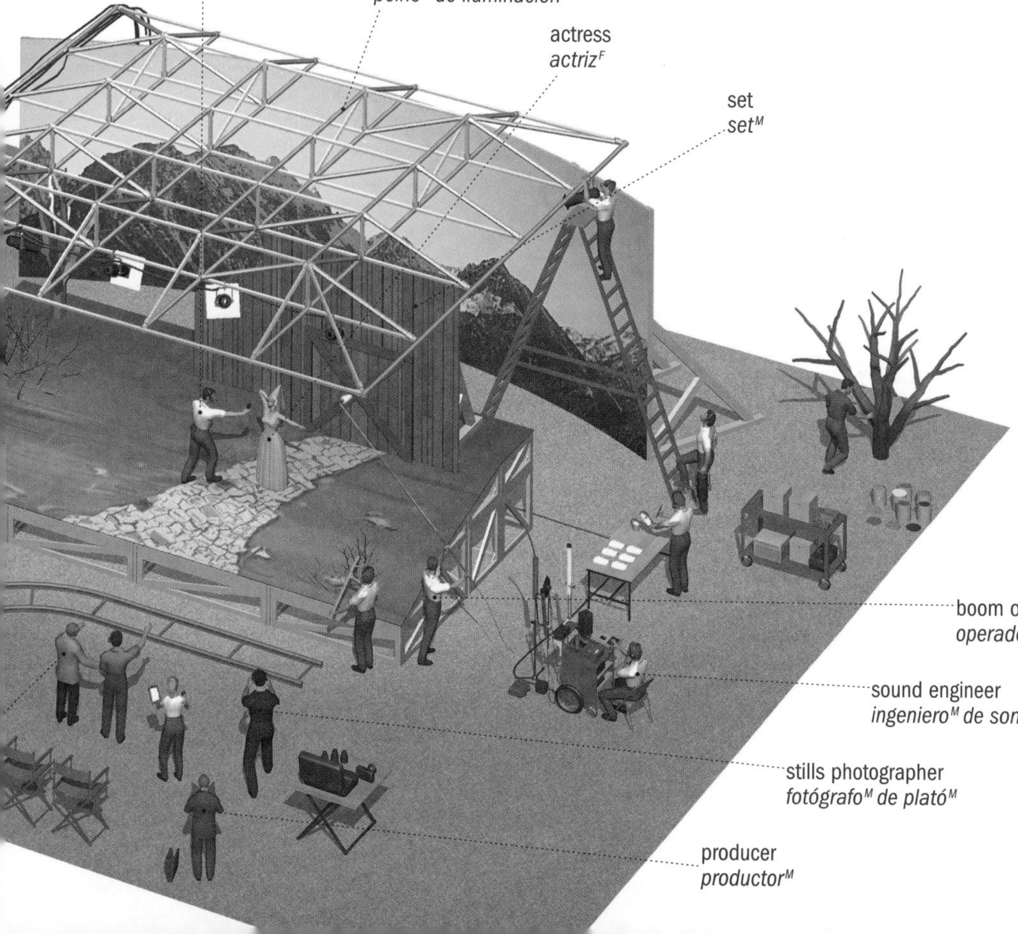

director of photography
*director*M *de fotografía*F

lighting grid
*peine*M *de iluminación*F

actress
*actriz*F

set
*set*M

boom operator
*operador*M *de jirafa*F

sound engineer
*ingeniero*M *de sonido*M

stills photographer
*fotógrafo*M *de plató*M

producer
*productor*M

clarinet
clarinete^M

city *n, pl* **cities** : ciudad *f*
civic *adj* : cívico — **civics** *ns*
 & pl : civismo *m*
civil *adj* : civil — **civilian** *n* : civil *mf*
 — **civility** *n, pl* **-ties** : cortesía *f*
 — **civilization** *n* : civilización *f* —
 civilize *vt* **-lized; -lizing** : civilizar
clad *adj* **clad in** : vestido de
claim *vt* **1** DEMAND : reclamar **2** MAINTAIN
 : afirmar, sostener **3 claim responsibility**
 : atribuirse la responsabilidad —
 claim *n* **1** DEMAND : demanda *f*,
 reclamación *f* **2** ASSERTION : afirmación *f*
clam *n* : almeja *f*
clamber *vi* : trepar (con torpeza)
clammy *adj* **-mier; -est** :
 húmedo y algo frío
clamor *n* : clamor *m* — **clamor** *vi* : clamar
clamp *n* : abrazadera *f* — **clamp** *vt*
 : sujetar con abrazaderas — *vi*
 clamp down on : reprimir
clan *n* : clan *m*
clandestine *adj* : clandestino
clang *n* : ruido *m* metálico
clap *v* **clapped; clapping** *vt* **1** : aplaudir
 2 clap one's hands : dar palmadas
 — *vi* : aplaudir — **clap** *n* : palmada *f*
clarify *vt* **-fied; -fying** : aclarar

— **clarification** *n* : clarificación *f*
▸ **clarinet** *n* : clarinete *m*
clarity *n* : claridad *f*
clash *vi* **1** : chocar, enfrentarse **2** CONFLICT
 : estar en conflicto — **clash** *n* **1** CRASH
 : choque *m* **2** CONFLICT : conflicto *m*
clasp *n* : broche *m*, cierre *m* —
 clasp *vt* **1** : abrazar (a una persona),
 agarrar (una cosa) **2** FASTEN : abrochar
class *n* : clase *f*
classic *or* **classical** *adj* : clásico
 — **classic** *n* : clásico *m*
classify *vt* **-fied; -fying** : clasificar
 — **classification** *n* : clasificación *f* —
 classified *adj* RESTRICTED : secreto
classmate *n* : compañero *m*,
 -ra *f* de clase
classroom *n* : aula *f*, salón *m* de clase
clatter *vi* : hacer ruido —
 clatter *n* : estrépito *m*
clause *n* : cláusula *f*
claustrophobia *n* : claustrofobia *f*
claw *n* : garra *f*, uña *f* (de un gato), pinza *f*
 (de un crustáceo) — **claw** *v* : arañar
clay *n* : arcilla *f*
clean *adj* **1** : limpio **2** UNADULTERATED
 : puro **3** SPOTLESS : impecable —
 clean *vt* : limpiar — **clean** *adv* :
 limpio — **cleaner** *n* **1** : limpiador *m*,
 -dora *f* **2** DRY CLEANER : tintorería *f* —
 cleanliness *n* : limpieza *f* — **cleanse** *vt*
 cleansed; cleansing : limpiar, purificar
clear *adj* **1** : claro **2** TRANSPARENT
 : transparente **3** UNOBSTRUCTED :
 despejado, libre — **clear** *vt* **1** : despejar
 (una superficie), desatascar (un tubo,
 etc.) **2** EXONERATE : absolver **3** : saltar
 por encima de (un obstáculo) **4 clear**
 the table : levantar la mesa **5 clear**
 up RESOLVE : aclarar, resolver — *vi* **1**
 clear up BRIGHTEN : despejarse (dícese
 del tiempo, etc.) **2 clear up** VANISH :
 desaparecer (dícese de una infección,
 etc.) — **clear** *adv* **1 make oneself clear**
 : explicarse **2 stand clear !** : ¡aléjate! —
 clearance *n* **1** SPACE : espacio *m* (libre) **2**
 AUTHORIZATION : autorización *f* **3 clearance**
 sale : liquidación *f* — **clearing** *n* :
 claro *m* — **clearly** *adv* **1** DISTINCTLY :
 claramente **2** OBVIOUSLY : obviamente
cleaver *n* : cuchillo *m* de carnicero
clef *n* : clave *f*
cleft *n* : hendidura *f*, grieta *f*
clement *adj* : clemente —
 clemency *n* : clemencia *f*

clench *vt* : apretar
clergy *n, pl* **-gies** : clero *m* —
 clergyman *n, pl* **-men** : clérigo *m*
 — **clerical** *adj* **1** : clerical **2 clergy**
 work : trabajo *m* de oficina
clerk *n* **1** : oficinista *mf*; empleado *m*,
 -da *f* de oficina **2** SALESPERSON
 : dependiente *m*, -ta *f*
clever *adj* **1** SKILLFUL : ingenioso, hábil **2**
 SMART : listo, inteligente — **cleverly** *adv* :
 ingeniosamente — **cleverness** *n* **1** SKILL
 : ingenio *m* **2** INTELLIGENCE : inteligencia *f*
cliché *n* : cliché *m*
click *vt* : chasquear — *vi* **1** :
 chasquear **2** GET ALONG : llevarse
 bien — **click** *n* : chasquido *m*
client *n* : cliente *m*, -ta *f* —
 clientele *n* : clientela *f*
cliff *n* : acantilado *m*
climate *n* : clima *m*
climax *n* : clímax *m*, punto *m* culminante
climb *vt* : escalar, subir a, trepar a
 — *vi* **1** RISE : subir **2** *or* **climb up** :
 subirse, treparse — **climb** *n* : subida *f*
clinch *vt* : cerrar (un acuerdo, etc.)
cling *vi* **clung; clinging** :
 adherirse, pegarse
clinic *n* : clínica *f* — **clinical** *adj* : clínico
clink *vi* : tintinear
clip *vt* **clipped; clipping 1** CUT : cortar,
 recortar **2** FASTEN : sujetar (con un clip)
 — **clip** *n* **1** FASTENER : clip *m* **2 at a good**
 clip : a buen trote **3** → **paper clip** —
 clippers *npl* **1** : maquinilla *f* para cortar
 el pelo **2** *or* **nail clippers** : cortauñas *m*
cloak *n* : capa *f*
clock 1 : reloj *m* (de pared) **2 around**
 the clock : las veinticuatro horas —
 clockwise *adv & adj* : en el sentido de
 las agujas del reloj — **clockwork** *n* **1**
 : mecanismo *m* de relojería **2 like**
 clockwork : con precisión
clog *n* : zueco *m* — **clog** *v* **clogged;**
 clogging *vt* : atascar, obstruir
 — *vi or* **clog up** : atascarse
cloister *n* : claustro *m*
close¹ *v* **closed; closing** *vt* : cerrar — *vi* **1**
 : cerrarse **2** TERMINATE : terminar **3 close**
 in : acercarse — **close** *n* : final *m*
close² *adj* **closer; closest 1** NEAR :
 cercano, próximo **2** INTIMATE : íntimo **3**
 STRICT : estricto **4** STUFFY : sofocante **5 a**
 close game : un juego reñido — **close** *adv*
 : cerca, de cerca — **closely** *adv* : cerca,
 de cerca — **closeness** *n* **1** NEARNESS

: cercanía *f* **2** INTIMACY : intimidad *f*
closet *n* : armario *m*, clóset *m*, *Lat*
closure *n* : cierre *m*
clot *n* : coágulo *m* — **clot** *v*
 clotted; clotting *vt* : coagular,
 cuajar — *vi* : coagularse
cloth *n*, *pl* **cloths 1** FABRIC :
 tela *f* **2** RAG : trapo *m*
clothe *vt* **clothed** *or* **clad; clothing** : vestir
 — **clothes** *npl* **1** : ropa *f* **2 put on one's**
 clothes : vestirse — **clothespin** *n* : pinza *f*
 (para la ropa) — **clothing** *n* : ropa *f*
cloud *n* : nube *f* — **cloud** *vt* : nublar
 — *vi or* **cloud over** : nublarse —
 cloudy *adj* **cloudier; -est** : nublado
clout *n* **1** BLOW : golpe *m*, tortazo *m*
 fam **2** INFLUENCE : influencia *f*
clove *n* **1** : clavo *m* **2** : diente *m* (de ajo)
clover *n* : trébol *m*
clown *n* : payaso *m*, -sa *f* — **clown**
 or **clown around** *vi* : payasear
cloying *adj* : empalagoso
club *n* **1** : garrote *m*, porra *f* **2**
 ASSOCIATION : club *m* **3 clubs** *mpl* :

tréboles *mpl* (en los naipes) — **club** *vt*
 clubbed; clubbing : aporrear
cluck *vi* : cloquear
clue *n* **1** : pista *f*, indicio *m* **2 I haven't**
 got a clue : no tengo la menor idea
clump *n* : grupo *m* (de arbustos)
clumsy *adj* **-sier; -est** : torpe
 — **clumsiness** *n* : torpeza *f*
cluster *n* : grupo *m*, racimo *m* (de
 uvas, etc.) — **cluster** *vi* : agruparse
clutch *vt* : agarrar, asir — *vi*
 clutch at : tratar de agarrarse
 de — **clutch** *n* : embrague *m*,
 clutch *m*, *Lat* (de un automóvil)
clutter *vt* : llenar desordenadamente
 — **clutter** *n* : desorden *m*, revoltijo *m*
coach *n* **1** CARRIAGE : carruaje *m*,
 carroza *f* **2** : vagón *m* de pasajeros
 (de un tren) **3** BUS : autobús *m* **4** :
 pasaje *m* aéreo de segunda clase
 5 TRAINER : entrenador *m*, -dora *f*
 — *vt* : entrenar (un atleta), dar
 clases particulares a (un alumno)
coagulate *v* **-lated; -lating** *vt* :

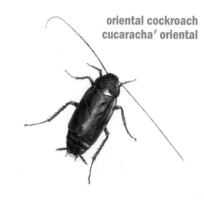

coagular — *vi* : coagularse
coal *n* : carbón *m*
coalition *n* : coalición *f*
coarse *adj* **coarser; -est 1** : tosco, basto
 2 CRUDE, VULGAR : grosero, ordinario —
 coarseness *n* : aspereza *f*, tosquedad *f*
coast *n* : costa *f* — **coast** *vi* : ir
 en punto muerto (dícese de un
 automóvil), deslizarse (dícese de una
 bicicleta) — **coastal** *adj* : costero
coaster *n* : posavasos *m*
coast guard *n* : guardacostas *mpl*
coastline *n* : litoral *m*
coat *n* **1** : abrigo *m* **2** : pelaje *m* (de un
 animal) **3** : mano *f* (de pintura) — **coat** *vt*
 : cubrir, revestir — **coating** *n* : capa *f* —
 coat of arms *n* : escudo *m* de armas
coax *vt* : engatusar
cob → **corncob**
cobblestone *n* : adoquín *m*
cobweb *n* : telaraña *f*
cocaine *n* : cocaína *f*
cock *n* **1** ROOSTER : gallo *m* **2** FAUCET
 : grifo *m* **3** : martillo *m* (de un arma
 de fuego) — **cock** *vt* **1** : amartillar (un
 arma de fuego) **2 cock one's head** :
 ladear la cabeza — **cockeyed** *adj* **1**
 ASKEW : ladeado **2** ABSURD : absurdo
cockpit *n* : cabina *f*
cockroach *n* : cucaracha *f*
cocktail *n* : coctel *m*, cóctel *m*
cocky *adj* **cockier; -est** :
 engreído, arrogante
cocoa *n* **1** : cacao *m* **2** :
 chocolate *m* (bebida)
coconut *n* : coco *m*
cocoon *n* : capullo *m*
cod *ns & pl* : bacalao *m*

colors
colores *M*

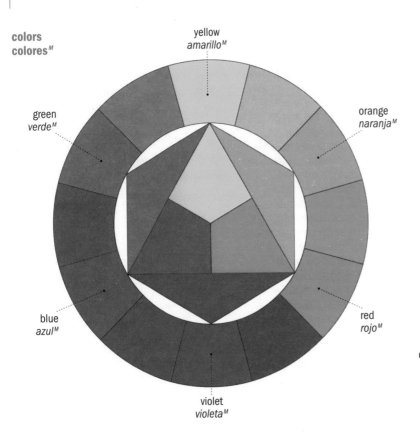

green
verde *M*

yellow
amarillo *M*

orange
naranja *M*

blue
azul *M*

red
rojo *M*

violet
violeta *M*

coddle *vt* **-dled; -dling** : mimar
code *n* : código *m*
coeducational *adj* : mixto
coerce *vt* **-erced; -ercing** : coaccionar,
  forzar — **coercion** *n* : coacción *f*
coffee *n* : café *m* —
  coffeepot *n* : cafetera *f*
coffer *n* : cofre *m*
coffin *n* : ataúd *m*, féretro *m*
cog *n* : diente *m* (de una rueda)
cogent *adj* : convincente, persuasivo
cognac *n* : coñac *m*
cogwheel *n* : rueda *f* dentada
coherent *adj* : coherente
coil *vt* : enrollar — *vi* : enrollarse —
  coil *n* **1** ROLL : rollo *m* **2** : tirabuzón *m*
  (de pelo), espiral *f* (de humo)
coin *n* : moneda *f* — **coin** *vt* : acuñar
coincide *vi* **-cided; -ciding** : coincidir —
  coincidence *n* : coincidencia *f*, casualidad *f*
  — **coincidental** *adj* : casual, fortuito
coke *n* : coque *m* (combustible)
colander *n* : colador *m*

cold *adj* **1** : frío **2 be cold** : tener frío
  3 it's cold today : hace frío hoy —
  cold *n* **1** : frío *m* **2** : resfriado *m* (en
  medicina) **3 catch a cold** : resfriarse
coleslaw *n* : ensalada *f* de col
colic *n* : cólico *m*
collaborate *vi* **-rated; -rating** : colaborar
  — **collaboration** *n* : colaboración *f* —
  collaborator *n* : colaborador *m*, -dora *f*
collapse *vi* **-lapsed; -lapsing** **1** :
  derrumbarse, hundirse **2** : sufrir un
  colapso (físico o mental) — **collapse** *n* **1**
  FALL : derrumbamiento *m* **2** BREAKDOWN :
  colapso *m* — **collapsible** *adj* : plegable
collar *n* : cuello *m* (de camisa,
  etc.) , collar *m* (para animales)
  — **collarbone** *n* : clavícula *f*
colleague *n* : colega *mf*
collect *vt* **1** GATHER : reunir **2** :
  coleccionar, juntar (timbres, etc.)
  3 : recaudar (fondos, etc.) — *vi* **1**
  ACCUMULATE : acumularse, juntarse **2**
  CONGREGATE : congregarse, reunirse

— **collect** *adv* **call collect** : llamar
  a cobro revertido, llamar por cobrar
  Lat — **collection** *n* **1** : colección *f* **2**
  : colecta *f* (de contribuciones)
  — **collective** *adj* : colectivo —
collector *n* **1** : coleccionista *mf* **2** :
  cobrador *m*, -dora *f* (de deudas)
college *n* **1** : instituto *m* (a nivel
  universitario) **2** : colegio *m* (electoral, etc.)
collide *vi* **-lided; -liding** :
  chocar, colisionar — **collision** *n*
  : choque *m*, colisión *f*
colloquial *adj* : coloquial, familiar
cologne *n* : colonia *f*
Colombian *adj* : colombiano
colon[1] *n, pl* **colons** *or* **cola** :
  colon *m* (en anatomía)
colon[2] *n, pl* **colons** : dos puntos *mpl*
  (signo de puntuación)
colonel *n* : coronel *m*
colony *n, pl* **-nies** : colonia *f* —
  colonial *adj* : colonial — **colonize** *vt*
  -nized; -nizing : colonizar
▸ **color** *or Brit* **colour** *n* : color *m* —
  color *vt* : colorear, pintar — *vi* BLUSH :
  sonrojarse — **color–blind** *or Brit* **colour-
  blind** *adj* : daltónico — **colored** *or Brit*
  coloured *adj* : de color — **colorful** *or
  Brit* **colourful** *adj* **1** : de vivos colores **2**
  PICTURESQUE : pintoresco — **colorless**
  or Brit **colourless** *adj* : incoloro
colossal *adj* : colosal
colt *n* : potro *m*
column *n* : columna *f* —
  columnist *n* : columnista *mf*
coma *n* : coma *m*
comb *n* **1** : peine *m* **2** : cresta *f*
  (de un gallo) — **comb** *vt* : peinar
combat *n* : combate *m* — **combat** *vt*
  -bated *or* **-batted; -bating** *or* **-batting** :
  combatir — **combatant** *n* : combatiente *mf*
combine *v* **-bined; -bining** *vt* :
  combinar — *vi* : combinarse —
  combine *n* HARVESTER : cosechadora *f*
  — **combination** *n* : combinación *f*
combustion *n* : combustión *f*
come *vi* **came; come; coming** **1** : venir
  2 ARRIVE : llegar **3 come about** : suceder
  4 come back : regresar, volver **5 come
  from** : venir de, provenir de **6 come in**
  : entrar **7 come out** : salir **8 come to**
  REVIVE : volver en sí **9 come on!** : ¡ándale!
  10 come up OCCUR : surgir **11 how
  come?** : ¿por qué? — **comeback** *n* **1**
  RETURN : retorno *m* **2** RETORT : réplica *f*

comedy *n, pl* **-dies** : comedia *f* —
comedian *n* : cómico *m*, -ca *f*
comet *n* : cometa *m*
comfort *vt* : consolar — **comfort** *n* **1**
: comodidad *f* **2** SOLACE : consuelo *m*
— **comfortable** *adj* : cómodo
comic *or* **comical** *adj* : cómico —
comic *n* **1** COMEDIAN : cómico *m*,
-ca *f* **2** *or* **comic book** : revista *f*
de historietas, cómic *m* — **comic**
strip *n* : tira *f* cómica, historieta *f*
coming *adj* : próximo, que viene
comma *n* : coma *f*
command *vt* **1** ORDER : ordenar, mandar
2 : estar al mando de (un barco, etc.) **3**
command respect : inspirar (el) respeto
— *vi* : dar órdenes — **command** *n* **1**
ORDER : orden *f* **2** LEADERSHIP : mando *m* **3**
MASTERY : maestría *f*, dominio *m* —
commander *n* : comandante *mf* —
commandment *n* : mandamiento *m*
commemorate *vt* **-rated; -rating** :
conmemorar — **commemoration** *n*
: conmemoración *f*
commence *v* **-menced;**
-mencing : comenzar, empezar
— **commencement** *n* **1** BEGINNING
: comienzo *m* **2** GRADUATION :
ceremonia *f* de graduación
commend *vt* **1** ENTRUST :
encomendar **2** PRAISE : alabar —
commendable *adj* : loable
comment *n* : comentario *m*,
observación *f* — **comment** *vi* : hacer
comentarios — **commentary** *n*,
pl **-taries** : comentario *m* —
commentator *n* : comentarista *mf*
commerce *n* : comercio *m*
— **commercial** *adj* : comercial
— **commerce** *n* : anuncio *m*,
aviso *m*, *Lat* — **commercialize** *vt*
-ized; -izing : comercializar
commiserate *vi* **-ated;**
-ating : compadecerse
commission *n* : comisión *f* —
commission *vt* : encargar (una
obra de arte) — **commissioner** *n*
: comisario *m*, -ria *f*
commit *vt* **-mitted; -mitting 1** ENTRUST
: confiar **2** : cometer (un crimen) **3** :
internar (a algn en un hospital) **4 commit**
oneself : comprometerse **5 commit**
to memory : aprender de memoria
— **commitment** *n* : compromiso *m*
committee *n* : comité *m*, comisión *f*

commodity *n, pl* **-ties** : artículo *m*
de comercio, producto *m*
common *adj* **1** : común **2** ORDINARY
: ordinario, común y corriente —
common *n* **in common** : en común
— **commonly** *adv* : comúnmente —
commonplace *adj* : común, banal —
common sense *n* : sentido *m* común
commotion *n* : alboroto *m*, jaleo *m*
commune[1] *n* : comuna *f* —
communal *adj* : comunal
commune[2] *vi* **-muned; -muning**
commune with : comunicarse con
communicate *v* **-cated; -cating** *vt*
: comunicar — *vi* : comunicarse —
communicable *adj* : transmisible —
communication *n* : comunicación *f* —
communicative *adj* : comunicativo
communion *n* : comunión *f*
Communism *n* : comunismo *m*
— **Communist** *adj* : comunista —
Communism *n* : comunista *mf*
community *n, pl* **-ties** : comunidad *f*

commute *v* **-muted; -muting** *vt* :
conmutar, reducir (una sentencia) — *vi*
: viajar de la residencia al trabajo
compact *adj* : compacto — **compact** *n* **1**
or **compact car** : auto *m* compacto
2 *or* **powder compact** : polvera *f* —
compact disc *n* : disco *m* compacto
companion *n* : compañero *m*, -ra *f* —
companionship *n* : compañerismo *m*
company *n, pl* **-nies 1** :
compañía *f* **2** GUESTS : visita *f*
compare *v* **-pared; -paring** *vt* : comparar
— *vi* **compare with** : poderse comparar
con — **comparable** *adj* : comparable —
comparative *adj* : comparativo, relativo
— **comparison** *n* : comparación *f*
compartment *n* : compartimento *m*
▶ **compass** *n* **1** : compás *m* **2 points of**
the compass : puntos *mpl* cardinales
compassion *n* : compasión *f* —
compassionate *adj* : compasivo
compatible *adj* : compatible, afín —
compatibility *n* : compatibilidad *f*

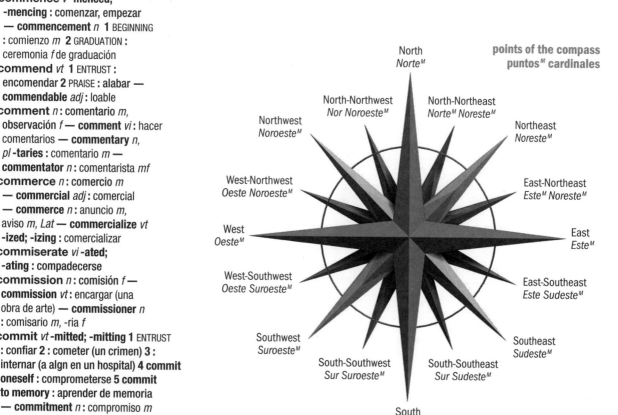

points of the compass
puntos[M] **cardinales**

North
Norte[M]

North-Northwest
Nor Noroeste[M]

North-Northeast
Norte[M] *Noreste*[M]

Northwest
Noroeste[M]

Northeast
Noreste[M]

West-Northwest
Oeste Noroeste[M]

East-Northeast
Este[M] *Noreste*[M]

West
Oeste[M]

East
Este[M]

West-Southwest
Oeste Suroeste[M]

East-Southeast
Este Sudeste[M]

Southwest
Suroeste[M]

Southeast
Sudeste[M]

South-Southwest
Sur Suroeste[M]

South-Southeast
Sur Sudeste[M]

South
Sur[M]

compel vt -pelled; -pelling : obligar
— compelling adj : convincente
compensate v -sated;
-sating vi compensate for :
compensar — vt : indemnizar,
compensar — compensation n :
compensación f, indemnización f
compete vi -peted; -peting : competir
— competent adj : competente —
competition n 1 : competencia f 2
CONTEST : concurso m — competitor n
: competidor m, -dora f
compile vt -piled; -piling
: compilar, recopilar
complacency n : satisfacción f
consigo mismo — complacent adj
: satisfecho de sí mismo
complain vi : quejarse — complaint n 1
: queja f 2 AILMENT : enfermedad f
complement n : complemento m
— complement vt : complementar —
complementary adj : complementario
complete adj -pleter; -est 1 WHOLE :
completo, entero 2 FINISHED : terminado
3 TOTAL : total — complete vt
-pleted; -pleting : completar —
completion n : conclusión f
complex adj : complejo —
complex n : complejo m
complexion n : cutis m, tez f
complexity n, pl -ties : complejidad f
compliance n 1 : acatamiento m 2
in compliance with : conforme
a — compliant adj : sumiso
complicate vt -cated; -cating
: complicar — complicated adj
: complicado — complication n
: complicación f
compliment n 1 : cumplido m 2
compliments npl : saludos mpl
— compliment vt : felicitar
— complimentary adj 1
FLATTERING : halagador, halagüeño
2 FREE : de cortesía, gratis
comply vi -plied; -plying comply
with : cumplir, obedecer
component n : componente m
compose vt -posed; -posing 1 :
componer 2 compose oneself : serenarse
— composer n : compositor m, -tora f —
composition n 1 : composición f 2 ESSAY
: ensayo m — composure n : calma f
compound¹ vt 1 COMPOSE :
componer 2 : agravar (un problema,
etc.) — compound adj : compuesto

— compound n : compuesto m
compound² n ENCLOSURE : recinto m
comprehend vt : comprender —
comprehension n : comprensión f
— comprehensive adj 1 INCLUSIVE
: inclusivo 2 BROAD : amplio
compress vt : comprimir —
compression n : compresión f
comprise vt -prised;
-prising : comprender
compromise n : acuerdo m, arreglo m
— compromise v -mised; -mising vi :
llegar a un acuerdo — vt : comprometer
compulsion n 1 COERCION :
coacción f 2 URGE : impulso m —
compulsive adj : compulsivo —
compulsory adj : obligatorio
compute vt -puted; -puting : computar

— computer n : computadora f,
computador m, ordenador m Spain —
computerize vt -ized; -izing : informatizar
comrade n : camarada mf
con vt conned; conning : estafar —
con n 1 SWINDLE : estafa f 2 the pros
and cons : los pros y los contras
concave adj : cóncavo
conceal vt : ocultar
concede vt -ceded; -ceding
: conceder, admitir
conceit n : vanidad f —
conceited adj : engreído
conceive v -ceived; -ceiving vt :
concebir — vi conceive of : concebir
— conceivable adj : concebible
concentrate v -trated; -trating vt
: concentrar — vi : concentrarse

condiments
condimentos^M

Worcestershire sauce
salsa^F Worcertershire

balsamic vinegar
vinagre^M balsámico

rice vinegar
vinagre^M de arroz^M

ketchup
ketchup^M

American mustard
mostaza^F americana

table salt
sal^F de mesa^F

— **concentration** *n* : concentración *f*
concept *n* : concepto *m* —
conception *n* : concepción *f*
concern *vt* **1** : concernir **2 concern oneself about** : preocuparse por —
concern *n* **1** AFFAIR : asunto *m* **2** WORRY : preocupación *f* **3** BUSINESS : negocio *m*
— **concerned** *adj* **1** ANXIOUS : ansioso **2 as far as I'm concerned** : en cuanto a mí — **concerning** *prep* : con respecto a
concert *n* : concierto *m* —
concerted *adj* : concertado
concession *n* : concesión *f*
concise *adj* : conciso
conclude *v* **-cluded; -cluding** : concluir — **conclusion** *n* : conclusión *f* — **conclusive** *adj* : concluyente
concoct *vt* **1** PREPARE : confeccionar **2** DEVISE : inventarse, tramar — **concoction** *n* : mezcla *f*, brebaje *m*
concourse *n* : vestíbulo *m*, salón *m*
concrete *adj* : concreto — **concrete** *n* : hormigón *m*, concreto *m*, *Lat*
concur *vi* **concurred; concurring** AGREE : estar de acuerdo
concussion *n* : conmoción *f* cerebral
condemn *vt* : condenar — **condemnation** *n* : condenación *f*
condense *v* **-densed; -densing** *vt* : condensar — *vi* : condensarse — **condensation** *n* : condensación *f*
condescending *adj* : condescendiente
condiment *n* : condimento *m*
condition *n* **1** : condición *f* **2 in good condition** : en buen estado — **conditional** *adj* : condicional
condolences *npl* : pésame *m*
condom *n* : condón *m*
condominium *n*, *pl* **-ums** : condominio *m*, *Lat*
condone *vt* **-doned; -doning** : aprobar
conducive *adj* : propicio, favorable
conduct *n* : conducta *f* — **conduct** *vt* **1** DIRECT, GUIDE : conducir, dirigir **2** CARRY OUT : llevar a cabo **3 conduct oneself** : conducirse, comportarse — **conductor** *n* : revisor *m*, -sora *f* (en un tren); cobrador *m*, -dora *f* (en un autobús); director *m*, -tora *f* (de una orquesta)
cone *n* **1** : cono *m* **2** *or* **ice–cream cone** : cucurucho *m*, barquillo *m*, *Lat*
confection *n* : dulce *m*
confederation *n* : confederación *f*
confer *v* **-ferred; -ferring** *vt* : conferir, otorgar — *vi* **confer with** : consultar

cone
cono *M*

— **conference** *n* : conferencia *f*
confess *vt* : confesar — *vi* **1** : confesarse **2 confess to** : confesar, admitir — **confession** *n* : confesión *f*
confetti *n* : confeti *m*
confide *v* **-fided; -fiding** : confiar — **confidence** *n* **1** TRUST : confianza *f* **2** SELF-ASSURANCE : confianza *f* en sí mismo **3** SECRET : confidencia *f* — **confident** *adj* **1** SURE : seguro **2** SELF-ASSURED : confiado, seguro de sí mismo — **confidential** *adj* : confidencial
confine *vt* **-fined; -fining 1** LIMIT : confinar, limitar **2** IMPRISON : encerrar — **confines** *npl* : confines *mpl*
confirm *vt* : confirmar — **confirmation** *n* : confirmación *f* — **confirmed** *adj* : inveterado
confiscate *vt* **-cated; -cating** : confiscar
conflict *n* : conflicto *m* — **conflict** *vi* : estar en conflicto, oponerse
conform *vi* **1** COMPLY : ajustarse **2 conform with** : corresponder a — **conformity** *n*, *pl* **-ties** : conformidad *f*
confound *vt* : confundir, desconcertar
confront *vt* : afrontar, encarar — **confrontation** *n* : confrontación *f*
confuse *vt* **-fused; -fusing** : confundir — **confusing** *adj* : confuso, desconcertante — **confusion** *n* : confusión *f*, desconcierto *m*
congeal *vi* : coagularse
congenial *adj* : agradable
congested *adj* : congestionado — **congestion** *n* : congestión *f*
congratulate *vt* **-lated; -lating** : felicitar — **congratulations** *npl* : felicitaciones *fpl*
congregate *vi* **-gated; -gating** : congregarse — **congregation** *n* : feligreses *mpl* (en religión)

congress *n* : congreso *m* — **congressional** *adj* : del congreso — **congressman** *n*, *pl* **-men** : congresista *mf*
conjecture *n* : conjetura *f*, presunción *f* — **conjecture** *v* **-tured; -turing** *vt* : conjeturar — *vi* : hacer conjeturas
conjugal *adj* : conyugal
conjugate *vt* **-gated; -gating** : conjugar — **conjugation** *n* : conjugación *f*
conjunction *n* **1** : conjunción *f* **2 in conjunction with** : en combinación con
conjure *v* **-jured; -juring** *vi* : hacer juegos de manos — **conjure** *vt* *or* **conjure up** : evocar
connect *vi* : conectarse — *vt* **1** JOIN : conectar, juntar **2** ASSOCIATE : asociar — **connection** *n* **1** : conexión *f* **2** : enlace *m* (con un tren, etc.) **3 connects** *npl* : relaciones *fpl* (personas)
connoisseur *n* : conocedor *m*, -dora *f*
connote *vt* **-noted; -noting** : connotar, implicar
conquer *vt* : conquistar — **conqueror** *n* : conquistador *m*, -dora *f* — **conquest** *n* : conquista *f*
conscience *n* : conciencia *f* — **conscientious** *adj* : concienzudo
conscious *adj* **1** AWARE : consciente **2** INTENTIONAL : intencional — **consciously** *adv* : deliberadamente — **consciousness** *n* **1** AWARENESS : conciencia *f* **2 lose consciousness** : perder el conocimiento
consecrate *vt* **-crated; -crating** : consagrar — **consecration** *n* : consagración *f*
consecutive *adj* : consecutivo, sucesivo
consensus *n* : consenso *m*
consent *vi* : consentir — **consent** *n* : consentimiento *m*
consequence *n* **1** : consecuencia *f* **2 of no consequence** : sin importancia — **consequent** *adj* : consiguiente — **consequently** *adv* : por consiguiente
conserve *vt* **-served; -serving** : conservar, preservar — **conservation** *n* : conservación *f* — **conservative** *adj* **1** : conservador **2** CAUTIOUS : moderado, prudente — **conserve** *n* : conservador *m*, -dora *f* — **conservatory** *n*, *pl* **-ries** : conservatorio *m*
consider *vt* **1** : considerar **2 all things considered** : teniéndolo todo en cuenta — **considerable** *adj* : considerable — **considerate** *adj* : considerado

— **consideration** *n* **1** : consideración *f* **2**
take into consideration : tener en cuenta
— **considering** *prep* : teniendo en cuenta
consign *vt* **1** : relegar **2** SEND : enviar
— **consignment** *n* : envío *m*
consist *vi* **1 consist in** : consistir
en **2 consist of** : constar de,
componerse de — **consistency** *n*,
pl -**cies 1** TEXTURE : consistencia *f* **2**
COHERENCE : coherencia *f* **3** UNIFORMITY
: regularidad *f* — **consistent** *adj* **1**
UNCHANGING : constante, regular **2**
consistent with : consecuente con
console *vt* -**soled; -soling** : consolar
— **consolation** *n* **1** : consuelo *m* **2**
console prize : premio *m* de consolación
consolidate *vt* -**dated; -dating**
: consolidar — **consolidation** *n*

: consolidación *f*
consonant *n* : consonante *f*
conspicuous *adj* **1** OBVIOUS : visible,
evidente **2** STRIKING : llamativo —
conspicuously *adv* : de manera llama-tiva
conspire *vi* -**spired; -spiring** : conspirar
— **conspiracy** *n, pl* -**cies** : conspiración *f*
constant *adj* : constante —
constantly *adv* : constantemente
▸ **constellation** *n* : constelación *f*
constipated *adj* : estreñido —
constipation *n* : estreñimiento *m*
constituent *n* **1** COMPONENT
: componente *m* **2** VOTER :
elector *m*, -tora *f;* votante *mf*
constitute *vt* -**tuted; -tuting** : constituir
— **constitution** *n* : constitución *f* —
constitutional *adj* : constitucional

constraint *n* : restricción *f,* limitación *f*
construct *vt* : construir —
construction *n* : construcción *f* —
constructive *adj* : constructivo
construe *vt* -**strued;**
-**struing** : interpretar
consul *n* : cónsul *mf* —
consulate *n* : consulado *m*
consult *v* : consultar — **consultant** *n*
: asesor *m*, -sora *f;* consultor *m*, -tora *f*
— **consultation** *n* : consulta *f*
consume *vt* -**sumed; -suming** :
consumir — **consumer** *n* : consumidor *m*,
-dora *f* — **consumption** *n* : consumo *m*
contact *n* : contacto *m* — **contact** *vt*
: ponerse en contacto con — **contact**
lens *n* : lente *mf* (de contacto)
contagious *adj* : contagioso

constellations of the Northern hemisphere
constelaciones *F* **del hemisferio** *M* **boreal**

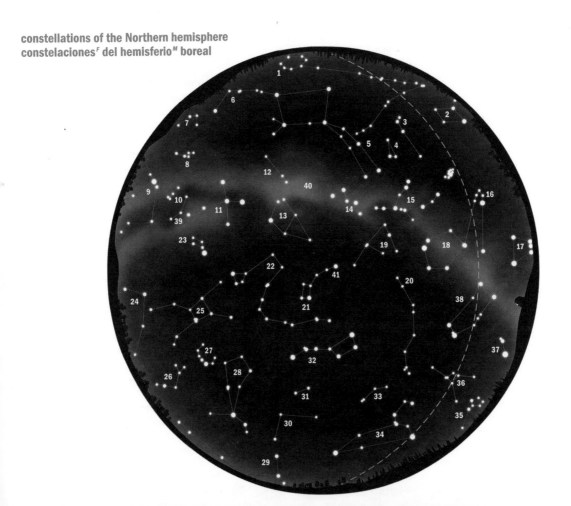

contain *vt* **1** : contener **2 contain
oneself** : contenerse — **container** *n*
: recipiente *m*, envase *m*
contaminate *vt* **-nated; -nating**
: contaminar — **contamination** *n*
: contaminación *f*
contemplate *v* **-plated; -plating** *vt* **1**
: contemplar **2** CONSIDER : considerar,
pensar en — *vi* : reflexionar —
contemplation *n* : contemplación *f*
contemporary *adj* : contemporáneo
— **contemporary** *n, pl* **-raries**
: contemporáneo *m*, -nea *f*
contempt *n* : desprecio *m* —
contemptible *adj* : despreciable —
contemptuous *adj* : desdeñoso
contend *vi* **1** COMPETE : contender,
competir **2 contend with** : enfrentarse

a — *vt* : sostener, afirmar —
contender *n* : contendiente *mf*
content[1] *n* **1** : contenido *m* **2 table
of contents** : índice *m* de materias
content[2] *adj* : contento — **content** *vt*
content oneself with : contentarse con
— **contented** *adj* : satisfecho, contento
contention *n* **1** DISPUTE : disputa *f* **2**
OPINION : argumento *m*, opinión *f*
contentment *n* : satisfacción *f*
contest *vt* : disputar — **contest** *n* **1**
STRUGGLE : contienda *f* **2**
COMPETITION : concurso *m*,
competencia *f* — **contestant** *n* :
concursante *mf*, contendiente *mf*
context *n* : contexto *m*
continent *n* : continente *m* —
continental *adj* : continental

contingency *n, pl* **-cies** : contingencia *f*
continue *v* **-tinued; -tinuing** : continuar
— **continual** *adj* : continuo, constante
— **continuation** *n* : continuación *f* —
continuity *n, pl* **-ties** : continuidad *f*
— **continuous** *adj* : continuo
contort *vt* : retorcer —
contortion *n* : contorsión *f*
contour *n* **1** : contorno *m* **2** *or*
contour line : curva *f* de nivel
contraband *n* : contrabando *m*
contraception *n* : anticoncepción *f*
— **contraceptive** *adj* : anticonceptivo
— **contraception** *n* : anticonceptivo *m*
contract *n* : contrato *m* — **contract** *vt*
: contraer — *vi* : contraerse —
contraction *n* : contracción *f* —
contractor *n* : contratista *mf*

1	Pisces *Piscis*[M]	12	Lacerta *Lagarto*[M]	23	Lyra *Lira*[F]	34	Leo *León*[M]
2	Cetus *Ballena*[F]	13	Cepheus *Cefeo*[M]	24	Ophiuchus *Ofiuco*[M]	35	Hydra *Hidra*[F] Hembra
3	Aries *Aries*[M]	14	Cassiopeia *Casiopea*[F]	25	Hercules *Hércules*[M]	36	Cancer *Cáncer*[M]
4	Triangulum *Triángulo*[M]	15	Perseus *Perseo*[M]	26	Serpens *Serpiente*[F]	37	Canis Minor *Can*[M] Menor
5	Andromeda *Andrómeda*[F]	16	Taurus *Tauro*[M]	27	Corona Borealis *Corona*[F] Boreal	38	Gemini *Géminis*[F]
6	Pegasus *Pegaso*[M]	17	Orion *Orión*[M]	28	Boötes *Boyero*[M]	39	Vulpecula *Zorra*[F]
7	Equuleus *Caballo*[M] Menor	18	Auriga *Cochero*[M]	29	Virgo *Virgo*[F]	40	Milky Way *Vía*[F] Láctea
8	Delphinus *Delfín*[M]	19	Camelopardalis *Jirafa*[F]	30	Coma Berenices *Cabellera*[F] de Berenice	41	North Star *Estrella*[F] Polar
9	Aquila *Águila*[F]	20	Lynx *Lince*[M]	31	Canes Venatici *Lebreles*[M]		
10	Sagitta *Flecha*[F]	21	Ursa Minor *Osa*[F] Menor	32	Ursa Major *Osa*[F] Mayor		
11	Cygnus *Cisne*[M]	22	Draco *Dragón*[M]	33	Leo Minor *León*[M] Menor		

contradiction *n* : contradicción *f*
— **contradict** *vt* : contradecir —
contradictory *adj* : contradictorio
contraption *n* : artilugio *m*, artefacto *m*
contrary *n*, *pl* -**traries 1** : contrario
2 on the contrary : al contrario —
contrary *adj* **1** : contrario, opuesto
2 contrary to : en contra de
contrast *v* : contrastar —
contrast *n* : contraste *m*
contribute *v* -**uted; -uting** : contribuir
— **contribution** *n* : contribución *f* —
contributor *n* **1** : contribuyente *mf* **2** :
colaborador *m*, -dora *f* (en periodismo)
contrite *adj* : arrepentido
contrive *vt* -**trived; -triving 1**
DEVISE : idear **2 contrive to do**
something : lograr hacer algo
control *vt* -**trolled; -trolling** :
controlar — **control** *n* **1** : control *m* **2**
controls *npl* : mandos *mpl*
controversy *n*, *pl* -**sies** : controversia *f*
— **controversial** *adj* : polémico
convalescence *n* : convalecencia *f*
— **convalescent** *adj* : convaleciente —
convalescence *n* : convaleciente *mf*
convene *v* -**vened; -vening** *vt*
: convocar — *vi* : reunirse
convenience *n* : conveniencia *f*,
comodidad *f* — **convenient** *adj*
: conveniente
convent *n* : convento *m*
convention *n* : convención *f* —
conventional *adj* : convencional
converge *vi* -**verged; -verging**
: converger, convergir
converse[1] *vi* -**versed;**
-**versing** : conversar —
conversation *n* : conversación *f* —
conversational *adj* : familiar
converse[2] *adj* : contrario, opuesto
— **conversely** *adv* : a la inversa
conversion *n* : conversión *f*
— **convert** *vt* : convertir — *vi* :
convertirse — **convertible** *adj*
: convertible — **convertible** *n* :
descapotable *m*, convertible *m*, *Lat*
convex *adj* : convexo
convey *vt* **1** TRANSPORT : llevar,
transportar **2** TRANSMIT : comunicar
convict *vt* : declarar culpable a —
convict *n* : presidiario *m*, -ria *f* —
conviction *n* **1** : condena *f* (de un
acusado) **2** BELIEF : convicción *f*
convince *vt* -**vinced; -vincing**

: convencer — **convincing** *adj*
: convincente
convoke *vt* -**voked; -voking** : convocar
convoluted *adj* : complicado
convulsion *n* : convulsión *f* —
convulsive *adj* : convulsivo
cook *n* : cocinero *m*, -ra *f* — **cook** *vi* :
cocinar, guisar — *vt* : preparar (comida)
— **cookbook** *n* : libro *m* de cocina
cookie *or* **cooky** *n*, *pl* -**ies**
: galleta *f* (dulce)
cooking *n* : cocina *f*
cool *adj* **1** : fresco **2** CALM : tranquilo **3**
UNFRIENDLY : frío — **cool** *vt* : enfriar — *vi*
: enfriarse — **cool** *n* **1** : fresco *m* **2**
COMPOSURE : calma *f* — **cooler** *n* : nevera *f*
portátil — **coolness** *n* : frescura *f*
coop *n* : gallinero *m* — **coop** *vt*
or **coop up** : encerrar
cooperate *vi* -**ated; -ating** : cooperar
— **cooperation** *n* : cooperación *f*
— **cooperative** *adj* : cooperativo
coordinate *v* -**nated; -nating** *vt*
: coordinar — **coordination** *n*
: coordinación *f*
cop *n* **1** : poli *mf fam* **2 the**
cops : la poli *fam*
cope *vi* **coped; coping 1** : arreglárselas
2 cope with : hacer frente a, poder con
copier *n* : fotocopiadora *f*
copious *adj* : copioso
copper *n* : cobre *m*
copy *n*, *pl* **copies 1** : copia *f* **2** :
ejemplar *m* (de un libro), número *m*
(de una revista) — **copy** *vt* **copied;**
copying 1 DUPLICATE : hacer una
copia de **2** IMITATE : copiar —
copyright *n* : derechos *mpl* de autor
coral *n* : coral *m*
cord *n* **1** : cuerda *f* **2** *or* **electric**
cord : cable *m* (eléctrico)
cordial *adj* : cordial
corduroy *n* : pana *f*
core *n* **1** : corazón *m* (de una fruta)
2 CENTER : núcleo *m*, centro *m*
cork *n* : corcho *m* — **corkscrew** *n*
: sacacorchos *m*
corn *n* **1** : grano *m* **2** *or* **Indian**
corn : maíz *m* **3** : callo *m* (del
pie) — **corncob** *n* : mazorca *f*
corner *n* : ángulo *m*, rincón *m* (en
una habitación), esquina *f* (de una
intersección) — **corner** *vt* **1** TRAP
: acorralar **2** MONOPOLIZE : acaparar
(un mercado) — **cornerstone** *n*

: piedra *f* angular
cornmeal *n* : harina *f* de maíz
— **cornstarch** *n* : maicena *f*
corny *adj* : cursi, sentimental
coronary *n*, *pl* -**naries** :
trombosis *f* coronaria
coronation *n* : coronación *f*
corporal *n* : cabo *m*
corporation *n* : sociedad *f* anónima,
compañía *f* — **corporate** *adj* : corporativo
corps *n*, *pl* **corps** : cuerpo *m*
corpse *n* : cadáver *m*
corpulent *adj* : obeso, gordo
corpuscle *n* : glóbulo *m*
corral *n* : corral *m* — **corral** *vt*
-**ralled; -ralling** : acorralar
correct *vt* : corregir — **correct** *adj* :
correcto — **correction** *n* : corrección *f*
correlation *n* : correlación *f*
correspond *vi* **1** WRITE : corresponderse
2 correspond to : corresponder a —
correspondence *n* : correspondencia *f*
corridor *n* : pasillo *m*
corroborate *vt* -**rated;**
-**rating** : corroborar
corrode *v* -**roded; -roding** *vt* : corroer
— *vi* : corroerse — **corrosion** *n* :
corrosión *f* — **corrosive** *adj* : corrosivo
corrugated *adj* : ondulado
corrupt *vt* : corromper —
corrupt *adj* : corrupto, corrompido
— **corruption** *n* : corrupción *f*
corset *n* : corsé *m*
cosmetic *n* : cosmético *m* —
cosmetic *adj* : cosmético
cosmic *adj* : cósmico
cosmopolitan *adj* : cosmopolita
cosmos *n* : cosmos *m*
cost *n* : costo *m*, coste *m* — **cost** *vi* **cost;**
costing 1 : costar **2 how much does it**
cost? : ¿cuánto cuesta?, ¿cuánto vale?
Costa Rican *adj* : costarricense
costly *adj* : costoso
costume *n* **1** OUTFIT : traje *m* **2**
DISGUISE : disfraz *m*
cot *n* : catre *m*
cottage *n* : casita *f* (de campo) —
cottage cheese *n* : requesón *m*
cotton *n* : algodón *m*
couch *n* : sofá *m*
cough *vi* : toser — **cough** *n* : tos *f*
could → **can 1**
council *n* **1** : concejo *m* **2** *or* **city**
council : ayuntamiento *m* — **councillor**
or **councilor** *n* : concejal *m*, -jala *f*

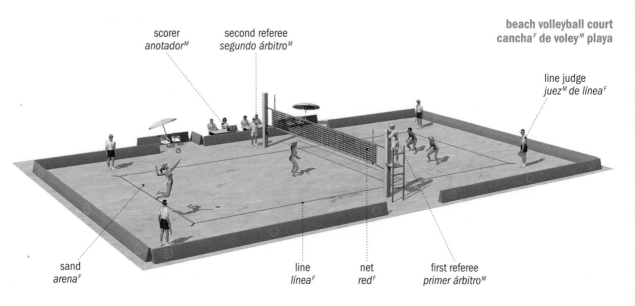

beach volleyball court
cancha^F **de voley**^{M} **playa**

scorer
anotador^M

second referee
segundo árbitro^M

line judge
juez^M *de línea*^{F}

sand
arena^F

line
línea^F

net
red^F

first referee
primer árbitro^M

counsel *n* **1** ADVICE : consejo *m* **2** LAWYER : abogado *m*, -da *f* — **counsel** *vt* **-seled** *or* **-selled; -seling** *or* **-selling** : aconsejar — **counselor** *or* **counsellor** *n* : consejero *m*, -ra *f*
count^1 *vt* : contar — *vi* **1** : contar **2 count on** : contar con **3 that doesn't count** : eso no vale — **count** *n* **1** : recuento *m* **2 keep count of** : llevar la cuenta de
count^2 *n* : conde *m* (noble)
counter^1 *n* **1** : mostrador *m* (de un negocio) **2** TOKEN : ficha *f* (de un juego)
counter^2 *vt* : oponerse a — *vi* : contraatacar — **counter** *adv* **counter to** : contrario a — **counteract** *vt* : contrarrestar — **counterattack** *n* : contraataque *m* — **counterbalance** *n* : con-trapeso *m* — **counterclockwise** *adv* & *adj* : en sentido opuesto a las agujas del reloj — **counterfeit** *vt* : falsificar — **counterfeit** *adj* : falsificado — **counterfeit** *n* : falsificación *f* — **counterpart** *n* : homólogo *m* (de una persona), equivalente *m* (de una cosa) — **counterproductive** *adj* : contraproducente
countess *n* : condesa *f*
countless *adj* : incontable, innumerable
country *n*, *pl* **-tries 1** NATION : país *m* **2** COUNTRYSIDE : campo *m* — **country** *adj* : campestre, rural — **countryman** *n*, *pl* **-men** *or* **fellow**

countryman : compatriota *mf* — **countryside** *n* : campo *m*, campiña *f*
county *n*, *pl* **-ties** : condado *m*
coup *n*, *pl* **coups** *or* **coup d'etat** : golpe *m* (de estado)
couple *n* **1** : pareja *f* (de personas) **2 a couple of** : un par de — **couple** *vt* **-pled; -pling** : acoplar, unir
coupon *n* : cupón *m*
courage *n* : valor *m* — **courageous** *adj* : valiente
courier *n* : mensajero *m*, -ra *f*
course *n* **1** : curso *m* **2** : plato *m* (de una cena) **3** *or* **golf course** : campo *m* de golf **4 in the course of** : en el transcurso de **5 of course** : desde luego, por supuesto
▸ **court** *n* **1** : corte *f* (de un rey, etc.) **2** : cancha *f*, pista *f* (en deportes) **3** TRIBUNAL : corte *f*, tribunal *m* — **court** *vt* : cortejar
courteous *adj* : cortés — **courtesy** *n*, *pl* **-sies** : cortesía *f*
courthouse *n* : palacio *m* de justicia, juzgado *m* — **courtroom** *n* : sala *f* (de un tribunal)
courtship *n* : cortejo *m*, noviazgo *m*
courtyard *n* : patio *m*
cousin *n* : primo *m*, -ma *f*
cove *n* : ensenada *f*, cala *f*
covenant *n* : pacto *m*, convenio *m*
cover *vt* **1** : cubrir **2** *or* **cover up** : encubrir, ocultar **3** TREAT : tratar — **cover** *n* **1** : cubierta *f* **2** SHELTER :

abrigo *m*, refugio *m* **3** LID : tapa *f* **4** : cubierta *f* (de un libro), portada *f* (de una revista) **5 covers** *npl* BEDCLOTHES : mantas *fpl*, cobijas *fpl Lat* **6 take cover** : ponerse a cubierto **7 under cover of** : al amparo de — **coverage** *n* : cobertura *f* — **covert** *adj* : encubierto — **cover-up** *n* : encubrimiento *m*
covet *vt* : codiciar — **covetous** *adj* : codicioso
cow *n* : vaca *f* — **cow** *vt* : intimidar, acobardar
coward *n* : cobarde *mf* — **cowardice** *n* : cobardía *f* — **cowardly** *adj* : cobarde
cowboy *n* : vaquero *m*
cower *vi* : encogerse (de miedo)
coy *adj* : tímido y coqueto
coyote *n*, *pl* **coyotes** *or* **coyote** : coyote *m*
cozy *adj* **-zier; -est** : acogedor
crab *n* : cangrejo *m*, jaiba *f Lat*
crack *vt* **1** SPLIT : rajar, partir **2** : cascar (nueces, huevos) **3** : chasquear (un látigo, etc.) **4 crack down on** : tomar medidas enérgicas contra — *vi* **1** SPLIT : rajarse, agrietarse **2** : chasquear (dícese de un látigo) **3 crack up** : sufrir una crisis nerviosa — **crack** *n* **1** CRACKING : chasquido *m*, crujido *m* **2** CREVICE : raja *f*, grieta *f* **3 have a crack at** : intentar
cracker *n* : galleta *f* (de soda, etc.)
crackle *vi* **-led; -ling** : crepitar,

chisporrotear — **crackle** n :
crujido m, chisporroteo m
cradle n : cuna f — **cradle** vt
-dled; -dling : acunar
craft n **1** TRADE : oficio m **2** CUNNING
: astucia f **3** → **craftsmanship 4** pl
usually **craft** BOAT : embarcación f —
craftsman n, pl **-men** : artesano m,
-na f — **craftsmanship** n :
artesanía f, destreza f — **crafty;** adj
craftier; -est : astuto, taimado
crag n : peñasco m
cram v **crammed; cramming** vt **1**
STUFF : embutir **2 cram with** : atiborrar
de — vi : estudiar a última hora
cramp n **1** : calambre m,
espasmo m (de los músculos) **2**
cramps npl : retorcijones mpl
cranberry n, pl **-berries** :
arándano m (rojo y agrio)
crane n **1** : grulla f (ave) **2** : grúa f
(máquina) — **crane** vt **craned;**
craning : estirar (el cuello)
crank n **1** : manivela f **2** ECCENTRIC
: excéntrico m, -ca f — **cranky** adj
crankier; -est : malhumorado
crash vi **1** : caerse con estrépito
2 COLLIDE : estrellarse, chocar
— vt : estrellar — **crash** n **1** DIN :
estrépito m **2** COLLISION : choque m
crass adj : burdo, grosero

crate n : cajón m (de madera)
crater n : cráter m
crave vt **craved; craving** : ansiar
— **craving** n : ansia f
crawl vi : arrastrarse, gatear (dícese de un
bebé) — **crawl** n **at a crawl** : a paso lento
crayon n : lápiz m de cera
craze n : moda f pasajera, manía f
crazy adj **-zier; -est 1** : loco **2 go crazy** :
volverse loco — **craziness** n : locura f
creak vi : chirriar, crujir —
creak n : chirrido m, crujido m
cream n : crema f, nata f Spain —
cream cheese n : queso m crema —
creamy adj **creamier; -est** : cremoso
crease n : pliegue m, raya f (del pantalón)
— **crease** vt **creased; creasing** :
plegar, poner una raya en (el pantalón)
create vt **-ated; -ating** : crear —
creation n : creación f — **creative** adj :
creativo — **creator** n : creador m, -dora f
creature n : criatura f, animal m
credence n **lend credence**
to : dar crédito a
credentials npl : credenciales fpl
credible adj : creíble —
credibility n : credibilidad f
credit n **1** : crédito m **2** RECOGNITION
: reconocimiento m **3 be a credit to** :
ser el orgullo de — **credit** vt **1** BELIEVE :
creer **2** : abonar (en una cuenta) **3 credit**

someone with something : atribuir algo a
algn — **credit card** n : tarjeta f de crédito
credulous adj : crédulo
creed n : credo m
creek n : arroyo m, riachuelo m
creep vi **crept; creeping 1** CRAWL :
arrastrarse **2** SLINK : ir a hurtadillas —
creep n **1** CRAWL : paso m lento **2 the**
creeps : escalofríos mpl — **creeping** adj
creep plant : planta f trepadora
cremate vt **-mated; -mating** : incinerar
crescent n : media luna f
cress n : berro m
crest n : cresta f —
crestfallen adj : alicaído
crevice n : grieta f
crew n **1** : tripulación f (de una
nave) **2** TEAM : equipo m
▸ **crib** n : cuna f (de un bebé)
cricket n **1** : grillo m (insecto)
2 : críquet m (juego)
crime n : crimen m — **criminal** adj :
criminal — **criminal** n : criminal mf
crimp vt : rizar
crimson n : carmesí m
cringe vi **cringed; cringing** : encogerse
crinkle vt **-kled; -kling** : arrugar
cripple vt **-pled; -pling 1** DISABLE :
lisiar, dejar inválido **2** INCAPACITATE
: inutilizar, paralizar
crisis n, pl **crises** : crisis f
crisp adj **1** CRUNCHY : crujiente **2** :
frío y vigorizante (dícese del aire) —
crispy adj **crispier; -est** : crujiente
crisscross vt : entrecruzar
criterion n, pl **-ria** : criterio m
critic n : crítico m, -ca f — **critical** adj
: crítico — **criticism** n : crítica f —
criticize vt **-cized; -cizing** : criticar
croak vi : croar
crock n : vasija f de barro —
crockery n : vajilla f, loza f
▸ **crocodile** n : cocodrilo m
crony n, pl **-nies** : amigote m fam
crook n **1** STAFF : cayado m **2** THIEF :
ratero m, -ra f; ladrón m, -drona f **3** BEND :
pliegue m — **crooked** adj **1** BENT : torcido,
chueco Lat **2** DISHONEST : deshonesto
crop n **1** WHIP : fusta f **2** HARVEST :
cosecha f **3** : cultivo m (de maíz, tabaco,
etc.) — **crop** v **cropped; cropping** vt TRIM
: recortar, cortar — vi **crop up** : surgir
cross n **1** : cruz f **2** HYBRID : cruce m
— **cross** vt **1** : cruzar, atravesar **2**
CROSSBREED : cruzar **3** or **cross out** :

crib
cunaF

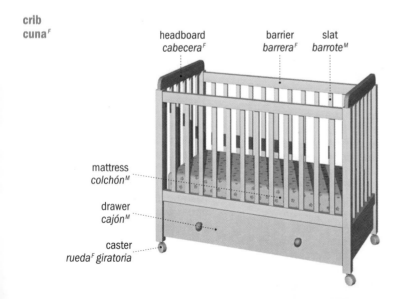

headboard
cabecera F

barrier
barrera F

slat
barrote M

mattress
colchón M

drawer
cajón M

caster
rueda F giratoria

alligator
aligátor[M]

crocodile
cocodrilo[M]

crocodile and others crocodilians
cocodrilo[M] y demás crocodiles[M]

caiman
caimán[M]

tachar — **cross** *adj* **1** : que atraviesa **2** ANGRY : enojado — **crossbreed** *vt* **-bred; -breeding** : cruzar — **cross–examine** *vt* : interrogar — **cross–eyed** *adj* : bizco — **cross fire** *n* : fuego *m* cruzado — **crossing** *n* **1** INTERSECTION : cruce *m*, paso *m* **2** VOYAGE : travesía *f* (del mar) — **cross–reference** *n* : referencia *f* — **crossroads** *n* : cruce *m* — **cross section** *n* **1** : corte *m* transversal **2** SAMPLE : muestra *f* representativa — **crosswalk** *n* : cruce *m* peatonal, paso *m* de peatones — **crossword puzzle** *n* : crucigrama *m*
crotch *n* : entrepierna *f*
crouch *vi* : agacharse
crouton *n* : crutón *m*
crow *n* : cuervo *m* — **crow** *vi* **crowed** *or Brit* **crew; crowing** : cacarear
crowbar *n* : palanca *f*
crowd *vi* : amontonarse — *vt* : atestar, llenar — **crowd** *n* : multitud *f*, muchedumbre *f*
crown *n* **1** : corona *f* **2** : cima *f* (de una colina) — **crown** *vt* : coronar
crucial *adj* : crucial
crucify *vt* **-fied; -fying** : crucificar — **crucifix** *n* : crucifijo *m* — **crucifixion** *n* : crucifixión *f*
crude *adj* **cruder; -est 1** RAW : crudo **2** VULGAR : grosero **3** ROUGH : tosco, rudo
cruel *adj* **-eler** *or* **-eller; -elest** *or* **-ellest** : cruel — **cruelty** *n*, *pl* **-ties** : crueldad *f*
cruet *n* : vinagrera *f*

cruise *vi* **cruised; cruising 1** : hacer un crucero **2** : ir a velocidad de crucero — **cruise** *n* : crucero *m* — **cruiser** *n* **1** WARSHIP : crucero *m* **2** : patrulla *f* (de policía)
crumb *n* : miga *f*, migaja *f*
crumble *v* **-bled; -bling** *vt* : desmenuzar — *vi* : desmenuzarse, desmoronarse
crumple *vt* **-pled; -pling** : arrugar
crunch *vt* : ronzar (con los dientes), hacer crujir (con los pies, etc.) — **crunchy** *adj* **crunchier; -est** : crujiente
crusade *n* : cruzada *f*
crush *vt* : aplastar, apachurrar *Lat* — **crush** *n* **have a crush on** : estar chiflado por
crust *n* : corteza *f*
crutch *n* : muleta *f*
crux *n* : quid *m*
cry *vi* **cried; crying 1** SHOUT : gritar **2** WEEP : llorar — **cry** *n*, *pl* **cries** : grito *m*
crypt *n* : cripta *f*
crystal *n* : cristal *m*
cub *n* : cachorro *m*, -rra *f*
Cuban *adj* : cubano
cube *n* : cubo *m* — **cubic** *adj* : cúbico
cubicle *n* : cubículo *m*
cuckoo *n* : cuco *m*, cuclillo *m*
cucumber *n* : pepino *m*
cuddle *v* **-dled; -dling** *vi* : acurrucarse, abrazarse — *vt* : abrazar
cudgel *n* : porra *f* — **cudgel** *vt* **-geled** *or* **-gelled; -geling** *or* **-gelling** : aporrear

cue[1] *n* SIGNAL : señal *f*
cue[2] *n* : taco *m* (de billar)
cuff[1] **1** : puño *m* (de una camisa) **2 cuffs** *npl* → **handcuffs**
cuff[2] *vt* : bofetear — **cuff** *n* SLAP : bofetada *f*
cuisine *n* : cocina *f*
culinary *adj* : culinario
cull *vt* : seleccionar, entresacar
culminate *vi* **-nated; -nating** : culminar — **culmination** *n* : culminación *f*
culprit *n* : culpable *mf*
cult *n* : culto *m*
cultivate *vt* **-vated; -vating** : cultivar — **cultivation** *n* : cultivo *m*
culture *n* **1** : cultura *f* **2** : cultivo *m* (en biología) — **cultural** *adj* : cultural — **cultured** *adj* : culto
cumbersome *adj* : torpe (y pesado), difícil de manejar
cumulative *adj* : acumulativo
cunning *adj* : astuto, taimado — **cunning** *n* : astucia *f*
cup *n* **1** : taza *f* **2** TROPHY : copa *f*
cupboard *n* : alacena *f*, armario *m*
curator *n* : conservador *m*, -dora *f*; director *m*, -tora *f*
curb *n* **1** RESTRAINT : freno *m* **2** : borde *m* de la acera — **curb** *vt* : refrenar
curdle *v* **-dled; -dling** *vi* : cuajarse — *vt* : cuajar
cure *n* : cura *f*, remedio *m* — **cure** *vt* **cured; curing** : curar

hydrologic cycle
ciclo^M *hidrológico*

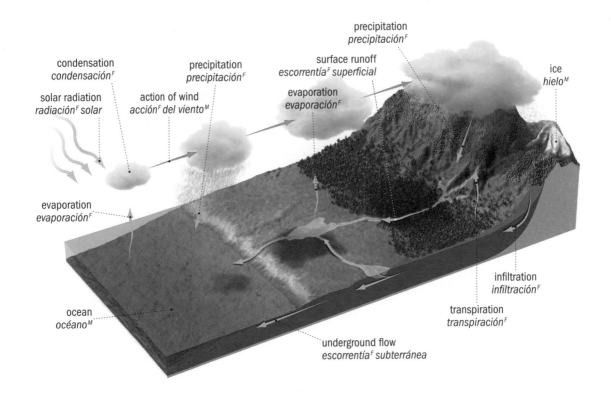

precipitation
precipitación^F

condensation
condensación^F

precipitation
precipitación^F

surface runoff
escorrentía^F *superficial*

ice
hielo^M

solar radiation
radiación^F *solar*

action of wind
acción^F *del viento*^M

evaporation
evaporación^F

evaporation
evaporación^F

infiltration
infiltración^F

ocean
océano^M

transpiration
transpiración^F

underground flow
escorrentía^F *subterránea*

---

curfew *n* : toque *m* de queda
curious *adj* : curioso — **curio** *n*,
pl **-rios** : curiosidad *f* — **curiosity** *n*,
pl **-ties** : curiosidad *f*
curl *vt* **1** : rizar **2** COIL : enrollar, enroscar
— *vi* **1** : rizarse **2 curl up** : acurrucarse
— **curl** *n* : rizo *m* — **curler** *n* : rulo *m*
— **curly** *adj* **curlier; -est** : rizado
currant *n* **1** : grosella *f* (fruta)
2 RAISIN : pasa *f* de Corinto
currency *n, pl* **-cies 1** MONEY
: moneda *f* **2 gain currency**
: ganar aceptación
current *adj* **1** PRESENT : actual **2** PREVALENT
: corriente — **current** *n* : corriente *f*
curriculum *n, pl* **-la** : plan *m* de estudios
curry *n, pl* **-ries** : curry *m*
curse *n* : maldición *f* — **curse** *v*
cursed; cursing : maldecir
cursor *n* : cursor *m*
cursory *adj* : superficial
curt *adj* : corto, seco

curtail *vt* : acortar
curtain *n* : cortina *f* (de una
ventana), telón *m* (en un teatro)
curtsy *vi* **-sied** *or* **-seyed; -sying**
or **-seying** : hacer una reverencia
— **curtsy** *n* : reverencia *f*
curve *v* **curved; curving** *vi* : hacer una
curva — *vt* : encorvar — **curve** *n* : curva *f*
cushion *n* : cojín *m* —
cushion *vt* : amortiguar
custard *n* : natillas *fpl*
custody *n, pl* **-dies 1** : custodia *f* **2 be in
custody** : estar detenido — **custodian** *n*
: custodio *m*, -dia *f*; guardián, -diana *f*
custom *n* : costumbre *f* — **customary** *adj*
: habitual, acostumbrado — **customer** *n* :
cliente *m*, -ta *f* — **customs** *npl* : aduana *f*
cut *v* **cut; cutting** *vt* **1** : cortar **2** REDUCE :
reducir, rebajar **3 cut oneself** : cortarse
4 cut up : cortar en pedazos — *vi* **1** :
cortar **2 cut in** : interrumpir — **cut** *n* **1** :
corte *m* **2** REDUCTION : rebaja *f*, reducción *f*

cute *adj* **cuter; -est** : mono *fam*, lindo
cutlery *n* : cubiertos *mpl*
cutlet *n* : chuleta *f*
cutting *adj* : cortante, mordaz
cyanide *n* : cianuro *m*
▸ **cycle** *n* **1** : ciclo *m* **2** BICYCLE :
bicicleta *f* — **cycle** *vi* **-cled; -cling** :
ir en bicicleta — **cyclic** *or* cyclical *adj*
: cíclico — **cyclist** *n* : ciclista *mf*
cyclone *n* : ciclón *m*
cylinder *n* : cilindro *m* —
cylindrical *adj* : cilíndrico
cymbal *n* : platillo *m*, címbalo *m*
cynic *n* : cínico *m*, -ca *f* — **cynical** *adj*
: cínico — **cynicism** *n* : cinismo *m*
cypress *n* : ciprés *m*
cyst *n* : quiste *m*
czar *n* : zar *m*
Czech *adj* : checo — **Czech** *n*
: checo *m* (idioma)

d *n, pl* **d's** *or* **ds** : d *f,* cuarta
letra del alfabeto inglés
dab *n* : toque *m* — **dab** *vt*
 dabbed; dabbing : dar toques
 ligeros a, aplicar suavemente
dabble *vi* **-bled; -bling dabble in** :
 interesarse superficialmente en —
 dabbler *n* : aficionado *m,* -da *f*
dad *n* : papá *m fam* — **daddy** *n,*
 pl **-dies** : papá *m fam*
daffodil *n* : narciso *m*
dagger *n* : daga *f,* puñal *m*
daily *adj* : diario — **daily** *adv* : diariamente
dainty *adj* **-tier; -est** : delicado
dairy *n, pl* **-ies 1** : lechería *f* (tienda)
 2 *or* **dairy farm** : granja *f* lechera
▸ **daisy** *n, pl* **-sies** : margarita *f*
dam *n* : presa *f* — **dam** *vt*
 dammed; damming : represar
damage *n* **1** : daño *m,* perjuicio *m* **2**
 damages *npl* : daños y perjuicios *mpl*
 — **damage** *vt* **-aged; -aging** : dañar
damn *vt* **1** CONDEMN : condenar **2**
 CURSE : maldecir — **damn** *n* **not give**
 a damn : no importarse un comino *fam*
 — **damn** *or* damned *adj* : maldito *fam*
damp *adj* : húmedo

 — **dampen** *vt* **1** MOISTEN : humedecer
 2 DISCOURAGE : desalentar, desanimar
 — **dampness** *n* : humedad *f*
dance *v* **danced; dancing** :
 bailar — **dance** *n* : baile *m* —
 dancer *n* : bailarín *m,* -rina *f*
dandelion *n* : diente *m* de león
dandruff *n* : caspa *f*
dandy *adj* **-dier; -est** : de
 primera, excelente
danger *n* : peligro *m* —
 dangerous *adj* : peligroso
dangle *v* **-gled; -gling** *vi* HANG :
 colgar, pender — *vt* : hacer oscilar
Danish *adj* : danés — **Danish** *n*
 : danés *m* (idioma)
dank *adj* : frío y húmedo
dare *v* **dared; daring** *vt* : desafiar — *vi* :
 osar — **dare** *n* : desafío *m* — **daredevil** *n*
 : persona *f* temeraria — **daring** *adj* :
 atrevido, audaz — **daring** *n* : audacia *f*
dark *adj* **1** : oscuro **2** : moreno
 (dícese del pelo o de la piel) **3** GLOOMY
 : sombrio **4 get dark** : hacerse de
 noche — **darken** *vt* : oscurecer — *vi* :
 oscurecerse — **darkness** *n* : oscuridad *f*
darling *n* BELOVED : querido *m,*

daisy
margarita *F*

 -da *f* — **darling** *adj* : querido
darn *vt* : zurcir — **darn** *adj* : maldito *fam*
▸ **dart** *n* **1** : dardo *m* **2 darts** *npl* : juego *m*
 de dardos — **dart** *vi* : precipitarse
dash *vt* **1** SMASH : romper **2** HURL : lanzar **3**
 dash off : hacer (algo) rápidamente — *vi*
 : lanzarse, irse corriendo — **dash** *n* **1** :
 guión *m* largo (signo de puntuación) **2** PINCH
 : poquito *m,* pizca *f* **3** RACE : carrera *f* —
 dashboard *n* : tablero *m* de instrumentos
 — **dashing** *adj* : gallardo, apuesto
data *ns & pl* : datos *mpl* —
 database *n* : base *f* de datos
date¹ *n* : dátil *m* (fruta)
date² *n* **1** : fecha *f* **2** APPOINTMENT :
 cita *f* — **date** *v* **dated; dating** *vt* **1**
 : fechar (una carta, etc.) **2** : salir con
 (algn) — *vi* **date from** : datar de
 — **dated** *adj* : pasado de moda
daub *vt* : embadurnar
daughter *n* : hija *f* — **daughter–in–**
 law *n, pl* **daughters–in–law** : nuera *f*
daunt *vt* : intimidar
dawdle *vi* **-dled; -dling** :
 entretenerse, perder tiempo
dawn *vi* **1** : amanecer **2 it dawned**
 on him that : cayó en la cuenta de
 que — **dawn** *n* : amanecer *m*
day *n* **1** : día *m* **2** *or* **working day** :
 jornada *f* **3 the day before** : el día
 anterior **4 the day before yesterday** :
 anteayer **5 the day after** : el día siguiente
 6 the day after tomorrow : pasada
 mañana — **daybreak** *n* : amanecer *m* —
 daydream *n* : ensueño *m* — **daydream** *vi*
 : soñar despierto — **daylight** *n* :
 luz *f* del día — **daytime** *n* : día *m*
daze *vt* **dazed; dazing** : aturdir

darts
juego *M* **de dardos** *M*

dartboard
diana *F*

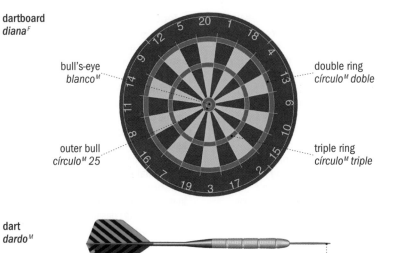

bull's-eye
blanco *M*

double ring
círculo *M* **doble**

outer bull
círculo *M* **25**

triple ring
círculo *M* **triple**

dart
dardo *M*

flight
volador *M*

point
punta *F*

decanter
garrafa^F

— **daze** *n* **in a daze** : aturdido
dazzle *vt* **-zled; -zling** : deslumbrar
dead *adj* **1** LIFELESS : muerto **2** NUMB :
entumecido — **dead** *n* **1 in the dead
of night** : en plena noche **2 the dead** :
los muertos — **dead** *adv* ABSOLUTELY :
absolutamente — **deaden** *vt* **1** : atenuar
(dolores) **2** MUFFLE : amortiguar — **dead
end** *n* : callejón *m* sin salida — **deadline** *n*
: fecha *f* límite — **deadlock** *n* : punto *m*
muerto — **deadly** *adj* **-lier; -est 1** :
mortal, letal **2** ACCURATE : certero, preciso
deaf *adj* : sordo — **deafen** *vt* :
ensordecer — **deafness** *n* : sordera *f*
deal *n* **1** TRANSACTION : trato *m*,
transacción *f* **2** : reparto *m* (de naipes)
3 a good deal : mucho — **deal** *v* **dealt;
dealing** *vt* **1** : dar **2** : repartir, dar (naipes)
3 deal a blow : asestar un golpe — *vi* **1**
: dar, repartir (en juegos de naipes) **2 deal
in** : comerciar en **3 deal with** CONCERN :
tratar de **4 deal with someone** : tratar
con algn — **dealer** *n* : comerciante *mf*
— **dealings** *npl* : trato *m*, relaciones *fpl*
dean *n* : decano *m*, -na *f*
dear *adj* : querido — **dear** *n* :
querido *m*, -da *f* — **dearly** *adv* **1** :
mucho **2 pay dear** : pagar caro
death *n* : muerte *f*

debar *vt* : excluir
debate *n* : debate *m*, discusión *f* —
debate *vt* **-bated; -bating** : debatir, discutir
debit *vt* : adeudar, cargar —
debit *n* : débito *m*, debe *m*
debris *n*, *pl* **-bris** : escombros *mpl*
debt *n* : deuda *f* — **debtor** *n*
: deudor *m*, -dora *f*
debunk *vt* : desmentir
debut *n* : debut *m* — **debut** *vi* : debutar
decade *n* : década *f*
decadence *n* : decadencia *f* —
decadent *adj* : decadente
decal *n* : calcomanía *f*
▸ **decanter** *n* : licorera *f*
decapitate *vt* **-tated; -tating** : decapitar
decay *vi* **1** DECOMPOSE : descomponerse
2 DETERIORATE : deteriorarse **3** : cariarse
(dícese de los dientes) — **decay** *n* **1** :
descomposición *f* **2** : deterioro *m* (de un
edificio, etc.) **3** : caries *f* (de los dientes)
deceased *adj* : difunto — **deceased** *n*
the deceased : el difunto, la difunta
deceive *vt* **-ceived; -ceiving** :
engañar — **deceit** *n* : engaño *m*
— **deceitful** *adj* : engañoso
December *n* : diciembre *m*
decent *adj* **1** : decente **2** KIND : bueno,
amable — **decency** *n*, *pl* **-cies** : decencia *f*
deception *n* : engaño *m* —
deceptive *adj* : engañoso
decide *v* **-cided; -ciding** *vt* : decidir
— *vi* : decidirse — **decided** *adj* **1**
UNQUESTIONABLE : indudable **2** RESOLUTE :
decidido — **decidedly** *adv* **1** DEFINITELY :
decididamente **2** RESOLUTELY : con decisión
decimal *adj* : decimal — **decimal** *n*
: número *m* decimal — **decimal
point** *n* : coma *f* decimal
decipher *vt* : descifrar
decision *n* : decisión *f* — **decisive** *adj* **1**
RESOLUTE : decidido **2** CONCLUSIVE : decisivo
deck *n* **1** : cubierta *f* (de un barco)
2 *or* **deck of cards** : baraja *f* (de
naipes) **3** TERRACE : entarimado *m*
declare *vt* **-clared; -claring** : declarar
— **declaration** *n* : declaración *f*
decline *v* **-clined; -clining** *vt* REFUSE
: declinar, rehusar — *vi* DECREASE :
disminuir — **decline** *n* **1** DETERIORATION
: decadencia *f*, deterioro *m* **2**
DECREASE : disminución *f*
decode *vt* **-coded; -coding** : descodificar
decompose *vt* **-posed; -posing** :
descomponer — *vi* : descomponerse

decongestant *n* : descongestionante *m*
decorate *vt* **-rated; -rating** : decorar
— **decor** *or* décor *n* : decoración *f*
— **decoration** *n* : decoración *f* —
decorator *n* : decorador *m*, -dora *f*
decoy *n* : señuelo *m*
decrease *v* **-creased; -creasing** :
disminuir — **decrease** *n* : disminución *f*
decree *n* : decreto *m* — **decree** *vt*
-creed; -creeing : decretar
decrepit *adj* **1** FEEBLE : decrépito
2 DILAPIDATED : ruinoso
dedicate *vt* **-cated; -cating 1** : dedicar
2 dedicate oneself to : consagrarse
a — **dedication** *n* **1** DEVOTION :
dedicación *f* **2** INSCRIPTION : dedicatoria *f*
deduce *vt* **-duced; -ducing** :
deducir — **deduct** *vt* : deducir
— **deduction** *n* : deducción *f*
deed *n* : acción *f*, hecho *m*
deem *vt* : considerar, juzgar
deep *adj* : hondo, profundo —
deep *adv* **1** DEEPLY : profundamente
2 deep down : en el fondo **3 dig deep**
: cavar hondo — **deepen** *vt* : ahondar
— *vi* : hacerse más profundo —
deeply *adv* : hondo, profundamente
deer *ns & pl* : ciervo *m*
deface *vt* **-faced; -facing** : desfigurar
default *n* **by default** : en rebeldía —
default *vi* **1 default on** : no pagar (una
deuda) **2** : no presentarse (en deportes)
defeat *vt* **1** BEAT : vencer, derrotar **2**
FRUSTRATE : frustrar — **defeat** *n* : derrota *f*
defect *n* : defecto *m* — **defect** *vi* :
desertar — **defective** *adj* : defectuoso
defend *vt* : defender — **defendant** *n*
: acusado *m*, -da *f* — **defense** *or* Brit
defence *n* : defensa *f* — **defenseless**
or Brit **defenceless** *adj* : indefenso —
defensive *adj* : defensivo — **defend** *n*
on the defend : a la defensiva
defer *v* **-ferred; -ferring** *vt* : diferir,
aplazar — *vi* **defer to** : deferir a
— **deference** *n* : deferencia *f* —
deferential *adj* : deferente
defiance *n* **1** : desafío *m* **2**
in defiance of : a despecho de
— **defiant** *adj* : desafiante
deficiency *n*, *pl* **-cies** : deficiencia *f*
— **deficient** *adj* : deficiente
deficit *n* : déficit *m*
defile *vt* **-filed; -filing 1** DIRTY :
ensuciar **2** DESECRATE : profanar
define *vt* **-fined; -fining** : definir

— **definite** *adj* **1** : definido **2** CERTAIN : seguro, incuestionable — **definition** *n* : definición *f* — **definitive** *adj* : definitivo

deflate *v* **-flated; -flating** *vt* : desinflar (una llanta, etc.) — *vi* : desinflarse

deflect *vt* : desviar — *vi* : desviarse

deform *vt* : deformar — **deformity** *n, pl* **-ties** : deformidad *f*

defraud *vt* : defraudar

defrost *vt* : descongelar — *vi* : descongelarse

deft *adj* : hábil, diestro

defy *vt* **-fied; -fying 1** CHALLENGE : desafiar **2** RESIST : resistir

degenerate *vi* : degenerar — **degenerate** *adj* : degenerado

degrade *vt* **-graded; -grading** : degradar — **degrading** *adj* : degradante

degree *n* **1** : grado *m* **2** *or* **academic degree** : título *m*

dehydrate *vt* **-drated; -drating** : deshidratar

deign *vi* **deign to** : dignarse (a)

deity *n, pl* **-ties** : deidad *f*

dejected *adj* : abatido

— **dejection** *n* : abatimiento *m*

delay *n* : retraso *m* — **delay** *vt* **1** POSTPONE : aplazar **2** HOLD UP : retrasar — *vi* : demorar

delectable *adj* : delicioso

delegate *n* : delegado *m*, -da *f* — **delegate** *v* **-gated; -gating** : delegar — **delegation** *n* : delegación *f*

delete *vt* **-leted; -leting** : borrar

deliberate *v* **-ated; -ating** *vt* : deliberar sobre — *vi* : deliberar — **deliberate** *adj* : deliberado — **deliberately** *adv* INTENTIONALLY : a propósito — **deliberation** *n* : deliberación *f*

delicacy *n, pl* **-cies 1** : delicadeza *f* **2** FOOD : manjar *m*, exquisitez *f* — **delicate** *adj* : delicado

▸ **delicatessen** *n* : charcutería *f*

delicious *adj* : delicioso

delight *n* : placer *m*, deleite *m* — **delight** *vt* : deleitar, encantar — *vi* **delight in** : deleitarse con — **delightful** *adj* : delicioso, encantador

delinquent *adj* : delincuente — **delinquent** *n* : delincuente *mf*

delirious *adj* : delirante — **delirium** *n* : delirio *m*

deliver *vt* **1** DISTRIBUTE : entregar, repartir **2** FREE : liberar **3** : asistir en el parto de (un niño) **4** : pronunciar (un discurso, etc.) **5** DEAL : asestar (un golpe, etc.) — **delivery** *n, pl* **-eries 1** DISTRIBUTION : entrega *f*, reparto *m* **2** LIBERATION : liberación *f* **3** CHILDBIRTH : parto *m*, alumbramiento *m*

delude *vt* **-luded; -luding 1** : engañar **2 delude oneself** : engañarse

deluge *n* : diluvio *m*

delusion *n* : ilusión *f*

deluxe *adj* : de lujo

delve *vi* **delved; delving 1** : escarbar **2 delve into** PROBE : investigar

demand *n* **1** REQUEST : petición *f* **2** CLAIM : reclamación *f*, exigencia *f* **3** → **supply** — **demand** *vt* : exigir — **demanding** *adj* : exigente

demean *vt* **demean oneself** : rebajarse

demeanor *n* : comportamiento *m*

demented *adj* : demente, loco

demise *n* : fallecimiento *m*

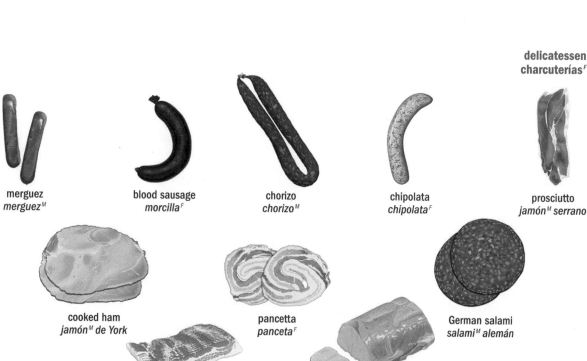

delicatessen
charcuterías[F]

merguez
merguez[M]

blood sausage
morcilla[F]

chorizo
chorizo[M]

chipolata
chipolata[F]

prosciutto
jamón[M] *serrano*

cooked ham
jamón[M] *de York*

pancetta
panceta[F]

German salami
salami[M] *alemán*

bacon
bacón[M] *americano*

Canadian bacon
bacón[M] *canadiense*

democracy *n, pl* **-cies** : democracia *f*
— **democrat** *n* : demócrata *mf* —
democratic *adj* : democrático

demolish *vt* : demoler —
demolition *n* : demolición *f*

demon *n* : demonio *m*

demonstrate *v* **-strated; -strating** *vt* :
demostrar — *vi* RALLY : manifestarse —
demonstration *n* **1** : demostración *f* **2**
RALLY : manifestación *f*

demoralize *vt* **-ized;**
-izing : desmoralizar

demote *vt* **-moted; -moting**
: bajar de categoría

demure *adj* : recatado

den *n* LAIR : guarida *f*

denial *n* **1** : negación *f*, rechazo *m* **2**
REFUSAL : denegación *f*

denim *n* : tela *f* vaquera, mezclilla *f Lat*

denomination *n* **1** : confesión *f*
(religiosa) **2** : valor *m* (de una moneda)

denounce *vt* **-nounced;**
-nouncing : denunciar

dense *adj* **denser; -est 1** THICK
: denso **2** STUPID : estúpido —
density *n, pl* **-ties** : densidad *f*

dent *vt* : abollar — **dent** *n* : abolladura *f*

dental *adj* : dental — **dental floss** *n* :
hilo *m* dental — **dentist** *n* : dentista *mf*
— **dentures** *npl* : dentadura *f* postiza

deny *vt* **-nied; -nying 1** :
negar **2** REFUSE : denegar

deodorant *n* : desodorante *m*

depart *vi* **1** : salir **2 depart from**
: apartarse de (la verdad, etc.)

department *n* : sección *f* (de una
tienda, etc.), departamento *m* (de
una empresa, etc.), ministerio *m*
(del gobierno) — **department**
store *n* : grandes almacenes *mpl*

departure *n* **1** : salida *f* **2**
DEVIATION : desviación *f*

depend *vi* **1 depend on** : depender
de **2 depend on someone** : contar con
algn **3 that depends** : eso depende —
dependable *adj* : digno de confianza
— **dependence** *n* : dependencia *f*
— **dependent** *adj* : dependiente

depict *vt* **1** PORTRAY : representar
2 DESCRIBE : describir

deplete *vt* **-pleted; -pleting**
: agotar, reducir

deplore *vt* **-plored; -ploring** : deplorar,
lamentar — **deplorable** *adj* : lamentable

deploy *vt* : desplegar

deport *vt* : deportar, expulsar (de un
país) — **deportation** *n* : deportación *f*

depose *vt* **-posed; -posing** : deponer

deposit *vt* **-ited; -iting** : depositar
— **deposit** *n* **1** : depósito *m* **2**
DOWN PAYMENT : entrega *f* inicial

depot *n* **1** WAREHOUSE : almacén *m*,
depósito *m* **2** STATION : terminal *mf*

depreciate *vi* **-ated; -ating** : depreciarse
— **depreciation** *n* : depreciación *f*

depress *vt* **1** : deprimir **2** PRESS :
apretar — **depressed** *adj* : abatido,
deprimido — **depressing** *adj* : deprimente
— **depression** *n* : depresión *f*

deprive *vt* **-prived; -priving** : privar

depth *n, pl* **depths 1** : profundidad *f* **2**
in the depths of night : en lo
más profundo de la noche

deputy *n, pl* **-ties** : suplente *mf;*
sustituto *m*, -ta *f*

digestive system
aparato^M **digestivo**

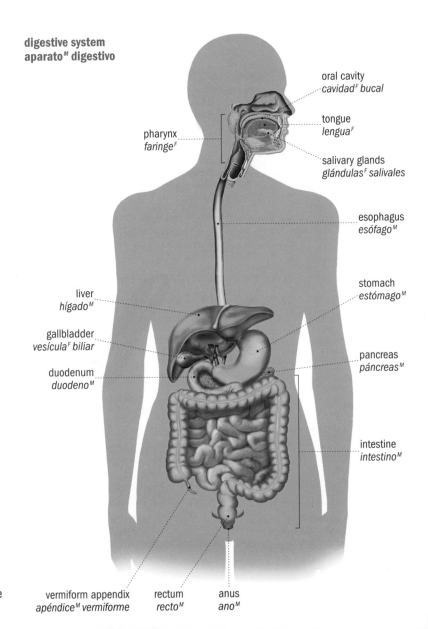

digestive system
aparato^M digestivo

oral cavity
cavidad^F bucal

tongue
lengua^F

salivary glands
glándulas^F salivales

pharynx
faringe^F

esophagus
esófago^M

stomach
estómago^M

liver
hígado^M

gallbladder
vesícula^F biliar

duodenum
duodeno^M

pancreas
páncreas^M

intestine
intestino^M

vermiform appendix
apéndice^M vermiforme

rectum
recto^M

anus
ano^M

derail *vt* : hacer descarrilar
deranged *adj* : trastornado
derelict *adj* : abandonado
deride *vt* **-rided; -riding** : burlarse de — **derision** *n* : mofa *f*
derive *vi* **-rived; -riving** : derivar — **derivation** *n* : derivación *f*
derogatory *adj* : despectivo
descend *v* : descender, bajar — **descendant** *n* : descendiente *mf* — **descent** *n* **1** : descenso *m* **2** LINEAGE : descendencia *f*
describe *vt* **-scribed; -scribing** : describir — **description** *n* : descripción *f* — **descriptive** *adj* : descriptivo
desecrate *vt* **-crated; -crating** : profanar
desert *n* : desierto *m* — **desert** *adj* **desert island** : isla *f* desierta — **desert** *vt* : abandonar — *vi* : desertar — **deserter** *n* : desertor *m*, -tora *f*
deserve *vt* **-served; -serving** : merecer
design *vt* **1** DEVISE : diseñar **2** PLAN : proyectar — **design** *n* **1** : diseño *m* **2** PLAN : plan *m*, proyecto *m*
designate *vt* **-nated; -nating** : nombrar, designar
designer *n* : diseñador *m*, -dora *f*
desire *vt* **-sired; -siring** : desear — **desire** *n* : deseo *m* — **desirable** *adj* : deseable
desk *n* : escritorio *m*, pupitre *m* (en la escuela)
desolate *adj* : desolado
despair *vi* : desesperar — **despair** *n* : desesperación *f*
desperate *adj* : desesperado — **desperation** *n* : desesperación *f*
despise *vt* **-spised; -spising** : despreciar — **despicable** *adj* : despreciable
despite *prep* : a pesar de
despondent *adj* : desanimado
dessert *n* : postre *m*
destination *n* : destino *m* — **destined** *adj* **1** : destinado **2** **destined for** : con destino a — **destiny** *n*, *pl* **-nies** : destino *m*
destitute *adj* : indigente
destroy *vt* : destruir — **destruction** *n* : destrucción *f* — **destructive** *adj* : destructivo
detach *vt* : separar — **detached** *adj* **1** : separado **2** IMPARTIAL : objetivo
detail *n* **1** : detalle *m* **2** **go into detail** : entrar en detalles — **detail** *vt* : detallar — **detailed** *adj* : detallado

detain *vt* **1** : detener (un prisionero) **2** DELAY : entretener
detect *vt* : detectar — **detection** *n* : detección *f*, descubrimiento *m* — **detective** *n* : detective *mf*
detention *n* : detención *m*
deter *vt* **-terred; -terring** : disuadir
detergent *n* : detergente *m*
deteriorate *vi* **-rated; -rating** : deteriorarse — **deterioration** *n* : deterioro *m*
determine *vt* **-mined; -mining** : determinar — **determined** *adj* RESOLUTE : decidido — **determination** *n* : determinación *f*
deterrent *n* : medida *f* disuasiva
detest *vt* : detestar — **detestable** *adj* : odioso
detonate *v* **-nated; -nating** *vt* : hacer detonar — *vi* EXPLODE : detonar, estallar — **detonation** *n* : detonación *f*
detour *n* **1** : desviación *f* **2** **make a detour** : dar un rodeo — **detour** *vi* : desviarse
detract *vi* **detract from** : aminorar, restar importancia a
detrimental *adj* : perjudicial
devalue *vt* **-ued; -uing** : devaluar
devastate *vt* **-tated; -tating** : devastar — **devastating** *adj* : devastador — **devastation** *n* : devastación *f*
develop *vt* **1** : desarrollar **2** **develop an illness** : contraer una enfermedad — *vi* **1** GROW : desarrollarse **2** HAPPEN : aparecer — **development** *n* : desarrollo *m*
deviate *v* **-ated; -ating** *vi* : desviarse — **deviation** *n* : desviación *f*
device *n* : dispositivo *m*, mecanismo *m*
devil *n* : diablo *m*, demonio *m* — **devilish** *adj* : diabólico
devious *adj* **1** CRAFTY : taimado **2** WINDING : tortuoso
devise *vt* **-vised; -vising** : idear, concebir
devoid *adj* **devoid of** : desprovisto de
devote *vt* **-voted; -voting** : consagrar, dedicar — **devoted** *adj* : leal — **devotee** *n* : devoto *m*, -ta *f* — **devotion** *n* **1** : devoción *f*, dedicación *f* **2** : oración *f* (en religión)
devour *vt* : devorar
devout *adj* : devoto
dew *n* : rocío *m*
dexterity *n*, *pl* **-ties** : destreza *f*
diabetes *n* : diabetes *f* — **diabetic** *adj* : diabético — **diabetic** *n* : diabético *m*, -ca *f*

diabolic *or* diabolical *adj* : diabólico
diagnosis *n*, *pl* **-noses** : diagnóstico *m* — **diagnose** *vt* **-nosed; -nosing** : diagnosticar — **diagnostic** *adj* : diagnóstico
diagonal *adj* : diagonal, en diagonal — **diagonal** *n* : diagonal *f*
diagram *n* : diagrama *m*
dial *n* : esfera *f* (de un reloj), dial *m* (de un radio, etc.) — **dial** *v* **dialed** *or* **dialled; dialing** *or* **dialling** : marcar
dialect *n* : dialecto *m*
dialogue *n* : diálogo *m*
diameter *n* : diámetro *m*
diamond *n* **1** : diamante *m* **2** : rombo *m* (forma) **3** *or* **baseball diamond** : cuadro *m*, diamante *m*
diaper *n* : pañal *m*
diaphragm *n* : diafragma *m*
diarrhea *n* : diarrea *f*
diary *n*, *pl* **-ries** : diario *m*
dice *ns* & *pl* : dados *mpl* (juego)
dictate *vt* **-tated; -tating** : dictar — **dictation** *n* : dictado *m* — **dictator** *n* : dictador *m*, -dora *f* — **dictatorship** *n* : dictadura *f*
dictionary *n*, *pl* **-naries** : diccionario *m*
did → **do**
die[1] *vi* **died; dying** **1** : morir **2** **die down** : amainar, disminuir **3** **die out** : extinguirse **4** **be dying for** : morirse por
die[2] *n* **1** *pl* **dice** : dado *m* (para jugar) **2** *pl* **dies** MOLD : molde *m*
diesel *n* : diesel *m*
diet *n* **1** FOOD : alimentación *f* **2** **go on a diet** : ponerse a régimen — **diet** *vi* : estar a régimen
differ *vi* **-ferred; -ferring** **1** : diferir, ser distinto **2** DISAGREE : no estar de acuerdo — **difference** *n* : diferencia *f* — **different** *adj* : distinto, diferente — **differentiate** *v* **-ated; -ating** *vt* : diferenciar — *vi* : distinguir — **differently** *adv* : de otra manera
difficult *adj* : difícil — **difficulty** *n*, *pl* **-ties** : dificultad *f*
diffident *adj* : tímido, que falta confianza
dig *v* **dug; digging** *vt* **1** : cavar **2** **dig up** : desenterrar — *vi* : cavar — **dig** *n* **1** GIBE : pulla *f* **2** EXCAVATION : excavación *f*
digest *n* : resumen *m* — **digest** *vt* **1** : digerir **2** SUMMARIZE : resumir — **digestible** *adj* : digerible — **digestion** *n* : digestión *f* — **digestive** *adj* : digestivo
digit *n* **1** NUMERAL : dígito *m*, número *m* **2**

dinosaurs
dinosaurios ^M

diplodocus
diplodocus ^M

stegosaurus
stegosaurus ^M

brachiosaurus
brachiosaurus ^M

FINGER TOE : **dedo** *m* — **digital** *adj* : digital
dignity *n, pl* **-ties** : dignidad *f* —
  dignified *adj* : digno, decoroso
digress *vi* : desviarse del tema,
  divagar — **digression** *n* : digresión *f*
dike *n* : dique *m*
dilapidated *adj* : ruinoso
dilate *v* **-lated; -lating** *vt* :
  dilatar — *vi* : dilatarse
dilemma *n* : dilema *m*
diligence *n* : diligencia *f* —
  diligent *adj* : diligente
dilute *vt* **-luted; -luting** : diluir
dim *v* **dimmed; dimming** *vt* :
  atenuar — *vi* : irse atenuando

— **dim** *adj* **dimmer; dimmest 1**
  DARK : oscuro **2** FAINT : débil, tenue
dime *n* : moneda *f* de diez centavos
dimension *n* : dimensión *f*
diminish *v* : disminuir
diminutive *adj* : diminuto
dimple *n* : hoyuelo *m*
din *n* : estrépito *m*
dine *vi* **dined; dining** : cenar —
  diner *n* **1** : comensal *mf* (persona)
  2 : cafetería *f* (restaurante)
dingy *adj* **-gier; -est** : sucio, deslucido
dinner *n* : cena *f*, comida *f*
▸ **dinosaur** *n* : dinosaurio *m*
dint *n* **by dint of** : a fuerza de

dip *v* **dipped; dipping** *vt* : mojar
  — *vi* : bajar, descender — **dip** *n* **1**
  DROP : descenso *m*, caída *f* **2** SWIM
  : chapuzón *m* **3** SAUCE : salsa *f*
diploma *n, pl* **-mas** : diploma *m*
diplomacy *n* : diplomacia *f* —
  diplomat *n* : diplomático *m*, -ca *f*
  — **diplomatic** *adj* : diplomático
dire *adj* **direr; direst 1** : grave,
  terrible **2** EXTREME : extremo
direct *vt* **1** : dirigir **2** ORDER : mandar
  — **direct** *adj* **1** STRAIGHT : directo
  2 FRANK : franco — **direct** *adv* :
  directamente — **direct current** *n* :
  corriente *f* continua — **direction** *n* **1**

triceratops
triceratops M

ankylosaurus
ankylosaurus M

parasauroloph
parasaurolophus M

tyrannosaurus
tyrannosaurus M

: dirección *f* **2 ask directions** : pedir indicaciones — **directly** *adv* **1** STRAIGHT : directamente **2** IMMEDIATELY : en seguida — **director** *n* **1** : director *m*, -tora *f* **2 board of directors** : directorio *m* — **directory** *n, pl* **-ries** : guía *f* (telefónica)
dirt *n* **1** : suciedad *f* **2** SOIL : tierra *f* — **dirty** *adj* **dirtier; -est 1** : sucio **2** INDECENT : obsceno, cochino *fam*
disability *n, pl* **-ties** : minusvalía *f*, invalidez *f* — **disable** *vt* **-abled; -abling** : incapacitar — **disabled** *adj* : minusválido
disadvantage *n* : desventaja *f*
disagree *vi* **1** : no estar de acuerdo (con algn) **2** CONFLICT : no coincidir

— **disagreeable** *adj* : desagradable — **disagreement** *n* **1** : desacuerdo *m* **2** ARGUMENT : discusión *f*
disappear *vi* : desaparecer — **disappearance** *n* : desaparición *f*
disappoint *vt* : decepcionar, desilusionar — **disappointment** *n* : decepción *f*, desilusión *f*
disapprove *vi* **-proved; -proving disapprove of** : desaprobar — **disapproval** *n* : desaprobación *f*
disarm *vt* : desarmar — **disarmament** *n* : desarme *m*
disarray *n* : desorden *m*
disaster *n* : desastre *m*

— **disastrous** *adj* : desastroso
disbelief *n* : incredulidad *f*
disc → **disk**
discard *vt* : desechar, deshacerse de
discern *vt* : percibir, discernir — **discernible** *adj* : perceptible
discharge *vt* **-charged; -charging 1** UNLOAD : descargar **2** RELEASE : liberar, poner en libertad **3** DISMISS : despedir **4** CARRY OUT : cumplir con (una obligación) — **discharge** *n* **1** : descarga *f* (de electricidad), emisión *f* (de humo, etc.) **2** DISMISSAL : despido *m* **3** RELEASE : alta *f* (de un paciente), puesta *f* en libertad (de un preso) **4** : supuración *f* (en medicina)

disciple *n* : discípulo *m*, -la *f*
discipline *n* **1** : disciplina *f* **2** PUNISHMENT : castigo *m* — **discipline** *vt* -plined; -plining **1** CONTROL : disciplinar **2** PUNISH : castigar
disclaim *vt* : negar
disclose *vt* -closed; -closing : revelar — **disclosure** *n* : revelación *f*
discomfort *n* **1** : incomodidad *f* **2** PAIN : malestar *m* **3** UNEASINESS : inquietud *f*
disconcert *vt* : desconcertar
disconnect *vt* : desconectar
disconsolate *adj* : desconsolado
discontented *adj* : descontento
discontinue *vt* -ued; -uing : suspender, descontinuar
discount *n* : descuento *m*, rebaja *f* — **discount** *vt* **1** : descontar (precios) **2** DISREGARD : descartar
discourage *vt* -aged; -aging : desalentar, desanimar — **discouragement** *n* : desánimo *m*, desaliento *m*
discover *vt* : descubrir — **discovery** *n*, *pl* -ries : descubrimiento *m*
discredit *vt* : desacreditar — **discredit** *n* : descrédito *m*
discreet *adj* : discreto
discrepancy *n*, *pl* -cies : discrepancia *f*
discretion *n* : discreción *f*
discriminate *vi* -nated; -nating **1** **discriminate against** : discriminar **2** **discriminate between** : distinguir entre — **discrimination** *n* **1** PREJUDICE : discriminación *f* **2** DISCERNMENT : discernimiento *m*
discuss *vt* : hablar de, discutir — **discussion** *n* : discusión *f*
disdain *n* : desdén *m* — **disdain** *vt* : desdeñar
disease *n* : enfermedad *f* — **diseased** *adj* : enfermo
disembark *vi* : desembarcar
disengage *vt* -gaged; -gaging **1** RELEASE : soltar **2** **disengage the clutch** : desembragar
disentangle *vt* -gled; -gling : desenredar
disfavor *n* : desaprobación *f*
disfigure *vt* -ured; -uring : desfigurar
disgrace *vt* -graced; -gracing : deshonrar — **disgrace** *n* **1** DISHONOR : deshonra *f* **2** SHAME : vergüenza *f* — **disgraceful** *adj* : vergonzoso, deshonroso
disgruntled *adj* : descontento
disguise *vt* -guised; -guising :

disfrazar — **disguise** *n* : disfraz *m*
disgust *n* : asco *m*, repugnancia *f* — **disgust** *vt* : asquear — **disgusting** *adj* : asqueroso
dish *n* **1** : plato *m* **2** *or* **serving dish** : fuente *f* **3** **wash the dishes** : lavar los platos — **dish** *vt* *or* **dish up** : servir — **dishcloth** *n* : paño *m* de cocina (para secar), trapo *m* de fregar (para lavar)
dishearten *vt* : desanimar
disheveled *or* **dishevelled** *adj* : desaliñado, despeinado (dícese del pelo)
dishonest *adj* : deshonesto — **dishonesty** *n*, *pl* -ties : falta *f* de honradez
dishonor *n* : deshonra *f* — **dishonor** *vt* : deshonrar — **dishonorable** *adj* : deshonroso
dishwasher *n* : lavaplatos *m*, lavavajillas *m*
disillusion *vt* : desilusionar — **disillusionment** *n* : desilusión *f*
disinfect *vt* : desinfectar — **disinfectant** *n* : desinfectante *m*
disintegrate *vi* -grated; -grating : desintegrarse
disinterested *adj* : desinteresado
disk *or* disc *n* : disco *m*
dislike *n* : aversión *f*, antipatía *f* — **dislike** *vt* -liked; -liking **1** : tener aversión a **2** **I dislike dancing** : no me gusta bailar
dislocate *vt* -cated; -cating : dislocar
dislodge *vt* -lodged; -lodging : sacar, desalojar
disloyal *adj* : desleal — **disloyalty** *n*, *pl* -ties : deslealtad *f*
dismal *adj* : sombrío, deprimente
dismantle *vt* -tled; -tling : desmontar, desarmar
dismay *vt* : consternar — **dismay** *n* : consternación *f*
dismiss *vt* **1** DISCHARGE : despedir, destituir **2** REJECT : descartar, rechazar — **dismissal** *n* **1** : despido *m* (de un empleado), destitución *f* (de un funcionario) **2** REJECTION : rechazo *m*
dismount *vi* : desmontar
disobey *v* : desobedecer — **disobedience** *n* : desobediencia *f* — **disobedient** *adj* : desobediente
disorder *n* **1** : desorden *m* **2** AILMENT : afección *f*, problema *m* — **disorderly** *adj* : desordenado
disorganize *vt* -nized; -nizing : desorganizar
disown *vt* : renegar de

dispassionate *adj* : desapasionado
dispatch *vt* : despachar, enviar
dispel *vt* -pelled; -pelling : disipar
dispensation *n* EXEMPTION : exención *m*, dispensa *f*
dispense *v* -pensed; -pensing *vt* : repartir, distribuir — *vi* **dispense with** : prescindir de
disperse *v* -persed; -persing *vt* : dispersar — *vi* : dispersarse
displace *vt* -placed; -placing **1** : desplazar **2** REPLACE : reemplazar
display *vt* **1** EXHIBIT : exponer, exhibir **2** **display anger** : manifestar la ira — **display** *n* : muestra *f*, exposición *f*
displease *vt* -pleased; -pleasing : desagradar — **displeasure** *n* : desagrado *m*
dispose *v* -posed; -posing *vt* : disponer — *vi* **dispose of** : deshacerse de — **disposable** *adj* : desechable — **disposal** *n* **1** REMOVAL : eliminación *f* **2** **have at one's disposal** : tener a su disposición — **disposition** *n* **1** ARRANGEMENT : disposición *f* **2** TEMPERAMENT : temperamento *m*, carácter *m*
disprove *vt* -proved; -proving : refutar
dispute *v* -puted; -putting *vt* QUESTION : cuestionar — *vi* ARGUE : discutir — **dispute** *n* : disputa *f*, conflicto *m*
disqualification *n* : descalificación *f* — **disqualify** *vt* -fied; -fying : descalificar
disregard *vt* : ignorar, hacer caso omiso de — **disregard** *n* : indiferencia *f*
disrepair *n* : mal estado *m*
disreputable *adj* : de mala fama
disrespect *n* : falta *f* de respeto — **disrespectful** *adj* : irrespetuoso
disrupt *vt* : trastornar, perturbar — **disruption** *n* : trastorno *m*
dissatisfaction *n* : descontento *m* — **dissatisfied** *adj* : descontento
dissect *vt* : disecar
disseminate *vt* -nated; -nating : diseminar, difundir
dissent *vi* : disentir — **dissent** *n* : disentimiento *m*
dissertation THESIS : tesis *f*
disservice *n* **do a disservice to** : no hacer justicia a
dissident *n* : disidente *mf*
dissimilar *adj* : distinto
dissipate *vt* -pated; -pating **1** DISPEL : disipar **2** SQUANDER : desperdiciar

scuba diver
buceador^M

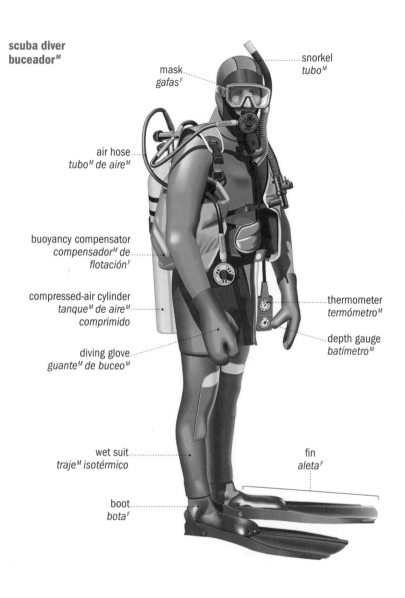

snorkel
tubo^M

mask
gafas^F

air hose
tubo^M *de aire*^M

buoyancy compensator
compensador^M *de*
flotación^F

compressed-air cylinder
tanque^M *de aire*^M
comprimido

diving glove
guante^M *de buceo*^M

thermometer
termómetro^M

depth gauge
batímetro^M

wet suit
traje^M *isotérmico*

fin
aleta^F

boot
bota^F

---

zona *f*, barrio *m* (de una ciudad)
2 : distrito *m* (zona política)
distrust *n* : desconfianza *f* —
distrust *vt* : desconfiar de
disturb *vt* **1** BOTHER : molestar, perturbar
2 WORRY : inquietar — **disturbance** *n* **1**
COMMOTION : alboroto *m*, disturbio *m* **2**
INTERRUPTION : interrupción *f*
disuse *n* **fall into disuse** : caer en desuso
ditch *n* : zanja *f*, cuneta *f* — **ditch** *vt*
DISCARD : deshacerse de, botar
ditto *n*, *pl* **-tos 1** : ídem *m* **2**
ditto marks : comillas *fpl*
dive *vi* **dived** *or* **dove; dived; diving 1** :
zambullirse, tirarse al agua **2** DESCEND :
bajar en picada (dícese de un avión, etc.)
— **dive** *n* **1** : zambullida *f*, clavado *m*,
Lat **2** DESCENT : descenso *m* en picada
— **diver** *n* : saltador *m*, -dora *f*
diverge *vi* **-verged; -verging** : divergir
diverse *adj* : diverso — **diversify** *v* **-fied;**
-fying *vt* : diversificar — *vi* : diversificarse
diversion *n* **1** : desviación *f* **2**
AMUSEMENT : diversión *f*, distracción *f*
diversity *n*, *pl* **-ties** : diversidad *f*
divert *vt* **1** : desviar **2** DISTRACT
: distraer **3** AMUSE : divertir
divide *v* **-vided; -viding** *vt* :
dividir — *vi* : dividirse
dividend *n* : dividendo *m*
divine *adj* **-viner; -est** : divino —
divinity *n*, *pl* **-ties** : divinidad *f*
division *n* : división *f*
divorce *n* : divorcio *m* — **divorce** *v*
-vorced; -vorcing *vt* : divorciar — *vi* :
divorciarse — **divorcée** *n* : divorciada *f*
divulge *vt* **-vulged; -vulging**
: revelar, divulgar
dizzy *adj* **dizzier; -est 1** : mareado **2 a**
dizzy speed : una velocidad vertiginosa
— **dizziness** *n* : mareo *m*, vértigo *m*
DNA *n* : AND *m*
do *v* **did; done; doing; does** *vt* **1** :
hacer **2** PREPARE : preparar — *vi* **1**
BEHAVE : hacer **2** FARE : estar, ir, andar
3 SUFFICE : ser suficiente **4 do away**
with : abolir, eliminar **5 how are you**
doing? : ¿cómo estás? — *v aux* **1**
(*used in interrogative sentences*) **do**
you know her? : ¿la conoces? **2** (*used*
in negative statements) **I don't know**
: yo no se **3** (*used as a substitute verb*
to avoid repetition) **do you speak**
English? yes, I do : ¿habla inglés? sí
dock *n* : muelle *m* — **dock** *vt* :

---

dissolve *v* **-solved; -solving** *vt*
: disolver — *vi* : disolverse
dissuade *vt* **-suaded; -suading** : disuadir
distance *n* **1** : distancia *f* **2**
in the distance : a lo lejos
— **distant** *adj* : distante
distaste *n* : desagrado *m* —
distasteful *adj* : desagradable
distend *vt* : dilatar — *vi* : dilatarse
distill *or Brit* **distil** *vt* **-tilled;**
-tilling : destilar
distinct *adj* **1** DIFFERENT : distinto
2 CLEAR : claro — **distinction** *n* :
distinción *f* — **distinctive** *adj* : distintivo

distinguish *vt* : distinguir —
distinguished *adj* : distinguido
distort *vt* : deformar, distorsionar
— **distortion** *n* : deformación *f*
distract *vt* : distraer —
distraction *n* : distracción *f*
distraught *adj* : muy afligido
distress *n* **1** : angustia *f*, aflicción *f* **2**
in distress : en peligro — **distress** *vt*
: afligir — **distressing** *adj* : penoso
distribute *vt* **-uted; -uting** : distribuir,
repartir — **distribution** *n* : distribución *f*
— **distributor** *n* : distribuidor *m*, -dora *f*
district *n* **1** REGION : región *f*,

descontar dinero de (un sueldo)
— *vi* ANCHOR : fondear, atracar
doctor *n* **1** : doctor *m*, -tora *f*
(en derecho, etc.) **2** PHYSICIAN :
médico *m*, -ca; doctor *m*, -tora *f* —
doctor *vt* ALTER : alterar, falsificar
doctrine *n* : doctrina *f*
document *n* : documento *m* —
document *vt* : documentar —
documentary *n*, *pl* **-ries** : documental *m*
dodge *n* : artimaña *f*, truco *m* —
dodge *v* **dodged; dodging** *vt* : esquivar,
eludir — *vi* : echarse a un lado
doe *n*, *pl* **does** *or* **doe** : gama *f*, cierva *f*
does → **do**
dog *n* : perro *m*, -rra *f* — **dog** *vt* **dogged;**
dogging : perseguir — **dogged** *adj* : tenaz
dogma *n* : dogma *m* —
dogmatic *adj* : dogmático
doily *n*, *pl* **-lies** : tapete *m*
doings *npl* : actividades *fpl*
doldrums *npl* **be in the**
doldrums : estar abatido

dole *n* : subsidio *m* de desempleo —
dole *vt* **doled; doling** *or* **dole out** : repartir
doleful *adj* : triste, lúgubre
doll *n* : muñeco *m*, -ca *f*
dollar *n* : dólar *m*
dolphin *n* : delfín *m*
domain *n* **1** TERRITORY : dominio *m* **2**
FIELD : campo *m*, esfera *f*
dome *n* : cúpula *f*
domestic *adj* **1** : doméstico **2**
INTERNAL : nacional — **domestic** *n*
SERVANT : empleado *m* doméstico,
empleada *f* doméstica — **domesticate** *vt*
-cated; -cating : domesticar
domination *n* : dominación *f*
— **dominant** *adj* : dominante —
dominate *v* **-nated; -nating** : dominar
— **domineer** *vi* : dominar, tiranizar
dominos *n* : dominó *m* (juego)
donate *vt* **-nated; -nating** : donar, hacer
un donativo de — **donation** *n* : donativo *m*
done → **do** — **done** *adj* **1** FINISHED :
terminado, hecho **2** COOKED : cocido

donkey *n*, *pl* **-keys** : burro *m*
donor *n* : donante *mf*
don't (*contraction of* **do not**) → **do**
doodle *v* **-dled; -dling** : garabatear
— **doodle** *n* : garabato *m*
doom *n* : perdición *f*, fatalidad *f*
— **doom** *vt* : condenar
door *n* **1** : puerta *f* **2** ENTRANCE :
entrada *f* — **doorbell** *n* : timbre *m* —
doorknob *n* : pomo *m* — **doorman** *n*,
pl **-men** : portero *m* — **doormat** *n* :
felpudo *m* — **doorstep** *n* : umbral *m*
— **doorway** *n* : entrada *f*, portal *m*
dope *n* **1** DRUG : droga *f* **2** IDIOT : idiota *mf*
— **dope** *vt* **doped; doping** : drogar
dormant *adj* : inactivo, latente
dormitory *n*, *pl* **-ries** : dormitorio *m*
dose *n* : dosis *f* — **dosage** *n* : dosis *f*
dot *n* **1** : punto *m* **2 on the dot** : en punto
dote *vi* **doted; doting dote on** : adorar
double *adj* : doble — **double** *v* **-bled;**
-bling *vt* : doblar — *vi* : doblarse —
double *adv* : (el) doble — **double** *n*
: doble *mf* — **double bass** *n* :
contrabajo *m* — **double–cross** *vt* :
traicionar — **doubly** *adv* : doblemente
doubt *vt* **1** : dudar **2** DISTRUST :
desconfiar de, dudar de — **doubt** *n*
: duda *f* — **doubtful** *adj* : dudoso
— **doubtless** *adv* : sin duda
dough *n* : masa *f* — **doughnut** *n*
: rosquilla *f*, dona *f Lat*
douse *vt* **doused; dousing** **1** DRENCH :
empapar, mojar **2** EXTINGUISH : apagar
dove[1] → **dive**
dove[2] *n* : paloma *f*
dowdy *adj* **dowdier; -est** : poco elegante
down *adv* **1** DOWNWARD : hacia abajo
2 come/go down : bajar **3 down here**
: aquí abajo **4 fall down** : caer **5 lie**
down : acostarse **6 sit down** : sentarse
— **down** *prep* **1** ALONG : a lo largo de **2**
THROUGH : a través de **3 down the hill** :
cuesta abajo — **down** *adj* **1** DESCENDING
: de bajada **2** DOWNCAST : abatido —
down *n* : plumón *m* — **downcast** *adj*
: triste, abatido — **downfall** *n* : ruina *f*
— **downhearted** *adj* : desanimado
— **downhill** *adv & adj* : cuesta abajo
— **down payment** *n* : entrega *f* inicial
— **downpour** *n* : chaparrón *m* —
downright *adv* : absolutamente —
downright *adj* : absoluto, categórico —
downstairs *adv* : abajo — **downstairs** *adj*
: de abajo — **downstream** *adv* : río abajo

dresses and skirts
vestidos[M] **y faldas**[F]

shirtwaist dress
vestido[M] *camisero*

drop waist dress
vestido[M] *de talle*[M] *bajo*

sarong
falda[F] *sarong*[M]

sundress
vestido[M] *de tirantes*[M]

jumper
pichi[M]

kilt
falda[F] *escocesa*

dragonfly
libélula^F

— **down–to–earth** adj : realista — **downtown** n : centro m (de la ciudad) — **downtown** adv : al centro, en el centro — **downtown** adj : del centro — **downward** or downwards adv & adj : hacia abajo
dowry n, pl -ries : dote f
doze vi dozed; dozing : dormitar
dozen n, pl dozens or dozen : docena f
drab adj drabber; drabbest : monótono, apagado
draft n 1 : corriente f de aire 2 or rough draft : borrador m 3 : conscripción f (militar) 4 or draft beer : cerveza f de barril — **draft** vt 1 SKETCH : hacer el borrador de 2 CONSCRIPT : reclutar — **drafty** adj draftier; -est : con corrientes de aire
drag v dragged; dragging vt 1 : arrastrar 2 DREDGE : dragar — vi : arrastrar(se) — **drag** n 1 RESISTANCE : resistencia f (aerodinámica) 2 BORE : pesadez f, plomo m fam
dragon n : dragón m —
dragonfly n, pl -flies : libélula f
drain vt 1 EMPTY : vaciar, drenar 2 EXHAUST : agotar — vi 1 : escurrir(se) (se dice de los platos) 2 or drain away : desaparecer poco a poco — **drain** n 1 : desagüe m 2 SEWER : alcantarilla f 3 DEPLETION : agotamiento m — **drainage** n : drenaje m — **drainpipe** n : tubo m de desagüe
drama n : drama m — **dramatic** adj : dramático — **dramatist** n : dramaturgo m, -ga f — **dramatize** vt -tized; -tizing : dramatizar
drank → drink
drape vt draped; draping 1 COVER : cubrir (con tela) 2 HANG : drapear — **drapes** npl CURTAINS : cortinas fpl
drastic adj : drástico
draught → draft
draw v drew; drawn; drawing vt 1 PULL : tirar de 2 ATTRACT : atraer 3 SKETCH : dibujar, trazar 4 : sacar (una espada, etc.) 5 draw a conclusion : llegar a una conclusión 6 draw up DRAFT : redactar — vi 1 SKETCH : dibujar 2 draw near : acercarse — **draw** n 1 DRAWING : sorteo m 2 TIE : empate m 3 ATTRACTION : atracción f — **drawback** n : desventaja f — **drawer** n : gaveta f, cajón m (en un mueble) — **drawing** n 1 LOTTERY : sorteo m 2 SKETCH : dibujo m
drawl n : habla f lenta y con vocales prolongadas

dread vt : temer — **dread** n : pavor m, temor m — **dreadful** adj : espantoso, terrible
dream n : sueño m — **dream** v dreamed or dreamt; dreaming vi : soñar — vt 1 : soñar 2 dream up : idear — **dreamer** n : soñador m, -dora f — **dreamy** adj dreamier; -est : soñador
dreary adj -rier; -est : sombrío, deprimente
dredge vt dredged; dredging : dragar — **dredge** n : draga f
dregs npl : heces fpl
drench vt : empapar
dress vt 1 : vestir 2 : preparar (pollo o pescado), aliñar (ensalada) — vi 1 : vestirse 2 dress up : ponerse elegante — **dress** n 1 CLOTHING : ropa f 2 : vestido m (de mujer) — **dresser** n : cómoda f con espejo — **dressing** n 1 : aliño m (de ensalada), relleno m (de pollo) 2 BANDAGE : vendaje m — **dressmaker** n : modista mf — **dressy** adj dressier; -est : elegante
drew → draw
dribble vi -bled; -bling 1 DRIP : gotear 2 DROOL : babear 3 : driblar (en basquetbol) — **dribble** n 1 TRICKLE : goteo m, hilo m 2 DROOL : baba f
drier, driest → dry
drift n 1 MOVEMENT : movimiento m 2 HEAP : montón m (de arena, etc.), ventisquero m (de nieve) 3 MEANING : sentido m — **drift** vi 1 : ir a la deriva 2 ACCUMULATE : amontonarse
drill n 1 : taladro m 2 : ejercicio m (en educación), simulacro m (de incendio, etc.) — **drill** vt 1 : perforar, taladrar 2 TRAIN : instruir por repetición — vi drill for : perforar en busca de
drink v drank; drunk or drank; drinking : beber — **drink** n : bebida f
drip vi dripped; dripping : gotear — **drip** n 1 DROP : gota f 2 DRIPPING : goteo m
drive v drove; driven; driving vt 1 : manejar 2 IMPEL : impulsar 3 drive crazy : volver loco 4 drive someone to (do something) : llevar a algn a (hacer algo) — vi : manejar, conducir — **drive** n 1 : paseo m (en coche) 2 CAMPAIGN : campaña f 3 VIGOR : energía f 4 NEED : instinto m
drivel n : tonterías fpl
driver n : conductor m, -tora f; chofer m
driveway n : camino m de entrada
drizzle n : llovizna f — **drizzle** vi

-zled; -zling : lloviznar
drone n 1 BEE : zángano m 2 HUM : zumbido m — **drone** vi droned; droning 1 BUZZ : zumbar 2 or drone on : hablar con monotonía
drool vi : babear — **drool** n : baba f
droop vi : inclinarse (dícese de la cabeza), encorvarse (dícese de los escombros), marchitarse (dícese de las flores)
drop n 1 : gota f (de líquido) 2 DECLINE, FALL : caída f — **drop** v dropped; dropping vt 1 : dejar caer 2 LOWER : bajar 3 ABANDON : abandonar, dejar 4 drop off LEAVE : dejar — vi 1 FALL : caer(se) 2 DECREASE : bajar, descender 3 drop by or drop in : pasar
drought n : sequía f
drove → drive
droves n in droves : en manada
drown vt : ahogar — vi : ahogarse
drowsy adj drowsier; -est : somnoliento
drudgery n, pl -eries : trabajo m pesado
drug n 1 MEDICATION : medicamento m 2 NARCOTIC : droga f, estupefaciente m — **drug** vt drugged; drugging : drogar — **drugstore** n : farmacia f
drum n 1 : tambor m 2 or oil drum : bidón m (de petróleo) — **drum** v drummed; drumming vi : tocar el tambor — vt : tamborilear con (los dedos, etc.) — **drumstick** n 1 : palillo m (de tambor) 2 : muslo m (de pollo)
drunk → drink — ~ adj : borracho — ~ or drunkard n : borracho m, -cha f — **drunken** adj : borracho, ebrio
dry adj drier; driest : seco — **dry** v dried; drying vt : secar — vi : secarse — **dry–clean** vt : limpiar en seco — **dry cleaner** n : tintorería f (servicio) — **dry cleaning** n : limpieza f en seco — **dryer** n : secadora f — **dryness** n : sequedad f, aridez f
dual adj : doble
dub vt dubbed; dubbing 1 CALL :

downtown
centro^M **ciudad**^F

cathedral
catedral^F

convention center
palacio^M *de congresos*^M

office tower
torre^F *de oficinas*^F

square
plaza^F

park
parque^M

railroad station
estación^F *de ferrocarriles*^M

planetarium
planetario^M

street
calle^F

railroad track
vía^F *ferroviaria*

delivery ramp
rampa^F *de mercancías*^F

freeway
autopista^F

boulevard
bulevar^M

hotel
hotel^M

restaurant
restaurante^M

skyscraper
rascacielos^M

church
iglesia^F

high-rise apartment
torre^F *de apartamentos*^M

parking lot
área^F *de estacionamiento*^M

office building
edificio^M *de oficinas*^F

museum
museo^M

commercial premises
centro^M *comercial*

stadium
estadio^M

dunes
dunas^F

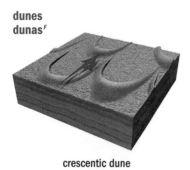

crescentic dune
barján^M

star dune
duna^F *en estrella*^F

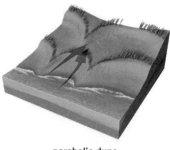

parabolic dune
duna^F *parabólica*

longitudinal dunes
dunas^F *longitudinales*

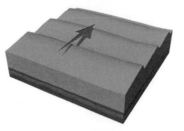

transverse dunes
dunas^F *transversales*

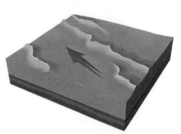

chain of dunes
cadena^F *de dunas*^F

apodar **2** : doblar (una película)

dubious *adj* **1** UNCERTAIN : dudoso
 2 QUESTIONABLE : sospechoso

duchess *n* : duquesa *f*

duck *n, pl* **duck** *or* **ducks** : pato *m*,
 -ta *f* — **duck** *vt* **1** LOWER : agachar,
 bajar **2** EVADE : eludir, esquivar — *vi* :
 agacharse — **duckling** *n* : patito *m*, -ta *f*

duct *n* : conducto *m*

due *adj* **1** PAYABLE : pagadero **2**
 APPROPRIATE : debido, apropiado **3**
 EXPECTED : esperado **4 due to** : debido a
 — **due** *n* **1 give someone their due** :
 hacer justicia a algn **2 dues** *npl* : cuota *f*
 — **due** *adv* **due east** : justo al este

duel *n* : duelo *m*

duet *n* : dúo *m*

dug → **dig**

duke *n* : duque *m*

dull *adj* **1** STUPID : torpe **2** BLUNT :
 desafilado **3** BORING : aburrido **4**
 LACKLUSTER : apagado — **dull** *vt* :
 entorpecer (los sentidos), aliviar (el dolor)

dumb *adj* **1** MUTE : mudo
 2 STUPID : estúpido

dumbfound *or* dumfound *vt*
 : dejar sin habla

dummy *n, pl* **-mies 1** SHAM
 : imitación *f* **2** MANNEQUIN :
 maniquí *m* **3** IDIOT : tonto *m*, -ta *f*

dump *vt* : descargar, verter — **dump** *n* **1**
 : vertedero *m*, tiradero *m*, *Lat* **2 down
 in the dumps** : triste, deprimido

dumpling *n* : bola *f* de masa hervida

dumpy *adj* **dumpier; -est** : regordete

dunce *n* : burro *m*, -rra *f* *fam*

▸ **dune** *n* : duna *f*

dung *n* **1** : excrementos *mpl* **2**
 MANURE : estiércol *m*

dungarees *npl* JEANS :
 vaqueros *mpl*, jeans *mpl*

dungeon *n* : calabozo *m*

dunk *vt* : mojar

duo *n, pl* **duos** : dúo *m*

dupe *vt* **duped; duping** : engañar
 — **dupe** *n* : inocentón *m*, -tona *f*

duplex *n* : casa *f* de dos
 viviendas, dúplex *m*

duplicate *adj* : duplicado — **duplicate** *vt*
 -cated; -cating : duplicar, hacer copias
 de — **duplicate** *n* : duplicado *m*, copia *f*

durable *adj* : duradero

duration *n* : duración *f*

duress *n* : coacción *f*

during *prep* : durante

dusk *n* : anochecer *m*, crepúsculo *m*

dust *n* : polvo *m* — **dust** *vt* **1** : quitar
 el polvo a **2** SPRINKLE : espolvorear
 — **dustpan** *n* : recogedor *m* —
 dusty *adj* **dustier; -est** : polvoriento

Dutch *adj* : holandés — **Dutch** *n* **1**
 : holandés *m* (idioma) **2 the
 Dutch** : los holandeses

duty *n, pl* **-ties 1** OBLIGATION : deber *m* **2**
 TAX : impuesto *m* **3 on duty** : de
 servicio — **dutiful** *adj* : obediente

dwarf *n, pl* **dwarfs** *or* **dwarves** : enano *m*,
 -na *f* — **dwarf** *vt* : hacer parecer pequeño

dwell *vi* **dwelled** *or* **dwelt; dwelling 1**
 RESIDE : morar, vivir **2 dwell on** : pensar
 demasiado en — **dweller** *n* : habitante *mf*
 — **dwelling** *n* : morada *f*, vivienda *f*

dwindle *vi* **-dled; -dling** : disminuir

dye *n* : tinte *m* — **dye** *vt*
 dyed; dyeing : teñir

dying → **die**¹

dynamic *adj* : dinámico

dynamite *n* : dinamita *f*

dynamo *n, pl* **-mos** : dínamo *m*

dynasty *n, pl* **-ties** : dinastía *f*

dysentery *n, pl* **-teries** : disentería *f*

e *n*, *pl* **e's** *or* **es** : e *f*, quinta
letra del alfabeto inglés

each *adj* : cada — **each** *pron* **1** : cada
uno *m*, cada una *f* **2 each other** : el uno
al otro **3 they hate each other** : se odian
— **each** *adv* : cada uno, por persona

eager *adj* **1** ENTHUSIASTIC : entusiasta **2**
IMPATIENT : impaciente — **eagerness** *n*
: entusiasmo *m*, impaciencia *f*

▸ **eagle** *n* : águila *f*

ear *n* **1** : oreja *f* **2 ear of corn** : mazorca *f*,
choclo *m*, *Lat* — **eardrum** *n* : tímpano *m*

earl *n* : conde *m*

earlobe *n* : lóbulo *m* de la oreja

early *adv* **earlier; -est 1** : temprano **2 as**
early as possible : lo más pronto posible
3 ten minutes early : diez minutos de
adelanto — **early** *adj* **earlier; -est 1** FIRST
: primero **2** ANCIENT : primitivo, antiguo **3**
an early death : una muerte prematura **4**
be early : llegar temprano **5 in the early**
spring : a principios de la primavera

earmark *vt* : destinar

earn *vt* **1** : ganar **2** DESERVE : merecer

earnest *adj* : serio — **earnest** *n*
in earnest : en serio

earnings *npl* **1** WAGES : ingresos *mpl* **2**
PROFITS : ganancias *fpl*

earphone *n* : audífono *m*

earring *n* : pendiente *m*, arete *m*, *Lat*

earshot *n* **within earshot**
: al alcance del oído

▸ **earth** *n* : tierra *f* — **earthenware** *n* : loza *f*
— **earthly** *adj* : terrenal — **earthquake** *n*
: terremoto *m* — **earthworm** *n* : lombriz *f*
(de tierra) — **earthy** *adj* **earthier; -est**

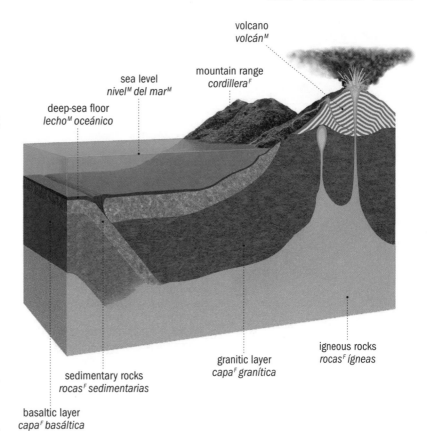

section of the Earth's crust
corte^M **de la corteza**^F **terrestre**

volcano
volcán^M

mountain range
cordillera^F

sea level
nivel^M *del mar*^M

deep-sea floor
lecho^M *oceánico*

igneous rocks
rocas^F *ígneas*

granitic layer
capa^F *granítica*

sedimentary rocks
rocas^F *sedimentarias*

basaltic layer
capa^F *basáltica*

eagle
águila^F

1 : terroso **2** COARSE CRUDE : grosero

ease *n* **1** FACILITY : facilidad *f* **2**
COMFORT : comodidad *f* **3 feel at**
ease : sentir cómodo — **ease** *v*
eased; easing *vt* **1** ALLEVIATE : aliviar,
calmar **2** FACILITATE : facilitar — *vi* **1**
: calmarse **2 ease up** : disminuir

easel *n* : caballete *m*

easily *adv* **1** : fácilmente, con facilidad **2**
UNQUESTIONABLY : con mucho, de lejos *Lat*

east *adv* : al este — **east** *adj*
: este, del este — **east** *n* **1** :
este *m* **2 the East** : el Oriente

Easter *n* : Pascua *f*

easterly *adv & adj* : del este

eastern *adj* **1** : del este **2**
Eastern : oriental, del este

easy *adj* **easier; -est 1** : fácil **2**
RELAXED : relajado — **easygoing** *adj*
: tolerante, relajado

eat *v* **ate; eaten; eating** *vt* : comer
— *vi* **1** : comer **2 eat into** CORRODE :
corroer **3 eat into** DEPLETE : comerse
— **eatable** *adj* : comestible

eaves *npl* : alero *m* —
eavesdrop *vi* **-dropped; -dropping**
: escuchar a escondidas

ebb *n* : reflujo *m* — **ebb** *vi* **1** : bajar
(dícese de la marea) **2** DECLINE : decaer

ebony *n*, *pl* **-nies** : ébano *m*

eccentric *adj* : excéntrico —
eccentric *n* : ecéntrico *m*, -ca *f* —
eccentricity *n*, *pl* **-ties** : excentricidad *f*

echo *n*, *pl* **echoes** : eco *m* —
echo *v* **echoed; echoing** *vt* : repetir
— *vi* : hacer eco, resonar

eel
anguila^F

eclipse *n* : eclipse *m* — **eclipse** *vt*
eclipsed; eclipsing : eclipsar
ecology *n, pl* -gies : ecología *f*
— **ecological** *adj* : ecológico
economy *n, pl* -mies : economía *f*
— **economic** *or* economical *adj*
: económico — **economics** *n*
: economía *f* — **economist** *n* :
economista *mf* — **economize** *v*
-mized; -mizing : economizar
ecstasy *n, pl* -sies : éxtasis *m*
— **ecstatic** *adj* : extático
Ecuadoran *or* Ecuadorean *or*
Ecuadorian *adj* : ecuatoriano
edge *n* **1** BORDER : borde *m* **2** :
filo *m* (de un cuchillo) **3** ADVANTAGE :
ventaja *f* — **edge** *v* **edged; edging** *vt*
: bordear, ribetear — *vi* : avanzar poco
a poco — **edgewise** *adv* : de lado —
edgy *adj* **edgier; -est** : nervioso
edible *adj* : comestible
edit *vt* **1** : editar, redactar, corregir **2**
edit out : suprimir, cortar — **edition** *n* :
edición *f* — **editor** *n* : director *m*, -tora *f*
(de un periódico); redactor *m*, -tora *f* (de
un libro) — **editorial** *n* : editorial *m*
educate *vt* -cated; -cating **1** TEACH
: educar, instruir **2** INFORM : informar

— **education** *n* : educación *f* —
educational *adj* **1** : educativo,
instructivo **2** TEACHING : docente —
educator *n* : educador *m*, -dora *f*
▸ **eel** *n* : anguila *f*
eerie *adj* -rier; -est : extraño
e inquietante, misterioso
effect *n* **1** : efecto *m* **2 go into effect**
: entrar en vigor — **effect** *vt* : efectuar,
llevar a cabo — **effective** *adj* **1** :
eficaz **2** ACTUAL : efectivo, vigente
— **effectiveness** *n* : eficacia *f*
effeminate *adj* : afeminado
effervescent *adj* : efervescente
efficient *adj* : eficiente —
efficiency *n, pl* -cies : eficiencia *f*
effort *n* **1** : esfuerzo *m* **2 it's not**
worth the effort : no vale la pena —
effortless *adj* : fácil, sin esfuerzo
egg *n* : huevo *m* — **egg** *vt* **egg on** :
▸ incitar — **eggplant** *n* : berenjena *f*
— **eggshell** *n* : cascarón *m*
ego *n, pl* **egos 1** SELF : ego *m*,
yo *m* **2** SELF-ESTEEM : amor *m* propio
— **egotism** *n* : egotismo *m* —
egotist *n* : egotista *mf* — **egotistic**
or egotistical *adj* : egotista
eiderdown *n* **1** DOWN : plumón *m* **2**
COMFORTER : edredón *m*
eight *n* : ocho *m* — **eight** *adj* : ocho
— **eight hundred** *n* : ochocientos *m*
eighteen *n* : dieciocho *m* — **eighteen** *adj*
: dieciocho — **eighteenth** *adj* :
decimoctavo — **eighteenth** *n* **1** :
decimoctavo *m*, -va *f* (en una serie) **2** :
dieciochoavo *m*, dieciochoava parte *f*
eighth *n* **1** : octavo *m*, -va *f* (en
una serie) **2** : octavo *m*, octava
parte *f* — **eighth** *adj* : octavo
eighty *n, pl* **eighties** : ochenta *m*
— **eighty** *adj* : ochenta
either *adj* **1** : cualquiera (de los
dos) **2** (*in negative constructions*) :
ninguno (de los dos) **3** EACH : cada
— **either** *pron* **1** : cualquiera *mf* (de
los dos) **2** (*in negative constructions*) :
ninguno *m*, -na *f* (de los dos) **3** *or* **either**
one : algún *m*, alguna *f* — **either** *conj* **1**
: o **2** (*in negative constructions*) : ni
eject *vt* : expulsar, expeler
eke *vt* **eked; eking** *or* **eke out**
: ganar a duras penas
elaborate *adj* **1** DETAILED :
detallado **2** COMPLEX : complicado
— **elaborate** *v* -rated; -rating *vt* :

elaborar — *vi* : entrar en detalles
elapse *vi* **elapsed; elapsing** : transcurrir
elastic *adj* : elástico — **elastic** *n* **1**
: elástico *m* **2** RUBBER BAND :
goma *f* (elástica) — **elasticity** *n*,
pl -ties : elasticidad *f*
elated *adj* : regocijado
elbow *n* : codo *m*
elder *adj* : mayor — **elder** *n* **1** :
mayor *mf* **2** : anciano *m*, -na *f* (de un tribu,
etc.) — **elderly** *adj* : mayor, anciano
elect *vt* : elegir — **elect** *adj* : electo —
election *n* : elección *f* — **electoral** *adj* :
electoral — **electorate** *n* : electorado *m*
electricity *n, pl* -ties : electricidad *f*
— **electric** *or* electrical *adj* : eléctrico
— **electrician** *n* : electricista *mf*
— **electrify** *vt* -fied; -fying :
electrificar — **electrocute** *vt*
-cuted; -cuting : electrocutar
electron *n* : electrón *m* — **electronic** *adj* :
electrónico — **electronic mail** *n* : correo *m*
electrónico — **electronics** *n* : electrónica *f*
elegant *adj* : elegante —
elegance *n* : elegancia *f*
element *n* **1** : elemento *m* **2**
elements *npl* BASICS : elementos *mpl*,
rudimentos *mpl* — **elementary** *adj*
: elemental — **elementary**
school *n* : escuela *f* primaria
elephant *n* : elefante *m*, -ta *f*
elevate *vt* -vated; -vating : elevar
▸ — **elevator** *n* : ascensor *m*
eleven *n* : once *m* — **eleven** *adj* :
once — **eleventh** *adj* : undécimo —
eleventh *n* **1** : undécimo *m*, -ma *f* (en
una serie) **2** : onceavo *m*, onceava parte *f*
elf *n, pl* **elves** : duende *m*

eggplant
berenjena^F

elicit *vt* : provocar
eligible *adj* : elegible
eliminate *vt* -nated; -nating : eliminar — **elimination** *n* : eliminación *f*
elite *n* : elite *f*
elk *n* : alce *m* (de Europa), uapití *m* (de América)
elliptical *or* **elliptic** *adj* : elíptico
elm *n* : olmo *m*
elongate *vt* -gated; -gating : alargar
elope *vi* **eloped; eloping** : fugarse — **elopement** *n* : fuga *f*
eloquence *n* : elocuencia *f* — **eloquent** *adj* : elocuente
else *adv* **1 how else ?** : ¿de qué otro modo? **2 where else ?** : ¿en qué otro sitio? **3 or else** : si no, de lo contrario — **else** *adj* **1 everyone else** : todos los demás **2 nobody else** : ningún otro, nadie más **3 nothing else** : nada más **4 what else ?** : ¿qué más? — **elsewhere** *adv* : en otra parte
elude *vt* **eluded; eluding** : eludir, esquivar — **elusive** *adj* : esquivo
elves → **elf**
emaciated *adj* : esquálido, demacrado
E–mail → **electronic mail**
emanate *vi* -nated; -nating : emanar
emancipate *vt* -pated; -pating : emancipar — **emancipation** *n* : emancipación *f*
embalm *vt* : embalsamar
embankment *n* : terraplén *m*, dique *m* (de un río)
embargo *n, pl* -goes : embargo *m*
embark *vt* : embarcar — *vi* **1** : embarcarse **2 embark upon** : emprender — **embarkation** *n* : embarque *m*, embarco *m*
embarrass *vt* : avergonzar — **embarrassing** *adj* : embarazoso — **embarrassment** *n* : vergüenza *f*
embassy *n, pl* -sies : embajada *f*
embed *vt* -bedded; -bedding : incrustar, enterrar
embellish *vt* : adornar, embellecer — **embellishment** *n* : adorno *m*
embers *npl* : ascuas *fpl*
embezzle *vt* -zled; -zling : desfalcar, malversar — **embezzlement** *n* : desfalco *m*, malversación *f*
emblem *n* : emblema *m*
embody *vt* -bodied; -bodying : encarnar, personificar
emboss *vt* : repujar, grabar en relieve

embrace *v* -braced; -bracing *vt* : abrazar — *vi* : abrazarse — **embrace** *n* : abrazo *m*
embroider *vt* : bordar — **embroidery** *n, pl* -deries : bordado *m*
embryo *n, pl* **embryos** : embrión *m*
emerald *n* : esmeralda *f*
emerge *vi* **emerged; emerging** : salir, aparecer — **emergence** *n* : aparición *f*
emergency *n, pl* -cies **1** : emergencia *f* **2 emergency exit** : salida *f* de emergencia **3 emergency room** : sala *f* de urgencias, sala *f* de guardia
emery *n, pl* -eries **1** : esmeril *m* **2 emery board** : lima *f* de uñas
emigrant *n* : emigrante *mf* — **emigrate** *vi* -grated; -grating : emigrar — **emigration** *n* : emigración *f*
eminence *n* : eminencia *f* — **eminent** *adj* : eminente

emission *n* : emisión *f* — **emit** *vt* **emitted; emitting** : emitir
emotion *n* : emoción *f* — **emotional** *adj* **1** : emocional **2** MOVING : emotivo
emperor *n* : emperador *m*
emphasis *n, pl* -phases : énfasis *m* — **emphasize** *vt* -sized; -sizing : subrayar, hacer hincapié en — **emphatic** *adj* : enérgico, categórico
empire *n* : imperio *m*
employ *vt* : emplear — **employee** *n* : empleado *m*, -da *f* — **employer** *n* : patrón *m*, -trona *f*; empleador *m*, -dora *f* — **employment** *n* : trabajo *m*, empleo *m*
empower *vt* : autorizar
empress *n* : emperatriz *f*
empty *adj* **emptier; -est 1** : vacío **2** MEANINGLESS : vano — **empty** *v*

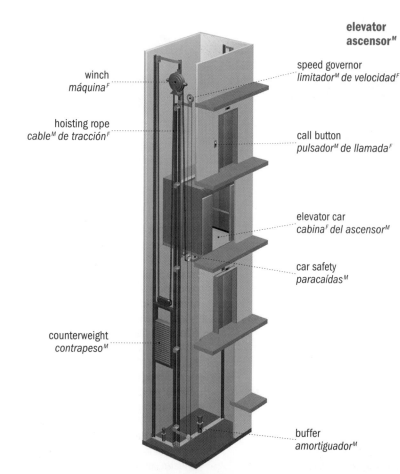

elevator
ascensor^M

winch
máquina^F

hoisting rope
cable^M *de tracción*^{F}

counterweight
contrapeso^M

speed governor
limitador^M *de velocidad*^{F}

call button
pulsador^M *de llamada*^{F}

elevator car
cabina^F *del ascensor*^{M}

car safety
paracaídas^M

buffer
amortiguador^M

medical equipment
equipo^M **médico**

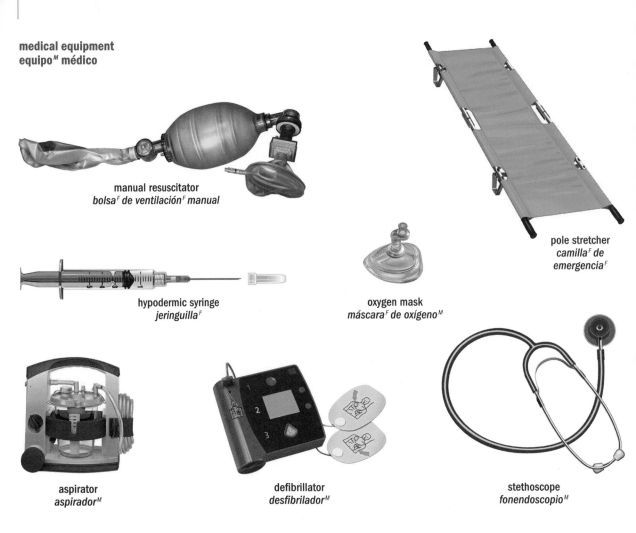

manual resuscitator
bolsa^F *de ventilación*^F *manual*

hypodermic syringe
jeringuilla^F

oxygen mask
máscara^F *de oxígeno*^M

pole stretcher
camilla^F *de*
emergencia^F

aspirator
aspirador^M

defibrillator
desfibrilador^M

stethoscope
fonendoscopio^M

-tied; -tying *vt* : vaciar — *vi* :
vaciarse — **emptiness** *n* : vacío *m*
emulate *vt* **-lated; -lating** : emular
enable *vt* **-abled; -abling** :
hacer posible, permitir
enact *vt* **1** : promulgar (un ley o un
decreto) **2** PERFORM : representar
enamel *n* : esmalte *m*
encampment *n* : campamento *m*
encase *vt* **-cased; -casing**
: encerrar, revestir
enchant *vt* : encantar — **enchanting** *adj* :
encantador — **enchantment** *n* : encanto *m*
encircle *vt* **-cled; -cling** : rodear
enclose *vt* **-closed; -closing 1** SURROUND
: encerrar, cercar **2** INCLUDE : adjuntar
(a una carta) — **enclosure** *n* **1** AREA :

recinto *m* **2** : anexo *m* (con una carta)
encompass *vt* **1** ENCIRCLE :
cercar **2** INCLUDE : abarcar
encore *n* : bis *m*
encounter *vt* : encontrar —
encounter *n* : encuentro *m*
encourage *vt* **-aged; -aging 1** :
animar, alentar **2** FOSTER : promover,
fomentar — **encouragement** *n* **1** :
aliento *m* **2** PROMOTION : fomento *m*
encroach *vi* **encroach on** : invadir,
usurpar, quitar (el tiempo)
encyclopedia *n* : enciclopedia *f*
end *n* **1** : fin **2** EXTREMITY : extremo *m*,
punta *f* **3 come to an end** : llegar a
su fin **4 in the end** : por fin — **end** *vt* :
terminar, poner fin a — *vi* : terminar(se)

endanger *vt* : poner en peligro
endearing *adj* : simpático
endeavor *or Brit* **endeavour** *vt*
endeavor to : esforzarse por —
endeavor *n* : esfuerzo *m*
ending *n* : final *m*, desenlace *m*
endive *n* : endibia *f*, endivia *f*
endless *adj* **1** INTERMINABLE : interminable
2 INNUMERABLE : innumerable **3 endless**
possibilities : posibilidades *fpl* infinitas
endorse *vt* **-dorsed; -dorsing 1** SIGN
: endosar **2** APPROVE : aprobar —
endorsement *n* APPROVAL : aprobación *f*
endow *vt* : dotar
endure *v* **-dured; -during** *vt* :
soportar, aguantar — *vi* LAST : durar
— **endurance** *n* : resistencia *f*

enemy *n, pl* **-mies** : enemigo *m*, -ga *f*

energy *n, pl* **-gies** : energía *f*
— **energetic** *adj* : enérgico

enforce *vt* **-forced; -forcing 1**
: hacer cumplir (un ley, etc.) **2**
IMPOSE : imponer — **enforced** *adj*
: forzoso — **enforcement** *n* :
imposición *f* del cumplimiento

engage *v* **-gaged; -gaging** *vt* **1** :
captar, atraer (la atención, etc.) **2**
engage the clutch : embragar — *vi*
engage in : dedicarse a, entrar en —
engagement *n* **1** APPOINTMENT : cita *f*,
hora *f* **2** BETROTHAL : compromiso *m*
— **engaging** *adj* : atractivo

engine *n* **1** : motor *m* **2** LOCOMOTIVE
: locomotora *f* — **engineer** *n* **1** :
ingeniero *m*, -ra *f* **2** : maquinista *mf*
(de locomotoras) — **engineer** *vt* **1**
CONSTRUCT : construir **2** CONTRIVE :
tramar — **engineering** *n* : ingeniería *f*

English *adj* : inglés — **English** *n* :
inglés *m* (idioma) — **Englishman** *n* :
inglés *m* — **Englishwoman** *n* : inglesa *f*

engrave *vt* **-graved; -graving** :
grabar — **engraving** *n* : grabado *m*

engross *vt* : absorber

engulf *vt* : envolver

enhance *vt* **-hanced; -hancing**
: aumentar, mejorar

enjoy *vt* **1** : disfrutar, gozar de **2 enjoy**
oneself : divertirse — **enjoyable** *adj* :
agradable — **enjoyment** *n* : placer *m*

enlarge *v* **-larged; -larging** *vt* :
agrandar, ampliar — *vi* **1** : agrandarse
2 enlarge upon : extenderse sobre
— **enlargement** *n* : ampliación *f*

enlighten *vt* : aclarar, iluminar

enlist *vt* **1** ENROLL : alistar **2** OBTAIN
: conseguir — *vi* : alistarse

enliven *vt* : animar

enmity *n, pl* **-ties** : enemistad *f*

enormous *adj* : enorme

enough *adj* : bastante, suficiente
— **enough** *adv* : bastante —
enough *pron* **1** : (lo) suficiente, (lo)
bastante **2 it's not enough** : no basta
3 I've had enough ! : ¡estoy harto!

enquire, enquiry → **inquire inquiry**

enrage *vt* **-raged; -raging** : enfurecer

enrich *vt* : enriquecer

enroll *or* **enrol** *v* **-rolled; -rolling** *vt*
: matricular, inscribir — *vi* :
matricularse, inscribirse

ensemble *n* : conjunto *m*

ensign *n* **1** FLAG : enseña *f* **2**
: alférez *mf* (de fragata)

enslave *vt* **-slaved; -slaving** : esclavizar

ensue *vi* **-sued; -suing** : seguir, resultar

ensure *vt* **-sured; -suring** : asegurar

entail *vt* : suponer, conllevar

entangle *vt* **-gled; -gling** : enredar
— **entanglement** *n* : enredo *m*

enter *vt* **1** : entrar en **2** RECORD : inscribir
— *vi* **1** : entrar **2 enter into** : firmar (un
acuerdo), entablar (negociaciones, etc.)

enterprise *n* **1** : empresa *f* **2**
INITIATIVE : iniciativa *f* —
enterprising *adj* : emprendedor

entertain *vt* **1** AMUSE : entretener, divertir
2 CONSIDER : considerar **3 entertain guests**
: recibir invitados — **entertainment** *n*
: entretenimiento *m*, diversión *f*

enthrall *or* **enthral** *vt* **-thralled;**
-thralling : cautivar, embelesar

enthusiasm *n* : entusiasmo *m*
— **enthusiast** *n* : entusiasta *mf* —
enthusiastic *adj* : entusiasta

entice *vt* **-ticed; -ticing** : atraer, tentar

entire *adj* : entero, completo —
entirely *adv* : completamente —
entirety *n, pl* **-ties** : totalidad *f*

entitle *vt* **-tled; -tling 1** NAME :
titular **2** AUTHORIZE : dar derecho a
— **entitlement** *n* : derecho *m*

entity *n, pl* **-ties** : entidad *f*

entrails *npl* : entrañas *fpl*, vísceras *fpl*

entrance[1] *vt* **-tranced; -trancing**
: encantar, fascinar

entrance[2] *n* : entrada *f* —
entrant *n* : participante *mf*

entreat *vt* : suplicar

entrée *or* **entree** *n* : plato *m* principal

entrepreneur *n* : empresario *m*, -ria *f*

entrust *vt* : confiar

entry *n, pl* **-tries 1** ENTRANCE : entrada *f* **2**
NOTATION : entrada *f*, anotación *f*

enumerate *vt* **-ated; -ating** : enumerar

enunciate *vt* **-ated; -ating 1** STATE
: enunciar **2** PRONOUNCE : articular

envelop *vt* : envolver —
envelope *n* : sobre *m*

envious *adj* : envidioso —
enviously *adv* : con envidia

environment *n* : medio *m* ambiente
— **environmental** *adj* : ambiental —
environmentalist *n* : ecologista *mf*

envision *vt* : prever, imaginar

envoy *n* : enviado *m*, -da *f*

envy *n, pl* **envies** : envidia *f*

— **envy** *vt* **-vied; -vying** : envidiar

enzyme *n* : enzima *f*

epic *adj* : épico — **epic** *n* : epopeya *f*

epidemic *n* : epidemia *f* —
epidemic *adj* : epidémico

epilepsy *n, pl* **-sies** : epilepsia *f*
— **epileptic** *adj* : epiléptico —
epilepsy *n* : epiléptico *m*, -ca *f*

episode *n* : episodio *m*

epitaph *n* : epitafio *m*

epitome *n* : personificación *f* —
epitomize *vt* **-mized; -mizing** : ser
la personificación de, personificar

epoch *n* : época *f*

equal *adj* **1** SAME : igual **2 be equal to** :
estar a la altura de (una tarea, etc.) —
equal *n* : igual *mf* — **equal** *vt* **equaled**
or **equalled; equaling** *or* **equalling 1** :
igualar **2** : ser igual a (en matemáticas)
— **equality** *n, pl* **-ties** : igualdad *f* —
equalize *vt* **-ized; -izing** : igualar —
equally *adv* **1** : igualmente **2 equal**
important : igual de importante

equate *vt* **equated; equating equate with**
: equiparar con — **equation** *n* : ecuación *f*

equator *n* : ecuador *m*

equilibrium *n, pl* **-riums**
or **-ria** : equilibrio *m*

equinox *n* : equinoccio *m*

equip *vt* **equipped; equipping** :
▸ equipar — **equipment** *n* : equipo *m*

equity *n, pl* **-ties 1** FAIRNESS :
equidad *f* **2 equities** *npl* STOCKS
: acciones *fpl* ordinarias

equivalent *adj* : equivalente —
equivalent *n* : equivalente *m*

era *n* : era *f*, época *f*

eradicate *vt* **-cated; -cating** : erradicar

erase *vt* **erased; erasing** : borrar —
eraser *n* : goma *f* de borrar, borrador *m*

erect *adj* : erguido — **erect** *vt* : erigir,
levantar — **erection** *n* **1** BUILDING :
construcción *f* **2** : erección *f* (en fisiología)

erode *vt* **eroded; eroding** : erosionar
(el suelo), corroer (metales) —
erosion *n* : erosión *f*, corrosión *f*

erotic *adj* : erótico

err *vi* : equivocarse, errar

errand *n* : mandado *m*, recado *m* Spain

erratic *adj* : errático, irregular

error *n* : error *m* —
erroneous *adj* : erróneo

erupt *vi* **1** : hacer erupción (dícese de un
volcán) **2** : estallar (dícese de la cólera, la
violencia, etc.) — **eruption** *n* : erupción *f*

escalate *vi* -lated; -lating : intensificarse
escalator *n* : escalera *f* mecánica
escapade *n* : aventura *f*
escape *v* -caped; -caping *vt* : escapar
a, evitar — *vi* : escaparse, fugarse
— **escape** *n* **1** : fuga *f* **2 escape
from reality** : evasión *f* de la realidad
— **escapee** *n* : fugitivo *m*, -va *f*
escort *n* **1** GUARD : escolta *f* **2** COMPANION
: acompañante *mf* — **escort** *vt* **1** :
escoltar **2** ACCOMPANY : acompañar
Eskimo *adj* : esquimal
especially *adv* : especialmente
espionage *n* : espionaje *m*
espresso *n*, *pl* -sos : café *m* exprés
essay *n* : ensayo *m* (literario),
composición *f* (académica)
essence *n* : esencia *f* — **essential** *adj*
: esencial — **essence** *n* **1** : elemento *m*

esencial **2 the essences** : lo indispensable
establish *vt* : establecer —
establishment *n* : establecimiento *m*
estate *n* **1** POSSESSIONS : bienes *mpl* **2**
LAND, PROPERTY : finca *f*
esteem *n* : estima *f* — **esteem** *vt* : estimar
esthetic → **aesthetic**
estimate *vt* -mated; -mating : calcular,
estimar — **estimate** *n* **1** : cálculo *m*
(aproximado) **2** *or* **estimate of costs**
: presupuesto *m* — **estimation** *n* **1**
JUDGMENT : juicio *m* **2** ESTEEM : estima *f*
estuary *n*, *pl* -aries : estuario *m*, ría *f*
eternal *adj* : eterno — **eternity** *n*,
pl -ties : eternidad *f*
ether *n* : éter *m*
ethical *adj* : ético — **ethics** *ns*
& pl : ética *f*, moralidad *f*
ethnic *adj* : étnico

etiquette *n* : etiqueta *f*
Eucharist *n* : Eucaristía *f*
eulogy *n*, *pl* -gies : elogio *m*, panegírico *m*
euphemism *n* : eufemismo *m*
euphoria *n* : euforia *f*
European *adj* : europeo
evacuate *vt* -ated; -ating : evacuar
— **evacuation** *n* : evacuación *f*
evade *vt* evaded; evading : evadir, eludir
evaluate *vt* -ated; -ating : evaluar
evaporate *vi* -rated; -rating : evaporarse
evasion *n* : evasión *f* —
evasive *adj* : evasivo
eve *n* : víspera *f*
even *adj* **1** REGULAR, STEADY : regular,
constante **2** LEVEL : plano, llano **3**
SMOOTH : liso **4** EQUAL : igual **5 even
number** : número *m* par **6 get even
with** : desquitarse con — **even** *adv* **1**

evolution
evolución^F **de las especies**^F

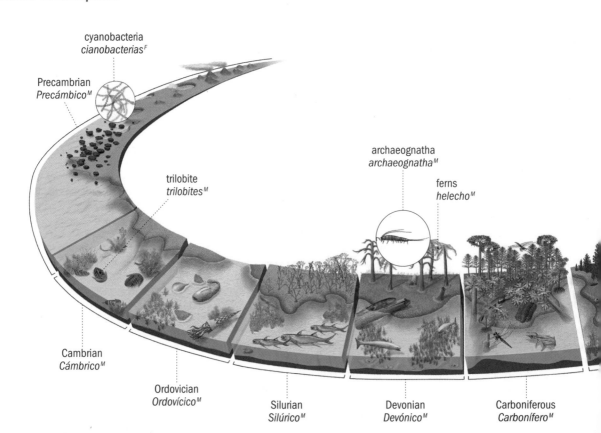

cyanobacteria
cianobacterias^F

Precambrian
Precámbrico^M

trilobite
trilobites^M

archaeognatha
archaeognatha^M

ferns
helecho^M

Cambrian
Cámbrico^M

Ordovician
Ordovícico^M

Silurian
Silúrico^M

Devonian
Devónico^M

Carboniferous
Carbonífero^M

: hasta, incluso **2 even better** : aún mejor, todavía mejor **3 even if** : aunque **4 even so** : aun así — **even** *vt* : igualar *vi or* **even out** : nivelarse
evening *n* : tarde *f*, noche *f*
event *n* **1** : acontecimiento *m*, suceso *m* **2** : prueba *f* (en deportes) **3 in the event of** : en caso de — **eventful** *adj* : lleno de incidentes
eventual *adj* : final — **eventuality** *n*, *pl* **-ties** : eventualidad *f* — **eventually** *adv* : al fin, finalmente
ever *adv* **1** ALWAYS : siempre **2 ever since** : desde entonces **3 hardly ever** : casi nunca **4 have you ever done it?** : ¿lo has hecho alguna vez?
evergreen *n* : planta *f* de hoja perenne
everlasting *adj* : eterno
every *adj* **1** EACH : cada **2 every month**

: todos los meses **3 every other day** : cada dos días — **everybody** *pron* : todos *mpl*, -das *fpl;* todo el mundo — **everyday** *adj* : cotidiano, de todos los días — **everyone** → **everybody** — **everything** *pron* : todo — **everywhere** *adv* : en todas partes, por todas partes
evict *vt* : desahuciar, desalojar — **eviction** *n* : desahucio *m*
evidence *n* **1** PROOF : pruebas *fpl* **2** TESTIMONY : testimonio *m*, declaración *f* — **evident** *adj* : evidente — **evidently** *adv* **1** OBVIOUSLY : obviamente **2** APPARENTLY : evidentemente, al parecer
evil *adj* **eviler** *or* **eviller; evilest** *or* **evillest** : malvado, malo — **evil** *n* : mal *m*, maldad *f*
evoke *vt* **evoked; evoking** : evocar
▸ **evolution** *n* : evolución *f*, desarrollo *m* — **evolve** *vi* **evolved; evolving**

: evolucionar, desarrollarse
exact *adj* : exacto, preciso — **exact** *vt* : exigir — **exacting** *adj* : exigente — **exactly** *adv* : exactamente
exaggerate *v* **-ated; -ating** : exagerar — **exaggeration** *n* : exageración *f*
examine *vt* **-ined; -ining 1** : examinar **2** INSPECT : revisar **3** QUESTION : interrogar — **exam** *n* : examen *m* — **examination** *n* : examen *m*
example *n* : ejemplo *m*
exasperate *vt* **-ated; -ating** : exasperar — **exasperation** *n* : exasperación *f*
excavate *vt* **-vated; -vating** : excavar — **excavation** *n* : excavación *f*
exceed *vt* : exceder, sobrepasar — **exceedingly** *adv* : extremadamente
excel *v* **-celled; -celling** *vi* : sobresalir — *vt* SURPASS : superar — **excellence** *n* :

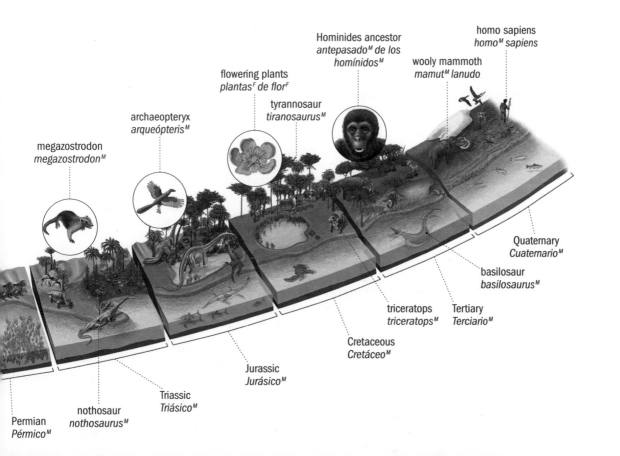

homo sapiens
*homo*ᴹ sapiens

Hominides ancestor
*antepasado*ᴹ *de los homínidos*ᴹ

wooly mammoth
*mamut*ᴹ *lanudo*

flowering plants
*plantas*ᶠ *de flor*ᶠ

tyrannosaur
*tiranosaurus*ᴹ

archaeopteryx
*arqueópteris*ᴹ

megazostrodon
*megazostrodon*ᴹ

Quaternary
*Cuaternario*ᴹ

basilosaur
*basilosaurus*ᴹ

triceratops
*triceratops*ᴹ

Tertiary
*Terciario*ᴹ

Cretaceous
*Cretáceo*ᴹ

Jurassic
*Jurásico*ᴹ

Triassic
*Triásico*ᴹ

nothosaur
*nothosaurus*ᴹ

Permian
*Pérmico*ᴹ

excelencia f — **excellent** adj : excelente

except prep or **except for** : excepto, menos, salvo — **except** vt : exceptuar — **exception** n : excepción f — **exceptional** adj : excepcional

excerpt n : extracto m

excess n : exceso m — **excess** adj : excesivo, de sobra — **excessive** adj : excesivo

exchange n 1 : intercambio m 2 : cambio m (en finanzas) — **exchange** vt -changed; -changing : cambiar, intercambiar

excise n **excise tax** : impuesto m interno, impuesto m sobre el consumo

excite vt -cited; -citing : excitar, emocionar — **excited** adj : excitado, entusiasmado — **excitement** n : entusiasmo m, emoción f

exclaim v : exclamar — **exclamation** n : exclamación f — **exclamation point** n : signo m de admiración

exclude vt -cluded; -cluding : excluir — **excluding** prep : excepto, con excepción de — **exclusion** n : exclusión f — **exclusive** adj : exclusivo

excrement n : excremento m

excruciating adj : insoportable, atroz

excursion n : excursión f

excuse vt -cused; -cusing 1 : perdonar 2 **excuse me** : perdóne, perdón — **excuse** n : excusa f

execute vt -cuted; -cuting : ejecutar — **execution** n : ejecución f — **executioner** n : verdugo m

executive adj : ejecutivo — **executive** n 1 MANAGER : ejecutivo m, -va f 2 or **executive branch** : poder m ejecutivo

exemplify vt -fied; -fying : ejemplificar — **exemplary** adj : ejemplar

exempt adj : exento — **exempt** vt : dispensar — **exemption** n : exención f

exercise n : ejercicio m — **exercise** v -cised; -cising vt USE : ejercer, hacer uso de — vi : hacer ejercicio

exert vt 1 : ejercer 2 **exert oneself** : esforzarse — **exertion** n : esfuerzo m

exhale v -haled; -haling : exhalar

exhaust vt : agotar — **exhaust** n 1 or **exhaust fumes** : gases mpl de escape 2 or **exhaust pipe** : tubo m de escape — **exhaustion** n : agotamiento m — **exhaustive** adj : exhaustivo

exhibit vt 1 DISPLAY : exponer 2 SHOW : mostrar — **exhibit** n 1 : objeto m expuesto 2 EXHIBITION : exposición f — **exhibition** n : exposición f

exhilarate vt -rated; -rating : alegrar — **exhilaration** n : regocijo m

exile n 1 : exilio m 2 OUTCAST : exiliado m, -da f — **exile** vt **exiled; exiling** : exiliar

exist vi : existir — **existence** n : existencia f — **existing** adj : existente

exit n : salida f — **exit** vi : salir

exodus n : éxodo m

exonerate vt -ated; -ating : exonerar, disculpar

exorbitant adj : exorbitante, excesivo

exotic adj : exótico

expand vt 1 : ampliar, extender 2 : dilatar (metales, etc.) — vi 1 : ampliarse, extenderse 2 : dilatarse (dícese de metales, etc.) — **expanse** n : extensión f — **expansion** n : expansión f

expatriate n : expatriado m, -da f — **expatriate** adj : expatriado

expect vt 1 : esperar 2 REQUIRE : contar con — vi **be expecting** : estar embarazada — **expectancy** n, pl -cies : esperanza f — **expectant** adj 1 : expectante 2 **expectant mother** : futura madre f — **expectation** n : esperanza f

expedient adj : conveniente — **expedient** n : expediente m, recurso m

expedition n : expedición f

expel vt -pelled; -pelling : expulsar (a una persona), expeler (humo, etc.)

expend vt : gastar — **expendable** adj : prescindible — **expenditure** n : gasto m — **expense** n 1 : gasto m 2 expends npl : gastos mpl, expensas fpl 3 **at the expense of** : a expensas de — **expensive** adj : caro

experience n : experiencia f — **experience** vt -enced; -encing : experimentar — **experienced** adj : experimentado — **experiment** n : experimento m — **experience** vi : experimentar — **experimental** adj : experimental

expert adj : experto — **expert** n : experto m, -ta f — **expertise** n : pericia f, competencia f

expire vi -pired; -piring 1 : caducar, vencer 2 DIE : expirar, morir — **expiration** n : vencimiento m, caducidad f

explain vt : explicar — **explanation** n : explicación f — **explanatory** adj : explicativo

explicit adj : explícito

explode v -ploded; -ploding vt : hacer explotar — vi : explotar, estallar

exploit n : hazaña f, proeza f — **exploit** vt : explotar — **exploitation** n : explotación f

exploration n : exploración f — **explore** vt -plored; -ploring : explorar — **explorer** n : explorador m, -dora f

explosion n : explosión f — **explosive** adj : explosivo — **explosion** n : explosivo m

export vt : exportar — **export** n : exportación f

expose vt -posed; -posing 1 : exponer 2 REVEAL : descubrir, revelar — **exposed** adj : expuesto, al descubierto — **exposure** n : exposición f

express adj 1 SPECIFIC : expreso, específico 2 FAST : expreso, rápido — **express** adv : por correo urgente — **express** n or **express train** : expreso m — **express** vt : expresar — **expression** n : expresión f — **expressive** adj : expresivo — **expressly** adv : expresamente — **expressway** n : autopista f

expulsion n : expulsión f

exquisite adj : exquisito

extend vt 1 STRETCH : extender 2 LENGTHEN : prolongar 3 ENLARGE : ampliar 4 **extend one's hand** : tender la mano — vi : extenderse — **extension** n 1 : extensión f 2 LENGTHENING : prolongación f 3 ANNEX : ampliación f, anexo m 4 **extension cord** : alargador m — **extensive** adj : extenso — **extent** n 1 SIZE : extensión f 2 DEGREE : alcance m, grado m 3 **to a certain extent** : hasta cierto punto

extenuating adj **extenuating circumstances** : circunstancias fpl atenuantes

exterior adj : exterior — **exterior** n : exterior m

exterminate vt -nated; -nating : exterminar — **extermination** n : exterminación f

external adj : externo — **externally** adv : exteriormente

extinct adj : extinto — **extinction** n : extinción f

extinguish vt : extinguir, apagar — **extinguisher** n : extintor m

extol vt -tolled; -tolling : ensalzar, alabar

extort vt : arrancar (algo a algn) por la fuerza — **extortion** n : extorsión f

extra adj : suplementario, de más — **extra** n : extra m — **extra** adv 1 : extra,

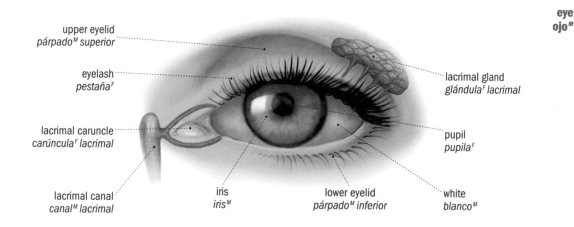

upper eyelid
párpado^M superior

eyelash
pestaña^F

lacrimal caruncle
carúncula^F lacrimal

lacrimal gland
glándula^F lacrimal

pupil
pupila^F

lacrimal canal
canal^M lacrimal

iris
iris^M

lower eyelid
párpado^M inferior

white
blanco^M

más **2 extra special** : super especial
extract *vt* : extraer, sacar — **extract** *n* :
extracto *m* — **extraction** *n* : extracción *f*
extracurricular *adj* : extracurricular
extradite *vt* -**dited**; -**diting** : extraditar
extraordinary *adj* : extraordinario
extraterrestrial *adj* : extraterrestre —
extraterrestrial *n* : extraterrestre *mf*
extravagant *adj* **1** WASTEFUL
: despilfarrador, derrochador **2**
EXAGGERATED : extravagante, exagerado
— **extravagance** *n* **1** WASTEFULNESS :
derroche *m*, despilfarro *m* **2** LUXURY :
lujo *m* **3** EXAGGERATION : extravagancia *f*
extreme *adj* : extremo — **extreme** *n*
: extremo *m* — **extremely** *adv* :
extremadamente — **extremity** *n*,
pl -**ties** : extremidad *f*
extricate *vt* -**cated**; -**cating**
: librar, (lograr) sacar
extrovert *n* : extrovertido *m*, -da *f*
— **extroverted** *adj* : extrovertido
exuberant *adj* **1** JOYOUS :
eufórico **2** LUSH : exuberante —
exuberance *n* **1** JOYOUSNESS :
euforia *f* **2** VIGOR : exuberancia *f*
exult *vi* : exultar
eye *n* **1** : ojo *m* **2** VISION : visión *f*,
vista *f* **3** GLANCE : mirada *f* — **eye** *vt* **eyed**;
eyeing *or* **eying** : mirar — **eyeball** *n* :
globo *m* ocular — **eyebrow** *n* : ceja *f* —
eyeglasses *npl* : anteojos *mpl*, lentes *mpl*
— **eyelash** *n* : pestaña *f* — **eyelid** *n*
: párpado *m* — **eyesight** *n* : vista *f*,
visión *f* — **eyesore** *n* : monstruosidad *f*
— **eyewitness** *n* : testigo *mf* ocular

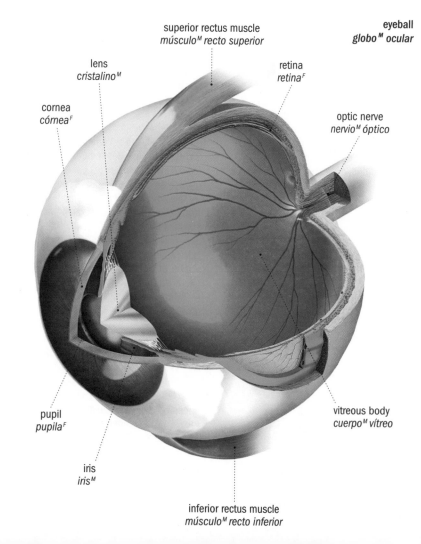

eyeball
globo^M ocular

superior rectus muscle
músculo^M recto superior

lens
cristalino^M

retina
retina^F

cornea
córnea^F

optic nerve
nervio^M óptico

pupil
pupila^F

iris
iris^M

vitreous body
cuerpo^M vítreo

inferior rectus muscle
músculo^M recto inferior

f *n, pl* **f's** *or* **fs** : f, sexta letra del alfabeto inglés

fable *n* : fábula *f*

fabric *n* : tela *f*, tejido *m*

fabulous *adj* : fabuloso

facade *n* : fachada *f*

face *n* **1** : ccra *f*, rostro *m* (de una persona) **2** APPEARANCE : fisonomía *f*, aspecto *m* **3** : cara *f* (de una moneda), fachada *f* (de un edificio) **4 face value** : valor *m* nominal **5 in the face of** : en medio de, ante **6 lose face** : desprestigiarse **7 make faces** : hacer muecas — **face faced; facing** *vt* **1** : estar frente a **2** CONFRONT : enfrentarse a **3** OVERLOOK : dar a — *vi* **face to the north** : mirar hacia el norte — **facedown** *adv* : boca abajo — **faceless** *adj* : anónimo — **face–lift** *n* : estiramiento *m* facial

facet *n* : faceta *f*

face–to–face *adv & adj* : cara a cara

facial *adj* : de la cara, facial — **facial** *n* : limpieza *f* de cutis

facetious *adj* : gracioso, burlón

facility *n, pl* **-ties 1** EASE : facilidad *f* **2** CENTER : centro *m* **3 facilities** *npl* : comodidades *fpl*, servicios *mpl*

facsimile *n* : facsímile *m*, facsímil *m*

fact *n* **1** : hecho *m* **2 in fact** : en realidad, de hecho

faction *n* : facción *m*, bando *m*

factor *n* : factor *m*

factory *n, pl* **-ries** : fábrica *f*

factual *adj* : basado en hechos

faculty *n, pl* **-ties** : facultad *f*

fad *n* : moda *f* pasajera, manía *f*

fade *v* **faded; fading** *vi* **1** WITHER : marchitarse **2** DISCOLOR : desteñirse, decolorarse **3** DIM : apagarse **4** VANISH : desvanecerse — *vt* : desteñir

fail *vi* **1** : fracasar (dícese de una empresa, un matrimonio, etc.) **2** BREAK DOWN : fallar **3 fail in** : faltar a, no cumplir con **4** FLUNK : suspender *Spain*, ser reprobado *Lat* **5 fail to do something** : no hacer algo — *vt* **1** DISAPPOINT : fallar **2** FLUNK : suspender *Spain*, reprobar *Lat* — **fail** *n* **without fail** : sin falta —

failing *n* : defecto *m* — **failure** *n* **1** : fracaso *m* **2** BREAKDOWN : falla *f*

faint *adj* **1** WEAK : débil **2** INDISTINCT : tenue, indistinto **3 feel faint** : estar mareado — **faint** *vi* : desmayarse — **faint** *n* : desmayo *m* —

fainthearted *adj* : cobarde, pusilánime — **faintly** *adv* **1** WEAKLY : débilmente **2** SLIGHTLY : ligeramente, levemente

fair[1] *n* : feria *f*

fair[2] *adj* **1** BEAUTIFUL : bello, hermoso **2** : bueno (dícese del tiempo) **3** JUST : justo **4** : rubio (dícese del pelo), blanco (dícese de la tez) **5** ADEQUATE : adecuado — **fair** *adv* **play fair** : jugar limpio — **fairly** *adv* **1** JUSTLY : justamente **2** QUITE : bastante — **fairness** *n* : justicia *f*

▸ **fairy** *n, pl* **fairies 1** : hada *f* **2 fairy tale** : cuento *m* de hadas

faith *n, pl* **faiths** : fe *f* — **faithful** *adj* : fiel — **faithfully** *adv* : fielmente — **faithfulness** *n* : fidelidad *f*

fake *v* **faked; faking** *vt* **1** FALSIFY : falsificar, falsear **2** FEIGN : fingir — *vi* PRETEND : fingir — **fake** *adj* : falso — **fake** *n* **1** IMITATION : falsificación *f* **2** IMPOSTOR : impostor *m*, -tora *f*

▸ **falcon** *n* : halcón *m*

fall *vi* **fell; fallen; falling 1** : caer, bajar (dícese de los precios), descender (dícese de la temperatura) **2 fall asleep** : dormirse **3 fall back** : retirarse **4 fall back on** : recurrir a **5 fall down** : caerse **6 fall in love** : enamorarse **7 fall out** QUARREL : pelearse **8 fall through** : fracasar — **fall** *n* **1** : caída *f*, bajada *f* (de precios), descenso *m* (de temperatura) **2** AUTUMN : otoño *m* **3**

falls *npl* WATERFALL : cascada *f*, catarata *f*

fallacy *n, pl* **-cies** : concepto *m* erróneo

fallible *adj* : falible

fallow *adj* **lie fallow** : estar en barbecho

false *adj* **falser; falsest 1** : falso **2 false alarm** : falsa alarma *f* **3 false teeth** : dentadura *f* postiza — **falsehood** *n* : mentira — **falseness** *n* : falsedad *f* — **falsify** *vt* **-fied; fying** : falsificar, falsear

falter *vi* **-tered; -tering 1** STUMBLE : tambalearse **2** WAVER : vacilar

fame *n* : fama *f*

familiar *adj* **1** : familiar **2 be familiar with** : estar familiarizado con — **familiarity** *n, pl* **-ties** : familiaridad *f* — **familiarize** *vt* **-ized; -izing** **familiarize oneself** : familiarizarse

family *n, pl* **-lies** : familia *f*

famine *n* : hambre *f*, hambruna *f*

famished *adj* : famélico

famous *adj* : famoso

▸ **fan** *n* **1** : ventilador *m*, abanico *m* **2** : aficionado *m*, -da *f* (a un pasatiempo); admirador *m*, -dora *f* (de una persona) — **fan** *vt* **fanned; fanning** : abanicar (a una persona), avivar (un fuego)

fanatic *or* **fanatical** *adj* : fanático — **fanatic** *n* : fanático *m*, -ca *f* — **fanaticism** *n* : fanatismo *m*

fancy *vt* **-cied; -cying 1** IMAGINE : imaginarse **2** DESIRE : apetecerle (algo a uno) — **fancy** *adj* **-cier; -est 1** ELABORATE : elaborado **2** LUXURIOUS : lujoso, elegante — **fancy** *n, pl* **-cies 1** WHIM : capricho *m* **2** IMAGINATION : imaginación *f* **3 take a fancy to** : aficionarse a (una cosa), tomar cariño a (una persona) — **fanciful** *adj* **1** CAPRICIOUS : caprichoso **2** IMAGINATIVE : imaginativo

fanfare *n* : fanfarria *f*

fang *n* : colmillo *m* (de un animal), diente *m* (de una serpiente)

fantasy *n, pl* **-sies** : fantasía *f* — **fantasize** *vi* **-sized; -sizing** : fantasear — **fantastic** *adj* : fantástico

far *adv* **farther** *or* **further; farthest** *or* **furthest 1** : lejos **2** MUCH : muy, mucho **3 as far as** : hasta (un lugar), con respecto a (un tema) **4 by far** : con mucho **5 far and wide** : por todas partes **6 far away** : a lo lejos **7 far from it!** : ¡todo lo contrario! **8 so far** : hasta ahora, todavía — **far** *adj* **farther** *or* **further; farthest** *or* **furthest 1** REMOTE : lejano **2** EXTREME : extremo — **faraway** *adj* : remoto, lejano

farce *n* : farsa *f*

fairy
hada*F*

ceiling fan
ventilador^M de techo^M

fare *vi* **fared; faring** : irle a
uno — **fare** *n* **1** : precio *m* del
pasaje **2** FOOD : comida *f*
farewell *n* : despedida *f* —
farewell *adj* : de despedida
far–fetched *adj* : improbable, exagerado
farm *n* : granja *f,* hacienda *f* — **farm** *vt* :
cultivar (la tierra), criar (animales) — *vi* :
ser agricultor — **farmer** *n* : agricultor *m,*
-tora *f;* granjero *m,* -jera *f* — **farmhand** *n*
: peón *m* — **farmhouse** *n* : granja *f,* casa *f*
de hacienda — **farming** *n* : agricultura *f,*
cultivo *m* (de plantas), crianza *f* (de
animales) — **farmyard** *n* : corral *m*
far–off *adj* : lejano
far–reaching *adj* : de gran alcance
farsighted *adj* **1** : hipermétrope
2 PRUDENT : previsor
farther *adv* **1** : más lejos **2** MORE : más
— *adj* : más lejano — **farthest** *adv* **1** : lo
más lejjs **2** MOST : más — *adj* : más lejano
fascinate *vt* **-nated; -nating** : fascinar
— **fascination** *n* : fascinación *f*
fascism *n* : fascismo *m* — **fascist** *adj*
: fascista — **fascism** *n* : fascista *mf*
fashion *n* **1** MANNER : manera *f* **2** STYLE
: moda *f* **3 out of fashion** : pasada de
moda — **fashionable** *adj* : de moda
fast[1] *vi* : ayunar — **fast** *n* : ayuno *m*
fast[2] *adj* **1** SWIFT : rápido **2** SECURE :
firme, seguro **3** : adelantado (dícese
de un reloj) **4 fast friends** : amigos *mpl*
leales — **fast** *adv* **1** SECURELY :
firmemente **2** SWIFTLY : rápidamente **3**

fast asleep : profundamente dormido
fasten *vt* : sujetar (papeles, etc.),
abrochar (una blusa, etc.), cerrar
(una maleta, etc.) — *vi* : abrocharse,
cerrar — **fastener** *n* : cierre *m*
fat *adj* **fatter; fattest 1** : gordo **2**
THICK : grueso — **fat** *n* : grasa *f*
fatal *adj* **1** : mortal **2** FATEFUL
: fatal, fatídico — **fatality** *n,*
pl **-ties** : víctima *f* mortal
fate *n* **1** : destino *m* **2** LOT :
suerte *f* — **fateful** *adj* : fatídico
father *n* : padre *m* — **father** *vt* : engendrar
— **fatherhood** *n* : paternidad *f* —
father–in–law *n, pl* **fathers–in–law** :
suegro *m* — **fatherly** *adj* : paternal
fathom *vt* : comprender
fatigue *n* : fatiga *f* — **fatigue** *vt*
-tigued; -tiguing : fatigar
fatten *vt* : engordar —
fattening *adj* : que engorda
fatty *adj* **fattier; -est** : graso
faucet *n* : llave *f Lat,* grifo *m Spain*
fault *n* **1** FLAW : defecto *m* **2**
RESPONSIBILITY : culpa *f* **3** : falla *f*
(geológica) — *vt* : encontrar defectos
a — **faultless** *adj* : impecable —
faulty *adj* **faultier; -est** : defectuoso
fauna *n* : fauna *f*
favor *or Brit* **favour** *n* **1** : favor *m* **2**
in favor of : a favor de — **favor** *vt* **1** :
favorecer **2** SUPPORT : estar a favor de
3 PREFER : preferir — **favorable** *or Brit*
favourable *adj* : favorable — **favorite**

or Brit **favourite** *n* : favorito *m,* -ta *f* —
favorite *adj* : favorito — **favoritism** *or*
Brit **favouritism** *n* : favoritismo *m*
fawn[1] *vi* **fawn over** : adular
fawn[2] *n* : cervato *m*
fax *n* : fax *m* — **fax** *vt* :
faxear, enviar por fax
fear *v* : temer — **fear** *n* **1** : miedo *m,*
temor *m* **2 for fear of** : por temor
a — **fearful** *adj* **1** FRIGHTENING :
espantoso **2** AFRAID : temeroso
feasible *adj* : viable, factible
feast *n* **1** BANQUET : banquete *m,*
festín *m* **2** FESTIVAL : fiesta *f* —
feast *vi* **1** : banquetear **2 feast**
upon : darse un festín de
feat *n* : hazaña *f*
feather *n* : pluma *f*
feature *n* **1** : rasgo *m* (de la cara) **2**
CHARACTERISTIC : característica *f* **3** :
artículo *m* (en un periódico) **4 feature**
film : largometraje *m* — *v* **-tured;**
-turing *vt* **1** PRESENT : presentar **2**
EMPHASIZE : destacar — *vi* : figurar
February *n* : febrero *m*
feces *npl* : excremento *mpl*
federal *adj* : federal —
federation *n* : federación *f*
fed up *adj* : harto
fee *n* **1** : honorarios *mpl* **2**
entrance fee : entrada *f*
feeble *adj* **-bler; -blest 1** : débil **2 a**
feeble excuse : una pobre excusa
feed *v* **fed; feeding** *vt* **1** : dar de comer
a, alimentar **2** SUPPLY : alimentar — *vi* :

falcon
halcón^M

comer, alimentarse — **feed** n : pienso m
feel v **felt; feeling** vt **1** : sentir (una
sensación, etc.) **2** TOUCH : tocar, palpar
3 BELIEVE : **creer** — vi **1** : sentirse (bien,
cansado, etc.) **2** SEEM : parecer **3 feel hot/
thirsty** : tener calor/sed **4 feel like doing**
: tener ganas de hacer — **feel** n : tacto m,
sensación f — **feeling** n **1** SENSATION :
sensación f **2** EMOTION : sentimiento m **3**
OPINION : opinión f **4 hurt someone's
feelings** : herir los sentimientos de algn
feet → **foot**
feign vt : fingir
feline adj : felino — **feline** n
: felino m, -na f
fell[1] → **fall**
fell[2] vt : talar (un árbol)
fellow n **1** COMPANION : compañero m,
-ra f **2** MEMBER : socio m, -cia f **3**
MAN : tipo m — **fellowship** n **1** :
compañerismo m **2** ASSOCIATION :
fraternidad f **3** GRANT : beca f
felon n : criminal mf — **felony** n,
pl **-nies** : delito m grave
felt[1] → **feel**
felt[2] n : fieltro m

female adj : femenino — **female** n **1**
: hembra f (animal) **2** WOMAN : mujer f
feminine adj : femenino — **femininity** n
: femineidad f — **feminism** n :
feminismo m — **feminist** adj : feminista
— **feminist** n : feminista mf
fence n : cerca f, valla f, cerco m, Lat
— **fence** v **fenced; fencing** vt or **fence
in** : vallar, cercar — vi : hacer esgrima
▸ — **fencing** n : esgrima m (deporte)
fend vt **fend off** : rechazar (un enemigo),
eludir (una pregunta) — vi **fend for
oneself** : valerse por sí mismo
fender n : guardabarros mpl
fennel n : hinojo m
ferment v : fermentar —
fermentation n : fermentación f
fern n : helecho m
ferocious adj : feroz —
ferocity n : ferocidad f
ferret n : hurón m — **ferret** vt
ferret out : descubrir
Ferris wheel n : noria f
ferry vt **-ried; -rying** : transportar
— **ferry** n, pl **-ries** : ferry m
fertile adj : fértil — **fertility** n :

fertilidad f — **fertilize** vt **-ized; -izing**
: fecundar (un huevo), abonar (el suelo)
— **fertilizer** n : fertilizante m, abono m
fervent adj : ferviente — **fervor**
or Brit **fervour** n : fervor m
fester vi : enconarse
festival n **1** : fiesta f **2 film festival** :
festival m de cine — **festive** adj : festivo
— **festivity** n, pl **-ties** : festividad f
fetch vt **1** : ir a buscar **2** :
venderse por (un precio)
fête n : fiesta f
fetid adj : fétido
fetish n : fetiche m
fetters npl : grillos mpl —
fetter vt : encadenar
fetus n : feto m
feud n : enemistad f (entre
familiares) — **feud** vi : pelear
feudal adj : feudal —
feudalism n : feudalismo m
fever n : fiebre f — **feverish** adj : febril
few adj **1** : pocos **2 a few times** : varias
veces — **few** pron **1** : pocos **2 a few** :
algunos, unos cuantos **3 quite a few** :
muchos — **fewer** adj & pron : menos

fencing
esgrima[M]

fencer
esgrimista[M]

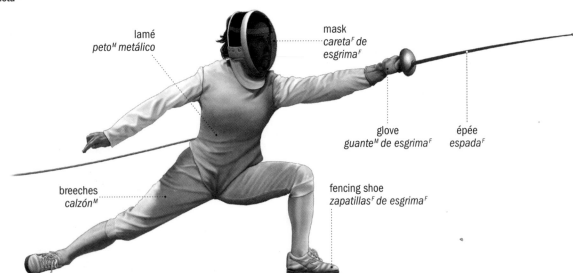

lamé
peto[M] metálico

mask
careta[F] de
esgrima[F]

glove
guante[M] de esgrima[F]

épée
espada[F]

breeches
calzón[M]

fencing shoe
zapatillas[F] de esgrima[F]

fiancé, fiancée *n* : prometido *m*,
-da *f*; novio *m*, -via *f*
fiasco *n, pl* **-coes** : fiasco *m*
fib *n* : mentirilla *f* — **fib** *vi* **fibbed;**
fibbing : decir mentirillas
fiber *or* **fibre** *n* : fibra *f* — **fiberglass** *n* :
fibra *f* de vidrio — **fibrous** *adj* : fibroso
fickle *adj* : inconstante
fiction *n* : ficción *f* — **fictional**
or fictitious *adj* : ficticio
fiddle *n* : violín *m* — **fiddle** *vi*
-dled; -dling 1 : tocar el violín **2**
fiddle with : juguetear con
fidelity *n, pl* **-ties** : fidelidad *f*
fidget *vi* **1** : estarse inquieto, moverse
2 fidget with : juguetear con —
fidgety *adj* : inquieto, nervioso
field *n* : campo *m* — **field** *vt* : interceptar
(una pelota), sortear (una pregunta) — **field**
glasses *n* : binoculares *mpl*, gemelos *mpl*
— **field trip** *n* : viaje *m* de estudio
fiend *n* **1** : demonio *m* **2** FANATIC :
fanático *m*, -ca *f* — **fiendish** *adj* : diabólico
fierce *adj* **fiercer; -est 1** : feroz **2**
INTENSE : fuerte (dícese del viento),
acalorado (dícese de un debate)

— **fierceness** *n* : ferocidad *f*
fiery *adj* **fierier; -est 1** BURNING :
llameante **2** SPIRITED : ardiente, fogoso
— **fieriness** *n* : pasión *f*, ardor *m*
fifteen *n* : quince *m* — **fifteen** *adj*
: quince — **fifteenth** *adj* :
decimoquinto — **fifteenth** *n* **1** :
decimoquinto *m*, -ta *f* (en una serie)
2 : quinceavo *m* (en matemáticas)
fifth *n* **1** : quinto *m*, -ta *f* (en
una serie) **2** : quinto *m* (en
matemáticas) — **fifth** *adj* : quinto
fiftieth *adj* : quincuagésimo —
fiftieth *n* **1** : quincuagésimo *m*,
-ma *f* (en una serie) **2** :
cincuentavo *m* (en matemáticas)
fifty *n, pl* **-ties** : cincuenta *m* —
fifty *adj* : cincuenta — **fifty–fifty** *adv*
: a medias, mitad y mitad — **fifty–**
fifty *adj* a fifty–fifty chance : un
cincuenta por ciento de posibilidades
fig *n* : higo *m*
fight *v* **fought; fighting** *vi* **1** BATTLE
: luchar **2** QUARREL : pelear **3 fight**
back : defenderse — *vt* : luchar
contra — **fight** *n* **1** STRUGGLE :

lucha *f* **2** QUARREL : pelea *f* —
fighter *n* **1** : luchador *m*, -dora *f* **2**
or **fighter plane** : avión *m* de caza
figment *n* **figment of the imagination**
: producto *m* de la imaginación
figurative *adj* : figurado
figure *n* **1** NUMBER : número *m*, cifra *f* **2**
PERSON, SHAPE : figura *f* · **3 figure of**
speech : figura *f* retórica **4 watch one's**
figure : cuidar la línea — **figure** *v* **-ured;**
-uring *vt* : calcular — *vi* **1** : figurar **2 that**
figures! : ¡no me extraña! — **figurehead** *n*
: testaferro *m* — **figure out** *vt* **1**
UNDERSTAND : entender **2** RESOLVE : resolver
file[1] *n* : lima *f* (instrumento) —
file *vt* **filed; filing** : limar
file[2] *vt* **filed; filing 1** : archivar
(documentos) **2 file charges** : presentar
cargos — **file** *n* : archivo *m*
file[3] *n* LINE : fila *f* — **file** *vi* **file in/**
out : entrar/salir en fila
fill *vt* **1** : llenar, rellenar **2** : cumplir con
(un requisito) **3** : tapar (un agujero),
empastar (un diente) — *vi* **1 fill in for**
: reemplazar **2** *or* **fill up** : llenarse —
fill *n* **1 eat one's fill** : comer lo suficiente

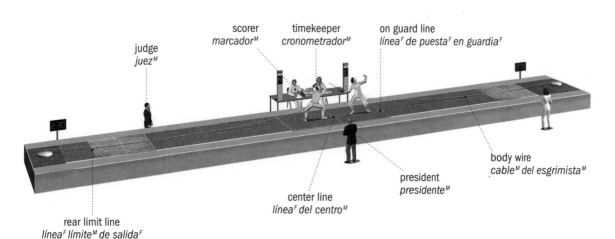

piste
pista[F] *de esgrima*[F]

judge
juez[M]

scorer
marcador[M]

timekeeper
cronometrador[M]

on guard line
línea[F] *de puesta*[F] *en guardia*[F]

body wire
cable[M] *del esgrimista*[M]

president
presidente[M]

center line
línea[F] *del centro*[M]

rear limit line
línea[F] *límite*[M] *de salida*[F]

2 have one's fill of : estar harto de
fillet *n* : filete *m*
filling *n* **1** : relleno *m* **2** :
empaste *m* (de dientes) **3 filling
station** → **service station**
filly *n, pl* **-lies** : potra *f*
film *n* : película *f* — **film** *vt* : filmar
filter *n* : filtro *m* — **filter** *vt* : filtrar
filth *n* : mugre *f* — **filthy** *adj* **filthier;
-est 1** : mugriento **2** OBSCENE : obsceno
fin *n* : aleta *f*
final *adj* **1** LAST : último **2** DEFINITIVE :
definitivo **3** ULTIMATE : final — **final** *n* **1**
: final *f* (en deportes) **2 finals** *npl* :
exámenes *mpl* finales — **finalist** *n* :
finalista *mf* — **finalize** *vt* **-ized; -izing**
: finalizar — **finally** *adv* : finalmente
finance *n* **1** : finanzas *fpl* **2
finances** *npl* : recursos *mpl* financieros
— **finance** *vt* **-nanced; -nancing** :
financiar — **financial** *adj* : financiero
— **financially** *adv* : económicamente
find *vt* **found; finding 1** LOCATE :
encontrar **2** REALIZE : darse cuenta
de **3 find guilty** : declarar culpable
4 *or* **find out** : descubrir — *vi* **find
out** : enterarse — **find** *n* : hallazgo *m*
— **findings** *n* **1** FIND : hallazgo *m* **2
findings** *npl* : conclusiones *fpl*
fine[1] *n* : multa *f* — **fine** *vt*
fined; fining : multar
fine[2] *adj* **finer; -est 1** DELICATE : fino **2**
EXCELLENT : excelente **3** SUBTLE : sutil **4** :

bueno (dícese del tiempo) **5 fine print** :
letra *f* menuda **6 it's fine with me** : me
parece bien — **fine** *adv* OK : bien — **fine
arts** *npl* : bellas artes *fpl* — **finely** *adv* **1**
EXCELLENTLY : excelentemente **2** PRECISELY
: con precisión **3** MINUTELY : fino, menudo
finger *n* : dedo *m* — **finger** *vt* : tocar,
toquetear — **fingernail** *n* : uña *f*
— **fingerprint** *n* : huella *f* digital —
fingertip *n* : punta *f* del dedo
finicky *adj* : maniático, mañoso *Lat*
finish *v* : acabar, terminar — **finish** *n* **1**
END : fin *m*, final *m* **2** *or* **finish line**
: meta *f* **3** SURFACE : acabado *m*
finite *adj* : finito
fir *n* : abeto *m*
fire *n* **1** : fuego *m* **2** CONFLAGRATION :
incendio *m* **3 catch fire** : incendiarse
(dícese de bosques, etc.), prenderse
(dícese de fósforos, etc.) **4 on fire** :
en llamas **5 open fire on** : abrir fuego
sobre — **fire** *vt* **fired; firing 1** DISMISS
: despedir **2** SHOOT : disparar — *vi* :
disparar — **fire alarm** *n* : alarma *f*
contra incendios — **firearm** *n* : arma *f*
de fuego — **firecracker** *n* : petardo *m*
— **fire engine** *n* : carro *m* de bomberos
Lat, coche *m* de bomberos *Spain* —
fire escape *n* : escalera *f* de incendios
— **fire extinguisher** *n* : extintor *m* (de
incendios) — **firefighter** *n* : bombero *m*,
-ra *f* — **firefly** *n, pl* **-flies** : luciérnaga *f*
— **firehouse** → **fire station** —
fireman *n, pl* **-men** → **firefighter** —
fireplace *n* : hogar *m*, chimenea *f* —
fireproof *adj* : ignífugo — **fireside** *n* :
hogar *m* — **fire station** *n* : estación *f* de
bomberos *Lat*, parque *m* de bomberos
Spain — **firewood** *n* : leña *f* —
fireworks *npl* : fuegos *mpl* artificiales
firm[1] *n* : empresa *f*
firm[2] *adj* : firme — **firmly** *adv* :
firmemente — **firmness** *n* : firmeza *f*
first *adj* **1** : primero **2 at first sight** : a
primera vista **3 for the first time** : por
primera vez — **first** *adv* **1** : primero **2
first and foremost** : ante todo **3 first
of all** : en primer lugar — **first** *n* **1** :
primero *m*, -ra *f* **2 at first** : al principio
— **first aid** *n* : primeros auxilios *mpl* —
first–class *adv* : en primera — **first–
class** *adj* : de primera *f* — **firsthand** *adv*
: directamente — **first** *adj* : de primera
mano — **firstly** *adv* : en primer lugar
— **first name** *n* : nombre *m* de pila

— **first–rate** *adj* → **first–class**
fiscal *adj* : fiscal
fish *n, pl* **fish** *or* **fishes** : pez *m* (vivo),
pescado *m* (para comer) — **fish** *vi* **1** :
pescar **2 fish for** SEEK : buscar **3 go fishing**
: ir de pesca — **fisherman** *n, pl* **-men**
: pescador *m*, -dora *f* — **fishhook** *n*
: anzuelo *m* — **fishing** *n* : pesca *f* —
fishing pole *n* : caña *f* de pescar — **fish
market** *n* : pescadería *f* — **fishy**; *adj*
fishier; -est 1 : a pescado (dícese de
sabores, etc.) **2** SUSPICIOUS : sospechoso
fist *n* : puño *m*
fit[1] *n* **1** : ataque *m* **2 he had
a fit** : le dio un ataque
fit[2] *adj* **fitter; fittest 1** SUITABLE : apropiado
2 HEALTHY : en forma **3 be fit for** : ser
apto para — **fit** *v* **fitted; fitting** *vt* **1** :
encajar en (un hueco, etc.) **2** *(relating
to clothing)* : quedar bien a **3** SUIT : ser
apropiado para **4** MATCH : coincidir con
5 *or* **fit out** : equipar — *vi* **1** : caber (en
una caja, etc.), encajar (en un hueco,
etc.) **2** *or* **fit in** BELONG : encajar **3 this
dress doesn't fit** : este vestido no me
queda bien — **fit** *n* **it's a good fit** : me
queda bien — **fitful** *adj* : irregular —
fitness *n* **1** HEALTH : salud *f* **2** SUITABILITY
: idoneidad *f* — **fitting** *adj* : apropiado
five *n* : cinco *m* — **five** *adj* : cinco
— **five hundred** *n* : quinientos *m*
— **five hundred** *adj* : quinientos
fix *vt* **1** ATTACH : fijar, sujetar **2** REPAIR :
arreglar **3** PREPARE : preparar — **fix** *n*
PREDICAMENT : aprieto *m*, apuro *m* —
fixed *adj* : fijo — **fixture** *n* : instalación *f*
fizz *vi* : burbujear — **fizz** *n*
: efervescencia *f*
fizzle *vi* **-zled; -zling** *or* **fizzle
out** : quedar en nada
flabbergasted *adj* :
estupefacto, pasmado
flabby *adj* **-bier; -est** : fofo
flaccid *adj* : fláccido
flag[1] *vi* WEAKEN : flaquear
flag[2] *n* : bandera *f* — **flag** *vt* **flagged;
flagging** *or* **flag down** : hacer señales
de parada a — **flagpole** *n* : asta *f*
flagrant *adj* : flagrante
flair *n* : don *m*, facilidad *f*
flake *n* : copo *m* (de nieve), escama *f*
(de pintura, de la piel) — **flake** *vi*
flaked; flaking : pelarse
flamboyant *adj* : extravagante
flame *n* **1** : llama *f* **2 burst into**

flamingo
flamenco[M]

flames : estallar en llamas 3 **go
up in flames** : incendiarse
▸ flamingo *n*, *pl* **-gos** : flamenco *m*
flammable *adj* : inflamable
flank *n* : ijado *m* (de un animal), flanco *m*
(militar) — **flank** *vt* : flanquear
flannel *n* : franela *f*
flap *n* : solapa *f* (de un sobre, un
libro, etc.), tapa *f* (de un recipiente)
— **flap** *v* **flapped; flapping** *vi* :
agitarse — *vt* : batir, agitar
flapjack → **pancake**
flare *vi* **flared; flaring 1 flare up** BLAZE
: llamear **2 flare up** EXPLODE, ERUPT :
estallar, explotar — **flare** *n* **1** BLAZE :
llamarada *f* **2** SIGNAL : (luz *f* de) bengala *f*
flash *vi* **1** : brillar, destellar **2 flash past** :
pasar como un rayo — *vt* **1** : dirigir (una
luz) **2** SHOW : mostrar **3 flash a smile** :
sonreír — **flash** *n* **1** : destello *m* **2 flash
of lightning** : relámpago *m* **3 in a flash**
: de repente — **flashlight** *n* : linterna *f*
— **flashy** *adj* **flashier; -est** : ostentoso
flask *n* : frasco *m*
flat *adj* **flatter; flattest 1** LEVEL : plano,
llano **2** DOWNRIGHT : categórico **3** FIXED :
fijo **4** MONOTONOUS : monótono **5** : bemol
(en la música) **6 flat tire** : neumático *m*
desinflado — **flat** *n* **1** : bemol *m* (en la
música) **2** *Brit* APARTMENT : apartamento *m*,
departamento *m*, *Lat* **3** PUNCTURE :
pinchazo *m* — **flat** *adv* **1 flat broke** :
pelado **2 in one hour flat** : en una hora
justa — **flatly** *adv* : categóricamente —
flat–out *adj* **1** : frenético **2** DOWNRIGHT
: categórico — **flatten** *vt* **1** LEVEL :
aplanar, allanar **2** KNOCK DOWN : arrasar
flatter *vt* **1** : halagar **2** BECOME :
favorecer — **flatterer** *n* : adulador *m*,
-dora *f* — **flattering** *adj* **1** : halagador
2 BECOMING : favorecedor —
flattery *n*, *pl* **-ries** : halagos *mpl*
flaunt *vt* : hacer alarde de
flavor *or Brit* **flavour** *n* : gusto *m*, sabor *m*
— **flavor** *vt* : sazonar — **flavorful** *or Brit*
flavourful *adj* : sabroso — **flavoring** *or*
Brit **flavouring** *n* : condimento *m*, sazón *f*
flaw *n* : defecto *m* —
flawless *adj* : perfecto
flax *n* : lino *m*
flea *n* : pulga *f*
fleck *n* **1** PARTICLE : mota *f* **2** SPOT : pinta *f*
flee *v* **fled; fleeing** *vi* : huir — *vt* : huir de
fleece *n* : vellón *m* — **fleece** *vt*
fleeced; fleecing 1 SHEAR :

esquilar **2** DEFRAUD : desplumar
fleet *n* : flota *f*
fleeting *adj* : fugaz
Flemish *adj* : flamenco
flesh *n* **1** : carne *f* **2** PULP : pulpa *f* **3**
in the flesh : en persona — **fleshy** *adj*
fleshier; -est 1 : gordo **2** PULPY : carnoso
flew → **fly**
flex *vt* : flexionar — **flexibility** *n*, *pl* **-ties**
: flexibilidad *f* — **flexible** *adj* : flexible
flick *n* : golpecito *m* — **flick** *vt* : dar un
golpecito a — *vi* **flick through** : hojear
flicker *vi* : parpadear — **flicker** *n* **1**
: parpadeo *m* **2 a flicker of
hope** : un rayo de esperanza
flier *n* **1** AVIATOR : aviador *m*, -dora *f* **2** *or*
flyer LEAFLET : folleto *m*, volante *m*, *Lat*
flight[1] *n* **1** : vuelo *m* **2** TRAJECTORY :
trayectoria *f* **3 flight of stairs** : tramo *m*
flight[2] *n* ESCAPE : huida *f*
flimsy *adj* **flimsier; -est 1** LIGHT
: ligero **2** SHAKY : poco sólido **3 a
flimsy excuse** : una excusa floja
flinch *vi* **flinch from** : encogerse ante
fling *vt* **flung; flinging 1** : arrojar
2 fling open : abrir de un golpe
— **fling** *n* **1** AFFAIR : aventura *f* **2**
have a fling at : intentar
flint *n* : pedernal *m*
flip *v* **flipped; flipping** *vt* **1** *or* **flip
over** : dar la vuelta a **2 flip a coin** :
echarlo a cara o cruz — *vi* **1** *or* **flip
over** : volcarse **2 flip through** : hojear
— **flip** *n* SOMERSAULT : voltereta *f*
flippant *adj* : ligero, frívolo
flipper *n* : aleta *f*
flirt *vi* : coquetear — **flirt** *n* : coqueto *m*,
-ta *f* — **flirtatious** *adj* : coqueto
flit *vi* **flitted; flitting** : revolotear
float *n* **1** : flotador *m* **2** : carroza *f*
(en un desfile) — **float** *vi* :
flotar — *vt* : hacer flotar
flock *n* : rebaño *m* (de ovejas), bandada *f*
(de pájaros) — **flock** *vi* : congregarse
flog *vt* **flogged; flogging** : azotar
flood *n* **1** : inundación *f* **2** : torrente *m*
(de palabras, de lágrimas, etc.) —
flood *vt* : inundar — **floodlight** *n* : foco *m*
floor *n* **1** : suelo *m*, piso *m*, *Lat* **2**
STORY : piso *m* **3 dance floor** : pista *f*
de baile **4 ground floor** : planta *f*
baja — **floor** *vt* **1** KNOCK DOWN :
derribar **2** NONPLUS : desconcertar —
floorboard *n* : tabla *f* del suelo
flop *vi* **flopped; flopping 1** FLAP : agitarse

2 COLLAPSE : dejarse caer **3** FAIL :
fracasar — **flop** *n* FAILURE : fracaso *m* —
floppy *adj* **-pier; -est** : flojo, flexible —
floppy disk *n* : diskette *m*, disquete *m*
flora *n* : flora *f* — **floral** *adj* : floral —
florid *adj* **1** FLOWERY : florido **2** RUDDY
: rojizo — **florist** *n* : florista *mf*
floss *n* → **dental floss**
flounder[1] *n*, *pl* **flounder** *or*
flounders : platija *f*
flounder[2] *vi* **1** *or* **flounder
about** : resbalarse, revolcarse **2**
: titubear (en un discurso)
flour *n* : harina *f*
flourish *vi* : florecer — *vt* BRANDISH
: blandir — **flourish** *n* : floritura *f*
— **flourishing** *adj* : floreciente
flout *vt* : desacatar, burlarse de
flow *vi* : fluir, correr — **flow** *n* **1** :
flujo *m*, circulación *f* **2** : corriente *f*
(de información, etc.)
flower *n* : flor *f* — **flower** *vi* : florecer —
flowered *adj* : floreado — **flowerpot** *n*
: maceta *f* — **flowery** *adj* : florido
flown → **fly**
flu *n* : gripe *f*
fluctuate *vi* **-ated; -ating** : fluctuar
— **fluctuation** *n* : fluctuación *f*
fluency *n* : fluidez *f* — **fluent** *adj* **1**
: fluido **2 be fluent in** : hablar con
fluidez — **fluently** *adv* : con fluidez
fluff *n* : pelusa *f* — **fluffy** *adj*
fluffier; -est : de pelusa, velloso
fluid *adj* : fluido — **fluid** *n* : fluido *m*
flung → **fling**
flunk *vt* : reprobar *Lat*, suspender *Spain*
— *vi* : ser reprobado *Lat*, suspender *Spain*
fluorescence *n* : fluorescencia *f*
— **fluorescent** *adj* : fluorescente
flurry *n*, *pl* **-ries 1** GUST : ráfaga *f* **2**
or **snow flurry** : nevisca *f* **3 flurry of
questions** : aluvión *m* de preguntas
flush *vi* BLUSH : ruborizarse, sonrojarse
— *vt* **flush the toilet** : tirar de la
cadena, jalarle a la cadena *Lat* —
flush *n* BLUSH : rubor *m*, sonrojo *m* —
flush *adj* **flush with** : a nivel con, a ras
de — **flush** *adv* : al mismo nivel, a ras
fluster *vt* : poner nervioso
flute *n* : flauta *f*
flutter *vi* **1** FLIT : revolotear **2** WAVE
: ondear **3** *or* **flutter about** : ir y
venir — **flutter** *n* **1** : revoloteo *m*
(de alas) **2** STIR : revuelo *m*
flux *n* **be in a state of flux** :

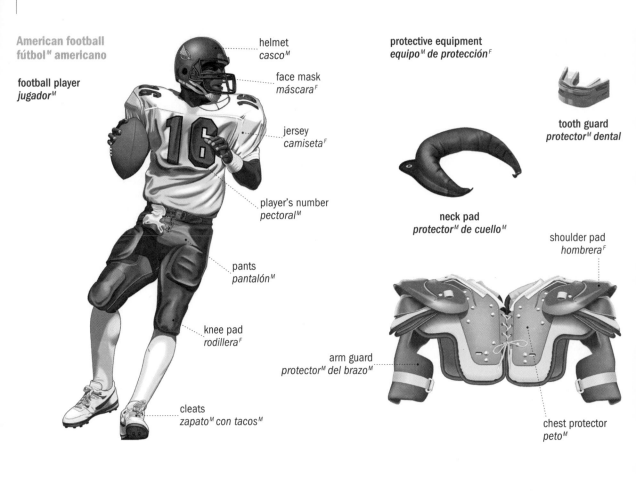

American football
fútbol^M americano

football player
jugador^M

helmet
casco^M

face mask
máscara^F

jersey
camiseta^F

player's number
pectoral^M

pants
pantalón^M

knee pad
rodillera^F

cleats
zapato^M con tacos^M

protective equipment
equipo^M de protección^F

tooth guard
protector^M dental

neck pad
protector^M de cuello^M

shoulder pad
hombrera^F

arm guard
protector^M del brazo^M

chest protector
peto^M

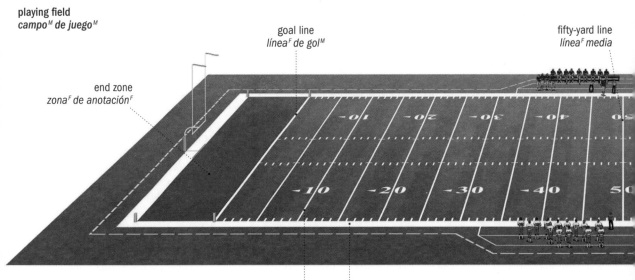

playing field
campo^M de juego^M

goal line
línea^F de gol^M

fifty-yard line
línea^F media

end zone
zona^F de anotación^F

yard line
línea^F yardas^F

sideline
banda^F

cambiar continuamente

fly[1] *v* **flew; flown; flying** *vi* **1** : volar **2** TRAVEL : ir en avión **3** WAVE : ondear **4** RUSH : correr **5 fly by** : pasar volando — *vt* **1** PILOT : pilotar **2** : hacer volar (una cometa), enarbolar (una bandera) —

fly *n, pl* **flies** : bragueta *f* (de un pantalón)

fly[2] *n, pl* **flies** : mosca *f* (insecto)

flyer → **flier**

flying saucer *n* : platillo *m* volador *Lat*, platillo *m* volante *Spain*

flyswatter *n* : matamoscas *m*

foal *n* : potro *m*, -tra *f*

foam *n* : espuma *f* — **foam** *vi* : hacer espuma — **foamy** *adj* **foamier; -est** : espumoso

focus *n, pl* **-ci 1** : foco *m* **2 be in focus** : estar enfocado **3 focus of attention** : centro *m* de atención — **focus** *v* **-cused** *or* **-cussed; -cusing** *or* **-cussing** *vt* **1** : enfocar **2** : centrar (la atención, etc.) — *vi* **focus on** : enfocar (con los ojos), concentrarse en (con la mente)

fodder *n* : forraje *m*

foe *n* : enemigo *m*, -ga *f*

fog *n* : niebla *f* — **fog** *v* **fogged; fogging** *vt* : empañar — *vi or* **fog up** : empañarse — **foggy** *adj* **foggier; -est** : nebuloso — **foghorn** *n* : sirena *f* de niebla

foil[1] *vt* : frustrar

foil[2] *n or* **aluminum foil** : papel *m* de aluminio

fold[1] *n* **1** : redil *m* (para ovejas) **2 return to the fold** : volver al redil

fold[2] *vt* **1** : doblar, plegar **2 fold one's arms** : cruzar los brazos — *vi* **1** *or* **fold up** : doblarse, plegarse **2** FAIL : fracasar — **fold** *n* : pliegue *m* — **folder** *n* : carpeta *f*

foliage *n* : follaje *m*

folk *n, pl* **folk** *or* **folks 1** : gente *f* **2 folks** *npl* PARENTS : padres *mpl* — **folk** *adj* **1** : popular **2 folk dance** : danza *f* folklórica — **folklore** *n* : folklore *m*

follow *vt* **1** : seguir **2** UNDERSTAND : entender **3 follow up** : seguir — *vi* **1** : seguir **2** UNDERSTAND : entender **3 follow up on** : seguir con — **follower** *n* : seguidor *m*, -dora *f* — **following** *adj* : siguiente — **following** *n* : seguidores *mpl* — **following** *prep* : después de

folly *n, pl* **-lies** : locura *f*

fond *adj* **1** : cariñoso **2 be fond of something** : ser aficionado a algo **3 be fond of someone** : tener cariño a algn

fondle *vt* **-dled; -dling** : acariciar

fondness *n* **1** LOVE : cariño *m* **2** LIKING : afición *f*

food *n* : comida *f*, alimento *m* — **foodstuffs** *npl* : comestibles *mpl*

fool *n* **1** : idiota *mf* **2** JESTER : bufón *m*, -fona *f* — **fool** *vi* **1** JOKE : bromear **2 fool around** : perder el tiempo — *vt* TRICK : engañar — **foolhardy** *adj* : temerario — **foolish** *adj* : tonto — **foolishness** *n* : tontería *f* — **foolproof** *adj* : infalible

▸ **foot** *n, pl* **feet** : pie *m* — **footage** *n* : secuencias *fpl* (cinemáticas) — **football** *n* : fútbol *m* americano — **footbridge** *n* : pasarela *f*, puente *m* peatonal — **foothills** *npl* : estribaciones *fpl* — **foothold** *n* : punto *m* de apoyo — **footing** *n* **1** BALANCE : equilibrio *m* **2 on equal footing** : en igualdad — **footlights** *npl* : candilejas *fpl* — **footnote** *n* : nota *f* al pie de la página — **footpath** *n* : sendero *m* — **footprint** *n* : huella *f* — **footstep** *n* : paso *m* — **footstool** *n* : escabel *m* — **footwear** *n* : calzado *m*

for *prep* **1** (*indicating purpose, etc.*) : para **2** (*indicating motivation, etc.*) : por **3** (*indicating duration*) : durante **4 we walked for 3 miles** : andamos 3 millas **5** AS FOR : con respecto a — **for** *conj* : puesto que, porque

forage *n* : forraje *m* — **forage** *vi* **-aged; -aging 1** : forrajear **2 forage for** : buscar

foray *n* : incursión *f*

forbid *vt* **-bade** *or* **-bad; -bidden; -bidding** : prohibir — **forbidding** *adj* : intimidante, severo

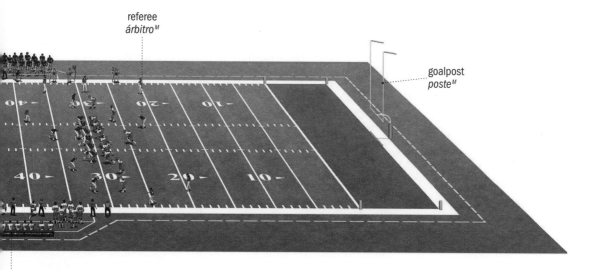

referee
árbitro[M]

goalpost
poste[M]

players' bench
banquillo[M] *de jugadores*[M]

force *n* **1** : fuerza *f* **2 by force** : por la fuerza **3 in force** : en vigor, en vigencia **4 armed forces** : fuerzas *fpl* armadas — **force** *vt* **forced; forcing 1** : forzar **2** OBLIGATE : obligar — **forced** *adj* : forzado, forzoso — **forceful** *adj* : fuerte, enérgetico

forceps *ns & pl* : fórceps *m*

forcibly *adv* : por la fuerza

ford *n* : vado *m* — **ford** *vt* : vadear

fore *n* **come to the fore** : empezar a destacarse

forearm *n* : antebrazo *m*

foreboding *n* : premonición *f*, presentimiento *m*

forecast *vt* **-cast; -casting** : predecir, pronosticar — **forecast** *n* : predicción *f*, pronóstico *m*

forefathers *n* : antepasados *mpl*

forefinger *n* : índice *m*, dedo *m* índice

forefront *n* **at/in the forefront** : a la vanguardia

forego → **forgo**

foregone *adj* **foregone conclusion** : resultado *m* inevitable

foreground *n* : primer plano *m*

forehead *n* : frente *f*

foreign *adj* **1** : extranjero **2 foreign trade** : comercio *m* exterior — **foreigner** *n* : extranjero *m*, -ra *f*

foreman *n, pl* **-men** : capataz *mf*

foremost *adj* : principal — **foremost** *adv* **first and foremost** : ante todo

forensic *adj* : forense

forerunner *n* : precursor *m*, -sora *f*

foresee *vt* **-saw; -seen; -seeing** : prever — **foreseeable** *adj* : previsible

foreshadow *vt* : presagiar

foresight *n* : previsión *f*

forest *n* : bosque *m* — **forestry** *n* : silvicultura *f*

foretaste *n* : anticipo *m*

foretell *vt* **-told; -telling** : predecir

forethought *n* : reflexión *f* previa

forever *adv* **1** ETERNALLY : para siempre **2** CONTINUALLY : siempre, constantemente

forewarn *vt* : advertir, prevenir

foreword *n* : prólogo *m*

forfeit *n* **1** PENALTY : pena *f* **2** : prenda *f* (en un juego) — **forfeit** *vt* : perder

forge *n* : forja *f* — **forge** *v* **forged; forging** *vt* **1** : forjar (metal, etc.) **2** COUNTERFEIT : falsificar — *vi* **forge ahead** : avanzar, seguir adelante — **forger** *n* : falsificador *m*, -dora *f* — **forgery** *n, pl* **-eries** : falsificación *f*

forget *v* **-got; -gotten** *or* **-got; -getting** *vt* : olvidar, olvidarse de — *vi* **1** : olvidarse **2 I forgot** : se me olvidó — **forgetful** *adj* : olvidadizo

forgive *vt* **-gave; -given; -giving** : perdonar — **forgiveness** *n* : perdón *m*

forgo *or* **forego** *vt* **-went; -gone; -going** : privarse de, renunciar a

fork *n* **1** : tenedor *m* **2** PITCHFORK : horca *f* **3** : bifurcación *f* (de un camino, etc.) — *vi* : ramificarse, bifurcarse — *vt* **fork over** : desembolsar

forlorn *adj* : triste

form *n* **1** : forma *f* **2** DOCUMENT : formulario *m* **3** KIND : tipo *m* — **form** *vt* **1** : formar **2 form a habit** : adquirir un hábito — *vi* : formarse

formal *adj* : formal — **formal** *n* **1** BALL : baile *m* (formal) **2** *or* **formal dress** : traje *m* de etiqueta — **formality** *n, pl* **-ties** : formalidad *f*

format *n* : formato *m* — **format** *vt* **-matted; -matting** : formatear

formation *n* **1** : formación *f* **2** SHAPE : forma *f*

former *adj* **1** PREVIOUS : antiguo, anterior **2** : primero (de dos) — **formerly** *adv* : anteriormente, antes

formidable *adj* : formidable

formula *n, pl* **-las** *or* **-lae 1** : fórmula *f* **2** *or* **baby formula** : preparado *m* para biberón

forsake *vt* **-sook; -saken; -saking** : abandonar

fort *n* : fuerte *m*

forth *adv* **1 and so forth** : etcétera **2 back and forth** → **back 3 from this day forth** : de hoy en adelante — **forthcoming** *adj* **1** COMING : próximo **2** OPEN : comunicativo — **forthright** *adj* : directo, franco

fortieth *adj* : cuadragésimo — **fortieth** *n* **1** : cuadragésimo *m*, -ma *f* (en una serie) **2** : cuarentavo *m*, cuarentava parte *f*

fortify *vt* **-fied; -fying** : fortificar — **fortification** *n* : fortificación *f*

fortitude *n* : fortaleza *f*

fortnight *n* : quince días *mpl*, quincena *f*

fortress *n* : fortaleza *f*

fortunate *adj* : afortunado — **fortunately** *adv* : afortunadamente — **fortune** *n* : fortuna *f* — **fortune–teller** *n* : adivino *m*, -na *f*

forty *n, pl* **forties** : cuarenta *m* — **forty** *adj* : cuarenta

forum *n, pl* **-rums** : foro *m*

forward *adj* **1** : hacia adelante (en dirección), delantero (en posición) **2** BRASH : descarado — **forward** *adv* **1** : (hacia) adelante **2 from this day forward** : de aquí en adelante — **forward** *vt* : remitir, enviar — **forward** *n* : delantero *m*, -ra *f* (en deportes) — **forwards** *adv* → **forward**

fossil *n* : fósil *m*

foster *adj* : adoptivo — **foster** *vt* : promover, fomentar

fought → **fight**

foul *adj* **1** REPULSIVE : asqueroso **2 foul language** : palabrotas *fpl* **3 foul play** : actos *mpl* criminales **4 foul weather** : mal tiempo *m* — **foul** *n* : falta *f* (en deportes) — **foul** *vi* : cometer faltas (en deportes) — *vt* : ensuciar

found[1] → **find**

found[2] *vt* : fundar, establecer — **foundation** *n* **1** : fundación *f* **2** BASIS : fundamento *m* **3** : cimientos *mpl* (de un edificio)

founder[1] *n* : fundador *m*, -dora *f*

founder[2] *vi* SINK : hundirse

fountain *n* : fuente *f*

four *n* : cuatro *m* — **four** *adj* : cuatro — **fourfold** *adj* : cuadruple — **four hundred** *adj* : cuatrocientos — **four hundred** *n* : cuatrocientos *m*

fourteen *n* : catorce *m* — **fourteen** *adj* : catorce — **fourteenth** *adj* : decimocuarto — **fourteenth** *n* **1** : decimocuarto *m*, -ta *f* (en una serie) **2** : catorceavo *m*, catorceava parte *f*

fourth *n* **1** : cuarto *m*, -ta *f* (en una serie) **2** : cuarto *m*, cuarta parte *f* — **fourth** *adj* : cuarto

fowl *n, pl* **fowl** *or* **fowls** : ave *f*

fox *n, pl* **foxes** : zorro *m*, -ra *f* — **fox** *vt* TRICK : engañar — **foxy** *adj* **foxier; -est** SHREWD : astuto

foyer *n* : vestíbulo *m*

fraction *n* : fracción *f*

fracture *n* : fractura *f* — **fracture** *vt* **-tured; -turing** : fracturar

fragile *adj* : frágil

fragment *n* : fragmento *m*

fragrant *adj* : fragante — **fragrance** *n* : fragancia *f*, aroma *m*

frail *adj* : débil, delicado

frame *vt* **framed; framing 1** ENCLOSE : enmarcar **2** COMPOSE, DRAFT : formular **3** INCRIMINATE : incriminar — **frame** *n* **1** : armazón *mf* (de un edificio, etc.) **2** :

marco *m* (de un cuadro, una puerta,
etc.) **3** *or* **frames** *npl* : montura *f* (para
anteojos) **4 frame of mind** : estado *m*
de ánimo — **framework** *n* : armazón *f*
franc *n* : franco *m*
frank *adj* : franco — **frankly** *adv* :
francamente — **frankness** *n* : franqueza *f*
frantic *adj* : frenético
fraternal *adj* : fraterno, fraternal
— **fraternity** *n*, *pl* **-ties** :
fraternidad *f* — **fraternize** *vi*
-nized; -nizing : confraternizar
fraud *n* **1** DECEIT : fraude *m* **2**
IMPOSTOR : impostor *m*, **-tora** *f* —
fraudulent *adj* : fraudulento
fraught *adj* **fraught with** :
lleno de, cargado de
fray[1] *n* **1 join the fray** : salir a la palestra
2 return to the fray : volver a la carga
fray[2] *vt* : crispar (los nervios)
— *vi* : deshilacharse
freak *n* **1** ODDITY : fenómeno *m* **2**
ENTHUSIAST : entusiasta *mf* —
freakish *adj* : anormal
freckle *n* : peca *f*
free *adj* **freer; freest 1** : libre **2** *or* **free of
charge** : gratuito, gratis **3** LOOSE : suelto
— **free** *vt* **freed; freeing 1** : liberar, poner
en libertad **2** RELEASE, UNFASTEN : soltar,
desatar — **free** *adv* *or* **for free** : gratis —
freedom *n* : libertad *f* — **freelance** *adj*
: por cuenta propia — **freely** *adv* **1** :
libremente **2** LAVISHLY : con generosidad
— **freeway** *n* : autopista *f* — **free
will** *n* **1** : libre albedrío *m* **2 of one's
own free will** : por su propia voluntad
freeze *v* **froze; frozen; freezing** *vi* **1** :
congelarse, helarse **2** STOP : quedarse
inmóvil — *vt* : helar (agua, etc.),
congelar (alimentos, precios, etc.)
— **freeze–dry** *vt* **-dried; -drying** :
liofilizar — **freezer** *n* : congelador *m*
— **freezing** *adj* **1** CHILLY : helado **2 it's
freezing!** : ¡hace un frío espantoso!
freight *n* **1** SHIPPING : porte *m*,
flete *m*, *Lat* **2** CARGO : carga *f*
French *adj* : francés — **French** *n* **1** :
francés *m* (idioma) **2 the French** *npl* : los
franceses — **Frenchman** *n* : francés *m*
— **Frenchwoman** *n* : francesa *f* —
french fries *npl* : papas *fpl* fritas
frenetic *adj* : frenético
frenzy *n*, *pl* **-zies** : frenesí *m*
— **frenzied** *adj* : frenético
frequent *vt* : frecuentar — **frequent** *adj*

frog
rana^F

nostril
narina^F

eyeball
globo^M ocular

tympanum
tímpano^M

hind limb
pata^F trasera

mouth
boca^F

digit
dedo^M

webbed foot
dedo^M palmeado

: frecuente — **frequency** *n*, *pl* **-cies**
: frecuencia *f* — **frequently** *adv*
: a menudo, frecuentemente
fresco *n*, *pl* **-coes** : fresco *m*
fresh *adj* **1** : fresco **2** IMPUDENT :
descarado **3** CLEAN : limpio **4** NEW :
nuevo **5 fresh water** : agua *m* dulce —
freshen *vt* : refrescar — *vi* **freshen up**
: arreglarse — **freshly** *adv* : recién —
freshman *n*, *pl* **-men** : estudiante *mf* de
primer año — **freshness** *n* : frescura *f*
fret *vi* **fretted; fretting** : preocuparse
— **fretful** *adj* : nervioso, irritable
friar *n* : fraile *m*
friction *n* : fricción *f*
Friday *n* : viernes *m*
friend *n* : amigo *m*, **-ga** *f* —
friendliness *n* : simpatía *f* —
friendly *adj* **-lier; -est** : simpático,
amable — **friendship** *n* : amistad *f*
frigate *n* : fragata *f*
fright *n* : miedo *m*, susto *m* —
frighten *vt* : asustar, espantar —
frightened *adj* **1** : asustado, temeroso
2 be frightened of : tener miedo de
— **frightening** *adj* : espantoso —
frightful *adj* : espantoso, terrible
frigid *adj* : frío, glacial
frill *n* **1** RUFFLE : volante *m* **2**
LUXURY : lujo *m*
fringe *n* **1** : fleco *m* **2** EDGE : periferia *f*,

margen *m* **3 fringe benefits** :
incentivos *mpl*, extras *mpl*
frisk *vt* SEARCH : cachear, registrar —
frisky *adj* **friskier; -est** : retozón, juguetón
fritter *n* : buñuelo *m* — **fritter** *vt*
or **fritter away** : malgastar
(dinero), desperdiciar (tiempo)
frivolous *adj* : frívolo —
frivolity *n*, *pl* **-ties** : frivolidad *f*
frizzy *adj* **frizzier; -est** : rizado, crespo
fro *adv* **to and fro** → **to**
frock *n* : vestido *m*
▶ **frog** *n* **1** : rana *f* **2 have a frog in
one's throat** : tener carraspera
frolic *vi* **-icked; -icking** : retozar
from *prep* **1** : de **2** (*indicating a starting
point*) : desde **3** (*indicating a cause*) : de,
por **4 from now on** : a partir de ahora
front *n* **1** : parte *f* delantera **2** : delantera *f*
(de un vestido, etc.), fachada *f* (de
un edificio), frente *m* (military) **3 cold
front** : frente *m* frío **4 in front of** :
delante de, adelante de *Lat* — **front** *vi*
or **front on** : dar a, estar orientado a
— **front** *adj* **1** : delantero, de adelante
2 the front row : la primera fila
frontier *n* : frontera *f*
frost *n* **1** : helada *f* **2** : escarcha *f* (en una
superficie) — **frost** *vt* ICE : bañar (pasteles)
— **frostbite** *n* : congelación *f* — **frosting** *n*
ICING : baño *m* — **frosty** *adj* **frostier; -est 1**

: cubierto de escarcha **2** CHILLY : helado, frío
froth *n, pl* **froths** : espuma *f* —
  frothy; *adj* **frothier; -est** : espumoso
frown *vi* **1** : fruncir el ceño, fruncir
  el entrecejo **2 frown at** : mirar con
  ceño **3 frown upon** : desaprobar
  — **frown** *n* : ceño *m* (fruncido)
froze, frozen → **freeze**
frugal *adj* : frugal
fruit *n* **1** : fruta *f* **2** PRODUCT, RESULT
  : fruto *m* — **fruitcake** *n* : pastel *m* de
  frutas — **fruitful** *adj* : fructífero —
  fruition *n* **come to fruition** : realizarse
  — **fruitless** *adj* : infructuoso — **fruity** *adj*
  fruitier; -est : (con sabor) a fruta
frustrate *vt* **-trated; -trating** :
  frustrar — **frustrating** *adj* : frustrante
  — **frustration** *n* : frustración *f*
fry *vt* **fried; frying** : freír — **fry** *n,*
  pl **fries 1 small fry** : gente *f* de poca
  monta **2 fries** *npl* → **french fries**
  — **frying pan** *n* : sartén *mf*
fudge *n* : dulce *m* blando
  de chocolate y leche
fuel *n* : combustible *m* — **fuel** *vt* **-eled**
  or **-elled; -eling** *or* **-elling 1** : alimentar
  (un horno), abastecer de combustible
  (un avión) **2** STIMULATE : estimular
fugitive *n* : fugitivo *m*, -va *f*
fulfill *or* **fulfil** *vt* **-filled; -filling 1**
  : cumplir con (una obligación),
  desarrollar (potencial) **2** FILL,
  MEET : cumplir — **fulfillment** *n* **1**
  ACCOMPLISHMENT : cumplimiento *m* **2**
  SATISFACTION : satisfacción *f*
full *adj* **1** FILLED : lleno **2** COMPLETE :
  complete, detallado **3** : redondo (dícese
  de la cara), amplio (dícese de ropa) **4**
  at full speed : a toda velocidad **5 in**
  full bloom : en plena flor — **full** *adv* **1**
  DIRECTLY : de lleno **2 know full well** : saber
  muy bien — **full** *n* **1 pay in full** : pagar
  en su totalidad **2 to the full** : al máximo
  — **full–fledged** *adj* : hecho y derecho —
  fully *adv* **1** COMPLETELY : completamente
  2 AT LEAST : al menos, por lo menos
fumble *vi* **-bled; -bling 1**
  RUMMAGE : hurgar **2 fumble**
  with : manejar con torpeza
fume *vi* **fumed; fuming 1** SMOKE :
  echar humo, humear **2** RAGE : estar
  furioso — **fumes** *npl* : gases *mpl*
fumigate *vt* **-gated; -gating** : fumigar
fun *n* **1** AMUSEMENT : diversión *f* **2 have**
  fun : divertirse **3 make fun of** : reírse
  de, burlarse de — **fun** *adj* : divertido
function *n* **1** : función *f* **2** GATHERING :
  recepción *f*, reunión *f* social — **function** *vi*

fur animals
animales^M **de piel**^{F}

stone marten
garduña^F

fennec
fenec^M

mink
visón^M

marten
marta^M

mongoose
mangosta^F

woodchuck
marmota^F

weasel
comadreja^F

chipmunk
ardilla^F *listada*

ferret
hurón^M

squirrel
ardilla^F

pika
pica^F

hare
liebre^F

raccoon
mapache^M

koala
koala^M

lemur
lémur^M

wolverine
glotón^M

beaver
castor^M

: funcionar — **functional** *adj* : funcional
fund *n* **1** : fondo *m* **2 funds** *npl* RESOURCES
: fondos *mpl* — **fund** *vt* : financiar
fundamental *adj* : fundamental —
fundamentals *npl* : fundamentos *mpl*
funeral *adj* : funeral, fúnebre — **funeral** *n*
: funeral *m*, funerales *mpl* — **funeral**
home *or* **funeral parlor** *n* : funeraria *f*
fungus *n*, *pl* **fungi** : hongo *m*
funnel *n* **1** : embudo *m* **2**
SMOKESTACK : chimenea *f*
funny *adj* **funnier; -est 1** : divertido,
gracioso **2** STRANGE : extraño, raro
— **funnies** *npl* : tiras *fpl* cómicas
▸ **fur** *n* **1** : pelaje *m*, pelo *m* (de un
animal) **2** *or* **fur coat** : (prenda *f*
de) piel *f* — **fur** *adj* : de piel
furious *adj* : furioso
furnace *n* : horno *m*
furnish *vt* **1** SUPPLY : proveer **2** : amueblar
(una casa, etc.) — **furnishings** *npl* :
muebles *mpl*, mobiliario *m* — **furniture** *n*
: muebles *mpl*, mobiliario *m*
furrow *n* : surco *m*
furry *adj* **furrier; -est** : peludo
(dícese de un animal), de peluche
(dícese de un juguete, etc.)
further *adv* **1** FARTHER : más lejos
2 MOREOVER : además **3** MORE : más
— **further** *vt* : promover, fomentar
— **further** *adj* **1** FARTHER : más
lejano **2** ADDITIONAL : adicional, más
3 until further notice : hasta
nuevo aviso — **furthermore** *adv* :
además — **furthest** → **farthest**
furtive *adj* : furtivo
fury *n*, *pl* **-ries** : furia *f*
fuse¹ *or* **fuze** *n* : mecha *f*
(de una bomba, etc.)
fuse² *v* **fused; fusing** *vt* **1** MELT : fundir **2**
UNITE : fusionar — *vi* : fundirse, fusionarse
— **fuse** *n* **1** : fusible *m* **2 blow a fuse** :
fundir un fusible — **fusion** *n* : fusión *f*
fuss *n* **1** : jaleo *m*, alboroto *m* **2**
make a fuss : armar un escándalo
— **fuss** *vi* **1** WORRY : preocuparse **2**
COMPLAIN : quejarse — **fussy** *adj* **fussier;**
-est 1 IRRITABLE : irritable **2** ELABORATE
: recargado **3** FINICKY : quisquilloso
futile *adj* : inútil, vano —
futility *n*, *pl* **-ties** : inutilidad *f*
future *adj* : futuro — **future** *n* : futuro *m*
fuze → **fuse**¹
fuzz *n* : pelusa *f* — **fuzzy** *adj* **fuzzier;**
-est 1 FURRY : con pelusa, peludo **2**
BLURRY : borroso **3** VAGUE : confuso

g *n, pl* **g's** *or* **gs** : g *f*, séptima
letra del alfabeto inglés
gab *vi* **gabbed; gabbing** : charlar,
cotorrear *fam* — **gab** *n* CHATTER : charla *f*
gable *n* : aguilón *m*
gadget *n* : artilugio *m*
gag *v* **gagged; gagging** *vt* : amordazar
— *vi* CHOKE : atragantarse — **gag** *n* **1**
: mordaza *f* **2** JOKE : chiste *m*
gage → **gauge**
gaiety *n, pl* **-eties** : alegría *f* —
gaily *adv* : alegremente
gain *n* **1** PROFIT : ganancia *f* **2**
INCREASE : aumento *m* — **gain** *vt* **1**
OBTAIN : ganar, adquirir **2 gain weight**

: aumentar de peso — *vi* **1** PROFIT :
beneficiarse **2** : adelantar(se) (dícese
de un reloj) — **gainful** *adj* : lucrativo
gait *n* : modo *m* de andar
gala *n* : fiesta *f*
galaxy *n, pl* **-axies** : galaxia *f*
gale *n* **1** : vendaval *f* **2 gales
of laughter** : carcajadas *fpl*
gall *n* **have the gall to** :
tener el descaro de
gallant *adj* **1** BRAVE : valiente
2 CHIVALROUS : galante
gallbladder *n* : vesícula *f* biliar
gallery *n, pl* **-leries** : galería *f*

gallon *n* : galón *m*
gallop *vi* : galopar — **gallop** *n* : galope *m*
gallows *n, pl* **-lows** *or* **-lowses** : horca *f*
gallstone *n* : cálculo *m* biliar
galore *adj* : en abundancia
galoshes *n, pl* : galochas *fpl*, chanclos *mpl*
galvanize *vt* **-nized; -nizing** : galvanizar
gamble *v* **-bled; -bling** *vi* : jugar
— *vt* : jugarse — **gamble** *n* **1**
BET : apuesta *f* **2** RISK : riesga *f* —
gambler *n* : jugador *m*, -dora *f*
game *n* **1** : juego *m* **2** MATCH :
partido *m* **3** *or* **game animals** : caza *f*
— **game** *adj* READY : listo, dispuesto
gamut *n* : gama *f*

garden
jardín^M

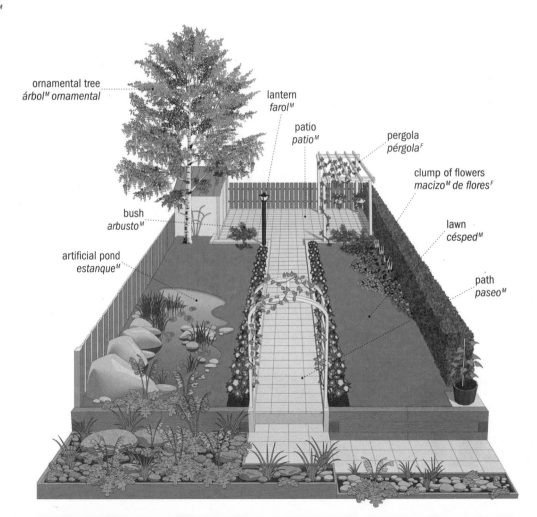

ornamental tree
árbol^M ornamental

lantern
farol^M

patio
patio^M

pergola
pérgola^F

clump of flowers
macizo^M de flores^F

bush
arbusto^M

lawn
césped^M

artificial pond
estanque^M

path
paseo^M

gang *n* : banda *f*, pandilla *f* —
  gang *vi* **gang up on** : unirse contra
gangplank *n* : pasarela *f*
gangrene *n* : gangrena *f*
gangster *n* : gángster *mf*
gangway *n* → **gangplank**
gap *n* **1** OPENING : espacio *m* **2** INTERVAL
  : intervalo *m* **3** DISPARITY : brecha *f*,
  distancia *f* **4** DEFICIENCY : laguna *f*
gape *vi* **gaped; gaping 1** OPEN : estar
  abierto **2** STARE : mirar boquiabierto
garage *n* : garaje *m* — **garage** *vt*
  -raged; -raging : dejar en un garaje
garb *n* : vestido *m*
garbage *n* : basura *f* — **garbage**
  can *n* : cubo *m* de la basura
garble *vt* **-bled; -bling** : tergiversar —
  garbled *adj* : confuso, incomprensible
garden *n* : jardín *m* — **garden** *vi* : trabajar
  en el jardín — **gardener** *n* : jardinero *m*,
  -ra *f* — **gardening** *n* : jardinería *f*
gargle *vi* **-gled; -gling** : hacer gárgaras
garish *adj* : chillón
garland *n* : guirnalda *f*
garlic *n* : ajo *m*
garment *n* : prenda *f*
garnish *vt* : guarnecer — **garnish** *n*
  : adorno *m*, guarnición *f*
garret *n* : buhardilla *f*
garrison *n* : guarnición *f*
garrulous *adj* : charlatán, parlanchín
garter *n* : liga *f*
gas *n, pl* **gases 1** : gas *m* **2** GASOLINE
  : gasolina *f* — **gas** *v* **gassed;**
  gassing *vt* : asfixiar con gas — *vi* **gas**
  up : llenar el tanque con gasolina
gash *n* : tajo *m* — **gash** *vt* :
  hacer un tajo en, cortar
gasket *n* : junta *f*
gasoline *n* : gasolina *f*
gasp *vi* **1** : dar un grito ahogado **2** PANT
  : jadear — **gasp** *n* : grito *m* ahogado
gas station *n* : gasolinera *f*
gastric *adj* : gástrico
gastronomy *n* : gastronomía *f*
gate *n* **1** DOOR : puerta *f* **2** BARRIER :
  barrera *f* — **gateway** *n* : puerta *f*
gather *vt* **1** ASSEMBLE : reunir **2**
  COLLECT : recoger **3** CONCLUDE : deducir
  4 : fruncir (una tela) **5 gather speed**
  : acelerar — *vi* : reunirse (dícese de
  personas), acumularse (dícese de
  cosas) — **gathering** *n* : reunión *f*
gaudy *adj* **gaudier; -est** :
  chillón, llamativo

gauge *n* **1** INDICATOR : indicador *m* **2**
  CALIBER : calibre *m* — **gauge** *vt*
  gauged; gauging 1 MEASURE : medir
  2 ESTIMATE : calcular, evaluar
gaunt *adj* : demacrado, descarnado
gauze *n* : gasa *f*
gave → **give**
gawky *adj* **gawkier; -est** : desgarbado
gay *adj* **1** : alegre **2** HOMOSEXUAL
  : gay, homosexual
gaze *vi* **gazed; gazing** : mirar
  (fijamente) — **gaze** *n* : mirada *f*
gazelle *n* : gacela *f*
gazette *n* : gaceta *f*
gear *n* **1** EQUIPMENT : equipo *m* **2**
  POSSESSIONS : efectos *mpl* personales
  3 : marcha *f* (de un vehículo) **4** *or* **gear**
  wheel : rueda *f* dentada — **gear** *vt*
  : orientar, adaptar — *vi* **gear up** :
  prepararse — **gearshift** *n* : palanca *f* de
  cambio, palanca *f* de velocidades *Lat*
geese → **goose**
gelatin *n* : gelatina *f*
gem *n* : gema *f*, piedra *f* preciosa —
  gemstone *n* : piedra *f* preciosa
gender *n* **1** SEX : sexo *m* **2** :
  género *m* (en la gramática)
gene *n* : gen *m*, gene *m*
genealogy *n, pl* **-gies** : genealogía *f*

general *adj* : general — **general** *n* **1**
  : general *mf* (militar) **2 in general**
  : en general, por lo general —
  generalize *v* **-ized; -izing** : generalizar
  — **generally** *adv* : generalmente, en
  general — **general practitioner** *n*
  : médico *m*, -ca *f* de cabecera
generate *vt* **-ated; -ating** : generar
  — **generation** *n* : generación *f* —
  generator *n* : generador *m*
generous *adj* **1** : generoso **2**
  AMPLE : abundante — **generosity** *n,*
  pl **-ties** : generosidad *f*
genetic *adj* : genético —
  genetics *n* : genética *f*
genial *adj* : afable, simpático
genital *adj* : genital —
  genitals *npl* : genitales *mpl*
genius *n* : genio *m*
genocide *n* : genocidio *m*
genteel *adj* : refinado
gentle *adj* **-tler; -tlest 1** MILD : suave,
  dulce **2** LIGHT : ligero **3 a gentle hint** :
  una indirecta discreta — **gentleman** *n,*
  pl **-men 1** MAN : caballero *m*, señor *m* **2 a**
  perfect gentleman : un perfecto caballero
  — **gentleness** *n* : delicadeza *f*, ternura *f*
genuine *adj* **1** AUTHENTIC : verdadero,
  auténtico **2** SINCERE : sincero
geography *n, pl* **-phies** :

geography: Earth coordinate system
geografía: sistema*ᴹ* de coordenadas*ᶠ* terrestres

North Pole
*polo*ᴹ Norte

Arctic Circle
*círculo*ᴹ *polar Ártico*

Northern Hemisphere
*hemisferio*ᴹ *Norte*

Tropic of Cancer
*trópico*ᴹ *de Cáncer*

Equator
*ecuador*ᴹ

Southern Hemisphere
*hemisferio*ᴹ *Sur*

Tropic of Capricorn
*trópico*ᴹ *de Capricornio*ᴹ

Antarctic Circle
*Círculo*ᴹ *polar Antártico*

South Pole
*polo*ᴹ *Sur*

giraffe •
jirafa*ᶠ*

geografía *f* — **geographic** *or*
geographical *adj* : geográfico
geology *n* : geología *f* — **geologic**
or **geological** *adj* : geológico
geometry *n, pl* **-tries** : geometría *f* —
geometric *or* **geometrical** *adj* : geométrico
geranium *n* : geranio *m*
geriatric *adj* : geriátrico —
geriatrics *n* : geriatría *f*
germ *n* **1** : germen *m* **2**
MICROBE : microbio *m*
German *adj* : alemán —
German *n* : alemán *m* (idioma)
germinate *v* **-nated; -nating** *vi* :
germinar — *vt* : hacer germinar
gestation *n* : gestación *f*
gesture *n* : gesto *m* — **gesture** *vi*
-tured; -turing 1 : hacer gestos
2 gesture to : hacer señas a
get *v* **got; got** *or* **gotten; getting** *vt* **1**
OBTAIN : conseguir, obtener **2** RECEIVE :
recibir **3** EARN : ganar **4** FETCH : traer **5**
CATCH : coger, agarrar *Lat* **6** UNDERSTAND :
entender **7** PREPARE : preparar **8 get one's**
hair cut : cortarse el pelo **9 get someone**
to do something : lograr que uno haga
algo **1 0 have got** : tener **1 1 have got**
to : tener que — *vi* **1** BECOME : ponerse,
hacerse **2** GO MOVE : ir **3** PROGRESS :
avanzar **4 get ahead** : progresar **5**
get at MEAN : querer decir **6 get away**

: escaparse **7 get away with** : salir
impune de **8 get back at** : desquitarse
con **9 get by** : arreglárselas **1 0 get**
home : llegar a casa **11 get out** : salir
1 2 get over : reponerse de, consolarse
de **1 3 get together** : reunirse **14 get**
up : levantarse — **getaway** *n* : fuga *f*,
huida *f* — **get–together** *n* : reunión *f*
geyser *n* : géiser *m*
ghastly *adj* **-lier; -est** :
horrible, espantoso
ghetto *n, pl* **-tos** *or* **-toes** : gueto *m*
ghost *n* : fantasma *f*, espectro *m*
— **ghostly** *adv* : fantasmal
giant *n* : gigante *m*, -ta *f* —
giant *adj* : gigantesco
gibberish *n* : galimatías *m*, jerigonza *f*
gibe *vi* **gibed; gibing gibe at** : mofarse
de — **gibe** *n* : pulla *f*, mofa *f*
giblets *npl* : menudillos *mpl*
giddy *adj* **-dier; -est** : mareado,
vertiginoso — **giddiness** *n* : vértigo *m*
gift *n* **1** PRESENT : regalo *m* **2** TALENT :
don *m* — **gifted** *adj* : talentoso, de talento
gigantic *adj* : gigantesco
giggle *vi* **-gled; -gling** : reírse
tontamente — **giggle** *n* : risa *f* tonta
gild *vt* **gilded** *or* **gilt; gilding** : dorar
gill *n* : agalla *f*, branquia *f*
gilt *adj* : dorado
gimmick *n* : truco *m*, ardid *m*
gin *n* : ginebra *f*
ginger *n* : jengibre *m* — **ginger ale** *n* :
refresco *m* de jengibre — **gingerbread** *n*
: pan *m* de jengibre — **gingerly** *adv*
: con cuidado, cautelosamente
▸ **giraffe** *n* : jirafa *f*
girder *n* : viga *f*
girdle *n* CORSET : faja *f*
girl *n* **1** : niña *f*, muchacha *f*, chica *f*
— **girlfriend** *n* : novia *f*, amiga *f*
girth *n* : circunferencia *f*
gist *n* **get the gist of** :
comprender lo esencial de
give *v* **gave; given; giving** *vt* **1** : dar **2**
INDICATE : señalar **3** PRESENT : presentar
4 give away : regalar **5 give back** :
devolver **6 give out** : repartir **7 give up**
smoking : dejar de fumar — *vi* **1** YIELD :
ceder **2** COLLAPSE : romperse **3 give out**
: agotarse **4 give up** : rendirse — **give** *n*
: elasticidad *f* — **given** *adj* **1** SPECIFIED :
determinado **2** INCLINED : dado, inclinado
— **given name** *n* : nombre *m* de pila
glacier *n* : glaciar *m*

glad *adj* **gladder; gladdest 1** : alegre,
contento **2 be glad** : alegrarse **3 glad to**
meet you! : ¡mucho gusto! — **gladden** *vt*
: alegrar — **gladly** *adv* : con mucho
gusto — **gladness** *n* : alegría *f*, gozo *m*
glade *n* : claro *m*
glamor *or* **glamour** *n* : atractivo *m*,
encanto *m* — **glamorous** *adj* : atractivo
glance *vi* **glanced; glancing 1**
glance at : mirar, dar un vistazo
a **2 glance off** : rebotar en —
glance *n* : mirada *f*, vistazo *m*
gland *n* : glándula *f*
glare *vi* **glared; glaring 1** : brillar,
relumbrar **2 glare at** : lanzar una
mirada feroz a — **glare** *n* **1** : luz *f*
deslumbrante **2** STARE : mirada *f*
feroz — **glaring** *adj* **1** BRIGHT :
deslumbrante **2** FLAGRANT : flagrante
glass *n* **1** : vidrio *m*, cristal *m* **2 a glass**
of milk : un vaso de leche **3 glasses** *npl*
SPECTACLES : anteojos *mpl*, lentes *fpl* —
glass *adj* : de vidrio — **glassware** *n* :
cristalería *f* — **glassy** *adj* **glassier; -est 1**
: vítreo **2 glassy eyes** : ojos *mpl* vidriosos
glaze *vt* **glazed; glazing 1** : poner vidrios
a (una ventana, etc.) **2** : vidriar (cerámica)
3 ICE : glasear — **glaze** *n* **1** : vidriado *m*,
barniz *m* (de cerámica) **2** ICING : glaseado *m*
gleam *n* **1** : destello *m* **2 a gleam**
of hope : un rayo de esperanza
— **gleam** *vi* : destellar, relucir
glee *n* : alegría *f* — **gleeful** *adj*
: lleno de alegría
glib *adj* **glibber; glibbest 1** : de mucha
labia **2 a glib reply** : una respuesta
simplista — **glibly** *adv* : con mucha labia
glide *vi* **glided; gliding** : deslizarse
(en una superficie), planear (en el
▸ aire) — **glider** *n* : planeador *m*
glimmer *vi* : brillar con luz trémula —
glimmer *n* : luz *f* trémula, luz *f* tenue
glimpse *vt* **glimpsed; glimpsing** :
vislumbrar — **glimpse** *n* : vislumbre *f*
glint *vi* : destellar — **glint** *n* : destello *m*
glisten *vi* : brillar
glitter *vi* : relucir, brillar
gloat *vi* **gloat over** : regodearse con
globe *n* : globo *m* — **global** *adj*
: global, mundial
gloom *n* **1** DARKNESS : oscuridad *f* **2**
SADNESS : tristeza *f* — **gloomy** *adj*
gloomier; -est 1 DARK : sombrío,
tenebroso **2** DISMAL : deprimente,
lúgubre **3** PESSIMISTIC : pesimista

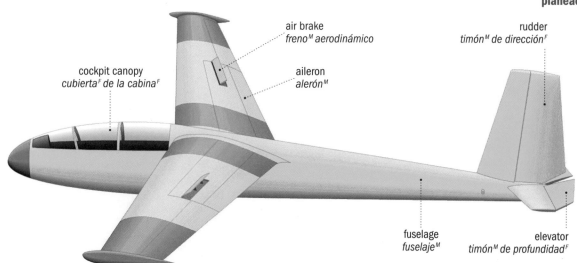

glider
planeador^M

air brake
freno^M *aerodinámico*

rudder
timón^M *de dirección*^F

cockpit canopy
cubierta^F *de la cabina*^F

aileron
alerón^M

fuselage
fuselaje^M

elevator
timón^M *de profundidad*^F

---

glory *n, pl* **-ries** : gloria *f* —
 glorify *vt* **-fied; -fying** : glorificar —
 glorious *adj* : glorioso, espléndido
gloss *n* : lustre *m*, brillo *m* —
 gloss *vt* **gloss over** : minimizar
 (la importancia de algo)
glossary *n, pl* **-ries** : glosario *m*
glossy *adj* **glossier; -est**
 : lustroso, brillante
glove *n* : guante *m*
glow *vi* **1** : brillar, resplandecer **2**
 glow with health : rebosar de salud
 — **glow** *n* : resplandor *m*, brillo *m*
glue *n* : pegamento *m*, cola *f* — **glue** *vt*
 glued; gluing *or* **glueing** : pegar
glum *adj* **glummer; glummest**
 : sombrío, triste
glut *n* : superabundancia *f*, exceso *m*
glutton *n* : glotón *m*, -tona *f* —
 gluttonous *adj* : glotón — **gluttony** *n,*
 pl **-tonies** : glotonería *f*
gnarled *adj* : nudoso
gnash *vt* **gnash one's teeth** :
 hacer rechinar los dientes
gnat *n* : jején *m*
gnaw *vt* : roer
go *v* **went; gone; going; goes** *vi* **1** : ir **2**
 LEAVE : irse, salir **3** EXTEND : ir, extenderse
 4 SELL : venderse **5** FUNCTION : funcionar,
 marchar **6** DISAPPEAR : desaparecer **7 go**

back on one's word : faltar a su palabra
8 go crazy : volverse loco **9 go for** LIKE
 : gustar **10 go off** EXPLODE : estallar **1 1**
go with MATCH : armonizar con **1 2 go**
without : pasar sin — *v aux* **be going**
to : ir a — **go** *n, pl* **goes 1 be on the**
go : no parar **2 have a go at** : intentar
goad *vt* : aguijonear (un animal),
 incitar (a una persona)
goal *n* **1** AIM : meta *m*, objetivo *m* **2** :
 gol *m* (en deportes) — **goalkeeper** *or*
 goalie *n* : portero *m*, -ra *f;* arquero *m*, -ra *f*
goat *n* : cabra *f*
goatee *n* : barbita *f* de chivo
gobble *vt* **-bled; -bling** *or*
 gobble up : engullir
goblet *n* : copa *f*
goblin *n* : duende *m*
god *n* **1** : dios *m* **2 God** : Dios *m* —
 goddess *n* : diosa *f* — **godchild** *n,*
 pl **-children** : ahijado *m*, -da *f*
 — **godfather** *n* : padrino *m* —
 godmother *n* : madrina *f* —
 godparents *npl* : padrinos *mpl* —
 godsend *n* : bendición *f* (del cielo)
goes → **go**
goggles *npl* : gafas *fpl*
 (protectoras), anteojos *mpl*
goings-on *npl* : sucesos *mpl*
gold *n* : oro *m* — **golden** *adj* **1** :

(hecho) de oro **2** : dorado, de color
 oro — **goldfish** *n* : pez *m* de colores
 — **goldsmith** *n* : orfebre *mf*
golf *n* : golf *m* — **golf** *vi* : jugar
 (al) golf — **golf ball** *n* : pelota *f* de
 golf — **golf course** *n* : campo *m*
 de golf — **golfer** *n* : golfista *mf*
gone *adj* **1** : ido, pasado **2** DEAD :
 muerto **3** LOST : desaparecido
good *adj* **better; best 1** : bueno **2** KIND
 : amable **3 good afternoon (evening)**
 : buenas tardes **4 be good at** : tener
 facilidad para **5 feel good** : sentirse
 bien **6 good for a cold** : beneficioso
 para los resfriados **7 have a good time**
 : divertirse **8 good morning** : buenos
 días **9 good night** : buenas noches
 — **good** *n* **1** : bien *m* **2** GOODNESS
 : bondad *f* **3 goods** *npl* PROPERTY
 : bienes *mpl* **4 goods** *npl* WARES :
 mercancías *fpl*, mercaderías *fpl* **5 for**
good : para siempre — **good** *adv* : bien
 — **good-bye** *or* good-by *n* : adiós *m*
 — **Good Friday** *n* : Viernes *m* Santo
 — **good-looking** *adj* : bello, guapo
 — **goodness** *n* **1** : bondad *f* **2 thank**
goodness ! : ¡gracias a Dios!, ¡menos
 mal! — **goodwill** *n* : buena voluntad *f*
 — **goody** *n, pl* **goodies** : golosina *f*
gooey *adj* **gooier; gooiest** : pegajoso

natural greenhouse effect
efecto^M invernadero^M natural

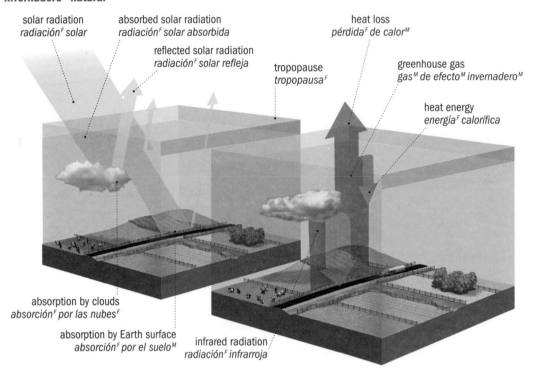

solar radiation
radiación^F solar

absorbed solar radiation
radiación^F solar absorbida

reflected solar radiation
radiación^F solar refleja

heat loss
pérdida^F de calor^M

tropopause
tropopausa^F

greenhouse gas
gas^M de efecto^M invernadero^M

heat energy
energía^F calorífica

absorption by clouds
absorción^F por las nubes^F

absorption by Earth surface
absorción^F por el suelo^M

infrared radiation
radiación^F infrarroja

---

goof *n* : pifia *f fam* — **goof** *vi* **1**
or **goof up** : cometer un error **2**
goof around : hacer tonterías
goose *n, pl* **geese** : ganso *m*, -sa *f*;
oca *f* — **goose bumps** *or* **goose**
pimples *npl* : carne *f* de gallina
gopher *n* : taltuza *f*
gore[1] *n* BLOOD : sangre *f*
gore[2] *vt* **gored; goring** : cornear
gorge *n* RAVINE : cañon *m* — **gorge** *vt*
gorged; gorging gorge oneself : hartarse
gorgeous *adj* : magnífico, espléndido
▸ **gorilla** *n* : gorila *m*
gory *adj* **gorier; -est** : sangriento
gospel *n* **1** : evangelio *m* **2**
the Gospel : el Evangelio
gossip *n* **1** : chismoso *m*, -sa *f*
(persona) **2** RUMOR : chisme *m* —
gossip *vi* : chismear, contar chismes
— **gossipy** *adj* : chismoso
got → **get**
Gothic *adj* : gótico
gotten → **get**
gourmet *n* : gastrónomo *m*, -ma *f*

gout *n* : gota *f*
govern *v* : gobernar — **governess** *n* :
institutriz *f* — **government** *n* : gobierno *m*
— **governor** *n* : gobernador *m*, -dora *f*
gown *n* **1** : vestido *m* **2** : toga *f*
(de magistrados, etc.)
grab *v* **grabbed; grabbing** *vt*
: agarrar, arrebatar
grace *n* **1** : gracia *f* **2 say grace** :
bendecir la mesa — **grace** *vt* **graced;**
gracing 1 HONOR : honrar **2** ADORN :
adornar — **graceful** *adj* : lleno de gracia,
grácil — **gracious** *adj* : cortés, gentil
grade *n* **1** QUALITY : calidad *f* **2** RANK
: grado *m*, rango *m* (militar) **3** YEAR :
grado *m*, año *m* (a la escuela) **4** MARK
: nota *f* **5** SLOPE : cuesta *f* — **grade** *vt*
graded; grading 1 CLASSIFY : clasificar
2 MARK : calificar (exámenes, etc.) —
grade school → **elementary school**
gradual *adj* : gradual — **gradually** *adv*
: gradualmente, poco a poco
graduate *n* : licenciado *m*, -da *f* (de la
universidad), bachiller *mf* (de la escuela

secundaria) — **graduate** *v* **-ated; -ating** *vi*
: graduarse, licenciarse — *vt* CALIBRATE :
graduar — **graduation** *n* : graduación *f*
graffiti *npl* : graffiti *mpl*
graft *n* : injerto *m* — **graft** *vt* : injertar
grain *n* **1** : grano *m* **2** CEREALS
: cereales *mpl* **3** : veta *f*,
vena *f* (de madera)
gram *n* : gramo *m*
grammar *n* : gramática *f* — **grammar**
school → **elementary school**
grand *adj* **1** : magnífico, espléndido **2**
FABULOUS, GREAT : fabuloso, estupendo
— **grandchild** *n, pl* **-children** : nieto *m*,
-ta *f* — **granddaughter** *n* : nieta *f*
— **grandeur** *n* : grandiosidad *f* —
grandfather *n* : abuelo *m* — **grandiose** *adj*
: grandioso — **grandmother** *n* :
abuela *f* — **grandparents** *npl* :
abuelos *mpl* — **grandson** *n* : nieto *m*
— **grandstand** *n* : tribuna *f*
granite *n* : granito *m*
grant *vt* **1** : conceder **2** ADMIT : reconocer,
admitir **3 take for granted** : dar (algo)

por sentado — **grant** *n* **1** SUBSIDY : subvención *f* **2** SCHOLARSHIP : beca *f*

grape *n* : uva *f*

grapefruit *n* : toronja *f*, pomelo *m*

grapevine *n* **1** : vid *f*, parra *f* **2 I heard it through the grapevine** : me lo dijo un pajarito *fam*

graph *n* : gráfica *f*, gráfico *m* — **graphic** *adj* : gráfico

grapple *vi* **-pled; -pling grapple with** : forcejear con (una persona), luchar con (un problema)

grasp *vt* **1** : agarrar **2** UNDERSTAND : comprender, captar — **grasp** *n* **1** : agarre *m* **2** UNDERSTANDING : comprensión *f* **3** REACH : alcance *m*

grass *n* **1** : hierba *f* (planta) **2** LAWN : césped *m*, pasto *m*, *Lat* — **grasshopper** *n* : saltamontes *m* — **grassy** *adj* **grassier; -est** : cubierto de hierba

grate[1] *v* **grated; -ing** *vt* **1** : rallar (en cocina) **2 grate one's teeth** : hacer rechinar los dientes — *vi* RASP : chirriar

grate[2] *n* GRATING : reja *f*, rejilla *f*

grateful *adj* : agradecido — **gratefully** *adv* : con agradecimiento — **gratefulness** *n* : gratitud *f*, agradecimiento *m*

grater *n* : rallador *m*

gratify *vt* **-fied; -fying 1** PLEASE : complacer **2** SATISFY : satisfacer

grating *n* : reja *f*, rejilla *f*

gratitude *n* : gratitud *f*

gratuitous *adj* : gratuito

grave[1] *n* : tumba *f*, sepultura *f*

grave[2] *adj* **graver; -est** : grave

gravel *n* : grava *f*, gravilla *f*

gravestone *n* : lápida *f* — **graveyard** *n* : cementerio *m*

gravity *n, pl* **-ties** : gravedad *f*

gravy *n, pl* **-vies** : salsa *f* (preparada con jugo de carne)

gray *adj* **1** : gris **2 gray hair** : pelo *m* canoso — **gray** *n* : gris *m* — **gray** *vi or* **turn gray** : encanecer, ponerse gris

graze[1] *vi* **grazed; grazing** : pastar, pacer

graze[2] *vt* **1** TOUCH : rozar **2** SCRATCH : rasguñarse

grease *n* : grasa *f* — **grease** *vt* **greased; greasing** : engrasar — **greasy** *adj* **greasier; -est 1** : grasiento **2** OILY : graso, grasoso

great *adj* **1** : grande **2** FANTASTIC : estupendo, fabuloso — **great-grandchild** *n, pl* **-children** : bisnieto *m*, -ta *f* — **great-grandfather** *n* : bisabuelo *m* — **great-grandmother** *n* : bisabuela *f* — **greatly** *adv* **1** MUCH : mucho **2** VERY : muy — **greatness** *n* : grandeza *f*

greed *n* **1** : codicia *f*, avaricia *f* **2** GLUTTONY : glotonería *f* — **greedily** *adv* : con avaricia — **greedy** *adj* **greedier; -est 1** : codicioso, avaro **2** GLUTTONOUS : glotón

Greek *adj* : griego — **Greek** *n* : griego *m* (idioma)

green *adj* **1** : verde **2** INEXPERIENCED : novato — **green** *n* **1** : verde *m* (color) **2 greens** *npl* : verduras *fpl* — **greenery** *n, pl* **-eries** : vegetación *f* — **greenhouse** *n* : invernadero *m*

greet *vt* **1** : saludar **2** WELCOME : recibir — **greeting** *n* **1** : saludo *m* **2 greets** *npl* REGARDS : saludos *mpl*, recuerdos *mpl*

gregarious *adj* : sociable

grenade *n* : granada *f*

grew → **grow**

grey → **gray**

greyhound *n* : galgo *m*

grid *n* **1** GRATING : rejilla *f* **2** NETWORK : red *f* **3** : cuadriculado *m* (de un mapa)

griddle *n* : plancha *f*

grief *n* : dolor *m*, pesar *m* — **grievance** *n* : queja *f* — **grieve** *v* **grieved; grieving** *vt* : entristecer — *vi* **grief for** : llorar (a), lamentar — **grievous** *adj* : grave, doloroso

grill *vt* **1** : asar a la parrilla **2** INTERROGATE : interrogar — **grill** *n* : parrilla *f* (para cocinar) — **grille** *or* **grill** GRATING *n* : reja *f*, rejilla *f*

grim *adj* **grimmer; grimmest 1** STERN : severo **2** GLOOMY : sombrío

grimace *n* : mueca *f* — **grimace** *vi* **-maced; -macing** : hacer muecas

grime *n* : mugre *f*, suciedad *f* — **grimy** *adj* **grimier; -est** : mugriento, sucio

grin *vi* **grinned; grinning** : sonreír (abiertamente) — **grin** *n* : sonrisa *f* (abierta)

grind *v* **ground; grinding** *vt* **1** : moler (el café, etc.) **2** SHARPEN : afilar **3 grind one's teeth** : rechinar los dientes — *vi* : rechinar — **grind** *n* **the daily grind** : la rutina diaria — **grinder** *n* : molinillo *m*

grip *vt* **gripped; gripping 1** : agarrar, asir **2** INTEREST : captar el interés de — **grip** *n* **1** GRASP : agarre *m* **2** CONTROL : control *m*, dominio *m* **3** HANDLE : empuñadura *f* **4 come to grips with** : llegar a entender de

gripe *vi* **griped; griping** : quejarse — **gripe** *n* : queja *f*

grisly *adj* **-lier; -est** :

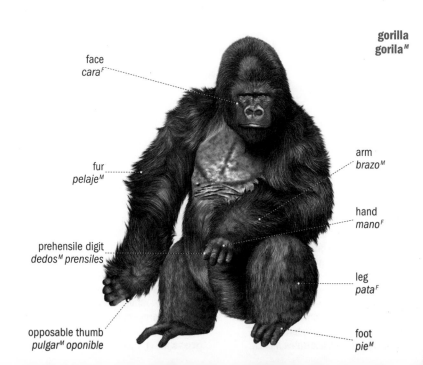

gorilla
gorila[M]

face
cara[F]

fur
pelaje[M]

prehensile digit
dedos[M] prensiles

opposable thumb
pulgar[M] oponible

arm
brazo[M]

hand
mano[F]

leg
pata[F]

foot
pie[M]

gymnastics: event platform
gimnasia^F

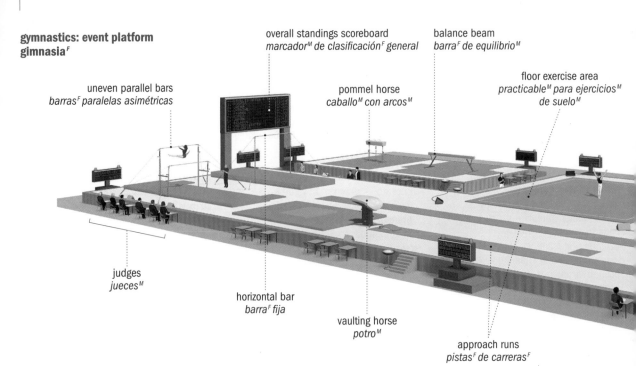

overall standings scoreboard
marcador^M de clasificación^F general

balance beam
barra^F de equilibrio^M

uneven parallel bars
barras^F paralelas asimétricas

floor exercise area
*practicable^M para ejercicios^M
de suelo^M*

pommel horse
caballo^M con arcos^M

judges
jueces^M

horizontal bar
barra^F fija

vaulting horse
potro^M

approach runs
pistas^F de carreras^F

parallel bars
barras^F paralelas

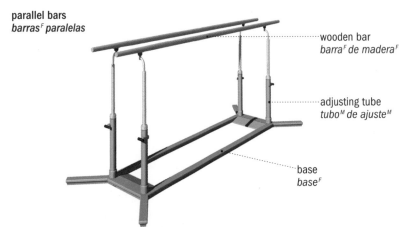

wooden bar
barra^F de madera^F

adjusting tube
tubo^M de ajuste^M

base
base^F

---

obeso **3** TOTAL : bruto **4** VULGAR : grosero,
basto — **gross** *n* **1** *or* **gross income** :
ingresos *mpl* brutos **2** *pl* **gross** : gruesa *f*
(12 docenas) — **grossly** *adv* **1** EXTREMELY
: enormemente **2** CRUDELY : groseramente
grotesque *adj* : grotesco
grouch *n* : gruñón *m*, -ñona *f fam* —
grouchy *adj* **grouchier; -est** : gruñon *fam*
ground¹ → **grind**
ground² *n* **1** : suelo *m*, tierra *f* **2** *or*
grounds LAND : terreno *m* **3 grounds**
REASON : razón *f*, motivos *mpl* **4**
grounds DREGS : pozo *m* (de café) —
ground *vt* **1** BASE : fundar, basar **2** :
conectar a tierra (un aparato eléctrico)
3 : restringir (un avión o un piloto) a la
tierra — **groundhog** *n* : marmota *f* (de
América) — **groundless** *adj* : infundado
— **groundwork** *n* : trabajo *m* preparatorio
group *n* : grupo *m* — **group** *vt* : agrupar
— *vi* *or* **group together** : agruparse
grove *n* : arboleda *f*
grovel *vi* **-eled** *or* **-elled; -eling** *or*
-elling : arrastrarse, humillarse
grow *v* **grew; grown; growing** *vi* **1** :
crecer **2** INCREASE : aumentar **3** BECOME

---

espeluznante, horrible
gristle *n* : cartílago *m*
grit *n* **1** : arena *f*, grava *f* **2** GUTS :
agallas *fpl fam* **3 grits** *npl* : sémola *f*
de maíz — **grit** *vt* **gritted; gritting**
grit one's teeth : acorazarse
groan *vi* : gemir — **groan** *n* : gemido *m*
grocery *n, pl* **-ceries 1** *or* **grocery
store** : tienda *f* de comestibles, tienda *f*
de abarrotes *Lat* **2 groceries** *npl* :
comestibles *mpl*, abarrotes *mpl Lat*

— **grocer** *n* : tendero *m*, -ra *f*
groggy *adj* **-gier; -est** :
atontado, grogui *fam*
groin *n* : ingle *f*
groom *n* BRIDEGROOM : novio *m*
— **groom** *vt* **1** : almohazar (un
animal) **2** PREPARE : preparar
groove *n* : ranura *f*, surco *m*
grope *vi* **groped; groping 1** : andar a
tientas **2 grope for** : buscar a tientas
gross *adj* **1** SERIOUS : grave **2** OBESE :

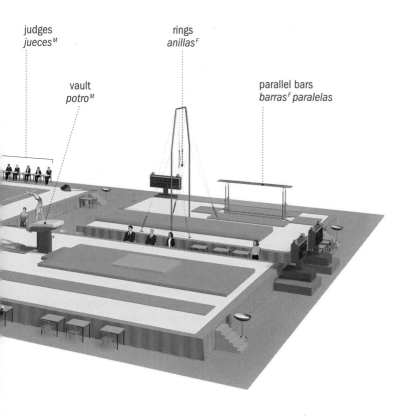

judges
jueces^M

rings
anillas^F

vault
potro^M

parallel bars
barras^F *paralelas*

: volverse, ponerse **4 grow dark :**
oscurecerse **5 grow up :** hacerse
mayor — *vt* **1** CULTIVATE : cultivar
2 : dejarse crecer (el pelo, etc.) —
grower *n* : cultivador *m*, -dora *f*
growl *vi* : gruñir — **growl** *n* : gruñido *m*
grown–up *adj* : mayor — **grown–
up** *n* : persona *f* mayor
growth *n* **1** : crecimiento *m* **2**
INCREASE : aumento *m* **3** DEVELOPMENT
: desarrollo *m* **4** TUMOR : tumor *m*
grub *n* **1** LARVA : larva *f* **2** FOOD : comida *f*
grubby *adj* **grubbier; -est**
: mugriento, sucio
grudge *vt* **grudged; grudging** :
dar de mala gana — **grudge** *n*
hold a grudge : guardar rencor
grueling *or* **gruelling** *adj* :
extenuante, agotador
gruesome *adj* : horripilante
gruff *adj* **1** BRUSQUE : brusco
2 HOARSE : bronco
grumble *vi* **-bled; -bling** :
refunfuñar, rezongar
grumpy *adj* **grumpier; -est** :
malhumorado, gruñón *fam*

grunt *vi* : gruñir — **grunt** *n* : gruñido *m*
guarantee *n* : garantía *f* — **guarantee** *vt*
-teed; -teeing : garantizar
guard *n* **1** : guardia *f* **2** PRECAUTION :
protección *f* — **guard** *vt* : proteger, vigilar
— *vi* **guard against** : protegerse contra
— **guardian** *n* **1** : tutor *m*, -tora *f* (de
niños) **2** PROTECTOR : guardián *m*, -diana *f*
guava *n* : guayaba *f*
guerrilla *or* guerilla *n* **1** :
guerrillero *m*, -ra *f* **2 guerrilla
warfare** : guerra *f* de guerrillas
guess *vt* **1** : adivinar **2** SUPPOSE :
suponer, creer — *vi* **guess at** : adivinar
— **guess** *n* : conjetura *f*, suposición *f*
guest *n* **1** : invitado *m*, -da *f* **2**
: huésped *mf* (a un hotel)
guide *n* : guía *mf* (persona), guía *f*
(libro, etc.) — **guide** *vt* **guided;
guiding** : guiar — **guidance** *n* :
orientación *f* — **guidebook** *n* : guía *f*
— **guideline** *n* : pauta *f*, directriz *f*
guild *n* : gremio *m*
guile *n* : astucia *f*
guilt *n* : culpa *f*, culpabilidad *f* —
guilty *adj* **guiltier; -est** : culpable

guinea pig *n* : conejillo *m*
de Indias, cobaya *f*
guise *n* : apariencia *f*
guitar *n* : guitarra *f*
gulf *n* **1** : golfo *m* **2** ABYSS : abismo *m*
gull *n* : gaviota *f*
gullet *n* **1** THROAT : garganta *f* **2**
ESOPHAGUS : esófago *m*
gullible *adj* : crédulo
gully *n*, *pl* **-lies** : barranco *m*
gulp *vt or* **gulp down** : tragarse, engullir
— *vi* : tragar saliva — **gulp** *n* : trago *m*
gum¹ *n* : encía *f* (de la boca)
gum² *n* **1** : resina *f* (de plantas) **2** CHEWING
GUM : goma *f* de mascar, chicle *m*
gumption *n* : iniciativa *f*, agallas *fpl fam*
gun *n* **1** FIREARM : arma *f* de fuego **2**
or **spray gun** : pistola *f* **3** → **cannon,
pistol, revolver, rifle** — **gun** *vt* **gunned;
gunning 1** *or* **gun down** : matar a tiros,
asesinar **2 gun the engine** : acelerar (el
motor) — **gunboat** *n* : cañonero *m* —
gunfire *n* : disparos *mpl* — **gunman** *n*,
pl **-men** : pistolero *m*, gatillero *m*,
Lat — **gunpowder** *n* : pólvora *f* —
gunshot *n* : disparo *m*, tiro *m*
gurgle *vi* **-gled; -gling 1** : borbotar,
gorgotear **2** : gorjear (dícese de un niño)
gush *vi* **1** SPOUT : salir a chorros **2 gush
with praise** : deshacerse en elogios
gust *n* : ráfaga *f*
gusto *n*, *pl* **gustoes** : entusiasmo *m*
gusty *adj* **gustier; -est** :
racheado, ventoso
gut *n* **1** : intestino *m* **2 guts** *npl*
INNARDS : tripas *fpl* **3 guts** *npl* COURAGE
: agallas *fpl fam* — **gut** *vt* **gutted;
gutting 1** EVISCERATE : destripar (un
pollo, etc.), limpiar (un pescado) **2** :
destruir el interior de (un edificio)
gutter *n* : canaleta *f* (de un techo),
cuneta *f* (de una calle)
guy *n* : tipo *m fam*
guzzle *vt* **-zled; -zling** :
chupar *fam*, tragar
gym *or* **gymnasium** *n*, *pl* **-siums** *or* **-sia** :
gimnasio *m* — **gymnast** *n* : gimnasta *mf*
▸ — **gymnastics** *ns & pl* : gimnasia *f*
gynecology *n* : ginecología *f* —
gynecologist *n* : ginecólogo *m*, -ga *f*
gyp *vt* **gypped; gypping** : estafar, timar
Gypsy *n*, *pl* **-sies** : gitano *m*, -na *f*
gyrate *vi* **-rated; -rating** : girar

h *n, pl* **h's** *or* **hs** : h *f*, octava letra del alfabeto inglés

habit *n* **1** CUSTOM : hábito *m*, costumbre *f* **2** : hábito *m* (religioso)

habitat *n* : hábitat *m*

habitual *adj* **1** CUSTOMARY : habitual **2** INVETERATE : empedernido

hack[1] *n* **1** : caballo *m* de alquiler **2** *or* **hack writer** : escritorzuelo *m*, -la *f*

hack[2] *vt* : cortar — *vi or* **hack into** : piratear (un sistema informático)

hackneyed *adj* : manido, trillado

hacksaw *n* : sierra *f* para metales

had → **have**

haddock *ns & pl* : eglefino *m*

hadn't (*contraction of* **had not**) → **have**

hag *n* : bruja *f*

haggard *adj* : demacrado

haggle *vi* **-gled; -gling** : regatear

hail[1] *vt* **1** GREET : saludar **2** : llamar (un taxi)

hail[2] *n* : granizo *m* (en meteorología) — **hail** *vi* : granizar — **hailstone** *n* : piedra *f* de granizo

hair *n* **1** : pelo *m*, cabello *m* **2** : vello *m* (en las piernas, etc.) — **hairbrush** *n* : cepillo *m* (para el pelo) — **haircut** *n* **1** : corte *m* de pelo **2 get a haircut** : cortarse el pelo — **hairdo** *n, pl* **-dos** : peinado *m* — **hairdresser** *n* : peluquero *m*, -ra *f* — **hairless** *adj* : sin pelo, calvo — **hairpin** *n* : horquilla *f* — **hair–raising** *adj* : espeluznante — **hairstyle** → **hairdo** — **hair spray** *n* : laca *f* (para el pelo) — **hairy** *adj* **hairier; -est** : peludo, velludo

hale *adj* : saludable, robusto

half *n, pl* **halves 1** : mitad *f* **2** *or* **halftime** : tiempo *m* (en deportes) **3 in half** : por la mitad — **half** *adj* **1** : medio **2 half an hour** : una media hora — **half** *adv* : medio — **half brother** *n* : medio hermano *m*, hermanastro *m* — **halfhearted** *adj* : sin ánimo, poco entusiasta — **half sister** *n* : media hermana *f*, hermanastra *f* — **halfway** *adv* : a medio camino — **half** *adj* : medio

halibut *ns & pl* : halibut *m*

hall *n* **1** HALLWAY : corredor *m*, pasillo *m* **2** AUDITORIUM : sala *f* **3** LOBBY : vestíbulo *m* **4** DORMITORY : residencia *f* universitaria

hallmark *n* : sello *m* (distintivo)

Halloween *n* : víspera *f* de Todos los Santos

hallucination *n* : alucinación *f*

hallway *n* **1** ENTRANCE : entrada *f* **2** CORRIDOR : corredor *m*, pasillo *m*

halo *n, pl* **-los** *or* **-loes** : aureola *f*, halo *m*

halt *n* **1 call a halt to** : poner fin a **2 come to a halt** : pararse — **halt** *vi* : pararse — *vt* : parar

halve *vt* **halved; halving 1** DIVIDE : partir por la mitad **2** REDUCE : reducir a la mitad — **halves** → **half**

ham *n* : jamón *m*

hamburger *or* **hamburg** *n* **1** : carne *f* molida **2** *or* **hamburger patty** : hamburguesa *f*

hammer *n* : martillo *m* — **hammer** *v* : martillar, martillear

hammock *n* : hamaca *f*

hamper[1] *vt* : obstaculizar, dificultar

hamper[2] *n* : cesto *m*, canasta *f* (para ropa sucia)

hamster *n* : hámster *m*

hand *n* **1** : mano *f* **2** : manecilla *f*, aguja *f* (de un reloj, etc.) **3** HANDWRITING : letra *f*, escritura *f* **4** WORKER : obrero *m*,

---

handbags
bolsos[M]

accordion bag
bolso[M] *de fuelle*[M]

shoulder bag
bolso[M] *de bandolera*[F]

duffel bag
bolso[M] *de viaje*[M]

tote bag
bolsa[F] *de lona*[F]

satchel bag
bolso[M] *clásico*

drawstring bag
bolso[M] *tipo*
cubo[M]

-ra f **5 by hand** : a mano **6 lend a
hand** : echar una mano **7 on hand** : a
mano, disponible **8 on the other hand**
: por otro lado — **hand** vt **1** : pasar,
dar **2 hand out** : distribuir **3 hand over**
: entregar — **handbag** n : cartera f
Lat, bolso m Spain — **handbook** n
: manual m — **handcuffs** npl :
esposas fpl — **handful** n : puñado m
— **handgun** n : pistola f, revólver m
handicap n **1** : minusvalía f (física) **2** :
hándicap m (en deportes) — **handicap** vt
-capped; -capping 1 : asignar un handicap
a (en deportes) **2** HAMPER : obstaculizar
— **handicapped** adj : minusválido
handicrafts npl : artesanía(s) f(pl)
handiwork n : trabajo m (manual)
handkerchief n, pl **-chiefs** : pañuelo m
handle n : asa m (de una taza, etc.),
mango m (de un utensilio), pomo m (de
una puerta), tirador m (de un cajón) —
handle vt **-dled; -dling 1** TOUCH : tocar **2**
MANAGE : tratar, manejar — **handlebars** npl
: manillar m, manubrio m, Lat
handmade adj : hecho a mano
handout n **1** ALMS : dádiva f,
limosna f **2** LEAFLET : folleto m
handrail n : pasamanos m
handshake n : apretón m de manos
handsome adj **-somer; -est 1**
ATTRACTIVE : apuesto, guapo **2** GENEROUS
: generoso **3** SIZABLE : considerable
handwriting n : letra f, escritura f —
handwritten adj : escrito a mano
handy adj **handier; -est 1** NEARBY
: a mano **2** USEFUL : práctico, útil **3**
DEFT : habilidoso — **handyman** n,
pl **-men** : hombre m habilidoso
hang v **hung; hanging** vt **1** : colgar **2** (past
tense often **hanged**) EXECUTE : ahorcar **3**
hang one's head : bajar la cabeza — vi **1**
: colgar, pender **2** : caer (dícese de la
ropa, etc.) **3 hang up on someone** : colgar
a alln — **hang** n **1** DRAPE : caída f **2**
get the hang of : agarrar la onda de
hangar n : hangar m
hanger n : percha f, gancho m
(para ropa) Lat
hangover n : resaca f
hanker vi **hanker for** : tener ansias de
— **hankering** n : ansia f, anhelo m
haphazard adj : casual, fortuito
happen vi **1** : pasar, suceder, ocurrir **2**
happen to do something : hacer algo por
casualidad **3 it so happens that…** : da

la casualidad de que… — **happening** n
: suceso m, acontecimiento m
happy adj **-pier; -est 1** : feliz **2 be
happy** : alegrarse **3 be happy with** :
estar contento con **4 be happy to do
something** : hacer algo con mucho
gusto — **happily** adv : alegremente —
happiness n : felicidad f — **happy–
go–lucky** adj : despreocupado
harass vt : acosar —
harassment n : acoso m
harbor or Brit **harbour** n : puerto m
— vt **1** SHELTER : albergar **2 harbor a
grudge against** : guardar rencor a
hard adj **1** : duro **2** DIFFICULT : difícil **3**
be a hard worker : ser muy trabajador
4 hard liquor : bebidas fpl fuertes **5**
hard water : agua f dura — **hard** adv **1**
FORCEFULLY : fuerte **2 work hard** : trabajar
duro **3 take something hard** : tomarse
algo muy mal — **harden** vt : endurecer
— **hardheaded** adj : testarudo, terco
— **hard–hearted** adj : duro de corazón
— **hardly** adv **1** : apenas **2 hardly
ever** : casi nunca — **hardness** n **1** :

dureza f **2** DIFFICULTY : dificultad f —
hardship n : dificultad f — **hardware** n **1** :
ferretería f **2** : hardware m (en informática)
— **hardworking** adj : trabajador
hardy adj **-dier; -est** : fuerte
(dícese de personas), resistente
(dícese de las plantas)
hare n, pl **hare** or **hares** : liebre f
harm n : daño m — **harm** vt : hacer daño a
(una persona), dañar (una cosa), perjudicar
(la reputación de algn, etc.) — **harmful** adj
: perjudicial — **harmless** adj : inofensivo
harmonica n : armónica f
harmony n, pl **-nies** : armonía f
— **harmonious** adj : armonioso —
harmonize v **-nized; -nizing** : armonizar
harness n : arnés m — **harness** vt **1**
: enjaezar **2** UTILIZE : utilizar
▸ **harp** n : arpa m — **harp** vi
harp on : insistir sobre
harpoon n : arpón m
harpsichord n : clavicémbalo m
harsh adj **1** ROUGH : áspero **2** SEVERE :
duro, severo **3** : fuerte (dícese de una
luz), discordante (dícese de sonidos)

harp
arpa F

crown
corona F

tuning peg
clavija F

shoulder
hombrera F

string
cuerda F

soundboard
tabla F armónica

pillar
columna F

sound box
caja F de resonancia F

pedal
pedal M

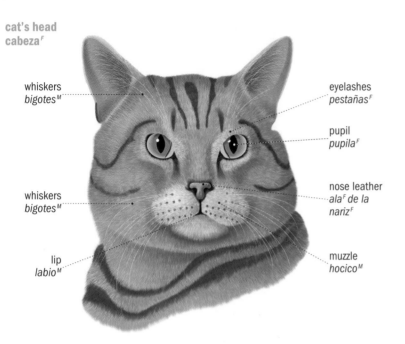

cat's head
cabeza^F

whiskers
bigotes^M

whiskers
bigotes^M

lip
labio^M

eyelashes
pestañas^F

pupil
pupila^F

nose leather
ala^F *de la
nariz*^F

muzzle
hocico^M

— **harshness** *n* : severidad *f*
harvest *n* : cosecha *f* —
harvest *v* : cosechar
has → **have**
hash *vt* **1** CHOP : picar **2 hash over** DISCUSS
: discutir — **hash** *n* : picadillo *m* (comida)
hasn't (*contraction of* **has not**) → **has**
hassle *n* : problemas *mpl*, lío *m* —
hassle *vt* **-sled; -sling** : fastidiar
haste *n* **1** : prisa *f*, apuro *m*, *Lat* **2
make haste** : darse prisa, apurarse
Lat — **hasten** *vt* : acelerar — *vi* :
apresurarse, apurarse *Lat* — **hasty** *adj*
hastier; -est : precipitado
hat *n* : sombrero *m*
hatch *n* : escotilla *f* — **hatch** *vt* **1**
: empollar (huevos) **2** CONCOCT :
tramar — *vi* : salir del cascarón
hatchet *n* : hacha *f*
hate *n* : odio *m* — **hate** *vt* **hated; hating**
: odiar, aborrecer — **hateful** *adj* : odioso,
aborrecible — **hatred** *n* : odio *m*
haughty *adj* **-tier; -est** : altanero, altivo
haul *vt* : arrastrar, jalar *Lat* — **haul** *n* **1**
CATCH : redada *f* (de peces) **2** LOOT :
botín *m* **3 a long haul** : un trayecto largo
haunch *n* : cadera *f* (de una
persona), anca *f* (de un animal)

haunt *vt* **1** : frecuentar, rondar **2**
TROUBLE : inquietar — **haunt** *n* : sitio *m*
predilecto — **haunted** *adj* : embrujado
have *v* **had; having; has** *vt* **1** : tener
2 CONSUME : comer, tomar **3** ALLOW :
permitir **4** : dar (una fiesta, etc.), convocar
(una reunión) **5 have one's hair cut**
: cortarse el pelo **6 have something
done** : mandar hacer algo — *v aux* **1**
: haber **2 have just done something** :
acabar de hacer algo **4 you've finished,
haven't you?** : has terminado, ¿no?
haven *n* : refugio *m*
havoc *n* : estragos *mpl*
hawk[1] *n* : halcón *m*
hawk[2] *vt* : pregonar (mercancías)
hay *n* : heno *m* — **hay fever** *n* : fiebre *f*
del heno — **haystack** *n* : almiar *m* —
haywire *adj* **go haywire** : estropearse
hazard *n* : peligro *m*, riesgo *m* —
hazard *vt* : arriesgar, aventurar —
hazardous *adj* : arriesgado, peligroso
haze *n* : bruma *f*, neblina *f*
hazel *n* : color *m* avellana —
hazelnut *n* : avellana *f*
hazy *adj* **hazier; -est** : nebuloso
he *pron* : él
▸ **head** *n* **1** : cabeza *f* **2** END TOP : cabeza *f*

(de un clavo, etc.), cabecera *f* (de una
mesa) **3** LEADER : jefe *m*, -fa *f* **4 be out
of one's head** : estar loco **5 come to a
head** : llegar a un punto crítico **6 heads or
tails** : cara o cruz **7 per head** : por cabeza
— **head** *adj* MAIN : principal — **head** *vt* :
encabezar — *vi* : dirigirse — **headache** *n* :
dolor *m* de cabeza — **headband** *n* : cinta *f*
del pelo — **headdress** *n* : tocado *m* —
headfirst *adv* : de cabeza — **heading** *n* :
encabezamiento *m*, título *m* — **headland** *n*
: cabo *m* — **headlight** *n* : faro *m* —
headline *n* : titular *m* — **headlong** *adv* **1**
HEADFIRST : de cabeza **2** HASTILY :
precipitadamente — **headmaster** *n* :
director *m* — **headmistress** *n* : directora *f*
— **head-on** *adv & adj* : de frente —
headphones *npl* : auriculares *mpl*,
audífonos *mpl Lat* — **headquarters** *ns
& pl* : oficina *f* central (de una compañía),
cuartel *m* general (de los militares) —
head start *n* : ventaja *f* — **headstrong** *adj*
: testarudo, obstinado — **headwaiter** *n* :
jefe *m*, -fa *f* de comedor — **headway** *n* **1**
: progreso *m* **2 make headway** : avanzar
— **heady** *adj* **headier; -est** : embriagador
heal *vt* : curar — *vi* : cicatrizar
health *n* : salud *f* — **healthy** *adj*
healthier; -est : sano, saludable
heap *n* : montón *m* — **heap** *vt* : amontonar
hear *v* **heard; hearing** *vt* : oír — *vi* **1**
: oír **2 hear about** : enterarse de **3
hear from** : tener noticias de —
hearing *n* **1** : oído *m* **2** : vista *f* (en un
tribunal) — **hearing aid** *n* : audífono *m*
— **hearsay** *n* : rumores *mpl*
hearse *n* : coche *m* fúnebre
heart *n* **1** : corazón *m* **2 at heart** :
en el fondo **3 by heart** : de memoria
4 lose heart : descorazonarse **5 take
heart** : animarse — **heartache** *n* :
pena *f*, dolor *m* — **heart attack** *n*
: infarto *m*, ataque *m* al corazón —
heartbeat *n* : latido *m* (del corazón) —
heartbreak *n* : congoja *f*, angustia *f*
— **heartbroken** *adj* : desconsolado
— **heartburn** *n* : acidez *f* estomacal
hearth *n* : hogar *m*
heartily *adv* : de buena gana
heartless *adj* : de mal corazón, cruel
hearty *adj* **heartier; -est 1** :
cordial, caluroso **2** : abundante
(dícese de una comida)
heat *vt* : calentar — *vi* **or heat up** :
calentarse — **heat** *n* **1** : calor *m* **2**

HEATING : calefacción *f* — **heated** *adj* : acalorado — **heater** *n* : calentador *m*
heath *n* : brezal *m*
heathen *adj* : pagano — **heathen** *n*, *pl* **-thens** *or* **-then** : pagano *m*, -na *f*
heather *n* : brezo *m*
heave *v* **heaved** *or* **hove**; **heaving** *vt* **1** LIFT : levantar (con esfuerzo) **2** HURL : lanzar, tirar **3 heave a sigh** : suspirar — **heave** *vi or* **heave up** : levantarse
heaven *n* : cielo *m* — **heavenly** *adj* **1** : celestial **2 heavenly body** : cuerpo *m* celeste
heavy *adj* **heavier; -est 1** : pesado **2** INTENSE : fuerte **3 heavy sigh** : suspiro *m* profundo **4 heavy traffic** : tráfico *m* denso — **heavily** *adv* **1** : pesadamente **2** EXCESSIVELY : mucho — **heaviness** *n* : peso *m*, pesadez *f* — **heavyweight** *n* : peso *m* pesado
Hebrew *adj* : hebreo — **Hebrew** *n*

: hebreo *m* (idioma)
heckle *vt* **-led; -ling** : interrumpir (a un orador) con preguntas molestas
hectic *adj* : agitado, ajetreado
he'd (*contraction of* **he had** *or* **he would**) → **have, would**
hedge *n* : seto *m* vivo — **hedge** *v* **hedged; hedging** *vt* **hedge one's bets** : cubrirse — *vi* : contestar con evasivas — **hedgehog** *n* : erizo *m*
heed *vt* : prestar atención a, hacer caso de — **heed** *n* **take heed** : tener cuidado — **heedless** *adj* **be heedless of** : hacer caso omiso de
heel *n* : talón *m* (del pie), tacón *m* (de un zapato)
hefty *adj* **heftier; -est** : robusto y pesado
heifer *n* : novilla *f*
height *n* **1** : estatura *f* (de una persona), altura *f* (de un objeto) **2** PEAK : cumbre *f* **3 the height of folly** : el colmo de la locura **4 what is your height ?** : ¿cuánto mides?

— **heighten** *vt* : aumentar, intensificar
heir *n* : heredero *m*, -ra *f* — **heiress** *n* : heredera *f* — **heirloom** *n* : reliquia *f* de familia
held → **hold**
▸ **helicopter** *n* : helicóptero *m*
hell *n* : infierno *m* — **hellish** *adj* : infernal
he'll (*contraction of* **he shall** *or* **he will**) → **shall, will**
hello *interj* : ¡hola!
helm *n* : timón *m*
helmet *n* : casco *m*
help *vt* **1** : ayudar **2 help oneself** : servirse **3 I can't help it** : no lo puedo remediar — **help** *n* **1** : ayuda *f* **2** STAFF : personal *m* **3 help!** : ¡socorro!, ¡auxilio! — **helper** *n* : ayudante *mf* — **helpful** *adj* **1** OBLIGING : servicial, amable **2** USEFUL : útil — **helping** *n* : porción *f* — **helpless** *adj* **1** POWERLESS : incapaz **2** DEFENSELESS : indefenso
hem *n* : dobladillo *m* — **hem** *vt*

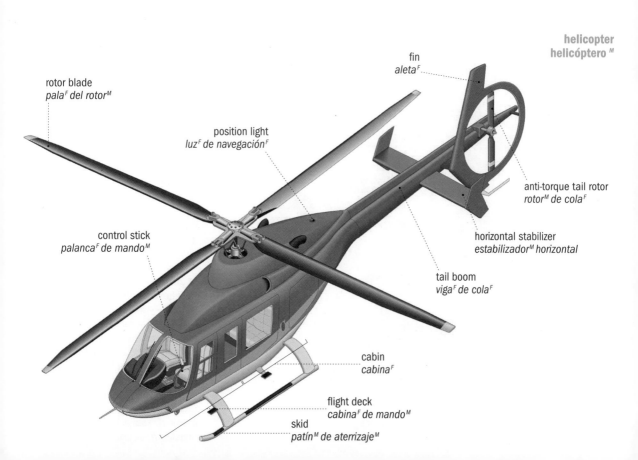

helicopter
helicóptero ^M

rotor blade
pala^F del rotor^M

fin
aleta^F

position light
luz^F de navegación^F

anti-torque tail rotor
rotor^M de cola^F

control stick
palanca^F de mando^M

horizontal stabilizer
estabilizador^M horizontal

tail boom
viga^F de cola^F

cabin
cabina^F

flight deck
cabina^F de mando^M

skid
patín^M de aterrizaje^M

hemmed; hemming hem in : encerrar
▸ **hemisphere** *n* : hemisferio *m*
hemorrhage *n* : hemorragia *f*
hemorrhoids *npl* : hemorroides *fpl*, almorranas *fpl*
hemp *n* : cáñamo *m*
hen *n* : gallina *f*
hence *adv* **1** : de aquí, de ahí **2** THEREFORE : por lo tanto **3 ten years hence** : de aquí a 10 años — **henceforth** *adv* : de ahora en adelante
henpeck *vt* : dominar (al marido)
hepatitis *n, pl* **-titides** : hepatitis *f*
her *adj* : su, sus — **her** *pron* **1** (*used as direct object*) : la **2** (*used as indirect object*) : le, se **3** (*used as object of a preposition*) : ella
herald *vt* : anunciar
herb *n* : hierba *f*
herd *n* : manada *f* — **herd** *vt* : conducir (en manada) — *vi* or **herd together** : reunir
here *adv* **1** : aquí, acá **2 here you are!** : ¡toma! — **hereabouts** *or* hereabout *adv* : por aquí (cerca) — **hereafter** *adv* : en el

futuro — **hereby** *adv* : por este medio
hereditary *adj* : hereditario — **heredity** *n* : herencia *f*
heresy *n, pl* **-sies** : herejía *f*
herewith *adv* : adjunto
heritage *n* **1** : herencia *f* **2** : patrimonio *m* (nacional)
hermit *n* : ermitaño *m*, -ña *f*
hernia *n, pl* **-nias** *or* **-niae** : hernia *f*
hero *n, pl* **-roes** : héroe *m* — **heroic** *adj* : heroico — **heroine** *n* : heroína *f* — **heroism** *n* : heroísmo *m*
▸ **heron** *n* : garza *f*
herring *n, pl* **-ring** *or* **-rings** : arenque *m*
hers *pron* **1** : (el) suyo, (la) suya, (los) suyos, (las) suyas **2 some friends of hers** : unos amigos suyos, unos amigos de ella — **herself** *pron* **1** (*used reflexively*) : se **2** (*used emphatically*) : ella misma
he's (*contraction of* **he is** *or* **he has**) → **be, have**
hesitant *adj* : titubeante, vacilante — **hesitate** *vi* **-tated; -tating** : vacilar, titubear — **hesitation** *n* : vacilación *f*, titubeo *m*

heron
garza^M

heterosexual *adj* : heterosexual — **heterosexual** *n* : heterosexual *mf*
hexagon *n* : hexágono *m*
hey *interj* : ¡eh!, ¡oye!
heyday *n* : auge *m*, apogeo *m*
hi *interj* : ¡hola!
hibernate *vi* **-nated; -nating** : hibernar
hiccup *n* **have the hiccups** : tener hipo — **hiccup** *vi* **-cuped; -cuping** : tener hipo
hide^1 *n* : piel *f*, cuero *m*
hide^2 *v* **hid; hidden** *or* **hid; hiding** *vt* **1** : esconder **2** : ocultar (motivos, etc.) — *vi* : esconderse — **hide–and–seek** *n* : escondite *m*, escondidas *fpl Lat*
hideous *adj* : horrible, espantoso
hideout *n* : escondite *m*, guarida *f*
hierarchy *n, pl* **-chies** : jerarquía *f* — **hierarchical** *adj* : jerárquico
high *adj* **1** : alto **2** INTOXICATED : borracho, drogado **3 a high voice** : una voz aguda **4 it's two feet high** : tiene dos pies de alto **5 high winds** : fuertes vientos *mpl* — **high** *adv* : alto — **high** *n* : récord *m*, máximo *m* — **higher** *adj* **1** : superior **2 higher education** : enseñanza *f* superior — **highlight** *n* : punto *m* culminante — **highly** *adv* **1** VERY : muy, sumamente **2 think highly of** : tener en mucho a — **Highness** *n* **His/Her Highness** : Su Alteza *f* — **high school** *n* : escuela *f* superior, escuela *f* secundaria — **high–strung** *adj* : nervioso, excitable — **highway** *n* : carretera *f*
hijack *vt* : secuestrar — **hijacker** *n* : secuestrador *m*, -dora *f*

hive
colmena^F

roof
techo^M

exit cone
respiradero^M

honeycomb
panal^M

frame
bastidor^M

cell
celdilla^F

queen ex-cluder
separador^M
de reinas^F

alighting board
estribo^M

entrance
entrada^F

— **hijacking** *n* : secuestro *m*

hike *v* **hiked; hiking** *vi* : ir de caminata
— *vt or* **hike up** RAISE : subir —
hike *n* : caminata *f*, excursión *f*
— **hiker** *n* : excursionista *mf*

hilarious *adj* : muy divertido
— **hilarity** *n* : hilaridad *f*

hill *n* **1** : colina *f*, cerro *m* **2** SLOPE :
cuesta *f* — **hillside** *n* : ladera *f*, cuesta *f*
— **hilly** *adj* **hillier; -est** : accidentado

hilt *n* : puño *m*

him *pron* **1** (*used as direct object*) :
lo **2** (*used as indirect object*) : le, se
3 (*used as object of a preposition*) : él
— **himself** *pron* **1** (*used reflexively*) :
se **2** (*used emphatically*) : él mismo

hind *adj* : trasero, posterior

hinder *vt* : dificultar, estorbar —
hindrance *n* : obstáculo *m*

hindsight *n* **in hindsight**
: en retrospectiva

Hindu *adj* : hindú

hinge *n* : bisagra *f*, gozne *m* — **hinge** *vi*
hinged; hinging hinge on : depender de

hint *n* **1** : indirecta *f* **2** TIP : consejo *m* **3**
TRACE : asomo *m*, toque *m* — **hint** *vt* :
dar a entender — *vi* **hint at** : insinuar

hip *n* : cadera *f*

hippopotamus *n*, *pl* **-muses**
or **-mi** : hipopótamo *m*

hemispheres
hemisferios
hemispheres
hemisferios^M

Northern Hemisphere
hemisferio^M *Norte*

Southern Hemisphere
hemisferio^M *Sur*

hire *n* **1** : alquiler *m* **2 for hire** : se
alquila — **hire** *vt* **hired; hiring 1** EMPLOY
: contratar, emplear **2** RENT : alquilar

his *adj* : su, sus, de él — **his** *pron* **1**
: (el) suyo, (la) suya, (los) suyos, (las)
suyas **2 some friends of his** : unos
amigos suyos, unos amigos de él

Hispanic *adj* : hispano, hispánico

hiss *vi* : silbar — *n* : silbido *m*

history *n*, *pl* **-ries 1** : historia *f* **2**
BACKGROUND : historial *m* — **historian** *n*
: historiador *m*, -dora *f* — **historic**
or historical *adj* : histórico

hit *v* **hit; hitting** *vt* **1** : golpear, pegar **2** :
dar (con un proyectil) **3** AFFECT : afectar **4**
REACH : alcanzar **5 the car hit a tree** : el
coche chocó contra un árbol — *vi* : pegar
— **hit** *n* **1** : golpe *m* **2** SUCCESS : éxito *m*

hitch *vt* **1** ATTACH : enganchar **2** *or* **hitch
up** RAISE : subirse **3 hitch a ride** : hacer
autostop — **hitch** *n* PROBLEM : problema *m*
— **hitchhike** *vi* **-hiked; -hiking** : hacer
autostop — **hitchhiker** *n* : autostopista *mf*

hitherto *adv* : hasta ahora

HIV *n* : VIH *m*, virus *m* del sida

hive *n* : colmena *f*

hives *ns & pl* : urticaria *f*

hoard *n* : tesoro *m* (de dinero), reserva *f*
(de provisiones) — **hoard** *vt* : acumular

hoarse *adj* **hoarser; -est** : ronco

hoax *n* : engaño *m*

hobble *vi* **-bled; -bling** : cojear

hobby *n*, *pl* **-bies** : pasatiempo *m*

hobo *n*, *pl* **-boes** : vagabundo *m*, -da *f*

hockey *n* : hockey *m*

hippopotamus
hipopótamo^M

hoe *n* : azada *f* — **hoe** *vt*
hoed; hoeing : azadonar

hog *n* : cerdo *m* — **hog** *vt* **hogged;
hogging** MONOPOLIZE : acaparar

hoist *vt* **1** : izar (una vela, etc.) **2**
LIFT : levantar — **hoist** *n* : grúa *f*

hold^1 *n* : bodega *f* (en un barco o un avión)

hold^2 *v* **held; holding** *vt* **1** GRIP : agarrar
2 POSSESS : tener **3** SUPPORT : sostener **4**
: celebrar (una reunión, etc.), mantener
(una conversación) **5** CONTAIN : contener
6 CONSIDER : considerar **7** *or* **hold back**
: detener **8 hold hands** : agarrarse de
la mano **9 hold up** ROB : atracar **1 0
hold up** DELAY : retrasar — *vi* **1** LAST
: durar, continuar **2** APPLY : ser válido
— **hold** *n* **1** GRIP : agarre *m* **2 get hold
of** : conseguir **3 get hold of oneself** :
controlarse — **holder** *n* : tenedor *m*,
-dora *f* — **holdup** *n* **1** ROBBERY :
atraco *m* **2** DELAY : retraso *m*, demora *f*

hole *n* : agujero *m*, hoyo *m*

holiday *n* **1** : día *m* feriado, fiesta *f* **2**
Brit VACATION : vacaciones *fpl*

holiness *n* : santidad *f*

holler *vi* : gritar — **holler** *n* : grito *m*

hollow *n* **1** : hueco *m* **2** VALLEY :
hondonada *f* — **hollow** *adj* **-lower;
-est 1** : hueco **2** FALSE : vacío, falso —
hollow *vt or* **hollow out** : ahuecar

holly *n*, *pl* **-lies** : acebo *m*

holocaust *n* : holocausto *m*

holster *n* : pistolera *f*

holy *adj* **-lier; -est** : santo, sagrado

homage *n* : homenaje *m*

hooves
pezuñas_F_

one-toed hoof
pezuña _F_ _de un pesuño_ _M_

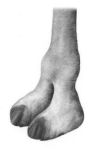

two-toed hoof
pezuña _F_ _de dos pesuños_ _M_

three-toed hoof
pezuña _F_ _de tres pesuños_ _M_

four-toed hoof
pezuña _F_ _de cuatro pesuños_ _M_

home _n_ **1** : casa _f_ **2** FAMILY : hogar _m_ **3** INSTITUTION : residencia _f,_ asilo _m_ **4 at home and abroad** : dentro y fuera del país — **home** _adv_ **go home** : ir a casa — **homeland** _n_ : patria _f_ — **homeless** _adj_ : sin hogar — **homely** _adj_ **-lier; -est 1** DOMESTIC : casero **2** UGLY : feo — **homemade** _adj_ : casero, hecho en casa — **homemaker** _n_ : ama _f_ de casa — **home run** _n_ : jonrón _m_ — **homesick** _adj_ **be homesick** : echar de menos a la familia — **homeward** _adj_ : de vuelta, de regreso — **homework** _n_ : tarea _f,_ deberes _mpl_ — **homey** _adj_ **homier; -est** : hogareño, acogedor **homicide** _n_ : homicidio _m_ **homogeneous** _adj_ : homogéneo — **homosexual** _adj_ : homosexual — **homosexual** _n_ : homosexual _mf_ — **homosexuality** _n_ : homosexualidad _f_ **honest** _adj_ **1** : honrado **2** FRANK : sincero — **honestly** _adv_ : sinceramente

— **honesty** _n, pl_ **-ties** : honradez _f_ **honey** _n, pl_ **-eys** : miel _f_ — **honeycomb** _n_ : panal _m_ — **honeymoon** _n_ : luna _f_ de miel **honk** _vi_ : tocar la bocina — **honk** _n_ : bocinazo _m_ **honor** _or Brit_ **honour** _n_ : honor _m_ — **honor** _vt_ **1** : honrar **2** : aceptar (un cheque, etc.), cumplir con (una promesa) — **honorable** _or Brit_ **honourable** _adj_ : honorable, honroso — **honorary** _adj_ : honorario **hood** _n_ **1** : capucha _f_ (de un abrigo, etc.) **2** : capó _m_ (de un automóvil) **hoodlum** _n_ : matón _m_ **hoodwink** _vt_ : engañar
▸ **hoof** _n, pl_ **hooves** _or_ **hoofs** : pezuña _f_ (de una vaca, etc.) , casco _m_ (de un caballo) **hook** _n_ **1** : gancho _m_ **2** _or_ **hook and eye** : corchete _m_ **3** → **fishhook 4 off the hook** : descolgado — **hook** _vt_ : enganchar — _vi_ : engancharse **hoop** _n_ : aro _m_

hooray → **hurrah**
hoot _vi_ **1** : ulular (dícese de un búho) **2 hoot with laughter** : reírse a carcajadas — **hoot** _n_ **1** : ululato _m_ (de un búho) **2 I don't give a hoot** : me importa un comino **hop**[1] _vi_ **hopped; hopping** : saltar a la pata coja — **hop** _n_ : salto _m_ a la pata coja **hop**[2] _n_ **hops** : lúpulo _m_ (planta) **hope** _v_ **hoped; hoping** _vi_ : esperar — _vt_ : esperar que — **hope** _n_ : esperanza _f_ — **hopeful** _adj_ : esperanzado — **hopefully** _adv_ **1** : con esperanza **2 hopefully it will help** : se espera que ayude — **hopeless** _adj_ : desesperado — **hopelessly** _adv_ : desesperadamente **horde** _n_ : horda _f_ **horizon** _n_ : horizonte _m_ — **horizontal** _adj_ : horizontal **hormone** _n_ : hormona _f_ **horn** _n_ **1** : cuerno _m_ (de un animal) **2** : trompa _f_ (instrumento musical) **3** : bocina _f,_ claxon _m_ (de un vehículo) **hornet** _n_ : avispón _m_ **horoscope** _n_ : horóscopo _m_ **horror** _n_ : horror _m_ — **horrendous** _adj_ : horrendo — **horrible** _adj_ : horrible — **horrid** _adj_ : horroroso, horrible — **horrify** _vt_ **-fied; -fying** : horrorizar **hors d'oeuvre** _n, pl_ **hors d'oeuvres** : entremés _m_
▸ **horse** _n_ : caballo _m_ — **horseback** _n_ **on horseback** : a caballo — **horsefly** _n, pl_ **-flies** : tábano _m_ — **horseman** _n, pl_ **-men** : jinete _m_ — **horseplay** _n_ : payasadas _fpl_ — **horsepower** _n_ : caballo _m_ de fuerza — **horseradish** _n_ : rábano _m_ picante — **horseshoe** _n_ : herradura _f_ — **horsewoman** _n, pl_ **-women** : jinete _f_ **horticulture** _n_ : horticultura _f_ **hose** _n_ **1** _pl_ **hoses** : manguera _f,_ manga _f_ **2 hose** _npl_ STOCKINGS : medias _fpl_ — **hose** _vt_ **hosed; hosing** : regar (con manguera) — **hosiery** _n_ : calcetería _f_ **hospice** _n_ : hospicio _m_ **hospital** _n_ : hospital _m_ — **hospitable** _adj_ : hospitalario — **hospitality** _n, pl_ **-ties** : hospitalidad _f_ — **hospitalize** _vt_ **-ized; -izing** : hospitalizar **host**[1] _n_ **a host of** : toda una serie de **host**[2] _n_ **1** : anfitrión _m,_ -triona _f_ **2** : presentador _m,_ -dora _f_ (de televisión, etc.) — **host** _vt_ : presentar (un programa de televisión, etc.) **host**[3] _n_ EUCHARIST : hostia _f,_ Eucaristía _f_ **hostage** _n_ : rehén _m_ **hostel** _n or_ **youth hostel** :

albergue *m* juvenil

hostess *n* : anfitriona *f*

hostile *adj* : hostil — **hostility** *n*,
pl **-ties** : hostilidad *f*

hot *adj* **hotter; hottest 1** : caliente,
caluroso (dícese del tiempo), cálido
(dícese del clima) **2** SPICY : picante
3 feel hot : tener calor **4 have a
hot temper** : tener mal genio **5 hot
news** : noticias *fpl* de última hora
6 it's hot today : hace calor

hot dog *n* : perro *m* caliente

hotel *n* : hotel *m*

hotheaded *adj* : exaltado

hound *n* : perro *m* (de caza) —
hound *vt* : acosar, perseguir

hour *n* : hora *f* — **hourglass** *n* :
reloj *m* de arena — **hourly** *adv*
& *adj* : cada hora, por hora

house *n, pl* **houses 1** : casa *f* **2** :
cámara *f* (del gobierno) **3 publishing
house** : editorial *f* — **house** *vt* **housed;
housing** : albergar — **houseboat** *n* :
casa *f* flotante — **housefly** *n, pl* **-flies**

: mosca *f* común — **household** *adj* **1** :
doméstico **2 household name** : nombre *m*
muy conocido — **household** *n* : casa *f*
— **housekeeper** *n* : ama *f* de llaves —
housekeeping *n* : gobierno *m* de la casa
— **housewarming** *n* : fiesta *f* de estreno
de una casa — **housewife** *n, pl* **-wives**
: ama *f* de casa — **housework** *n* :
faenas *fpl* domésticas — **housing** *n* **1** :
viviendas *fpl* **2** CASE : caja *f* protectora

hove → **heave**

hovel *n* : casucha *f*, tugurio *m*

hover *vi* **1** : cernerse **2**
hover about : rondar

how *adv* **1** : cómo **2** (*used in
exclamations*) : qué **3 how are you?** :
¿cómo está Ud.? **4 how come** : por qué
5 how much : cuánto **6 how do you
do?** : mucho gusto **7 how old are you?** :
¿cuántos años tienes? — **how** *conj* : como

however *conj* **1** : de cualquier manera
que **2 however you like** : como quieras
— **however** *adv* **1** NEVERTHELESS : sin
embargo, no obstante **2 however difficult**

it is : por difícil que sea **3 however
hard I try** : por más que me esfuerce

howl *vi* : aullar — **howl** *n* : aullido *m*

hub *n* **1** CENTER : centro *m* **2**
: cubo *m* (de una rueda)

hubbub *n* : alboroto *m*, jaleo *m*

hubcap *n* : tapacubos *m*

huddle *vi* **-dled; -dling** *or*
huddle together : apiñarse

hue *n* : color *m*, tono *m*

huff *n* **be in a huff** : estar enojado

hug *vt* **hugged; hugging** :
abrazar — **hug** *n* : abrazo *m*

huge *adj* **huger; hugest** :
inmenso, enorme

hull *n* : casco *m* (de un barco, etc.)

hum *v* **hummed; humming** *vi* **1** :
tararear **2** BUZZ : zumbar — *vt* : tararear
(una melodía) — **hum** *n* : zumbido *m*

human *adj* : humano — **human** *n* :
(ser *m*) humano *m* — **humane** *adj*
: humano, humanitario —
humanitarian *adj* : humanitario —
humanity *n, pl* **-ties** : humanidad *f*

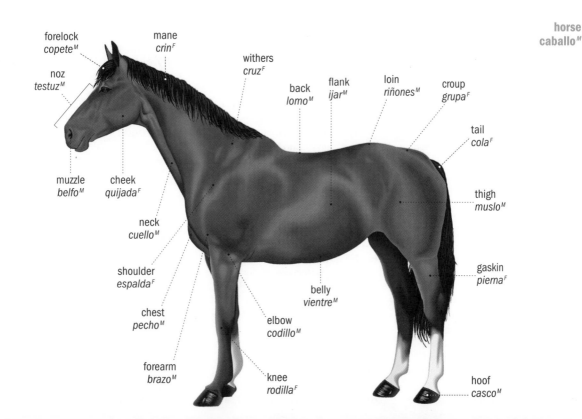

horse
caballo*M*

forelock
copete*M*

mane
crin*F*

withers
cruz*F*

noz
testuz*M*

back
lomo*M*

flank
ijar*M*

loin
riñones*M*

croup
grupa*F*

tail
cola*F*

muzzle
belfo*M*

cheek
quijada*F*

thigh
muslo*M*

neck
cuello*M*

shoulder
espalda*F*

belly
vientre*M*

gaskin
pierna*F*

chest
pecho*M*

elbow
codillo*M*

forearm
brazo*M*

knee
rodilla*F*

hoof
casco*M*

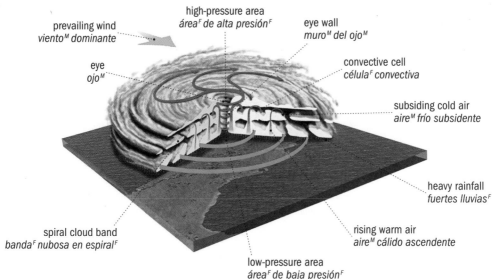

prevailing wind
viento^M *dominante*

high-pressure area
área^F *de alta presión*^{F}

eye wall
muro^M *del ojo*^{M}

eye
ojo^M

convective cell
célula^F *convectiva*

subsiding cold air
aire^M *frío subsidente*

heavy rainfall
fuertes lluvias^F

spiral cloud band
banda^F *nubosa en espiral*^{F}

rising warm air
aire^M *cálido ascendente*

low-pressure area
área^F *de baja presión*^{F}

---

humble *vt* **-bled; -bling 1 :** humillar **2 humble oneself :** humillarse — **humble** *adj* **-bler; -blest :** humilde
humdrum *adj* **:** monótono, rutinario
humid *adj* **:** húmedo — **humidity** *n*, *pl* **-ties :** humedad *f*
humiliate *vt* **-ated; -ating :** humillar — **humiliating** *adj* **:** humillante — **humiliation** *n* **:** humillación *f* — **humility** *n* **:** humildad *f*
humor *or Brit* **humour** *n* **:** humor *m* — **humor** *vt* **:** seguir la corriente a, complacer — **humorous** *adj* **:** humorístico, cómico
hump *n* **:** joroba *f*
hunch *vi or* **hunch over :** encorvarse — **hunch** *n* **:** presentimiento *m*
hundred *adj* **:** cien, ciento — **hundred** *n*, *pl* **-dreds** *or* **-dred :** ciento *m* — **hundredth** *adj* **:** centésimo — **hundredth** *n* **1 :** centésimo *m*, -ma *f* (en una serie) **2 :** centésimo *m* (en matemáticas)
hung → **hang**
Hungarian *adj* **:** húngaro — **Hungarian** *n* **:** húngaro *m* (idioma)
hunger *n* **:** hambre *m* — **hunger** *vi* **1 :** tener hambre **2 hunger for :** ansiar, anhelar — **hungry** *adj* **-grier; -est 1 :** hambriento **2 be hungry :** tener hambre
hunk *n* **:** pedazo *m* (grande)
hunt *vt* **1 :** cazar **2 hunt for :** buscar

— **hunt** *n* **1 :** caza *f*, cacería *f* **2 SEARCH :** búsqueda *f*, busca *f* — **hunter** *n* **:** cazador *m*, -dora *f* — **hunting** *n* **1 :** caza *f* **2 go hunting :** ir de caza
hurdle *n* **1 :** valla *f* (en deportes) **2 OBSTACLE :** obstáculo *m*
hurl *vt* **:** lanzar, arrojar
hurrah *interj* **:** ¡hurra!
▸ **hurricane** *n* **:** huracán *m*
hurry *n* **:** prisa *f*, apuro *f Lat* — *v* **-ried; -rying** *vi* **:** darse prisa, apurarse *Lat* — *vt* **:** apurar, dar prisa a — **hurried** *adj* **:** apresurado — **hurriedly** *adv* **:** apresuradamente, de prisa
hurt *v* **hurt; hurting** *vt* **1 INJURE :** hacer daño a, lastimar **2 OFFEND :** ofender, herir — *vi* **1 :** doler **2 my foot hurts :** me duele el pie — **hurt** *n* **1 INJURY :** herida *f* **2 DISTRESS :** dolor *m*, pena *f* — **hurtful** *adj* **:** hiriente, doloroso
hurtle *vi* **-tled; -tling :** lanzarse, precipitarse
husband *n* **:** esposo *m*, marido *m*
hush *vt* **:** hacer callar, acallar — **hush** *n* **:** silencio *m*
husk *n* **:** cáscara *f*
husky^1 *adj* **-kier; -est HOARSE :** ronco
husky^2 *n*, *pl* **-kies :** perro *m*, -rra *f* esquimal
husky^3 *adj* **BURLY :** fornido
hustle *v* **-tled; -tling** *vt* **:** dar prisa

a, apurar *Lat* — *vi* **:** darse prisa, apurarse *Lat* — **hustle** *n* **hustle and bustle :** aaetreo *m*, bullicio *m*
hut *n* **:** cabaña *f*
hutch *n or* **rabbit hutch :** conejera *f*
hyacinth *n* **:** jacinto *m*
hybrid *n* **:** híbrido *m* — **hybrid** *adj* **:** híbrido
hydrant *n or* **fire hydrant :** boca *f* de incendios
hydraulic *adj* **:** hidráulico
hydroelectric *adj* **:** hidroeléctrico
hydrogen *n* **:** hidrógeno *m*
hyena *n* **:** hiena *f*
hygiene *n* **:** higiene *f* — **hygienic** *adj* **:** higiénico
hymn *n* **:** himno *m*
hyperactive *adj* **:** hiperactivo
hyphen *n* **:** guión *m*
hypnosis *n*, *pl* **-noses :** hipnosis *f* — **hypnotic** *adj* **:** hipnótico — **hypnotism** *n* **:** hipnotismo *m* — **hypnotize** *vt* **-tized; -tizing :** hipnotizar
hypochondriac *n* **:** hipocondríaco *m*, -ca *f*
hypocrisy *n*, *pl* **-sies :** hipocresía *f* — **hypocrite** *n* **:** hipócrita *mf* — **hypocritical** *adj* **:** hipócrita
hypothesis *n*, *pl* **-eses :** hipótesis *f* — **hypothetical** *adj* **:** hipotético
hysteria *n* **:** histeria *f*, histerismo *m* — **hysterical** *adj* **:** histérico

i *n, pl* **i's** *or* **is** : i *f,* novena letra del alfabeto inglés

I *pron* : yo

ice *n* : hielo *m* — **ice** *v* **iced; icing** *vt* **1** FREEZE : congelar **2** CHILL : enfriar **3** : bañar (pasteles, etc.) — **ice** *vi or* **ice up** : helarse, congelarse — **iceberg** *n* : iceberg *m* — **icebox** → **refrigerator** — **ice–cold** *adj* : helado — **ice cream** *n* : helado *m* — **ice cube** *n* : cubito *m* de hielo — **ice–skate** *vi* **-skated; -skating** : patinar — **ice skate** *n* : patín *m* de cuchilla — **icicle** *n* : carámbano *m* — **icing** *n* : baño *m*

icon *n* : icono *m*

icy *adj* **icier; -est 1** : cubierto de hielo (dícese de pavimento, etc.) **2** FREEZING : helado

I'd (*contraction of* **I should** *or* **I would**) → **should, would**

idea *n* : idea *f*

ideal *adj* : ideal — **ideal** *n* : ideal *m* — **idealist** *n* : idealista *mf* — **idealistic** *adj* : idealista — **idealize** *vt* **-ized; -izing** : idealizar

identity *n, pl* **-ties** : identidad *f* — **identical** *adj* : idéntico — **identify** *v* **-fied; -fying** *vt* : identificar — *vi* **identify with** : identificarse con — **identification** *n* **1** : identificación *f* **2** **identification card** : carnet *m,* carné *m*

ideology *n, pl* **-gies** : ideología *f* — **ideological** *adj* : ideológico

idiocy *n, pl* **-cies** : idiotez *f*

idiom *n* EXPRESSION : modismo *m* — **idiomatic** *adj* : idiomático

idiosyncrasy *n, pl* **-sies** : idiosincrasia *f*

idiot *n* : idiota *mf* — **idiotic** *adj* : idiota

idle *adj* **idler; idlest 1** LAZY : haragán, holgazán **2** INACTIVE : parado (dícese de una máquina) **3** UNEMPLOYED : desocupado **4** VAIN : frívolo, vano **5 out of idle curiosity**

player's skate
patín^M *de jugador*^M

goalkeeper's skate
patín^M *del portero*^M

figure skate
patín^M *para figuras*^F

clapskate
patín^M *de pista*^F *larga*

short track skate
patín^M *de pista*^F *corta*

igloo
iglú *M*

: por pura curiosidad — **idle** *v* **idled; idling** *vi* : andar al ralentí (dícese de un motor) — *vt* **idle away the hours** : pasar el rato — **idleness** *n* : ociosidad *f*

idol *n* : ídolo *m* — **idolize** *vt* **-ized; -izing** : idolatrar

idyllic *adj* : idílico

if *conj* **1** : si **2** THOUGH : aunque, si bien **3 if so** : si es así

▸ **igloo** *n, pl* **-loos** : iglú *m*

ignite *v* **-nited; -niting** *vt* : encender — *vi* : encenderse — **ignition** *n* **1** : ignición *f* **2** *or* **ignition switch** : encendido *m*

ignore *vt* **-nored; -noring** : ignorar, no hacer caso de — **ignorance** *n* : ignorancia *f* — **ignorant** *adj* **1** : ignorante **2 be ignorant of** : desconocer, ignorar

ilk *n* : tipo *m,* clase *f*

ill *adj* **worse; worst 1** SICK : enfermo

2 BAD : malo — *adv* **worse; worst** : mal — **ill–advised** *adj* : imprudente — **ill at ease** *adj* : incómodo

I'll (*contraction of* **I shall** *or* **I will**) → **shall, will**

illegal *adj* : ilegal

illegible *adj* : ilegible

illegitimate *adj* : ilegítimo — **illegitimacy** *n* : ilegitimidad *f*

illicit *adj* : ilícito

illiterate *adj* : analfabeto — **illiteracy** *n, pl* **-cies** : analfabetismo *m*

ill–mannered *adj* : descortés, maleducado

ill–natured *adj* : de mal genio

illness *n* : enfermedad *f*

illogical *adj* : ilógico

ill–treat *vt* : maltratar

ice hockey
hockey ^M sobre hielo ^M

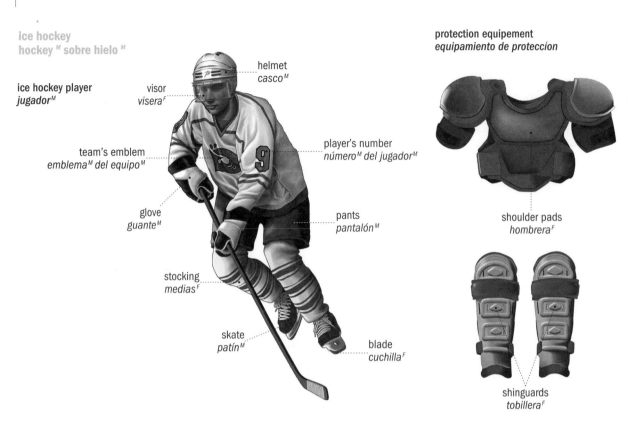

ice hockey player
jugador^M

helmet
casco^M

visor
visera^F

player's number
número^M del jugador^M

team's emblem
emblema^M del equipo^M

glove
guante^M

pants
pantalón^M

stocking
medias^F

skate
patín^M

blade
cuchilla^F

protection equipement
equipamiento de proteccíon

shoulder pads
hombrera^F

shinguards
tobillera^F

pista^F
rink

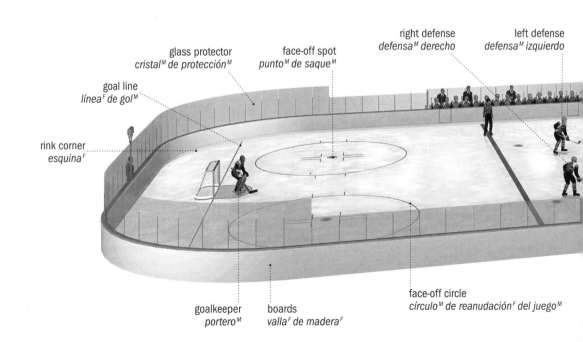

glass protector
cristal^M de protección^M

face-off spot
punto^M de saque^M

right defense
defensa^M derecho

left defense
defensa^M izquierdo

goal line
línea^F de gol^M

rink corner
esquina^F

goalkeeper
portero^M

boards
valla^F de madera^F

face-off circle
círculo^M de reanudación^F del juego^M

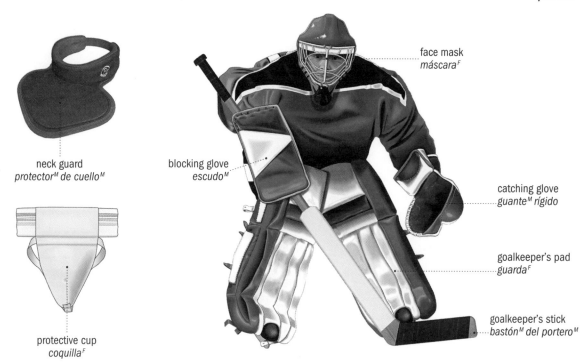

neck guard
protector^M *de cuello*^M

face mask
máscara^F

blocking glove
escudo^M

catching glove
guante^M *rígido*

goalkeeper's pad
guarda^F

goalkeeper's stick
bastón^M *del portero*^M

protective cup
coquilla^F

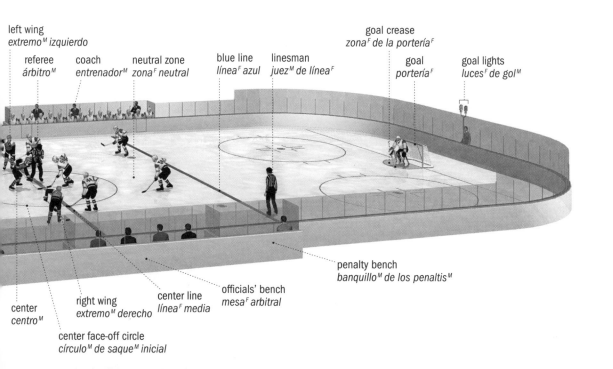

left wing
extremo^M *izquierdo*

goal crease
zona^F *de la portería*^F

referee
árbitro^M

coach
entrenador^M

neutral zone
zona^F *neutral*

blue line
línea^F *azul*

linesman
juez^M *de línea*^F

goal
portería^F

goal lights
luces^F *de gol*^M

penalty bench
banquillo^M *de los penaltis*^M

center
centro^M

right wing
extremo^M *derecho*

center line
línea^F *media*

officials' bench
mesa^F *arbitral*

center face-off circle
círculo^M *de saque*^M *inicial*

illuminate *vt* **-nated; -nating** : iluminar —
— illumination *n* : iluminación *f*
illusion *n* : ilusión *f* —
illusory *adj* : ilusorio
illustrate *v* **-trated; -trating** : ilustrar —
illustration *n* **1** : ilustración *f* **2** EXAMPLE :
ejemplo *m* — **illustrative** *adj* : ilustrativo
illustrious *adj* : ilustre, glorioso
ill will *n* : animadversión *f*, mala voluntad *f*
I'm (*contraction of* **I am**) → **be**
image *n* : imagen *f* — **imaginary** *adj*
: imaginario — **imagination** *n* :
imaginación *f* — **imaginative** *adj*
: imaginativo — **imagine** *vt*
-ined; -ining : imaginar(se)
imbalance *n* : desequilibrio *m*
imbecile *n* : imbécil *mf*
imbue *vt* **-bued; -buing** : imbuir
imitation *n* : imitación *f* — **imitation** *adj*
: de imitación, artificial — **imitate** *vt*
-tated; -tating : imitar, remedar —
imitator *n* : imitador *m*, -dora *f*
immaculate *adj* : inmaculado
immaterial *adj* : irrelevante,
sin importancia
immature *adj* : inmaduro —
immaturity *n, pl* **-ties** : inmadurez *f*
immediate *adj* : inmediato —
immediately *adv* : inmediatamente
immense *adj* : inmenso —
immensity *n, pl* **-ties** : inmensidad *f*
immerse *vt* **-mersed; -mersing** :
sumergir — **immersion** *n* : inmersión *f*
immigrate *vi* **-grated; -grating** :
inmigrar — **immigrant** *n* : inmigrante *mf*
— **immigration** *n* : inmigración *f*
imminent *adj* : inminente —
imminence *n* : inminencia *f*
immobile *adj* : inmóvil — **immobilize** *vt*
-lized; -lizing : inmovilizar
immoral *adj* : inmoral — **immorality** *n*,
pl **-ties** : inmoralidad *f*
immortal *adj* : inmortal —
immortal *n* : inmortal *mf* —
immortality *n* : inmortalidad *f*
immune *adj* : inmune — **immunity** *n*,
pl **-ties** : inmunidad *f* — **immunization** *n*
: inmunización *f* — **immunize** *vt*
-nized; -nizing : inmunizar
imp *n* RASCAL : diablillo *m*
impact *n* : impacto *m*
impair *vt* : dañar, perjudicar
impart *vt* : impartir (información),
conferir (una calidad, etc.)
impartial *adj* : imparcial

illumination: lights
iluminación ᶠ: lámparas ᶠ

swivel wall lamp
*lámpara*ᶠ *orientable de pared*ᶠ

table lamp
*lámpara*ᶠ *de mesa*ᶠ

desk lamp
*lámpara*ᶠ *de escritorio*ᴹ

chandelier
*araña*ᶠ

adjustable lamp
*flexo*ᴹ

ceiling fitting
*plafón*ᴹ

clamp spotlight
*lámpara*ᶠ *de pinza*ᶠ

floor lamp
lámpara^F de pie^M

post lantern
farola^F

— **impartiality** *n, pl* **-ties** : imparcialidad *f*
impassable *adj* : intransitable
impasse *n* : impasse *m*
impassioned *adj* : apasionado
impassive *adj* : impasible
impatience *n* : impaciencia *f*
— **impatient** *adj* : impaciente —
impatiently *adv* : con impaciencia
impeccable *adj* : impecable
impede *vt* **-peded; -peding** :
dificultar — **impediment** *n* :
impedimento *m*, obstáculo *m*
impel *vt* **-pelled; -pelling** : impeler
impending *adj* : inminente
impenetrable *adj* : impenetrable
imperative *adj* **1** COMMANDING :
imperativo **2** NECESSARY : imprescindible
— **imperative** *n* : imperativo *m*
imperceptible *adj* : imperceptible
imperfection *n* : imperfección *f* —
imperfect *adj* : imperfecto — **imperfect** *n*
or **imperfect tense** : imperfecto *m*
imperial *adj* : imperial —
imperialism *n* : imperialismo *m*
— **imperious** *adj* : imperioso
impersonal *adj* : impersonal
impersonate *vt* **-ated; -ating**
: hacerse pasar por, imitar —
impersonation *n* : imitación *f* —
impersonator *n* : imitador *m*, -dora *f*
impertinent *adj* : impertinente —
impertinence *n* : impertinencia *f*
impervious *adj* **impervious**
to : impermeable a
impetuous *adj* : impetuoso, impulsivo
impetus *n* : ímpetu *m*, impulso *m*
impinge *vi* **-pinged; -pinging**
impinge on : afectara, incidir en
impish *adj* : pícaro, travieso
implant *vt* : implantar
implausible *adj* : inverosímil
implement *n* : instrumento *m*,
implemento *m, Lat* — **implement** *vt*
: poner en práctica
implicate *vt* **-cated; -cating**
: implicar — **implication** *n* **1**
INVOLVEMENT : implicación *f* **2**
CONSEQUENCE : consecuencia *f* **3 by**
implication : de forma indirecta
implicit *adj* **1** : implícito **2** UNQUESTIONING
: absoluto, incondicional
implore *vt* **-plored; -ploring**
: implorar, suplicar
imply *vt* **-plied; -plying 1** HINT :
insinuar **2** ENTAIL : implicar

impolite *adj* : descortés, maleducado
import *vt* : importar (mercancías)
— **important** *adj* : importante —
importance *n* : importancia *f* —
importation *n* : importación *f* —
importer *n* : importador *m*, -dora *f*
impose *v* **-posed; -posing** *vt*
: imponer — *vi* **impose on** :
importunar, molestar — **imposing** *adj*
: imponente — **imposition** *n* **1**
ENFORCEMENT : imposición *f* **2 be**
an imposition on : molestar
impossible *adj* : imposible —
impossibility *n, pl* **-ties** : imposibilidad *f*
impostor *or* imposter *n* :
impostor *m*, -tora *f*
impotent *adj* : impotente —
impotence *n* : impotencia *f*
impound *vt* : incautar, embargar
impoverished *adj* : empobrecido
impracticable *adj* : impracticable
impractical *adj* : poco práctico
imprecise *adj* : impreciso —
imprecision *n* : imprecisión *f*
impregnable *adj* : impenetrable
impregnate *vt* **-nated; -nating 1** :
impregnar **2** FERTILIZE : fecundar
impress *vt* **1** : causar una buena
impresión a **2** AFFECT : impresionar
3 impress something on someone :
recalcar algo a algn — *vi* : impresionar
— **impression** *n* : impresión *f* —
impressionable *adj* : impresionable
— **impressive** *adj* : impresionante
imprint *vt* : imprimir — **imprint** *n*
MARK : impresión *f*, huella *f*
imprison *vt* : encarcelar —
imprisonment *n* : encarcelamiento *m*
improbable *adj* : improbable —
improbability *n, pl* **-ties** : improbabilidad *f*
impromptu *adj* : improvisado
improper *adj* **1** UNSEEMLY : indecoroso
2 INCORRECT : impropio — **impropriety** *n*,
pl **-eties** : inconveniencia *f*
improve *v* **-proved; -proving** : mejorar
— **improvement** *n* : mejora *f*
improvise *v* **-vised; -vising** : improvisar
— **improvisation** *n* : improvisación *f*
impudent *adj* : insolente —
impudence *n* : insolencia *f*
impulse *n* **1** : impulso *m* **2**
on impulse : sin reflexionar —
impulsive *adj* : impulsivo —
impulsiveness *n* : impulsividad *f*
impunity *n* **1** : impunidad *f* **2**

infants and children's clothing
ropa ^F de niños ^M

tank top
camiseta^F

shorts
pantalón^M *corto*

training set
conjunto^M *deportivo*

pajamas
pijama^M

crossover back straps overalls
pantalones^M *de peto*^M

snowsuit
traje^M *para nieve*^F

---

with impunity : impunemente

impure *adj* : impuro — **impurity** *n*, *pl* **-ties** : impureza *f*

in *prep* **1** : en **2** DURING : por, en *Lat* **3** WITHIN : dentro de **4 dressed in red** : vestido de rojo **5 in the rain** : bajo la lluvia **6 in the sun** : al sol **7 in this way** : de esta manera **8 the best in the world** : el mejor del mundo **9 written in ink/French** : escrito con tinta/en francés — *adv* **1** INSIDE : dentro, adentro **2 be in** : estar (en casa) **3 be in on** : participar en **4 come in!** : ¡entre!, ¡pase! **5 he's in for a shock** : se va a llevar un shock — **in** *adj* : de moda

inability *n*, *pl* **-ties** : incapacidad *f*

inaccessible *adj* : inaccesible

inaccurate *n* : inexacto

inactive *n* : inactivo — **inactivity** *n*, *pl* **-ties** : inactividad *f*

inadequate *adj* : insuficiente

inadvertently *adv* : sin querer

inadvisable *adj* : desaconsejable

inane *adj* **inaner; -est** : estúpido, tonto

inanimate *adj* : inanimado

inapplicable *adj* : inaplicable

inappropriate *adj* : impropio, inoportuno

inarticulate *adj* : incapaz de expresarse

inasmuch as *conj* : ya que, puesto que

inattentive *adj* : poco atento

inaudible *adj* : inaudible

inaugural *adj* **1** : inaugural **2 inaugural address** : discurso *m* de investidura

— **inaugurate** *vt* **-rated; -rating 1** : investir (a un presidente, etc.) **2** BEGIN : inaugurar — **inauguration** *n* : investidura *f* (de una persona), inauguración *f* (de un edificio, etc.)

inborn *adj* : innato

inbred *adj* INNATE : innato

incalculable *adj* : incalculable

incapable *adj* : incapaz — **incapacitate** *vt* **-tated; -tating** : incapacitar — **incapacity** *n*, *pl* **-ties** : incapacidad *f*

incarcerate *vt* **-ated; -ating** : encarcelar

incarnate *adj* : encarnado — **incarnation** *n* : encarnación *f*

incendiary *adj* : incendiario

incense¹ *n* : incienso *m*

incense² *vt* **-censed; -censing** : indignar, enfurecer

incentive *n* : incentivo *m*

inception *n* : comienzo *m*, principio *m*

incessant *adj* : incesante

incest *n* : incesto *m* — **incestuous** *adj* : incestuoso

inch *n* : pulgada *f* — **inch** *v* : avanzar poco a poco

incident *n* : incidente *m* — **incidence** *n* : índice *m* (de crímenes, etc.) — **incidental** *adj* **1** MINOR : incidental **2** CHANCE : casual — **incidentally** *adv* : a propósito

incinerate *vt* **-ated; -ating** : incinerar

— **incinerator** *n* : incinerador *m*

incision *n* : incisión *f*

incite *vt* **-cited; -citing** : incitar, instigar

incline *v* **-clined; -clining** *vt* **1** BEND : inclinar **2 be inclineed to** : inclinarse a, tender a — **incline** *vi* : inclinarse — **incline** *n* : pendiente *f* — **inclination** *n* **1** : inclinación *f* **2** DESIRE : deseo *m*, ganas *fpl*

include *vt* **-cluded; -cluding** : incluir — **inclusion** *n* : inclusión *f* — **inclusive** *adj* : inclusivo

incognito *adv & adj* : de incógnito

incoherent *adj* : incoherente — **incoherence** *n* : incoherencia *f*

income *n* : ingresos *mpl* — **income tax** *n* : impuesto *m* sobre la renta

incomparable *adj* : incomparable

incompatible *adj* : incompatible

incompetent *adj* : incompetente — **incompetence** *n* : incompetencia *f*

incomplete *adj* : incompleto

incomprehensible *adj* : incomprensible

inconceivable *adj* : inconcebible

inconclusive *adj* : no concluyente

incongruous *adj* : incongruente

inconsiderate *adj* : desconsiderado

inconsistent *adj* **1** : inconsecuente **2 be inconsistent with** : no concordar con — **inconsistency** *n*, *pl* **-cies** : inconsecuencia *f*

inconspicuous *adj* : que no llama la atención

inconvenient *adj* : incómodo, inconveniente — **inconvenience** *n* **1** BOTHER : incomodidad *f*, molestia *f* **2** DRAWBACK : inconveniente *m* — **inconvenient** *vt* **-nienced; -niencing** *vt* : importunar, molestar

incorporate *vt* **-rated; -rating** : incorporar

incorrect *adj* : incorrecto

increase *n* : aumento *m* — **increase** *v* **-creased; -creasing** : aumentar — **increasingly** *adv* : cada vez más

incredible *adj* : increíble

incredulous *adj* : incrédulo

incriminate *vt* **-nated; -nating** : incriminar

incubator *n* : incubadora *f*

incumbent *n* : titular *mf*

incur *vt* **incurred; incurring** : provocar (al enojo, etc.), incurrir en (gastos)

incurable *adj* : incurable

indebted *adj* **1** : endeudado **2 be indebted to someone** : estar en deuda con algn

indecent *adj* : indecente — **indecency** *n, pl* **-cies** : indecencia *f*

indecisive *adj* : indeciso

indeed *adv* **1** TRULY : verdaderamente, sin duda **2** IN FACT : en efecto **3 indeed?** : ¿de veras?

indefinite *adj* **1** : indefinido **2** VAGUE : impreciso — **indefinitely** *adv* : indefinidamente

indelible *adj* : indeleble

indent *vt* : sangrar (un párrafo) — **indentation** *n* DENT, NOTCH : mella *f*

independent *adj* : independiente — **independence** *n* : independencia *f*

indescribable *adj* : indescriptible

indestructible *adj* : indestructible

index *n, pl* **-dexes** *or* **-dices** : índice *m* — **index** *vt* : incluir en un índice — **index finger** *n* : dedo *m* índice

Indian *adj* : indio *m*, -dia *f*

indication *n* : indicio *m*, señal *f* — **indicate** *vt* **-cated; -cating** : indicar — **indicative** *adj* : indicativo — **indicator** *n* : indicador *m*

indict *vt* : acusar (de un crimen) — **indictment** *n* : acusación *f*

indifferent *adj* **1** : indiferente **2** MEDIOCRE : mediocre — **indifference** *n* : indiferencia *f*

indigenous *adj* : indígena

indigestion *n* : indigestión *f*

— **indigestible** *adj* : indigesto

indignation *n* : indignación *f* — **indignant** *adj* : indignado — **indignity** *n, pl* **-ties** : indignidad *f*

indigo *n, pl* **-gos** *or* **-goes** : añil *m*

indirect *adj* : indirecto

indiscreet *adj* : indiscreto — **indiscretion** *n* : indiscreción *f*

indiscriminate *adj* : indiscriminado

indispensable *adj* : indispensable, imprescindible

indisputable *adj* : indiscutible

indistinct *adj* : indistinto

individual *adj* **1** : individual **2** PARTICULAR : particular — **individual** *n* : individuo *m* — **individuality** *n, pl* **-ties** : individualidad *f* — **individually** *adv* : individualmente

indoctrinate *vt* **-nated; -nating** : adoctrinar — **indoctrination** *n* : adoctrinamiento *m*

indoor *adj* **1** : (de) interior **2 indoor plant** : planta *f* de interior **3 indoor pool** : piscina *f* cubierta **4 indoor sports** : deportes *mpl* bajo techo — **indoors** *adv* : adentro, dentro

induce *vt* **-duced; -ducing** **1** : inducir **2** CAUSE : provocar — **inducement** *n* : incentivo *m*

indulge *v* **-dulged; -dulging** *vt* **1** GRATIFY : satisfacer **2** PAMPER : consentir — *vi* **indulge in** : permitirse — **indulgence** *n* **1** : indulgencia *f* **2** SATISFYING : satisfacción *f* — **indulgent** *adj* : indulgente

industry *n, pl* **-tries** **1** : industria *f* **2** DILIGENCE : diligencia *f* — **industrial** *adj* : industrial — **industrialize** *vt* **-ized; -izing** : industrializar — **industrious** *adj* : diligente, trabajador

inebriated *adj* : ebrio, embriagado

inedible *adj* : no comestible

ineffective *adj* **1** : ineficaz **2** INCOMPETENT : incompetente — **ineffectual** *adj* : inútil, ineficaz

inefficient *adj* **1** : ineficiente **2** INCOMPETENT : incompetente — **inefficiency** *n, pl* **-cies** : ineficiencia *f*

ineligible *adj* : ineligible

inept *adj* **1** : inepto **2 inept at** : incapaz para

inequality *n, pl* **-ties** : desigualdad *f*

inert *adj* : inerte — **inertia** *n* : inercia *f*

inescapable *adj* : ineludible

inevitable *adj* : inevitable — **inevitably** *adv* : inevitablemente

inexcusable *adj* : inexcusable

inexpensive *adj* : barato, económico

inexperienced *adj* : inexperto

inexplicable *adj* : inexplicable

infallible *adj* : infalible

infamous *adj* : infame

infancy *n, pl* **-cies** : infancia *f* — ▸ **infant** *n* : bebé *m*; niño *m*, -ña *f* — **infantile** *adj* : infantil

infantry *n, pl* **-tries** : infantería *f*

infatuated *adj* **be infatuated with** : estar encaprichado con — **infatuation** *n* : encaprichamiento *m*

infect *vt* : infectar — **infection** *n* : infección *f* — **infectious** *adj* : contagioso

infer *vt* **inferred; inferring** : deducir, inferir — **inference** *n* : deducción *f*

inferior *adj* : inferior — **inferior** *n* : inferior *mf* — **inferiority** *n, pl* **-ties** : inferioridad *f*

infernal *adj* : infernal — **inferno** *n, pl* **-nos** : infierno *m*

infertile *adj* : estéril — **infertility** *n* : esterilidad *f*

infest *vt* : infestar

infidelity *n, pl* **-ties** : infidelidad *f*

infiltrate *v* **-trated; -trating** *vt* : infiltrar — *vi* : infiltrarse

infinite *adj* : infinito

infinitive *n* : infinitivo *m*

infinity *n, pl* **-ties** **1** : infinito *m* **2 an infinity of** : una infinidad de

infirm *adj* : enfermizo, endeble — **infirmary** *n, pl* **-ries** : enfermería *f* — **infirmity** *n, pl* **-ties** **1** FRAILTY : endeblez *f* **2** AILMENT : enfermedad *f*

inflame *vt* **-flamed; -flaming** : inflamar — **inflammable** *adj* : inflamable — **inflammation** *n* : inflamación *f* — **inflammatory** *adj* : inflamatorio

inflate *vt* **-flated; -flating** : inflar — **inflation** *n* : inflación *f* — **inflationary** *adj* : inflacionario, inflacionista

inflexible *adj* : inflexible

inflict *vt* : infligir

influence *n* **1** : influencia *f* **2 under the influence** : embriagado — **influence** *vt* **-enced; -encing** : influir en, influenciar — **influential** *adj* : influyente

influenza *n* : gripe *f*, influenza *f*

influx *n* : afluencia *f*

inform *vt* **1** : informar **2 keep me informed** : manténme al corriente — *vi* **inform on** : delatar, denunciar

informal *adj* **1** : informal **2** : familiar (dícese del lenguaje) — **informality** *n*,

writing instruments
instrumentos ᴹ para escribir

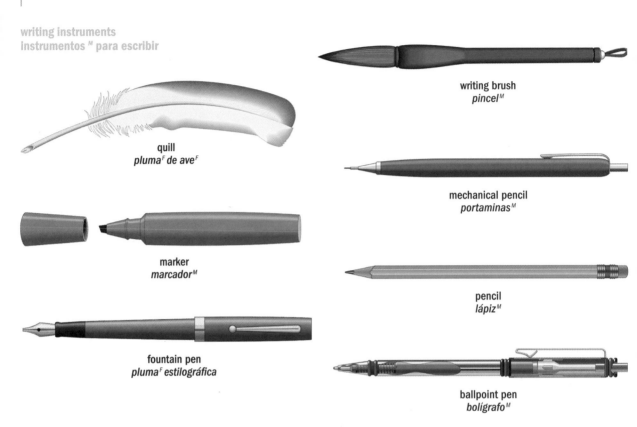

quill
*pluma*ᶠ *de ave*ᶠ

marker
*marcador*ᴹ

fountain pen
*pluma*ᶠ *estilográfica*

writing brush
*pincel*ᴹ

mechanical pencil
*portaminas*ᴹ

pencil
*lápiz*ᴹ

ballpoint pen
*bolígrafo*ᴹ

pl **-ties** : falta *f* de cereeonia —
  informally *adv* : de manera informal
information *n* : información *f*
  — **informative** *adj* : informativo
  — **informer** *n* : informante *mf*
infrared *adj* : infrarrojo
infrastructure *n* : infraestructura *f*
infrequent *adj* : infrequente —
  infrequently *adv* : raramente
infringe *v* **-fringed; -fringing** *vt* :
  infringir — *vi* **infringe on** : violar
  — **infringement** *n* : violación *f*
infuriate *vt* **-ated; -ating** :
  enfurecer, poner furioso —
  infuriating *adj* : exasperante
infuse *vt* **-fused; -fusing** : infundir
  — **infusion** *n* : infusión *f*
ingenious *adj* : ingenioso —
  ingenuity *n, pl* **-ities** : ingenio
ingenuous *adj* : ingenuo
ingest *vt* : ingerir
ingot *n* : lingote *m*
ingrained *adj* : arraigado

ingratiate *vt* **-ated; -ating ingratiate
  oneself with** : congraciarse con
ingratitude *n* : ingratitud *f*
ingredient *n* : ingrediente *m*
ingrown *adj* **ingrown nail**
  : uña *f* encarnada
inhabit *vt* : habitar —
  inhabitant *n* : habitante *mf*
inhale *v* **-haled; -haling** *vt* :
  inhalar, aspirar — *vi* : inspirar
inherent *adj* : inherente —
  inherently *adv* : intrínsecamente
inherit *vt* : heredar —
  inheritance *n* : herencia *f*
inhibit *vt* IMPEDE : inhibir —
  inhibition *n* : inhibición *f*
inhuman *adj* : inhumano —
  inhumane *adj* : inhumano —
  inhumanity *n, pl* **-ties** : inhumanidad *f*
initial *adj* : inicial — *n* : inicial *f*
  — *vt* **-tialed** *or* **-tialled; -tialing** *or*
  -tialling : poner las iniciales a
initiate *vt* **-ated; -ating 1** BEGIN : iniciar

2 initiate someone into something :
  iniciar a algn en algo — **initiation** *n* :
  iniciación *f* — **initiative** *n* : iniciativa *f*
inject *vt* : inyectar —
  injection *n* : inyección *f*
injure *vt* **-jured; -juring 1** : herir **2**
  injure oneself : hacerse daño —
  injurious *adj* : perjudicial — **injury** *n*,
  pl **-ries 1** : herida *f* **2** HARM : perjuicio *m*
injustice *n* : injusticia *f*
ink *n* : tinta *f* — **inkwell** *n* : tintero *m*
inland *adj* : interior — **inland** *adv*
  : hacia el interior, tierra adentro
in–laws *npl* : suegros *mpl*
inlet *n* : ensenada *f*, cala *f*
inmate *n* **1** PATIENT : paciente *mf* **2**
  PRISONER : preso *m*, -sa *f*
inn *n* : posada *f*, hostería *f*
innards *npl* : entrañas *fpl*, tripas *fpl fam*
innate *adj* : innato
inner *adj* : interior, interno —
  innermost *adj* : más íntimo, más profundo
inning *n* : entrada *f*

innocent *adj* : inocente — **innocent** *n* :
inocente *mf* — **innocence** *n* : inocencia *f*
innocuous *adj* : inocuo
innovate *vi* -**vated; -vating** : innovar
— **innovation** *n* : innovación *f*
— **innovative** *a dj* : innovador —
innovator *n* : innovador *m*, -dora *f*
innuendo *n, pl* -**dos** *or* -**does**
: insinuación *f*, indirecta *f*
innumerable *adj* : innumerable
inoculate *vt* -**lated; -lating** : inocular
— **inoculation** *n* : inoculación *f*
inoffensive *adj* : inofensivo
inpatient *n* : paciente *mf* hospitalizado
input *n* **1** : contribución *f* **2** : entrada *f*
(de datos) — **input** *vt* -**putted** *or*
-**put; -putting** : entrar (datos, etc.)
inquire *v* -**quired; -quiring** *vt* :
preguntar — *vi* **1 inquire about** :
informarse sobre **2 inquire into** :
investigar — **inquiry** *n, pl* -**ries 1**
QUESTION : pregunta *f* **2** INVESTIGATION
: investigación *f* — **inquisition** *n* :
inquisición *f* — **inquisitive** *adj* : curioso
insane *adj* : loco — **insanity** *n,*
pl -**ties** : locura *f*
insatiable *adj* : insaciable
inscribe *vt* -**scribed; -scribing** :
inscribir — **inscription** *n* : inscripción *f*
inscrutable *adj* : inescrutable
insect *n* : insecto *m* —
insecticide *n* : insecticida *m*
insecure *adj* : inseguro, poco seguro
— **insecurity** *n, pl* -**ties** : inseguridad *f*
insensitive *adj* : insensible —
insensitivity *n, pl* -**ties** : insensibilidad *f*
inseparable *adj* : inseparable
insert *vt* : insertar (texto),
introducir (una moneda, etc.)
inside *n* **1** : interior *m* **2 inside out**
: al revés — *adv* : dentro, adentro —
inside *adj* : interior — **inside** *prep* **1**
or **inside of** : dentro de **2 inside an**
hour : en menos de una hora
insidious *adj* : insidioso
insight *n* : perspicacia *f*
insignia *or* insigne *n, pl* -**nia** *or*
-**nias** : insignia *f*, enseña *f*
insignificant *adj* : insignificante
insincere *adj* : insincero
insinuate *vt* -**ated; -ating** : insinuar
— **insinuation** *n* : insinuación *f*
insipid *adj* : insípido
insist *v* : insistir —
insistent *adj* : insistente

insofar as *conj* : en la medida en que
insole *n* : plantilla *f*
insolent *adj* : insolente —
insolence *n* : insolencia *f*
insolvent *adj* : insolvente
insomnia *n* : insomnio *m*
inspect *vt* : inspeccionar, revisar
— **inspection** *n* : inspección *f* —
inspector *n* : inspector *m*, -tora *f*
inspire *vt* -**spired; -spiring** : inspirar
— **inspiration** *n* : inspiración *f* —
inspirational *adj* : inspirador
instability *n, pl* -**ties** : inestabilidad *f*
install *vt* -**stalled; -stalling** : instalar
— **installation** *n* : instalación *f*
— **installment** *n* **1** PAYMENT :
plazo *m*, cuota *f* **2** : entrega *f* (de
una publicación o telenovela)
instance *n* **1** : ejemplo *m* **2**
for instance : por ejemplo **3 in**
this instance : en este caso
instant *n* : instante *m* — **instant** *adj* **1**
IMMEDIATE : inmediato **2 instant coffee** :
café *m* instantáneo — **instantaneous** *adj*
: instantáneo — **instantly** *adv* :
al instante, instantáneamente
instead *adv* **1** : en cambio **2 I went**
instead : fui en su lugar — **instead**
of *prep* : en vez de, en lugar de
instep *n* : empeine *m*
instigate *vt* -**gated; -gating** : instigar
a — **instigation** *n* : instigación *f* —
instigator *n* : instigador *m*, -dora *f*
instill *or* Brit **instil** *vt* -**stilled;**
-**stilling** : inculcar, infundir
instinct *n* : instinto *m* — **instinctive**
or **instinctual** *adj* : instintivo
institute *vt* -**tuted; -tuting 1** : instituir
2 INITIATE : iniciar — **institute** *n* :
instituto *m* — **institution** *n* : institución *f*
instruct *vt* **1** : instruir **2** COMMAND :
mandar — **instruction** *n* : instrucción *f*
— **instructor** *n* : instructor *m*, -tora *f*
▸ instrument *n* : instrumento *m* —
instrumental *adj* **1** : instrumental
2 be instrument in : jugar un
papel fundamental en
insubordinate *adj* : insubordinado —
insubordination *n* : insubordinación *f*
insufferable *adj* : insoportable
insufficient *adj* : insuficiente
insular *adj* **1** : insular **2** NARROW-
MINDED : estrecho de miras
insulate *vt* -**lated; -lating** : aislar
— **insulation** *n* : aislamiento *m*

insulin *n* : insulina *f*
insult *vt* : insultar — **insult** *n* : insulto *m*
— **insulting** *adj* : insultante, ofensivo
insure *vt* -**sured; -suring** : asegurar
— **insurance** *n* : seguro *m*
insurmountable *adj* : insuperable
intact *adj* : intacto
intake *n* : consumo *m* (de alimentos),
entrada *f* (de aire, etc.)
intangible *adj* : intangible
integral *adj* : integral
integrate *v* -**grated; -grating** *vt*
: integrar — *vi* : integrarse
integrity *n* : integridad *f*
intellect *n* : intelecto *m* — **intellectual** *adj*
: intelectual — **intellectual** *n* :
intelectual *mf* — **intelligence** *n* :
inteligencia *f* — **intelligent** *adj* :
inteligente — **intelligible** *adj* : inteligible
intend *vt* **1 be intended for** : ser para
2 intend to do : pensar hacer, tener
la intención de hacer — **intended** *adj*
: intencionado, deliberado
intense *adj* : intenso — **intensely** *adv* :
sumamente, profundamente — **intensify** *v*
-**fied; -fying** *vt* : intensificar — *vi* :
intensificarse — **intensity** *n, pl* -**ties** :
intensidad *f* — **intensive** *adj* : intensivo
intent *n* : intención *f* — **intent** *adj* **1** :
atento, concentrado **2 intent on doing** :
resuelto a hacer — **intention** *n* : intención *f*
— **intentional** *adj* : intencional, deliberado
— **intently** *adv* : atentamente, fijamente
interact *vi* **1** : interactuar **2 interact**
with : relacionarse con — **interaction** *n* :
interacción *f* — **interactive** *adj* : interactivo
intercede *vi* -**ceded; -ceding** : interceder
intercept *vt* : interceptar
interchange *vt* -**changed; -changing**
: intercambiar — **interchange** *n* **1** :
intercambio *m* **2** JUNCTION : enlace *m* —
interchangeable *adj* : intercambiable
intercourse *n* : relaciones *fpl* (sexuales)
interest *n* : interés *m* — **interest** *vt* :
interesar — **interested** *adj* : interesado
— **interesting** *adj* : interesante
interface *n* : interfaz *mf* (de
una computadora)
interfere *vi* -**fered; -fering 1 interfere in** :
entrometerse en, interferir en **2 interfere**
with DISRUPT : afectar (una actividad, etc.)
— **interference** *n* **1** : interferencia *f* **2**
: intromisión *f* (en el radio, etc.)
interim *n* **1** : interín *m* **2 in**
the interim : mientras tanto

— **interim** *adj* : interino, provisional
interior *adj* : interior —
  interior *n* : interior *m*
interjection *n* : interjección *f*
interlock *vt* : engranar
interloper *n* : intruso *m*, -sa *f*
interlude *n* 1 : intervalo *m* 2 :
  interludio *m* (en música, etc.)
intermediate *adj* : intermedio
  — **intermediary** *n, pl* -aries
  : intermediario *m*, -ria *f*
interminable *adj* : interminable
intermission *n* : intervalo *m*,
  intermedio *m*
intermittent *adj* : intermitente
intern[1] *vt* : confinar

intern[2] *vi* : hacer las prácticas
  — **intern** *n* : interno *m*, -na *f*
internal *adj* : interno
international *adj* : internacional
interpret *vt* : interpretar —
  interpretation *n* : interpretación *f*
  — **interpreter** *n* : intérprete *mf*
interrogate *vt* -gated; -gating
  : interrogar — **interrogation** *n*
  QUESTIONING : interrogatorio *m* —
  interrogative *adj* : interrogativo
interrupt *v* : interrumpir —
  interruption *n* : interrupción *f*
intersect *vt* : cruzarr(dícese de
  calles), cortar (dícese de líneas) — *vi*
  : cruzarse, cortarse — **intersection** *n*

  : cruce *m*, intersección *f*
intersperse *vt* -spersed;
  -spersing : intercalar
interstate *n or* **interstate highway**
  : carretera *f* interestatal
intertwine *vi* -twined;
  -twining : entrelazarse
interval *n* : intervalo *m*
intervene *vi* -vened; -vening 1 :
  intervenir 2 ELAPSE : transcurrir, pasar
  — **intervention** *n* : intervención *f*
interview *n* : entrevista *f* — **interview** *vt*
  : entrevistar — **interviewer** *n*
  : entrevistador *m*, -dora *f*
intestine *n* : intestino *m* —
  intestinal *adj* : intestinal

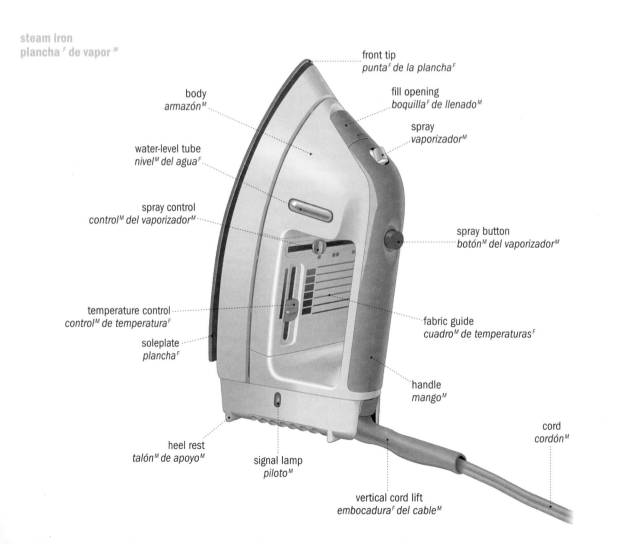

steam iron
plancha^F de vapor^M

front tip
punta^F *de la plancha*^F

body
armazón^M

fill opening
boquilla^F *de llenado*^M

spray
vaporizador^M

water-level tube
nivel^M *del agua*^F

spray control
control^M *del vaporizador*^M

spray button
botón^M *del vaporizador*^M

temperature control
control^M *de temperatura*^F

fabric guide
cuadro^M *de temperaturas*^F

soleplate
plancha^F

handle
mango^M

cord
cordón^M

heel rest
talón^M *de apoyo*^M

signal lamp
piloto^M

vertical cord lift
embocadura^F *del cable*^M

intimate[1] *vt* **-mated; -mating**
: insinuar, dar a entender
intimate[2] *adj* : íntimo —
intimacy *n, pl* **-cies** : intimidad *f*
intimidate *vt* **-dated; -dating** : intimidar
— **intimidation** *n* : intimidación *f*
into *prep* **1** : en, a **2 bump into** :
darse contra **3** (*used in mathematics*)
3 into 12 : 12 dividido por 3
intolerable *adj* : intolerable —
intolerance *n* : intolerancia *f* —
intolerant *adj* : intolerante
intoxicate *vt* **-cated; -cating** :
embriagar — **intoxicated** *adj* **1** :
embriagado **2 intoxicate with** : ebrio de
intransitive *adj* : intransitivo
intravenous *adj* : intravenoso
intrepid *adj* : intrépido
intricate *adj* : complicado, intrincado
— **intricacy** *n, pl* **-cies** : complejidad *f*
intrigue *n* : intriga *f* — **intrigue** *v*
-trigued; -triguing : intrigar —
intriguing *adj* : intrigante
intrinsic *adj* : intrínseco
introduce *vt* **-duced; -ducing 1** :
introducir **2** : presentar (a una persona)
— **introduction** *n* **1** : introducción *f* **2**
: presentación *f* (de una persona) —
introductory *adj* : introductorio
introvert *n* : introvertido *m*, -da *f*
— **introverted** *adj* : introvertido
intrude *vi* **-truded; -truding 1** :
entrometerse **2 intrude on someone**
: molestar a algn — **intruder** *n* :
intruso *m*, -sa *f* — **intrusion** *n* :
intrusión *f* — **intrusive** *adj* : intruso
intuition *n* : intuición *f* —
intuitive *adj* : intuitivo
inundate *vt* **-dated; -dating** : inundar
invade *vt* **-vaded; -vading** : invadir
invalid[1] *adj* : inválido
invalid[2] *n* : inválido *m*, -da *f*
invaluable *adj* : inestimable,
invalorable *Lat*
invariable *adj* : invariable
invasion *n* : invasión *f*
invent *vt* : inventar — **invention** *n* :
invención *f* — **inventive** *adj* : inventivo
— **inventor** *n* : inventor *m*, -tora *f*
inventory *n, pl* **-ries** : inventario *m*
invert *vt* : invertir
invertebrate *adj* : invertebrado —
invertebrate *n* : invertebrado *m*
invest *vt* : invertir
investigate *v* **-gated; -gating** : investigar

— **investigation** *n* : investigación *f* —
investigator *n* : investigador *m*, -dora *f*
investment *n* : inversión *f* —
investor *n* : inversor *m*, -sora *f*
inveterate *adj* : inveterado
invigorating *adj* : vigorizante
invincible *adj* : invencible
invisible *adj* : invisible
invitation *n* : invitación *f* — **invite** *vt*
-vited; -viting 1 : invitar **2** SEEK : buscar
(problemas, etc.) — **inviting** *adj* : atrayente
invoice *n* : factura *f*
invoke *vt* **-voked; -voking** : invocar
involuntary *adj* : involuntario
involve *vt* **-volved; -volving 1**
CONCERN : concernir, afectar **2** ENTAIL
: suponer — **involved** *adj* **1** COMPLEX
: complicado **2** CONCERNED : afectado
— **involvement** *n* : participación *f*
invulnerable *adj* : invulnerable
inward *adj* INNER : interior, interno
— **inward** *or* inwards *adv* : hacia
adentro, hacia el interior
iodine *n* : yodo *m*, tintura *f* de yodo
ion *n* : ion *m*
iota *n* : pizca *f*, ápice *m*
IOU *n* : pagaré *m*, vale *m*
Iranian *adj* : iraní
Iraqi *adj* : iraquí
ire *n* : ira *f* — **irate** *adj* : furioso
iris *n, pl* **irises** *or* **irides 1** : iris *m*
(del ojo) **2** : lirio *m* (planta)
Irish *adj* : irlandés
irksome *adj* : irritante, fastidioso
▸ **iron** *n* **1** : hierro *m*, fierro *m*, *Lat*
(metal) **2** : plancha *f* (para la
ropa) — **iron** *v* : planchar
ironic *or* **ironical** *adj* : irónico
ironing board *n* : tabla *f* (de planchar)
irony *n, pl* **-nies** : ironía *f*
irrational *adj* : irracional
irreconcilable *adj* : irreconciliable
irrefutable *adj* : irrefutable
irregular *adj* : irregular —
irregularity *n, pl* **-ties** : irregularidad *f*
irrelevant *adj* : irrelevante
irreparable *adj* : irreparable
irreplaceable *adj* : irreemplazable
irresistible *adj* : irresistible
irresolute *adj* : irresoluto
irrespective of *prep* :
sin tener en cuenta
irresponsible *adj* : irresponsable
— **irresponsibility** *n, pl* **-ties**
: irresponsabilidad *f*

irreverent *adj* : irreverente
irreversible *adj* : irreversible, irrevocable
irrigate *vt* **-gated; -gating** : irrigar, regar
— **irrigation** *n* : irrigación *f*, riego *m*
irritate *vt* **-tated; -tating** : irritar —
irritable *adj* : irritable — **irritably** *adv*
: con irritación — **irritating** *adj* :
irritante — **irritation** *n* : irritación *f*
is → **be**
Islam *n* : el Islam — **Islamic** *adj* : islámico
island *n* : isla *f* — **isle** *n* : isla *f*
isolate *vt* **-lated; -lating** : aislar
— **isolation** *n* : aislamiento *m*
Israeli *adj* : israelí
issue *n* **1** MATTER : asunto *m*, cuestión *f* **2**
: número *m* (de una revista, etc.) **3 make
an issue of** : insistir demasiado sobre **4
take issue with** : disentir de — **issue** *v*
-sued; -suing *vi* **issue from** : surgir de
— *vt* **1** : emitir (sellos, etc.), distribuir
(provisiones, etc.) **2** PUBLISH : publicar
isthmus *n* : istmo *m*
it *pron* **1** (*as subject*) : él, ella **2** (*as indirect
object*) : le, se **3** (*as direct object*) : lo, la **4**
(*as object of a preposition*) : él, ella **5 it's
raining** : está lloviendo **6 it's 8 o'clock**
: son las ocho **7 it's hot out** : hace calor
8 it is necessary : es necesario **9 who
is it?** : ¿quién es? **10 it's me** : soy yo
Italian *adj* : italiano — **Italian** *n*
: italiano *m* (idioma)
italics *n* : cursiva *f*
itch *vi* **1** : picar **2 be itching to** :
morirse por — **itch** *n* : picazón *f* —
itchy *adj* **itchier; -est** : que pica
it'd (*contraction of* **it had** *or* **it
would**) → **have, would**
item *n* **1** : artículo *m* **2** : punto *m* (en una
agenda) **3 item of clothing** : prenda *f* de
vestir **4 news item** : noticia *f* — **itemize** *vt*
-ized; -izing : detallar, enumerar
itinerant *adj* : ambulante
itinerary *n, pl* **-aries** : itinerario *m*
it'll (*contraction of* **it shall** *or*
it will) → **shall, will**
its *adj* : su, sus
it's (*contraction of* **it is** *or*
it has) → **be, have**
itself *pron* **1** (*used reflexively*) : se **2**
(*used for emphasis*) : (él) mismo, (ella)
misma, sí (mismo) **3 by itself** : solo
I've (*contraction of* **I have**) → **have**
ivory *n, pl* **-ries** : marfil *m*
ivy *n, pl* **ivies** : hiedra *f*

J

j *n, pl* **j's** *or* **js** : j *f*, décima letra del alfabeto inglés

jab *vt* **jabbed; jabbing 1** PIERCE : pinchar **2** POKE : golpear (con la punta de algo) — **jab** *n* **1** PRICK : pinchazo *m* **2** POKE : golpe *m* abrupto

jabber *vi* : farfullar

jack *n* **1** : gato *m* (mecanismo) **2** : sota *f* (de naipes) — **jack** *vt or* **jack up 1** : levantar (con un gato) **2** INCREASE : subir

jackal *n* : chacal *m*

jackass *n* : asno *m*, burro *m*

jacket *n* **1** : chaqueta *f,* **2** : sobrecubierta *f* (de un libro), carátula *f* (de un disco)

jackhammer *n* : martillo *m* neumático

jackknife *n* : navaja *f* — **jackknife** *vi* **-knifed; -knifing** : plegarse (dícese de un camión)

jack-o'-lantern *n* : linterna *f* hecha de una calabaza

jackpot *n* : premio *m* gordo

jaded *adj* **1** TIRED : agotado **2** BORED : hastiado

jagged *adj* : dentado

jail *n* : cárcel *f* — **jail** *vt* : encarcelar — **jailer** *or* **jailor** *n* : carcelero *m*, -ra *f*

jalapeño *n* : jalapeño *m, Lat*

jam¹ *v* **jammed; jamming** *vt* **1** CRAM : apiñar, embutir **2** BLOCK : atascar, atorar — *vi* : atascarse, atrancarse — **jam** *n* **1** *or* **traffic jam** : embotellamiento *m* (de tráfico) **2** FIX : lío *m*, aprieto *m*

jam² *n* PRESERVES : mermelada *f*

jangle *v* **-gled; -gling** *vi* : hacer un ruido metálico — *vt* : hacer sonar — **jangle** *n* : ruido *m* metálico

janitor *n* : portero *m*, -ra *f;* conserje *mf*

January *n* : enero *m*

Japanese *adj* : japonés — **Japanese** *n* : japonés *m* (idioma)

jar¹ *v* **jarred; jarring** *vi* **1** GRATE : chirriar **2** CLASH : desentonar **3** **jar on** IRRITATE : crispar, enervar (a algn) — *vt* JOLT : sacudir — **jar** *n* : sacudida *f*

jar² *n* : tarro *m*

jargon *n* : jerga *f*

jaundice *n* : ictericia *f*

jaunt *n* : excursión *f*

jaunty *adj* **-tier; -est** : garboso, desenvuelto

jaw *n* : mandíbula *f* (de una persona), quijada *f* (de un animal) — **jawbone** *n* : mandíbula *f*, quijada *f*

jay *n* : arrendajo *m*

jazz *n* : jazz *m* — **jazz** *vt or* **jazz up** : animar, alegrar — **jazzy** *adj* **jazzier; -est** FLASHY : llamativo

jealous *adj* : celoso — **jealousy** *n* : celos *mpl*, envidia *f*

jeans *npl* : jeans *mpl*, vaqueros *mpl*

jeer *vt* **1** BOO : abuchear **2** MOCK : mofarse de — *vi* **jeer at** : mofarse de — **jeer** *n* : mofa *f*

jell *vi* : cuajar

jelly *n, pl* **-lies** : jalea *f* — **jellyfish** *n* : medusa *f*

jeopardy *n* : peligro *m*, riesgo *m* — **jeopardize** *vt* **-dized; -dizing** : arriesgar, poner en peligro

jerk *n* **1** JOLT : sacudida *f* brusca **2** FOOL : idiota *mf* — **jerk** *vt* : sacudir — *vi* JOLT : dar sacudidas

jersey *n, pl* **-seys** : jersey *m*

jest *n* : broma *f* — **jest** *vi* : bromear — **jester** *n* : bufón *m*

Jesus *n* : Jesús *m*

jet *n* **1** STREAM : chorro *m* **2** *or* **jet airplane** : avión *m* a reacción, reactor *m* — **jet-propelled** *adj* : a reacción

jettison *vt* **1** : echar al mar **2** DISCARD : deshacerse de

jetty *n, pl* **-ties** : desembarcadero *m*, muelle *m*

jewel *n* **1** : joya *f* **2** GEM : piedra *f* preciosa — **jeweler** *or* **jeweller** *n* : joyero *m*, -ra *f* — **jewelry** *n* : joyas *fpl*, alhajas *fpl*

Jewish *adj* : judío

jibe *vi* **jibed; jibing** AGREE : concordar

jiffy *n, pl* **-fies** : santiamén *m*, segundo *m*

jig *n* : giga *f*

jiggle *vt* **-gled; -gling** : sacudir, zarandear — **jiggle** *n* : sacudida *f*

jigsaw *n* **1** : sierra *f* de vaivén **2** *or* **jigsaw puzzle** : rompecabezas *m*

jilt *vt* : dejar plantado

jingle *v* **-gled; -gling** *vi* : tintinear — *vt* : hacer sonar — **jingle** *n* TINKLE : tintineo *m*

jinx *n* CURSE : maldición *f*

jitters *npl* **have the jitters** : estar nervioso — **jittery** *adj* : nervioso

job *n* **1** EMPLOYMENT : empleo *m*, trabajo *m* **2** TASK : trabajo *m*

jockey *n, pl* **-eys** : jockey *mf*

jog *v* **jogged; jogging** *vt* **jog someone's memory** : refrescar la memoria a algn — *vi* : hacer

juggler
malabarista*F*

footing — **jogging** *n* : footing *m*

join *vt* **1** UNITE : unir, juntar **2** MEET : reunirse con **3** : hacerse socio de (una organización, etc.) — *vi* **1** *or* **join together** : unirse **2** : hacerse socio (de una organización, etc.)

joint *n* **1** : articulación *f* (en anatomía) **2** JUNCTURE : juntura *f*, unión *f* — **joint** *adj* : conjunto — **jointly** *adv* : conjuntamente

joke *n* : chiste *m*, broma *f* — **joke** *vi* **joked; joking** : bromear — **joker** *n* **1** : bromista *mf* **2** : comodín *m* (en los naipes)

jolly *adj* **-lier; -est** : alegre, jovial

jolt *vt* : sacudir — **jolt** *n* **1** : sacudida *f* brusca **2** SHOCK : golpe *m* (emocional)

jostle *v* **-tled; -tling** *vt* : empujar, dar empujones — *vi* : empujarse

jot *vt* **jotted; jotting** *or* **jot down** : anotar, apuntar

journal *n* **1** DIARY : diario *m* **2** PERIODICAL : revista *f* — **journalism** *n* : periodismo *m* — **journalist** *n* : periodista *mf*

journey *n, pl* **-neys** : viaje *m* — **journey** *vi* **-neyed; -neying** : viajar

jovial *adj* : jovial

joy *n* : alegría *f* — **joyful** *adj* : alegre, feliz — **joyous** *adj* : jubiloso, alegre

jubilant *adj* : jubiloso — **jubilee** *n* : aniversario *m* especial

Judaism *n* : judaísmo *m*

judge *vt* **judged; judging** : juzgar — **judge** *n* : juez *mf* — **judgment**

or judgement *n* **1** RULING : fallo *m*, sentencia *f* **2** VIEW : juicio *m*
judicial *adj* : judicial —
judicious *adj* : juicioso
jug *n* : jarra *f*
juggle *vi* **-gled; -gling** : hacer juegos malabares — **juggler** *n* : malabarista *mf*
jugular vein *n* : vena *f* yugular
juice *n* : jugo *m* — **juicy** *adj* **juicier; -est** : jugoso
jukebox *n* : máquina *f* de discos
July *n* : julio *m*
jumble *vt* **-bled; -bling** : mezclar — **jumble** *n* : revoltijo *m*
jumbo *adj* : gigante
jump *vi* **1** LEAP : saltar **2** START : sobresaltarse **3** RISE : subir de un golpe **4 jump at** : no dejar escapar (una oportunidad, etc.) — *vt* : saltar — **jump** *n* **1** LEAP : salto *m* **2** INCREASE : aumento *m* — **jumper** *n* **1** : saltador *m*, -dora *f* (en deportes) **2** : jumper *m* (vestido) — **jumpy** *adj* **jumpier; -est** : nervioso
junction *n* **1** JOINING : unión *f* **2** : cruce *m* (de calles), empalme *m* (de un

ferrocarril) — **juncture** *n* : coyuntura *f*
June *n* : junio *m*
jungle *n* : selva *f*
junior *adj* **1** YOUNGER : más joven **2** SUBORDINATE : subalterno — **junior** *n* **1** : persona *f* de menor edad **2** SUBORDINATE : subalterno *m*, -na *f* **3** : estudiante *mf* de penúltimo año
junk *n* : trastos *mpl* (viejos) — **junk** *vt* : echar a la basura
junta *n* : junta *f* (militar)
jurisdiction *n* : jurisdicción *f*
jury *n*, *pl* **-ries** : jurado *m* — **juror** *n* : jurado *mf*
just *adj* : justo — **just** *adv* **1** BARELY : apenas **2** EXACTLY : exactamente **3** ONLY : sólo, solamente **4 just now** : ahora mismo **5 she has just left** : acaba de salir **6 we were just leaving** : justo íbamos a salir
justice *n* **1** : justicia *f* **2** JUDGE : juez *mf*
justify *vt* **-fied; -fying** : justificar — **justification** *n* : justificación *f*
jut *vi* **jutted; jutting** *or* **jut out** : sobresalir
juvenile *adj* **1** YOUNG : juvenil **2** CHILDISH : infantil — **juvenile** *n* : menor *mf*

juxtapose *vt* **-posed; -posing** : yuxtaponer
k *n*, *pl* **k's** *or* **ks** : k *f*, undécima letra del alfabeto inglés
kaleidoscope *n* : calidoscopio *m*
▸ **kangaroo** *n*, *pl* **-roos** : canguro *m*
karat *n* : quilate *m*
karate *n* : karate *m*
keel *n* : quilla *f* — **keel** *vi* *or* **keel over** : volcarse (dícese de un barco), desplomarse (dícese de una persona)
keen *adj* **1** SHARP : afilado **2** PENETRATING : cortante, penetrante **3** ENTHUSIASTIC : entusiasta **4 keen eyesight** : visión *f* aguda
keep *v* **kept; keeping** *vt* **1** : guardar **2** : cumplir (una promesa), acudir a (una cita) **3** DETAIN : hacer quedar, detener **4** PREVENT : impedir **5 keep up** : mantener — *vi* **1** REMAIN : mantenerse **2** LAST : conservarse **3** *or* **keep on** CONTINUE : no dejar — **keep** *n* **1 earn one's keep** :

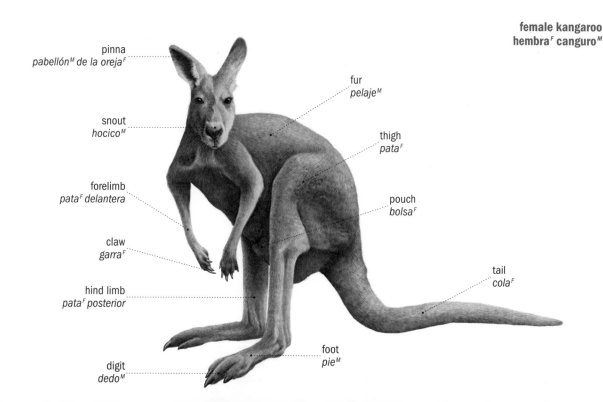

female kangaroo
hembra[F] **canguro**[M]

pinna
pabellón[M] *de la oreja*[F]

fur
pelaje[M]

snout
hocico[M]

thigh
pata[F]

forelimb
pata[F] *delantera*

pouch
bolsa[F]

claw
garra[F]

tail
cola[F]

hind limb
pata[F] *posterior*

foot
pie[M]

digit
dedo[M]

first aid kit
botiquín^M

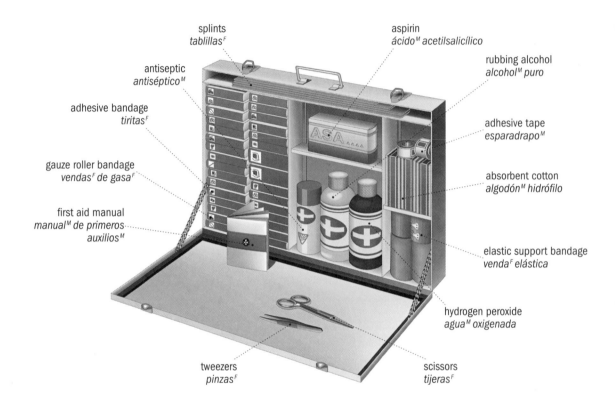

splints
tablillas^F

aspirin
ácido^M acetilsalicílico

antiseptic
antiséptico^M

rubbing alcohol
alcohol^M puro

adhesive bandage
tiritas^F

adhesive tape
esparadrapo^M

gauze roller bandage
vendas^F de gasa^F

absorbent cotton
algodón^M hidrófilo

first aid manual
manual^M de primeros
auxilios^M

elastic support bandage
venda^F elástica

hydrogen peroxide
agua^M oxigenada

tweezers
pinzas^F

scissors
tijeras^F

---

ganarse el pan **2 for keeps** : para siempre — **keeper** *n* : guarda *mf* — **keeping** *n* **1** CARE : cuidado *m* **2 in keeping with** : de acuerdo con — **keepsake** *n* : recuerdo *m*
keg *n* : barril *m*
kennel *n* : caseta *f* para perros, perrera *f*
kept → **keep**
kerchief *n* : pañuelo *m*
kernel *n* **1** : almendra *f* **2** CORE : meollo *m*
kerosene *or* **kerosine** *n* : queroseno *m*
ketchup *n* : salsa *f* de tomate
kettle *n* : hervidor *m*, tetera *f* (para hervir)
key *n* **1** : llave *f* **2** : tecla *f* (de un piano o una máquina) — **key** *vt* **be keyed up** : estar nervioso — **key** *adj* : clave — **keyboard** *n* : teclado *m* — **keyhole** *n* : ojo *m* (de la cerradura) — **keynote** *n* : tónica *f* — **key ring** *n* : llavero *m*
khaki *adj* : caqui

kick *vt* **1** : dar una patada a **2 kick out** : echar a patadas — *vi* **1** : dar patadas (dícese de una persona), cocear (dícese de un animal) **2** RECOIL : dar un culatazo — **kick** *n* **1** : patada *f*, coz *f* (de un animal) **2** RECOIL : culatazo *m* **3** PLEASURE, THRILL : placer *m*
kid *n* **1** GOAT : chivo *m*, -va *f*; cabrito *m* **2** CHILD : niño *m*, -ña *f* — **kid** *v* **kidded**; **kidding** *vi or* **kid around** : bromear — *vt* TEASE : tomar el pelo a — **kidnap** *vt* **-napped** *or* **-naped**; **-napping** *or* **-naping** : secuestrar, raptar
kidney *n, pl* **-neys** : riñón *m*
kidney bean *n* : frijol *m*
kill *vt* **1** : matar **2** DESTROY : acabar con **3 kill time** : matar el tiempo — **kill** *n* **1** KILLING : matanza *f* **2** PREY : presa *f* — **killer** *n* : asesino *m*, -na *f* — **killing** *n* **1**

: matanza *f* **2** MURDER : asesinato *m*
kiln *n* : horno *m*
kilo *n, pl* **-los** : kilo *m* — **kilogram** *n* : kilogramo *m* — **kilometer** *n* : kilómetro *m* — **kilowatt** *n* : kilovatio *m*
kin *n* : parientes *mpl*
kind *n* : tipo *m*, clase *f* — **kind** *adj* : amable
kindergarten *n* : jardín *m* infantil, jardín *m* de niños *Lat*
kindhearted *adj* : de buen corazón
kindle *vt* **-dled**; **-dling 1** : encender (un fuego) **2** AROUSE : despertar
kindly *adj* **-lier**; **-est** : bondadoso, amable — **kindly** *adv* **1** : amablemente **2 take kindly to** : aceptar de buena gana **3 we kindly ask you not smoke** : les rogamos que no fumen — **kindness** *n* : bondad *f*

multipurpose knife
navaja*F* multiusos

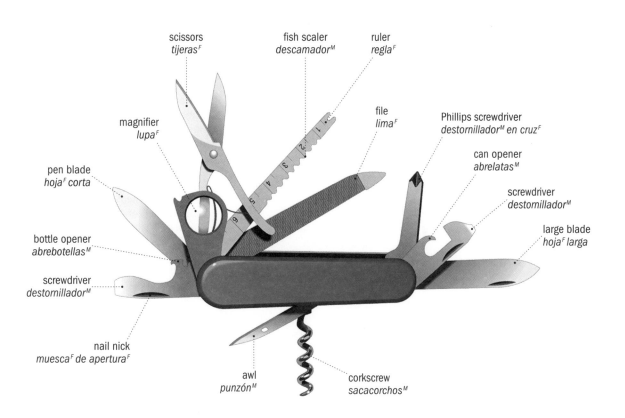

scissors
tijeras*F*

fish scaler
descamador*M*

ruler
regla*F*

magnifier
lupa*F*

file
lima*F*

Phillips screwdriver
destornillador*M* en cruz*F*

can opener
abrelatas*M*

pen blade
hoja*F* corta

screwdriver
destornillador*M*

bottle opener
abrebotellas*M*

large blade
hoja*F* larga

screwdriver
destornillador*M*

nail nick
muesca*F* de apertura*F*

awl
punzón*M*

corkscrew
sacacorchos*M*

— kind of *adv* SOMEWHAT : un tanto, algo
kindred *adj* **1** : emparentado **2**
  kindred spirit : alma *f* gemela
king *n* : rey *m* — **kingdom** *n* : reino *m*
kink *n* **1** TWIST : vuelta *f*,
  curva *f* **2** FLAW : problema *m*
kinship *n* : parentesco *m*
kiss *vt* : besar — *vi* : besarse
  — **kiss** *n* : beso *m*
▶ **kit** *n* **1** : juego *m*, kit *m* **2 first–**
  aid kit : botiquín *m* **3 tool kit**
  : caja *f* de herramientas
kitchen *n* : cocina *f*
kite *n* : cometa *f*, papalote *m*, *Lat*
kitten *n* : gatito *m*, -ta *f* — **kitty** *n*,
  pl **-ties** FUND : fondo *m* común
knack *n* : maña *f*, facilidad *f*
knapsack *n* : mochila *f*

knead *vt* **1** : amasar, sobar
  2 MASSAGE : masajear
knee *n* : rodilla *f* — **kneecap** *n* : rótula *f*
kneel *vi* **knelt** *or* **kneeled;**
  kneeling : arrodillarse
knew → **know**
knickknack *n* : chuchería *f*
▶ **knife** *n*, *pl* **knives** : cuchillo *m* —
  knife *vt* **knifed; knifing** : acuchillar
knight *n* **1** : caballero *m* **2** : caballo *m* (en
  ajedrez) — **knighthood** *n* : título *m* de Sir
knit *v* **knit** *or* **knitted; knitting** *v* :
  tejer — **knit** *n* : prenda *f* tejida
knob *n* : tirador *m*, botón *m*, perilla *f Lat*
knock *vt* **1** : golpear **2** CRITICIZE : criticar
  3 knock down : derribar, echar al
  suelo — *vi* **1** : dar un golpe, llamar (a
  la puerta) **2** COLLIDE : darse, chocar —
knock *n* : golpe *m*, llamada *f* (a la puerta)

knot *n* : nudo *m* — **knot** *vt* **knotted;**
  knotting : anudar — **knotty** *adj*
  -tier; -est 1 : nudoso **2** : enredado
  (dícese de un problema)
know *v* **knew; known; knowing** *vt* **1**
  : saber **2** : conocer (a una persona,
  un lugar) **3 know how to** : saber — *vi*
  : saber — **knowing** *adj* : cómplice
  — **knowingly** *adv* **1** : de manera
  cómplice **2** DELIBERATELY : a sabiendas
  — **know–it–all** *n* : sabelotodo *mf fam*
  — **knowledge** *n* **1** : conocimiento *m* **2**
  LEARNING : conocimientos *mpl*, saber *m* —
  knowledgeable *adj* : informado, entendido
knuckle *n* : nudillo *m*
Koran *n* **the Koran** : el Corán *m*
Korean *adj* : coreano *m*, -na *f* —
  Korean *n* : coreano *m* (idioma)
kosher *adj* : aprobado por la ley judía

laboratory equipment
material^M de laboratorio^M

petri dish
cápsula^F de Petri

graduated cylinder
probeta^F graduada

beaker
cubeta^F de precipitación^M

test tube
tubo^M de ensayo^M

serological pipette
pipeta^F

gas burner
mechero^M de gas^M

wash bottle
frasco^M lavador

round-bottom flask
balón^M

I *n, pl* **I's** *or* **Is** : I *f,* duodécima
letra del alfabeto inglés
lab → **laboratory**
label *n* **1** TAG : etiqueta *f* **2** BRAND :
marca *f* — **label** *vt* **-beled** *or* **-belled;**
-beling *or* **-belling** : etiquetar
labor *n* **1** : trabajo *m* **2** WORKERS :
mano *f* de obra **3 in labor** : de parto
— **labor** *vi* **1** : trabajar **2** STRUGGLE
: avanzar penosamente — *vt*
BELABOR : insistir en (un punto)
▸ **laboratory** *n, pl* **-ries** : laboratorio *m*
laborer *n* : trabajador *m,* -dora *f*
laborious *adj* : laborioso
lace *n* **1** : encaje *m* **2** SHOELACE :
cordón *m* (de zapatos), agujeta *f Lat* —
lace *vt* **laced; lacing 1** TIE : atar **2 be laced**
with : echar licor a (una bebida, etc.)
lacerate *vt* **-ated; -ating** : lacerar
lack *vt* : carecer de, no tener
— *vi* **be lacking** : faltar —
lack *n* : falta *f,* carencia *f*
lackadaisical *adj* : apático, indolente
lackluster *adj* : sin brillo, apagado
laconic *adj* : lacónico
lacquer *n* : laca *f*
lacrosse *n* : lacrosse *f*
lacy *adj* **lacier; -est** : como de encaje
lad *n* : muchacho *m,* niño *m*
ladder *n* : escalera *f*
laden *adj* : cargado
ladle *n* : cucharón *m* — **ladle** *vt*
-dled; -dling : servir con cucharón
lady *n, pl* **-dies** : señora *f,* dama *f*
— **ladybug** *n* : mariquita *f* —
ladylike *adj* : elegante, como señora
lag *n* **1** DELAY : retraso *m* **2** INTERVAL
: intervalo *m* — **lag** *vi* **lagged;**
lagging : quedarse atrás, rezagarse
lager *n* : cerveza *f* rubia
lagoon *n* : laguna *f*
laid *pp* → **lay 1**
lain *pp* → **lie 1**
lair *n* : guarida *f*
lake *n* : lago *m*
lamb *n* : cordero *m*
lame *adj* **lamer; lamest 1** : cojo,
renco **2 a lame excuse** : una
excusa poco convincente
lament *vt* **1** MOURN : llorar **2** DEPLORE
: lamentar — **lament** *n* : lamento *m*
— **lamentable** *adj* : lamentable
laminate *vt* **-nated; -nating** : laminar
lamp *n* : lámpara *f* — **lamppost** *n* :
farol *m* — **lampshade** *n* : pantalla *f*

lance *n* : lanza *f* — **lance** *vt* **lanced;**
  lancing : abrir con lanceta (en medecina)
land *n* **1** : tierra *f* **2**COUNTRY : país *m* **3**
  or **plot of land** : terreno *m* — **land** *vt* **1**
  : desembarcar (pasajeros de un barco),
  hacer aterrizar (un avión) **2** CATCH : sacar
  (un pez) del agua **3** SECURE : conseguir
  (empleo, etc.) — *vi* **1** : aterrizar
  (dícese de un avión) **2** FALL : caer —
  landing *n* **1** : aterrizaje *m* (de aviones) **2** :
  desembarco *m* (de barcos) **3** : descanso *m*
  (de una escalera) — **landlady** *n, pl* **-dies**
  : casera *f* — **landlord** *n* : casero *m* —
  landmark *n* **1** : punto *m* de referencia
  2 MONUMENT : monumento *m* histórico
  — **landowner** *n* : hacendado *m*, -da *f*;

terrateniente *mf* — **landscape** *n* :
  paisaje *m* — **landscape** *vt* **-scaped;**
  -scaping : ajardinar — **landslide** *n* **1**
  : desprendimiento *m* de tierras **2** *or*
  landslide victory : victoria *f* arrolladora
lane *n* **1** : carril *m* (de una carretera)
  2 PATH, ROAD : camino *m*
language *n* **1** : idioma *m*,
  lengua *f* **2** SPEECH : lenguaje *m*
languid *adj* : lánguido —
  languish *vi* : languidecer
lanky *adj* **lankier; -est** :
  delgado, larguirucho *fam*
lantern *n* : linterna *f*
lap *n* **1** : regazo *m* (de una persona)
  2 : vuelta *f* (en deportes) — **lap** *v*

lapped; lapping *vt or* **lap up** : beber a
  lengüetadas — *vi* **lap against** : lamer
lapel *n* : solapa *f*
lapse *n* **1** : lapsus *m*, falla *f* (de
  memoria, etc.) **2** INTERVAL : lapso *m*,
  intervalo *m* — **lapse** *vi* **lapsed;**
  lapsing 1 EXPIRE : caducar **2** ELAPSE :
  transcurrir, pasar **3 lapse into** : caer en
▸ **laptop** *adj* : portátil
larceny *n, pl* **-nies** : robo *m*
lard *n* : manteca *f* de cerdo
large *adj* **larger; largest 1** : grande **2 at**
  large : en libertad **3 by and large** : por lo
  general — **largely** *adv* : en gran parte
lark *n* **1** : alondra *f* (pájaro) **2**
  for a lark : por divertirse

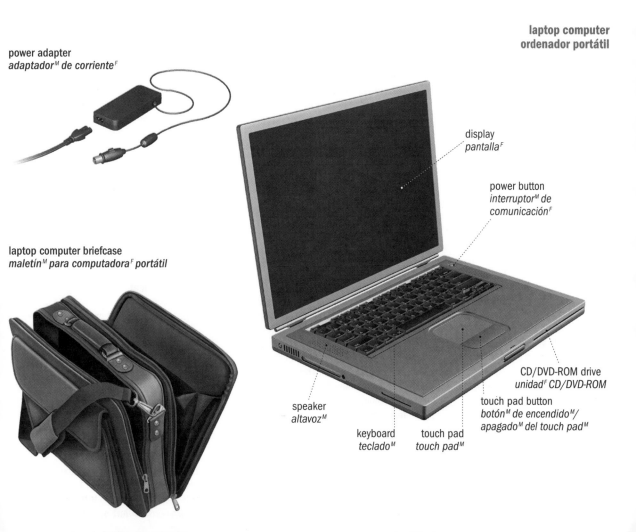

laptop computer
ordenador portátil

power adapter
adaptador^M de corriente^F

laptop computer briefcase
maletín^M para computadora^F portátil

display
pantalla^F

power button
interruptor^M de
comunicación^F

CD/DVD-ROM drive
unidad^F CD/DVD-ROM

touch pad button
botón^M de encendido^M/
apagado^M del touch pad^M

speaker
altavoz^M

keyboard
teclado^M

touch pad
touch pad^M

lemon
limón^M

larva n, pl **-vae** : larva f
larynx n, pl **-rynges** or **-ynxes** :
laringe f — **laryngitis** n : laringitis f
lasagna n : lasaña f
laser n : láser m
lash vt **1** WHIP : azotar **2** BIND : amarrar
— vi **lash out at** : arremeter contra
— **lash** n **1** BLOW : latigazo m (con
un látigo) **2** EYELASH : pestaña f
lass or lassie n : muchacha f, chica f
lasso n, pl **-sos** or **-soes** : lazo m
last vi : durar — **last** n **1** : último m,
-ma f **2 at last** : por fin, finalmente —
last adv **1** : por última vez, en último lugar
2 arrive last : llegar el último — **last** adj **1**
: último **2 last year** : el año pasado —
lastly adv : por último, finalmente
latch n : picaporte m, pestillo m
late adj **later; latest 1** : tarde **2** : avanzado
(dícese de la hora) **3** DECEASED : difunto **4**
RECENT : reciente — **late** adv **later; latest**
: tarde — **lately** adv : recientemente,
últimamente — **lateness** n **1** :
retraso m **2** : lo avanzado (de la hora)
latent adj : latente
lateral adj : lateral
latest n **at the latest** : a más tardar
lathe n : torno m
lather n : espuma f — **lather** vt :
enjabonar — vi : hacer espuma
Latin–American adj : latinoamericano
latitude n : latitud f
latter adj **1** : último **2** SECOND :
segundo — **latter** pron **the latter**
: éste, ésta, éstos pl, **éstas** pl
lattice n : enrejado m

laugh vi : reír(se) — **laugh** n : risa f
— **laughable** adj : risible, ridículo
— **laughter** n : risa f, risas fpl
launch vt : lanzar — **launch** n
: lanzamiento m
launder vt **1** : lavar y planchar (ropa) **2**
: blanquear, lavar (dinero) — **laundry** n,
pl **-dries 1** : ropa f sucia **2** : lavandería f
(servicio) **3 do the laundry** : lavar la ropa
lava n : lava f
lavatory n, pl **-ries** BATHROOM :
baño m, cuarto m de baño
lavender n : lavanda f
lavish adj **1** EXTRAVAGANT : pródigo
2 ABUNDANT : abundante **3** LUXURIOUS
: lujoso — **lavish** vt : prodigar
law n **1** : ley f **2** : derecho m (profesión,
etc.) **3 practice law** : ejercer la abogacía
— **lawful** adj : legal, legítimo
▸ **lawn** n : césped m — **lawn**
mower n : cortadora f de césped
lawsuit n : pleito m
lawyer n : abogado m, -da f
lax adj : poco estricto, relajado
laxative n : laxante m
lay¹ vt **laid; laying 1** PLACE PUT : poner,
colocar **2 lay eggs** : poner huevos **3**
lay off : dispedir (un empleado) **4 lay**
out PRESENT : presentar, exponer **5 lay**
out DESIGN : diseñar (el trazado de)
lay² pp → **lie 1**
lay³ adj **1** SECULAR : laico **2**
NONPROFESSIONAL : lego, profano
layer n : capa f
layman n, pl **-men** : lego m,
laico m (en religión)
layout n ARRANGEMENT : disposición f
lazy adj **-zier; -est** : perezoso
— **laziness** n : pereza f
lead¹ vt **led; leading 1** GUIDE : conducir
2 DIRECT : dirigir **3** HEAD : encabezar, ir
al frente de — vi : llevar, conducir (a
algo) — **lead** n **1** : delantera f **2 follow**
someone's lead : seguir el ejemplo de algn
lead² n **1** : plomo m (metal) **2**
GRAPHITE : mina f — **leaden** adj **1**
: de plomo **2** HEAVY : pesado
leader n : jefe m, -fa f — **leadership** n
: mando m, dirección f
leaf n, pl **leaves 1** : hoja f **2 turn over**
a new leaf : hacer borrón y cuenta
nueva — **leaf** vi **leaf through** : hojear
(un libro, etc.) — **leaflet** n : folleto m
league n **1** : liga f **2 be in league**
with : estar confabulado con

leak vt **1** : dejar escapar (un líquido o
un gas) **2** : filtrar (información) — vi **1**
: gotear, escaparse (dícese de un
líquido o un gas) **2** : filtrarse (dícese de
información) — **leak** n **1** : agujero m
(de un cubo, etc.), gotera f (de un techo)
2 : fuga f, escape m (de un líquido o un
gas) **3** : filtración f (de información) —
leaky adj **leakier; -est** : que hace agua
lean¹ v **leaned** or Brit **leant; leaning** vi **1**
BEND : inclinarse **2 lean against** :
apoyarse contra — vt : apoyar
lean² adj **1** THIN : delgado **2** : sin
grasa (dícese de la carne)
leaning n : inclinación f
leanness n : delgadez f (de una
persona), lo magro (de la carne)
leap vi **leapt** or **leaped; leaping** : saltar,
brincar — **leap** n : salto m, brinco m
— **leap year** n : año m bisiesto
learn v **learned; learning** : aprender
— **learned** adj : sabio, erudito —
learner n : principiante mf, estudiante mf
— **learning** n : erudición f, saber m
lease n : contrato m de arrendamiento
— **lease** vt **leased; leasing** : arrendar
leash n : correa f
least adj **1** : menor **2** SLIGHTEST
: más minimo — **least** n **1 at**
least : por lo menos **2 the least** : lo
menos **3 to say the least** : por no
decir más — **least** adv : menos
leather n : cuero m
leave v **left; leaving** vt **1** : dejar **2** :
salir(se) de (un lugar) **3 leave out** : omitir
— vi DEPART : irse — **leave** n **1** or **leave**
of absence : permiso m, licencia f **2**
take one's leave : despedirse
leaves → **leaf**
lecture n **1** TALK : conferencia f **2**
REPRIMAND : sermón m, reprimenda f —
lecture v **-tured; -turing** vt : sermonear
— vi : dar clase, dar una conferencia
led pp → **lead 1**
ledge n : antepecho m (de una ventana),
saliente m (de una montaña)
leech n : sanguijuela f
leek n : puerro m
leer vi : lanzar una mirada lasciva
— **leer** n : mirada f lasciva
leery adj : receloso
leeway n : libertad f de acción , margen m
left¹ → **leave**
left² adj : izquierdo — **left** adv : a
la izquierda — **left** n : izquierda f

— **left–handed** *adj* : zurdo
leftovers *npl* : restos *mpl*, sobras *fpl*
leg *n* **1** : pierna *f* (de una persona,
de ropa), pata *f* (de un animal, de
muebles) **2** : etapa *f* (de un viaje)
legacy *n*, *pl* **-cies** : legado *m*
legal *adj* **1** LAWFUL : legítimo,
legal **2** JUDICIAL : legal, jurídico —
legality *n*, *pl* **-ties** : legalidad *f* —
legalize *vt* **-ized; -izing** : legalizar
legend *n* : leyenda *f* —
legendary *adj* : lengendario
legible *adj* : legible
legion *n* : legión *f*
legislate *vi* **-lated; -lating** : legislar
— **legislation** *n* : legislación *f* —
legislative *adj* : legislativo, legislador —
legislature *n* : asamblea *f* legislativa
legitimate *adj* : legítimo —
legitimacy *n* : legitimidad *f*
leisure *n* **1** : ocio *m*, tiempo *m* libre **2**
at your leisure : cuando te venga bien
— **leisurely** *adj & adv* : lento, sin prisas
▸ **lemon** *n* : limón *m* —
lemonade *n* : limonada *f*
lend *vt* **lent; lending** : prestar
length *n* **1** : largo *m* **2** DURATION :
duración *f* **3 at length** FINALLY : por fin **4**
at length : EXTENSIVELY : extensamente
5 go to any lengths : hacer todo lo
posible — **lengthen** *vt* **1** : alargar **2**
PROLONG : prolongar — *vi* : alargarse —
lengthways *or* lengthwise *adv* : a o largo
— **lengthy** *adj* **lengthier; -est** : largo
lenient *adj* : indulgente —
leniency *n*, *pl* **-cies** : indulgencia *f*
lens *n* **1** : cristalino *m* (del ojo) **2** : lente *mf*
(de un instrumento) **3** → **contact lens**
Lent *n* : Cuaresma *f*
lentil *n* : lenteja *f*
leopard *n* : leopardo *m*
leotard *n* : leotardo *m*, malla *f*
lesbian *n* : lesbiana *f*
less *adv* (*comparative of* **little**) : menos
— **less** *adj* (*comparative of* **little**)
: menos — **less** *pron* : menos —
less *prep* MINUS : menos — **lessen** *v*
: disminuir — **lesser** *adj* : menor
lesson *n* **1** CLASS : clase *f*, curso *m* **2**
learn one's lesson : aprender la lección
lest *conj* **lest we forget** :
para que no olvidemos
let *vt* **let; letting 1** ALLOW : dejar,
permitir **2** RENT : alquilar **3 let's go!**
: ¡vamos!, ¡vámonos! **4 let down**

DISAPPOINT : fallar **5 let in** : dejar
entrar **6 let off** FORGIVE : perdonar **7**
let up ABATE : amainar, disminuir
letdown *n* : chasco *m*, decepción *f*
lethal *adj* : letal
lethargic *adj* : letárgico
let's (*contraction of* **let us**) → **let**
letter *n* **1** : carta *f* **2** : letra *f* (del alfabeto)
lettuce *n* : lechuga *f*
letup *n* : pausa *f*, descanso *m*
leukemia *n* : leucemia *f*
level *n* **1** : nivel *m* **2 be on the level** :
ser honrado — **level** *vt* **-eled** *or* **-elled;**
-eling *or* **-elling 1** : nivelar **2** AIM :
apuntar **3** RAZE : arrasar — **level** *adj* **1**
FLAT : llano, plano **2** : nivel (de altura) —
levelheaded *adj* : sensato, equilibrado
lever *n* : palanca *f* — **leverage** *n* **1**
: apalancamiento *m* (en física)
2 INFLUENCE : influencia *f*
levity *n* : ligereza *f*
levy *n*, *pl* **levies** : impuesto *m*

— **levy** *vt* **levied; levying** :
imponer, exigir (un impuesto)
lewd *adj* : lascivo
lexicon *n*, *pl* **-ica** *or* **-icons**
: léxico *m*, lexicón *m*
liable *adj* **1** : responsable **2** LIKELY :
probable **3** SUSCEPTIBLE : propenso
— **liability** *n*, *pl* **-ties 1** RESPONSIBILITY
: responsabilidad *f* **2** DRAWBACK
: desventaja *f* **3 liabilities** *npl*
DEBTS : deudas *fpl*, pasivo *m*
liaison *n* **1** : enlace *m* **2**
AFFAIR : amorío *m*
liar *n* : mentiroso *m*, -sa *f*
libel *n* : libelo *m*, difamación *f*
— **libel** *vt* **-beled** *or* **-belled;**
-beling *or* **-belling** : difamar
liberal *adj* : liberal — **liberal** *n* : liberal *mf*
liberate *vt* **-ated; -ating** : liberar
— **liberation** *n* : liberación *f*
liberty *n*, *pl* **-ties** : libertad *f*
library *n*, *pl* **-braries** : biblioteca *f*

power lawn mower
cortadora^F **del césped**

starter
motor^M *de arranque*^M

motor
motor^M

grass catcher
recogedor^M

lighthouse
faro^M

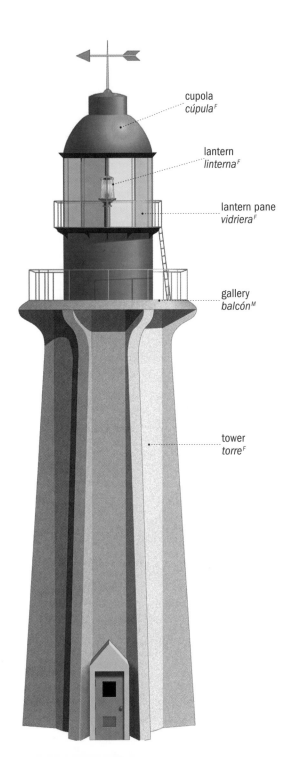

cupola
cúpula^F

lantern
linterna^F

lantern pane
vidriera^F

gallery
balcón^M

tower
torre^F

— **librarian** *n* : bibliotecario *m*, -ria *f*
lice → **louse**
license *or* licence *n* **1** PERMIT :
licencia *f* **2** FREEDOM : libertad *f* **3**
AUTHORIZATION : permiso *m* — **license** *vt*
licensed; licensing : autorizar
lick *vt* **1** : lamer **2** DEFEAT : dar una
paliza a *fam* — **lick** *n* : lamida *f*
licorice *n* : regaliz *m*
lid *n* **1** : tapa *f* **2** EYELID : párpado *m*
lie¹ *vi* **lay; lain; lying 1** *or* **lie**
down : acostarse, echarse **2**
BE : estar, encontrarse
lie² *vi* **lied; lying** : mentir — **lie** *n* : mentira *f*
lieutenant *n* : teniente *mf*
life *n, pl* **lives** : vida *f* — **lifeboat** *n* :
bote *m* salvavidas — **lifeguard** *n* :
socorrista *mf* — **lifeless** *adj* : sin vida
— **lifelike** *adj* : natural, realista —
lifelong *adj* : de toda la vida — **life**
preserver *n* : salvavidas *m* — **lifestyle** *n*
: estilo *m* de vida — **lifetime** *n* : vida *f*
lift *vt* **1** RAISE : levantar **2** STEAL : robar
— *vi* **1** CLEAR UP : despejarse **2** *or* **lift**
off : despegar (dícese de un avión, etc.)
— **lift** *n* **1** LIFTING : levantamiento *m* **2**
give someone a lift : llevar en coche
a algn — **liftoff** *n* : despegue *m*
light¹ *n* **1** : luz *f* **2** LAMP : lámpara *f* **3**
HEADLIGHT : faro *m* **4 do you have a**
light? : ¿tienes fuego? — **light** *adj* **1**
BRIGHT : bien iluminado **2** : claro (dícese
de los colores), rubio (dícese del pelo)
— **light** *v* **lit** *or* **lighted; lighting** *vt* **1**
: encender (un fuego) **2** ILLUMINATE :
iluminar — *vi or* **light up** : iluminarse
— **lightbulb** *n* : bombilla *f*, bombillo *m*,
Lat — **lighten** *vt* BRIGHTEN : iluminar —
▸ **lighter** *n* : encendedor *m* — **lighthouse** *n*
: faro *m* — **lighting** *n* : alumbrado *m*
— **lightning** *n* : relámpago *m*, rayo *m*
— **light–year** *n* : año *m* luz
light² *adj* : ligero — **lighten** *vt* : aligerar —
lightly *adv* **1** : suavemente **2 let off lightly**
: tratar con indulgencia — **lightness** *n*
: ligereza *f* — **lightweight** *adj* : ligero
like¹ *v* **liked; liking** *vt* **1** : gustarle
(a uno) **2** WANT : querer — *vi* **if**
you like : si quieres — **likes** *npl*
: preferencias *fpl*, gustos *mpl* —
likable *or* **likeable** *adj* : simpático
like² *adj* SIMILAR : parecido — **like** *prep*
: como — **like** *conj* **1** AS : como **2** AS IF :
como si — **likelihood** *n* : probabilidad *f* —
likely *adj* **-lier; -est** : probable — **liken** *vt*

: comparar — **likeness** *n* : semejanza *f*,
parecido *m* — **likewise** *adv* **1** :
lo mismo **2** ALSO : también

liking *n* : afición *f* (por una cosa),
simpatía *f* (por una persona)

lilac *n* : lila *f*

lily *n*, *pl* **lilies** : lirio *m*, azucena *f* — **lily
of the valley** *n* : lirio *m* de los valles

lima bean *n* : frijol *m* de media luna

limb *n* **1** : miembro *m* (en anatomía)
2 : rama *f* (de un árbol)

limber *vi or* **limber up** : calentarse, hacer
ejercicios preliminares — **limber** *adj* : ágil

limbo *n*, *pl* **-bos** : limbo *m*

▸ **lime** *n* : lima *f*, limón *m* verde *Lat*

limelight *n* **be in the limelight**
: estar en el candelero

limerick *n* : poema *m* jocoso
de cinco versos

limestone *n* : (piedra *f*) caliza *f*

limit *n* : límite *m* — **limit** *vt* : limitar,
restringir — **limitation** *n* : limitación *f*,
restricción *f* — **limited** *adj* : limitado

limousine *n* : limusina *f*

limp[1] *vi* : cojear — **limp** *n* : cojera *f*

limp[2] *adj* : flojo, fláccido

line *n* **1** : línea *f* **2** ROPE : cuerda *f* **3**
ROW : fila *f* **4** QUEUE : cola *f* **5** WRINKLE
: arruga *f* **6 drop a line** : mándar unas
líneas — **line** *v* **lined; lining** *vt* **1**
: forrar (un vestido, etc.), cubrir (las
paredes, etc.) **2** MARK : rayar, trazar
líneas en **3** BORDER : bordear — *vi*
line up : ponerse en fila, hacer cola

lineage *n* : linaje *m*

linear *adj* : lineal

linen *n* : lino *m*

liner *n* **1** LINING : forro *m* **2** SHIP
: buque *m*, transatlántico *m*

lineup *n* **1** *or* **police lineup** : fila *f* de
sospechosos **2** : alineación *f* (en deportes)

linger *vi* **1** : quedarse, entretenerse
2 PERSIST : persistir

lingerie *n* : ropa *f* íntima
femenina, lencería *f*

lingo *n*, *pl* **-goes** JARGON : jerga *f*

linguistics *n* : lingüística *f* — **linguist** *n* :
lingüista *mf* — **linguistic** *adj* : lingüístico

lining *n* : forro *m*

link *n* **1** : eslabón *m* (de una cadena)
2 BOND : lazo *m* **3** CONNECTION :
conexión *f* — **link** *vt* : enlazar, conectar
— *vi* **link up** : unirse, conectar

linoleum *n* : linóleo *m*

lint *n* : pelusa *f*

lion *n* : león *m* — **lioness** *n* : leona *f*

lip *n* **1** : labio *m* **2** EDGE : borde *m*
— **lipstick** *n* : lápiz *m* de labios

liqueur *n* : licor *m*

liquid *adj* : líquido — **liquid** *n* : líquido *m*
— **liquidate** *vt* **-dated; -dating** :
liquidar — **liquidation** *n* : liquidación *f*

liquor *n* : bebidas *fpl* alcohólicas

lisp *vi* : cecear — **lisp** *n* : ceceo *m*

list[1] *n* : lista *f* — **list** *vt* **1** ENUMERATE
: hacer una lista de, enumerar **2**
INCLUDE : incluir (en una lista)

list[2] *vi* : escorar (dícese de un barco)

listen *vi* **1** : escuchar **2 listen to** HEED :
hacer caso de **3 listen to reason** : atender
a razones — **listener** *n* : oyente *mf*

listless *adj* : apático

lit *pp* → **light**

litany *n*, *pl* **-nies** : letanía *f*

liter *n* : litro *m*

literacy *n* : alfabetismo *m*

literal *adj* : literal — **literally** *adv*
: literalmente, al pie de la letra

literate *adj* : alfabetizado

literature *n* : literatura *f* —
literary *adj* : literario

lithe *adj* : ágil y grácil

litigation *n* : litigio *m*

litre → **liter**

litter *n* **1** RUBBISH : basura *f* **2** : camada *f*
(de animales) **3** *or* **kitty litter** : arena *f*,
higiénica — **litter** *vt* : tirar basura
en, ensuciar — *vi* : tirar basura

little *adj* **littler** *or* **less** *or* **lesser; littlest** *or*
least 1 SMALL : pequeño **2 a little** SOME
: un poco de **3 he speaks little English**
: habla poco inglés — **little** *adv* **less;
least** : poco — **little** *pron* **1** : poco *m*,
-ca *f* **2 little by little** : poco a poco

llama
llama*F*

liturgy *n*, *pl* **-gies** : liturgia *f* —
liturgical *adj* : litúrgico

live *vi* **lived; living 1** : vivir **2** RESIDE : residir
3 live on : vivir de — *vt* : vivir, llevar
(una vida) — **live** *adj* **1** : vivo **2** : con
corriente (dícese de cables eléctricos) **3** :
en vivo, en directo (dícese de programas
de televisión, etc.) — **livelihood** *n* :
sustento *m*, medio *m* de vida — **lively** *adj*
-lier; -est : animado, alegre — **liven** *vt*
or **liven up** : animar — *vi* : animarse

liver *n* : hígado *m*

livestock *n* : ganado *m*

livid *adj* **1** : lívido **2** ENRAGED : furioso

living *adj* : vivo — **living** *n* **make
a living** : ganarse la vida — **living
room** *n* : living *m*, sala *f* (de estar)

lizard *n* : lagarto *m*

▸ **llama** *n* : llama *f*

load *n* **1** CARGO : carga *f* **2** BURDEN
: carga *f*, peso *m* **3 loads of** : un
montón de — **load** *vt* : cargar

loaf[1] *n*, *pl* **loaves** : pan *m*, barra *f* (de pan)

loaf[2] *vi* : holgazanear — **loafer** *n* **1** :
holgazán *m*, -zana *f* **2** : mocasín *m* (zapato)

loan *n* : préstamo *m* — **loan** *vt* : prestar

loathe *vt* **loathed; loathing** : odiar
— **loathsome** *adj* : odioso

lobby *n*, *pl* **-bies 1** : vestíbulo *m* **2**
or **political lobby** : grupo *m* de
presión, lobby *m* — **lobby** *v* **-bied;
-bying** *vt* : ejercer presión sobre

lobe *n* : lóbulo *m*

lobster *n* : langosta *f*

local *adj* : local — **local** *n* **the locals** : los

lime
lima*F*

lock
esclusa^F

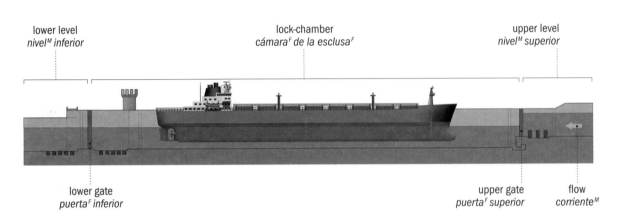

lower level
nivel^M *inferior*

lock-chamber
cámara^F *de la esclusa*^F

upper level
nivel^M *superior*

lower gate
puerta^F *inferior*

upper gate
puerta^F *superior*

flow
corriente^M

---

vecinos del lugar — **locale** *n* : escenario *m*
— **locality** *n, pl* **-ties** : localidad *f*
locate *vt* **-cated; -cating 1** SITUATE
: situar, ubicar **2** FIND : localizar —
location *n* : situación *f*, lugar *m*
lock¹ *n* : mechón *m* (de pelo)
▸ **lock**² *n* **1** : cerradura *f* (de una puerta,
etc.) **2** : esclusa *f* (de un canal) —
lock *vt* **1** : cerrar (con llave) **2** *or*
lock up CONFINE : encerrar — *vi* **1**
: cerrarse con llave **2** : bloquearse
(dícese de una rueda, etc.) — **locker** *n*
: armario *m* — **locket** *n* : medallón *m*
— **locksmith** *n* : cerrajero *m*, -ra *f*
locomotive *n* : locomotora *f*
locust *n* : langosta *f*, chapulín *m, Lat*
lodge *v* **lodged; lodging** *vt* **1** HOUSE :
hospedar, alojar **2** FILE : presentar — *vi*
: hospedarse, alojarse — **lodge** *n* :
pabellón *m* — **lodger** *n* : huésped *m*,
-peda *f* — **lodging** *n* **1** : alojamiento *m* **2**
lodges *npl* : habitaciones *fpl*
loft *n* **1** : desván *m* (en una casa) **2**
HAYLOFT : pajar *m* — **lofty** *adj* **loftier; -est**
1 : noble, elevado **2** HAUGHTY : altanero
log *n* **1** : tronco *m*, leño *m* **2** RECORD
: diario *m* — **log** *vi* **logged; logging**
1 : talar (árboles) **2** RECORD : registrar,
anotar **3 log on** : entrar (en el sistema)
4 log off : salir (del sistema) —
logger *n* : leñador *m*, -dora *f*
logic *n* : lógica *f* — **logical** *adj* : lógico
— **logistics** *ns & pl* : logística *f*
logo *n, pl* **logos** : logotipo *m*

loin *n* : lomo *m*
loiter *vi* : vagar, holgazanear
lollipop *or* **lollypop** *n* :
pirulí *m*, chupete *m, Lat*
lone *adj* : solitario — **loneliness** *n* :
soledad *f* — **lonely** *adj* **-lier; -est** :
solitario, solo — **loner** *n* : solitario *m*,
-ria *f* — **lonesome** *adj* : solo, solitario
long¹ *adj* **longer; longest** : largo —
long *adv* **1** : mucho tiempo **2 all
day long** : todo el día **3 as long as** :
mientras **4 no longer** : ya no **5 so long!**
: ¡hasta luego!, ¡adiós! — **long** *n* **1**
before long : dentro de poco **2 the
long and the short** : lo esencial
long² *vi* **long for** : anhelar, desear
longevity *n* : longevidad *f*
longing *n* : ansia *f*, anhelo *m*
longitude *n* : longitud *f*
look *vi* **1** : mirar **2** SEEM : parecer **3 look
after** : cuidar (de) **4 look for** EXPECT :
esperar **5 look for** SEEK : buscar **6 look
into** : investigar **7 look out** : tener cuidado
8 look over EXAMINE : revisar **9 look up
to** : respetar — *vt* : mirar — **look** *n* **1**
: mirada *f* **2** APPEARANCE : aspecto *m*,
aire *m* — **lookout** *n* **1** : puesto *m* de
observación **2** WATCHMAN : vigía *mf* **3 be
on the lookout for** : estar al acecho de
loom¹ *n* : telar *m*
loom² *vi* **1** APPEAR : aparecer, surgir
2 APPROACH : ser inminente
loop *n* : lazada *f*, lazo *m* — **loop** *vt* : hacer
lazadas con — **loophole** *n* : escapatoria *f*

loose *adj* **looser; -est 1** MOVABLE : flojo,
suelto **2** SLACK : flojo **3** ROOMY : holgado
4 APPROXIMATE : libre, aproximado **5**
FREE : suelto **6** IMMORAL : relajado —
loosely *adv* **1** : sin apretar **2** ROUGHLY :
aproximadamente — **loosen** *vt* : aflojar
loot *n* : botín *m* — **loot** *vt* : saquear,
robar — **looter** *n* : saqueador *m*,
-dora *f* — **looting** *n* : saqueo *m*
lop *vt* **lopped; lopping** : cortar, podar
lopsided *adj* : torcido, chueco *Lat*
lord *n* **1** : señor *m*, noble *m* **2
the Lord** : el Señor
lore *n* : saber *m* popular, tradición *f*
lose *v* **lost; losing** *vt* **1** : perder **2 lose
one's way** : perderse **3 lose time** :
atrasarse (dícese de un reloj) — *vi* :
perder — **loser** *n* : perdedor *m*, -dora *f*
— **loss** *n* **1** : pérdida *f* **2** DEFEAT :
derrota *f* **3 be at a loss for words** :
no encontrar palabras — **lost** *adj* **1**
: perdido **2 get lost** : perderse
lot *n* **1** FATE : suerte *f* **2** PLOT : solar *m* **3
a lot of** *or* **lots of** : mucho, un montón de
lotion *n* : loción *f*
lottery *n, pl* **-teries** : lotería *f*
loud *adj* **1** : alto, fuerte **2** NOISY : ruidoso
3 FLASHY : llamativo — **loud** *adv* **1** : fuerte
2 out loud : en voz alta — **loudly** *adv* : en
voz alta — **loudspeaker** *n* : altavoz *m*
lounge *vi* **lounged; lounging 1** :
repantigarse **2** *or* **lounge about** :
holgazanear — **lounge** *n* : salón *m*
louse *n, pl* **lice** : piojo *m*

— **lousy ;** *adj* **lousier; -est 1 :**
piojoso **2** BAD **:** pésimo, muy malo
love *n* **1 :** amor *m* **2 fall in love :**
enamorarse — **love** *v* **loved; loving**
: querer, amar — **lovable** *adj* **:**
adorable, amoroso *Lat* — **lovely** *adj*
-lier; -est : lindo, precioso — **lover** *n*
: amante *mf* — **loving** *adj* **:** cariñoso
low *adj* **lower; -est 1 :** bajo **2** SCARCE
: escaso **3** DEPRESSED **:** deprimido —
low *adv* **1 :** bajo **2 turn the lights down**
low : bajar las luces — **low** *n* **1 :** punto *m*
bajo **2** *or* **low gear :** primera velocidad *f*
— **lower** *adj* **:** inferior, más bajo — **low** *vt*
: bajar — **lowly** *adj* **-lier; -est :** humilde
loyal *adj* **:** leal, fiel — **loyalty** *n,*
pl **-ties :** lealtad *f*
lozenge *n* **:** pastilla *f*
lubricate *vt* **-cated; -cating :**
lubricar — **lubricant** *n* **:** lubricante *m*
— **lubrication** *n* **:** lubricación *f*
lucid *adj* **:** lúcido — **lucidity** *n* **:** lucidez *f*
luck *n* **1 :** suerte *f* **2 good luck! :** ¡buena
suerte! — **luckily** *adv* **:** afortunadamente
— **lucky** *adj* **luckier; -est 1 :** afortunado
2 luck charm : amuleto *m* (de la suerte)
lucrative *adj* **:** lucrativo
ludicrous *adj* **:** ridículo, absurdo
lug *vt* **lugged; lugging :** arrastrar
▸ **luggage** *n* **:** equipaje *m*
lukewarm *adj* **:** tibio
lull *vt* **1** CALM **:** calmar **2 lull to**
sleep : adormecer — **lull** *n* **:**
período *m* de calma, pausa *f*
lullaby *n, pl* **-bies :** canción *f*
de cuna, nana *f*
lumber *n* **:** madera *f* —
lumberjack *n* **:** leñador *m,* -dora *f*
luminous *adj* **:** luminoso

lynx
lince *M*

luggage
equipaje *M*

carry-on bag
bolso *M* *de viaje* *M*

luggage carrier
carrito *M* *portamaletas* *M*

upright suitcase
maleta *F* *vertical*

garment bag
portatrajes *M*

lump *n* **1** CHUNK, PIECE **:** pedazo *m,*
trozo *m* **2** SWELLING **:** bulto *m* **3 :**
grumo *m* (en un líquido) — **lump** *vt*
or **lump together :** juntar, agrupar —
lumpy *adj* **lumpier; -est :** grumoso
(dícese de una salsa), lleno de
bultos (dícese de un colchón)
lunacy *n, pl* **-cies :** locura *f*
lunar *adj* **:** lunar
lunatic *n* **:** loco *m,* -ca *f*
lunch *n* **:** almuerzo *m,* comida *f*
— **lunch** *vi* **:** almorzar, comer —
luncheon *n* **:** comida *f,* almuerzo *m*
lung *n* **:** pulmón *m*
lunge *vi* **lunged; lunging 1 :** lanzarse
2 lunge at : arremeter contre
lurch[1] *vi* **1** STAGGER **:** tambalearse **2 :**
dar bandazos (dícese de un vehículo)
lurch[2] *n* **leave in a lurch :**
dejar en la estacada
lure *n* **1** BAIT **:** señuelo *m* **2** ATTRACTION **:**

atractivo *m* — **lure** *vt* **lured; luring :** atraer
lurid *adj* **1** GRUESOME **:** espeluznante
2 SENSATIONAL **:** sensacionalista
3 GAUDY **:** chillón
lurk *vi* **:** estar al acecho
luscious *adj* **:** delicioso, exquisito
lush *adj* **:** exuberante, suntuoso
lust *n* **1 :** lujuria *f* **2** CRAVING **:** ansia *f,*
anhelo *m* — **lust** *vi* **lust after :** desear (a
una persona), codiciar (riquezas, etc.)
luster *or* **lustre** *n* **:** lustre *m*
lusty *adj* **lustier; -est :** fuerte, vigoroso
luxurious *adj* **:** lujoso —
luxury *n, pl* **-ries :** lujo *m*
lye *n* **:** lejía *f*
lying → **lie**
lynch *vt* **:** linchar
▸ **lynx** *n* **:** lince *m*
lyric *or* **lyrical** *adj* **:** lírico — **lyrics** *npl*
: letra *f* (de una canción)

physical map
mapa^M **físico**

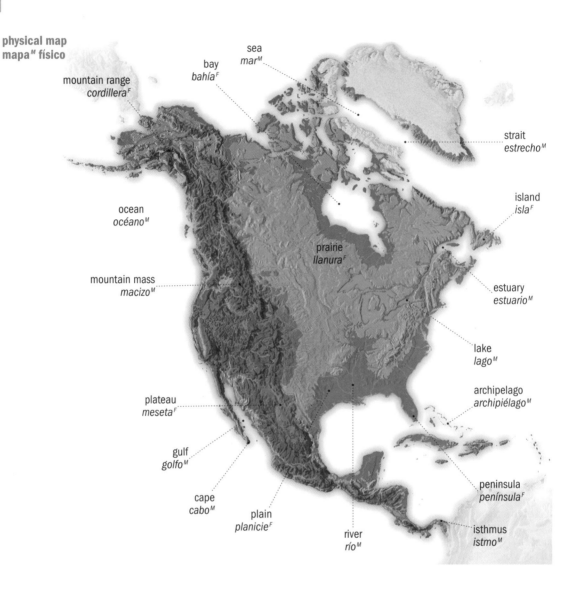

mountain range
cordillera^F

bay
bahía^F

sea
mar^M

strait
estrecho^M

ocean
océano^M

island
isla^F

prairie
llanura^F

mountain mass
macizo^M

estuary
estuario^M

lake
lago^M

archipelago
archipiélago^M

plateau
meseta^F

gulf
golfo^M

peninsula
península^F

cape
cabo^M

plain
planicie^F

river
río^M

isthmus
istmo^M

---

m *n, pl* **m's** *or* **ms** : m *f*, decimotercera
letra del alfabeto inglés

ma'am → **madam**

macabre *adj* : macabro

macaroni *n* : macarrones *mpl*

mace *n* **1** : maza *f* (arma o
símbolo) **2** : macis *f* (especia)

machete *n* : machete *m*

machine *n* : máquina *f* — **machinery** *n,*
pl **-eries 1** : maquinaria *f* **2** WORKS
: mecanismo *m* — **machine**
gun *n* : ametralladora *f*

mad *adj* **madder; maddest 1** INSANE : loco
2 FOOLISH : insensato **3** ANGRY : furioso

madam *n, pl* **mesdames** : señora *f*

madden *vt* : enfurecer

made → **make**

madly *adv* : como un loco, locamente
— **madman** *n, pl* **-men** : loco *m*
— **madness** *n* : locura *f*

Mafia *n* : Mafia *f*

magazine *n* **1** PERIODICAL : revista *f* **2**
: recámara *f* (de un arma de fuego)

maggot *n* : gusano *m*

magic *n* : magia *f* — **magic**
or **magical** *adj* : mágico —
magician *n* : mago *m*, -ga *f*

magistrate *n* : magistrado *m*, -da *f*

magnanimous *adj* : magnánimo

magnate *n* : magnate *mf*

magnet *n* : imán *m* — **magnetic** *adj*
: magnético — **magnetism** *n* :
magnetismo *m* — **magnetize** *vt*
-tized; -tizing : magnetizar

magnificent *adj* : magnífico —
magnificence *n* : magnificencia *f*

magnify *vt* **-fied; -fying 1** ENLARGE
: ampliar **2** EXAGGERATE : **exagerar**
— **magnifying glass** *n* : lupa *f*

magnitude *n* : magnitud *f*

magnolia *n* : magnolia *f*

mahogany *n, pl* **-nies** : caoba *f*

maid *n* : sirvienta *f*, criada *f*, muchacha *f* — **maiden** *adj* FIRST : inaugural —

maiden name *n* : nombre *m* de soltera

mail *n* **1** : correo *m* **2** LETTERS : correspondencia *f* — **mail** *vt* : enviar por correo — **mailbox** *n* : buzón *m* — **mailman** *n, pl* -**men** : cartero *m*

maim *vt* : mutilar

main *n* : tubería *f* principal (de agua o gas), cable *m* principal (de un circuito) — **main** *adj* : principal — **mainframe** *n* : computadora *f* central — **mainland** *n* : continente *m* — **mainly** *adv* : principalmente — **mainstay** *n* : sostén *m* (principal) — **mainstream** *n* : corriente *f* principal — **mainstream** *adj* : dominante, convencional

maintain *vt* : mantener — **maintenance** *n* : mantenimiento *m*

maize *n* : maíz *m*

majestic *adj* : majestuoso — **majesty** *n, pl* -**ties** : majestad *f*

major *adj* **1** : muy importante, principal **2** : mayor (en música) — **major** *n* **1** : mayor *mf*, comandante *mf* (en las fuerzas armadas) **2** : especialidad *f* (universitaria) — **major** *vi* -**jored**; -**joring** : especializarse — **majority** *n, pl* -**ties** : mayoría *f*

make *v* **made; making** *vt* **1** : hacer **2** MANUFACTURE : **fabricar 3** CONSTITUTE : constituir **4** PREPARE : preparar **5** RENDER : **poner 6** COMPEL : obligar **7** **make a decision** : tomar una decisión **8 make a living** : ganar la vida — *vi* **1 make do** : arreglárselas **2 make for** : dirigirse a **3 make good** SUCCEED : tener éxito — **make** *n* BRAND : marca *f* — **make–believe** *n* : fantasía *f* — **make–believe** *adj* : imaginario — **make out** *vt* **1** : hacer (un cheque, etc.) **2** DISCERN : distinguir **3** UNDERSTAND : comprender — *vi* **how did you make?** : ¿qué tal te fue? — **maker** *n* MANUFACTURER : fabricante *mf* — **makeshift** *adj* : improvisado — **makeup** *n* **1** COMPOSITION : composición *f* **2** COSMETICS : maquillaje *m* — **make up** *vt* **1** PREPARE : preparar **2** INVENT : inventar **3** CONSTITUTE : formar — *vi* RECONCILE : hacer las paces

maladjusted *adj* : inadaptado

malaria *n* : malaria *f*, paludismo *m*

male *n* : macho *m* (de animales o plantas), varón *m* (de personas) — **male** *adj* **1** : macho **2** MASCULINE : masculino

malevolent *adj* : malévolo

malfunction *vi* : funcionar mal — **malfunction** *n* : mal funcionamiento *m*

malice *n* : mala intención *f*, rencor *m* — **malicious** *adj* : malicioso

malign *adj* : maligno — **malign** *vt* : calumniar

malignant *adj* : maligno

mall *n or* **shopping mall** : centro *m* comercial

malleable *adj* : maleable

mallet *n* : mazo *m*

malnutrition *n* : desnutrición *f*

malpractice *n* : mala práctica *f*, negligencia *f*

malt *n* : malta *f*

mama *or* mamma *n* : mamá *f*

mammal *n* : mamífero *m*

mammogram *n* : mamografía *f*

mammoth *adj* : gigantesco

man *n, pl* **men** : hombre *m* — **man** *vt* **manned; manning** : tripular (un barco o avión), encargarse de (un servicio)

manage *v* -**aged; -aging** *vt* **1** HANDLE : manejar **2** DIRECT : administrar, dirigir — *vi* COPE : arreglárselas — **manageable** *adj* : manejable — **management** *n* : dirección *f* — **manager** *n* : director *m*, -tora *f*; gerente *mf* — **managerial** *adj* : directivo

mandarin *n or* **mandarin orange** : mandarina *f*

mandate *n* : mandato *m* — **mandatory** *adj* : obligatorio

mane *n* : crin *f* (de un caballo), melena *f* (de un león)

maneuver *n* : maniobra *f* — **maneuver** *v* -**vered; -vering** : maniobrar

mangle *vt* -**gled; -gling** : destrozar

mango *n, pl* -**goes** : mango *m*

mangy *adj* **mangier; -est** : sarnoso

manhandle *vi* -**dled; -dling** : maltratar

manhole *n* : boca *f* de alcantarilla

manhood *n* **1** : madurez *f* (de un hombre) **2** VIRILITY : virilidad *f*

mania *n* : manía *f* — **maniac** *n* : maníaco *m*, -ca *f*

manicure *n* : manicura *f* — **manicure** *vt* -**cured; -curing** : hacer la manicura a

manifest *adj* : manifiesto, patente — **manifest** *vt* : manifestar — **manifesto** *n, pl* -**tos** *or* -**toes** : manifiesto *m*

manipulate *vt* -**lated; -lating** : manipular — **manipulation** *n* : manipulación *f*

mankind *n* : género *m* humano, humanidad *f*

maple
arce *M*

manly *adj* -**lier; -est** : viril — **manliness** *n* : virilidad *f*

man–made *adj* : artificial

mannequin *n* : maniquí *m*

manner *n* **1** : manera *f* **2** KIND : clase *f* **3** **manners** *npl* ETIQUETTE : modales *mpl*, educación *f* — **mannerism** *n* : peculiaridad *f* (de una persona)

manoeuvre *Brit* → **maneuver**

manor *n* : casa *f* solariega

manpower *n* : mano *f* de obra

mansion *n* : mansión *f*

manslaughter *n* : homicidio *m* sin premeditación

mantel *or* **mantelpiece** *n* : repisa *f* de la chimenea

manual *adj* : manual — **manual** *n* : manual *m*

manufacture *n* : fabricación *f* — **manufacture** *vt* -**tured; -turing** : fabricar — **manufacturer** *n* : fabricante *mf*

manure *n* : estiércol *m*

manuscript *n* : manuscrito *m*

many *adj* **more; most 1** : muchos **2 as many** : tantos **3 how many** : cuántos **4 too many** : demasiados — **many** *pron* : muchos *pl*, -chas *pl*

▸ **map** *n* : mapa *m* — **map** *vt* **mapped; mapping 1** : trazar el mapa de **2** *or* **map out** : planear, proyectar

▸ **maple** *n* : arce *m*

mar *vt* **marred; marring** : estropear
marathon *n* : maratón *m*
marble *n* **1** : mármol *m* **2 marbles** *npl* : canicas *fpl* (para jugar)
march *n* : marcha *f* — **march** *vi* : marchar, desfilar
March *n* : marzo *m*
mare *n* : yegua *f*
margarine *n* : margarina *f*
margin *n* : margen *m* — **marginal** *adj* : marginal
marigold *n* : caléndula *f*
marijuana *n* : marihuana *f*
marinate *vt* **-nated; -nating** : marinar
marine *adj* : marino — **marine** *n* : soldado *m* de marina
marionette *n* : marioneta *f*
marital *adj* **1** : matrimonial **2 marital status** : estado *m* civil
maritime *adj* : marítimo
mark *n* **1** : marca *f* **2** STAIN : mancha *f* **3** IMPRINT : huella *f* **4** TARGET : blanco *m* **5** GRADE : nota *f* — **mark** *vt* **1** : marcar **2** STAIN : manchar **3** POINT OUT : señalar **4** : calificar (un examen, etc.) **5** COMMEMORATE : conmemorar **6** CARACTERIZE : caracterizar **7 mark off** : delimitar — **marked** *adj* : marcado, notable — **markedly** *adv* : notablemente — **marker** *n* : marcador *m*
market *n* : mercado *m* — **market** *vt* : vender, comercializar — **marketable** *adj* : vendible — **marketplace** *n* : mercado *m*
marksman *n, pl* **-men** : tirador *m* — **marksmanship** *n* : puntería *f*
marmalade *n* : mermelada *f*
maroon[1] *vt* : abandonar, aislar
maroon[2] *n* : rojo *m* oscuro
marquee *n* CANOPY : marquesina *f*
marriage *n* **1** : matrimonio *m* **2** WEDDING : casamiento *m*, boda *f* — **married** *adj* **1** : casado **2 get married** : casarse
marrow *n* : médula *f*, tuétano *m*
marry *v* **-ried; -rying** *vt* **1** : casar **2** WED : casarse con — *vi* : casarse
Mars *n* : Marte *m*
marsh *n* **1** : pantano *m* **2** *or* **salt marsh** : marisma *f*
marshal *n* : mariscal *m* (en el ejército); jefe *m*, -fa *f* (de policía, de bomberos, etc.) — **marshal** *vt* **-shaled** *or* **-shalled; -shaling** *or* **-shalling** : poner en orden (los pensamientos, etc.), reunir (las tropas)
marshmallow *n* : malvavisco *m*
marshy *adj* **marshier; -est** : pantanoso
mart *n* : mercado *m*

martial *adj* : marcial
martyr *n* : mártir *mf* — **martyr** *vt* : martirizar
marvel *n* : maravilla *f* — **marvel** *vi* **-veled** *or* **-velled; -veling** *or* **-velling** : maravillarse — **marvelous** *or* **marvellous** *adj* : maravilloso
mascara *n* : rímel *m*
mascot *n* : mascota *f*
masculine *adj* : masculino — **masculinity** *n* : masculinidad *f*
mash *vt* **1** CRUSH : aplastar, majar **2** PUREE : hacer puré de — **mashed potatoes** *npl* : puré *m* de patatas, puré *m* de papas *Lat*
mask *n* : máscara *f* — **mask** *vt* : enmascarar
masochism *n* : masoquismo *m* — **masochist** *n* : masoquista *mf* — **masochistic** *adj* : masoquista
mason *n* : albañil *mf* — **masonry** *n, pl* **-ries** : albañilería *f*
masquerade *n* : mascarada *f* — **masquerade** *vi* **-aded; -ading masquerade as** : disfrazarse de, hacerse pasar por
mass *n* **1** : masa *f* **2** MULTITUDE : cantidad *f* **3 the masses** : las masas
Mass *n* : misa *f*
massacre *n* : masacre *f* — **massacre** *vt* **-cred; -cring** : masacrar
massage *n* : masaje *m* — **massage** *vt* **-saged; -saging** : dar masaje a, masajear — **masseur** *n* : masajista *m* — **masseuse** *n* : masajista *f*
massive *adj* **1** BULKY, SOLID : macizo **2** HUGE : enorme, masivo
mast *n* : mástil *m*
master *n* **1** : amo *m*, señor *m* (de la casa) **2** EXPERT : maestro *m*, -tra *f* **3 master's degree** : maestría *f* — **master** *vt* : dominar — **masterful** *adj* : magistral — **masterpiece** *n* : obra *f* maestra — **mastery** *n* : maestría *f*
masturbate *v* **-bated; -bating** *vi* : masturbarse — **masturbation** *n* : masturbación *f*
mat *n* **1** DOORMAT : felpudo *m* **2** RUG : estera *f*
matador *n* : matador *m*
match *n* **1** EQUAL : igual *mf* **2** : fósforo *m*, cerilla *f* (para encender) **3** GAME : partido *m*, combate *m* (en boxeo) **4 be a good match** : hacer buena pareja — **match** *vt* **1** *or* **match up** : emparejar **2** EQUAL : igualar **3** :

combinar con, hacer juego con (ropa, colores, etc.) — *vi* : concordar, coincidir
mate *n* **1** COMPANION : compañero *m*, -ra *f*; amigo *m*, -ga *f* **2** : macho *m*, hembra *f* (de animales) — **mate** *vi* **mated; mating** : aparearse
material *adj* **1** : material **2** IMPORTANT : importante — **material** *n* **1** : material *m* **2** CLOTH : tela *f*, tejido *m* — **materialistic** *adj* : materialista — **materialize** *vi* **-ized; -izing** : aparecer
maternal *adj* : maternal — **maternity** *n, pl* **-ties** : maternidad *f* — **maternal** *adj* **1** : de maternidad **2 maternal clothes** : ropa *f* de futura mamá
math → **mathematics**
mathematics *ns & pl* : matemáticas *fpl* — **mathematical** *adj* : matemático — **mathematician** *n* : matemático *m*, -ca *f*
matinee *or* **matinée** *n* : matiné(e) *f*, fonción *f* de tarde
matrimony *n* : matrimonio *m* — **matrimonial** *adj* : matrimonial
matrix *n, pl* **-trices** *or* **-trixes** : matriz *f*
matte *adj* : mate
matter *n* **1** SUBSTANCE : materia *f* **2** QUESTION : asunto *m*, cuestión *f* **3 as a matter of fact** : en efecto, en realidad **4 for that matter** : de hecho **5 to make matters worse** : para colmo de males **6 what's the matter?** : ¿qué pasa? — **matter** *vi* : importar
mattress *n* : colchón *m*
mature *adj* **-turer; -est** : maduro — **mature** *vi* **-tured; -turing** : madurar — **maturity** *n* : madurez *f*
maul *vt* : maltratar, aporrear
mauve *n* : malva *m*
maxim *n* : máxima *f*
maximum *n, pl* **-ma** *or* **-mums** : máximo *m* — **maximum** *adj* : máximo — **maximize** *vt* **-mized; -mizing** : llevar al máximo
may *v aux past* **might** *present s & pl* **may** **1** : poder **2 come what may** : pase lo que pase **3 it may happen** : puede pasar **4 may the best man win** : que gane el mejor
May *n* : mayo *m*
maybe *adv* : quizás, tal vez
mayhem *n* : alboroto *m*
mayonnaise *n* : mayonesa *f*
mayor *n* : alcalde *m*, -desa *f*
maze *n* : laberinto *m*
me *pron* **1** : me **2 for me** : para mí

3 give it to me! : ¡dámelo! **4 it's me**
: soy yo **5 with me** : conmigo
meadow *n* : prado *m*, pradera *f*
meager *or* **meagre** *adj* : escaso
meal *n* **1** : comida *f* **2** : harina *f* (de maíz,
etc.) — **mealtime** *n* : hora *f* de comer
mean[1] *vt* **meant; meaning 1** SIGNIFY
: querer decir **2** INTEND : querer,
tener la intención de **3 be meant**
for : estar destinado a **4 he didn't**
mean it : no lo dijo en serio
mean[2] *adj* **1** UNKIND : malo **2** STINGY :
mezquino, tacaño **3** HUMBLE : humilde
mean[3] *adj* AVERAGE : medio
— **mean** *n* : promedio *m*
meander *vi* **-dered; -dering 1** WIND
: serpentear **2** WANDER : vagar
meaning *n* : significado *m*, sentido *m*
— **meaningful** *adj* : significativo —
meaningless *adj* : sin sentido
meanness *n* **1** UNKINDNESS :
maldad *f* **2** STINGINESS : mezquindad *f*
means *n* **1** : medio *m* **2 by all means** :
por supuesto **3 by means of** : por medio
de **4 by no means** : de ninguna manera
meantime *n* **1** : interín *m* **2 in**
the meantime : mientras tanto —
meantime *adv* → **meanwhile**

meanwhile *adv* : mientras tanto
— **meanwhile** *n* → **meantime**
measles *npl* : sarampión *m*
measly *adj* **-slier; -est** : miserable, misero
measure *n* : medida *f* — **measure** *v*
-sured; -suring : medir —
measurable *adj* : mensurable —
measurement *n* : medida *f* — **measure**
up *vi* **measure up to** : estar a la altura de
▸ **meat** *n* : carne *f* — **meatball** *n* :
albóndiga *f* — **meaty** *adj* **meatier; -est**
1 : carnoso **2** SUBSTANTIAL : sustancioso
mechanic *n* : mecánico *m*, -ca *f*
— **mechanical** *adj* : mecánico —
mechanics *ns & pl* **1** : mecánica *f* **2**
WORKINGS : mecanismo *m* —
mechanism *n* : mecanismo *m* —
mechanize *vt* **-nized; -nizing** : mecanizar
medal *n* : medalla *f* —
medallion *n* : medallón *m*
meddle *vi* **-dled; -dling** : entrometerse
media *or* **mass media** *npl* :
medios *mpl* de comunicación
median *adj* : medio
mediate *vi* **-ated; -ating** : mediar
— **mediation** *n* : mediación *f* —
mediator *n* : mediador *m*, -dora *f*
medical *adj* : médico — **medicated** *adj*

: medicinal — **medication** *n* :
medicamento *m* — **medicinal** *adj* :
medicinal — **medicine** *n* **1** : medicina *f* **2**
MEDICATION : medicina *f*, medicamento *m*
medieval *or* **mediaeval** *adj* : medieval
mediocre *adj* : mediocre —
mediocrity *n, pl* **-ties** : mediocridad *f*
meditate *vi* **-tated; -tating** : meditar
— **meditation** *n* : meditación *f*
medium *n, pl* **-diums** *or* **-dia 1**
MEANS : medio *m* **2** MEAN : punto *m*
medio, término *m* medio **3** →
media — **medium** *adj* : mediano
medley *n, pl* **-leys 1** : mezcla *f* **2**
: popurrí *m* (de canciones)
meek *adj* : dócil
meet *v* **met; meeting** *vt* **1** ENCOUNTER :
encontrarse con **2** SATISFY : satisfacer
3 pleased to meet you : encantado
de conocerlo — *vi* **1** : encontrarse **2**
ASSEMBLE : **reunirse 3** BE INTRODUCED
: conocerse — **meet** *n* : encuentro *m*
— **meeting** *n* : reunión *f*
megabyte *n* : megabyte *m*
megaphone *n* : megáfono *m*
melancholy *n, pl* **-cholies** : melancolía *f*
— **melancholy** *adj* : melancólico, triste
mellow *adj* **1** : suave, dulce **2** CALM :

cuts of meat
cortes de carne[F]

ground beef
carne[F] *picada*

pork chop
chuleta[F]

steak
bistec[M]

chop
chuleta[F]

back ribs
costillar[M]

roast
asado[M]

smoked ham
jamón[M] *ahumado*

apacible 3 : maduro (dícese de frutas), añejo (dícese de vinos) — **mellow** *vt* : suavizar, endulzar — *vi* : suavizarse

melody *n*, *pl* **-dies** : melodía *f*

melon *n* : melón *m*

melt *vi* : derretirse, fundirse — *vt* : derretir

member *n* : miembro *m* — **membership** *n* 1 : calidad *f* de miembro 2 MEMBERS : miembros *mpl*

membrane *n* : membrana *f*

memory *n*, *pl* **-ries** 1 : memoria *f* 2 RECOLLECTION : recuerdo *m* — **memento** *n*, *pl* **-tos** *or* **-toes** : recuerdo *m* — **memo** *n*, *pl* **memos** *or* **memorandum** *n*, *pl* **-dums** *or* **-da** : memorándum *m* — **memoirs** *npl* : memorias *fpl* — **memorable** *adj* : memorable — **memorial** *adj* : conmemorativo — **memory** *n* : monumento *m* (conmemorativo) — **memorize** *vt* **-rized; -rizing** : aprender de memoria

men → **man**

menace *n* : amenaza *f* — **menace** *vt* **-aced; -acing** : amenazar — **menacing** *adj* : amenazador

mend *vt* 1 : reparar, arreglar 2 DARN : zurcir — *vi* HEAL : curarse

menial *adj* : servil, bajo

meningitis *n*, *pl* **-gitides** : meningitis *f*

menopause *n* : menopausia *f*

menstruate *vi* **-ated; -ating** : menstruar — **menstruation** *n* : menstruación *f*

mental *adj* : mental — **mentality** *n*, *pl* **-ties** : mentalidad *f*

mention *n* : mención *f* — **mention** *vt* 1 : mencionar 2 **don't mention it!** : ¡de nada!, ¡no hay de qué!

menu *n* : menú *m*

meow *n* : maullido *m*, miau *m* — **meow** *vi* : maullar

mercenary *n*, *pl* **-naries** : mercenario *m*, -ria *f* — **mercenary** *adj* : mercenario

merchant *n* : comerciante *mf* — **merchandise** *n* : mercancía *f*, mercadería *f*

merciful *adj* : misericordioso, compasivo — **merciless** *adj* : despiadado

mercury *n*, *pl* **-ries** : mercurio *m*

Mercury *n* : Mercurio *m*

mercy *n*, *pl* **-cies** 1 : misericordia *f*, compasión *f* 2 **at the mercy of** : a merced de

mere *adj*, *superlative* **merest** : mero, simple — **merely** *adv* : simplemente

merge *v* **merged; merging** *vi* : unirse, fusionarse (dícese de las compañías),

confluir (dícese de los ríos, las calles, etc.) — *vt* : unir, fusionar, combinar — **merger** *n* : unión *f*, fusión *f*

merit *n* : mérito *m* — **merit** *vt* : merecer

mermaid *n* : sirena *f*

merry *adj* **-rier; -est** : alegre — **merry–go–round** *n* : tiovivo *m*

mesa *n* : mesa *f*

mesh *n* : malla *f*

mesmerize *vt* **-ized; -izing** : hipnotizar

mess *n* 1 : desorden *m* 2 MUDDLE : lío *m* 3 : rancho *m* (militar) — **mess** *vt* 1 *or* **mess up** SOIL : ensuciar 2 **mess up** DISARRANGE : desordenar 3 **mess up** BUNGLE : echar a perder — *vi* 1 **mess around** PUTTER : entretenerse 2 **mess with** PROVOKE : meterse con

message *n* : mensaje *m* — **messenger** *n* : mensajero *m*, -ra *f*

messy *adj* **messier; -est** : desordenado, sucio

met → **meet**

metabolism *n* : metabolismo *m*

metal *n* : metal *m* — **metallic** *adj* : metálico

metamorphosis *n*, *pl* **-phoses** : metamorfosis *f*

metaphor *n* : metáfora *f*

meteor *n* : meteoro *m* — **meteorological** *adj* : meteorológico — **meteorologist** *n* : meteorólogo *m*, -ga *f* — **meteorology** *n* : meteorología *f*

meter *or Brit* **metre** *n* 1 : metro *m* 2 : contador *m* (de electricidad, etc.)

method *n* : método *m* — **methodical** *adj* : metódico

meticulous *adj* : meticuloso

metric *or* **metrical** *adj* : métrico

metropolis *n* : metrópoli *f* — **metropolitan** *adj* : metropolitano

Mexican *adj* : mexicano

mice → **mouse**

microbe *n* : microbio *m*

microfilm *n* : microfilm *m*

microphone *n* : micrófono *m*

microscope *n* : microscopio *m* — **microscopic** *adj* : microscópico

microwave *n or* **microwave oven** : microondas *m*

mid *adj* 1 **mid morning** : a media mañana 2 **in mid-August** : a mediados de agosto 3 **she is in her mid thirties** : tiene alrededor de 35 años — **midair** *n* **in midair** : en el aire — **midday** *n* : mediodía *m*

middle *adj* : de en medio, del medio

— **middle** *n* 1 : medio *m*, centro *m* 2 **in the middle of** : en medio de (un espacio), a mitad de (una actividad) 3 **in the middle of the month** : a mediados del mes — **middle–aged** *adj* : de mediana edad — **Middle Ages** *npl* : Edad *f* Media — **middle class** *n* : clase *f* media — **middleman** *n*, *pl* **-men** : intermediario *m*, -ria *f*

midget *n* : enano *m*, -na *f*

midnight *n* : medianoche *f*

midriff *n* : diafragma *m*

midst *n* 1 **in the midst of** : en medio de 2 **in our midst** : entre nosotros

midsummer *n* : pleno verano *m*

midway *adv* : a mitad de camino, a medio camino

midwife *n*, *pl* **-wives** : comadrona *f*

midwinter *n* : pleno invierno *m*

miff *vt* : ofender

might[1] (*used to express permission or possibility or as a polite alternative to* **may**) → **may**

might[2] *n* : fuerza *f*, poder *m* — **mighty** *adj* **mightier; -est** 1 : fuerte, poderoso 2 GREAT : enorme — **might** *adv* : muy

migraine *n* : jaqueca *f*, migraña *f*

migrate *vi* **-grated; -grating** : emigrar — **migrant** *n* : trabajador *m*, -dora *f* ambulante

mild *adj* 1 GENTLE : suave 2 LIGHT : leve 3 **a mild climate** : una clima templada

mildew *n* : moho *m*

mildly *adv* : ligeramente, suavemente — **mildness** *n* : apacibilidad *f* (de personas), suavedad *f* (de sabores, etc.)

mile *n* : milla *f* — **mileage** *n* : distancia *f* recorrida (en millas), kilometraje *m* — **milestone** *n* : hito *m*

military *adj* : militar — **military** *n* **the military** : las fuerzas armadas — **militant** *adj* : militante — **militant** *n* : militante *mf* — **militia** *n* : milicia *f*

milk *n* : leche *f* — **milk** *vt* 1 : ordeñar (una vaca, etc.) 2 EXPLOIT : explotar — **milky** *adj* **milkier; -est** : lechoso — **Milky Way** *n* **the Milky Way** : la Vía Láctea

mill *n* 1 : molino *m* 2 FACTORY : fábrica *f* 3 GRINDER : molinillo *m* — **mill** *vt* : moler — *vi or* **mill about** : arremolinarse

millennium *n*, *pl* **-nia** *or* **-niums** : milenio *m*

miller *n* : molinero *m*, -ra *f*

milligram *n* : miligramo *m* — **millimeter** *or Brit* **millimetre** *n* : milímetro *m*

million *n*, *pl* **millions** *or* **million** 1 :

millón *m* **2 a million people** : un millón de personas — **million** *adj* **a million** : un millón de — **millionaire** *n* : millonario *m*, -ria *f* — **millionth** *adj* : millonésimo
mime *n* **1** : mimo *mf* **2** PANTOMIME : pantomima *f* — **mime** *v* **mimed; miming** *vt* : imitar — *vi* : hacer la mímica — **mimic** *vt* **-icked; -icking** : imitar, remedar — **mimic** *n* : imitador *m*, -dora *f* — **mimicry** *n, pl* **-ries** : imitación *f*
mince *v* **minced; mincing** *vt* **1** : picar, moler **2 not to mince one's words** : no tener pelos en la lengua
mind *n* **1** : mente *f* **2** INTELLECT : capacidad *f* intelectual **3** OPINION : opinión *f* **4** REASON : razón *f* **5 have a mind to** : tener intención de — **mind** *vt* **1** TEND : cuidar **2** OBEY : obedecer **3** WATCH : tener cuidado con **4 I don't mind the heat** : no me molesta el calor — *vi* **1** OBEY : obedecer **2 I don't mind** : no me importa, me es igual — **mindful** *adj* : atento — **mindless** *adj* **1** SENSELESS : estúpido, sin sentido **2** DULL : aburrido

mine[1] *pron* **1** : (el) mío, (la) mía, (los) míos, (las) mías **2 a friend of mine** : un amigo mío
mine[2] *n* : mina *f* — **mine** *vt* **mined; mining 1** : extraer (oro, etc.) **2** : minar (con artefactos explosivos) — **minefield** *n* : campo *m* de minas — **miner** *n* : minero *m*, -ra *f*
mineral *n* : mineral *m*
mingle *v* **-gled; -gling** *vt* : mezclar — *vi* **1** : mezclarse **2** : circular (a una fiesta, etc.)
miniature *n* : miniatura *f* — **miniature** *adj* : en miniatura
minimal *adj* : mínimo — **minimize** *vt* **-mized; -mizing** : minimizar — **minimum** *adj* : mínimo — **minimum** *n, pl* **-ma** *or* **-mums** : mínimo *m*
mining *n* : minería *f*
minister *n* **1** : pastor *m*, -tora *f* (de una iglesia) **2** : ministro *m*, -tra *f* (en política) — **minister** *vi* **minister to** : cuidar (de), atender a — **ministerial** *adj* : ministerial — **ministry** *n, pl* **-tries** : ministerio *m*
mink *n, pl* **mink** *or* **minks** : visón *m*

minnow *n, pl* **-nows** : pececillo *m* de agua dulce
minor *adj* **1** : menor **2** INSIGNIFICANT : sin importancia — **minor** *n* **1** : menor *mf* (de edad) **2** : asignatura *f* secundaria (de estudios) — **minority** *n, pl* **-ties** : minoría *f*
mint[1] *n* **1** : menta *f* (planta) **2** : pastilla *f* de menta (dulce)
mint[2] *n* **1 the U.S. Mint** : la casa de la moneda de los EE.UU. **2 be worth a mint** : valer un dineral — **mint** *vt* : acuñar — **mint** *adj* **in mint condition** : como nuevo
minus *prep* **1** : menos **2** WITHOUT : sin — **minus** *n or* **minus sign** : signo *m* de menos
minuscule *adj* : minúsculo
minute[1] *n* **1** : minuto *m* **2** MOMENT : momento *m* **3 minutes** *npl* : actas *fpl* (de una reunión)
minute[2] *adj* **-nuter; -est 1** TINY : diminuto, minúsculo **2** DETAILED : minucioso
miracle *n* : milagro *m* — **miraculous** *adj* : milagroso
mirage *n* : espejismo *m*
mire *n* : lodo *m*, fango *m*

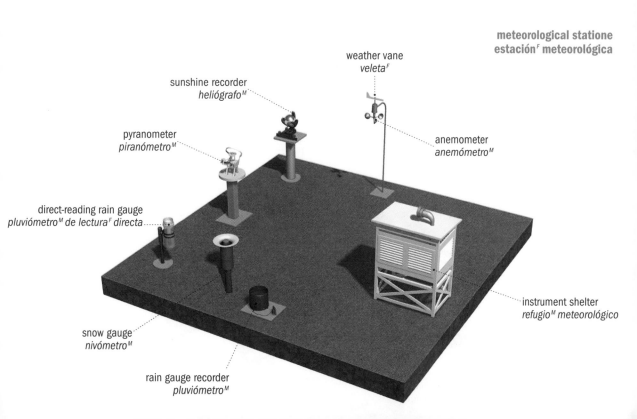

meteorological statione
estación[F] **meteorológica**

weather vane
veleta[F]

sunshine recorder
heliógrafo[M]

anemometer
anemómetro[M]

pyranometer
piranómetro[M]

direct-reading rain gauge
pluviómetro[M] *de lectura*[F] *directa*

instrument shelter
refugio[M] *meteorológico*

snow gauge
nivómetro[M]

rain gauge recorder
pluviómetro[M]

mirror *n* : espejo *m* — **mirror** *vt* : reflejar

mirth *n* : alegría *f*, risas *fpl*

misapprehension *n* : malentendido *m*

misbehave *vi* **-haved; -having** : portarse mal — **misbehavior** *n* : mala conducta *f*

miscalculate *v* **-lated; -lating** : calcular mal

miscarriage *n* **1** : aborto *m* **2 miscarriage of justice** : error *m* judicial

miscellaneous *adj* : diverso, vario

mischief *n* : travesuras *fpl* — **mischievous** *adj* : travieso

misconception *n* : concepto *m* erróneo

misconduct *n* : mala conducta *f*

misdeed *n* : fechoría *f*

misdemeanor *n* : delito *m* menor

miser *n* : avaro *m*, -ra *f*; tacaño *m*, -ña *f*

miserable *adj* **1** UNHAPPY : triste **2** WRETCHED : miserable **3 miserable weather** : tiempo *m* malo

miserly *adj* : mezquino

misery *n*, *pl* **-eries 1** : sufrimiento *m* **2** WRETCHEDNESS : miseria *f*

misfire *vi* **-fired; -firing** : fallar

misfit *n* : inadaptado *m*, -da *f*

misfortune *n* : desgracia *f*

misgiving *n* : duda *f*

misguided *adj* : descaminado, equivocado

mishap *n* : contratiempo *m*

misinform *vt* : informar mal

misinterpret *vt* : interpretar mal

misjudge *vt* **-judged; -judging** : juzgar mal

mislay *vt* **-laid; -laying** : extraviar, perder

mislead *vt* **-led; -leading** : engañar — **misleading** *adj* : engañoso

misnomer *n* : nombre *m* inapropiado

misplace *vt* **-placed; -placing** : extraviar, perder

misprint *n* : errata *f*, error *m* de imprenta

miss *vt* **1** : errar, faltar **2** OVERLOOK : pasar por alto **3** : perder (una oportunidad, un vuelo, etc.) **4** AVOID : evitar **5** OMIT : saltarse **6 I miss you** : te echo de menos — **miss** *n* **1** : fallo *m* (de un tiro, etc.) **2** FAILURE : fracaso *m*

Miss *n* : señorita *f*

missile *n* **1** : misil *m* **2** PROJECTILE : proyectil *m*

missing *adj* : perdido, desaparecido

mission *n* : misión *f* — **missionary** *n*, *pl* **-aries** : misionero *m*, -ra *f*

misspell *vt* : escribir mal

mist *n* : neblina *f*, bruma *f*

mistake *vt* **mistook; mistaken; -taking 1** MISINTERPRET : entender mal **2** CONFUSE : confundir — **mistake** *n* **1** : error *m* **2 make a mistake** : equivocarse — **mistaken** *adj* : equivocado

mister *n* : señor *m*

mistletoe *n* : muérdago *m*

mistreat *vt* : maltratar

mistress *n* **1** : dueña *f*, señora *f* (de una casa) **2** LOVER : amante *f*

mistrust *n* : desconfianza *f* — **mistrust** *vt* : desconfiar de

misty *adj* **mistier; -est** : neblinoso, nebuloso

misunderstand *vt* **-stood; -standing** : entender mal — **misunderstanding** *n* : malentendido *m*

misuse *vt* **-used; -using 1** : emplear mal **2** MISTREAT : maltratar — **misuse** *n*

: mal empleo *m*, abuso *m*

mitigate *vt* **-gated; -gating** : mitigar

mitt *n* : manopla *f*, guante *m* (de béisbol) — **mitten** *n* : manopla *f*, mitón *m*

mix *vt* **1** : mezclar **2 mix up** : confundir — *vi* : mezclarse — **mix** *n* : mezcla *f* — **mixture** *n* : mezcla *f* — **mix- up** *n* : confusión *f*, lío *m fam*

moan *n* : gemido *m* — **moan** *vi* : gemir

mob *n* : muchedumbre *f* — **mob** *vt* **mobbed; mobbing** : acosar

mobile *adj* : móvil — **mobile** *n* : móvil *m* — **mobile home** *n* : caravana *f* — **mobility** *n* : movilidad *f* — **mobilize** *vt* **-lized; -lizing** : movilizar

moccasin *n* : mocasín *m*

mock *vt* : burlarse de, mofarse de — **mock** *adj* : falso — **mockery** *n*, *pl* **-eries** : burla *f* — **mock-up** *n* : maqueta *f*

mode *n* **1** : modo *m* **2** FASHION : moda *f*

model *n* **1** : modelo *m* **2** MOCK-UP : maqueta *f* **3** : modelo *mf* (persona) — **model** *v* **-eled** *or* **-elled; -eling** *or* **-elling** *vt* **1** SHAPE : modelar **2** WEAR : lucir — *vi* : trabajar de modelo — **model** *adj* : modelo

modem *n* : módem *m*

moderate *adj* : moderado — **moderate** *n* : moderado *m*, -da *f* — **moderate** *v* **-ated; -ating** *vt* : moderar — *vi* : moderarse — **moderation** *n* : moderación *f* — **moderator** *n* : moderador *m*, -dora *f*

modern *adj* : moderno — **modernize** *vt* **-ized; -izing** : modernizar

modest *adj* : modesto — **modesty** *n* : modestia *f*

modify *vt* **-fied; -fying** : modificar

mole
topo^M

fur
pelaje^M

eye
ojo^M

snout
hocico^M

tail
cola^F

forelimb
pata^F anterior

claw
garra^F

hind limb
pata^F posterior

monkeys and apes
monos^M y simios^M

tamarin
tamarino^M

gibbon
gibón^M

orangutan
orangután^M

marmoset
tití^M

chimpanzee
chimpancé^M

macaque
macaco^M

moist *adj* : húmedo — **moisten** *vt* :
humedecer — **moisture** *n* : humedad *f*
— **moisturizer** *n* : crema *f* hidratante
molar *n* : muela *f*
molasses *n* : melaza *f*
mold[1] *n* FORM : molde *m* —
mold *vt* : moldear, formar
mold[2] *n* FUNGUS : moho *m* —
moldy *adj* **moldier; -est** : mohoso
mole[1] *n* : lunar *m* (en la piel)
▸ **mole**[2] *n* : topo *m* (animal)
molecule *n* : molécula *f*
molest *vt* **1** HARASS : importunar
2 : abusar (sexualmente)
molten *adj* : fundido

mom *n* : mamá *f*
moment *n* : momento *m* —
momentarily *adv* **1** : momentáneamente
2 SOON : dentro de poco, pronto —
momentary *adj* : momentáneo
momentous *adj* : muy importante
momentum *n, pl* **-ta** *or* **-tums**
1 : momento *m* (en física)
2 IMPETUS : ímpetu *m*
monarch *n* : monarca *mf* —
monarchy *n, pl* **-chies** : monarquía *f*
monastery *n, pl* **-teries** : monasterio *m*
Monday *n* : lunes *m*
money *n, pl* **-eys** *or* **-ies** : dinero *m*
— **monetary** *adj* : monetario

— **money order** *n* : giro *m* postal
mongrel *n* : perro *m* mestizo
monitor *n* : monitor *m* (de
una computadora, etc.) —
monitor *vt* : controlar
monk *n* : monje *m*
▸ **monkey** *n, pl* **-keys** : mono *m*, -na *f*
— **monkey wrench** *n* : llave *f* inglesa
monogram *n* : monograma *m*
monologue *n* : monólogo *m*
monopoly *n, pl* **-lies** : monopolio *m* —
monopolize *vt* **-lized; -lizing** : monopolizar
monotonous *adj* : monótono
— **monotony** *n* : monotonía *f*
monster *n* : monstruo *m*

Moon
Luna^F

lunar features
superficie^F lunar

bay
bahía^F

cliff
risco^M

sea
mar^M

lake
lago^M

highland
continente^M

ocean
océano^M

crater
cráter^M

cirque
circo^M

mountain range
cordillera^F

phases of the Moon
fases^F de la Luna^F

new moon
Luna^F nueva

full moon
Luna^F llena

new crescent
Luna^F creciente

waning gibbous
tercer octante^M

first quarter
cuarto^M creciente

last quarter
cuarto^M menguante

waxing gibbous
quinto octante^M

old crescent
Luna^F menguante

— **monstrosity** *n, pl* **-ties** :
monstruosidad *f* — **monstrous** *adj* **1**
: monstruoso **2** HUGE : gigantesco
month *n* : mes *m* — **monthly** *adv* :
mensualmente — **monthly** *adj* : mensual
monument *n* : monumento *m* —
monumental *adj* : monumental
moo *vi* : mugir — **moo** *n* : mugido *m*
mood *n* : humor *m* — **moody** *adj*
moodier; -est 1 GLOOMY : melancólico,
deprimido **2** IRRITABLE : malhumorado **3**
TEMPERAMENTAL : de humor variable
▸ **moon** *n* : luna *f* — **moonlight** *n*
: luz *f* de la luna
moor^1 *n* : brezal *m*, páramo *m*
moor^2 *vt* : amarrar — **mooring** *n*

DOCK : atracadero *m*
moose *ns & pl* : alce *m*
moot *adj* : discutible
mop *n* **1** : trapeador *m Lat*, fregona *f*
Spain **2** *or* **mop of hair** : pelambrera *f*
— **mop** *vt* **mopped; mopping** :
trapear *Lat*, pasar la fregona a *Spain*
mope *vi* **moped; moping**
: andar deprimido
moped *n* : ciclomotor *m*
moral *adj* : moral — **moral** *n* **1** :
moraleja *f* (de un cuento, etc.) **2 morals** *npl*
: moral *f*, moralidad *f* — **morale** *n* : moral *f*
— **morality** *n, pl* **-ties** : moralidad *f*
morbid *adj* : morboso
more *adj* : más — **more** *adv* **1** : más **2**

more and more : cada vez más **3 more**
or less : más o menos **4 once more** : una
vez más — **more** *n* : más *m* — **more** *pron*
: más — **moreover** *adv* : además
morgue *n* : depósito *m* de cadáveres
morning *n* **1** : mañana *f* **2 good**
morning! : ¡buenos días! **3 in**
the morning : por la mañana
moron *n* : estúpido *m*, -da *f*; imbécil *mf*
morose *adj* : malhumorado
morphine *n* : morfina *f*
morsel *n* **1** BITE : bocado *m* **2**
FRAGMENT : pedazo *m*
mortal *adj* : mortal — **mortal** *n* :
mortal *mf* — **mortality** *n* : mortalidad *f*
mortar *n* : mortero *m*

mortgage *n* : hipoteca *f* — **mortgage** *vt* -gaged; -gaging : hipotecar
mortify *vt* -fied; -fying **1** : mortificar **2** HUMILIATE : avergonzar
mosaic *n* : mosaico *m*
Moslem → **Muslim**
mosque *n* : mezquita *f*
mosquito *n, pl* -toes : mosquito *m*, zancudo *m*, *Lat*
moss *n* : musgo *m*
most *adj* **1** : la mayoría de, la mayor parte de **2 (the) most** : más — **most** *adv* : más — **most** *n* : más *m*, máximo *m* — **most** *pron* : la mayoría, la mayor parte — **mostly** *adv* **1** MAINLY : en su mayor parte, principalmente **2** USUALLY : normalmente
motel *n* : motel *m*
moth *n* : palomilla *f*, polilla *f*
mother *n* : madre *f* — **mother** *vt* **1** : cuidar de **2** SPOIL : mimar — **motherhood** *n* : maternidad *f* — **mother–in–law** *n, pl* **mothers–in–law** : suegra *f* — **motherly** *adj* : maternal — **mother–of–pearl** *n* : nácar *m*
motif *n* : motivo *m*
motion *n* **1** : movimiento *m* **2** PROPOSAL : moción *f* **3 set in motion** : poner en marcha — **motion** *vi* **motion to someone** : hacer una señal a algn — **motionless** *adj* : inmóvil — **motion picture** *n* : película *f*
motive *n* : motivo *m* — **motivate** *vt* -vated; -vating : motivar — **motivation** *n* : motivación *f*
motor *n* : motor *m* — **motorbike** *n* : motocicleta *f* (pequeña), moto *f* — **motorboat** *n* : lancha *f* motora — **motorcycle** *n* : motocicleta *f* — **motorcyclist** *n* : motociclista *mf* — **motorist** *n* : automovilista *mf*, motorista *mf Lat*
motto *n, pl* -toes : lema *m*
mould → **mold**
mound *n* **1** PILE : montón *m* **2** HILL : montículo *m*
mount[1] *n* **1** HORSE : montura *f* **2** SUPPORT : soporte *m* — **mount** *vt* : montar (un caballo, etc.), subir (una escalera) — *vi* INCREASE : aumentar
mount[2] *n* HILL : monte *m* — **mountain** *n* : montaña *f* — **mountainous** *adj* : montañoso
mourn *vt* : llorar (por) — *vi* : lamentarse — **mourner** *n* : doliente *mf* — **mournful** *adj* : triste — **mourning** *n* : luto *m*

mouse *n, pl* **mice** : ratón *m* — **mousetrap** *n* : ratonera *f*
moustache → **mustache**
▸ **mouth** *n* : boca *f* (de una persona o un animal), desembocadura *f* (de un río) — **mouthful** *n* : bocado *m* — **mouthpiece** *n* : boquilla *f* (de un instrumento musical)
move *v* **moved; moving** *vi* **1** GO : ir **2** RELOCATE : mudarse **3** STIR : moverse **4** ACT : tomar medidas — *vt* **1** : mover **2** AFFECT : conmover **3** TRANSPORT : transportar, trasladar **4** PROPOSE : proponer — **move** *n* **1** MOVEMENT : movimiento *m* **2** RELOCATION : mudanza *f* **3** STEP : medida *f* — **movable** *or* **moveable** *adj* : movible, móvil — **movement** *n* : movimiento *m*
movie *n* **1** : película *f* **2** movies *npl* : cine *m*
mow *vt* **mowed; mowed** *or* **mown; mowing** : cortar (la hierba) — **mower** → **lawn mower**
Mr. *n, pl* **Messrs.** : señor *m*
Mrs. *n, pl* **Mesdames** : señora *f*
Ms. *n* : señora *f*, señorita *f*
much *adj* **more; most** : mucho — **much** *adv* **more; most 1** : mucho **2** as

much as : tanto como **3 how much?** : ¿cuánto? **4 too much** : demasiado — **much** *pron* : mucho, -cha
muck *n* **1** DIRT : mugre *f*, suciedad *f* **2** MANURE : estiércol *m*
mucus *n* : mucosidad *f*
mud *n* : barro *m*, lodo *m*
muddle *v* -dled; -dling *vt* **1** CONFUSE : confundir **2** JUMBLE : desordenar — *vi* **muddle through** : arreglárselas — **muddle** *n* : confusión *f*, lío *m fam*
muddy *adj* -dier; -est : fangoso, lleno de barro
muffin *n* : mollete *m*
muffle *vt* -fled; -fling : amortiguar (un sonido) — **muffler** *n* **1** SCARF : bufanda *f* **2** : silenciador *m*, mofle *m*, *Lat* (de un automóvil)
mug *n* CUP : tazón *m* — **mug** *vt* : asaltar, atracar — **mugger** *n* : atracador *m*, -dora *f*
muggy *adj* -gier; -est : bochornoso
mule *n* : mula *f*
mull *vt or* **mull over** : reflexionar sobre
multicolored *adj* : multicolor
multimedia *adj* : multimedia
multinational *adj* : multinacional

mouth
boca*F*

superior dental arch
arco[M] *dentario superior*

gum
encía[F]

hard palate
bóveda[F] *palatina*

palatine tonsil
amígdala[F]

uvula
úvula[F]

inferior dental arch
arco[M] *dentario inferior*

upper lip
labio[M] *superior*

tongue
lengua[F]

lower lip
labio[M] *inferior*

mushrooms
hongos^M

chanterelle
rebozuelo^M

truffle
trufa^F

cultivated mushroom
champiñón^M

oyster mushroom
orellana^F

shiitake mushroom
shiitake^M

saffron milk cap
níscalo^M

porcini
porcini^M

morel
morilla^F

royal agaric
oronja^F

multiple *adj* : múltiple — **multiple** *n* : múltiplo *m* — **multiplication** *n* : multiplicación *f* — **multiply** *v* -plied; -plying *vt* : multiplicar — *vi* : multiplicarse
multitude *n* : multitud *f*
mum *adj* **keep mum** : guardar silencio
mumble *v* -bled; -bling *vt* : mascullar — *vi* : hablar entre dientes
mummy *n*, *pl* -mies : momia *f*
mumps *ns & pl* : paperas *fpl*
munch *v* : mascar, masticar
mundane *adj* : rutinario, ordinario

municipal *adj* : municipal — **municipality** *n*, *pl* -ties : municipio *m*
munitions *npl* : municiónes *fpl*
mural *n* : mural *m*
murder *n* : asesinato *m*, homicidio *m* — **murder** *vt* : asesinar, atar — *vi* : matar — **murderer** *n* : asesino *m*, -na *f*; homicida *mf* — **murderous** *adj* : asesino, homicida
murky *adj* -kier; -est : turbio, oscuro
murmur *n* : murmullo *m* — **murmur** *v* : mumurar
muscle *n* : músculo *m* — **muscle** *vi*

-cled; -cling *or* **muscle in** : meterse por la fuerza en — **muscular** *adj* **1** : muscular **2** STRONG : musculoso
muse^1 *n* : musa *f*
muse^2 *vi* **mused; musing** : meditar
museum *n* : museo *m*
▸ **mushroom** *n* **1** : hongo *m*, seta *f* **2** : champiñón *m* (en la cocina) — **mushroom** *vi* GROW : crecer rápidamente, multiplicarse
mushy *adj* **mushier; -est 1** SOFT : blando **2** MAWKISH : sensiblero
music *n* : música *f* — **musical** *adj* : musical — **music** *n* : comedia *f* musical — **musician** *n* : músico *m*, -ca *f*
Muslim *adj* : musulmán — **Muslim** *n* : musulmán *m*, -mana *f*
muslin *n* : muselina *f*
mussel *n* : mejillón *m*
must *v aux* **1** : deber, tener que **2 you must come** : tienes que venir **3 you must be tired** : debes (de) estar cansado — **must** *n* : necesidad *f*
mustache *n* : bigote *m*, bigotes *mpl*
mustang *n* : mustang *m*
mustard *n* : mostaza *f*
muster *vt* **1** : reunir **2** *or* **muster up** : armarse de, cobrar (valor, fuerzas, etc.)
musty *adj* **mustier; -est** : que huele a cerrado
mute *adj* **muter; mutest** : mudo — **mute** *n* : mudo *m*, -da *f*
mutilate *vt* -lated; -lating : mutilar
mutiny *n*, *pl* -nies : motín *m* — **mutiny** *vi* -nied; -nying : amotinarse
mutter *vi* : murmurar
mutton *n* : carne *f* de carnero
mutual *adj* **1** : mutuo **2** COMMON : común — **mutually** *adv* : mutuamente
muzzle *n* **1** SNOUT : hocico *m* **2** : bozal *m* (para un perro, etc.) **3** : boca *f* (de un arma de fuego) — **muzzle** *vt* -zled; -zling : poner un bozal a (un animal)
my *adj* : mi
myopia *n* : miopía *f* — **myopic** *adj* : miope
myself *pron* **1** (*reflexive*) : me **2** (*emphatic*) : yo mismo **3 by myself** : solo
mystery *n*, *pl* -teries : misterio *m* — **mysterious** *adj* : misterioso
mystic *adj or* **mystical** : místico
mystify *vt* -fied; -fying : dejar perplejo, confundir
mystique *n* : aura *f* de misterio
myth *n* : mito *m* — **mythical** *adj* : mítico

n *n, pl* **n's** *or* **ns** : n *f,* decimocuarta
  letra del alfabeto inglés
nab *vt* **nabbed; nabbing 1** ARREST
  : pescar *fam* **2** GRAB : agarrar
nag *v* **nagged; nagging** *vi* COMPLAIN
  : quejarse — *vt* **1** ANNOY : fastidiar,
  dar la lata a **2** SCOLD : regañar
  — **nagging** *adj* : persistente
nail *n* **1** : clavo *m* **2** : uña *f* (de un
  dedo) — **nail** *vt or* **nail down** : clavar
  — **nail file** *n* : lima *f* de uñas
naive *or* **naïve** *adj* **-iver; -est** : ingenuo
  — **naïveté** *n* : ingenuidad *f*
naked *adj* **1** : desnudo **2 the**
  naked truth : la pura verdad **3 to**
  the naked eye : a simple vista
name *n* **1** : nombre *m* **2** REPUTATION :

fama *f* **3 what is your name?** : ¿cómo
  se llama? **4** → **first name, surname**
  — **name** *vt* **named; naming 1** : poner
  nombre a **2** APPOINT : nombrar **3 name a**
  price : fijar un precio — **nameless** *adj*
  : anónimo — **namely** *adv* : a saber
  — **namesake** *n* : tocayo *m,* -ya *f*
nap[1] *vi* **napped; napping** : echarse
  una siesta — **nap** *n* : siesta *f*
nap[2] *n* : pelo *m* (de una tela)
nape *n or* **nape of the neck** : nuca *f*
napkin *n* **1** : servilleta *f* **2**
  → **sanitary napkin**
narcotic *n* : narcótico *m,*
  estupefaciente *m*
narrate *vt* **-rated; -rating** : narrar
  — **narration** *n* : narración *f*

— **narrative** *n* : narración *f* —
  narrator *n* : narrador *m,* -dora *f*
narrow *adj* **1** : estrecho, angosto **2**
  RESTRICTED : limitado — **narrow** *vi*
  : estrecharse — *vt* **1** : estrechar
  2 *or* **narrow down** : limitar —
  narrowly *adv* : por poco — **narrow–**
  minded *adj* : de miras estrechas
▸ **nasal** *adj* : nasal
nasty *adj* **-tier; -est 1** MEAN : malo, cruel
  2 UNPLEASANT : desagradable **3** REPUGNANT
  : asqueroso — **nastiness** *n* : maldad *f*
nation *n* : nación *f* — **national** *adj*
  : nacional — **nationalism** *n* :
  nacionalismo *m* — **nationality** *n,*
  pl **-ties** : nacionalidad *f* — **nationalize** *vt*
  -ized; -izing : nacionalizar

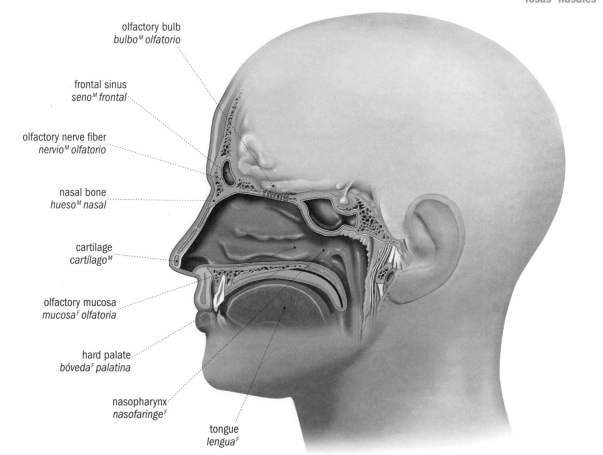

nasal cavity
fosas[F] nasales

olfactory bulb
bulbo[M] olfatorio

frontal sinus
seno[M] frontal

olfactory nerve fiber
nervio[M] olfatorio

nasal bone
hueso[M] nasal

cartilage
cartílago[M]

olfactory mucosa
mucosa[F] olfatoria

hard palate
bóveda[F] palatina

nasopharynx
nasofaringe[F]

tongue
lengua[F]

— **nationwide** *adj* : por todo el país
native *adj* **1** : natal (dícese de un país, etc.) **2** INNATE : innato **3 native language** : lengua *f* materna — **native** *n* **1** : nativo *m*, -va *f* **2 be a native of** : ser natural de — **Native American** : indio *m* americano, india *f* americana — **nativity** *n*, *pl* **-ties the Nativity** : la Navidad
nature *n* **1** : naturaleza *f* **2** KIND : índole *f*, clase *f* **3** DISPOSITION : carácter *m*, natural *m* — **natural** *adj* : natural — **naturalize** *vt* **-ized; -izing** : naturalizar — **naturally** *adv* : naturalmente
naught *n* **1** NOTHING : nada *f* **2** ZERO : cero *m*
naughty *adj* **-tier; -est 1** : travieso, pícaro **2** RISQUÉ : picante
nausea *n* : náuseas *fpl* — **nauseating** *adj* : nauseabundo — **nauseous** *adj* **1 feel nausea** : sentir náuseas **2** SICKENING : nauseabundo
nautical *adj* : náutico
naval *adj* : naval
nave *n* : nave *f* (de una iglesia)

navel *n* : ombligo *m*
navigate *v* **-gated; -gating** *vi* : navegar — *vt* **1** : gobernar (un barco), pilotar (un avión) **2** : navegar por (un río, etc.) — **navigable** *adj* : navegable — **navigation** *n* : navegación *f* — **navigator** *n* : navegante *mf*
navy *n*, *pl* **-vies 1** : marina *f* de guerra **2** *or* **navy blue** : azul *m* marino
near *adv* : cerca — **near** *prep* : cerca de — **near** *adj* : cercano, próximo — **near** *vt* : acercarre a — **nearby** *adv* : cerca — **nearby** *adj* : cercano — **nearly** *adv* : casi — **nearsighted** *adj* : miope, corto de vista
neat *adj* **1** TIDY : muy arreglado **2** CLEVER : hábil, ingenioso — **neatly** *adv* **1** : ordenadamente **2** CLEVERLY : hábilmente — **neatness** *n* : pulcritud *f*, orden *m*
nebulous *adj* : nebuloso
necessary *adj* : necesario — **necessarily** *adv* : necesariamente — **necessitate** *vt* **-tated; -tating** : exigir, requerir — **necessity** *n*, *pl* **-ties 1** : necesidad *f* **2 necessities** *npl*

: cosas *fpl* indispensables
neck *n* **1** : cuello *m* (de una persona o una botella), pescuezo *m* (de un animal) **2** COLLAR : cuello *m* — **necklace** *n* : collar *m* — **necktie** *n* : corbata *f*
nectar *n* : néctar *m*
nectarine *n* : nectarina *f*
need *n* **1** : necesidad *f* **2 if need be** : si hace falta — **need** *vt* **1** : necesitar, exigir **2 need to** : tener que — *v aux* : tener que
needle *n* : aguja *f* — **needle** *vt* **-dled; -dling** : pinchar
needless *adj* **1** : innecesario **2 needless to say** : de más está decir
needlework *n* : bordado *m*
needn't (*contraction of* **need not**) → **need**
needy *adj* **needier; -est** : necesitado
negative *adj* : negativo — **negative** *n* **1** : negación *f* (en gramática) **2** : negativo *m* (en fotografía)
neglect *vt* : descuidar — **neglect** *n* : descuido *m*, abandono *m*
negligee *n* : negligé *m*
negligence *n* : negligencia *f*, descuido *m*

newspaper
periódico[M]

front page
primera plana[F]

nameplate
nombre[M] *del periódico*[M]

front picture
foto[F] *de primera plana*[F]

article
artículo[M]

headline
titular[M]

deck
subtítulo[M]

literary supplement
suplemento[M] *literario*

color supplement
suplemento[M] *a color*[M]

nervous system: brain
sistema^M nervioso: cerebro^M

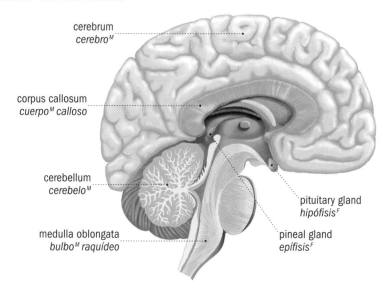

cerebrum
cerebro^M

corpus callosum
cuerpo^M calloso

cerebellum
cerebelo^M

medulla oblongata
bulbo^M raquídeo

pituitary gland
hipófisis^F

pineal gland
epífisis^F

— **negligent** *adj* : negligente, descuidado
negligible *adj* : insignificante
negotiate *v* -ated; -ating : negociar
— **negotiable** *adj* : negociable —
negotiation *n* : negociación *f* —
negotiator *n* : negociador *m*, -dora *f*
Negro *n, pl* -groes *sometimes considered offensive* : negro *m*, -gra *f*
neigh *vi* : relinchar — **neigh** *n* : relincho *m*
neighbor *or Brit* **neighbour** *n* :
vecino *m*, -na *f* — **neighborhood** *or Brit* **neighbourhood** *n* 1 : barrio *m*,
vecindario *m* 2 **in the neighborhood of** : alrededor de — **neighborly** *or Brit* **neighbourly** *adv* : amable
neither *conj* 1 neither…nor : ni… ni 2 **neither am/do I** : yo tampoco
— **neither** *pron* : ninguno, -na —
neither *adj* : ninguno (de los dos)
neon *n* : neón *m*
nephew *n* : sobrino *m*
Neptune *n* : Neptuno *m*
nerve *n* 1 : nervio *m* 2 COURAGE : coraje *m* 3 GALL : descaro *m* 4
nerves *npl* JITTERS : nervios *mpl*
— **nervous** *adj* : nervioso —
nervousness *n* : nerviosismo *m* —
nervy *adj* **nervier; -est** : descarado
nest *n* : nido *m* — **nest** *vi* : anidar

nestle *vi* -tled; -tling : acurrucarse
net[1] *n* : red *f* — **net** *vt* **netted; netting** : pescar, atrapar (con una red)
net[2] *adj* : neto — **net** *vt* **netted; netting** YIELD : producir neto
nettle *n* : ortiga *f*
network *n* : red *f*
neurology *n* : neurología *f*
neurosis *n, pl* -roses : neurosis *f*
— **neurotic** *adj* : neurótico
neuter *adj* : neutro — **neuter** *vt* : castrar
neutral *n* : punto *m* muerto (de un automóvil) — **neutral** *adj* 1 : neutral
2 : neutro (en electrotecnia o química)
— **neutrality** *n* : neutralidad *f* —
neutralize *vt* -ized; -izing : neutralizar
neutron *n* : neutrón *m*
never *adv* 1 : nunca, jamás 2 NOT : no
3 **never again** : nunca más 4 **never mind** : no importa — **nevermore** *adv*
: nunca jamás — **nevertheless** *adv*
: sin embargo, no obstante
new *adj* : nuevo — **newborn** *adj*
: recién nacido — **newcomer** *n* :
recién llegado *m*, -da *f* — **newly** *adv* :
recién, recientemente — **newlywed** *n*
: recién casado *m*, -da *f* — **news** *n* :
noticias *fpl* — **newscast** *n* : noticiario *m*,
noticiero *m*, *Lat* — **newscaster** *n* :

presentador *m*, -dora *f* (de un noticiario)
— **newsletter** *n* : boletín *m* informativo
▸ — **newspaper** *n* : periódico *m*, diario *m*
— **newsstand** *n* : puesto *m* de periódicos
newt *n* : tritón *m*
New Year's Day *n* : día *m* del Año Nuevo
next *adj* 1 : próximo 2 FOLLOWING :
siguiente — **next** *adv* 1 : la próxima
vez 2 AFTERWARD : después, luego 3
NOW : ahora — **next–door** *adj* : de
al lado — **next to** *adv* ALMOST : casi
— **next to** *prep* BESIDE : al lado de
nib *n* : plumilla *f*
nibble *vt* -bled; -bling : mordisquear
Nicaraguan *adj* : nicaragüense
nice *adj* **nicer; nicest** 1 PLEASANT :
agradable, bueno 2 KIND : amable —
nicely *adv* 1 WELL : bien 2 KINDLY :
amablemente — **niceness** *n* : amabilidad *f*
— **niceties** *npl* : detalles *mpl*, sutilezas *fpl*
niche *n* 1 : nicho *m* 2 **find one's niche** : hacerse su hueco
nick *n* 1 : corte *m* pequeño, muesca *f* 2
in the nick of time : justo a tiempo
— **nick** *vt* : hacer una muesca en
nickel *n* 1 : níquel *m* (metal) 2 :
moneda *f* de cinco centavos
nickname *n* : apodo *m*,
sobrenombre *m* — **nickname** *vt*
-named; -naming : apodar

nicotine *n* : nicotina *f*
niece *n* : sobrina *f*
niggling *adj* **1** PETTY : insignificante **2** PERSISTENT : constante
night *n* **1** : noche *f* **2 at night** : de noche **3 last night** : anoche **4 tomorrow night** : mañana por la noche — **nightclub** *n* : club *m* nocturno — **nightfall** *n* : anochecer *m* — **nightgown** *n* : camisón *m* (de noche) — **nightly** *adj* : de todas las noches — **nightly** *adv* : cada noche — **nightmare** *n* : pesadilla *f* — **nighttime** *n* : noche *f*
nil *n* NOTHING : nada *f*
nimble *adj* **-bler; -blest** : ágil
nine *adj* : nueve — **nine** *n* : nueve *m* — **nine hundred** *adj* : novecientos — **nine hundred** *n* : novecientos *m* —
nineteen *adj* : diecinueve — **nineteen** *n* : diecinueve *m* — **nineteenth** *adj* : decimonoveno, decimonono — **nineteenth** *n* **1** : decimonoveno *m*, -na *f*; decimonono *m*, -na *f* (en una serie) **2** : diecinueveavo *m* (en matemáticas) — **ninetieth** *adj* : nonagésimo — **ninetieth** *n* **1** : nonagésimo *m*, -ma *f* (en una serie) **2** : noventavo *m* (en matemáticas) — **ninety** *adj* : noventa — **ninety** *n*, *pl* **-ties** : noventa *m* — **ninth** *adj* : noveno — **ninth** *n* **1** : noveno *m*, -na *f* (en una serie) **2** : noveno *m* (en matemáticas)
nip *vt* **nipped; nipping 1** PINCH : pellizcar **2** BITE : mordisquear **3 nip in the bud** : cortar de raíz — **nip** *n* **1** PINCH : pellizco *m* **2** NIBBLE : mordisco *m*
nipple *n* **1** : pezón *m* (de una mujer) **2** : tetilla *f* (de un hombre o un biberón)
nitrogen *n* : nitrógen *m*
nitwit *n* : idiota *mf*
no *adv* : no — **no** *adj* **1** : ninguno **2 I have no money** : no tengo dinero **3 it's no trouble** : no es ningún problema **4 no smoking** : prohibido fumar — **no** *n*, *pl* **noes** *or* **nos** : no *m*
noble *adj* **-bler; -blest** : noble — **noble** *n* : noble *mf* — **nobility** *n* : nobleza *f*
nobody *pron* : nadie
nocturnal *adj* : nocturno
nod *v* **nodded; nodding** *vi* **1** *or* **nod yes** : asentir con la cabeza **2 nod off** : dormirse — *vt* **nod one's head** : asentir con la cabeza — **nod** *n* : señal *m* con la cabeza
noes → **no**
noise *n* : ruido *m* — **noisily** *adv* : ruidosamente — **noisy** *adj*

noisier; -est : ruidoso
nomad *n* : nómada *mf* —
nomadic *adj* : nómada
nominal *adj* : nominal
nominate *vt* **-nated; -nating 1** : proponer, postular *Lat* **2** APPOINT : nombrar —
nomination *n* **1** : propuesta *f*, postulación *f* *Lat* **2** APPOINTMENT : nombramiento *m*
nonalcoholic *adj* : no alcohólico
nonchalant *adj* : despreocupado
noncommissioned officer *n* : suboficial *mf*
noncommittal *adj* : evasivo
nondescript *adj* : anodino, soso
none *pron* **1** : ninguno, ninguna **2 there are none left** : no hay más — **none** *adv* **1 be none the worse** : no sufrir daño alguno **2 none too happy** : nada contento **3 none too soon** : a buena hora
nonentity *n*, *pl* **-ties** : persona *f* insignificante
nonetheless *adv* : sin embargo, no obstante
nonexistent *adj* : inexistente
nonfat *adj* : sin grasa
nonfiction *n* : no ficción *f*
nonprofit *adj* : sin fines lucrativos
nonsense *n* : tonterías *fpl*, disparates *mpl* — **nonsensical** *adj* : absurdo
nonsmoker *n* : no fumador *m*, -dora *f*
nonstop *adj* : directo — **nonstop** *adv* : sin parar
noodle *n* : fideo *m*
nook *n* : rincón *m*
noon *n* : mediodía *m*
no one *pron* : nadie
noose *n* **1** : dogal *m*, soga *f* **2** LASSO : lazo *m*
nor *conj* **1** neither…nor : ni… ni **2 nor I** : yo tampoco
norm *n* **1** : norma *f* **2 the norm** : lo normal — **normal** *adj* : normal — **normality** *n* : normalidad *f* — **normally** *adv* : normalmente
north *adv* : al norte — **north** *adj* : norte, del norte — **north** *n* **1** : norte *m* **2 the North** : el Norte — **North American** *adj* : norteamericano — **northeast** *adv* : hacia el nordeste — **northeast** *adj* : nordeste, del nordeste — **northeast** *n* : nordeste *m*, noreste *m* — **northeastern** *adj* : nordeste, del nordeste — **northerly** *adj* : del norte — **northern** *adj* : del norte, norteño — **northwest** *adv* : hacia el noroeste — **northwest** *adj* : noroeste, del noroeste

— **northwest** *n* : noroeste *m* —
northwestern *adj* : noroeste, del noroeste
Norwegian *adj* : noruego
nose *n* **1** : nariz *f* (de una persona), hocico *m* (de un animal) **2 blow one's nose** : sonarse las narices — **nose** *vi* **nosed; nosing** *or* **nose around** : meter las narices — **nosebleed** *n* : hemorragia *f* nasal — **nosedive** *n* : descenso *m* en picada
nostalgia *n* : nostalgia *f* — **nostalgic** *adj* : nostálgico
nostril *n* : ventana *f* de la nariz
nosy *or* **nosey** *adj* **nosier; -est** : entrometido
not *adv* **1** : no **2 he's not tired** : no esta cansado **3 I hope not** : espero que no **4 not … anything** : no…nada
notable *adj* : notable — **notable** *n* : personaje *m* — **notably** *adv* : notablemente
notary public *n*, *pl* **notaries public** *or* **notary publics** : notario *m*, -ria *f*
▸ **notation** *n* : anotación *f*
notch *n* : muesca *f*, corte *m* — **notch** *vt* : hacer un corte en
note *vt* **noted; noting 1** NOTICE : observar, notar **2** RECORD : anotar — **note** *n* **1** : nota *f* **2 of note** : destacado **3 take note of** : prestar atención a **4 take notes** : apuntar — **notebook** *n* : libreta *f*, cuaderno *m* — **noted** *adj* : renombrado, célebre — **noteworthy** *adj* : notable
nothing *pron* **1** : nada **2 be nothing but** : no ser más que **3 for nothing** FREE : gratis — **nothing** *n* **1** ZERO : zero *m* **2** TRIFLE : nimiedad *f*
notice *n* **1** SIGN : letrero *m*, aviso *m* **2 at a moment's notice** : sin previo aviso **3 be given one's notice** : ser despedido **4 take notice of** : prestar atención a — **notice** *vt* **-ticed; -ticing** : notar — **noticeable** *adj* : perceptible, evidente
notify *vt* **-fied; -fying** : notificar, avisar — **notification** *n* : notificación *f*, aviso *m*
notion *n* **1** : noción *f*, idea *f* **2** notions *npl* : artículos *mpl* de mercería
notorious *adj* : de mala fama — **notoriety** *n* : mala fama *f*, notoriedad *f*
notwithstanding *prep* : a pesar de, no obstante — **notwithstanding** *adv* : sin embargo — **notwithstanding** *conj* : a pesar de que
nougat *n* : turrón *m*
nought → **naught**

musical notation
notación^F musical

musical notation
notación^F musical

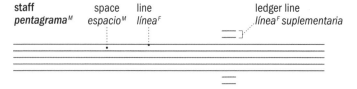

staff · space · line · ledger line
pentagrama^M · *espacio^M* · *línea^F* · *línea^F suplementaria*

clefs
claves^F

G clef · F clef · C clef
clave^F de sol^M · *clave^F de fa^M* · *clave^F de do^M*

scale
escala^F

C · D · E · F · G · A · B · C
do(C) · *re(D)* · *mi(E)* · *fa(F)* · *sol(G)* · *la(A)* · *si(B)* · *do(C)*

note symbols
valores^M de las notas^F musicales

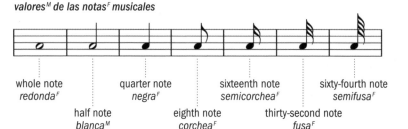

whole note · quarter note · sixteenth note · sixty-fourth note
redonda^F · *negra^F* · *semicorchea^F* · *semifusa^F*

half note · eighth note · thirty-second note
blanca^M · *corchea^F* · *fusa^F*

---

noun *n* : nombre *m*, sustantivo *m*

nourish *vt* : nutrir — **nourishing** *adj* : nutritivo — **nourishment** *n* : alimento *m*

novel *adj* : original, novedoso — **novel** *n* : novela *f* — **novelist** *n* : novelista *mf* — **novelty** *n, pl* **-ties** : novedad *f*

November *n* : noviembre *m*

novice *n* : novato *m*, -ta *f*; principiante *mf*

now *adv* **1** : ahora **2** THEN : entonces **3** from now on : de ahora en adelante **4** now and then : de vez en cuando **5** right now : ahora mismo — **now** *conj* *or* **now that** : ahora que, ya que — **now** *n* **1 a year from now** : dentro de un año **2 by now** : ya **3 until now** : hasta ahora — **nowadays** *adv* : hoy en día

nowhere *adv* **1** (*indicating location*) : por ninguna parte, por ningún lado **2** (*indicating motion*) : a ninguna parte, a ningún lado **3 I'm nowhere near finished** : aún me falta mucho para terminar **4 it's nowhere near here** : queda bastante lejos de aquí — **nowhere** *n* : ninguna parte *f*

nozzle *n* : boca *f* (de una manguera, etc.)

nuance *n* : matiz *m*

nucleus *n, pl* **-clei** : núcleo *m* — **nuclear** *adj* : nuclear

nude *adj* **nuder; nudest** : desnudo — **nude** *n* : desnudo *m*

nudge *vt* **nudged; nudging** : dar un codazo a — **nudge** *n* : toque *m* (con el codo)

nudity *n* : desnudez *f*

nugget *n* : pepita *f* (de oro, etc.)

nuisance *n* **1** ANNOYANCE : fastidio *m*, molestia *f* **2** PEST : pesado *m*, -da *f fam*

null *adj* **null and void** : nulo y sin efecto

numb *adj* **1** : entumecido, dormido **2 numb with fear** : paralizado de miedo — **numb** *vt* : entumecer, adormecer

number *n* **1** : número *m* **2 a number of** : varios — **number** *vt* **1** : numerar **2** INCLUDE : contar, incluir **3** TOTAL : ascender a

numeral *n* : número *m* — **numeric** *or* **numerical** *adj* : numérico — **numerous** *adj* : numeroso

nun *n* : monja *f*

nuptial *adj* : nupcial

nurse *n* **1** : enfermero *m*, -ra *f* **2** → **nursemaid** — **nurse** *vt* **nursed; nursing 1** : cuidar (de), atender **2** SUCKLE : amamantar — **nursemaid** *n* : niñera *f* — **nursery** *n, pl* **-eries 1** : cuarto *m* de los niños **2** *or* **day nursery** : guardería *f* **3** : vivero *m* (de plantas) — **nursing home** *n* : asilo *m* de ancianos

nurture *vt* **-tured; -turing 1** NOURISH : nutrir **2** EDUCATE : criar, educar **3** FOSTER : alimentar

nut *n* **1** : nuez *f* **2** LUNATIC : loco *m*, -ca *f* **3** ENTHUSIAST : fanático *m*, -ca *f* **4 nuts and bolts** : tuercas y tornillos — **nutcracker** *n* : cascanueces *m*

nutmeg *n* : nuez *f* moscada

nutrient *n* : nutriente *m*

nutrition *n* : nutrición *f* — **nutritional** *adj* : nutritivo — **nutritious** *adj* : nutritivo

nuts *adj* : loco

nutshell *n* **1** : cáscara *f* de nuez **2 in a nutshell** : en pocas palabras

nutty *adj* **-tier; -tiest** : loco

nuzzle *v* **-zled; -zling** *vi* : acurrucarse — *vt* : acariciar con el hocico

nylon *n* **1** : nilón *m* **2 nylons** *npl* : medias *fpl* de nilón

nymph *n* : ninfa *f*

o *n, pl* **o's** *or* **os 1** : o *f*, decimoquinta letra del alfabeto inglés **2** ZERO : cero *m*

O → **oh**

oaf *n* : zoquete *m*

▸ **oak** *n, pl* **oaks** *or* **oak** : roble *m*

oar *n* : remo *m*

oasis *n, pl* **oases** : oasis *m*

oath *n, pl* **oaths 1** : juramento *m* **2** SWEARWORD : palabrota *f*

oats *npl* : avena *f* — **oatmeal** *n* : harina *f* de avena

obedient *adj* : obediente — **obedience** *n* : obediencia *f*

obese *adj* : obeso — **obesity** *n* : obesidad *f*

obey *v* **obeyed; obeying** : obedecer

obituary *n, pl* **-aries** : obituario *m*

object *n* **1** : objeto *m* **2** AIM : objetivo *m* **3** : complemento *m* (en gramática) — **object** *vt* : objetar — *vi* **object to** : oponerse a — **objection** *n* : objeción *f* — **objectionable** *adj* : desagradable — **objective** *adj* : objetivo — **objective** *n* : objetivo *m*

oblige *vt* **obliged; obliging 1** : obligar **2**

be much obliged : estar muy agradecido **3 oblige someone** : hacer un favor a algn — **obligation** *n* : obligación *f* — **obligatory** *adj* : obligatorio — **obliging** *adj* : atento, servicial

oblique *adj* **1** SLANTING : oblicuo **2** INDIRECT : indirecto

obliterate *vt* **-ated; -ating 1** ERASE : borrar **2** DESTROY : arrasar

oblivion *n* : olvido *m* — **oblivious** *adj* : inconsciente

oblong *adj* : oblongo — **oblong** *n* : rectángulo *m*

obnoxious *adj* : odioso

oboe *n* : oboe *m*

obscene *adj* : obsceno — **obscenity** *n, pl* **-ties** : obscenidad *f*

obscurity *n, pl* **-ties** : oscuridad *f* — **obscure** *adj* : oscuro — **obscurity** *vt* **-scured; -scuring 1** DARKEN : oscurecer **2** HIDE : ocultar

observe *v* **-served; -serving** *vt* : observar — *vi* WATCH : mirar — **observance** *n* **1** : observancia *f* **2 religious observes** : prácticas *fpl*

religiosas — **observant** *adj* : observador — **observation** *n* : observación *f* — **observatory** *n, pl* **-ries** : observatorio *m*

obsess *vt* : obsesionar — **obsession** *n* : obsesión *f* — **obsessive** *adj* : obsesivo

obsolete *adj* : obsoleto, desusado

obstacle *n* : obstáculo *m*

obstetrics *n* : obstetricia *f*

obstinate *adj* : obstinado

obstruct *vt* **1** BLOCK : obstruir **2** HINDER : obstaculizar — **obstruction** *n* : obstrucción *f*

obtain *vt* : obtener, conseguir — **obtainable** *adj* : asequible

obtrusive *adj* : entrometido (dícese de las personas), demasiado prominente (dícese de las cosas)

obtuse *adj* : obtuso

obvious *adj* : obvio, evidente — **obviously** *adv* **1** CLEARLY : obviamente **2** OF COURSE : claro, por supuesto

occasion *n* **1** : ocasión *f* **2 on occasion** : de vez en cuando — **occasion** *vt* : ocasionar — **occasional** *adj* : poco frecuente, ocasional — **occasionally** *adv* : de vez en cuando

occult *adj* : oculto

occupy *vt* **-pied; -pying 1** : ocupar **2 occupy oneself** : entretenerse — **occupancy** *n, pl* **-cies** : ocupación *f* — **occupant** *n* : ocupante *mf* — **occupation** *n* : ocupación *f* — **occupational** *adj* : profesional

occur *vi* **occurred; occurring 1** : ocurrir **2** APPEAR : encontrarse **3 occur to someone** : ocurrirse a algn — **occurrence** *n* **1** EVENT : acontecimiento *m*, suceso *m* **2** INCIDENCE : incidencia *f*

ocean *n* : océano *m*

ocher *or* **ochre** *n* : ocre *m*

o'clock *adv* **1 at 6 o'clock** : a las seis **2 it's one o'clock** : es la una **3 it's ten o'clock** : son las diez

octagon *n* : octágono *m* — **octagonal** *adj* : octagonal

octave *n* : octava *f*

October *n* : octubre *m*

octopus *n, pl* **-puses** *or* **-pi** : pulpo *m*

oculist *n* : oculista *mf*

odd *adj* **1** STRANGE : extraño, raro **2** : sin pareja (dícese de un calcetín, etc.) **3 forty odd years** : cuarenta y tantos años **4 odd jobs** : algunos trabajos *mpl* **5 odd number** : número *m* impar — **oddity** *n, pl* **-ties** : rareza *f* — **oddly** *adv* : de manera extraña

oak
roble *M*

onions
cebollas^F

yellow onion
cebolla^F amarilla

red onion
cebolla^F roja

pearl onion
cebolleta^F

white onion
cebolla^F blanca

green onion
cebolla^F tierna

— **odds** *npl* **1** CHANCES : probabilidades *fpl*
2 at odds : en desacuerdo **3 five to one
odds** : cinco contra uno (en apuestas) —
odds and ends *npl* : cosas *fpl* sueltas
ode *n* : oda *f*
odious *adj* : odioso
odor *or Brit* **odour** *n* : olor *m* — **odorless**
or Brit **odourless** *adj* : inodoro
of *prep* **1** : de **2 five minutes of
ten** : las diez menos cinco **3 the
eighth of April** : el ocho de abril
off *adv* **1 be off** LEAVE : irse **2 cut off** :
cortar **3 day off** : día *m* de descanso **4
fall off** : caerse **5 doze off** : dormirse
6 far off : lejos **7 off and on** : de vez
en cuando **8 shut off** : apagar **9 ten
miles off** : a diez millas de aquí —
off *prep* **1** : de **2 be off duty** : estar libre
3 off center : descentrado — **off** *adj* **1**
CANCELED : cancelado **2** OUT : apagado **3
an off chance** : una posibilidad remota
offend *vt* : ofender — **offender** *n* :
delincuente *mf* — **offense** *or* **offence** *n* **1**
AFFRONT : afrenta *f* **2** ASSAULT : ataque *m* **3** :
ofensiva *f* (en deportes) **4** CRIME : delito *m* **5**
take offense : ofenderse — **offensive** *adj*
: ofensivo — **offensive** *n* : ofensiva *f*
offer *vt* : ofrecer — **offer** *n* : oferta *f*
— **offering** *n* : ofrenda *f*
offhand *adv* : de improviso, en este
momento — **offhand** *adj* : improvisado
office *n* **1** : oficina *f* **2** POSITION : cargo *m*
3 run for office : presentarse como
candiiato — **officer** *n* **1** : oficial *mf*
2 *or* **police office** : agente *mf* (de
policía) — **official** *n* : funcionario *m*,
-ria *f* — **office** *adj* : oficial
offing *n* **in the offing** : en perspectiva
offset *vt* **-set; -setting** : compensar
offshore *adv* : a una distancia de la costa
offspring *ns & pl* : prole *f*, progenie *f*
often *adv* **1** : muchas veces, a
menudo, con frecuencia **2 every
so often** : de vez en cuando
ogle *vt* **ogled; ogling** :
comerse con los ojos
ogre *n* : ogro *m*
oh *interj* **1** : ¡oh!, ¡ah! **2 oh no!** : ¡ay
no! **3 oh really?** : ¿de veras?
oil *n* **1** : aceite *m* **2** PETROLEUM : petróleo *m*
3 *or* **oil painting** : óleo *m* — **oil** *vt* :
lubricar — **oilskin** *n* : hule *m* — **oily** *adj*
oilier; -est : aceitoso, grasiento
ointment *n* : ungüento *m*, pomada *f*
OK *or* okay *adv* **1** : muy bien **2** OK! :

¡de acuerdo!, ¡bueno! — **OK** *adj* **1** ALL
RIGHT : bien **2 it's OK with me** : por
mí no hay problema — **OK** *n* : visto *m*
bueno — **OK** *vt* **OK'd** *or* **okayed; OK'ing**
or **okaying** : dar el visto bueno a
okra *n* : quingombó *m*
old *adj* **1** : viejo **2** FORMER : antiguo **3 any
old** : cualquier **4 be ten years old** : tener
diez años (de edad) **5 old age** : vejez *f*
6 old man : anciano *m* **7 old woman** :
anciana *f* — **old** *n* **the old** : los viejos, los
ancianos — **old-fashioned** *adj* : anticuado
olive *n* **1** : aceituna *f* (fruta) **2** *or*
olive green : verde *m* oliva
Olympic *adj* : olímpico —
Olympics *npl* **the Olympic** : las
Olimpiadas, las Olimpíadas
omelet *or* **omelette** *n* : omelette *mf*
Lat, tortilla *f* francesa *Spain*
omen *n* : agüero *m* — **ominous** *adj*
: ominoso, de mal agüero
omit *vt* **omitted; omitting** : omitir
— **omission** *n* : omisión *f*
omnipotent *adj* : omnipotente
on *prep* **1** : en **2** ABOUT : sobre **3 on foot**
: a pie **4 on Monday** : el lunes **5 on the
right** : a la derecha **6 on vacation** : de
vacaciones **7 talk on the phone** : hablar
por teléfono — **on** *adv* **1 and so on** :

etcétera **2 from that moment on** : a partir
de ese momento **3 keep on** : seguir **4 later
on** : más tarde **5 on and on** : sin parar **6
put on** : ponerse (ropa), poner (música,
etc.) **7 turn on** : encender (una luz, etc.),
abrir (una llave) — **on** *adj* **1** : encendido
(dícese de luces, etc.), abierto (dícese de
llaves) **2 be on to** : estar enterado de
once *adv* **1** : una vez **2** FORMERLY
: antes — **once** *n* **1 at once**
TOGETHER : al mismo tiempo **2 at
once** IMMEDIATELY : inmediatamente
— **once** *conj* : una vez que
oncoming *adj* : que viene
one *adj* **1** : un, uno **2** ONLY : único **3** *or* **one
and the same** : el mismo — **one** *n* **1** :
uno *m* (número) **2 one by one** : uno a uno
— **one** *pron* **1** : uno, una **2 one another** : el
uno al otro **3 one never knows** : nunca se
sabe **4 that one** : aquél, aquella **5 which
one?** : ¿cuál? — **oneself** *pron* **1** (*used
reflexively*) : se **2** (*used after prepositions*)
: sí mismo, sí misma **3** (*used emphatically*)
: uno mismo, una misma **4 by oneself**
: solo — **one-sided** *adj* **1** UNEQUAL :
desigual **2** BIASED : parcial — **one-way** *adj*
1 : de sentido único (dícese de una calle)
2 one-way ticket : boleto *m* de ida
ongoing *adj* : en curso, corrinte
▸ **onion** *n* : cebolla *f*

symphony orchestra
orquestra^F sinfónica

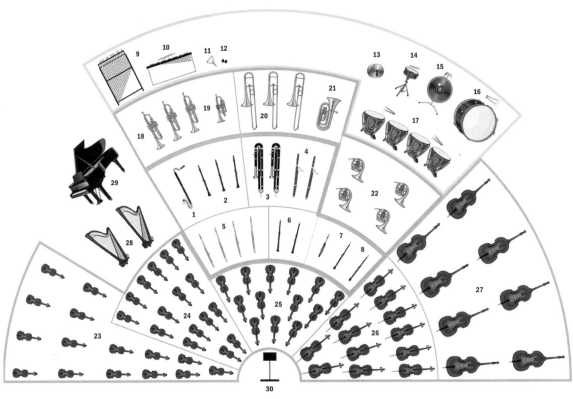

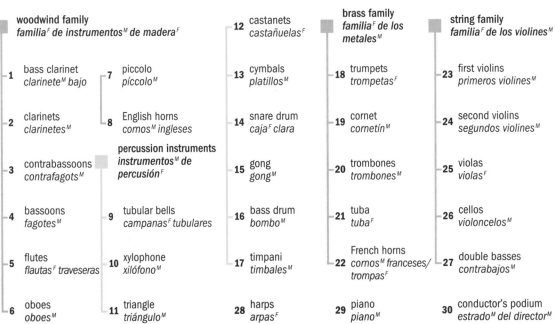

woodwind family
familia^F de instrumentos^M de madera^F

- **1** bass clarinet
  clarinete^M bajo

- **2** clarinets
  clarinetes^M

- **3** contrabassoons
  contrafagots^M

- **4** bassoons
  fagotes^M

- **5** flutes
  flautas^F traveseras

- **6** oboes
  oboes^M

- **7** piccolo
  píccolo^M

- **8** English horns
  cornos^M ingleses

percussion instruments
instrumentos^M de percusión^F

- **9** tubular bells
  campanas^F tubulares

- **10** xylophone
  xilófono^M

- **11** triangle
  triángulo^M

- **12** castanets
  castañuelas^F

- **13** cymbals
  platillos^M

- **14** snare drum
  caja^F clara

- **15** gong
  gong^M

- **16** bass drum
  bombo^M

- **17** timpani
  timbales^M

- **28** harps
  arpas^F

brass family
familia^F de los metales^M

- **18** trumpets
  trompetas^F

- **19** cornet
  cornetín^M

- **20** trombones
  trombones^M

- **21** tuba
  tuba^F

- **22** French horns
  cornos^M franceses/trompas^F

- **29** piano
  piano^M

string family
familia^F de los violines^M

- **23** first violins
  primeros violines^M

- **24** second violins
  segundos violines^M

- **25** violas
  violas^F

- **26** cellos
  violoncelos^M

- **27** double basses
  contrabajos^M

- **30** conductor's podium
  estrado^M del director^M

only *adj* : único — **only** *adv* **1** : sólo, solamente **2 if only** : ojalá, por lo menos — **only** *conj* BUT : pero

onset *n* : comienzo *m*, llegada *f*

onslaught *n* : ataque *m*, arremetida *f*

onto *prep* : sobre

onus *n* : responsabilidad *f*

onward *adv & adj* : hacia adelante

onyx *n* : ónix *m*

ooze *v* **oozed; oozing** : rezumar

opal *n* : ópalo *m*

opaque *adj* : opaco

open *adj* **1** : abierto **2** AVAILABLE : vacante, libre **3 an open question** : una cuestión pendiente — **open** *vt* : abrir — *vi* **1** : abrirse **2** BEGIN : comenzar — **open** *n* **in the open 1** OUTDOORS : al aire libre **2** KNOWN : sacado a la luz — **open–air** *adj* : al aire libre — **opener** *n* **1** : abridor *m* **2** *or* **bottle open** : abrebotellas *m* **3** *or* **can opener** : abrelatas *m* — **opening** *n* **1** : abertura *f* **2** BEGINNING : comienzo *m*, apertura *f* **3** OPPORTUNITY : opportunidad *f* — **openly** *adv* : abiertamente

opera *n* : ópera *f*

operate *v* **-ated; -ating** *vi* **1** FUNCTION : funcionar **2 operate on someone** : operar a algn — *vt* **1** : hacer funcionar (una máquina) **2** MANAGE : dirigir, manejar — **operation** *n* **1** : operación *f* **2** FUNCTIONING : funcionamiento *m* — **operational** *adj* : operacional — **operative** *adj* : en vigor — **operator** *n* **1** : operador *m*, -dora *f* **2** *or* **machine operator** : operario *m*, -ria *f*

opinion *n* : opinión *f* — **opinionated** *adj* : dogmático

opium *n* : opio *m*

opossum *n* : zarigüeya *f*, oposum *m*

opponent *n* : adversario *m*, -ria *f*; contrincante *mf* (en deportes)

opportunity *n*, *pl* **-ties** : oportunidad *f* — **opportune** *adj* : oportuno — **opportunist** *n* : oportunista *mf*

oppose *vt* **-posed; -posing** : oponerse a — **opposed** *adj* **oppose to** : en contra de

opposite *adj* **1** FACING : de enfrente **2** CONTRARY : opuesto — **opposite** *n* **the opposite** : lo contrario, lo opuesto — **opposite** *adv* : enfrente — **opposite** *prep* : enfrente de, frente a — **opposition** *n* **1** : oposición *f* **2 in opposition to** : en contra de

oppress *vt* : oprimir — **oppression** *n* : opresión *f* — **oppressive** *adj* **1** : opresivo **2** STIFLING : agobiante

— **oppressor** *n* : opresor *m*, -sora *f*

opt *vi* **opt for** : optar por

optic *or* **optical** *adj* : óptico — **optician** *n* : óptico *m*, -ca *f*

optimism *n* : optimismo *m* — **optimist** *n* : optimista *mf* — **optimistic** *adj* : optimista

optimum *n*, *pl* **-ma** : lo óptimo, lo ideal

option *n* **1** : opción *f* **2 have no option** : no tenerr más remedio — **optional** *adj* : facultativo, opcional

opulence *n* : opulencia *f* — **opulent** *adj* : opulento

or *conj* **1** (*indicating an alternative*) : o (u *before* o- *or* ho-) **2** (*following a negative*) : ni **3 or else** : si no

oracle *n* : oráculo *m*

oral *adj* : oral

▶ **orange** *n* **1** : naranja *f* (fruta) **2** : naranja *m* (color)

orator *n* : orador *m*, -dora *f*

orbit *n* : órbita *f* — **orbit** *vt* : girar alrededor de — *vi* : orbitar

orchard *n* : huerto *m*

▶ **orchestra** *n* : orquesta *f*

orchid *n* : orquídea *f*

ordain *vt* **1** : ordenar (un sacerdote, etc.) **2** DECREE : decretar

ordeal *n* : prueba *f* dura

order *vt* **1** : ordenar **2** : pedir (mercancías, etc.) — *vi* : hacer un pedido — **order** *n*

1 ARRANGEMENT : orden *m* **2** COMMAND : orden *f* **3** REQUEST : pedido *m* **4** : orden *f* (religiosa) **5 in order that** : para que **6 in order to** : para **7 out of order** : averiado, descompuesto *Lat* — **orderly** *adj* : ordenado — **orderly** *n*, *pl* **-lies 1** : ordenanza *m* (en el ejército) **2** : camillero *m* (en un hospital)

ordinary *adj* **1** : normal, corriente **2** MEDIOCRE : ordinario — **ordinarily** *adv* : generalmente

ore *n* : mena *f*

oregano *n* : orégano *m*

organ *n* : órgano *m* — **organic** *adj* : orgánico — **organism** *n* : organismo *m* — **organist** *n* : organista *mf* — **organize** *vt* **-nized; -nizing** : organizar — **organization** *n* : organización *f* — **organizer** *n* : organizador *m*, -dora *f*

orgasm *n* : orgasmo *m*

orgy *n*, *pl* **-gies** : orgía *f*

Orient *n* **the Orient** : el Oriente — **orient** *vt* : orientar — **oriental** *adj* : del Oriente, oriental — **orientation** *n* : orientación *f*

orifice *n* : orificio *m*

origin *n* : origen *m* — **original** *n* : original *m* — **origin** *adj* : original — **originality** *n* : originalidad *f*

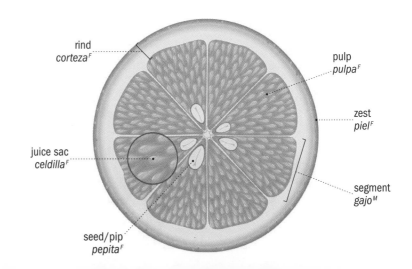

section of an orange
corteᴹ **de una naranja**ᶠ

rind
*corteza*ᶠ

pulp
*pulpa*ᶠ

zest
*piel*ᶠ

juice sac
*celdilla*ᶠ

seed/pip
*pepita*ᶠ

segment
*gajo*ᴹ

— **originally** *adv* : originariamente
— **originate** *v* -nated; -nating *vt*
: originar — *vi* **1** : originarse **2**
originate from : provenir de —
originator *n* : creador *m*, -dora *f*
ornament *n* : adorno *m* — **ornament** *vt*
: adornar — **ornamental** *adj* :
ornamental, de adorno — **ornate** *adj*
: elaborado, adornado
ornithology *n*, *pl* -gies : ornitología *f*
orphan *n* : huérfano *m*, -na *f*
— **orphan** *vt* : dejar huérfano —
orphanage *n* : orfelinato *m*, orfanato *m*
orthodox *adj* : ortodoxo —
orthodoxy *n*, *pl* -doxies : ortodoxia *f*
orthopedic *adj* : ortopédico
oscillation *n* : oscilación *f* —
oscillate *vi* -lated; -lating : oscilar
ostensible *adj* : aparente, ostensible
ostentation *n* : ostentación *f* —
ostentatious *adj* : ostentoso
osteopath *n* : osteópata *f*
ostracism *n* : ostracismo *m* —
ostracize *vt* -cized; -cizing : aislar
ostrich *n* : avestruz *m*
other *adj* **1** : otro **2 every other day** : cada
dos días **3 on the other hand** : por otra
parte, por otro lado — **other** *pron* **1** : otro,
otra **2 the others** : los otros, las otras, los
demás, las demás — **other than** *prep* :
aparte de, fuera de — **otherwise** *adv* **1**
: eso aparte, por lo demás **2** DIFFERENTLY
: de otro modo **3** OR ELSE : si no
▸ **otter** *n* : nutria *f*
ought *v aux* **1** : deber **2 you ought to**
have done it : deberías haberlo hecho

ounce *n* : onza *f*
our *adj* : nuestro — **ours** *pron* **1** : (el)
nuestro, (la) nuestra, (los) nuestros, (las)
nuestras **2 a friend of ours** : un amigo
nuestro — **ourselves** *pron* **1** (*used*
reflexively) : nos **2** (*used after prepositions*)
: nosotros, nosotras **3** (*used for emphasis*)
: nosotros mismos, nosotras mismas
oust *vt* : desbancar
out *adv* **1** OUTSIDE : fuera, afuera **2 cry**
out : gritar **3 eat out** : comer afuera **4**
go out : salir **5 look out** : mirar para
afuera **6 run out of** : agotar **7 turn out**
: apagar (una luz) **8 take out** REMOVE :
sacar — **out** *prep* → **out of** — **out** *adj*
1 ABSENT : ausente **2** UNFASHIONABLE
: fuera de moda **3** EXTINGUISHED :
apagado **4 the sun is out** : hace sol
outboard motor *n* :
motor *m* fuera de borde
outbreak *n* : brote *m* (de una
enfermedad), comienzo *m* (de guerra)
outburst *n* : arranque *m*, arrebato *m*
outcast *n* : paria *mf*
outcome *n* : resultado *m*
outcry *n*, *pl* -cries : protesta *f*
outdated *adj* : anticuado
outdo *vt* -did; -done; -doing;
-does : superar
outdoor *adj* : al aire libre —
outdoors *adv* : al aire libre
outer *adj* : exterior — **outer**
space *n* : espacio *m* exterior
outfit *n* **1** EQUIPMENT : equipo *m* **2**
CLOTHES : conjunto *m* — **outfit** *vt*
-fitted; -fitting EQUIP : equipar

outgoing *adj* **1** SOCIABLE : extrovertido
2 outgoing mail : correo *m* (para
enviar) **3 outgoing president** :
presidente *m*, -ta *f* saliente
outgrow *vt* -grew; -grown;
-growing : crecer más que
outing *n* : excursión *f*
outlandish *adj* : estrafalario
outlast *vt* : durar más que
outlaw *n* : forajido *m*, -da *f* —
outlaw *vt* : declarar ilegal
outlay *n* : desembolso *m*
outlet *n* **1** EXIT : salida *f* **2** RELEASE :
desahogo *m* **3** *or* **electrical outlet**
: toma *f* de corriente **4** *or* **retail**
outlet : tienda *f* al por menor
outline *n* **1** CONTOUR : contorno *m*
2 SKETCH : bosquejo *m*, boceto *m* **3**
SUMMARY : esquema *m* — **outline** *vt*
-lined; -lining **1** SKETCH : bosquejar
2 EXPLAIN : delinear, esbozar
outlive *vt* -lived; -living : sobrevivir a
outlook *n* **1** PROSPECTS : perspectivas *fpl*
2 VIEWPOINT : punto *m* de vista
outlying *adj* : alejado, distante
outmoded *adj* : pasado
de moda, anticuado
outnumber *vt* : superar en número a
out of *prep* **1** FROM : de **2** THROUGH :
por **3** WITHOUT : sin **4 out of curiosity**
: por curiosidad **5 out of control** :
fuera de control **6 one out of four**
: uno de cada cuatro — **out–of–**
date *adj* : anticuado — **out–of–door**
or **out–of–doors** *adj* → **outdoor**
outpatient *n* : paciente *m* externo
outpost *n* : puesto *m* avanzado
output *n* **1** : producción *f*, rendimiento *m*
2 : salida *f* (informática) — **output** *vt*
-putted *or* -put; -putting : producir
outrage *n* **1** : atrocidad *f*, escándalo *m*
2 ANGER : ira *f*, indignación *f* —
outrage *vt* -raged; -raging : ultrajar
— **outrageous** *adj* : escandaloso
outright *adv* **1** COMPLETELY : por
completo **2** INSTANTLY : en el acto —
outright *adj* : completo, absoluto
outset *n* : comienzo *m*, principio *m*
outside *n* **1** : exterior *m* **2 from the**
outside : desde fuera, desde afuera
— **outside** *adj* **1** : exterior, externo **2**
an outside chance : una posibilidad
remota — **outside** *adv* : fuera, afuera
— **outside** *prep* *or* **outside of** : fuera
de — **outsider** *n* : forastero *m*, -ra *f*
outskirts *npl* : afueras *fpl*,

river otter
nutria^F

alrededores *mpl*

outspoken *adj* : franco, directo

outstanding *adj* **1** UNPAID : pendiente
2 EXCELLENT : excepcional

outstretched *adj* : extendido

outstrip *vt* **-stripped** *or* **-stript;**
-stripping : aventajar

outward *adj* **1** : hacia afuera
2 EXTERNAL : externo, external
— **outward** *or* **outwards** *adv* :
hacia afuera — **outwardly** *adv*
APPARENTLY : aparentemente

outweigh *vt* : pesar más que

outwit *vt* **-witted; -witting**
: ser más listo que

oval *n* : óvalo *m* — **oval** *adj* : ovalado

ovary *n*, *pl* **-ries** : ovario *m*

ovation *n* : ovación *f*

oven *n* : horno *m*

over *adv* **1** ABOVE : por encima **2** AGAIN :
otra vez, de nuevo **3** MORE : más **4 all over**
: por todas partes **5 ask over** : invitar **6
cross over** : cruzar **7 fall over** : caerse **8
over and over** : una y otra vez **9 over here**
: aquí **10 over there** : allí — **over** *prep* **1**
ABOVE, UPON : encima de, sobre **2** ACROSS
: por encima de, sobre **3** DURING : en,
durante **4 fight over** : pelearse por **5 over
$5** : más de $5 **6 over the phone** : por
teléfono — **over** *adj* : terminado, acabado

overall *adv* GENERALLY : en general
— *adj* : total, en conjunto —
overalls *npl* : overol *m*, *Lat*

overbearing *adj* : dominante, imperioso

overboard *adv* **fall overboard**
: caer al agua

overburden *vt* : sobrecargar

overcast *adj* : nublado

overcharge *vt* **-charged;**
-charging : cobrar demasiado

overcoat *n* : abrigo *m*

overcome *v* **-came; -come;**
-coming *vt* **1** CONQUER : vencer **2**
OVERWHELM : agobiar — *vi* : vencer

overcook *vt* : cocer demasiado

overcrowded *adj* : abarrotado de gente

overdo *vt* **-did; -done; -doing; -does**
1 : hacer demasiado **2** EXAGGERATE
: exagerar **3** → **overcook**

overdose *n* : sobredosis *f*

overdraw *vt* **-drew; -drawn; -drawing**
: girar en descubierto — **overdraft** *n*
: sobregiro *m*, descubierto *m*

overdue *adj* : fuera de plazo
(dícese de pagos, libros, etc.)

overeat *vi* **-ate; -eaten; -eating**

: comer demasiado

overestimate *vt* **-mated;**
-mating : sobreestimar

overflow *vt* : desbordar — *vi*
: desbordarse — **overflow** *n* :
desbordamiento *m* (de un río)

overgrown *adj* : cubierto
(de malas hierbas, etc.)

overhand *adv* : por encima de la cabeza

overhang *v* **-hung; -hanging** : sobresalir

overhaul *vt* : revisar (un motor, etc.)

overhead *adv* : por encima
— **overhead** *adj* : de arriba —
overhead *n* : gastos *mpl* generales

overhear *vt* **-heard; -hearing**
: oír por casualidad

overheat *vt* : calentar demasiado
— *vi* : recalentarse

overjoyed *adj* : encantado

overland *adv & adj* : por tierra

overlap *v* **-lapped; -lapping** *vt* :
traslapar — *vi* : traslaparse

overload *vt* : sobrecargar

overlook *vt* **1** : dar a (un jardín, el
mar, etc.) **2** MISS : pasar por alto

overly *adv* : demasiado

overnight *adv* **1** : por la noche
2 SUDDENLY : de la noche a la
mañana — **overnight** *adj* **1** : de
noche **2** SUDDEN : repentino

overpass *n* : paso *m* elevado

overpopulated *adj* : superpoblado

overpower *vt* **1** SUBDUE : dominar
2 OVERWHELM : agobiar, abrumar

overrated *adj* : sobreestimado

override *vt* **-rode; -ridden;**
-riding 1 : predominar sobre **2** :
anular (una decisión, etc.)

overrule *vt* **-ruled; -ruling** : anular (una
decisión), rechazar (una protesta)

overrun *vt* **-ran; -running 1** INVADE
: invadir **2** EXCEED : exceder

overseas *adv* : en el extranjero —
overseas *adj* : extranjero, exterior

oversee *vt* **-saw; -seen;**
-seeing : supervisar

overshadow *vt* : eclipsar

oversight *n* : descuido *m*

oversleep *vi* **-slept; -sleeping**
: quedarse dormido

overstep *vt* **-stepped;**
-stepping : sobrepasar

overt *adj* : manifiesto

overtake *vt* **-took; -taken; -taking 1**
PASS : adelantar **2** SURPASS : superar

overthrow *vt* **-threw; -thrown;**

great horned owl
búho^*M* **real**

-throwing : derrocar

overtime *n* **1** : horas *fpl* extras (de
trabajo) **2** : prórroga *f* (en deportes)

overtone *n* SUGGESTION :
tinte *m*, insinuación *f*

overture *n* : obertura *f* (en música)

overturn *vt* **1** : dar la vuelta a **2**
NULLIFY : anular — *vi* : volcar

overweight *adj* : demasiado gordo

overwhelm *vt* **1** : abrumar,
agobiar **2** : aplastar (a un
enemigo) — **overwhelming** *adj*
: abrumador, apabullante

overwork *vt* : hacer trabajar demasiado
— *vi* : trabajar demasiado

overwrought *adj* : alterado, sobreexitado

owe *vt* **owed; owing** : deber —
owing to *prep* : debido a

▸ **owl** *n* : búho *m*

own *adj* : propio — **own** *vt* : poseer, tener
— *vi* **own up** : confesar — **own** *pron* **1**
my (your, his/her/their, our) **own** : el mío,
la mía; el tuyo, la tuya; el suyo, la suya; el
nuestro, la nuestra **2 be on one's own** :
estar solo **3 to each his own** : cada uno
a lo suyo — **owner** *n* : propietario *m*,
-ria *f* — **ownership** *n* : propiedad *f*

ox *n*, *pl* **oxen** : buey *m*

oxygen *n* : oxígeno *m*

oyster *n* : ostra *f*

ozone *n* : ozono *m*

p *n, pl* **p's** *or* **ps** : p *f*, decimosexta letra del alfabeto inglés

pace *n* **1** STEP : paso *m* **2** RATE : ritmo *m* **3 keep pace with** : andar al mismo paso que — **pace** *vi* **paced; pacing** *or* **pace up and down** : caminar de arriba para abajo

pacify *vt* **-fied; -fying** : apaciguar — **pacifier** *n* : chupete *m* — **pacifist** *n* : pacifista *mf*

pack *n* **1** BUNDLE : fardo *m* **2** BACKPACK : mochila *f* **3** PACKAGE : paquete *m* **4** : baraja *f* (de naipes) **5** : manada *f* (de lobos, etc.), jauría *f* (de perros) — **pack** *vt* **1** PACKAGE : empaquetar **2** FILL : llenar **3** : hacer (una maleta) — *vi* : hacer las maletas — **package** *vt* **-aged; -aging** : empaquetar — **pack** *n* : paquete *m* — **packet** *n* : paquete *m*

pact *n* : pacto *m*, acuerdo *m*

pad *n* **1** CUSHION : almohadilla *f* **2** TABLET : bloc *m* (de papel) **3** *or* **ink pad** : tampón *m* **4 launching pad** : plataforma *f* (de lanzamiento) — **pad** *vt* **padded; padding** : rellenar — **padding** *n* **1** : relleno *m* **2** : paja *f* (en un discurso, etc.)

paddle *n* **1** : canalete *m* (de una canoa) **2** : pala *f*, paleta *f* (en deportes)

parrot
loro *M*

— **paddle** *vt* **-dled; -dling** : hacer avanzar (una canoa) con canalete

padlock *n* : candado *m* — **padlock** *vt* : cerrar con candado

pagan *n* : pagano *m*, -na *f* — **pagan** *adj* : pagano

page[1] *vt* **paged; paging** : llamar por altavoz

page[2] *n* : página *f* (de un libro, etc.)

pageant *n* : espectáculo *m* — **pageantry** *n* : pompa *f*, boato *m*

paid → **pay**

pail *n* : cubo *m* *Spain*, cubeta *f Lat*

pain *n* **1** : dolor *m* **2** : pena *f* (mental) **3 pains** *npl* EFFORT : esfuerzos *mpl* — **pain** *vt* : doler — **painful** *adj* : doloroso — **painkiller** *n* : analgésico *m* — **painless** *adj* : indoloro, sin dolor — **painstaking** *adj* : meticuloso, esmerado

paint *v* : pintar — **paint** *n* : pintura *f* — **paintbrush** *n* : pincel *m* (de un artista), brocha *f* (para pintar casas, etc.) — **painter** *n* : pintor *m*, -tora *f* — **painting** *n* : pintura *f*

pair *n* **1** : par *m* **2** COUPLE : pareja *f* — **pair** *vt* : emparejar

pajamas *npl* : pijama *m*, piyama *mf Lat*

Pakistani *adj* : paquistaní

pal *n* : amigo *m*, -ga *f*

palace *n* : palacio *m*

palate *n* : paladar *m* — **palatable** *adj* : sabroso

pale *adj* **paler; palest 1** PALLID : pálido **2** : claro (dícese de los colores, etc.) — **pale** *vi* **paled; paling** : palidecer — **paleness** *n* : palidez *f*

Palestinian *adj* : palestino

palette *n* : paleta *f*

pallbearer *n* : portador *m*, -dora *f* del féretro

pallid *adj* : pálido — **pallor** *n* : palidez *f*

palm[1] *n* : palma *f* (de la mano)

palm[2] *or* **palm tree** : palmera *f* — **Palm Sunday** *n* : Domingo *m* de Ramos

palpitate *vi* **-tated; -tating** : palpitar — **palpitation** *n* : palpitación *f*

paltry *adj* **-trier; -est** : mísero, mezquino

pamper *vt* : mimar

pamphlet *n* : panfleto *m*, folleto *m*

pan *n* **1** SAUCEPAN : cacerola *f* **2** FRYING PAN : sartén *mf* — **pan** *vt* **panned; panning** CRITICIZE : poner por los suelos

pancake *n* : crepe *mf*, panqueque *m, Lat*

panda *n* : panda *mf*

pandemonium *n* : pandemonio *m*

pander *vi* **pander to** : complacer a

pane *n* : cristal *m*, vidrio *m*

panel *n* **1** : panel *m* **2** GROUP : jurado *m* **3** *or* **instrument panel** : tablero *m* (de instrumentos) — **panel** *vt* **-eled** *or* **-elled; -eling** *or* **-elling** : adornar con paneles — **paneling** *n* : paneles *mpl*

pang *n* : punzada *f*

panic *n* : pánico *m* — **panic** *v* **-icked; -icking** *vt* : llenar del pánico — *vi* : ser presa del pánico — **panicky** *adj* : presa de pánico

panorama *n* : panorama *m* — **panoramic** *adj* : panorámico

pansy *n, pl* **-sies** : pensamiento *m*

pant *vi* : jadear, resoplar

panther *n* : pantera *f*

panties *npl* : bragas *fpl Spain*, calzones *mpl Lat*

pantomime *n* : pantomima *f*

pantry *n, pl* **-tries** : despensa *f*

pants *npl* TROUSERS : pantalón *m*, pantalones *mpl*

papa *n* : papá *m fam*

papal *adj* : papal

papaya *n* : papaya *f*

paper *n* **1** : papel *m* **2** DOCUMENT : documento *m* **3** NEWSPAPER : periódico *m* — **paper** *vt* WALLPAPER : empapelar — **paper** *adj* : de papel — **paperback** *n* : libro *m* en rústica — **paper clip** *n* : clip *m*, sujetapapeles *m* — **paperweight** *n* : pisapapeles *m* — **paperwork** *n* : papeleo *m*

paprika *n* : pimentón *m*

par *n* **1** : par *m* (en golf) **2 below par** : debajo de la par **3 on a par with** : al nivel de

parable *n* : parábola *f*

▸ **parachute** *n* : paracaídas *m* — **parachute** *vi* **-chuted; -chuting** : lanzarse en paracaídas

parade *n* **1** : desfile *m* **2** DISPLAY : alarde *m* — **parade** *v* **-raded; -rading** *vi* MARCH : desfilar — *vt* DISPLAY : hacer alarde de

paradise *n* : paraíso *m*

paradox *n* : paradoja *f* — **paradoxical** *adj* : paradójico

paraffin *n* : parafina *f*

paragraph *n* : párrafo *m*

Paraguayan *adj* : paraguayo

parakeet *n* : periquito *m*

parallel *adj* : paralelo — **parallel** *n* **1** : paralelo *m* (en geografía) **2** SIMILARITY

: paralelismo *m*, semejanza *f* —
parallel *vt* : ser paralelo a
paralysis *n*, *pl* **-yses** : parálisis *f* —
 paralyze *or Brit* **paralise** *vt* **-lyzed** *or Brit*
 -lised; -lyzing *or Brit* **-lising** : paralizar
parameter *n* : parámetro *m*
paramount *adj* **of paramount**
 importance : de suma importancia
paranoia *n* : paranoia *f* —
 paranoid *adj* : paranoico
paraphernalia *ns & pl* : parafernalia *f*
paraphrase *n* : paráfrasis *f*
 — paraphrase *vt* **-phrased;**
 -phrasing : parafrasear
paraplegic *n* : parapléjico *m*, -ca *f*
parasite *n* : parásito *m*
paratrooper *n* : paracaidista *mf* (militar)
parcel *n* : paquete *m*
parch *vt* : resecar
parchment *n* : pergamino *m*
pardon *n* **1** : perdón *m* **2** REPRIEVE
 : indulto *m* **3 I beg your pardon** :
 perdone Ud., disculpe Ud. *Lat* —
 pardon *vt* **1** : perdonar **2** REPRIEVE

: indultar (a un delincuente)
parent *n* **1** : madre *f*, padre *m* **2**
 parents *npl* : padres *mpl* —
 parental *adj* : de los padres
parenthesis *n*, *pl* **-theses** : paréntesis *m*
parish *n* : parroquia *f* —
 parishioner *n* : feligrés *m*, -gresa *f*
parity *n*, *pl* **-ties** : igualdad *f*
park *n* : parque *m* — **park** *v* :
 estacionar, parquear *Lat*
parka *n* : parka *f*
parking *n* : estacionamiento *m*
parliament *n* : parlamento *m* —
 parliamentary *adj* : parlamentario
parlor *or Brit* **parlour** *n* : salón *m*
parochial *adj* **1** : parroquial **2**
 PROVINCIAL : de miras estrechas
parody *n*, *pl* **-dies** : parodia *f* —
 parody *vt* **-died; -dying** : parodiar
parole *n* : libertad *f* condicional
▸ **parrot** *n* : loro *m*, papagayo *m*
parry *vt* **-ried; -rying 1** : parar (un golpe)
 2 EVADE : eludir (una pregunta, etc.)
parsley *n* : perejil *m*

parsnip *n* : chirivía *f*
parson *n* : clérigo *m*
part *n* **1** : parte *f* **2** PIECE : pieza *f* **3** ROLE :
 papel *m* **4** : raya *f* (del pelo) — **part** *vi* **1**
 or **part company** : separarse **2 part with**
 : dehacerse de — *vt* SEPARATE : separar
partake *vi* **-took; -taken; -taking**
 partake in : participar en
partial *adj* **1** : parcial **2 be**
 partial to : ser aficionado a
participate *vi* **-pated; -pating** : participar
 — participant *n* : participante *mf*
participle *n* : participio *m*
particle *n* : partícula *f*
particular *adj* **1** : particular **2** FUSSY
 : exigente — **particular** *n* **1 in**
 particular : en particular, en especial
 2 particulars *npl* DETAILS : detalles *mpl*
 — particularly *adv* : especialmente
partisan *n* : partidario *m*, -ria *f*
partition *n* **1** DISTRIBUTION : partición *f* **2**
 DIVIDER : tabique *m* — **partition** *vt* : dividir
partly *adv* : en parte
partner *n* **1** : pareja *f* (en un juego,

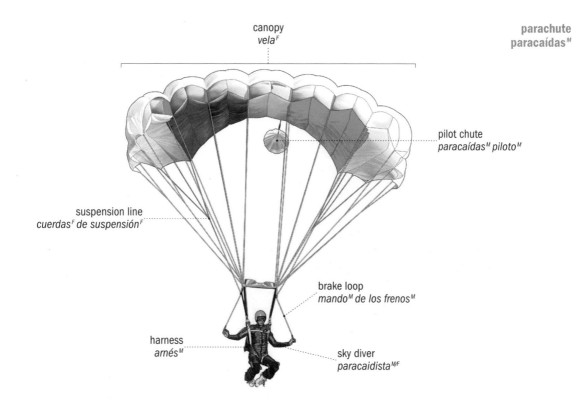

canopy
vela^F

parachute
paracaídas^M

pilot chute
paracaídas^M *piloto*^M

suspension line
cuerdas^F *de suspensión*^F

brake loop
mando^M *de los frenos*^M

harness
arnés^M

sky diver
paracaidista^{MF}

etc.) **2** or **business partner** : socio m,
-cia f — **partnership** n : asociación f
party n, pl **-ties 1** : partido m (político) **2**
GATHERING : fiesta f **3** GROUP : grupo m
pass vi **1** : pasar **2** CEASE : pasarse **3** :
aprobar (en un examen) **4** or **pass away**
DIE : morir **5 pass for** : pasar por **6 pass
out** FAINT : desmayarse — vt **1** : pasar **2**
or **pass in front of** : pasar por **3** OVERTAKE
: adelantar **4** : aprobar (un examen, una
ley, etc.) **5 pass down** : transmitir —
pass n **1** PERMIT : pase m, permiso m **2** :
pase m (en deportes) **3** or **mountain pass**
: paso m de montaña — **passable** adj **1**
ADEQUATE : adecuado **2** : transitable (dícese
de un camino, etc.) — **passage** n **1** :
paso m **2** CORRIDOR : pasillo m (dentro
de un edificio), pasaje m (entre edificios)
3 VOYAGE : travesía f (por el mar) —
passageway n : pasillo m, corredor m
passenger n : pasajero m, -ra f
passerby n, pl **passersby** : transeúnte mf
passion n : pasión f —
passionate adj : apasionado
passive adj : pasivo
Passover n : Pascua f (en el judaísmo)

passport n : pasaporte m
password n : contraseña f
past adj **1** : pasado **2** FORMER : anterior
3 the past few months : los últimos
meses — **past** prep **1** IN FRONT OF : por
delante de **2** BEYOND : más allá de **3 half
past two** : las dos y media — **past** n :
pasado m — **past** adv : por delante
pasta n : pasta f
paste n **1** : pasta f **2** GLUE : engrudo m
— **paste** vt **pasted; pasting** : pegar
pastel n : pastel m — **pastel** adj : pastel
pasteurize vt **-ized; -izing** : pasteurizar
pastime n : pasatiempo m
pastor n : pastor m, -tora f
pastry n, pl **-ries** : pasteles mpl
pasture n : pasto m
pasty adj **pastier; -est 1** DOUGHY
: pastoso **2** PALLID : pálido
pat n **1** : palmadita f **2 a pat of butter**
: una porción de mantequilla — **pat** vt
patted; patting : dar palmaditas a
— **pat** adv **have down pat** : saberse
de memoria — **pat** adj GLIB : fácil
patch n **1** : parche m, remiendo m (para
la ropa) **2** SPOT : mancha f, trozo m **3**

PLOT : parcela f (de tierra) — **patch** vt **1**
MEND : remendar **2 patch up** : arreglar
— **patchy** adj **patchier; -est 1** : desigual
2 INCOMPLETE : parcial, incompleto
patent adj **1** or patented : patentado **2**
OBVIOUS : patente, evidente — **patent** n
: patente f — **patent** vt : patentar
paternal adj **1** FATHERLY : paternal
2 paternal grandmother : abuela f
paterna — **paternity** n : paternidad f
path n **1** TRACK, TRAIL : camino m,
sendero m **2** COURSE : trayectoria f
pathetic adj : patético
pathology n, pl **-gies** : patología f
pathway n : camino m, sendero m
patience n : paciencia f — **patient** adj
: paciente — **patience** n : paciente mf
— **patiently** adv : con paciencia
patio n, pl **-tios** : patio m
patriot n : patriota mf —
patriotic adj : patriótico
patrol n : patrulla f — **patrol** v
-trolled; -trolling : patrullar
patron n **1** SPONSOR : patrocinador m,
-dora f **2** CUSTOMER : cliente m, -ta f
— **patronage** n **1** SPONSORSHIP :
patrocinio m **2** CLIENTELE : clientela f
— **patronize** vt **-ized; -izing 1** :
ser cliente de (una tienda, etc.) **2** :
tratar (a algn) con condescencia
patter n : tamborileo m (de la
lluvia), correteo m (de los pies)
pattern n **1** MODEL : modelo m **2**
DESIGN : diseño m **3** STANDARD : pauta f,
modo m **4** : patrón m (en costura) —
pattern vt : basar (en un modelo)
paunch n : panza f
pause n : pausa f — **pause** vi
paused; pausing : hacer una pausa
pave vt **paved; paving** : pavimentar
— **pavement** n : pavimento m
pavilion n : pabellón m
paw n **1** : pata f **2** : garra f (de un
gato) — **paw** vt : tocar con la pata
pawn[1] n : peón m (en ajedrez)
pawn[2] vt : empeñar — **pawnbroker** n
: prestamista mf — **pawnshop** n
: casa f de empeños
pay v **paid; paying** vt **1** : pagar **2 pay
attention** : prestar atención **3 pay back** :
devolver **4 pay one's respects** : presentar
uno sus respetos **5 pay a visit** : hacer una
visita — vi **1** : pagar **2 crime doesn't
pay** : no hay crimen sin castigo —
pay n : paga f — **payable** adj : pagadero

pelican
pelícano[M]

— **paycheck** *n* : cheque *m* del sueldo —
payment *n* **1** : pago *m* **2** INSTALLMENT :
plazo *m*, cuota *f Lat* — **payroll** *n* : nómina *f*
PC *n*, *pl* **PCs** *or* **PC's** : PC *mf*,
computadora *f* personal
pea *n* : guisante *m*, arveja *f Lat*
peace *n* : paz *f* — **peaceful** *adj* **1**
: pacífico **2** CALM : tranquilo
peach *n* : melocotón *m*, durazno *m*, *Lat*
peacock *n* : pavo *m* real
peak *n* **1** SUMMIT : cumbre *f*, cima *f*,
pico *m* (de una montaña) **2** APEX :
nivel *m* máximo — **peak** *adj* : máximo
— **peak** *vi* : alcanzar su nivel máximo
peal *n* **1** : repique *m* **2 peals**
of laughter : carcajadas *fpl*
peanut *n* : cacahuete *m*, maní *m*, *Lat*
pear *n* : pera *f*
pearl *n* : perla *f*
peasant *n* : campesino *m*, -na *f*
peat *n* : turba *f*
pebble *n* : guijarro *m*
pecan *n* : pacana *f*, nuez *f Lat*
peck *vt* : picar, picotear — **peck** *n* **1** :
picotazo *m* (de un pájaro) **2** KISS : besito
peculiar *adj* **1** DISTINCTIVE : peculiar,
característico **2** STRANGE : extraño,
raro — **peculiarity** *n*, *pl* **-ties 1** :
peculiaridad *f* **2** ODDITY : rareza *f*
pedal *n* : pedal *m* — **pedal** *vi* **-aled** *or*
-alled; -aling *or* **-alling** : pedalear
pedantic *adj* : pedante
peddle *vt* **-dled; -dling** : vender
en las calles — **peddler** *n* :
vendedor *m*, -dora *f* ambulante

pedestal *n* : pedestal *m*
pedestrian *n* : peatón *m*, -tona *f*
— **pedestrian** *adj* **pedestrian**
crossing : paso *m* de peatones
pediatrics *ns & pl* : pediatría *f* —
pediatrician *n* : pediatra *mf*
pedigree *n* : pedigrí *m* (de un
animal), linaje *m* (de una persona)
peek *vi* : mirar a hurtadillas —
peek *n* : miradita *f* (furtiva)
peel *vt* : pelar (fruta, etc.) — *vi* : pelarse
(dícese de la piel), desconcharse (dícese
de la pintura) — **peel** *n* : piel *f*, cáscara *f*
peep[1] *vi* CHEEP : piar — **peep** *n*
: pío *m* (de un pajarito)
peep[2] *vi* **1** PEEK : mirar a hurtadillas
2 *or* **peep out** : asomar — **peep** *n*
GLANCE : mirada *f* (furtiva)
peer[1] *n* : par *mf*
peer[2] *vi* : mirar (con atención)
peeve *vt* : irritar — **peevish** *adj*
: malhumorado
peg *n* **1** : clavija *f* **2** HOOK : gancho *m*
▸ **pelican** *n* : pelícano *m*
pellet *n* **1** : bolita *f* **2** SHOT : perdigón *m*
pelt[1] *n* : piel *f* (de un animal)
pelt[2] *vt* : lanzar (algo a algn)
pelvis *n*, *pl* **-vises** *or* **-ves** :
pelvis *f* — **pelvic** *adj* : pélvico

pen[1] *vt* **penned; penning** ENCLOSE :
encerrar — **pen** *n* : corral *m*, redil *m*
pen[2] *n* **1** *or* **ballpoint pen** : bolígrafo *m* **2**
or **fountain pen** : pluma *f*
penal *adj* : penal — **penalize** *vt*
-ized; -izing : penalizar — **penalty** *n*,
pl **-ties 1** : pena *f*, castigo *m* **2**
: penalty *m* (en deportes)
penance *n* : penitencia *f*
pencil *n* : lápiz *m* — **pencil**
sharpener *n* : sacapuntas *m*
pendant *n* : colgante *m*
pending *adj* : pendiente —
pending *prep* : en espera de
penetrate *v* **-trated; -trating** : penetrar
— **penetrating** *adj* : penetrante —
penetration *n* : penetración *f*
penguin *n* : pingüino *m*
penicillin *n* : penicilina *f*
peninsula *n* : península *f*
penis *n*, *pl* **-nes** *or* **-nises** : pene *m*
penitentiary *n*, *pl* **-ries** : penitenciaría *f*
pen name *n* : seudónimo *m*
pennant *n* : banderín *m*
penny *n*, *pl* **-nies** *or* **pence** : centavo *m* (de
los Estados Unidos), penique *m* (del Reino
Unido) — **penniless** *adj* : sin un centavo
pension *n* : pensión *m*, jubilación *f*
pensive *adj* : pensativo

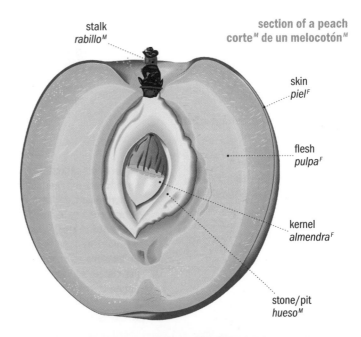

stalk
rabillo[M]

section of a peach
corte[M] de un melocotón[M]

skin
piel[F]

flesh
pulpa[F]

kernel
almendra[F]

stone/pit
hueso[M]

pentagon *n* : pentágono *m*
penthouse *n* : ático *m*
pent–up *adj* : reprimido
people *ns & pl* **1 people** *npl* : gente *f*,
personas *fpl* **2** *pl* **peoples** : pueblo *m*
pep *n* : energía *f*, vigor *m* —
 pep *vt or* **pep up** : animar
pepper *n* **1** : pimienta *f*
(condimento) **2** : pimiento *m* (fruta)
— **peppermint** *n* : menta *f*
per *prep* **1** : por **2** ACCORDING TO :
según **3 per day** : al día **4 miles
per hour** : millas *fpl* por hora
perceive *vt* -ceived; -ceiving : percibir
percent *adv* : por ciento —
 percentage *n* : porcentaje *m*
perception *n* : percepción *f* —
 perceptive *adj* : perspicaz
perch[1] *n* : percha *f* (para los
pájaros) — **perch** *vi* : posarse
perch[2] *n* : perca *f* (pez)
percolate *vi* -lated; -lating : filtrarse
— **percolator** *n* : cafetera *f* de filtro
percussion *n* : percusión *f*
perennial *adj* : perenne —
 perennial *n* : planta *f* perenne
perfect *adj* : perfecto — **perfect** *vt* :
perfeccionar — **perfection** *n* : perfección *f*
— **perfectionist** *n* : perfeccionista *mf*
perforate *vt* -rated; -rating : perforar
perform *vt* **1** CARRY OUT : realizar,
hacer **2** : representar (una obra teatral),
interpretar (una obra musical) — *vi* **1**
FUNCTION : funcionar **2** ACT : actuar
— **performance** *n* **1** : realización *f* **2**
INTERPRETATION : interpretación *f* **3**
PRESENTATION : representación *f*
— **performer** *n* : actor *m*, -triz *f*;
intérprete *mf* (de música)
perfume *n* : perfume *m*
perhaps *adv* : tal vez, quizá, quizás
peril *n* : peligro *m* —
 perilous *adj* : peligroso
perimeter *n* : perímetro *m*
period *n* **1** : período *m* (de tiempo)
2 : punto *m* (en puntuación) **3** ERA :
época *f* — **periodic** *adj* : periódico
— **periodical** *n* : revista *f*
peripheral *adj* : periférico
perish *vi* : perecer — **perishable** *adj*
: perecedero — **perishables** *npl*
: productos *mpl* perecederos
perjury *n* : perjurio *m*
perk *vi* **perk up** : animarse,
reanimarse — **perk** *n* : extra *m*

photographic accessories
accesorios^M fotográficos

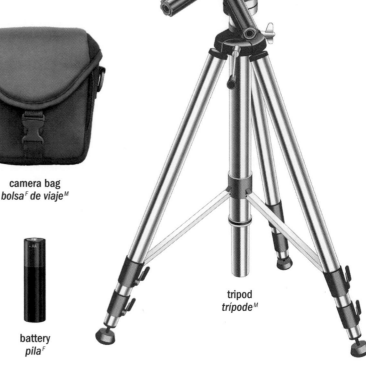

waterproof case
estuche^M sumergible

camera bag
bolsa^F de viaje^M

battery
pila^F

tripod
trípode^M

— **perky** *adj* **perkier; -est** : alegre
permanence *n* : permanencia *f*
— **permanent** *adj* : permanente —
 permanence *n* : permanente *f*
permeate *v* -ated; -ating : penetrar
permission *n* : permiso *m* —
 permissible *adj* : permisible —
 permissive *adj* : permisivo —
 permit *vt* -mitted; -mitting : permitir
— **permission** *n* : permiso *m*
peroxide *n* : peróxido *m*

perpendicular *adj* : perpendicular
perpetrate *vt* -trated; -trating
: cometer — **perpetrator** *n* :
autor *m*, -tora *f* (de un delito)
perpetual *adj* : perpetuo
perplex *vt* : dejar perplejo —
 perplexing *adj* : desconcertante —
 perplexity *n, pl* **-ties** : perplejidad *f*
persecute *vt* -cuted; -cuting : perseguir
— **persecution** *n* : persecución *f*
persevere *vi* -vered; -vering : perseverar

— **perseverance** n : perseverancia f
persist vi : persistir —
  persistence n : persistencia f —
  persistent adj : persistente
person n : persona f — **personal** adj
  : personal — **personality** n, pl -ties
  : personalidad f — **personally** adv
  : personalmente, en persona —
  personnel n : personal m
perspective n : perspectiva f
perspiration n : transpiración f —
  perspire vi -spired; -spiring : transpirar
persuade vt -suaded; -suading :
  persuadir — **persuasion** n : persuasión f
pertain vi **pertain to** : estar relacionado
  con — **pertinent** adj : pertinente
perturb vt : perturbar
Peruvian adj : peruano
pervade vt -vaded; -vading : penetrar
  — **pervasive** adj : penetrante
perverse adj **1** CORRUPT : perverso
  2 STUBBORN : obstinado —
  pervert n : pervertido m, -da f
peso n, pl -sos : peso m
pessimism n : pesimismo m
  — **pessimist** n : pesimista mf —
  pessimistic adj : pesimista
pest n **1** : insecto m nocivo, animal m
  nocivo **2** : peste f fam (persona)
pester vt -tered; -tering : molestar
pesticide n : pesticida m
pet n **1** : animal m doméstico **2**
  FAVORITE : favorito m, -ta f — **pet** vt
  petted; petting : acariciar
petal n : pétalo m
petite adj : chiquita
petition n : petición f — **petition** vt
  : dirigir una petición a
petrify vt -fied; -fying : petrificar
petroleum n : petróleo m
petticoat n : enagua f, fondo m, Lat
petty adj -tier; -est **1** UNIMPORTANT :
  insignificante, nimio **2** MEAN : mezquino
  — **pettiness** n : mezquindad f
petulant adj : irritable, de mal genio
pew n : banco m (de iglesia)
pewter n : peltre m
phallic adj : fálico
phantom n : fantasma m
pharmacy n, pl -cies : farmacia f —
  pharmacist n : farmacéutico m, -ca f
phase n : fase f — **phase** vt
  phased; phasing 1 phase in :
  introducir progresivamente **2 phase
  out** : retirar progresivamente

phenomenon n, pl -na
  or -nons : fenómeno m —
  phenomenal adj : fenomenal
philanthropy n, pl -pies : filantropía f
  — **philanthropist** n : filántropo m, -pa f
philosophy n, pl -phies : filosofía f
  — **philosopher** n : filósofo m, -fa f
phlegm n : flema f
phobia n : fobia f
phone → **telephone**
phonetic adj : fonético
phony or **phoney** adj -nier; -est : falso
  — **phony** n, pl -nies : farsante mf
phosphorus n : fósforo m
photo n, pl -tos : foto f — **photocopier** n :
  fotocopiadora f — **photocopy** n, pl -copies
  : fotocopia f — **photocopy** vt -copied;
  -copying : fotocopiar — **photograph** n
  : fotografía f, foto f — **photograph** vt
  : fotografiar — **photographer** n :
▸ fotógrafo m, -fa f — photographic adj :
  fotográfico — **photography** n : fotografía f
phrase n : frase f — **phrase** vt
  phrased; phrasing : expresar
physical adj : físico — **physical** n
  : reconocimiento m médico
physician n : médico m, -ca f
physics ns & pl : física f —
  physicist n : físico m, -ca f
physiology n : fisiología f
physique n : físico m
piano n, pl -anos : piano m
  — **pianist** n : pianista mf
pick vt **1** CHOOSE : escoger **2** GATHER
  : recoger **3** REMOVE : quitar (poco a
  poco) **4 pick a fight** : buscar camorra
  — vi **1 pick and choose** : ser exigente
  2 pick on : meterse con — **pick** n **1**
  CHOICE : selección f **2** or **pickax** :
  pico m **3 the pick of** : lo mejor de
picket n **1** STAKE : estaca f **2** or **picket
  line** : piquete m — **picket** v : piquetear
pickle n **1** : pepinillo m (encurtido)
  2 JAM : lío m fam, apuro m —
  pickle vt -led; -ling : encurtir
pickpocket n : carterista mf
pickup n **1** IMPROVEMENT : mejora f **2**
  or **pickup truck** : camioneta f — **pick
  up** vt **1** LIFT : levantar **2** TIDY : arreglar,
  ordenar — vi IMPROVE : mejorar
picnic n : picnic m — **picnic** vi
  -nicked; -nicking : ir de picnic
picture n **1** PAINTING : cuadro m **2**
  DRAWING : dibujo m **3** PHOTO :
  fotografía f **4** IMAGE : imagen f **5** MOVIE :

película f — **picture** vt -tured; -turing **1**
  DEPICT : representar **2** IMAGINE : imaginarse
  — **picturesque** adj : pintoresco
pie n : pastel m (con fruta o carne),
  empanada f (con carne)
piece n **1** : pieza f **2** FRAGMENT :
  trozo m, pedazo m **3 a piece of advice**
  : un consejo — **piece** vt **pieced;
  piecing** or **piece together** : juntar,
  componer — **piecemeal** adv : poco a
  poco — **piece** adj : poco sistemático
pier n : muelle m
pierce vt **pierced; piercing** : perforar
  — **piercing** adj : penetrante
piety n, pl -eties : piedad f
pig n : cerdo m, -da f; puerco m, -ca f
pigeon n : paloma f —
  pigeonhole n : casilla f
piggyback adv & adj : a cuestas
pigment n : pigmento m
pigpen n : pocilga f
pigtail n : coleta f, trenza f
pile[1] n HEAP : montón m, pila f — **pile** v
  piled; piling vt : amontonar, apilar — vi
  pile up : amontonarse, acumularse
pile[2] n NAP : pelo m (de telas)
pilfer vt : robar, hurtar
pilgrim n : peregrino m, -na f —
  pilgrimage n : peregrinación f
pill n : pastilla f, píldora f
pillage n : saqueo m — **pillage** vt
  -laged; -laging : saquear
pillar n : pilar m, columna f
pillow n : almohada f — **pillowcase** n
  : funda f (de almohada)
pilot n : piloto mf — **pilot** vt : pilotar,
  pilotear — **pilot light** n : piloto m
pimp n : proxeneta m
pimple n : grano m
pin n **1** : alfiler m **2** BROOCH : broche m **3**
  or **bowling pin** : bolo m — **pin** vt **pinned;
  pinning 1** FASTEN : prender, sujetar (con
  alfileres) **2** or **pin down** : inmovilizar
pincers npl : tenazas fpl
pinch vt **1** : pellizcar **2** STEAL : robar — vi
  : apretar — **pinch** n **1** : pellizco m **2** BIT
  : pizca f **3 in a pinch** : en caso necesario
pine[1] n : pino m (árbol)
pine[2] vi **pined; pining 1** LANGUISH :
  languidecer **2 pine for** : suspirar por
pineapple n : piña f, ananás m
pink n : rosa m, rosado m —
  pink adj : rosa, rosado
pinnacle n : pináculo m
pinpoint vt : localizar, precisar

pint *n* : pinta *f*
pioneer *n* : pionero *m*, -ra *f*
pious *adj* : piadoso
pipe *n* **1** : tubo *m*, caño *m* **2** : pipa *f* (para fumar) — **pipeline** *n* **1** : conducto *m*, oleoducto *m* (para petróleo)
piquant *adj* : picante
pique *n* : resentimiento *m*
pirate *n* : pirata *mf*
pistachio *n*, *pl* **-chios** : pistacho *m*
pistol *n* : pistola *f*
piston *n* : pistón *m*
pit *n* **1** HOLE : hoyo *m*, fosa *f* **2** MINE : mina *f* **3** : hueso *m* (de una fruta) **4 pit of the stomach** : boca *f* del estómago — **pit** *vt* **pitted; pitting 1** : marcar de hoyos **2** : deshuesar (una fruta) **3 pit against** : enfrentar a
pitch *vt* **1** : armar (una tienda) **2** THROW : lanzar — *vi* **1** *or* **pitch forward** : caerse **2** LURCH : cabecear (dícese de un barco o un avión) — **pitch** *n* **1** DEGREE, LEVEL : grado *m*, punto *m* **2** TONE : tono *m* **3** THROW : lanzamiento *m* **4** *or* **sales pitch** : presentación *f* (de un vendedor)
pitcher *n* **1** JUG : jarro *m* **2** :

lanzador *m*, -dora *f* (en béisbol, etc.)
pitchfork *n* : horquilla *f*, horca *f*
pitfall *n* : riesgo *m*, dificultad *f*
pith *n* **1** : médula *f* (de un hueso, etc.) **2** CORE : meollo *m* — **pithy** *adj* **pithier; -est** : conciso y sustancioso
pity *n*, *pl* **pities 1** COMPASSION : compasión *f* **2 what a pity!** : ¡qué lástima! — **pity** *vt* **pitied; pitying** : compadecerse de — **pitiful** *adj* : lastimoso — **pitiless** *adj* : despiadado
pivot *n* : pivote *m* — **pivot** *vi* **1** : girar sobre un eje **2 pivot on** : depender de
pizza *n* : pizza *f*
placard *n* POSTER : cartel *m*, póster *m*
placate *vt* **-cated; -cating** : apaciguar
place *n* **1** : sitio *m*, lugar *m* **2** SEAT : asiento *m* **3** POSITION : puesto *m* **4** ROLE : papel *m* **5 take place** : tener lugar **6 take the place of** : sustituir a — **place** *vt* **placed; placing 1** PUT SET : poner, colocar **2** IDENTIFY : identificar, recordar **3 place an order** : hacer un pedido — **placement** *n* : colocación *f*
placid *adj* : plácido, tranquilo
plagiarism *n* : plagio *m* — **plagiarize** *vt*

-rized; -rizing : plagiar
plague *n* **1** : plaga *f* (de insectos, etc.) **2** : peste *f* (en medicina)
plaid *n* : tela *f* escocesa — **plaid** *adj* : escocés
plain *adj* **1** SIMPLE : sencillo **2** CLEAR : claro, evidente **3** CANDID : franco **4** HOMELY : poco atractivo **5 in plain sight** : a la vista (de todos) — **plain** *n* : llanura *f*, planicie *f* — **plainly** *adv* **1** CLEARLY : claramente **2** FRANKLY : francamente **3** SIMPLY : sencillamente
plaintiff *n* : demandante *mf*
plan *n* **1** : plan *m*, proyecto *m* **2** DIAGRAM : plano *m* — **plan** *v* **planned; planning** *vt* **1** : planear, proyectar **2** INTEND : tener planeado — *vi* : hacer planes
plane[1] *n* **1** LEVEL : plano *m*, nivel *m* **2** AIRPLANE : avión *m*
plane[2] *n or* **carpenter's plane** : cepillo *m*
▸ **planet** *n* : planeta *f*
plank *n* : tabla *f*
planning *n* : planificación *f*
plant *vt* : plantar (flores, árboles), sembrar (semillas) — **plant** *n* **1** : planta *f* **2** FACTORY : fábrica *f*

planets, satellites and dwarf planets
planetas^M, satélites^M y planetas^F enanos

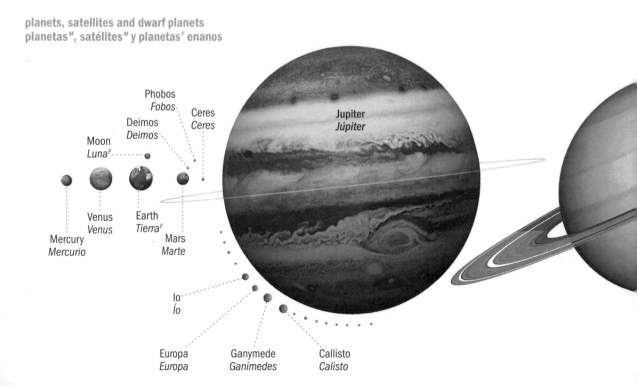

Phobos
Fobos
Ceres
Ceres
Deimos
Deimos
Moon
Luna^F
Jupiter
Júpiter
Venus
Venus
Earth
Tierra^F
Mars
Marte
Mercury
Mercurio
Io
Ío
Europa
Europa
Ganymede
Ganimedes
Callisto
Calisto

plantain *n* : plátano *m* (grande)
plantation *n* : plantación *f*
plaque *n* : placa *f*
plaster *n* : yeso *m* — **plaster** *vt* **1**
: enyesar **2** COVER : cubrir —
plaster cast *n* : escayola *f*
plastic *adj* **1** : de plástico **2** FLEXIBLE
: plástico, flexible **3 plastic surgery** :
cirugía *f* plástica — **plastic** *n* : plástico *m*
plate *n* **1** SHEET : placa *f* **2** DISH :
plato *m* **3** ILLUSTRATION : lámina *f* —
plate *vt* **plated; plating** : chapar (en metal)
plateau *n, pl* **-teaus** *or* **-teaux** : meseta *f*
platform *n* **1** : plataforma *f* **2** : andén *m*
(de una estación de ferrocarril) **3** *or*
political platform : programa *m* electoral
platinum *n* : platino *m*
platitude *n* : lugar *m* común
platoon *n* : sección *f* (en el ejército)
platter *n* : fuente *f*
plausible *adj* : creíble, verosímil
play *n* **1** : juego *m* **2** DRAMA : obra *f* de
teatro — **play** *vi* **1** : jugar **2 play in a**
band : tocar en un grupo — *vt* **1** : jugar
(deportes, etc.), jugar a (juegos) **2** : tocar
(música o un instrumento) **3 play the role**

of : representar el papel de — **player** *n* **1**
: jugador *m*, -dora *f* **2** ACTOR : actor *m*,
actriz *f* **3** MUSICIAN : músico *m*, -ca *f* —
playful *adj* : juguetón — **playground** *n*
: patio *m* de recreo — **playing card** *n*
: naipe *m*, carta *f* — **playmate** *n* :
compañero *m*, -ra *f* de juego — **play–off** *n*
: desempate *m* — **playpen** *n* : corral *m*
(para niños) — **plaything** *n* : juguete *m*
— **playwright** *n* : dramaturgo *m*, -ga *f*
plea *n* **1** : acto *m* de declararse
(en derecho) **2** APPEAL : ruego *m*,
súplica *f* — **plead** *v* **pleaded** *or*
pled; pleading *vi* **1 plead for** :
suplicar **2 plead guilty** : declararse
culpable **3 plead not guilty** : negar la
acusación — *vt* **1** : alegar, pretextar
2 plead a case : defender un caso
pleasant *adj* : agradable, grato —
please *v* **pleased; pleasing** *vt* **1**
GRATIFY : complacer **2** SATISFY :
satisfacer — *vi* **1** : agradar **2 do as**
you please : haz lo que quieras —
please *adv* : por favor — **pleased** *adj*
: contento — **pleasing** *adj* : agradable
— **pleasure** *n* : placer *m*, gusto *m*

pleat *vt* : plisar — **pleat** *n* : pliegue *m*
pledge *n* **1** SECURITY : prenda *f* **2**
PROMISE : promesa *f* — **pledge** *vt*
pledged; pledging 1 PAWN :
empeñar **2** PROMISE : prometer
plenty *n* **1** : abundancia *f* **2**
plenty of time : tiempo *m* de sobra
— **plentiful** *adj* : abundante
pliable *adj* : flexible
pliers *npl* : alicates *mpl*
plight *n* : situación *f* difícil
plod *vi* **plodded; plodding 1** :
caminar con paso pesado **2** DRUDGE
: trabajar laboriosamente
plot *n* **1** LOT : parcela *f* **2** : argumento *m*
(de una novela, etc.) **3** CONSPIRACY :
complot *m*, intriga *f* — **plot** *v* **plotted;**
plotting *vt* : tramar (un plan), trazar (una
gráfica, etc.) — *vi* CONSPIRE : conspirar
plow *or* **plough** *n* **1** : arado *m* **2**
→ **snowplow** — **plow** *v* : arar
ploy *n* : estratagema *f*
pluck *vt* **1** : arrancar **2** : desplumar (un
pollo, etc.) **3** : recoger (flores) **4 pluck**
one's eyebrows : depilarse las cejas
plug *n* **1** STOPPER : tapón *m* **2** :

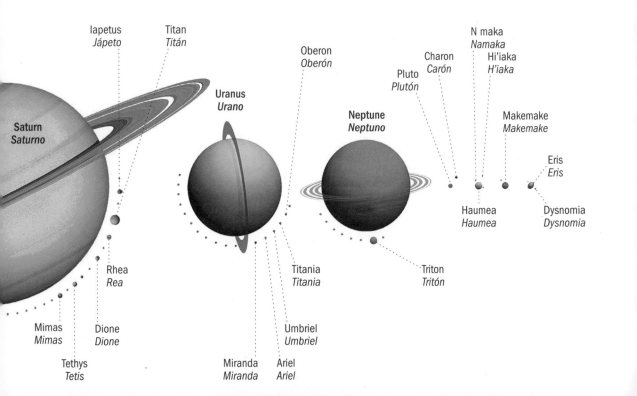

porcupine
puerco^M espín

enchufe m (eléctrico) — **plug** vt **plugged;
plugging 1** BLOCK : tapar **2** ADVERTISE :
dar publicidad a **3 plug in** : enchufar
plum n : ciruela f
plumb adj : a plomo, vertical —
  plumber n : fontanero m, -ra f; plomero m,
  -ra f Lat — **plumbing** n **1** : fontanería f,
  plomería f Lat **2** PIPES : cañerías fpl
plume n : pluma f
plummet vi : caer en picado
plump adj : rechoncho fam
plunder vi : saquear, robar
  — **plunder** n : botín m
plunge v **plunged; plunging** vt **1** IMMERSE
  : sumergir **2** THRUST : hundir — vi **1** :
  zambullirse (en el agua) **2** DESCEND :
  descender en picada — **plunge** n **1** DIVE :
  zambullida f **2** DROP : descenso m abrupto
plural adj : plural — **plural** n : plural m
plus adj : positivo — **plus** n **1**
  or **plus sign** : signo m (de) más **2**
  ADVANTAGE : ventaja f — **plus** $prep$
  : más — **plus** $conj$: y, además
plush n : felpa f — **plush** adj **1** :
  de felpa **2** LUXURIOUS : lujoso
plutonium n : plutonio m
ply vt **plied; plying 1** : ejercer
  (un oficio) **2 ply with questions**
  : acosar con preguntas
plywood n : contrachapado m
pneumatic adj : neumático
pneumonia n : pulmonía f
poach[1] vt : cocer a fuego lento
poach[2] vt or **poach game** : cazar
  ilegalmente — **poacher** n : cazador m
  furtivo, cazadora f furtiva
pocket n : bolsillo m — **pocket** vt
  : meterse en el bolsillo —
  pocketbook n : cartera f, bolsa f Lat

— **pocketknife** n, pl **-knives** : navaja f
pod n : vaina f
poem n : poema m — **poet** n :
  poeta mf — **poetic** or **poetical** adj
  : poético — **poetry** n : poesía f
poignant adj : conmovedor
point n **1** : punto m **2** PURPOSE :
  sentido m **3** TIP : punta f **4** FEATURE :
  cualidad f **5 be beside the point** : no
  venir al caso **6 there's no point …** :
  no sirve de nada… — **point** vt **1** AIM :
  apuntar **2** or **point out** : señalar, indicar
  — vi **point at** : señalar (con el dedo)
  — **point–blank** adv : a quemarropa
  — **pointer** n **1** NEEDLE : aguja f **2** :
  perro m de muestra **3** TIP : consejo m
  — **pointless** adj : inútil — **point of
  view** n : perspectiva f, punto m de vista
poise n **1** : elegancia f **2**
  COMPOSURE : aplomo m
poison n : veneno m — **poison** vt
  : envenenar — **poisonous** adj :
  venenoso (dícese de una culebra, etc.),
  tóxico (dícese de una sustancia)

poisonous mushrooms
hongo^M venenoso

fly agaric
$falsa\ oronja^F$

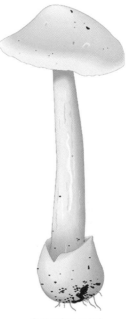

destroying angel
$amanita^F\ virosa$

poke vt **poked; poking 1** JAB : golpear
  (con la punta de algo), dar **2** THRUST :
  introducir, asomar — **poke** n : golpe m
  abrupto (con la punta de algo)
poker[1] n : atizador m (para el fuego)
poker[2] n : póquer m (juego de naipes)
polar adj : polar — **polar bear** n
  : oso m blanco — **polarize** vt
  -ized; -izing : polarizar
pole[1] n : palo m, poste m
pole[2] n : polo m (en geografía)
police vt **-liced; -licing** : mantener el
  orden en — **police** ns & pl **the police**
  : la policía — **policeman** n, pl **-men** :
  policía m — **police officer** n : policía mf,
  agente mf de policía — **policewoman** n,
  pl **-women** : (mujer f) policía f
policy n, pl **-cies 1** : política f **2** or
  insurance policy : póliza f de seguros
polio or poliomyelitis n :
  polio f, poliomielitis f
polish vt **1** : pulir **2** : limpiar (zapatos),
  encerar (un suelo) — **polish** n **1**
  LUSTER : brillo m, lustre m **2** : betún m

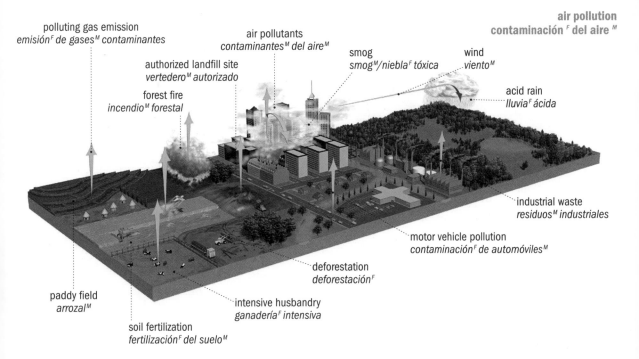

air pollution
contaminación *F* **del aire** *M*

polluting gas emission
emisión F de gases M contaminantes

air pollutants
contaminantes M del aire M

smog
smog M/niebla F tóxica

wind
viento M

authorized landfill site
vertedero M autorizado

acid rain
lluvia F ácida

forest fire
incendio M forestal

industrial waste
residuos M industriales

motor vehicle pollution
contaminación F de automóviles M

deforestation
deforestación F

paddy field
arrozal M

intensive husbandry
ganadería F intensiva

soil fertilization
fertilización F del suelo M

(para zapatos), cera *f* (para suelos y muebles), esmalte *m* (para las uñas)
Polish *adj* : polaco — **Polish** *n* : polaco *m* (idioma)
polite *adj* **-liter; -est** : cortés — **politeness** *n* : cortesía *f*
political *adj* : político — **politician** *n* : político *m*, -ca *f* — **politics** *ns & pl* : política *f*
polka *n* : polka *f* — **polka dot** *n* : lunar *m*
poll *n* **1** : encuesta *f*, sondeo *m* **2 the polls** : las urnas — **poll** *vt* **1** : obtener (votos) **2** CANVASS : encuestar, sondear
pollen *n* : polen *m*
pollute *vt* **-luted; -luting** : contaminar
▸ — **pollution** *n* : contaminación *f*
polyester *n* : poliéster *m*
polygon *n* : polígono *m*
pomegranate *n* : granada *f*
pomp *n* : pompa *f* — **pompous** *adj* : pomposo
pond *n* : charca *f* (natural), estanque *m* (artificial)
ponder *vt* : considerar — *vi* **ponder over** : reflexionar sobre
pony *n*, *pl* **-nies** : poni *m* — **ponytail** *n* : cola *f* de caballo

poodle *n* : caniche *m*
pool *n* **1** PUDDLE : charco *m* **2** : fondo *m* común (de recursos) **3** BILLIARDS : billar *m* **4** *or* **swimming pool** : piscina *f* — **pool** *vt* : hacer un fondo común de
poor *adj* **1** : pobre **2** INFERIOR : malo **3 the poor** : los pobres — **poorly** *adv* : mal
pop[1] *v* **popped; popping** *vt* **1** : hacer reventar **2 pop something into** : meter algo en — *vi* **1** BURST : reventarse, estallar **2 pop in** : entrar (un momento) **3 pop out** : saltar (dícese de los ojos) **4 pop up** APPEAR : aparecer — **pop** *n* **1** : ruido *m* seco **2** → **soda pop**
pop[2] *n* *or* **pop music** : música *f* popular
popcorn *n* : palomitas *fpl*
pope *n* : papa *m*
poplar *n* : álamo *m*
▸ **poppy** *n*, *pl* **-pies** : amapola *f*
popular *adj* : popular — **popularity** *n* : popularidad *f* — **popularize** *vt* **-ized; -izing** : popularizar
populate *vt* **-lated; -lating** : poblar — **population** *n* : población *f*
porcelain *n* : porcelana *f*
porch *n* : porche *m*
▸ **porcupine** *n* : puerco *m* espín

pore[1] *vi* **pored; poring pore over** : estudiar esmeradamente
pore[2] *n* : poro *m*
pork *n* : carne *f* de cerdo
pornography *n* : pornografía *f* — **pornographic** *adj* : pornográfico
porous *adj* : poroso
porpoise *n* : marsopa *f*
porridge *n* : avena *f* (cocida), gachas *fpl* (de avena)

poppy
amapola *F*

postal service network
red^F de correos^M pública

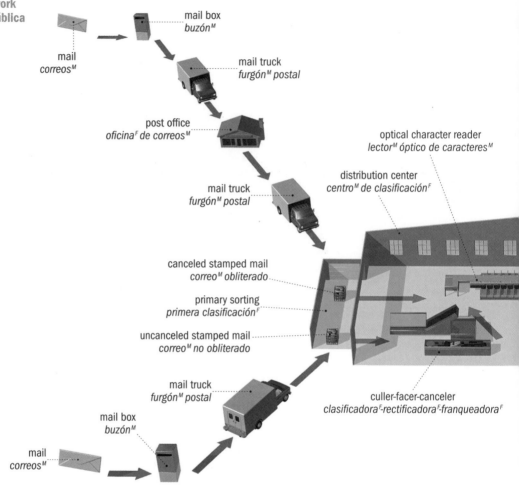

mail
correos^M

mail box
buzón^M

mail truck
furgón^M postal

post office
oficina^F de correos^M

optical character reader
lector^M óptico de caracteres^M

distribution center
centro^M de clasificación^F

mail truck
furgón^M postal

canceled stamped mail
correo^M obliterado

primary sorting
primera clasificación^F

uncanceled stamped mail
correo^M no obliterado

mail truck
furgón^M postal

mail box
buzón^M

mail
correos^M

culler-facer-canceler
clasificadora^F-rectificadora^F-franqueadora^F

---

port¹ *n* HARBOR : puerto *m*
port² *n or* **port side** : babor *m*
port³ *n* : oporto *m* (vino)
portable *adj* : portátil
portent *n* : presagio *m*
porter *n* : maletero *m*,
 mozo *m* (de estación)
portfolio *n, pl* **-lios** : cartera *f*
porthole *n* : portilla *f*
portion *n* : porción *f*
portrait *n* : retrato *m*
portray *vt* 1 : representar, retratar
 2 : interpretar (un personaje)
Portuguese *adj* : portugués —
 Portuguese *n* : portugués *m* (idioma)

pose *v* **posed; posing** *vt* : plantear
 (una pregunta, etc.), representar (una
 amenaza) — *vi* 1 : posar 2 **pose as** :
 hacerse pasar por — **pose** *n* : pose *f*
posh *adj* : elegante, de lujo
position *n* 1 : posición *f* 2 JOB :
 puesto *m* — **position** *vt* : colocar, situar
positive *adj* 1 : positivo
 2 CERTAIN : seguro
possess *vt* : poseer — **possession** *n* 1
 : posesión *f* 2 possesss *npl* BELONGINGS :
 bienes *mpl* — **possessive** *adj* : posesivo
possible *adj* : posible —
 possibility *n, pl* **-ties** : posibilidad *f*
 — **possibly** *adv* : posiblemente

post¹ *n* POLE : poste *m*, palo *m*
post² *n* POSITION : puesto *m*
post³ *n* MAIL : cartas *fpl* — **post** *vt* 1
 : echar al correo 2 **keep posted** :
 tener al corriente — **postage** *n* :
▸ franqueo *m* — **postal** *adj* : postal
 — **postcard** *n* : tarjeta *f* postal
poster *n* : cartel *m*
posterity *n* : posteridad *f*
posthumous *adj* : póstumo
postman → **mailman** — **post**
 office *n* : oficina *f* de correos
postpone *vt* **-poned; -poning** : aplazar
 — **postponement** *n* : aplazamiento *m*
postscript *n* : posdata *f*

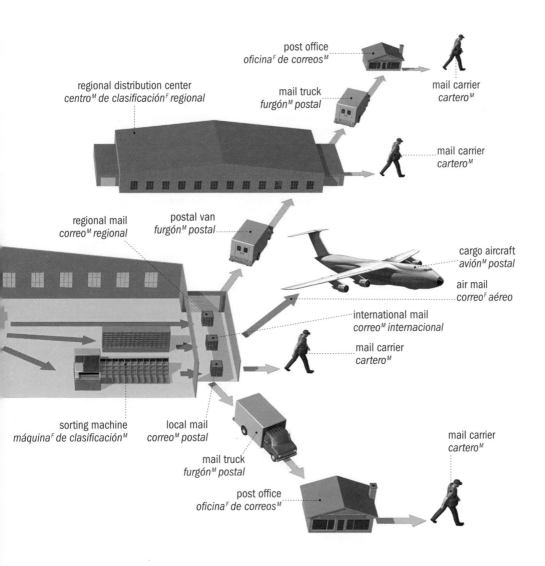

post office
*oficina*ᶠ *de correos*ᴹ

regional distribution center
*centro*ᴹ *de clasificación*ᶠ *regional*

mail truck
*furgón*ᴹ *postal*

mail carrier
*cartero*ᴹ

mail carrier
*cartero*ᴹ

regional mail
*correo*ᴹ *regional*

postal van
*furgón*ᴹ *postal*

cargo aircraft
*avión*ᴹ *postal*

air mail
*correo*ᶠ *aéreo*

international mail
*correo*ᴹ *internacional*

mail carrier
*cartero*ᴹ

sorting machine
*máquina*ᶠ *de clasificación*ᴹ

local mail
*correo*ᴹ *postal*

mail carrier
*cartero*ᴹ

mail truck
*furgón*ᴹ *postal*

post office
*oficina*ᶠ *de correos*ᴹ

---

posture *n* : postura *f*
postwar *adj* : de (la) posguerra
pot *n* **1** : olla *f* (de cocina) **2**
  FLOWERPOT : maceta *f* **3 pots**
  and pans : cacharros *mpl*
potassium *n* : potasio *m*
potato *n, pl* **-toes** : patata *f*, papa *f Lat*
potent *adj* **1** POWERFUL :
  poderoso **2** EFFECTIVE : eficaz
potential *adj* : potencial —
  potential *n* : potencial *m*
pothole *n* : bache *m*
potion *n* : poción *f*
pottery *n, pl* **-teries** : cerámica *f*
pouch *n* **1** BAG : bolsa *f* pequeña

2 : bolsa *f* (de un animal)
poultry *n* : aves *fpl* de corral
pounce *vi* **pounced;**
  pouncing : abalanzarse
pound¹ *n* : libra *f* (unidad
  de dinero o de peso)
pound² *n or* **dog pound** : perrera *f*
pound³ *vt* **1** CRUSH : machacar
  2 HIT : golpear — *vi* : palpitar
  (dícese del corazón)
pour *vt* : verter — *vi* **1** FLOW : fluir, salir **2**
  it's pouring : está lloviendo a cántaros
pout *vi* : hacer pucheros —
  pout *n* : puchero *m*
poverty *n* : pobreza *f*

powder *vt* **1** : empolvar **2** CRUSH :
  pulverizar — **powder** *n* **1** : polvo *m* **2**
  or **face powder** : polvos *mpl* —
  powdery *adj* : polvoriento
power *n* **1** CONTROL : poder *m* **2** ABILITY
  : capacidad *f* **3** STRENGTH : fuerza *f* **4** :
  potencia *f* (política) **5** ENERGY : energía *f* **6**
  ELECTRICITY : electricidad *f* — **power** *vt*
  : impulsar — **powerful** *adj* : poderoso
  — **powerless** *adj* : impotente
practical *adj* : práctico —
  practically *adv* : casi, prácticamente
practice *or* practise *v* **-ticed** *or* **-tised;**
  -ticing *or* **-tising** *vt* **1** : practicar **2** :
  ejercer (una profesión) — *vi* : practicar

— **practice** n 1 : práctica f 2 CUSTOM : costumbre f 3 : ejercicio m (de una profesión) 4 **be out of practice** : no estar en forma — **practitioner** n 1 : profesional mf 2 **general practice** : médico m, -ca f de medicina general

pragmatic adj : pragmático

prairie n : pradera f

praise vt **praised; praising** : elogiar, alabar — **praise** n : elogio m, alabanza f — **praiseworthy** adj : loable

prance vi **pranced; prancing** : hacer cabriolas

prank n : travesura f

prawn n : gamba f

pray vi 1 : rezar 2 **pray for** : rogar — **prayer** n : oración f

preach v : predicar — **preacher** n MINISTER : pastor m, -tora f

precarious adj : precario

precaution n : precaución f

precede vt **-ceded; -ceding** : preceder a — **precedence** n : precedencia f — **precedent** n : precedente m

precinct n 1 DISTRICT : distrito m 2 precincts npl : recinto m

precious adj : precioso

precipice n : precipicio m

precipitate vt **-tated; -tating** : precipitar — **precipitation** n 1 HASTE : precipitación f 2 : precipitaciones fpl (en meteorología)

precise adj : preciso — **precisely** adv : precisamente — **precision** n : precisión f

preclude vt **-cluded; -cluding** 1 PREVENT : impedir 2 EXCLUDE : excluir

precocious adj : precoz

preconceived adj : preconcebido

predator n : depredador m

predecessor n : antecesor m, -sora f; predecesor m, -sora f

predicament n : apuro m

predict vt : pronosticar, predecir — **predictable** adj : previsible — **prediction** n : pronóstico m, predicción f

predispose vt **-posed; -posing** : predisponer

predominant adj : predominante

preeminent adj : preeminente

preempt vt : adelantarse a (un ataque, etc.)

preen vt 1 : arreglarse (las plumas) 2 **preen oneself** : acicalarse

prefabricated adj : prefabricado

preface n : prefacio m, prólogo m

prefer vt **-ferred; -ferring** : preferir — **preferable** adj : preferible — **preference** n : preferencia f — **preferential** adj : preferente

prefix n : prefijo m

pregnancy n, pl **-cies** : embarazo m — **pregnant** adj : embarazada

prehistoric or prehistorical adj : prehistórico

prejudice n 1 BIAS : prejuicio m 2 HARM : perjuicio m — **prejudice** vt **-diced; -dicing** 1 BIAS : predisponer 2 HARM : perjudicar — **prejudiced** adj : parcial

preliminary adj : preliminar

prelude n : preludio m

premarital adj : prematrimonial

premature adj : prematuro

premeditated adj : premeditado

premier adj : principal — **premier** n PRIME MINISTER : primer ministro m, primera ministra f

premiere n : estreno m

premise n 1 : premisa f (de un argumento) 2 premises npl : recinto m, local m

premium n 1 : premio m 2 or **insurance premium** : prima f (de seguro)

preoccupied adj : preocupado

prepare v **-pared; -paring** vt : preparar — vi : prepararse — **preparation** n 1 : preparación f 2 **preparations** npl ARRANGEMENTS : preparativos mpl — **preparatory** adj : preparatorio

prepay vt **-paid; -paying** : pagar por adelantado

preposition n : preposición f

preposterous adj : absurdo, ridículo

prerequisite n : requisito m previo

prerogative n : prerrogativa f

prescribe vt **-scribed; -scribing** 1 : prescribir 2 : recetar (en medicina) — **prescription** n : receta f

presence n : presencia f

present[1] adj 1 CURRENT : actual 2 **be present at** : estar presente en — **present** n 1 : presente m 2 **at present** : actualmente

present[2] n GIFT : regalo m — **present** vt 1 INTRODUCE : presentar 2 GIVE : entregar — **presentation** n 1 : presentación f 2 or **presentation ceremony** : ceremonia f de entrega

presently adv 1 SOON : dentro de poco 2 NOW : actualmente

preserve vt **-served; -serving**

1 : conservar 2 MAINTAIN : mantener — **preserve** n 1 JAM : confitura f 2 or **game preserve** : coto m de caza — **preservation** n : preservación f, conservación f — **preservative** n : conservante m

president n : presidente m, -ta f — **presidency** n, pl **-cies** : presidencia f — **presidential** adj : presidencial

press n : prensa f — **pressure** vt 1 : apretar 2 IRON : planchar — vi 1 : apretar 2 URGE : presionar — **pressing** adj : urgente — **pressure** n : presión f — **pressure** vt **-sured; -suring** : presionar, apremiar

prestige n : prestigio m — **prestigious** adj : prestigioso

presume vt **-sumed; -suming** : presumir — **presumably** adv : es de suponer, supuestamente — **presumption** n : presunción f — **presumptuous** adj : presuntuoso

pretend vt 1 CLAIM : pretender 2 FEIGN : fingir — vi : fingir — **pretense** or **pretence** n 1 CLAIM : pretensión f 2 **under false pretenses** : con pretextos falsos — **pretentious** adj : pretencioso

pretext n : pretexto m

pretty adj **-tier; -est** : lindo, bonito — **pretty** adv FAIRLY : bastante

pretzel n : galleta f salada

prevail vi 1 TRIUMPH : prevalecer 2 PREDOMINATE : predominar 3 **prevail upon** : persuadir — **prevalent** adj : extendido

prevent vt : impedir — **prevention** n : prevención f — **preventive** adj : preventivo

preview n : preestreno m

previous adj : previo, anterior — **previously** adv : anteriormente

prey n, pl **preys** : presa f — **prey on** vt 1 : alimentarse de 2 **prey on one's mind** : atormentar a algn

price n : precio m — **price** vt **priced; pricing** : poner un precio a — **priceless** adj : inestimable

prick n : pinchazo m — **prick** vt 1 : pinchar 2 **prick up one's ears** : levantar las orejas — **prickly** adj : espinoso

pride n : orgullo m — **pride** vt **prided; priding pride oneself on** : enorgullecerse de

priest n : sacerdote m — **priesthood** n : sacerdocio m

prim adj **primmer; primmest** : remilgado

primary adj 1 FIRST : primario 2 PRINCIPAL : principal — **primarily** adv

precipitation: forms of rain
precipitaciones*F*: formas*F* de lluvia*F*

drizzle
*llovizna*F

light rain
*lluvia*F *ligera*

moderate rain
*lluvia*F *moderada*

heavy rain
*lluvia*F *intensa*

: principalmente
prime[1] *vt* **primed; priming 1** : cebar (un arma de fuego, etc.) **2** PREPARE : preparar
prime[2] *n* **the prime of one's life** : la flor de la vida — **prime** *adj* **1** MAIN : principal, primero **2** EXCELLENT : excelente — **prime minister** *n* : primero ministro *m*, primera ministra *f*
primer[1] *n* : base *f* (de pintura)
primer[2] *n* READER : cartilla *f*
primitive *adj* : primitivo
primrose *n* : primavera *f*
prince *n* : príncipe *m* — **princess** *n* : princesa *f*
principal *adj* : principal — **principal** *n* : director *m*, -tora *f* (de un colegio)
principle *n* : principio *m*
print *n* **1** MARK : huella *f* **2** LETTERING : letra *f* **3** ENGRAVING : grabado *m* **4** : estampado *m* (de tela) **5** : copia *f* (en fotografía) **6 out of print** : agotado — **print** *vt* : imprimir (libros, etc.) — *vi* : escribir con letra de molde — **printer** *n* **1** : impresor *m*, -sora *f* (persona) **2** : impresora *f* (máquina) — **printing** *n* **1** : impresión *f* **2** : imprenta *f* (profesión) **3** LETTERING : letras *fpl* de molde
prior *adj* **1** : previo **2 prior to** : antes de — **priority** *n*, *pl* **-ties** : prioridad *f*
prison *n* : prisión *f*, cárcel *f* — **prisoner** *n* **1** : preso *m*, -sa *f* **2 prisoner of war** : prisionero *m*, -ra *f* de guerra
privacy *n*, *pl* **-cies** : intimidad *f* — **private** *adj* **1** : privado **2** SECRET :

secreto — **privacy** *n* : soldado *m* raso — **privately** *adv* : en privado
privilege *n* : privilegio *m* — **privileged** *adj* : privilegiado
prize *n* : premio *m* — **prize** *adj* : premiado — **prize** *vt* **prized; prizing** : valorar, apreciar — **prizefighter** *n* : boxeador *m*, -dora *f* profesional — **prizewinning** *adj* : premiado
pro *n* **1** → **professional 2 the pros and cons** : los pros y los contras
probability *n*, *pl* **-ties** : probabilidad *f* — **probable** *adj* : probable — **probably** *adv* : probablemente
probation *n* **1** : período *m* de prueba (de un empleado, etc.) **2** : libertad *f* condicional (de un preso)
probe *n* **1** : sonda *f* (en medicina, etc.) **2** INVESTIGATION : investigación *f* — **probe** *vt* **probed; probing 1** : sondar **2** INVESTIGATE : investigar
problem *n* : problema *m*
procedure *n* : procedimiento *m*
proceed *vi* **1** ACT : proceder **2** CONTINUE : continuar **3** ADVANCE : avanzar — **proceedings** *npl* **1** EVENTS : actos *mpl* **2** : proceso *m* (en derecho) — **proceeds** *npl* : ganancias *fpl*
process *n*, *pl* **-cesses 1** : proceso *m* **2 in the process of** : en vías de — **process** *vt* : procesar — **procession** *n* : desfile *m*
proclaim *vt* : proclamar — **proclamation** *n* : proclamación *f*

procrastinate *vi* **-nated; -nating** : demorar, aplazar
procure *vt* **-cured; -curing** : obtener
prod *vt* **prodded; prodding** : pinchar, aguijonear
prodigal *adj* : pródigo
prodigy *n*, *pl* **-gies** : prodigio *m*
produce *vt* **-duced; -ducing 1** : producir **2** CAUSE : causar **3** SHOW : presentar, mostrar **4** : poner en escena (una obra de teatro) — **produce** *n* : productos *mpl* agrícolas — **producer** *n* : productor *m*, -tora *f* — **product** *n* : producto *m* — **productive** *adj* : productivo
profane *adj* **1** : profano **2** IRREVERENT : blasfemo — **profanity** *n*, *pl* **-ties** : blasfemia *f*
profess *vt* : profesar — **profession** *n* : profesión *f* — **professional** *adj* : profesional — **profess** *n* : profesional *mf* — **professor** *n* : profesor *m*, -sora *f*
proficiency *n* : competencia *f* — **proficient** *adj* : competente
profile *n* **1** : perfil *m* **2 keep a low profile** : no llamar la atención
profit *n* : beneficio *m*, ganancia *f* — **profit** *vi* : sacar provecho (de), beneficiarse (de) — **profitable** *adj* : provechoso
profound *adj* : profundo
profuse *adj* : profuso — **profusion** *n* : profusión *f*
prognosis *n*, *pl* **-noses** : pronóstico *m*
program *n* : programa *m* — **program** *vt* **-grammed** *or* **-gramed;**

-**gramming** *or* -**graming** : programar

progress *n* **1** : progreso *m* **2** ADVANCE
: avance *m* — **progress** *vi* : progresar,
avanzar — **progressive** *adj* **1** :
progresista (dícese de la política,
etc.) **2** INCREASING : progresiva

prohibit *vt* : prohibir —
prohibition *n* : prohibición *f*

project *n* : proyecto *m* — **project** *vt*
: proyectar — *vi* PROTRUDE : sobresalir
— **projectile** *n* : proyectil *m* —
projection *n* **1** : proyección *f* **2**
PROTRUSION : saliente *m* —
projector *n* : proyector *m*

proliferate *vi* -**ated**; -**ating** : proliferar
— **proliferation** *n* : proliferación *f*
— **prolific** *adj* : prolífico

prologue *n* : prólogo *m*

prolong *vt* : prolongar

prom *n* : baile *m* formal (en un colegio)

prominent *adj* : prominente —
prominence *n* **1** : prominencia *f* **2**
IMPORTANCE : eminencia *f*

promiscuous *adj* : promiscuo

promise *n* : promesa *f*

— **promise** *v* -**ised**; -**ising** : prometer
— **promising** *adj* : prometedor

promote *vt* -**moted**; -**moting** **1** :
ascender (a un alumno o un empleado)
2 FURTHER : promover, fomentar **3**
ADVERTISE : promocionar — **promoter** *n*
: promotor *m*, -tora *f*; empresario *m*,
-ria *f* (en deportes) — **promotion** *n* **1** :
ascenso *m* (de un alumno o un empleado)
2 ADVERTISING : publicidad *f*, propaganda *f*

prompt *vt* **1** INCITE : provocar (una cosa),
inducir (a una persona) **2** : apuntar
(a un actor, etc.) — **prompt** *adj* **1**
: rápido **2** PUNCTUAL : puntual

prone *adj* **1** : boca abajo, decúbito
prono **2 be prone to** : ser propenso a

prong *n* : punta *f*, diente *m*

pronoun *n* : pronombre *m*

pronounce *vt* -**nounced**;
-**nouncing** : pronunciar —
pronouncement *n* : declaración *f* —
pronunciation *n* : pronunciación *f*

proof *n* : prueba *f* — **proof** *adj* **proof
against** : a prueba de — **proofread** *vt*
-**read**; -**reading** : corregir

prop *n* **1** SUPPORT : puntal *m*, apoyo *m* **2**
: accesorio *m* (en teatro) — **prop** *vt*
propped; **propping 1 prop against** :
apoyar contra **2 prop up** SUPPORT : apoyar

propaganda *n* : propaganda *f*

propagate *v* -**gated**; -**gating** *vt*
: propagar — *vi* : propagarse

propel *vt* -**pelled**; -**pelling** :
propulsar — **propeller** *n* : hélice *f*

propensity *n*, *pl* -**ties** : propensión *f*

proper *adj* **1** SUITABLE : apropiado **2** REAL :
verdadero **3** CORRECT : correcto **4** GENTEEL
: cortés **5 proper name** : nombre *m*
propio — **properly** *adv* : correctamente

property *n*, *pl* -**ties** **1** : propiedad *f* **2**
BUILDING : inmueble *m* **3**
LAND LOT : parcela *f*

prophet *n* : profeta *m*, profetisa *f*
— **prophecy** *n*, *pl* -**cies** : profecía *f*
— **prophesy** *v* -**sied**; -**sying** *vt* :
profetizar — *vi* : hacer profecías
— **prophetic** *adj* : profético

proportion *n* **1** : proporción *f* **2** SHARE :
parte *f* — **proportional** *adj* : proporcional
— **proportionate** *adj* : proporcional

pruning and cutting tools
herramientas para cortar y podar

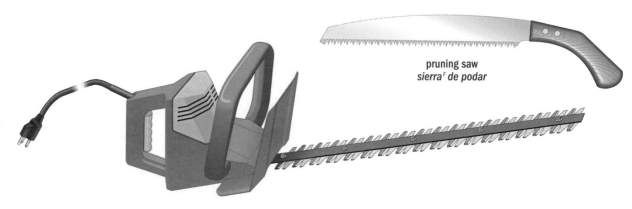

pruning saw
sierra^F de podar

hedge trimmer
cortasetos^M eléctrico

ax
hacha^F

pruning shears
tijeras^F de podar

proposal *n* : propuesta *f*
propose *v* **-posed; -posing** *vt* **1**
  SUGGEST : proponer **2 propose to**
  do something : pensar hacer algo
  — *vi* : proponer matrimonio —
proposition *n* : proposición *f*
proprietor *n* : propietario *m*, -ria *f*
propriety *n, pl* **-eties** :
  decencia *f*, decoro *m*
propulsion *n* : propulsión *f*
prose *n* : prosa *f*
prosecute *vt* **-cuted; -cuting** : procesar
  — **prosecution** *n* **1** : procesamiento *m* **2**
  the prosecute : la acusación —
prosecutor *n* : acusador *m*, -dora *f*
prospect *n* **1** : perspectiva *f* **2**
  POSSIBILITY : posibilidad *f* —
prospective *adj* : futuro, posible
prosper *vi* : prosperar — **prosperity** *n* :
  prosperidad *f* — **prosperous** *adj* : próspero
prostitute *n* : prostituta *f* —
prostitution *n* : prostitución *f*
prostrate *adj* : postrado
protagonist *n* : protagonista *mf*
protect *vt* : proteger — **protection** *n* :
  protección *f* — **protective** *adj* : protector
  — **protector** *n* : protector *m*, -tora *f*
protégé *n* : protegido *m*, -da *f*
protein *n* : proteína *f*
protest *n* : protesta *f* — **protest** *vt* :
  protestar mdash} *vi* **protest against**
  : protestar contra — **Protestant** *n*
  : protestante *mf* — **protester** *or*
  protestor *n* : manifestante *mf*
protocol *n* : protocolo *m*
prototype *n* : prototipo *m*
protract *vt* : prolongar
protrude *vi* **-truded; -truding** : sobresalir
proud *adj* : orgulloso
prove *v* **proved; proved** *or* **proven;**
  proving *vt* : probar — *vi* : resultar
proverb *n* : proverbio *m*, refrán *m*
  — **proverbial** *adj* : proverbial
provide *v* **-vided; -viding** *vt* : proveer
  — *vi* **provide for** SUPPORT : mantener
  — **provided** *or* **provided that** *conj*
  : con tal (de) que, siempre que —
providence *n* : providencia *f*
province *n* **1** : provincia *f* **2**
  SPHERE : campo *m*, competencia *f*
  — **provincial** *adj* : provinciano
provision *n* **1** : provisión *f*,
  suministro *m* **2** STIPULATION :
  condición *f* **3** provisions *npl* : víveres *mpl*
  — **provisional** *adj* : provisional

— **proviso** *n, pl* **-sos** *or* **-soes** : condición *f*
provoke *vt* **-voked; -voking** : provocar
  — **provocation** *n* : provocación *f* —
provocative *adj* : provocador, provocativo
prow *n* : proa *f*
prowess *n* **1** BRAVERY :
  valor *m* **2** SKILL : habilidad *f*
prowl *vi* : merodear, rondar — *vt*
  : merodear por — **prowler** *n*
  : merodeador *m*, -dora *f*
proximity *n* : proximidad *f* — **proxy** *n,*
  pl **proxies by proxy** : por poder
prude *n* : mojigato *m*, -ta *f*
prudence *n* : prudencia *f* —
prudent *adj* : prudente
prune¹ *n* : ciruela *f* pasa
▸ **prune²** *vt* **pruned; pruning** :
  podar (arbustos, etc.)
pry *v* **pried; prying** *vi* **pry into**
  : entrometerse en — *vt or* **pry**
  open : abrir (a la fuerza)
psalm *n* : salmo *m*
pseudonym *n* : seudónimo *m*
psychiatry *n* : psiquiatría *f* —
  psychiatric *adj* : psiquiátrico —
  psychiatrist *n* : psiquiatra *mf*
psychic *adj* : psíquico
psychoanalysis *n, pl* **-yses** :
  psicoanálisis *m* — **psychoanalyst** *n* :
  psicoanalista *mf* — **psychoanalyze** *vt*
  -lyzed; -lyzing : psicoanalizar
psychology *n, pl* **-gies** : psicología *f*
  — **psychological** *adj* : psicológico —
  psychologist *n* : psicólogo *m*, -ga *f*
psychopath *n* : psicópata *mf*
psychotherapy *n, pl* **-pies**
  : psicoterapia *f*
psychotic *adj* : psicótico
puberty *n* : pubertad *f*
pubic *adj* : púbico
public *adj* : público — **public** *n* : público *m*
  — **publication** *n* : publicación *f* —
publicity *n* : publicidad *f* — **publicize** *vt*
  -cized; -cizing : publicitar, divulgar
publish *vt* : publicar — **publisher** *n* **1**
  : editor *m*, -tora *f* (persona) **2** :
  casa *f* editorial (negocio)
pucker *vt* : fruncir, arrugar
  — *vi* : arrugarse
pudding *n* : budín *m*, pudín *m*
puddle *n* : charco *m*
pudgy *adj* **pudgier; -est** : rechoncho *fam*
Puerto Rican *adj* : puertorriqueño
puff *vi* **1** BLOW : soplar **2** PANT : resoplar
  3 puff up SWELL : hincharse — *vt* **puff**

Halloween pumpkin
calabaza*f* de Halloween

out : hinchar — **puff** *n* **1** : bocanada *f*
  (de humo) **2** : chupada *f* (a un cigarrillo)
  3 *or* **cream puff** : pastelito *m* de
  crema **4** *or* **powder puff** : borla *f* —
puffy *adj* **puffier; -est** : hinchado
pull *vt* **1** : tirar de **2** EXTRACT : sacar
  3 TEAR : desgarrarse (un músculo,
  etc.) **4 pull off** REMOVE : quitar **5 pull**
  oneself together : calmarse **6 pull up**
  : levantar, subir — *vi* **1** : tirar **2 pull**
  through RECOVER : reponerse **3 pull**
  together COOPERATE : reunir **4 pull up**
  STOP : parar — **pull** *n* **1** : tirón *m* **2**
  INFLUENCE : influencia *f* — **pulley** *n,*
  pl **-leys** : polea *f* — **pullover** *n* : suéter *m*
pulp *n* **1** : pulpa *f* (de frutas, etc.) **2**
  or **wood pulp** : pasta *f* de papel
pulpit *n* : púlpito *m*
pulsate *vi* **-sated; -sating** :
  palpitar — **pulse** *n* : pulso *m*
pulverize *vt* **-ized; -izing** : pulverizar
pummel *vt* **-meled; -meling** : aporrear
pump¹ *n* : bomba *f* — **pump** *vt* **1**
  : bombear **2 pump up** : inflar
pump² *n* SHOE : zapato *m* de tacón
pumpernickel *n* : pan *m*
  negro de centeno
▸ **pumpkin** *n* : calabaza *f*, zapallo *m*, *Lat*
pun *n* : juego *m* de palabras
  — **pun** *vi* **punned; punning** :
  hacer juegos de palabras
punch¹ *vt* **1** : dar un puñetazo a **2**
  PERFORATE : perforar (papeles, etc.),
  picar (un boleto) — **punch** *n* **1**
  : golpe *m*, puñetazo *m* **2** *or*
paper punch : perforadora *f*

pyramid
pirámide[F]

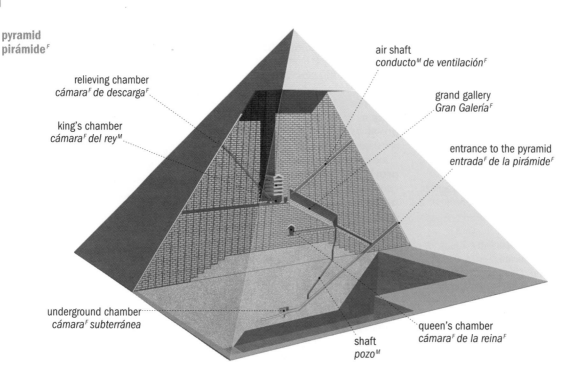

relieving chamber
cámara[F] *de descarga*[F]

king's chamber
cámara[F] *del rey*[M]

air shaft
conducto[M] *de ventilación*[F]

grand gallery
Gran Galería[F]

entrance to the pyramid
entrada[F] *de la pirámide*[F]

underground chamber
cámara[F] *subterránea*

shaft
pozo[M]

queen's chamber
cámara[F] *de la reina*[F]

---

punch[2] *n* : ponche *m* (bebida)
punctual *adj* : puntual —
　punctuality *n* : puntualidad *f*
punctuate *vt* -ated; -ating : puntuar
　— **punctuation** *n* : puntuación *f*
puncture *n* : pinchazo *m*,
　ponchadura *f Lat* — **puncture** *vt*
　-tured; -turing : pinchar, ponchar *Lat*
pungent *adj* : acre
punish *vt* : castigar — **punishment** *n*
　: castigo *m* — **punitive** *adj* : punitivo
puny *adj* -nier; -est : enclenque
pup *n* : cachorro *m*, -rra *f* (de un
　perro); cría *f* (de otros animales)
pupil[1] *n* : alumno *m*, -na *f* (de colegio)
pupil[2] *n* : pupila *f* (del ojo)
puppet *n* : títere *m*
puppy *n, pl* -**pies** : cachorro *m*, -rra *f*
purchase *vt* -chased; -chasing :
　comprar — **purchase** *n* : compra *f*
pure *adj* purer; purest : puro
puree *n* : puré *m*
purely *adv* : puramente
purgatory *n, pl* -ries : purgatorio *m*
　— **purge** *vt* **purged; purging** :
　purgar — **purgatory** *n* : purga *f*
purify *vt* -fied; -fying : purificar

— **purification** *n* : purificación *f*
puritanical *adj* : puritano
purity *n* : pureza *f*
purple *n* : morado *m*
purport *vt* **purport to be** : pretender ser
purpose *n* **1** : propósito *m* **2** RESOLUTION
　: determinación *f* **3 on purpose** : a
　propósito — **purposeful** *adj* : resuelto
　— **purposely** *adv* : a propósito
purr *n* : ronroneo *m* — **purr** *vi* : ronronear
purse *n* **1** *or* **change purse** :
　monedero *m* **2** HANDBAG : cartera *f*,
　bolso *m Spain*, bolsa *f Lat* —
　purse *vt* **pursed; pursing** : fruncir
pursue *vt* -**sued; -suing 1** CHASE :
　perseguir **2** SEEK : buscar — **pursuer** *n*
　: perseguidor *m*, -dora *f* — **pursuit** *n* **1**
　CHASE : persecución *f* **2** SEARCH :
　búsqueda *f* **3** OCCUPATION : actividad *f*
pus *n* : pus *m*
push *vt* **1** SHOVE : empujar **2** PRESS
　: apretar **3** URGE : presionar **4 push**
　around BULLY : mangonear — *vi* **1** :
　empujar **2 push for** : presionar para
　— **push** *n* **1** SHOVE : empujón *m* **2**
　DRIVE : dinamismo *m* **3** EFFORT :
　esfuerzo *m* — **pushy** *adj* **pushier;**

-est : mandón, prepotente
pussy *n, pl* **pussies** : gatito *m*,
　-ta *f;* minino *m*, -na *f*
put *v* put; putting *vt* **1** : poner **2** INSERT
　: meter **3** EXPRESS : decir **4 put one's**
　mind to something : proponerse hacer
　algo — *vi* **put up with** : aguantar — **put**
　away *vt* **1** STORE : guardar **2** *or* **put aside** :
　dejar a un lado — **put down** *vt* **1** SUPPRESS
　: aplastar, sofocar **2** ATTRIBUTE : atribuir
　— **put off** *vt* DEFER : aplazar, posponer —
　put on *vt* **1** ASSUME : adoptar **2** PRESENT :
　presentar (una obra de teatro, etc.) **3** WEAR
　: ponerse — **put out** *vt* INCONVENIENCE :
　incomodar — **put up** *vt* **1** BUILD : construir
　2 LODGE : alojar **3** PROVIDE : poner (dinero)
putrefy *vi* -fied; -fying : pudrirse
putty *n, pl* -ties : masilla *f*
puzzle *v* -zled; -zling *vt* : confundir,
　dejar perplejo — *vi* **puzzle over** :
　tratar de descifrar — **puzzle** *n* **1** :
　rompecabezas *m* **2** MYSTERY : enigma *m*
pylon *n* : pilón *m*
▸ **pyramid** *n* : pirámide *f*
python *n* : pitón *f*

q *n, pl* **q's** *or* **qs** : q *f*, decimoséptima letra del alfabeto inglés

quack[1] *vi* : graznar (dícese del pato) — **quack** *n* : graznido *m*

quack[2] *n* CHARLATAN : charlatán *m*, -tana *f*

quadruple *v* -**pled; -pling** *vt* : cuadruplicar — *vi* : cuadruplicarse

quagmire *n* : atolladero *m*

quail *n, pl* **quail** *or* **quails** : codorniz *f*

quaint *adj* **1** ODD : curioso **2** PICTURESQUE : pintoresco

quake *vi* **quaked; quaking** : temblar — **quake** *n* → **earthquake**

qualify *v* -**fied; -fying** *vt* **1** LIMIT : matizar **2** : calificar (en gramática) **3** EQUIP : habilitar — *vi* **1** : titularse (de abogado, etc.) **2** : clasificarse (en deportes) — **qualification** *n* **1** REQUIREMENT : requisito *m* **2** qualifys *npl* ABILITY : capacidad *f* **3 without qualification** : sin reservas — **qualified** *adj* : capacitado

quality *n, pl* -**ties 1** : calidad *f* **2** PROPERTY : cualidad *f*

qualm *n* **1** DOUBT : duda *f* **2 have no qualms about** : no tener ningún escrúpulo en

quandary *n, pl* -**ries** : dilema *m*

quantity *n, pl* -**ties** : cantidad *f*

quarantine *n* : cuarentena *f* — **quarantine** *vt* -**tined; -tining** : poner en cuarentena

quarrel *n* : pelea *f*, riña *f*

— **quarrel** *vi* -**reled** *or* -**relled; -reling** *or* -**relling** : pelearse, reñir

— **quarrelsome** *adj* : pendenciero

quarry[1] *n, pl* **quarries** PREY : presa *f*

quarry[2] *n, pl* **quarries** EXCAVATION : cantera *f*

quart *n* : cuarto *m* de galón

quarter *n* **1** : cuarto *m* (en matemáticas) **2** : moneda *f* de 25 centavos **3** DISTRICT : barrio *m* **4 quarter after three** : las tres y cuarto **5 quarters** *npl* LODGING : alojamiento *m* — **quarter** *vt* **1** : dividir en cuatro partes **2** : acuartelar (tropas) — **quarterly** *adv* : cada tres meses — **quarterly** *adj* : trimestral — **quarterly** *n, pl* -**lies** : publicación *f* trimestral

quartet *n* : cuarteto *m*

quartz *n* : cuarzo *m*

quash *vt* **1** ANNUL : anular **2** SUPPRESS : aplastar, sofocar

quaver *vi* : temblar

quay *n* : muelle *m*

queasy *adj* -**sier; -est** : mareado

queen *n* : reina *f*

queer *adj* ODD : extraño

quell *vt* SUPPRESS : sofocar, aplastar

quench *vt* **1** EXTINGUISH : apagar **2 quench one's thirst** : quitar la sed

query *n, pl* -**ries** : pregunta *f* — **query** *vt* -**ried; -rying 1** ASK : preguntar **2** QUESTION : cuestionar

quest *n* : búsqueda *f*

question *n* **1** QUERY : pregunta *f* **2** ISSUE : cuestión *f* **3 be out of the question** : ser indiscutible **4 call into question** : poner en duda **5 without question** : sin duda — **question** *vt* **1** ASK : preguntar **2** DOUBT : cuestionar **3** INTERROGATE : interrogar — *vi* : preguntar — **questionable** *adj* : discutible — **question mark** *n* : signo *m* de interrogación — **questionnaire** *n* : cuestionario *m*

queue *n* : cola *f* — **queue** *vi* **queued; queuing** *or* **queueing** : hacer cola

quibble *vi* -**bled; -bling** : discutir, quejarse por nimiedades

quick *adj* **1** : rápido **2** CLEVER : agudo — **quick** *n* **to the quick** : en lo vivo — **quick** *adv* : rápidamente — **quicken** *vt* : acelerar — **quickly** *adv* : rápidamente — **quicksand** *n* : arena *f* movediza — **quick–tempered** *adj* : irascible — **quick–witted** *adj* : agudo

quiet *n* **1** : silencio *m* **2** CALM : tranquilidad *f* — **quiet** *adj* **1** : silencioso **2** CALM : tranquilo **3** RESERVED : callado **4** : discreto (dícese de colores, etc.) — **quiet** *vt* **1** SILENCE : hacer callar **2** CALM : calmar — *vi or* **quiet down** : calmarse — **quietly** *adv* **1** : silenciosamente **2** CALMLY : tranquilamente

quilt *n* : edredón *m*

▸ **quintet** *n* : quinteto *m*

quip *n* : ocurrencia *f*, salida *f* — **quip** *vt* **quipped; quipping** : decir bromeando

quirk *n* : peculiaridad *f*

quit *v* **quit; quitting** *vt* **1** LEAVE : dejar, abandonar **2 quit doing** : dejar de hacer — *vi* **1** STOP : parar **2** RESIGN : dimitir, renunciar

quite *adv* **1** COMPLETELY : completamente **2** RATHER : bastante

quits *adj* **call it quits** : quedar en paz

quiver *vi* : temblar

quiz *n, pl* **quizzes** TEST : prueba *f* — **quiz** *vt* **quizzed; quizzing** : interrogar

quota *n* : cuota *f*, cupo *m*

quotation *n* **1** : cita *f* **2** ESTIMATE : presupuesto *m* — **quotation marks** *npl* : comillas *fpl* — **quote** *vt* **quoted; quoting 1** CITE : citar **2** : cotizar (en finanzas) — **quote** *n* **1** → **quotation 2 quotes** *npl* → **quotation marks**

quotient *n* : cociente *m*

quintet
quinteto[M]

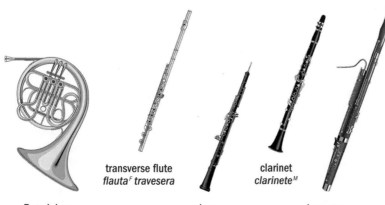

French horn
corno[M] *francés/trompa*[F]

transverse flute
flauta[F] *travesera*

oboe
oboe[M]

clarinet
clarinete[M]

bassoon
fagot[M]

r *n, pl* **r's** *or* **rs** : r *f*, decimoctava letra del alfabeto inglés

rabbi *n* : rabino *m*, -na *f*

▸ **rabbit** *n, pl* **-bit** *or* **-bits** : conejo *m*, -ja *f*

rabble *n* : chusma *f*, populacho *m*

rabies *ns & pl* : rabia *f* — **rabid** *adj* **1** : rabioso **2** FANATIC : fanático

raccoon *n, pl* **-coon** *or* **-coons** : mapache *m*

race[1] *n* **1** : raza *f* **2 human race** : género *m* humano

race[2] *n* : carrera *f* (competitiva) — **race** *vi* **raced; racing 1** : correr (en una carrera) **2** RUSH : ir corriendo — **racehorse** *n* : caballo *m* de carreras — **racetrack** *n* : pista *f* (de carreras)

racial *adj* : racial — **racism** *n* : racismo *m* — **racist** *n* : racista *mf*

rack *n* **1** SHELF : estante *m* **2 luggage rack** : portaequipajes *m* — **rack** *vt* **1 racked with** : atormentado por **2 rack one's brains** : devanarse los sesos

racket[1] *n* : raqueta *f* (en deportes)

racket[2] *n* **1** DIN : alboroto *m*, bulla *f* **2** SWINDLE : estafa *f*

racy *adj* **racier; -est** : subido de tono, picante

radar *n* : radar *m*

radiant *adj* : radiante — **radiance** *n* : resplandor *m* — **radiate** *v* **-ated; -ating** *vt* : irradiar — *vi* **1** : irradiar **2** *or* **radiant out** : extenderse (desde un centro) — **radiation** *n* : radiación *f* — **radiator** *n* : radiador *m*

radical *adj* : radical — **radical** *n* : radical *mf*

radii → **radius**

radio *n, pl* **-dios** : radio *mf* (aparato), radio *f* (medio) — **radio** *vt* : transmitir por radio — **radioactive** *adj* : radioactivo, radiactivo

radish *n* : rábano *m*

radius *n, pl* **radii** : radio *m*

raffle *vt* **-fled; -fling** : rifar — **raffle** *n* : rifa *f*

raft *n* : balsa *f*

rafter *n* : cabrio *m*

rag *n* **1** : trapo *m* **2 rags** *npl* TATTERS : harapos *mpl*, andrajos *mpl*

rage *n* **1** : cólera *f*, rabia *f* **2 be all the rage** : hacer furor — **rage** *vi* **raged; raging 1** : estar furioso **2** : bramar (dícese del viento, etc.)

ragged *adj* **1** UNEVEN : irregular **2** TATTERED : andrajoso, harapiento

raid *n* **1** : invasión *f* (militar) **2** : asalto *m* (por delincuentes), redada *f* (por la policía) — **raid** *vt* **1** INVADE : invadir **2** ROB : asaltar **3** : hacer una redada en (dícese de la policía) — **raider** *n* ATTACKER : asaltante *mf*

rail[1] *vi* **rail at someone** : recriminar a algn

rail[2] *n* **1** BAR : barra *f* **2** HANDRAIL : pasamanos *m* **3** TRACK : riel *m* **4 by rail** : por ferrocarril — **railing** *n* **1** : baranda *f* (de un balcón), pasamanos *m* (de una escalera) **2** RAILS : reja *f* — **railroad** *n* : errocarril *m* — **railway** → **railroad**

rain *n* : lluvia *f* — **rain** *vi* : llover — **rainbow** *n* : arco *m* iris — **raincoat** *n* : impermeable *m* — **rainfall** *n* : precipitación *f* — **rainy** *adj* **rainier; -est** : lluvioso

raise *vt* **raised; raising 1** : levantar **2** COLLECT : recaudar **3** REAR : criar **4** GROW : cultivar **5** INCREASE : aumentar **6** : sacar (objeciones, etc.) — **raise** *n* : aumento *m*

raisin *n* : pasa *f*

rake *n* : rastrillo *m* — **rake** *vt* **raked; raking** : rastrillar

rally *v* **-lied; -lying** *vi* **1** : unirse, reunirse **2** RECOVER : recuperarse — *vt* : conseguir (apoyo), unir a (la gente) — **rally** *n, pl* **-lies** : reunión *f*, mitin *m*

ram *n* : carnero *m* (animal) — **ram** *vt* **rammed; ramming 1** CRAM : meter con fuerza **2** *or* **ram into** : chocar contra

RAM *n* : RAM *f*

ramble *vi* **-bled; -bling 1** WANDER : pasear **2** *or* **ramble on** : divagar

section of a raspberry
corte*ᴹ* de una frambuesa*ᶠ*

peduncle
pedúnculo*ᴹ*

seed
semilla*ᶠ*

sepal
sépalo*ᴹ*

drupelet
drupéola*ᶠ*

receptacle
receptáculo*ᴹ*

— **ramble** *n* : paseo *m*, excursión *f*

▸ **ramp** *n* : rampa *f*

rampage *vi* **-paged; -paging** : andar arrasando todo — **rampage** *n* : frenesí *m* (de violencia)

rampant *adj* : desenfrenado

rampart *n* : muralla *f*

ramshackle *adj* : destartalado

ran → **run**

ranch *n* : hacienda *f* — **rancher** *n* : hacendado *m*, -da *f*

rancid *adj* : rancio

rancor *n* : rencor *m*

random *adj* **1** : aleatorio **2 at random** : al azar

rang → **ring**

range *n* **1** GRASSLAND : pradera *f* **2** STOVE : cocina *f* **3** VARIETY : gama *f* **4** SCOPE : amplitud *f* **5** *or* **mountain range** : cordillera *f* — **range** *vi* **ranged; ranging 1** EXTEND : extenderse **2 range from… to…** : variar entre…y… — **ranger** *n* *or* **forest ranger** : guardabosque *mf*

rank[1] *adj* **1** SMELLY : fétido

rabbit
conejo*ᴹ*

2 OUTRIGHT : **completo**
rank^2 *n* **1** ROW : **fila** *f* **2** : **rango** *m* (militar)
3 ranks *npl* : **soldados** *mpl* **rasos 4 the**
rank and file : **las bases** — **rank** *vt*
RATE : **clasificar** — *vi* : **clasificarse**
rankle *vi* **-kled; -kling** :
causar rencor, doler
ransack *vt* **1** SEARCH :
registrar 2 LOOT : **saquear**
ransom *n* : **rescate** *m* —
ransom *vt* : **rescatar**
rant *vi or* **rant and rave** : **despotricar**
rap^1 *n* KNOCK : **golpecito** *m* — **rap** *v*
rapped; rapping : **golpear**
rap^2 *n or* **rap music** : **rap** *m*
rapacious *adj* : **rapaz**
rape *vt* **raped; raping** : **violar**
— **rape** *n* : **violación** *f*
rapid *adj* : **rápido** —
rapids *npl* : **rápidos** *mpl*
rapist *n* : **violador** *m*, **-dora** *f*
rapport *n* **have a good rapport**
: **entenderse bien**
rapt *adj* : **absorto, embelesado**
rapture *n* : **éxtasis** *m*
rare *adj* **rarer; rarest 1** FINE : **excepcional**
2 UNCOMMON : **raro 3** : **poco cocido**

(dícese de la carne) — **rarely** *adv* :
raramente — **rarity** *n*, *pl* **-ties** : **rareza** *f*
rascal *n* : **pillo** *m*, **-lla** *f*; **pícaro** *m*, **-ra** *f*
rash^1 *adj* : **imprudente, precipitado**
rash^2 *n* : **sarpullido** *m*, **erupción** *f*
rasp *vt* SCRAPE : **raspar** —
rasp *n* : **escofina** *f*
▸ **raspberry** *n*, *pl* **-ries** : **frambuesa** *f*
rat *n* : **rata** *f*
rate *n* **1** PACE : **velocidad** *f*, **ritmo** *m* **2** :
tipo *m*, **tasa** *m* (de interés, etc.) **3** PRICE :
tarifa *f* **4 at any rate** : **de todos modos**
5 birth rate : **índice** *m* **de natalidad**
— **rate** *vt* **rated; rating 1** REGARD :
considerar 2 DESERVE : **merecer**
rather *adv* **1** FAIRLY : **bastante**
2 I'd rather… : **prefiero… 3**
or **rather** : **o mejor dicho**
ratify *vt* **-fied; -fying** : **ratificar** —
ratification *n* : **ratificación** *f*
rating *n* **1** : **clasificación** *f* **2**
ratings *npl* : **índice** *m* **de audiencia**
ratio *n*, *pl* **-tios** : **proporción** *f*
ration *n* **1** : **ración** *f* **2 rations** *npl*
PROVISIONS : **víveres** *mpl* — **ration** *vt*
rationed; rationing : **racionar**
rational *adj* : **racional** — **rationale** *n*

: **lógica** *f*, **razones** *fpl* — **rationalize** *vt*
-ized; -izing : **racionalizar**
rattle *v* **-tled; -tling** *vi* : **traquetear**
— *vt* **1** SHAKE : **agitar 2** UPSET :
desconcertar 3 rattle off : **decir de**
corrido — **rattle** *n* **1** : **traqueteo** *m* **2**
or **baby's rattle** : **sonajero** *m* —
rattlesnake *n* : **serpiente** *f* **de cascabel**
raucous *adj* **1** HOARSE : **ronco**
2 BOISTEROUS : **bullicioso**
ravage *vt* **-aged; -aging** : **estragar,**
asolar — **ravages** *npl* : **estragos** *mpl*
rave *vi* **raved; raving 1** : **delirar 2 rave**
about : **hablar con entusiasmo sobre**
raven *n* : **cuervo** *m*
ravenous *adj* **1** HUNGRY :
hambriento 2 VORACIOUS : **voraz**
ravine *n* : **barranco** *m*
ravishing *adj* : **encantador**
raw *adj* **rawer; rawest 1** UNCOOKED : **crudo**
2 INEXPERIENCED : **inexperto 3** CHAFED :
en carne viva 4 : **frío y húmedo** (dícese
del tiempo) **5 raw deal** : **trato** *m* **injusto**
6 raw materials : **materias** *fpl* **primas**
ray *n* : **rayo** *m*
rayon *n* : **rayón** *m*
raze *vt* **razed; razing** : **arrasar**

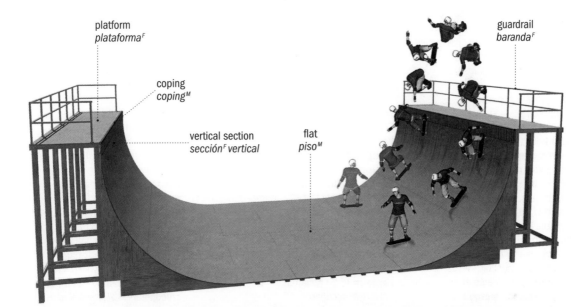

skateboarding ramp
medio tubo^M para skateboard^M

platform
plataforma^F

coping
coping^M

vertical section
sección^F vertical

flat
piso^M

guardrail
baranda^F

razor *n* : maquinilla *f* de afeitar —
razor blade *n* : hoja *f* de afeitar
reach *vt* **1** : alcanzar **2** *or* **reach out**
: extender **3** : llegar a (un acuerdo,
un límite, etc.) **4** CONTACT : contactar
— *vi* **1** : extenderse **2 reach for**
: tratar de agarrar — **reach** *n* **1** :
alcance *m* **2 within reach** : al alcance
react *vi* : reaccionar — **reaction** *n* :
reacción *f* — **reactionary** *adj* : reaccionario
— **react** *n*, *pl* **-ries** : reaccionario *m*,
-ria *f* — **reactor** *n* : reactor *m*
read *v* **read; reading** *vt* **1** : leer
2 INTERPRET : interpretar **3** SAY :
decir **4** INDICATE : marcar — *vi* **1** :
leer **2 it reads as follows** : dice lo
siguiente — **readable** *adj* : legible
— **reader** *n* : lector *m*, -tora *f*
readily *adv* **1** WILLINGLY : de buena
gana **2** EASILY : fácilmente
reading *n* : lectura *f*
readjust *vt* : reajustar — *vi*
: volverse a adaptar
ready *adj* **readier; -est 1** : listo, preparado
2 WILLING : dispuesto **3** AVAILABLE :
disponible **4 get ready** : prepararse —
ready *vt* **readied; readying** : preparar
real *adj* **1** : verdadero, real **2**
GENUINE : auténtico — **real** *adv* VERY
: muy — **real estate** *n* : propiedad *f*
inmobiliaria, bienes *mpl* raíces —
realism *n* : realismo *m* — **realist** *n* :
realista *mf* — **realistic** *adj* : realista
— **reality** *n*, *pl* **-ties** : realidad *f*
realize *vt* **-ized; -izing 1** : darse cuenta
de **2** ACHIEVE : realizar — **realization** *n* **1** :
comprensión *f* **2** FULFILLMENT : realización *f*
really *adv* : verdaderamente
realm *n* **1** KINGDOM : reino *m* **2**
SPHERE : esfera *f*
ream *n* : resma *f* (de papel)
reap *v* : cosechar
reappear *vi* : reaparecer
rear[1] *vt* **1** RAISE : levantar **2** : criar (niños,
etc.) — *vi or* **rear up** : encabritarse
rear[2] *n* **1** BACK : parte *f* de atrás
2 BUTTOCKS : trasero *m fam* —
rear *adj* : trasero, posterior
rearrange *vt* **-ranged; -ranging**
: reorganizar, cambiar
reason *n* : razón *f* — **reason** *vt*
THINK : pensar — *vi* : razonar —
reasonable *adj* : razonable —
reasoning *n* : razonamiento *m*
reassure *vt* **-sured; -suring** :

tranquilizar — **reassurance** *n* :
(palabras *fpl* de) consuelo *m*
rebate *n* : reembolso *m*
rebel *n* : rebelde *mf* — **rebel** *vi* **-belled;**
-belling : rebelarse — **rebellion** *n* :
rebelión *f* — **rebellious** *adj* : rebelde
rebirth *n* : renacimiento *m*
rebound *vi* : rebotar —
rebound *n* : rebote *m*
rebuff *vt* : rechazar — **rebuff** *n* : desaire *m*
rebuild *vt* **-built; -building** : reconstruir
rebuke *vt* **-buked; -buking** : reprender
— **rebuke** *n* : reprimenda *f*
rebut *vt* **-butted; -butting** : rebatir
— **rebuttal** *n* : refutación *f*
recall *vt* **1** : llamar (al servicio,
etc.) **2** REMEMBER : recordar **3**
REVOKE : revocar — **recall** *n* **1** :
retirada *f* **2** MEMORY : memoria *f*
recant *vi* : retractarse
recapitulate *v* **-lated;**
-lating : recapitular
recapture *vt* **-tured; -turing 1**
: recobrar **2** RELIVE : revivir
recede *vi* **-ceded; -ceding** : retirarse
receipt *n* **1** : recibo *m* **2**
receipts *npl* : ingresos *mpl*
receive *vt* **-ceived; -ceiving** : recibir —
receiver *n* **1** : receptor *m* (de radio, etc.)
2 *or* **telephone receiver** : auricular *m*
recent *adj* : reciente —
recently *adv* : recientemente
receptacle *n* : receptáculo *m*,
recipiente *m*
reception *n* : recepción *f* —
receptionist *n* : recepcionista *mf*
— **receptive** *adj* : receptivo
recess *n* **1** ALCOVE : hueco *m* **2** :
recreo *m* (escolar) **3** ADJOURNMENT :
suspensión *f* de actividades *Spain*,
receso *m*, *Lat* — **recession** *n* : recesión *f*
recharge *vt* **-charged; -charging** :
recargar — **rechargeable** *adj* : recargable
recipe *n* : receta *f*
recipient *n* : recipiente *mf*
reciprocal *adj* : recíproco
recite *vt* **-cited; -citing 1** : recitar
(un poema, etc.) **2** LIST : enumerar
— **recital** *n* : recital *m*
reckless *adj* : imprudente —
recklessness *n* : imprudencia *f*
reckon *vt* **1** COMPUTE : calcular **2** CONSIDER
: considerar — **reckoning** *n* : cálculos *mpl*
reclaim *vt* **1** : reclamar **2**
RECOVER : recuperar

recline *vi* **-clined; -clining** :
reclinarse — **reclining** *adj* : reclinable
(dícese de un asiento, etc.)
recluse *n* : solitario *m*, -ria *f*
recognition *n* : reconocimiento *m*
— **recognizable** *adj* : reconocible —
recognize *vt* **-nized; -nizing** : reconocer
recoil *vi* : retroceder — **recoil** *n* :
culatazo *m* (de un arma de fuego)
recollect *v* : recordar —
recollection *n* : recuerdo *m*
recommend *vt* : recomendar —
recommendation *n* : recomendación *f*
reconcile *v* **-ciled; -ciling** *vt* **1** :
reconciliar (personas), conciliar (datos,
etc.) **2 reconcile oneself to** : resignarse
a — *vi* MAKE UP : reconciliarse —
reconciliation *n* : reconciliación *f*
reconnaissance *n* :
reconocimiento *m* (militar)
reconsider *vt* : reconsiderar
reconstruct *vt* : reconstruir
record *vt* **1** WRITE DOWN : anotar,
apuntar **2** REGISTER : registrar **3** :
grabar (música, etc.) — **record** *n* **1**
DOCUMENT : documento *m* **2** REGISTER
: registro *m* **3** HISTORY : historial *m* **4**
: disco *m* (de música, etc.) **5 criminal**
record : antecedentes *mpl* penales **6**
world record : récord *m* mundial —
recorder *n* **1** : flauta *f* dulce **2** *or* **tape**
recorder : grabadora *f* — **recording** *n* :
disco *m* — **record player** *n* : tocadiscos *m*
recount[1] *vt* NARRATE : narrar, relatar
recount[2] *vt* : volver a contar (votos,
etc.) **recount** — *n* : recuento *m*
recourse *n* **1** : recurso *m* **2**
have recourse to : recurrir a
recover *vt* : recobrar — *vi* RECUPERATE
: recuperarse — **recovery** *n*,
pl **-eries** : recuperación *f*
recreation *n* : recreo *m* —
recreational *adj* : de recreo
recruit *vt* : reclutar — **recruit** *n*
: recluta *mf* — **recruitment** *n*
: reclutamiento *m*
rectangle *n* : rectángulo *m* —
rectangular *adj* : rectangular
rectify *vt* **-fied; -fying** : rectificar
rector *n* **1** : párroco *m* (clérigo) **2** :
rector *m*, -tora *f* (de una universidad)
— **rectory** *n*, *pl* **-ries** : rectoría *f*
rectum *n*, *pl* **-tums** *or* **-ta** : recto *m*
recuperate *v* **-ated; -ating** *vt*
: recuperar — *vi* : recuperarse

— **recuperation** *n* : recuperación *f*
recur *vi* **-curred; -curring** : repetirse
— **recurrence** *n* : repetición *f* —
recurrent *adj* : que se repite
recycle *vt* **-cled; -cling** : reciclar
red *adj* : rojo — **red** *n* : rojo *m*
— **redden** *vt* : enrojecer — *vi* :
enrojecerse — **reddish** *adj* : rojizo
redecorate *vt* **-rated; -rating**
: pintar de nuevo
redeem *vt* **1** SAVE : salvar, rescatar
2 : desempeñar (de un monte de
piedad) **3** : canjear (cupones, etc.)
— **redemption** *n* : redención *f*
red–handed *adv or adj* : con
las manos en la masa
redhead *n* : pelirrojo *m*, -ja *f*
red–hot *adj* : al rojo vivo

redness *n* : rojez *f*
redo *vt* **-did; -done; -doing**
: hacer de nuevo
redouble *vt* **-bled; -bling** : redoblar
red tape *n* : papeleo *m*
reduce *v* **-duced; -ducing** *vt* :
reducir — *vi* SLIM : adelgazar
— **reduction** *n* : reducción *f*
redundant *adj* : redundante
reed *n* **1** : caña *f* **2** : lengüeta *f*
(de un instrumento)
reef *n* : arrecife *m*
reek *vi* : apestar
reel *n* : carrete *m* (de hilo, etc.)
— **reel** *vt* **1 reel in** : enrollar (un
sedal), sacar (un pez) del agua **2 reel
off** : enumerar — *vi* **1** SPIN : dar
vueltas **2** STAGGER : tambalearse

reestablish *vt* : restablecer
refer *v* **-ferred; -ferring** *vt* **1**
DIRECT : enviar, mandar **2** SUBMIT
: remitir — *vi* **refer to 1** MENTION :
referirse a **2** CONSULT : consultar
referee *n* : árbitro *m*, -tra *f* —
referee *v* **-eed; -eeing** : arbitrar
reference *n* **1** : referencia *f* **2**
CONSULTATION : consulta *f* **3** *or*
reference book : libro *m* de consulta
4 in reference to : con referencia a
refill *vt* : rellenar — **refill** *n* : recambio *m*
refine *vt* **-fined; -fining** : refinar
— **refined** *adj* : refinado —
refinement *n* : refinamiento *m* —
refinery *n, pl* **-eries** : refinería *f*
reflect *vt* : reflejar — *vi* **1** : reflejarse
2 reflect badly on : desacreditar **3
reflect upon** : reflexionar sobre —
reflection *n* **1** : reflexión *f* **2** IMAGE :
reflejo *m* — **reflector** *n* : reflector *m*
reflex *n* : reflejo *m*
reflexive *adj* : reflexivo
reform *vt* : reformar — *vi* :
reformarse — **reform** *n* : reforma *f* —
reformer *n* : reformador *m*, -dora *f*
refrain[1] *vi* **refrain from** : abstenerse de
refrain[2] *n* : estribillo *m* (en música)
refresh *vt* : refrescar —
refreshments *npl* : refrigerio *m*
refrigerate *vt* **-ated; -ating** : refrigerar
— **refrigeration** *n* : refrigeración *f*
▸ — refrigerator *n* : nevera *f*,
refrigerador *m* Lat, frigorífico *m* Spain
refuel *v* **-eled** *or* **-elled; -eling** *or* **-elling** *vt*
: llenar de carburante — *vi* : repostar
refuge *n* : refugio *m* — **refugee** *n*
: refugiado *m*, -da *f*
refund *vt* : reembolsar —
refund *n* : reembolso *m*
refurbish *vt* : renovar, restaurar
reuse[1] *v* **-fused; -fusing** *vt* **1** :
rehusar, rechazar **2 refuse to do
something** : negarse a hacer algo — *vi*
: negarse — **refusal** *n* : negativa *f*
refuse[2] *n* : residuos *mpl*, desperdicios *mpl*
refute *vt* **-futed; -futing** : refutar
regain *vt* : recuperar, recobrar
regal *adj* : regio, majestuoso —
regalia *n* : ropaje *m*, insignias *fpl*
regard *n* **1** : consideración *f* **2** ESTEEM :
estima *f* **3 in this regard** : en este sentido
4 regards *npl* : saludos *mpl* **5 with
regard to** : respecto a — **regard** *vt* **1** :
mirar (con recelo, etc.) **2** HEED : tener en

refrigerator
frigorífico[M]

water dispenser
dispensador[M] *de agua*[F]

butter compartment
compartimiento[M]
para mantequilla[F]

refrigerator
compartment
espacio[M] *interior*

dairy compartment
compartimiento[M]
para lácteos[M]

meat keeper
cajón[M] *para carnes*[F]

freezer compartment
congelador[M] *incorporado*

crisper
cesto[M] *para verdura*[F]

reindeer
reno[M]

cuenta **3** ESTEEM : estimar **4 as regards** : en lo que se refiere a **5 regard as** : considerar — **regarding** prep : respecto a — **regardless** adv : a pesar de todo — **regardless of** prep **1** : sin tener en cuenta **2** IN SPITE OF : a pesar de
regent n : regente mf
regime n : régimen m — **regimen** n : régimen m
regiment n : regimiento m
region n : región f — **regional** adj : regional
register n : registro m — **register** vt **1** : registrar (a personas), matricular (vehículos) **2** SHOW : marcar, manifestar **3** : certificar (correo) — vi ENROLL : inscribirse, matricularse — **registrar** n : registrador m, -dora f oficial — **registration** n **1** : inscripción f, matriculación f **2** or **registration number** : número m de matrícula — **registry** n, pl **-tries** : registro m
regret vt **-gretted; -gretting** : lamentar — **regret** n **1** REMORSE : arrepentimiento m **2** SORROW : pesar m — **regrettable** adj : lamentable
regular adj **1** : regular **2** CUSTOMARY : habitual — **regular** n : cliente mf habitual — **regularity** n, pl **-ties** : regularidad f — **regularly** adv : regularmente — **regulate** vt **-lated; -lating** : regular — **regulation** n **1**

CONTROL : regulación f **2** RULE : regla f
rehabilitate vt **-tated; -tating** : rehabilitar — **rehabilitation** n : rehabilitación f
rehearse v **-hearsed; -hearsing** : ensayar — **rehearsal** n : ensayo m
reign n : reinado m — **reign** vi : reinar
reimburse vt **-bursed; -bursing** : reembolsar — **reimbursement** n : reembolso m
rein n : rienda f
reincarnation n : reencarnación f
▸ **reindeer** n : reno m
reinforce vt **-forced; -forcing** : reforzar — **reinforcement** n : refuerzo m
reinstate vt **-stated; -stating** **1** : restablecer **2** : restituir (a algn en su cargo)
reiterate vt **-ated; -ating** : reiterar
reject vt : rechazar — **rejection** n : rechazo m
rejoice vi **-joiced; -joicing** : regocijarse
rejuvenate vt **-nated; -nating** : rejuvenecer
rekindle vt **-dled; -dling** : reavivar
relapse n : recaída f — **relapse** vi **-lapsed; -lapsing** : recaer
relate v **-lated; -lating** vt **1** TELL : relatar **2** ASSOCIATE : relacionar — vi **relate to 1** CONCERN : estar relacionado con **2** UNDERSTAND : identificarse con **3** : relacionarse con (socialmente) — **related** adj **related to** : emparentado con — **relation** n **1** CONNECTION : relación f **2** RELATIVE : pariente mf **3 in relation to** : en relación con **4 relates** npl : relaciones fpl — **relationship** n **1** : relación f **2** KINSHIP : parentesco m — **relative** n : pariente mf — **relative** adj : relativo — **relatively** adv : relativamente
relax vt : relajar — vi : relajarse — **relaxation** n **1** : relajación f **2** RECREATION : esparcimiento m
relay n **1** : relevo m **2** or **relay race** : carrera f de relevos — **relay** vt **-layed; -laying** : transmitir
release vt **-leased; -leasing 1** FREE : liberar, poner en libertad **2** : soltar (un freno, etc.) **3** EMIT : despedir **4** : sacar (un libro, etc.), estrenar (una película) — **release** n **1** : liberación f **2** : estreno m (de una película), publicación f (de un libro) **3** : fuga f (de gases)
relegate vt **-gated; -gating** : relegar
relent vi : ceder — **relentless** adj

: implacable
relevant adj : pertinente — **relevance** n : pertinencia f
reliable adj : fiable (dícese de personas), fidedigno (dícese de información, etc.) — **reliability** n, pl **-ties** : fiabilidad f (de una cosa), responsabilidad f (de una persona) — **reliance** n **1** : dependencia f **2** TRUST : confianza f — **reliant** adj : dependente
relic n : reliquia f
relief n **1** : alivio m **2** AID : ayuda f **3** : relieve m (en la escultura) **4** REPLACEMENT : relevo m — **relieve** vt **-lieved; -lieving 1** : aliviar **2** REPLACE : relevar (a algn) **3 relieve someone of** : liberar a algn de
religion n : religión f — **religious** adj : religioso
relinquish vt : renunciar a, abandonar
relish n **1** : salsa f (condimento) **2 with relish** : con gusto — **relish** vt : saborear
relocate vt **-cated; -cating** : trasladar — vi : trasladarse — **relocation** n : traslado m
reluctance n : reticencia f, desgana f — **reluctant** adj : reacio, reticente — **reluctantly** adv : a regañadientes
rely vi **-lied; -lying rely on 1** DEPEND ON : depender de **2** TRUST : confiar (en)
remain vi **1** : quedar **2** STAY : quedarse **3** CONTINUE : seguir, continuar — **remainder** n : resto m — **remains** npl : restos mpl
remark n : comentario m, observación f — **remark** vt : observar — vi **remark on** : observar — **remarkable** adj : extraordinario, notable
remedy n, pl **-dies** : remedio m — **remedy** vt **-died; -dying** : remediar — **remedial** adj : correctivo
remember vt **1** : acordarse de, recordar **2 remember to** : acordarse de — vi : acordarse, recordar — **remembrance** n : recuerdo m
remind vt : recordar — **reminder** n : recordatorio m
reminiscence n : recuerdo m, reminiscencia f — **reminisce** vi **-nisced; -niscing** : rememorar los viejos tiempos — **reminiscent** adj **be reminiscence of** : recordar
remiss adj : negligente, remiso
remit vt **-mitted; -mitting 1** PARDON : perdonar **2** : enviar (dinero) — **remission** n : remisión f
remnant n **1** : resto m **2**

TRACE : **vestigio** *m*
remorse *n* : remordimiento *m* —
  remorseful *adj* : arrepentido
remote *adj* **-moter; -est 1** : remoto
  2 ALOOF : distante **3 remote from** :
▸ apartado de, alejado de — remote
  control *n* : control *m* remoto —
  remotely *adv* SLIGHTLY : remotamente
remove *vt* **-moved; -moving 1** : quitar
  (una tapa, etc.), quitarse (ropa) **2**
  EXTRACT : sacar **3** DISMISS : destituir **4**
  ELIMINATE : eliminar — **removable** *adj* :
  separable, de quita y pon — **removal** *n* **1**
  : eliminación *f* **2** EXTRACTION : extracción *f*
remunerate *vt* **-ated; -ating** : remunerar
render *vt* **1** : rendir (homenaje),
  prestar (ayuda) **2** MAKE : hacer
  3 TRANSLATE : traducir
rendezvous *ns & pl* : cita *f*
rendition *n* : interpretación *f*
renegade *n* : renegado *m*, **-da** *f*
renew *vt* **1** : renovar **2** RESUME :
  reanudar — **renewal** *n* : renovación *f*
renounce *vt* **-nounced;**
  -nouncing : renunciar a
renovate *vt* **-vated; -vating** : renovar
  — **renovation** *n* : renovación *f*
renown *n* : renombre *m* —
  renowned *adj* : célebre, renombrado
rent *n* **1** : alquiler *m*, arrendamiento *m*,
  renta *f* **2 for rent** : se alquila
  — **rent** *vt* : alquilar — **rental** *n* :
  alquiler *m* — **rental** *adj* : de alquiler
  — **renter** *n* : arrendatario *m*, **-ria** *f*
renunciation *n* : renuncia *f*
reopen *vt* : volver a abrir
reorganize *vt* **-nized; -nizing** :
  reorganizar — **reorganization** *n*
  : reorganización *f*
repair *vt* : reparar, arreglar —
  repair *n* **1** : reparación *f*, arreglo *m* **2**
  in bad repair : en mal estado
repay *vt* **-paid; -paying 1** : devolver
  (dinero), pagar (una deuda) **2** :
  corresponder a (un favor, etc.)
repeal *vt* : abrogar, revocar —
  repeal *n* : abrogación *f*, revocación *f*
repeat *vt* : repetir — **repeat** *n* : repetición *f*
  — **repeatedly** *adv* : repetidas veces
repel *vt* **-pelled; -pelling** : repeler
  — **repellent** *n* : repelente *m*
repent *vi* : arrepentirse —
  repentance *n* : arrepentimiento *m*
repercussion *n* : repercusión *f*
repertoire *n* : repertorio *m*

remote control
control^M remoto

display
pantalla^F

menu button
botón^M de menú^M

select button
botón^M de selección^F

stop button
botón^M de stop^M

volume control
control^M de volumen^M

channel selector controls
selector^M de canales^M

function buttons
botones^M de función^F

navigation button
botón^M de navegación^F

track search/fast operation buttons
cambio^M de pista^F/lectura^F rápida

pause/still button
pausa^F/imagen^F fija

play button
funcionamiento^M

channel scan button
botones^M de búsqueda de canales^M

mute
sordina^F

on-off button
interruptor^M

repetition *n* : repetición *f* —
  repetitious *adj* : repetitivo —
  repetitive *adj* : repetitivo
replace *vt* **-placed; -placing 1** : reponer
  2 SUBSTITUTE : reemplazar, sustituir **3**
  EXCHANGE : cambiar — **replacement** *n* **1** :
  sustitución *f* **2** : sustituto *m*, **-ta** *f* (persona)
  3 *or* **replacement part** : repuesto *m*
replenish *vt* **1** : reponer **2** REFILL : rellenar
replete *adj* **replete with** : repleto de
replica *n* : réplica *f*
reply *vi* **-plied; -plying** :
  contestar, responder — **reply** *n*,
  pl **-plies** : respuesta *f*
report *n* **1** : informe *m* **2** RUMOR
  : rumor *m* **3** *or* **news report** :
  reportaje *m* **4 weather report** : boletín *m*

meteorológico — **report** *vt* **1** RELATE :
  anunciar **2 report a crime** : denunciar
  un delito **3** *or* **report on** : informar sobre
  — *vi* **1** : informar **2 report for duty** :
  presentarse — **report card** *n* : boletín *m*
  de calificaciones — **reportedly** *adv*
  : según se dice — **reporter** *n* :
  periodista *mf*; reportero *m*, **-ra** *f*
repose *vi* **-posed; -posing** :
  reposar — **repose** *n* : reposo *m*
reprehensible *adj* : reprensible
represent *vt* **1** : representar
  2 PORTRAY : presentar —
  representation *n* : representación *f*
  — **representative** *adj* : representativo
  — **represent** *n* : representante *mf*
repress *vt* : reprimir

— **repression** n : represión f
reprieve n : indulto m
reprimand n : reprimenda f —
   reprimand vt : reprender
reprint vt : reimprimir —
   reprint n : reedición f
reprisal n : represalia f
reproach n 1 : reproche m 2 **beyond**
   reproach : irreprochable — **reproach** vt :
reprochar — **reproachful** adj : de reproche
reproduce v -duced; -ducing vt :
reproducir — vi : reproducirse —
   reproduction n : reproducción f —
   reproductive adj : reproductor
reproof n : reprobación f
reptile n : reptil m
republic n : república f —
   republican n : republicano m, -na f
   — **republican** adj : republicano
repudiate vt -ated; -ating : repudiar
repugnant adj : repugnante, asqueroso
   — **repugnance** n : repugnancia f
repulse vt -pulsed; -pulsing : repeler,
rechazar — **repulsive** adj : repulsivo
reputation n : reputación f —
   reputable adj : de confianza, acreditado
   — **reputed** adj : supuesto
request n : petición f — **request** vt : pedir
requiem n : réquiem m
require vt -quired; -quiring 1 CALL
   FOR : requerir 2 NEED : necesitar
   — **requirement** n 1 NEED :
necesidad f 2 DEMAND : requisito m
   — **requisite** adj : necesario
resale n : reventa f
rescind vt : rescindir (un contrato),
revocar (una ley, etc.)
rescue vt -cued; -cuing : rescatar,
salvar — **rescue** n : rescate m —
rescuer n : salvador m, -dora f
research n : investigación f —
   research vt : investigar — **researcher** n
   : investigador m, -dora f
resemble vt -sembled;
   -sembling : parecerse a —
   resemblance n : parecido m
resent vt : resentirse de, ofenderse
por — **resentful** adj : resentido —
resentment n : resentimiento m
reserve vt -servee; -serving :
reservar — **reserve** n 1 : reserva f 2
reserves npl : reservas fpl (militares) —
reservation n : reserva f — **reserved** adj
: reservado — **reservoir** n : embalse m
reset vt -set; -setting : volver

a poner (un reloj, etc.)
residence n : residencia f — **reside** vi
   -sided; -siding : residir — **resident** adj
   : residente — **residence** n : residente mf
   — **residential** adj : residencial
residue n : residuo m
resign vt 1 QUIT : dimitir 2 **resign oneself**
   to : resignarse a — **resignation** n 1 :
dimisión f 2 ACCEPTANCE : resignación f
resilient adj 1 : resistente (dícese
de personas) 2 ELASTIC : elástico
   — **resilience** n 1 : resistencia f 2
ELASTICITY : elasticidad f
resin n : resina f
resist vt : resistir — vi : resistirse
   — **resistance** n : resistencia f
   — **resistant** adj : resistente
resolve vt -solved; -solving : resolver —
   resolve n : resolución f — **resolution** n 1
   : resolución f 2 DECISION, INTENTION :
propósito m — **resolute** adj : resuelto
resonance n : resonancia f —
   resonant adj : resonante
resort n 1 RECOURSE : recurso m 2
   or **tourist resort** : centro m turístico
   — **resort** vi **resort to** : recurrir a
resounding adj 1 RESONANT :
resonante 2 ABSOLUTE : rotundo
resource n : recurso m —
   resourceful adj : ingenioso
respect n 1 ESTEEM : respeto m 2 **in**
   some respects : en algún sentido 3
   pay one's respects : presentar uno
sus respetos 4 **with respect to** : (con)
respecto a — **respect** vt : respetar
   — **respectable** adj : respetable
   — **respectful** adj : respetuoso
   — **respective** adj : respectivo —
respectively adv : respectivamente
respiration n : respiración f —
   respiratory adj : respiratorio
respite n : respiro m
response n : respuesta f — **respond** vi
   : responder — **responsibility** n,
pl -ties : responsabilidad f —
   responsible adj : responsable —
responsive adj : sensible, receptivo
rest[1] n 1 : descanso m 2 SUPPORT :
apoyo m 3 : silencio m (en música) —
   rest vi 1 : descansar 2 LEAN : apoyarse 3
rest on DEPEND ON : depender de — vt 1
RELAX : descansar 2 LEAN : apoyar
rest[2] n REMAINDER : resto m
restaurant n : restaurante m
restful adj : tranquilo, apacible

restitution n : restitución f
restless adj : inquieto, agitado
restore vt -stored; -storing 1
   RETURN : devolver 2 REESTABLISH :
restablecer 3 REPAIR : restaurar —
   restoration n 1 : restablecimiento m 2
REPAIR : restauración f
restrain vt 1 : contener 2 **restrain**
   oneself : contenerse — **restrained** adj
   : comedido, moderado — **restraint** n 1
   : restricción f 2 SELF-CONTROL :
moderación f, control m de sí mismo
restriction n : restricción f — **restrict** vt
   : restringir — **restricted** adj : restringido
   — **restrictive** adj : restrictivo
result vi : resultar — **result** n 1
   : resultado m 2 **as a result of**
   : como consecuencia de
resume v -sumed; -suming vt :
reanudar — vi : reanudarse
résumé or **resume** or **resumé** n
   : currículum m (vitae)
resumption n : reanudación f
resurgence n : resurgimiento m
resurrection n : resurrección f
   — **resurrect** vt : resucitar
resuscitate vt -tated; -tating : resucitar
retail vt : vender al por menor — **retail** n
   : venta f al por menor — **retail** adj :
detallista, minorista — **retail** adv :
al detalle, al por menor — **retailer** n
   : detallista mf, minorista mf
retain vt : retener
retaliate vi -ated; -ating : tomar
represalias — **retaliation** n
   : represalias fpl
retard vt : retardar, retrasar —
   retarded adj : retrasado
retention n : retención f
reticence n : reticencia f —
   reticent adj : reticente
retina n, pl -nas or -nae : retina f
retinue n : séquito m
retire vi -tired; -tiring 1 WITHDRAW
   : retirarse 2 : jubilarse, retirarse
(de un trabajo) 3 : acostarse (en la
cama) — **retirement** n : jubilación f
   — **retiring** adj SHY : retraído
retort vt : replicar — **retort** n : réplica f
retrace vt -traced; -tracing **retrace**
   one's steps : volver sobre sus pasos
retract vt 1 WITHDRAW : retirar 2 :
retraer (garras, etc.) — vi : retractarse
retrain vt : reciclar
retreat n 1 : retirada f 2 REFUGE :

rice
arroz^M

rice
arroz^M

wild rice
arroz^M silvestre

refugio *m* — **retreat** *vi* : retirarse
retribution *n* : castigo *m*
retrieve *vt* **-trieved; -trieving 1** :
cobrar, recuperar **2** RESCUE : salvar
— **retrieval** *n* : recuperación *f* —
retriever *n* : perro *m* cobrador
retroactive *adj* : retroactivo
retrospect *n* **in retrospect**
: mirando hacia atrás —
retrospective *adj* : retrospectivo
return *vi* **1** : volver, regresar **2** REAPPEAR
: reaparecer — *vt* **1** : devolver **2** YIELD
: producir — **return** *n* **1** : regreso *m*,
vuelta *f* **2** : devolución *f* (de algo prestado)
3 YIELD : rendimiento *m* **4 in return for** : a
cambio de **5** *or* **tax return** : declaración *f*
de impuestos — **return** *adj* : de vuelta
reunite *vt* **-nited; -niting** : reunir
— **reunion** *n* : reunión *f*
revamp *vt* : renovar
reveal *vt* **1** : revelar **2** SHOW : dejar ver
revel *vi* **-eled** *or* **-elled; -eling** *or*
-elling revel in : deleitarse en
revelation *n* : revelación *f*
revelry *n, pl* **-ries** : jolgorio *m*,
regocijos *mpl*
revenge *vt* **-venged; -venging** :
vengar — **revenge** *n* **1** : venganza *f* **2**
take revenge on : vengarse de
revenue *n* : ingresos *mpl*
reverberate *vi* **-ated; -ating**
: retumbar, resonar
reverence *n* : reverencia *f*,
veneración *f* — **revere** *vt* **-vered;**
-vering : venerar — **reverend** *adj* :

reverendo — **reverent** *adj* : reverente
reverie *n, pl* **-eries** : ensueño *m*
reverse *adj* : inverso, contrario —
reverse *v* **-versed; -versing** *vt* **1** :
invertir **2** : cambiar (una política), revocar
(una decisión) **3** : dar marcha atrás
a (un automóvil) — *vi* : invertirse —
reverse *n* **1** BACK : dorso *m*, revés *m* **2**
or **reverse gear** : marcha *f* atrás **3 the**
reverse : lo contrario — **reversible** *adj* :
reversible — **reversal** *n* **1** : inversión *f* **2**
CHANGE : cambio *m* total **3** SETBACK
: revés *m* — **revert** *vi* : revertir
review *n* **1** : revisión *f* **2** OVERVIEW
: resumen *m* **3** CRITIQUE : reseña *f*,
crítica *f* **4** : repaso *m* (para un examen)
— **review** *vt* **1** EXAMINE : examinar
2 : repasar (una lección) **3** CRITIQUE :
reseñar — **reviewer** *n* : crítico *m*, -ca *f*
revile *vt* **-viled; -viling** : injuriar
revise *vt* **-vised; -vising 1** : modificar
(una política, etc.) **2** : revisar, corregir
(una publicación) — **revision** *n*
: corrección *f*, modificación *f*
revive *v* **-vived; -viving** *vt* **1** :
reanimar, reactivar **2** : resucitar (a
una persona) **3** RESTORE : restablecer
— *vi* **1** : reanimarse, reactivarse **2**
COME TO : volver en sí — **revival** *n*
: reanimación *f*, reactivación *f*
revoke *vt* **-voked; -voking** : revocar
revolt *vi* : rebelarse, sublevarse — *vt*
: dar asco a — **revolt** *n* : revuelta *f*,
sublevación *f* — **revolting** *adj* : asqueroso
revolution *n* : revolución *f*

— **revolutionary** *adj* : revolucionario
— **revolution** *n, pl* **-aries** :
revolucionario *m*, -ria *f* — **revolutionize** *vt*
-ized; -izing : revolucionar
revolve *v* **-volved; -volving** *vt*
: hacer girar — *vi* : girar
revolver *n* : revólver *m*
revue *n* : revista *f* (teatral)
revulsion *n* : repugnancia *f*
reward *vt* : recompensar —
reward *n* : recompensa *f*
rewrite *vt* **-wrote; -written;**
-writing : volver a escribir
rhetoric *n* : retórica *f* —
rhetorical *adj* : retórico
rheumatism *n* : reumatismo *m*
— **rheumatic** *adj* : reumático
rhino *n, pl* **-no** *or* **-nos** → **rhinoceros**
— **rhinoceros** *n, pl* **-noceroses** *or*
-noceros *or* **-noceri** : rinoceronte *m*
rhubarb *n* : ruibarbo *m*
rhyme *n* **1** : rima *f* **2** VERSE :
verso *m* (en rima) — **rhyme** *vi*
rhymed; rhyming : rimar
rhythm *n* : ritmo *m* — **rhythmic**
or **rhythmical** *adj* : rítmico
rib *n* : costilla *f* — **rib** *vt*
TEASE : tomar el pelo a
ribbon *n* : cinta *f*
▸ **rice** *n* : arroz *m*
rich *adj* **1** : rico **2 rich foods** :
comidas *fpl* pesadas — **riches** *npl* :
riquezas *fpl* — **richness** *n* : riqueza *f*
rickety *adj* : desvencijado, destartalado
ricochet *n* : rebote *m* —
ricochet *vi* **-cheted** *or* -chetted;
-cheting *or* -chetting : rebotar
rid *vt* **rid; ridding 1** : librar **2 get rid of**
: deshacerse de — **riddance** *n* **good**
riddance! : ¡adiós y buen viaje!
riddle[1] *n* : acertijo *m*, adivinanza *f*
riddle[2] *vt* **-dled; -dling 1** : acribillar
2 riddled with : lleno de
ride *v* **rode; ridden; riding** *vt* **1** :
montar (a caballo, en bicicleta),
ir (en autobús, etc.) **2** TRAVERSE :
recorrer — *vi* **1** *or* **ride horseback** :
montar a caballo **2** : ir (en auto, etc.)
— **ride** *n* **1** : paseo *m*, vuelta *f* **2** :
aparato *m* (en un parque de diversiones)
— **rider** *n* **1** : jinete *mf* (a caballo) **2**
CYCLIST : ciclista *mf*, motociclista *mf*
ridge *n* : cadena *f* (de montañas)
ridiculous *adj* : ridículo —
ridicule *n* : burlas *fpl* — **ridiculous** *vt*

speed skating rinks
pistas^F de patinaje

short track
pista^F corta

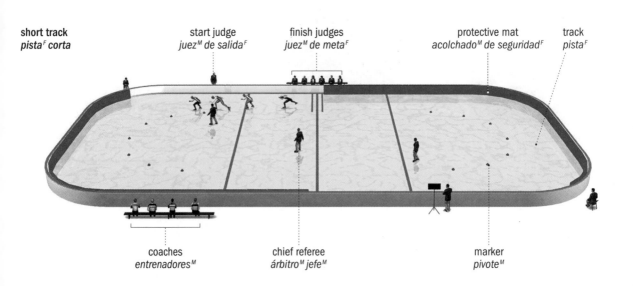

start judge
juez^M de salida^F

finish judges
juez^M de meta^F

protective mat
acolchado^M de seguridad^F

track
pista^F

coaches
entrenadores^M

chief referee
árbitro^M jefe^M

marker
pivote^M

long track
pista^F larga

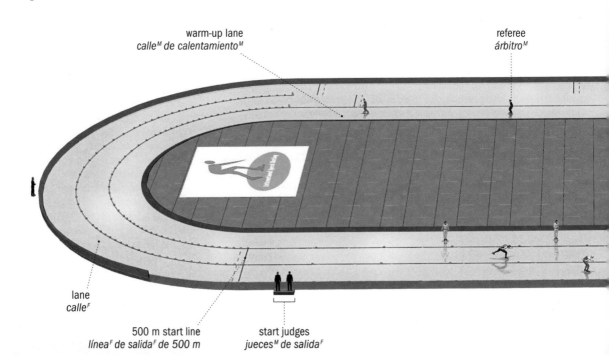

warm-up lane
calle^M de calentamiento^M

referee
árbitro^M

lane
calle^F

500 m start line
línea^F de salida^F de 500 m

start judges
jueces^M de salida^F

-culed; -culing : ridiculizar

rife *adj* **1** : extendido **2 be rife with** : estar plagado de

rifle[1] *vi* **-fled; -fling rifle through** : revolver

rifle[2] *n* : rifle *m*, fusil *m*

rift *n* **1** : grieta *f* **2** : ruptura *f* (entre personas)

rig[1] *vt* : amañar (una elección)

rig[2] *vt* **rigged; rigging 1** : aparejar (un barco) **2** EQUIP : equipar **3** *or* **rig out** DRESS : vestir **4** *or* **rig up** CONSTRUCT : construir — **rig** *n* **1** : aparejo *m* (de un barco) **2** *or* **oil rig** : plataforma *f* petrolífera — **rigging** *n* : aparejo *m*

right *adj* **1** JUST : bueno, justo **2** CORRECT : correcto **3** APPROPRIATE : apropiado, adecuado **4** STRAIGHT : recto **5 be right** : tener razón **6** → **right–hand** — **right** *n* **1** GOOD : bien *m* **2** ENTITLEMENT : derecho *m* **3 on the right** : a la derecha **4** *or* **right side** : derecha *f* — **right** *adv* **1** WELL : bien **2** PRECISELY : justo **3** DIRECTLY : derecho **4** IMMEDIATELY : inmediatamente **5** COMPLETELY : completamente **6** *or to* **the right** : a la derecha — **right** *vt* **1** STRAIGHTEN : enderezar **2 right a wrong** : reparar un daño — **right angle** *n* : ángulo *m* recto — **righteous** *adj* : recto,

honrado — **rightful** *adj* : legítimo — **right–hand** *adj* : derecho — **right–handed** *adj* : diestro — **rightly** *adv* **1** : justamente **2** CORRECTLY : correctamente — **right–wing** *adj* : derechista

rigid *adj* : rígido

rigor *or Brit* **rigour** *n* : rigor *m* — **rigorous** *adj* : riguroso

rim *n* **1** EDGE : borde *m* **2** : llanta *f* (de una rueda) **3** : montura *f* (de anteojos)

rind *n* : corteza *f*

ring[1] *v* **rang; rung; ringing** *vi* **1** : sonar (dícese de un timbre, etc.) **2** RESOUND : resonar — *vt* : tocar (un timbre, etc.) — **ring** *n* **1** : toque *m* (de un timbre, etc.) **2** CALL : llamada *f* (por teléfono)

ring[2] *n* **1** : anillo *m*, sortija *f* **2** BAND, HOOP : aro *m* **3** CIRCLE : círculo *m* **4** *or* **boxing ring** : cuadrilátero *m* **5** NETWORK : red *f* — **ring** *vt* : cercar, rodear — **ringleader** *n* : cabecilla *mf*

ringlet *n* : rizo *m*, bucle *m*

▸ **rink** *n* : pista *f* (de patinaje)

rinse *vt* **rinsed; rinsing** : enjuagar — **rinse** *n* : enjuague *m*

riot *n* : disturbio *m* — **riot** *vi* : causar disturbios — **rioter** *n* : alborotador *m*, -dora *f*

rip *v* **ripped; ripping** *vt* **1** : rasgar, desgarrar **2 rip off** : arrancar — *vi* : rasgarse — **rip** *n* : rasgón *m*, desgarrón *m*

ripe *adj* **riper; ripest 1** : maduro **2 ripe for** : listo por — **ripen** *v* : madurar — **ripeness** *n* : madurez *f*

rip–off *n* : timo *m fam*

ripple *v* **-pled; -pling** *vi* : rizarse (dícese de agua) — *vt* : rizar — **ripple** *n* : onda *f*, rizo *m*

rise *vi* **rose; risen; rising 1** GET UP : levantarse **2** : salir (dícese del sol, etc.) **3** ASCEND : subir **4** INCREASE : aumentar **5 rise up** REBEL : sublevarse — **rise** *n* **1** ASCENT : subida *f* **2** INCREASE : aumento *m* **3** SLOPE : cuesta *f* — **riser** *n* **1 early riser** : madrugador *m*, -dora *f* **2 late riser** : dormilón *m*, -lona *f*

risk *n* : riesgo *m* — **risk** *vt* : arriesgar — **risky** *adj* **riskier; -est** : arriesgado, riesgoso *Lat*

rite *n* : rito *m* — **ritual** *adj* : ritual — **rite** *n* : ritual *m*

rival *n* : rival *mf* — **rival** *adj* : rival — **rival** *vt* **-valed** *or* **-valled; -valing** *or* **-valling** : rivalizar con — **rivalry** *n, pl* **-ries** : rivalidad *f*

river *n* : río *m*

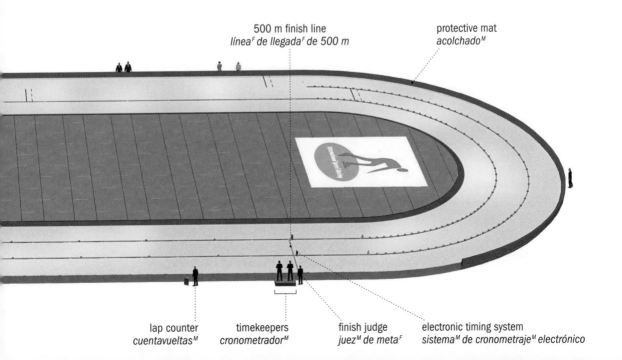

500 m finish line
línea[F] *de llegada*[F] *de 500 m*

protective mat
acolchado[M]

lap counter
cuentavueltas[M]

timekeepers
cronometrador[M]

finish judge
juez[M] *de meta*[F]

electronic timing system
sistema[M] *de cronometraje*[M] *electrónico*

rivet *n* : remache *m* — **rivet** *vt* **1** :
remachar **2** FIX : fijar (los ojos, etc.) **3**
be riveted by : estar fascinado con
roach → **cockroach**
▸ **road** *n* **1** : **carretera** *f* **2** STREET : calle *f* **3**
PATH : camino *m* — **roadblock** *n* :
control *m* — **roadside** *n* : borde *m* de la
carretera — **roadway** *n* : carretera *f*
roam *vi* : vagar — *vt* : vagar por
roar *vi* **1** : rugir **2** roar with laughter :
reírse a carcajadas — *vt* : decir a gritos
— **roar** *n* : rugido *m* (de un animal),
estruendo *m* (de un avión, etc.)
roast *vt* : asar (carne, etc.),
tostar (café, etc.) — *vi* : asarse

— **roast** *n* : asado *m* — **roast** *adj* :
asado — **roast beef** *n* : rosbif *m*
rob *v* **robbed; robbing** *vt* **1** : robar
2 rob of : privar de — *vi* : robar
— **robber** *n* : ladrón *m*, -drona *f* —
robbery *n, pl* **-beries** : robo *m*
robe *n* **1** : toga *f* (de un magistrado,
etc.) **2** → **bathrobe**
robin *n* : petirrojo *m*
robot *n* : robot *m*
robust *adj* : robusto
rock[1] *vt* **1** : acunar (a un niño),
mecer (una cuna) **2** SHAKE : sacudir
— *vi* : mecerse — **rock** *n or*
rock music : música *f* rock

rock[2] *n* **1** : roca *f* (sustancia) **2** BOULDER
: peña *f*, peñasco *m* **3** STONE : piedra *f*
rocket *n* : cohete *m*
rocking chair *n* : mecedora *f*
rocky *adj* **rockier; -est 1** : rocoso
2 SHAKY : tambaleante
rod *n* **1** : varilla *f* **2** *or* **fishing**
rod : caña *f* de pescar
rode → **ride**
rodent *n* : roedor *m*
rodeo *n, pl* **-deos** : rodeo *m*
roe *n* : hueva *f*
rogue *n* : pícaro *m*, -ra *f*
role *n* : papel *m*

section of a road
corte*M* de una calle*F*

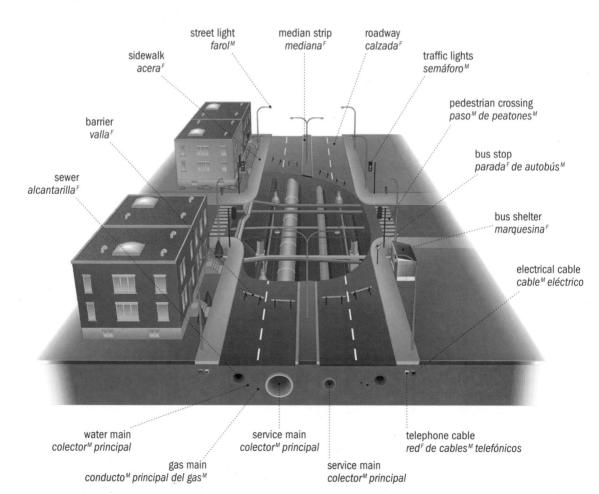

street light
farol*M*

median strip
mediana*F*

roadway
calzada*F*

sidewalk
acera*F*

traffic lights
semáforo*M*

pedestrian crossing
paso*M* de peatones*M*

barrier
valla*F*

bus stop
parada*F* de autobús*M*

sewer
alcantarilla*F*

bus shelter
marquesina*F*

electrical cable
cable*M* eléctrico

water main
colector*M* principal

service main
colector*M* principal

telephone cable
red*F* de cables*M* telefónicos

gas main
conducto*M* principal del gas*M*

service main
colector*M* principal

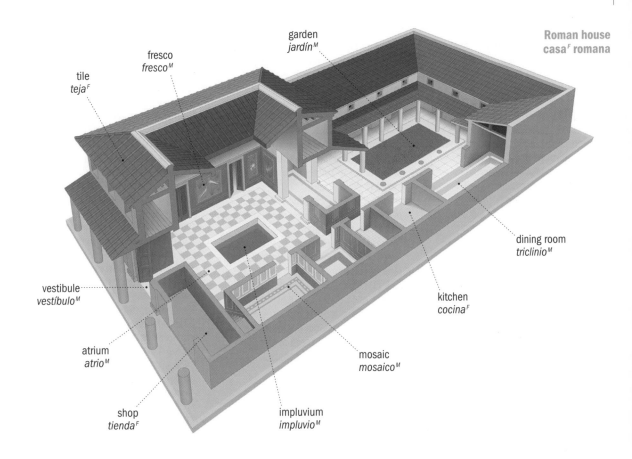

Roman house
casa^F **romana**

garden
jardín^M

fresco
fresco^M

tile
teja^F

dining room
triclinio^M

kitchen
cocina^F

vestibule
vestíbulo^M

atrium
atrio^M

mosaic
mosaico^M

shop
tienda^F

impluvium
impluvio^M

roll *n* **1** : rollo *m* (de película, etc.)
2 LIST : lista *f* **3** : redoble *m* (de un
tamboo) **4** SWAYING : balanceo *m* **5**
BUN : **pancito** *m Lat*, **panecillo** *m Spain*
— **roll** *vt* **1** : hacer rodar **2** *or* **roll out** :
estirar (masa) **3 roll up** : enrollar (papel,
etc.), arremangar (una manga) — *vi* **1** :
rodar **2** SWAY : balancearse **3 roll around**
: revolcarse **4 roll over** : darse la vuelta
— **roller** *n* **1** : rodillo *m* **2** CURLER :
rulo *m* — **roller coaster** *n* : montaña *f*
rusa — **roller–skate** *vi* **-skated;**
-skating : patinar (sobre ruedas) —
roller skate *n* : patín *m* (de ruedas)
▸ **Roman** *adj* : romano — **Roman**
Catholic *adj* : católico
romance *n* **1** : novela *f* romántica
2 AFFAIR : romance *m*
Romanian *adj* : rumano —
Romanian *n* : rumano *m* (idioma)
romantic *adj* : romántico
romp *n* : retozo *m* — **romp** *vi* : retozar

roof *n, pl* **roofs 1** : tejado *m*,
techo *m* **2 roof of the mouth** :
paladar *m* — **roofing** *n* : techumbre *f*
— **rooftop** *n* : tejado *m*, techo *m*
rook¹ *n* : grajo *m* (ave)
rook² *n* : torre *f* (en ajedrez)
rookie *n* : novato *m*, -ta *f*
room *n* **1** : cuarto *m*, habitación *f* **2**
BEDROOM : dormitorio *m* **3** SPACE
: espacio *m* **4** OPPORTUNITY :
posibilidad *f* — **roommate** *n* :
compañero *m*, -ra *f* de cuarto —
roomy *adj* **roomier; -est** : espacioso
roost *n* : percha *f* — **roost** *vi* :
▸ posarse — **rooster** *n* : gallo *m*
root¹ *n* : raíz *f* — **root** *vt* **root out** : extirpar
root² *vi* **root around in** : hurgar en
root³ *vi* **root for** SUPPORT : alentar
rope *n* : cuerda *f* — **rope** *vt* **roped; roping**
1 : atar (con cuerda) **2 rope off** : acordonar
rosary *n, pl* **-ries** : rosario *m*
rose¹ → **rise**

rooster
gallo^M

rose[2] *n* : rosa *f* (flor), rosa *m* (color) —
  rose *adj* : rosa — **rosebush** *n* : rosal *m*
▸ **rosemary** *n, pl* **-maries** : romero *m*
Rosh Hashanah *n* : el Año Nuevo judío
roster *n* : lista *f*
rostrum *n, pl* **-tra** *or* **-trums** : tribuna *f*
rosy *adj* **rosier; -est 1** : sonrosado
  2 PROMISING : halagüeno
rot *v* **rotted; rotting** *vi* : pudrirse — *vt*
  : pudrir — **rot** *n* : putrefacción *f*
rotary *adj* : rotativo — **rotary** *n*
  : rotonda *f*, glorieta *f Spain*
rotate *v* **-tated; -tating** *vi* : girar
  — *vt* **1** : girar **2** ALTERNATE : alternar
  — **rotation** *n* : rotación *f*
rote *n* **by rote** : de memoria
rotor *n* : rotor *m*
rotten *adj* **1** : podrido **2** BAD : malo
rouge *n* : colorete *m*
rough *adj* **1** COARSE : áspero **2** RUGGED
  : accidentado **3** CHOPPY : agitado **4**
  DIFFICULT : duro **5** FORCEFUL : brusco **6**
  APPROXIMATE : aproximado **7** UNREFINED
  : tosco **8 rough draft** : borrador *m* —
  rough *vt* **1** → **roughen 2 rough up**
  BEAT : dar una paliza a — **roughage** *n* :
  fibra *f* — **roughen** *vt* : poner áspero — *vi*
  : ponerse áspero — **roughly** *adv* **1** :
  bruscamente **2** ABOUT : aproximadamente
  — **roughness** *n* COARSENESS : aspereza *f*
roulette *n* : ruleta *f*
round *adj* : redondo — **round** *adv* →
  around — **round** *n* **1** : círculo *m* **2**
  : ronda *f* (de bebidas, negociaciones,
  etc.) **3** : asalto *m* (en boxeo), vuelta *f*
  (en juegos) **4 round of applause** :
  aplauso *m* **5 rounds** *npl* : visitas *fpl* (de
  un médico), rondas *fpl* (de un policía, etc.)
  — **round** *vt* **1** TURN : doblar **2 round off**
  : redondear **3 round off** *or* **round out**
  COMPLETE : rematar **4 round up** GATHER
  : reunir (personas), rodear (ganado) —
  round *prep* → **around** — **roundabout** *adj*
  : indirecto — **round–trip** *n* : viaje *m* de
  ida y vuelta — **roundup** *n* : rodeo *m* (de
  animales), redada *f* (de delincuentes, etc.)
rouse *vt* **roused; rousing 1** AWAKEN
  : despertar **2** EXCITE : excitar
rout *n* : derrota *f* aplastante
  — **rout** *vt* : derrotar
route *n* **1** : ruta *f* **2** *or* **delivery**
  route : recorrido *m*
routine *n* : rutina *f* —
  routine *adj* : rutinario
rove *v* **roved; roving** *vi* : errar,

  vagar — *vt* : errar por
row[1] *vt* **1** : llevar a remo **2 row**
  a boat : remar — *vi* : remar
row[2] *n* **1** : fila *f* (de gente o asientos),
  hilera *f* (de casas, etc.) **2 in a**
  row SUCCESSIVELY : seguido
row[3] *n* **1** RACKET : bulla *f* **2**
  QUARREL : pelea *f*
rowboat *n* : bote *m* de remos
rowdy *adj* **-dier; -est** : escandaloso,
  alborotador — **rowdy** *n, pl* **-dies**
  : alborotador *m*, -dora *f*
royal *adj* : real — **royalty** *n,*
  pl **-ties 1** : realeza *f* **2 royalties** *npl*
  : derechos *mpl* de autor
rub *v* **rubbed; rubbing** *vt* **1** : frotar **2**
  CHAFE : rozar **3 rub in** : aplicar frotando
  — *vi* **1 rub against** : rozar **2 rub off** :
  salir (al frotar) — **rub** *n* : frotamiento *m*
rubber *n* **1** : goma *f*, caucho *m* **2**
  rubbers *npl* : chanclos *mpl* —
  rubber band *n* : goma *f* (elástica)
  — **rubber stamp** *n* : sello *m* (de
  goma) — **rubbery** *adj* : gomoso
rubbish *n* **1** : basura *f* **2**
  NONSENSE : tonterías *fpl*
rubble *n* : escombros *mpl*
ruby *n, pl* **-bies** : rubí *m*
rudder *n* : timón *m*
ruddy *adj* **-dier; -est** : rubicundo
rude *adj* **ruder; rudest 1** IMPOLITE
  : grosero, mal educado **2** ABRUPT :
  brusco — **rudely** *adv* : groseramente
  — **rudeness** *n* : mala educación *f*
rudiment *n* : rudimento *m* —
  rudimentary *adj* : rudimentario
rue *vt* **rued; ruing** : lamentar —
  rueful *adj* : triste, arrepentido
ruffle *vt* **-fled; -fling 1** : despeinar (pelo),
  erizar (plumas) **2** VEX : alterar, contrariar
  — **ruffle** *n* : volante *m* (de un vestido, etc.)
rug *n* : alfombra *f*, tapete *m*
rugged *adj* **1** : escabroso (dícese del
  terreno), escarpado (dícese de montañas)
  2 HARSH : duro **3** STURDY : fuerte
ruin *n* : ruina *f* — **ruin** *vt* : arruinar
rule *n* **1** : regla *f* **2** CONTROL :
  dominio *m* **3 as a rule** : por lo general
  — **rule** *v* **ruled; ruling** *vt* **1** GOVERN :
  gobernar **2** : fallar (dícese de un juez)
  3 rule out : descartar — *vi* : gobernar,
  reinar — **ruler** *n* **1** : gobernante *mf;*
  soberano *m*, -na *f* **2** : regla *f* (para
  medir) — **ruling** *n* VERDICT : fallo *m*
rum *n* : ron *m*

Rumanian → **Romanian**
rumble *vi* **-bled; -bling 1** : retumbar **2** :
  hacer ruidos (dícese del estómago) —
  rumble *n* : retumbo *m*, estruendo *m*
rummage *vi* **-maged; -maging** : hurgar
rumor *n* : rumor *m* — **rumor** *vt*
  be rumored : rumorearse
rump *n* **1** : grupa *f* (de un animal) **2**
  rump steak : filete *m* de cadera
rumpus *n* : lío *m*, jaleo *m fam*
run *v* **ran; run; running** *vi* **1** : correr **2**
  FUNCTION : funcionar **3** LAST : durar **4** :
  desteñir (dícese de colores) **5** EXTEND
  : correr, extenderse **6** : presentarse
  (como candidato) **7 run away** : huir **8**
  run into ENCOUNTER : tropezar con **9**
  run into HIT : chocar contra **10 run late**
  : ir retrasado **11 run out of** : quedarse
  sin **12 run over** : atropellar — *vt* **1** :
  correr **2** OPERATE : hacer funcionar **3** :
  hacer correr (agua) **4** MANAGE : dirigir
  5 run a fever : tener fiebre — **run** *n* **1**
  : carrera *f* **2** TRIP : viaje *m*, paseo *m* (en
  coche) **3** SERIES : serie *f* **4 in the long run**
  : a la larga **5 in the short run** : a corto
  plazo — **runaway** *n* : fugitivo *m*, -va *f*
  — **runaway** *adj* : fugitivo — **rundown** *n*
  : resumen *m* — **run–down** *adj* **1** :
  destartalado **2** EXHAUSTED : agotado
rung[1] → **ring**[1]
rung[2] *n* : peldaño *m* (de una escalera, etc.)
runner *n* **1** : corredor *m*, -dora *f* **2** :
  patín *m* (de un trineo), riel *m* (de un cajón,
  etc.) — **runner–up** *n, pl* **runners–up** :
  subcampeón *m*, -peona *f* — **running** *adj* **1**
  FLOWING : corriente **2** CONTINUOUS :
  continuo **3** CONSECUTIVE : seguido
runt *n* : animal *m* más pequeño
  (de una camada)
runway *n* : pista *f* de aterrizaje
rupture *n* : ruptura *f* — **rupture** *v* **-tured;**
  -turing *vt* : romper — *vi* : reventar
rural *adj* : rural
ruse *n* : ardid *m*
rush[1] *n* : junco *m* (planta)
rush[2] *vi* : ir de prisa — *vt* **1** : apresurar,
  apurar **2** ATTACK : asaltar **3** : llevar
  rápidamente (al hospital, etc.) —
  rush *n* **1** : prisa *f*, apuro *m* **2** : ráfaga *f*
  (de aire), torrente *m* (de agua) — **rush** *adj*
  : urgente — **rush hour** *n* : hora *f* punta
russet *n* : color *m* rojizo
Russian *adj* : ruso — **Russian** *n*
  : ruso *m* (idioma)
rust *n* : herrumbre *f*, óxido *m* —
  rust *vi* : oxidarse — *vt* : oxidar

rustic *adj* : rústico
rustle *v* -tled; -tling *vt* **1** : hacer susurrar **2** : robar (ganado) — *vi* :

susurrar — **rustle** *n* : susurro *m*
rusty *adj* **rustier; -est** : oxidado
rut *n* **1** : surco *m* **2 be in a rut**

: ser esclavo de la rutina
ruthless *adj* : despiadado, cruel
rye *n* : centeno *m*

rosemary and ohers herbs
romero *M* **y otras hierbas** *F* **aromáticas**

parsley
perejil M

chervil
perifollo M

coriander
cilantro M

rosemary
romero M

dill
eneldo M

anise
anís M

sweet bay
laurel M

oregano
orégano M

tarragon
estragón M

basil
albahaca F

sage
salvia F

thyme
tomillo M

mint
hierbabuena F

hyssop
hisopo M

borage
borraja F

lovage
alheña F

savory
ajedrea F

lemon balm
melisa F

sailboat
velero^M

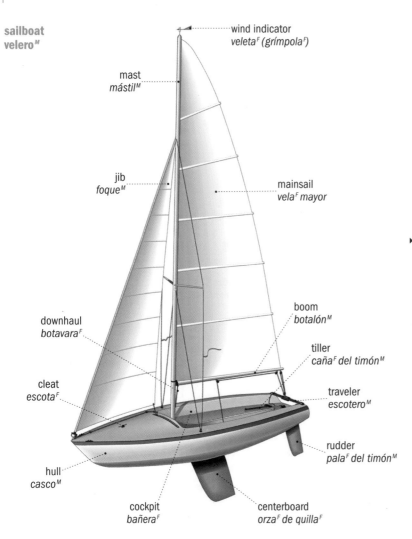

wind indicator
veleta^F *(grímpola*^F*)*

mast
mástil^M

jib
foque^M

mainsail
vela^F *mayor*

boom
botalón^M

downhaul
botavara^F

tiller
caña^F *del timón*^M

cleat
escota^F

traveler
escotero^M

rudder
pala^F *del timón*^M

hull
casco^M

cockpit
bañera^F

centerboard
orza^F *de quilla*^F

---

peligro **2 arrive safe** : llegar sin novedad
— **safety** *n, pl* **-ties** : seguridad *f* —
safety belt *n* : cinturón *m* de seguridad
— **safety pin** *n* : imperdible *m*
saffron *n* : azafrán *m*
sag *vi* **sagged; sagging 1** : combarse
2 GIVE : aflojarse **3** FLAG : flaquear
saga *n* : saga *f*
sage¹ *n* : salvia *f* (planta)
sage² *adj* **sager; -est** : sabio
— **sage** *n* : sabio *m*, -bia *f*
said → **say**
sail *n* **1** : vela *f* (de un barco) **2 go for a**
sail : salir a navegar **3 set sail** : zarpar
— **sail** *vi* : navegar — *vt* : gobernar (un
▸ barco), navegar (el mar) — **sailboat** *n*
: velero *m* — **sailor** *n* : marinero *m*
saint *n* : santo *m*, -ta *f* — **saintly** *adj*
saintlier; -est : santo
sake *n* **1 for goodness' sake!** : ¡por
Dios! **2 for the sake of** : por (el bien de)
salad *n* : ensalada *f*
salamander *n* : salamandra *f*
salami *n* : salami *m*
salary *n, pl* **-ries** : sueldo *m*
sale *n* **1** : venta *f* **2 for sale** : se vende
3 on sale : de rebaja — **salesman** *n*,
pl **-men** : vendedor *m*, dependiente *m*
— **saleswoman** *n, pl* **-women** :
vendedora *f*, dependienta *f*
salient *adj* : saliente
saliva *n* : saliva *f*
sallow *adj* : amarillento, cetrino
salmon *ns & pl* : salmón *m*
salon *n* → **beauty salon**
saloon *n* : bar *m*
salsa *n* : salsa *f* mexicana, salsa *f* picante
salt *n* : sal *f* — **salt** *vt* : salar —
saltwater *adj* : de agua salada —
salty *adj* **saltier; -est** : salado
salute *v* **-luted; -luting** *vt* : saludar — *vi*
: hacer un saludo — **salute** *n* : saludo *m*
salvage *n* : salvamento *m* —
salvage *vt* **-vaged; -vaging** : salvar
salvation *n* : salvación *f*
salve *n* : ungüento *m*
same *adj* **1** : mismo **2 be the same (as)**
: ser igual (que) **3 the same thing (as)**
: la misma cosa (que) — **same** *pron* **1**
all the same : igual **2 the same** : lo
mismo — **same** *adv* **the same** : igual
sample *n* : muestra *f* — **sample** *vt*
-pled; -pling : probar
sanatorium *n, pl* **-riums**
or **-ria** : sanatorio *m*

---

s *n, pl* **s's** *or* **ss** : s *f*, decimonovena
letra del alfabeto inglés
Sabbath *n* **1** : sábado *m* (día santo judío)
2 : domingo *m* (día santo cristiano)
sabotage *n* : sabotaje *m* — **sabotage** *vt*
-taged; -taging : sabotear
saccharin *n* : sacarina *f*
sack *n* : saco *m* — **sack** *vt* **1** FIRE
: despedir **2** PLUNDER : saquear
sacrament *n* : sacramento *m*
sacred *adj* : sagrado
sacrifice *n* : sacrificio *m* — **sacrifice** *vt*
-ficed; -ficing : sacrificar
sacrilege *n* : sacrilegio *m* —
sacrilegious *adj* : sacrílego

sad *adj* **sadder; saddest** : triste
— **sadden** *vt* : entristecer
saddle *n* : silla *f* (de montar) —
saddle *vt* **-dled; -dling 1** : ensillar (un
caballo, etc.) **2 saddle someone with**
something : cargar a algn con algo
sadistic *adj* : sádico
sadness *n* : tristeza *f*
safari *n* : safari *m*
safe *adj* **safer; safest 1** : seguro **2**
UNHARMED : ileso **3** CAREFUL : prudente
4 safe and sound : sano y salvo —
safe *n* : caja *f* fuerte — **safeguard** *n*
: salvaguarda *f* — **safeguard** *vt* :
salvaguardar — **safely** *adv* **1** : sin

sanctify *vt* **-fied; -fying** : santificar
sanction *n* : sanción *f* —
  sanction *vt* : sancionar
sanctity *n, pl* **-ties** : santidad *f*
sanctuary *n, pl* **-aries** : santuario *m*
sand *n* : arena *f* — **sand** *vt* : lijar (madera)
sandal *n* : sandalia *f*
sandpaper *n* : papel *m* de lija
  — **sandpaper** *vt* : lijar
sandwich *n* : sandwich *m*,
  bocadillo *m Spain* — **sandwich** *vt*
  sandwich between : meter entre
sandy *adj* **sandier; -est** : arenoso
sane *adj* **saner; sanest 1** :
  cuerdo **2** SENSIBLE : sensato
sang → **sing**
sanitarium *n, pl* **-iums** *or*
  -ia → **sanatorium**
sanitary *adj* **1** : sanitario **2**
  HYGIENIC : higiénico — **sanitary**
  napkin *n* : compresa *f* (higiénica)
  — **sanitation** *n* : sanidad *f*
sanity *n* : cordura *f*
sank → **sink**
Santa Claus *n* : Papá *m* Noel
sap[1] *n* **1** : savia *f* (de una planta)
  2 SUCKER : inocentón *m*, -tona *f*
sap[2] *vt* **sapped; sapping** :
  minar (la fuerza, etc.)
sapphire *n* : zafiro *m*
sarcasm *n* : sarcasmo *m* —
  sarcastic *adj* : sarcástico
sardine *n* : sardina *f*
sash *n* : faja *f* (de un vestido) ,
  fajín *m* (de un uniforme)
sat → **sit**
satanic *adj* : satánico
satchel *n* : cartera *f*
satellite *n* : satélite *m*
satin *n* : raso *m*
satire *n* : sátira *f* — **satiric**
  or **satirical** *adj* : satírico
satisfaction *n* : satisfacción *f* —
  satisfactory *adj* : satisfactorio — **satisfy** *v*
  -fied; -fying *vt* **1** : satisfacer **2** CONVINCE :
  convencer — **satisfying** *adj* : satisfactorio
saturate *vt* **-rated; -rating 1** :
  saturar **2** DRENCH : empapar —
  saturation *n* : saturación *f*
Saturday *n* : sábado *m*
Saturn *n* : Saturno *m*
sauce *n* : salsa *f* — **saucepan** *n*
  : cacerola *f* — **saucer** *n* :
  platillo *m* — **saucy** *adj* **saucier;**
  -est IMPUDENT : descarado

sauna *n* : sauna *mf*
saunter *vi* : pasear
sausage *n* : salchicha *f*
sauté *vt* **-téed** *or* **-téd;**
  -téing : saltear, sofreír
savage *adj* : salvaje, feroz
  — **savage** *n* : salvaje *mf* —
  savagery *n, pl* **-ries** : ferocidad *f*
save *vt* **saved; saving 1** RESCUE : salvar
  2 RESERVE : guardar **3** : ahorrar (dinero,
  tiempo, etc.) — **save** *prep* EXCEPT : salvo
savior *n* : salvador *m*, -dora *f*
savor *vt* : saborear — **savory** *adj* : sabroso
saw[1] → **see**
saw[2] *n* : sierra *f* — **saw** *vt* **sawed;**
  sawed *or* **sawn; sawing** : serrar —
  sawdust *n* : serrín *m*, aserrín *m*
▸ **saxophone** *n* : saxofón *m*
say *v* **said; saying; says** *vt* **1** : decir **2**
  INDICATE : marcar (dícese de relojes,
  etc.) — *vi* **1** : decir **2** **that is to say** : es
  decir — **say** *n, pl* **says 1 have no say** :
  no tener ni voz ni voto **2 have one's say**
  : dar su opinión — **saying** *n* : refrán *m*
scab *n* **1** : costra *f* (en una herida)

2 STRIKEBREAKER : esquirol *mf*
scaffold *n* : andamio *m* (en construcción)
scald *vt* : escaldar
scale[1] *n* : balanza *f* (para pesar)
scale[2] *n* : escama *f* (de un pez, etc.) —
  scale *vt* **scaled; scaling** : escamar
scale[3] *vt* **scaled; scaling 1** CLIMB :
  escalar **2 scale down** : reducir —
  scale *n* : escala *f* (musical, salarial, etc.)
scallion *n* : cebolleta *f*
scallop *n* : vieira *f*
scalp *n* : cuero *m* cabelludo
scam *n* : estafa *f*, timo *m fam*
scamper *vi* **scamper away**
  : irse corriendo
scan *vt* **scanned; scanning 1**
  : escandir (versos) **2** EXAMINE :
  escudriñar **3** SKIM : echar un vistazo
  a **4** : escanear (en informática)
scandal *n* **1** : escándalo *m* **2**
  GOSSIP : habladurías *fpl* —
  scandalous *adj* : escandaloso
Scandinavian *adj* : escandinavo
scant *adj* : escaso
scapegoat *n* : chivo *m* expiatorio

saxophone
saxofón[M]

mouthpiece
boquilla[F]

palm lever
palanca[F]

bell
pabellón[M]

reed
lengüeta[F]

bellkey
llave[F]

body
cuerpo[M]

key/finger button
botón[M] de la llave[F]

thumb rest
gancho[M] del pulgar[M]

scar n : cicatriz f — **scar** v **scarred; scarring** vt : dejar una cicatriz en — vi : cicatrizar

scarce adj **scarcer; -est** : escaso — **scarcely** adv : apenas — **scarcity** n, pl **-ties** : escasez f

scare vt **scared; scaring 1** : asustar **2 be scared of** : tener miedo a — **scare** n **1** FRIGHT : susto m **2** ALARM : pánico m — **scarecrow** n : espantapájaros m, espantajo m

scarf n, pl **scarves** or **scarfs 1** : bufanda f **2** KERCHIEF : pañuelo m

scarlet adj : escarlata — **scarlet fever** n : escarlatina f

scary adj **scarier; -est** : que da miedo

scathing adj : mordaz

scatter vt **1** STREW : esparcir **2** DISPERSE : dispersar — vi : dispersarse

scavenger n : carroñero m, -ra f (animal)

scenario n, pl **-ios 1** : guión m (cinemático) **2 the worst-case scenario** : el peor de los casos

scene n **1** : escena f **2 behind the scenes** : entre bastidores **3 make a scene** : armar un escándalo — **scenery** n, pl **-eries 1** : decorado m **2** LANDSCAPE : paisaje m — **scenic** adj : pintoresco

scent n **1** : aroma m **2** PERFUME : perfume m **3** TRAIL : rastro m — **scented** adj : perfumado

sceptic → **skeptic**

schedule n **1** : programa m **2** TIMETABLE : horario m **3 behind schedule** : atrasado, con retraso **4 on schedule** : según lo previsto — **schedule** vt **-uled; -uling** : planear, programar

scheme n **1** PLAN : plan m **2** PLOT : intriga f **3** DESIGN : esquema f — **scheme** vi **schemed; scheming** : intrigar

schism n : cisma m

schizophrenia n : esquizofrenia f — **schizophrenic** adj : esquizofrénico

scholar n : erudito m, -ta f — **scholarly** adj : erudito — **scholarship** n **1** : erudición f **2** GRANT : beca f

school[1] n : banco m (de peces)

school[2] n **1** : escuela f **2** COLLEGE : universidad f **3** DEPARTMENT : facultad f — **school** vt : instruir — **schoolboy** n : colegial m — **schoolgirl** n : colegiala f — **schoolteacher** n → **teacher**

science n : ciencia f — **scientific** adj : científico — **scientist** n : científico m, -ca f

scissors npl : tijeras fpl

scoff vi **scoff at** : burlarse de, mofarse de

scold vt : regañar

scoop n **1** : pala f **2** : noticia f exclusiva (en periodismo) — **scoop** vt **1** : sacar (con pala) **2 scoop out** : ahuecar **3 scoop up** : recoger

scoot vi : ir rápidamente — **scooter** n **1** : patinete m **2** or **motor scooter** : escúter m

scope n **1** RANGE : alcance m **2** OPPORTUNITY : posibilidades fpl

scorch vt : chamuscar

score n, pl **scores 1** : tanteo m (en deportes) **2** RATING : puntuación f **3** : partitura f (musical) **4** or pl **score** TWENTY : veintena f **5 keep score** : llevar la cuenta **6 on that score** : en ese sentido — **score** v **scored; scoring** vt **1** : marcar, anotarse Lat (un tanto) **2** : sacar (una nota) — vi : marcar (en deportes)

scorn n : desdén m — **scorn** vt : desdeñar — **scornful** adj : desdeñoso

scorpion n : alacrán m, escorpión m

Scot n : escocés m, -cesa f — **Scotch** adj → **Scottish** — **Scot** n or **Scot whiskey** : whisky m escocés — **Scottish** adj : escocés

scoundrel n : sinvergüenza mf

scour vt **1** SCRUB : fregar **2** SEARCH : registrar

scourge n : azote m

scout n : explorador m, -dora f

scowl vi : fruncir el ceño — **scowl** n : ceño m fruncido

scram vi **scrammed; scramming** : largarse

scramble v **-bled; -bling** vi **1** CLAMBER : trepar **2 scramble for** : pelearse por — vt : mezclar — **scramble** n : rebatiña f, pelea f — **scrambled eggs** npl : huevos mpl revueltos

scrap[1] n **1** PIECE : pedazo m **2** or **scrap metal** : chatarra f **3 scraps** npl : sobras — **scrap** vt **scrapped; scrapping** : desechar

scrap[2] n FIGHT : pelea f

scrapbook n : álbum m de recortes

scrape v **scraped; scraping** vt **1** : rascar **2** : rasparse (la rodilla, etc.) **3** or **scrape off** : raspar **4 scrape together** : reunir — vi **1** RUB : rozar **2 scrape by** : arreglárselas — **scrape** n **1** : rasguño m **2** PREDICAMENT : apuro m

scratch vt **1** CLAW : arañar **2** MARK : rayar **3** : rascarse (la cabeza, etc.) **4 scratch out** : tachar — **scratch** n **1** : arañazo m **2** MARK : rayón m **3 start**

from scratch : empezar desde cero

scrawl v : garabatear — **scrawl** n : garabato m

scrawny adj **scrawnier; -est** : escuálido

scream vi : gritar, chillar — **scream** n : grito m, chillido m

screech n **1** : chillido m (de personas) **2** : chirrido m (de frenos, etc.) — **screech** vi **1** : chillar **2** : chirriar (dícese de los frenos, etc.)

screen n **1** : pantalla f **2** PARTITION : mampara f **3** or **window screen** : mosquitero m — **screen** vt **1** SHIELD : proteger **2** HIDE : ocultar **3** : seleccionar (candidatos, etc.)

screw n : tornillo m — **screw** vt **1** : atornillar **2 screw up** RUIN : fastidiar — **screwdriver** n : destornillador m

scribble v **-bled; -bling** : garabatear — **scribble** n : garabato m

script n **1** HANDWRITING : escritura f **2** : guión m (de cine, etc.) — **scripture** n **1** : escritos mpl sagrados **2 the Scriptures** npl : las Escrituras fpl

scroll n : rollo m (de pergamino, etc.)

scrounge v **scrounged; scrounging** vt : gorrear fam — vi **scrounge around for something** : andar buscando algo

scrub[1] n UNDERBRUSH : maleza f

scrub[2] vt **scrubbed; scrubbing** SCOUR : fregar — **scrub** n : fregado m

scruff n **by the scruff of the neck** : por el pescuezo

scruple n : escrúpulo m — **scrupulous** adj : escrupuloso

scrutiny n, pl **-nies** : análisis m cuidadoso — **scrutinize** vt **-nized; -nizing** : escudriñar

scuff vt : raspar, rayar

scuffle n : refriega f

sculpture n : escultura f — **sculpt** v : esculpir — **sculptor** n : escultor m, -tora f

scum n **1** FROTH : espuma f **2** : escoria f (dícese de personas)

scurry vi **-ried; -rying** : corretear

scuttle[1] n : cubo m (para carbón)

scuttle[2] vt **-tled; -tling** : hundir (un barco)

scuttle[3] vi SCAMPER : corretear

sea n **1** : mar mf **2 at sea** : en el mar — **sea** adj : del mar — **seafarer** n : marinero m — **seafood** n : mariscos mpl — **seagull** n : gaviota f

seal[1] n : foca f (animal)

seal[2] n **1** STAMP : sello m **2** CLOSURE : cierre m (hermético) — **seal** vt : sellar

seam n **1** : costura f **2** VEIN : veta f

seaman n, pl **-men** : marinero m

seamy adj **seamier; -est** : sórdido

seaplane n : hidroavión m

seaport n : puerto m marítimo

search vt : registrar — vi **search for** : buscar — **search** n **1** : registro m **2** HUNT : búsqueda f — **searchlight** n : reflector m

seashell n : concha f (marina) — **seashore** n : orilla f del mar — **seasick** adj **1** : mareado **2 be seasick** : marearse — **seasickness** n : mareo m

season n **1** : estación f (del año) **2** : temporada f (en deportes, etc.) — **season** vt **1** FLAVOR : sazonar **2** : secar (madera) — **seasonal** adj : estacional — **seasoned** adj EXPERIENCED : veterano — **seasoning** n : condimento m

seat n **1** : asiento m **2** : fondillos mpl (de un pantalón) **3** BUTTOCKS : trasero m **4** CENTER : sede f — **seat** vt **1 be seated** : sentarse **2 the bus seats 30** : el autobús tiene cabida para 30 — **seat belt** n : cinturón m de seguridad

seaweed n : alga f marina

secede vi **-ceded; -ceding** : separarse (de una nación, etc.)

secluded adj : aislado — **seclusion** n : aislamiento m

second adj : segundo — **second** or **secondly** adv : en segundo lugar — **second** n **1** : segundo m, -da f **2** MOMENT : segundo m **3 have seconds** : repetir (en una comida) — **second** vt : secundar — **secondary** adj : secundario — **secondhand** adj : de segunda mano — **second–rate** adj : mediocre

secret adj : secreto — **secret** n : secreto m — **secrecy** n, pl **-cies** : secreto m

secretary n, pl **-taries 1** : secretario m, -ria f **2** : ministro m, -tra f (del gobierno)

secretion n : secreción f — **secrete** vt **-creted; -creting** : secretar

secretive adj : reservado — **secretly** adv : en secreto

sect n : secta f

section n : sección f, parte f

sector n : sector m

secular adj : secular

security n, pl **-ties 1** : seguridad f **2** GUARANTEE : garantía f **3 securities** npl : valores mpl — **secure** adj **-curer; -est** : seguro — **security** vt **-cured; -curing** **1** FASTEN : asegurar **2** GET : conseguir

sedan n : sedán m

sedate adj : sosegado

sedative adj : sedante — **sedative** n : sedante m

sedentary adj : sedentario

sediment n : sedimento m

seduce vt **-duced; -ducing** : seducir — **seduction** n : seducción f — **seductive** adj : seductor

see v **saw; seen; seeing** vt **1** : ver **2** UNDERSTAND : entender **3** ESCORT : acompañar **4 see someone off** : despedirse de algn **5 see something**

through : llevar algo a cabo **6 see you later!** : ¡hasta luego! — vi **1** : ver **2** UNDERSTAND : entender **3 let's see** : vamos a ver **4 see to** : ocuparse de

seed n, pl **seed** or **seeds 1** : semilla f **2** SOURCE : germen m — **seedy** adj **seedier; -est** SQUALID : sórdido

seek v **sought; seeking** vt **1** or **seek out** : buscar **2** REQUEST : pedir **3 seek to** : tratar de — vi SEARCH : buscar

seem vi : parecer

seep vi : filtrarse

seesaw n : balancín m

seaweeds
algas marinas

structure of an alga
estructura de un alga

receptacle
receptáculo

thallus
talo

aerocyst
aerocisto

midrib
nervio central

green alga
alga verde

red alga
alga roja

brown alga
alga parda

seethe *vi* **seethed; seething**
: rabiar, estar furioso
segment *n* : segmento *m*
segregate *vt* **-gated; -gating** : segregar
— **segregation** *n* : segregación *f*
seize *v* **seized; seizing** *vt* **1** GRASP :
agarrar **2** CAPTURE : tomar **3** : aprovechar
(una oportunidad) — *vi or* **seize up** :
agarrotarse — **seizure** *n* **1** CAPTURE
: toma *f* **2** : ataque *m* (en medicina)
seldom *adv* : pocas veces, raramente
select *adj* : selecto — **select** *vt* :
seleccionar — **selection** *n* : selección *f*
— **selective** *adj* : selectivo
self *n, pl* **selves 1** : ser *m* **2 her better self**
: su lado bueno — **self–addressed** *adj*
: con la dirección del remitente — **self–**
assured *adj* : seguro de sí mismo —
self–centered *adj* : egocéntrico — **self–**
confidence *n* : confianza *f* en sí mismo
— **self–confident** *adj* : seguro de sí
mismo — **self–conscious** *adj* : cohibido
— **self–control** *n* : dominio *m* de sí mismo
— **self–defense** *n* : defensa *f* propia —
self–employed *adj* : que trabaja por cuenta
propia — **self–esteem** *n* : amor *m* propio
— **self–evident** *adj* : evidente — **self–**
help *n* : autoayuda *f* — **self–important** *adj*
: presumido — **self–interest** *n* : interés *m*
personal — **selfish** *adj* : egoísta —
selfishness *n* : egoísmo *m* — **selfless** *adj*
: desinteresado — **self–pity** *n, pl* **-ties**
: autocompasión *f* — **self–portrait** *n* :
autorretrato *m* — **self–respect** *n* : amor *m*
propio — **self–righteous** *adj* : santurrón
— **self–service** *adj* : de autoservicio
— **self–sufficient** *adj* : autosuficiente
— **self–taught** *adj* : autodidacta
sell *v* **sold; selling** *vt* : vender — *vi* :
venderse — **seller** *n* : vendedor *m*, -dora *f*
selves → **self**
semantics *ns & pl* : semántica *f*
semblance *n* : apariencia *f*
semester *n* : semestre *m*
semicolon *n* : punto y coma *m*
semifinal *n* : semifinal *f*
seminary *n, pl* **-naries** : seminario *m*
— **seminar** *n* : seminario *m*
senate *n* : senado *m* — **senator** *n*
: senador *m*, -dora *f*
send *vt* **sent; sending 1** : mandar,
enviar **2 send away for** : pedir **3**
send back : devolver (mercancías,
etc.) **4 send for** : mandar a buscar
— **sender** *n* : remitente *mf*

senile *adj* : senil — **senility** *n* : senilidad *f*
senior *n* **1** SUPERIOR : superior *m* **2**
: estudiante *mf* de último año (en
educación) **3** *or* **senior citizen** :
persona *f* mayor **4 be someone's senior**
: ser mayor que algn — **senior** *adj* **1**
: superior (en rango) **2** ELDER : mayor
— **seniority** *n* : antigüedad *f*
sensation *n* : sensación *f* —
sensational *adj* : sensacional
sense *n* **1** : sentido *m* **2** FEELING
: sensación *f* **3** COMMON SENSE :
sentido *m* común **4 make sense** :
tener sentido — **sense** *vt* **sensed;**
sensing : sentir — **senseless** *adj* **1** :
sin sentido **2** UNCONSCIOUS : inconsciente
— **sensible** *adj* : sensato, práctico —
sensibility *n, pl* **-ties** : sensibilidad *f*
— **sensitive** *adj* **1** : sensible **2** TOUCHY
: susceptible — **sensitivity** *n, pl* **-ties**
: sensibilidad *f* — **sensual** *adj* :
sensual — **sensuous** *adj* : sensual
sent → **send**
sentence *n* **1** : frase *f* **2** JUDGMENT
: sentencia *f* — **sentence** *vt*
-tenced; -tencing : sentenciar
sentiment *n* **1** : sentimiento *m* **2**
BELIEF : opinión *f* — **sentimental** *adj*
: sentimental — **sentimentality** *n,*
pl **-ties** : sentimentalismo *m*
sentry *n, pl* **-tries** : centinela *m*
separation *n* : separación *f* —
separate *v* **-rated; -rating** *vt* **1** : separar
2 DISTINGUISH : distinguir — *vi* : separarse
— **separation** *adj* **1** : separado **2**
DETACHED : aparte **3** DISTINCT : distinto
— **separately** *adv* : por separado
September *n* : septiembre *m,*
setiembre *m*
sequel *n* **1** : continuación *f* **2**
CONSEQUENCE : secuela *f*
sequence *n* **1** ORDER : orden *m* **2** :
secuencia *f* (de números o escenas)
Serb *or* **Serbian** *adj* : serbio
serene *adj* : sereno —
serenity *n* : serenidad *f*
sergeant *n* : sargento *mf*
serial *adj* : seriado — **serial** *n* : serial *m*
— **series** *n, pl* **series** : serie *f*
serious *adj* : serio — **seriously** *adv* **1**
: seriamente **2** GRAVELY : gravemente
3 take seriously : tomar en serio
sermon *n* : sermón *m*
serpent *n* : serpiente *f*
servant *n* : criado *m*, -da *f*

serve *v* **served; serving** *vi* **1** : servir
2 : sacar (en deportes) **3 serve as**
: servir de — *vt* **1** : servir **2 serve**
time : cumplir una condena —
server *n* **1** WAITER : camarero *m,*
-ra *f* **2** : servidor *m* (en informática)
service *n* **1** : servicio *m* **2** CEREMONY
: oficio *m* **3** MAINTENANCE : revisión *f* **4**
armed services : fuerzas *fpl* armadas
— **service** *vt* **-viced; -vicing** : revisar (un
vehículo, etc.) — **serviceman** *n, pl* **-men** :
militar *m* — **service station** *n* : estación *f*
de servicio — **serving** *n* : porción *f*, ración *f*
session *n* : sesión *f*
set *n* **1** : juego *m* (de platos, etc.) **2** :
set *m* (en tenis, etc.) **3** *or* **stage set** :
decorado *m* **4 television set** : aparato *m*
de televisión — **set** *v* **set; setting** *vt* **1**
or **set down** : poner **2** : poner en hora
(un reloj) **3** FIX : fijar (una fecha, etc.) **4**
set fire to : prender fuego a **5 set free** :
poner en libertad **6 set off** : hacer sonar
(una alarma), hacer estallar (una bomba)
7 set out to (do something) : proponerse
(hacer algo) **8 set up** ASSEMBLE : montar,
armar **9 set up** ESTABLISH : establecer
— *vi* **1** : cuajarse (dícese de la gelatina,
etc.), fraguar (dícese del cemento) **2** :
ponerse (dícese del sol, etc.) **3 set in**
BEGIN : empezar **4 set off** *or* **set out** :
salir (de viaje) — **set** *adj* **1** FIXED : fijo
2 READY : listo, preparado — **setback** *n*
: revés *m* — **setting** *n* **1** : posición *f*
(de un control) **2** MOUNTING : engaste *m*
(de joyas) **3** SCENE : escenario *m*
settle *v* **settled; settling** *vi* **1** : asentarse
(dícese de polvo, colonos, etc.) **2 settle**
down RELAX : calmarse **3 settle for** :
conformarse con **4 settle in** : instalarse
— *vt* **1** DECIDE : fijar, decidir **2** RESOLVE :
resolver **3** PAY : pagar **4** CALM : calmar **5**
COLONIZE : colonizar — **settlement** *n* **1**
PAYMENT : pago *m* **2** COLONY : colonia *f,*
poblado *m* **3** AGREEMENT : acuerdo *m*
— **settler** *n* : colono *m*, -na *f*
seven *adj* : siete — **seven** *n* : siete *m*
— **seven hundred** *adj* : setecientos —
seven hundred *n* : setecientos *m* —
seventeen *adj* : diecisiete — **seventeen** *n*
: diecisiete *m* — **seventeenth** *adj* :
decimoséptimo — **seventeenth** *n* **1** :
decimoséptimo *m*, -ma *f* (en una serie)
2 : diecisieteavo *m* (en matemáticas) —
seventh *adj* : séptimo — **seventh** *n* **1**
: séptimo *m*, -ma *f* (en una serie) **2**

: séptimo *m* (en matemáticas) —
seventieth *adj* : septuagésimo —
seventieth *n* **1** : septuagésimo *m*,
-ma *f* (en una serie) **2** : setentavo *m* (en
matemáticas) — **seventy** *adj* : setenta
— **seventy** *n, pl* **-ties** : setenta *m*
sever *vt* **-ered; -ering** : cortar, romper
several *adj* : varios —
several *pron* : varios, varias
severance *n* : ruptura *f*
severe *adj* **severer; -est 1** : severo **2**
SERIOUS : grave — **severely** *adv* **1** :
severamente **2** SERIOUSLY : gravemente
— **severity** *n* **1** : severidad *f* **2**
SERIOUSNESS : gravedad *f*
sew *v* **sewed; sewn** *or*
sewed; sewing : coser
sewer *n* : cloaca *f* — **sewage** *n*
: aguas *fpl* negras
sewing *n* : costura *f*
sex *n* **1** : sexo *m* **2** INTERCOURSE :
relaciones *fpl* sexuales — **sexism** *n*
: sexismo *m* — **sexist** *adj* : sexista —
sexual *adj* : sexual — **sexuality** *n* :
sexualidad *f* — **sexy** *adj* **sexier; -est** : sexy
shabby *adj* **shabbier; -est 1** WORN :
gastado **2** UNFAIR : malo, injusto

shack *n* : choza *f*
shackle *n* : grillete *m*
shade *n* **1** : sombra *f* **2** : tono *m* (de
un color) **3** NUANCE : matiz *m* **4** *or*
lampshade : pantalla *f* **5** *or* window
shade : persiana *f* — **shade** *vt* **shaded;
shading** : proteger de la luz — **shadow** *n*
: sombra *f* — **shadowy** *adj* INDISTINCT
: vago — **shady** *adj* **shadier; -est 1** :
sombreado **2** DISREPUTABLE : sospechoso
shaft *n* **1** : asta *f* (de una flecha, etc.)
2 HANDLE : mango *m* **3** AXLE : eje *m* **4** :
rayo *m* (de luz) **5** *or* mine shaft : pozo *m*
shaggy *adj* **shaggier; -est** : peludo
shake *v* **shook; shaken; shaking** *vt* **1**
: sacudir **2** MIX : agitar **3** shake hands
with someone : dar la mano a algn
4 shake one's head : negar con la
cabeza **5** shake up UPSET : afectar — *vi*
: temblar — **shake** *n* **1** : sacudida *f* **2**
→ handshake — **shaker** *n* **1** salt
shaker : salero *m* **2** pepper shaker :
pimentero *m* — **shaky** *adj* **shakier; -est**
1 : tembloroso **2** UNSTABLE : poco firme
shall *v aux past* **should; pres sing & pl**
shall 1 (*expressing volition or futurity*) →
will 2 (*expressing possibility or obligation*)

→ **should 3 shall we go? : ¿nos vamos?**
shallow *adj* **1** : poco profundo
2 SUPERFICIAL : superficial
sham *n* : farsa *f* — **sham** *v*
shammed; shamming : fingir
shambles *ns & pl* : caos *m*, desorden *m*
shame *n* **1** : vergüenza *f* **2** what a
shame! : ¡qué lástima! — **shame** *vt*
shamed; shaming : avergonzar
— **shameful** *adj* : vergonzoso —
shameless *adj* : desvergonzado
shampoo *vt* : lavar (el pelo) —
shampoo *n, pl* **-poos** : champú *m*
shamrock *n* : trébol *m*
shan't (*contraction of shall not*) → **shall**
shape *v* **shaped; shaping** *vt* **1** :
formar **2** DETERMINE : determinar **3** be
shaped like : tener forma de — *vi or*
shape up : tomar forma — **shape** *n* **1**
: forma *f* **2** get in shape : ponerse en
forma — **shapeless** *adj* : informe
share *n* **1** : porción *f* **2** : acción *f*
(en una compañía) — **share** *v*
shared; sharing *vt* **1** : compartir **2**
DIVIDE : dividir — *vi* : compartir —
shareholder *n* : accionista *mf*
▸ **shark** *n* : tiburón *m*

**shark
tiburón**^M

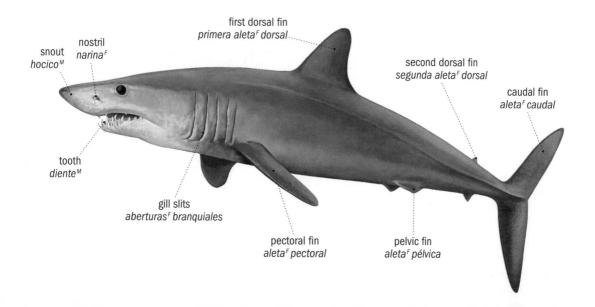

snout
hocico^M

nostril
narina^F

first dorsal fin
primera aleta^F *dorsal*

second dorsal fin
segunda aleta^F *dorsal*

caudal fin
aleta^F *caudal*

tooth
diente^M

gill slits
aberturas^F *branquiales*

pectoral fin
aleta^F *pectoral*

pelvic fin
aleta^F *pélvica*

sharp *adj* **1** : afilado **2** POINTY : puntiagudo **3** ACUTE : agudo **4** HARSH : duro, severo **5** CLEAR : nítido **6** : sostenido (en música) **7 a sharp curve** : una curva cerrada — **sharp** *adv* **at two o'clock sharp** : a las dos en punto — **sharp** *n* : sostenido (en música) — **sharpen** *vt* : afilar (un cuchillo, etc.), sacar punta a (un lápiz) — **sharpener** *n* **1** *or* **knife sharpener** : afilador *m* **2** *or* **pencil sharpener** : sacapuntas *m* — **sharply** *adv* : bruscamente

shatter *vt* **1** : hacer añicos **2** DEVASTATE : destrozar — *vi* : hacerse añicos

shave *v* **shaved; shaved** *or* **shaven; shaving** *vt* **1** : afeitar **2** SLICE : cortar — *vi* : afeitarse — **shave** *n* : afeitada *f* — **shaver** *n* : máquina *f* de afeitar

shawl *n* : chal *m*

she *pron* : ella

sheaf *n, pl* **sheaves 1** : gavilla *f* **2** : fajo *m* (de papeles)

shear *vt* **sheared; sheared** *or* **shorn; shearing** : esquilar — **shears** *npl* : tijeras *fpl* (grandes)

sheath *n, pl* **sheaths** : funda *f*, vaina *f*

shed[1] *v* **shed; shedding** *vt* **1** : derramar (lágrimas, etc.) **2** : mudar (de piel, etc.), quitarse (ropa) **3 shed light on** : aclarar

shed[2] *n* : cobertizo *m*

she'd (*contraction of* **she had** *or* **she would**) → **have, would**

sheen *n* : brillo *m*, lustre *m*

sheep *n, pl* **sheep** : oveja *f* — **sheepish** *adj* : avergonzado

sheer *adj* **1** THIN : transparente **2** PURE : puro **3** STEEP : escarpado

sheet *n* **1** : sábana *f* (de la cama) **2** : hoja *f* (de papel) **3** : capa *f* (de hielo, etc.) **4** PLATE : placa *f*, lámina *f*

shelf *n, pl* **shelves** : estante *m*

▸ **shell** *n* **1** : concha *f* **2** : caparazón *m* (de un crustáceo, etc.) **3** : cáscara *f* (de un huevo, etc.) **4** : armazón *mf* (de un edificio, etc.) **5** POD : vaína *f* **6** MISSILE : proyectil *m* — **shell** *vt* **1** : pelar (nueces, etc.) **2** BOMBARD : bombardear

she'll (*contraction of* **she shall** *or* **she will**) → **shall, will**

shellfish *n* : marisco *m*

shelter *n* **1** : refugio *m* **2 take shelter** : refugiarse — **shelter** *vt* **1** PROTECT : proteger **2** HARBOR : albergar

shelve *vt* **shelved; shelving** DEFER : dar carpetazo a

shepherd *n* : pastor *m* — **shepherd** *vt* GUIDE : conducir, guiar

sherbet *n* : sorbete *m*

sheriff *n* : sheriff *mf*

sherry *n, pl* **-ries** : jerez *m*

she's (*contraction of* **she is** *or* **she has**) → **be, have**

shield *n* : escudo *m* — **shield** *vt* : proteger

shier, shiest → **shy**

shift *vt* **1** MOVE : mover **2** SWITCH : transferir — *vi* **1** CHANGE : cambiar **2** MOVE : moverse **3** *or* **shift gears** : cambiar de velocidad — **shift** *n* **1** CHANGE : cambio *m* **2** : turno *m* (de trabajo) — **shiftless** *adj* : holgazán — **shifty** *adj* **shiftier; -est** : sospechoso

shimmer *vi* : brillar, relucir

shin *n* : espinilla *f*

shine *v* **shone** *or* **shined; shining** *vi* : brillar — *vt* **1** : alumbrar (una luz) **2** POLISH : sacar brillo a — **shine** *n* : brillo *m*

shingle *n* : teja *f* plana y delgada (en construcción) — **shingle** *vt* **-gled; -gling** : techar — **shingles** *npl* : herpes *m*

shiny *adj* **shinier; -est** : brillante

▸ **ship** *n* **1** : barco *m*, buque *m* **2** → **spaceship** — **ship** *vt* **shipped; shipping** : transportar, enviar (por barco) — **shipbuilding** *n* : construcción *f* naval — **shipment** *n* : envío *m* — **shipping** *n* **1** : transporte *m* **2** SHIPS : barcos *mpl* — **shipshape** *adj* : ordenado — **shipwreck** *n* : naufragio *m* — **ship** *vt* **be shiped** : naufragar — **shipyard** *n* : astillero *m*

shirk *vt* : esquivar

shirt *n* : camisa *f*

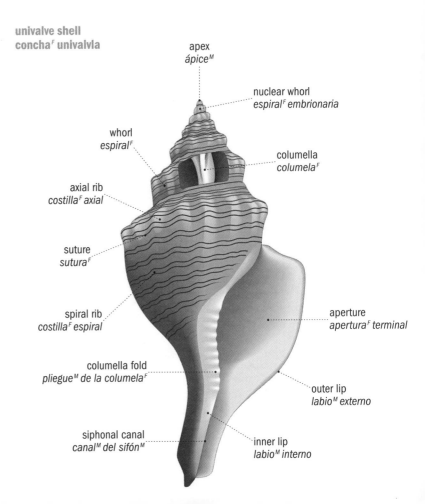

univalve shell
concha[F] univalvia

apex
ápice[M]

nuclear whorl
espiral[F] embrionaria

whorl
espiral[F]

columella
columela[F]

axial rib
costilla[F] axial

suture
sutura[F]

spiral rib
costilla[F] espiral

aperture
apertura[F] terminal

columella fold
pliegue[M] de la columela[F]

outer lip
labio[M] externo

siphonal canal
canal[M] del sifón[M]

inner lip
labio[M] interno

shiver *vi* : temblar (del frío, etc.)
— **shiver** *n* : escalofrío *m*

shoal *n* : banco *m*

shock *n* **1** IMPACT : choque *m* **2** SURPRISE,
UPSET : golpe *m* emocional **3** : shock *m* (en
medicina) **4** *or* **electric shock** : descarga *f*
(eléctrica) — **shock** *vt* : escandalizar
— **shock absorber** *n* : amortiguador *m*
— **shocking** *adj* : escandaloso

shoddy *adj* **shoddier; -est**
: de mala calidad

shoe *n* : zapato *m* — **shoe** *vt* **shod;**
shoeing : herrar (un caballo) —
shoelace *n* : cordón *m* (de zapato) —
shoemaker *n* : zapatero *m*, -ra *f*

shone → **shine**

shook → **shake**

shoot *v* **shot; shooting** *vt* **1** : disparar
2 : echar (una mirada) **3** PHOTOGRAPH :
fotografiar **4** FILM : rodar — *vi* **1** : disparar
2 shoot by : pasar como una bala —
shoot *n* : brote *m*, retoño *m* (de una planta)
— **shooting star** *n* : estrella *f* fugaz

shop *n* **1** : tienda *f* **2** WORKSHOP :
taller *m* — **shop** *vi* **shopped; shopping**
1 : hacer compras **2 go shopping** : ir de
compras — **shopkeeper** *n* : tendero *m*,
-ra *f* — **shoplift** *vi* : hurtar mercancía
(en tiendas) — **shoplifter** *n* : ladrón *m*,
-drona *f* (que roba en tiendas) —
shopper *n* : comprador *m*, -dora *f*

shore *n* : orilla *f*

shorn → **shear**

short *adj* **1** : corto **2** : bajo (de estatura)
3 CURT : brusco **4 a short time ago** :
hace poco **5 be short of** : estar corto
de — **short** *adv* **1 stop short** : parar
en seco **2 fall short** : quedarse corto
— **shortage** *n* : escasez *f*, carencia *f*
— **shortcake** *n* : tarta *f* de fruta —
shortcoming *n* : defecto *m* — **shortcut** *n*
: atajo *m* — **shorten** *vt* : acortar —
shorthand *n* : taquigrafía *f* — **short–**
lived *adj* : efímero — **shortly** *adv* : dentro
de poco — **shortness** *n* **1** : lo corto (de
una cosa), baja estatura *f* (de una persona)
2 short of breath : falta *f* de aliento —
shorts *npl* : shorts *mpl*, pantalones *mpl*
cortos — **shortsighted** → **nearsighted**

shot *n* **1** : disparo *m*, tiro *m* **2** :
tiro *m* (en deportes) **3** ATTEMPT :
intento *m* **4** PHOTOGRAPH : foto *f* **5**
INJECTION : inyección *f* **6** : trago *m*
(de licor) — **shotgun** *n* : escopeta *f*

should *past of* **shall 1 if she should**

call : si llama **2 I should have gone** :
debería haber ido **3 they should arrive**
soon : deben llegar pronto **4 what**
should we do? : ¿qué hacemos?

shoulder *n* **1** : hombro *m* **2** : arcén *m*
(de una carretera) — **shoulder** *vt* :
cargar con (la responsabilidad, etc.)
— **shoulder blade** *n* : omóplato *m*

shouldn't (*contraction of*
should not) → **should**

shout *v* : gritar — **shout** *n* : grito *m*

shove *v* **shoved; shoving** : empujar
— **shove** *n* : empujón *m*

shovel *n* : pala *f* — **shovel** *vt* **-veled**

or **-velled; -veling** *or* **-velling 1**
: mover (tierra, etc.) con una pala
2 DIG : cavar (con una pala)

show *v* **showed; shown** *or* **showed;**
showing *vt* **1** : mostrar **2** TEACH : enseñar
3 PROVE : demostrar **4** ESCORT : acompañar
5 : proyectar (una película), dar (un
programa de televisión) **6 show off** :
hacer alarde de — *vi* **1** : notarse, verse
2 show off : lucirse **3 show up** ARRIVE :
aparecer — **show** *n* **1** : demostración *f* **2**
EXHIBITION : exposición *f* **3** : espectáculo *m*
(teatral), programa *m* (de televisión, etc.)
— **showdown** *n* : confrontación *f*

ancient ships
barcos^M **antiguos**

galley
galera^F

caravel
carabela^F

longship
dragón^M vikingo

galleon
galeón^M

shower *n* **1** : ducha *f* **2** : chaparrón *m* (en meteorología) **3** PARTY : fiesta *f* — **shower** *vt* **1** SPRAY : regar **2 shower someone with** : colmar a algn de — *vi* **1** : ducharse **2** RAIN : llover

showy *adj* **showier; -est** : llamativo, ostentoso

shrank → **shrink**

shrapnel *ns & pl* : metralla *f*

shred *n* **1** : tira *f* (de tela, etc.) **2** IOTA : pizca *f* — **shred** *vt* **shredded; shredding 1** : hacer tiras **2** GRATE : rallar

shrewd *adj* : astuto

shriek *vi* : chillar — **shriek** *n* : chillido *m*, alarido *m*

shrill *adj* : agudo, estridente

shrimp *n* : camarón *m*

shrine *n* **1** TOMB : sepulcro *m* **2** SANCTUARY : santuario *m*

shrink *v* **shrank; shrunk** *or* **shrunken; shrinking** *vt* : encoger — *vi* **1** : encogerse (dícese de ropa), reducirse (dícese de números, etc.) **2** *or* **shrink back** : retroceder

shrivel *vi* **-veled** *or* **-velled; -veling** *or* **-velling** *or* **shrivel up** : arrugarse, marchitarse

shroud *n* **1** : sudario *m*, mortaja *f* **2** VEIL : velo *m* — **shroud** *vt* : envolver

shrub *n* : arbusto *m*, mata *f*

shrug *vi* **shrugged; shrugging** : encogerse de hombros

shrunk → **shrink**

shudder *vi* : estremecerse — **shudder** *n* : estremecimiento *m*

shuffle *v* **-fled; -fling** *vt* : barajar (naipes), revolver (papeles, etc.) — *vi* : caminar arrastrando los pies

shun *vi* **shunned; shunning** : evitar, esquivar

shut *v* **shut; shutting** *vt* **1** CLOSE : cerrar **2 shut off** → **turn off 3 shut up** CONFINE : encerrar — *vi* **1** *or* **shut down** : cerrarse **2 shut up!** : ¡cállate! — **shutter** *n* **1** *or* **window shutter** : contraventana *f* **2** : obturador *m* (de una cámara)

shuttle *n* **1** : lanzadera *f* (para tejer) **2** *or* **shuttle bus** : autobús *m* (de corto recorrido) **3** → **space shuttle** — **shuttle** *v* **-tled; -tling** *vt* : transportar — *vi* : ir y venir

shy *adj* **shier** *or* **shyer; shiest** *or* **shyest** : tímido — **shy** *vi* **shied; shying** *or* **shy away** : retroceder — **shyness** *n* : timidez *f*

sibling *n* : hermano *m*, hermana *f*

sick *adj* **1** : enfermo **2 be sick** VOMIT : vomitar **3 be sick of** : estar harto de **4 feel sick** : tener náuseas — **sicken** *vt* DISGUST : dar asco a — **sickening** *adj* : nauseabundo

sickle *n* : hoz *f*

sickly *adj* **sicklier; -est 1** UNHEALTHY : enfermizo **2** → **sickening** — **sickness** *n* : enfermedad *f*

side *n* **1** : lado *m* **2** : costado *m* (de una persona), ijada *f* (de un animal) **3** : parte *f* (en una disputa, etc.) **4 side by side** : uno al lado de otro **5 take sides** : tomar partido — **side** *vi* **side with** : ponerse de parte de — **sideboard** *n* : aparador *m* — **sideburns** *npl* : patillas *fpl* — **side effect** *n* : efecto *m* secundario — **sideline** *n* : línea *f* de banda (en deportes) — **sidestep** *vt* - **stepped; -stepping** : eludir, esquivar — **sidetrack** *vt* **get sidetracked** : distraerse — **sidewalk** *n* : acera *f* — **sideways** *adj & adv* : de lado — **siding** *n* : revestimiento *m* exterior

siege *n* : sitio *m*

sieve *n* : tamiz *m*, cedazo *m*

sift *vt* **1** : cerner, tamizar **2** *or* **sift through** : pasar por el tamiz

sigh *vi* : suspirar — **sigh** *n* : suspiro *m*

sight *n* **1** : vista *f* **2** SPECTACLE : espectáculo *m* **3** : lugar *m* de interés (turístico) **4 catch sight of** : avistar — **sight** *vt* : avistar — **sightseer** *n* : turista *mf*

sign *n* **1** : signo *m* **2** NOTICE : letrero *m* **3** GESTURE : seña *f*, señal *f* — **sign** *vt* : firmar (un cheque, etc.) — *vi* **1** : firmar **2 sign up** ENROLL : inscribirse

signal *n* : señal *f* — **signal** *v* **-naled** *or* **-nalled; -naling** *or* **-nalling** *vt* **1** : hacer señas a **2** INDICATE : señalar — *vi* **1** : hacer señas **2** : señalizar (en un vehículo)

signature *n* : firma *f*

significance *n* **1** : significado *m* **2** IMPORTANCE : importancia *f* — **significant** *adj* : importante — **signify** *vt* **-fied; -fying** : significar

sign language *n* : lenguaje *m* gestual — **signpost** *n* : poste *m* indicador

silence *n* : silencio *m* — **silence** *vt* **-lenced; -lencing** : silenciar — **silent** *adj* **1** : silencioso **2** MUM : callado **3** : mudo (dícese de películas y letras)

silhouette *n* : silueta *f* — **silhouette** *vt* **-etted; -etting be silhouetted against** : perfilarse contra

silicon *n* : silicio *m*

silk *n* : seda *f* — **silky** *adj*

silkier; -est : sedoso

sill *n* : alféizar *m* (de una ventana), umbral *m* (de una puerta)

silly *adj* **sillier; -est** : tonto, estúpido

silt *n* : cieno *m*

silver *n* **1** : plata *f* **2** → **silverware** — **silver** *adj* : de plata — **silverware** *n* : plata *f* — **silvery** *adj* : plateado

similar *adj* : similar, parecido — **similarity** *n*, *pl* **-ties** : semejanza *f*, parecido *m*

simmer *v* : hervir a fuego lento

simple *adj* **simpler; -plest 1** : simple **2** EASY : sencillo — **simplicity** *n* : simplicidad *f*, sencillez *f* — **simplify** *vt* **-fied; -fying** : simplificar — **simply** *adv* **1** : sencillamente **2** ABSOLUTELY : realmente

simulate *vt* **-lated; -lating** : simular

simultaneous *adj* : simultáneo

sin *n* : pecado *m* — **sin** *vi* **sinned; sinning** : pecar

since *adv* **1** *or* **since then** : desde entonces **2 long since** : hace mucho — **since** *conj* **1** : desde que **2** BECAUSE : ya que, como **3 it's been years since…** : hace años que… — **since** *prep* : desde

sincere *adj* **-cerer; -est** : sincero — **sincerely** *adv* : sinceramente — **sincerity** *n* : sinceridad *f*

sinful *adj* : pecador (dícese de las personas), pecaminoso (dícese de las acciones)

sing *v* **sang** *or* **sung; sung; singing** : cantar

singe *vt* **singed; singeing** : chamuscar

singer *n* : cantante *mf*

single *adj* **1** : solo, único **2** UNMARRIED : soltero **3 every single day** : cada día, todos los días — **single** *n* **1** : soltero *m*, -ra *f* **2** *or* **single room** : habitación *f* individual — **single** *vt* **-gled; -gling single out 1** SELECT : escoger **2** DISTINGUISH : señalar — **single-handed** *adj* : sin ayuda, solo

singular *adj* : singular — **singular** *n* : singular *m*

sinister *adj* : siniestro

sink *v* **sank** *or* **sunk; sunk; sinking** *vi* **1** : hundirse (en un líquido) **2** DROP : bajar, caer — *vt* **1** : hundir **2 sink something into** : clavar algo en — **sink** *n* **1** *or* **kitchen sink** : fregadero *m* **2** *or* **bathroom sink** : lavabo *m*, lavamanos *m*

sinner *n* : pecador *m*, -dora *f*

sip *v* **sipped; sipping** *vt* : sorber — *vi*

skeleton: anterior view
esqueleto^M: vista^F anterior

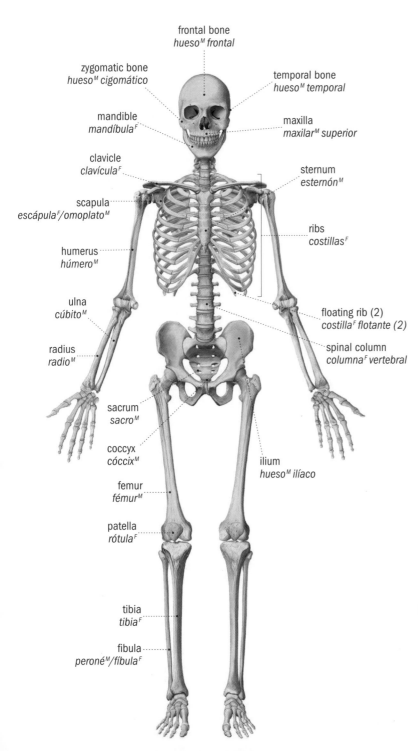

frontal bone
hueso^M frontal

zygomatic bone
hueso^M cigomático

temporal bone
hueso^M temporal

mandible
mandíbula^F

maxilla
maxilar^M superior

clavicle
clavícula^F

sternum
esternón^M

scapula
escápula^F/omoplato^M

ribs
costillas^F

humerus
húmero^M

ulna
cúbito^M

floating rib (2)
costilla^F flotante (2)

radius
radio^M

spinal column
columna^F vertebral

sacrum
sacro^M

coccyx
cóccix^M

ilium
hueso^M ilíaco

femur
fémur^M

patella
rótula^F

tibia
tibia^F

fibula
peroné^M/fíbula^F

: beber a sorbos — **sip** n : sorbo m
siphon n : sifón m — **siphon** vt
: sacar con sifón
sir n **1** (in titles) : sir m **2** (as a
form of address) : señor m **3**
Dear Sir : Estimado señor
siren n : sirena f
sirloin n : solomillo m
sissy n, pl **-sies** : mariquita mf fam
sister n : hermana f — **sister–in–**
law n, pl **sisters–in–law** : cuñada f
sit v **sat; sitting** vi **1** or **sit down** :
sentarse **2** LIE : estar (ubicado) **3**
MEET : estar en sesión **4** or **sit up**
: incorporarse — vt : sentar
site n **1** : sitio m, lugar m **2** LOT : solar m
sitting room → **living room**
sitter → **baby–sitter**
situated adj : ubicado, situado
— **situation** n : situación f
six adj : seis — **six** n : seis m — **six**
hundred adj : seiscientos — **six**
hundred n : seiscientos m — **sixteen** adj
: dieciséis — **sixteen** n : dieciséis m
— **sixteenth** adj : decimosexto —
sixteenth n **1** : decimosexto m, -ta f
(en una serie) **2** : dieciseisavo m,
dieciseisava parte f — **sixth** adj : sexto
— **sixth** n **1** : sexto m, -ta f (en una
serie) **2** : sexto m (en matemáticas) —
sixtieth adj : sexagésimo — **sixtieth** n **1**
: sexagésimo m, -ma f (en una serie) **2** :
sesentavo m (en matemáticas) — **sixty** adj
: sesenta — **sixty** n, pl **-ties** : sesenta m
size n **1** : tamaño m, talla f (de
ropa), número m (de zapatos) **2**
EXTENT : magnitud f — **size** vt **sized;**
sizing size up : evaluar — **sizable**
or **sizeable** adj : considerable
sizzle vi **-zled; -zling** : chisporrotear
skate[1] n : raya f (pez)
skate[2] n : patín m — **skate** vi
skated; skating : patinar —
skateboard n : monopatín m —
skater n : patinador m, -dora f
▸ **skeleton** n : esqueleto m
skeptic n : escéptico m, -ca f
— **skeptical** adj : escéptico —
skepticism n : escepticismo m
sketch n **1** : esbozo m, bosquejo m **2**
SKIT : sketch m — **sketch** vt : bosquejar
— vi : hacer bosquejos — **sketchy** adj
sketchier; -est : incompleto
skewer n : brocheta f, broqueta f
ski n, pl **skis** : esquí m — **ski** vi

skunk
mofeta^F

skied; skiing : esquiar

skid n : derrape m, patinazo m — **skid** vi
skidded; skidding : derrapar, patinar

skier n : esquiador m, -dora f

skill n 1 : habilidad f, destreza f 2
TECHNIQUE : técnica f — **skilled** adj : hábil

skillet n : sartén mf

skillful adj : hábil, diestro

skim vt **skimmed; skimming** 1 :
espumar (sopa, etc.), descremar (leche)
2 : pasar rozando (una superficie) 3
or **skim through** : echar un vistazo
a — **skim** adj : descremado

skimp vi **skimp on** : escatimar —
skimpy adj **skimpier; -est** 1 : exiguo,
escaso 2 : brevísimo (dícese de ropa)

skin n : piel f — **skin** vt **skinned;**
skinning : despellejar — **skin**
diving n : buceo m, submarinismo m
— **skinny** adj **skinnier; -est** : flaco

skip v **skipped; skipping** vi : ir
brincando — vt OMIT : saltarse
— **skip** n : brinco m, salto m

skipper n : capitán m, -tana f

skirmish n : escaramuza f

skirt n : falda f — **skirt** vt 1 BORDER
: bordear 2 EVADE : eludir

skull n : cráneo m (de una persona
viva) , calavera f (de un esqueleto)

▸ **skunk** n : mofeta f, zorrillo m, Lat

▸ **sky** n, pl **skies** : cielo m —
skylight n : claraboya f, tragaluz m
— **skyline** n : horizonte m —
skyscraper n : rascacielos m

slab n : bloque m (de piedra, etc.)

slack adj 1 LOOSE : flojo 2 CARELESS
: descuidado — **slack** n 1 **take up**
the slack : tensar (una cuerda, etc.)
2 **slacks** npl : pantalones mpl —
slacken vt : aflojar — vi : aflojarse

slain → **slay**

slam n : golpe m, portazo m (de
una puerta) — **slam** v **slammed;**
slamming vt 1 or **slam down** :
tirar, plantar 2 or **slam shut** : cerrar
de golpe 3 **slam the door** : dar un
portazo — vi 1 : cerrarse de golpe
2 **slam into** : chocar contra

slander vt : calumniar, difamar —
slander n : calumnia f, difamación f

slang n : argot m

slant n : inclinación f —
slant vi : inclinarse

slap vt **slapped; slapping** 1 : dar una
bofetada a 2 **slap someone on the back**
: dar una palmada en la espalda a algn
— **slap** n : bofetada f, cachetada f Lat

slash vt 1 : hacer un tajo en 2 :
rebajar (precios) drásticamente
— **slash** n : tajo m

slat n : tablilla f

slate n : pizarra f

slaughter n : matanza f —
slaughter vt 1 : matar (animales)
2 MASSACRE : masacrar —
slaughterhouse n : matadero m

slave n : esclavo m, -va f — **slave** vi
slaved; slaving : trabajar como un
burro — **slavery** n : esclavitud f

Slavic adj : eslavo

slay vt **slew; slain; slaying** : asesinar

sleazy adj **sleazier; -est** : sórdido

sled n : trineo m

sledgehammer n : almádena f

sleek adj : liso y brillante

sleep n 1 : sueño m 2 **go to sleep** :
dormirse — **sleep** vi **slept; sleeping** :
dormir — **sleeper** n **be a light sleeper**
: tener el sueño ligero — **sleepless** adj
have a sleepless night : pasar la
noche en blanco — **sleepwalker** n
: sonámbulo m, -la f — **sleepy** adj
sleepier; -est 1 : somnoliento,
soñoliento 2 **be sleepy** : tener sueño

sleet n : aguanieve f —
sleet vi : caer aguanieve

sleeve n : manga f —
sleeveless adj : sin mangas

sleigh n : trineo m

slender adj : delgado

slew → **slay**

slice vt **sliced; slicing** : cortar —
slice n : trozo m, rebanada f (de
pan, etc.) , tajada f (de carne)

slick adj SLIPPERY : resbaladizo,
resbaloso Lat

slide v **slid; sliding** vi : deslizarse — vt :
deslizar — **slide** n 1 : deslizamiento m 2
: tobogán m (para niños) 3 : diapositiva f
(fotográfica) 4 DECLINE : descenso m

slier, sliest → **sly**

slight adj 1 : ligero, leve 2 SLENDER
: delgado — **slight** vt : desairar —
slightly adv : ligeramente, un poco

slim adj **slimmer; slimmest** 1 : delgado 2
a slim chance : escasas posibilidades fpl
— **slim** v **slimmed; slimming** : adelgazar

slime n 1 : baba f (de un caracol,
etc.) 2 MUD : limo m — **slimy** adj
slimier; -est : viscoso

sling vt **slung; slinging** 1 THROW :
lanzar 2 HANG : colgar — **sling** n 1 :
honda f 2 : cabestrillo m (en medicina)
— **slingshot** n : tirachinas m

slink vi **slunk; slinking** :
andar furtivamente

slip¹ v **slipped; slipping** vi 1 SLIDE
: resbalarse 2 **let something slip**
: dejar escapar algo 3 **slip away** :
escabullirse 4 **slip up** : equivocarse
— vt 1 : deslizar 2 **slip into** : ponerse
(una prenda) 3 **it slipped my mind**
: se me olvidó — **slip** n 1 MISTAKE :
error m, desliz m 2 **slip of the tongue**
: lapsus m 3 PETTICOAT : enagua f

slip² n **slip of paper** : papelito m

slipper n : zapatilla f, pantufla f

slippery adj **slipperier; -est** :
resbaladizo, resbaloso Lat

slit n 1 OPENING : rendija f 2 CUT : corte m,
raja f — **slit** vt **slit; slitting** : cortar

slither vi : deslizarse

sliver n : astilla f

slogan n : eslogan m

slop v **slopped; slopping** vt :
derramar — vi : derramarse

slope vi **sloped; sloping** : inclinarse
— **slope** n : pendiente f, declive m

sloppy adj **sloppier; -est** 1 CARELESS :
descuidado 2 UNKEMPT : desaliñado

slot n : ranura f

sloth n : pereza f

slouch vi : andar con los hombros
caídos (en una silla)

slovenly *adj* : desaliñado

slow *adj* **1** : lento **2 be slow** : estar atrasado (dícese de un reloj) — **slow** *adv* → **slowly** — **slow** *vt* : retrasar, retardar — *vi or* **slow down** : ir más despacio — **slowly** *adv* : lentamente, despacio — **slowness** *n* : lentitud *f*

sludge *n* SEWAGE : aguas *fpl* negras

slug[1] *n* **1** : babosa *f* (molusco) **2** BULLET : bala *f* **3** TOKEN : ficha *f*

slug[2] *vt* **slugged; slugging** : pegar un porrazo a

sluggish *adj* : lento

slum *n* : barrio *m* bajo

slumber *vi* : dormir — **slumber** *n* : sueño *m*

slump *vi* **1** DROP : bajar **2** COLLAPSE : dejarse caer **3** → **slouch** — **slump** *n* : bajón *m*

slung → **sling**

slunk → **slink**

slur[1] *n* ASPERSION : calumnia *f*, difamación *f*

slur[2] *vt* **slurred; slurring** : arrastrar (las palabras)

slurp *v* : beber haciendo ruido — **slurp** *n* : sorbo *m* (ruidoso)

slush *n* : nieve *f* medio derretida

sly *adj* **slier; sliest 1** : astuto, taimado **2 on the sly** : a escondidas

smack[1] *vi* **smack of** : oler a

smack[2] *vt* **1** : pegar una bofetada a **2** KISS : besar **3 smack one's lips** : relamerse — **smack** *n* : **1** SLAP : bofetada *f* **2** KISS : beso *m* — **smack** *adv* : justo, exactamente

small *adj* : pequeño, chico — **smallpox** *n* : viruela *f*

smart *adj* **1** : listo, inteligente **2** STYLISH : elegante — **smart** *vi* STING : escocer — **smartly** *adv* : elegantemente

smash *n* **1** BLOW : golpe *m* **2** COLLISION : choque *m* **3** BANG CRASH : estrépito *m* — **smash** *vt* **1** BREAK : romper **2** DESTROY : aplastar — *vi* **1** SHATTER : hacerse pedazos **2 smash into** : estrellarse contra

smattering *n* : nociones *fpl*

smear *n* : mancha *f* — **smear** *vt* **1** : embadurnar (de pinta, etc.), untar (de aceite, etc.) **2** SMUDGE : manchar

smell *v* **smelled** *or* **smelt; smelling** : oler — **smell** *n* **1** : (sentido *m* del) olfato *m* **2** ODOR : olor *m* — **smelly** *adj* **smellier; -est** : maloliente

smelt *vt* : fundir

smile *vi* **smiled; smiling** : sonreír — **smile** *n* : sonrisa *f*

smirk *vi* : sonreír con suficiencia — **smirk** *n* : sonrisa *f* satisfecha

smitten *adj* **be smitten with** : estar enamorado de

smith → **blacksmith**

smock *n* : blusón *m*, bata *f*

smog *n* : smog *m*

smoke *n* : humo *m* — **smoke** *v* **smoked; smoking** *vi* **1** : humear (dícese de fuegos, etc.) **2** : fumar (dícese de personas) — *vt* **1** : ahumar (carne, etc.) **2** : fumar (cigarrillos) — **smoker** *n* : fumador *m*, -dora *f* — **smokestack** *n* : chimenea *f* — **smoky** *adj* **smokier; -est 1** : lleno de humo **2** : a humo (dícese de sabores, etc.)

smolder *vi* : arder (sin llama)

smooth *adj* **1** : liso (dícese de superficies), suave (dícese de movimientos), tranquilo (dícese del mar) **2** : sin grumos (dícese de salsas, etc.) — **smooth** *vt* : alisar — **smoothly** *adv* : suavemente — **smoothness** *n* : suavidad *f*

smother *vt* : asfixiar (a algn), sofocar (llamas, etc.)

smudge *v* **smudged; smudging** *vt* : emborronar — *vi* : correrse — **smudge** *n* : mancha *f*, borrón *m*

smug *adj* **smugger; smuggest** : suficiente

smuggle *vt* **-gled; -gling** : pasar de contrabando — **smuggler** *n* : contrabandista *mf*

snack *n* : refrigerio *m*, tentempié *m fam*

snag *n* : problema *m* — **snag** *v* **snagged; snagging** *vt* : enganchar — *vi* : engancharse

snail *n* : caracol *m*

snake *n* : culebra *f*, serpiente *f*

snap *v* **snapped; snapping** *vi* **1** BREAK : romperse **2** : intentar morder (dícese de un perro, etc.) **3 snap at** : contestar bruscamente a — *vt* **1** BREAK : romper **2 snap one's fingers** : chasquear los dedos **3 snap open/shut** : abrir/cerrar de golpe — **snap** *n* **1** : chasquido *m* **2** FASTENER : broche *m* (de presión) **3 be a snap** : ser facilísimo — **snappy** *adj* **snappier; -est 1** FAST : rápido **2** STYLISH : elegante — **snapshot** *n* : instantánea *f*

snare *n* : trampa *f* — **snare** *vt* **snared; snaring** : atrapar

snarl[1] *vi* TANGLE : enmarañar, enredar — **snarl** *n* : enredo *m*, maraña *f*

snarl[2] *vi* GROWL : gruñir — *n* : gruñido *m*

snatch *vt* : arrebatar

sneak *vi* : ir a hurtadillas — *vt* : hacer furtivamente — **sneak** *n* : soplón *m*, -plona *f fam* — **sneakers** *npl* : tenis *mpl*, zapatillas *fpl* — **sneaky** *adj* **sneakier; -est** : solapado

sneer *vi* : sonreír con desprecio — **sneer** *n* : sonrisa *f* de desprecio

sneeze *vi* **sneezed; sneezing** :

stormy sky
cielo[M] **turbulento**

cloud
nube[F]

lightning
rayo[M]

rainbow
arco[M] iris

rain
lluvia[F]

soccer
futbol^M

soccer player
futbolista ^{M/F}

jersey
camiseta^F

shorts
pantalones^M

shin guard
espinillera^F

sock
calcetín^M

soccer ball
balón^M *de fútbol*^M

estornudar — **sneeze** *n* : estornudo *m*
snide *adj* : sarcástico
sniff *vi* : oler — *vt* **1** : oler **2** →
sniffle — **sniff** *n* : aspiración *f* por
la nariz — **sniffle** *vi* **-fled; -fling**
: sorberse la nariz — **sniffles** *npl*
have the sniffles : estar resfriado
snip *n* : tijeretada *f* — **snip** *vt* **snipped;**
snipping : cortar (con tijeras)
snivel *vi* **-veled** *or* **-velled; -veling**
or **-velling** : lloriquear
snob *n* : esnob *mf* — **snobbish** *adj* : esnob
snoop *vi* : husmear — **snoop** *n*
: fisgón *m*, -gona *f*
snooze *vi* **snoozed; snoozing** : dormitar
— **snooze** *n* : siestecita *f*, siestita *f*
snore *vi* **snored; snoring** : roncar
— **snore** *n* : ronquido *m*
snort *vi* : bufar — **snort** *n* : bufido *m*
snout *n* : hocico *m*, morro *m*
snow *n* : nieve *f* — **snow** *vi* : nevar —
snowfall *n* : nevada *f* — **snowflake** *n*
: copo *m* de nieve — **snowman** *n* :
muñeco *m* de nieve — **snowplow** *n* :
quitanieves *m* — **snowshoe** *n* : raqueta *f*
(para nieve) — **snowstorm** *n* : tormenta *f*
de nieve — **snowy** *adj* **snowier; -est 1**
a snowy day : un día nevoso **2 snowy**

soccer field
campo^M *de fútbol*^M

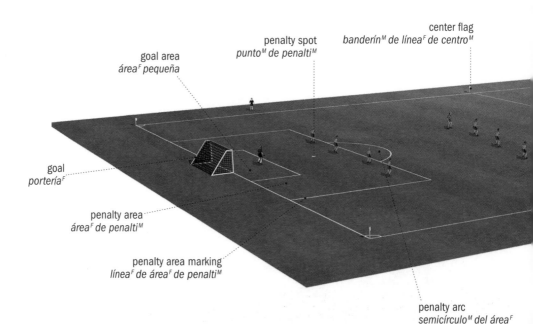

center flag
banderín^M *de línea*^F *de centro*^M

penalty spot
punto^M *de penalti*^M

goal area
área^F *pequeña*

goal
portería^F

penalty area
área^F *de penalti*^M

penalty area marking
línea^F *de área*^F *de penalti*^M

penalty arc
semicírculo^M *del área*^F

mountains : montañas *fpl* nevadas
snub *vt* **snubbed; snubbing** :
desairar — **snub** *n* : desaire *m*
snuff *vt or* **snuff out** : apagar
snug *adj* **snugger; snuggest 1** : cómodo
2 TIGHT : ajustado — **snuggle** *vi*
-gled; -gling : acurrucarse
so *adv* **1** LIKEWISE : también **2** THUS : así
3 THEREFORE : por lo tanto **4** *or* **so much**
: tanto **5** *or* **so very** : tan **6 and so on**
: etcétera **7 I think so** : creo que sí **8**
I told you so : te lo dije — **so** *conj* **1**
THEREFORE : así que **2** *or* **so that** : para
que **3 so what?** : ¿y qué? — **so** *adj* TRUE
: cierto — **so** *pron or* **so** : más o menos
soak *vi* : estar en remojo — *vt* **1**
: poner en remojo **2 soak up** :
absorber — **soak** *n* : remojo *m*
soap *n* : jabón *m* — **soap** *vt or*
soap up : enjabonar — **soapy**
adj **soapier; -est** : jabonoso
soar *vi* **1** : planear **2**
SKYROCKET : dispararse
sob *vi* **sobbed; sobbing** : sollozar
— **sob** *n* : sollozo *m*
sober *adj* **1** : sobrio **2** SERIOUS : serio
— **sobriety** *n* **1** : sobriedad *f* **2**
SERIOUSNESS : seriedad *f*

so–called *adj* : supuesto, presunto
▸ **soccer** *n* : futbol *m*, fútbol *m*
social *adj* : social — **social** *n* : reunión *f*
social — **sociable** *adj* : sociable —
socialism *n* : socialismo *m* — **socialist** *n*
: socialista *mf* — **socialist** *adj* :
socialista — **socialize** *v* **-ized; -izing** *vt*
: socializar — *vi* **socialize with** :
alternar con — **society** *n*, *pl* **-eties** :
sociedad *f* — **sociology** *n* : sociología *f*
sock[1] *n*, *pl* **socks** *or* **sox** : calcetín *m*
sock[2] *vt* : pegar, golpear —
sock *n* PUNCH : puñetazo *m*
socket *n* **1** *or* **electric socket** :
enchufe *m*, toma *f* de corriente **2**
or **eye socket** : órbita *f*, cuenca *f* **3**
: glena *f* (de una articulación)
soda *n* **1** *or* **soda pop** : refresco *m*,
gaseosa *f* **2** *or* **soda water** : soda *f*
sodium *n* : sodio *m*
sofa *n* : sofá *m*
soft *adj* **1** : blando **2** SMOOTH : suave
— **softball** *n* : softbol *m* — **soft**
drink *n* : refresco *m* — **soften** *vt* **1**
: ablandar **2** EASE, SMOOTH : suavizar
— *vi* **1** : ablandarse **2** EASE : suavizarse
— **softly** *adv* : suavemente —
software *n* : software *m*

soggy *adj* **soggier; -est** : empapado
soil *vt* : ensuciar — **soil** *n* DIRT : tierra *f*
solace *n* : consuelo *m*
solar *adj* : solar
sold → **sell**
solder *n* : soldadura *f* — **solder** *vt* : soldar
soldier *n* : soldado *mf*
sole[1] *n* : lenguado *m* (pez)
sole[2] *n* : planta *f* (del pie),
suela *f* (de un zapato)
sole[3] *adj* : único — **solely** *adv*
: únicamente, sólo
solemn *adj* : solemne — **solemnity** *n*,
pl **-ties** : solemnidad *f*
solicit *vt* : solicitar
solid *adj* **1** : sólido **2** UNBROKEN :
continuo **3 solid gold** : oro *m* macizo **4**
two solid hours : dos horas seguidas
— **solid** *n* : sólido *m* — **solidarity** *n*
: solidaridad *f* — **solidify** *v* **-fied;**
-fying *vt* : solidificar — *vi* : solidificarse
— **solidity** *n*, *pl* **-ties** : solidez *f*
solitary *adj* : solitario —
solitude *n* : soledad *f*
solo *n*, *pl* **solos** : solo *m* —
soloist *n* : solista *mf*
solution *n* : solución *f* — **soluble** *adj*
: soluble — **solve** *vt* **solved; solving**

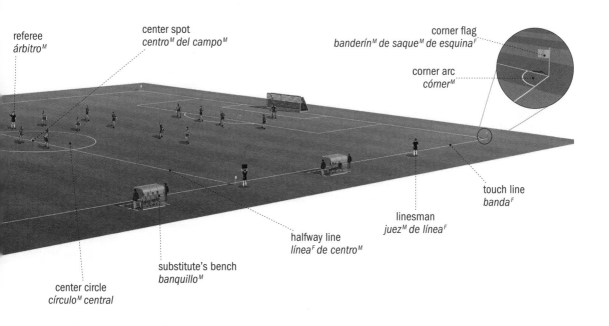

referee
árbitro[M]

center spot
centro[M] *del campo*[M]

corner flag
banderín[M] *de saque*[M] *de esquina*[F]

corner arc
córner[M]

touch line
banda[F]

linesman
juez[M] *de línea*[F]

halfway line
línea[F] *de centro*[M]

substitute's bench
banquillo[M]

center circle
círculo[M] *central*

: resolver — **solvent** *n* : solvente *m*

somber *adj* : sombrío

some *adj* **1** (*of unspecified identity*) : un **2** (*of an unspecified amount*) : algo de, un poco de **3** (*of an unspecified number*) : unos **4** CERTAIN : algunos **5 that was some game!** : ¡fue un partidazo! — **some** *pron* **1** SEVERAL : algunos, unos **2** PART : un poco, algo — **some** *adv* **some twenty people** : unas veinte personas — **somebody** *pron* : alguien — **someday** *adv* : algún día — **somehow** *adv* **1** : de algún modo **2 somehow or other** : de alguna manera u otra — **someone** *pron* : alguien

somersault *n* : voltereta *f*, salto *m* mortal

something *pron* **1** : algo **2 something else** : otra cosa — **sometime** *adv* **1** : algún día, en algún momento **2 sometime next month** : (durante) el mes que viene — **sometimes** *adv* : a veces — **somewhat** *adv* : algo — **somewhere** *adv* **1** : en alguna parte, en algún lado **2 somewhere around** : alrededor de **3 somewhere else** → **elsewhere**

son *n* : hijo *m*

song *n* : canción *f*

son-in-law *n*, *pl* **sons-in-law** : yerno *m*

sonnet *n* : soneto *m*

soon *adv* **1** : pronto **2** SHORTLY : dentro de poco **3 as soon as** : en cuanto **4 as soon as possible** : lo más pronto posible **5 soon after** : poco después **6 sooner or later** : tarde o temprano **7 the sooner the better** : cuanto antes mejor

soot *n* : hollín *m*

soothe *vt* **soothed; soothing 1** CALM : calmar **2** RELIEVE : aliviar

sop *vt* **sopped; sopping sop up** : absorber

sophistication *n* : sofisticación *f* — **sophisticated** *adj* : sofisticado

sophomore *n* : estudiante *mf* de segundo año

soprano *n*, *pl* **-nos** : soprano *mf*

sorcerer *n* : hechicero *m*, brujo *m* — **sorcery** *n* : hechicería *f*, brujería *f*

sordid *adj* : sórdido

sore *adj* **sorer; sorest 1** : dolorido **2** ANGRY : enfadado **3 sore throat** : dolor *m* de garganta **4 I have a sore throat** : me duele la garganta — **sore** *n* : llaga *f* — **sorely** *adv* : muchísimo — **soreness** *n* : dolor *m*

sorrow *n* : pesar *m*, pena *f* — **sorry** *adj* **sorrier; -est 1** PITIFUL

: lamentable **2 feel sorry for** : compadecer **3 I'm sorry** : lo siento

sort *n* **1** : tipo *m*, clase *f* **2 a sort of** : una especie de — **sort** *vt* : clasificar — **sort of** *adv* **1** SOMEWHAT : algo **2** MORE OR LESS : más o menos

SOS *n* : SOS *m*

so-so *adj & adv* : así así *fam*

soufflé *n* : suflé *m*

sought → **seek**

soul *n* : alma *f*

sound[1] *adj* **1** HEALTHY : sano **2** FIRM : sólido **3** SENSIBLE : lógico **4 a sound sleep** : un sueño profundo **5 safe and sound** : sano y salvo

sound[2] *n* : sonido *m* — *vt* : hacer sonar, tocar (una trompeta, etc.) — *vi* **1** : sonar **2** SEEM : parecer

sound[3] *n* CHANNEL : brazo *m* de mar — **sound** *vt* **1** : sondar (en navegación) **2** *or* **sound out** : sondear

soundly *adv* **1** SOLIDLY : sólidamente **2** DEEPLY : profundamente

soundproof *adj* : insonorizado

soup *n* : sopa *f*

sour *adj* **1** : agrio **2 sour milk** : leche *f* cortada — **sour** *vt* : agriar

source *n* : fuente *f*, origen *m*

south *adv* : al sur — **south** *adj* : (del) sur — **south** *n* : sur *m* — **South African** *adj* : sudafricano — **South American** *adj* : sudamericano — **southeast** *adv* : hacia el sureste — **southeast** *adj* : (del) sureste — **southeast** *n* : sureste *m*, sudeste *m* — **southeastern** *adj* → **southeast** — **southerly** *adv & adj* : del sur — **southern** *adj* : del sur, meridional — **southwest** *adv* : hacia el suroeste — **southwest** *adj* : (del) suroeste — **southwest** *n* : suroeste *m*, sudoeste *m* — **southwestern** *adj* → **southwest**

souvenir *n* : recuerdo *m*

sovereign *n* : soberano *m*, -na *f* — **sovereign** *adj* : soberano — **sovereignty** *n*, *pl* **-ties** : soberanía *f*

Soviet *adj* : soviético

sow[1] *n* : cerda *f*

sow[2] *vt* **sowed; sown** *or* **sowed; sowing** : sembrar

sox → **sock**

soybean *n* : soya *f*, soja *f*

spa *n* : balneario *m*

space *n* **1** : espacio *m* **2** ROOM, SPOT : sitio *m*, lugar *m* — **space** *vt* **spaced; spacing** : espaciar — **spaceship** *n*

: nave *f* espacial — **space shuttle** *n* : transbordador *m* espacial —

spacious *adj* : espacioso, amplio

spade[1] *n* SHOVEL : pala *f*

spade[2] *n* : pica *f* (naipe)

spaghetti *n* : espaguetis *mpl*

span *n* **1** PERIOD : espacio *m* **2** : luz *f* (entre dos soportes) — **span** *vt* **spanned; spanning 1** : abarcar (un período) **2** CROSS : extenderse sobre

Spaniard *n* : español *m*, -ñola *f*

spaniel *n* : spaniel *m*

Spanish *adj* : español — **Spanish** *n* : español *m* (idioma)

spank *vt* : dar palmadas a (en las nalgas)

spar *vi* **sparred; sparring** : entrenarse (en boxeo)

spare *vt* **spared; sparing 1** PARDON : perdonar **2** SAVE : ahorrar **3 can you spare a dollar?** : ¿me das un dólar? **4 I can't spare the time** : no tengo tiempo **5 spare no expense** : no reparar en gastos **6 to spare** : de sobra — **spare** *adj* **1** : de repuesto **2** EXCESS : de más **3** LEAN : delgado — **spare** *n* *or* **spare part** : repuesto *m* — **spare time** *n* : tiempo *m* libre — **sparing** *adj* : parco, económico

spark *n* : chispa *f* — **spark** *vi* : chispear, echar chispas — *vt* : despertar (interés), provocar (crítica) — **sparkle** *vi* **-kled; -kling** : destellar, centellear — **sparkle** *n* : destello *m*, centelleo *m* — **spark plug** *n* : bujía *f*

sparrow *n* : gorrión *m*

sparse *adj* **sparser; -est** : escaso

spasm *n* : espasmo *m*

spat[1] → **spit**

spat[2] *n* QUARREL : disputa *f*, pelea *f*

spatter *vt* : salpicar

spawn *vi* : desovar — *vt* : engendrar, producir — **spawn** *n* : hueva *f*

speak *v* **spoke; spoken; speaking** *vi* **1** : hablar **2 speak out against** : denunciar **3 speak up** : hablar más alto **4 speak up for** : defender — *vt* **1** : decir **2** : hablar (un idioma) — **speaker** *n* **1** ORATOR : orador *m*, -dora *f* **2** : hablante *mf* (de un idioma) **3** LOUDSPEAKER : altavoz *m*

spear *n* : lanza *f* — **spearhead** *n* : punta *f* de lanza — **spearhead** *vt* : encabezar — **spearmint** *n* : menta *f* verde

special *adj* : especial — **specialist** *n* : especialista *mf* — **specialization** *n* : especialización *f* — **specialize** *vi* **-ized; -izing** : especializarse

— **specially** *adv* : especialmente —
specialty *n, pl* **-ties** : especialidad *f*
species *ns & pl* : especie *f*
specify *vt* **-fied; -fying** : especificar
— **specific** *adj* : específico —
specifically *adv* **1** : específicamente
2 EXPLICITLY : expresamente —
specification *n* : especificación *f*
specimen *n* : espécimen *m*
speck *n* **1** SPOT : **mancha** *f* **2** BIT :
mota *f* — **speckled** *adj* : moteado
spectacle *n* **1** : espectáculo *m* **2**
spectacles *npl* GLASSES : gafas *fpl*,
lentes *fpl*, anteojos *mpl* —
spectacular *adj* : espectacular —
spectator *n* : espectador *m*, -dora *f*
specter *or* **spectre** *n* : espectro *m*
spectrum *n, pl* **-tra** *or* **-trums 1** :
espectro *m* **2** RANGE : gama *f*
speculation *n* : especulación *f*
speech *n* **1** : habla *f* **2** ADDRESS :
discurso *m* — **speechless** *adj* : mudo
speed *n* **1** : rapidez *f* **2** VELOCITY
: velocidad *f* — **speed** *v* **sped** *or*
speeded; speeding *vi* **1** : conducir
a exceso de velocidad **2 speed off**
: irse a toda velocidad **3 speed up** :
acelerarse — *vt or* **speed up** : acelerar
— **speed limit** *n* : velocidad *f* máxima
— **speedometer** *n* : velocímetro *m* —
speedy *adj* **speedier, -est** : rápido
spell[1] *vt* **1** : escribir (las letras de) **2** *or*
spell out : deletrear **3** MEAN : significar
spell[2] *n* ENCHANTMENT : hechizo *m*
spell[3] *n* : período *m* (de tiempo)
spellbound *adj* : embelesado
spelling *n* : ortografía *f*
spend *vt* **spent; spending 1** : gastar
(dinero) **2** : pasar (las vacaciones, etc.)
3 spend time on : dedicar tiempo a
sperm *n, pl* **sperm** *or*
sperms : esperma *mf*
spew *vt* : vomitar, arrojar (lava, etc.)
sphere *n* : esfera *f* —
spherical *adj* : esférico
spice *n* : especia *f* — **spice** *vt* **spiced;**
spicing : condimentar, sazonar —
spicy *adj* **spicier; -est** : picante
spider *n* : araña *f*
spigot *n* : grifo *m* Spain, llave *f* Lat
spike *n* **1** : clavo *m* (grande) **2** POINT
: punta *f* — **spiky** *adj* : puntiagudo
spill *vt* : derramar — *vi* : derramarse
spin *v* **spun; spinning** *vi* : girar — *vt* **1**
: hilar (lana, etc.) **2** TWIRL : hacer girar

— **spin** *n* **1** : vuelta *f*, giro *m* **2 go**
for a spin : dar una vuelta (en auto)
spinach *n* : espinacas *fpl*
spinal cord *n* : médula *f* espinal
spindle *n* : huso *m* (para hilar) —
spindly *adj* : larguirucho *fam*
spine *n* **1** : columna *f* vertebral **2**
QUILL : púa *f* **3** THORN : espina *f* **4**
: lomo *m* (de un libro)
spinster *n* : soltera *f*
spiral *adj* : de espiral, en espiral —
spiral *n* : espiral *f* — **spiral** *vi* **-raled** *or*
-ralled; -raling *or* **-ralling** : ir en espiral
spire *n* : aguja *f*
spirit *n* **1** : espíritu *m* **2 in good**
spirits : animado **3** spirits *npl* :
licores *mpl* — **spirited** *adj* : animado
— **spiritual** *adj* : espiritual —
spirituality *n, pl* **-ties** : espiritualidad *f*
spit[1] *n* ROTISSERIE : asador *m*
spit[2] *v* **spit** *or* **spat; spitting** :
escupir — *n* SALIVA : saliva *f*
spite *n* **1** : rencor *m* **2 in spite of** : a
pesar de — **spite** *vt* **spited; spiting** :
fastidiar — **spiteful** *adj* : rencoroso
spittle *n* : saliva *f*
splash *vt* : salpicar — *vi* **1** : salpicar **2** *or*
splash about : chapotear — **splash** *n* **1** :
salpicadura *f* **2** : mancha *f* (de color, etc.)
splatter → **spatter**
spleen *n* : bazo *m* (órgano)
splendor *n* : esplendor *m* —
splendid *adj* : espléndido
splint *n* : tablilla *f*
splinter *n* : astilla *f* — *vi* : astillarse
split *v* **split; splitting** *vt* **1** : partir BURST
: reventar **3** *or* **split up** : dividir — *vi* **1** :
partirse, rajarse **2** *or* **split up** : dividirse
— **split** *n* **1** CRACK : rajadura *f* **2** *or* **split**
seam : descosido *m* **3** DIVISION : división *f*
splurge *vi* **splurged; splurging**
: derrochar dinero
spoil *vt* **spoiled** *or* **spoilt; spoiling 1**
RUIN : estropear **2** PAMPER : consentir,
mimar — **spoils** *npl* : botín *m*
spoke[1] → **speak**
spoke[2] *n* : rayo *m* (de una rueda)
spoken → **speak**
spokesman *n, pl* **-men** : portavoz *mf* —
spokeswoman *n, pl* **-women** : portavoz *f*
sponge *n* : esponja *f* — **sponge** *vt*
sponged; sponging : limpiar
con una esponja — **spongy** *adj*
spongier; -est : esponjoso
sponsor *n* : patrocinador *m*,

-dora *f* — **sponsor** *vt* : patrocinar
— **sponsorship** *n* : patrocinio *m*
spontaneity *n* : espontaneidad *f*
— **spontaneous** *adj* : espontáneo
spooky *adj* **spookier; -est** : espeluzante
spool *n* : carrete *m*
spoon *n* : cuchara *f* —
spoonful *n* : cucharada *f*
sporadic *adj* : esporádico
spore *n* : espora *f*
sport *n* **1** : deporte *m* **2 be a good**
sport : tener espíritu deportivo —
sportsman *n, pl* **-men** : deportista *m* —
sportswoman *n, pl* **-women** : deportista *f*
— **sporty**; *adj* **sportier; -est** : deportivo
spot *n* **1** : mancha *f* **2** DOT : punto *m* **3**
PLACE : lugar *m*, sitio *m* **4 in a tight**
spot : en apuros **5 on the spot**
INSTANTLY : en ese mismo momento
— **spot** *vt* **spotted; spotting 1** STAIN
: manchar **2** DETECT, NOTICE : ver,
descubrir — **spotless** *adj* : impecable —
spotlight *n* **1** : foco *m*, reflector *m* **2 be**
in the spot : ser el centro de atención
— **spotty** *adj* **spottier; -est** : irregular
spouse *n* : cónyuge *mf*
spout *vi* : salir a chorros —
spout *n* **1** : pico *m* (de una jarra,
etc.) **2** STREAM : chorro *m*
sprain *n* : esguince *m* — **sprain** *vt*
: sufrir un esguince en
sprawl *vi* **1** : repantigarse (en un
sillón, etc.) **2** EXTEND : extenderse
— **sprawl** *n* : extensión *f*
spray[1] *n* BOUQUET : ramillete *m*
spray[2] *n* **1** MIST : rocío *m* **2** *or* **aerosol**
spray : spray *m* **3** *or* **spray bottle** :
atomizador *m* — **spray** *vt* : rociar (una
superficie), pulverizar (un líquido)
spread *v* **spread; spreading** *vt* **1** :
propagar (enfermedades), difundir
(noticias, etc.) **2** *or* **spread out** : extender
3 : untar (con mantequilla, etc.) — *vi* **1** :
propagarse, difundirse **2** *or* **spread out** :
extenderse — **spread** *n* **1** : propagación *f*,
difusión *f* **2** PASTE : pasta *f* (para untar)
— **spreadsheet** *n* : hoja *f* de cálculo
spree *n* **go on a spree** : ir de juerga *fam*
sprig *n* : ramito *m*
sprightly *adj* **sprightlier; -est** : vivo
spring *v* **sprang** *or* **sprung; sprung;**
springing *vi* **1** : saltar **2 spring from** :
surgir de **3 spring up** : surgir — *vt* **1**
ACTIVATE : accionar **2 spring a leak** : hacer
agua **3 spring something on someone** :

squashes
calabaza^F

pattypan squash
calabaza^F bonetera amarilla

straightneck squash
calabaza^F de cuello^M largo

crookneck squash
calabaza^F de cuello^M retorcido

vegetable marrow
calabacín^M

spaghetti squash
calabaza^F romana

zucchini
calabacín^M

acorn squash
calabaza^F bonetera

buttercup squash
calabaza^F botón^M de oro^M

sorprender a algn con algo — **spring** *n* **1** : manantial *m* (de aguas) **2** : primavera *f* (estación) **3** LEAP : salto *m* **4** RESILIENCE : elasticidad *f* **5** : resorte *m* (mecanismo) **6** *or* bedspring : muelle *m* — **springboard** *n* : trampolín *m* — **springtime** *n* : primavera *f* — **springy** *adj* **springier; -est** : mullido

sprinkle *vt* **-kled; -kling 1** : salpicar, rociar **2** DUST : espolvorear — **sprinkle** *n* : llovizna *f* — **sprinkler** *n* : aspersor *m*

sprint *vi* **1** : correr **2** : esprintar (en deportes) — **sprint** *n* : esprint *m* (en deportes)

sprout *vi* : brotar — **sprout** *n* : brote *m*

spruce¹ *vt* **spruced; sprucing**
  spruce up : arreglar

spruce² *n* : picea *f* (árbol)

spry *adj* **sprier** *or* **spryer; spriest** *or* **spryest** : ágil, activo

spun → **spin**

spur *n* **1** : espuela *f* **2** STIMULUS : acicate *m* **3** **on the spur of the moment** : sin pensarlo — **spur** *vt* **spurred; spurring** *or* **spur on 1** : espolear (un caballo) **2** MOTIVATE : motivar

spurn *vt* : desdeñar, rechazar

spurt¹ *vi* : salir a chorros
  — **spurt** *n* : chorro *m*

spurt² *n* **1** : arranque *m* (de energía, etc.) **2 work in spurts** : trabajar por rachas

spy *v* **spied; spying** *vt* : ver, divisar
  — *vi* **spy on someone** : espiar a algn — **spy** *n* : espía *mf*

squabble *n* : riña *f*, pelea *f* —
  squabble *vi* **-bled; -bling** : reñir, pelearse

squad *n* : pelotón *m* (militar), brigada *f* (de policías)

squadron *n* : escuadrón *m* (de soldados), escuadra *f* (de aviones o naves)

squalid *adj* : miserable

squall *n* : turbión *m*

squalor *n* : miseria *f*

squander *vt* : derrochar (dinero, etc.), desperdiciar (oportunidades, etc.)

square *n* **1** : cuadrado *m* **2** : plaza *f* (de una ciudad) — **square** *adj* **squarer; -est 1** : cuadrado **2** HONEST : justo **3** EVEN : en paz **4 a square meal** : una comida decente — **square** *vt* **squared; squaring 1** : elevar al cuadrado (un número) **2** : saldar (una cuenta) — **square root** *n* : raíz *f* cuadrada

squash¹ *vt* **1** : aplastar **2** : acallar (protestas, etc.) — **squash** *n* : squash *m* (deporte)

▸ **squash**² *n, pl* **squashes** *or* **squash** : calabaza *f* (vegetal)

squat *vi* **squatted; squatting 1** *or* **squat down** : ponerse en cuclillas **2** : ocupar un lugar sin derecho — **squat** *adj* **squatter; squattest** : achaparrado

squawk n : graznido m —
squawk vi : graznar
squeak vi **1** : chillar **2** CREAK :
chirriar — **squeak** n **1** : chillido m **2**
CREAK : chirrido m — **squeaky** adj
squeakier; -est : chirriante
squeal vi **1** : chillar (dícese de
personas, etc.), chirriar (dícese de
frenos, etc.) **2** PROTEST : quejarse
— **squeal** n : chillido m (de una
persona), chirrido m (de frenos, etc.)
squeamish adj : impresionable, delicado
squeeze vt **squeezed; squeezing**
1 : apretar **2** : exprimir (frutas,
etc.) **3** : extraer (jugo, etc.) —
squeeze n : apretón m
squid n, pl **squid** or **squids** : calamar m
squint vi : entrecerrar los ojos
— **squint** n : estrabismo m
squirm vi : retorcerse
squirrel n : ardilla f

squirt vt : lanzar un chorro de — vi :
salir a chorros — **squirt** n : chorrito m
stab n **1** : puñalada f **2 stab of**
pain : pinchazo m **3 take a stab at** :
intentar — **stab** vt **stabbed; stabbing**
1 KNIFE : apuñalar **2** STICK : clavar
stable n **1** : establo m (para ganado)
2 or **horse stable** : caballeriza f —
stable adj **-bler; -blest** : estable —
stability n, pl **-ties** : estabilidad f —
stabilize vt **-lized; -lizing** : estabilizar
stack n : montón m, pila f —
stack vt : amontonar, apilar
stadium n, pl **-dia** or **-diums** : estadio m
staff n, pl **staffs** or **staves 1** :
bastón m **2** pl **staffs** PERSONNEL
: personal m **3** pl **staffs** :
pentagrama m (en música) —
staff vt : proveer de personal
stag n, pl **stags** or **stag** : ciervo m,
venado m — **stag** adj : sólo para

hombres — **stag** adv **go stag** : ir solo
stage n **1** : escenario m (de un teatro)
2 PHASE : etapa f **3 the stage** : el
teatro — **stage** vt **staged; staging 1**
: poner en escena **2** ARRANGE : montar
— **stagecoach** n : diligencia f
stagger vi : tambalearse — vt **1**
: escalonar (turnos, etc.) **2 be**
staggered by : quedarse estupefacto
por — **stagger** n : tambaleo m —
staggering adj : asombroso
stagnant adj : estancado — **stagnate** vi
-nated; -nating : estancarse
stain vt **1** : manchar **2** : teñir
(madera) — **stain** n **1** : mancha f **2**
DYE : tinte m, tintura f — **stainless**
steel n : acero m inoxidable
▸ **stair** n **1** STEP : escalón m, peldaño m **2**
stairs npl : escalera(s) f(pl) —
staircase n : escalera(s) f(pl) —
stairway n : escalera(s) f(pl)

stairs
escaleraF

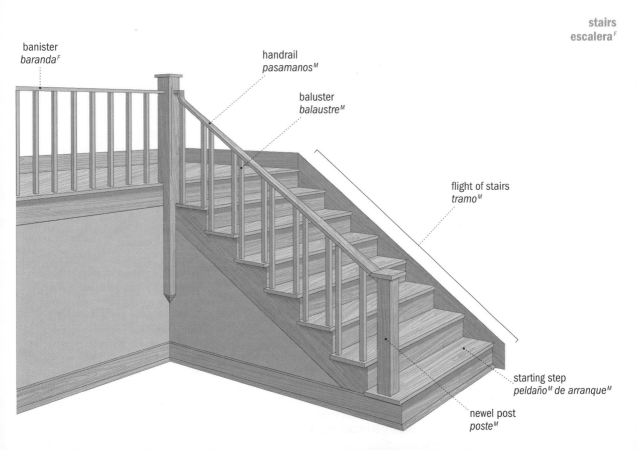

banister
*baranda*F

handrail
*pasamanos*M

baluster
*balaustre*M

flight of stairs
*tramo*M

starting step
*peldaño*M *de arranque*M

newel post
*poste*M

stake *n* **1** POST : estaca *f* **2** BET : apuesta *f* **3** INTEREST : intereses *mpl* **4 be at stake** : estar en juego — **stake** *vt* **staked; staking 1** : estacar **2** BET : jugarse **3 stake a claim to** : reclamar

stale *adj* **staler; stalest 1** : duro (dícese del pan) **2** OLD : viejo **3** STUFFY : viciado

stalk[1] *n* : tallo *m* (de una planta)

stalk[2] *vt* : acechar — *vi or* **stalk off** : irse con altivez

stall[1] *n* **1** : compartimiento *m* (de un establo) **2** STAND : puesto *m* — **stall** *vt* : parar (un motor) — *vi* : pararse

stall[2] *vt* DELAY : entretener — *vi* : andar con rodeos

stallion *n* : caballo *m* semental

stalwart *adj* **1** STRONG : fornido **2 stalwart supporter** : partidario *m* leal

stamina *n* : resistencia *f*

stammer *vi* : tartamudear — **stammer** *n* : tartamudeo *m*

stamp *n* **1** SEAL : sello *m* **2** DIE : cuño *m* **3** *or* **postage stamp** : sello *m*, estampilla *f Lat*, timbre *m*, *Lat* — **stamp** *vt* **1** : franquear (una carta) **2** IMPRINT : sellar **3** MINT : acuñar **4 stamp one's foot** : dar una patada (en el suelo)

stampede *n* : estampida *f* — **stampede** *vi* **-peded; -peding** : salir en estampida

stance *n* : postura *f*

stand *v* **stood; standing** *vi* **1** : estar de pie, estar parado *Lat* **2** BE : estar **3** CONTINUE : seguir vigente **4** LIE, REST : reposar **5 stand aside** *or* **stand back** : apartarse **6 stand out** : sobresalir **7** *or* **stand up** : ponerse de pie, pararse *Lat* — *vt* **1** PLACE : poner, colocar **2** ENDURE : soportar **3 stand a chance** : tener una posibilidad — **stand by** *vt* **1** : mantener (una promesa, etc.) **2** SUPPORT : apoyar — **stand for** *vt* **1** MEAN : significar **2** PERMIT : permitir — **stand up** *vi* **1 stand up for** : defender **2 stand up to** : resistir a — **stand** *n* **1** RESISTANCE : resistencia *f* **2** STALL : puesto *m* **3** BASE : base *f* **4** POSITION : posición *f* **5 stands** *npl* : tribuna *f*

standard *n* **1** : norma *f* **2** BANNER : estandarte *m* **3** CRITERION : criterio *m* **4 standard of living** : nivel *m* de vida — **standard** *adj* : estándar — **standardize** *vt* **-ized; -izing** : estandarizar

standing *n* **1** RANK : posición *f* **2** DURATION : duración *f*

standpoint *n* : punto *m* de vista

starfish
estrella[F] **de mar**

spine
espina[F]

arm
brazo[M]

central disk
disco[M] *central*

eyespot
mancha[F] *ocular*

tube foot
pie[M] *ambulacral*

standstill *n* **1 be at a standstill** : estar paralizado **2 come to a standstill** : pararse

stank → **stink**

stanza *n* : estrofa *f*

staple[1] *n* : producto *m* principal — **staple** *adj* : principal, básico

staple[2] *n* : grapa *f* (para papeles) — **staple** *vt* **-pled; -pling** : grapar, engrapar *Lat* — **stapler** *n* : grapadora *f*, engrapadora *f Lat*

star *n* : estrella *f* — **star** *v* **starred; starring** *vt* FEATURE : estar protagonizado por — *vi* **star in** : protagonizar

starboard *n* : estribor *m*

starch *vt* : almidonar — **starch** *n* **1** : almidón *m* **2** : fécula *f* (comida)

stardom *n* : estrellato *m*

stare *vi* **stared; staring** : mirar fijamente — **stare** *n* : mirada *f* fija

▸ **starfish** *n* : estrella *f* de mar

stark *adj* **1** PLAIN : austero **2** HARSH : severo, duro **3** SHARP : marcado — **stark** *adv* **1** : completamente **2 stark naked** : en cueros (vivos)

starlight *n* : luz *f* de las estrellas

▸ **starling** *n* : estornino *m*

starry *adj* **starrier; -est** : estrellado

start *vi* **1** : empezar, comenzar **2** SET OUT : salir **3** JUMP : sobresaltarse **4** *or* **start up** : arrancar — *vt* **1** : empezar, comenzar **2** CAUSE : provocar **3** *or* **start up** ESTABLISH : montar **4** *or* **start up** : arrancar (un motor, etc.) — **start** *n* **1** : principio *m* **2 get an early start** : salir temprano **3 give someone a start** : asustar a algn — **starter** *n* : motor *m* de arranque (de un vehículo)

startle *vt* **-tled; -tling** : asustar

starve *v* **starved; starving** *vi* : morirse de hambre — *vt* : privar de comida — **starvation** *n* : inanición *f*, hambre *f*

stash *vt* : esconder

state *n* **1** : estado *m* **2 the States** : los Estados Unidos — **state** *vt* **stated; stating 1** SAY : decir **2** REPORT : exponer — **stately** *adj* **statelier; -est** : majestuoso — **statement** *n* **1** : declaración *f* **2** *or* **bank statement** : estado *m* de cuenta — **statesman** *n*, *pl* **-men** : estadista *mf*

static *adj* : estático — **static** *n* : estática *f*

station *n* **1** : estación *f* (de trenes, etc.) **2** RANK : condición *f* (social) **3** : canal *m* (de televisión), emisora *f* (de radio) **4** → **fire station, police station** — *vt* : apostar, estacionar — **stationary** *adj* : estacionario

stationery n : papel m y
sobres mpl (para cartas)

station wagon n : camioneta f (familiar)

statistic n : estadística f —
statistical adj : estadístico

statue n : estatua f

stature n : estatura f, talla f

status n **1** : situación f **2** or
social status : estatus m **3**
marital status : estado m civil

statute n : estatuto m

staunch adj : leal

stave vt **staved** or **stove; staving 1**
stave in : romper **2 stave off** : evitar

staves → **staff**

stay[1] vi **1** REMAIN : quedarse, permanecer
2 LODGE : alojarse **3 stay awake** :
mantenerse despierto **4 stay in** :
quedarse en casa — vt : suspender (una
ejecución, etc.) — **stay** n **1** : estancia f,
estadía f Lat **2** SUSPENSION : suspensión f

stay[2] n SUPPORT : soporte m

stead n **1 in someone's stead** : en
lugar de algn **2 stand someone in**
good stead : ser muy útil a algn —
steadfast adj **1** FIRM : firme **2** LOYAL : leal,
fiel — **steadily** adv **1** : progresivamente **2**
INCESSANTLY : sin parar **3** FIXEDLY : fijamente
— **steady** adj **steadier; -est 1** FIRM, SURE
: firme, seguro **2** FIXED : fijo **3** DEPENDABLE
: responsable **4** CONSTANT : constante
— **steady** vt **steadied; steadying 1** :
mantener firme **2** : calmar (los nervios)

steak n : bistec m, filete m

steal v **stole; stolen; stealing** vt : robar
— vi **1** : robar **2 steal away** : escabullirse

stealth n : sigilo m — **stealthy** adj
stealthier; -est : furtivo, sigiloso

steam n **1** : vapor m **2 let off steam** :
desahogarse — **steam** vi : echar vapor
— vt **1** : cocer al vapor **2 steam up** :
empañar — **steam engine** n : motor m
de vapor — **steamship** n : (barco m de)
vapor m — **steamy** adj **steamier; -est**
1 : lleno de vapor **2** PASSIONATE : tórrido

steel n : acero m — **steel** vt **steel oneself**
: armarse de valor — **steel** adj : de acero

steep[1] adj **1** : empinado **2**
CONSIDERABLE : considerable **3** :
muy alto (dícese de precios)

steep[2] vt : dejar (té, etc.) en infusión

steeple n : aguja f, campanario m

steer[1] n : buey m

steer[2] vt : dirigir (un auto, etc.), pilotear
(un barco) — **steering wheel** n : volante

stem[1] n : tallo m (de una planta),
pie m (de una copa) — **stem** vi
stem from : provenir de

stem[2] vt **stemmed; stemming**
: contener, detener

stench n : hedor m, mal olor m

stencil n : plantilla f (para marcar)

step n **1** : paso m **2** RUNG, STAIR :
escalón m **3 step by step** : paso por
paso **4 take steps** : tomar medidas
5 watch your step : mira por dónde
caminas — **step** vi **stepped; stepping**
1 : dar un paso **2 step back** : retoceder
3 step down RESIGN : retirarse **4 step**
in : intervenir **5 step out** : salir (por un
momento) **6 step this way** : pase por
aquí — **step up** vt INCREASE : aumentar

stepbrother n : hermanastro m
— **stepdaughter** n : hijastra f —
stepfather n : padrastro m

stepladder n : escalera f de tijera

stepmother n : madrastra f
— **stepsister** n : hermanastra f
— **stepson** n : hijastro m

stereo n, pl **stereos** : estéreo m
— **stereo** adj : estéreo

stereotype vt **-typed; -typing**
: estereotipar — **stereotype** n
: estereotipo m

sterile adj : estéril — **sterility** n
: esterilidad f — **sterilization** n
: esterilización f — **sterilize** vt
-ized; -izing : esterilizar

sterling adj : excelente —
sterling silver : plata f de ley

stern[1] adj : severo, adusto

stern[2] n : popa f

stethoscope n : estetoscopio m

stew n : estofado m, guiso m —
stew vt : estofar, guisar — vi **1**
: cocer **2** FRET : preocuparse

steward n **1** : administrador m,
-dora f **2** : auxiliar m de vuelo
(en un avión) **3** : camarero m (en
un barco) — **stewardess** n **1** :
auxiliar f de vuelo, azafata f (en un
avión) **2** : camarera f (en un barco)

stick[1] n **1** : palo m **2** TWIG : ramita f
(suelta) **3** WALKING STICK : bastón m

stick[2] v **stuck; sticking** vt **1** : pegar **2**
STAB : clavar **3** PUT : poner **4 stick out** :
sacar (la lengua, etc.) — vi **1** : pegarse **2**
JAM : atascarse **3 stick around** : quedarse
4 stick out PROTRUDE : sobresalir **5**
stick out SHOW : asomar **6 stick up** :

sobresalir **7 stick up for** : defender
— **sticker** n : etiqueta f adhesiva —
stickler n **be a stick for** : insistir mucho
en — **sticky** adj **stickier; -est** : pegajoso

stiff adj **1** RIGID : rígido, tieso **2** STILTED
: forzado **3** STRONG : fuerte **4** DIFFICULT
: difícil **5** : entumecido (dícese de
músculos) — **stiffen** vt : fortalecer,
hacer más duro — vi **1** HARDEN :
endurecerse **2** : entumecerse (dícese de
músculos) — **stiffness** n : rigidez f

stifle vt **-fled; -fling** : sofocar

stigmatize vt **-tized;**
-tizing : estigmatizar

still adj **1** : inmóvil **2** SILENT : callado —
still adv **1** : todavía, aún **2** NEVERTHELESS
: de todos modos, aún así **3 sit still!** :
¡quédate quieto! — **still** n : quietud f,
calma f — **stillborn** adj : nacido muerto
— **stillness** n : calma f, silencio m

stilt n : zanco m — **stilted** adj : forzado

stimulate vt **-lated; -lating** : estimular
— **stimulant** n : estimulante m —
stimulation n : estimulación f —
stimulus n, pl **-li** : estímulo m

sting v **stung; stinging** : picar — **sting** n
: picadura f — **stinger** n : aguijón m

stingy adj **stingier; -est** : tacaño
— **stinginess** n : tacañería f

stink vi **stank** or **stunk; stunk;**
stinking : apestar, oler mal —
stink n : hedor m, peste f fam

stint vi **stint on** : escatimar
— **stint** n : período m

stipulate vt **-lated; -lating** : estipular

stir v **stirred; stirring** vt **1** : remover,

starling
estornino[M]

stork
cigüeña[F]

revolver **2** MOVE : mover **3** INCITE : incitar
4 *or* **stir up** : despertar (memorias, etc.),
provocar (ira, etc.) — *vi* : moverse,
agitarse — **stir** *n* COMMOTION : revuelo *m*
stirrup *n* : estribo *m*
stitch *n* **1** : puntada *f* **2** PAIN : punzada *f*
(en el costado) — **stitch** *v* : coser
stock *n* **1** INVENTORY : existencias *fpl* **2**
SECURITIES : acciones *fpl* **3** ANCESTRY
: linaje *m*, estirpe *f* **4** BROTH :
caldo *m* **5 out of stock** : agotado **6**
take stock of : evaluar — **stock** *vt*
: surtir, abastecer — *vi* **stock up on**
: abastecerse de — **stockbroker** *n*
: corredor *m*, -dora *f* de bolsa
stocking *n* : media *f*
stock market *n* : bolsa *f* — **stockpile** *n*
: reservas *fpl* — **stock** *vt* **-piled;**
-piling : almacenar — **stocky** *adj*
stockier; -est : robusto, fornido
stodgy *adj* **stodgier; -est 1** DULL :
pesado **2** OLD-FASHIONED : anticuado
stoic *n* : estoico *m*, -ca *f* —
stoic *or* **stoical** *adj* : estoico —
stoicism *n* : estoicismo *m*
stoke *vt* **stoked; stoking** :
echar carbón o leña a
stole[1] → **steal**
stole[2] *n* : estola *f*
stolen → **steal**
stomach *n* : estómago *m* —
stomach *vt* : aguantar, soportar

— **stomachache** *n* : dolor *m* de estómago
stone *n* **1** : piedra *f* **2** : hueso *m*
(de una fruta) — **stone** *vt* **stoned;**
stoning : apedrear — **stony** *adj*
stonier; -est 1 : pedregoso **2 a stone**
silence : un silencio sepulcral
stood → **stand**
stool *n* : taburete *m*
stoop *vi* **1** : agacharse **2 stoop**
to : rebajarse a — **stoop** *n* **have**
a stoop : ser encorvado
stop *v* **stopped; stopping** *vt* **1** PLUG : tapar
2 PREVENT : impedir **3** HALT : parar, detener
4 CEASE : dejar de — *vi* **1** : detenerse,
parar **2** CEASE : cesar, dejar **3 stop by** :
visitar — **stop** *n* **1** : parada *f*, alto *m* **2**
come to a stop : pararse, detenerse **3**
put a stop to : poner fin a — **stopgap** *n*
: arreglo *m* provisorio — **stoplight** *n*
: semáforo *m* — **stoppage** *n or* **work**
stoppage : paro *m* — **stopper** *n* : tapón *m*
store *vt* **stored; storing** : guardar
(comida, etc.), almacenar (datos,
mercancías, etc.) — **store** *n* **1** SUPPLY :
reserva *f* **2** SHOP : tienda *f* — **storage** *n*
: almacenamiento *m* — **storehouse** *n* :
almacén *m* — **storekeeper** *n* : tendero *m*,
-ra *f* — **storeroom** *n* : almacén *m*
▸ **stork** *n* : cigüeña *f*
storm *n* : tormenta *f*, tempestad *f*
— **storm** *vi* **1** RAGE : ponerse furioso
2 storm in/out : entrar/salir furioso
— *vt* ATTACK : asaltar — **stormy** *adj*
stormier; -est : tormentoso
story[1] *n, pl* **stories 1** TALE : cuento *m* **2**
ACCOUNT : historia *f* **3** RUMOR : rumor *m*
story[2] *n* FLOOR : piso *m*, planta *f*
stout *adj* **1** BRAVE : valiente **2** RESOLUTE :
tenaz **3** STURDY : fuerte **4** FAT : corpulento
stove[1] *n* **1** : estufa *f* (para
calentar) **2** RANGE : cocina *f*
stove[2] → **stave**
stow *vt* **1** : guardar **2** LOAD : cargar
— *vi* **stow away** : viajar de polizón
— **stowaway** *n* : polizón *m*
straddle *vt* **-dled; -dling** :
sentarse a horcajadas sobre
straggle *vi* **-gled; -gling** :
rezagarse, quedarse atrás —
straggler *n* : rezagado *m*, -da *f*
straight *adj* **1** : recto, derecho **2** : lacio
(dícese del pelo) **3** HONEST : franco **4** TIDY
: arreglado — **straight** *adv* **1** DIRECTLY
: derecho **2** EXACTLY : justo **3** CLEARLY :
con claridad **4** FRANKLY : con franqueza

— **straightaway** *adv* : inmediatamente —
straighten *vt* **1** : enderezar **2 straighten**
up : arreglar — **straightforward** *adj* **1**
FRANK : franco **2** CLEAR : claro, sencillo
strain[1] *n* LINEAGE : linaje *m* **2**
STREAK : veta *f* **3** VARIETY : variedad *f* **4**
strains *npl* : acordes *mpl* (de música)
strain[2] *vt* **1** : forzar (la vista o la voz)
2 FILTER : colar **3** : tensar (relaciones,
etc.) **4 strain a muscle** : sufrir un
esguince **5 strain oneself** : hacerse
daño — *vi* : esforzarse (por) —
strain *n* **1** STRESS : tensión *f* **2** SPRAIN :
esguince *m* — **strainer** *n* : colador *m*
strait *n* **1** : estrecho *m* **2 in dire**
straits : en grandes apuros
strand[1] *vt* **be stranded** :
quedar(se) varado
strand[2] *n* **1** : hebra *f* **2 a**
strand of hair : un pelo
strange *adj* **stranger; -est 1** : extraño,
raro **2** UNFAMILIAR : desconocido —
strangely *adv* : de manera extraña
— **strangeness** *n* **1** : rareza *f* **2**
UNFAMILIARITY : lo desconocido —
stranger *n* : desconocido *m*, -da *f*
strangle *vt* **-gled; -gling** : estrangular
strap *n* **1** : correa *f* **2 or shoulder**
strap : tirante *m* — **strap** *vt* **strapped;**
strapping : sujetar con una correa
— **strapless** *n* : sin tirantes —
strapping *adj* : robusto, fornido
strategy *n, pl* **-gies** : estrategia *f*
— **strategic** *adj* : estratégico
straw *n* **1** : paja *f* **2 or drinking straw**
: pajita *f* **3 the last straw** : el colmo
strawberry *n, pl* **-ries** : fresa *f*
stray *n* : animal *m* perdido —
stray *vi* **1** : perderse, extraviarse **2** :
apartarse (de un grupo, etc.) **3** DEVIATE
: desviarse — **stray** *adj* : perdido
streak *n* **1** : raya *f* **2** VEIN : veta *f* **3**
streak of luck : racha *f* de suerte — *vi*
streak by : pasar como una flecha
stream *n* **1** : arroyo *m*, riachuelo *m* **2**
FLOW : chorro *m*, corriente *f* —
stream *vi* : correr — **streamer** *n* **1**
PENNANT : banderín *m* **2** : serpentina *f*
(de papel) — **streamlined** *adj* **1** :
aerodinámico **2** EFFICIENT : eficiente
street *n* : calle *f* — **streetcar** *n* :
tranvía *m* — **streetlight** *n* : farol *m*
strength *n* **1** : fuerza *f* **2** FORTITUDE :
fortaleza *f* **3** TOUGHNESS : resistencia *f*,
solidez *f* **4** INTENSITY : intensidad *f* **5**

strengths and weaknesses : virtudes y defectos — **strengthen** vt **1** : fortalecer **2** REINFORCE : reforzar **3** INTENSIFY : intensificar

strenuous adj **1** : enérgico **2** ARDUOUS : duro, riguroso

stress n **1** : tensión f **2** EMPHASIS : énfasis m **3** : acento m (en lingüística) — **stress** vt **1** EMPHASIZE : enfatizar **2** or **stress out** : estresar — **stressful** adj : estresante

stretch vt **1** : estirar (músculos, elástico, etc.) **2** EXTEND : extender **3 stretch the truth** : forzar la verdad — vi **1** : estirarse **2** EXTEND : extenderse — **stretch** n **1** : extensión f **2** ELASTICITY : elasticidad f **3** EXPANSE : tramo m **4** : período m (de tiempo) — **stretcher** n : camilla f

strew vt **strewed; strewed** or **strewn; strewing** : esparcir (semillas, etc.), desparramar (papeles, etc.)

stricken adj **stricken with** : aquejado de (una enfermedad), afligido por (tristeza, etc.)

strict adj : estricto — **strictly** adv **strict speaking** : en rigor

stride vi **strode; stridden; striding** : ir dando zancadas — **stride** n **1** : zancada f **2 make great strides** : hacer grandes progresos

strident adj : estridente

strife n : conflictos mpl

strike v **struck; struck; striking** vt **1** HIT : golpear **2** or **strike against** : chocar contra **3** or **strike out** DELETE : tachar **4** : dar (la hora) **5** IMPRESS : impresionar **6** : descubrir (oro o petróleo) **7 it strikes me as…** : me parece… **8 strike up** START : entablar — vi **1** : golpear **2** ATTACK : atacar **3** : declararse en huelga **4** : sobrevenir (dícese de una enfermedad, etc.) — **strike** n **1** BLOW : golpe m **2** : huelga f, paro m, Lat (de trabajadores) **3** ATTACK : ataque m — **strikebreaker** n : esquirol mf — **striker** n : huelgista mf — **striking** adj : notable, llamativo

string n **1** : cordel m **2** : sarta f (de perlas, insultos, etc.), serie f (de eventos, etc.) **3 strings** npl : cuerdas fpl (en música) — **string** vt **strung; stringing** **1** : ensartar **2** or **string up** : colgar — **string bean** n : habichuela f verde

stringent adj : estricto, severo

strip[1] v **stripped; stripping** vt **1** REMOVE : quitar **2** UNDRESS : desnudar **3 strip someone of something** : despojar a algn

de algo — vi UNDRESS : desnudarse

strip[2] n : tira f

stripe n : raya f, lista f — **striped** adj : a rayas, rayado

strive vi **strove; striven** or **strived; striving** **1 strive for** : luchar por **2 strive to** : esforzarse por

strode → **stride**

stroke vt **stroked; stroking** : acariciar — **stroke** n **1** : golpe m **2** : derrame m cerebral (en medicina)

stroll vi : pasearse — **stroll** n : paseo m — **stroller** n : cochecito m (para niños)

strong adj : fuerte — **stronghold** n : bastión m — **strongly** adv **1** DEEPLY : profundamente **2** WHOLEHEARTEDLY : totalmente **3** VIGOROUSLY : enérgicamente

strove → **strive**

struck → **strike**

structure n : estructura f — **structural** adj : estructural

struggle vi **-gled; -gling 1** : forcejear **2** STRIVE : luchar — **struggle** n : lucha f

strum vt **strummed; strumming** : rasguear

strung → **string**

strut vi **strutted; strutting** : pavonearse — **strut** n : puntal m (en construcción)

stub n : colilla f (de un cigarrillo), cabo m (de un lápiz, etc.), talón m (de un cheque) — **stub** vt **stubbed; stubbing** **stub one's toe** : darse en el dedo

stubble n : barba f de varios días

stubborn adj **1** : terco, obstinado **2** PERSISTENT : tenaz

stucco n, pl **stuccos** or **stuccoes** : estuco m

stuck → **stick** — **stuck-up** adj : engreído, creído fam

stud[1] n : semental m (animal)

stud[2] n **1** NAIL, TACK : tachuela f, tachón m **2** or **stud earring** : arete m Lat, pendiente m Spain **3** : montante m (en construcción)

student n : estudiante mf; alumno m, -na f (de un colegio) — **studio** n, pl **studios** : estudio m — **study** n, pl **studies** : estudio m — **study** v **studied; studying** : estudiar — **studious** adj : estudioso

stuff n **1** : cosas fpl **2** MATTER, SUBSTANCE : cosa f **3 know one's stuff** : ser experto — **stuff** vt **1** FILL : rellenar **2** CRAM : meter — **stuffing** n : relleno m — **stuffy** adj **stuffier; -est 1** STODGY : pesado, aburrido

2 : tapado (dícese de la nariz) **3 stuffy rooms** : salas fpl mal ventiladas

stumble vi **-bled; -bling 1** : tropezar **2 stumble across** or upon : tropezar con

stump n **1** : muñón m (de una pierna, etc.) **2** or **tree stump** : tocón m — **stump** vt : dejar perplejo

stun vt **stunned; stunning 1** : aturdir (con un golpe) **2** ASTONISH : dejar atónito

stung → **sting**

stunk → **stink**

stunning adj **1** : increíble, sensacional **2** STRIKING : imponente

stunt[1] vt : atrofiar

stunt[2] n : proeza f (acrobática)

stupendous adj : estupendo

stupid adj **1** : estúpido **2** SILLY : tonto, bobo — **stupidity** n : tontería f, estupidez f

sturdy adj **sturdier; -est 1** : fuerte, resistente **2** ROBUST : robusto

stutter vi : tartamudear — **stutter** n : tartamudeo m

sty n **1** pl **sties** PIGPEN : pocilga f **2** pl **sties** or **styes** : orzuelo m (en el ojo)

style n **1** : estilo m **2** FASHION : moda f **3 be in style** : estar de moda — **style** vt **styled; styling** : peinar (pelo), diseñar (vestidos, etc.) — **stylish** adj : elegante, chic — **stylist** n : estilista mf

suave adj : refinado y afable

sub[1] vi **subbed; subbing** → **substitute** — **sub** n → **substitute**

sub[2] n → **submarine**

subconscious adj : subconsciente — **subconscious** n : subconsciente m

subdivide vt **-vided; -viding** : subdividir — **subdivision** n : subdivisión f

subdue vt **-dued; -duing 1** CONQUER : sojuzgar **2** CONTROL : dominar **3** SOFTEN : atenuar — **subdued** adj : apagado

subject n **1** : sujeto m **2** : súbdito m, -ta f (de un gobierno) **3** TOPIC : tema m — **subject** adj **1** : sometido **2 subject to** : sujeto a — **subject** vt **subject to** : someter a — **subjective** adj : subjetivo

subjunctive n : subjuntivo m — **subjunctive** adj : subjuntivo

sublime adj : sublime

submarine adj : submarino — **submarine** n : submarino m

submerge v **-merged; -merging** vt : sumergir — vi : sumergirse

submit v **-mitted; -mitting** vi **1** YIELD : rendirse **2 submit to** : someterse a — vt : presentar — **submission** n **1** :

Sun
Sol^M

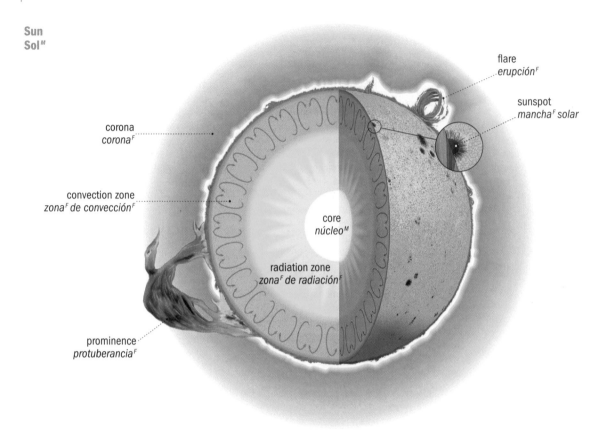

corona
corona^F

convection zone
zona^F *de convección*^F

core
núcleo^M

radiation zone
zona^F *de radiación*^F

prominence
protuberancia^F

flare
erupción^F

sunspot
mancha^F *solar*

---

sumisión *f* **2** PRESENTATION **:** presentación *f*
— **submissive** *adj* **:** sumiso
subordinate *adj* **:** subordinado
— **subordinate** *n* **:** subordinado *m,*
-da *f* — **subordinate** *vt* **-nated;**
-nating : subordinar
subpoena *n* **:** citación *f*
subscribe *vi* **-scribed; -scribing**
subscribe to : suscribirse a (una revista,
etc.), suscribir (una opinión, etc.) —
subscriber *n* **:** suscriptor *m,* -tora *f* (de
una revista, etc.); abonado *m,* -da *f* (de un
servicio) — **subscription** *n* **:** suscripción *f*
subsequent *adj* **1 :** subsiguiente
2 subsequent to : posterior a —
subsequently *adv* **:** posteriormente
subservient *adj* **:** servil
subside *vi* **-sided; -siding 1** SINK
: hundirse **2 :** amainar (dícese
de tormentas, pasiones, etc.),
remitir (dícese de fiebres, etc.)
subsidiary *adj* **:** secundario

— **subsidiary** *n, pl* **-ries :** filial *f*
subsidy *n, pl* **-dies :** subvención *f*
— **subsidize** *vt* **-dized;**
-dizing : subvencionar
subsistence *n* **:** subsistencia *f*
— **subsist** *vi* **:** subsistir
substance *n* **:** sustancia *f*
substandard *adj* **:** inferior
substantial *adj* **1** CONSIDERABLE **:**
considerable **2** STURDY **:** sólido **3 :**
sustancioso (dícese de una comida, etc.)
— **substantially** *adv* **:** considerablemente
substitute *n* **:** sustituto *m,* -ta *f* (de
una persona); sucedáneo *m* (de una
cosa) — **substitute** *vt* **-tuted; -tuting :**
sustituir — **substitution** *n* **:** sustitución *f*
subterranean *adj* **:** subterráneo
subtitle *n* **:** subtítulo *m*
subtle *adj* **-tler; -tlest :** sutil —
subtlety *n, pl* **-ties :** sutileza *f*
subtraction *n* **:** resta *f* —
subtract *vt* **:** restar

suburb *n* **1 :** barrio *m* residencial,
suburbio *m* **2 the suburbs :** las
afueras — **suburban** *adj* **:** de
las afueras (de una ciudad)
subversion *n* **:** subversión *f* —
subversive *adj* **:** subversivo
subway *n* **:** metro *m*
succeed *vt* **:** suceder a — *vi* **:** tener
éxito (dícese de personas), dar resultado
(dícese de planes, etc.) — **success** *n*
: éxito *m* — **successful** *adj* **:** de éxito,
exitoso *Lat* — **successfully** *adv* **:** con éxito
succession *n* **1 :** sucesión *f* **2 in**
succession : sucesivamente, seguidos
— **successive** *adj* **:** sucesivo —
successor *n* **:** sucesor *m,* -sora *f*
succinct *adj* **:** sucinto
succulent *adj* **:** suculento
succumb *vi* **:** sucumbir
such *adj* **1 :** tal **2 such as :** como **3 such**
a pity! : ¡qué lástima! — **such** *pron* **1 :**
tal **2 and such :** y cosas por el estilo **3 as**

such : como tal — **such** *adv* **1** VERY : muy **2 such a nice man!** : ¡qué hombre tan simpático! **3 such that** : de tal manera que

suck *vt* **1** *or* **suck on** : chupar **2** *or* **suck up** : sorber (bebidas), aspirar (con una máquina) — **sucker** *n* **1** SHOOT : chupón *m* **2** FOOL : imbécil *mf* — **suckle** *vt* **-led; -ling** : amamantar — **suction** *n* : succión *f*

sudden *adj* **1** : repentino **2 all of a sudden** : de repente — **suddenly** *adv* : de repente

suds *npl* : espuma *f* (de jabón)

sue *vt* **sued; suing** : demandar (por)

suede *n* : ante *m*, gamuza *f*

suet *n* : sebo *m*

suffer *vi* : sufrir — *vt* **1** : sufrir **2** BEAR : tolerar — **suffering** *n* : sufrimiento *m*

suffice *vi* **-ficed; -ficing** : bastar — **sufficient** *adj* : suficiente — **sufficiently** *adv* : (lo) suficientemente

suffix *n* : sufijo *m*

suffocate *v* **-cated; -cating** *vt* : asfixiar — *vi* : asfixiarse — **suffocation** *n* : asfixia *f*

suffrage *n* : sufragio *m*

sugar *n* : azúcar *mf* — **sugarcane** *n* : caña *f* de azúcar — **sugary** *adj* : azucarado

suggestion *n* **1** : sugerencia *f* **2** TRACE : indicio *m* — **suggest** *vt* **1** : sugerir **2** INDICATE : indicar

suicide *n* **1** : suicidio *m* (acto) **2** : suicida *mf* (persona) — **suicidal** *adj* : suicida

suit *n* **1** LAWSUIT : pleito *m* **2** : traje *m* (ropa) **3** : palo *m* (de naipes) — **suit** *vt* **1** ADAPT : adaptar **2** BEFIT : ser apropiado para **3 suit someone** : convenir a algn (dícese de fechas, etc.), quedar bien a algn (dícese de ropa) — **suitable** *adj* : apropiado — **suitcase** *n* : maleta *f*, valija *f* *Lat*

suite *n* **1** : suite *f* (de habitaciones) **2** : juego *m* (de muebles)

suitor *n* : pretendiente *m*

sulfur *n* : azufre *m*

sulk *vi* : enfurruñarse *fam* — **sulky** *adj* **sulkier; -est** : malhumorado

sullen *adj* : hosco

sultry *adj* **sultrier; -est 1** : bochornoso **2** SENSUAL : sensual

sum *n* : suma *f* — **sum** *vt* **summed; summing sum up** : resumir — **summarize** *v* **-rized; -rizing** : resumir — **summary** *n*, *pl* **-ries** : resumen *m*

summer *n* : verano *m*

summit *n* : cumbre *f*

summon *vt* **1** : llamar (a algn), convocar (una reunión) **2** : citar (en derecho) — **summons** *n*, *pl* **summonses** SUBPOENA : citación *f*

sumptuous *adj* : suntuoso

▸ **sun** *n* : sol *m* — **sunbathe** *vi* **-bathed; -bathing** : tomar el sol — **sunbeam** *n* : rayo *m* de sol — **sunburn** *n* : quemadura *f* de sol

Sunday *n* : domingo *m*

sundry *adj* : varios, diversos

sunflower *n* : girasol *m*

sung → **sing**

sunglasses *npl* : gafas *fpl* de sol, lentes *mpl* de sol

sunk → **sink** — **sunken** *adj* : hundido

sunlight *n* : (luz *f* del) sol *m* — **sunny** *adj* **-nier; -est** : soleado — **sunrise** *n* : salida *f* del sol — **sunset** *n* : puesta *f* del sol — **sunshine** *n* : sol *m*, luz *f* del sol — **suntan** *n* : bronceado *m*

super *adj* : súper *fam*

superb *adj* : magnífico, espléndido

superficial *adj* : superficial

superfluous *adj* : superfluo

superimpose *vt* **-posed; -posing** : sobreponer

superintendent *n* **1** : superintendente *mf* (de policía) **2** *or* **building superintendent** : portero *m*, -ra *f* **3** *or* **school superintendent** : director *m*, -tora *f* (de un colegio)

superior *adj* : superior — **superior** *n* : superior *m* — **superiority** *n*, *pl* **-ties** : superioridad *f*

superlative *adj* **1** : superlativo (en gramática) **2** EXCELLENT : excepcional — **superlative** *n* : superlativo *m*

supermarket *n* : supermercado *m*

supernatural *adj* : sobrenatural

superpower *n* : superpotencia *f*

supersede *vt* **-seded; -seding** : reemplazar, suplantar

supersonic *adj* : supersónico

superstition *n* : superstición *f* — **superstitious** *adj* : supersticioso

supervisor *n* : supervisor *m*, -sora *f* — **supervise** *vt* **-vised; -vising** : supervisar — **supervision** *n* : supervisión *f* — **supervisory** *adj* : de supervisor

supper *n* : cena *f*, comida *f*

supplant *vt* : suplantar

supple *adj* **-pler; -plest** : flexible

supplement *n* : suplemento *m* — **supplement** *vt* : complementar

— **supplementary** *adj* : suplementario

supply *vt* **-plied; -plying 1** : suministrar **2 supply with** : proveer de — **supply** *n*, *pl* **-plies 1** : suministro *m*, provisión *f* **2 supply and demand** : oferta y demanda **3 supplies** *npl* PROVISIONS : provisiones *fpl*, víveres *mpl* — **supplier** *n* : proveedor *m*, -dora *f*

support *vt* **1** BACK : apoyar **2** : mantener (una familia, etc.) **3** PROP UP : sostener — **support** *n* **1** : apoyo *m* (moral), ayuda *f* (económica) **2** PROP : soporte *m* — **supporter** *n* : partidario *m*, -ria *f*

suppose *vt* **-posed; -posing 1** : suponer **2 be supposed to (do something)** : tener que (hacer algo) — **supposedly** *adv* : supuestamente

suppress *vt* **1** : reprimir **2** : suprimir (noticias, etc.) — **suppression** *n* **1** : represión *f* **2** : supresión *f* (de información)

supreme *adj* : supremo — **supremacy** *n*, *pl* **-cies** : supremacía *f*

sure *adj* **surer; -est 1** : seguro **2 make sure that** : asegurarse de que — **sure** *adv* **1** OF COURSE : por supuesto, claro **2 it sure is hot!** : ¡qué calor! — **surely** *adv* : seguramente

surfing *n* : surf *m*, surfing *m*

surface *n* : superficie *f* — **surface** *v* **-faced; -facing** *vi* : salir a la superficie — *vt* : revestir

surfeit *n* : exceso *m*

surfing *n* : surf *m*, surfing *m*

surge *vi* **surged; surging 1** SWELL : hincharse (dícese del mar) **2** SWARM : moverse en tropel — **surge** *n* **1** : oleaje *m* (del mar), oleada *f* (de gente) **2** INCREASE : aumento *m* (súbito)

surgeon *n* : cirujano *m*, -na *f* — **surgery** *n*, *pl* **-geries** : cirugía *f* — **surgical** *adj* : quirúrgico

surly *adj* **surlier; -est** : hosco, arisco

surmount *vt* : superar

surname *n* : apellido *m*

surpass *vt* : superar

surplus *n* : excedente *m*

surprise *n* **1** : sorpresa *f* **2 take by surprise** : sorprender — **surprise** *vt* **-prised; -prising** : sorprender — **surprising** *adj* : sorprendente

surrender *vt* : entregar, rendir — *vi* : rendirse — **surrender** *n* : rendición *m* (de una ciudad, etc.), entrega *f* (de posesiones)

surrogate *n* : sustituto *m*

surround *vt* : rodear — **surroundings** *npl* : ambiente *m*

surveillance *n* : vigilancia *f*
survey *vt* **-veyed; -veying 1** : medir (un solar) **2** INSPECT : inspeccionar **3** POLL : sondear — **survey** *n, pl* **-veys 1** INSPECTION : inspección *f* **2** : medición *f* (de un solar) **3** POLL : encuesta *f*, sondeo *m* — **surveyor** *n* : agrimensor *m*, -sora *f*
survive *v* **-vived; -viving** *vi* : sobrevivir — *vt* : sobrevivir a — **survival** *n* : supervivencia *f* — **survivor** *n* : superviviente *mf*
susceptible *adj* **susceptible to** : propenso a — **susceptibility** *n, pl* **-ties** : propensión *f* (a enfermedades, etc.)
suspect *adj* : sospechoso — **suspect** *n* : sospechoso *m*, -sa *f* — **suspect** *vt* : sospechar (algo), sospechar de (algn)
suspend *vt* : suspender — **suspense** *n* **1** : incertidumbre *m* **2** : suspenso *m Lat*, suspense *m Spain* (en el cine, etc.) — **suspension** *n* : suspensión *f*
suspicion *n* : sospecha *f* — **suspicious** *adj* **1** QUESTIONABLE : sospechoso **2** DISTRUSTFUL : suspicaz
sustain *vt* **1** : sostener **2** SUFFER : sufrir
swagger *vi* : pavonearse
swallow[1] *v* : tragar — **swallow** *n* : trago *m*
swallow[2] *n* : golondrina *f* (pájaro)
swam → **swim**
swamp *n* : pantano *m*, ciénaga *f* — **swamp** *vt* : inundar — **swampy** *adj* **swampier; -est** : pantanoso, cenagoso
swan *n* : cisne *f*
swap *vt* **swapped; swapping 1** : intercambiar **2 swap something for something** : cambiar algo por algo **3 swap something with someone** : cambiar algo a algn — **swap** *n* : cambio *m*
swarm *n* : enjambre *m* — **swarm** *vi* : enjambrar
swat *vt* **swatted; swatting** : aplastar (un insecto)
sway *n* **1** : balanceo *m* **2** INFLUENCE : influjo *m* — **sway** *vi* : balancearse — *vt* : influir en
swear *v* **swore; sworn; swearing** *vi* **1** : jurar **2** CURSE : decir palabrotas — *vt* : jurar — **swearword** *n* : palabrota *f*
sweat *vi* **sweat** *or* **sweated; sweating** : sudar — **sweat** *n* : sudor *m* — **sweater** *n* : suéter *m* — **sweatshirt** *n* : sudadera *f* — **sweaty** *adj* **sweatier; -est** : sudado
Swedish *adj* : sueco — **Swedish** *n* : sueco *m* (idioma)
sweep *v* **swept; sweeping** *vt* **1** :

barrer **2 sweep aside** : apartar **3 sweep through** : extenderse por — *vi* : barrer — **sweep** *n* **1** : barrido *m* **2** : movimiento *m* circular (de la mano, etc.) **3** SCOPE : alcance *m* — **sweeping** *adj* **1** WIDE : amplio **2** EXTENSIVE : extenso — **sweepstakes** *ns & pl* : lotería *f*
sweet *adj* **1** : dulce PLEASANT : agradable — **sweet** *n* : dulce *m* — **sweeten** *vt* : endulzar — **sweetener** *n* : endulzante *m* — **sweetheart** *n* **1** : novio *m*, -via *f* **2** (*used as a form of address*) : cariño *m* — **sweetness** *n* : dulzura *f* — **sweet potato** *n* : batata *f*, boniato *m*
swell *vi* **swelled; swelled** *or* **swollen; swelling 1** *or* **swell up** : hincharse **2** INCREASE : aumentar, crecer — **swell** *n* : oleaje *m* (del mar) — **swelling** *n* : hinchazón *f*
sweltering *adj* : sofocante
swept → **sweep**
swerve *vi* **swerved; swerving** : virar bruscamente
swift *adj* : rápido — **swiftly** *adv* : rápidamente
swig *n* : trago *m* — **swig** *vi* **swigged; swigging** : beber a tragos
swim *vi* **swam; swum; swimming 1** : nadar **2** REEL : dar vueltas — **swim** *n* **1** : baño *m* **2 go for a swim** : ir a nadar — **swimmer** *n* : nadador *m*, -dora *f*
swindle *vt* **-dled; -dling** : estafar, timar — **swindle** *n* : estafa *f*, timo *m fam*
swine *ns & pl* : cerdo *m*, -da *f*
swing *v* **swung; swinging** *vt* **1** : balancear, hacer oscilar **2** MANAGE : arreglar — *vi* **1** : balancearse, oscilar **2** SWIVEL : girar — **swing** *n* **1** : vaivén *m*, balanceo *m* **2** SHIFT : cambio *m* **3** : columpio *m* (para niños) **4 in full swing** : en pleno proceso
swipe *v* **swiped; swiping** *vt* STEAL : birlar *fam*, robar — *vi* **swipe at** : intentar pegar
swirl *vi* : arremolinarse — **swirl** *n* **1** EDDY : remolino *m* **2** SPIRAL : espiral *f*
swish *vt* : agitar (haciendo un sonido) — *vi* **1** RUSTLE : hacer frufrú **2 swish by** : pasar silbando
Swiss *adj* : suizo
switch *n* **1** WHIP : vara *f* **2** CHANGE : cambio *m* **3** : interruptor *m*, llave *f* (de la luz, etc.) — **switch** *vt* **1** CHANGE : cambiar de **2** EXCHANGE : intercambiar **3 switch on** : encender, prender *Lat* **4 switch off** : apagar — *vi* **1** : sacudir (la

cola, etc.) **2** CHANGE : cambiar **3** SWAP : intercambiarse — **switchboard** *n* : centralita *f*, conmutador *m*, *Lat*
swivel *vi* **-veled** *or* **-velled; -veling** *or* **-velling** : girar (sobre un pivote)
swollen → **swell**
swoon *vi* : desvanecerse
swoop *vi* **swoop down on** : abatirse sobre — **swoop** *n* : descenso *m* en picada
sword *n* : espada *f*
swordfish *n* : pez *m* espada
swore, sworn → **swear**
swum → **swim**
swung → **swing**
syllable *n* : sílaba *f*
syllabus *n, pl* **-bi** *or* **-buses** : programa *m* (de estudios)
symbol *n* : símbolo *m* — **symbolic** *adj* : simbólico — **symbolism** *n* : simbolismo *m* — **symbolize** *vt* **-ized; -izing** : simbolizar
symmetry *n, pl* **-tries** : simetría *f* — **symmetrical** *adj* : simétrico
sympathy *n, pl* **-thies 1** COMPASSION : compasión *f* **2** UNDERSTANDING : comprensión *f* **3** CONDOLENCES : pésame *m* **4 sympathies** *npl* LOYALTY : simpatías *fpl* — **sympathize** *vi* **-thized; -thizing 1 sympathize with** PITY : compadecerse de **2 sympathize with** UNDERSTAND : cooprender — **sympathetic** *adj* **1** COMPASSIONATE : compasivo **2** UNDERSTANDING : comprensivo
symphony *n, pl* **-nies** : sinfonía *f*
symposium *n, pl* **-sia** *or* **-siums** : simposio *m*
symptom *n* : síntoma *m* — **symptomatic** *adj* : sintomático
synagogue *n* : sinagoga *f*
synchronize *vt* **-nized; -nizing** : sincronizar
syndrome *n* : síndrome *m*
synonym *n* : sinónimo *m* — **synonymous** *adj* : sinónimo
synopsis *n, pl* **-opses** : sinopsis *f*
syntax *n* : sintaxis *f*
synthesis *n, pl* **-theses** : síntesis *f* — **synthesize** *vt* **-sized; -sizing** : sintetizar — **synthetic** *adj* : sintético
syphilis *n* : sífilis *f*
Syrian *adj* : sirio
syringe *n* : jeringa *f*, jeringuilla *f*
syrup *n* : jarabe *m*
system *n* **1** : sistema *m* **2** BODY : organismo *m* **3 digestive system** : aparato *m* digestivo — **systematic** *adj* : sistemático

t *n pl* **t's** *or* **ts** : t *f*, vigésima letra del alfabeto inglés

tab *n* **1** TAG : etiqueta *f* **2** FLAP : lengüeta *f* **3** ACCOUNT : cuenta *f* **4 keep tabs on** : vigilar

▸ **table** *n* **1** : mesa *f* **2** LIST : tabla *f* **3 table of contents** : índice *m* de materias — **tablecloth** *n* : mantel *m* — **tablespoon** *n* **1** : cuchara *f* grande **2** : cucharada *f* (cantidad)

tablet *n* **1** PAD : bloc *m* **2** PILL : pastilla *f* **3** *or* **stone tablet** : lápida *f*

tabloid *n* : tabloide *m*

taboo *adj* : tabú — **taboo** *n* : tabú *m*

tacit *adj* : tácito

taciturn *adj* : taciturno

tack *vt* **1** : fijar con tachuelas **2 tack on** ADD : añadir — **tack** *n* **1** : tachuela *f* **2 change tack** : cambiar de rumbo

tackle *n* **1** GEAR : aparejo *m* **2** : placaje *m*, tacle *m*, *Lat* (acción) — **tackle** *vt* **-led; -ling 1** : placar, taclear *Lat* **2** CONFRONT : abordar

tacky *adj* **tackier; -est 1** : pegajoso **2** GAUDY : de mal gusto

tact *n* : tacto *m* — **tactful** *adj* : diplomático, discreto

tactical *adj* : táctico — **tactic** *n* : táctica *f* — **tactics** *ns & pl* : táctica *f*

tactless *adj* : indiscreto

tadpole *n* : renacuajo *m*

tag[1] *n* LABEL : etiqueta *f* — **tag** *v* **tagged; tagging** *vt* : etiquetar — *vi* **tag along with someone** : acompañar a algn

tag[2] *vt* : tocar (en varios juegos)

tail *n* **1** : cola *f* **2 tails** *npl* : cruz *f* (de una moneda) — **tail** *vt* FOLLOW : seguir

tailor *n* : sastre *m*, -tra *f* — **tailor** *vt* **1** : confeccionar (ropa) **2** ADAPT : adaptar

taint *vt* : contaminar

take *v* **took; taken; taking** *vt* **1** : tomar **2** BRING : llevar **3** REMOVE : sacar **4** BEAR : soportar, aguantar **5** ACCEPT : aceptar **6 I take it that...** : supongo que... **7 take a bath** : bañarse **8 take a walk** : dar un paseo **9 take back** : retirar (palabras, etc.) **10 take in** ALTER : achicar **11 take in** GRASP : entender **12 take in** TRICK : engañar **13 take off** REMOVE : quitar, quitarse (ropa) **14 take on** : asumir (una responsabilidad, etc.) **15 take out** : sacar **16 take over** : tomar el poder de **17 take place** : tener lugar **18 take up** SHORTEN : acortar **19 take up** OCCUPY : ocupar — *vi* **1** : prender (dícese de una vacuna, etc.) **2 take off** : despegar (dícese de aviones, etc.) **3 take over** : asumir el mando — **take** *n* **1** PROCEEDS : ingresos *mpl* **2** : toma *f* (en el cine) — **takeoff** *n* : despegue *m* (de un avión, etc.) — **takeover** *n* : toma *f* (de poder, etc.), adquisición *f* (de una empresa)

talcum powder *n* : polvos *mpl* de talco

tale *n* : cuento *m*

talent *n* : talento *m* — **talented** *adj* : talentoso

talk *vi* **1** : hablar **2 talk about** : hablar de **3 talk to/with** : hablar con — *vt* **1** SPEAK : hablar **2 talk over** : hablar de, discutir — **talk** *n* **1** CHAT : conversación *f* **2** SPEECH : charla *f* — **talkative** *adj* : hablador

tall *adj* **1** : alto **2 how tall are you?** : ¿cuánto mides?

tally *n pl* **-lies** : cuenta *f* — **tally** *v* **-lied; -lying** *vt* RECKON : calcular — *vi* MATCH : concordar, cuadrar

talon *n* : garra *f*

tambourine *n* : pandereta *f*

tame *adj* **tamer; -est 1** : domesticado **2** DOCILE : manso **3** DULL : insípido, soso — **tame** *vt* **tamed; taming** : domar

tamper *vi* **tamper with** : forzar (una cerradura), amañar (documentos, etc.)

tampon *n* : tampón *m*

tan *v* **tanned; tanning** *vt* : curtir (cuero) — *vi* : broncearse — **tan** *n* **1** SUNTAN : bronceado *m* **2** : (color *m*) café *m* con leche

tang *n* : sabor *m* fuerte

tangent *n* : tangente *f*

tangerine *n* : mandarina *f*

tangible *adj* : tangible

tangle *v* **-gled; -gling** *vt* : enredar — *vi* : enredarse — **tangle** *n* : enredo *m*

tango *n pl* **-gos** : tango *m*

tank *n* **1** : tanque *m*, depósito *m* **2** : tanque *m* (militar) — **tanker** *n* **1** : buque *m* tanque **2** *or* **tanker truck** : camión *m* cisterna

tantalizing *adj* : tentador

tantrum *n* **throw a tantrum** : hacer un berrinche

tap[1] *n* FAUCET : llave *f*, grifo *m* *Spain* — **tap** *vt* **tapped; tapping 1** : sacar (un líquido, etc.), sangrar (un

serving cart
mesita[F] *de servicio*[M]

nest of tables
juego[M] *de mesas*[F]

extension table
mesa[F] *plegable*

árbol) **2** : intervenir (un teléfono)
tap² *vt* **tapped; tapping** STRIKE
: tocar, dar un golpecito en —
tap *n* : golpecito *m*, toque *m*
tape *n* : cinta *f* — **tape** *vt* **taped; taping**
1 : pegar con cinta **2** RECORD : grabar
— **tape measure** *n* : cinta *f* métrica
taper *n* : vela *f* (larga) —
taper *vi* **1** NARROW : estrecharse
2 *or* **taper off** : disminuir
tapestry *n pl* **-tries** : tapiz *m*
tar *n* : alquitrán *m* — **tar** *vt*
tarred; tarring : alquitranar
tarantula *n* : tarántula *f*
target *n* **1** : blanco *m* **2** GOAL : objetivo *m*
tariff *n* : tarifa *f*, arancel *m*
tarnish *vt* **1** : deslustrar **2** : empañar (una
reputación, etc.) — *vi* : deslustrarse
tart¹ *adj* SOUR : ácido, agrio
tart² *n* : pastel *m*
tartan *n* : tartán *m*
task *n* : tarea *f*
tassel *n* : borla *f*
taste *v* **tasted; tasting** *vt* TRY : probar
— *vi* **1** : saber **2 taste like** : saber a —
taste *n* **1** FLAVOR : gusto *m*, sabor *m* **2**
have a taste of : probar **3 in good/bad**
taste : de buen/mal gusto — **tasteful** *adj*
: de buen gusto — **tasteless** *adj* **1** :
sin sabor **2** COARSE : de mal gusto —
tasty *adj* **tastier; -est** : sabroso
tatters *npl* : harapos *mpl* —
tattered *adj* : harapiento
tattle *vi* **-tled; -tling tattle on**
someone : acusar a algn
tattoo *vt* : tatuar — **tattoo** *n* : tatuaje *m*
taught → **teach**
taunt *n* : pulla *f*, burla *f* — **taunt** *vt*
: mofarse de, burlarse de
taut *adj* : tirante, tenso
tavern *n* : taberna *f*
tax *vt* **1** : gravar **2** STRAIN : poner a prueba
— **tax** *n* **1** : impuesto *m* **2** BURDEN :
carga *f* — **taxable** *adj* : imponible —
taxation *n* : impuestos *mpl* — **tax–**
exempt *adj* : libre de impuestos
taxi *n pl* **taxis** : taxi *m* — **taxi** *vi* **taxied;**
taxiing *or* **taxying; taxis** *or* **taxies** :
rodar por la pista (dícese de un avión)
taxpayer *n* : contribuyente *mf*
tea *n* : té *m*
teach *v* **taught; teaching** *vt* : enseñar,
dar clases de (una asignatura) — *vi* :
dar clases — **teacher** *n* : profesor *m*,
-sora *f*; maestro *m*, -tra *f* (de niños

pequeños) — **teaching** *n* : enseñanza *f*
teacup *n* : taza *f* de té
team *n* : equipo *m* — **team** *vi or*
team up : asociarse — **teammate** *n*
: compañero *m*, -ra *f* de equipo —
teamwork *n* : trabajo *m* de equipo
teapot *n* : tetera *f*
tear¹ *v* **tore; torn; tearing** *vt* **1** :
romper, rasgar **2 tear apart** : destrozar
3 tear down : derribar **4 tear off** *or*
tear out : arrancar **5 tear up** : romper
(papel, etc.) — *vi* **1** : romperse,
rasgarse **2** RUSH : ir a toda velocidad
— **tear** *n* : desgarro *m*, rasgón *m*
tear² *n* : lágrima *f* — **tearful** *adj* : lloroso
tease *vt* **teased; teasing 1** : tomar el
pelo a, burlarse de **2** ANNOY : fastidiar
teaspoon *n* **1** : cucharita *f* **2**
: cucharadita *f* (cantidad)
technical *adj* : técnico —
technicality *n pl* **-ties** : detalle *m* técnico
— **technically** *adv* : técnicamente
— **technician** *n* : técnico *m*, -ca *f*
technique *n* : técnica *f*
technological *adj* : tecnológico —
technology *n pl* **-gies** : tecnología *f*
teddy bear *n* : oso *m* de peluche
tedious *adj* : tedioso, aburrido
— **tedium** *n* : tedio *m*
tee *n* : tee *m* (en deportes)
teem *vi* **1** POUR : llover a cántaros **2**
be teeming with : estar repleto de
teenage *or* **teenaged** *adj* : adolescente
— **teenager** *n* : adolescente *mf*
— **teens** *npl* : adolescencia *f*
teepee → **tepee**
teeter *vi* : tambalearse
teeth → **tooth** — **teethe** *vi* **teethed;**
teething : echar los dientes
telecommunication *n* :
telecomunicación *f*
telegram *n* : telegrama *m*
telegraph *n* : telégrafo *m* —
telegraph *v* : telegrafiar
telephone *n* : teléfono *m* — **telephone** *v*
-phoned; -phoning : llamar por teléfono
telescope *n* : telescopio *m*
televise *vt* **-vised; -vising** : televisar
— **television** *n* : televisión *f*
tell *v* **told; telling** *vt* **1** : decir **2** RELATE
: contar **3** DISTINGUISH : distinguir **4 tell**
someone off : regañar a algn — *vi* **1** :
decir **2** KNOW : saber **3** SHOW : tener efecto
4 tell on someone : acusar a algn —
teller *n or* **bank teller** : cajero *m*, -ra *f*

temp *n* : empleado *m*, -da *f* temporal
temper *vt* MODERATE : temperar —
temper *n* **1** MOOD : humor *m* **2 have**
a bad temper : tener mal genio **3 lose**
one's temper : perder los estribos —
temperament *n* : temperamento *m* —
temperamental *adj* : temperamental
— **temperate** *adj* **1** : moderado **2**
temperate zone : zona *f* templada
temperature *n* **1** : temperatura *f* **2**
have a temperature : tener fiebre
tempest *n* : tempestad *f*
temple *n* **1** : templo *m* **2** :
sien *f* (en anatomía)
tempo *n pl* **-pi** *or* **-pos 1** :
tempo *m* **2** PACE : ritmo *m*
temporarily *adv* : temporalmente
— **temporary** *adj* : temporal
tempt *vt* : tentar —
temptation *n* : tentación *f*
ten *adj* : diez — **ten** *n* : diez *m*
tenacity *n* : tenacidad *f* —
tenacious *adj* : tenaz
tenant *n* : inquilino *m*, -na *f*;
arrendatario *m*, -ria *f*
tend¹ *vt* MIND : cuidar
tend² *vi* **tend to** : tender a —
tendency *n pl* **-cies** : tendencia *f*
tender¹ *adj* **1** : tierno **2** PAINFUL : dolorido
tender² *vt* : presentar —
tender *n* **1** : oferta *f* **2 legal tender**
: moneda *f* de curso legal
tenderloin *n* : lomo *f* (de cerdo o vaca)
tenderness *n* : ternura *f*
tendon *n* : tendón *m*
tenet *n* : principio *m*
tennis *n* : tenis *m*
tenor *n* : tenor *m*
tense¹ *n* : tiempo *m* (de un verbo)
tense² *v* **tensed; tensing** *vt* : tensar
— *vi* : tensarse — **tense** *adj* **tenser;**
tensest : tenso — **tension** *n* : tensión *f*
tent *n* : tienda *f* de campaña
tentacle *n* : tentáculo *m*
tentative *adj* **1** HESITANT : vacilante
2 PROVISIONAL : provisional
tenth *adj* : décimo — **tenth** *n* **1** :
décimo *m*, -ma *f* (en una serie) **2**
: décimo *m* (en matemáticas)
tenuous *adj* : tenue, endeble
tepid *adj* : tibio
term *n* **1** WORD : término *m* **2** PERIOD :
período *m* **3 be on good terms** : tener
buenas relaciones **4 in terms of** : con
respecto a — **term** *vt* : calificar de

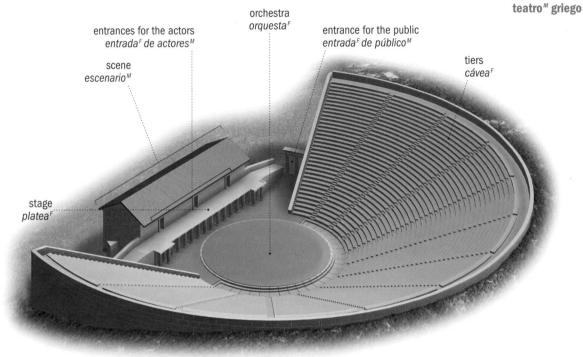

orchestra
orquesta^F

entrances for the actors
entrada^F *de actores*^M

entrance for the public
entrada^F *de público*^M

scene
escenario^M

tiers
cávea^F

stage
platea^F

---

terminal *adj* : terminal — **terminal** *n* **1** : terminal *m* **2** *or* **bus terminal** : terminal *f*

terminate *v* **-nated; -nating** *vi* : terminar(se) — *vt* : poner fin a — **termination** *n* : terminación *f*

termite *n* : termita *f*

terrace *n* : terraza *f*

terrain *n* : terreno *m*

terrestrial *adj* : terrestre

terrible *adj* : espantoso, terrible — **terribly** *adv* : terriblemente

terrier *n* : terrier *mf*

terrific *adj* **1** HUGE : tremendo **2** EXCELLENT : estupendo

terrify *vt* **-fied; -fying** : aterrar, aterrorizar — **terrifying** *adj* : aterrador

territory *n pl* **-ries** : territorio *m* — **territorial** *adj* : territorial

terror *n* : terror *m* — **terrorism** *n* : terrorismo *m* — **terrorist** *n* : terrorista *mf* — **terrorize** *vt* **-ized; -izing** : aterrorizar

terse *adj* **terser; tersest** : seco, lacónico

test *n* **1** TRIAL : prueba *f* **2** EXAM : examen *m*, prueba *f* **3** : análisis *m* (en medicina) — **test** *vt* **1** TRY : probar **2**

QUIZ : examinar **3** : analizar (la sangre, etc.), examinar (los ojos, etc.)

testament *n* **1** WILL : testamento *m* **2** **the Old/New Testament** : el Antiguo/Nuevo Testamento

testicle *n* : testículo *m*

testify *v* **-fied; -fying** : testificar

testimony *n pl* **-nies** : testimonio *m*

test tube *n* : probeta *f*, tubo *m* de ensayo

tetanus *n* : tétano *m*

tether *vt* : atar

text *n* : texto *m* — **textbook** *n* : libro *m* de texto

textile *n* : textil *m*

texture *n* : textura *f*

than *conj & prep* : que, de (con cantidades)

thank *vt* **1** : agradecer, dar (las) gracias a **2** **thank you!** : ¡gracias! — **thankful** *adj* : agradecido — **thankfully** *adv* **1** : con agradecimiento **2** FORTUNATELY : gracias a Dios — **thanks** *npl* **1** : agradecimiento *m* **2** **thank!** : ¡gracias!

Thanksgiving *n* : día *m* de Acción de Gracias

that *pron pl* **those 1** : ése, ésa, eso **2** (*more distant*) : aquél, aquélla, aquello **3** **is that you?** : ¿eres tú? **4** **like that** : así **5** **that is...** : es decir... **6** **those who...** : los que... — **that** *conj* : que — **that** *adj pl* **those 1** : ese, esa **2** (*more distant*) : aquel, aquella **3** **that one** : ése, ésa — **that** *adv* : tan

thatched *adj* : con techo de paja

thaw *vt* : descongelar (alimentos), derretir (hielo) — *vi* **1** : descongelarse **2** MELT : derretirse — **thaw** *n* : deshielo *m*

the *art* **1** : el, la, los, las **2** PER : por — **the** *adv* **1** **the sooner the better** : cuanto más pronto, mejor **2** **I like this one the best** : éste es el que más me gusta

▶ **theater** *or* **theatre** *n* : teatro *m* — **theatrical** *adj* : teatral

theft *n* : robo *m*, hurto *m*

their *adj* : su, sus, de ellos, de ellas — **theers** *pron* **1** : (el) suyo, (la) suya, (los) suyos, (las) suyas **2** **some friends of their** : unos amigos suyos, unos amigos de ellos

them *pron* **1** (*used as direct object*) : los, las **2** (*used as indirect*

thermometer
termómetro^M

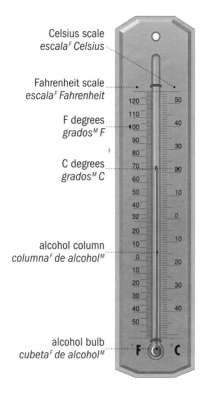

Celsius scale
escala^F *Celsius*

Fahrenheit scale
escala^F *Fahrenheit*

F degrees
grados^M *F*

C degrees
grados^M *C*

alcohol column
columna^F *de alcohol*^{M}

alcohol bulb
cubeta^F *de alcohol*^{M}

object) : les, se **3** (*used as object of a preposition*) : ellos, ellas

theme *n* **1** : tema *m* **2** ESSAY : trabajo *m* (escrito)

themselves *pron* **1** (*used reflexively*) : se **2** (*used emphatically*) : ellos mismos, ellas mismas **3** (*used after a preposition*) : sí (mismos), sí (mismas)

then *adv* **1** : entonces **2** NEXT : luego, después **3** BESIDES : además — **then** *adj* : entonces

thence *adv* : de ahí (en adelante)

theology *n pl* **-gies** : teología *f* — **theological** *adj* : teológico

theorem *n* : teorema *m* — **theoretical** *adj* : teórico — **theory** *n pl* **-ries** : teoría *f*

therapeutic *adj* : terapéutico — **therapist** *n* : terapeuta *mf* — **therapy** *n pl* **-pies** : terapia *f*

there *adv* **1** *or* **over there** : allí, allá **2** *or* **right there** : ahí **3 in there** : ahí (dentro) **4 there, it's done!** : ¡listo! **5 up/down**

there : ahí arriba/abajo **6 who's there?** : ¿quién es? — **there** *pron* **1 there is/ are** : hay **2 there are three of us** : somos tres — **thereabouts** *or* **thereabout** *adv* or **thereabouts** : por ahí — **thereafter** *adv* : después — **thereby** *adv* : así — **therefore** *adv* : por lo tanto

thermal *adj* : térmico

▸ **thermometer** *n* : termómetro *m*

thermos *n* : termo *m*

thermostat *n* : termostato *m*

thesaurus *n pl* **-sauri** *or* **-sauruses** : diccionario *m* de sinónimos

these → **this**

thesis *n pl* **theses** : tesis *f*

they *pron* **1** : ellos, ellas **2 where are they?** : ¿dónde están? **3 as they say** : como dicen — **they'd** (*contraction of* **they had** *or* **they would**) → **have, would** — **they'll** (*contraction of* **they shall** *or* **they will**) → **shall, will** — **they're** (*contraction of* **they are**) → **be** — **they've** (*contraction of* **they have**) → **have**

thick *adj* **1** : grueso **2** DENSE : espeso **3 a thick accent** : un acento marcado **4 it's two inches thick** : tiene dos pulgadas de grosor — **thick** *n* **in the thick of** : en medio de — **thicken** *vt* : espesar — *vi* : espesarse — **thicket** *n* : matorral *m* — **thickness** *n* : grosor *m*, espesor *m*

thief *n pl* **thieves** : ladrón *m*, -drona *f*

thigh *n* : muslo *m*

thimble *n* : dedal *m*

thin *adj* **thinner; -est 1** : delgado **2** : ralo (dícese del pelo) **3** WATERY : claro, aguado **4** FINE : fino — **thin** *v* **thinned; thinning** *vt* DILUTE : diluir — *vi* : ralear (dícese del pelo)

thing *n* **1** : cosa *f* **2 for one thing** : en primer lugar **3 how are things?** : ¿qué tal? **4 it's a good thing that…** : menos mal que… **5 the important thing is…** : lo importante es…

think *v* **thought; thinking** *vt* **1** : pensar **2** BELIEVE : creer **3 think up** : idear — *vi* **1** : pensar **2 think about** *or* **think of** CONSIDER : pensar en **3 think of** REMEMBER : acordarse de **4 what do you think of it?** : ¿qué te parece? — **thinker** *n* : pensador *m*, -dora *f*

third *adj* : tercero — **third** *or* **thirdly** *adv* : en tercer lugar — **third** *n* **1** : tercero *m*, -ra *f* (en una serie) **2** : tercero *m* (en matemáticas) — **Third World** *n* : Tercer Mundo *m*

thirst *n* : sed *f* — **thirsty** *adj* **thirstier;**

-est 1 : sediento **2 be thirsty** : tener sed

thirteen *adj* : trece — **thirteen** *n* : trece *m* — **thirteenth** *adj* : décimo tercero — **thirteenth** *n* **1** : decimotercero *m*, -ra *f* (en una serie) **2** : treceavo *m* (en matemáticas)

thirty *adj* : treinta — **thirty** *n pl* **thirties** : treinta *m* — **thirtieth** *adj* : trigésimo — **thirtieth** *n* **1** : trigésimo *m*, -ma *f* (en una serie) **2** : treintavo *m* (en matemáticas)

this *pron pl* **these 1** : éste, ésta, esto **2 like this** : así — **this** *adj pl* **these 1** : este, esta **2 this one** : éste, ésta **3 this way** : por aquí — **this** *adv* **this big** : así de grande **this big** : así de grande

thistle *n* : cardo *m*

thong *n* **1** : correa *f* **2** SANDAL : chancla *f*

thorn *n* : espina *f* — **thorny** *adj* : espinoso

thorough *adj* **1** : meticuloso **2** COMPLETE : completo — **thoroughly** *adv* **1** : a fondo **2** COMPLETELY : completamente — **thoroughbred** *adj* : de pura sangre — **thoroughfare** *n* : vía *f* pública

those → **that**

though *conj* : aunque — **though** *adv* **1** : sin embargo **2 as though** : como si

thought → **think** — **thought** *n* **1** : pensamiento *m* **2** IDEA : idea *f* — **thoughtful** *adj* **1** : pensativo **2** KIND : amable — **thoughtless** *adj* **1** CARELESS : descuidado **2** RUDE : desconsiderado

thousand *adj* : mil — **thousand** *n pl* **-sands** *or* **-sand** : mil *m* — **thousandth** *adj* : milésimo — **thousandth** *n* **1** : milésimo *m*, -ma *f* (en una serie) **2** : milésimo *m* (en matemáticas)

thrash *vt* : dar una paliza a — *vi or* **thrash around** : agitarse, revolcarse

thread *n* **1** : hilo *m* **2** : rosca *f* (de un tornillo) — **thread** *vt* : enhilar (una aguja), ensartar (cuentas) — **threadbare** *adj* : raído

threat *n* : amenaza *f* — **threaten** *v* : amenazar — **threatening** *adj* : amenazador

three *adj* : tres — **three** *n* : tres *m* — **three hundred** *adj* : trescientos — **three hundred** *n* : trescientos *m*

threshold *n* : umbral *m*

threw → **throw**

thrift *n* : frugalidad *f* — **thrifty** *adj* **thriftier; -est** : económico, frugal

thrill *vt* : emocionar — **thrill** *n* : emoción *f* — **thriller** *n* : película *f* de suspense *Spain*, película *f* de suspenso *Lat* — **thrilling** *adj* : emocionante

thrive *vi* **throve** *or* **thrived; thriven 1**

FLOURISH : **florecer 2** PROSPER : **prosperar**
throat *n* : garganta *f*
throb *vi* **throbbed; throbbing 1** PULSATE
: palpitar **2** VIBRATE : **vibrar 3 throb**
with pain : tener un dolor punzante
throes *npl* **1** PANGS : agonía *f* **2**
in the throes of : en medio de
throne *n* : trono *m*
throng *n* : muchedumbre *f,* multitud *f*
throttle *vt* **-tled; -tling** : estrangular
— **throttle** *n* : válvula *f* reguladora
through *prep* **1** : por, a través de **2**
BETWEEN : **entre 3** BECAUSE OF : a causa
de **4** DURING : durante **5** → **throughout**
6 Monday through Friday : de lunes a
viernes — **through** *adv* **1** : de un lado a
otro (en el espacio), de principio a fin (en
el tiempo) **2** COMPLETELY : completamente
— **through** *adj* **1 be through** : haber
terminado **2 through traffic** : tráfico *m* de
paso — **throughout** *prep* : por todo (un
lugar), a lo largo de (un período de tiempo)
throw *v* **threw; thrown; throwing** *vt* **1** :
tirar, lanzar **2** : proyectar (una sombra) **3**
CONFUSE : desconcertar **4 throw a party**
: dar una fiesta **5 throw away** *or* **throw**
out : tirar, botar *Lat* — *vi* **throw up** VOMIT :
vomitar — **throw** *n* : tiro *m,* lanzamiento *m*
thrush *n* : tordo *m,* zorzal *m*
thrust *vt* **thrust; thrusting 1** : empujar
(bruscamente) **2** PLUNGE : clavar **3**
thrust upon : imponer a — **thrust** *n* **1** :
empujón *m* **2** : estocada *f* (en esgrima)
thud *n* : ruido *m* sordo
thug *n* : matón *m*
thumb *n* : (dedo *m*) pulgar *m* —
thumb *vt or* **thumb through** : hojear
— **thumbnail** *n* : uña *f* del pulgar —
thumbtack *n* : tachuela *f,* chinche *f Lat*
thump *vt* : golpear — *vi* : latir
con fuerza (dícese del corazón)
— **thump** *n* : ruido *m* sordo
thunder *n* : truenos *mpl* —
thunder *vi* : tronar — *vt* SHOUT :
bramar — **thunderbolt** *n* : rayo *m*
— **thunderous** *adj* : atronador —
thunderstorm *n* : tormenta *f* eléctrica
Thursday *n* : jueves *m*
thus *adv* **1** : así **2** THEREFORE : por lo tanto
thwart *vt* : frustrar
thyme *n* : tomillo *m*
thyroid *n* : tiroides *mf*
tiara *n* : diadema *f*
tic *n* : tic *m* (nervioso)
tick[1] *n* : garrapata *f* (insecto)

tick[2] *n* **1** : tictac *m* (sonido) **2** CHECK
: marca *f* — **tick** *vi* : hacer tictac
— *vt* **1** *or* **tick off** CHECK : marcar
2 tick off ANNOY : fastidiar
ticket *n* **1** : pasaje *m* (de avión),
billete *m Spain* (de tren, avión, etc.),
boleto *m, Lat* (de tren o autobús) **2** :
entrada *f* (al teatro, etc.) **3** FINE : multa *f*
tickle *v* **-led; -ling** *vt* **1** : hacer cosquillas
a **2** AMUSE : divertir — *vi* : picar —
tickle *n* : cosquilleo *m* — **ticklish** *adj* **1**
: cosquilloso **2** TRICKY : delicado
tidal wave *n* : maremoto *m*
tidbit *n* MORSEL : golosina *f*
tide *n* : marea *f* — **tide** *vt* **tided; tiding**
tide over : ayudar a superar un apuro
tidy *adj* **-dier; -est** : ordenado,
arreglado — **tidy** *vt* **-died; -dying**
or **tidy up** : ordenar, arreglar
tie *n* **1** : atadura *f,* cordón *m* **2** BOND
: lazo *m* **3** : empate *m* (en deportes)
4 NECKTIE : corbata *f* — **tie** *v* **tied;**
tying *or* **tieing** *vt* **1** : atar, amarrar
Lat **2 tie a knot** : hacer un nudo
— *vi* : empatar (en deportes)

tier *n* : nivel *m,* piso (de un pastel),
grada *f* (de un estadio)
▸ **tiger** *n* : tigre *m*
tight *adj* **1** : apretado **2** SNUG : ajustado,
ceñido **3** TAUT : tirante **4** STINGY :
agarrado **5** SCARCE : escaso **6 a tight**
seal : un cierre hermético **7 a tight**
spot : un aprieto — **tight** *adv* **closed**
tight : bien cerrado — **tighten** *vt* **1** :
apretar **2** TENSE : tensar **3** : hacer más
estricto (reglas, etc.) — **tightly** *adv* :
bien, fuerte — **tightrope** *n* : cuerda *f* floja
— **tights** *npl* : leotardo *m,* mallas *fpl*
tile *n* **1** : azulejo *m,* baldosa *f* (de
piso) **2** *or* **roofing tile** : teja *f* — **tile** *vt*
tiled; tiling 1 : revestir de azulejos,
embaldosar (un piso) **2** : tejar (un techo)
till[1] *prep & conj* → **until**
till[2] *vt* : cultivar
till[3] *n* : caja *f* (registradora)
tilt *n* **1** : inclinación *f* **2 at full**
tilt : a toda velocidad — **tilt** *vt*
: inclinar — *vi* : inclinarse
timber *n* **1** : madera *f* (para
construcción) **2** BEAM : viga *f*

tiger
tigreᴹ

high-speed train
tren de alta velocidadᶠ

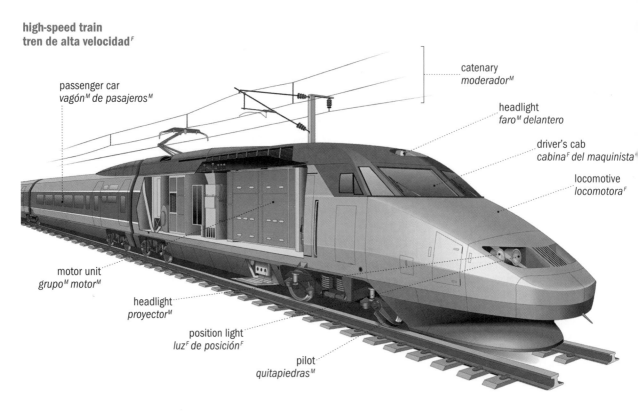

catenary
*moderador*ᴹ

passenger car
*vagón*ᴹ *de pasajeros*ᴹ

headlight
*faro*ᴹ *delantero*

driver's cab
*cabina*ᶠ *del maquinista*

locomotive
*locomotora*ᶠ

motor unit
*grupo*ᴹ *motor*ᴹ

headlight
*proyector*ᴹ

position light
*luz*ᶠ *de posición*ᶠ

pilot
*quitapiedras*ᴹ

---

timbre *n* : timbre *m*

time *n* **1** : tiempo *m* **2** AGE : época *f* **3** : compás *m* (en música) **4 at times** : a veces **5 at this time** : en este momento **6 for the time being** : por el momento **7 from time to time** : de vez en cuando **8 have a good time** : pasarlo bien **9 many times** : muchas veces **10 on time** : a tiempo **11 time after time** : una y otra vez **12 what time is it?** : ¿qué hora es? — **time** *vt* **timed; timing** : tomar el tiempo a (algn), cronometrar (una carrera, etc.) — **timeless** *adj* : eterno — **timely** *adj* **-lier; -est** : oportuno — **timer** *n* : temporizador *m*, avisador *m* (de cocina) — **times** *prep* **3 times 4 is 12** : 3 por 4 son 12 — **timetable** *n* : horario *m*

timid *adj* : tímido

tin *n* **1** : estaño *m* **2** CAN : lata *f*, bote *m* *Spain* — **tinfoil** *n* : papel *m* (de) aluminio

tinge *vt* **tinged; tingeing** *or* **tinging** : matizar — **tinge** *n* **1** TINT : matiz *m* **2** TOUCH : dejo *m*

tingle *vi* **-gled; -gling** : sentir (un)

hormigueo — **tingle** *n* : hormigueo *m*

tinker *vi* **tinker with** : intentar arreglar (con pequeños ajustes)

tinkle *vi* **-kled; -kling** : tintinear — **tinkle** *n* : tintineo *m*

tint *n* : tinte *m* — **tint** *vt* : teñir

tiny *adj* **-nier; -est** : diminuto, minúsculo

tip¹ *v* **tipped; tipping** *vt* **1** TILT : inclinar **2** *or* **tip over** : volcar — *vi* : inclinarse

tip² *n* END : punta *f*

tip³ *n* ADVICE : consejo *m* — **tip** *vt* **tip off** : avisar

tip⁴ *vt* : dar una propina a — **tip** *n* GRATUITY : propina *f*

tipsy *adj* **-sier; -est** : achispado

tiptoe *n* **on tiptoe** : de puntillas — **tiptoe** *vi* **-toed; -toeing** : caminar de puntillas

tip–top *adj* : excelente

tire¹ *n* : neumático *m*, llanta *f Lat*

tire² *v* **tired; tiring** *vt* : cansar — *vi* : cansarse — **tired** *adj* **1 tire of** : cansado de, harto de **2 tire out** : agotado — **tireless** *adj* : incansable

— **tiresome** *adj* : pesado

tissue *n* **1** : pañuelo *m* de papel **2** : tejido *m* (en biología)

title *n* : título *m* — **title** *vt* **-tled; -tling** : titular

to *prep* **1** : a **2** TOWARD : hacia **3** IN ORDER TO : para **4** UP TO : hasta **5 a quarter to seven** : las siete menos cuarto **6 be nice to them** : trátalos bien **7 ten to the box** : diez por caja **8 the mate to this shoe** : el compañero de este zapato **9 two to four years old** : entre dos y cuatro años de edad **10 want to do** : querer hacer — **to** *adv* **1 come to** : volver en sí **2 to and fro** : de un lado a otro

toad *n* : sapo *m*

toast *vt* **1** : tostar (pan, etc.) **2** : brindar por (una persona) — **toast** *n* **1** : pan *m* tostado, tostadas *fpl* **2** DRINK : brindis *m* — **toaster** *n* : tostador *m*

tobacco *n pl* **-cos** : tabaco *m*

toboggan *n* : tobogán *m*

today *adv* : hoy — **today** *n* : hoy *m*

toddler *n* : niño *m* pequeño, niña *f*

pequeña (que comienza a caminar)
toe *n* : dedo *m* (del pie) —
toenail *n* : uña *f* (del pie)
together *adv* **1** : juntos **2**
together with : junto con
toil *n* : trabajo *m* duro —
toil *vi* : trabajar duro
toilet *n* **1** BATHROOM : baño *m*,
servicio *m* **2** : inodoro *m* (instalación)
— **toilet paper** *n* : papel *m* higiénico —
toiletries *npl* : artículos *mpl* de tocador
token *n* **1** SIGN : muestra *f* **2** MEMENTO :
recuerdo *m* **3** : ficha *f* (para un tren, etc.)
told → **tell**
tolerable *adj* : tolerable — **tolerance** *n*
: tolerancia *f* — **tolerant** *adj* : tolerante
— **tolerate** *vt* -**ated; -ating** : tolerar
toll[1] *n* **1** : peaje *m* **2 death**
toll : número *m* de muertos **3**
take a toll on : afectar
toll[2] *vi* RING : tocar, doblar
— **toll** *n* : tañido *m*
tomato *n pl* -**toes** : tomate *m*
tomb *n* : tumba *f*, sepulcro *m*
— **tombstone** *n* : lápida *f*
tome *n* : tomo *m*
tomorrow *adv* : mañana —
tomorrow *n* : mañana *m*
ton *n* : tonelada *f*
tone *n* : tono *m* — **tone** *vt* **toned;**
toning *or* **tone down** : atenuar
tongs *npl* : tenazas *fpl*
tongue *n* : lengua *f*
tonic *n* **1** : tónico *m* **2** *or*
tonic water : tónica *f*
tonight *adv* : esta noche —
tonight *n* : esta noche *f*
tonsil *n* : amígdala *f*
too *adv* **1** ALSO : también **2**
EXCESSIVELY : demasiado
took → **take**
tool *n* : herramienta *f* — **toolbox** *n*
: caja *f* de herramientas
toot *vt* : sonar (un claxon, etc.) — **toot** *n* **1**
WHISTLE : pitido *m* **2** HONK : bocinazo *m*
tooth *n pl* **teeth** : diente *m* — **toothache** *n*
: dolor *m* de muelas — **toothbrush** *n* :
cepillo *m* de dientes — **toothpaste** *n* :
pasta *f* de dientes, pasta *f* dentífrica
top[1] *n* **1** : parte *f* superior **2** SUMMIT
: cima *f*, cumbre *f* **3** COVER : tapa *f*,
cubierta *f* **4 on top of** : encima de —
top *vt* **topped; topping 1** COVER : rematar
(un edificio, etc.), bañar (un pastel, etc.)
2 SURPASS : superar **3 top off** : llenar

— **top** *adj* **1** : de arriba, superior **2** BEST :
mejor **3 a top executive** : un alto ejecutivo
top[2] *n* : trompo *m* (juguete)
topic *n* : tema *m* — **topical** *adj*
: de interés actual
topmost *adj* : más alto
topple *v* -**pled; -pling** *vi* : caerse — *vt* **1**
OVERTURN : volcar **2** OVERTHROW : derrocar
torch *n* : antorcha *f*
tore → **tear**[1]
torment *n* : tormento *m* —
torment *vt* : atormentar
torn → **tear**[1]
tornado *n pl* -**does** *or* -**dos** : tornado *m*
torpedo *n pl* -**does** : torpedo *m*
— **torpedo** *vt* : torpedear
torrent *n* : torrente *m*
torrid *adj* : tórrido
torso *n pl* -**sos** *or* -**si** : torso *m*
tortilla *n* : tortilla *f*
tortoise *n* : tortuga *f* (terrestre) —
tortoiseshell *n* : carey *m*, concha *f*
tortuous *adj* : tortuoso
torture *n* : tortura *f* — **torture** *vt*
-**tured; -turing** : torturar
toss *vt* **1** : tirar, lanzar **2** : mezclar (una
ensalada) — *vi* **toss and turn** : dar
vueltas — **toss** *n* : lanzamiento *m*
tot *n* : pequeño *m*, -ña *f*
total *adj* : total — **total** *n* : total *m*
— **total** *vt* -**taled** *or* -**talled;**
-**taling** *or* -**talling 1** : ascender a
2 *or* **total up** : totalizar, sumar
totalitarian *adj* : totalitario
tote *vt* **toted; toting** : llevar
totter *vi* : tambalearse
touch *vt* **1** : tocar **2** MOVE : conmover
3 AFFECT : afectar **4 touch up** : retocar
— *vi* : tocarse — **touch** *n* **1** : tacto *m*
(sentido) **2** HINT : toque *m* **3** BIT : pizca *f* **4**
keep in touch : mantenerse en contacto
5 lose one's touch : perder la habilidad
— **touchdown** *n* : touchdown *m* —
touchy *adj* **touchier; -est 1** : delicado **2 be**
touchy about : picarse a la mención de
tough *adj* **1** : duro **2** STRONG : fuerte **3**
STRICT : severo **4** DIFFICULT : difícil —
toughen *vt* *or* **tough up** : endurecer — *vi*
: endurecerse — **toughness** *n* : dureza *f*
tour *n* **1** : viaje *m* (por un país, etc.),
visita *f* (a un museo, etc.) **2** : gira *f* (de
un equipo, etc.) — **tour** *vi* **1** TRAVEL
: viajar **2** : hacer una gira (dícese
de equipos, etc.) — *vt* : viajar por,
recorrer — **tourist** *n* : turista *mf*

tournament *n* : torneo *m*
tousle *vt* -**sled; -sling** : despeinar
tout *vt* : promocionar
tow *vt* : remolcar — **tow** *n* : remolque *m*
toward *or* **towards** *prep* : hacia
towel *n* : toalla *f*
tower *n* : torre *f* — **tower** *vi* **tower over** :
descollar sobre — **towering** *adj* : altísimo
town *n* **1** VILLAGE : pueblo *m* **2** CITY :
ciudad *f* — **township** *n* : municipio *m*
tow truck *n* : grúa *f*
toxic *adj* : tóxico
toy *n* : juguete *m* — **toy** *vi*
toy with : juguetear con
trace *n* **1** SIGN : rastro *m*, señal *f* **2**
HINT : dejo *m* — **trace** *vt* **traced;**
tracing 1 : calcar (un dibujo, etc.)
2 DRAW : trazar **3** FIND : localizar
track *n* **1** : pista *f* **2** PATH : sendero *m* **3**
or **railroad track** : vía *f* (férrea) **4**
keep track of : llevar la cuenta de —
track *vt* TRAIL : seguir la pista de
tract[1] *n* **1** EXPANSE : extensión *f* **2**
: tracto *m* (en anatomía)
tract[2] *n* PAMPHLET : folleto *m*
traction *n* : tracción *f*
tractor *n* **1** : tractor *m* **2** *or* tractor-
trailer : camión *m* (con remolque)
trade *n* **1** PROFESSION : oficio *m* **2**
COMMERCE : comercio *m* **3** INDUSTRY
: industria *f* **4** EXCHANGE : cambio *m*
— **trade** *v* **traded; trading** *vi* :
comerciar — *vt* **trade something with**
someone : cambiar algo a algn —
trademark *n* : marca *f* registrada
tradition *n* : tradición *f* —
traditional *adj* : tradicional
traffic *n* : tráfico *m* — **traffic** *vi*
trafficked; trafficking traffic in : traficar
con — **traffic light** *n* : semáforo *m*
tragedy *n pl* -**dies** : tragedia *f*
— **tragic** *adj* : trágico
trail *vi* **1** DRAG : arrastrar **2** LAG : rezagarse
3 trail off : apagarse — *vt* **1** DRAG :
arrastrar **2** PURSUE : seguir la pista de
— **trail** *n* **1** : rastro *m*, huellas *fpl* **2**
PATH : sendero *m* — **trailer** *n* **1** :
remolque *m* **2** : caravana *f* (vivienda)
▸ **train** *n* **1** : tren *m* **2** : cola *f* (de un
vestido) **3** SERIES : serie *f* **4 train of**
thought : hilo *m* (de las ideas) —
train *vt* **1** : adiestrar, entrenar (atletas,
etc.) **2** AIM : apuntar — *vi* : prepararse,
entrenarse (en deportes, etc.) —
trainer *n* : entrenador *m*, -dora *f*

trait *n* : rasgo *m*

traitor *n* : traidor *m*, -dora *f*

tramp *vi* : caminar (pesadamente) — **tramp** *n* VAGRANT : vagabundo *m*, -da *f*

trample *vt* **-pled; -pling** : pisotear

▸ **trampoline** *n* : trampolín *m*

trance *n* : trance *m*

tranquillity *or* **tranquility** *n* : tranquilidad *f* — **tranquil** *adj* : tranquilo — **tranquilize** *vt* **-ized; -izing** : tranquilizar — **tranquilizer** *n* : tranquilizante *m*

transaction *n* : transacción *f*

transatlantic *adj* : transatlántico

transcend *vt* **1** : ir más allá de **2** OVERCOME : superar

transcribe *vt* **-scribed; -scribing** : transcribir — **transcript** *n* : transcripción *f*

transfer *v* **-ferred; -ferring** *vt* **1** : transferir (fondos, etc.) **2** : trasladar (a un empleado, etc.) — *vi* **1** : cambiarse (de escuelas, etc.) **2** : hacer transbordo (entre trenes, etc.) — **transfer** *n* **1** : transferencia *f* (de fondos, etc.), traslado *m* (de una persona) **2** : boleto *m* (para hacer transbordo) **3** DECAL : calcomanía *f*

transform *vt* : transformar — **transformation** *n* : transformación *f*

transfusion *n* : transfusión *f*

transgression *n* : transgresión *f*

— **transgress** *vt* : transgredir

transient *adj* : pasajero

transit *n* **1** : tránsito *m* **2** TRANSPORTATION : transporte *m* — **transition** *n* : transición *f* — **transitive** *adj* : transitivo — **transitory** *adj* : transitorio

translate *vt* **-lated; -lating** : traducir — **translation** *n* : traducción *f* — **translator** *n* : traductor *m*, -tora *f*

translucent *adj* : translúcido

transmit *vt* **-mitted; -mitting** : transmitir — **transmission** *n* : transmisión *f* — **transmitter** *n* : transmisor *m*

transparent *adj* : transparente — **transparency** *n pl* **-cies** : transparencia *f*

transpire *vi* **-spired; -spiring 1** TURN OUT : resultar **2** HAPPEN : suceder

transplant *vt* : trasplantar — **transplant** *n* : trasplante *m*

transport *vt* : transportar — **transport** *n* : transporte *m* — **transportation** *n* : transporte *m*

transpose *vt* **-posed; -posing 1** : trasponer **2** : transportar (en música)

trap *n* : trampa *f* — **trap** *vt* **trapped; trapping** : atrapar — **trapdoor** *n* : trampilla *f*

trapeze *n* : trapecio *m*

trappings *npl* : adornos *mpl*, atavíos *mpl*

trash *n* : basura *f*

trauma *n* : trauma *m* — **traumatic** *adj* : traumático

travel *vi* **-eled** *or* **-elled; -eling** *or* **-elling 1** : viajar **2** MOVE : desplazarse — **travel** *n* : viajes *mpl* — **traveler** *or* **traveller** *n* : viajero *m*, -ra *f*

traverse *vt* **-versed; -versing** : atravesar

travesty *n pl* **-ties** : parodia *f*

trawl *vi* : pescar (con red de arrastre) — **trawler** *n* : barco *m* de pesca

tray *n* : bandeja *f*

treachery *n pl* **-eries** : traición *f* — **treacherous** *adj* **1** : traidor **2** DANGEROUS : peligroso

tread *v* **trod; trodden** *or* **trod; treading** *vt* **1** *or* **tread on** : pisar **2 tread water** : flotar — *vi* **1** STEP : pisar **2** WALK : caminar — **tread** *n* **1** STEP : paso *m* **2** : banda *f* de rodadura (de un neumático) — **treadmill** *n* : rueda *f* de andar

treason *n* : traición *f* (a la patria)

treasure *n* : tesoro *m* — **treasure** *vt* **-sured; -suring** : apreciar — **treasurer** *n* : tesorero *m*, -ra *f* — **treasury** *n pl* **-suries** : erario *m*, tesoro *m*

treat *vt* **1** : tratar **2** CONSIDER : considerar **3 treat someone to (dinner, etc.)** : invitar a algn (a cenar, etc.) — **treat** *n* **1** : gusto *m*,

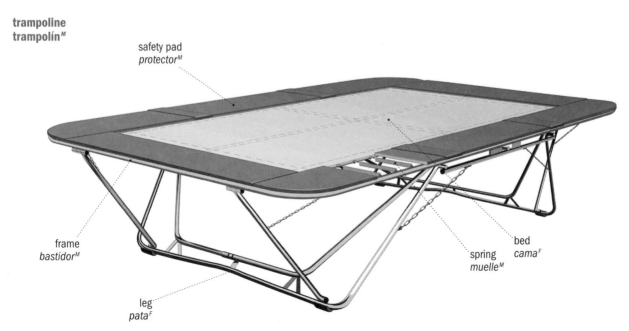

trampoline
trampolín*M*

safety pad
protector*M*

frame
bastidor*M*

leg
pata*F*

spring
muelle*M*

bed
cama*F*

placer *m* **2 it's my treat** : invito yo
treatise *n* : tratado *m*
treatment *n* : tratamiento *m*
treaty *n pl* **-ties** : tratado *m*
treble *adj* **1** TRIPLE : triple **2** : de tiple
(en música) — **treble** *vt* **-bled; -bling** :
triplicar — **treble clef** : clave *f* de sol
▸ **tree** *n* : árbol *m*
trek *vi* **trekked; trekking** : viajar (con
dificultad) — **trek** *n* : viaje *m* difícil
trellis *n* : enrejado *m*
tremble *vi* **-bled; -bling** : temblar
tremendous *adj* : tremendo
tremor *n* : temblor *m*
trench *n* **1** : zanja *f* **2** :
trinchera *f* (militar)
trend *n* **1** : tendencia *f* **2** FASHION : **moda** *f*
— **trendy** *adj* **trendier; -est** : de moda
trepidation *n* : inquietud *f*
trespass *vi* : entrar ilegalmente
(en propiedad ajena)
trial *n* **1** : juicio *m*, proceso *m* **2**
TEST : prueba *f* **3** ORDEAL : dura
prueba *f* — **trial** *adj* : de prueba
triangle *n* : triángulo *m* —
triangular *adj* : triangular
tribe *n* : tribu *f* — **tribal** *adj* : tribal
tribulation *n* : tribulación *f*
tribunal *n* : tribunal *m*
tribute *n* : tributo *m* — **tributary** *n pl*
-taries : afluente *m*
trick *n* **1** : trampa *f* **2** PRANK :
broma *f* **3** KNACK, FEAT : truco *m* **4**
: baza *f* (en naipes) — **trick** *vt* :
engañar — **trickery** *n* : engaño *m*
trickle *vi* **-led; -ling** : gotear
— **trickle** *n* : goteo *m*
tricky *adj* **trickier; -est 1** SLY : astuto,
taimado **2** DIFFICULT : difícil
tricycle *n* : triciclo *m*
trifle *n* **1** TRIVIALITY : nimiedad *f* **2 a trifle** :
un poco — **trifle** *vi* **-fled; -fling trifle with**
: jugar con — **trifling** *adj* : insignificante
trigger *n* : gatillo *m* — **trigger** *vt*
: causar, provocar
trill *n* : trino *m* — **trill** *vi* : trinar
trillion *n* : billón *m*
trilogy *n pl* **-gies** : trilogía *f*
trim *vt* **trimmed; trimming 1** : recortar
2 ADORN : adornar — **trim** *adj* **trimmer;**
trimmest 1 SLIM : esbelto **2** NEAT :
arreglado — **trim** *n* **1** : recorte *m* **2**
DECORATION : adornos *mpl* **3 in trim** :
en buena forma — **trimming** *npl* **1** :
adornos *mpl* **2** GARNISH : guarnición *f*

Trinity *n* : Trinidad *f*
trinket *n* : chuchería *f*
trio *n pl* **trios** : trío *m*
trip *v* **tripped; tripping** *vi* **1** : caminar
(a paso ligero) **2** STUMBLE : tropezar **3**
trip up : equivocarse — *vt* **1** ACTIVATE
: activar **2 trip someone** : hacer una
zancadilla a algn **3 trip someone up**
: hacer equivocar a algn — **trip** *n* **1**
: viaje *m* **2** STUMBLE : traspié *m*
tripe *n* **1** : mondongo *m*, callos *mpl* **2**
NONSENSE : tonterías *fpl*
triple *vt* **-pled; -pling** : triplicar — **triple** *n*

: triple *m* — **triple** *adj* : triple — **triplet** *n* :
trillizo *m*, -za *f* — **triplicate** *n* : triplicado *m*
tripod *n* : trípode *m*
trite *adj* **triter; tritest** : trillado
triumph *n* : triunfo *m* — **triumph** *vi*
: triunfar — **triumphal** *adj* : triunfal
— **triumphant** *adj* : triunfante
trivial *adj* : trivial — **trivia** *ns & pl*
: trivialidades *fpl* — **triviality** *n pl*
-ties : trivialidad *f*
trod, trodden → **tread**
trolley *n pl* **-leys** : tranvía *m*
trombone *n* : trombón *m*

structure of a tree
anatomíaᶠ **de un árbol**ᴹ

foliage
*follaje*ᴹ

branches
*ramaje*ᴹ

top
*cima*ᶠ

branch
*rama*ᶠ

crown
*copa*ᶠ

twig
*ramilla*ᶠ

limb
*rama*ᶠ *madre*

bole
*base*ᶠ *del tronco*ᴹ

trunk
*tronco*ᴹ

shallow root
*raíces*ᶠ *superficiales*

radicle
*radícula*ᶠ

taproot
*raíz*ᶠ *primaria*

root-hair zone
*zona*ᶠ *de pelos*ᴹ
absorbentes

trucks
camiónes^M

tow truck
grúa^F *remolque*

concrete mixer truck
hormigonera^F

garbage truck
compactadora^F

septic truck
aspiradora^F *de fangos*^{M}

street sweeper
barredora^F

tank truck
camión^M *cisterna*^{F}

box van
camioneta^F

dump truck
camión^M *basculante*

tuna
atún^M

tuna
atún^M

troop *n* **1** : escuadrón *m* (de caballería), compañía *f* (de soldados) **2 troops** *npl* : tropas *fpl* — **troop** *vi*
troop in/out : entrar/salir en tropel — **trooper** *n* **1** : soldado *m* **2** *or* **state trooper** : policía *mf* estatal
trophy *n pl* **-phies** : trofeo *m*
tropic *n* **1** : trópico *m* **2 the tropics** : el trópico — **tropic** *or* **tropical** *adj* : tropical
trot *n* : trote *m* — **trot** *vi* **trotted; trotting** : trotar
trouble *v* **-bled; -bling** *vt* **1** WORRY : preocupar **2** BOTHER : molestar — *vi* : molestarse — **trouble** *n* **1** PROBLEMS : problemas *mpl* **2** EFFORT : molestia *f* **3 be in trouble** : estar en apuros **4 get in trouble** : meterse en problemas **5 I had trouble doing it** : me costó hacerlo — **troublemaker** *n* : alborotador *m*, -dora *f* — **troublesome** *adj* : problemático
trough *n pl* **troughs 1** : depresión *f* **2** *or* **feeding trough** : comedero *m* **3** *or* **drinking trough** : bebedero *m*
troupe *n* : compañía *f* (de teatro)
trousers *npl* : pantalón *m*, pantalones *mpl*
trout *n pl* **trout** : trucha *f*
trowel *n* : paleta *f* (de albañil), desplantador *m* (de jardinero)
truant *n* : alumno *m*, -na *f* que falta a clase
truce *n* : tregua *f*
truck *vt* : transportar en camión — **truck** *n* **1** : camión *m* **2** CART : carro *m* — **trucker** *n* : camionero *m*, -ra *f*
trudge *vi* **trudged; trudging** : caminar a paso pesado
true *adj* **truer; truest 1** : verdadero **2** LOYAL : fiel **3** GENUINE : auténtico **4 be true** : ser cierto, ser verdad
truffle *n* : trufa *f*
truly *adv* : verdaderamente
trump *n* : triunfo *m* (en naipes)
trumpet *n* : trompeta *f*
trunk *n* **1** STEM, TORSO : tronco *m* **2** : trompa *f* (de un elefante) **3** : baúl *m* (equipaje) **4** : maletero *m* (de un auto) **5 trunks** *npl* : traje *m* de baño (de hombre)
truss *n* **1** FRAMEWORK : armazón *m* **2** : braguero *m* (en medicina)
trust *n* **1** CONFIDENCE : confianza *f* **2** HOPE : esperanza *f* **3** CREDIT : crédito *m* **4** : trust *m* (en finanzas) **5 in trust** : en fideicomiso — **trust** *vi* **1** : confiar **2** HOPE : esperar — *vt* **1** : confiar en, fiarse de (en frases negativas) **2 trust someone**

with something : confiar algo a algn — **trustee** *n* : fideicomisario *m*, -ria *f* — **trustworthy** *adj* : digno de confianza
truth *n pl* **truths** : verdad *f* — **truthful** *adj* : sincero, veraz
try *v* **tried; trying** *vt* **1** ATTEMPT : tratar (de), intentar **2** : juzgar (un caso, etc.) **3** TEST : poner a prueba **4** *or* **try out** : probar **5 try on** : probarse (ropa) — *vi* : hacer un esfuerzo — **try** *n pl* **tries** : intento *m* — **trying** *adj* **1** ANNOYING : irritante, pesado **2** DIFFICULT : duro — **tryout** *n* : prueba *f*
tsar → **czar**
T–shirt *n* : camiseta *f*
tub *n* **1** : cuba *f*, tina *f* **2** CONTAINER : envase *m* **3** BATHTUB : bañera *f*
tuba *n* : tuba *f*
tube *n* **1** : tubo *m* **2** *or* **inner tube** : cámara *f* **3 the tube** : la tele
tuberculosis *n pl* **-loses** : tuberculosis *f*
tubing *n* : tubería *f* — **tubular** *adj* : tubular
tuck *vt* **1** : meter **2 tuck away** : guardar **3 tuck in** : meter por dentro (una blusa, etc.) **4 tuck someone in** : arropar a algn — **tuck** *n* : jareta *f*
Tuesday *n* : martes *m*
tuft *n* : mechón *m* (de pelo), penacho *m* (de plumas)
tug *vt* **tugged; tugging** *or* **tug at** : tirar de, jalar de — **tug** *n* : tirón *m*, jalón *m* — **tugboat** *n* : remolcador *m* — **tug–of–war** *n pl* **tugs–of–war** : tira y afloja *m*
tuition *n* **1** : enseñanza *f* **2** *or* **tuition fees** : matrícula *f*
tulip *n* : tulipán *m*
tumble *vi* **-bled; -bling** : caerse — **tumble** *n* : caída *f* — **tumbler** : vaso *m* (sin pie)
tummy *n pl* **-mies** : barriga *f*, panza *f*
tumor *n* : tumor *m*
tumult *n* : tumulto *m* — **tumultuous** *adj* : tumultuoso
tuna *n pl* **-na** *or* **-nas** : atún *m*

tune *n* **1** MELODY : melodía *f* **2** SONG : tonada *f* **3 in tune** : afinado **4 out of tune** : desafinado — **tune** *v* **tuned; tuning** *vt* : afinar — *vi* **tune in** : sintonizar — **tuner** *n* **1** : afinador *m*, -dora *f* (de pianos, etc.) **2** : sintonizador *m* (de un receptor)
tunic *n* : túnica *f*
tunnel *n* : túnel *m* — **tunnel** *vi* **-neled** *or* **-nelled; -neling** *or* **-nelling** : hacer un túnel
turban *n* : turbante *m*
turbine *n* : turbina *f*
turbulent *adj* : turbulento — **turbulence** *n* : turbulencia *f*
turf *n* **1** GRASS : césped *m* **2** SOD : tepe *m*
turgid *adj* : ampuloso (dícese de prosa, etc.)
turkey *n pl* **-keys** : pavo *m*
turmoil *n* : confusión *f*
turn *vt* **1** : hacer girar (una rueda, etc.), volver (la cabeza, una página, etc.) **2** : dar la vuelta a (una esquina) **3** SPRAIN : torcer **4 turn down** REFUSE : rechazar **5 turn down** LOWER : bajar **6 turn in** : entregar **7 turn off** : cerrar (una llave), apagar (la luz, etc.) **8 turn on** : abrir (una llave), encender, prender *Lat* (la luz, etc.) **9 turn out** EXPEL : echar **10 turn out** PRODUCE : producir **11 turn out** → **turn off 12** *or* **turn over** FLIP : dar la vuelta a, voltear *Lat* **13 turn over** TRANSFER : entregar **14 turn someone's stomach** : revolver el estómago a algn **15 turn something into something** : convertir algo en algo **16 turn up** RAISE : subir — *vi* **1** ROTATE : girar, dar vueltas **2** BECOME : ponerse **3** SOUR : agriarse **4** RESORT : recurrir **5** *or* **turn around** : darse la vuelta, volverse **6 turn into** : convertirse en **7 turn left** : doblar a la izquierda **8 turn out** COME : acudir **9 turn out** RESULT : resultar **10 turn up** APPEAR : aparecer — **turn** *n* **1** : vuelta *f* **2** CHANGE : cambio *m* **3** CURVE :

typography
tipografía[F]

characters of a font
caracteres[M] de una fundición[F]

sans serif type
tipo[M] sans serif

serif type
tipo[M] serif

abcdefghijklmnopqrstuvwxyz 0123456789

abcdefghijklmnopqrstuvwxyz 0123456789

shape of characters
forma[F] de los caracteres[M]

ABCDEF

ABCDEF

abcdef

abcdef

uppercase
mayúscula

small capital
versalita

lowercase
minúscula

italic
cursiva

weight
tamaño[M]

a a a a a

a a a a

extra-light
extra-fina

light
fina

medium
media

semi-bold
semi-negrita

bold
negrita

extra-bold
extra-negrita

black
negro

---

curva f **4 do a good turn** : hacer un favor
5 whose turn is it? : ¿a quién le toca?
turnip n : nabo m
turnout n : concurrencia f —
  turnover n **1** : tartaleta f (postre) **2** :
  volumen m (de ventas) **3** : movimiento f
  (de personal) — **turnpike** n : carretera f de
  peaje — **turntable** n : plato m giratorio
turpentine n : trementina f
turquoise n : turquesa f
turret n **1** : torrecilla f **2** :
  torreta f (de un tanque, etc.)
turtle n : tortuga f (marina) —
  turtleneck n : cuello m de tortuga
tusk n : colmillo m
tussle n : pelea f — **tussle** vi
  -sled; -sling : pelearse
tutor n : profesor m, -sora f particular
  — **tutor** vt : dar clases particulares a
tuxedo n pl **-dos** or **-does** :
  esmoquin m, smoking m
TV → **television**
twang n **1** : tañido m **2** :
  acento m nasal (de la voz)
tweak vt : pellizcar —
  tweak n : pellizco m
tweed n : tweed m

tweet n : gorjeo m, pío m — **tweet** vi : piar
tweezers npl : pinzas fpl
twelve adj : doce — **twelve** n : doce m —
  twelfth adj : duodécimo — **twelfth** n **1**
  : duodécimo m, -ma f (en una serie)
  2 : doceavo m (en matemáticas)
twenty adj : veinte — **twenty** n pl **-ties** :
  veinte m — **twentieth** adj : vigésimo —
  twentieth n **1** : vigésimo m, -ma f (en una
  serie) **2** : veinteavo m (en matemáticas)
twice adv **1** : dos veces **2 twice
  as much/many as** : el doble de
  (algo), el doble que (algn)
twig n : ramita f
twilight n : crepúsculo m
twin n : gemelo m, -la f; mellizo m,
  -za f — **twin** adj : gemelo, mellizo
twine n : cordel m, bramante m Spain
twinge n : punzada f
twinkle vi **-kled; -kling 1** : centellear **2** :
  brillar (dícese de los ojos) — **twinkle** n
  : centelleo m, brillo m (de los ojos)
twirl vt : girar, dar vueltas a — vi : girar,
  dar vueltas — **twirl** n : giro m, vuelta f
twist vt **1** : retorcer **2** TURN : girar **3**
  SPRAIN : torcerse **4** : tergiversar (palabras)
  — vi **1** : retorcerse **2** COIL : enrollarse

3 : serpentear (entre montañas, etc.)
  — **twist** n **1** BEND : vuelta f **2** TURN
  : giro m **3 twist of lemon** : rodajita f
  de limón — **twister** → **tornado**
twitch vi : moverse
  (espasmódicamente) — **twitch** n
  nervous twitch : tic m nervioso
two adj : dos — **two** n pl **twos** : dos m
  — **twofold** adj : doble — **twofold** adv :
  al doble — **two hundred** adj : doscientos
  — **two hundred** n : doscientos m
tycoon n : magnate mf
tying → **tie**
type n : tipo m — **type** v **typed;
  typing** : escribir a máquina —
  typewritten adj : escrito a máquina —
  typewriter n : máquina f de escribir
typhoon n : tifón m
typical adj : típico, característico —
  typify vt **-fied; -fying** : tipificar
typist n : mecanógrafo m, -fa f
▸ **typography** n : tipografía f
tyranny n pl **-nies** : tiranía f —
  tyrant n : tirano m, -na f
tzar → **czar**

u *n, pl* **u's** *or* **us** : u *f,* vigésima
primera letra del alfabeto inglés
udder *n* : ubre *f*
UFO (*unidentified flying object*) *n,*
pl **UFO's** *or* **UFOs** : ovni *m,* OVNI *m*
ugly *adj* **uglier; -est** : feo —
ugliness *n* : fealdad *f*
ulcer *n* : úlcera *f*
ulterior *adj* **ulterior motive**
: segunda intención *f*
ultimate *adj* **1** FINAL : final, último
2 UTMOST : máximo **3** FUNDAMENTAL
: fundamental — **ultimately** *adv* **1**
FINALLY : por último, finalmente
2 EVENTUALLY : a la larga
ultimatum *n, pl* **-tums** *or*
-ta : ultimátum *m*
ultraviolet *adj* : ultravioleta
umbilical cord *n* : cordón *m* umbilical
▶ **umbrella** *n* : paraguas *m*
umpire *n* : árbitro *m,* -tra *f* —
umpire *vt* **-pired; -piring** : arbitrar
umpteenth *adj* : enésimo
unable *adj* **1** : incapaz **2 be**
unable to : no poder
unabridged *adj* : íntegro
unacceptable *adj* : inaceptable
unaccountable *adj* : inexplicable
unaccustomed *adj* **be unaccustomed**
to : no estar acostumbrado a
unadulterated *adj* : puro

unaffected *adj* **1** : no afectado **2**
NATURAL : sin afectación, natural
unafraid *adj* : sin miedo
unaided *adj* : sin ayuda
unanimous *adj* : unánime
unannounced *adj* : sin dar aviso
unarmed *adj* : desarmado
unassuming *adj* : modesto,
sin pretensiones
unattached *adj* **1** : suelto
2 UNMARRIED : soltero
unattractive *adj* : poco atractivo
unauthorized *adj* : no autorizado
unavailable *adj* : no disponible
unavoidable *adj* : inevitable
unaware *adj* **1** : inconsciente **2 be**
unaware of : ignorar — **unawares** *adv*
catch someone unawares :
agarrar a algn desprevenido
unbalanced *adj* : desequilibrado
unbearable *adj* : inaguantable,
insoportable
unbelievable *adj* : increíble
unbending *adj* : inflexible
unbiased *adj* : imparcial
unborn *adj* : aún no nacido
unbreakable *adj* : irrompible
unbridled *adj* : desenfrenado
unbroken *adj* **1** INTACT : intacto
2 CONTINUOUS : continuo
unbutton *vt* : desabrochar, desabotonar

uncalled–for *adj* :
inapropiado, innecesario
uncanny *adj* **-nier; -est** :
extraño, misterioso
unceasing *adj* : incesante
unceremonious *adj* **1** INFORMAL :
poco ceremonioso **2** ABRUPT : brusco
uncertain *adj* **1** : incierto **2 in no**
uncertain terms : de forma vehemente
— **uncertainty** *n, pl* **-ties** : incertidumbre *f*
unchanged *adj* : igual, sin alterar
— **unchanging** *adj* : inmutable
uncivilized *adj* : incivilizado
uncle *n* : tío *m*
unclear *adj* : poco claro
uncomfortable *adj* **1** : incómodo **2**
DISCONCERTING : inquietante, desagradable
uncommon *adj* : raro
uncompromising *adj* : intransigente
unconcerned *adj* : indiferente
unconditional *adj* : incondicional
unconscious *adj* : inconsciente
unconstitutional *adj* : inconstitucional
uncontrollable *adj* : incontrolable
unconventional *adj* : poco convencional
uncouth *adj* : grosero
uncover *vt* **1** : destapar
2 REVEAL : descubrir
undecided *adj* : indeciso
undeniable *adj* : innegable
under *adv* **1** : debajo **2** LESS : menos **3** *or*
under anesthetic : bajo los efectos de la
anestesia — **under** *prep* **1** BELOW BENEATH
: debajo de, abajo de **2 under 20 minutes**
: menos de 20 minutos **3 under the**
circumstances : dadas las circunstancias
underage *adj* : menor de edad
underclothes → **underwear**
undercover *adj* : secreto
undercurrent *n* : tendencia *f* oculta
underdeveloped *adj* : subdesarrollado
underestimate *vt* **-mated;**
-mating : subestimar
underfoot *adv* : bajo los pies
undergo *vt* **-went; -gone;**
-going : sufrir, experimentar
undergraduate *n* : estudiante *m*
universitario, estudiante *f* universitaria
underground *adv* **1** : bajo tierra **2 go**
underground : pasar a la clandestinidad
— **underground** *adj* **1** : subterráneo
2 SECRET : secreto, clandestino —
underground *n* : movimiento *m* clandestino
undergrowth *n* : maleza *f*
underhanded *adj* SLY : solapado

umbrella
paraguas^M

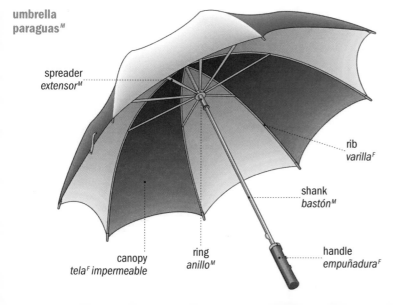

spreader
extensor^M

rib
varilla^F

shank
bastón^M

canopy
tela^F impermeable

ring
anillo^M

handle
empuñadura^F

underline *vt* -lined; -lining : subrayar
underlying *adj* : subyacente
undermine *vt* -mined;
-mining : socavar, minar
underneath *adv* : debajo, abajo —
underneath *prep* : debajo de, abajo de *Lat*
underpants *npl* : calzoncillos *mpl*,
calzones *mpl Lat*
underpass *n* : paso *m* inferior
underprivileged *adj* : desfavorecido
underrate *vt* -rated; -rating : subestimar
undershirt *n* : camiseta *f*
understand *v* -stood; -standing
: comprender, entender —
understandable *adj* : comprensible
— **understanding** *adj* : comprensivo,
compasivo — **understand** *n* 1 :
comprensión *f* 2 AGREEMENT : acuerdo *m*
understatement *n* that's an
understatement : decir sólo
eso es quedarse corto
understudy *n, pl* -dies :
sobresaliente *mf* (en el teatro)
undertake *vt* -took; -taken; -taking :

emprender (una tarea), encargarse de
(una responsabilidad) — **undertaker** *n*
: director *m*, -tora *f* de una funeraria —
undertaking *n* : empresa *f*, tarea *f*
undertone *n* 1 : voz *f* baja
2 SUGGESTION : matiz *m*
undertow *n* : resaca *f*
underwater *adj* : submarino —
underwater *adv* : debajo (del agua)
under way *adv* get under
: ponerse en marcha
underwear *n* : ropa *f* interior
underwent → **undergo**
underworld *n* the underworld
CRIMINALS : la hampa, los bajos fondos
underwriter *n* : asegurador *m*, -dora *f*
undesirable *adj* : indeseable
undeveloped *adj* : sin desarrollar
undignified *adj* : indecoroso
undisputed *adj* : indiscutible
undo *vt* -did; -done; -doing 1 UNFASTEN :
deshacer, desatar 2 : reparar (daños, etc.)
undoubtedly *adv* : indudablemente
undress *vt* : desnudar — *vi* : desnudarse

undue *adj* : indebido, excesivo
undulate *vi* -lated; -lating : ondular
unduly *adv* : excesivamente
undying *adj* : eterno
unearth *vt* : desenterrar
unearthly *adj* -lier; -est :
sobrenatural, de otro mundo
uneasy *adj* -easier; -est 1 AWKWARD :
incómodo 2 WORRIED : inquieto 3 RESTLESS
: agitado — **uneasily** *adv* : inquietamente
— **uneasiness** *n* : inquietud *f*
uneducated *adj* : inculto
unemployed *adj* : desempleado —
unemployment *n* : desempleo *m*
unerring *adj* : infalible
unethical *adj* : poco ético
uneven *adj* 1 : desigual 2 :
impar (dícese de un número)
unexpected *adj* : inesperado
unfailing *adj* 1 CONSTANT : constante
2 INEXHAUSTIBLE : inagotable
unfair *adj* : injusto — **unfairly** *adv* :
injustamente — **unfairness** *n* : injusticia *f*
unfaithful *adj* : infiel

International System of Units (SI)
sistema*F* internacional de unidades*F*

measurement of frequency
unidadF de medidaF de frecuenciaF

Hz
hertz
hercioM

measurement of electric potential difference
unidadF de medidaF de la diferenciaF de potencialM eléctrico

V
volt
voltioM, voltM

measurement of energy
unidadF de medidaF de energíaF

J
joule
julioM

measurement of power
unidadF de medidaF de potenciaF eléctrica

W
watt
vatioM

measurement of pressure
unidadF de medidaF de presiónF

Pa
pascal
pascalM

measurement of force
unidadF de medidaF de fuerzaF

N
newton
newtonM

measurement of length
unidadF de medidaF de longitudF

m
meter
metroM

measurement of thermodynamic temperature
unidadF de medidaF de temperaturaF termodinámica

K
kelvin
kelvinM

measurement of mass
unidadF de medidaF de masaF

kg
kilogram
kilogramoM

— **unfaithfulness** *n* : infidelidad *f*
unfamiliar *adj* **1** : desconocido **2**
  be unfamiliar with : desconocer
unfasten *vt* **1** : desabrochar (ropa, etc.)
  2 UNDO : desatar (una cuerda, etc.)
unfavorable *adj* : desfavorable
unfeeling *adj* : insensible
unfinished *adj* : sin terminar
unfit *adj* **1** UNSUITABLE : impropio
  2 UNSUITED : no apto, incapaz
unfold *vt* **1** : desplegar, desdoblar
  2 REVEAL : revelar (un plan, etc.)
  — *vi* **1** : extenderse, desplegarse
  2 DEVELOP : desarrollarse
unforeseen *adj* : imprevisto
unforgettable *adj* : inolvidable
unforgivable *adj* : imperdonable
unfortunate *adj* **1** UNLUCKY :
  desgraciado, desafortunado **2**
  INAPPROPRIATE : inoportuno —
  unfortunately *adv* : desgraciadamente
unfounded *adj* : infundado
unfriendly *adj* **-lier; -est** : poco amistoso
unfurl *vt* : desplegar
unfurnished *adj* : desamueblado
ungainly *adj* : desgarbado
ungodly *adj* **1** : impío **2 an ungodly**
  hour : una hora intempestiva
ungrateful *adj* : desagradecido
unhappy *adj* **-pier; -est 1** SAD : infeliz,
  triste **2** UNFORTUNATE : desafortunado
  — **unhappily** *adv* **1** SADLY : tristemente
  2 UNFORTUNATELY : desgraciadamente
  — **unhappiness** *n* : tristeza *f*
unharmed *adj* : salvo, ileso
unhealthy *adj* **-thier; -est 1** :
  malsano **2** SICKLY : enfermizo
unheard–of *adj* : sin precedente, insólito
unhook *vt* : desenganchar
unhurt *adj* : ileso
unicorn *n* : unicornio *m*
unification *n* : unificación *f*
uniform *adj* : uniforme — **uniform** *n*
  : uniforme *m* — **uniformity** *n*,
  pl **-ties** : uniformidad *f*
unify *vt* **-fied; -fying** : unificar
unilateral *adj* : unilateral
unimaginable *adj* : inconcebible
unimportant *adj* : insignificante
uninhabited *adj* :
  deshabitado, despoblado
uninjured *adj* : ileso
unintentional *adj* : involuntario
union *n* **1** : unión *f* **2** *or* **labor union**
  : sindicato *m*, gremio *m*, *Lat*

unique *adj* : único — **uniquely** *adv*
  EXCEPTIONALLY : excepcionalmente
unison *n* **in unison** : al unísono
▸ **unit** *n* **1** : unidad *f* **2** : módulo *m*
  (de un mobiliario)
unite *v* **united; uniting** *vt* : unir
  — *vi* : unirse — **unity** *n*, *pl* **-ties 1** :
  unidad *f* **2** HARMONY : acuerdo *m*
universe *n* : universo *m* —
  universal *adj* : universal
university *n*, *pl* **-ties** : universidad *f*
unjust *adj* : injusto —
  unjustified *adj* : injustificado
unkempt *adj* **1** : descuidado, desaseado
  2 : despeinado (dícese del pelo)
unkind *adj* : poco amable,
  cruel — **unkindness** *n* : falta *f*
  de amabilidad, crueldad *f*
unknown *adj* : desconocido
unlawful *adj* : ilegal
unless *conj* : a menos que, a no ser que
unlike *adj* : diferente — **unlike** *prep*
  : a diferencia de — **unlikelihood** *n*
  : improbabilidad *f* — **unlikely** *adj*
  -lier; -est : improbable
unlimited *adj* : ilimitado
unload *v* : descargar
unlock *vt* : abrir (con llave)
unlucky *adj* **-luckier; -est 1** UNFORTUNATE
  : desgraciado **2** : de mala suerte
  (dícese de un número, etc.)
unmarried *adj* : soltero
unmask *vt* : desenmascarar
unmistakable *adj* : inconfundible
unnatural *adj* **1** : anormal **2**
  AFFECTED : afectado, forzado
unnecessary *adj* : innecesario —
  unnecessarily *adv* : innecesariamente
unnerving *adj* : desconcertante
unnoticed *adj* : inadvertido
unobtainable *adj* : inasequible
unobtrusive *adj* : discreto
unofficial *adj* : no oficial
unorthodox *adj* : poco ortodoxo
unpack *vt* **1** : desempaquetar,
  desempacar *Lat* (un paquete,
  etc.) **2** : deshacer (una maleta)
  — *vi* : deshacer las maletas
unparalleled *adj* : sin igual
unpleasant *adj* : desagradable
unplug *vt* **-plugged; -plugging**
  : desconectar, desenchufar
unpopular *adj* : poco popular
unprecedented *adj* : sin precedente
unpredictable *adj* : imprevisible

unprepared *adj* **1** : no preparado
  2 UNREADY : desprevenido
unqualified *adj* **1** : no calificado,
  sin título **2** COMPLETE : absoluto
unquestionable *adj* : indiscutible
  — **unquestioning** *adj* : incondicional
unravel *v* **-eled** *or* **-elled; -eling**
  or **-elling** *vt* : desenmarañar
  — *vi* : deshacerse
unreal *adj* : irreal —
  unrealistic *adj* : poco realista
unreasonable *adj* **1** : irrazonable
  2 EXCESSIVE : excesivo
unrecognizable *adj* : irreconocible
unrelated *adj* : no relacionado
unrelenting *adj* : implacable
unreliable *adj* : que no es de fiar
unrepentant *adj* : impenitente
unrest *n* **1** : inquietud *f*, malestar *m* **2**
  or **political unrest** : disturbios *mpl*
unripe *adj* : verde, no maduro
unrivaled *or* unrivalled *adj* :
  incomparable, sin par
unroll *vt* : desenrollar — *vi* : desenrollarse
unruly *adj* : indisciplinado
unsafe *adj* : inseguro
unsaid *adj* : sin decir
unsanitary *adj* : antihigiénico
unsatisfactory *adj* : insatisfactorio
unscathed *adj* : ileso
unscrew *vt* : destornillar
unscrupulous *adj* : sin escrúpulos
unseemly *adj* **-lier; -est** : indecoroso
unseen *adj* **1** : no visto **2**
  UNNOTICED : inadvertido
unselfish *adj* : desinteresado
unsettle *vt* **-tled; -tling** DISTURB :
  perturbar — **unsettled** *adj* **1** CHANGEABLE
  : inestable **2** DISTURBED : agitado, inquieto
  3 : variable (dícese del tiempo)
unsightly *adj* : feo
unskilled *adj* : no calificado —
  unskillful *adj* : torpe, poco hábil
unsociable *adj* : poco sociable
unsound *adj* **1** : defectuoso, erróneo
  2 of unsound mind : demente
unspeakable *adj* **1** : indecible
  2 TERRIBLE : atroz
unstable *adj* : inestable
unsteady *adj* **1** : inestable
  2 SHAKY : tembloroso
unsuccessful *adj* **1** : fracasado **2**
  be unsuccessful : no tener éxito
unsuitable *adj* **1** : inadecuado **2**
  INCONVENIENT : inconveniente

unsure *adj* : inseguro

unsuspecting *adj* : confiado

unsympathetic *adj* : indiferente

unthinkable *adj* : inconcebible

untidy *adj* : desordenado (dícese de una sala, etc.), desaliñado (dícese de una persona)

untie *vt* **-tied; -tying** *or* **-tieing** : desatar

until *prep* : hasta — **until** *conj* : hasta que

untimely *adj* **1** PREMATURE : prematuro **2** INOPPORTUNE : inoportuno

untold *adj* : incalculable

untoward *adj* **1** ADVERSE : adverso **2** IMPROPER : indecoroso

untroubled *adj* **1** : tranquilo **2 be untroubled by** : no estar afectado por

untrue *adj* : falso

unused *adj* **1** NEW : nuevo **2 be unused to** : no estar acustumbrado a

unusual *adj* : poco común, insólito — **unusually** *adv* : excepcionalmente

unveil *vt* : descubrir, revelar

unwanted *adj* : superfluo (dícese de un objeto), no deseado (dícese de un niño, etc.)

unwarranted *adj* : injustificado

unwelcome *adj* : inoportuno, molesto

unwell *adj* **be unwell** : sentirse mal

unwieldy *adj* : difícil de manejar

unwilling *adj* : poco dispuesto — **unwillingly** *adv* : de mala gana

unwind *v* **-wound; -winding** *vt* : desenrollar — *vi* **1** : desenrollarse **2** RELAX : relajarse

unwise *adj* : imprudente

unworthy *adj* **be unworthy of** : no ser digno de

unwrap *vt* **-wrapped; -wrapping** : desenvolver

up *adv* **1** ABOVE : arriba **2** UPWARDS : hacia arriba **3 ten miles farther up** : diez millas más adelante **4 up here/ there** : aquí/allí arriba **5 up north** : en el norte **6 up until** : hasta — **up** *adj* **1** AWAKE : levantado **2** FINISHED : terminado **3 be up against** : enfrentarse con **4 be up on** : estar al corriente de **5 it's up to you** : depende de tí **6 prices are up** : los precios han aumentado **7 the sun is up** : ha salido el sol **8 what's up?** : ¿qué pasa? — **up** *prep* **1 go up the river** : ir río arriba **2 go up the stairs** : subir la escalera **3 up the coast** : a lo largo de la costa — **up** *v* **upped; upping; ups** *vt* : aumentar — *vi* **she up and left** : agarró y se fue

upbringing *n* : educación *f*

upcoming *adj* : próximo

update *vt* **-dated; -dating** : poner al día, actualizar — **update** *n* : puesta *f* al día

upgrade *vt* **-graded; -grading** : elevar la categoría de (un puesto, etc.), mejorar (una facilidad, etc.)

upheaval *n* : trastorno *m*

uphill *adv* : cuesta arriba — **uphill** *adj* **1** : en subida **2 be an uphill battle** : ser muy difícil

uphold *vt* **-held; -holding** : sostener, apoyar

upholstery *n, pl* **-steries** : tapicería *f*

upkeep *n* : mantenimiento *m*

upon *prep* **1** : en, sobre **2 upon leaving** : al salir

upper *adj* : superior — **upper** *n* : parte *f* superior (del calzado, etc.)

uppercase *adj* : mayúsculo

upper class *n* : clase *f* alta

upper hand *n* : ventaja *f*, dominio *m*

uppermost *adj* : más alto

upright *adj* **1** VERTICAL : vertical **2** ERECT : derecho **3** JUST : recto, honesto — **upright** *n* : montante *m*, poste *m*

uprising *n* : insurrección *f*, revuelta *f*

uproar *n* COMMOTION : alboroto *m*

uproot *vt* : desarraigar

upset *vt* **-set; -setting 1** OVERTURN : volcar **2** DISTRESS : alterar, inquietar **3** DISRUPT : trastornar — **upset** *adj* **1** DISTRESSED : alterado **2 have an upset stomach** : estar mal del estómago — **upset** *n* : trastorno *m*

upshot *n* : resultado *m* final

upside down *adv* **1** : al revés **2 turn upside down** : volver — **upside-down** *adj* : al revés

upstairs *adv* : arriba — **upstairs** *adj* : de arriba — **upstairs** *ns & pl* : piso *m* de arriba

upstart *n* : advenedizo *m*, -za *f*

kitchen utensils
utensilios[M] **de cocina**[F]

kitchen timer
minutero[M]

muffin pan
molde[M] *para magdalenas*[F]

colander
escurridor[M]

ice cream scoop
cuchara[F] *para servir helado*[M]

rotary cheese grater
rallador[M] *cilíndrico de queso*[M]

cutting board
tabla[F] *de cortar*

upstream *adv* : río arriba

upswing *n* **be on the upswing**
: estar mejorándose

up–to–date *adj* **1** : corriente,
al día **2** MODERN : moderno

uptown *adv* : hacia la parte alta de la
ciudad, hacia el distrito residencial

upturn *n* : mejora *f*, auge *m* (económico)

upward *or* upwards *adv* : hacia arriba —
upward *adj* : ascendente, hacia arriba

uranium *n* : uranio *m*

urban *adj* : urbano

urbane *adj* : urbano, cortés

urge *vt* **urged; urging 1** PRESS : instar,
exhortar **2 urge on** : animar — **urge** *n*
: impulso *m*, ganas *fpl* — **urgency** *n*,
pl **-cies** : urgencia *f* — **urgent** *adj* **1**
: urgente **2 be urgent** : urgir

urine *n* : orina *f* — **urinate** *vi*
-nated; -nating : orinar

urn *n* : urna *f*

Uruguayan *adj* : uruguayo

us *pron* **1** (*as direct or indirect object*)
: nos **2** (*as object of a preposition*) :
nosotros, nosotras **3 both of us** : nosotros
dos **4 it's us!** : ¡somos nosotros!

usage *n* : uso *m*

use *v* **used; using** *vt* **1** : usar **2** CONSUME
: consumir, tomar (drogas, etc.) **3 use up**
: agotar, consumir — *vi* **1 she used to
dance** : acostumbraba bailar **2 winters
used to be colder** : los inviernos solían
ser más fríos — **use** *n* **1** : uso *m* **2 have
no use for** : no necesitar **3 have the use of**
: poder usar, tener acceso a **4 it's no use!**
: ¡es inútil! — **used** *adj* **1** SECONDHAND :
usado **2 be used to** : estar acostumbrado
a — **useful** *adj* : útil, práctico —
usefulness *n* : utilidad *f* — **useless** *adj*
: inútil — **user** *n* : usuario *m*, -ria *f*

usher *vt* **1** : acompañar, conducir **2
usher in** : hacer entrar — **usher** *n*

: acomodador *m*, -dora *f*

usual *adj* **1** : habitual, usual **2
as usual** : como de costumbre
— **usually** *adv* : usualmente

usurp *vt* : usurpar

▸ **utensil** *n* : utensilio *m*

uterus *n*, *pl* **uteri** : útero *m*, matriz *f*

utility *n*, *pl* **-ties 1** : utilidad *f* **2** *or* **public
utility** : empresa *f* de servicio público

utilize *vt* **-lized; -lizing** : utilizar

utmost *adj* **1** FARTHEST : extremo **2
of the utmost importance** : de suma
importancia — **utmost** *n* **do one's
utmost** : hacer todo lo posible

utopia *n* : utopía *f* — **utopian** *adj* : utópico

utter[1] *adj* : absoluto, completo

utter[2] *vt* : decir, pronunciar (palabras) —
utterance *n* : declaración *f*, expresión *f*

utterly *adv* : completamente, totalmente

cookie cutters
moldes[M] *de pastas*[F]

stoner
deshuesador[M]

spaghetti tongs
pinzas[F] *para espagueti*[M]

nutcracker
cascanueces[M]

apple corer
descorazonador[M]

rolling pin
rodillo[M]

measuring beaker
vaso[M] *medidor*

food mill
pasapurés[M]

salad spinner
secadora[F] *de ensalada*[F]

kitchen scale
báscula[F] *de cocina*[F]

v *n, pl* **v's** *or* **vs** : v *f*, vigésima segunda letra del alfabeto inglés

vacant *adj* **1** AVAILABLE : **libre 2** UNOCCUPIED : **desocupado 3** : vacante (dícese de un puesto) **4** : ausente (dícese de una mirada) — **vacancy** *n, pl* **-cies 1** : (puesto *m*) vacante *f* **2** : habitación *f* libre (en un hotel, etc.)

vacate *vt* **-cated; -cating** : desalojar, desocupar

vacation *n* : vacaciones *fpl*

vaccination *n* : vacunación *f* — **vaccinate** *vt* **-nated; -nating** : vacunar — **vaccine** *n* : vacuna *f*

vacuum *n, pl* **vacuums** *or* **vacua** : vacío *m* ▸ — **vacuum** *vt* : pasar la aspiradora por — **vacuum cleaner** *n* : aspiradora *f*

vagina *n, pl* **-nae** *or* **-nas** : vagina *f*

vagrant *n* : vagabundo *m*, -da *f*

vague *adj* **vaguer; -est** : vago, indistinto

vain *adj* **1** CONCEITED : **vanidoso 2 in vain** : en vano

valentine *n* : tarjeta *f* del día de San Valentín

valiant *adj* : valiente, valeroso

valid *adj* : válido — **validate** *vt* **-dated; -dating** : validar — **validity** *n* : validez *f*

valley *n, pl* **-leys** : valle *m*

valor *n* : valor *m*, valentía *f*

value *n* : valor *m* — **value** *vt* **-ued; -uing** : valorar — **valuable** *adj* : valioso — **valuables** *npl* : objetos *mpl* de valor

valve *n* : válvula *f*

vampire *n* : vampiro *m*

van *n* : furgoneta *f*, camioneta *f*

vandal *n* : vándalo *m* — **vandalism** *n* : vandalismo *m* — **vandalize** *vt* : destrozar, destruir

vane *n or* **weather vane** : veleta *f*

vanguard *n* : vanguardia *f*

vanilla *n* : vainilla *f*

vanish *vi* : desaparecer

vanity *n, pl* **-ties 1** : vanidad *f* **2** *or* **vanity table** : tocador *m*

vantage point *n* : posición *f* ventajosa

vapor *n* : vapor *m*

variable *adj* : variable — **variable** *n* : variable *f* — **variance** *n* **at variance with** : en desacuerdo con — **variant** *n* : variante *f* — **variation** *n* : variación *f* — **varied** *adj* : variado — **variegated** *adj* : abigarrado, multicolor — **variety** *n, pl* **-ties 1** : variedad *f* **2** ASSORTMENT : surtido *m* **3** SORT : clase *f* — **various** *adj* : varios, diversos

varnish *n* : barniz *f* — **varnish** *vt* : barnizar

vary *v* **varied; varying** : variar

vase *n* **1** : jarrón *m* **2** *or* **flower vase** : florero *m*

vast *adj* : vasto, enorme — **vastness** *n* : inmensidad *f*

vat *n* : cuba *f*

vault[1] *vi* LEAP : **saltar** — **vault** *n* : salto *m*

vault[2] *n* **1** DOME : **bóveda** *f* **2** *or* **bank vault** : cámara *f* acorazada, bóveda *f* de seguridad *Lat* **3** CRYPT : **cripta** *f*

VCR (*videocassette recorder*) *n* : video *m*

veal *n* : (carne *f* de) ternera *f*

veer *vi* : virar

vegetable *adj* : vegetal — **vegetable** *n* **1** : vegetal *m* (planta) **2 vegetables** *npl* : verduras *fpl* — **vegetarian** *n* : vegetariano *mf* — **vegetation** *n* : vegetación *f*

vehemence *n* : vehemencia *f* — **vehement** *adj* : vehemente

vehicle *n* : vehículo *m*

veil *n* : velo *m* — **veil** *vt* **1** : cubrir con un velo **2** CONCEAL : **velar**

vein *n* **1** : vena *f* **2** : veta *f* (de un mineral, etc.)

velocity *n, pl* **-ties** : velocidad *f*

velvet *n* : terciopelo *m* — **velvety** *adj* : aterciopelado

vending machine *vt* : máquina *f* expendedora

vendor *n* : vendedor *m*, -dora *f*

veneer *n* **1** : chapa *f* **2** FACADE : **apariencia** *f*

venerable *adj* : venerable — **venerate** *vt* **-ated; -ating** : venerar — **veneration** *n* : veneración *f*

venereal *adj* : venéreo

venetian blind *n* : persiana *f* veneciana

Venezuelan *adj* : venezolano

vengeance *n* **1** : venganza *f* **2 take vengeance on** : vengarse de — **vengeful** *adj* : vengativo

venison *n* : (carne *f* de) venado *m*

venom *n* : veneno *m* — **venomous** *adj* : venenoso

vent *vt* : desahogar — **vent** *n* **1** *or* **air vent** : rejilla *f* de ventilación **2** OUTLET : **desahogo** *m* — **ventilate** *vt* **-lated; -lating** : ventilar — **ventilation** *n* : ventilación *f* — **ventilator** *n* : ventilador *m*

ventriloquist *n* : ventrílocuo *m*, -cua *f*

venture *v* **-tured; -turing** *vt* **1** RISK : **arriesgar 2** : aventurar (una opinión, etc.) — *vi* : atreverse — **venture** *n*

or **business venture** : empresa *f*

venue *n* : lugar *m*

Venus *n* : Venus *m*

veranda *or* **verandah** *n* : veranda *f*

verb *n* : verbo *m* — **verbal** *adj* : verbal — **verbatim** *adv* : palabra por palabra — **verbatim** *adj* : literal — **verbose** *adj* : verboso

verdict *n* **1** : veredicto *m* **2** OPINION : **opinión** *f*

verge *n* **1** : borde *m* **2 on the verge of** : a punto de (hacer algo), al borde de (algo) — **verge** *vi* **verged; verging verge on** : rayar en

verify *vt* **-fied; -fying** : verificar — **verification** *n* : verificación *f*

vermin *ns & pl* : alimañas *fpl*

vermouth *n* : vermut *m*

versatile *adj* : versátil — **versatility** *n* : versatilidad *f*

verse *n* **1** LINE : **verso** *m* **2** POETRY : poesía *f* **3** : versículo *m* (en la Biblia) — **versed** *adj* **be well versed in** : ser muy versado en

version *n* : versión *f*

versus *prep* : versus

vertebra *n, pl* **-brae** *or* **-bras** : vértebra *f*

vertical *adj* : vertical — **vertical** *n* : vertical *f*

vertigo *n, pl* **-goes** *or* **-gos** : vértigo *m*

verve *n* : brío *m*

very *adv* **1** : muy **2 at the very least** : por lo menos **3 the very same thing** : la misma cosa **4 very much** : mucho **5 very well** : muy bien — **very** *adj* **verier; -est 1** PRECISE, SAME : **mismo 2** MERE : **solo, mero 3 the very thing** : justo lo que hacía falta

vessel *n* **1** CONTAINER : **recipiente** *m* **2** SHIP : **nave** *f*, buque *m* **3** *or* **blood vessel** : vaso *m* sanguíneo

vest *n* **1** : chaleco *m* **2** *Brit* UNDERSHIRT : **camiseta** *f*

vestibule *n* : vestíbulo *m*

vestige *n* : vestigio *m*

vet *n* **1** → **veterinarian 2** → **veteran**

veteran *n* : veterano *m*, -na *f*

veterinarian *n* : veterinario *m*, -ria *f* — **veterinary** *adj* : veterinario

veto *n, pl* **-toes** : veto *m* — **veto** *vt* : vetar

vex *vt* ANNOY : **irritar**

via *prep* : por, vía

viable *adj* : viable

viaduct *n* : viaducto *m*

vial *n* : frasco *m*

vibrant *adj* : vibrante

vegetables
verduras^F

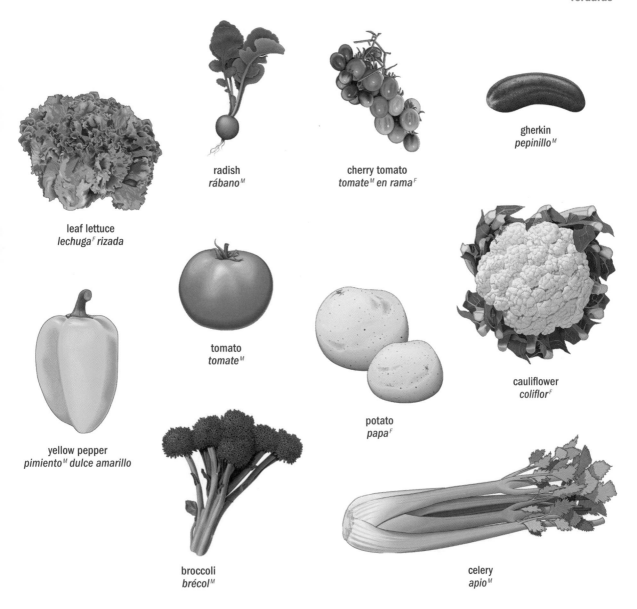

gherkin
pepinillo^M

radish
rábano^M

cherry tomato
tomate^M *en rama*^F

leaf lettuce
lechuga^F *rizada*

tomato
tomate^M

potato
papa^F

cauliflower
coliflor^F

yellow pepper
pimiento^M *dulce amarillo*

broccoli
brécol^M

celery
apio^M

— **vibrate** *vi* -brated; -brating :
vibrar — **vibration** *n* : vibración *f*
vicar *n* : vicario *m*, -ria *f*
vicarious *adj* : indirecto
vice *n* : vicio *m*
vice president *n* : vicepresidente *m*, -ta *f*
vice versa *adv* : viceversa

vicinity *n, pl* -ties **1** : inmediaciones *fpl* **2**
in the vicinity of ABOUT : alrededor de
vicious *adj* **1** SAVAGE : feroz
2 MALICIOUS : malicioso
victim *n* : víctima *f*
victor *n* : vencedor *m*, -dora *f*
victory *n, pl* -ries : victoria *f*

— **victorious** *adj* : victorioso
video *n* : video *m*, vídeo *m*
Spain — **video** *adj* : de video —
videocassette *n* : videocasete *m* —
videotape *n* : videocinta *f* — **video** *vt*
-taped; -taping : videograbar
vie *vi* **vied; vying** : competir

volleyball
voleibol[M]

court
cancha[F]

players' bench
banquillo[M] *de jugadores*[M]

scorer
anotador[M]

net
red[F]

sideline
banda[F]

attack line
línea[F] *de ataque*[M]

attack zone
zona[F] *de ataque*[M]

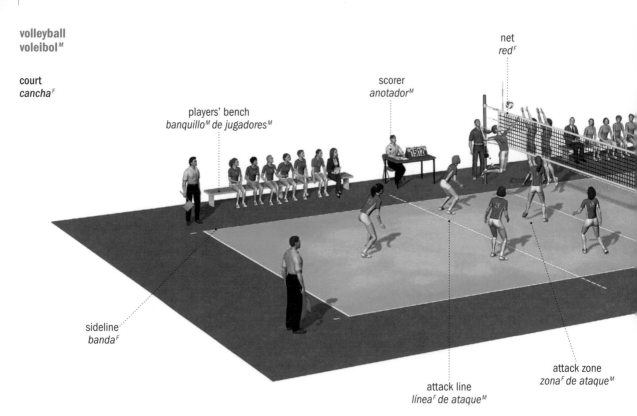

Vietnamese *adj* : vietnamita
view *n* **1** : vista *f* **2** OPINION : opinión *f* **3**
  come into view : aparecer **4 in view**
  of : en vista de (que) — **view** *vt* **1** :
  ver **2** CONSIDER : considerar — **viewer** *n*
  or **television viewer** : televidente *mf*
  — **viewpoint** *n* : punto *m* de vista
vigil *n* : vela *f* — **vigilance** *n* :
  vigilancia *f* — **vigilant** *adj* : vigilante
vigor *or Brit* **vigour** *n* : vigor *m*
  — **vigorous** *adj* **1** : enérgico
  2 ROBUST : vigoroso
Viking *n* : vikingo *m*, -ga *f*
vile *adj* **viler; vilest 1** : vil **2** REVOLTING
  : asqueroso **3** TERRIBLE : horrible
villa *n* : casa *f* de campo
village *n* : pueblo *m* (grande),
  aldea *f* (pequeña) — **villager** *n*
  : vecino *m*, -na *f* (de un pueblo);
  aldeano *m*, -na *f* (de una aldea)
villain *n* : villano *m*, -na *f*

vindicate *vt* **-cated; -cating 1** :
  vindicar **2** JUSTIFY : justificar
vindictive *adj* : vengativo
vine *n* **1** : enredadera *f* **2** GRAPEVINE : vid *f*
vinegar *n* : vinagre *m*
vineyard *n* : viña *f*, viñedo *m*
vintage *n* **1** : cosecha *f* (de vino) **2**
  ERA : época *f* — **vintage** *adj* **1** : añejo
  (dícese de un vino) **2** CLASSIC : de época
vinyl *n* : vinilo
viola *n* : viola *f*
violate *vt* **-lated; -lating** : violar
  — **violation** *n* : violación *f*
violence *n* : violencia *f* —
  violent *adj* : violento
violet *n* : violeta *f* (flor), violeta *m* (color)
violin *n* : violín *m* — **violinist** *n* :
  violinista *mf* — **violoncello** → **cello**
VIP *n, pl* **VIPs** : VIP *mf*
viper *n* : víbora *f*
virgin *n* : virgen *mf* — **virgin** *adj* **1** :

virgen (dícese de la lana, etc.) **2** CHASTE
  : virginal — **virginity** *n* : virginidad *f*
virile *adj* : viril — **virility** *n* : virilidad *f*
virtual *adj* : virtual —
  virtually *adv* : prácticamente
virtue *n* **1** : virtud *f* **2 by**
  virtue of : en virtud de
virtuoso *n, pl* **-sos** *or* **-si**
  : virtuoso *m*, -sa *f*
virtuous *adj* : virtuoso
virulent *adj* : virulento
virus *n* : virus *m*
visa *n* : visado *m*, visa *f Lat*
vis–à–vis *prep* : con respecto a
viscous *adj* : viscoso
vise *n* : torno *m* de banco
visible *adj* **1** : visible **2** NOTICEABLE
  : evidente — **visibility** *n*,
  pl **-ties** : visibilidad *f*
vision *n* **1** : visión *f* **2 have visions of** :
  imaginarse — **visionary** *adj* : visionario

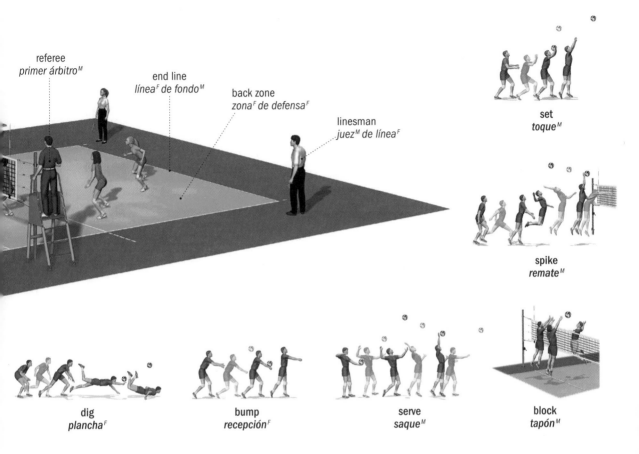

referee
*primer árbitro*ᴹ

end line
*línea*ᶠ *de fondo*ᴹ

back zone
*zona*ᶠ *de defensa*ᶠ

linesman
*juez*ᴹ *de línea*ᶠ

set
*toque*ᴹ

spike
*remate*ᴹ

dig
*plancha*ᶠ

bump
*recepción*ᶠ

serve
*saque*ᴹ

block
*tapón*ᴹ

— **vision** *n, pl* **-ries** : visionario *m*, -ria *f*
visit *vt* : visitar — *vi* **1** : hacer una
  visita **2 be visiting** : estar de visita
  — **visit** *n* : visita *f* — **visitor** *n* **1**
  : visitante *mf* **2** GUEST : visita *f*
visor *n* : visera *f*
vista *n* : vista *f*
visual *adj* : visual — **visualize** *vt*
  -ized; -izing : visualizar
vital *adj* **1** : vital **2** CRUCIAL : esencial —
  vitality *n, pl* **-ties** : vitalidad *f*, energía *f*
vitamin *n* : vitamina *f*
vivacious *adj* : vivaz, animado
vivid *adj* : vivo (dícese de colores),
  vívido (dícese de sueños, etc.)
vocabulary *n, pl* **-laries** : vocabulario *m*
vocal *adj* **1** : vocal **2** OUTSPOKEN :
  vociferante — **vocal cords** *npl* :
  cuerdas *fpl* vocales — **vocalist** *n*
  : cantante *mf*, vocalista *mf*
vocation *n* : vocación *f*

— **vocational** *adj* : profesional
vociferous *adj* : vociferante, ruidoso
vodka *n* : vodka *m*
vogue *n* **1** : moda *f*, boga *f* **2 be in**
  vogue : estar de moda, estar en boga
voice *n* : voz *f* — **voice** *vt*
  voiced; voicing : expresar
void *adj* **1** INVALID : nulo **2 void of** : falto
  de — **void** *n* : vacío *m* — **void** *vt* : anular
volatile *adj* : volátil —
  volatility *n* : volatilidad *f*
volcano *n, pl* **-noes** *or* **-nos** : volcán *m*
  — **volcanic** *adj* : volcánico
volition *n* **of one's own volition**
  : por voluntad propia
volley *n, pl* **-leys 1** : descarga *f* (de tiros)
  2 : torrente *m* (de insultos, etc.) **3** : volea *f*
▸ (en deportes) — **volleyball** *n* : voleibol *m*
volt *n* : voltio *m* — **voltage** *n* : voltaje *m*
voluble *adj* : locuaz
volume *n* : volumen *m*

— **voluminous** *adj* : voluminoso
voluntary *adj* : voluntario — **volunteer** *n*
  : voluntario *m*, -ria *f* — **volunteer** *vt* :
  ofrecer — *vi* **volunteer to** : ofrecerse a
voluptuous *adj* : voluptuoso
vomit *n* : vómito *m* — **vomit** *v* : vomitar
voracious *adj* : voraz
vote *n* **1** : voto *m* **2** SUFFRAGE : derecho *m*
  al voto — **vote** *vi* **voted; voting** : votar —
  voter *n* : votante *mf* — **voting** *n* : votación *f*
vouch *vi* **vouch for** : responder de (algo),
  responder por (algn) — **voucher** *n* : vale *m*
vow *n* : voto *m* — **vow** *vt* : jurar
vowel *n* : vocal *m*
voyage *n* : viaje *m*
vulgar *adj* **1** COMMON : ordinario
  2 CRUDE : grosero, vulgar —
  vulgarity *n, pl* **-ties** : vulgaridad *f*
vulnerable *adj* : vulnerable —
  vulnerability *n, pl* **-ties** : vulnerabilidad *f*
vulture *n* : buitre *m*
vying → **vie**

walrus
morsa *f*

w *n, pl* **w's** *or* **ws** : w *f,* vigésima
tercera letra del alfabeto inglés
wad *n* : taco *m* (de papel,
etc.), fajo *m* (de billetes)
waddle *vi* **-dled; -dling** :
andar como un pato
wade *v* **waded; wading** *vi* : caminar por
el agua — *vt or* **wade across** : vadear
wafer *n* : barquillo *m*
waffle *n* : gofre *m Spain,* wafle *m, Lat*
waft *vt* : llevar por el aire — *vi* : flotar
wag *v* **wagged; wagging** *vt* :
menear — *vi* : menearse
wage *n or* **wages** *npl* : salario *m*
— **wage** *vt* **waged; waging**
wage war : hacer la guerra
wager *n* : apuesta *f* — **wager** *v* : apostar
wagon *n* **1** CART : carrito *m* **2**
→ **station wagon**
waif *n* : niño *m* abandonado
wail *vi* : lamentarse — **wail** *n* : lamento *m*
waist *n* : cintura *f* — **waistline** *n* : cintura *f*
wait *vi* : esperar — *vt* **1** AWAIT : esperar **2**
wait tables : servir a la mesa — **wait** *n* **1**
: espera *f* **2 lie in wait** : estar al acecho
— **waiter** *n* : camarero *m,* mozo *m, Lat*
— **waiting room** *n* : sala *f* de espera —
waitress *n* : camarera *f,* moza *f Lat*
waive *vt* **waived; waiving** : renunciar
a — **waiver** *n* : renuncia *f*
wake[1] *v* **woke; woken** *or* **waked;**
waking *vi or* **wake up** : despertarse
— *vt* : despertar — **wake** *n* :
velatorio *m* (de un difunto)
wake[2] *n* **1** : estela *f* (de un barco) **2 in the**
wake of : tras, como consecuencia de
waken *vt* : despertar — *vi* : despertarse

walk *vi* **1** : caminar, andar **2** STROLL :
pasear **3 too far to walk** : demasiado
lejos para ir a pie — *vt* **1** : caminar por **2**
: sacar a pasear (a un perro) — **walk** *n* **1**
: paseo *m* **2** PATH : camino *m* **3** GAIT :
andar *m* — **walker** *n* **1** : paseante *mf* **2**
HIKER : excursionista *mf* — **walking**
stick *n* : bastón *m* — **walkout** *n* STRIKE
: huelga *f* — **walk out** *vi* **1** STRIKE :
declararse en huelga **2** LEAVE : salir,
irse **3 walk out on** : abandonar
wall *n* : muro *m* (exterior), pared *f*
(interior), muralla *f* (de una ciudad)
wallet *n* : billetera *f,* cartera *f*
wallflower *n* **be a wallflower**
: comer pavo
wallop *vt* : pegar fuerte —
wallop *n* : golpe *m* fuerte
wallow *vi* : revolcarse
wallpaper *n* : papel *m* pintado
— **wallpaper** *vt* : empapelar
walnut *n* : nuez *f*
▶ walrus *n, pl* **-rus** *or* **-ruses** : morsa *f*
waltz *n* : vals *m* — **waltz** *vi* : valsar
wan *adj* **wanner; -est** : pálido
wand *n* : varita *f* (mágica)
wander *vi* **1** : vagar, pasear **2**
STRAY : divagar — *vt* : pasear por —
wanderer *n* : vagabundo *m,* -da *f* —
wanderlust *n* : pasión *f* por viajar
wane *vi* **waned; waning** :
menguar — **wane** *n* **be on the**
wane : estar disminuyendo
want *vt* **1** DESIRE : querer **2** NEED
: necesitar **3** LACK : carecer de —
want *n* **1** NEED : necesidad *f* **2**
LACK : falta *f* **3** DESIRE : deseo *m* —
wanting *adj* **be wanting** : carecer
wanton *adj* **1** LEWD : lascivo **2 wanton**
cruelty : crueldad *f* despiadada
war *n* : guerra *f*
ward *n* **1** : sala *f* (de un hospital, etc.)
2 : distrito *m* electoral **3** : pupilo *m,*
-la *f* (de un tutor, etc.) — **ward** *vt*
ward off : protegerse contra —
warden *n* **1** : guardián *m,* -diana *f* **2**
or **game warden** : guardabosque *mf* **3**
or **prison warden** : alcaide *m*
wardrobe *n* **1** CLOSET : armario *m* **2**
CLOTHES : vestuario *m*
warehouse *n* : almacén *m,* bodega *f*
Lat — **wares** *npl* : mercancías *fpl*
warfare *n* : guerra *f*
warily *adv* : cautelosamente
warlike *adj* : belicoso

warm *adj* **1** : caliente **2** LUKEWARM : tibio
3 CARING : cariñoso **4 I feel warm** : tengo
calor **5 warm clothes** : ropa *f* de abrigo
— **warm** *vt or* **warm up** : calentar — *vi* **1**
or **warm up** : calentarse **2 warm to** :
tomar simpatía a (algn), entusiasmarse con
(algo) — **warm-blooded** *adj* : de sangre
caliente — **warmhearted** *adj* : cariñoso
— **warmly** *adv* **1** : calurosamente **2 dress**
warmly : abrigarse — **warmth** *n* **1** :
calor *m* **2** AFFECTION : cariño *m,* afecto *m*
warn *vt* : advertir, avisar —
warning *n* : advertencia *f,* aviso *m*
warp *vt* **1** : alabear (madera, etc.) **2**
DISTORT : deformar — *vi* : alabearse
warrant *n* **1** : autorización *f* **2**
arrest warrant : orden *f* judicial
— **warrant** *vt* : justificar —
warranty *n, pl* **-ties** : garantía *f*
warrior *n* : guerrero *m,* -ra *f*
warship *n* : buque *m* de guerra
wart *n* : verruga *f*

watches
relojes *M*

digital watch
reloj *M* *digital*

analog watch
reloj *M* de pulsera *F*

wartime *n* : tiempo *m* de guerra
wary *adj* **warier; -est** : cauteloso
was → **be**
wash *vt* **1** : lavar(se) **2** CARRY : arrastrar **3**
wash away : llevarse **4 wash over** : bañar
— *vi* : lavarse — **wash** *n* **1** : lavado *m* **2**
LAUNDRY : ropa *f* sucia — **washable** *adj*
: lavable — **washcloth** *n* : toallita *f*
(para lavarse) — **washed–out** *adj* **1** :
desvaído (dícese de colores) **2** EXHAUSTED
: agotado — **washer** *n* **1** → **washing**
machine 2 : arandela *f* (de una llave,
etc.) — **washing machine** *n* : máquina *f*
de lavar, lavadora *f* — **washroom** *n*
: servicios *mpl* (públicos), baño *m*
wasn't (*contraction of* **was not**) → **be**
wasp *n* : avispa *f*
waste *v* **wasted; wasting** *vt* **1** :
desperdiciar, derrochar, malgastar
2 waste time : perder tiempo — *vi*
or **waste away** : consumirse —
waste *adj* : de desecho — **waste** *n* **1** :
derroche *m*, desperdicio *m* **2** RUBBISH :
desechos *mpl* **3 a waste of time** : una
pérdida de tiempo — **wastebasket** *n* :
papelera *f* — **wasteful** *adj* : derrochador
— **wasteland** *n* : yermo *m*
▸ **watch** *vi* **1** : mirar **2** *or* **keep watch**
: velar **3 watch out!** : ¡ten cuidado!,
¡ojo! — *vt* **1** : mirar **2** *or* **watch over**
: vigilar, cuidar **3 watch what you do**
: ten cuidado con lo que haces —
watch *n* **1** reloj *m* **2** SURVEILLANCE :
vigilancia *f* **3** LOOKOUT : guardia *mf*
— **watchdog** *n* : perro *m* guardián —
watchful *adj* : vigilante — **watchman** *n,*
pl **-men** : vigilante *m*, guarda *m* —
watchword *n* : santo *m* y seña
water *n* : agua *f* — **water** *vt* **1** : regar
(el jardín, etc.) **2 water down** DILUTE :
diluir, aguar — *vi* **1** : lagrimar (dícese de
los ojos) **2 my mouth is watering** : se
me hace agua la boca — **watercolor** *n*
: acuarela *f* — **watercress** *n* : berro *m*
— **waterfall** *n* : cascada *f*, salto *m*
de agua — **water lily** *n* : nenúfar *m*
— **waterlogged** *adj* : lleno de agua,
▸ empapado — **watermelon** *n* : sandía *f*
— **waterpower** *n* : energía *f* hidráulica
— **waterproof** *adj* : impermeable —
watershed *n* **1** : cuenca *f* (de un río) **2**
: momento *m* crítico — **waterskiing** *n*
: esquí *m* acuático — **watertight** *adj* :
hermético — **waterway** *n* : vía *f* navegable
— **waterworks** *npl* : central *f* de

abastecimiento de agua — **watery** *adj* **1**
: acuoso **2** DILUTED : aguado, diluido **3**
WASHED–OUT : desvaído (dícese de colores)
watt *n* : vatio *m* — **wattage** *n* : vataje *m*
wave *v* **waved; waving** *vi* **1** : saludar
con la mano **2** : flotar (dícese de una
bandera) — *vt* **1** SHAKE : agitar **2** CURL
: ondular **3** SIGNAL : hacer señas a (con
la mano) — **wave** *n* **1** : ola *f* (de agua)
2 CURL : onda *f* **3** : onda *f* (en física) **4** :
señal *f* (con la mano) **5** SURGE : oleada *f*
— **wavelength** *n* : longitud *f* de onda
waver *vi* : vacilar
wax[1] *vi* : crecer (dícese de la luna)
wax[2] *n* : cera *f* (para pisos, etc.)
— **wax** *vt* : encerar — **waxy** *adj*
waxier; -est : ceroso
way *n* **1** : camino *m* **2** MEANS : manera *f*,
modo *m* **3 by the way** : a propósito,
por cierto **4 by way of** : vía, pasando
por **5 come a long way** : hacer grandes
progresos **6 get in the way** : meterse en
el camino **7 get one's own way** : salirse
uno con la suya **8 mend one's ways** :
dejar las malas costumbres **9 out of**
the way REMOTE : remoto, recóndito **10**
which way did he go? : ¿por dónde fue?
we *pron* : nosotros, nosotras
weak *adj* **1** : débil **2** DILUTED : aguado
3 a weak excuse : una excusa poco
convincente — **weaken** *vt* : debilitar — *vi*
: debilitarse — **weakling** *n* : debilucho *m,*
-cha *f* — **weakly** *adv* : débilmente —
weakly *adj* **weaklier; -est** : enfermizo

— **weakness** *n* **1** : debilidad *f* **2**
FLAW : flaqueza *f*, punto *m* débil
wealth *n* : riqueza *f* — **wealthy** *adj*
wealthier; -est : rico
wean *vt* : destetar
weapon *n* : arma *f*
wear *v* **wore; worn; wearing** *vt* **1** : llevar
(ropa, etc.), calzar (zapatos) **2** *or* **wear**
away : desgastar **3 wear oneself out**
: agotarse **4 wear out** : gastar — *vi* **1**
LAST : durar **2 wear off** : desaparecer
3 wear out : gastarse — **wear** *n* **1**
USE : uso *m* **2** CLOTHING : ropa *f* **3 be**
the worse for wear : estar deteriorado
— **wear and tear** *n* : desgaste *m*
weary *adj* **-rier; -est** : cansado —
weary *v* **-ried; -rying** *vt* : cansar — *vi* :
cansarse — **weariness** *n* : cansancio *m*
— **wearisome** *adj* : cansado
weasel *n* : comadreja *f*
weather *n* : tiempo *m* — **weather** *vt* **1**
WEAR : erosionar, desgastar **2** ENDURE,
OVERCOME : superar — **weather–**
beaten *adj* : curtido — **weatherman** *n,*
pl **-men** : meteorólogo *m*, -ga *f*
— **weather vane** *n* : valeta *f*
weave *v* **wove** *or* **weaved; woven** *or*
weaved; weaving *vt* **1** : tejer (tela) **2**
INTERLACE : entretejer **3 weave one's way**
: abrirse camino — *vi* : tejer — **weave** *n*
: tejido *m* — **weaver** *n* : tejedor *m*, -dora *f*
web *n* **1** : telaraña *f* (de araña)
2 : membrana *f* interdigital (de
aves) **3** NETWORK : red *f*

watermelon
sandía[F]

whales and other marine mammals
balllenas*F* y otras mamiferos*M* acuáticos

porpoise
*marsopa*F

narwhal
*narval*M

dolphin
*delfín*M

killer whale
*orca*F

northern right whale
*ballena*F *franca del norte*M

sperm whale
*cachalote*M

wed *v* **wedded; wedding** *vt* :
casarse con — *vi* : casarse
we'd (*contraction of* **we had, we should,**
or **we would**) → **have, should, would**
wedding *n* : boda *f*, casamiento *m*
wedge *n* **1** : cuña *f* **2** PIECE : porción *f*,
trozo *m* — **wedge** *vt* **wedged; wedging**
1 : apretar (con una cuña) **2** CRAM : meter
Wednesday *n* : miércoles *m*
wee *adj* **1** : pequeñito **2 in the**
wee hours : a las altas horas
weed *n* : mala hierba *f* — **weed** *vt* **1**
: desherbar **2 weed out** : eliminar
week *n* : semana *f* — **weekday** *n*
: día *m* laborable — **weekend** *n* :
fin *m* de semana — **weekly** *adv* :
semanalmente — **weekly** *adj* : semanal
— **weekly** *n, pl* **-lies** : semanario *m*
weep *v* **wept; weeping** : llorar —
weeping willow *n* : sauce *m* llorón —
weepy *adj* **weepier; -est** : lloroso
weigh *vt* **1** : pesar **2** CONSIDER :
sopesar **3 weigh down** : sobrecargar
(con una carga), abrumar (con
preocupaciones, etc.) — *vi* : pesar
weight *n* **1** : peso *m* **2 gain weight** :
engordar **3 lose weight** : adelgazar —
weighty *adj* **weightier; -est 1** HEAVY :
pesado **2** IMPORTANT : importante, de peso
weird *adj* **1** : misterioso

2 STRANGE : extraño
welcome *vt* **-comed; -coming** : dar la
bienvenida a, recibir — **welcome** *adj* **1**
: bienvenido **2 you're welcome** : de nada
— **welcome** *n* : bienvenida *f*, acojida *f*
weld *v* : soldar
welfare *n* **1** WELL-BEING : bienestar *m* **2**
AID : asistencia *f* social
well[1] *adv* **better; best 1** : bien **2**
CONSIDERABLY : bastante **3 as well** :
también **4 as well as** : además de
— **well** *adj* : bien — **well** *interj* **1**
(*used to introduce a remark*) : bueno
2 (*used to express surprise*) : ¡vaya!
well[2] *n* : pozo *m* — **well** *vi or*
well up : brotar, manar
we'll (*contraction of* **we shall**
or **we will**) → **shall, will**
well–being *n* : bienestar *m* — **well–**
bred *adj* : fino, bien educado — **well–**
done *adj* **1** : bien hecho **2** : bien cocido
(dícese de la carne, etc.) — **well–**
known *adj* : famoso, bien conocido —
well–meaning *adj* : bienintencionado
— **well–off** *adj* : acomodado — **well–**
rounded *adj* : completo — **well–**
to–do *adj* : próspero, adinerado
Welsh *adj* : galés — **Welsh** *n* **1** : galés *m*
(idioma) **2 the Welsh** : los galeses
went → **go**

wept → **weep**
were → **be**
we're (*contraction of* **we are**) → **be**
weren't (*contraction of* **were not**) → **be**
west *adv* : al oeste — **west** *adj* : oeste, del
oeste — **west** *n* **1** : oeste *m* **2 the West**
: el Oeste, el Occidente — **westerly** *adv*
& *adj* : del oeste — **western** *adj* **1** :
del oeste **2 Western** : occidental —
Westerner *n* : habitante *mf* del oeste —
westward *adv* & *adj* : hacia el oeste
wet *adj* **wetter; wettest 1** : mojado **2**
RAINY : lluvioso **3 wet paint** : pintura *f*
fresca — **wet** *vt* **wet** *or* **wetted;**
wetting : mojar, humedecer
we've (*contraction of* **we have**) → **have**
whack *vt* : golpear fuertemente
— **whack** *n* : golpe *m* fuerte
▸ **whale** *n, pl* **whales** *or* **whale** : ballena *f*
wharf *n, pl* **wharves** : muelle *m*,
embarcadero *m*
what *adj* **1** (*used in questions and*
exclamations) : qué **2** WHATEVER : cualquier
— **what** *pron* **1** (*used in questions*) :
qué **2** (*used in indirect statements*) : lo
que, que **3 what does it cost?** : ¿cuánto
cuesta? **4 what for?** : ¿por qué? **5 what**
if : y si — **whatever** *adj* **1** : cualquier **2**
there's no chance whatever : no hay
ninguna posibilidad **3 nothing whatever**

humpback whale
ballena[F] *jorobada*

beluga whale
ballena[F] *blanca*

: nada en absoluto — **whatever** pron **1**
ANYTHING : lo que **2** (used in questions) :
qué **3 whatever it may be** : sea lo que sea
— **whatsoever** adj & pron → **whatever**
wheat n : trigo m
wheedle vt **-dled; -dling** : engatusar
wheel n **1** : rueda f **2** or **steering**
wheel : volante m (de automóviles,
etc.), timón m (de barcos) — **wheel** vt
: empujar (algo sobre ruedas) — vi
or **wheel around** : darse la vuelta
— **wheelbarrow** n : carretilla f —
wheelchair n : silla f de ruedas
wheeze vi **wheezed; wheezing** :
resollar — **wheeze** n : resuello m
when adv : cuándo — **when** conj **1**
: cuando **2 the days when I clean
the house** : los días (en) que limpio
la casa — **when** pron : cuándo —
whenever adv : cuando sea —
whenever conj **1** : cada vez que **2
whenever you like** : cuando quieras
where adv **1** : dónde **2 where are you
going?** : ¿adónde vas? — **where** conj
& pron : donde — **whereabouts** adv :
(por) dónde — **whereabouts** ns & pl
: paradero m — **wherever** adv **1** : en

cualquier parte **2** WHERE : dónde, adónde
— **wherever** conj : dondequiera que
whet vt **whetted; whetting 1** : afilar **2
whet the appetite** : estimular el apetito
whether conj **1** : si **2 we doubt
whether he'll show up** : dudamos
que aparezca **3 whether you like it
or not** : tanto si quieras como si no
which adj **1** : qué, cuál **2 in which
case** : en cuyo caso — **which** pron **1**
(used in questions) : cuál **2** (used in
relative clauses) : que, el (la) cual
— **whichever** adj : cualquier —
whichever pron : el (la) que, cualquiera que
whiff n **1** PUFF : soplo m **2**
SMELL : olorcillo m
while n **1** : rato m **2 be worth one's
while** : valer la pena **3 in a while** : dentro
de poco — **while** conj **1** : mientras **2**
WHEREAS : mientras que **3** ALTHOUGH :
aunque — **while** vt **whiled; whiling**
while away the time : matar el tiempo
whim n : capricho m, antojo m
whimper vi : lloriquear —
whimper n : quejido m
whimsical adj : caprichoso, fantasioso
whine vi **whined; whining 1** :

gimotear 2 COMPLAIN : quejarse —
whine n : quejido m, gemido m
whip v **whipped; whipping** vt **1** : azotar
2 BEAT : batir (huevos, crema, etc.) **3
whip up** AROUSE : avivar, despertar — vi
FLAP : agitarse — **whip** n : látigo m
whir vi **whirred; whirring** : zumbar
— **whir** n : zumbido m
whirl vi **1** : dar vueltas, girar **2** or
whirl about : arremolinarse —
whirl n **1** : giro m **2** SWIRL : torbellino m
— **whirlpool** n : remolino m —
whirlwind n : torbellino m
whisk vt **1** : batir **2 whisk away** :
llevarse — **whisk** n or **egg whisk** :
batidor m — **whisk broom** n : escobilla f
whisker n **1** : pelo m (de la barba) **2**
whiskers npl : bigotes mpl (de animales)
whiskey or whisky n, pl **-keys**
or **-kies** : whisky m
whisper vi : cuchichear, susurrar — vt
: susurrar — **whisper** n : susurro m
whistle v **-tled; -tling** vi **1** : silbar,
chiflar Lat **2** : pitar (dícese de un tren,
etc.) — vt : silbar — **whistle** n **1**
: silbido m, chiflido m (sonido) **2** :
silbato m, pito m (instrumento)
white adj **whiter; -est** : blanco —
white n **1** : blanco m (color) **2** : clara f (de
huevos) **3** or **white person** : blanco m,
-ca f — **white–collar** adj **1** : de oficina
2 white–collar worker : oficinista mf —
whiten vt : blanquear — **whiteness** n :
blancura f — **whitewash** vt **1** : enjalbegar
2 CONCEAL : encubrir (un escándalo,
etc.) — **whitewash** n **1** : jalbegue m,
lechada f **2** COVER-UP : encubrimiento m
whittle vt **-tled; -tling 1** : tallar
(madera) **2** or **whittle down** : reducir
whiz or whizz vi **whizzed; whizzing 1** BUZZ
: zumbar **2 whiz by** : pasar muy rápido —
whiz or whizz n, pl **whizzes** : zumbido m
— **whiz kid** n : joven m prometedor
who pron **1** (used in direct and
indirect questions) : quién **2** (used
in relative clauses) : que, quien —
whodunit n : novela f policíaca —
whoever pron **1** : quienquiera que,
quien **2** (used in questions) : quién
whole adj **1** : entero **2** INTACT :
intacto **3 a whole lot** : muchísimo —
whole n **1** : todo m **2 as a whole** : en
conjunto **3 on the whole** : en general
— **wholehearted** adj : sincero —
wholesale n : venta f al por mayor

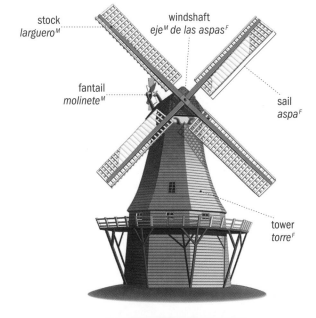

windmill: smock mill
molino^M de viento^M: molino^M de plataforma^F

stock
larguero^M

windshaft
eje^M de las aspas^F

fantail
molinete^M

sail
aspa^F

tower
torre^F

structure of a window
estructura^f **de una ventana**^f

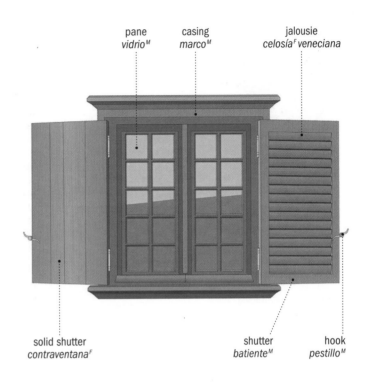

pane
vidrio^M

casing
marco^M

jalousie
celosía^F *veneciana*

solid shutter
contraventana^F

shutter
batiente^M

hook
pestillo^M

— **whole** *adj* **1** : al por mayor **2 whole slaughter** : matanza *f* sistemática — **whole** *adv* : al por mayor — **wholesaler** *n* : mayorista *mf* — **wholesome** *adj* : sano — **whole wheat** *adj* : de trigo integral — **wholly** *adv* : completamente

whom *pron* **1** (*used in direct questions*) : a quién **2** (*used in indirect questions*) : de quién, con quién, en quién **3** (*used in relative clauses*) : que, a quien

whooping cough *n* : tos *f* ferina

whore *n* : puta *f*

whose *adj* **1** (*used in questions*) : de quién **2** (*used in relative clauses*) : cuyo — **whose** *pron* : de quién

why *adv* : por qué — **why** *n*, *pl* **whys** : porqué *m* — **why** *conj* : por qué — **why** *interj* (*used to express surprise*) : ¡vaya!, ¡mira!

wick *n* : mecha *f*

wicked *adj* **1** : malo, malvado **2** MISCHIEVOUS : travieso **3** TERRIBLE : terrible, horrible — **wickedness** *n* : maldad *f*

wicker *n* : mimbre *m* — **wicker** *adj* : de mimbre

wide *adj* **wider; widest 1** : ancho **2** VAST : amplio, extenso **3** *or* **wide of the mark** : desviado — **wide** *adv* **1 wide apart** : muy separados **2 far and wide** : por todas partes **3 wide open** : abierto de par en par — **wide–awake** *adj* : (completamente) despierto — **widely** *adv* : extensivamente — **widespread** *adj* : extendido

widow *n* : viuda *f* — **widow** *vt* : dejar viuda — **widower** *n* : viudo *m*

width *n* : ancho *m*, anchura *f*

wield *vt* **1** : usar, manejar **2** EXERT : ejercer

wiener → **frankfurter**

wife *n*, *pl* **wives** : esposa *f*, mujer *f*

wig *n* : peluca *f*

wiggle *v* **-gled; -gling** *vt* : menear, contonear — *vi* : menearse — **wiggle** *n* : meneo *m*

wigwam *n* : wigwam *m*

wild *adj* **1** : salvaje **2** DESOLATE : agreste **3** UNRULY : desenfrenado **4** RANDOM : al azar **5** FRANTIC : frenético **6** OUTRAGEOUS : extravagante — **wild** *adv* **1** → **wildly 2 run wild** : volver al estado silvestre (dícese de las plantas), desmandarse (dícese de los niños) — **wildcat** *n* : gato *m* montés — **wilderness** *n* : yermo *m*, desierto *m* — **wildfire** *n* **1** : fuego *m* descontrolado **2 spread like wildfire** : propagarse como un reguero de pólvora — **wildflower** *n*

: flor *f* silvestre — **wildlife** *n* : fauna *f* — **wildly** *adv* **1** FRANTICALLY : frenéticamente **2** EXTREMELY : locamente

will¹ *v past* **would;** *pres sing & pl* **will** *vi* WISH : querer — *v aux* **1 tomorrow we will go shopping** : mañana iremos de compras **2 he will get angry over nothing** : se pone furioso por cualquier cosa **3 I will go despite them** : iré a pesar de ellos **4 I won't do it** : no lo haré **5 that will be the mailman** : eso ha de ser el cartero **6 the couch will hold three people** : en el sofá cabrán tres personas **7 accidents will happen** : los accidentes ocurrirán **8 you will do as I say** : harás lo que digo

will² *n* **1** : voluntad *f* **2** TESTAMENT : testamento *m* **3 free will** : libre albedrío *m* — **willful** *or* **wilful** *adj* **1** OBSTINATE : terco **2** INTENTIONAL : intencionado — **willing** *adj* **1** : complaciente **2 to be willing to** : estar dispuesto a — **willingly** *adv* : con gusto — **willingness** *n* : buena voluntad *f*

willow *n* : sauce *m*

willpower *n* : fuerza *f* de voluntad

wilt *vi* : marchitarse

wily *adj* **wilier; -est** : artero, astuto

win *v* **won; winning** *vi* : ganar — *vt* **1** : ganar, conseguir **2 win over** : ganarse a — **win** *n* : triunfo *m*, victoria *f*

wince *vi* **winced; wincing** : hacer una mueca de dolor — **wince** *n* : mueca *f* de dolor

winch *n* : torno *m*

wind¹ *n* **1** : viento *m* **2** BREATH : aliento *m* **3** FLATULENCE : flatulencia *f* **4 get wind of** : enterarse de

wind² *v* **wound; winding** *vi* : serpentear — *vt* **1** COIL : enrollar **2 wind a clock** : dar cuerda a un reloj

windfall *n* : beneficio *m* imprevisto

winding *adj* : tortuoso

wind instrument *n* : instrumento *m* de viento

▸ **windmill** *n* : molino *m* de viento

▸ **window** *n* : ventana *f* (de un edificio

woodpecker
pájaro^M **carpintero**

o una computadora), ventanilla *f* (de
un vehículo), vitrina *f* (de una tienda)
— **windowpane** *n* : vidrio *m* —
windowsill *n* : repisa *f* de la ventana
windpipe *n* : tráquea *f*
windshield *n* **1** : parabrisas *m* **2**
windshield wiper : limpiaparabrisas *m*
window–shop *vi* **-shopped;**
-shopping : mirar las vitrinas
wind up *vt* : terminar, concluir
— *vi* : terminar, acabar —
windup *n* : conclusión *f*
windy *adj* **windier; -est 1** : ventoso
2 it's windy : hace viento
wine *n* : vino *m* — **wine cellar** *n* : bodega *f*
wing *n* **1** : ala *f* **2 under**
someone's wing : bajo el cargo
de algn — **winged** *adj* : alado
wink *vi* : guiñar — **wink** *n* **1** : guiño *m* **2**
not sleep a wink : no pegar el ojo
winner *n* : ganador *m*, -dora *f* —
winning *adj* **1** : ganador **2** CHARMING :
encantador — **winnings** *npl* : ganancias *fpl*
winter *n* : invierno *m* — **winter** *adj* :
invernal, de invierno — **wintergreen** *n*
: gaulteria *f* — **wintertime** *n* :
invierno *m* — **wintry** *adj* **wintrier;**
-est : invernal, de invierno
wipe *vt* **wiped; wiping 1** : limpiar **2 wipe**
away : enjugar (lágrimas), borrar (una
memoria) **3 wipe out** : aniquilar, destruir

— **wipe** *n* : pasada *f* (con un trapo, etc.)
wire *n* **1** : allmbre *m* **2** : cable *m*
(eléctrico o telefónico) **3** TELEGRAM
: telegrama *m* — **wire** *vt* **-wired;**
wiring 1 : instalar el cableado en (una
casa, etc.) **2** BIND : atar con alambre **3**
TELEGRAPH : enviar un telegrama a —
wireless *adj* : inalámbrico — **wiring** *n*
: cableado *m* — **wiry** *adj* **wirier; -est**
1 : hirsuto, tieso (dícese del pelo) **2** :
esbelto y musculoso (dícese del cuerpo)
wisdom *n* : sabiduría *f* — **wisdom**
tooth *n* : muela *f* de juicio
wise *adj* **wiser; wisest 1** : sabio **2** SENSIBLE
: prudente — **wisecrack** *n* : broma *f*,
chiste *m* — **wisely** *adv* : sabiamente
wish *vt* **1** : desear **2 wish someone**
well : desear lo mejor a algn — *vi* **1**
: pedir (como deseo) **2 as you wish** :
como quieras — **wish** *n* **1** : deseo *m* **2**
best wishes : muchos recuerdos —
wishbone *n* : espoleta *f* — **wishful** *adj* **1** :
deseoso **2 wishful thinking** : ilusiones *fpl*
wishy–washy *adj* : insípido, soso
wisp *n* **1** : mechón *m* (de pelo)
2 : voluta *f* (de humo)
wistful *adj* : melancólico
wit *n* **1** CLEVERNESS : ingenio *m* **2**
HUMOR : agudeza *f* **3 at one's wit's**
end : desesperado **4 scared out of**
one's wits : muerto de miedo
witch *n* : bruja *f* — **witchcraft** *n*
: brujería *f*, hechicería *f*
with *prep* **1** : con **2 I'm going with you** :
voy contigo **3 it varies with the season**
: varía según la estación **4 the girl with**

red hair : la muchacha de pelo rojo **5**
with all his work, the business failed : a
pesar de su trabajo, el negocio fracasó
withdraw *v* **-drew; -drawn;**
-drawing *vt* : retirar — *vi* : apartarse
— **withdrawal** *n* **1** : retirada *f* **2**
: abandono (de drogas, etc.) —
withdrawn *adj* : introvertido
wither *vi* : marchitarse
withhold *vt* **-held; -holding** : retener
(fondos), negar (permiso, etc.)
within *adv* : dentro — **within** *prep* **1** :
dentro de **2** (*in expressions of distance*)
: a menos de **3** (*in expressions of time*)
: dentro de, en menos de **4 within**
reach : al alcance de la mano
without *adv* **do without** : pasar
sin algo — **without** *prep* : sin
withstand *vt* **-stood; -standing 1**
BEAR : aguantar **2** RESIST : resistir
witness *n* **1** : testigo *mf* **2** EVIDENCE
: testimonio *m* **3 bear witness** :
atestiguar — **witness** *vt* **1** SEE : ser
testigo de **2** : atestiguar (una firma, etc.)
witticism *n* : agudeza *f*, ocurrencia *f*
witty *adj* **-tier; -est** : ingenioso, ocurrente
wives → **wife**
wizard *n* **1** : mago *m*, brujo *m* **2 a math**
wizard : un genio de matemáticas
wizened *adj* : arrugado
wobble *vi* **-bled; -bling 1** :
tambalearse **2** : temblar (dícese de
la voz, etc.) — **wobbly** *adj* : cojo
woe *n* **1** : aflicción *f* **2 woes** *npl* TROUBLES
: penas *fpl* — **woeful** *adj* : triste
woke, woken → **wake**
▸ **wolf** *n*, *pl* **wolves** : lobo *m*, -ba *f* —
wolf *vt or* **wolf down** : engullir
woman *n*, *pl* **women** : mujer *f*
— **womanly** *adj* : femenino
womb *n* : útero *m*, matriz *f*
won → **win**
wonder *n* **1** MARVEL : maravilla *f* **2**
AMAZEMENT : asombro *m* — **wonder** *v*
: preguntarse — **wonderful** *adj*
: maravilloso, estupendo
won't (*contraction of* **will not**) → **will**
woo *vt* **1** COURT : cortejar **2** : buscar el
apoyo de (clientes, votantes, etc.)
▸ **wood** *n* **1** : madera *f* (materia) **2** FIREWOOD
: leña *f* **3** *or* **woods** *npl* FOREST : bosque *m*
— **wood** *adj* : de madera — **woodchuck** *n*
: marmota *f* de América — **wooded** *adj*
: arbolado, boscoso — **wooden** *adj* : de
▸ madera — **woodpecker** *n* : pájaro *m*

wolf
lobo^M

wood carving: tools and steps
talla^F en madera^F: utensilios^M y etapas^F

drawing
diseño^M

riffler
bruñidor^M *con rascador*^M

knife
cuchillo^M *de contornear*

roughing out
desbaste^M

block cutter
escoplo^M *redondo*

carving
talla^F

firmer chisel
formón^M

finishing
acabado^M

rasp
escofina^F

carpintero — **woodshed** n : leñera f — **woodwind** n : instrumento m de viento de madera — **woodwork** n : carpintería f
wool n : lana f — **woolen** or **woollen** adj : de lana — **wool** n 1 : lana f (tela) 2 **wools** npl : prendas fpl de lana — **woolly** adj **-lier; -est** : lanudo
word n 1 : palabra f 2 NEWS : noticias fpl 3 **words** npl : letra f (de una canción, etc.) 4 **have words with** : reñir con 5 **just say the word** : no tienes que decirlo 6 **keep one's word** : cumplir su palabra — **word** vt : expresar — **word processing** n : procesamiento m de textos — **word processor** n : procesador m de textos — **wordy** adj **wordier; -est** : prolijo
wore → **wear**
work n 1 LABOR : trabajo m 2 EMPLOYMENT : trabajo m, empleo m 3 : obra f (de arte, etc.) 4 **works** npl FACTORY : fábrica f 5 **works** npl MECHANISM : mecanismo m — **work** v **worked** or **wrought; working** vt 1 : hacer trabajar (a una persona) 2 : manejar, operar (una máquina, etc.) — vi 1 : trabajar 2 FUNCTION : funcionar 3 : surtir efecto (dícese de una droga), resultar (dícese de una idea, etc.) — **worked up** adj : nervioso — **worker** n : trabajador m, -dora f; obrero m, -ra f — **working** adj 1 : que trabaja (dícese de personas), de trabajo (dícese de la ropa, etc.) 2 **to be in working order** : funcionar bien — **working class** n : clase f obrera — **workingman** n, pl **-men** : obrero m — **workman** n, pl **-men** 1 : obrero m 2 ARTISAN : artesano m — **workmanship** n : artesanía f, destreza f — **workout** n : ejercicios mpl (físicos) — **work out** vt 1 DEVELOP : elaborar 2 SOLVE : resolver — vi 1 TURN OUT : resultar 2 SUCCEED : lograr, salir bien 3 EXERCISE : hacer ejercicio — **workshop** n : taller m — **work up** vt 1 EXCITE : ponerse como loco 2 GENERATE : desarrollar
world n : mundo m 2 **think the world of someone** : tener a algn en alta estima — **world** adj : mundial, del mundo — **worldly** adj : mundano — **worldwide** adv : en todo el mundo — **worldwide** adj : global, mundial
worm n 1 : gusano m, lombriz f 2 **worms** npl : lombrices fpl (parásitos)
worn → **wear** — **worn-out** adj 1 USED : gastado 2 TIRED : agotado
worry v **-ried; -rying** vt : preocupar, inquietar — vi : preocuparse, inquietarse

— **worry** n, pl **-ries** : preocupación f — **worried** adj : preocupado — **worrisome** adj : inquietante
worse adv (comparative of bad or of ill) : peor — **worse** adj (comparative of bad or of ill) 1 : peor 2 **from bad to worse** : de mal en peor 3 **get worse** : empeorar — **worse** n 1 **the worse** : el (la) peor, lo peor 2 **take a turn for the worse** : ponerse peor — **worsen** v : empeorar
worship v **-shiped** or **-shipped; -shiping** or **-shipping** vt : adorar — vi : practicar una religión — **worship** n : adoración f, culto m — **worshiper** or **worshipper** n : adorador m, -dora f
worst adv (superlative of ill or of bad or badly) : peor — **worst** adj (superlative of bad or of ill) : peor — **worst** n **the worst** : lo peor, el (la) peor
worth n 1 : valor m (monetario) 2 MERIT : mérito m, valía f 3 **ten dollars' worth of gas** : diez dólares de gasolina — **worth** prep 1 **it's worth $10** : vale $10 2 **it's worth doing** : vale la pena hacerlo — **worthless** adj 1 : sin valor 2 USELESS : inútil — **worthwhile** adj : que vale la pena — **worthy** adj **-thier; -est** : digno
would past of will 1 **he would often take his children to the park** : solía llevar a sus hijos al parque 2 **I would go if I had the money** : iría yo si tuviera el dinero 3 **I would rather go alone** : preferiría ir sola 4 **she would have won if she hadn't tripped** : habría ganado si no hubiera tropezado 5 **would you kindly help me with this?** : ¿tendría la bondad de ayudarme con esto? — **would-be** adj **a would-be poet** : un aspirante a poeta — **wouldn't** (contraction of **would not**) → **would**
wound[1] n : herida f — **wound** vt : herir
wound[2] → **wind**
wove, woven → **weave**
wrangle vi **-gled; -gling** : reñir — **wrangle** n : riña f, disputa f
wrap vt **wrapped; wrapping** 1 : envolver 2 **wrap up** FINISH : dar fin a — **wrap** n 1 : prenda f que envuelve (como un chal) 2 WRAPPER : envoltura f — **wrapper** n : envoltura f, envoltorio m — **wrapping** n : envoltura f, envoltorio m
wrath n : ira f, cólera f — **wrathful** adj : iracundo
wreath n, pl **wreaths** : corona f (de flores, etc.)

wreck n 1 WRECKAGE : restos mpl 2 RUIN : ruina f, desastre m 3 **be a nervous wreck** : tener los nervios destrozados — **wreck** vt : destrozar (un automóvil), naufragar (un barco) — **wreckage** n : restos mpl (de un buque naufragado, etc.), ruinas fpl (de un edificio)
wren n : chochín m
wrench vt 1 PULL : arrancar (de un tirón) 2 SPRAIN TWIST : torcerse — **wrench** n 1 TUG : tirón m, jalón m 2 SPRAIN : torcedura f 3 or **monkey wrench** : llave f inglesa
wrestle vi **-tled; -tling** : luchar — **wrestler** n : luchador m, -dora f — **wrestling** n : lucha f
wretch n : desgraciado m, -da f — **wretched** adj 1 : miserable 2 **wretch weather** : tiempo m espantoso
wriggle vi **-gled; -gling** : retorcerse, menearse
wring vt **wrung; wringing** 1 or **wring out** : escurrir (el lavado, etc.) 2 TWIST : retorcer 3 EXTRACT : arrancar (información, etc.)
wrinkle n : arruga f — **wrinkle** v **-kled; -kling** vt : arrugar — vi : arrugarse
wrist n : muñeca f — **wristwatch** n : reloj m de pulsera
writ n : orden f (judicial)
write v **wrote; written; writing** : escribir — **write down** vt : apuntar, anotar — **write off** vt CANCEL : cancelar — **writer** n : escritor m, -tora f
writhe vi **writhed; writhing** : retorcerse
writing n : escritura f
wrong n 1 INJUSTICE : injusticia f, mal m 2 : agravio m (en derecho) 3 **be in the wrong** : haber hecho mal — **wrong** adj **wronger; wrongest** 1 : malo 2 UNSUITABLE : inadecuado, inapropiado 3 INCORRECT : incorrecto, equivocado 4 **be wrong** : no tener razón — **wrong** adv : mal, incorrectamente — **wrong** vt **wronged; wronging** : ofender, ser injusto con — **wrongful** adj 1 UNJUST : injusto 2 UNLAWFUL : ilegal — **wrongly** adv 1 UNJUSTLY : injustamente 2 INCORRECTLY : mal
wrote → **write**
wrought iron n : hierro m forjado
wrung → **wring**
wry adj **wrier; wriest** : irónico, sardónico (dícese del humor)

X

x *n*, *pl* x's *or* xs : x *f*, vigésima
cuarta letra del alfabeto inglés
xenophobia *n* : xenofobia *f*
Xmas *n* : Navidad *f*
▸ **X ray** *n* **1** : rayo *m* X **2** *or* **X photograph**
: radiografía *f* — **x–ray** *vt* : radiografiar
xylophone *n* : xilófono *m*

Y

y *n*, *pl* y's *or* ys : y *f*, vigésima
quinta letra del alfabeto inglés
yacht *n* : yate *m*
yam *n* **1** : ñame *m* **2** SWEET
POTATO : batata *f*, boniato *m*

yank *vt* : tirar de, jalar *Lat* —
yank *n* : tirón *m*, jalón *m*, *Lat*
Yankee *n* : yanqui *mf*
yap *vi* **yapped; yapping** : ladrar
— **yap** *n* : ladrido *m*
yard *n* **1** : yarda *f* (medida) **2**
COURTYARD : patio *m* **3** : jardín *m* (de
una casa) — **yardstick** *n* **1** : vara *f*
(de medir) **2** CRITERION : criterio *m*
yarn *n* **1** : hilado *m* **2** TALE
: historia *f*, cuento *m*
yawn *vi* : bostezar — **yawn** *n* : bostezo *m*
year *n* **1** : año *m* **2 she's ten years
old** : tiene diez años **3 I haven't seen
them in years** : hace siglos que no
los veo — **yearbook** *n* : anuario *m* —
yearling *n* : animal *m* menor de dos

años — **yearly** *adv* **1** : anualmente
2 three times yearly : tres veces
al año — **yearly** *adj* : anual
yearn *vi* : anhelar — **yearning** *n*
: anhelo *m*, ansia *f*
yeast *n* : levadura *f*
yell *vi* : gritar, chillar — *vt* : gritar
— **yell** *n* : grito *m*, chillido *m*
yellow *adj* : amarillo — **yellow** *n* :
amarillo *m* — **yellowish** *adj* : amarillento
yelp *n* : gañido *m* — **yelp** *vi* : dar un gañido
yes *adv* **1** : sí **2 say yes** : decir
que sí — **yes** *n* : sí *m*
yesterday *adv* : ayer —
yesterday *n* **1** : ayer *m* **2 the day
before yesterday** : anteayer
yet *adv* **1** : aún, todavía **2 has he**

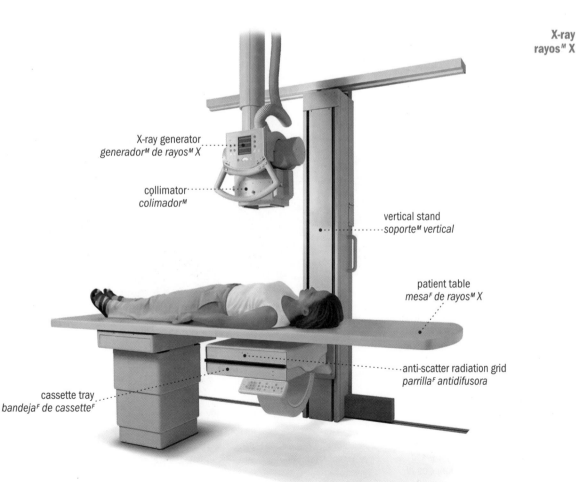

X-ray
rayosᴹ **X**

X-ray generator
generadorᴹ de rayosᴹ X

collimator
colimadorᴹ

vertical stand
soporteᴹ vertical

patient table
mesaᶠ de rayosᴹ X

anti-scatter radiation grid
parrillaᶠ antidifusora

cassette tray
bandejaᶠ de cassetteᶠ

come yet? : ¿ya ha venido? **3 not yet**
: todavía no **4 yet more problems** :
más problemas aún **5** NEVERTHELESS
: sin embargo — **yet** *conj* : pero
yield *vt* **1** PRODUCE : producir **2**
yield the right of way : ceder el
paso — *vi* : ceder — **yield** *n* :
rendimiento *m*, rédito *m* (en finanzas)
yoga *n* : yoga *m*
yogurt *n* : yogur *m*, yogurt *m*
yoke *n* : yugo *m*
yolk *n* : yema *f* (de un huevo)
you *pron* **1** (*used as subject — familiar*) :
tú; vos (*in some Latin American countries*);
ustedes *pl*; vosotros, vosotras *pl Spain* **2**
(*used as subject — formal*) : usted,
ustedes *pl* **3** (*used as indirect object
— familiar*) : te, les *pl* (se *before lo, la,
los, las*) , os *pl Spain* **4** (*used as indirect
object — formal*) : lo (*Spain sometimes*
le), la; los (*Spain sometimes* les), las / **5**
(*used after a preposition — familiar*) : ti;
vos (*in some Latin American countries*);
ustedes *pl*; vosotros, vosotras *pl Spain* **6**
(*used after a preposition — formal*) :
usted, ustedes *pl* **7 with you** (*familiar*)
: contigo; con ustedes *pl*; con vosotros,
con vosotras *pl Spain* **8 with you** (*formal*)
: con usted, con ustedes *pl* **9 you
never know** : nunca se sabe — **you'd**
(*contraction of* **you had** *or* **you would**)
→ **have, would** — **you'll** (*contraction
of* **you shall** *or* **you will**) → **shall, will**
young *adj* **younger; youngest 1** : joven
2 my younger brother : mi hermano
menor **3 she is the youngest** : es la
más pequeña **4 the young** : los jóvenes
— **young** *npl* : jóvenes *mfpl* (de los
humanos), crías *fpl* (de los animales) —
youngster *n* : chico *m*, -ca *f*; joven *mf*
your *adj* **1** (*familiar singular*) : tu **2**
(*familiar plural*) su, vuestro *Spain* **3**
(*formal*) : su **4 on your left** : a la izquierda
you're (*contraction of* **you are**) → **be**
yours *pron* **1** (*belonging to one person
— familiar*) : (el) tuyo, (la) tuya, (los)
tuyos, (las) tuyas **2** (*belonging to more
than one person — familiar*) : (el) suyo,
(la) suya, (los) suyos, (las) suyas; (el)
vuestro, (la) vuestra, (los) vuestros,
(las) vuestras *Spain* **3** (*formal*) : (el)
suyo, (la) suya, (los) suyos, (las) suyas
yourself *pron, pl* **yourselves 1** (*used
reflexively — familiar*) : te, se *pl*, os *pl
Spain* **2** (*used reflexively — formal*) : se **3**
(*used for emphasis*) : tú mismo, tú misma;

usted mismo, usted misma; ustedes
mismos, ustedes mismas *pl*; vosotros
mismos, vosotras mismas *pl Spain*
youth *n, pl* **youths 1** : juventud *f* **2**
BOY : joven *m* **3 today's youth** : los
jóvenes de hoy — **youthful** *adj* **1** :
juvenil, de juventud **2** YOUNG : joven
you've (*contraction of* **you have**) → **have**
yowl *vi* : aullar — **yowl** *n* : aullido *m*
yucca *n* : yuca *f*
Yugoslavian *adj* : yugoslavo
yule *n* CHRISTMAS : Navidad *f* —
yuletide *n* : Navidades *fpl*

z *n, pl* **z's** *or* **zs** : z *f*, vigésima
sexta letra del alfabeto inglés
zany *adj* **-nier; -est** : alocado, disparatado
zeal *n* : fervor *m*, celo *m* —
zealous *adj* : entusiasta

zebra *n* : cebra *f*
zenith *n* **1** : cenit *m* (en
astronomía) **2** PEAK : apogeo *m*
zero *n, pl* **-ros** : cero *m*
zest *n* **1** : gusto *m* **2** FLAVOR : sazón *f*
zigzag *n* : zigzag *m* — **zigzag** *vi*
-zagged; -zagging : zigzaguear
zinc *n* : cinc *m*, zinc *m*
zip *v* **zipped; zipping** *vt or* **zip up** :
cerrar la cremallera de, cerrar el cierre
de *Lat* — *vi* SPEED : pasarse volando
— **zip code** *n* : código *m* postal —
zipper *n* : cremallera *f*, cierre *m Lat*
zodiac *n* : zodíaco *m*
zone *n* : zona *f*
zoo *n, pl* **zoos** : zoológico *m*, zoo *m*
— **zoology** *n* : zoología *f*
zoom *vi* : zumbar, ir volando — **zoom** *n* **1**
: zumbido *m* **2** *or* **zoom lens** : zoom *m*
zucchini *n, pl* **-ni** *or* **-nis** :
calabacín *m*, calabacita *f Lat*

zoom and other lenses
zoom y otros objetivosᴹ

macro lens
*objetivo*ᴹ *macro*

wide-angle lens
*objetivo*ᴹ *gran angular*ᴹ

zoom lens
*objetivo*ᴹ *zoom*ᴹ

IPA PRONUNCIATION SYMBOLS
International Phonetic Alphabet

M-W PRONUNCIATION SYMBOLS
Merriam-Webster Phonetic System

VOWELS

æ	ask, bat, glad
ɑ	cot, bomb
a	*New England* **au**nt, *British* **a**sk, gl**a**ss, *Spanish* c**a**sa
ɛ	egg, bet, fed
ə	about, javelin, Alabama
ə	when italicized as in *ə*l, *ə*m, *ə*n, indicates a syllabic pronunciation of the consonant as in bott**le**, pris**m**, butt**on**
i	very, any, thirty, *Spanish* pi**ñ**a
i:	eat, bead, bee
ɪ	id, bid, pit
o	Ohio, yellower, potat**o**, *Spanish* **ó**valo
o:	oats, own, zone, blow
ɔ	awl, maul, caught, paw
ʊ	sure, should, could
u:	boot, few, coo
ʌ	under, putt, bud
eɪ	eight, wade, bay
aɪ	ice, bite, tie
aʊ	out, gown, plow
ɔɪ	oyster, coil, boy
:	indicates that the preceding vowel is long. Long vowels are almost always diphthongs in English, but not in Spanish.

CONSONANTS

b	**b**aby, la**b**or, ca**b**
d	**d**ay, rea**d**y, ki**d**
dʒ	**j**ust, ba**dg**er, fu**dg**e
ð	**th**en, ei**th**er, ba**th**e
f	**f**oe, tou**gh**, bu**ff**
g	**g**o, bi**gg**er, ba**g**
h	**h**ot, a**h**a
j	**y**es, vine**y**ard
k	**c**at, **k**eep, la**c**quer, flo**ck**
l	**l**aw, ho**ll**ow, boi**l**
m	**m**at, he**m**p, ha**mm**er, ri**m**
n	**n**ew, te**n**t, te**n**or, ru**n**
ŋ	ru**ng**, ha**ng**, swi**ng**er
p	**p**ay, la**p**se, to**p**
r	**r**ope, bu**r**n, ta**r**
s	**s**ad, mi**s**t, ki**ss**
ʃ	**sh**oe, mi**ss**ion, slu**sh**
t	**t**oe, bu**tt**on, ma**t**
t̬	indicates that some speakers of English pronounce this sound as a voiced alveolar flap [ɾ], as in la**t**er, ca**tt**y, ba**tt**le
tʃ	**ch**oose, ba**tch**
θ	**th**in, e**th**er, ba**th**
v	**v**at, ne**v**er, ca**v**e
w	**w**et, soft**w**are
z	**z**oo, ea**s**y, bu**zz**
ʒ	a**z**ure, bei**g**e
h, k, *p, t*	when italicized indicate sounds which are present in the pronunciation of some speakers of English but absent in the pronunciation of others, so that *whence* [ˈʍɛn*t*s] can be pronounced as [ˈhwɛns], [ˈʍɛnts], [ˈwɛnts], or [ˈwɛns].

STRESS MARKS

ˈ	high stress **pen**manship
ˌ	low stress penman**ship**

M-W column

ə	banana, collide, abut; raised \ᵊ\ in \ᵊl, ᵊn\ as in battle, cotton
ˈə, ˌə	humbug, abut
ər	operation, further
a	map, patch
ā	day, fate
ä	bother, cot, father
aù	now, out
b	baby, rib
ch	chin, catch
d	did, adder
e	set, red
ē	beat, nosebleed, easy
f	fifty, cuff
g	go, big
h	hat, ahead
hw	whale
i	tip, banish
ī	site, buy
j	job, edge
k	kin, cook
l	lily, cool
m	murmur, dim
n	nine, own
ŋ	sing, singer, finger, ink
ō	bone, hollow
ȯ	saw, cork
ȯi	toy, sawing
p	pepper, lip
r	rarity
s	source, less
sh	shy, mission
t	tie, attack
th	thin, ether
t̲h̲	then, either
ü	boot, few \ˈfyü\
u̇	put, pure \ˈpyu̇r\
v	vivid, give
w	we, away
y	yard, cue \ˈkyü\
z	zone, raise
zh	vision, pleasure
\	slant line used in pairs to mark the beginning and end of a transcription
( )	indicates sounds which are present in the pronunciation of some speakers of English but absent in the pronunciation of others

STRESS MARKS

ˈ	mark at the beginning of a syllable that has primary (strongest) stress: \ˈpenmənˌship\
ˌ	mark at the beginning of a syllable that has secondary (next-strongest) stress: \ˈpenmənˌship\

ENGLISH WORD	IPA	M-W	ENGLISH WORD	IPA	M-W
abandon	[ə'bændən]	\ə'bandⁿn\	adjacent	[ə'dʒeɪsənt]	\ə'jāsⁿnt\
abbreviate	[ə'bri:vi,eɪt]	\ə'brēvē,āt\	adjective	['ædʒɪktɪv]	\'ajiktiv\
abdomen	['æbdəmən; æb'do:mən]	\'abdəmən; ab'dōmən\	adjust	[ə'dʒʌst]	\ə'jəst\
ability	[ə'bɪləti]	\ə'bilətē\	admire	[æd'maɪr]	\ad'mīr\
able	['eɪbəl]	\'ābⁿl\	admit	[æd'mɪt, əd-]	\ad'mit, əd-\
abnormal	[æb'nɔrməl]	\ab'nórməl\	adolescent	[,ædəl'ɛsənt]	\,adⁿl'esⁿnt\
aboard	[ə'bord]	\ə'bōrd\	adopt	[ə'dɑpt]	\ə'däpt\
abort	[ə'bɔrt]	\ə'bórt\	adore	[ə'dor]	\ə'dōr\
abound	[ə'baʊnd]	\ə'baùnd\	adorn	[ə'dɔrn]	\ə'dórn\
about	[ə'baʊt]	\ə'baùt\	adult	[ə'dʌlt, 'æ,dʌlt]	\ə'dəlt, 'a,dəlt\
above	[ə'bʌv]	\ə'bəv\	advance	[æd'vænts, əd-]	\ad'van(t)s, əd-\
abroad	[ə'brɔd]	\ə'bród\	advantage	[əd'væntɪdʒ, æd-]	\əd'vantij, ad-\
absence	['æbsənts]	\'absⁿn(t)s\	adventure	[æd'vɛntʃər, əd-]	\ad'venchər, əd-\
absolute	['æbsə,lu:t]	\'absə,lüt\	adverb	['æd,vərb]	\'ad,vərb\
absorb	[əb'zɔrb, æb-, -'sɔrb]	\əb'zórb, ab-, -'sórb\	adversity	[æd'vərsəti, əd-]	\ad'vərsətē, əd-\
abstract	[æb'strækt, 'æb,-]	\ab'strakt, 'ab,-\	advertise	['ædvər,taɪz]	\'advər,tīz\
absurd	[əb'sərd, -'zərd]	\əb'sərd, -'zərd\	advice	[æd'vaɪs]	\ad'vīs\
abundant	[ə'bʌndənt]	\ə'bəndⁿnt\	advise	[æd'vaɪz, əd-]	\ad'vīz, əd-\
abuse	[ə'bju:z; ə'bju:s]	\ə'byüz; ə'byüs\	aerial	['æriəl]	\'arēəl\
academy	[ə'kædəmi]	\ə'kadəmē\	aerobics	[,ær'o:bɪks]	\,ar'ōbiks\
accelerate	[ɪk'sɛlə,reɪt, æk-]	\ik'selə,rāt, ak-\	affair	[ə'fær]	\ə'far\
accent	['æk,sɛnt, æk'sɛnt]	\'ak,sent, ak'sent\	affect	[ə'fɛkt, æ-]	\ə'fekt, a-\
accept	[ɪk'sɛpt, æk-]	\ik'sept, ak-\	affirm	[ə'fərm]	\ə'fərm\
access	['æk,sɛs]	\'ak,ses\	afflict	[ə'flɪkt]	\ə'flikt\
accident	['æksədənt]	\'aksədənt\	afford	[ə'ford]	\ə'fōrd\
acclaim	[ə'kleɪm]	\ə'klām\	afraid	[ə'freɪd]	\ə'frād\
accommodate	[ə'kɑmə,deɪt]	\ə'kämə,dāt\	African	['æfrɪkən]	\'afrikⁿn\
accompany	[ə'kʌmpəni, -'kɑm-]	\ə'kəmpənē, -'käm-\	after	['æftər]	\'aftər\
accomplish	[ə'kɑmplɪʃ, -'kʌm-]	\ə'kämplish, -'kəm-\	afternoon	[,æftər'nu:n]	\,aftər'nün\
accordion	[ə'kɔrdiən]	\ə'kórdēən\	afterward	['æftərwərd]	\'aftərwərd\
account	[ə'kaʊnt]	\ə'kaùnt\	again	[ə'gɛn, -'gɪn]	\ə'gen, -'gin\
accuse	[ə'kju:z]	\ə'kyüz\	against	[ə'gɛntst, -'gɪntst]	\ə'gen(t)st, -'gin(t)st\
ace	['eɪs]	\'ās\	age	['eɪdʒ]	\'āj\
ache	['eɪk]	\'āk\	agency	['eɪdʒəntsi]	\'ājⁿn(t)sē\
achieve	[ə'tʃi:v]	\ə'chēv\	agenda	[ə'dʒɛndə]	\ə'jendə\
acid	['æsəd]	\'asəd\	agent	['eɪdʒənt]	\'ājⁿnt\
acknowledge	[ɪk'nɑlɪdʒ, æk-]	\ik'nälij, ak-\	aggression	[ə'grɛʃən]	\ə'greshⁿn\
acne	['ækni]	\'aknē\	agile	['ædʒəl]	\'ajⁿl\
acorn	['eɪ,kɔrn, -kərn]	\'ā,kórn, -kərn\	agitate	['ædʒə,teɪt]	\'ajə,tāt\
acquire	[ə'kwaɪr]	\ə'kwīr\	ago	[ə'go:]	\ə'gō\
acrobat	['ækrə,bæt]	\'akrə,bat\	agony	['ægəni]	\'agənē\
across	[ə'krɔs]	\ə'krós\	agree	[ə'gri:]	\ə'grē\
act	['ækt]	\'akt\	agriculture	['ægrɪ,kʌltʃər]	\'agri,kəlchər\
action	['ækʃən]	\'akshⁿn\	ahead	[ə'hɛd]	\ə'hed\
activate	['æktə,veɪt]	\'aktə,vāt\	aid	['eɪd]	\'ād\
active	['æktɪv]	\'aktiv\	aim	['eɪm]	\'ām\
actor	['æktər]	\'aktər\	air	['ær]	\'ar\
actual	['æktʃuəl]	\'ak(t)chúəl\	ajar	[ə'dʒɑr]	\ə'jär\
acupuncture	['ækju,pʌŋktʃər]	\'akyù,pəŋk(t)chər\	alarm	[ə'lɑrm]	\ə'lärm\
acute	[ə'kju:t]	\ə'kyüt\	album	['ælbəm]	\'albəm\
adapt	[ə'dæpt]	\ə'dapt\	alcohol	['ælkə,hɔl]	\'alkə,hól\
add	['æd]	\'ad\	alert	[ə'lərt]	\ə'lərt\
addict	['ædɪkt]	\'adikt\	alga	['ælgə]	\'algə\
addition	[ə'dɪʃən]	\ə'dishⁿn\	algebra	['ældʒəbrə]	\'aljəbrə\
address	[ə'drɛs; 'æ,drɛs]	\ə'dres; 'a,dres\	alien	['eɪliən]	\'ālēən\
adhere	[æd'hɪr, əd-]	\ad'hir, əd-\	align	[ə'laɪn]	\ə'līn\

ENGLISH WORD	IPA	M-W	ENGLISH WORD	IPA	M-W
alike	[əˈlaɪk]	\əˈlīk\	annual	[ˈænjʊəl]	\ˈanyu̇əl\
alive	[əˈlaɪv]	\əˈlīv\	anonymous	[əˈnɑnəməs]	\əˈnänəməs\
all	[ˈɔl]	\ȯl\	another	[əˈnʌðər]	\əˈnəthər\
allergy	[ˈælərdʒi]	\ˈalərjē\	answer	[ˈæntsər]	\ˈan(t)sər\
alley	[ˈæli]	\ˈalē\	ant	[ˈænt]	\ˈant\
alliance	[əˈlaɪənts]	\əˈlīən(t)s\	antarctic	[æntˈɑrktɪk, -ˈɑrtɪk]	\antˈärktik, -ˈärtik\
alligator	[ˈæləˌgeɪtər]	\ˈaləˌgātər\	antenna	[ænˈtɛnə]	\anˈtenə\
allow	[əˈlaʊ]	\əˈlau̇\	anthem	[ˈænθəm]	\ˈanthəm\
ally	[əˈlaɪ, ˈæˌlaɪ]	\əˈlī, ˈaˌlī\	anthropology	[ˌænθrəˈpɑlədʒi]	\ˌanthrəˈpäləjē\
almanac	[ˈɔlməˌnæk, ˈæl-]	\ˈȯlməˌnak, ˈal-\	antibiotic	[ˌæntɪbaɪˈɑtɪk]	\ˌantēbīˈätik\
almond	[ˈɑmənd, ˈɑl-, ˈæ-, ˈæl-]	\ˈämənd, ˈäl-, ˈa-, ˈal-\	anticipate	[ænˈtɪsəˌpeɪt]	\anˈtisəˌpāt\
almost	[ˈɔlˌmoːst, ɔlˈmoːst]	\ˈȯlˌmōst, ȯlˈmōst\	antipathy	[ænˈtɪpəθi]	\anˈtipəthē\
alone	[əˈloːn]	\əˈlōn\	antiquity	[ænˈtɪkwəti]	\anˈtikwətē\
along	[əˈlɔŋ]	\əˈlȯŋ\	antisocial	[ˌæntiˈsoːʃəl, ˌæntaɪ-]	\ˌantēˈsōshᵊl, ˌantī-\
aloud	[əˈlaʊd]	\əˈlau̇d\	antonym	[ˈæntəˌnɪm]	\ˈantəˌnim\
alphabet	[ˈælfəˌbɛt]	\ˈalfəˌbet\	anxiety	[æŋkˈzaɪəti]	\aŋ(k)ˈzīətē\
already	[ɔlˈrɛdi]	\ȯlˈredē\	any	[ˈɛni]	\ˈenē\
also	[ˈɔlˌsoː]	\ˈȯlˌsō\	anyhow	[ˈɛniˌhaʊ]	\ˈenēˌhau̇\
altar	[ˈɔltər]	\ˈȯltər\	anymore	[ˌɛniˈmor]	\ˌenēˈmȯr\
alter	[ˈɔltər]	\ˈȯltər\	anyone	[ˈɛniˌwʌn]	\ˈenēˌwən\
alteration	[ˌɔltəˈreɪʃən]	\ˌȯltəˈrāshᵊn\	anything	[ˈɛniˌθɪŋ]	\ˈenēˌthiŋ\
alternate	[ˈɔltərnət, ˈɔltərˌneɪt]	\ˈȯltərnət, ˈȯltərˌnāt\	anytime	[ˈɛniˌtaɪm]	\ˈenēˌtīm\
although	[ɔlˈðoː]	\ȯlˈthō\	anywhere	[ˈɛniˌhwɛr]	\ˈenēˌ(h)wer\
altitude	[ˈæltəˌtuːd, -ˌtjuːd]	\ˈaltəˌtüd, -ˌtyüd\	apart	[əˈpɑrt]	\əˈpärt\
altogether	[ˌɔltəˈgɛðər]	\ˌȯltəˈgethər\	apartment	[əˈpɑrtmənt]	\əˈpärtmənt\
always	[ˈɔlwɪz, -ˌweɪz]	\ˈȯlwēz, -ˌwāz\	apostrophe	[əˈpɑstrəˌfiː]	\əˈpästrəˌfē\
amateur	[ˈæmətʃər]	\ˈaməchər\	apparent	[əˈpærənt]	\əˈparənt\
amaze	[əˈmeɪz]	\əˈmāz\	apparition	[ˌæpəˈrɪʃən]	\ˌapəˈrishᵊn\
ambassador	[æmˈbæsədər]	\amˈbasədər\	appear	[əˈpɪr]	\əˈpir\
ambition	[æmˈbɪʃən]	\amˈbishᵊn\	appendix	[əˈpɛndɪks]	\əˈpendiks\
ambulance	[ˈæmbjələnts]	\ˈambyəlᵊn(t)s\	appetite	[ˈæpəˌtaɪt]	\ˈapəˌtīt\
amen	[ˈeɪmɛn, ˈɑ-]	\ˈāˌmen, ˈä-\	applause	[əˈplɔz]	\əˈplȯz\
American	[əˈmɛrɪkən]	\əˈmerikᵊn\	apple	[ˈæpəl]	\ˈapᵊl\
amiss	[əˈmɪs]	\əˈmis\	appliance	[əˈplaɪənts]	\əˈplīən(t)s\
amnesia	[æmˈniːʒə]	\amˈnēzhə\	apply	[əˈplaɪ]	\əˈplī\
among	[əˈmʌŋ]	\əˈməŋ\	appoint	[əˈpɔɪnt]	\əˈpȯint\
amount	[əˈmaʊnt]	\əˈmau̇nt\	appreciate	[əˈpriːʃiˌeɪt, -ˈprɪ-]	\əˈprēshēˌāt, -ˈpri-\
amphibian	[æmˈfɪbiən]	\amˈfibēən\	apprentice	[əˈprɛntɪs]	\əˈprentis\
amuse	[əˈmjuːz]	\əˈmyüz\	approach	[əˈproːtʃ]	\əˈprōch\
analyze	[ˈænəˌlaɪz]	\ˈanəˌlīz\	appropriate	[əˈproːpriˌeɪt, əˈproːpriət]	
anatomy	[əˈnætəmi]	\əˈnatəmē\			\əˈprōprēˌāt, əˈprōprēət\
ancestor	[ˈænˌsɛstər]	\ˈanˌsestər\	approve	[əˈpruːv]	\əˈprüv\
anchor	[ˈæŋkər]	\ˈaŋkər\	approximate	[əˈprɑksəmət, əˈprɑksəˌmeɪt]	
ancient	[ˈeɪntʃənt]	\ˈān(t)chᵊnt\			\əˈpräksəmət, əˈpräksəˌmāt\
and	[ˈænd]	\ˈand\	apricot	[ˈæprəˌkɑt, ˈeɪ-]	\ˈaprəˌkät, ˈā-\
angel	[ˈeɪndʒəl]	\ˈānjəl\	April	[ˈeɪprəl]	\ˈāprəl\
anger	[ˈæŋgər]	\ˈaŋgər\	apron	[ˈeɪprən]	\ˈāprᵊn\
angle	[ˈæŋgəl]	\ˈaŋgəl\	apt	[ˈæpt]	\ˈapt\
angry	[ˈæŋgri]	\ˈaŋgrē\	aquarium	[əˈkwæriəm]	\əˈkwarēəm\
anguish	[ˈæŋgwɪʃ]	\ˈaŋgwish\	aquatic	[əˈkwɑtɪk, -ˈkwæ-]	\əˈkwätik, -ˈkwa-\
animal	[ˈænəməl]	\ˈanəmᵊl\	aqueduct	[ˈækwəˌdʌkt]	\ˈakwəˌdəkt\
ankle	[ˈæŋkəl]	\ˈaŋkᵊl\	Arab	[ˈærəb]	\ˈarəb\
anniversary	[ˌænəˈvɜrsəri]	\ˌanəˈvərsərē\	arch	[ˈɑrtʃ]	\ˈärch\
annotate	[ˈænəˌteɪt]	\ˈanəˌtāt\	archipelago	[ˌɑrkəˈpɛləˌgoː, ˌɑrtʃə-]	\ˌärkəˈpeləˌgō, ˌärchə-\
announce	[əˈnaʊnts]	\əˈnau̇n(t)s\	architecture	[ˈɑrkəˌtɛktʃər]	\ˈärkəˌtek(t)chər\
annoy	[əˈnɔɪ]	\əˈnȯi\	archives	[ˈɑrˌkaɪvz]	\ˈärˌkīvz\

ENGLISH WORD	IPA	M-W	ENGLISH WORD	IPA	M-W
arctic	[ˈɑrktɪk, ˈɑrt-]	\ˈärktik, ˈärt-\	athlete	[ˈæθˌliːt]	\ˈathˌlēt\
area	[ˈæriə]	\ˈarēə\	atlas	[ˈætləs]	\ˈatləs\
arena	[əˈriːnə]	\əˈrēnə\	atmosphere	[ˈætməˌsfɪr]	\ˈatməˌsfir\
Argentine	[ˈɑrdʒənˌtaɪn, -ˌtiːn]	\ˈärjənˌtīn, -ˌtēn\	atom	[ˈætəm]	\ˈatəm\
argue	[ˈɑrˌgjuː]	\ˈärˌgyü\	atomizer	[ˈætəˌmaɪzər]	\ˈatəˌmīzər\
arid	[ˈærəd]	\ˈarəd\	atrophy	[ˈætrəfi]	\ˈatrəfē\
arise	[əˈraɪz]	\əˈrīz\	attach	[əˈtætʃ]	\əˈtach\
arithmetic	[əˈrɪθməˌtɪk]	\əˈrithməˌtik\	attack	[əˈtæk]	\əˈtak\
arm	[ˈɑrm]	\ˈärm\	attempt	[əˈtɛmpt]	\əˈtempt\
armpit	[ˈɑrmˌpɪt]	\ˈärmˌpit\	attend	[əˈtɛnd]	\əˈtend\
army	[ˈɑrmi]	\ˈärmē\	attention	[əˈtɛntʃən]	\əˈtenchᵊn\
aroma	[əˈroːmə]	\əˈrōmə\	attitude	[ˈætəˌtuːd, -ˌtjuːd]	\ˈatəˌtüd, -ˌtyüd\
around	[əˈraʊnd]	\əˈraúnd\	attract	[əˈtrækt]	\əˈtrakt\
arrange	[əˈreɪndʒ]	\əˈrānj\	audacity	[ɔˈdæsəti]	\ȯˈdasətē\
arrest	[əˈrɛst]	\əˈrest\	audible	[ˈɔdəbəl]	\ˈȯdəbᵊl\
arrive	[əˈraɪv]	\əˈrīv\	audience	[ˈɔdiənts]	\ˈȯdēən(t)s\
arrow	[ˈæro]	\ˈarō\	audiovisual	[ˌɔdioˈvɪʒuəl]	\ˌȯdēōˈvizhúəl\
art	[ˈɑrt]	\ˈärt\	audition	[ɔˈdɪʃən]	\ȯˈdishᵊn\
artery	[ˈɑrtəri]	\ˈärtərē\	August	[ˈɔgəst]	\ˈȯgəst\
arthritis	[ɑrˈθraɪtəs]	\ärˈthrītəs\	aunt	[ˈænt, ˈɑnt]	\ˈant, ˈänt\
artichoke	[ˈɑrtəˌtʃoːk]	\ˈärtəˌchōk\	Australian	[ɔˈstreɪljən]	\ȯˈstrālyən\
article	[ˈɑrtɪkəl]	\ˈärtikᵊl\	authentic	[əˈθɛntɪk, ɔ-]	\əˈthentik, ȯ-\
articulate	[ɑrˈtɪkjəˌleɪt]	\ärˈtikyəˌlāt\	author	[ˈɔθər]	\ˈȯthər\
artificial	[ˌɑrtəˈfɪʃəl]	\ˌärtəˈfishᵊl\	authority	[əˈθɔrəti, ɔ-]	\əˈthȯrətē, ȯ-\
artillery	[ɑrˈtɪləri]	\ärˈtilərē\	autobiography	[ˌɔtəbaɪˈɑgrəfi]	\ˌȯtōbīˈägrəfē\
artist	[ˈɑrtɪst]	\ˈärtist\	autograph	[ˈɔtəˌgræf]	\ˈȯtəˌgraf\
as	[ˈæz]	\ˈaz\	automatic	[ˌɔtəˈmætɪk]	\ˌȯtəˈmatik\
ash	[ˈæʃ]	\ˈash\	autonomy	[ɔˈtɑnəmi]	\ȯˈtänəmē\
ashamed	[əˈʃeɪmd]	\əˈshāmd\	autopsy	[ˈɔˌtɑpsi, -təp-]	\ˈȯˌtäpsē, -təp-\
ashore	[əˈʃor]	\əˈshōr\	autumn	[ˈɔtəm]	\ˈȯtəm\
ashtray	[ˈæʃˌtreɪ]	\ˈashˌtrā\	auxiliary	[ɔgˈzɪljəri, -ˈzɪləri]	\ȯgˈzilyərē, -ˈzilərē\
Asian	[ˈeɪʒən, -ʃən]	\ˈāzhᵊn, -shᵊn\	available	[əˈveɪləbəl]	\əˈvāləbᵊl\
aside	[əˈsaɪd]	\əˈsīd\	avenge	[əˈvɛndʒ]	\əˈvenj\
ask	[ˈæsk]	\ˈask\	avenue	[ˈævəˌnuː, -ˌnjuː]	\ˈavəˌnü, -ˌnyü\
asleep	[əˈsliːp]	\əˈslēp\	average	[ˈævrɪdʒ, ˈævə-]	\ˈavrij, ˈavə-\
asparagus	[əˈspærəgəs]	\əˈsparəgəs\	aviation	[ˌeɪviˈeɪʃən]	\ˌāvēˈāshᵊn\
aspect	[ˈæˌspɛkt]	\ˈaˌspekt\	avocado	[ˌævəˈkɑdo, ˌɑvə-]	\ˌavəˈkädō, ˌävə-\
asphalt	[ˈæsˌfɔlt]	\ˈasˌfȯlt\	avoid	[əˈvɔɪd]	\əˈvȯid\
aspire	[əˈspaɪr]	\əˈspīr\	awake	[əˈweɪk]	\əˈwāk\
aspirin	[ˈæsprən, ˈæspə-]	\ˈasprən, ˈaspə-\	aware	[əˈwær]	\əˈwar\
assault	[əˈsɔlt]	\əˈsȯlt\	away	[əˈweɪ]	\əˈwā\
assign	[əˈsaɪn]	\əˈsīn\	awful	[ˈɔfəl]	\ˈȯfᵊl\
assist	[əˈsɪst]	\əˈsist\	awhile	[əˈhwaɪl]	\əˈ(h)wīl\
associate	[əˈsoːʃiˌeɪt]	\əˈsōshēˌāt\	awkward	[ˈɔkwərd]	\ˈȯkwərd\
assume	[əˈsuːm]	\əˈsüm\	axis	[ˈæksɪs]	\ˈaksis\
assure	[əˈʃʊr]	\əˈshùr\	baby	[ˈbeɪbi]	\ˈbābē\
asterisk	[ˈæstəˌrɪsk]	\ˈastəˌrisk\	baby-sit	[ˈbeɪbiˌsɪt]	\ˈbābēˌsit\
asthma	[ˈæzmə]	\ˈazmə\	bachelor	[ˈbætʃələr]	\ˈbachələr\
astonish	[əˈstɑnɪʃ]	\əˈstänish\	back	[ˈbæk]	\ˈbak\
astrology	[əˈstrɑlədʒi]	\əˈsträləjē\	bacon	[ˈbeɪkən]	\ˈbākᵊn\
astronaut	[ˈæstrəˌnɔt]	\ˈastrəˌnȯt\	bacteria	[bækˈtɪriə]	\bakˈtirēə\
astronomy	[əˈstrɑnəmi]	\əˈstränəmē\	bad	[ˈbæd]	\ˈbad\
astute	[əˈstuːt, -ˈstjuːt]	\əˈstüt, -ˈstyüt\	badly	[ˈbædli]	\ˈbadlē\
asylum	[əˈsaɪləm]	\əˈsīləm\	bag	[ˈbæg]	\ˈbag\
at	[ˈæt]	\ˈat\	baggage	[ˈbægɪdʒ]	\ˈbagij\
atheist	[ˈeɪθiɪst]	\ˈāthēist\	bail	[ˈbeɪl]	\ˈbāl\

ENGLISH WORD	IPA	M-W	ENGLISH WORD	IPA	M-W
bake	[ˈbeɪk]	\ˈbāk\	beast	[ˈbiːst]	\ˈbēst\
balance	[ˈbælənts]	\ˈbalən(t)s\	beat	[ˈbiːt]	\ˈbēt\
balcony	[ˈbælkəni]	\ˈbalkənē\	beauty	[ˈbjuːti]	\ˈbyütē\
bald	[ˈbɔld]	\ˈbȯld\	beaver	[ˈbiːvər]	\ˈbēvər\
ball	[ˈbɔl]	\ˈbȯl\	because	[bɪˈkʌz, -ˈkɔz]	\biˈkəz, -ˈkȯz\
ballad	[ˈbæləd]	\ˈbaləd\	become	[bɪˈkʌm]	\biˈkəm\
ballerina	[ˌbæləˈriːnə]	\ˌbaləˈrēnə\	bed	[ˈbɛd]	\ˈbed\
ballet	[bæˈleɪ, ˈbæˌleɪ]	\baˈlā, ˈbaˌlā\	bee	[ˈbiː]	\ˈbē\
ballpoint pen	[ˈbɔlˌpɔɪnt]	\ˈbȯlˌpȯint\	beech	[ˈbiːtʃ]	\ˈbēch\
bamboo	[bæmˈbuː]	\bamˈbü\	beef	[ˈbiːf]	\ˈbēf\
banana	[bəˈnænə]	\bəˈnanə\	beeline	[ˈbiːˌlaɪn]	\ˈbēˌlīn\
band	[ˈbænd]	\ˈband\	beep	[ˈbiːp]	\ˈbēp\
bandage	[ˈbændɪdʒ]	\ˈbandij\	beer	[ˈbɪr]	\ˈbir\
bandit	[ˈbændət]	\ˈbandət\	beet	[ˈbiːt]	\ˈbēt\
bang	[ˈbæŋ]	\ˈbaŋ\	beetle	[ˈbiːtəl]	\ˈbētᵊl\
bangle	[ˈbæŋgəl]	\ˈbaŋgᵊl\	before	[bɪˈfor]	\biˈfōr\
banister	[ˈbænəstər]	\ˈbanəstər\	beg	[ˈbɛg]	\ˈbeg\
bank	[ˈbæŋk]	\ˈbaŋk\	begin	[bɪˈgɪn]	\biˈgin\
banner	[ˈbænər]	\ˈbanər\	behalf	[bɪˈhæf, -ˈhaf]	\biˈhaf, -ˈhäf\
banquet	[ˈbæŋkwət]	\ˈbaŋkwət\	behave	[bɪˈheɪv]	\biˈhāv\
baptize	[bæpˈtaɪz, ˈbæpˌtaɪz]	\bapˈtīz, ˈbapˌtīz\	behind	[bɪˈhaɪnd]	\biˈhīnd\
bar	[ˈbɑr]	\ˈbär\	behold	[bɪˈhoːld]	\biˈhōld\
barbarian	[bɑrˈbæriən]	\bärˈbarēən\	beige	[ˈbeɪʒ]	\ˈbāzh\
barbecue	[ˈbɑrbɪˌkjuː]	\ˈbärbiˌkyü\	being	[ˈbiːɪŋ]	\ˈbēiŋ\
barber	[ˈbɑrbər]	\ˈbärbər\	belated	[bɪˈleɪtəd]	\biˈlātəd\
bare	[ˈbær]	\ˈbar\	Belgian	[ˈbɛldʒən]	\ˈbeljᵊn\
bargain	[ˈbɑrgən]	\ˈbärgən\	belie	[bɪˈlaɪ]	\biˈlī\
bark	[ˈbɑrk]	\ˈbärk\	belief	[bəˈliːf]	\bəˈlēf\
barley	[ˈbɑrli]	\ˈbärlē\	bell	[ˈbɛl]	\ˈbel\
barracks	[ˈbærəks]	\ˈbarəks\	belly	[ˈbɛli]	\ˈbelē\
barrel	[ˈbærəl]	\ˈbarəl\	belong	[bɪˈlɔŋ]	\biˈlȯŋ\
barrier	[ˈbæriər]	\ˈbarēər\	beloved	[bɪˈlʌvəd, -ˈlʌvd]	\biˈləvəd, -ˈləvd\
bartender	[ˈbɑrˌtɛndər]	\ˈbärˌtendər\	below	[bɪˈloː]	\biˈlō\
base	[ˈbeɪs]	\ˈbās\	belt	[ˈbɛlt]	\ˈbelt\
baseball	[ˈbeɪsˌbɔl]	\ˈbāsˌbȯl\	bench	[ˈbɛntʃ]	\ˈbench\
basement	[ˈbeɪsmənt]	\ˈbāsmənt\	bend	[ˈbɛnd]	\ˈbend\
basic	[ˈbeɪsɪk]	\ˈbāsik\	beneath	[bɪˈniːθ]	\biˈnēth\
basil	[ˈbeɪzəl, ˈbæzəl]	\ˈbāzᵊl, ˈbazᵊl\	benediction	[ˌbɛnəˈdɪkʃən]	\ˌbenəˈdikshᵊn\
basis	[ˈbeɪsəs]	\ˈbāsəs\	benefit	[ˈbɛnəfɪt]	\ˈbenəfit\
basket	[ˈbæskət]	\ˈbaskət\	berry	[ˈbɛri]	\ˈberē\
bat	[ˈbæt]	\ˈbat\	beside	[bɪˈsaɪd]	\biˈsīd\
batch	[ˈbætʃ]	\ˈbach\	best	[ˈbɛst]	\ˈbest\
bath	[ˈbæθ, ˈbɑθ]	\ˈbath, ˈbäth\	bestow	[bɪˈstoː]	\biˈstō\
baton	[bəˈtɑn]	\bəˈtän\	bet	[ˈbɛt]	\ˈbet\
battery	[ˈbætəri]	\ˈbatərē\	betray	[bɪˈtreɪ]	\biˈtrā\
battle	[ˈbætəl]	\ˈbatᵊl\	better	[ˈbɛtər]	\ˈbetər\
bay	[ˈbeɪ]	\ˈbā\	between	[bɪˈtwiːn]	\biˈtwēn\
bazaar	[bəˈzɑr]	\bəˈzär\	beverage	[ˈbɛvrɪdʒ, ˈbɛvə-]	\ˈbevrij, ˈbevə-\
be	[ˈbiː]	\ˈbē\	beware	[bɪˈwær]	\biˈwar\
beach	[ˈbiːtʃ]	\ˈbēch\	bewitch	[bɪˈwɪtʃ]	\biˈwich\
beak	[ˈbiːk]	\ˈbēk\	beyond	[biˈjɑnd]	\bēˈyänd\
beam	[ˈbiːm]	\ˈbēm\	bib	[ˈbɪb]	\ˈbib\
bean	[ˈbiːn]	\ˈbēn\	Bible	[ˈbaɪbəl]	\ˈbībᵊl\
bear	[ˈbær]	\ˈbar\	bicycle	[ˈbaɪsɪkəl, -ˌsɪ-]	\ˈbīsikᵊl, -ˌsi-\
beard	[ˈbɪrd]	\ˈbird\	big	[ˈbɪg]	\ˈbig\
bearing	[ˈbærɪŋ]	\ˈbariŋ\	bike	[ˈbaɪk]	\ˈbīk\

ENGLISH WORD	IPA	M-W	ENGLISH WORD	IPA	M-W
bikini	[bə'ki:ni]	\bə'kēnē\	bonfire	['bɑn͵faɪr]	\bän͵fīr\
bile	['baɪl]	\bīl\	bonus	['bo:nəs]	\bōnəs\
bill	['bɪl]	\bil\	bony	['bo:ni]	\bōnē\
billiards	['bɪljərdz]	\bilyərdz\	book	['bʊk]	\bu̇k\
billion	['bɪljən]	\bilyən\	boom	['bu:m]	\büm\
bind	['baɪnd]	\bīnd\	boost	['bu:st]	\büst\
bingo	['bɪŋ͵go:]	\biŋ͵gō\	boot	['bu:t]	\büt\
binoculars	[bə'nɑkjələrz, baɪ-]	\bə'näkyələrz, bī-\	booth	['bu:θ]	\büth\
biography	[baɪ'ɑgrəfi, bi:-]	\bī'ägrəfē, bē-\	border	['bordər]	\bȯrdər\
biology	[baɪ'ɑlədʒi]	\bī'äləjē\	bore	['bor]	\bōr\
birch	['bərtʃ]	\bərch\	born	['bɔrn]	\bȯrn\
bird	['bərd]	\bərd\	borrow	['bɑro]	\bärō\
birth	['bərθ]	\bərth\	Bosnian	['bɑzniən, 'bɔz-]	\bäznēən, bȯz-\
biscuit	['bɪskət]	\biskət\	bosom	['bʊzəm, 'bu:-]	\bu̇zəm, bü-\
bishop	['bɪʃəp]	\bishəp\	boss	['bɔs]	\bȯs\
bit	['bɪt]	\bit\	botany	['bɑtəni]	\bätᵊnē\
bite	['baɪt]	\bīt\	both	['bo:θ]	\bōth\
bitter	['bɪtər]	\bitər\	bother	['bɑðər]	\bäthər\
black	['blæk]	\blak\	bottle	['bɑtəl]	\bätᵊl\
bladder	['blædər]	\bladər\	bottom	['bɑtəm]	\bätəm\
blade	['bleɪd]	\blād\	bough	['baʊ]	\bau̇\
blame	['bleɪm]	\blām\	bound	['baʊnd]	\bau̇nd\
blank	['blæŋk]	\blaŋk\	boundary	['baʊndri, -dəri]	\bau̇ndrē, -dərē\
blanket	['blæŋkət]	\blaŋkət\	bow	['baʊ, 'bo:]	\bau̇; bō\
blazer	['bleɪzər]	\blāzər\	bowels	['baʊəlz]	\bau̇əls\
bleach	['bli:tʃ]	\blēch\	bowl	['bo:l]	\bōl\
bleed	['bli:d]	\blēd\	box	['bɑks]	\bäks\
blend	['blɛnd]	\blend\	boy	['bɔɪ]	\bȯi\
bless	['blɛs]	\bles\	boyfriend	['bɔɪ͵frɛnd]	\bȯi͵frend\
blindness	['blaɪndnəs]	\blīndnəs\	brace	['breɪs]	\brās\
blink	['blɪŋk]	\bliŋk\	bracket	['brækət]	\brakət\
bliss	['blɪs]	\blis\	braille	['breɪl]	\brāl\
blister	['blɪstər]	\blistər\	brain	['breɪn]	\brān\
blizzard	['blɪzərd]	\blizərd\	brake	['breɪk]	\brāk\
block	['blɑk]	\bläk\	branch	['bræntʃ]	\branch\
blood	['blʌd]	\bləd\	brand	['brænd]	\brand\
blossom	['blɑsəm]	\bläsᵊm\	brave	['breɪv]	\brāv\
blouse	['blaʊs, 'blaʊz]	\blau̇s, blau̇z\	Brazilian	[brə'zɪljən]	\brə'zilyən\
blow	['blo:]	\blō\	bread	['brɛd]	\bred\
blue	['blu:]	\blü\	breadth	['brɛtθ]	\bretth\
bluff	['blʌf]	\bləf\	break	['breɪk]	\brāk\
blur	['blər]	\blər\	breakfast	['brɛkfəst]	\brekfəst\
blurb	['blərb]	\blərb\	breast	['brɛst]	\brest\
blush	['blʌʃ]	\bləsh\	breath	['brɛθ]	\breth\
boar	['bor]	\bōr\	breed	['bri:d]	\brēd\
board	['bord]	\bōrd\	breeze	['bri:z]	\brēz\
boast	['bo:st]	\bōst\	brewery	['bru:əri, 'brori]	\brüərē, bru̇rē\
boat	['bo:t]	\bōt\	bribe	['braɪb]	\brīb\
body	['bɑdi]	\bädē\	brick	['brɪk]	\brik\
boil	['bɔɪl]	\bȯil\	bride	['braɪd]	\brīd\
bold	['bo:ld]	\bōld\	bridge	['brɪdʒ]	\brij\
Bolivian	[bə'lɪviən]	\bə'livēən\	brief	['bri:f]	\brēf\
bolt	['bo:lt]	\bōlt\	bright	['braɪt]	\brīt\
bomb	['bɑm]	\bäm\	brilliant	['brɪljənt]	\brilyənt\
bond	['bɑnd]	\bänd\	bring	['brɪŋ]	\briŋ\
bone	['bo:n]	\bōn\	British	['brɪtɪʃ]	\british\

ENGLISH WORD	IPA	M-W	ENGLISH WORD	IPA	M-W
broad	[ˈbrɔd]	\ˈbród\	bypass	[ˈbaɪˌpæs]	\ˈbī̩pas\
broadcast	[ˈbrɔdˌkæst]	\ˈbród̩kast\	bystander	[ˈbaɪˌstændər]	\ˈbī̩standər\
broaden	[ˈbrɔdən]	\ˈbród³n\	byte	[ˈbaɪt]	\ˈbīt\
broccoli	[ˈbrɑkəli]	\ˈbräkᵊlē\	byword	[ˈbaɪˌwərd]	\ˈbī̩wərd\
brochure	[broˈʃʊr]	\brōˈshùr\	cab	[ˈkæb]	\ˈkab\
broil	[ˈbrɔɪl]	\ˈbróil\	cabin	[ˈkæbən]	\ˈkab³n\
broken	[ˈbro:kən]	\ˈbrōk³n\	cable	[ˈkeɪbəl]	\ˈkāb³l\
brook	[ˈbrʊk]	\ˈbrúk\	cactus	[ˈkæktəs]	\ˈkaktəs\
broom	[ˈbru:m, ˈbrʊm]	\ˈbrüm, ˈbrùm\	cadet	[kəˈdɛt]	\kəˈdet\
broth	[ˈbrɔθ]	\ˈbróth\	cage	[ˈkeɪdʒ]	\ˈkāj\
brother	[ˈbrʌðər]	\ˈbrᵊthᵊr\	cake	[ˈkeɪk]	\ˈkāk\
brow	[ˈbraʊ]	\ˈbraú\	calcium	[ˈkælsiəm]	\ˈkalsēəm\
brown	[ˈbraʊn]	\ˈbraùn\	calculate	[ˈkælkjəˌleɪt]	\ˈkalkyə̩lāt\
brush	[ˈbrʌʃ]	\ˈbrəsh\	calendar	[ˈkæləndər]	\ˈkaləndər\
bubble	[ˈbʌbəl]	\ˈbəb³l\	calf	[ˈkæf, ˈkɑf]	\ˈkaf, ˈkäf\
buck	[ˈbʌk]	\ˈbək\	call	[ˈkɔl]	\ˈkól\
bucket	[ˈbʌkət]	\ˈbəkət\	calm	[ˈkɑm, ˈkɑlm]	\ˈkäm, ˈkälm\
buckle	[ˈbʌkəl]	\ˈbək³l\	calorie	[ˈkæləri]	\ˈkalərē\
Buddhism	[ˈbu:ˌdɪzəm, ˈbʊ-]	\ˈbü̩dizəm, ˈbù-\	camel	[ˈkæməl]	\ˈkam³l\
buddy	[ˈbʌdi]	\ˈbədē\	camera	[ˈkæmrə, ˈkæmərə]	\ˈkamrə, ˈkamərə\
budge	[ˈbʌdʒ]	\ˈbəj\	camp	[ˈkæmp]	\ˈkamp\
budget	[ˈbʌdʒət]	\ˈbəjət\	campaign	[kæmˈpeɪn]	\kamˈpān\
buffalo	[ˈbʌfəˌlo:]	\ˈbəfə̩lō\	camping	[ˈkæmpɪŋ]	\ˈkampiŋ\
buffet	[ˌbʌˈfeɪ, ˌbu:-]	\ˌbəˈfā, ˌbü-\	campus	[ˈkæmpəs]	\ˈkampəs\
bug	[ˈbʌg]	\ˈbəg\	can	[ˈkæn]	\ˈkan\
build	[ˈbɪld]	\ˈbild\	Canadian	[kəˈneɪdiən]	\kəˈnādēən\
bulb	[ˈbʌlb]	\ˈbəlb\	canal	[kəˈnæl]	\kəˈnal\
bulk	[ˈbʌlk]	\ˈbəlk\	canary	[kəˈnɛri]	\kəˈnerē\
bull	[ˈbʊl]	\ˈbúl\	cancel	[ˈkæntsəl]	\ˈkan(t)s³l\
bullet	[ˈbʊlət]	\ˈbúlət\	cancer	[ˈkæntsər]	\ˈkan(t)sər\
bulletin	[ˈbʊlətən, -lətən]	\ˈbúlət³n, -lətən\	candid	[ˈkændɪd]	\ˈkandid\
bullfight	[ˈbʊlˌfaɪt]	\ˈbúl̩fīt\	candidate	[ˈkændəˌdeɪt, -dət]	\ˈkandə̩dāt, -dət\
bully	[ˈbʊli]	\ˈbúlē\	candle	[ˈkændəl]	\ˈkand³l\
bump	[ˈbʌmp]	\ˈbəmp\	candy	[ˈkændi]	\ˈkandē\
bunch	[ˈbʌntʃ]	\ˈbənch\	cane	[ˈkeɪn]	\ˈkān\
bunny	[ˈbʌni]	\ˈbənē\	canine	[ˈkeɪˌnaɪn]	\ˈkā̩nīn\
burden	[ˈbərdən]	\ˈbərd³n\	cannibal	[ˈkænəbəl]	\ˈkanəb³l\
bureau	[ˈbjʊro]	\ˈbyùrō\	cannon	[ˈkænən]	\ˈkanən\
burglar	[ˈbərglər]	\ˈbərglər\	canoe	[kəˈnu:]	\kəˈnü\
burial	[ˈbɛriəl]	\ˈberēəl\	canon	[ˈkænən]	\ˈkanən\
burn	[ˈbərn]	\ˈbərn\	canteen	[kænˈti:n]	\kanˈtēn\
burst	[ˈbərst]	\ˈbərst\	canvas	[ˈkænvəs]	\ˈkanvəs\
bury	[ˈbɛri]	\ˈberē\	cap	[ˈkæp]	\ˈkap\
bus	[ˈbʌs]	\ˈbəs\	capable	[ˈkeɪpəbəl]	\ˈkāpəb³l\
bush	[ˈbʊʃ]	\ˈbùsh\	capacity	[kəˈpæsəti]	\kəˈpasətē\
busily	[ˈbɪzəli]	\ˈbizəlē\	capital	[ˈkæpətəl]	\ˈkapət³l\
business	[ˈbɪznəs, -nəz]	\ˈbiznəs, -nəz\	capitol	[ˈkæpətəl]	\ˈkapət³l\
busy	[ˈbɪzi]	\ˈbizē\	capsule	[ˈkæpsəl, -ˌsu:l]	\ˈkaps³l, -ˌsül\
but	[ˈbʌt]	\ˈbət\	captain	[ˈkæptən]	\ˈkapt³n\
butcher	[ˈbʊtʃər]	\ˈbùchər\	caption	[ˈkæpʃən]	\ˈkapsh³n\
butter	[ˈbʌtər]	\ˈbətər\	captivate	[ˈkæptəˌveɪt]	\ˈkaptə̩vāt\
butterfly	[ˈbʌtərˌflaɪ]	\ˈbətər̩flī\	capture	[ˈkæpʃər]	\ˈkapshər\
button	[ˈbʌtən]	\ˈbət³n\	car	[ˈkɑr]	\ˈkär\
buy	[ˈbaɪ]	\ˈbī\	caramel	[ˈkɑrməl; ˈkærəməl, -ˌmɛl]	\ˈkärm³l; ˈkarəm³l, -ˌmel\
buzz	[ˈbʌz]	\ˈbəz\			
by	[ˈbaɪ]	\ˈbī\	caravan	[ˈkærəˌvæn]	\ˈkarə̩van\

ENGLISH WORD	IPA	M-W	ENGLISH WORD	IPA	M-W
card	[ˈkɑrd]	\ˈkärd\	chair	[ˈtʃɛr]	\ˈcher\
cardiac	[ˈkɑrdiˌæk]	\ˈkärdēˌak\	chalk	[ˈtʃɔk]	\ˈchók\
cardinal	[ˈkɑrdənəl]	\ˈkärdᵊnəl\	challenge	[ˈtʃælɪndʒ]	\ˈchalinj\
care	[ˈkær]	\ˈkar\	champagne	[ʃæmˈpeɪn]	\shamˈpān\
career	[kəˈrɪr]	\kəˈrir\	champion	[ˈtʃæmpiən]	\ˈchampēən\
carefree	[ˈkærˌfriː, ˌkærˈ-]	\ˈkarˌfrē, ˌkarˈ-\	chance	[ˈtʃænts]	\ˈchan(t)s\
careful	[ˈkærfəl]	\ˈkarfᵊl\	change	[ˈtʃeɪndʒ]	\ˈchānj\
caress	[kəˈrɛs]	\kəˈres\	channel	[ˈtʃænəl]	\ˈchanᵊl\
caricature	[ˈkærɪkəˌtʃʊr]	\ˈkarikəˌchùr\	chaos	[ˈkeɪˌɑs]	\ˈkāˌäs\
caring	[ˈkærɪŋ]	\ˈkariŋ\	chapel	[ˈtʃæpəl]	\ˈchapᵊl\
carnival	[ˈkɑrnəvəl]	\ˈkärnəvᵊl\	chapter	[ˈtʃæptər]	\ˈchaptər\
carol	[ˈkærəl]	\ˈkarəl\	character	[ˈkærɪktər]	\ˈkariktər\
carpenter	[ˈkɑrpəntər]	\ˈkärpᵊntər\	charge	[ˈtʃɑrdʒ]	\ˈchärj\
carpet	[ˈkɑrpət]	\ˈkärpət\	charity	[ˈtʃærəti]	\ˈcharətē\
carriage	[ˈkærɪdʒ]	\ˈkarij\	charm	[ˈtʃɑrm]	\ˈchärm\
carrot	[ˈkærət]	\ˈkarət\	charter	[ˈtʃɑrtər]	\ˈchärtər\
carry	[ˈkæri]	\ˈkarē\	chat	[ˈtʃæt]	\ˈchat\
carton	[ˈkɑrtən]	\ˈkärtᵊn\	cheap	[ˈtʃiːp]	\ˈchēp\
cartoon	[kɑrˈtuːn]	\kärˈtün\	cheat	[ˈtʃiːt]	\ˈchēt\
cash	[ˈkæʃ]	\ˈkash\	check	[ˈtʃɛk]	\ˈchek\
cashier	[kæˈʃɪr]	\kaˈshir\	checkers	[ˈtʃɛkərz]	\ˈchekərz\
cassette	[kəˈsɛt, kæ-]	\kəˈset, ka-\	checkup	[ˈtʃɛkˌʌp]	\ˈchekˌəp\
castle	[ˈkæsəl]	\ˈkasᵊl\	cheek	[ˈtʃiːk]	\ˈchēk\
casual	[ˈkæʒʊəl]	\ˈkazhùəl\	cheer	[ˈtʃɪr]	\ˈchir\
cat	[ˈkæt]	\ˈkat\	cheese	[ˈtʃiːz]	\ˈchēz\
catch	[ˈkætʃ, ˈkɛtʃ]	\ˈkach, ˈkech\	chef	[ˈʃɛf]	\ˈshef\
category	[ˈkætəˌgori]	\ˈkatəˌgōrē\	chemist	[ˈkɛmɪst]	\ˈkemist\
cathedral	[kəˈθiːdrəl]	\kəˈthēdrəl\	cherish	[ˈtʃɛrɪʃ]	\ˈcherish\
catholic	[ˈkæθəlɪk]	\ˈkathəlik\	cherry	[ˈtʃɛri]	\ˈcherē\
cattle	[ˈkætəl]	\ˈkatᵊl\	chess	[ˈtʃɛs]	\ˈches\
cause	[ˈkɔz]	\ˈkóz\	chest	[ˈtʃɛst]	\ˈchest\
caution	[ˈkɔʃən]	\ˈkóshᵊn\	chestnut	[ˈtʃɛstˌnʌt]	\ˈches(t)ˌnət\
cave	[ˈkeɪv]	\ˈkāv\	chew	[ˈtʃuː]	\ˈchü\
cavern	[ˈkævərn]	\ˈkavərn\	chic	[ˈʃiːk]	\ˈshēk\
cavity	[ˈkævəti]	\ˈkavətē\	chicken	[ˈtʃɪkən]	\ˈchikᵊn\
CD	[ˌsiːˈdiː]	\ˌsēˈdē\	chief	[ˈtʃiːf]	\ˈchēf\
cease	[ˈsiːs]	\ˈsēs\	child	[ˈtʃaɪld]	\ˈchīld\
ceiling	[ˈsiːlɪŋ]	\ˈsēliŋ\	Chilean	[ˈtʃɪliən, tʃɪˈleɪən]	\ˈchilēən, chiˈlāən\
celebrate	[ˈsɛləˌbreɪt]	\ˈseləˌbrāt\	chill	[ˈtʃɪl]	\ˈchil\
celery	[ˈsɛləri]	\ˈselərē\	chimney	[ˈtʃɪmni]	\ˈchimnē\
cell	[ˈsɛl]	\ˈsel\	chin	[ˈtʃɪn]	\ˈchin\
cellar	[ˈsɛlər]	\ˈselər\	Chinese	[tʃaɪˈniːz, -ˈniːs]	\chīˈnēz, -ˈnēs\
cellular	[ˈsɛljələr]	\ˈselyələr\	chip	[ˈtʃɪp]	\ˈchip\
cement	[sɪˈmɛnt]	\siˈment\	chocolate	[ˈtʃɑkələt, ˈtʃɔk-]	\ˈchäkələt, ˈchók-\
cemetery	[ˈsɛməˌtɛri]	\ˈseməˌterē\	choice	[ˈtʃɔɪs]	\ˈchóis\
cent	[ˈsɛnt]	\ˈsent\	choir	[ˈkwaɪr]	\ˈkwīr\
centigrade	[ˈsɛntəˌgreɪd, ˈsɑn-]	\ˈsentəˌgrād, ˈsän-\	choke	[ˈtʃoːk]	\ˈchōk\
centimeter	[ˈsɛntəˌmiːtər, ˈsɑn-]	\ˈsentəˌmētər, ˈsän-\	choose	[ˈtʃuːz]	\ˈchüz\
central	[ˈsɛntrəl]	\ˈsentrəl\	chop	[ˈtʃɑp]	\ˈchäp\
century	[ˈsɛntʃəri]	\ˈsenchərē\	chopsticks	[ˈtʃɑpˌstɪks]	\ˈchäpˌstiks\
ceramics	[səˈræmɪks]	\səˈramiks\	chorus	[ˈkorəs]	\ˈkōrəs\
cereal	[ˈsɪriəl]	\ˈsirēəl\	Christian	[ˈkrɪstʃən]	\ˈkrischᵊn\
ceremony	[ˈsɛrəˌmoːni]	\ˈserəˌmōnē\	Christmas	[ˈkrɪsməs]	\ˈkrisməs\
certain	[ˈsərtən]	\ˈsərtᵊn\	chronic	[ˈkrɑnɪk]	\ˈkränik\
certify	[ˈsərtəˌfaɪ]	\ˈsərtəˌfī\	chronology	[krəˈnɑlədʒi]	\krəˈnäləjē\
chain	[ˈtʃeɪn]	\ˈchān\	chubby	[ˈtʃʌbi]	\ˈchəbē\

ENGLISH WORD	IPA	M-W	ENGLISH WORD	IPA	M-W
chunk	[ˈtʃʌŋk]	\ˈchəŋk\	coal	[ˈkoːl]	\ˈkōl\
church	[ˈtʃərtʃ]	\ˈchərch\	coast	[ˈkoːst]	\ˈkōst\
chute	[ˈʃuːt]	\ˈshüt\	coastline	[ˈkoːstˌlaɪn]	\ˈkōstˌlīn\
cigarette	[ˌsɪgəˈrɛt, ˈsɪgəˌrɛt]	\ˌsigəˈret, ˈsigəˌret\	coat	[ˈkoːt]	\ˈkōt\
cinema	[ˈsɪnəmə]	\ˈsinəmə\	cobweb	[ˈkɑbˌwɛb]	\ˈkäbˌweb\
cinnamon	[ˈsɪnəmən]	\ˈsinəmən\	cockroach	[ˈkɑkˌroːtʃ]	\ˈkäkˌrōch\
cipher	[ˈsaɪfər]	\ˈsīfər\	cocoa	[ˈkoːˌkoː]	\ˈkōˌkō\
circle	[ˈsərkəl]	\ˈsərkᵊl\	coconut	[ˈkoːkəˌnʌt]	\ˈkōkəˌnət\
circuit	[ˈsərkət]	\ˈsərkət\	cod	[ˈkɑd]	\ˈkäd\
circular	[ˈsərkjələr]	\ˈsərkyələr\	code	[ˈkoːd]	\ˈkōd\
circulate	[ˈsərkjəˌleɪt]	\ˈsərkyəˌlāt\	coffee	[ˈkɔfi]	\ˈkófē\
circumference	[sərˈkʌmpfrənts]	\sərˈkəm(p)frən(t)s\	coffin	[ˈkɔfən]	\ˈkófᵊn\
circumstance	[ˈsərkəmˌstænts]	\ˈsərkᵊmˌstan(t)s\	coil	[ˈkɔɪl]	\ˈkóil\
circus	[ˈsərkəs]	\ˈsərkəs\	coin	[ˈkɔɪn]	\ˈkóin\
cite	[ˈsaɪt]	\ˈsīt\	coincide	[ˌkoːɪnˈsaɪd, ˈkoːɪnˌsaɪd]	\ˌkōinˈsīd, ˈkōinˌsīd\
citizen	[ˈsɪtəzən]	\ˈsitəzᵊn\	cold	[ˈkoːld]	\ˈkōld\
city	[ˈsɪti]	\ˈsitē\	coleslaw	[ˈkoːlˌslɔ]	\ˈkōlˌsló\
civic	[ˈsɪvɪk]	\ˈsivik\	collapse	[kəˈlæps]	\kəˈlaps\
civil	[ˈsɪvəl]	\ˈsivᵊl\	collar	[ˈkɑlər]	\ˈkälər\
claim	[ˈkleɪm]	\ˈklām\	collect	[kəˈlɛkt]	\kəˈlekt\
clap	[ˈklæp]	\ˈklap\	college	[ˈkɑlɪdʒ]	\ˈkälij\
clarify	[ˈklærəˌfaɪ]	\ˈklarəˌfī\	Colombian	[kəˈlʌmbiən]	\kəˈləmbēən\
clarinet	[ˌklærəˈnɛt]	\ˌklarəˈnet\	colon	[ˈkoːlən]	\ˈkōlən\
clash	[ˈklæʃ]	\ˈklash\	column	[ˈkɑləm]	\ˈkäləm\
class	[ˈklæs]	\ˈklas\	coma	[ˈkoːmə]	\ˈkōmə\
classic	[ˈklæsɪk]	\ˈklasik\	comb	[ˈkoːm]	\ˈkōm\
classify	[ˈklæsəˌfaɪ]	\ˈklasəˌfī\	combat	[ˈkɑmˌbæt; kəmˈbæt]	\ˈkämˌbat; kəmˈbat\
classmate	[ˈklæsˌmeɪt]	\ˈklasˌmāt\	combine	[kəmˈbaɪn]	\kəmˈbīn\
classroom	[ˈklæsˌruːm]	\ˈklasˌrüm\	come	[ˈkʌm]	\ˈkəm\
claw	[ˈklɔ]	\ˈkló\	comedy	[ˈkɑmədi]	\ˈkämədē\
clean	[ˈkliːn]	\ˈklēn\	comet	[ˈkɑmət]	\ˈkämət\
clear	[ˈklɪr]	\ˈklir\	comfortable	[ˈkʌmpfərtəbəl, ˈkʌmpftə-]	
clef	[ˈklɛf]	\ˈklef\			\ˈkəm(p)fərtəbᵊl, ˈkəm(p)ftə-\
clerk	[ˈklərk, British ˈklɑrk]	\ˈklərk, British ˈklärk\	comic	[ˈkɑmɪk]	\ˈkämik\
clever	[ˈklɛvər]	\ˈklevər\	command	[kəˈmænd]	\kəˈmand\
click	[ˈklɪk]	\ˈklik\	commemorate	[kəˈmɛməˌreɪt]	\kəˈmeməˌrāt\
client	[ˈklaɪənt]	\ˈklīənt\	comment	[ˈkɑˌmɛnt]	\ˈkäˌment\
climate	[ˈklaɪmət]	\ˈklīmət\	commerce	[ˈkɑmərs]	\ˈkämərs\
climax	[ˈklaɪˌmæks]	\ˈklīˌmaks\	commission	[kəˈmɪʃən]	\kəˈmishᵊn\
climb	[ˈklaɪm]	\ˈklīm\	commit	[kəˈmɪt]	\kəˈmit\
clinic	[ˈklɪnɪk]	\ˈklinik\	committee	[kəˈmɪti]	\kəˈmitē\
clip	[ˈklɪp]	\ˈklip\	common	[ˈkɑmən]	\ˈkämᵊn\
clock	[ˈklɑk]	\ˈkläk\	communicate	[kəˈmjuːnəˌkeɪt]	\kəˈmyünəˌkāt\
clockwork	[ˈklɑkˌwərk]	\ˈkläkˌwərk\	communion	[kəˈmjuːnjən]	\kəˈmyünyən\
close	[ˈkloːz; ˈkloːs]	\ˈklōz; ˈklōs\	community	[kəˈmjuːnəti]	\kəˈmyünətē\
closet	[ˈklɑzət]	\ˈkläzət\	compact	[kəmˈpækt, ˈkɑmˌpækt]	\kəmˈpakt, ˈkämˌpakt\
cloth	[ˈklɔθ]	\ˈklóth\	company	[ˈkʌmpəni]	\ˈkəmpənē\
clothe	[ˈkloːð]	\ˈklōth\	compare	[kəmˈpær]	\kəmˈpar\
cloud	[ˈklaʊd]	\ˈklaúd\	compass	[ˈkʌmpəs, ˈkɑm-]	\ˈkəmpəs, ˈkäm-\
clover	[ˈkloːvər]	\ˈklōvər\	compassion	[kəmˈpæʃən]	\kəmˈpashᵊn\
clown	[ˈklaʊn]	\ˈklaún\	compel	[kəmˈpɛl]	\kəmˈpel\
club	[ˈklʌb]	\ˈkləb\	compensate	[ˈkɑmpənˌseɪt]	\ˈkämpᵊnˌsāt\
clue	[ˈkluː]	\ˈklü\	compete	[kəmˈpiːt]	\kəmˈpēt\
clumsy	[ˈklʌmzi]	\ˈkləmzē\	complain	[kəmˈpleɪn]	\kəmˈplān\
clutch	[ˈklʌtʃ]	\ˈkləch\	complement	[ˈkɑmpləmənt; ˈkɑmpləˌmɛnt]	
coach	[ˈkoːtʃ]	\ˈkōch\			\ˈkämpləmənt; ˈkämpləˌment\

ENGLISH WORD	IPA	M-W	ENGLISH WORD	IPA	M-W
complete	[kəm'pli:t]	\kəm'plēt\	context	['kan,tɛkst]	\'kän,tekst\
complex	[kam'plɛks, 'kam,plɛks]		continent	['kantənənt]	\'känt³nənt\
		\käm'pleks; 'käm,pleks\	continue	[kən'tɪnju:]	\kən'tinyü\
complexion	[kəm'plɛkʃən]	\kəm'pleksh³n\	contract	['kan,trækt; kən'trækt]	\'kän,trakt; kən'trakt\
complicate	['kamplə,keɪt]	\'kämplə,kāt\	contradiction	[,kantrə'dɪkʃən]	\,käntrə'diksh³n\
compliment	['kampləmənt, -,mɛnt]	\'kämpləmənt, -,ment\	contrary	['kan,trɛri]	\'kän,trerē\
compose	[kəm'po:z]	\kəm'pōz\	contribute	[kən'trɪbjət]	\kən'tribyət\
compound	[kam'paʊnd, 'kam,paʊnd]		control	[kən'tro:l]	\kən'trōl\
		\käm'paund, 'käm,paund\	convene	[kən'vi:n]	\kən'vēn\
comprehend	[,kamprɪ'hɛnd]	\,kämpri'hend\	conversation	[,kanvər'seɪʃən]	\,känvər'sāsh³n\
compromise	['kamprə,maɪz]	\'kämprə,mīz\	convert	[kən'vərt]	\kən'vərt\
computer	[kəm'pju:tər]	\kəm'pyütər\	convex	[kan'vɛks, 'kan,-, kən'-]	\kän'veks, 'kän,-, kən'-\
conceal	[kən'si:l]	\kən'sēl\	conviction	[kən'vɪkʃən]	\kən'viksh³n\
concede	[kən'si:d]	\kən'sēd\	convince	[kən'vɪn(t)s]	\kən'vin(t)s\
concentrate	['kant sən,treɪt]	\'kän(t)s³n,trāt\	convoke	[kən'vo:k]	\kən'vōk\
concept	['kan,sɛpt]	\'kän,sept\	cook	['kʊk]	\'kůk\
concern	[kən'sərn]	\kən'sərn\	cool	['ku:l]	\'kül\
concert	['kan,sərt]	\'kän,sərt\	cooperate	[ko'apə,reɪt]	\kō'äpə,rāt\
conclude	[kən'klu:d]	\kən'klüd\	coordinate	[ko'ordən,eɪt]	\kō'ȯrd³n,āt\
concrete	[kan'kri:t, 'kan,kri:t]	\kän'krēt, 'kän,krēt\	cope	['ko:p]	\'kōp\
condemn	[kən'dɛm]	\kən'dem\	copier	['kapiər]	\'käpēər\
condiment	['kandəmənt]	\'kändəmənt\	copy	['kapi]	\'käpē\
condition	[kən'dɪʃən]	\kən'dish³n\	cord	['kord]	\'kȯrd\
conduct	['kan,dʌkt; kən'dʌkt]	\'kän,dəkt; kən'dəkt\	cordial	['kordʒəl]	\'kȯrj³l\
cone	['ko:n]	\'kōn\	core	['kor]	\'kōr\
conference	['kanfrənts, -fərənts]	\'känfr³n(t)s, -fər³n(t)s\	corn	['korn]	\'kȯrn\
confess	[kən'fɛs]	\kən'fes\	corner	['kornər]	\'kȯrnər\
confidence	['kanfədənts]	\'känfəd³n(t)s\	coronary	['korə,nɛri]	\'kȯrə,nerē\
confirm	[kən'fərm]	\kən'fərm\	coronation	[,korə'neɪʃən]	\,kȯrə'nāsh³n\
conflict	['kan,flɪkt; kən'flɪkt]	\'kän,flikt; kən'flikt\	corps	['kor]	\'kōr\
confuse	[kən'fju:z]	\kən'fyüz\	corpse	['korps]	\'kȯrps\
congested	[kən'dʒɛstəd]	\kən'jestəd\	correct	[kə'rɛkt]	\kə'rekt\
congratulate	[kən'grædʒə,leɪt, -'grætʃə-]		correspond	[,korə'spand]	\,kȯrə'spänd\
		\kən'grajə,lāt, -'grachə-\	corridor	['korədər, -,dor]	\'kȯrədər, -,dȯr\
congress	['kaŋgrəs]	\'käŋgrəs\	corruption	[kə'rʌpʃən]	\kə'rəpsh³n\
conjunction	[kən'dʒʌŋkʃən]	\kən'jəŋksh³n\	cosmetic	[kaz'mɛtɪk]	\käz'metik\
connect	[kə'nɛkt]	\kə'nekt\	cosmos	['kazməs, -,mo:s, -,mas]	\'käzməs, -,mōs, -,mäs\
conscience	['kantʃənts]	\'känch³n(t)s\	cost	['kost]	\'kȯst\
conscious	['kantʃəs]	\'känchəs\	Costa Rican	[,kostə'ri:kən]	\,kȯstə'rēkən\
consequence	['kantsə,kwɛnt s, -kwənts]		costume	['kas,tu:m, -,tju:m]	\'käs,tüm, -,tyüm\
		\'kän(t)sə,kwen(t)s, -kwən(t)s\	cottage	['katɪdʒ]	\'kätij\
conservative	[kən'sərvətɪv]	\kən'sərvətēv\	cotton	['katən]	\'kät³n\
consider	[kən'sɪdər]	\kən'sidər\	couch	['kaʊtʃ]	\'kaůch\
consist	[kən'sɪst]	\kən'sist\	cough	['kof]	\'kȯf\
console	[kən'so:l]	\kən'sōl\	counsel	['kaʊntsəl]	\'kaůn(t)s³l\
constant	['kantstənt]	\'kän(t)st³nt\	count	['kaʊnt]	\'kaůnt\
constitute	['kantstə,tu:t, -,tju:t]	\'kän(t)stə,tüt, -,tyüt\	counter	['kaʊntər]	\'kaůntər\
construct	[kən'strʌkt]	\kən'strəkt\	countless	['kaʊntləs]	\'kaůntləs\
consult	[kən'sʌlt]	\kən'səlt\	country	['kʌntri]	\'kəntrē\
consume	[kən'su:m]	\kən'süm\	couple	['kʌpə l]	\'kəp³l\
contact	['kan,tækt, kən'-]	\'kän,takt, kən'-\	courage	['kərɪdʒ]	\'kərij\
contain	[kən'teɪn]	\kən'tān\	course	['kors]	\'kōrs\
contaminate	[kən'tæmə,neɪt]	\kən'tamə,nāt\	court	['kort]	\'kȯrt\
contemporary	[kən'tɛmpə,rɛri]	\kən'tempə,rerē\	courtesy	['kərtəsi]	\'kərtəsē\
content	['kan,tɛnt; kən'tɛnt]	\'kän,tent; kən'tent\	courtyard	['kort,jard]	\'kȯrt,yärd\
contest	[kən'tɛst; 'kan,tɛst]	\kən'test; 'kän,test\	cousin	['kʌzən]	\'kəz³n\

ENGLISH WORD	IPA	M-W	ENGLISH WORD	IPA	M-W
cover	[ˈkʌvər]	\ˈkəvər\	cupboard	[ˈkʌbərd]	\ˈkəbərd\
cow	[ˈkaʊ]	\ˈkaủ\	curb	[ˈkərb]	\ˈkərb\
coward	[ˈkaʊərd]	\ˈkaủərd\	cure	[ˈkjʊr]	\ˈkyủr\
cowboy	[ˈkaʊˌbɔɪ]	\ˈkaủˌbói\	curious	[ˈkjʊriəs]	\ˈkyủrēəs\
crab	[ˈkræb]	\ˈkrab\	curl	[ˈkərl]	\ˈkərl\
crack	[ˈkræk]	\ˈkrak\	currency	[ˈkərənt si]	\ˈkərən(t)sē\
cracker	[ˈkrækər]	\ˈkrakər\	current	[ˈkərənt]	\ˈkərənt\
cradle	[ˈkreɪdəl]	\ˈkrād³l\	curriculum	[kəˈrɪkjələm]	\kəˈrikyələm\
craft	[ˈkræft]	\ˈkraft\	curtain	[ˈkərtən]	\ˈkərt³n\
cramp	[ˈkræmp]	\ˈkramp\	curve	[ˈkərv]	\ˈkərv\
crane	[ˈkreɪn]	\ˈkrān\	cushion	[ˈkʊʃən]	\ˈkủsh³n\
crash	[ˈkræʃ]	\ˈkrash\	custom	[ˈkʌstəm]	\ˈkəst³m\
crawl	[ˈkrɔl]	\ˈkról\	cut	[ˈkʌt]	\ˈkət\
crayon	[ˈkreɪˌɑn, -ən]	\ˈkrāˌän, -ən\	cute	[ˈkjuːt]	\ˈkyüt\
crazy	[ˈkreɪzi]	\ˈkrāzē\	cutlery	[ˈkʌtləri]	\ˈkətlərē\
cream	[ˈkriːm]	\ˈkrēm\	cutlet	[ˈkʌtlət]	\ˈkətlət\
create	[kriˈeɪt]	\krēˈāt\	cutting	[ˈkʌtɪŋ]	\ˈkətiŋ\
creature	[ˈkriːtʃər]	\ˈkrēchər\	cycle	[ˈsaɪkəl]	\ˈsīk³l\
credit	[ˈkrɛdɪt]	\ˈkredit\	cynic	[ˈsɪnɪk]	\ˈsinik\
creek	[ˈkriːk, ˈkrɪk]	\ˈkrēk, ˈkrik\	Czech	[ˈtʃɛk]	\ˈchek\
creep	[ˈkriːp]	\ˈkrēp\	dad	[ˈdæd]	\ˈdad\
crew	[ˈkruː]	\ˈkrü\	daily	[ˈdeɪli]	\ˈdālē\
crib	[ˈkrɪb]	\ˈkrib\	daisy	[ˈdeɪzi]	\ˈdāzē\
cricket	[ˈkrɪkət]	\ˈkrikət\	damage	[ˈdæmɪdʒ]	\ˈdamij\
crime	[ˈkraɪm]	\ˈkrīm\	damn	[ˈdæm]	\ˈdam\
crinkle	[ˈkrɪŋkəl]	\ˈkriŋk³l\	damp	[ˈdæmp]	\ˈdamp\
cripple	[ˈkrɪpəl]	\ˈkrip³l\	dance	[ˈdænt s]	\ˈdan(t)s\
crisis	[ˈkraɪsɪs]	\ˈkrīsis\	dandruff	[ˈdændrəf]	\ˈdandrəf\
crisp	[ˈkrɪsp]	\ˈkrisp\	danger	[ˈdeɪndʒər]	\ˈdānjər\
criterion	[kraɪˈtɪriən]	\krīˈtirēən\	Danish	[ˈdeɪnɪʃ]	\ˈdānish\
critic	[ˈkrɪtɪk]	\ˈkritik\	daring	[ˈdærɪŋ]	\ˈdariŋ\
crocodile	[ˈkrɑkəˌdaɪl]	\ˈkräkəˌdīl\	dark	[ˈdɑrk]	\ˈdärk\
crop	[ˈkrɑp]	\ˈkräp\	dart	[ˈdɑrt]	\ˈdärt\
cross	[ˈkrɔs]	\ˈkrós\	dash	[ˈdæʃ]	\ˈdash\
crow	[ˈkroː]	\ˈkrō\	data	[ˈdeɪtə, ˈdæ-, ˈdɑ-]	\ˈdātə, ˈda-, ˈdä-\
crowd	[ˈkraʊd]	\ˈkraủd\	date	[ˈdeɪt]	\ˈdāt\
crucial	[ˈkruːʃəl]	\ˈkrüsh³l\	daughter	[ˈdɔtər]	\ˈdótər\
crucifix	[ˈkruːsəˌfɪks]	\ˈkrüsəˌfiks\	dawn	[ˈdɔn]	\ˈdón\
crude	[ˈkruːd]	\ˈkrüd\	day	[ˈdeɪ]	\ˈdā\
cruel	[ˈkruːəl]	\ˈkrüəl\	daze	[ˈdeɪz]	\ˈdāz\
cruise	[ˈkruːz]	\ˈkrüz\	dead	[ˈdɛd]	\ˈded\
crumb	[ˈkrʌm]	\ˈkrəm\	deaf	[ˈdɛf]	\ˈdef\
crumble	[ˈkrʌmbəl]	\ˈkrəmb³l\	deal	[ˈdiːl]	\ˈdēl\
crunch	[ˈkrʌntʃ]	\ˈkrənch\	death	[ˈdɛθ]	\ˈdeth\
crush	[ˈkrʌʃ]	\ˈkrəsh\	debate	[diˈbeɪt]	\dēˈbāt\
crutch	[ˈkrʌtʃ]	\ˈkrəch\	debt	[ˈdɛt]	\ˈdet\
cry	[ˈkraɪ]	\ˈkrī\	decade	[ˈdɛˌkeɪd, dɛˈkeɪd]	\ˈdeˌkād, deˈkād\
crystal	[ˈkrɪstəl]	\ˈkrist³l\	decal	[ˈdiːˌkæl, diˈkæl]	\ˈdēˌkal, dēˈkal\
Cuban	[ˈkjuːbən]	\ˈkyüb³n\	deceive	[diˈsiːv]	\dēˈsēv\
cube	[ˈkjuːb]	\ˈkyüb\	December	[diˈsɛmbər]	\dēˈsembər\
cucumber	[ˈkjuːˌkʌmbər]	\ˈkyüˌkəmbər\	decent	[ˈdiːsənt]	\ˈdēs³nt\
cue	[ˈkjuː]	\ˈkyü\	deception	[diˈsɛpʃən]	\dēˈsepsh³n\
cuff	[ˈkʌf]	\ˈkəf\	decide	[diˈsaɪd]	\dēˈsīd\
cultivate	[ˈkʌltəˌveɪt]	\ˈkəltəˌvāt\	decimal	[ˈdɛsəməl]	\ˈdesəm³l\
culture	[ˈkʌltʃər]	\ˈkəlchər\	decision	[dɪˈsɪʒən]	\diˈsizh³n\
cup	[ˈkʌp]	\ˈkəp\	deck	[ˈdɛk]	\ˈdek\

ENGLISH WORD	IPA	M-W	ENGLISH WORD	IPA	M-W
declare	[dɪˈklær]	\dēˈklar\	despondent	[dɪˈspɑndənt]	\dēˈspändənt\
decorate	[ˈdɛkəˌreɪt]	\ˈdekəˌrāt\	dessert	[dɪˈzərt]	\dēˈzərt\
decrease	[dɪˈkriːs; ˈdiːˌkriːs]	\dēˈkrēs; ˈdēˌkrēs\	destination	[ˌdɛstəˈneɪʃən]	\ˌdestəˈnāshən\
decree	[dɪˈkriː]	\dēˈkrē\	destroy	[dɪˈstrɔɪ]	\dēˈstrói\
dedicate	[ˈdɛdɪˌkeɪt]	\ˈdediˌkāt\	detergent	[dɪˈtərdʒənt]	\dēˈtərjənt\
deduce	[dɪˈduːs]	\dēˈdüs\	deteriorate	[dɪˈtɪriəˌreɪt]	\dēˈtirēəˌrāt\
deduct	[dɪˈdʌkt]	\dēˈdəkt\	determine	[dɪˈtərmən]	\dēˈtərmən\
deed	[ˈdiːd]	\ˈdēd\	detest	[dɪˈtɛst]	\dēˈtest\
deep	[ˈdiːp]	\ˈdēp\	devalue	[dɪˈvælˌjuː]	\dēˈvalˌyü\
deer	[ˈdɪr]	\ˈdir\	develop	[dɪˈvɛləp]	\dēˈveləp\
defeat	[dɪˈfiːt]	\dēˈfēt\	device	[dɪˈvaɪs]	\dēˈvīs\
defect	[ˈdiːˌfɛkt; dɪˈfɛkt]	\ˈdēˌfekt; dēˈfekt\	devil	[ˈdɛvəl]	\ˈdevəl\
defend	[dɪˈfɛnd]	\dēˈfend\	devise	[dɪˈvaɪz]	\dēˈvīz\
defer	[dɪˈfər]	\dēˈfər\	devoid	[dɪˈvɔɪd]	\dēˈvóid\
defiance	[dɪˈfaɪənts]	\dēˈfīən(t)s\	dexterity	[dɛkˈstɛrəti]	\dekˈsterətē\
define	[dɪˈfaɪn]	\dēˈfīn\	diagnosis	[ˌdaɪɡˈnoːsɪs]	\ˌdīigˈnōsis\
deflect	[dɪˈflɛkt]	\dēˈflekt\	diagonal	[daɪˈæɡənəl]	\dīˈagənəl\
defy	[dɪˈfaɪ]	\dēˈfī\	diagram	[ˈdaɪəˌɡræm]	\ˈdīəˌgram\
degree	[dɪˈɡriː]	\dēˈgrē\	dial	[ˈdaɪl]	\ˈdīl\
dehydrate	[dɪˈhaɪˌdreɪt]	\dēˈhīˌdrāt\	dialect	[ˈdaɪəˌlɛkt]	\ˈdīəˌlekt\
delay	[dɪˈleɪ]	\dēˈlā\	dialogue	[ˈdaɪəˌlɔɡ]	\ˈdīəˌlóg\
delegate	[ˈdɛlɪɡət, -ˌɡeɪt]	\ˈdeligət, -ˌgāt\	diamond	[ˈdaɪmənd, ˈdaɪə-]	\ˈdīmənd, ˈdīə-\
delicacy	[ˈdɛlɪkəsi]	\ˈdelikəsē\	diaper	[ˈdaɪpər, ˈdaɪə-]	\ˈdīpər, ˈdīə-\
delicatessen	[ˌdɛlɪkəˈtɛsən]	\ˌdelikəˈtesən\	diaphragm	[ˈdaɪəˌfræm]	\ˈdīəˌfram\
delicious	[dɪˈlɪʃəs]	\dēˈlishəs\	diary	[ˈdaɪəri]	\ˈdīərē\
delightful	[dɪˈlaɪtfəl]	\dɪˈlītfəl\	dice	[ˈdaɪs]	\ˈdīs\
delinquent	[dɪˈlɪŋkwənt]	\dēˈliŋkwənt\	dictate	[ˈdɪkˌteɪt, dɪkˈteɪt]	\ˈdikˌtāt, dikˈtāt\
deliver	[dɪˈlɪvər]	\dēˈlivər\	dictionary	[ˈdɪkʃəˌnɛri]	\ˈdikshəˌnerē\
demise	[dɪˈmaɪz]	\dɪˈmīz\	die	[ˈdaɪ]	\ˈdī\
democracy	[dɪˈmɑkrəsi]	\dēˈmäkrəsē\	differ	[ˈdɪfər]	\ˈdifər\
demon	[ˈdiːmən]	\ˈdēmən\	difficult	[ˈdɪfɪˌkʌlt]	\ˈdifiˌkəlt\
demonstrate	[ˈdɛmənˌstreɪt]	\ˈdemənˌstrāt\	dig	[ˈdɪɡ]	\ˈdig\
denial	[dɪˈnaɪəl]	\dēˈnīəl\	digest	[ˈdaɪˌdʒɛst; daɪˈdʒɛst]	\ˈdīˌjest; dīˈjest\
denounce	[dɪˈnaʊnts]	\dēˈnaún(t)s\	digit	[ˈdɪdʒət]	\ˈdijət\
dentist	[ˈdɛntɪst]	\ˈdentist\	digress	[daɪˈɡrɛs, də-]	\dīˈgres, də-\
deny	[dɪˈnaɪ]	\dēˈnī\	dilate	[daɪˈleɪt, ˈdaɪˌleɪt]	\dīˈlāt, ˈdīˌlāt\
deodorant	[dɪˈoːdərənt]	\dēˈōdərənt\	dilemma	[dɪˈlɛmə]	\diˈlemə\
department	[dɪˈpɑrtmənt]	\dēˈpärtmənt\	dimension	[dəˈmɛntʃən, daɪ-]	\dəˈmenchən, dī-\
depend	[dɪˈpɛnd]	\dēˈpend\	dinner	[ˈdɪnər]	\ˈdinər\
deplete	[dɪˈpliːt]	\dēˈplēt\	dint	[ˈdɪnt]	\ˈdint\
deplorable	[dɪˈplorəbəl]	\dēˈplōrəbəl\	diploma	[dəˈploːmə]	\dəˈplōmə\
deposit	[dɪˈpazət]	\dēˈpäzət\	diplomacy	[dəˈploːməsi]	\dəˈplōməsē\
depress	[dɪˈprɛs]	\dēˈpres\	direct	[dəˈrɛkt, daɪ-]	\dəˈrekt, dī-\
deprive	[dɪˈpraɪv]	\dēˈprīv\	dirty	[ˈdərti]	\ˈdərtē\
depth	[ˈdɛpθ]	\ˈdepth\	disability	[ˌdɪsəˈbɪləti]	\ˌdisəˈbilətē\
deranged	[dɪˈreɪndʒd]	\dēˈrānjd\	disadvantage	[ˌdɪsədˈvæntɪdʒ]	\ˌdisədˈvantij\
descendant	[dɪˈsɛndənt]	\dēˈsendənt\	disagreeable	[ˌdɪsəˈɡriːəbəl]	\ˌdisəˈgrēəbəl\
describe	[dɪˈskraɪb]	\dēˈskrīb\	disappear	[ˌdɪsəˈpɪr]	\ˌdisəˈpir\
deserve	[dɪˈzərv]	\dēˈzərv\	disaster	[dɪˈzæstər]	\diˈzastər\
design	[dɪˈzaɪn]	\dēˈzīn\	discharge	[dɪsˈtʃɑrdʒ, ˈdɪsˌ-]	\disˈchärj, ˈdisˌ-\
designate	[ˈdɛzɪɡˌneɪt]	\ˈdezigˌnāt\	disciple	[dɪˈsaɪpəl]	\diˈsīpəl\
designer	[dɪˈzaɪnər]	\dēˈzīnər\	discipline	[ˈdɪsəplən]	\ˈdisəplən\
desire	[dɪˈzaɪr]	\dēˈzīr\	disclose	[dɪsˈkloːz]	\disˈklōz\
desk	[ˈdɛsk]	\ˈdesk\	discomfort	[dɪsˈkʌmfərt]	\disˈkəmfərt\
despair	[dɪˈspær]	\dēˈspar\	disconnect	[ˌdɪskəˈnɛkt]	\ˌdiskəˈnekt\
desperation	[ˌdɛspəˈreɪʃən]	\ˌdespəˈrāshən\	discount	[ˈdɪsˌkaʊnt, dɪsˈ-]	\ˈdisˌkaúnt, disˈ-\

ENGLISH WORD	IPA	M-W	ENGLISH WORD	IPA	M-W
discourage	[dɪsˈkərɪdʒ]	\disˈkərij\	dogma	[ˈdɔgmə]	\ˈdógmə\
discover	[dɪsˈkʌvər]	\disˈkəvər\	doll	[ˈdɑl, ˈdɔl]	\ˈdäl, ˈdól\
discreet	[dɪsˈkriːt]	\disˈkrēt\	dollar	[ˈdɑlər]	\ˈdälər\
discretion	[dɪsˈkrɛʃən]	\disˈkreshᵊn\	dolphin	[ˈdɑlfən, ˈdɔl-]	\ˈdälfən, ˈdól-\
discriminate	[dɪsˈkrɪmə,neɪt]	\disˈkrimə,nāt\	domain	[doˈmeɪn, də-]	\doˈmān, də-\
discuss	[dɪsˈkʌs]	\disˈkəs\	domination	[,dɑmə'neɪʃən]	\,dämə'nāshᵊn\
disease	[dɪˈziːz]	\diˈzēz\	donate	[ˈdoːˌneɪt, doˈ-]	\ˈdōˌnāt, dōˈ-\
disgust	[dɪˈskʌst]	\diˈskəst\	done	[ˈdʌn]	\ˈdən\
dish	[ˈdɪʃ]	\ˈdish\	donkey	[ˈdɑŋki, ˈdʌŋ-]	\ˈdäŋkē, ˈdəŋ-\
dishonest	[dɪˈsɑnəst]	\diˈsänəst\	donor	[ˈdoːnər]	\ˈdōnər\
dishwasher	[ˈdɪʃ,wɔʃər]	\ˈdish,wóshər\	door	[ˈdor]	\ˈdor\
disillusion	[,dɪsəˈluːʒən]	\,disəˈlüzhᵊn\	dormitory	[ˈdɔrmə,tori]	\ˈdórmə,tōrē\
dislike	[dɪsˈlaɪk]	\disˈlīk\	dose	[ˈdoːs]	\ˈdōs\
disloyal	[dɪsˈlɔɪəl]	\disˈlóiəl\	dot	[ˈdɑt]	\ˈdät\
dismiss	[dɪsˈmɪs]	\disˈmis\	double	[ˈdʌbəl]	\ˈdəbᵊl\
disorder	[dɪsˈɔrdər]	\disˈórdər\	doubt	[ˈdaʊt]	\ˈdaút\
disorganize	[dɪsˈɔrgə,naɪz]	\disˈórgə,nīz\	dough	[ˈdoː]	\ˈdō\
dispel	[dɪsˈpɛl]	\disˈpel\	dove	[ˈdoːv]	\ˈdōv\
dispense	[dɪsˈpɛnts]	\disˈpen(t)s\	dove	[ˈdʌv]	\ˈdəv\
disperse	[dɪsˈpərs]	\disˈpərs\	down	[ˈdaʊn]	\ˈdaún\
displace	[dɪsˈpleɪs]	\disˈplās\	dozen	[ˈdʌzən]	\ˈdəzᵊn\
display	[dɪsˈpleɪ]	\disˈplā\	draft	[ˈdræft, ˈdraft]	\ˈdraft, ˈdräft\
displease	[dɪsˈpliːz]	\disˈplēz\	drag	[ˈdræg]	\ˈdrag\
disposal	[dɪsˈpoːzəl]	\disˈpōzᵊl\	drain	[ˈdreɪn]	\ˈdrān\
dispute	[dɪsˈpjuːt]	\disˈpyüt\	drama	[ˈdrɑmə, ˈdræ-]	\ˈdrämə, ˈdra-\
disqualification	[dɪsˌkwɑləfəˈkeɪʃən]	\dis,kwäləfəˈkäshᵊn\	drastic	[ˈdræstɪk]	\ˈdrastik\
disrespectful	[,dɪsrɪˈspɛktfəl]	\,disriˈspektfᵊl\	draw	[ˈdrɔ]	\ˈdró\
disruption	[dɪsˈrʌpʃən]	\disˈrəpshᵊn\	dread	[ˈdrɛd]	\ˈdred\
dissolve	[dɪˈzɑlv]	\diˈzälv\	dream	[ˈdriːm]	\ˈdrēm\
distance	[ˈdɪstənts]	\ˈdistən(t)s\	dress	[ˈdrɛs]	\ˈdres\
distinct	[dɪˈstɪŋkt]	\diˈstiŋkt\	drill	[ˈdrɪl]	\ˈdril\
distinguish	[dɪsˈtɪŋgwɪʃ]	\disˈtiŋgwish\	drink	[ˈdrɪŋk]	\ˈdriŋk\
distract	[dɪˈstrækt]	\diˈstrakt\	drive	[ˈdraɪv]	\ˈdrīv\
distress	[dɪˈstrɛs]	\diˈstres\	driver	[ˈdraɪvər]	\ˈdrīvər\
distribute	[dɪˈstrɪ,bjuːt, -bjʊt]	\diˈstri,byüt, -byut\	drizzle	[ˈdrɪzəl]	\ˈdrizᵊl\
district	[ˈdɪs,trɪkt]	\ˈdis,trikt\	drool	[ˈdruːl]	\ˈdrül\
distrust	[dɪsˈtrʌst]	\disˈtrəst\	drop	[ˈdrɑp]	\ˈdräp\
disturbance	[dɪˈstərbənts]	\diˈstərbən(t)s\	drown	[ˈdraʊn]	\ˈdraún\
disuse	[dɪsˈjuːs]	\disˈyüs\	drugstore	[ˈdrʌg,stor]	\ˈdrəg,stōr\
ditto	[ˈdɪto]	\ˈditō\	drum	[ˈdrʌm]	\ˈdrəm\
diverse	[daɪˈvərs, də-, ˈdaɪ,vərs]	\dīˈvərs, də-, ˈdī,vərs\	drunk	[ˈdrʌŋk]	\ˈdrəŋk\
diversity	[daɪˈvərsəti, də-]	\dīˈvərsətē, də-\	dry	[ˈdraɪ]	\ˈdrī\
divert	[dəˈvərt, daɪ-]	\dəˈvərt, dī-\	duck	[ˈdʌk]	\ˈdək\
divide	[dəˈvaɪd]	\dəˈvīd\	due	[ˈduː, ˈdjuː]	\ˈdü, ˈdyü\
dividend	[ˈdɪvə,dɛnd, -dənd]	\ˈdivə,dend, -dənd\	duel	[ˈduːəl, ˈdjuː-]	\ˈdüəl, ˈdyü-\
division	[dɪˈvɪʒən]	\diˈvizhᵊn\	dull	[ˈdʌl]	\ˈdəl\
divorce	[dəˈvors]	\dəˈvōrs\	duplicate	[ˈduː,plɪ,keɪt]	\ˈdüpli,kāt\
divulge	[dəˈvʌldʒ, daɪ-]	\dəˈvəlj, dī-\	durable	[ˈdʊrəbəl, ˈdjʊr-]	\ˈdurəbəl, ˈdyur-\
dizzy	[ˈdɪzi]	\ˈdizē\	duration	[dʊˈreɪʃən, djʊ-]	\duˈrāshᵊn, dyú-\
DNA	[,diːˌɛnˈeɪ]	\,dē,en'ā\	during	[ˈdʊrɪŋ, ˈdjʊr-]	\ˈduriŋ, ˈdyur-\
do	[ˈduː]	\ˈdü\	dusk	[ˈdʌsk]	\ˈdəsk\
doctor	[ˈdɑktər]	\ˈdäktər\	dust	[ˈdʌst]	\ˈdəst\
doctrine	[ˈdɑktrɪn]	\ˈdäktrin\	Dutch	[ˈdʌtʃ]	\ˈdəch\
document	[ˈdɑkjʊmənt, -,mɛnt]	\ˈdäkyùmənt, -,ment\	dwarf	[ˈdwɔrf]	\ˈdwórf\
dodge	[ˈdɑdʒ]	\ˈdäj\	dynamic	[daɪˈnæmɪk]	\dīˈnamik\
dog	[ˈdɔg, ˈdɑg]	\ˈdóg, ˈdäg\	each	[ˈiːtʃ]	\ˈēch\

ENGLISH WORD	IPA	M-W	ENGLISH WORD	IPA	M-W
eager	[ˈiːgər]	\ˈēgər\	emotion	[iˈmoːʃən]	\ēˈmōshən\
eagle	[ˈiːgəl]	\ˈēgəl\	emphasis	[ˈɛmfəsɪs]	\ˈemfəsis\
ear	[ˈɪr]	\ˈir\	employ	[ɪmˈplɔɪ, ɛm-]	\imˈplói, em-\
early	[ˈərli]	\ˈərlē\	empty	[ˈɛmpti]	\ˈemptē\
earn	[ˈərn]	\ˈərn\	enable	[ɪˈneɪbəl, ɛ-]	\iˈnābᵊl, e-\
earnings	[ˈərnɪŋz]	\ˈərniŋz\	enclose	[ɪnˈkloːz, ɛn-]	\inˈklōz, en-\
earphone	[ˈɪrˌfoːn]	\ˈirˌfōn\	encourage	[ɪnˈkərɪdʒ, ɛn-]	\inˈkərij, en-\
earring	[ˈɪrˌrɪŋ]	\ˈirˌriŋ\	encyclopedia	[ɪnˌsaɪkləˈpiːdiə, ɛn-]	\inˌsīkləˈpēdēə, en-\
earth	[ˈərθ]	\ˈərth\	end	[ˈɛnd]	\ˈend\
ease	[ˈiːz]	\ˈēz\	ending	[ˈɛndɪŋ]	\ˈendiŋ\
easily	[ˈiːzəli]	\ˈēzəlē\	endless	[ˈɛndləs]	\ˈendləs\
east	[ˈiːst]	\ˈēst\	endure	[ɪnˈdʊr, ɛn-, -ˈdjʊr]	\inˈdür, en-, -ˈdyür\
easy	[ˈiːzi]	\ˈēzē\	enemy	[ˈɛnəmi]	\ˈenəmē\
eat	[ˈiːt]	\ˈēt\	energy	[ˈɛnərdʒi]	\ˈenərjē\
echo	[ˈɛˌkoː]	\ˈeˌkō\	engage	[ɪnˈgeɪdʒ, ɛn-]	\inˈgāj, en-\
eclipse	[ɪˈklɪps]	\iˈklips\	engine	[ˈɛndʒən]	\ˈenjᵊn\
ecology	[iˈkalədʒi, ɛ-]	\ēˈkäləjē, e-\	English	[ˈɪŋglɪʃ, ˈɪŋlɪʃ]	\ˈiŋglish, ˈiŋlish\
economy	[iˈkanə mi]	\ēˈkänəmē\	enhance	[ɪnˈhænts, ɛn-]	\inˈhan(t)s, en-\
Ecuadoran	[ˌɛkwəˈdorən]	\ˌekwəˈdōrən\	enjoy	[ɪnˈdʒɔɪ, ɛn-]	\inˈjói, en-\
edge	[ˈɛdʒ]	\ˈej\	enlarge	[ɪnˈlardʒ, ɛn-]	\inˈlärj, en-\
edit	[ˈɛdɪt]	\ˈedit\	enlist	[ɪnˈlɪst, ɛn-]	\inˈlist, en-\
educate	[ˈɛdʒəˌkeɪt]	\ˈejəˌkāt\	enormous	[ɪˈnɔrməs]	\iˈnórməs\
effect	[ɪˈfɛkt]	\iˈfekt\	enough	[ɪˈnʌf]	\iˈnəf\
efficient	[ɪˈfɪʃənt]	\iˈfishᵊnt\	enrage	[ɪnˈreɪdʒ, ɛn-]	\inˈrāj, en-\
effort	[ˈɛfərt]	\ˈefərt\	enrich	[ɪnˈrɪtʃ, ɛn-]	\inˈrich, en-\
egg	[ˈɛg]	\ˈeg\	ensure	[ɪnˈʃʊr, ɛn-]	\inˈshür, en-\
eight	[ˈeɪt]	\ˈāt\	entail	[ɪnˈteɪl, ɛn-]	\inˈtāl, en-\
eighteen	[eitˈtiːn]	\ātˈtēn\	entangle	[ɪnˈtæŋgəl, ɛn-]	\inˈtaŋᵊl, en-\
eighth	[ˈeɪtθ]	\ˈātth\	enter	[ˈɛntər]	\ˈentər\
eighty	[ˈeɪti]	\ˈātē\	enterprise	[ˈɛntərˌpraɪz]	\ˈentərˌprīz\
either	[ˈiːðər, ˈaɪ-]	\ˈēthᵊr, ˈī-\	entertain	[ˌɛntərˈteɪn]	\ˌentərˈtān\
eject	[iˈdʒɛkt]	\ēˈjekt\	enthusiasm	[ɪnˈθuːziˌæzəm]	\inˈthüzēˌazᵊm\
elaborate	[iˈlæbərət; iˈlæbəˌreɪt]	\ēˈlabərət; ēˈlabəˌrāt\	entire	[ɪnˈtaɪr, ɛn-]	\inˈtīr, en-\
elastic	[iˈlæstɪk]	\ēˈlastik\	entitle	[ɪnˈtaɪtəl, ɛn-]	\inˈtītᵊl, en-\
elbow	[ˈɛlˌboː]	\ˈelˌbō\	entity	[ˈɛntəti]	\ˈentətē\
elder	[ˈɛldər]	\ˈeldər\	entrance	[ɪnˈtrænts; ˈɛntrənts]	\inˈtran(t)s; ˈentrᵊn(t)s\
elect	[iˈlɛkt]	\ēˈlekt\	entrust	[ɪnˈtrʌst, ɛn-]	\inˈtrəst, en-\
electricity	[iˌlɛkˈtrɪsəti]	\ē̞ˌlekˈtrisətē\	entry	[ˈɛntri]	\ˈentrē\
electronic	[iˌlɛkˈtranɪk]	\ē̞ˌlekˈtränik\	envelop	[ɪnˈvɛləp, ɛn-]	\inˈveləp, en-\
elegant	[ˈɛlɪgə nt]	\ˈeligᵊnt\	envious	[ˈɛnviəs]	\ˈenvēəs\
element	[ˈɛləmənt]	\ˈeləmənt\	environment	[ɪnˈvaɪrənmənt]	\inˈvīrənmənt-\
elephant	[ˈɛləfənt]	\ˈeləfᵊnt\	envy	[ˈɛnvi]	\ˈenvē\
elevate	[ˈɛləˌveɪt]	\ˈeləˌvāt\	enzyme	[ˈɛnˌzaɪm]	\ˈenˌzīm\
eleven	[ɪˈlɛvən]	\iˈlevᵊn\	epidemic	[ˌɛpəˈdɛmɪk]	\ˌepəˈdemik\
eliminate	[ɪˈlɪməˌneɪt]	\iˈliməˌnāt\	episode	[ˈɛpəˌsoːd]	\ˈepəˌsōd\
elliptical	[ɪˈlɪptɪkəl, ɛ-]	\iˈliptikᵊl, e-\	epoch	[ˈɛpək, ˈɛˌpak, ˈiːˌpak]	\ˈepək, ˈeˌpäk, ˈēˌpäk\
elm	[ˈɛlm]	\ˈelm\	equal	[ˈiːkwəl]	\ˈēkwəl\
else	[ˈɛls]	\ˈels\	equation	[ɪˈkweɪʒən]	\iˈkwāzhᵊn\
embark	[ɪmˈbark, ɛm-]	\imˈbärk, em-\	equator	[ɪˈkweɪtər]	\iˈkwātər\
embarrass	[ɪmˈbærəs, ɛm-]	\imˈbarəs, em-\	equipment	[ɪˈkwɪpmənt]	\iˈkwipmənt\
embrace	[ɪmˈbreɪs, ɛm-]	\imˈbrās, em-\	equivalent	[ɪˈkwɪvələnt]	\iˈkwivᵊlənt\
embryo	[ˈɛmbriˌoː]	\ˈembrēˌō\	era	[ˈɪrə, ˈɛrə, ˈiːrə]	\ˈirə, ˈerə, ˈērə\
emerald	[ˈɛmrəld, ˈɛmə-]	\ˈemrəld, ˈemə-\	erase	[ɪˈreɪs]	\iˈrās\
emerge	[iˈmərdʒ]	\ēˈmərj\	errand	[ˈɛrənd]	\ˈerənd\
emergency	[iˈmərdʒəntsi]	\ēˈmərjᵊn(t)sē\	error	[ˈɛrər]	\ˈerər\
emigrant	[ˈɛmɪgrənt]	\ˈemigrᵊnt\	eruption	[ɪˈrʌpʃən]	\iˈrəpshᵊn\

ENGLISH WORD	IPA	M-W	ENGLISH WORD	IPA	M-W
escalator	[ˈɛskəˌleɪtər]	\ˈeskəˌlātər\	external	[ɪkˈstərnəl, ɛk-]	\ikˈstərnᵊl, ek-\
escape	[ɪˈskeɪp, ɛ-]	\iˈskāp, e-\	extra	[ˈɛkstrə]	\ˈekstrə\
Eskimo	[ˈɛskəˌmoː]	\ˈeskəˌmō\	extraordinary	[ɪkˈstrɔrdənˌɛri, ˌɛkstrəˈɔrd-]	
especially	[ɪˈspɛʃəli]	\iˈspeshˑlē\			\ikˈstrȯrdᵊnˌerē, ˌekstrəˈȯrd-\
espresso	[ɛˈsprɛˌsoː]	\eˈspreˌsō\	extreme	[ɪkˈstriːm, ɛk-]	\ikˈstrēm, ek-\
essay	[ˈɛˌseɪ]	\ˈeˌsā\	extrovert	[ˈɛkstrəˌvərt]	\ˈekstrəˌvərt\
essence	[ˈɛsənts]	\ˈesᵊn(t)s\	eye	[ˈaɪ]	\ˈī\
establish	[ɪˈstæblɪʃ, ɛ-]	\iˈstablish, e-\	fable	[ˈfeɪbəl]	\ˈfābᵊl\
estimate	[ˈɛstəˌmeɪt, -mət]	\ˈestəˌmāt, -mət\	fabric	[ˈfæbrɪk]	\ˈfabrik\
eternal	[ɪˈtərnəl, iː-]	\iˈtərnᵊl, ē-\	fabulous	[ˈfæbjələs]	\ˈfabyələs\
ethics	[ˈɛθɪks]	\ˈethiks\	facade	[fəˈsad]	\fəˈsäd\
ethnic	[ˈɛθnɪk]	\ˈethnik\	face	[ˈfeɪs]	\ˈfās\
European	[ˌjuːrəˈpiːən, -piːn]	\ˌyu̇rəˈpēən, -pēn\	facial	[ˈfeɪʃəl]	\ˈfāshᵊl\
evaluate	[ɪˈvæljuˌeɪt]	\iˈvalyu̇ˌāt\	facetious	[fəˈsiːʃəs]	\fəˈsēshəs\
eve	[ˈiːv]	\ˈēv\	facility	[fəˈsɪləti]	\fəˈsilətē\
even	[ˈiːvən]	\ˈēvᵊn\	facsimile	[fækˈsɪməli]	\fakˈsiməlē\
evening	[ˈiːvnɪŋ]	\ˈēvniŋ\	fact	[ˈfækt]	\ˈfakt\
event	[ɪˈvɛnt]	\iˈvent\	faction	[ˈfækʃən]	\ˈfakshᵊn\
ever	[ˈɛvər]	\ˈevər\	factor	[ˈfæktər]	\ˈfaktər\
every	[ˈɛvri]	\ˈevrē\	factory	[ˈfæktəri]	\ˈfaktərē\
evidence	[ˈɛvədənts]	\ˈevədən(t)s\	faculty	[ˈfækəlti]	\ˈfakᵊltē\
evil	[ˈiːvəl, -vɪl]	\ˈēvᵊl, -vil\	fad	[ˈfæd]	\ˈfad\
evolution	[ˌɛvəˈluːʃən, ˌiː-]	\ˌevəˈlüshᵊn, ē-\	fail	[ˈfeɪl]	\ˈfāl\
exact	[ɪgˈzækt, ɛg-]	\igˈzakt, eg-\	faint	[ˈfeɪnt]	\ˈfānt\
exaggerate	[ɪgˈzædʒəˌreɪt, ɛg-]	\igˈzajəˌrāt, eg-\	fair	[ˈfær]	\ˈfar\
examine	[ɪgˈzæmən, ɛg-]	\igˈzamᵊn, eg-\	fairy	[ˈfæri]	\ˈfarē\
example	[ɪgˈzæmpəl, ɛg-]	\igˈzampᵊl, eg-\	faith	[ˈfeɪθ]	\ˈfāth\
excellent	[ˈɛksələnt]	\ˈeksᵊlənt\	fall	[ˈfɔl]	\ˈfȯl\
except	[ɪkˈsɛpt]	\ikˈsept\	false	[ˈfɔls]	\ˈfȯls\
excess	[ɪkˈsɛs, ˈɛkˌsɛs]	\ikˈses, ˈekˌses\	fame	[ˈfeɪm]	\ˈfām\
exchange	[ɪksˈtʃeɪndʒ, ɛks-; ˈɛksˌtʃeɪndʒ]		familiar	[fəˈmɪljər]	\fəˈmilyər\
		\iksˈchānj, eks-; ˈeksˌchānj\	family	[ˈfæmli, ˈfæmə-]	\ˈfamlē, ˈfamə-\
excite	[ɪkˈsaɪt, ɛk-]	\ikˈsīt, ek-\	famous	[ˈfeɪməs]	\ˈfāməs\
exclaim	[ɪksˈkleɪm, ɛk-]	\iksˈklām, ek-\	fan	[ˈfæn]	\ˈfan\
excluding	[ɪksˈkluːdɪŋ, ɛks-]	\iksˈklüdiŋ, eks-\	fantasy	[ˈfæntəsi]	\ˈfantəsē\
excuse	[ɪkˈskjuːz, ɛk-; ɪkˈskjuːs]		far	[ˈfar]	\ˈfär\
		\ikˈskyüz, ek-; ikˈskyüs\	farewell	[færˈwɛl]	\farˈwel\
execute	[ˈɛksɪˌkjuːt]	\ˈeksiˌkyüt\	farm	[ˈfarm]	\ˈfärm\
executive	[ɪgˈzɛkjətɪv, ɛg-]	\igˈzekyətiv, eg-\	fascinate	[ˈfæsəˌneɪt]	\ˈfasᵊnˌāt\
exercise	[ˈɛksərˌsaɪz]	\ˈeksərˌsīz\	fashion	[ˈfæʃən]	\ˈfashᵊn\
exhaust	[ɪgˈzɔst, ɛg-]	\igˈzȯst, eg-\	fast	[ˈfæst]	\ˈfast\
exhibit	[ɪgˈzɪbət, ɛg-]	\igˈzibət, eg-\	fasten	[ˈfæsən]	\ˈfasᵊn\
exist	[ɪgˈzɪst, ɛg-]	\igˈzist, eg-\	fat	[ˈfæt]	\ˈfat\
exit	[ˈɛgzət, ˈɛksət]	\ˈegzət, ˈeksət\	fatal	[ˈfeɪtəl]	\ˈfātᵊl\
expect	[ɪkˈspɛkt, ɛk-]	\ikˈspekt, ek-\	fate	[ˈfeɪt]	\ˈfāt\
expedition	[ˌɛkspəˈdɪʃən]	\ˌekspəˈdishᵊn\	father	[ˈfaðər]	\ˈfäthər\
expend	[ɪkˈspɛnd, ɛk-]	\ikˈspend, ek-\	fatigue	[fəˈtiːg]	\fəˈtēg\
experience	[ɪkˈspɪriənts, ɛk-]	\ikˈspirēən(t)s, ek-\	fatten	[ˈfætən]	\ˈfatᵊn\
expert	[ˈɛkˌspərt, ɪkˈspərt]	\ˈekˌspərt, ikˈspərt\	faucet	[ˈfɔsət]	\ˈfȯsət\
expire	[ɪkˈspaɪr, ɛk-]	\ikˈspīr, ek-\	fault	[ˈfɔlt]	\ˈfȯlt\
explain	[ɪkˈspleɪn, ɛk-]	\ikˈsplān, ek-\	fauna	[ˈfɔnə]	\ˈfȯnə\
export	[ɛkˈsport, ˈɛkˌsport]	\ekˈspōrt, ˈekˌspōrt\	fear	[ˈfɪr]	\ˈfir\
expose	[ɪkˈspoːz, ɛk-]	\ikˈspōz, ek-\	feasible	[ˈfiːzəbəl]	\ˈfēzəbᵊl\
express	[ɪkˈsprɛs, ɛk-]	\ikˈspres, ek-\	feast	[ˈfiːst]	\ˈfēst\
extend	[ɪkˈstɛnd, ɛk-]	\ikˈstend, ek-\	feat	[ˈfiːt]	\ˈfēt\
exterior	[ɛkˈstɪriər]	\ekˈstirēər\	feather	[ˈfɛðər]	\ˈfethər\

ENGLISH WORD	IPA	M-W	ENGLISH WORD	IPA	M-W
feature	[ˈfiːtʃər]	\ˈfēchər\	flier	[ˈflaɪər]	\ˈflīər\
February	[ˈfɛbjʊˌɛri, ˈfɛbru-]	\ˈfebyùˌerē, ˈfebrù-\	flight	[ˈflaɪt]	\ˈflīt\
fee	[ˈfiː]	\ˈfē\	flipper	[ˈflɪpər]	\ˈflipər\
feeble	[ˈfiːbəl]	\ˈfēbᵊl\	float	[ˈfloːt]	\ˈflōt\
feed	[ˈfiːd]	\ˈfēd\	flock	[ˈflɑk]	\ˈfläk\
feel	[ˈfiːl]	\ˈfēl\	flood	[ˈflʌd]	\ˈfləd\
female	[ˈfiːˌmeɪl]	\ˈfēˌmāl\	floor	[ˈflor]	\ˈflōr\
feminine	[ˈfɛmənən]	\ˈfemənən\	flour	[ˈflaʊər]	\ˈflaùər\
fence	[ˈfɛnts]	\ˈfen(t)s\	flourish	[ˈflərɪʃ]	\ˈflərish\
fender	[ˈfɛndər]	\ˈfendər\	flow	[ˈfloː]	\ˈflō\
ferment	[fərˈmɛnt]	\fərˈment\	flower	[ˈflaʊər]	\ˈflaùər\
fertility	[fərˈtɪləti]	\fərˈtilətē\	flu	[ˈfluː]	\ˈflü\
festive	[ˈfɛstɪv]	\ˈfestiv\	fluctuate	[ˈflʌktʃʊˌeɪt]	\ˈfləkchùˌāt\
fever	[ˈfiːvər]	\ˈfēvər\	fluency	[ˈfluːəntsi]	\ˈflüən(t)sē\
few	[ˈfjuː]	\ˈfyü\	fluid	[ˈfluːɪd]	\ˈflüid\
fiction	[ˈfɪkʃən]	\ˈfikshᵊn\	flush	[ˈflʌʃ]	\ˈfləsh\
fidelity	[fəˈdɛləti, faɪ-]	\fəˈdelətē, fī-\	flute	[ˈfluːt]	\ˈflüt\
field	[ˈfiːld]	\ˈfēld\	fly	[ˈflaɪ]	\ˈflī\
fifteen	[fɪfˈtiːn]	\fifˈtēn\	foamy	[ˈfoːmi]	\ˈfōmē\
fifth	[ˈfɪfθ]	\ˈfifth\	focus	[ˈfoːkəs]	\ˈfōkəs\
fifty	[ˈfɪfti]	\ˈfiftē\	fog	[ˈfɔg, ˈfɑg]	\ˈfòg, ˈfäg\
fight	[ˈfaɪt]	\ˈfīt\	fold	[ˈfoːld]	\ˈfōld\
figure	[ˈfɪgjər, -gər]	\ˈfigyər, -gər\	folklore	[ˈfoːkˌlor]	\ˈfōkˌlōr\
file	[ˈfaɪl]	\ˈfīl\	follow	[ˈfɑlo]	\ˈfälō\
fill	[ˈfɪl]	\ˈfil\	fondness	[ˈfɑndnəs]	\ˈfändnəs\
film	[ˈfɪlm]	\ˈfilm\	food	[ˈfuːd]	\ˈfüd\
filter	[ˈfɪltər]	\ˈfiltər\	fool	[ˈfuːl]	\ˈfül\
fin	[ˈfɪn]	\ˈfin\	foot	[ˈfʊt]	\ˈfùt\
final	[ˈfaɪnəl]	\ˈfīnᵊl\	for	[ˈfɔr]	\ˈfòr\
finance	[fəˈnænts, ˈfaɪˌnænts]	\fəˈnan(t)s, ˈfīˌnan(t)s\	forbid	[fərˈbɪd]	\fərˈbid\
find	[ˈfaɪnd]	\ˈfīnd\	force	[ˈfors]	\ˈfōrs\
fine	[ˈfaɪn]	\ˈfīn\	forearm	[ˈforˌɑrm]	\ˈfōrˌärm\
finger	[ˈfɪŋgər]	\ˈfiŋgər\	forecast	[ˈforˌkæst]	\ˈfōrˌkast\
finish	[ˈfɪnɪʃ]	\ˈfinish\	forefinger	[ˈforˌfɪŋgər]	\ˈfōrˌfiŋgər\
finite	[ˈfaɪˌnaɪt]	\ˈfīˌnīt\	forefront	[ˈforˌfrʌnt]	\ˈfōrˌfrənt\
fire	[ˈfaɪr]	\ˈfīr\	forehead	[ˈforəd, ˈforˌhɛd]	\ˈfòrəd, ˈfōrˌhed\
firm	[ˈfərm]	\ˈfərm\	foreign	[ˈfɔrən]	\ˈfòrən\
first	[ˈfərst]	\ˈfərst\	forest	[ˈfɔrəst]	\ˈfòrəst\
fiscal	[ˈfɪskəl]	\ˈfiskᵊl\	foretell	[forˈtɛl]	\fōrˈtel\
fish	[ˈfɪʃ]	\ˈfish\	forever	[fɔrˈɛvər]	\fòrˈevər\
fit	[ˈfɪt]	\ˈfit\	forfeit	[ˈfɔrfət]	\ˈfòrfət\
five	[ˈfaɪv]	\ˈfīv\	forge	[ˈfordʒ]	\ˈfōrj\
fix	[ˈfɪks]	\ˈfiks\	forget	[fərˈgɛt]	\fərˈget\
flag	[ˈflæg]	\ˈflag\	forgive	[fərˈgɪv]	\fərˈgiv\
flame	[ˈfleɪm]	\ˈflām\	form	[ˈfɔrm]	\ˈfòrm\
flammable	[ˈflæməbəl]	\ˈflaməbᵊl\	formal	[ˈfɔrməl]	\ˈfòrmᵊl\
flap	[ˈflæp]	\ˈflap\	formation	[fɔrˈmeɪʃən]	\fòrˈmāshᵊn\
flash	[ˈflæʃ]	\ˈflash\	former	[ˈfɔrmər]	\ˈfòrmər\
flatter	[ˈflætər]	\ˈflatər\	formula	[ˈfɔrmjələ]	\ˈfòrmyələ\
flaw	[ˈflɔ]	\ˈflò\	fortunate	[ˈfɔrtʃənət]	\ˈfòrchᵊnət\
flea	[ˈfliː]	\ˈflē\	forty	[ˈfɔrti]	\ˈfòrtē\
flee	[ˈfliː]	\ˈflē\	forward	[ˈfɔrwərd]	\ˈfòrwərd\
fleet	[ˈfliːt]	\ˈflēt\	foul	[ˈfaʊl]	\ˈfaùl\
fleeting	[ˈfliːtɪŋ]	\ˈflētiŋ\	found	[ˈfaʊnd]	\ˈfaùnd\
Flemish	[ˈflɛmɪʃ]	\ˈflemish\	fountain	[ˈfaʊntən]	\ˈfaùntᵊn\
flexibility	[ˌflɛksəˈbɪləti]	\ˌfleksəˈbilətē\	four	[ˈfor]	\ˈfōr\

ENGLISH WORD	IPA	M-W	ENGLISH WORD	IPA	M-W
fourteen	[for'ti:n]	\fȯr'tēn\	gamble	['gæmbəl]	\'gambᵊl\
fourth	['forθ]	\'fȯrth\	game	['geɪm]	\'gām\
fox	['faks]	\'fäks\	gang	['gæŋ]	\'gaŋ\
fraction	['frækʃən]	\'frakshᵊn\	gap	['gæp]	\'gap\
fracture	['fræktʃər]	\'frakchər\	garage	[gə'raʒ, -'radʒ]	\gə'räzh, -'räj\
fragile	['frædʒəl, -ˌdʒaɪl]	\'frajəl, -ˌjīl\	garbage	['garbɪdʒ]	\'gärbij\
fragment	['frægmənt]	\'fragmənt\	garden	['gardən]	\'gärdᵊn\
fragrance	['freɪgrənts]	\'frāgrᵊn(t)s\	garlic	['garlɪk]	\'gärlik\
frail	['freɪl]	\'frāl\	gas	['gæs]	\'gas\
frame	['freɪm]	\'frām\	gasoline	['gæsəˌli:n, ˌgæsə'-]	\'gasəˌlēn, ˌgasə'-\
frank	['fræŋk]	\'fraŋk\	gasp	['gæsp]	\'gasp\
fraternal	[frə'tərnəl]	\frə'tərnᵊl\	gate	['geɪt]	\'gāt\
freckle	['frɛkəl]	\'frekᵊl\	gather	['gæðər]	\'gathər\
free	['fri:]	\'frē\	gauze	['gɔz]	\'gȯz\
freeze	['fri:z]	\'frēz\	gay	['geɪ]	\'gā\
French	['frɛntʃ]	\'fren(t)ch\	gaze	['geɪz]	\'gāz\
frequent	[fri'kwɛnt, 'fri:kwənt]	\frē'kwent, 'frēkwənt\	gear	['gɪr]	\'gir\
fresh	['frɛʃ]	\'fresh\	gelatin	['dʒɛlətən]	\'jelətᵊn\
friction	['frɪkʃən]	\'frikshᵊn\	gender	['dʒɛndər]	\'jendər\
Friday	['fraɪˌdeɪ, -di]	\'frīˌdā, -dē\	gene	['dʒi:n]	\'jēn\
friend	['frɛnd]	\'frend\	genealogy	[ˌdʒi:ni'alədʒi, ˌdʒɛ-, -'æ-]	
fright	['fraɪt]	\'frīt\			\ˌjēnē'äləjē, je-, -'a-\
frill	['frɪl]	\'fril\	general	['dʒɛnrəl, 'dʒɛnə-]	\'jenrəl, 'jenə-\
frisk	['frɪsk]	\'frisk\	generate	['dʒɛnəˌreɪt]	\'jenəˌrāt\
frivolous	['frɪvələs]	\'frivələs\	generous	['dʒɛnərəs]	\'jenərəs\
frog	['frɔg, 'frag]	\'frȯg, 'fräg\	genial	['dʒi:niəl]	\'jēnēəl\
from	['frʌm, 'fram]	\'frəm, 'främ\	genius	['dʒi:njəs]	\'jēnyəs\
front	['frʌnt]	\'frənt\	gentle	['dʒɛntəl]	\'jentᵊl\
frontier	[ˌfrʌn'tɪr]	\ˌfrən'tir\	genuine	['dʒɛnjuwən]	\'jenyəwən\
frost	['frɔst]	\'frȯst\	geography	[dʒi'agrəfi]	\jē'ägrəfē\
froth	['frɔθ]	\'frȯth\	geology	[dʒi'alədʒi]	\jē'äləjē\
fruit	['fru:t]	\'früt\	geometry	[dʒi'amətri]	\jē'ämətrē\
frustrate	['frʌsˌtreɪt]	\'frəsˌtrāt\	geriatric	[ˌdʒɛri'ætrɪk]	\ˌjerē'atrik\
fry	['fraɪ]	\'frī\	German	['dʒərmən]	\'jərmən\
fuel	['fju:əl]	\'fyüəl\	gesture	['dʒɛstʃər]	\'jeschər\
fugitive	['fju:dʒətɪv]	\'fyüjətiv\	get	['gɛt]	\'get\
full	['fʊl, 'fʌl]	\'fu̇l, 'fəl\	ghost	['go:st]	\'gōst\
fun	['fʌn]	\'fən\	giant	['dʒaɪənt]	\'jīənt\
function	['fʌŋkʃən]	\'fəŋkshᵊn\	gift	['gɪft]	\'gift\
fund	['fʌnd]	\'fənd\	gigantic	[dʒaɪ'gæntɪk]	\jī'gantik\
fundamental	[ˌfʌndə'mɛntəl]	\ˌfəndə'mentᵊl\	gild	['gɪld]	\'gild\
funeral	['fju:nərəl]	\'fyünərəl\	ginger	['dʒɪndʒər]	\'jinjər\
fungus	['fʌŋgəs]	\'fəŋgəs\	giraffe	[dʒə'ræf]	\jə'raf\
funny	['fʌni]	\'fənē\	girl	['gərl]	\'gərl\
furious	['fjʊriəs]	\'fyu̇rēəs\	gist	['dʒɪst]	\'jist\
furnace	['fərnəs]	\'fərnəs\	give	['gɪv]	\'giv\
furnish	['fərnɪʃ]	\'fərnish\	glad	['glæd]	\'glad\
furry	['fəri]	\'fərē\	glance	['glænts]	\'glan(t)s\
furthermore	['fərðərˌmor]	\'fərthərˌmōr\	glare	['glær]	\'glar\
fuss	['fʌs]	\'fəs\	glass	['glæs]	\'glas\
future	['fju:tʃər]	\'fyüchər\	gleam	['gli:m]	\'glēm\
gain	['geɪn]	\'gān\	glide	['glaɪd]	\'glīd\
galaxy	['gæləksi]	\'galəksē\	glimmer	['glɪmər]	\'glimər\
gallery	['gæləri]	\'galərē\	globe	['glo:b]	\'glōb\
gallon	['gælən]	\'galᵊn\	gloom	['glu:m]	\'glüm\
gallop	['gæləp]	gloom	glory	['glori]	\'glōrē\

ENGLISH WORD	IPA	M-W	ENGLISH WORD	IPA	M-W
glossary	[ˈglɔsəri, ˈglɑ-]	\ˈglȯsərē, ˈglä-\	group	[ˈgru:p]	\ˈgrüp\
glove	[ˈglʌv]	\ˈgləv\	grove	[ˈgro:v]	\ˈgrōv\
glow	[ˈglo:]	\ˈglō\	grow	[ˈgro:]	\ˈgrō\
glue	[ˈglu:]	\ˈglü\	growl	[ˈgraʊl]	\ˈgraúl\
glum	[ˈglʌm]	\ˈgləm\	grown-up	[ˈgro:nˌəp]	\ˈgrōnˌəp\
go	[ˈgo:]	\ˈgō\	growth	[ˈgro:θ]	\ˈgrōth\
goal	[ˈgo:l]	\ˈgōl\	grumble	[ˈgrʌmbəl]	\ˈgrəmbᵊl\
goat	[ˈgo:t]	\ˈgōt\	grunt	[ˈgrʌnt]	\ˈgrənt\
god	[ˈgɑd, ˈgɔd]	\ˈgäd, ˈgȯd\	guarantee	[ˌgærənˈti:]	\ˌgarənˈtē\
gold	[ˈgo:ld]	\ˈgōld\	guard	[ˈgɑrd]	\ˈgärd\
golf	[ˈgɑlf, ˈgɔlf]	\ˈgälf, ˈgȯlf\	guess	[ˈgɛs]	\ˈges\
gone	[ˈgɔn]	\ˈgȯn\	guest	[ˈgɛst]	\ˈgest\
good	[ˈgʊd]	\ˈgúd\	guide	[ˈgaɪd]	\ˈgīd\
goose	[ˈgu:s]	\ˈgüs\	guilt	[ˈgɪlt]	\ˈgilt\
gorilla	[gəˈrɪlə]	\gəˈrilə\	guitar	[gəˈtɑr, gɪ-]	\gəˈtär, gi-\
gossip	[ˈgɑsɪp]	\ˈgäsip\	gulf	[ˈgʌlf]	\ˈgəlf\
gourmet	[ˈgʊrˌmeɪ, gʊrˈmeɪ]	\ˈgùrˌmā, gùrˈmā\	gull	[ˈgʌl]	\ˈgəl\
govern	[ˈgʌvərn]	\ˈgəvərn\	gulp	[ˈgʌlp]	\ˈgəlp\
gown	[ˈgaʊn]	\ˈgaún\	gum	[ˈgʌm]	\ˈgəm\
grace	[ˈgreɪs]	\ˈgrās\	gun	[ˈgʌn]	\ˈgən\
grade	[ˈgreɪd]	\ˈgrād\	gut	[ˈgʌt]	\ˈgət\
gradual	[ˈgrædʒʊəl]	\ˈgrajùəl\	guy	[ˈgaɪ]	\ˈgī\
graduate	[ˈgrædʒʊət; ˈgrædʒʊˌeɪt]	\ˈgrajùət; ˈgrajùˌāt\	gym	[ˈdʒɪm]	\ˈjim\
graffiti	[grəˈfi:ti, græ-]	\grəˈfētē, gra-\	habit	[ˈhæbɪt]	\ˈhabit\
grain	[ˈgreɪn]	\ˈgrān\	habitual	[həˈbɪtʃʊəl]	\həˈbichùəl\
gram	[ˈgræm]	\ˈgram\	hack	[ˈhæk]	\ˈhak\
grammar	[ˈgræmər]	\ˈgramər\	hail	[ˈheɪl]	\ˈhāl\
grand	[ˈgrænd]	\ˈgrand\	hair	[ˈhær]	\ˈhar\
grant	[ˈgrænt]	\ˈgrant\	hale	[ˈheɪl]	\ˈhāl\
grape	[ˈgreɪp]	\ˈgrāp\	half	[ˈhæf, ˈhaf]	\ˈhaf, ˈhäf\
grapefruit	[ˈgreɪpˌfru:t]	\ˈgrāpˌfrüt\	hall	[ˈhɔl]	\ˈhȯl\
graph	[ˈgræf]	\ˈgraf\	hallmark	[ˈhɔlˌmɑrk]	\ˈhȯlˌmärk\
grasp	[ˈgræsp]	\ˈgrasp\	Halloween	[ˌhæləˈwi:n, ˌhɑ-]	\ˌhaləˈwēn, ˌhä-\
grass	[ˈgræs]	\ˈgras\	hallucination	[həˌlu:sənˈeɪʃən]	\həˌlüsᵊnˈāshᵊn\
grateful	[ˈgreɪtfəl]	\ˈgrātfᵊl\	hallway	[ˈhɔlˌweɪ]	\ˈhȯlˌwā\
gratitude	[ˈgrætəˌtu:d, -ˌtju:d]	\ˈgratəˌtüd, -ˌtyüd\	halt	[ˈhɔlt]	\ˈhȯlt\
grave	[ˈgreɪv]	\ˈgrāv\	halve	[ˈhæv, ˈhav]	\ˈhav, ˈhäv\
graveyard	[ˈgreɪvˌjɑrd]	\ˈgrāvˌyärd\	ham	[ˈhæm]	\ˈham\
gravity	[ˈgrævəti]	\ˈgravətē\	hamburger	[ˈhæmˌbərgər]	\ˈhamˌbərgər\
gray	[ˈgreɪ]	\ˈgrā\	hammer	[ˈhæmər]	\ˈhamər\
grease	[ˈgri:s]	\ˈgrēs\	hammock	[ˈhæmək]	\ˈhamək\
great	[ˈgreɪt]	\ˈgrāt\	hamper	[ˈhæmpər]	\ˈhampər\
Greek	[ˈgri:k]	\ˈgrēk\	hamster	[ˈhæmpstər]	\ˈham(p)stər\
green	[ˈgri:n]	\ˈgrēn\	hand	[ˈhænd]	\ˈhand\
greet	[ˈgri:t]	\ˈgrēt\	handicap	[ˈhændiˌkæp]	\ˈhandēˌkap\
grid	[ˈgrɪd]	\ˈgrid\	handicrafts	[ˈhændiˌkræfts]	\ˈhandēˌkrafts\
grief	[ˈgri:f]	\ˈgrēf\	handkerchief	[ˈhæŋkərtʃəf, -ˌtʃi:f]	\ˈhaŋkərchəf, -ˌchēf\
grill	[ˈgrɪl]	\ˈgril\	handle	[ˈhændəl]	\ˈhandᵊl\
grim	[ˈgrɪm]	\ˈgrim\	handout	[ˈhændˌaʊt]	\ˈhandˌaút\
grime	[ˈgraɪm]	\ˈgrīm\	handrail	[ˈhændˌreɪl]	\ˈhandˌrāl\
grinder	[ˈgraɪndər]	\ˈgrīndər\	handshake	[ˈhændˌʃeɪk]	\ˈhandˌshāk\
grip	[ˈgrɪp]	\ˈgrip\	handsome	[ˈhæntsəm]	\ˈhan(t)sᵊm\
groan	[ˈgro:n]	\ˈgrōn\	handwriting	[ˈhændˌraɪtɪŋ]	\ˈhandˌrītiŋ\
groggy	[ˈgrɑgi]	\ˈgrägē\	hang	[ˈhæŋ]	\ˈhaŋ\
groom	[ˈgru:m, ˈgrʊm]	\ˈgrüm, ˈgrùm\	happen	[ˈhæpən]	\ˈhapᵊn\
ground	[ˈgraʊnd]	\ˈgraúnd\	happy	[ˈhæpi]	\ˈhapē\

ENGLISH WORD	IPA	M-W	ENGLISH WORD	IPA	M-W
hard	[ˈhɑrd]	\ˈhärd\	his	[ˈhɪz, ɪz]	\ˈhiz, iz\
hardy	[ˈhɑrdi]	\ˈhärdē\	Hispanic	[hɪˈspænɪk]	\hiˈspanik\
harm	[ˈhɑrm]	\ˈhärm\	history	[ˈhɪstəri]	\ˈhistərē\
harmony	[ˈhɑrməni]	\ˈhärmənē\	hit	[ˈhɪt]	\ˈhit\
harness	[ˈhɑrnəs]	\ˈhärnəs\	hoarse	[ˈhors]	\ˈhōrs\
harsh	[ˈhɑrʃ]	\ˈhärsh\	hobby	[ˈhabi]	\ˈhäbē\
harvest	[ˈhɑrvəst]	\ˈhärvəst\	hockey	[ˈhaki]	\ˈhäkē\
haste	[ˈheɪst]	\ˈhāst\	hog	[ˈhɔg, ˈhag]	\ˈhóg, ˈhäg\
hat	[ˈhæt]	\ˈhat\	hold	[ˈhoːld]	\ˈhōld\
hatchet	[ˈhætʃət]	\ˈhachət\	hole	[ˈhoːl]	\ˈhōl\
hate	[ˈheɪt]	\ˈhāt\	holiday	[ˈhalə,deɪ]	\ˈhälə,dā\
haughty	[ˈhɔti]	\ˈhótē\	hollow	[ˈha,loː]	\ˈhä,lō\
haul	[ˈhɔl]	\ˈhól\	holy	[ˈhoːli]	\ˈhōlē\
haunt	[ˈhɔnt]	\ˈhónt\	homage	[ˈamɪdʒ, ˈha-]	\ˈämij, ˈhä-\
have	[ˈhæv, ˈhæf]	\ˈhav, ˈhaf\	home	[ˈhoːm]	\ˈhōm\
haven	[ˈheɪvən]	\ˈhāvᵊn\	homicide	[ˈhamə,saɪd, ˈhoː-]	\ˈhämə,sīd, ˈhō-\
hawk	[ˈhɔk]	\ˈhók\	homogeneous	[ˌhoːməˈdʒiːniəs, -njəs]	\ˌhōməˈjēnēəs, -nyəs\
hazard	[ˈhæzərd]	\ˈhazərd\	honest	[ˈanəst]	\ˈänəst\
haze	[ˈheɪz]	\ˈhāz\	honey	[ˈhʌni]	\ˈhənē\
he	[ˈhiː]	\ˈhē\	hook	[ˈhʊk]	\ˈhük\
head	[ˈhɛd]	\ˈhed\	hope	[ˈhoːp]	\ˈhōp\
heal	[ˈhiːl]	\ˈhēl\	horizon	[həˈraɪzən]	\həˈrīzᵊn\
health	[ˈhɛlθ]	\ˈhelth\	hormone	[ˈhɔr,moːn]	\ˈhór,mōn\
hear	[ˈhɪr]	\ˈhir\	horn	[ˈhɔrn]	\ˈhórn\
heart	[ˈhɑrt]	\ˈhärt\	horoscope	[ˈhɔrə,skoːp]	\ˈhórə,skōp\
heat	[ˈhiːt]	\ˈhēt\	horror	[ˈhɔrər]	\ˈhórər\
heaven	[ˈhɛvən]	\ˈhevᵊn\	horse	[ˈhors]	\ˈhórs\
heavy	[ˈhɛvi]	\ˈhevē\	hose	[ˈhoːz]	\ˈhōz\
Hebrew	[ˈhiː,bruː]	\ˈhē,brü\	hospital	[ˈhas,pɪtəl]	\ˈhäs,pitᵊl\
heel	[ˈhiːl]	\ˈhēl\	host	[ˈhoːst]	\ˈhōst\
height	[ˈhaɪt]	\ˈhīt\	hostage	[ˈhastɪdʒ]	\ˈhästij\
heir	[ˈær]	\ˈar\	hostel	[ˈhastəl]	\ˈhästᵊl\
helicopter	[ˈhelə,kaptər]	\ˈhelə,käptər\	hot	[ˈhat]	\ˈhät\
hello	[həˈloː, hɛ-]	\həˈlō, he-\	hotel	[hoːˈtɛl]	\hōˈtel\
helmet	[ˈhɛlmət]	\ˈhelmət\	hound	[ˈhaʊnd]	\ˈhaúnd\
help	[ˈhɛlp]	\ˈhelp\	hour	[ˈaʊər]	\ˈaúər\
hem	[ˈhɛm]	\ˈhem\	house	[ˈhaʊs; ˈhaʊz]	\ˈhaús; ˈhaúz\
hemisphere	[ˈhɛmə,sfɪr]	\ˈhemə,sfir\	how	[ˈhaʊ]	\ˈhaú\
hen	[ˈhɛn]	\ˈhen\	however	[haʊˈɛvər]	\haúˈevər\
her	[ˈhər]	\ˈhər\	hug	[ˈhʌg]	\ˈhəg\
herb	[ˈərb, ˈhərb]	\ˈərb, ˈhərb\	human	[ˈhjuːmən, ˈjuː-]	\ˈhyümən, ˈyü-\
here	[ˈhɪr]	\ˈhir\	humble	[ˈhʌmbəl]	\ˈhəmbᵊl\
hero	[ˈhiː,roː, ˈhɪr,oː]	\ˈhē,rō, ˈhir,ō\	humid	[ˈhjuːməd, ˈjuː-]	\ˈhyüməd, ˈyü-\
hers	[ˈhərz]	\ˈhərz\	humiliate	[hjuːˈmɪli,eɪt, juː-]	\hyüˈmilē,āt, yü-\
hi	[ˈhaɪ]	\ˈhī\	hundred	[ˈhʌndrəd]	\ˈhəndrəd\
hiccup	[ˈhɪkəp]	\ˈhikəp\	Hungarian	[hʌŋˈgæriən]	\həŋˈgarēən\
hide	[ˈhaɪd]	\ˈhīd\	hunger	[ˈhʌŋgər]	\ˈhəŋgər\
hierarchy	[ˈhaɪə,rɑrki]	\ˈhīə,rärkē\	hunt	[ˈhʌnt]	\ˈhənt\
high	[ˈhaɪ]	\ˈhī\	hurdle	[ˈhərdəl]	\ˈhərdᵊl\
hiker	[ˈhaɪkər]	\ˈhīkər\	hurl	[ˈhərl]	\ˈhərl\
hill	[ˈhɪl]	\ˈhil\	hurrah	[hʊˈra, -ˈrɔ]	\húˈrä, -ˈró\
hilt	[ˈhɪlt]	\ˈhilt\	hurricane	[ˈhərə,keɪn]	\ˈhərə,kān\
him	[ˈhɪm, əm]	\ˈhim, əm\	hurry	[ˈhəri]	\ˈhərē\
Hindu	[ˈhɪn,duː]	\ˈhin,dü\	hurt	[ˈhərt]	\ˈhərt\
hinge	[ˈhɪndʒ]	\ˈhinj\	husband	[ˈhʌzbənd]	\ˈhəzbənd\
hip	[ˈhɪp]	\ˈhip\	hut	[ˈhʌt]	\ˈhət\

ENGLISH WORD	IPA	M-W	ENGLISH WORD	IPA	M-W
hygiene	[ˈhaɪˌdʒiːn]	\ˈhīˌjēn\	impossible	[ɪmˈpɑsəbəl]	\imˈpäsəbəl\
hymn	[ˈhɪm]	\ˈhim\	imprecise	[ˌɪmprɪˈsaɪs]	\impriˈsīs\
hyperactive	[ˌhaɪpərˈæktɪv]	\ˌhīpərˈaktiv\	impregnable	[ɪmˈprɛgnəbəl]	\imˈpregnəbəl\
hyphen	[ˈhaɪfən]	\ˈhīfᵊn\	impress	[ɪmˈprɛs]	\imˈpres\
hypothesis	[haɪˈpɑθəsɪs]	\hīˈpäthəsis\	improbable	[ɪmˈprɑbəbəl]	\imˈpräbəbəl\
hysteria	[hɪsˈtɛriə, -tɪr-]	\hisˈterēə, -tir-\	improve	[ɪmˈpruːv]	\imˈprüv\
ice	[ˈaɪs]	\ˈīs\	improvise	[ˈɪmprəˌvaɪz]	\ˈimprəˌvīz\
idea	[aɪˈdiːə]	\īˈdēə\	impulse	[ˈɪmˌpʌls]	\ˈimˌpəls\
ideal	[aɪˈdiːəl]	\īˈdēəl\	impure	[ɪmˈpjʊr]	\imˈpyür\
identity	[aɪˈdɛntəti]	\īˈdentətē\	in	[ˈɪn]	\ˈin\
ideology	[ˌaɪdiˈɑlədʒi, ˌɪ-]	\ˌīdēˈäləjē, ˌi-\	inability	[ˌɪnəˈbɪləti]	\ˌinəˈbilətē\
idiocy	[ˈɪdiəsi]	\ˈidēəsē\	inactive	[ɪnˈæktɪv]	\inˈaktiv\
idiom	[ˈɪdiəm]	\ˈidēəm\	inadequate	[ɪnˈædɪkwət]	\inˈadikwət\
idiot	[ˈɪdiət]	\ˈidēət\	inanimate	[ɪnˈænəmət]	\inˈanəmət\
idol	[ˈaɪdəl]	\ˈīdᵊl\	inappropriate	[ˌɪnəˈproːpriət]	\ˌinəˈprōprēət\
if	[ˈɪf]	\ˈif\	inaugurate	[ɪˈnɔgjəˌreɪt, -gə-]	\iˈnógyəˌrāt, -gə-\
ignore	[ɪgˈnor]	\igˈnōr\	incapable	[ɪnˈkeɪpəbəl]	\inˈkāpəbᵊl\
ill	[ˈɪl]	\ˈil\	incense	[ˈɪnˌsɛns]	\ˈinˌsen(t)s\
illegal	[ɪlˈliːgəl]	\ilˈlēgᵊl\	incense	[ɪnˈsɛns]	\inˈsen(t)s\
illegitimate	[ˌɪlɪˈdʒɪtəmət]	\ˌiliˈjitəmət\	inch	[ˈɪntʃ]	\ˈinch\
illiterate	[ɪlˈlɪtərət]	\ilˈlitərət\	incidentally	[ˌɪntsəˈdɛntəli, -ˈdɛntli]	
illogical	[ɪlˈlɑdʒɪkəl]	\ilˈläjikᵊl\			\ˌin(t)səˈdentᵊlē, -ˈdentlē\
illuminate	[ɪˈluːməˌneɪt]	\iˈlüməˌnāt\	incite	[ɪnˈsaɪt]	\inˈsīt\
illusion	[ɪˈluːʒən]	\iˈlüzhᵊn\	incline	[ɪnˈklaɪn; ˈɪnˌklaɪn]	\inˈklīn; ˈinˌklīn\
illustrate	[ˈɪləsˌtreɪt]	\ˈiləsˌtrāt\	include	[ɪnˈkluːd]	\inˈklüd\
illustrious	[ɪˈlʌstriəs]	\iˈləstrēəs\	incoherent	[ˌɪnkoˈhɪrənt, -ˈhɛr-]	\inkōˈhirənt, -ˈher-\
image	[ˈɪmɪdʒ]	\ˈimij\	income	[ˈɪnˌkʌm]	\ˈinˌkəm\
imbalance	[ɪmˈbælənts]	\imˈbalən(t)s\	incomparable	[ɪnˈkɑmpərəbəl]	\inˈkämpərəbᵊl\
imitation	[ˌɪməˈteɪʃən]	\ˌiməˈtāshᵊn\	incompetent	[ɪnˈkɑmpətənt]	\inˈkämpətənt\
immature	[ˌɪməˈtʃʊr, -ˈtjʊr, -ˈtʊr]		incomplete	[ˌɪnkəmˈpliːt]	\ˌinkəmˈplēt\
		\ˌiməˈchur, -ˈtyür, -ˈtür\	inconceivable	[ˌɪnkənˈsiːvəbəl]	\ˌinkənˈsēvəbᵊl\
immediate	[ɪˈmiːdiət]	\iˈmēdēət\	inconsiderate	[ˌɪnkənˈsɪdərət]	\ˌinkənˈsidərət\
immense	[ɪˈmɛnts]	\iˈmen(t)s\	inconvenient	[ˌɪnkənˈviːnjənt]	\ˌinkənˈvēnyənt\
immigrant	[ˈɪmɪgrənt]	\ˈimigrənt\	incorrect	[ˌɪnkəˈrɛkt]	\ˌinkəˈrekt\
imminent	[ˈɪmənənt]	\ˈimənənt\	increase	[ˈɪnˌkriːs, ɪnˈkriːs]	\ˈinˌkrēs, inˈkrēs\
immobile	[ɪmˈoːbəl]	\imˈōbᵊl\	incredible	[ɪnˈkrɛdəbəl]	\inˈkredəbᵊl\
immoral	[ɪˈmorəl]	\iˈmórəl\	incredulous	[ɪnˈkrɛdʒələs]	\inˈkrejələs\
impact	[ˈɪmˌpækt]	\ˈimˌpakt\	indebted	[ɪnˈdɛtəd]	\inˈdetəd\
impartial	[ɪmˈpɑrʃəl]	\imˈpärshᵊl\	indecisive	[ˌɪndɪˈsaɪsɪv]	\ˌindiˈsīsiv\
impatience	[ɪmˈpeɪʃənts]	\imˈpāshᵊn(t)s\	indefinite	[ɪnˈdɛfənət]	\inˈdefənət\
impeccable	[ɪmˈpɛkəbəl]	\imˈpekəbᵊl\	indelible	[ɪnˈdɛləbəl]	\inˈdeləbᵊl\
impede	[ɪmˈpiːd]	\imˈpēd\	independent	[ˌɪndəˈpɛndənt]	\ˌindəˈpendənt\
impending	[ɪmˈpɛndɪŋ]	\imˈpendiŋ\	index	[ˈɪnˌdɛks]	\ˈinˌdeks\
impenetrable	[ɪmˈpɛnətrəbəl]	\imˈpenətrəbᵊl\	Indian	[ˈɪndiən]	\ˈindēən\
imperative	[ɪmˈpɛrətɪv]	\imˈperətiv\	indication	[ˌɪndəˈkeɪʃən]	\ˌindəˈkāshᵊn\
imperceptible	[ˌɪmpərˈsɛptəbəl]	\ˌimpərˈseptəbᵊl\	indifferent	[ɪnˈdɪfrənt, -ˈdɪfə-]	\inˈdifrənt, -ˈdifə-\
imperfection	[ˌɪmˌpərˈfɛkʃən]	\imˌpərˈfekshᵊn\	indigenous	[ɪnˈdɪdʒənəs]	\inˈdijənəs\
imperialism	[ɪmˈpɪriəˌlɪzəm]	\imˈpirēəˌlizᵊm\	indigestion	[ˌɪndaɪˈdʒɛstʃən, -dɪ-]	\ˌindīˈjeschᵊn, -di-\
impersonal	[ɪmˈpərsənəl]	\imˈpərsᵊnəl\	indirect	[ˌɪndəˈrɛkt, -daɪ-]	\ˌindəˈrekt, -dī-\
impersonation	[ɪmˌpərsəˈneɪʃən]	\imˌpərsᵊnˈāshᵊn\	indiscreet	[ˌɪndɪˈskriːt]	\ˌindiˈskrēt\
implement	[ˈɪmpləmənt, -ˌmɛnt]	\ˈimpləmənt, -ˌment\	indiscriminate	[ˌɪndɪˈskrɪmənət]	\ˌindiˈskrimənət\
implicate	[ˈɪmpləˌkeɪt]	\ˈimpləˌkāt\	indispensable	[ˌɪndɪˈspɛntsəbəl]	\ˌindiˈspen(t)səbᵊl\
imply	[ɪmˈplaɪ]	\imˈplī\	indisputable	[ˌɪndɪˈspjuːtəbəl, ɪnˈdɪspjuˌtə-]	
impolite	[ˌɪmpəˈlaɪt]	\ˌimpəˈlīt\			\ˌindiˈspyütəbᵊl, inˈdispyùˌtə-\
import	[ɪmˈport]	\imˈpōrt\	individual	[ˌɪndəˈvɪdʒuəl]	\ˌindəˈvijùəl\
impose	[ɪmˈpoːz]	\imˈpōz\	induce	[ɪnˈduːs, -ˈdjuːs]	\inˈdüs, -ˈdyüs\

ENGLISH WORD	IPA	M-W	ENGLISH WORD	IPA	M-W
industry	[ˈɪndəstri]	\ˈindəstrē\	insert	[ɪnˈsərt]	\inˈsərt\
inequality	[ˌɪniˈkwɑləti]	\ˌiniˈkwälətē\	inside	[ɪnˈsaɪd, ˈɪnˌsaɪd]	\inˈsīd, ˈinˌsīd\
inescapable	[ˌɪniˈskeɪpəbəl]	\ˌiniˈskāpəˈl\	insignificant	[ˌɪnsɪɡˈnɪfɪkənt]	\ˌinsigˈnifikənt\
inevitable	[ɪˈnɛvətəbl]	\iˈnevətəbˈl\	insist	[ɪnˈsɪst]	\inˈsist\
inexplicable	[ˌɪnɪkˈsplɪkəbəl]	\ˌinikˈsplikəbˈl\	insomnia	[ɪnˈsɑmniə]	\inˈsämnēə\
infallible	[ɪnˈfæləbəl]	\inˈfaləbˈl\	inspection	[ɪnˈspɛkʃən]	\inˈspekshˈn\
infancy	[ˈɪnfənsi]	\ˈinfən(t)sē\	inspire	[ɪnˈspaɪr]	\inˈspīr\
infect	[ɪnˈfɛkt]	\inˈfekt\	install	[ɪnˈstɔl]	\inˈstól\
infer	[ɪnˈfər]	\inˈfər\	instance	[ˈɪnˈstənts]	\ˈin(t)stən(t)s\
inferior	[ɪnˈfɪriər]	\inˈfirēər\	instant	[ˈɪnˈstənt]	\ˈin(t)stənt\
infidelity	[ˌɪnfəˈdɛləti, -faɪ-]	\ˌinfəˈdelətē, -fī-\	institute	[ˈɪnˈstəˌtuːt, -ˌtjuːt]	\ˈin(t)stəˌtüt, -ˌtyüt\
infinite	[ˈɪnfənət]	\ˈinfənət\	instruct	[ɪnˈstrʌkt]	\inˈstrəkt\
infinitive	[ɪnˈfɪnətɪv]	\inˈfinətiv\	instrument	[ˈɪnˈstrəmənt]	\ˈin(t)strəmənt\
infinity	[ɪnˈfɪnəti]	\inˈfinətē\	insufficient	[ˌɪnsəˈfɪʃənt]	\ˌinsəˈfishənt\
infirmary	[ɪnˈfərməri]	\inˈfərmərē\	insulate	[ˈɪnˈsəˌleɪt]	\ˈin(t)səˌlāt\
inflame	[ɪnˈfleɪm]	\inˈflām\	insure	[ɪnˈʃʊr]	\inˈshùr\
inflation	[ɪnˈfleɪʃən]	\inˈflāshˈn\	intact	[ɪnˈtækt]	\inˈtakt\
inflexible	[ɪnˈflɛksɪbəl]	\inˈfleksibˈl\	intake	[ˈɪnˌteɪk]	\ˈinˌtāk\
influential	[ˌɪnfluˈɛntʃəl]	\ˌinflüˈenchˈl\	intangible	[ɪnˈtændʒəbəl]	\inˈtanjəbˈl\
influx	[ˈɪnˌflʌks]	\ˈinˌfləks\	integral	[ˈɪntɪɡrəl]	\ˈintigrəl\
inform	[ɪnˈfɔrm]	\inˈfórm\	integrate	[ˈɪntəˌɡreɪt]	\ˈintəˌgrāt\
informal	[ɪnˈfɔrməl]	\inˈfórmˈl\	integrity	[ɪnˈtɛɡrəti]	\inˈtegrətē\
information	[ˌɪnfərˈmeɪʃən]	\ˌinfərˈmāshˈn\	intellectual	[ˌɪntəˈlɛktʃuəl]	\ˌintəˈlekchúəl\
infrequently	[ɪnˈfriːkwəntli]	\inˈfrēkwəntlē\	intend	[ɪnˈtɛnd]	\inˈtend\
infuse	[ɪnˈfjuːz]	\inˈfyüz\	intense	[ɪnˈtɛnts]	\inˈten(t)s\
ingenious	[ɪnˈdʒiːnjəs]	\inˈjēnyəs\	intent	[ɪnˈtɛnt]	\inˈtent\
ingest	[ɪnˈdʒɛst]	\inˈjest\	interact	[ˌɪntərˈækt]	\ˌintərˈakt\
ingratitude	[ɪnˈɡrætəˌtuːd, -ˌtjuːd]	\inˈgratəˌtüd, -ˌtyüd\	intercede	[ˌɪntərˈsiːd]	\ˌintərˈsēd\
ingredient	[ɪnˈɡriːdiənt]	\inˈgrēdēənt\	interest	[ˈɪntrəst, -təˌrɛst]	\ˈintrəst, -təˌrest\
inhabit	[ɪnˈhæbət]	\inˈhabət\	interface	[ˈɪntərˌfeɪs]	\ˈintərˌfās\
inhale	[ɪnˈheɪl]	\inˈhāl\	interior	[ɪnˈtɪriər]	\inˈtirēər\
inherent	[ɪnˈhɪrənt, -ˈhɛr-]	\inˈhirənt, -ˈher-\	interjection	[ˌɪntərˈdʒɛkʃən]	\ˌintərˈjekshˈn\
inherit	[ɪnˈhɛrət]	\inˈherət\	interlude	[ˈɪntərˌluːd]	\ˈintərˌlüd\
inhibit	[ɪnˈhɪbət]	\inˈhibət\	intermediate	[ˌɪntərˈmiːdiət]	\ˌintərˈmēdēət\
inhuman	[ɪnˈhjuːmən, -ˈjuː-]	\inˈhyümən, -ˈyü-\	intermission	[ˌɪntərˈmɪʃən]	\ˌintərˈmishˈn\
initial	[ɪˈnɪʃəl]	\iˈnishˈl\	intermittent	[ˌɪntərˈmɪtənt]	\ˌintərˈmitˈnt\
initiate	[ɪˈnɪʃiˌeɪt]	\iˈnishēˌāt\	international	[ˌɪntərˈnæʃənəl]	\ˌintərˈnashənˈl\
inject	[ɪnˈdʒɛkt]	\inˈjekt\	interpret	[ɪnˈtərprət]	\inˈtərprət\
injure	[ˈɪndʒər]	\ˈinjər\	interrogate	[ɪnˈtɛrəˌɡeɪt]	\inˈterəˌgāt\
injustice	[ɪnˈdʒʌstəs]	\inˈjəstəs\	interrupt	[ˌɪntəˈrʌpt]	\ˌintəˈrəpt\
ink	[ˈɪŋk]	\ˈiŋk\	intersect	[ˌɪntərˈsɛkt]	\ˌintərˈsekt\
in-laws	[ˈɪnˌlɔz]	\ˈinˌlóz\	interval	[ˈɪntərvəl]	\ˈintərvəl\
inn	[ˈɪn]	\ˈin\	intervene	[ˌɪntərˈviːn]	\ˌintərˈvēn\
innate	[ɪˈneɪt]	\iˈnāt\	interview	[ˈɪntərˌvjuː]	\ˈintərˌvyü\
inner	[ˈɪnər]	\ˈinər\	intimate	[ˈɪntəˌmeɪt; ˈɪntəmət]	\ˈintəˌmāt; ˈintəmət\
inning	[ˈɪnɪŋ]	\ˈiniŋ\	into	[ˈɪnˌtuː]	\ˈinˌtü\
innocent	[ˈɪnəsənt]	\ˈinəsənt\	intolerant	[ɪnˈtɑlərənt]	\inˈtälərənt\
innovate	[ˈɪnəˌveɪt]	\ˈinəˌvāt\	intransitive	[ɪnˈtrænsətɪv, -ˈtrænzə-]	
inoffensive	[ˌɪnəˈfɛntsɪv]	\ˌinəˈfen(t)siv\			\inˈtran(t)sətiv, -ˈtranzə-\
input	[ˈɪnˌpʊt]	\ˈinˌpùt\	introduce	[ˌɪntrəˈduːs, -ˈdjuːs]	\ˌintrəˈdüs, -ˈdyüs\
inquire	[ɪnˈkwaɪr]	\inˈkwīr\	introvert	[ˈɪntrəˌvərt]	\ˈintrəˌvərt\
insane	[ɪnˈseɪn]	\inˈsān\	intuition	[ˌɪntʊˈɪʃən, -tjʊ-]	\ˌintùˈishˈn, -tyü-\
inscription	[ɪnˈskrɪpʃən]	\inˈskripshˈn\	invade	[ɪnˈveɪd]	\inˈvād\
insecure	[ˌɪnsɪˈkjʊr]	\ˌinsiˈkyùr\	invalid	[ɪnˈvæləd]	\inˈvaləd\
insensitive	[ɪnˈsɛntsətɪv]	\inˈsen(t)sətiv\	invalid	[ˈɪnvələd]	\ˈinvələd\
inseparable	[ɪnˈsɛpərəbəl]	\inˈsepərəbˈl\	invariable	[ɪnˈværiəbəl]	\inˈverēəbˈl\

ENGLISH WORD	IPA	M-W	ENGLISH WORD	IPA	M-W
invasion	[ɪn'veɪʒən]	\in'vāzhᵊn\	jersey	['dʒərzi]	\'jərzē\
invention	[ɪn'vɛntʃən]	\in'venchᵊn\	jet	['dʒɛt]	\'jet\
inventory	['ɪnvəntɔri]	\'invən,tórē\	jewel	['dʒuːəl]	\'jüəl\
invert	[ɪn'vərt]	\in'vərt\	Jewish	['dʒuːɪʃ]	\'jüish\
invertebrate	[ɪn'vərtəbrət, -ˌbreɪt]	\in'vərtəbrət, -ˌbrāt\	jiggle	['dʒɪgəl]	\'jigᵊl\
investigator	[ɪn'vɛstəˌgeɪtər]	\in'vestə,gātər\	jingle	['dʒɪŋgəl]	\'jingᵊl\
investment	[ɪn'vɛstmənt]	\in'vestmənt\	job	['dʒab]	\'jäb\
invitation	[ˌɪnvə'teɪʃən]	\,invə'tāshᵊn\	jockey	['dʒaki]	\'jäkē\
invoice	['ɪnˌvɔɪs]	\'in,vóis\	jog	['dʒag]	\'jäg\
involuntary	[ɪn'valənˌtɛri]	\in'välən,terē\	join	['dʒɔɪn]	\'jóin\
involve	[ɪn'valv]	\in'välv\	joint	['dʒɔɪnt]	\'jóint\
IOU	[ˌaɪˌo'juː]	\ˌī,ō'yü\	joke	['dʒoːk]	\'jōk\
Iranian	[ɪ'reɪniən, -'ræ-, -'ra-; aɪ'-]		jolly	['dʒali]	\'jälē\
		\i'rānēən, -'ra, -'rä-; ī'-\	jot	['dʒat]	\'jät\
Iraqi	[ɪ'raki, -'ræk-]	\i'räkē, -'rak-\	journal	['dʒərnəl]	\'jərnᵊl\
irate	[aɪ'reɪt]	\ī'rāt\	journey	['dʒərni]	\'jərnē\
iris	['aɪrəs]	\'īrəs\	jovial	['dʒoːviəl]	\'jōvēəl\
Irish	['aɪrɪʃ]	\'īrish\	joy	['dʒɔɪ]	\'jói\
iron	['aɪərn]	\'īərn\	Judaism	['dʒuːdəˌɪzəm, 'dʒuːdi-, 'dʒuːˌdeɪ-]	
ironic	[aɪ'ranɪk]	\ī'ränik\			\'jüdə,izəm, 'jüdē-, 'jüˌdā-\
irony	['aɪrəni]	\'īrənē\	judge	['dʒʌdʒ]	\'jəj\
irrational	[ɪ'ræʃənəl]	\i'rashᵊnᵊl\	judicial	[dʒʊ'dɪʃəl]	\jù'dishᵊl\
irregular	[ɪ'rɛgjələr]	\i'regyələr\	juice	['dʒuːs]	\'jüs\
irrelevant	[ɪ'rɛləvənt]	\i'reləvənt\	July	[dʒʊ'laɪ]	\jù'lī\
irresponsible	[ˌɪrɪ'spantsəbəl]	\,iri'spän(t)səbᵊl\	jumble	['dʒʌmbəl]	\'jəmbᵊl\
irreverent	[ɪ'rɛvərənt]	\i'revərənt\	jumbo	['dʒʌmˌboː]	\'jəm,bō\
irrigate	['ɪrəˌgeɪt]	\'irə,gāt\	jump	['dʒʌmp]	\'jəmp\
irritate	['ɪrəˌteɪt]	\'irə,tāt\	June	['dʒuːn]	\'jün\
Islamic	[ɪs'lamɪk, ɪz-, -'læ-]	\is'lämik, iz-, -'la-\	jungle	['dʒʌŋgəl]	\'jəngᵊl\
island	['aɪlənd]	\'īlənd\	junior	['dʒuːnjər]	\'jünyər\
isolate	['aɪsəˌleɪt]	\'īsə,lāt\	junk	['dʒʌŋk]	\'jəngk\
Israeli	[ɪz'reɪli]	\iz'rālē\	jury	['dʒʊri]	\'jùrē\
issue	['ɪˌʃuː]	\'i,shü\	just	['dʒʌst]	\'jəst\
isthmus	['ɪsməs]	\'isməs\	justice	['dʒʌstɪs]	\'jəstis\
it	['ɪt]	\'it\	justify	['dʒʌstəˌfaɪ]	\'jəstə,fī\
Italian	[ɪ'tæliən, aɪ-]	\i'talēən, ī-\	kangaroo	[ˌkæŋgə'ruː]	\ˌkangə'rü\
italics	[ɪ'tælɪks, aɪ-]	\i'taliks, ī-\	karate	[kə'rati]	\kə'rätē\
item	['aɪtəm]	\'ītəm\	keen	['kiːn]	\'kēn\
itinerant	[aɪ'tɪnərənt]	\ī'tinərənt\	keep	['kiːp]	\'kēp\
itinerary	[aɪ'tɪnəˌrɛri]	\ī'tinə,rerē\	kernel	['kərnəl]	\'kərnᵊl\
its	['ɪts]	\'its\	ketchup	['kɛtʃəp, 'kæ-]	\'kechəp, 'ka-\
itself	[ɪt'sɛlf]	\it'self\	key	['kiː]	\'kē\
jab	['dʒæb]	\'jab\	kick	['kɪk]	\'kik\
jack	['dʒæk]	\'jak\	kid	['kɪd]	\'kid\
jacket	['dʒækət]	\'jakət\	kidney	['kɪdni]	\'kidnē\
jail	['dʒeɪl]	\'jāl\	kill	['kɪl]	\'kil\
jam	['dʒæm]	\'jam\	kilo	['kiːˌloː]	\'kē,lō\
jangle	['dʒæŋgəl]	\'jangᵊl\	kin	['kɪn]	\'kin\
January	['dʒænjuˌɛri]	\'janyù,erē\	kind	['kaɪnd]	\'kīnd\
Japanese	[ˌdʒæpə'niːz, -'niːs]	\ˌjapə'nēz, -'nēs\	kindergarten	['kɪndərˌgartən, -dən]	\'kindər,gärtᵊn, -dᵊn\
jar	['dʒar]	\'jär\	kindle	['kɪndəl]	\'kindᵊl\
jargon	['dʒargən]	\'järgᵊn\	kindly	['kaɪndli]	\'kīndlē\
jaw	['dʒɔ]	\'jó\	kinship	['kɪnˌʃɪp]	\'kin,ship\
jazz	['dʒæz]	\'jaz\	kiss	['kɪs]	\'kis\
jealous	['dʒɛləs]	\'jeləs\	kit	['kɪt]	\'kit\
jeans	['dʒiːnz]	\'jēnz\	kitchen	['kɪtʃən]	\'kichᵊn\

ENGLISH WORD	IPA	M-W	ENGLISH WORD	IPA	M-W
knapsack	['næp,sæk]	\'nap,sak\	left	['lɛft]	\'left\
knead	['ni:d]	\'nēd\	leg	['lɛg]	\'leg\
knee	['ni:]	\'nē\	legal	['li:gəl]	\'lēg'l\
kneel	['ni:l]	\'nēl\	legible	['lɛdʒəbəl]	\'lejəb'l\
knife	['naɪf]	\'nīf\	legislate	['lɛdʒəs,leɪt]	\'lejəs,lāt\
knight	['naɪt]	\'nīt\	legitimate	[lɪ'dʒɪtəmət]	\li'jitəmət\
knit	['nɪt]	\'nit\	leisure	['li:ʒər, 'lɛ-]	\'lēzhər, 'le-\
knock	['nɑk]	\'näk\	lemon	['lɛmən]	\'lem'n\
knot	['nɑt]	\'nät\	lend	['lɛnd]	\'lend\
know	['no:]	\'nō\	length	['lɛŋkθ]	\'leŋ(k)th\
knuckle	['nʌkəl]	\'nək'l\	lens	['lɛnz]	\'lenz\
Korean	[kə'ri:ən]	\kə'rēən\	less	['lɛs]	\'les\
label	['leɪbəl]	\'lāb'l\	lesson	['lɛsən]	\'les'n\
labor	['leɪbər]	\'lābər\	let	['lɛt]	\'let\
laboratory	['læbrə,tori, lə'bɔrə-]	\'labrə,tōrē, lə'bȯrə-\	letter	['lɛtər]	\'letər\
lace	['leɪs]	\'lās\	lettuce	['lɛtəs]	\'letəs\
lack	['læk]	\'lak\	level	['lɛvəl]	\'lev'l\
ladder	['lædər]	\'ladər\	lever	['lɛvər, 'li:-]	\'levər, 'lē-\
lady	['leɪdi]	\'lādē\	liable	['laɪəbəl]	\'līəb'l\
lake	['leɪk]	\'lāk\	liberal	['lɪbrəl, 'lɪbərəl]	\'librəl, 'libərəl\
lamb	['læm]	\'lam\	liberate	['lɪbə,reɪt]	\'libə,rāt\
lame	['leɪm]	\'lām\	liberty	['lɪbərti]	\'libərtē\
lament	[lə'mɛnt]	\lə'ment\	library	['laɪ,brɛri]	\'lī,brerē\
lamp	['læmp]	\'lamp\	lie	['laɪ]	\'lī\
land	['lænd]	\'land\	life	['laɪf]	\'līf\
lane	['leɪn]	\'lān\	lift	['lɪft]	\'lift\
language	['læŋgwɪdʒ]	\'laŋgwij\	light	['laɪt]	\'līt\
laptop	['læp,tɑp]	\'lap,täp\	like	['laɪk]	\'līk\
large	['lɑrdʒ]	\'lärj\	limb	['lɪm]	\'lim\
lasagna	[lə'zɑnjə]	\lə'zänyə\	limit	['lɪmət]	\'limət\
laser	['leɪzər]	\'lāzər\	limp	['lɪmp]	\'limp\
lash	['læʃ]	\'lash\	line	['laɪn]	\'līn\
last	['læst]	\'last\	linguistics	[lɪŋ'gwɪstɪks]	\liŋ'gwistiks\
late	['leɪt]	\'lāt\	link	['lɪŋk]	\'liŋk\
Latin-American	['lætənə'mɛrəkən]	\'lat'nə'merək'n\	lion	['laɪən]	\'līən\
laugh	['læf]	\'laf\	lip	['lɪp]	\'lip\
launch	['lɔntʃ]	\'lȯnch\	liquid	['lɪkwəd]	\'likwəd\
launder	['lɔndər]	\'lȯndər\	list	['lɪst]	\'list\
lavatory	['lævə,tori]	\'lavə,tōrē\	listen	['lɪsən]	\'lis'n\
law	['lɔ]	\'lȯ\	liter	['li:tər]	\'lētər\
lawn	['lɔn]	\'lȯn\	literacy	['lɪtərəsi]	\'litərəsē\
lay	['leɪ]	\'lā\	literal	['lɪtərəl]	\'litərəl\
layer	['leɪər]	\'lāər\	literature	['lɪtərə,tʃʊr, -tʃər]	\'litərə,chùr, -chər\
lazy	['leɪzi]	\'lāzē\	little	['lɪtəl]	\'lit'l\
lead	['li:d]	\'lēd\	live	['lɪv, 'laɪv]	\'liv; 'līv\
lead	['lɛd]	\'led\	liver	['lɪvər]	\'livər\
leaf	['li:f]	\'lēf\	living	['lɪvɪŋ]	\'liviŋ\
league	['li:g]	\'lēg\	lizard	['lɪzərd]	\'lizərd\
lean	['li:n]	\'lēn\	load	['lo:d]	\'lōd\
leap	['li:p]	\'lēp\	loaf	['lo:f]	\'lōf\
learn	['lərn]	\'lərn\	loan	['lo:n]	\'lōn\
lease	['li:s]	\'lēs\	lobby	['lɑbi]	\'läbē\
least	['li:st]	\'lēst\	lobster	['lɑbstər]	\'läbstər\
leather	['lɛðər]	\'lethər\	local	['lo:kəl]	\'lōk'l\
leave	['li:v]	\'lēv\	locate	['lo:,keɪt, lo'keɪt]	\'lō,kāt, lō'kāt\
lecture	['lɛktʃər]	\'lekchər\	lock	['lɑk]	\'läk\

ENGLISH WORD	IPA	M-W	ENGLISH WORD	IPA	M-W
lodge	[ˈlɑdʒ]	\ˈläj\	manual	[ˈmænjʊəl]	\ˈmanyüəl\
loft	[ˈlɔft]	\ˈlóft\	manufacture	[ˌmænjəˈfæktʃər]	\ˌmanyəˈfakchər\
log	[ˈlɔg, ˈlɑg]	\ˈlòg, ˈläg\	many	[ˈmɛni]	\ˈmenē\
logic	[ˈlɑdʒɪk]	\ˈläjik\	map	[ˈmæp]	\ˈmap\
loin	[ˈlɔɪn]	\ˈlóin\	march	[ˈmɑrtʃ]	\ˈmärch\
lone	[ˈloːn]	\ˈlōn\	margarine	[ˈmɑrdʒərən]	\ˈmärjərən\
long	[ˈlɔŋ]	\ˈlòŋ\	margin	[ˈmɑrdʒən]	\ˈmärjᵊn\
longitude	[ˈlɑndʒəˌtuːd, -ˌtjuːd]	\ˈlänjəˌtüd, -ˌtyüd\	mark	[ˈmɑrk]	\ˈmärk\
look	[ˈlʊk]	\ˈlùk\	market	[ˈmɑrkət]	\ˈmärkət\
loom	[ˈluːm]	\ˈlüm\	marriage	[ˈmærɪdʒ]	\ˈmarij\
loose	[ˈluːs]	\ˈlüs\	marry	[ˈmæri]	\ˈmarē\
lord	[ˈlɔrd]	\ˈlórd\	Mars	[ˈmɑrz]	\ˈmärz\
lose	[ˈluːz]	\ˈlüz\	martyr	[ˈmɑrtər]	\ˈmärtər\
lot	[ˈlɑt]	\ˈlät\	marvel	[ˈmɑrvəl]	\ˈmärvᵊl\
lotion	[ˈloːʃən]	\ˈlōshᵊn\	masculine	[ˈmæskjələn]	\ˈmaskyələn\
lottery	[ˈlɑtəri]	\ˈlätərē\	mask	[ˈmæsk]	\ˈmask\
loud	[ˈlaʊd]	\ˈlaùd\	mass	[ˈmæs]	\ˈmas\
love	[ˈlʌv]	\ˈləv\	massage	[məˈsɑʒ, -ˈsɑdʒ]	\məˈsäzh, -ˈsäj\
low	[ˈloː]	\ˈlō\	massive	[ˈmæsɪv]	\ˈmasiv\
loyal	[ˈlɔɪəl]	\ˈlóiəl\	master	[ˈmæstər]	\ˈmastər\
lubricate	[ˈluːbrɪˌkeɪt]	\ˈlübriˌkāt\	match	[ˈmætʃ]	\ˈmach\
lucid	[ˈluːsəd]	\ˈlüsəd\	material	[məˈtiriəl]	\məˈtirēəl\
luck	[ˈlʌk]	\ˈlək\	maternal	[məˈtərnəl]	\məˈtərnᵊl\
luggage	[ˈlʌgɪdʒ]	\ˈləgij\	mathematics	[ˌmæθəˈmætɪks]	\ˌmathəˈmatiks\
lumber	[ˈlʌmbər]	\ˈləmbər\	matter	[ˈmætər]	\ˈmatər\
luminous	[ˈluːmənəs]	\ˈlümənəs\	mattress	[ˈmætrəs]	\ˈmatrəs\
lunar	[ˈluːnər]	\ˈlünər\	mature	[məˈtʊr, -ˈtjʊr, -ˈtʃʊr]	\məˈtùr, -ˈtyùr, -ˈchùr\
lunch	[ˈlʌntʃ]	\ˈlənch\	maximum	[ˈmæksəməm]	\ˈmaksəməm\
lung	[ˈlʌŋ]	\ˈləŋ\	may	[ˈmeɪ]	\ˈmā\
luxurious	[ˌlʌgˈʒʊriəs, ˌlʌkˈʃʊr-]		maybe	[ˈmeɪbi]	\ˈmābē\
		\ˌləgˈzhùrēəs, ˌləkˈshùr-\	mayonnaise	[ˈmeɪəˌneɪz]	\ˈmāəˌnāz\
machine	[məˈʃiːn]	\məˈshēn\	mayor	[ˈmeɪər, ˈmɛr]	\ˈmāər, ˈmer\
mad	[ˈmæd]	\ˈmad\	me	[ˈmiː]	\ˈmē\
madam	[ˈmædəm]	\ˈmadᵊm\	mean	[ˈmiːn]	\ˈmēn\
madness	[ˈmædnəs]	\ˈmadnəs\	meander	[miˈændər]	\mēˈandər\
magazine	[ˈmægəˌziːn]	\ˈmagəˌzēn\	meaning	[ˈmiːnɪŋ]	\ˈmēniŋ\
magic	[ˈmædʒɪk]	\ˈmajik\	means	[ˈmiːnz]	\ˈmēnz\
magnificent	[mægˈnɪfəsənt]	\magˈnifəsənt\	meanwhile	[ˈmiːnˌ(h)waɪl]	\ˈmēnˌ(h)wīl\
mail	[ˈmeɪl]	\ˈmāl\	measure	[ˈmɛʒər, ˈmeɪ-]	\ˈmezhər, ˈmā-\
main	[ˈmeɪn]	\ˈmān\	meat	[ˈmiːt]	\ˈmēt\
maintain	[meɪnˈteɪn]	\mānˈtān\	mechanic	[mɪˈkænɪk]	\miˈkanik\
majority	[məˈdʒɔrəti]	\məˈjórətē\	media	[ˈmiːdiə]	\ˈmēdēə\
make	[ˈmeɪk]	\ˈmāk\	medical	[ˈmɛdɪkəl]	\ˈmedikᵊl\
male	[ˈmeɪl]	\ˈmāl\	meditate	[ˈmɛdəˌteɪt]	\ˈmedəˌtāt\
malnutrition	[ˌmælnʊˈtrɪʃən, -njʊ-]	\ˌmalnùˈtrishᵊn, -nyü-\	meet	[ˈmiːt]	\ˈmēt\
mammal	[ˈmæməl]	\ˈmamᵊl\	megabyte	[ˈmɛgəˌbaɪt]	\ˈmegəˌbīt\
man	[ˈmæn]	\ˈman\	melancholy	[ˈmɛləˌnˌkɑli]	\ˈmelᵊnˌkälē\
manage	[ˈmænɪdʒ]	\ˈmanij\	melody	[ˈmɛlədi]	\ˈmelədē\
mandate	[ˈmænˌdeɪt]	\ˈmanˌdāt\	melon	[ˈmɛlən]	\ˈmelən\
maneuver	[məˈnuːvər, -ˈnjuː-]	\məˈnüvər, -ˈnyü-\	melt	[ˈmɛlt]	\ˈmelt\
mania	[ˈmeɪniə, -njə]	\ˈmānēə, -nyə\	member	[ˈmɛmbər]	\ˈmembər\
manipulate	[məˈnɪpjəˌleɪt]	\məˈnipyəˌlāt\	memory	[ˈmɛmri, ˈmɛmə-]	\ˈmemrē, ˈmemə-\
mankind	[ˈmænˈkaɪnd, -ˌkaɪnd]	\ˈmanˈkīnd, -ˌkīnd\	menace	[ˈmɛnəs]	\ˈmenəs\
manly	[ˈmænli]	\ˈmanlē\	mental	[ˈmɛntəl]	\ˈmentᵊl\
manner	[ˈmænər]	\ˈmanər\	mention	[ˈmɛntʃən]	\ˈmenchᵊn\
mansion	[ˈmæntʃən]	\ˈmanchᵊn\	menu	[ˈmɛnˌjuː]	\ˈmenˌyü\

ENGLISH WORD	IPA	M-W	ENGLISH WORD	IPA	M-W
merchant	[ˈmərtʃənt]	\ˈmərchᵊnt\	molar	[ˈmoːlər]	\ˈmōlər\
merciful	[ˈmərsɪfəl]	\ˈmərsifᵊl\	mom	[ˈmɑm, ˈmʌm]	\ˈmäm, ˈməm\
merge	[ˈmərdʒ]	\ˈmərj\	moment	[ˈmoːmənt]	\ˈmōmənt\
merit	[ˈmɛrət]	\ˈmerət\	Monday	[ˈmʌnˌdeɪ, -di]	\ˈmən͟ˌdā, -dē\
mess	[ˈmɛs]	\ˈmes\	money	[ˈmʌni]	\ˈmənē\
message	[ˈmɛsɪdʒ]	\ˈmesij\	monitor	[ˈmɑnətər]	\ˈmänətər\
metal	[ˈmɛtəl]	\ˈmetᵊl\	monkey	[ˈmʌŋki]	\ˈməŋkē\
metamorphosis	[ˌmɛtəˈmɔrfəsɪs]	\ˌmetəˈmȯrfəsis\	monologue	[ˈmɑnəˌlɔg]	\ˈmänəˌlȯg\
metaphor	[ˈmɛtəˌfɔr, -fər]	\ˈmetəˌfȯr, -fər\	month	[ˈmʌnθ]	\ˈmənth\
method	[ˈmɛθəd]	\ˈmethəd\	monument	[ˈmɑnjəmənt]	\ˈmänyəmənt\
metropolis	[məˈtrɑpələs]	\məˈträpələs\	moon	[ˈmuːn]	\ˈmün\
Mexican	[ˈmɛksɪkən]	\ˈmeksikᵊn\	mop	[ˈmɑp]	\ˈmäp\
microbe	[ˈmaɪˌkroːb]	\ˈmīˌkrōb\	moral	[ˈmɔrəl]	\ˈmȯrəl\
microphone	[ˈmaɪkrəˌfoːn]	\ˈmīkrəˌfōn\	more	[ˈmor]	\ˈmōr\
microscope	[ˈmaɪkrəˌskoːp]	\ˈmīkrəˌskōp\	morning	[ˈmɔrnɪŋ]	\ˈmȯrniŋ\
microwave	[ˈmaɪkrəˌweɪv]	\ˈmīkrəˌwāv\	mortal	[ˈmɔrtəl]	\ˈmȯrtᵊl\
mid	[ˈmɪd]	\ˈmid\	mortgage	[ˈmɔrgɪdʒ]	\ˈmȯrgij\
middle	[ˈmɪdəl]	\ˈmidᵊl\	mosque	[ˈmɑsk]	\ˈmäsk\
midnight	[ˈmɪdˌnaɪt]	\ˈmidˌnīt\	most	[ˈmoːst]	\ˈmōst\
might	[ˈmaɪt]	\ˈmīt\	mother	[ˈmʌðər]	\ˈməthər\
mile	[ˈmaɪl]	\ˈmīl\	motion	[ˈmoːʃən]	\ˈmōshᵊn\
military	[ˈmɪləˌtɛri]	\ˈmiləˌterē\	motive	[ˈmoːtɪv]	\ˈmōtiv\
milk	[ˈmɪlk]	\ˈmilk\	motor	[ˈmoːtər]	\ˈmōtər\
millennium	[məˈlɛniəm]	\məˈlenēəm\	mount	[ˈmaʊnt]	\ˈmaůnt\
million	[ˈmɪljən]	\ˈmilyən\	mourning	[ˈmornɪŋ]	\ˈmōrniŋ\
mimic	[ˈmɪmɪk]	\ˈmimik\	mouse	[ˈmaʊs]	\ˈmaůs\
mind	[ˈmaɪnd]	\ˈmīnd\	mouth	[ˈmaʊθ]	\ˈmaůth\
mine	[ˈmaɪn]	\ˈmīn\	move	[ˈmuːv]	\ˈmüv\
mineral	[ˈmɪnərəl]	\ˈminərəl\	movie	[ˈmuːvi]	\ˈmüvē\
minimize	[ˈmɪnəˌmaɪz]	\ˈminəˌmīz\	Mr.	[ˈmɪstər]	\ˈmistər\
minister	[ˈmɪnəstər]	\ˈminəstər\	Mrs.	[ˈmɪsəz, -səs, ˈmɪzəz, -zəs]	
minor	[ˈmaɪnər]	\ˈmīnər\			\ˈmisəz, -səs, ˈmizəz, -zəs\
mint	[ˈmɪnt]	\ˈmint\	Ms.	[ˈmɪz]	\ˈmiz\
minus	[ˈmaɪnəs]	\ˈmīnəs\	much	[ˈmʌtʃ]	\ˈməch\
minute	[maɪˈnuːt; ˈmɪnət]	\mīˈnüt; ˈminət\	mud	[ˈmʌd]	\ˈməd\
miracle	[ˈmɪrɪkəl]	\ˈmirikᵊl\	muddy	[ˈmʌdi]	\ˈmədē\
mirror	[ˈmɪrər]	\ˈmirər\	mug	[ˈmʌg]	\ˈməg\
mischief	[ˈmɪstʃəf]	\ˈmischəf\	multimedia	[ˌmʌltiˈmiːdiə, ˌmʌltaɪ-]	\ˌməltēˈmēdēə, ˌməltī-\
miss	[ˈmɪs]	\ˈmis\	multinational	[ˌmʌltiˈnæʃənəl, ˌmʌltaɪ-]	
missing	[ˈmɪsɪŋ]	\ˈmisiŋ\			\ˌməltēˈnashənᵊl, ˌməltī-\
mission	[ˈmɪʃən]	\ˈmishᵊn\	multiple	[ˈmʌltəpəl]	\ˈməltəpᵊl\
mist	[ˈmɪst]	\ˈmist\	multitude	[ˈmʌltəˌtuːd, -ˌtjuːd]	\ˈməltəˌtüd, -ˌtyüd\
mistake	[mɪˈsteɪk]	\miˈstāk\	municipal	[mjʊˈnɪsəpəl]	\myůˈnisəpəl\
mistreat	[mɪsˈtriːt]	\misˈtrēt\	muscle	[ˈmʌsəl]	\ˈməsᵊl\
misunderstanding	[ˌmɪsˌʌndərˈstændɪŋ]	\ˌmisˌəndərˈstandiŋ\	museum	[mjʊˈziːəm]	\myůˈzēəm\
mix	[ˈmɪks]	\ˈmiks\	mushroom	[ˈmʌʃˌruːm, -ˌrʊm]	\ˈməshˌrüm, -ˌrům\
moan	[ˈmoːn]	\ˈmōn\	music	[ˈmjuːzɪk]	\ˈmyüzik\
mobile	[ˈmoːbəl, -ˌbiːl, -ˌbaɪl]	\ˈmōbᵊl, -ˌbēl, -ˌbīl\	Muslim	[ˈmʌzləm, ˈmʊs-, ˈmʊz-]	\ˈməzləm, ˈműs-, ˈműz-\
moccasin	[ˈmɑkəsən]	\ˈmäkəsᵊn\	must	[ˈmʌst]	\ˈməst\
model	[ˈmɑdəl]	\ˈmädᵊl\	mustache	[ˈmʌˌstæʃ, mʌˈstæʃ]	\ˈməˌstash, məˈstash\
modem	[ˈmoːdəm, -ˌdɛm]	\ˈmōdəm, -ˌdem\	mute	[ˈmjuːt]	\ˈmyüt\
moderate	[ˈmɑdərət, -ˌreɪt]	\ˈmädərət, -ˌrāt\	mutiny	[ˈmjuːtəni]	\ˈmyütᵊnē\
modern	[ˈmɑdərn]	\ˈmädərn\	my	[ˈmaɪ]	\ˈmī\
modest	[ˈmɑdəst]	\ˈmädəst\	myself	[maɪˈsɛlf]	\mīˈself\
modify	[ˈmɑdəˌfaɪ]	\ˈmädəˌfī\	mystery	[ˈmɪstəri]	\ˈmistərē\
moist	[ˈmɔɪst]	\ˈmȯist\	myth	[ˈmɪθ]	\ˈmith\

ENGLISH WORD	IPA	M-W	ENGLISH WORD	IPA	M-W
nail	[ˈneɪl]	\ˈnāl\	norm	[ˈnɔrm]	\ˈnȯrm\
naked	[ˈneɪkəd]	\ˈnākəd\	north	[ˈnɔrθ]	\ˈnȯrth\
name	[ˈneɪm]	\ˈnām\	Norwegian	[nɔrˈwiːdʒən]	\nȯrˈwējⁿn\
nap	[ˈnæp]	\ˈnap\	nose	[ˈnoːz]	\ˈnōz\
nape	[ˈneɪp, ˈnæp]	\ˈnāp, ˈnap\	nostalgia	[naˈstældʒə, nə-]	\näˈstaljə, nə-\
napkin	[ˈnæpkən]	\ˈnapkən\	not	[ˈnat]	\ˈnät\
narrate	[ˈnærˌeɪt]	\ˈnarˌāt\	note	[ˈnoːt]	\ˈnōt\
narrow	[ˈnærˌoː]	\ˈnarˌō\	nothing	[ˈnʌθɪŋ]	\ˈnəthiŋ\
nasal	[ˈneɪzəl]	\ˈnāzᵊl\	notice	[ˈnoːtɪs]	\ˈnōtis\
nasty	[ˈnæsti]	\ˈnastē\	notion	[ˈnoːʃə n]	\ˈnōshⁿn\
nation	[ˈneɪʃən]	\ˈnāshⁿn\	noun	[ˈnaʊn]	\ˈnaun\
native	[ˈneɪtɪv]	\ˈnātiv\	nourish	[ˈnərɪʃ]	\ˈnərish\
nature	[ˈneɪtʃər]	\ˈnāchər\	novel	[ˈnavəl]	\ˈnävᵊl\
naughty	[ˈnɔti]	\ˈnȯtē\	November	[noˈvɛmbər]	\nōˈvembər\
naval	[ˈneɪvəl]	\ˈnāvᵊl\	now	[ˈnaʊ]	\ˈnau\
navel	[ˈneɪvəl]	\ˈnāvᵊl\	nowhere	[ˈnoːˌʰwɛr]	\ˈnōˌ(h)wer\
navigate	[ˈnævəˌgeɪt]	\ˈnavəˌgāt\	nuclear	[ˈnuːkliər, ˈnjuː-]	\ˈnüklēǝr, ˈnyü-\
near	[ˈnɪr]	\ˈnir\	nude	[ˈnuːd, ˈnjuːd]	\ˈnüd, ˈnyüd\
neat	[ˈniːt]	\ˈnēt\	number	[ˈnʌmbər]	\ˈnəmbər\
necessary	[ˈnɛsəˌsɛri]	\ˈnesəˌserē\	nun	[ˈnʌn]	\ˈnən\
neck	[ˈnɛk]	\ˈnek\	nurse	[ˈnərs]	\ˈnərs\
need	[ˈniːd]	\ˈnēd\	nurture	[ˈnərtʃər]	\ˈnərchər\
needle	[ˈniːdəl]	\ˈnēdᵊl\	nut	[ˈnʌt]	\ˈnət\
negative	[ˈnɛgətɪv]	\ˈnegətiv\	nutrition	[nuˈtrɪʃən, njʊ-]	\nùˈtrishⁿn, nyù-\
neglect	[nɪˈglɛkt]	\niˈglekt\	nylon	[ˈnaɪˌlan]	\ˈnīˌlän\
negotiate	[nɪˈgoːʃiˌeɪt]	\niˈgōshēˌāt\	oak	[ˈoːk]	\ˈōk\
Negro	[ˈniːˌgroː]	\ˈnēˌgrō\	oath	[ˈoːθ]	\ˈōth\
neither	[ˈniːðər, ˈnaɪ-]	\ˈnēthər, ˈnī-\	oats	[ˈoːts]	\ˈōts\
nephew	[ˈnɛˌfjuː]	\ˈneˌfyü\	obedient	[oˈbiːdiənt]	\ōˈbēdēənt\
nerve	[ˈnərv]	\ˈnərv\	obey	[oˈbeɪ]	\ōˈbā\
nest	[ˈnɛst]	\ˈnest\	object	[ˈabdʒɪkt; əbˈdʒɛkt]	\ˈäbjikt; əbˈjekt\
net	[ˈnɛt]	\ˈnet\	obligation	[ˌablǝˈgeɪʃən]	\ˌäbləˈgāshⁿn\
network	[ˈnɛtˌwərk]	\ˈnetˌwərk\	obscurity	[abˈskjʊrəti, əb-]	\äbˈskyùrətē, əb-\
neutral	[ˈnuːtrəl, ˈnjuː-]	\ˈnütrəl, ˈnyü-\	observe	[əbˈzərv]	\əbˈzərv\
never	[ˈnɛvər]	\ˈnevər\	obsession	[abˈsɛʃən, əb-]	\äbˈseshⁿn, əb-\
new	[ˈnuː, ˈnjuː]	\ˈnü, ˈnyü\	obstacle	[ˈabstɪkəl]	\ˈäbstikᵊl\
next	[ˈnɛkst]	\ˈnekst\	obtain	[əbˈteɪn]	\əbˈtān\
Nicaraguan	[ˌnɪkəˈragwən]	\ˌnikəˈrägwən\	obvious	[ˈabviəs]	\ˈäbvēəs\
nice	[ˈnaɪs]	\ˈnīs\	occasion	[əˈkeɪzən]	\əˈkāzhⁿn\
nickname	[ˈnɪkˌneɪm]	\ˈnikˌnām\	occult	[əˈkʌlt, ˈaˌkʌlt]	\əˈkəlt, ˈäˌkəlt\
niece	[ˈniːs]	\ˈnēs\	occupy	[ˈakjəˌpaɪ]	\ˈäkyəˌpī\
night	[ˈnaɪt]	\ˈnīt\	occur	[əˈkər]	\əˈkər\
nine	[ˈnaɪn]	\ˈnīn\	ocean	[ˈoːʃə n]	\ˈōshⁿn\
no	[ˈnoː]	\ˈnō\	October	[akˈtoːbər]	\äkˈtōbər\
nobody	[ˈnoːbədi, -ˌbadi]	\ˈnōbədē, -ˌbädē\	odd	[ˈad]	\ˈäd\
nod	[ˈnad]	\ˈnäd\	of	[ˈʌv, ˈav]	\ˈəv, ˈäv\
noise	[ˈnɔɪz]	\ˈnȯiz\	off	[ˈɔf]	\ˈȯf\
nominate	[ˈnaməˌneɪt]	\ˈnäməˌnāt\	offend	[əˈfɛnd]	\əˈfend\
none	[ˈnʌn]	\ˈnən\	offer	[ˈɔfər]	\ˈȯfər\
nonetheless	[ˌnʌnðəˈlɛs]	\ˌnənthəˈles\	office	[ˈɔfəs]	\ˈȯfəs\
nonsense	[ˈnanˌsɛnts, ˈnanˌtsənts]		often	[ˈɔfən, ˈɔftən]	\ˈȯfⁿn, ˈȯftⁿn\
		\ˈnänˌsen(t)s, ˈnän(t)sⁿn(t)s\	oh	[ˈoː]	\ˈō\
nonstop	[ˌnanˈstap]	\ˌnänˈstäp\	oil	[ˈɔɪl]	\ˈȯil\
noodle	[ˈnuːdəl]	\ˈnüdᵊl\	OK	[ˌoːˈkeɪ]	\ˌōˈkā\
noon	[ˈnuːn]	\ˈnün\	old	[ˈoːld]	\ˈōld\
nor	[ˈnɔr]	\ˈnȯr\	olive	[ˈalɪv, -ləv]	\ˈäliv, -ləv\

ENGLISH WORD	IPA	M-W	ENGLISH WORD	IPA	M-W
Olympic	[oˈlɪmpɪk]	\ōˈlimpik\	oven	[ˈʌvən]	\ˈəvᵊn\
omit	[oˈmɪt]	\ōˈmit\	over	[ˈoːvər]	\ˈōvər\
on	[ˈan, ˈɔn]	\ˈän, ˈȯn\	overall	[ˌoːvərˈɔl]	\ˌōvərˈȯl\
once	[ˈwʌnts]	\ˈwən(t)s\	overcoat	[ˈoːvərˌkoːt]	\ˈōvərˌkōt\
oncoming	[ˈanˌkʌmɪŋ, ˈɔn-]	\ˈänˌkəmiŋ, ˈȯn-\	overcome	[ˌoːvərˈkʌm]	\ˌōvərˈkəm\
one	[ˈwʌn]	\ˈwən\	overdo	[ˌoːvərˈduː]	\ˌōvərˈdü\
ongoing	[ˈanˌgoːɪŋ]	\ˈänˌgōiŋ\	overdose	[ˈoːvərˌdoːs]	\ˈōvərˌdōs\
onion	[ˈʌnjən]	\ˈənyən\	overdraft	[ˈoːvərˌdræft]	\ˈōvərˌdraft\
only	[ˈoːnli]	\ˈōnlē\	overhand	[ˈoːvərˌhænd]	\ˈōvərˌhand\
onto	[ˈanˌtuː, ˈɔn-]	\ˈänˌtü, ˈȯn-\	overhead	[ˌoːvərˈhɛd]	\ˌōvərˈhed\
open	[ˈoːpən]	\ˈōpᵊn\	overland	[ˈoːvərˌlænd, -lənd]	\ˈōvərˌland, -lənd\
operate	[ˈapəˌreɪt]	\ˈäpəˌrāt\	overlook	[ˌoːvərˈlʊk]	\ˌōvərˈlůk\
opinion	[əˈpɪnjən]	\əˈpinyən\	overly	[ˈoːvərli]	\ˈōvərlē\
opponent	[əˈpoːnənt]	\əˈpōnᵊnt\	overnight	[ˌoːvərˈnaɪt]	\ˌōvərˈnīt\
opportunity	[ˌapərˈtuːnəti, -ˈtjuː-]	\ˌäpərˈtünətē, -ˈtyü-\	overpass	[ˈoːvərˌpæs]	\ˈōvərˌpas\
oppose	[əˈpoːz]	\əˈpōz\	overseas	[ˌoːvərˈsiːz]	\ˌōvərˈsēz\
opposite	[ˈapəzət]	\ˈäpəzət\	oversleep	[ˌoːvərˈsliːp]	\ˌōvərˈslēp\
oppress	[əˈprɛs]	\əˈpres\	overt	[oˈvərt, ˈoːˌvərt]	\ōˈvərt, ˈōˌvərt\
optimism	[ˈaptəˌmɪzəm]	\ˈäptəˌmizᵊm\	overtake	[ˌoːvərˈteɪk]	\ˌōvərˈtāk\
option	[ˈapʃən]	\ˈäpshᵊn\	overtime	[ˈoːvərˌtaɪm]	\ˈōvərˌtīm\
or	[ˈɔr]	\ˈȯr\	overwhelm	[ˌoːvərˈʰwɛlm]	\ˌōvərˈ(h)welm\
oral	[ˈorəl]	\ˈōrəl\	owe	[ˈoː]	\ˈō\
orange	[ˈɔrɪndʒ]	\ˈȯrinj\	owl	[ˈaʊl]	\ˈaůl\
orchestra	[ˈɔrkəstrə]	\ˈȯrkəstrə\	own	[ˈoːn]	\ˈōn\
orchid	[ˈɔrkɪd]	\ˈȯrkid\	oxygen	[ˈaksɪdʒən]	\ˈäksijᵊn\
order	[ˈɔrdər]	\ˈȯrdər\	pace	[ˈpeɪs]	\ˈpās\
ordinary	[ˈɔrdənˌɛri]	\ˈȯrdᵊnˌerē\	pacify	[ˈpæsəˌfaɪ]	\ˈpasəˌfī\
organ	[ˈɔrgən]	\ˈȯrgᵊn\	pack	[ˈpæk]	\ˈpak\
origin	[ˈɔrədʒən]	\ˈȯrəjᵊn\	pact	[ˈpækt]	\ˈpakt\
ornament	[ˈɔrnəmənt]	\ˈȯrnəmənt\	pad	[ˈpæd]	\ˈpad\
orphan	[ˈɔrfən]	\ˈȯrfᵊn\	padlock	[ˈpædˌlak]	\ˈpadˌläk\
ostrich	[ˈastrɪtʃ, ˈɔs-]	\ˈästrich, ˈȯs-\	page	[ˈpeɪdʒ]	\ˈpāj\
other	[ˈʌðər]	\ˈəthər\	pain	[ˈpeɪn]	\ˈpān\
ought	[ˈɔt]	\ˈȯt\	paint	[ˈpeɪnt]	\ˈpānt\
ounce	[ˈaʊnts]	\ˈaůn(t)s\	pair	[ˈpær]	\ˈpar\
our	[ˈar, ˈaʊr]	\ˈär, ˈaůr\	pajamas	[pəˈdʒɑməz, -ˈdʒæ-]	\pəˈjäməz, -ˈja-\
out	[ˈaʊt]	\ˈaůt\	Pakistani	[ˌpækɪˈstæni, ˌpakɪˈstani]	
outcome	[ˈaʊtˌkʌm]	\ˈaůtˌkəm\			\ˌpakiˈstanē, ˌpäkiˈstänē\
outdo	[ˌaʊtˈduː]	\ˌaůtˈdü\	palace	[ˈpæləs]	\ˈpaləs\
outdoor	[ˈaʊtˈdor]	\ˈaůtˈdor\	palate	[ˈpælət]	\ˈpalət\
outer	[ˈaʊtər]	\ˈaůtər\	pale	[ˈpeɪl]	\ˈpāl\
outgoing	[ˈaʊtˌgoːɪŋ]	\ˈaůtˌgōiŋ\	Palestinian	[ˌpæləˈstɪniən]	\ˌpaləˈstinēən\
outlay	[ˈaʊtˌleɪ]	\ˈaůtˌlā\	palm	[ˈpam, ˈpalm]	\ˈpäm, ˈpälm\
outlet	[ˈaʊtˌlɛt, -lət]	\ˈaůtˌlet, -lət\	palpitate	[ˈpælpəˌteɪt]	\ˈpalpəˌtāt\
outline	[ˈaʊtˌlaɪn]	\ˈaůtˌlīn\	pan	[ˈpæn]	\ˈpan\
outlook	[ˈaʊtˌlʊk]	\ˈaůtˌlůk\	pancake	[ˈpænˌkeɪk]	\ˈpanˌkāk\
output	[ˈaʊtˌpʊt]	\ˈaůtˌpůt\	panic	[ˈpænɪk]	\ˈpanik\
outrage	[ˈaʊtˌreɪdʒ]	\ˈaůtˌrāj\	panorama	[ˌpænəˈræmə, -ˈra-]	\ˌpanəˈramə, -ˈrä-\
outright	[ˌaʊtˈraɪt]	\ˌaůtˈrīt\	panther	[ˈpænθər]	\ˈpanthər\
outset	[ˈaʊtˌsɛt]	\ˈaůtˌset\	pants	[ˈpænts]	\ˈpants\
outside	[ˌaʊtˈsaɪd, ˈaʊtˌ-]	\ˌaůtˈsīd, ˈaůtˌ-\	papaya	[pəˈpaɪə]	\pəˈpīə\
outskirts	[ˈaʊtˌskərts]	\ˈaůtˌskərts\	paper	[ˈpeɪpər]	\ˈpāpər\
outspoken	[ˌaʊtˈspoːkən]	\ˌaůtˈspōkᵊn\	paprika	[pəˈpriːkə, pæ-]	\pəˈprēkə, pa-\
outstanding	[ˌaʊtˈstændɪŋ]	\ˌaůtˈstandiŋ\	parachute	[ˈpærəˌʃuːt]	\ˈparəˌshüt\
outward	[ˈaʊtwərd]	\ˈaůtwərd\	paradise	[ˈpærəˌdaɪs, -ˌdaɪz]	\ˈparəˌdīs, -ˌdīz\
oval	[ˈoːvəl]	\ˈōvᵊl\	paragraph	[ˈpærəˌgræf]	\ˈparəˌgraf\

ENGLISH WORD	IPA	M-W	ENGLISH WORD	IPA	M-W
Paraguayan	[ˌpærəˈgwaɪən, -ˈgweɪ-]	\ˌparəˈgwīən, -ˈgwā-\	pedal	[ˈpɛdəl]	\ˈpedᵊl\
paralysis	[pəˈræləsɪs]	\pəˈraləsis\	pedestrian	[pəˈdɛstriən]	\pəˈdestrēən\
paratrooper	[ˈpærəˌtruːpər]	\ˈparəˌtrüpər\	pediatrician	[ˌpiːdiəˈtrɪʃən]	\ˌpēdēəˈtrishᵊn\
parcel	[ˈparsəl]	\ˈpärsᵊl\	peel	[ˈpiːl]	\ˈpēl\
pardon	[ˈpardn]	\ˈpärdᵊn\	pelt	[ˈpɛlt]	\ˈpelt\
parent	[ˈpærənt]	\ˈparənt\	pelvis	[ˈpɛlvɪs]	\ˈpelvis\
parenthesis	[pəˈrɛnθəsɪs]	\pəˈrenthəsis\	pen	[ˈpɛn]	\ˈpen\
parish	[ˈpærɪʃ]	\ˈparish\	penal	[ˈpiːnəl]	\ˈpēnᵊl\
park	[ˈpark]	\ˈpärk\	penance	[ˈpɛnənts]	\ˈpenᵊn(t)s\
parking	[ˈparkɪŋ]	\ˈpärkiŋ\	pencil	[ˈpɛntsəl]	\ˈpen(t)sᵊl\
parliament	[ˈparləmənt, ˈparljə-]	\ˈpärləmənt, ˈpärlyə-\	pending	[ˈpɛndɪŋ]	\ˈpendiŋ\
parole	[pəˈroːl]	\pəˈrōl\	penetrate	[ˈpɛnəˌtreɪt]	\ˈpenəˌtrāt\
parrot	[ˈpærət]	\ˈparət\	penicillin	[ˌpɛnəˈsɪlən]	\ˌpenəˈsilən\
parsley	[ˈparsli]	\ˈpärslē\	peninsula	[pəˈnɪntsələ, -ˈnɪntʃʊlə]	
part	[ˈpart]	\ˈpärt\			\pəˈnin(t)sələ, -ˈninchùlə\
partial	[ˈparʃəl]	\ˈpärshᵊl\	pension	[ˈpɛntʃən]	\ˈpenchᵊn\
participate	[pərˈtɪsəˌpeɪt, par-]	\pərˈtisəˌpāt, pär-\	pensive	[ˈpɛntsɪv]	\ˈpen(t)siv\
participle	[ˈpartəˌsɪpəl]	\ˈpärtəˌsipᵊl\	pentagon	[ˈpɛntəˌgan]	\ˈpentəˌgän\
particular	[parˈtɪkjələr]	\pärˈtikyələr\	people	[ˈpiːpəl]	\ˈpēpᵊl\
partition	[pərˈtɪʃən, par-]	\pərˈtishᵊn, pär-\	pepper	[ˈpɛpər]	\ˈpepər\
partner	[ˈpartnər]	\ˈpärtnər\	peppermint	[ˈpɛpərˌmɪnt]	\ˈpepərˌmint\
party	[ˈparti]	\ˈpärtē\	perceive	[pərˈsiːv]	\pərˈsēv\
pass	[ˈpæs]	\ˈpas\	percent	[pərˈsɛnt]	\pərˈsent\
passenger	[ˈpæsəndʒər]	\ˈpasᵊnjər\	perception	[pərˈsɛpʃən]	\pərˈsepshᵊn\
passion	[ˈpæʃən]	\ˈpashᵊn\	percussion	[pərˈkʌʃən]	\pərˈkəshᵊn\
passive	[ˈpæsɪv]	\ˈpasiv\	perfect	[ˈpərfɪkt; pərˈfɛkt]	\ˈpərfikt; pərˈfekt\
Passover	[ˈpæsˌoːvər]	\ˈpasˌōvər\	perforate	[ˈpərfəˌreɪt]	\ˈpərfəˌrāt\
passport	[ˈpæsˌport]	\ˈpasˌpōrt\	perform	[pərˈform]	\pərˈfórm\
password	[ˈpæsˌwərd]	\ˈpasˌwərd\	perfume	[ˈpərˌfjuːm, pər-]	\ˈpərˌfyüm, pər-\
past	[ˈpæst]	\ˈpast\	perhaps	[pərˈhæps]	\pərˈhaps\
paste	[ˈpeɪst]	\ˈpāst\	peril	[ˈpɛrəl]	\ˈperəl\
pastime	[ˈpæsˌtaɪm]	\ˈpasˌtīm\	period	[ˈpɪriəd]	\ˈpirēəd\
pastor	[ˈpæstər]	\ˈpastər\	peripheral	[pəˈrɪfərəl]	\pəˈrifərəl\
pasture	[ˈpæstʃər]	\ˈpaschər\	perish	[ˈpɛrɪʃ]	\ˈperish\
paternal	[pəˈtərnəl]	\pəˈtərnᵊl\	permanent	[ˈpərmənənt]	\ˈpərmənənt\
path	[ˈpæθ, ˈpaθ]	\ˈpath, ˈpäth\	permission	[pərˈmɪʃən]	\pərˈmishᵊn\
patience	[ˈpeɪʃənts]	\ˈpāshᵊn(t)s\	perpendicular	[ˌpərpənˈdɪkjələr]	\ˌpərpᵊnˈdikyələr\
patio	[ˈpætiˌoː]	\ˈpatēˌō\	persecute	[ˈpərsɪˌkjuːt]	\ˈpərsiˌkyüt\
patriot	[ˈpeɪtriət]	\ˈpātrēət\	person	[ˈpərsən]	\ˈpərsᵊn\
patrol	[pəˈtroːl]	\pəˈtrōl\	perspective	[pərˈspɛktɪv]	\pərˈspektiv\
pattern	[ˈpætərn]	\ˈpatərn\	persuade	[pərˈsweɪd]	\pərˈswād\
paunch	[ˈpɔntʃ]	\ˈpónch\	Peruvian	[pəˈruːviən]	\pəˈrüvēən\
pause	[ˈpɔz]	\ˈpóz\	perverse	[pərˈvərs]	\pərˈvərs\
pave	[ˈpeɪv]	\ˈpāv\	pessimist	[ˈpɛsəmɪst]	\ˈpesəmist\
pavilion	[pəˈvɪljən]	\pəˈvilyən\	petal	[ˈpɛtəl]	\ˈpetᵊl\
paw	[ˈpɔ]	\ˈpó\	petition	[pəˈtɪʃən]	\pəˈtishᵊn\
pawn	[ˈpɔn]	\ˈpón\	petroleum	[pəˈtroːliəm]	\pəˈtrōlēəm\
pay	[ˈpeɪ]	\ˈpā\	phenomenon	[fɪˈnaməˌnan, -nən]	\fiˈnäməˌnän, -nən\
pea	[ˈpiː]	\ˈpē\	philosophy	[fəˈlasəfi]	\fəˈläsəfē\
peace	[ˈpiːs]	\ˈpēs\	phobia	[ˈfoːbiə]	\ˈfōbēə\
peach	[ˈpiːtʃ]	\ˈpēch\	phosphorus	[ˈfasfərəs]	\ˈfäsfərəs\
peak	[ˈpiːk]	\ˈpēk\	photocopy	[ˈfoːtoˌkapi]	\ˈfōtōˌkäpē\
peanut	[ˈpiːˌnʌt]	\ˈpēˌnət\	phrase	[ˈfreɪz]	\ˈfrāz\
pear	[ˈpær]	\ˈpar\	physical	[ˈfɪzɪkəl]	\ˈfizikᵊl\
pearl	[ˈpərl]	\ˈpərl\	physics	[ˈfɪzɪks]	\ˈfiziks\
peasant	[ˈpɛzənt]	\ˈpezᵊnt\	physiology	[ˌfɪziˈalədʒi]	\ˌfizēˈäləjē\

ENGLISH WORD	IPA	M-W	ENGLISH WORD	IPA	M-W
physique	[fə'zi:k]	\fə'zēk\	poison	['pɔɪzən]	\'póizᵊn\
piano	[pi'æno:]	\pē'anō\	poker	['po:kər]	\'pōkər\
pick	['pɪk]	\'pik\	polarize	['po:lə,raɪz]	\'pōlə,rīz\
pickle	['pɪkəl]	\'pikᵊl\	pole	['po:l]	\'pōl\
picnic	['pɪk,nɪk]	\'pik,nik\	police	[pə'li:s]	\pə'lēs\
picture	['pɪktʃər]	\'pikchər\	policy	['paləsi]	\'päləsē\
pie	['paɪ]	\'pī\	polish	['palɪʃ]	\'pälish\
piece	['pi:s]	\'pēs\	Polish	['po:lɪʃ]	\'pōlish\
piety	['paɪəti]	\'pīətē\	polite	[pə'laɪt]	\pə'līt\
pig	['pɪg]	\'pig\	political	[pə'lɪtɪkəl]	\pə'litikᵊl\
pigeon	['pɪdʒən]	\'pijᵊn\	poll	['po:l]	\'pōl\
pigtail	['pɪg,teɪl]	\'pig,tāl\	pollute	[pə'lu:t]	\pə'lüt\
pile	['paɪl]	\'pīl\	pool	['pu:l]	\'pül\
pill	['pɪl]	\'pil\	poor	['pʊr, 'por]	\'pùr, 'pōr\
pillow	['pɪ,lo:]	\'pi,lō\	popcorn	['pap,kɔrn]	\'päp,kórn\
pilot	['paɪlət]	\'pīlət\	pope	['po:p]	\'pōp\
pin	['pɪn]	\'pin\	popular	['papjələr]	\'päpyələr\
pinch	['pɪntʃ]	\'pinch\	population	[,papjə'leɪʃən]	\,päpyə'lāshᵊn\
pineapple	['paɪn,æpəl]	\'pīn,apᵊl\	porcelain	['pɔrsələn]	\'pōrsələn\
pink	['pɪŋk]	\'piŋk\	port	['port]	\'pōrt\
pioneer	[,paɪə'nɪr]	\,pīə'nir\	portable	['portəbəl]	\'pōrtəbᵊl\
pipe	['paɪp]	\'pīp\	porter	['portər]	\'pōrtər\
pistol	['pɪstəl]	\'pistᵊl\	portion	['porʃən]	\'pōrshᵊn\
piston	['pɪstən]	\'pistᵊn\	portrait	['portrət, -,treɪt]	\'pōrtrət, -,trāt\
pit	['pɪt]	\'pit\	portray	[por'treɪ]	\pōr'trā\
pizza	['pi:tsə]	\'pētsə\	Portuguese	[,portʃə'gi:z, -'gi:s]	\,pōrchə'gēz, -'gēs\
place	['pleɪs]	\'plās\	pose	['po:z]	\'pōz\
plagiarism	['pleɪdʒə,rɪzəm]	\'plājə,rizᵊm\	position	[pə'zɪʃən]	\pə'zishᵊn\
plaid	['plæd]	\'plad\	positive	['pazətɪv]	\'päzətiv\
plain	['pleɪn]	\'plān\	possess	[pə'zɛs]	\pə'zes\
plan	['plæn]	\'plan\	possible	['pasəbəl]	\'päsəbᵊl\
plane	['pleɪn]	\'plān\	postal	['po:stəl]	\'pōstᵊl\
planet	['plænət]	\'planət\	poster	['po:stər]	\'pōstər\
plank	['plæŋk]	\'plaŋk\	postpone	[,po:st'po:n]	\,pōst'pōn\
planning	['plænɪŋ]	\'planiŋ\	postwar	[,po:st'wɔr]	\,pōst'wór\
plant	['plænt]	\'plant\	pot	['pat]	\'pät\
plantain	['plæntən]	\'plantᵊn\	potato	[pə'teɪto]	\pə'tātō\
plaque	['plæk]	\'plak\	pottery	['patəri]	\'pätərē\
plaster	['plæstər]	\'plastər\	pound	['paʊnd]	\'paùnd\
plastic	['plæstɪk]	\'plastik\	poverty	['pavərti]	\'pävərtē\
plate	['pleɪt]	\'plāt\	powder	['paʊdər]	\'paùdər\
platform	['plæt,fɔrm]	\'plat,fórm\	power	['paʊər]	\'paùər\
platter	['plætər]	\'platər\	practical	['præktɪkəl]	\'praktikᵊl\
play	['pleɪ]	\'plā\	prank	['præŋk]	\'praŋk\
pleasant	['plɛzənt]	\'plezənt\	pray	['preɪ]	\'prā\
pledge	['plɛdʒ]	\'plej\	preach	['pri:tʃ]	\'prēch\
plot	['plat]	\'plät\	precaution	[pri'kɔʃən]	\prē'kóshᵊn\
plug	['plʌg]	\'pləg\	precedent	['prɛsədənt]	\'presədənt\
plum	['plʌm]	\'pləm\	precious	['prɛʃəs]	\'preshəs\
plumber	['plʌmər]	\'pləmər\	precipitation	[pri,sɪpə'teɪʃən]	\prē,sipə'tāshᵊn\
plunge	['plʌndʒ]	\'plənj\	precise	[pri'saɪs]	\prē'sīs\
plural	['plʊrəl]	\'plùrəl\	precocious	[pri'ko:ʃəs]	\prē'kōshəs\
plus	['plʌs]	\'pləs\	predict	[pri'dɪkt]	\prē'dikt\
pocket	['pakət]	\'päkət\	predominant	[pri'damənənt]	\prē'dämᵊnənt\
poem	['po:əm]	\'pōəm\	preface	['prɛfəs]	\'prefəs\
point	['pɔɪnt]	\'póint\	prefer	[pri'fər]	\prē'fər\

ENGLISH WORD	IPA	M-W
prefix	[ˈpriˌfɪks]	\ˈprē͝ˌfiks\
pregnancy	[ˈprɛgnəntˌsi]	\ˈpregnən(t)sē\
prehistoric	[ˌpriːhɪsˈtɔrɪk]	\ˌprēhis'tórik\
prejudice	[ˈprɛdʒədəs]	\ˈprejədəs\
preliminary	[priˈlɪməˌnɛri]	\prēˈliməˌnerē\
premarital	[ˌpriːˈmærətəl]	\ˌprēˈmarətᵊl\
premature	[ˌpriːməˈtʊr, -ˈtjʊr, -ˈtʃʊr]	
		\ˌprēməˈtür, -ˈtyür, -ˈchür\
premise	[ˈprɛmɪs]	\ˈpremis\
premium	[ˈpriːmiəm]	\ˈprēmēəm\
prepare	[priˈpær]	\prēˈpar\
preposition	[ˌprɛpəˈzɪʃən]	\ˌprepəˈzish'n\
prescription	[priˈskrɪpʃən]	\prēˈskripsh'n\
presence	[ˈprɛzənts]	\ˈprez'n(t)s\
present	[ˈprɛzənt; priˈzɛnt]	\ˈprez'nt; prēˈzent\
preserve	[priˈzərv]	\prēˈzərv\
president	[ˈprɛzədənt]	\ˈprezədənt\
press	[ˈprɛs]	\ˈpres\
prestige	[prɛˈstiːʒ, -ˈstiːdʒ]	\preˈstēzh, -ˈstēj\
pretend	[priˈtɛnd]	\prēˈtend\
pretext	[ˈpriːˌtɛkst]	\ˈprēˌtekst\
pretty	[ˈprɪti]	\ˈpritē\
prevent	[priˈvɛnt]	\prēˈvent\
previously	[ˈpriːviəsli]	\ˈprēvēəslē\
price	[ˈpraɪs]	\ˈprīs\
prickly	[ˈprɪkəli]	\ˈprikᵊlē\
pride	[ˈpraɪd]	\ˈprīd\
priest	[ˈpriːst]	\ˈprēst\
primary	[ˈpraɪˌmɛri, ˈpraɪməri]	\ˈprīˌmerē, ˈprīmərē\
primitive	[ˈprɪmətɪv]	\ˈprimətiv\
principal	[ˈprɪntsəpəl]	\ˈprin(t)səpᵊl\
principle	[ˈprɪntsəpəl]	\ˈprin(t)səpᵊl\
print	[ˈprɪnt]	\ˈprint\
priority	[praɪˈɔrəti]	\prīˈórətē\
prison	[ˈprɪzən]	\ˈpriz'n\
privacy	[ˈpraɪvəsi]	\ˈprīvəsē\
privilege	[ˈprɪvlɪdʒ, ˈprɪvə-]	\ˈprivlij, ˈprivə-\
prize	[ˈpraɪz]	\ˈprīz\
pro	[ˈpriː]	\ˈprō\
probability	[ˌprabəˈbɪləti]	\ˌpräbəˈbilətē\
problem	[ˈprabləm]	\ˈpräbləm\
procedure	[prəˈsiːdʒər]	\prəˈsējər\
proceed	[proˈsiːd]	\prōˈsēd\
process	[ˈpraˌsɛs, ˈproː-]	\ˈpräˌses, ˈprō-\
proclaim	[proˈkleɪm]	\prōˈklām\
produce	[prəˈduːs, ˈproː-]	\prəˈdüs, ˈprō-\
profession	[prəˈfɛʃən]	\prəˈfesh'n\
profile	[ˈproːˌfaɪl]	\ˈprōˌfīl\
profit	[ˈprafət]	\ˈpräfət\
profound	[prəˈfaʊnd]	\prəˈfaúnd\
prognosis	[pragˈnoːsɪs]	\prägˈnōsis\
program	[ˈproːˌgræm, -grəm]	\ˈprōˌgram, -grəm\
progress	[ˈpragrəs, -ˌgrɛs; prəˈgrɛs]	
		\ˈprägrəs, -ˌgres; prəˈgres\
prohibit	[proˈhɪbət]	\prōˈhibət\

ENGLISH WORD	IPA	M-W
project	[ˈpraˌdʒɛkt, -dʒɪkt; prəˈdʒɛkt]	
		\ˈpräjekt, -jikt; prəˈjekt\
prologue	[ˈproːˌlɔg]	\ˈprōˌlóg\
prolong	[prəˈlɔŋ]	\prəˈlóŋ\
promise	[ˈpraməs]	\ˈpräməs\
promote	[prəˈmoːt]	\prəˈmōt\
prompt	[ˈprampt]	\ˈprämpt\
prong	[ˈprɔŋ]	\ˈpróŋ\
pronoun	[ˈproːˌnaʊn]	\ˈprōˌnaún\
pronounce	[prəˈnaʊnts]	\prəˈnaún(t)s\
proof	[ˈpruːf]	\ˈprüf\
propaganda	[ˌprapəˈgændə, ˌproː-]	\ˌpräpəˈgandə, ˌprō-\
propeller	[prəˈpɛlər]	\prəˈpelər\
property	[ˈprapərti]	\ˈpräpərtē\
proportion	[prəˈpɔrʃən]	\prəˈpórsh'n\
proposal	[prəˈpoːzəl]	\prəˈpōz'l\
propose	[prəˈpoːz]	\prəˈpōz\
proprietor	[prəˈpraɪətər]	\prəˈprīətər\
prose	[ˈproːz]	\ˈprōz\
prosecute	[ˈprasɪˌkjuːt]	\ˈpräsiˌkyüt\
prospect	[ˈpraˌspɛkt]	\ˈpräˌspekt\
prosper	[ˈpraspər]	\ˈpräspər\
protect	[prəˈtɛkt]	\prəˈtekt\
protest	[ˈproːˌtɛst; proˈtɛst]	\ˈprōˌtest; prōˈtest\
protrude	[proˈtruːd]	\prōˈtrüd\
proud	[ˈpraʊd]	\ˈpraúd\
prove	[ˈpruːv]	\ˈprüv\
proverb	[ˈpraˌvərb]	\ˈpräˌvərb\
provide	[prəˈvaɪd]	\prəˈvīd\
provision	[prəˈvɪʒən]	\prəˈvizh'n\
provoke	[prəˈvoːk]	\prəˈvōk\
proximity	[prakˈsɪməti]	\präkˈsimətē\
prudent	[ˈpruːdənt]	\ˈprüd'nt\
prune	[ˈpruːn]	\ˈprün\
pseudonym	[ˈsuːdəˌnɪm]	\ˈsüdəˌnim\
psychiatrist	[səˈkaɪətrɪst, saɪ-]	\səˈkīətrist, sī-\
psychology	[saɪˈkalədʒi]	\sīˈkäləjē\
puberty	[ˈpjuːbərti]	\ˈpyübərtē\
public	[ˈpʌblɪk]	\ˈpəblik\
publish	[ˈpʌblɪʃ]	\ˈpəblish\
pudding	[ˈpʊdɪŋ]	\ˈpùdiŋ\
puddle	[ˈpʌdəl]	\ˈpəd'l\
Puerto Rican	[ˌpwɛrtəˈriːkən, ˌpɔrtə-]	\ˌpwertəˈrēk'n, ˌpōrtə-\
pull	[ˈpʊl, ˈpʌl]	\ˈpúl, ˈpəl\
pulse	[ˈpʌls]	\ˈpəls\
pumpkin	[ˈpʌmpkɪn, ˈpʌŋkən]	\ˈpəmpkin, ˈpəŋk'n\
punch	[ˈpʌntʃ]	\ˈpənch\
punctual	[ˈpʌŋktʃʊəl]	\ˈpəŋkchùəl\
punctuation	[ˌpʌŋktʃʊˈeɪʃən]	\ˌpəŋkchùˈāsh'n\
punish	[ˈpʌnɪʃ]	\ˈpənish\
pupil	[ˈpjuːpəl]	\ˈpyüp'l\
puppet	[ˈpʌpət]	\ˈpəpət\
puppy	[ˈpʌpi]	\ˈpəpē\
purchase	[ˈpərtʃəs]	\ˈpərchəs\
pure	[ˈpjʊr]	\ˈpyür\
puree	[pjʊˈreɪ, -riː]	\pyùˈrā, -ˈrē\

ENGLISH WORD	IPA	M-W	ENGLISH WORD	IPA	M-W
purify	[ˈpjʊrəˌfaɪ]	\ˈpyùrəˌfī\	raw	[ˈrɔ]	\ˈrȯ\
purity	[ˈpjʊrəti]	\ˈpyùrətē\	ray	[ˈreɪ]	\ˈrā\
purple	[ˈpərpəl]	\ˈpərpᵊl\	razor	[ˈreɪzər]	\ˈrāzər\
purpose	[ˈpərpəs]	\ˈpərpəs\	reach	[ˈriːtʃ]	\ˈrēch\
purse	[ˈpərs]	\ˈpərs\	reaction	[riˈækʃən]	\rēˈakshᵊn\
pursue	[pərˈsuː]	\pərˈsü\	read	[ˈriːd]	\ˈrēd\
push	[ˈpʊʃ]	\ˈpùsh\	readily	[ˈrɛdəli]	\ˈredᵊlē\
quality	[ˈkwɑləti]	\ˈkwälətē\	ready	[ˈrɛdi]	redē
quantity	[ˈkwɑntəti]	\ˈkwäntətē\	real	[ˈriːl]	\ˈrēl\
quarrel	[ˈkwɔrəl]	\ˈkwȯrəl\	realize	[ˈriːəˌlaɪz]	\ˈrēəˌlīz\
quarter	[ˈkwɔrtər]	\ˈkwȯrtər\	really	[ˈrɪli, ˈriː-]	\ˈrilē, ˈrē-\
quartet	[kwɔrˈtɛt]	\kwȯrˈtet\	rear	[ˈrɪr]	\ˈrir\
queen	[ˈkwiːn]	\ˈkwēn\	rearrange	[ˌriːəˈreɪndʒ]	\ˌrēəˈrānj\
query	[ˈkwɪri, ˈkwɛr-]	\ˈkwirē, ˈkwer-\	reason	[ˈriːzən]	\ˈrēzᵊn\
quest	[ˈkwɛst]	\ˈkwest\	rebel	[ˈrɛbəl; rɪˈbɛl]	\ˈrebᵊl; riˈbel\
question	[ˈkwɛstʃən]	\ˈkweschᵊn\	rebuild	[ˌriːˈbɪld]	\ˌrēˈbild\
quick	[ˈkwɪk]	\ˈkwik\	recall	[riˈkɔl; ˈriːˌkɔl]	\rēˈkȯl; ˈrēˌkȯl\
quiet	[ˈkwaɪət]	\ˈkwīət\	receipt	[riˈsiːt]	\rēˈsēt\
quit	[ˈkwɪt]	\ˈkwit\	receive	[riˈsiːv]	\rēˈsēv\
quota	[ˈkwoːtə]	\ˈkwōtə\	recent	[ˈriːsənt]	\ˈrēsᵊnt\
quotation	[kwoˈteɪʃən]	\kwōˈtāshᵊn\	receptacle	[riˈsɛptɪkəl]	\rēˈseptikᵊl\
rabbit	[ˈræbət]	\ˈrabət\	reception	[riˈsɛpʃən]	\rēˈsepshᵊn\
race	[ˈreɪs]	\ˈrās\	recharge	[ˌriːˈtʃɑrdʒ]	\ˌrēˈchärj\
racial	[ˈreɪʃəl]	\ˈrāshᵊl\	recipe	[ˈrɛsəˌpiː]	\ˈresəˌpē\
rack	[ˈræk]	\ˈrak\	recipient	[riˈsɪpiənt]	\rēˈsipēənt\
racket	[ˈrækət]	\ˈrakət\	recite	[riˈsaɪt]	\rēˈsīt\
radar	[ˈreɪˌdɑr]	\ˈrāˌdär\	reckon	[ˈrɛkən]	\ˈrekᵊn\
radiance	[ˈreɪdiənts]	\ˈrādēən(t)s\	reclaim	[riˈkleɪm]	\rēˈklām\
radio	[ˈreɪdiˌoː]	\ˈrādēˌō\	recline	[riˈklaɪn]	\rēˈklīn\
raft	[ˈræft]	\ˈraft\	recognition	[ˌrɛkɪgˈnɪʃən]	\ˌrekigˈnishᵊn\
rag	[ˈræg]	\ˈrag\	recommend	[ˌrɛkəˈmɛnd]	\ˌrekəˈmend\
rage	[ˈreɪdʒ]	\ˈrāj\	reconsider	[ˌriːkənˈsɪdər]	\ˌrēkənˈsidər\
raid	[ˈreɪd]	\ˈrād\	record	[riˈkɔrd; ˈrɛkərd]	\rēˈkȯrd; ˈrekərd\
rail	[ˈreɪl]	\ˈrāl\	recover	[riˈkʌvər]	\rēˈkəvər\
rain	[ˈreɪn]	\ˈrān\	rectangle	[ˈrɛkˌtæŋgəl]	\ˈrekˌtangᵊl\
raise	[ˈreɪz]	\ˈrāz\	rector	[ˈrɛktər]	\ˈrektər\
raisin	[ˈreɪzən]	\ˈrāzᵊn\	recuperate	[riˈkuːpəˌreɪt, -ˈkjuː-]	\rēˈküpəˌrāt, -ˈkyü-\
rally	[ˈræli]	\ˈralē\	recur	[riˈkər]	\rēˈkər\
RAM	[ˈræm]	\ˈram\	recycle	[riˈsaɪkəl]	\rēˈsīkᵊl\
ramble	[ˈræmbəl]	\ˈrambᵊl\	red	[ˈrɛd]	\ˈred\
ramp	[ˈræmp]	\ˈramp\	redo	[ˌriːˈduː]	\ˌrēˈdü\
ranch	[ˈræntʃ]	\ˈranch\	reduce	[riˈduːs, -ˈdjuːs]	\rēˈdüs, -ˈdyüs\
random	[ˈrændəm]	\ˈrandəm\	refer	[riˈfər]	\rēˈfər\
range	[ˈreɪndʒ]	\ˈrānj\	referee	[ˌrɛfəˈriː]	\ˌrefəˈrē\
rank	[ˈræŋk]	\ˈraŋk\	refill	[ˌriːˈfɪl; ˈriːˌfɪl]	\ˌrēˈfil; ˈrēˌfil\
rap	[ˈræp]	\ˈrap\	reflect	[riˈflɛkt]	\rēˈflekt\
rapid	[ˈræpɪd]	\ˈrapid\	reflex	[ˈriːˌflɛks]	\ˈrēˌfleks\
rapport	[ræˈpor]	\raˈpōr\	reform	[riˈfɔrm]	\rēˈfȯrm\
rare	[ˈrær]	\ˈrar\	refrain	[riˈfreɪn]	\rēˈfrān\
rash	[ˈræʃ]	\ˈrash\	refresh	[riˈfrɛʃ]	\rēˈfresh\
raspberry	[ˈræzˌbɛri]	\ˈrazˌberē\	refrigerate	[riˈfrɪdʒəˌreɪt]	\rēˈfrijəˌrāt\
rat	[ˈræt]	\ˈrat\	refuel	[riːˈfjuːəl]	\rēˈfyüᵊl\
rate	[ˈreɪt]	\ˈrāt\	refund	[riˈfʌnd, ˈriːˌfʌnd]	\rēˈfənd, ˈrēˌfənd\
rather	[ˈræðər, ˈrʌ-, ˈrɑ-]	\ˈrathər, ˈrə-, ˈrä-\	refuse	[ˈrɛˌfjuːs, -ˌfjuːz]	\ˈreˌfyüs, -ˌfyüz\
rating	[ˈreɪtɪŋ]	\ˈrātiŋ\	regain	[riˈgeɪn]	\rēˈgān\
rational	[ˈræʃənəl]	\ˈrashənᵊl\	regard	[riˈgɑrd]	\rēˈgärd\

ENGLISH WORD	IPA	M-W	ENGLISH WORD	IPA	M-W
region	[ˈriːdʒən]	\ˈrējən\	restaurant	[ˈrestəˌrɑnt, -rənt]	\ˈrestəˌränt, -rənt\
register	[ˈrɛdʒəstər]	\ˈrejəstər\	restful	[ˈrɛstfəl]	\ˈrestfəl\
regret	[riˈgrɛt]	\rēˈgret\	restless	[ˈrɛstləs]	\ˈrestləs\
regular	[ˈrɛgjələr]	\ˈregyələr\	restore	[riˈstor]	\rēˈstȯr\
rehabilitate	[ˌriːhəˈbıləˌteɪt, ˌriːə-]	\ˌrēhəˈbiləˌtāt, ˌrēə-\	restrain	[riˈstreɪn]	\rēˈstrān\
rehearse	[riˈhərs]	\rēˈhərs\	restriction	[riˈstrıkʃən]	\rēˈstriksh³n\
reign	[ˈreɪn]	\ˈrān\	result	[riˈzʌlt]	\rēˈzəlt\
reinforce	[ˌriːənˈfors]	\ˌrēənˈfōrs\	resume	[riˈzuːm]	\rēˈzüm\
reject	[riˈdʒɛkt]	\rēˈjekt\	retire	[riˈtaɪr]	\rēˈtīr\
relate	[riˈleɪt]	\rēˈlāt\	retrieve	[riˈtriːv]	\rēˈtrēv\
relax	[riˈlæks]	\rēˈlaks\	return	[riˈtərn]	\rēˈtərn\
release	[riˈliːs]	\rēˈlēs\	reveal	[riˈviːl]	\rēˈvēl\
relevant	[ˈrɛləvənt]	\ˈreləvənt\	reverse	[riˈvərs]	\rēˈvərs\
reliable	[riˈlaɪəbəl]	\rēˈlīəb³l\	review	[riˈvjuː]	\rēˈvyü\
relief	[riˈliːf]	\rēˈlēf\	revise	[riˈvaɪz]	\rēˈvīz\
religion	[riˈlɪdʒən]	\rēˈlij³n\	revival	[riˈvaɪvəl]	\rēˈvīvəl\
remain	[riˈmeɪn]	\rēˈmān\	revolution	[ˌrɛvəˈluːʃən]	\ˌrevəˈlüsh³n\
remark	[riˈmɑrk]	\rēˈmärk\	reward	[riˈword]	\rēˈwȯrd\
remedy	[ˈrɛmədi]	\ˈremədē\	rewrite	[ˌriːˈraɪt]	\ˌrēˈrīt\
remember	[riˈmɛmbər]	\rēˈmembər\	rhyme	[ˈraɪm]	\ˈrīm\
remind	[riˈmaɪnd]	\rēˈmīnd\	rhythm	[ˈrɪðəm]	\ˈrith³m\
remote	[riˈmoːt]	\rēˈmōt\	rib	[ˈrɪb]	\ˈrib\
remove	[riˈmuːv]	\rēˈmüv\	ribbon	[ˈrɪbən]	\ˈrib³n\
rendition	[rɛnˈdɪʃən]	\renˈdish³n\	rice	[ˈraɪs]	\ˈrīs\
renew	[riˈnuː, -ˈnjuː]	\rēˈnü, -ˈnyü\	rich	[ˈrɪtʃ]	\ˈrich\
renovate	[ˈrɛnəˌveɪt]	\ˈrenəˌvāt\	rid	[ˈrɪd]	\ˈrid\
renown	[riˈnaʊn]	\rēˈnaùn\	riddle	[ˈrɪdəl]	\ˈrid³l\
rent	[ˈrɛnt]	\ˈrent\	ride	[ˈraɪd]	\ˈrīd\
repair	[riˈpær]	\rēˈpar\	ridiculous	[rəˈdɪkjələs]	\rəˈdikyələs\
repeat	[riˈpiːt]	\rēˈpēt\	rifle	[ˈraɪfəl]	\ˈrīf³l\
repetition	[ˌrɛpəˈtɪʃən]	\ˌrepəˈtish³n\	right	[ˈraɪt]	\ˈrīt\
replace	[riˈpleɪs]	\rēˈplās\	rigid	[ˈrɪdʒɪd]	\ˈrijid\
reply	[riˈplaɪ]	\rēˈplī\	ring	[ˈrɪŋ]	\ˈriŋ\
report	[riˈport]	\rēˈpōrt\	rink	[ˈrɪŋk]	\ˈriŋk\
represent	[ˌrɛprɪˈzɛnt]	\ˌrepriˈzent\	rinse	[ˈrɪnts]	\ˈrin(t)s\
repress	[riˈprɛs]	\rēˈpres\	ripe	[ˈraɪp]	\ˈrīp\
reproduce	[ˌriːprəˈduːs, -ˈdjuːs]	\ˌrēprəˈdüs, -ˈdyüs\	rise	[ˈraɪz]	\ˈrīz\
republic	[riˈpʌblɪk]	\rēˈpəblik\	risk	[ˈrɪsk]	\ˈrisk\
reputation	[ˌrɛpjəˈteɪʃən]	\ˌrepyəˈtāsh³n\	rival	[ˈraɪvəl]	\ˈrīv³l\
request	[riˈkwɛst]	\rēˈkwest\	river	[ˈrɪvər]	\ˈrivər\
require	[riˈkwaɪr]	\rēˈkwīr\	road	[ˈroːd]	\ˈrōd\
rescue	[ˈrɛsˌkjuː]	\ˈresˌkyü\	roast	[ˈroːst]	\ˈrōst\
research	[riˈsərtʃ, ˈriːˌsərtʃ]	\rēˈsərch, ˈrēˌsərch\	robot	[ˈroːˌbɑt, -bət]	\ˈrōˌbät, -bət\
resemble	[riˈzɛmbəl]	\rēˈzemb³l\	robust	[roˈbʌst, ˈroːˌbʌst]	\rōˈbəst, ˈrōˌbəst\
reserve	[riˈzərv]	\rēˈzərv\	rock	[ˈrɑk]	\ˈräk\
reset	[ˌriːˈsɛt]	\ˌrēˈset\	role	[ˈroːl]	\ˈrōl\
residence	[ˈrɛzədənts]	\ˈrezədən(t)s\	roll	[ˈroːl]	\ˈrōl\
resign	[riˈzaɪn]	\rēˈzīn\	romance	[roˈmænts, ˈroːˌmænts]	
resistant	[riˈzɪstənt]	\rēˈzist³nt\			\rōˈman(t)s, ˈrōˌman(t)s\
resolve	[riˈzɑlv]	\rēˈzälv\	Romanian	[rʊˈmeɪniən, ro-]	\rùˈmānēən, rō-\
resort	[riˈzort]	\rēˈzȯrt\	romantic	[roˈmæntɪk]	\rōˈmantik\
resource	[ˈriːˌsors, riˈsors]	\ˈrēˌsōrs, rēˈsōrs\	roof	[ˈruːf, ˈrʊf]	\ˈrüf, ˈrùf\
respect	[riˈspɛkt]	\rēˈspekt\	room	[ˈruːm, ˈrʊm]	\ˈrüm, ˈrùm\
respiration	[ˌrɛspəˈreɪʃən]	\ˌrespəˈrāsh³n\	rooster	[ˈruːstər, ˈrʊs-]	\ˈrüstər, ˈrùs-\
response	[riˈspɑnts]	\rēˈspän(t)s\	root	[ˈruːt, ˈrʊt]	\ˈrüt, ˈrùt\
rest	[ˈrɛst]	\ˈrest\	rope	[ˈroːp]	\ˈrōp\

ENGLISH WORD	IPA	M-W	ENGLISH WORD	IPA	M-W
rose	['ro:z]	\'rōz\	savage	['sævɪdʒ]	\'savij\
rotate	['ro:ˌteɪt]	\'rōˌtāt\	save	['seɪv]	\'sāv\
rough	['rʌf]	\'rəf\	saw	['sɔ]	\'sȯ\
round	['raʊnd]	\'raúnd\	say	['seɪ]	\'sā\
route	['ru:t, 'raʊt]	\'rüt, 'raút\	scale	['skeɪl]	\'skāl\
routine	[ru:'ti:n]	\rü'tēn\	scan	['skæn]	\'skan\
row	['ro:]	\'rō\	scandal	['skændəl]	\'skandᵊl\
row	['raʊ]	\'raú\	Scandinavian	[ˌskændə'neɪviən]	\ˌskandə'nāvēan\
rowdy	['raʊdi]	\'raúdē\	scar	['skɑr]	\'skär\
rub	['rʌb]	\'rəb\	scarce	['skɛrs]	\'skers\
rubber	['rʌbər]	\'rəbər\	scare	['skɛr]	\'sker\
rubbish	['rʌbɪʃ]	\'rəbish\	scarf	['skɑrf]	\'skärf\
rude	['ru:d]	\'rüd\	scene	['si:n]	\'sēn\
rug	['rʌg]	\'rəg\	schedule	['skɛˌdʒu:l, -dʒəl, *British* 'ʃɛdˌju:l]	
rugged	['rʌgəd]	\'rəgəd\			\'skeˌjül, -jəl, *British* 'shedˌyül\
ruin	['ru:ən]	\'rüən\	scheme	['ski:m]	\'skēm\
rule	['ru:l]	\'rül\	scholar	['skɑlər]	\'skälər\
rumor	['ru:mər]	\'rümər\	school	['sku:l]	\'skül\
run	['rʌn]	\'rən\	science	['saɪənts]	\'sīən(t)s\
runner	['rʌnər]	\'rənər\	scissors	['sɪzərz]	\'sizərz\
runway	['rʌnˌweɪ]	\'rənˌwā\	scoop	['sku:p]	\'sküp\
rupture	['rʌptʃər]	\'rəpchər\	scoot	['sku:t]	\'süt\
rural	['rʊrəl]	\'rúrəl\	scope	['sko:p]	\'skōp\
rush	['rʌʃ]	\'rəsh\	score	['skor]	\'skōr\
Russian	['rʌʃən]	\'rəshᵊn\	Scot	['skɑt]	\'skät\
sacred	['seɪkrəd]	\'sākrəd\	scout	['skaʊt]	\'skaút\
sacrifice	['sækrəˌfaɪs]	\'sakrəˌfīs\	scramble	['skræmbəl]	\'skrambᵊl\
sad	['sæd]	\'sad\	scrap	['skræp]	\'skrap\
sadness	['sædnəs]	\'sadnəs\	scrape	['skreɪp]	\'skrāp\
safe	['seɪf]	\'sāf\	scratch	['skrætʃ]	\'skrach\
sail	['seɪl]	\'sāl\	scream	['skri:m]	\'skrēm\
saint	['seɪnt, ˌseɪnt, sənt]	\'sānt, ˌsānt, sᵊnt\	screen	['skri:n]	\'skrēn\
sake	['seɪk]	\'sāk\	screw	['skru:]	\'skrü\
salad	['sæləd]	\'saləd\	script	['skrɪpt]	\'skript\
salary	['sæləri]	\'salərē\	scuff	['skʌf]	\'skəf\
sale	['seɪl]	\'sāl\	sculpture	['skʌlptʃər]	\'skəlpchər\
saliva	[sə'laɪvə]	\sə'līvə\	sea	['si:]	\'sē\
salt	['sɔlt]	\'sȯlt\	seal	['si:l]	\'sēl\
salvage	['sælvɪdʒ]	\'salvij\	search	['sərtʃ]	\'sərch\
salvation	[sæl'veɪʃən]	\sal'vāshᵊn\	season	['si:zən]	\'sēzᵊn\
same	['seɪm]	\'sām\	seat	['si:t]	\'sēt\
sample	['sæmpəl]	\'sampᵊl\	second	['sekənd]	\'sekənd\
sand	['sænd]	\'sand\	secret	['si:krət]	\'sēkrət\
sandal	['sændəl]	\'sandᵊl\	secretary	['sekrəˌteri]	\'sekrəˌterē\
sandwich	['sændˌwɪtʃ]	\'sandˌwich\	secretly	['si:krətli]	\'sēkrətlē\
sane	['seɪn]	\'sān\	sect	['sekt]	\'sekt\
sanitary	['sænəteri]	\'sanəterē\	section	['sekʃən]	\'sekshᵊn\
Santa Claus	['sæntəˌklɔz]	\'santəˌklȯz\	sector	['sektər]	\'sektər\
satellite	['sætəˌlaɪt]	\'satəˌlīt\	security	[sɪ'kjʊrəti]	\si'kyúrətē\
satire	['sæˌtaɪr]	\'saˌtīr\	see	['si:]	\'sē\
satisfaction	[ˌsætəs'fækʃən]	\ˌsatəs'fakshᵊn\	seed	['si:d]	\'sēd\
Saturday	['sætərˌdeɪ, -di]	\'satərˌdā, -dē\	seek	['si:k]	\'sēk\
Saturn	['sætərn]	\'satərn\	seem	['si:m]	\'sēm\
sauce	['sɔs]	\'sȯs\	segregate	['segrɪˌgeɪt]	\'segriˌgāt\
sauna	['sɔnə, 'saʊnə]	\'sȯnə, 'saúnə\	seldom	['seldəm]	\'seldəm\
sausage	['sɔsɪdʒ]	\'sȯsij\	select	[sə'lekt]	\sə'lekt\

ENGLISH WORD	IPA	M-W	ENGLISH WORD	IPA	M-W
self	[ˈsɛlf]	\ˈself\	shoot	[ˈʃuːt]	\ˈshüt\
sell	[ˈsɛl]	\ˈsel\	shop	[ˈʃap]	\ˈshäp\
semester	[səˈmɛstər]	\səˈmestər\	shore	[ˈʃor]	\ˈshōr\
semicolon	[ˈsɛmiˌkoːlən, ˈsɛˌmaɪ-]	\semēˌkōlən, ˈseˌmī-\	short	[ˈʃort]	\ˈshórt\
semifinal	[ˈsɛmiˌfaɪnəl, ˈsɛˌmaɪ-]	\semēˌfīnᵊl, ˈseˌmī-\	shot	[ˈʃat]	\ˈshät\
seminar	[ˈsɛməˌnɑr]	\ˈseməˌnär\	shoulder	[ˈʃoːldər]	\ˈshōldər\
senate	[ˈsɛnət]	\ˈsenət\	shout	[ˈʃaʊt]	\ˈshaút\
send	[ˈsɛnd]	\ˈsend\	shove	[ˈʃʌv]	\ˈshəv\
senior	[ˈsiːnjər]	\ˈsēnyər\	shovel	[ˈʃʌvəl]	\ˈshəvᵊl\
sensation	[sɛnˈseɪʃən]	\senˈsāshᵊn\	show	[ˈʃoː]	\ˈshō\
sense	[ˈsɛnts]	\ˈsen(t)s\	shower	[ˈʃaʊər]	\ˈshaúər\
sentence	[ˈsɛntənts, -ənz]	\ˈsentᵊn(t)s, -ᵊnz\	shrink	[ˈʃrɪŋk]	\ˈshriŋk\
sentiment	[ˈsɛntəmənt]	\ˈsentəmənt\	shrivel	[ˈʃrɪvəl]	\ˈshrivᵊl\
separation	[ˌsɛpəˈreɪʃən]	\ˌsepəˈrāshᵊn\	shuffle	[ˈʃʌfəl]	\ˈshəfᵊl\
September	[sɛpˈtɛmbər]	\sepˈtembər\	shun	[ˈʃʌn]	\ˈshən\
sequence	[ˈsiːkwənts]	\ˈsēkwən(t)s\	shut	[ˈʃʌt]	\ˈshət\
Serb	[ˈsərb]	\ˈsərb\	shy	[ˈʃaɪ]	\ˈshī\
serene	[səˈriːn]	\səˈrēn\	sick	[ˈsɪk]	\ˈsik\
sergeant	[ˈsɑrdʒənt]	\ˈsärjənt\	side	[ˈsaɪd]	\ˈsīd\
series	[ˈsɪrˌiːz]	\ˈsirˌēz\	sigh	[ˈsaɪ]	\ˈsī\
serious	[ˈsɪriəs]	\ˈsirēəs\	sight	[ˈsaɪt]	\ˈsīt\
sermon	[ˈsərmən]	\ˈsərmən\	sign	[ˈsaɪn]	\ˈsīn\
serve	[ˈsərv]	\ˈsərv\	signal	[ˈsɪgnəl]	\ˈsignᵊl\
service	[ˈsərvəs]	\ˈsərvəs\	signature	[ˈsɪgnəˌtʃʊr]	\ˈsignəˌchùr\
session	[ˈsɛʃən]	\ˈseshᵊn\	significance	[sɪgˈnɪfɪkənts]	\sigˈnifikən(t)s\
set	[ˈsɛt]	\ˈset\	silence	[ˈsaɪlənts]	\ˈsīlən(t)s\
settle	[ˈsɛtəl]	\ˈsetᵊl\	silk	[ˈsɪlk]	\ˈsilk\
seven	[ˈsɛvən]	\ˈsevᵊn\	silly	[ˈsɪli]	\ˈsilē\
several	[ˈsɛvrəl, ˈsɛvə-]	\ˈsevrəl, ˈsevə-\	silver	[ˈsɪlvər]	\ˈsilvər\
sew	[ˈsoː]	\ˈsō\	similar	[ˈsɪmələr]	\ˈsimələr\
sewing	[ˈsoːɪŋ]	\ˈsōiŋ\	simple	[ˈsɪmpəl]	\ˈsimpᵊl\
sex	[ˈsɛks]	\ˈseks\	simultaneous	[ˌsaɪməlˈteɪniəs]	\ˌsīməlˈtānēəs\
shade	[ˈʃeɪd]	\ˈshād\	sin	[ˈsɪn]	\ˈsin\
shake	[ˈʃeɪk]	\ˈshāk\	since	[ˈsɪnts]	\ˈsin(t)s\
shame	[ˈʃeɪm]	\ˈshām\	sincere	[sɪnˈsɪr]	\sinˈsir\
shampoo	[ʃæmˈpuː]	\shamˈpü\	sing	[ˈsɪŋ]	\ˈsiŋ\
shape	[ˈʃeɪp]	\ˈshāp\	singer	[ˈsɪŋər]	\ˈsiŋər\
share	[ˈʃɛr]	\ˈsher\	single	[ˈsɪŋgəl]	\ˈsiŋgᵊl\
shark	[ˈʃɑrk]	\ˈshärk\	singular	[ˈsɪŋgjələr]	\ˈsiŋgyələr\
sharp	[ˈʃɑrp]	\ˈshärp\	sink	[ˈsɪŋk]	\ˈsiŋk\
shave	[ˈʃeɪv]	\ˈshāv\	sinner	[ˈsɪnər]	\ˈsinər\
she	[ˈʃiː]	\ˈshē\	sir	[ˈsər]	\ˈsər\
sheet	[ˈʃiːt]	\ˈshēt\	sister	[ˈsɪstər]	\ˈsistər\
shelf	[ˈʃɛlf]	\ˈshelf\	sit	[ˈsɪt]	\ˈsit\
shell	[ˈʃɛl]	\ˈshel\	site	[ˈsaɪt]	\ˈsīt\
shepherd	[ˈʃɛpərd]	\ˈshepərd\	situation	[ˌsɪtʃʊˈeɪʃən]	\ˌsichùˈāshᵊn\
shield	[ˈʃiːld]	\ˈshēld\	six	[ˈsɪks]	\ˈsiks\
shift	[ˈʃɪft]	\ˈshift\	skate	[ˈskeɪt]	\ˈskāt\
shimmer	[ˈʃɪmər]	\ˈshimər\	skeleton	[ˈskɛlətən]	\ˈskelətᵊn\
shin	[ˈʃɪn]	\ˈshin\	sketch	[ˈskɛtʃ]	\ˈskech\
shine	[ˈʃaɪn]	\ˈshīn\	ski	[ˈskiː]	\ˈskē\
ship	[ˈʃɪp]	\ˈship\	skill	[ˈskɪl]	\ˈskil\
shirt	[ˈʃərt]	\ˈshərt\	skillful	[ˈskɪlfəl]	\ˈskilfᵊl\
shiver	[ˈʃɪvər]	\ˈshivər\	skin	[ˈskɪn]	\ˈskin\
shock	[ˈʃak]	\ˈshäk\	skip	[ˈskɪp]	\ˈskip\
shoe	[ˈʃuː]	\ˈshü\	skirt	[ˈskərt]	\ˈskərt\

ENGLISH WORD	IPA	M-W	ENGLISH WORD	IPA	M-W
skull	[ˈskʌl]	\ˈskəl\	son	[ˈsʌn]	\ˈsən\
sky	[ˈskaɪ]	\ˈskī\	song	[ˈsɔŋ]	\ˈsòŋ\
slap	[ˈslæp]	\ˈslap\	son-in-law	[ˈsʌnɪnˌlɔ]	\ˈsəninˌlò\
Slavic	[ˈslɑvɪk, ˈslæ-]	\ˈslävik, ˈsla-\	soon	[ˈsu:n]	\ˈsün\
sled	[ˈslɛd]	\ˈsled\	soothe	[ˈsu:ð]	\ˈsüth\
sleep	[ˈsli:p]	\ˈslēp\	sophomore	[ˈsɑfˌmor, ˈsɑfəˌmor]	\ˈsäfˌmōr, ˈsäfəˌmōr\
sleeve	[ˈsli:v]	\ˈslēv\	sore	[ˈsor]	\ˈsōr\
slender	[ˈslɛndər]	\ˈslendər\	sorry	[ˈsɑri]	\ˈsärē\
slice	[ˈslaɪs]	\ˈslīs\	sort	[ˈsɔrt]	\ˈsòrt\
slide	[ˈslaɪd]	\ˈslīd\	SOS	[ˌɛsˌoːˈɛs]	\ˌesˌōˈes\
slight	[ˈslaɪt]	\ˈslīt\	so-so	[ˈso:ˈso:]	\ˈsōˈsō\
slim	[ˈslɪm]	\ˈslim\	soul	[ˈso:l]	\ˈsōl\
slip	[ˈslɪp]	\ˈslip\	sound	[ˈsaʊnd]	\ˈsaùnd\
slipper	[ˈslɪpər]	\ˈslipər\	soundly	[ˈsaʊndli]	\ˈsaùndlē\
slit	[ˈslɪt]	\ˈslit\	soup	[ˈsu:p]	\ˈsüp\
slot	[ˈslɑt]	\ˈslät\	sour	[ˈsaʊər]	\ˈsaùər\
slow	[ˈslo:]	\ˈslō\	source	[ˈsors]	\ˈsōrs\
small	[ˈsmɔl]	\ˈsmòl\	south	[ˈsaʊθ]	\ˈsaùth\
smart	[ˈsmɑrt]	\ˈsmärt\	souvenir	[ˌsu:vəˈnɪr, ˈsu:vəˌ-]	\ˌsüvəˈnir, ˈsüvəˌ-\
smash	[ˈsmæʃ]	\ˈsmash\	space	[ˈspeɪs]	\ˈspās\
smell	[ˈsmɛl]	\ˈsmel\	spaghetti	[spəˈgɛti]	\spəˈgetē\
smile	[ˈsmaɪl]	\ˈsmīl\	Spaniard	[ˈspænjərd]	\ˈspanyərd\
smoke	[ˈsmo:k]	\ˈsmōk\	Spanish	[ˈspænɪʃ]	\ˈspanish\
smooth	[ˈsmu:ð]	\ˈsmüth\	spark	[ˈspɑrk]	\ˈspärk\
snack	[ˈsnæk]	\ˈsnak\	speak	[ˈspi:k]	\ˈspēk\
snake	[ˈsneɪk]	\ˈsnāk\	special	[ˈspɛʃəl]	\ˈspeshᵊl\
snappy	[ˈsnæpi]	\ˈsnapē\	species	[ˈspi:ˌʃi:z, -ˌsi:z]	\ˈspē͏ˌshēz, -ˌsēz\
snarl	[ˈsnɑrl]	\ˈsnärl\	specify	[ˈspɛsəˌfaɪ]	\ˈspesəˌfī\
sneakers	[ˈsni:kərz]	\ˈsnēkərz\	spectacle	[ˈspɛktɪkəl]	\ˈspektikᵊl\
sneaky	[ˈsni:ki]	\ˈsnēkē\	speech	[ˈspi:tʃ]	\ˈspēch\
sneeze	[ˈsni:z]	\ˈsnēz\	speed	[ˈspi:d]	\ˈspēd\
sniff	[ˈsnɪf]	\ˈsnif\	spell	[ˈspɛl]	\ˈspel\
snoop	[ˈsnu:p]	\ˈsnüp\	spelling	[ˈspɛlɪŋ]	\ˈspeliŋ\
snooze	[ˈsnu:z]	\ˈsnüz\	spend	[ˈspɛnd]	\ˈspend\
snore	[ˈsnor]	\ˈsnōr\	spice	[ˈspaɪs]	\ˈspīs\
snow	[ˈsno:]	\ˈsnō\	spider	[ˈspaɪdər]	\ˈspīdər\
so	[ˈso:]	\ˈsō\	spill	[ˈspɪl]	\ˈspil\
soap	[ˈso:p]	\ˈsōp\	spin	[ˈspɪn]	\ˈspin\
soccer	[ˈsɑkər]	\ˈsäkər\	spinach	[ˈspɪnɪtʃ]	\ˈspinich\
social	[ˈso:ʃəl]	\ˈsōshᵊl\	spine	[ˈspaɪn]	\ˈspīn\
sock	[ˈsɑk]	\ˈsäk\	spiral	[ˈspaɪrəl]	\ˈspīrᵊl\
socket	[ˈsɑkət]	\ˈsäkət\	spirit	[ˈspɪrət]	\ˈspirət\
soda	[ˈso:də]	\ˈsōdə\	spite	[ˈspaɪt]	\ˈspīt\
sofa	[ˈso:fə]	\ˈsōfə\	splash	[ˈsplæʃ]	\ˈsplash\
soft	[ˈsɔft]	\ˈsòft\	splendor	[ˈsplɛndər]	\ˈsplendər\
soggy	[ˈsɑgi]	\ˈsägē\	split	[ˈsplɪt]	\ˈsplit\
soil	[ˈsɔɪl]	\ˈsòil\	spoil	[ˈspɔɪl]	\ˈspòil\
solar	[ˈso:lər]	\ˈsōlər\	sponge	[ˈspʌndʒ]	\ˈspənj\
soldier	[ˈso:ldʒər]	\ˈsōljər\	sponsor	[ˈspɑntsər]	\ˈspän(t)sər\
sole	[ˈso:l]	\ˈsōl\	spontaneous	[spɑnˈteɪniəs]	\spänˈtānēəs\
solid	[ˈsɑləd]	\ˈsäləd\	spoon	[ˈspu:n]	\ˈspün\
solitary	[ˈsɑləˌtɛri]	\ˈsäləˌterē\	sport	[ˈsport]	\ˈspōrt\
solo	[ˈso:ˌlo:]	\ˈsōˌlō\	spot	[ˈspɑt]	\ˈspät\
solution	[səˈlu:ʃən]	\səˈlüshᵊn\	spouse	[ˈspaʊs]	\ˈspaùs\
some	[ˈsʌm]	\ˈsəm\	spray	[ˈspreɪ]	\ˈsprā\
something	[ˈsʌmθɪŋ]	\ˈsəmthiŋ\	spread	[ˈsprɛd]	\ˈspred\

ENGLISH WORD	IPA	M-W	ENGLISH WORD	IPA	M-W
spring	[ˈsprɪŋ]	\ˈspriŋ\	stock	[ˈstɑk]	\ˈstäk\
sprinkle	[ˈsprɪŋkəl]	\ˈspriŋkᵊl\	stocking	[ˈstɑkɪŋ]	\ˈstäkiŋ\
sprint	[ˈsprɪnt]	\ˈsprint\	stocky	[ˈstɑki]	\ˈstäkē\
sprout	[ˈspraʊt]	\ˈspraùt\	stomach	[ˈstʌmɪk]	\ˈstəmik\
spy	[ˈspaɪ]	\ˈspī\	stone	[ˈstoːn]	\ˈstōn\
squadron	[ˈskwɑdrən]	\ˈskwädrən\	stop	[ˈstɑp]	\ˈstäp\
square	[ˈskwær]	\ˈskwar\	store	[ˈstor]	\ˈstōr\
squeak	[ˈskwiːk]	\ˈskwēk\	storm	[ˈstɔrm]	\ˈstórm\
squeeze	[ˈskwiːz]	\ˈskwēz\	story	[ˈstori]	\ˈstōrē\
squirrel	[ˈskwərəl]	\ˈskwərᵊl\	stove	[ˈstoːv]	\ˈstōv\
stab	[ˈstæb]	\ˈstab\	straight	[ˈstreɪt]	\ˈstrāt\
stable	[ˈsteɪbəl]	\ˈstābᵊl\	strain	[ˈstreɪn]	\ˈstrān\
stadium	[ˈsteɪdiəm]	\ˈstādēəm\	strand	[ˈstrænd]	\ˈstrand\
staff	[ˈstæf]	\ˈstaf\	strange	[ˈstreɪndʒ]	\ˈstrānj\
stage	[ˈsteɪdʒ]	\ˈstāj\	strap	[ˈstræp]	\ˈstrap\
stagger	[ˈstægər]	\ˈstagər\	strategy	[ˈstrætədʒi]	\ˈstratəjē\
stair	[ˈstær]	\ˈstar\	strawberry	[ˈstrɔˌbɛri]	\ˈstrȯˌberē\
stalk	[ˈstɔk]	\ˈstȯk\	stream	[ˈstriːm]	\ˈstrēm\
stamp	[ˈstæmp]	\ˈstamp\	street	[ˈstriːt]	\ˈstrēt\
stand	[ˈstænd]	\ˈstand\	strength	[ˈstrɛŋkθ]	\ˈstreŋ(k)th\
standard	[ˈstændərd]	\ˈstandərd\	stress	[ˈstrɛs]	\ˈstres\
standing	[ˈstændɪŋ]	\ˈstandiŋ\	stretch	[ˈstrɛtʃ]	\ˈstrech\
standpoint	[ˈstændˌpɔɪnt]	\ˈstandˌpóint\	strict	[ˈstrɪkt]	\ˈstrikt\
star	[ˈstɑr]	\ˈstär\	strike	[ˈstraɪk]	\ˈstrīk\
stare	[ˈstær]	\ˈstar\	string	[ˈstrɪŋ]	\ˈstriŋ\
starlight	[ˈstɑrˌlaɪt]	\ˈstärˌlīt\	strip	[ˈstrɪp]	\ˈstrip\
starry	[ˈstɑri]	\ˈstärē\	stripe	[ˈstraɪp]	\ˈstrīp\
start	[ˈstɑrt]	\ˈstärt\	stroke	[ˈstroːk]	\ˈstrōk\
starve	[ˈstɑrv]	\ˈstärv\	stroll	[ˈstroːl]	\ˈstrōl\
state	[ˈsteɪt]	\ˈstāt\	strong	[ˈstrɔŋ]	\ˈstróŋ\
station	[ˈsteɪʃən]	\ˈstāshᵊn\	structure	[ˈstrʌktʃər]	\ˈstrəkchər\
statistic	[stəˈtɪstɪk]	\stəˈtistik\	struggle	[ˈstrʌgəl]	\ˈstrəgᵊl\
statue	[ˈstæˌtʃuː]	\ˈstaˌchü\	stubborn	[ˈstʌbərn]	\ˈstəbərn\
stature	[ˈstætʃər]	\ˈstachər\	student	[ˈstuːdənt, ˈstjuː-]	\ˈstüdᵊnt, ˈstyü-\
status	[ˈsteɪtəs, ˈstæ-]	\ˈstātəs, ˈsta-\	stuff	[ˈstʌf]	\ˈstəf\
stay	[ˈsteɪ]	\ˈstā\	stumble	[ˈstʌmbəl]	\ˈstəmbᵊl\
steady	[ˈstɛdi]	\ˈstedē\	stupid	[ˈstuːpəd, ˈstjuː-]	\ˈstüpəd, ˈstyü-\
steak	[ˈsteɪk]	\ˈstāk\	style	[ˈstaɪl]	\ˈstīl\
steal	[ˈstiːl]	\ˈstēl\	subconscious	[səbˈkɑntʃəs]	\səbˈkänchəs\
steam	[ˈstiːm]	\ˈstēm\	subject	[ˈsʌbdʒɪkt, səbˈdʒɛkt]	\ˈsəbjikt; səbˈjekt\
steel	[ˈstiːl]	\ˈstēl\	subordinate	[səˈbɔrdənət]	\səˈbórdᵊnət\
stem	[ˈstɛm]	\ˈstem\	subscribe	[səbˈskraɪb]	\səbˈskrīb\
step	[ˈstɛp]	\ˈstep\	substance	[ˈsʌbstənts]	\ˈsəbstən(t)s\
stereo	[ˈstɛriˌoː, ˈstɪr-]	\ˈsterēˌō, ˈstir-\	substitute	[ˈsʌbstəˌtuːt, -ˌtjuːt]	\ˈsəbstəˌtüt, -ˌtyüt\
sterile	[ˈstɛrəl]	\ˈsterəl\	subterranean	[ˌsʌbtəˈreɪniən]	\ˌsəbtəˈrānēən\
stern	[ˈstərn]	\ˈstərn\	subtitle	[ˈsʌbˌtaɪtəl]	\ˈsəbˌtītᵊl\
stew	[ˈstuː, ˈstjuː]	\ˈstü, ˈstyü\	subtle	[ˈsʌtəl]	\ˈsətᵊl\
stick	[ˈstɪk]	\ˈstik\	subtraction	[səbˈtrækʃən]	\səbˈtrakshᵊn\
stiff	[ˈstɪf]	\ˈstif\	suburb	[ˈsʌˌbərb]	\ˈsəˌbərb\
still	[ˈstɪl]	\ˈstil\	subway	[ˈsʌbˌweɪ]	\ˈsəbˌwā\
stimulate	[ˈstɪmjəˌleɪt]	\ˈstimyəˌlāt\	succeed	[səkˈsiːd]	\səkˈsēd\
sting	[ˈstɪŋ]	\ˈstiŋ\	such	[ˈsʌtʃ]	\ˈsəch\
stingy	[ˈstɪndʒi]	\ˈstinjē\	sudden	[ˈsʌdən]	\ˈsədᵊn\
stink	[ˈstɪŋk]	\ˈstiŋk\	suffer	[ˈsʌfər]	\ˈsəfər\
stir	[ˈstər]	\ˈstər\	sufficient	[səˈfɪʃənt]	\səˈfishənt\
stitch	[ˈstɪtʃ]	\ˈstich\	sugar	[ˈʃʊgər]	\ˈshùgər\

ENGLISH WORD	IPA	M-W	ENGLISH WORD	IPA	M-W
suggestion	[səgˈdʒɛstʃən, sə-]	\səgˈjeschən, sə-\	sword	[ˈsɔrd]	\ˈsȯrd\
suicide	[ˈsuːəˌsaɪd]	\ˈsüəˌsīd\	syllable	[ˈsɪləbəl]	\ˈsiləbᵊl\
suit	[ˈsuːt]	\ˈsüt\	symbol	[ˈsɪmbəl]	\ˈsimbᵊl\
suite	[ˈswiːt, ˈsuːt]	\ˈswēt, ˈsüt\	symmetry	[ˈsɪmətri]	\ˈsimətrē\
sulky	[ˈsʌlki]	\ˈsəlkē\	sympathy	[ˈsɪmpəθi]	\ˈsimpəthē\
sum	[ˈsʌm]	\ˈsəm\	symptom	[ˈsɪmptəm]	\ˈsimptəm\
summer	[ˈsʌmər]	\ˈsəmər\	synonym	[ˈsɪnəˌnɪm]	\ˈsinəˌnim\
summon	[ˈsʌmən]	\ˈsəmən\	Syrian	[ˈsɪriən]	\ˈsirēən\
sun	[ˈsʌn]	\ˈsən\	syrup	[ˈsərəp, ˈsɪrəp]	\ˈsərəp, ˈsirəp\
Sunday	[ˈsʌnˌdeɪ, -di]	\ˈsənˌdā, -dē\	system	[ˈsɪstəm]	\ˈsistəm\
superior	[suˈpɪriər]	\sùˈpirēər\	table	[ˈteɪbəl]	\ˈtābᵊl\
superlative	[suˈpərlətɪv]	\sùˈpərlətiv\	tablet	[ˈtæblət]	\ˈtablət\
supermarket	[ˈsuːpərˌmɑrkət]	\ˈsüpərˌmärkət\	taboo	[təˈbuː, tæ-]	\təˈbü, ta-\
supervisor	[ˈsuːpərˌvaɪzər]	\ˈsüpərˌvīzər\	tacit	[ˈtæsɪt]	\ˈtasit\
supper	[ˈsʌpər]	\ˈsəpər\	tact	[ˈtækt]	\ˈtakt\
supplement	[ˈsʌpləˌmɛnt]	\ˈsəpləˌment\	tactical	[ˈtæktɪkəl]	\ˈtaktikᵊl\
supply	[səˈplaɪ]	\səˈplī\	tag	[ˈtæg]	\ˈtag\
support	[səˈport]	\səˈpȯrt\	tail	[ˈteɪl]	\ˈtāl\
suppose	[səˈpoːz]	\səˈpōz\	tailor	[ˈteɪlər]	\ˈtālər\
suppress	[səˈprɛs]	\səˈpres\	take	[ˈteɪk]	\ˈtāk\
supreme	[suˈpriːm]	\sùˈprēm\	talcum powder	[ˈtælkəm]	\ˈtalkəm\
sure	[ˈʃʊr]	\ˈshu̇r\	tale	[ˈteɪl]	\ˈtāl\
surface	[ˈsərfəs]	\ˈsərfəs\	talent	[ˈtælənt]	\ˈtalənt\
surgeon	[ˈsərdʒən]	\ˈsərjᵊn\	talk	[ˈtɔk]	\ˈtȯk\
surname	[ˈsərˌneɪm]	\ˈsərˌnām\	tall	[ˈtɔl]	\ˈtȯl\
surpass	[sərˈpæs]	\sərˈpas\	tally	[ˈtæli]	\ˈtalē\
surprise	[səˈpraɪz, sər-]	\səˈprīz, sər-\	tampon	[ˈtæmˌpɑn]	\ˈtamˌpän\
surrender	[səˈrɛndər]	\səˈrendər\	tan	[ˈtæn]	\ˈtan\
surround	[səˈraʊnd]	\səˈrau̇nd\	tangle	[ˈtæŋgəl]	\ˈtaŋgᵊl\
survey	[sərˈveɪ; ˈsərˌveɪ]	\sərˈvā; ˈsərˌvā\	tank	[ˈtæŋk]	\ˈtaŋk\
survive	[sərˈvaɪv]	\sərˈvīv\	tape	[ˈteɪp]	\ˈtāp\
susceptible	[səˈsɛptəbəl]	\səˈseptəbᵊl\	target	[ˈtɑrgət]	\ˈtärgət\
suspect	[ˈsʌsˌpɛkt, səˈspɛkt]	\ˈsəsˌpekt, səˈspekt\	tariff	[ˈtærɪf]	\ˈtarif\
suspend	[səˈspɛnd]	\səˈspend\	tart	[ˈtɑrt]	\ˈtärt\
sustain	[səˈsteɪn]	\səˈstān\	tartan	[ˈtɑrtən]	\ˈtärtᵊn\
swallow	[ˈswɑloː]	\ˈswälō\	task	[ˈtæsk]	\ˈtask\
swamp	[ˈswɑmp]	\ˈswämp\	taste	[ˈteɪst]	\ˈtāst\
swan	[ˈswɑn]	\ˈswän\	tax	[ˈtæks]	\ˈtaks\
swap	[ˈswɑp]	\ˈswäp\	taxi	[ˈtæksi]	\ˈtaksē\
swarm	[ˈswɔrm]	\ˈswȯrm\	tea	[ˈtiː]	\ˈtē\
sway	[ˈsweɪ]	\ˈswā\	teach	[ˈtiːtʃ]	\ˈtēch\
swear	[ˈswær]	\ˈswar\	team	[ˈtiːm]	\ˈtēm\
sweat	[ˈswɛt]	\ˈswet\	tear	[ˈtær]	\ˈtar\
Swedish	[ˈswiːdɪʃ]	\ˈswēdish\	tear	[ˈtɪr]	\ˈtir\
sweep	[ˈswiːp]	\ˈswēp\	tease	[ˈtiːz]	\ˈtēz\
sweet	[ˈswiːt]	\ˈswēt\	teaspoon	[ˈtiːˌspuːn]	\ˈtēˌspün\
swell	[ˈswɛl]	\ˈswel\	technical	[ˈtɛknɪkəl]	\ˈteknikᵊl\
swift	[ˈswɪft]	\ˈswift\	technique	[tɛkˈniːk]	\tekˈnēk\
swim	[ˈswɪm]	\ˈswim\	technological	[ˌtɛknəˈlɑdʒɪkəl]	\ˌteknəˈläjikᵊl\
swindle	[ˈswɪndəl]	\ˈswindᵊl\	teddy bear	[ˈtɛdi]	\ˈtedē\
swing	[ˈswɪŋ]	\ˈswiŋ\	teenage	[ˈtiːnˌeɪdʒ]	\ˈtēnˌāj\
swirl	[ˈswərl]	\ˈswərl\	telecommunication	[ˌtɛləkəˌmjuːnəˈkeɪʃən]	\ˌteləkəˌmyünəˈkāshᵊn\
Swiss	[ˈswɪs]	\ˈswis\	telephone	[ˈtɛləˌfoːn]	\ˈteləˌfōn\
switch	[ˈswɪtʃ]	\ˈswich\	televise	[ˈtɛləˌvaɪz]	\ˈteləˌvīz\
swivel	[ˈswɪvəl]	\ˈswivᵊl\	tell	[ˈtɛl]	\ˈtel\
swoon	[ˈswuːn]	\ˈswün\			

ENGLISH WORD	IPA	M-W	ENGLISH WORD	IPA	M-W
temper	[ˈtɛmpər]	\ˈtempər\	thirst	[ˈθərst]	\ˈthərst\
temperature	[ˈtɛmpərˌtʃʊr, -prə-, -pərə-, -tʃər]		thirteen	[ˌθərˈtiːn]	\ˌthərˈtēn\
		\ˈtempərˌchúr, -prə-, -pərə-, -chər\	thirty	[ˈθərti]	\ˈthərtē\
tempest	[ˈtɛmpəst]	\ˈtempəst\	this	[ˈðɪs]	\ˈthis\
temple	[ˈtɛmpəl]	\ˈtempᵊl\	thorn	[ˈθɔrn]	\ˈthórn\
temporarily	[ˌtɛmpəˈrɛrəli]	\ˌtempəˈrerəlē\	though	[ˈðoː]	\ˈthō\
tempt	[ˈtɛmpt]	\ˈtempt\	thought	[ˈθɔt]	\ˈthót\
ten	[ˈtɛn]	\ˈten\	thousand	[ˈθaʊzənd]	\ˈthaúzᵊnd\
tend	[ˈtɛnd]	\ˈtend\	thread	[ˈθrɛd]	\ˈthred\
tender	[ˈtɛndər]	\ˈtendər\	threat	[ˈθrɛt]	\ˈthret\
tenderness	[ˈtɛndərnəs]	\ˈtendərnəs\	three	[ˈθriː]	\ˈthrē\
tennis	[ˈtɛnəs]	\ˈtenəs\	thrill	[ˈθrɪl]	\ˈthril\
tense	[ˈtɛnts]	\ˈten(t)s\	throat	[ˈθroːt]	\ˈthrōt\
tent	[ˈtɛnt]	\ˈtent\	through	[ˈθruː]	\ˈthrü\
tenth	[ˈtɛnθ]	\ˈtenth\	throw	[ˈθroː]	\ˈthrō\
term	[ˈtərm]	\ˈtərm\	thumb	[ˈθʌm]	\ˈthəm\
terminate	[ˈtərməˌneɪt]	\ˈtərməˌnāt\	thunder	[ˈθʌndər]	\ˈthəndər\
terrain	[təˈreɪn]	\təˈrān\	Thursday	[ˈθərzˌdeɪ, -di]	\ˈthərzˌdā, -dē\
terrible	[ˈtɛrəbəl]	\ˈterəbᵊl\	thus	[ˈðʌs]	\ˈthəs\
terrific	[təˈrɪfɪk]	\təˈrifik\	tic	[ˈtɪk]	\ˈtik\
terrify	[ˈtɛrəˌfaɪ]	\ˈterəˌfī\	tick	[ˈtɪk]	\ˈtik\
territory	[ˈtɛrəˌtori]	\ˈterəˌtōrē\	ticket	[ˈtɪkət]	\ˈtikət\
terror	[ˈtɛrər]	\ˈterər\	tie	[ˈtaɪ]	\ˈtī\
test	[ˈtɛst]	\ˈtest\	tiger	[ˈtaɪgər]	\ˈtīgər\
testament	[ˈtɛstəmənt]	\ˈtestəmənt\	tight	[ˈtaɪt]	\ˈtīt\
testify	[ˈtɛstəˌfaɪ]	\ˈtestəˌfī\	time	[ˈtaɪm]	\ˈtīm\
testimony	[ˈtɛstəˌmoːni]	\ˈtestəˌmōnē\	tiny	[ˈtaɪni]	\ˈtīnē\
text	[ˈtɛkst]	\ˈtekst\	tip	[ˈtɪp]	\ˈtip\
than	[ˈðæn]	\ˈthan\	tire	[ˈtaɪr]	\ˈtīr\
thank	[ˈθæŋk]	\ˈthank\	tissue	[ˈtɪˌʃuː]	\ˈtiˌshü\
Thanksgiving	[θæŋksˈgɪvɪŋ, ˈθæŋksˌ-]		title	[ˈtaɪtəl]	\ˈtītᵊl\
		\thanksˈgivin, ˈthanksˌ-\	to	[ˈtuː]	\ˈtü\
that	[ˈðæt]	\ˈthat\	toast	[ˈtoːst]	\ˈtōst\
the	[ðə, ðiː]	\thə, thē\	today	[təˈdeɪ]	\təˈdā\
their	[ˈðɛr]	\ˈther\	toe	[ˈtoː]	\ˈtō\
them	[ˈðɛm]	\ˈthem\	together	[təˈgɛðər]	\təˈgethər\
theme	[ˈθiːm]	\ˈthēm\	toilet	[ˈtɔɪlət]	\ˈtóilət\
themselves	[ðəmˈsɛlvz, ðɛm-]	\thəmˈselvz, them-\	token	[ˈtoːkən]	\ˈtōkᵊn\
then	[ˈðɛn]	\ˈthen\	tolerance	[ˈtalərənts]	\ˈtälərən(t)s\
thence	[ˈðɛnts, ˈθɛnts]	\ˈthen(t)s, ˈthen(t)s\	toll	[ˈtoːl]	\ˈtōl\
theology	[θiˈalədʒi]	\thēˈäləjē\	tomato	[təˈmeɪto, -ˈma-]	\təˈmātō, -ˈmä-\
theoretical	[ˌθiːəˈrɛtɪkəl]	\ˌthēəˈretikᵊl\	tomb	[ˈtuːm]	\ˈtüm\
therapeutic	[ˌθɛrəˈpjuːtɪk]	\ˌtherəˈpyütik\	tomorrow	[təˈmaro]	\təˈmärō\
there	[ˈðɛr]	\ˈthar\	ton	[ˈtʌn]	\ˈtən\
thermometer	[θərˈmamətər]	\thərˈmämətər\	tongue	[ˈtʌŋ]	\ˈtəŋ\
thermos	[ˈθərməs]	\ˈthərməs\	tonight	[təˈnaɪt]	\təˈnīt\
thesaurus	[θɪˈsɔrəs]	\thiˈsórəs\	too	[ˈtuː]	\ˈtü\
thesis	[ˈθiːsɪs]	\ˈthēsis\	tool	[ˈtuːl]	\ˈtül\
they	[ˈðeɪ]	\ˈthā\	tooth	[ˈtuːθ]	\ˈtüth\
thick	[ˈθɪk]	\ˈthik\	top	[ˈtap]	\ˈtäp\
thief	[ˈθiːf]	\ˈthēf\	topic	[ˈtapɪk]	\ˈtäpik\
thigh	[ˈθaɪ]	\ˈthī\	torment	[tɔrˈmɛnt, ˈtɔrˌ-]	\tórˈment, ˈtórˌ-\
thin	[ˈθɪn]	\ˈthin\	tornado	[tɔrˈneɪdo]	\tórˈnādo\
thing	[ˈθɪŋ]	\ˈthiŋ\	tortilla	[tɔrˈtiːjə]	\tórˈtēyə\
think	[ˈθɪŋk]	\ˈthiŋk\	tortoise	[ˈtɔrtəs]	\ˈtórtəs\
third	[ˈθərd]	\ˈthərd\	torture	[ˈtɔrtʃər]	\ˈtórchər\

ENGLISH WORD	IPA	M-W	ENGLISH WORD	IPA	M-W
total	[ˈtoːtəl]	\ˈtōtᵊl\	triumph	[ˈtraɪəmpf]	\ˈtrīəm(p)f\
touch	[ˈtʌtʃ]	\ˈtəch\	trivial	[ˈtrɪviəl]	\ˈtrivēəl\
tough	[ˈtʌf]	\ˈtəf\	troop	[ˈtruːp]	\ˈtrüp\
tour	[ˈtʊr]	\ˈtûr\	tropic	[ˈtrɑpɪk]	\ˈträpik\
toward	[ˈtord, təˈwɔrd]	\ˈtōrd, təˈwȯrd\	trot	[ˈtrɑt]	\ˈträt\
towel	[ˈtaʊəl]	\ˈtaủəl\	trouble	[ˈtrʌbəl]	\ˈtrəbᵊl\
tower	[ˈtaʊər]	\ˈtaủər\	trousers	[ˈtraʊzərz]	\ˈtraủzərz\
town	[ˈtaʊn]	\ˈtaủn\	truck	[ˈtrʌk]	\ˈtrək\
toxic	[ˈtɑksɪk]	\ˈtäksik\	true	[ˈtruː]	\ˈtrü\
toy	[ˈtɔɪ]	\ˈtȯi\	truly	[ˈtruːli]	\ˈtrülē\
trace	[ˈtreɪs]	\ˈtrās\	trumpet	[ˈtrʌmpət]	\ˈtrəmpət\
track	[ˈtræk]	\ˈtrak\	trunk	[ˈtrʌŋk]	\ˈtrəŋk\
trade	[ˈtreɪd]	\ˈtrād\	trust	[ˈtrʌst]	\ˈtrəst\
tradition	[trəˈdɪʃən]	\trəˈdishᵊn\	truth	[ˈtruːθ]	\ˈtrüth\
traffic	[ˈtræfɪk]	\ˈtrafik\	try	[ˈtraɪ]	\ˈtrī\
tragedy	[ˈtrædʒədi]	\ˈtrajədē\	T-shirt	[ˈtiːˌʃərt]	\ˈtēˌshərt\
trailer	[ˈtreɪlər]	\ˈtrālər\	tub	[ˈtʌb]	\ˈtəb\
train	[ˈtreɪn]	\ˈtrān\	tube	[ˈtuːb, ˈtjuːb]	\ˈtüb, ˈtyüb\
traitor	[ˈtreɪtər]	\ˈtrātər\	tuberculosis	[tʊˌbərkjəˈloːsɪs, tjʊ-]	\tủˌbərkyəˈlōsis, tyủ-\
trampoline	[ˌtræmpəˈliːn, ˈtræmpəˌ-]	\ˌtrampəˈlēn, ˈtrampəˌ-\	tubing	[ˈtuːbɪŋ, ˈtjuː-]	\ˈtübiŋ, ˈtyü-\
transatlantic	[ˌtræntsətˈlæntɪk, ˌtrænz-]		Tuesday	[ˈtuːzˌdeɪ, ˈtjuːz-, -di]	\ˈtüzˌdā, ˈtyüz-, -dē\
		\ˌtran(t)sətˈlantik, ˌtranz-\	tuition	[tuːˈɪʃən, tjuː-]	\tüˈishən, tyü-\
transfer	[træntsˈfər, ˈtræntsˌfər]		tulip	[ˈtuːlɪp, ˈtjuː-]	\ˈtülip, ˈtyü-\
		\tran(t)sˈfər, ˈtran(t)sˌfər\	tumble	[ˈtʌmbəl]	\ˈtəmbᵊl\
transform	[træntsˈfɔrm]	\tran(t)sˈfȯrm\	tumor	[ˈtuːmər, ˈtjuː-]	\ˈtümər, ˈtyü-\
transit	[ˈtræntsɪt, ˈtrænzɪt]	\ˈtran(t)sit, ˈtranzit\	tumult	[ˈtuːˌmʌlt, ˈtjuː-]	\ˈtüˌməlt, ˈtyü-\
translate	[træntsˈleɪt, trænz-; ˈtræntsˌ-, ˈtrænsˌ-]		tuna	[ˈtuːnə, ˈtjuː-]	\ˈtünə, ˈtyü-\
		\tran(t)sˈlāt, tranz-; ˈtran(t)sˌ-, ˈtransˌ-\	tune	[ˈtuːn, ˈtjuːn]	\ˈtün, ˈtyün\
transmit	[træntsˈmɪt, trænz-]	\tran(t)sˈmit, tranz-\	tunnel	[ˈtʌnəl]	\ˈtənᵊl\
transparent	[træntsˈpærənt]	\tran(t)sˈparənt\	turkey	[ˈtərki]	\ˈtərkē\
transport	[træntsˈport, ˈtræntsˌ-]		turn	[ˈtərn]	\ˈtərn\
		\tran(t)sˈpōrt, ˈtran(t)sˌ-\	turtle	[ˈtərtəl]	\ˈtərtᵊl\
trap	[ˈtræp]	\ˈtrap\	twelve	[ˈtwelv]	\ˈtwelv\
trash	[ˈtræʃ]	\ˈtrash\	twenty	[ˈtwʌnti, ˈtwɛn-]	\ˈtwəntē, ˈtwen-\
trauma	[ˈtrɔmə, ˈtraʊ-]	\ˈtrȯmə, ˈtraủ-\	twice	[ˈtwaɪs]	\ˈtwīs\
travel	[ˈtrævəl]	\ˈtravᵊl\	twilight	[ˈtwaɪˌlaɪt]	\ˈtwīˌlīt\
tray	[ˈtreɪ]	\ˈtrā\	twin	[ˈtwɪn]	\ˈtwin\
treason	[ˈtriːzən]	\ˈtrēzᵊn\	twinkle	[ˈtwɪŋkəl]	\ˈtwiŋkᵊl\
treasure	[ˈtrɛʒər, ˈtreɪ-]	\ˈtrezhər, ˈtrā-\	twist	[ˈtwɪst]	\ˈtwist\
treat	[ˈtriːt]	\ˈtrēt\	two	[ˈtuː]	\ˈtü\
treatment	[ˈtriːtmənt]	\ˈtrētmənt\	type	[ˈtaɪp]	\ˈtīp\
treaty	[ˈtriːti]	\ˈtrētē\	typical	[ˈtɪpɪkəl]	\ˈtipikᵊl\
tree	[ˈtriː]	\ˈtrē\	UFO	[ˌjuːˌɛfˈoː, ˈjuːˌfoː]	\ˌyüˌefˈō, ˈyüˌfō\
tremble	[ˈtrɛmbəl]	\ˈtrembᵊl\	ugly	[ˈʌgli]	\ˈəglē\
tremendous	[trɪˈmɛndəs]	\triˈmendəs\	ultimate	[ˈʌltəmət]	\ˈəltəmət\
trend	[ˈtrɛnd]	\ˈtrend\	umbrella	[ˌʌmˈbrɛlə]	\ˌəmˈbrelə\
trial	[ˈtraɪəl]	\ˈtrīəl\	umpire	[ˈʌmˌpaɪr]	\ˈəmˌpīr\
triangle	[ˈtraɪˌæŋgəl]	\ˈtrīˌaŋgᵊl\	unacceptable	[ˌʌnɪkˈsɛptəbəl]	\ˌənikˈseptəbᵊl\
tribe	[ˈtraɪb]	\ˈtrīb\	unafraid	[ˌʌnəˈfreɪd]	\ˌənəˈfrād\
trick	[ˈtrɪk]	\ˈtrik\	unattached	[ˌʌnəˈtætʃt]	\ˌənəˈtacht\
tricky	[ˈtrɪki]	\ˈtrikē\	unattractive	[ˌʌnəˈtræktɪv]	\ˌənəˈtraktiv\
tricycle	[ˈtraɪsəkəl, -ˌsɪkəl]	\ˈtrīsəkᵊl, -ˌsikᵊl\	unavailable	[ˌʌnəˈveɪləbəl]	\ˌənəˈvāləbᵊl\
trillion	[ˈtrɪljən]	\ˈtrilyən\	unavoidable	[ˌʌnəˈvɔɪdəbəl]	\ˌənəˈvȯidəbᵊl\
trim	[ˈtrɪm]	\ˈtrim\	unaware	[ˌʌnəˈwær]	\ˌənəˈwar\
trio	[ˈtriːˌoː]	\ˈtrēˌō\	unbalanced	[ˌʌnˈbæləntst]	\ˌənˈbalᵊn(t)st\
trip	[ˈtrɪp]	\ˈtrip\	unbearable	[ˌʌnˈbærəbəl]	\ˌənˈbarəbᵊl\

ENGLISH WORD	IPA	M-W	ENGLISH WORD	IPA	M-W
unbelievable	[ˌʌnbəˈliːvəbəl]	\ˌənbəˈlēvəbˌl\	unkempt	[ʌnˈkɛmpt]	\ˌənˈkempt\
unbending	[ʌnˈbɛndɪŋ]	\ˌənˈbendiŋ\	unknown	[ʌnˈnoːn]	\ˌənˈnōn\
unborn	[ʌnˈbɔrn]	\ˌənˈbȯrn\	unless	[ənˈlɛs]	\ənˈles\
unbreakable	[ʌnˈbreɪkəbəl]	\ˌənˈbrākəbˌl\	unlike	[ʌnˈlaɪk]	\ˌənˈlīk\
unbroken	[ʌnˈbroːkən]	\ˌənˈbrōkˌn\	unlimited	[ʌnˈlɪmətəd]	\ˌənˈlimətəd\
unbutton	[ʌnˈbʌtən]	\ˌənˈbətˌn\	unlock	[ʌnˈlɑk]	\ˌənˈläk\
uncalled-for	[ʌnˈkɔldˌfɔr]	\ˌənˈkȯldˌfȯr\	unlucky	[ʌnˈlʌki]	\ˌənˈləkē\
uncertain	[ʌnˈsərtə n]	\ˌənˈsərtˌn\	unmarried	[ʌnˈmærid]	\ˌənˈmarēd\
unchanged	[ʌnˈtʃeɪndʒd]	\ˌənˈchānjd\	unmistakable	[ˌʌnmɪˈsteɪkəbəl]	\ˌənmiˈstākəbˌl\
uncivilized	[ʌnˈsɪvəˌlaɪzd]	\ˌənˈsivəˌlīzd\	unnatural	[ʌnˈnætʃərəl]	\ˌənˈnachərəl\
uncle	[ˈʌŋkə l]	\ˈəŋkˌl\	unnecessary	[ʌnˈnɛsəˌsɛri]	\ˌənˈnesəˌserē\
unclear	[ʌnˈklɪr]	\ˌənˈklir\	unpleasant	[ʌnˈplɛzənt]	\ˌənˈplezˌnt\
uncomfortable	[ʌnˈkʌmpfərtəbəl]	\ˌənˈkəm(p)fərtəbˌl\	unreal	[ʌnˈriːl]	\ˌənˈrēl\
uncommon	[ʌnˈkɑmən]	\ˌənˈkämən\	unsanitary	[ʌnˈsænəˌtɛri]	\ˌənˈsanəˌterē\
unconcerned	[ˌʌnkənˈsərnd]	\ˌənkənˈsərnd\	unsettled	[ʌnˈsɛtəld]	\ˌənˈsetˌld\
unconditional	[ˌʌnkənˈdɪʃənəl]	\ˌənkənˈdishənˌl\	unstable	[ʌnˈsteɪbəl]	\ˌənˈstābˌl\
unconscious	[ʌnˈkɑntʃəs]	\ˌənˈkänchəs\	untidy	[ʌnˈtaɪdi]	\ˌənˈtīdē\
unconventional	[ˌʌnkənˈvɛntʃənəl]	\ˌənkənˈvenchənˌl\	untie	[ʌnˈtaɪ]	\ˌənˈtī\
uncover	[ʌnˈkʌvər]	\ˌənˈkəvər\	until	[ʌnˈtɪl]	\ˌənˈtil\
undecided	[ˌʌndiˈsaɪdəd]	\ˌəndēˈsīdəd\	untimely	[ʌnˈtaɪmli]	\ˌənˈtīmlē\
undeniable	[ˌʌndiˈnaɪəbəl]	\ˌəndēˈnīəbˌl\	untroubled	[ʌnˈtrʌbə ld]	\ˌənˈtrəbˌld\
under	[ˈʌndər]	\ˈəndər\	untrue	[ʌnˈtruː]	\ˌənˈtrü\
underdeveloped	[ˌʌndərdɪˈvɛləpt]	\ˌəndərdiˈveləpt\	unused	[ʌnˈjuzd]	\ˌənˈyüzd\
underground	[ˌʌndərˈgraund]	\ˌəndərˈgraünd\	unusual	[ʌnˈjuːʒʊəl]	\ˌənˈyüzhùəl\
underneath	[ˌʌndərˈniːθ]	\ˌəndərˈnēth\	unwanted	[ʌnˈwɑntəd]	\ˌənˈwäntəd\
undershirt	[ˈʌndərˌʃərt]	\ˈəndərˌshərt\	unwieldy	[ʌnˈwiːldi]	\ˌənˈwēldē\
understand	[ˌʌndərˈstænd]	\ˌəndərˈstand\	unwilling	[ʌnˈwɪlɪŋ]	\ˌənˈwiliŋ\
underwater	[ˌʌndərˈwɔtər, -ˈwɑ-]	\ˌəndərˈwȯtər, -ˈwä-\	unworthy	[ʌnˈwərði]	\ˌənˈwərthē\
undo	[ʌnˈduː]	\ˌənˈdü\	up	[ˈʌp]	\ˈəp\
undress	[ʌnˈdrɛs]	\ˌənˈdres\	update	[ʌpˈdeɪt; ˈʌpˌdeɪt]	\ˌəpˈdāt; ˈəpˌdāt\
uneasy	[ʌnˈiːzi]	\ˌənˈēzē\	upgrade	[ˈʌpˌgreɪd, ˌʌpˈ-]	\ˈəpˌgrād, ˌəpˈ-\
uneducated	[ʌnˈɛdʒəˌkeɪtəd]	\ˌənˈejəˌkātəd\	uphill	[ʌpˈhɪl]	\ˌəpˈhil\
unemployed	[ˌʌnɪmˈplɔɪd]	\ˌənimˈplȯid\	upon	[əˈpɑn, əˈpɔn]	\əˈpȯn, əˈpän\
unexpected	[ˌʌnɪkˈspɛktəd]	\ˌənikˈspektəd\	upper	[ˈʌpər]	\ˈəpər\
unfair	[ʌnˈfær]	\ˌənˈfar\	uppercase	[ˌʌpərˈkeɪs]	\ˌəpərˈkās\
unfaithful	[ʌnˈfeɪθfəl]	\ˌənˈfāthfˌl\	upright	[ˈʌpˌraɪt]	\ˈəpˌrīt\
unfasten	[ʌnˈfæsə n]	\ˌənˈfasˌn\	upset	[ʌpˈsɛt]	\ˌəpˈset\
unfavorable	[ʌnˈfeɪvərəbəl]	\ˌənˈfāvərəbˌl\	upside down	[ˌʌpˌsaɪdˈdaun]	\ˌəpˌsīdˈdaün\
unfeeling	[ʌnˈfiːlɪŋ]	\ˌənˈfēliŋ\	upstairs	[ˈʌpˌstærz, ˌʌpˈ-]	\ˈəpˌstarz, ˌəpˈ-\
unfit	[ʌnˈfɪt]	\ˌənˈfit\	upward	[ˈʌpwərd]	\ˈəpwərd\
unfold	[ʌnˈfoːld]	\ˌənˈfōld\	urban	[ˈərbən]	\ˈərbən\
unforgettable	[ˌʌnfərˈgɛtəbəl]	\ˌənfərˈgetəbˌl\	urgency	[ˈərdʒənˌsi]	\ˈərjˌn(t)sē\
unforgivable	[ˌʌnfərˈgɪvəbəl]	\ˌənfərˈgivəbˌl\	Uruguayan	[ˌʊrəˈgwaɪən, ˌjʊr-]	\ˌùrəˈgwīən, ˌyùr-\
unfortunate	[ʌnˈfɔrtʃənət]	\ˌənˈfȯrchənət\	us	[ˈʌs]	\ˈəs\
ungrateful	[ʌnˈgreɪtfəl]	\ˌənˈgrātfˌl\	usage	[ˈjuːsɪdʒ, -zɪdʒ]	\ˈyüsij, -zij\
unharmed	[ʌnˈhɑrmd]	\ˌənˈhärmd\	use	[ˈjuːz; ˈjuːs]	\ˈyüz; ˈyüs\
uniform	[ˈjuːnəˌfɔrm]	\ˈyünəˌfȯrm\	usher	[ˈʌʃər]	\ˈəshər\
unilateral	[ˌjuːnəˈlætərəl]	\ˌyünəˈlatərəl\	usual	[ˈjuːʒʊəl]	\ˈyüzhùəl\
uninhabited	[ˌʌnɪnˈhæbətəd]	\ˌəninˈhabətəd\	utility	[juːˈtɪləti]	\yüˈtilətē\
union	[ˈjuːnjən]	\ˈyünyən\	utilize	[ˈjuːtəlˌaɪz]	\ˈyütˌlˌīz\
unique	[jʊˈniːk]	\yùˈnēk\	vacant	[ˈveɪkə nt]	\ˈvākˌnt\
unit	[ˈjuːnɪt]	\ˈyünit\	vacate	[ˈveɪˌkeɪt]	\ˈvāˌkāt\
unite	[juːˈnaɪt]	\yùˈnīt\	vacation	[veɪˈkeɪʃən, və-]	\vāˈkāshˌn, və-\
universe	[ˈjuːnəˌvərs]	\ˈyünəˌvərs\	vaccine	[vækˈsiːn, ˈvækˌ-]	\vakˈsēn, ˈvakˌ-\
university	[ˌjuːnəˈvərsəti]	\ˌyünəˈvərsətē\	vacuum	[ˈvæˌkjuːm, -kjəm]	\ˈvaˌkyüm, -kyəm\
unjust	[ʌnˈdʒʌst]	\ˌənˈjəst\	vain	[ˈveɪn]	\ˈvān\

ENGLISH WORD	IPA	M-W	ENGLISH WORD	IPA	M-W
valid	[ˈvæləd]	\ˈvaləd\	vista	[ˈvɪstə]	\ˈvistə\
valley	[ˈvæli]	\ˈvalē\	visual	[ˈvɪʒʊəl]	\ˈvizhùəl\
value	[ˈvælˌju:]	\ˈvalˌyü\	vital	[ˈvaɪtəl]	\ˈvītᵊl\
van	[ˈvæn]	\ˈvan\	vitamin	[ˈvaɪtəmən]	\ˈvītəmən\
vanguard	[ˈvænˌgɑrd]	\ˈvanˌgärd\	vocabulary	[voˈkæbjəˌlɛri]	\vōˈkabyəˌlerē\
vanilla	[vəˈnɪlə, -ˈnɛ-]	\vəˈnilə, -ˈne-\	vocal	[ˈvoːkəl]	\ˈvōkᵊl\
vanity	[ˈvænəti]	\ˈvanətē\	vocation	[voˈkeɪʃən]	\vōˈkāshᵊn\
vapor	[ˈveɪpər]	\ˈvāpər\	vogue	[ˈvoːg]	\ˈvōg\
variable	[ˈvɛriəbəl]	\ˈverēəbᵊl\	voice	[ˈvɔɪs]	\ˈvóis\
vary	[ˈvɛri]	\ˈverē\	volley	[ˈvɑli]	\ˈvälē\
vase	[ˈveɪs, ˈveɪz, ˈvɑz]	\ˈvās, ˈvāz, ˈväz\	volume	[ˈvɑljəm, -ˌjuːm]	\ˈvälyəm, -ˌyüm\
VCR	[ˌviːˌsiːˈɑr]	\ˌvēˌsēˈär\	voluntary	[ˈvɑlənˌtɛri]	\ˈvälənˌterē\
vegetable	[ˈvɛdʒtəbəl, ˈvɛdʒətə-]	\ˈvejtəbᵊl, ˈvejətə-\	vomit	[ˈvɑmət]	\ˈvämət\
vehicle	[ˈviːəkəl, ˈviːˌhɪkəl]	\ˈvēəkᵊl, ˈvēˌhikᵊl\	vote	[ˈvoːt]	\ˈvōt\
veil	[ˈveɪl]	\ˈvāl\	vow	[ˈvæʊ]	\ˈvaú\
vein	[ˈveɪn]	\ˈvān\	vulnerable	[ˈvʌlnərəbəl]	\ˈvəlnərəbᵊl\
velocity	[vəˈlɑsəti]	\vəˈläsətē\	wade	[ˈweɪd]	\ˈwād\
venetian blind	[vəˈniːʃən-]	\vəˈnēshᵊn-\	waft	[ˈwɑft, ˈwæft]	\ˈwäft, ˈwaft\
Venezuelan	[ˌvɛnəˈzweɪlən, -zʊˈeɪ-]	\ˌvenəˈzwälən, -zùˈā-\	wage	[ˈweɪdʒ]	\ˈwāj\
vengeance	[ˈvɛndʒənts]	\ˈvenjᵊn(t)s\	wager	[ˈweɪdʒər]	\ˈwājər\
ventilate	[ˈvɛntəlˌeɪt]	\ˈventᵊlˌāt\	waist	[ˈweɪst]	\ˈwāst\
venture	[ˈvɛntʃər]	\ˈvenchər\	wait	[ˈweɪt]	\ˈwāt\
Venus	[ˈviːnəs]	\ˈvēnəs\	wake	[ˈweɪk]	\ˈwāk\
verb	[ˈvərb]	\ˈvərb\	waken	[ˈweɪkən]	\ˈwākᵊn\
verify	[ˈvɛrəˌfaɪ]	\ˈverəˌfī\	walk	[ˈwɔk]	\ˈwók\
versatile	[ˈvərsətəl]	\ˈvərsətᵊl\	wall	[ˈwɔl]	\ˈwól\
verse	[ˈvərs]	\ˈvərs\	wallet	[ˈwɑlət]	\ˈwälət\
version	[ˈvərʒən]	\ˈvərzhᵊn\	want	[ˈwɑnt, ˈwɔnt]	\ˈwänt, ˈwónt\
vertical	[ˈvərtɪkəl]	\ˈvərtikᵊl\	war	[ˈwɔr]	\ˈwór\
vertigo	[ˈvərtɪˌgoː]	\ˈvərtiˌgō\	wardrobe	[ˈwɔrdˌroːb]	\ˈwórdˌrōb\
very	[ˈvɛri]	\ˈverē\	warehouse	[ˈwærˌhaʊs]	\ˈwarˌhaús\
veteran	[ˈvɛtərən, ˈvɛtrən]	\ˈvetərən, ˈvetrən\	warm	[ˈwɔrm]	\ˈwórm\
veterinarian	[ˌvɛtərəˈnɛriən, ˌvɛtəˈnɛr-]		warn	[ˈwɔrn]	\ˈwórn\
		\ˌvetərəˈnerēən, ˌvetəˈner-\	warranty	[ˈwɔrənti, ˌwɔrənˈti:]	\ˈwórəntē, ˌwórənˈtē\
veto	[ˈviːto]	\ˈvētō\	wash	[ˈwɔʃ, ˈwɑʃ]	\ˈwósh, ˈwäsh\
vibrate	[ˈvaɪˌbreɪt]	\ˈvīˌbrāt\	wasp	[ˈwɑsp]	\ˈwäsp\
vice	[ˈvaɪs]	\ˈvīs\	waste	[ˈweɪst]	\ˈwāst\
victim	[ˈvɪktəm]	\ˈviktəm\	watch	[ˈwɑtʃ]	\ˈwäch\
victory	[ˈvɪktəri]	\ˈviktərē\	water	[ˈwɔtər, ˈwɑ-]	\ˈwótər, ˈwä-\
video	[ˈvɪdiˌoː]	\ˈvidēˌō\	wave	[ˈweɪv]	\ˈwāv\
Vietnamese	[viˌɛtnəˈmiːz, -ˈmiːs]	\ˈvēˌetnəˈmēz, -ˈmēs\	wax	[ˈwæks]	\ˈwaks\
view	[ˈvjuː]	\ˈvyü\	way	[ˈweɪ]	\ˈwā\
vigil	[ˈvɪdʒəl]	\ˈvijᵊl\	we	[ˈwiː]	\ˈwē\
vinegar	[ˈvɪnɪgər]	\ˈvinigər\	weak	[ˈwiːk]	\ˈwēk\
violate	[ˈvaɪəˌleɪt]	\ˈvīəˌlāt\	wealth	[ˈwɛlθ]	\ˈwelth\
violence	[ˈvaɪlənts, ˈvaɪə-]	\ˈvīlən(t)s, ˈvīə-\	weapon	[ˈwɛpən]	\ˈwepᵊn\
violet	[ˈvaɪlət, ˈvaɪə-]	\ˈvīlət, ˈvīə-\	wear	[ˈwær]	\ˈwar\
violin	[ˌvaɪəˈlɪn]	\ˌvīəˈlin\	weariness	[ˈwɪrinəs]	\ˈwirēnəs\
VIP	[ˌviːˌaɪˈpiː]	\ˌvēˌīˈpē\	weave	[ˈwiːv]	\ˈwēv\
virtual	[ˈvərtʃʊəl]	\ˈvərchùəl\	web	[ˈwɛb]	\ˈweb\
virtue	[ˈvərˌtʃuː]	\ˈvərˌchü\	wedding	[ˈwɛdɪŋ]	\ˈwediŋ\
virus	[ˈvaɪrəs]	\ˈvīrəs\	wedge	[ˈwɛdʒ]	\ˈwej\
visible	[ˈvɪzəbəl]	\ˈvizəbᵊl\	Wednesday	[ˈwɛnzˌdeɪ, -di]	\ˈwenzˌdā, -dē\
vision	[ˈvɪʒən]	\ˈvizhᵊn\	week	[ˈwiːk]	\ˈwēk\
visit	[ˈvɪzət]	\ˈvizət\	weep	[ˈwiːp]	\ˈwēp\
visor	[ˈvaɪzər]	\ˈvīzər\	weigh	[ˈweɪ]	\ˈwā\

ENGLISH WORD	IPA	M-W	ENGLISH WORD	IPA	M-W
weight	[ˈweɪt]	\ˈwāt\	witness	[ˈwɪtnəs]	\ˈwitnəs\
welcome	[ˈwɛlkəm]	\ˈwelkəm\	witticism	[ˈwɪtəˌsɪzəm]	\ˈwitəˌsizəm\
welfare	[ˈwɛlˌfær]	\ˈwelˌfar\	witty	[ˈwɪti]	\ˈwitē\
well	[ˈwɛl]	\ˈwel\	wolf	[ˈwʊlf]	\ˈwu̇lf\
well-being	[ˈwɛlˈbiːɪŋ]	\ˈwelˈbēiŋ\	woman	[ˈwʊmən]	\ˈwu̇mən\
Welsh	[ˈwɛlʃ]	\ˈwelsh\	wonder	[ˈwʌndər]	\ˈwəndər\
west	[ˈwɛst]	\ˈwest\	wood	[ˈwʊd]	\ˈwu̇d\
wet	[ˈwɛt]	\ˈwet\	wool	[ˈwʊl]	\ˈwu̇l\
whale	[ˈʰweɪl]	\ˈ(h)wāl\	word	[ˈwərd]	\ˈwərd\
what	[ˈʰwɑt, ˈʰwʌt]	\ˈ(h)wät, ˈ(h)wət\	work	[ˈwərk]	\ˈwərk\
wheat	[ˈʰwiːt]	\ˈ(h)wēt\	world	[ˈwərld]	\ˈwərld\
wheel	[ˈʰwiːl]	\ˈ(h)wēl\	worm	[ˈwərm]	\ˈwərm\
when	[ˈʰwɛn]	\ˈ(h)wen\	worry	[ˈwəri]	\ˈwərē\
where	[ˈʰwɛr]	\ˈ(h)wer\	worse	[ˈwərs]	\ˈwərs\
whether	[ˈʰwɛðər]	\ˈ(h)wethər\	worship	[ˈwərʃəp]	\ˈwərshəp\
which	[ˈʰwɪtʃ]	\ˈ(h)wich\	worst	[ˈwərst]	\ˈwərst\
while	[ˈʰwaɪl]	\ˈ(h)wīl\	worth	[ˈwərθ]	\ˈwərth\
whim	[ˈʰwɪm]	\ˈ(h)wim\	would	[ˈwʊd]	\ˈwu̇d\
whine	[ˈʰwaɪn]	\ˈ(h)wīn\	wound	[ˈwuːnd]	\ˈwünd\
whip	[ˈʰwɪp]	\ˈ(h)wip\	wound	[ˈwaʊnd]	\ˈwau̇nd\
whirlwind	[ˈʰwərlˌwɪnd]	\ˈ(h)wərlˌwind\	wrap	[ˈræp]	\ˈrap\
whisper	[ˈʰwɪspər]	\ˈ(h)wispər\	wreck	[ˈrɛk]	\ˈrek\
whistle	[ˈʰwɪsəl]	\ˈ(h)wisˀl\	wrench	[ˈrɛntʃ]	\ˈrench\
white	[ˈʰwaɪt]	\ˈ(h)wīt\	wrestle	[ˈrɛsəl]	\ˈresˀl\
who	[ˈhuː]	\ˈhü\	wretch	[ˈrɛtʃ]	\ˈrech\
whole	[ˈhoːl]	\ˈhōl\	wrinkle	[ˈrɪŋkəl]	\ˈriŋkˀl\
whom	[ˈhuːm]	\ˈhüm\	wrist	[ˈrɪst]	\ˈrist\
whose	[ˈhuːz]	\ˈhüz\	write	[ˈraɪt]	\ˈrīt\
why	[ˈʰwaɪ]	\ˈ(h)wī\	wrong	[ˈrɔŋ]	\ˈrȯŋ\
wide	[ˈwaɪd]	\ˈwīd\	X ray	[ˈɛksˌreɪ]	\ˈeksˌrā\
widow	[ˈwɪˌdoː]	\ˈwiˌdō\	yard	[ˈjɑrd]	\ˈyärd\
width	[ˈwɪdθ]	\ˈwidth\	yawn	[ˈjɔn]	\ˈyȯn\
wife	[ˈwaɪf]	\ˈwīf\	year	[ˈjɪr]	\ˈyir\
wig	[ˈwɪg]	\ˈwig\	yearn	[ˈjərn]	\ˈyərn\
wild	[ˈwaɪld]	\ˈwīld\	yellow	[ˈjɛlo]	\ˈyelō\
will	[ˈwɪl]	\ˈwil\	yes	[ˈjɛs]	\ˈyes\
win	[ˈwɪn]	\ˈwin\	yesterday	[ˈjɛstərˌdeɪ, -di]	\ˈyestərˌdā, -dē\
wind	[ˈwɪnd]	\ˈwind\	yet	[ˈjɛt]	\ˈyet\
wind	[ˈwaɪnd]	\ˈwīnd\	yield	[ˈjiːld]	\ˈyēld\
window	[ˈwɪnˌdoː]	\ˈwinˌdō\	yoga	[ˈjoːgə]	\ˈyōgə\
windpipe	[ˈwɪndˌpaɪp]	\ˈwindˌpīp\	yogurt	[ˈjoːgərt]	\ˈyōgərt\
windshield	[ˈwɪndˌʃiːld]	\ˈwindˌshēld\	yolk	[ˈjoːk]	\ˈyōk\
wing	[ˈwɪŋ]	\ˈwiŋ\	you	[ˈjuː]	\ˈyü\
wink	[ˈwɪŋk]	\ˈwiŋk\	young	[ˈjʌŋ]	\ˈyəŋ\
winner	[ˈwɪnər]	\ˈwinər\	your	[ˈjʊr, ˈjoːr, jər]	\ˈyu̇r, ˈyōr, yər\
winter	[ˈwɪntər]	\ˈwintər\	yours	[ˈjʊrz, ˈjoːrz]	\ˈyu̇rz, ˈyōrz\
wipe	[ˈwaɪp]	\ˈwīp\	yourself	[jərˈsɛlf]	\yərˈself\
wire	[ˈwaɪr]	\ˈwīr\	youth	[ˈjuːθ]	\ˈyüth\
wisdom	[ˈwɪzdəm]	\ˈwizdəm\	yucca	[ˈjʌkə]	\ˈyəkə\
wise	[ˈwaɪz]	\ˈwīz\	Yugoslavian	[ˌjuːgoˈslɑviən]	\ˌyügōˈslävēən\
wit	[ˈwɪt]	\ˈwit\	zeal	[ˈziːl]	\ˈzēl\
with	[ˈwɪð, ˈwɪθ]	\ˈwith, ˈwith\	zero	[ˈziːro, ˈzɪro]	\ˈzērō, ˈzirō\
withdraw	[wɪðˈdrɔ, wɪθ-]	\withˈdrȯ, with-\	zigzag	[ˈzɪgˌzæg]	\ˈzigˌzag\
within	[wɪðˈɪn, wɪθ-]	\withˈin, with-\	zipper	[ˈzɪpər]	\ˈzipər\
without	[wɪðˈaʊt, wɪθ-]	\withˈau̇t, with-\	zone	[ˈzoːn]	\ˈzōn\
withstand	[wɪθˈstænd, wɪð-]	\withˈstand, with-\	zoology	[zoˈɑlədʒi, zuː-]	\zōˈäləjē, zü-\